I0085632

Marriage

and

Divorce Records

from

Maine
Freewill Baptist
Publications

1819–1851

David C. Young
and
Elizabeth Keene Young

HERITAGE BOOKS
2016

HERITAGE BOOKS
AN IMPRINT OF HERITAGE BOOKS, INC.

Books, CDs, and more—Worldwide

For our listing of thousands of titles see our website
at
www.HeritageBooks.com

Published 2016 by
HERITAGE BOOKS, INC.
Publishing Division
5810 Ruatan Street
Berwyn Heights, Md. 20740

Copyright © 1994 David C. Young
and Elizabeth Keene Young

All rights reserved. No part of this book may be reproduced or
transmitted in any form or by any means, electronic or mechanical,
including photocopying, recording or by any information storage
and retrieval system without written permission from the author,
except for the inclusion of brief quotations in a review.

International Standard Book Numbers
Paperbound: 978-0-7884-0136-7
Clothbound: 978-0-7884-6328-0

CONTENTS

INTRODUCTION..v

ABBREVIATIONS AND TERMS...vi

INDEX OF GROOMS 3

INDEX OF BRIDES...359

LIST OF MINISTERS AND JUSTICES OF THE PEACE...............687

LOCATIONS 717

INTRODUCTION

We anticipate that this volume will be a valuable resource for genealogists, deed researchers, historians, geneticists and others. In Maine many marriages were not recorded until the 1830s; it was not required by law until 1892. The state of New Hampshire, according to George Sanborn, has even fewer sources for marriage records than Maine (i.e., Maine has county commissioner marriage records, which apparently New Hampshire does not).

In 1985, Robert L. Taylor and I compiled *Death Notices from Freewill Baptist Publications 1811-1851*. This book has been invaluable to many doing New England genealogical research, especially in Maine. As Mr. Taylor has been busy with other endeavors, my wife and I, with a great deal of help from our typist, Mrs. Richard Lane of Danville, Maine, embarked on compiling and indexing marriage and divorce records from Freewill Baptist publications. Out of the six Freewill Baptist publications we used in the first project only three were worthy of abstracting for this project. The records compiled were mostly marriage records with a few divorces. We consider statements such as: John Doe states "I will no longer pay any of my wife's debts because she has left my bed & board ...." to indicate a divorce. Most of the entries came from the *Morning Star* 1826-1851 at Bates College Library, Lewiston, Maine; followed by the *Maine Freewill Baptist Repository* 1843-1851 at the Shaker Library in New Gloucester, Maine and *The Religious Informer* 1819-1825 at Bates College and the University of Massachusetts at Amherst, Massachusetts. The *Maine Freewill Baptist Repository* was the only one of the collections in which we were unable to find all of the issues.

A citation at the end of each entry identifies the publication and issue date. As The *Religious Informer* was a monthly journal of more than ten pages we have added the page number to marriage records which were buried in the text. Thus, researchers with access to the papers in the original or microfilm form may use this volume as an index and refer to the newspapers for additional data.

You will find more information on newspapers in *Death Notices from Freewill Baptist Publications 1811-1851*, and *Vital Records from Maine Newspapers 1785-1820*.

Good luck and happy hunting.

David C. Young
P.O. Box 152
Danville, ME 04223

Marriage and Divorce Records

from

Freewill Baptist Publications

1819 - 1851

Marriage and Divorce Records from Freewill Baptist Publications 1819 - 1851

INDEX OF GROOMS

ABBEY M H Eld of Harrisburgh m SCOVELL Marietta of Poland NY on 4 Oct, WHITCHER H Eld *MS* 25 Oct 1843

ABBEY Stephen m MANCHESTER Rhoda on Jul 19, BROWN John Jr Esq *MS* 19 Jan 1842

ABBOTT Benjamin F of No 2 PLT, ME, m YOUNG Sarah M on Aug 4 1839 at Lexington, ME, ABBOT William Eld *MS* 5 Feb 1840

ABBOTT Stephen of Springfield m KIDDER Sarah of Newbury NH on 24 Jan, EMERY Amos Eld *MS* 10 Apr 1844

ABBOTT Thomas H m HUNTRESS Lydia L both of Effingham NH on 5 Dec in Effingham NH, HANSON Moses Eld *MS* 19 Dec 1849

ABBOTT William N m RICHARDSON Eunice H on Jan 13 in Mt Desert ME, BROWN John Jr Esq *MS* 19 Jan 1842

ABBOTT Albert P m HASKELL Rebecca both of Stow ME in Chatham NH, GUPTILL R W Esq *MS* 20 Feb 1850

ABBOTT Asa M m MOODY Sarah of Ossipee NH on 21 May at Ossipee, CHICK J Eld *MS* 13 Sept 1843

ABBOTT Benjamin F m MOORE Ann of New Market on 10 Apr at New Market NH, HUTCHINS E Eld *MS* 20 May 1842

ABBOTT E W m PATTERSON S A both of Hopkinton NH on 22 Dec 1847 in Hopkinton NH, DYER B Eld *MS* 26 Jan 1848

ABBOTT George m LEAVITT Dorcas of Scarboro' ME on 1 Dec 1844 at Saco ME, RAND J Eld *MS* 5 Feb 1845

ABBOTT Hiram C m CHASE Laura A on 28th ult at Conway NH, CRESSEY Rev *MFWBR* 6 Feb 1847

ABBOTT Horace P m HURD Olive at North Berwick ME, TRUE Ezekiel Eld *MS* 17 Feb 1847

ABBOTT John F m EMERSON Lucinda E of Ossipee NH on 9 Jul at Ossipee NH, CHICK J Eld *MS* 13 Sept 1843

ABBOTT Moses C m GOLDSMITH Harriet C both of Ossipee NH on 19 Dec in Ossipee, CHICK J Eld *MS* 15 Jan 1851

ABBOTT Nathan m SAYWAD Sally in Shapleigh, BODWELL Elisha *MS* 21 Apr 1830

ABBOTT Orin m CLARK Abiah W of New Market NH on 4 Nov 1846 at New Market NH, WATSON E Eld *MS* 20 Jan 1847

ABBOTT Orson of Pembroke m CLARK Elizabeth of Epsom on 25 Apr in Epsom, Van DAME B Eld *MS* 23 May 1838

ABBOTT Rufus L m WILLARD Nancy A both of Candia on 28 Oct 1848 in Manchester, CILLEY D P Eld *MS* 8 Nov 1848

ABBOTT Solomon Jr at Ossipee NH m HODGE Irena H, HOBBS A W Eld *MS* 12 Apr 1843

ABBOTT Solomon of Boston MA m MASON Hannah C on 25 Oct at Wolfboro NH, BLAISDELL William Eld *MS* 2 Nov 1842

ABBOTT Stephen G of Antrim m CHENEY Sarah B on 16 Apr in Holderness, ABBOTT Samuel Rev of Antrim *MS* 13 May 1846

ABBOTT William F of Belfast ME m SANBORN Mary A of Lowell MA on 15 Jul at Knox ME, HIGGINS Joseph Eld *MS* 4 Aug 1847

ABBOTT William H of North Berwick m REMICK Sophia M, FROST Isaac Eld *MS* 17 Jan 1844

ABBOTT William of Loudon m DWINELLS Nancy E of Canterbury on Mar 9, CLOUGH Jeremiah Eld *MS* 15 Apr 1840

ABBOTT William T m WHITTIER R Brenda on 29th ult at Hallowell ME *MFWBR* 8 Dec 1849

ABLEMAN G L m GRANDY Lavina both of Johnstown WT in Johnstown Rock Co WT, CARY R M Eld *MS* 8 Dec 1847

ABLEMAN Joseph C m GRANDY Amandy both of Johnstown WT in Johnstown Rock Co WT, CARY R M Eld *MS* 8 Dec 1847

ADAMS Andrew m SPEAR Evalina both of Farmersville NY on 2 Sept, JACKSON N A Eld *MS* 30 Sept 1846

ADAMS Benjamin Esq m SAWYER Eliza B at New Portland ME on 28th ult *MFWBR* 18 Aug 1849

ADAMS Benjamin of Campton LEAVITT Hannah D of Guilford on Dec 22, PINKHAM John Eld *MS* 29 Jan 1840

ADAMS Charles m HOYT Anna both of Readfield 8 Oct last, SPAULDING Joel Eld *MS* 10 Feb 1836

ADAMS Daniel of Norridgewock ME m RUSSELL Deborah L Mrs on 22nd inst at Madison ME *MFWBR* 8 Dec 1849

ADAMS Ebenezer of Limerick m HOBSON Lydia M of Buxton ME 11 Jan 1849, BAILEY J M Eld *MS* 24 Jan 1849

ADAMS Enoch C of Newbury NH m NOURSE Elizabeth B of Hopkinton on 26 Nov, HOLMES Hiram Eld *MS* 23 Dec 1846

ADAMS Ira A of Winslow VT m FRENCH Sarah of Unity NH on 30 Oct 1849 in Winslow VT, ADAMS A Eld *MS* 18 Apr 1849

ADAMS Israel G m WILSON Hannah P both of Bowdoin *MS* 28 Dec 1836

ADAMS Ivory of Wales ME m WATTS Joanna of Hallowell, FILES A Eld MA 7 Feb 1833

ADAMS Jacob of Wales ME m BRIDGES Eliza of Bridgeton on Thur last, BRIDGES A Eld *MS* 9 Mar 1831

ADAMS James F m SEVERY Miranda both of Stephentown NY 15 Mar in that place, COLEMAN J B Eld *MS* 24 Apr 1844

ADAMS James m CADY Eliza on 20 Feb at Pierpont NY, WHITFIELD William Eld *MS* 3 May 1843

ADAMS James m HOLLOWELL Rhoda on 27 Dec at Boothbay ME, ROBINSON N J Eld *MS* 1 Feb 1843

ADAMS James P m SAVERY Miranda on 15 Mar 1844 at Stephentown NY, COLEMAN I B Eld *MS* 24 Apr 1844

ADAMS James T of New Market m FURBER Mary J of Dover on Sabbath Morn last, SMITH E Rev *MS* 8 Nov 1837

ADAMS John F of Buxton ME m GOODALE Phebe I of Limington ME, MANSON B S Eld *MS* 7 Feb 1844

ADAMS Joseph P of Springfield MA m YOUNG Dorothy Y on 20th inst at Dover NH, HAYDEN L Rev *MS* 27 Apr 1842

ADAMS Levi H of Plainfield NY m CRUMB Mary on 4 Nov, CHANEY J Eld *MS* 17 Feb 1847

ADAMS Reuben L Esq Post Master of Lancaster m WENTWORTH Angelesia C of Jackson NH on 20 inst in Jackson NH, CRESSY E W Eld *MS* 3 Nov 1847

ADAMS Reuel B of Biddeford ME m JORDAN Lucy A of Saco ME, RAND J Eld *MS* 5 Feb 1845

ADAMS Thomas J m HARRIMAN Azula both of Bradford on 7 Nov 1848, WENTWORTH J J Eld of Bradford *MS* 11 Apr 1849

ADAMS William H m BICKFORD Isabella on 15 Apr at New Market, FROST D S Eld *MS* 28 Apr 1847

ADERSON [sic] Timothy m AYERS Betsey of Albany on 7 June at Conway NH, LONG L A Eld *MS* 23 June 1847

ADLE Cornelius of Readfield m DUDLEY Mary E of Augusta on 28 Sept at Hallowell ME, WEAVER Phillip Eld *MS* 7 Jan 1846

AINSWORTH Wyman H m WILDER Harriet A on 9 June 1842 at Varysburgh NY, ROLLINS D M Eld *MS* 29 June 1842

AKENS Jacob of Barnstead m LANGLEY Abigail L of Alton NH on 15 Sept, GARLAND D Eld *MS* 10 Oct 1844

ALBEE Wilmot of Alna m CURTIS Emeline E of Bath *MFWBR* 8 Sept 1849

ALBRIGHT William H m CARPENTER Eliza A of Sherburne on 17 Apr in Sherburne NY, GARDNER S D Eld *MS* 5 May 1846

ALBRO Emery Dea formerly of Warsaw NY to COFRIN Caroline of Springville NY on 14th Feb at the QM in Boston NY, PLUMB H N Eld *MS* 31 Mar 1847

ALCOTT Thomas J Col of York Mich m SWORD Betsey of Norway on 29 Sept in Norway NY *MS* 30 Oct 1850

ALDEN Shadrack m HURD Eleanor of Somersworth NH on 16th inst at Great Falls NH, CURTIS S Eld *MS* 29 Mar 1843

ALDRICH Cyrus L of Franconia m NOYES Mary of Lisbon NH on 14 Nov at Lisbon NH, GASKILL Silas Eld *MS* 22 Dec 1841

ALDRICH Hiram m THOMAS Salata both of Barnston CE on 8 Jan, SAWYER G Eld *MS* 19 Feb 1851

ALDRICH Horatio m HARRIS Laure both of Uxbridge on 1 Feb, BURLINGAME W W Eld *MS* 28 Feb 1838

ALDRICH John of Scituate m WINSOR Tabitha B of Providence RI, NOYES E Esq *MS* 8 Jan 1851

ALDRICH Lewis m CASS Judith both of Stanstead on Mar 16, MOULTON A W Eld *MS* 15 Apr 1840

ALDRICH O E Eld of Spencer m POST Emma A of LaGrange on 28 Mar in Oberlin Ohio, WHIPPLE H E Eld *MS* 24 Apr 1850

ALDRICH Robert m SOUTHWICK Elizabeth W on 2d inst, BURLIN-GAME M W Eld *MS* 16 Jan 1839

ALDRICH Samuel of Rochester m DUKE Sabrah J on 26 Jan at Datton, Cattaraugus Co NY *MS* 22 Mar 1837

ALDRICH Scuyler Eld of Mecca Ohio m HARDY Charlotte S on 5 Mar in Pierpont *MS* 24 Apr 1850

ALEXANDER Dan m THAYER Abigail both of Uxbridge on Thanksgiving Day in Mendon MA, BURLINGAME M W Eld *MS* 19 Dec 1838

ALEXANDER Isaac m SOUTHARD Frances L of Richmond ME at Bowdoinham ME, QUINNAM C Eld *MS* 6 Sept 1843

ALEXANDER Lewis P of Topsham m MOSLEY Margaret M of Bow-doin 13 Aug 1848, BEAN C Eld *MS* 17 Jan 1849

ALEXANDER Nehemiah C m CURRIER Hannah B both of Farming-ton in Farmington ME, CHANEY John Eld *MS* 13 Dec 1837

ALEXANDER Robert D m JACK Susan G of Litchfield ME on 21 Dec in the Union meeting house at Richmond Corner ME, QUINNAM C Eld *MS* 7 Jan 1846

ALEXANDER Willeby C m BLOOD Sarah A of Newbury VT on 13 Apr 1848 in Manchester, CILLEY D P Eld *MS* 26 Apr 1848

ALGER Alonzo W m BLAIR Malissa on 31 Dec 1846 at Richmond VT, DIKE O Eld *MS* 10 Mar 1847

ALLARD Daniel Jr m HASKELL Caroline H both of Dover on 3 inst, HUTCHINS E Eld *MS* 7 Aug 1850

ALLARD David M m PATCH Harriet both of Eaton on 2 Jul, RUN-NELS J Eld *MS* 5 Aug 1846

ALLARD Henry m VARNEY Mary J, DUNN R Eld in Great Falls *MS* 8 Dec 1847

ALLARD Levi of Albany m MOULTON Lucy of Tamworth NH on 4 Apr, MERRILL Wm S Eld *MS* 5 June 1850

ALLEN Amasa of Lee m PEASE Sophia of Parsonsfield ME on 10 Nov at Parsonsfield ME, JORDAN Z Eld *MS* 11 Dec 1844

ALLEN Amasa of Rochester m BLAISDELL Elizabeth A of Lebanon ME on 23 Jan, BLAISDELL Edward Eld *MS* 5 Feb 1851

ALLEN Amasa of Warren m STODDARD Roxanna of Brookfield in Tunbridge VT, SWETT David Eld *MS* 18 Apr 1838

ALLEN C G m BURBANK Elizabeth on 26th ult at Saco, NICHOLS J

ALLEN (Continued)
T G Rev *MFWBR* 10 Nov 1849

ALLEN Charles m JORDAN Eliza C of Biddeford ME on 19th inst *MFWBR* 28 Dec 1850

ALLEN Charles Capt m SKOLFIELD Ruth both of Harpswell ME, HERSEY L Eld *MS* 7 Oct 1846

ALLEN Charles m MILLS Elizabeth both of Sanford ME *MS* 24 Jan 1838

ALLEN Charles of Gilmanton m COPP Mary C of Pittsfield on 13 Nov at Pittsfield, DAVIS J B Eld *MS* 27 Nov 1844

ALLEN Charles of York ME m TRICKEY Adeline of Brookfield *MS* 23 Jan 1834

ALLEN Daniel Jr m BROCKWAY Sally Ann of Stephentown NY on 12 March at Stephentown NY, COLEMAN I B Eld *MS* 4 Oct 1843

ALLEN Dennis F of Farmington m FROST Mary Ann of Industry ME on 30 Mar, LENNAN John Eld *MS* 10 May 1837

ALLEN Elial m ALLEN Percis both of Winthrop ME on 9 Nov at Fayette ME *MS* 10 Feb 1836

ALLEN Ephraim m STODDARD A Miss on 30 Oct 1843 at Harrisburg NY, ABBEY M H Eld *MS* 7 Feb 1844

ALLEN George E of Portland m SOUTHWELL Mary A of Newburyport MA on 7th inst *MFWBR* 21 Dec 1850

ALLEN Henry B of Chelsea VT m WOODWARD Lucretia L on 21 ult, THURSTON Eld *MS* 13 Jul 1836

ALLEN Henry of Cornish m WILSON Betsey on 20th inst in Limerick, LIBBY Eld *MS* 26 Mar 1828

ALLEN Holman P m EARL Theodosia A both of Portland on 18 ult in Portland, MOULTON Eld *MS* 8 May 1844

ALLEN Ira B m AVERY Harriet E of Corinth VT on 2 Nov at Corinth VT, MOULTON F Eld *MS* 17 Feb 1847

ALLEN Isaac of Freeport m TOBEY Ellen Mrs of Pownal on 7 Apr in Brunswick ME, PURINTON A W Eld *MS* 15 May 1850

ALLEN John m ALLEN Rosannah both of Brunswick in Brunswick ME, LIBBY A Eld *MS* 23 Jan 1850

ALLEN Joseph G m JOSE Martha of Biddeford ME on 4th inst at Scarboro ME, STRICKLAND G G Rev *MFWBR* 15 June 1850

ALLEN Joseph H m GRIFFIN Hannah B at Danville, FULLONTON J Eld *MS* 1 Feb 1843 and *MS* 11 Jan 1843

ALLEN Joseph W m TENNEY Hannah J at Raymond ME, SMALL C Eld *MS* 8 June 1842

ALLEN Lemuel m CUMMINGS Cynthia both of Augusta in Augusta ME, CURTIS S Eld *MS* 24 Jan 1838

ALLEN Otis m McDONALS Ruth of Lowell on 20th inst, THURSTON N Eld *MS* 29 May 1839

ALLEN Reuben m BROWN Ruth M both of Warwick RI on 27 June 1848 in Gloucester RI, ALLEN R Eld *MS* 19 Jul 1848

ALLEN Samuel Esq m ABBOTT Joanna on 5th inst at Shapleigh ME
  MFWBR 18 Aug 1849
ALLEN Samuel of Enfield NH m BENNET Betsey of Strafford NH,
  PETTENGELL John Eld *MS* 1 Feb 1843
ALLEN Samuel of Parsonsfield ME m YOUNG Mercy of Freedom on
  28 Jan 1844, BUTLER O Eld *MS* 7 Feb 1844
ALLEN Theodore of Buxton m BROWN Ann on 19th inst, FLANDERS
  A Eld *MS* 27 Mar 1829
ALLEY Alonzo D of Eaton m THURSTON Hannah D of Parsonsfield
  ME in Freedom, RUNNELS J Eld *MS* 11 Nov 1846
ALLEY Ira m ALLEN Mary Eliza on 25 Apr at Cornish, RAND I Eld
  MS 29 May 1844
ALLEY Leavitt of Eaton m SMART Seftonah at Freedom NH, DAVIS
  Joseph Eld *MS* 3 May 1843
ALLS Jacob M m FRIZZLE Nancy J both of Colebrook NH on 22 Dec,
  BEAN Benaiah Eld *MS* 5 Jan 1848
ALMY Charles on 17 Mar m DROWN Phebe A at Saco ME, RAND J
  Eld *MS* 2 Apr 1845
AMBROSE Oliver L of Sandwich NH m COTTON Mary Jane of Moul-
  tonborough on 25 Nov 1847, BROOKS N Eld *MS* 1 Dec 1847
AMBROSE Samuel of Tamworth m CHESLEY Susan of Holderness,
  BROOKS N Eld *MS* 3 June 1846
AMES Charles formerly of Geauga Seminary Ohio m DANIELS Sarah
  Jane on 28 ult in Dover NH, HUTCHINS E Eld *MS* 3 Apr 1850
AMES Dexter N of Ferrisburg VT m BENEDICT Louisa A on 1 Jan
  1849 in Underhill VT, DIKE Orange Eld *MS* 21 Mar 1849
AMES Edmund m SMITH Clarisa Ann both of Norway ME, *MFWBR*
  13 Feb 1847
AMES Ira of Canton ME m TUCKER Lucretia A of Buckfield ME,
  ANDREWS Otis Eld *MS* 12 May 1847
AMES James M m BACHELDOR Abigail of Bridgewater on 17 Feb,
  TRUE Ezekiel Eld *MS* 26 Mar 1845
AMES Lotan m WATSON Mary Ann both of Lowell on 29 inst,
  THURSTON N Eld *MS* 16 May 1838
AMES Marston of Parsonsfield m TUCKER Mary on 14 inst in Ossi-
  pee, WALKER John Eld *MS* 24 May 1837
AMES Phinehas m SAUNDERS Jemima M of Dover ME on 4 Jul,
  GILMAN M Esq *MS* 24 Jul 1844
AMIDON Wm H H of Marshfield m MANN Louisa on Mar 10 at
  Randolph VT, CLAFLIN Jehiel Eld *MS* 25 Mar 1840
AMOS Martin m BRACKET Abigail both of Augusta ME on 2 Oct
  1847, DUDLEY Thomas J Eld *MS* 24 May 1848
ANSERSON - see ADERSON
ANDERSON George of Limington m EDWARDS Susan in Gorham,
  MS 27 Jan 1832
ANDERSON James m CHICK Patience in Berwick *MS* 27 Jan 1832

ANDERSON John B of Portland ME m MILLER/MILNER Frances at Shapleigh ME *MFWBR* 6/13 Jul 1850

ANDERSON John of Limington ME m COFFIN Albarous F on 25 Mar at Limerick, LORD D H Eld *MS* 6 Apr 1847

ANDERSON Moses m CHELLIS Hannah on 1 Dec at Kingston, FULLONTON J Eld *MS* 15 Dec 1841

ANDERSON Richard of Windham m LOWELL Mary A of Gorham ME on 26 ult in Gorham ME, LIBBY C O Eld *MS* 27 Mar 1850

ANDREW Abraham of Somersworth m WEBSTER Lucy of Newfield on 16th inst, LIBBY Elias Eld *MS* 26 Oct 1832

ANDREWS Daniel H of Pelham m NICOLS Lucy D of Lowell MA *MS* 3 May 1843

ANDREWS James L m FOWLER Roxanna both of Freedom on 2 Dec, BUTLER O Eld *MS* 22 Dec 1847

ANDREWS James m OSGOOD Mary D on 24th ult at Charlestown, WETHERBEE I J Eld *MS* 9 Dec 1846

ANDREWS John of Wales ME m CHADBOURNE Sarah B at Waterboro on 1st inst, GREY James Eld *MFWBR* 20 May 1848

ANDREWS Joseph of Goffstown m FRASIER Mary A on 14 May at Manchester, CILLEY D P Eld *MS* 31 May 1843

ANDREWS Levi of Exeter m HAYNES Louisa of Epsom NH on 23 Jan 1843, RAMSEY G P Eld *MS* 8 Feb 1843

ANDREWS Nathaniel of Waterboro' m GOODWILL Olive E of Berwick on 25 Sept at Palmyra ME, LANCY G Esq *MS* 15 Sept 1834

ANDREWS of Effingham m WHEELER Mereby on Jan 30 in Ossipee, EMERY James *MS* 9 Mar 1842

ANDREWS Oliver E m PARKMARD Mary A both of Great Falls on 19 Sept, BROOKS N Eld *MS* 25 Sept 1850

ANDREWS Simon m WHITTEMORE Mary Mrs on 10th inst at Biddeford, FARRINGTON Rev *MFWBR* 16 Oct 1847

ANDREWS Stephen m SEVERENCE Dorothy on 30 Oct 1842 at Lowell MA, SMART M M Eld *MS* 28 Dec 1842

ANDREWS Winthrop m PREBBLE Elizabeth on 12 Nov at Boothbay ME, MORRILL S P Eld *MS* 22 Jan 1845

ANDREWS William A m BROWNELL Ann M, NOYES E Eld *MS* 13 Nov 1850

ANDREWSON Joseph F of Raymond m GORDON Lucy of Candia on 25 Jan, DYER S B Eld *MS* 1 Feb 1843

ANDRUS Calvin N m YOUNG Lavinia H both of Chelsea VT on 31 Dec 1849, HENDERSON M C Eld *MS* 10 Apr 1850

ANGELL Eben Smith m THOMPSON Abby F on 22 Sept at North Scituate RI, BRADBURY A R Eld *MS* 18 Dec 1844

ANGELL Israel Col ae 86y m ANGELL Sarah ae 56y in Smithfield RI *MS* 18 May 1826

ANGELL Nathaniel m WATERMAN Laura on 20th ult at No Providence RI, HUTCHINS Elias Eld *MS* 24 Apr 1834

ANNES Wm S of Pittsfield m CATE Rosilla of Meredith on 9 Feb *MS* 27 Feb 1834

ANNIS George W of Methuen MA m HARRIMAN Augusta Ann of Groton on 6 Apr at Holderness, PETTENGILL John Eld *MS* 26 June 1839

ANNIS Sheldon H m NOYES Martha L both of Great Falls on 5 inst at Great Falls, CURTIS S Eld *MS* 22 Apr 1840

ANTHONY George W m DELAND Mary Ann of Hallowell at Hallowell ME, WEAVER Philip Eld *MS* 11 Mar 1846

APPLEBEE George m SHOREY Eliza T both of Great Falls on 30th ult at Great Falls, CAVERNO A Eld *MS* 6 Jan 1836

APPLEBY Joseph A of Brunswick m PIPER Elizabeth H of Great Falls at Great Falls *MFWBR* 25 Jan 1851

APPLETON Nathan D Esq m HALL Julia at Alfred *MS* 4 Jan 1827

ARCHIBALD Nathaniel of Poland ME on 11 Dec TENNEY Kesiah of Raymond ME, LIBBY James Eld *MS* 10 Feb 1847

ARCHILIES J B of Patton m EMERY Rachel of Hatley on 6 Jan, MOULTON A W Eld *MS* 15 Apr 1840

ARCHY Moazing m PRIEST Hannah both of Milo NY on 8th ult, MARKS David Eld *MS* 6 June 1833

ARLING George G m CLARK Frances E both of Rochester on 30 Nov in Rochester, WHITNEY G W Eld *MS* 1 Jan 1851

ARMSTRONG Charles m WHITNEY Isabel B of Portland ME on 6 Apr, MOULTON A K Eld *MS* 9 Jul 1845

ARMSTRONG Morey m CLARK Patience both of Plainfield NY on 5 Mar 1846 in Plainfield NY, CHANEY J Eld *MS* 29 Apr 1846

ARMSTRONG Sylvester m PROUTY Sophia on 6 Oct at Middlebury NY, PLUMB H N Eld *MS* 30 Dec 1846 & *MS* 27 Jan 1847

ARNOLD Samuel of Shirby m WHITMORE Betsey of Standish *MS* 21 Jan 1835

ARNOLD Sprague at East Randolph VT m BROOKS Clarissa of East Randolph SANBORN G Eld *MS* 4 Jan 1843

ARRINGTON James W m TALBOT Harriet both of Smithfield on 27 ult at Smithfield RI, BURLINGAME Wm Eld *MS* 10 Feb 1836

ASH William B m SPRAGUE Clarissa on 22 Feb at Manchester, CILLEY D P Eld *MS* 4 Mar 1846

ASHELY John of Greenfield m WAUGHN Betsy of Brunswick Ohio on 22 Oct in Brunswick, BEEBE W Eld *MS* 15 Jan 1851

ASHTON Joshua of Pierpont NY m HUTCHINSON Rosette, WHITFIELD W Eld at Pierpont NY *MS* 25 Feb 1846

ASPINWALL Ellis m CORSON Harriet C of Dover NH on 8th inst at Dover NH, HUTCHINS E Eld *MS* 11 Mar 1846

ATHERTON Joseph of Roxbury MA m EMERSON Sophrona of Candia on 3 inst, RUSSELL M Rev *MS* 30 Dec 1835

ATKINS Nathaniel of Westbrook m McCALLAR Jane of Falmouth on 13 Dec in Falmouth, BEAN C Eld *MS* 2 Jan 1839

ATKINSON Theodore Esq of Lawrence m PALMER Martha H of South
Berwick ME on 25th ult at South Berwick ME *MFWBR* 10 Nov
1849

ATWELL C W of Portland ME m YOUNG P H Miss of Meredith NH at
Meredith village NH *MFWBR* 24 Aug 1850

ATWOOD A P of Bangor ME m HUBBARD Sarah of South Berwick
ME at Frankfort ME *MFWBR* 13 Jul 1850

ATWOOD Jeduthan m THURSTON Mary E of Meredith NH, PITMAN
Stephen J Eld *MS* 11 Sept 1839

ATWOOD Mark Eld of Northwood NH m DAVIS Lovina of Jericho VT
on 19 Jan, STEVENS Rev *MS* 28 Jan 1846

ATWOOD Norman m MOORE Louisa both of Lincoln VT on 18 Sept
in Lincoln VT, ATWOOD M Eld *MS* 16 Oct 1850

AUBERY Albert of Burlington VT m 26 Jan 1848 JUDSON Lovina E
of Huntington in Huntington VT, DIKE Orange Eld *MS* 5 Apr 1848

AUGIR Franklin P Eld of Rochester Wis m BIXBY Lavinea I of Williamstown VT on 19 Sept 1847 in Williamstown VT, BIXBY L E
Eld *MS* 13 Oct 1847

AUGIR Orlando of East Troy Wis m MUNGER Lucy of Mukwanego on
25 Dec 1850, BELKNAP P W Eld *MS* 26 Mar 1851

AUSTIN David S m HATCH Emma both of No Berwick ME on 8 Mar
1848 in No Berwick ME, CLAY Daniel Eld *MS* 29 Mar 1848

AUSTIN Isaac N of Westford m DANIELS Diadamy E M C of Underhill
on 5 Feb in Jericho VT, FAY Edward Eld *MS* 25 Mar 1846

AUSTIN Oliver O m SPEARS Sarah Mrs of Gardiner on 25 Dec 1842
at West Gardiner, FROST Isaac Eld *MS* 18 Jan 1843

AUSTIN Samuel P m CLIFFORD Susan P both of Manchester on 25
Sept in Manchester, CILLEY D P Eld *MS* 13 Oct 1847

AUSTIN Stoten m VARNEY Sarah both of Dover NH, PERKINS J Rev
MS 13 May 1835

AUSTIN Thomas W of Danville ME m STARBIRD Frances of Poland
ME on 12 Mar 1843 at Poland ME, FAIRFIELD Smith Eld *MS* 5
Apr 1843

AUSTIN William B m LANE Lydia L both of Manchester on 13 Aug in
Manchester, CILLEY D P Eld *MS* 26 Aug 1846

AVERILL Gerry Cook on 8th inst at Portland ME m LOVIT Margaret
of Portland ME, MOULTON A K Eld *MS* 17 Apr 1844

AVERILL John P principal of the Institution at Woodstock CT to
CAVERNO Elizabeth A former teacher in Foxcroft Academy ME on
29 Nov at Charlestown MA, by CARVERNO A Eld *MS* 10 Dec 1845

AVERY Daniel E m RICHARDSON Abigail both of Sandwich on 8 Dec
MS 4 Jan 1837

AVERY David m CLOUGH Apphia S on 5th inst, BUZZELL H D Eld
in Alton *MS* 13 Feb 1834

AVERY John C of Sandwich m MASON Sarah M on 23 Nov, BLAKE
C E Eld *MS* 17 Dec 1845

AVERY Joshua E m MUDGETT Clarissa A on 27 Feb at Sandwich, BROOKS N Eld *MS* 12 Mar 1845

AVERY Joshua of Manchester m WIGGIN Susan of Warner on 26 Jul 1848 in Manchester, CILLEY D P Eld *MS* 16 Aug 1848

AVERY Oren m PALMER Exeaun both of Ellsworth NH on 23 Feb in Ellsworth NH, MORGAN S Eld *MS* 26 Mar 1851

AVERY Philander of Corinth m TILLOTSON Nancy of Topsham on 5 Dec 1841 in Topsham, SMITH A D Eld *MS* 16 Mar 1842

AVERY Samuel m SOUL Wealthy of Waterville ME at Waterville ME, LEWIS Daniel B Eld *MS* 25 Nov 1846

AYER Albion P m ESTES Eunice both of Westbrook ME on 6 Feb 1848 in Saccarappa ME, HARRIMAN D P Eld *MS* 16 Feb 1848

AYER Amaza L of Limerick ME m MOORE Caroline of Parsonsfield ME on 14 Sept in Parsonsfield ME, LORD D H Eld *MS* 27 Sept 1848

AYER Francis C of Frankfort m LIBBY Lucinda T of Brownfield on 12 ult in Brownfield, AYER Aaron Eld *MS* 27 Dec 1837

AYER James 3d m STRAW Cyrene in Newfield, KINSMAN E P Eld *MS* 26 Jul 1827

AYER John m TAYLOR Elizabeth B at Portsmouth on 2nd inst, TRUE Ezekial Eld *MS* 19 Feb 1840

AYER Joseph of Somersworth m DREW Sarah Ann of Barrington, SHERBURNE Samuel Eld *MS* 24 Sept 1834

AYER Moses C m FELCH Lois N both of Newbury on Nov 18, MOODY David Eld *MS* 12 Jan 1842

AYER Thomas L of Boston MA m WILSON Sarah A of Kittery ME on 16 inst, WETHERBY I J Eld *MS* 26 Apr 1843

AYERS Albert G m NILES Harriet O niece of Administrator on 16 Feb 1848 in Ogden NY, WHITCHER H Eld *MS* 8 Mar 1848

AYERS Levi m WELCH Sally both of Tuftonboro on 27 ult in Ossipee NH, WALKER John Eld *MS* 23 Aug 1837

AYERS Richard m LEIGHTON Susan on Sunday last at Dover, MARK Enoch Eld *MS* 6 Jan 1836

AYERS Stephen of Wolfborough m ROBERTS Tamson of Ossipee NH on 11 inst, CHICK J Eld *MS* 29 Sept 1847 & *MS* 16 Feb 1848

BABB Ashel m BERRY Lydia both of Strafford on 29th ult, PLACE E Eld *MS* 18 Feb 1835

BABB Davis m PEASLEY Jerusha of Alexander on 22 Dec at Alexander, BROWN A Eld *MS* 18 Jan 1843

BABB Ezekiel H m BABB Almira both of Strafford on 22 Oct 1848 in Strafford, HOLMES J C Eld *MS* 17 Jan 1849

BABB Horatio m DEMERIT Mary Ann Miss at Dover NH *MS* 21 Nov 1833

BABB Ira m HOLMES Mahala on 13 Jul at Barnstead *MS* 17 Aug 1836

BABB Isaac m GRANT Lydia of Dover on 29 Mar at Dover NH, SMITH A D Eld *MS* 28 Apr 1847

BABB Isaac W of Westbrook m JORDAN Sarah B of Gorham on 3 Aug at Gorham ME, LIBBY C O Eld *MS* 17 Sept 1845

BABB Joseph T m KIMBALL Abigail on 30 Jan at Strafford, PLACE E Eld *MS* 27 Mar 1844

BABB Moses M m PRESSEY Sophronia E both of Manchester on 3 Jan 1848 in Manchester, CILLEY D P Eld *MS* 19 Jan 1848

BABB Rufus of Scarboro' m BOOTHBAY Hannah of Parsonsfield ME on 6 Feb at Parsonsfield, JORDAN Z Eld *MS* 12 Mar 1845

BABB Thomas of New Durham m SAMPSON Abigail Mrs at Strafford, PLACE E Eld *MS* 27 Nov 1844

BABCOCK Edward A of Portland m FORSSKOL Elizabeth R of Saco on 16th inst at Saco, NICHOLS J T G Rev *MFWBR* 26 Oct 1850

BABCOCK George m BUFFINGTON Harriet both of New Albion NY on 10 inst *MS* 21 Dec 1836

BABCOCK George m on 4 Sept PATCHEN Eliza, GRIFFETH A Eld in Clayton NY *MS* 9 Oct 1850

BABCOCK Samuel m RICKER Mary C in Lowell MA *MS* 26 Oct 1836

BABCOCK Varnum M Jr m COLE Calista M of Nassau on 11th Sept at Stephentown NY, COLEMAN I B Eld *MS* 22 Oct 1845

BABCOCK William A m PELTON Harriet both of Leonardsville NY on 9 Sept in Leonardsville NY, CHANEY J Eld *MS* 30 Sept 1846

BACHELDER Daniel Jr m POTER (perhaps POTTER/PORTER) Lydia of Thorndike on 17 Sept 1848 at Brooks *MFWBR* 13 Jan 1849

BACHELDER George W m WELLS Abigail on 11 inst in Epsom, HOLMES H Eld *MS* 26 Apr 1837

BACHELDER Jonathan m LULL Phebe A on 11 Aug at Manchester NH, CILLEY D P Eld *MS* 20 Aug 1845

BACHELDER Nathaniel of Northampton m QUINBY Mary M Mrs of Dover on Tues last week, THURSTON N Eld *MS* 1 May 1834

BACHELDER Smith of Northwood m PAGE Huldah of Epsom NH, CILLEY D P Eld *MS* 31 Oct 1833

BACHELDER Thomas m CLEAVES Rhoda on 4th at Candia NH, CAVERNO A Rev *MFWBR* 24 Mar 1849

BACHELDOR James H of Ridgeway Orleans Co NY m WILLETS Ruth Jane of Rome Mich on 4 Jul at Rome, HERVEY Russell Eld *MS* 24 Jul 1839

BACHELDOR Lyman P of Holderness NH m COOPER Mary Jane of Sanford ME, STEVENS T Eld *MS* 25 Oct 1843

BACHELOR David S m TOWNSEND Mary C both of Franklin NH, KNOWLES E G Eld in Andover *MS* 21 June 1848

BACHELOR Joseph of Raymond m BEAN Sally, KIMBALL Eld at Candia *MS* 10 Sept 1834

BADGER James W m STINSON Asenath V on 2 Sept in Dracut, CURTIS S Eld *MS* 22 Sept 1847

BADGER Joseph Eld m PEAVY Mary Jane, who was b 26 Feb 1798, were m 1816 *RI* May 1820 p 77

BADGER Lewis D of Gilford m SWAIN Mary E of Meredith on 23 Feb in Meredith, PITMAN Stephen J Eld *MS* 1 May 1850

BADGER Wells M m BOND Lavina T both of Manchester on 21 Oct 1848 in Manchester, CILLEY D P Eld *MS* 8 Nov 1848

BAGLEY David Dea of West Topsham VT m MORSE Sabrina of West Plymouth NH on 24 Sept 1848 in West Topsham VT, CLIFFORD Aldin S Eld *MS* 4 Oct 1848

BAGLEY George R m TEBBETTS Eleanor M of Waterboro at Waterboro', WEST J D Eld *MFWBR* 18 Jan 1851

BAGLEY John A m DORE Mary of Great Falls NH at Great Falls NH, CURTIS S Eld *MS* 29 Mar 1843

BAGLEY Jonathan R of Plymouth NH m HOWLAND Martha I of Franconia NH on Dec 8th, GEORGE N K Eld *MS* 28 Dec 1842

BAGLEY Sewell D of Dixmont m DODGE Sarah L of Munroe on 26 ult in Munroe, FLETCHER Jabez Eld *MS* 15 Nov 1837

BAILEY Abner S of Mansfield m EMERY Elizabeth of Howland ME on 12 Jul in Howland ME, RUSSELL Stephen Eld *MS* 5 Aug 1846

BAILEY Alpha of Washington m JACOBS Hannah W of Manchester on 25 June in Manchester, CILLEY D P Eld *MS* 11 Jul 1849

BAILEY Chandler m WARD Elizabeth A on 27 Nov at Nottingham, NORRIS Rev *MS* 30 Dec 1846

BAILEY Charles of Woolwich m SHATTUCK Martha A of Wiscasset on 26 Dec 1850 in Woolwich ME, AVER A Eld *MS* 5 Feb 1851

BAILEY Elbridge A of Weare NH m TRUE Roxy Ann G on 26 Sept at Franklin, SHAW Elijah Eld *MS* 30 Oct 1844

BAILEY George m LANGMAID Sally of Yorkshire NY on 17 June at Yorkshire NY, JACKSON N A Eld *MS* 4 Aug 1847

BAILEY Giles Rev "pastor of Universalist Society" m BASSETT Mercy H of Dexter ME on 5th inst *MFWBR* 21 Dec 1850

BAILEY Henry D on 26 Oct m BACON Eliza A of Sutton, PECK Benjamin D Eld *MS* 18 Jan 1843

BAILEY James R m HOBSON Ethelinda on 14 inst *MS* 22 Sept 1847

BAILEY John B of Woolwich ME m BAILEY Rebecca G on 12th inst, PERKINS Seth W Eld *MS* 29 June 1842

BAILEY Joseph of Compton m MARTIN Jane of Stanstead LC on 15 May, MOULTON Abial Eld *MS* 20 Sept 1837

BAILEY Jotham C m WHITE Harriet Y of Wiscasset ME on 26 Sept 1848 in Wiscasset ME, PAGE E G Eld *MS* 4 Oct 1848

BAILEY Martin L of Cambridge (ME?) m GOULD Louisa of Dexter ME, MACE Jeremiah Rev *MS* 17 May 1843

BAILEY Mose m ROWLEY Susan both of Yorkshire NY on 13 inst in China NY, JACKSON N A Eld *MS* 26 Sept 1849

BAILEY Orlando H of Bedford m PARKER Lucy M of Manchester on 30 Sept in Manchester, CILLEY D P Eld *MS* 13 Oct 1847

BAILEY Paul m DAVIS Betsey of Epsom NH on 25 Nov at Epsom NH, "his 3rd wife, her 4th husband", RAMSEY G P Eld *MS* 22 Dec 1841

BAILEY Richard of Bartlett NH m JOHNSON Olive S of Conway NH on 16 Mar at Brownfield ME, HART E H Eld *MS* 30 Apr 1845

BAILEY Seth of Braintree m 4 inst FULLER Sapreta of West Brookfield VT, CLAFLIN Jehiel Eld in West Brookfield VT *MS* 14 Nov 1838

BAILEY Silas at Fairfield ME m WYMAN Ester E, LEWIS D B Eld *MS* 17 Apr 1844

BAILEY Terry m BAILEY Nancy both of Woolwich ME on 10 Apr in Woolwich ME, PERKINS Seth W Eld *MS* 20 June 1838

BAILEY Thomas of Dexter m KNIGHT Mary Mrs of Corinna ME on 30 Jan 1842 at Corinna ME, DAMMON I Eld *MS* 6 Apr 1842

BAILEY William C of Farmington m STICKNEY Mary Jane of Chesterville ME *MS* 27 Jul 1836

BAILEY William m KNIGHT Emeline both of Westbrook ME on 6 Feb 1850, WOODSUM WM Eld *MS* 20 Mar 1850

BAILEY William N m WISNER Mary of Charlestown MA on 17th June, WETHERBEE I J Eld *MS* 4 Aug 1847

BAKER Ahira Esq m ROSS Rhoda W both of Shapleigh ME on 3 Sept 1848 in Shapleigh ME, LITTLEFIELD W H Eld *MS* 20 Sept 1848

BAKER Ainus of Starksboro' m HAZZARD Irena of Huntington on 3 Jul at Huntington VT, DIKE Orange Eld *MS* 21 Sept 1842

BAKER Albion K P m RICHARDSON Emily both of Litchfield ME at Meeting House, QUINNAM C Eld in Litchfield ME *MS* 28 Mar 1849

BAKER Asa m COLLINS Phebe S both of Smithfield *MS* 8 June 1836

BAKER Bradford Y m MONTGOMERY Jane of Boothbay ME on 25 Jan, MORRILL S P Eld *MS* 4 Feb 1846

BAKER Edward of Lawrence m HUNT Sarepta E of Montpelier VT on 16 Nov 1847 in East Randolph VT, MOULTON F Eld *MS* 14 Feb 1849

BAKER Henry A m WOODCOCK Elizabeth both of Sidney on 8 inst in Waterville ME, BEAN G W Eld *MS* 7 Mar 1849

BAKER Horace m BLAKE Sally of Lisbon ME, AMES Eld *MS* 24 Sept 1834

BAKER Isaac L m WITHAM Tryphena both of Jackson ME on 11 Augin Jackson ME, RINES J N Eld *MS* 13 Nov 1850

BAKER James P Esq of Strong m HANNAFORD Mary of Cape Elizabeth ME 2 Jul Thursday eve, LIBBY C O Eld at Cape Elizabeth ME *MS* 15 Jul 1846

BAKER John Dr m TOWN Mary both of Weare NH on 1st ult*MS* 3 Oct 1833

BAKER Johnson C of China m JENKS Sarah S of Middlebury NY, ROLLIN D M L Eld *MS* 10 Aug 1842

BAKER Oscar E Eld m POWELL Jane A both of Marion on 13 Oct in Marion Ohio, BAKER George W Eld *MS* 27 Nov 1850

BAKER Otis m HAYES Lovina C both of Dover, CURTIS S Eld *MS* 1 Apr 1840

BAKER Perry at Middleville m TOMPKINS Margaret, SMITH O W Eld *MS* 29 Jan 1845

BAKER Peter H m KING Sarah A both of South Boston 10 Sept 1848, TUTTLE E Eld *MS* 4 Oct 1848

BAKER Stephen C of Holderness NH m CUMMINGS Susan J of Manchester NH on 3 Apr *MS* 19 Apr 1843

BAKER Thomas of Waterford ME m ROSS Adelia M of Harrison ME on 4 Jan in Harrison ME, LIBBY D Eld *MS* 19 Feb 1851

BAKESKEY Theodore m BARRY Eleanor both of Lowell in Lowell MA, THURSTON Nathaniel Eld *MS* 12 Apr 1837

BALDWIN Isaac m GLOVER Lucretia both of Bafford LC on 17 Jan, MOULTON A Eld of Stanstead LC *MS* 13 Apr 1842

BALDWIN Josiah M m BROWN Lourana both of Ashtabula Co on 9 Sept in Trumbull Ohio, COPP I B Eld *MS* 10 Oct 1849

BALDWIN Levi m CONVERS Lydia of Barnston on 1 Jan 1839 *MS* 17 Apr 1839

BALDWIN Oscar of Barnston m MAY Ruby of Stanstead EC on 7 Nov, *MS* 1 May 1844

BALL Alvinea m FOLSOM Clarissa P both of Manchester on 12 Aug 1847 in Manchester, CILLEY D P Eld *MS* 25 Aug 1847

BALL William Jr of Sebec m HANSON Charlotte A of Atkinson on Nov 4 at Atkinson, HATHAWAY L Eld *MS* 8 Jan 1840

BALLARD Josiah C of Westbrook m KNIGHT Lurana S on 20 Nov at Bridgton ME, WILLEY E C Eld *MS* 14 Jan 1846

BALLENGER John of East Liberty Logan Co Ohio m WILKIE Margaret on 2d Mar, HEALTH J D Eld *MS* 30 June 1847

BALLOU George m MONTGOMERY Nancy of Manchester NH on 5 Oct at Bedford, CILLEY D P Eld *MS* 15 Oct 1845

BANCROFT William m HOLBROKE Laura on 11 Nov 1841 at Farmerville, WINSOR Barnet Eld *MS* 15 Mar 1843

BANFILL Eli m JACKSON Elizabeth of Eaton on 13 Jan 1842 at Eaton, KNOWLES Samuel Eld *MS* 11 May 1842

BANGS E B Dr of Saco ME m BROOKS Mary J of Limerick ME on 25th ult in Limerick ME, FELCH A Rev *MFWBR* 13 Mar 1847

BANKS Esreff H m ATKINSON Lucinda M both of Saco ME on 3rd inst in Saco ME, BUNKER Rev *MFWBR* 13 Nov 1847

BANKS Israel of Parsonsfield ME m MOULTON Elvira of Sandwich NH on 24 June Sabbath eve in Sandwich, TASKER L B Eld *MS* 18 Jul 1849

BANKS Jacob of Parsonsfield m MULLOY Hannah of Limerick ME, LIBBY E Eld *MS* 27 May 1835

BANKS Lewis C of Oswego NY m CLAGGETT Charlotte Ann of Russel

BANKS (Continued)

Ohio on 7 Apr in Eldado Wis, KEEVILL E J E Eld *MS* 1 May 1850

BANKS Samuel Jr m HOBSON Mary G both of Hollis on 29 Dec 1850, BAILEY J M Eld in Hollis ME *MS* 22 Jan 1851

BARBER John A m DEVOE Lucy L at Bertrand Mich on 14 Sept 1848 at Bertrand, FELLOWS George Eld *MS* 8 Nov 1843

BARBER Marcus FOX Mary Ann of Three Mile Bay NY on 28 Mar at Three Mile Bay NY, PADDEN S B Eld *MS* 26 May 1847

BARBER William S m LEAVITT Lydia S of Guilford on 12 Nov at Alton NH, PINKHAM J Eld *MS* 18 Dec 1844

BARCLAY Cyrus P of Lowell MA m RUNDLETT Dorothy P on 17 Sept, WOODMAN J Eld *MS* 27 Sept 1843

BARCLEY Cyrus P m RUNDLETT Lydia S on 6 May at Dracut MA, CURTIS S Eld *MS* 2 June 1847

BARD Nathaniel m WOODARD Hannah on 13th inst at Lisbon ME, WITHAM John Eld *MS* 23 Oct 1839

BARKER Abijah m KNOX Julia Ann on 23 Sept of Clinton, BUKER Alvah J Eld *MS* 2 Dec 1846

BARKER Andrew H m JONES Ann H both of Unity NH on Jan 1st 1842 in Windsor VT, ADAMS Abel Eld *MS* 19 Jan 1842

BARKER Andrew H m GODFREY Betsey S both of Manchester on 6 Feb 1849 in Manchester, CILLEY D P Eld *MS* 14 Feb 1849

BARKER Dudley merchant of Alton NH m WILLEY Betsey of New Durham *MS* 8 Mar 1837

BARKER Francis m BALDWIN Maria on 10 Nov 1847 at Turtle Prairie Walwoth Co WT, CARY R M Eld *MS* 8 Dec 1847

BARKER John W merchant of Alton m POWERS Livona G of New Durham *MS* 8 Mar 1837

BARKER Joseph m ROBERTS Phebe T on 2 Apr in Lafayette WT, COOMBS A Eld *MS* 20 May 1846

BARKER Nathaniel Jr of Cornish ME m WEEKS Susannah of Parsonsfield ME, BUZZELL A Eld in Cornish *MS* 15 Apr 1840

BARKER William m PARMERTER Mrs both of Oneida Eaton Co Mich on 10 Jan 1849, CURRIER Samuel A *MS* 11 Apr 1849

BARKER William H m WEBSTER Sarah T both of Newport RI on 8 Mar in Newport RI, LORD D H Eld *MS* 8 Apr 1846

BARNARD Barzell m NOBLE Rebecca M both of Perry NY on March 15 1840 at Warsaw, PLUMB H N Eld *MS* 20 May 1840

BARNARD Cyrus G m LITTLEFIELD Joanna W of Wilmington MA at Wilmington MA, DURGIN J M Eld *MS* 18 May 1842

BARNARD Edward S of Nantucket m SMITH Mary G of Portland ME on 23rd at Portland, COX Eld *MFWBR* 2 Oct 1847

BARNES Benjamin Dover NH m KNAPP Martha K Miss of Newburyport *MS* 10 Apr 1834

BARNES George W m WEYMOUTH Mary both of Lowell MA on 30 Nov 1848 in Lowell MA, CURTIS S Eld *MS* 3 Jan 1849

BARNES Harmon of Greenwich MA m THURSTON Betsey of Pelham MA on 24 Mar, PIERCE Eld *MS* 6 Apr 1836

BARNES John Deacon m MEDCALF Eunice on 20 Feb in Freedom NY, WINSOR Barnet Eld *MS* 15 Mar 1843

BARNES Matthews L m BEADLE Angeline on 11 Oct at Cooperstown (NY?), PADDEN S B Eld *MS* 18 Dec 1844

BARNHAM George C of Portland ME m FOSS Olive B of Hollis on 13th inst at Hollis, BUZZELL Silas Esq *MFWBR* 19 Oct 1850

BARNS D A m PEAVY Louisa of Barnston on Jan 30, MOULTON A W Eld *MS* 15 Apr 1840

BARNS D S m STORY Lucy both of Compton on 9 Nov at Stanstead, *MS* 17 Feb 1836

BARON John m GAULT Sarah Ann on 13th inst at Boston MA, HOLMAN J W Eld *MS* 19 Jul 1843

BARRETT Benjamin m DANIEL Caroline A of Waterbury on 16 Sept at Waterbury VT, GRAY Ira Eld *MS* 2 Oct 1844

BARRETT Calvin of Springfield MA m HUNT Adelia M of Jackson ME on 7 Aug at Belchertown MA, PIERCE Luther Eld *MS* 31 Aug 1842

BARRETT William M m WADLEIGH Mary R of Manchester NH, BROOKS N Eld *MS* 15 Nov 1843

BARRETT William m CARD Abigail both of Portsmouth NH on 11 May in Portsmouth, CAVERNO A Eld *MS* 27 May 1846

BARRON Richard B m WALCOTT Julia Ann of Bath at Bath ME, HATHORN S Eld *MS* 19 Oct 1842

BARROWS Putnam m PORTER Mary on 9th inst at Dixmont ME *MFWBR* 29 June 1850

BARRY Ezra T of Loudon m FOSS Dorothy of Strafford NH in Strafford, PLACE E Eld *MS* 15 Nov 1837

BARTLET Joseiah Jr m BATCHELDER Eliza Ann both of Garland ME on 23 Nov in Garland, ROBINSON N J Eld *MS* 13 Dec 1837

BARTLET/BARTLETT Lewis m HOSE/HUSE Mary both of Weare on 14 Feb 1839, MOODY David Eld *MS* 12 Feb 1840

BARTLETT Abijah m STEPHENS Hannah O of Lowell MA on 17 Aug at Lowell MA, WOODMAN J Eld *MS* 19 Oct 1842

BARTLETT Ambrose H Capt of Waterville ME m DELANO Sophronia of Sidney ME on 15 inst at Augusta ME *MS* 28 Dec 1836

BARTLETT Belknap m FOLSOM Love on 1 Jan at Gilmanton, MOODY David Eld *MS* 18 Jan 1843

BARTLETT Benjamin F m RAYNOLD Olive E at Boston MA, HOLMAN J W Eld *MS* 19 Jul 1843

BARTLETT Broughton m LORD Mary A both of Boston MA in Boston MA, NOYES E Eld *MS* 4 Apr 1849

BARTLETT Enoch m TWOMBLY Ann B both of Monroe on 29 Nov in Jackson ME, RINES J N Eld *MS* 26 Dec 1849

BARTLETT James m DAVIS Elizabeth of Centre Harbor on 29th May

BARTLETT (Continued)
   at Meredith Bridge, BROOKS N Eld *MS* 5 June 1839
BARTLETT James P m HARRIS Frances Mary at Portsmouth NH
   MFWBR 29 June 1850
BARTLETT John A of Webster ME m WENTWORTH Sarah A of
   Boston on 23 Jan in Boston MA, DUNN R Eld *MS* 12 Feb 1851
BARTLETT John Col m LOCK Anna both of Deering NH on 16th ult,
   HARRIMAN David Eld *MS* 25 Apr 1833
BARTLETT John m ADAMS Sarah S both of Garland ME on 8 Oct
   1848 in Bangor ME, AMES M Eld *MS* 22 Nov 1848
BARTLETT Joseph M at Manchester NH m SEAVEY Susan L of
   Manchester NH, CILLEY D P Eld *MS* 23 Jul 1845
BARTLETT Joseph O D Eld of Wilmot m PRIEST Mary C of Notting-
   ham on 10 Oct at Deerfield, DYER S B Eld *MS* 17 Dec 1845
BARTLETT Michael m STOKES Dorothy on 19 Feb at Lowell MA,
   THURSTON N Eld *MS* 25 May 1842
BARTLETT Nehemiah of Garland ME m OLNEY Mary I of No Provi-
   dence on 25th ult at No Providence *MS* 9 Mar 1836
BARTON Albion of Rollinsford NH m CARR Elizabeth on 11th inst at
   Limerick ME, FREEMAN C Rev *MFWBR* 16 Nov 1850
BARTON George W m JOHNSON Margaret A on 25 Apr at Bath ME,
   HOBSON P M Eld *MS* 29 May 1844
BARTON Isaac N of Boston MA m HERRICK Mary C of Alfred ME on
   3d inst at Alfred ME *MFWBR* 25 Sept 1847
BARTON William m STEPHEN Abigail of Lynn MA on 30 Jul at Lynn
   MA, MERRILL William P *MS* 14 Aug 1844
BARWISE John of Garland ME m REED Charlotte H at Skowhegan
   ME *MFWBR* 13 Oct 1849
BASCOM Andrew P m TOMPKINS Adelia S of Hamilton on 16 Sept at
   Poolville NY, CARLNER S D Eld *MS* 11 Nov 1846
BASS Eleazer m MORSE Martha on 8 Feb 1843 at West Brookfield
   VT, CLAFFIN Jehiel Eld *MS* 14 June 1843
BASSETT Daniel Jr of Wolfboro' NH m CANNEY Eliza Jane of Dover
   NH on 1 Nov, CURTIS S Eld *MS* 9 Nov 1842
BASSIT Samuel at Epping m PEASLEY Hannah *MS* 2 Jul 1834
BATCH Frederick B of Lancaster NH m VINCENT Thankful H of
   Durham NH on 14 Mar 1848 in Durham NH, FROST D S Eld *MS*
   3 May 1848
BATCHELDER Alvin m LAWRENCE Sarah of Meredith NH on 26
   June at Meredith Bridge, BROOKS N Eld *MS* 13 June 1842
BATCHELDER Benjamin m FOSS Eleanor B both of Raymond on 11
   Jul in Raymond, HOLMES H Eld *MS* 1 Aug 1838
BATCHELDER Benjamin m SANBORN Arvilla W on 28 Nov at Mere-
   dith NH, PITMAN S J Eld *MS* 25 Dec 1844
BATCHELDER Eder D of Bridgewater m PLUMMER Mary Jane of
   Thornton on 28 Jan, MORGAN S Eld *MS* 26 Mar 1851

BATCHELDER Emery Capt m DEARBORN Dorathy Ann of Hampton on 18 inst in Hampton, HUTCHINS E Eld *MS* 26 Dec 1838

BATCHELDER George E of Chichester m LOCKE Abigail M of Boston MA on 7 Sept, CHASE William P Eld *MS* 24 Sept 1845

BATCHELDER Henry F merchant m ROGERS Lydia S both of Loudon on 5 Dec in Loudon, SARGENT W A Eld *MS* 26 Dec 1849

BATCHELDER Isaac 2d m MERROW Phebe A at Eaton, RUNNELS J Eld *MS* 30 June 1847

BATCHELDER J of Quinsey m WOODMAN H N of Meredith NH on 29 Nov in Meredith NH, BROOKS N Eld *MS* 26 Dec 1838

BATCHELDER James m FOX Lucy C of Raymond, CAVERNO A Rev *MFWBR* 24 Mar 1849

BATCHELDER James L m MASON Lydia of Hampton on 30 Dec at Hampton, BURBANK P S Eld *MS* 6 Jan 1847

BATCHELDER James S m SULLIVAN Louisa both of Manchester in Manchester, CILLEY D P Eld *MS* 15 Apr 1846

BATCHELDER Joseph of Northwood m HAYNES Eleanor of Nottingham, CILLEY D P Eld *MS* 20 Mar 1839

BATCHELDER Joshua C m BAKER Adaline both of Shapleigh on 4 Jul 1847 in Shapleigh, BAKER Ahira Esq *MS* 12 Jan 1848

BATCHELDER N G of Manchester m PRESCOTT Martha S of Meredith on 23 Jan in Lake Village, SINCLAIR J L Eld *MS* 13 Feb 1850

BATCHELDER Nathaniel Esq of No Hampton on 20 June m POWERS Mary Jane of New Market in New Market, EASTMAN C Allen Eld *MS* 3 Jul 1850

BATCHELDER Plummer P m NUTE Judith P Mrs on Dec 1848 in Candia, CAVERNO A Eld *MS* 10 Jan 1849

BATCHELDER Samuel Eaton at Phipsburg ME m BARTLETTE Drusilla on 16 Nov, SMITH O W Eld *MS* 1 Dec 1841

BATCHELDER Samuel S m RICKER Harriet A both of West Waterville ME at Fairfield ME, LEWIS D B Eld *MS* 20 Apr 1842

BATCHELDER Simon of Northwood m WALDRON Hannah B (after Simon's death she m[2] Elisha TASKER) *MS* 17 Feb 1847

BATCHELDER William W m SANBORN Ann W of Meredith NH on 4 Oct, PITMAN Stephen Eld *MS* 26 Oct 1842

BATES Alexander of Richmond m HALL Elizabeth Mrs of Litchfield ME on 17 Dec 1848 in Litchfield ME, QUINNAM C Eld *MS* 3 Jan 1849

BATES Alexander divorced 27 Jul 1832 BATES Polly *MS* 24 Aug 1832

BATES Charles D of Mecca m BRACKET Lodema of Bristol both formerly of Geauga Sem Ohio on 1 inst in Mecca Ohio, ALDRICH S Eld *MS* 23 Oct 1850

BATES Gilead m CROMWELL Hannah A both of Lowell on 2 Nov 1847 in Dracut, CURTIS S Eld *MS* 17 Nov 1847

BATES John m HOIT Mercy R of St Albans ME on 2 Nov at St Albans

BATES (Continued)

ME, COPP J B Eld *MS* 3 Dec 1845

BATES William of Bowdoinham m GEORGE Elizabeth of Richmond at Richmond, QUINNAM C Eld *MS* 21 Aug 1839

BATLEY Josiah W of Cumberland m WOOD Marcelia of Warwick RI, BURLINGAME M W Eld *MS* 24 Apr 1839

BATTY Caleb O m ARNOLD Adah both of Scituate on 8 Nov in No Scituate RI, ALLEN R Eld *MS* 1 Jan 1851

BAXTER John of Lowell MA m EVANS Ann Jeannette of Lowell MA on 16 Dec, CILLEY D P Eld *MS* 1 Jan 1845

BAXTER Zimri m SEAVEY Eunice Miss of Milton formerly of Cornish on 27th ult, TURNER N Esq *MS* 15 June 1832

BEACH Augustus of Saco ME m COOK Meriam of Somersworth NH on 6 inst at Great Falls, STEVENS T Eld *MS* 28 Nov 1838

BEACHMAN Asa Esq m QUARLES Abigail A on 23 Mar, CHICK J Eld of Ossipee NH *MS* 14 May 1845

BEACKER Aaron of Bowdoinham m LIBBY Ruth Ann of Richmond in Richmond, STINSON Robert Eld *MS* 17 Oct 1838

BEAK Thomas of Loudon m YEATON Susan of Chichester on 5 Mar in Loudon, CLOUGH Jeremiah Eld *MS* 15 Apr 1840

BEALE Nathaniel m ROBBINS Mary both of Phillips ME on 8 Apr 1849 in Phillips ME, PEASE A Eld *MS* 18 Apr 1849

BEALS Levi of Georgetown ME m RICHARDSON Nancy of Westport ME on 16 Nov, MORRILL S P Eld *MS* 4 Feb 1846

BEAN Alonzo E m EUER Augusta Ann on 19 Dec in Gilmanton, NORRIS J Eld *MS* 29 Jan 1851

BEAN Arlo C of Exeter ME m GOULD Sarah P of Dexter ME on 30th Mar, MACE Jeremiah Rev *MS* 17 May 1843

BEAN Benjamin Jr of Tuftonboro m PRAY Mary F of Ossipee NH on 15 Nov, FERNALD S P Eld *MS* 21 Dec 1836

BEAN Benjamin of Rollinsford m THORN Hannah of Standish ME on 19 inst in Dover, HUTCHINS E Eld *MS* 29 Aug 1849

BEAN Bradford of Waterboro m COFFIN Louisa Jane of Waterboro ME on 9th ult at Waterboro, EMERY E Eld *MFWBR* 6 Feb 1847

BEAN Charles Eld m DREW Salome on 4 inst in Newfield ME, BURBANK Samuel Eld *MS* 17 Oct 1838

BEAN Daniel of Exeter ME m AMES Lydia W of Corinth ME on 23 Sept 1847 in Garland ME, AMES M Eld *MS* 2 Feb 1848

BEAN Daniel m SHAW Lovinia on 22 Dec 1843 at Gilford, PINKHAM J Eld *MS* 12 Apr 1843

BEAN Francis E m THOMPSON Olive E both of Dover on 10 inst in Dover, HUTCHINS E Eld *MS* 17 Oct 1849

BEAN Francis G of Candia m SAWYER H Susan on 25 June in Deerfield, GARLAND G D Eld *MS* 8 Jul 1846

BEAN Freeman m BELLOWS Polly of Hartley on 14 Feb 1839 *MS* 17 Apr 1839

BEAN Freeman of Barnston m BELLOWS Nancy on 20 Mar of Stanstead LC, MOULTON A Eld *MS* 13 Apr 1842

BEAN Geo J m RUSSELL Charlotte both of Lowell on 25 Nov in Lowell, CURTIS S Eld *MS* 15 Dec 1847

BEAN George of Deerfield m PIKE Eliza G of Lowell MA, THURSTON N Eld *MS* 16 Sept 1835

BEAN George W Eld of Farmington ME m FOGG Perrfenda R at Readfield ME on 14 May, MORRILL S P Eld *MS* 12 June 1844

BEAN Hiram m MORGAN Delia on 8 Dec 1843 at Sutton NH, EMERY Amos Eld *MS* 10 Apr 1844

BEAN Horace F of Boston MA m LOCKE Adaline M of Sandwich NH, BROOKS N Eld *MS* 29 Jan 1845

BEAN Israel of Waterboro m THING Betsey on 24th ult, THURSTON Eld *MS* 21 Aug 1829

BEAN Jacob of No Sandwich m MARSTON Mary of Tamworth on 12 Nov, WEBBER Horace Eld *MS* 19 Dec 1838

BEAN James Jr m TRAFTON Hannah S both of Alfred ME in Springvale ME, LORD D H Eld *MS* 19 Sept 1838

BEAN James M of Newbury NH m BACHELDER Hannah D of Strafford on 26 Aug in Thetford VT, CLARK Eli Eld *MS* 21 Nov 1849

BEAN James M m MOULTON Miriam B on 20 Sept at Manchester, CILLEY D P Eld *MS* 1 Oct 1845

BEAN Jeremiah of Belmont m CAMMETT Sally of Waterboro ME on Sun evening last, CLARK Atherton Eld *MS* 4 Nov 1831

BEAN John C of Colebrook m GROUT Sarah J of Columbia on 25 Nov 1847 in Colebrook NH, BEAN Benaiah Eld *MS* 15 Dec 1847

BEAN John Jr m YOUNG Isabella of Somersworth NH at Berwick ME, CURTIS S Eld *MS* 8 June 1842

BEAN John m GILMAN Betsey both of Gilmanton on 6 Nov 1843, MOODY David Eld *MS* 24 Apr 1844

BEAN Jonathan H of Waterboro'ME at Lebanon m JONES Dorcas of Lebanon, LORD D H Eld *MS* 8 Dec 1841

BEAN Joseph m BRUNNING Hannah of Hatley on June 20, MOULTON Abial Eld *MS* 1 Jan 1840

BEAN Joseph m GOWEN Mary Mrs at Waterboro ME, EMERY Richard Eld *MFWBR* 23 Oct 1847 & *MS* 22 Dec 1847

BEAN Laomi m PICKERING Mary of Meredith NH, PITMAN Stephen J Eld *MS* 11 Sept 1839

BEAN Loammi of Gilford m DOCKHAM Sally, BROOKS N Eld *MS* 15 Nov 1843

BEAN Oran K of Danvers m SMALL Mary of DOVER NH on 6 inst in Lowell, THURSTON N Eld *MS* 14 June 1837

BEAN Richard 3d m WOODWARD Hannah both of Waterboro ME *MS* 16 Sept 1831

BEAN Rufus B m DAVIS Sarah L both of Effingham NH on 2 Apr *MS* 22 Apr 1846

BEAN Rufus L m COOK Laura A both of Rollinsford NH on 2 inst in Dover NH, HUTCHINS E Eld *MS* 5 Dec 1849

BEAN Samuel C of Vergenes m BRAY Charlotte A of Warren VT on 9 Jul, GRAY Ira Eld *MS* 2 Aug 1843

BEAN Samuel of Deerfield m FURBER Betsey of Northwood NH on 20 ult, CILLEY D P Eld *MS* 7 Oct 1835

BEAN Silas F m SEAVEY Ursula A both of Pittsfield NH *MS* 19 Oct 1836

BEAN Silas F of Tuftonborough m ABBOTT Mary Ann of Ossipee NH on 15 Mar 1848, CHICK John Eld in Ossipee *MS* 29 Mar 1848

BEAN Stephen D of Dover NH m PENDEXTER Mary Ann, HUTCHINS E Eld *MS* 7 June 1843

BEARDSLEE John S m FELLOWS Sarah of Haverhill MA on 14 Aug 1847 in Haverhill MA *MS* 6 Oct 1847

BEARDSLEY Ezra W m GRAVES Mary O both of Rochester Wis on 5 Sept in Rochester Racine Co Wis *MS* 17 Oct 1849

BEARDSLEY Smith H m DAVIS Augusta H on 15 June at Nottingham, SHERBURNE S Eld *MS* 2 Jul 1845

BEAU Daniel R of Raymond NH m GOULD Climena of Lowell MA on 9 Dec 1848 in Lowell MA, CURTIS S Eld *MS* 3 Jan 1849

BEBEE Geo W of New York City m COPP Mary S of Manchester on 19 May in Manchester, CILLEY D P Eld *MS* 30 May 1849

BECK George of Dover m MELLOON Huldah, PERKINS Seth W Eld *MS* 12 Nov 1845

BECK Joseph S Capt of Augusta ME m PUTNAM Mary Ann of Hallowell on 12 Sept in Hallowell, TOBIE E M Eld *MS* 4 Oct 1837

BECK Thomas F m SMITH Eliza both of Augusta *MS* 16 Nov 1836

BECK Thomas of Loudon m YEATON Susan of Chichester on Mar 5, CLOUGH Jeremiah Eld *MS* 15 Apr 1840

BECKER Martin F of Suriname South America m WALKER Caroline E of Manchester on 28 Mar 1850 in Manchester, CILLEY D P Eld *MS* 10 Apr 1850

BECKHAM James W m FLOYD Lovinah S at Biddeford ME *MFWBR* 28 Jul 1849

BECKWITH Christopher of New Lyme m CHAPEL Emeline S of Colebrook Ohio on 24 Feb in Colebrook Ohio, CLARK R Eld *MS* 24 Apr 1850

BEDEE Taylor of Poplin m SMITH Irena of Raymond *MS* 6 Feb 1839

BEDELL Isaiah M of Sanford me m ROBERTS Ellen E of Lyman on 1 June in Sanford, RAMSEY G P Eld *MS* 15 Jul 1846

BEDELL John H m HEARD Mary both of Sanford ME, SMALL C Eld *MS* 25 Jul 1849

BEEBE Hiram of Freedom, Cataraugus Co, NY m JACKSON Lucretia on 11 Dec 1834 *MS* 7 Jan 1835

BEEBE Sylvester m VINCENT Abby Ann on 20 Oct 1846 at Clayton NY, GRIFFETH Ansel Eld *MS* 10 Mar 1847

BEECH Israel B MD of Sharon Ohio m WIGGIN Emily C of Sandwich, BROOKS N Eld *MS* 16 Oct 1844

BEEDE David m VARNEY Elizabeth both of Dover at Great Falls NH,
CAVERNO A Eld *MS* 30 Dec 1835

BEEDE Hanson of Franklin m CHASE Mary Ann on Dec 14 at Bristol, BROWN Amos Eld *MS* 29 Jan 1840

BEEDE Moses V of Lowell MA m WIGGIN Mary D on evening 6 inst
in Durham, EASTMAN C Allen Eld *MS* 14 Feb 1849

BEEDE Samuel m SPAULDING Mary Miss on 25th ult in Dover NH,
MS 8 June 1832

BEEDE Samuel m SPAULDING Mary E at Dover NH, THURSTON
Nathaniel Eld *MS* 25 Apr 1833

BEEDE William of Dalton m SLEEPER Cynthia P of Gilmanton on 21
Nov at Sanbornton NH, MASON L Eld *MS* 31 Dec 1845

BEEDEL Joseph m HAM Jane both of Dover on 19 Nov 1848 in
Rochester, WHITNEY G W Eld *MS* 7 Feb 1849

BEEDLE Henry of Somersworth NH m BURBANK Mary Jane of
Parsonsfield ME on 25 Nov 1847 in Parsonsfield ME, JORDAN Z
Eld *MS* 12 Jan 1848

BEERS Elijah m STRAIT Martha both of Stephentown NY on 19 Oct
1848 in W Stephentown NY, COLMAN I B Eld *MS* 3 Jan 1849

BEERS Franklin m JONES Mercy R of Dracut MA on 28 Dec,
THURSTON N Eld *MS* 25 May 1842

BEERS Philo m MURPHREY Catherine of Nassau on 14 Nov 1846 at
Nassau, COLEMAN I B Eld *MS* 6 Jan 1847

BELKNAP P W of China on 1 Jan m KNOWLTON Charlotte A in
Portage NY, WHITCHER H Eld *MS* 29 Mar 1837

BELKNAP Philander W of Olina a preacher m KNOWLTON Charlotte
of Portage Alleghany Co NY on 9 Jan *MS* 22 Mar 1837

BELL John of Beverly MA m COOK Emeline of Manchester on 4 Mar
1850 in Manchester, CILLEY D P Eld *MS* 10 Apr 1850

BELLINGS Rufus of Clark Township CW m AMES Maria D of Fowler
NY in Fowler NY, JENKINS C Eld *MS* 15 Dec 1847

BEMIS Joseph K of Fryeburg ME m LIBBY Catherine R on 29 Dec
1844 at Brownfield ME, Hart E H Eld *MS* 12 Feb 1845

BENCH Frederick on Thursday last m CROOK Susan both of Great
Falls in Dover NH, SMITH Eleazer Rev *MS* 4 Oct 1837

BENCHAM Simon F of Ossipee NH m YOUNG Louisa W of Tuftonborough NH on 19 ult, CHICK John Eld *MS* 21 June 1837

BENCROFT Seneca C m CAMBURN Caroline both of Walworth in
Walworth NY, HOLMES D G Eld *MS* 16 Oct 1850

BENJAMIN David m VINCENT Laura Ann on 3 Jan at Norway *MS* 24
May 1843

BENJAMIN Henry F m MORSE Elvira C both of Manchester on 7
June in Manchester, CILLEY D P Eld *MS* 24 June 1846

BENJAMIN Samuel S m BENJAMIN Laura Ann Mrs on 16 Nov at

BENJAMIN (Continued)

Norway Herkimer Co NY, SMITH O W Eld *MS* 10 Dec 1845

BENNET Alden B m STEVENS Elizabeth at Lowell MA *MS* 21 Dec 1836

BENNET Benjamin m BOYD Elizabeth Jane of Boothbay on 3 Nov at Boothbay ME, ROBINSON N J Eld *MS* 29 Nov 1843

BENNET Levi W of Great Falls NH m SMITH Adaline of Salmon Falls on 21 Sept, BROOKS N Eld *MS* 25 Sept 1850

BENNET Rufus of Alfred ME m HANSON Lucy C of Sanford ME on 22 Dec at North Berwick ME, RAMSEY G P Eld *MS* 8 Jan 1845

BENNET Sylvester of Freedom NH m LANG Olive of Freedom on 21 Dec at Wakefield, HOLMES J C Eld *MS* 4 Jan 1843

BENNET Winthrop m BROWN Olive both of Dover on 29 ult in Dover, HUTCHINS E Eld *MS* 9 Oct 1850

BENNETT Albert of Alton m PIKE Hannah of Wolfborough on 29 Feb 1849 in Wolfborough, PARIS C Eld *MS* 18 Apr 1849

BENNETT Amos F m LITTLEFIELD Amy at Dracut MA, CURTIS S Eld *MS* 10 Sept 1845

BENNETT David m ELLIOT Judith of Dover on 4th inst at Dover NH, MOULTON A K Eld *MS* 14 Sept 1842

BENNETT Henry m INGRAM Kaltha of Putnam, Livingston Co Mich on 4 Jul, BUTTS Orry Eld *MS* 18 Sept 1839

BENNETT Henry m LULL Malinda L both of Manchester on 5 Dec in Manchester, CILLEY D P Eld *MS* 29 Dec 1847

BENNETT James M of Moultonboro NH m COOK Susan of Dover on 11 Nov in Sandwich, TASKER L B Eld *MS* 15 Jan 1851

BENNETT Joseph m SHAW Cyntha in Guilford, KNOWLES J D Eld *MS* 2 Jul 1834

BENNETT Joshua of Peacham VT m CARR Jennett of Manchester in Manchester, DAVIS J B Eld *MS* 26 Mar 1851

BENNETT Luther m VARNEY Samson on 22 Dec 1844 at Alton NH, PINKHAM J Eld *MS* 12 Feb 1845

BENNETT William I at Freedom m MOULTON Caroline M, GASKILL S Eld *MS* 21 Jan 1846

BENNETT William L of Bristol m DOLLOFF Laurett Jane of Meredith on 11 Nov 1847, PITMAN S J Eld *MS* 22 Dec 1847

BENSON Benjamin m LIBBY Ann M both of Gray ME on 5 Sept 1847 in Gray ME, LANCASTER David Eld *MS* 26 Jan 1848

BENSON Cyrus Ervin of Parsonsfield m COLE Amanda M on 29 Oct 1848 in S Parsonsfield ME, SMITH Wm Eld *MS* 8 Nov 1848

BENSON Elias P m LANDER Lucy A on 8 June in Waterville ME, BEAN G W Eld *MS* 29 Aug 1849

BENSON G D m FRENCH Susan on 22d inst at Saco NH, GRAHAM D M Rev *MFWBR* 28 Jul 1849

BENSON Geo B m CORNFORTH Elvira M both of Waterville on 14 Aug in Waterville ME, BEAN G W Eld *MS* 29 Aug 1849

BENSON George F of Bath ME m DENHAM Catharine of Bowdoin ME on 20 June 1848 in Bowdoin ME, WHITTEMORE John Esq *MS* 12 Jul 1848

BENSON Jabez C m FOSTER Zilphia of Gray ME on 14 Jan at Gray ME, REDLON A Eld *MS* 25 Feb 1846

BENSON James E of Parsonsfield ME m MOSES Martha J of Biddeford ME at Saco ME, BEAN C Eld *MS* 21 Dec 1842

BENSON James S m RICKER Sarah Ann of Buckfield ME on 7 Dec, HAYES Robert Eld *MS* 7 Jan 1846

BENSON Luther M m MITCHELL Sarah C both of Monroe on 14 Oct in Monroe ME, HAGGETT S M Eld *MS* 27 Nov 1850

BENTLEY James m MANWARREN Palmyra both of Sand Lake on morning of 6 ult, in Stephentown Renssalaer Co New York, COLEMAN J B Eld *MS* 17 Oct 1838

BENTON Albion P on 7 June m WADSWORTH Sarah S of Hiram, MANSON B S Eld *MS* 7 Feb 1844

BENTON Almon of Spencer NY m LEWIS Betsy F of Pharsalia NY on 20 ult in Pharsalia Chenango Co NY, CRANDALL J M Eld *MS* 9 Feb 1848

BERGIN Jasper m MARVIN Mariah both of Oneonta, WING A Eld *MS* 1 Dec 1847

BERMIS John m THOMPSON Arsina both of Dracut on 9 inst in even in Lowell, THURSTON N Eld *MS* 20 June 1838

BERRY Alexander S of Strafford m JENNESS Belinda of Rochester, PLACE E Eld *MS* 3 June 1835

BERRY Benjamin Jr of Strafford m HANSCOM Nancy of Somersworth NH on 25 May, PLACE E Eld *MS* 7 June 1843

BERRY Benjamin T of Strafford m FELKER Martha J of Barrington 15 Oct 1848 in Barrington, PLACE E Eld *MS* 15 Nov 1848

BERRY Daniel F m BERRY Judith, PLACE Eld in Strafford *MS* 9 Sept 1835

BERRY David m BROCK Betsey, PLACE Eld at Strafford *MS* 27 Jan 1836

BERRY Edward Jr m BOOKER Laura A of Lisbon ME on 11th inst, Little River village, Lincoln Co ME ELLIOTT J E Rev *MFWBR* 25 Jan 1851

BERRY Elvin of Strafford m last Thurs RICKER Balancha B of Dover, THURSTON N Eld *MS* 18 June 1834

BERRY Erastus A of Limington m MOORE Mary Jane of Parsonsfield ME on 2 Dec 1847 in Parsonsfield ME, JORDAN Z Eld *MS* 12 Jan 1848

BERRY Freeman of Barnstead m BERRY Judith of Sheffield VT on 1 Oct 1848 in Barnstead, GARLAND David Eld *MS* 15 Nov 1848

BERRY George Jr of Strafford m DANFORTH Mary of Somersworth on 22 Dec *MS* 11 Jan 1843

BERRY George m BUCK Melissa of Paris ME on 28 Jul 1844 at Paris

BERRY (Continued)

ME, SMITH Jacob S *MS* 25 Sept 1844

BERRY Henry C of Hartford ME m RICKER Charlotte M of Turner ME on 4 Sept, HAYES Robert Eld *MS* 7 Jan 1846

BERRY Ivory F m DEMERITT Mary Jane of Durham on 7th inst at Newmarket, HUTCHINS Elias Eld *MS* 18 Jan 1843

BERRY Ivory of Buxton m WOODMAN Mary J on 20th inst at Saco, STRICKLAND G G Rev *MFWBR* 29 Mar 1851

BERRY James m NASON Ursula both of Dover on 8 Oct in Dover, SMITH A D Eld *MS* 18 Oct 1848

BERRY James Monroe m CILLEY Arvilla Ann on 23 June at Manchester, CILLEY D P Eld *MS* 17 Jul 1844

BERRY John N m GLIDDEN Julia Ann both of Boston on 11 inst in Dover, SMITH A D Eld *MS* 14 Oct 1846

BERRY Jonathan of Sheffield m BICKINSEAL of Sutton VT on 30 Oct, HILL Mark Eld *MS* 11 Jan 1843

BERRY Joseph H m KNOWLTON Judith Ann both of Portsmouth on 22d ult, MARKS David Eld *MS* 9 JUly 1834

BERRY Jotham S of Portsmouth NH m WALLINGFORD Judith of Lebanon ME on 17 Apr, MERRILL William P Esq *MS* 21 May 1845

BERRY Levi G at Biddeford ME m NASON Phebe on 10 Mar 1844, MOULTON F Eld *MS* 3 Apr 1844

BERRY Morrill P m SMITH Urana F both of Roxbury on 7 inst, CURTIS S Eld in Roxbury *MS* 27 Mar 1850

BERRY Nahum m HURD Drusilla P both of Sheffield VT on 13 Apr 1848 in Sheffield VT, HILL M Eld *MS* 24 Jan 1849 & BERRY Nahum on 25 Apr 1848 m HURD Drusilla P both of Sheffield *MS* 28 June 1848

BERRY William M m SMITH Susan B of Boston on 27 Oct at Boston MA, GARLAND G D Eld *MS* 20 Nov 1844

BERWICK James A m DRESSER Adelaide P at Portland ME *MFWBR* 22 Feb 1851

BESSE Alexander m GOODWIN Hannah S on 22 Aug at Great Falls NH, CURTIS S Eld *MS* 9 Nov 1842

BIBBER Ezra of Portland ME m BEAMAN Mary R on 2nd inst at Portland ME, STREETER R Rev *MFWBR* 14 Aug 1847

BIBBER Joel m WILDER Wealthy J both of Portland ME, LIBBY Isaac Eld in Portland ME *MS* 24 May 1848

BICKET Barnard m MORRILL Rosanna both of Candia on 4 ult in Candia, HOLMES H Eld *MS* 17 Oct 1838

BICKFORD Abner S m STEVENS Thankful H on 3d inst at Saco, GRAHAM D M Rev *MFWBR* 9 Mar 1850

BICKFORD D Mr of Barrington m MESERVE Susan Mrs of Rochester NH at Rochester NH, HUTCHINSON S Eld *MS* 13 Jan 1847

BICKFORD Dodavah m QUINT Lydia on Sunday before last, PIPER Jonathan Esq *MS* 30 Apr 1828

BICKFORD Ebenezer m CLARK Ruth at Meredith NH *MS* 24 Aug 1836

BICKFORD George W Capt m STEWART Mary in Freedom, RUNNELS J Eld *MS* 9 Feb 1848

BICKFORD Horace P m BUSSEY Lydia A both of Newburgh ME on 18 Jan 1848, ALLEN Ebenezer Eld *MS* 15 Mar 1848

BICKFORD Ira H of Boston m BURNHAM Martha Ann of So Parsonsfield on 10 Sept in So Parsonsfield ME, WOODMAN J M Eld *MS* 7 Oct 1846

BICKFORD James of Saco ME m DAVIS Sophronia of Buxton ME on 13 inst, LIBBY Isaac Eld *MS* 29 Mar 1848

BICKFORD Jerome of Concord m WATSON Charlotte of Manchester on 22 Nov 1847 in Manchester, CILLEY D P Eld *MS* 8 Dec 1847

BICKFORD Newell J m WENTWORTH Clara R both of Great Falls NH on 26 Aug, BROODS N Eld *MS* 5 Sept 1849

BICKFORD Orin m HEATH Sally M both of Sheffield VT on 7 Sept 1848 in Sheffield VT, HILL M Eld *MS* 24 Jan 1849

BICKFORD Paul P m ALLARD Harriet B of Eaton on 1 Feb at Eaton NH, FLETCHER Jonathan Eld *MS* 11 Feb 1846

BICKFORD Robert m JENNESS Elizabeth both of Durham on 1 inst in Durham, CILLEY D P Eld *MS* 14 Nov 1838

BICKFORD Samuel of Rochester NH m FOSS Abby P of Strafford on 27 Nov at Strafford NH, PLACE E Eld (In the distribution of the "Bridal loaf" the printers were not forgotten) *MS* 3 Dec 1845

BICKFORD Stephen H m CHAMBERLAIN Miss of Dover on 24 Oct at Rochester, HUTCHINSON S Eld *MS* 25 Nov 1846

BICKFORD Thomas C of Wolfboro NH m PLUMMER Mehitabel of Wolfboro, HOLMES John C Eld *MS* 4 Sept 1844

BICKFORD Thomas m JENNESS Nancy both of Meredith, PITMAN Stephen J Eld *MS* 9 Mar 1842

BICKNELL Thomas m GATES Caroline on 11 Jan 1848 in Pierpont NY, WHITFIELD W Eld *MS* 15 Mar 1848

BIGELOW Ashbill of Worcester m RAMSDELL Charlotte of Washington on 16 Jul 1848 in Washington VT, HARTSHORN N Eld *MS* 25 Oct 1848

BIGELOW Sila of Chester m MORSE Zeruiah S of Solon on 30 Aug in Solon Ohio, BRANCH Daniel Eld *MS* 19 Sept 1849

BIGNALL James Eld formerly of Yates Quarterly Meeting m BREWER Sarah of Purma NY on 13 Sept at Purma NY, CRANE E F Eld *MS* 18 Oct 1843

BILLINS Joseph m GREEN Amanda both of Danby VT on 17 Oct in Danby VT, GREEN Orange Eld *MS* 7 Nov 1838

BINGHAM Albert Esq m in Belfast LANE Harriet F *MS* 8 Dec 1830

BINGHAM John m DANIELS Margaret M of Canaan ME on 9 Aug at Canaan ME, BUKER A J Eld *MS* 22 Oct 1845

BISBY Robert of Harmony m on 28 Oct 1849 MOSES Elvira of Well-

BISBY (Continued)

ington ME in Wellington ME, PRATT C S Eld *MS* 20 Mar 1850

BISHOP Cyrus of Nashua NH m BISBEE Celia D of Woonsocket RI on 21 inst in Woonsocket RI, TITUS C H Rev *MS* 4 Jul 1849

BISHOP George W m WEDGE Syrena on 10 June 1841 at Freedom NY, WINSOR Barnet Eld *MS* 15 Mar 1843

BISHOP Joseph W m NEWELL Lucy A on 25 Nov 1847 in Raymond, FULLONTON J Eld *MS* Dec 15 1847

BISHOP Naaman m BIDLON Mary both of Wayne, CURTIS Silas L Esq *MS* 12 Oct 1832

BISHOP Nicholas m GODDARD Marian both of New Lyme on 19 Nov 1848, HYDE Nelson Esq *MS* 3 Jan 1849

BITTEN William D of Linneus, Aroostook Co, ME m YOUNG Hannah H of Charleston ME on 17 Jul, HATHAWAY Leonard Eld *MS* 25 Sept 1839

BIXBY Levi R m MALOON Martha of Boston MA, HOLMAN J W Eld *MS* 19 Jul 1843

BIXBY Loren E Eld m LOYON Sybil of Rutland VT on 18 Jan at Pittsford VT, BIXBY N W Eld *MS* 7 Feb 1844

BIXBY Luther m STOWE Lydia of Morristown NY on 1 Jan at Morristown NY, ATWOOD M Eld *MS* 27 Mar 1844

BIXBY Newell W Eld of Waterbury Center m KNAPP Ruth of Huntington on 9 Nov at Starksboro' VT, BIXBY L E Eld *MS* 23 Nov 1842

BIXBY Urbane L m HOVEY Mary Ann both of Brookfield VT on Sunday 22 Apr at Meeting house in East Brookfield VT, HARRIS Lucius Eld *MS* 9 May 1849

BLACK John m LIBBY Sarah of Windham ME at Falmouth ME, PERKINS Seth W Eld *MS* 20 Dec 1843

BLACKMAR H Eld of Alabama NY m MORSE Louiza of Rushford NY on 13 June 1843, BELKNAP P W Eld *MS* 3 Jan 1844

BLACKSTONE William m FIELD Isabella J on 2d inst, MOULTON A K Eld *MS* 29 Nov 1843

BLAISDEL\BLAISDELL\BLASDEL

BLAISDELL C S m HANSON Hannah J on 29 June at Great Falls NH, WEBBER H Eld *MS* 18 Dec 1844

BLAISDELL Charles m SMITH Harriet of Charlestown MA at Charleston MA, JACKSON Daniel Eld *MS* 24 May 1843

BLAISDELL David 2nd of Lebanon ME m HORN Abigail of Rochester on 25th ult at Wolfboro, COLBY John T *MS* 4 Feb 1835

BLAISDELL Harvey of Strafford VT m LEWING Hannah of Lebanon NH on 31 Oct 1843, PETTENGILL J Eld *MS* 6 Mar 1844

BLAISDELL Henry Rev m THURSTON Abigail both of Eaton NH on 22 Mar 1849 in Eaton NH, MILLS James E Eld *MS* 4 Apr 1849

BLAISDELL Ira m BEAN Susan at Great Falls NH *MFWBR* 16 Oct 1847

BLAISDELL Ira m GOODWIN Mercy A, NOYES E Eld *MS* 6 Dec 1848

BLAISDELL Jacob m MANSEY Ann S at Gilford, PINKHAM John Eld *MS* 4 Oct 1843

BLAISDELL Jacob of Strafford VT m BROWN Sally, PETTENGELL John Eld *MS* 1 Feb 1843

BLAISDELL John 2d m TRAFTON Mary Ann at Fairfield ME, LEWIS D B Eld *MS* 17 Apr 1844

BLAISDELL John of Georgetown ME m MOOR Joanna on 14 Nov, SPINNEY Zina W Esq *MS* 11 Dec 1839

BLAISDELL Joseph of Dexter m MOOR Locina of Waterville ME *MS* 15 Mar 1837

BLAISDELL Joseph of Phipsburgh m MOORE Eleanor of Georgetown ME on 5 Oct at Georgetown ME, HINKLEY John Esq *MS* 2 Nov 1842

BLAISDELL Joseph of Rochester m MILLS Eliza of Lebanon on 27 Mar at Lebanon ME, BLAISDELL David Eld *MS* 13 Apr 1842

BLAISDELL Martin of Tamworth m ROBERTS Rebecca of Ossipee NH, JACKSON D Eld *MS* 20 Apr 1831

BLAISDELL Nehemiah of Jay m BERRY Louisa of Chesterville ME on 13 May at Chesterville ME, FOSTER John Eld *MS* 13 Jul 1832

BLAISDELL Nicholas C m SNELL Sally B both of Eaton on 22 Sept at Dover NH *MS* 3 Oct 1833

BLAISDELL Nicholas m FOOT Mary both of Phipsburgh ME, WHITTEN Samuel F Eld/BOYINTON John Rev in Phipsburgh "These marriages were inserted in our paper a few weeks since and said to have been solemnized by Elder Whitten, we have made correction" *MS* 25 Mar 1835 & *MS* 8 Apr 1835

BLAISDELL Samuel of Gilford m CORSON Mary of Lebanon ME 27 Sept in Lebanon ME, RICHARDS A Rev *MS* 7 Oct 1846

BLAISDELL Samuel S m SMITH Susan at Meredith NH *MS* 1 Feb 1843

BLAISDELL Thomas m DIXON Lydia of Lebanon ME on 12 Sept at Lebanon ME, COWELL D B Eld *MS* 23 Oct 1844

BLAISDELL Uriah Dea of Great Falls NH m MOORE Rebecca G of Concord in Concord ME, TURNER S Rev *MS* 3 Oct 1849

BLAKE Charles E m KNOWLTON Lucy A on 22 May at New Market NH, HUTCHINS E Eld *MS* 8 June 1842

BLAKE Francis of Brownfield ME m ROGERS Hannah of Newfield ME in Newfield, BURBANK Eld *MS* 6 Dec 1827

BLAKE Ithiel m FILES ESTER W both of Gorham on 28 ult in Gorham, DURGIN J M Eld *MS* 2 Jan 1839

BLAKE James H m MESSER Betsey both of Landaff NH on 10 May in Bath, MESSER Asa Eld *MS* 13 June 1838

BLAKE Jesse m HENRY Nancy at Roxbury MA, DAVIS J B Eld *MS* 17 Jul 1844

BLAKE Jesse m HARMON Mehitabel C both of Roxbury on 9 ult in Roxbury MA, CURTIS S Eld *MS* 5 June 1850

BLAKE John of Barnstead m BUZZELL Mary Jane Mrs of Guilford, BUZZELL H D Eld *MS* 19 Feb 1845

BLAKE Josiah of Barnstead m PERKINS Alice G of Strafford on 10 Sept 1848 in Strafford, HOLMES J C Eld *MS* 17 Jan 1849

BLAKE Mark m RILEY Martha J both of Kittery ME on 14 Nov in Kittery ME, PERKINS Seth W Eld *MS* 5 Dec 1849

BLAKE Thomas I of Ossipee m WILLIAMS Sally of Moultonboro' NH on 27 Nov 1847 in Ossipee NH, HART E H Eld *MS* 19 Apr 1848

BLAKE William m TERRY Rebecca both of Boston on 30 Jan in Boston MA, DUNN R Eld *MS* 12 Feb 1851

BLAKE William of Barrington m ROBERTS Joan of Strafford *MS* 21 Dec 1836

BLAKELY Silas S of Chelsea m BREWSTER Maris E of Brookfield on 16 June in Brookfield VT, HARRIS L T Eld *MS* 4 Jul 1849

BLANCHARD Abel m SAWYER Eliza A on 1st inst at Belgrade ME *MFWBR* 17 Mar 1849

BLANCHARD Ansel at Bowdoinham ME m GAUBERT Harriet of Richmond, QUINNAM C Eld *MS* 6 Apr 1842

BLANCHARD Levi m CHAFFEE Rhoda on 22 Mar in China NY, STEVENS S Rev *MS* 16 May 1838

BLANCHARD Thomas of Pittston m KNOX Patience of Gardiner at Gardiner, GOODRICH Barnard Eld *MS* 10 Apr 1839

BLAZO Ablert M m YOUNG Sarah A both of Middleton on 7 Jul in Middleton, BUTLER O Eld *MS* 7 Aug 1850

BLAZO Ebenezer Esq m GIBBS Elizabeth in Porter *MS* 24 June 1831

BLAZO Ebenezer of Bartlett m YOUNG Sally of Wakefield NH on 26 Dec at Ossipee NH, VARNEY M Eld *MFWBR* 13 Jan 1849

BLETHEN David of Durham (ME?) m BLETHEN Octavia on 26th Jan, BEAN C Eld *MS* 12 Feb 1845

BLETHEN Elias I m TARBOX Sirena both of Hollis ME on 25 Nov 1847 in Hollis ME, KENISTON Thomas Eld *MS* 5 Jan 1848

BLETHEN Joseph JONES Elanor on 20 Apr at Lewiston ME, KEENE J Jr Eld *MS* 7 June 1843

BLISS Albert T m BLISS Orlinda A both of Huston PA on 1 Sept in Huston PA, STILES Dutton Eld *MS* 16 Oct 1850

BLISS Clark of Norway NY m WINDOVER Almira of Ohio on 23 Dec at Middleville, SMITH O W Eld *MS* 29 Jan 1845

BLISS Orvis Z of Groton m McFARLAND Zetha, PECK Benjamin D Eld *MS* 18 Jan 1843

BLODGETT Joshua B of Newbury m ROGERS Rhoda G of Wendell on Feb 15th at New London, CROSS J Esq *MFWBR* 24 Mar 1849

BLOOD Jason G m WETHERBY Elizabeth both of Haverhill on Nov 27 in Haverhill *MS* 8 Apr 1846

BLOOD Oliver of Augusta m JONES Nancy M of Belgrade ME in Augusta, CURTIS S Eld *MS* 10 May 1837

BLOOD Stephen C m ELLISWORTH Sally S on 2 Mar at Wentworth,

BLOOD (Continued)

MESSER Asa Eld *MS* 16 Apr 1845

BLOSSOM Alden Dr of Boothbay m WILLEY Wealthy L of Bremen on 23 Oct in Edgecomb ME, PAGE E D Eld *MS* 27 Nov 1850

BLOSSOM Thomas D editor of *Hingham Gazette* m WHITON Susan A in Hingham *MS* 31 May 1837

BOCHART William m BASSART Amenda of Pierpont on 2 Mar, WHITFIELD William Eld *MS* 3 May 1843

BODGE Davis of Pittston m SHAW Mary A on 14 Nov, FAIRFIELD Smith Eld *MS* 8 Dec 1841

BODGE Isaac m PEARL Hannah both of Barrington on 12 ult, SHERBURNE S Eld *MS* 8 Apr 1835

BODGE James m MEADER Vienna of Rochester on 18th, MEADER J Eld *MS* 15 Oct 1845

BODGE Joseph of Portsmouth m BURLEIGH Sarah J in New Market*MS* 27 Mar 1834

BODGE William m MORRISON Mary on 9 Mar at Barrington, SHERBURNE S Eld *MS* 25 June 1845

BODLE William m SHEPHERD Mary at Lowell MA, THURSTON N Eld *MS* 18 Feb 1835

BODWELL Asa Esq m HILTON Tempy in Acton ME *MS* 21 Apr 1830

BODWELL Elisha A of Saco ME m ROBINSON Grace E of Sandwich on 14 Nov in Sandwich, TASKER L B Eld *MS* 26 Dec 1849

BOLO Rufus m YOUNG Susan at Milton, JONES Joseph Esq of Farmington *MS* 13 Feb 1834

BOLTER Amaziah H m BOOTHBY Lydia W at Unity ME, LEWIS Daniel B Eld *MS* 25 Nov 1846

BOLTON Thomas of Portland m TUTTLE Nancy M of Boston MA on 31st ult *MFWBR* 13 Jan 1849

BOND Seth of Ellenburgh NY m SHAW Ruth of Beckmantown Clinton Co NY on 10 inst in Ellenbourgh NY, PARKS R Eld *MS* 27 Mar 1850

BOODY Israel m FRY Mary Miss both of Limington ME on Thurs last in Limington, STROUT Simeon Esq *MS* 7 Dec 1826

BOODY John W m CHENEY Harriet of Lawrence on 4 Feb 1849, DAVIS J E Eld *MS* 7 Mar 1849

BOON William m STAPLES Sarah S on 22 Oct at the house of Col E STAPLES in Poolville NY, CARLNER S D Eld *MS* 11 Nov 1846

BOOTH Stephen D of Remson m TERRY Harriet of Newport NY on Oct 28, McKOON D W Eld *MS* 19 Jan 1842

BOOTHBY Alexander of Unity m GRAND Eliza D of Bridgton on 9 Apr 1849 in Unity, WATERMAN D Eld *MS* 25 Apr 1849

BOOTHBY Arthur m SCAMMON Rachel C on 11th inst at Saco ME, DWIGHT Rev *MFWBR* 24 Mar 1849

BOOTHBY Arthur 2d of Limington ME m PLUMMER Abigail of Portland ME on 11th inst at Portland ME, MOULTON A K Eld

BOOTHBY (Continued)
MS 20 Mar 1844

BOOTHBY Enoch of Buxton m JOHNSON Harriet of Gorham in Gorham, WHITE Eld MS 7 Feb 1828

BOOTHBY Leador/ Leander m WALKER Mary Ann of Limington ME on 5 May MFWBR 1 June 1850 & MS 29 May 1850

BOOTHBY William M of Saco ME m LIBBY Susan F of Scarboro' ME, on 13th inst at Scarboro' FAYBAN John D Esq MFWBR 22 Dec 1849

BORDMAN Joseph merchant m SMITH Sarah Ann at Exeter MS 26 Dec 1833

BOSS Charles Esq of Ashford NY m ROBBINS Betsey Mrs of Collins Eric Co on 29 Oct 1843, TAYNTOR O Eld MS 14 Feb 1844

BOSS Henry D of Scituate RI m SMITH John of Gloucester RI, BRADBURY Abby F Eld MS 18 Dec 1844

BOSS Horace of Ashford m RATHBON Eliza of Collins on 16 Jan, TAYNTOR O Eld MS 14 Feb 1844

BOSTON John m BROWN Elsoy on 27 ult in Raymond, PARKER L Eld MS 10 Oct 1849

BOSWELL William W of Newton NH m PARISH Mary J of Lowell on 27 Nov in Lowell, CURTIS S Eld MS 15 Dec 1847

BOSWORTH Isaac of Dedham MA m HASTY Susan of Limington ME on 30 Sept in Limington, STEVENS T Eld MS 21 Oct 1846

BOUKER Simeon of Exeter ME m BAKER Mary E of Attleborough MA on 1 Sept 1848 in Attleborough MA, CLARKE Gardner Eld MS 13 Sept 1848

BOWDITCH G Mr of Portland ME m LIBBY Olive of Limerick ME on 10th inst at Limerick, TRIPP L S Eld MFWBR 16 Sept 1848

BOWDMAN Abijah of Topsham ME m GOWELL Mary B of Bowdoin ME, FOLSOM P Eld MS 10 Feb 1847

BOWEN Allen m BOWEN Elizabeth S both of Rehoboth on 8 Nov 1847 in Attleborough MA, CLARKE G Eld MS 8 Dec 1847

BOWEN John m WEBBER Roxana of Holderness on 30 Oct at Holderness, WEBBER H Eld MS 17 Dec 1845

BOWERS Darius Bowers of Dracut MA m REED Ester V of Lowell MA on 20 Oct at Lowell MA, THURSTON N Eld MS 2 Nov 1842

BOWERS Frederick m CHELDON Clarinda both of Hamburg on 7 Oct in Hamburg NY, PLUMB H N Eld MS 20 Dec 1837

BOWERS James W of Whitestown m JONES Eliza A S Mrs of Sweden ME on 24 Oct 1847 in Whitestown NY, SMART M M Eld MS 1 Dec 1847

BOWLES Chandler of Lisbon m COGGSWELL Hannah S of Landaff NH on 19th ult, COGGSWELL G W Esq MS 18 May 1832

BOWLES David m DEXTER Mary Jane on 22 Dec, GASKILL Silas Eld MS 19 Apr 1843

BOWLES James of Dalton m BOWLES Louisa of Bethlehem on

BOWLES (Continued)

26 Dec 1849 in Bethlehem, BLAKE C E Eld *MS* 10 Apr 1850

BOWLES Levi m WALLACE Vienna on 23 Mar at Franconia, BLAKE C E Eld *MS* 28 Apr 1847

BOWMAN David 3d of Sidney ME m COTTLE Rhoda of Waterville ME, LEWIS Daniel B Eld *MS* 30 Nov 1842

BOWMAN Oren of Sidney m WILLIAMS Mary of Readfield ME, LEWIS Daniel B Eld *MS* 21 Jan 1846

BOYD James W m WITCRAFT Elizabeth H on 9 Feb 1850 in Peru Township Logan Co Ohio, HEATH J D Eld *MS* 27 Mar 1850

BOYD William m ROBINSON Sarah C on 27 Nov at Manchester, BROOKS John Eld *MS* 24 Dec 1845

BOYINGTON Royal m KNOWLES Joan C at Thornton, RUSSELL G W Eld *MS* 25 Mar 1840

BOYNTON Charles R m THOMPSON Lucy H both of Centre Harbor on 18 Dec 1849, PITMAN Stephen J Eld *MS* 18 Apr 1849

BOYNTON Colburn B of New Hampton m PERKINS Mary D of Centre Harbor on 1 Nov 1843, PITMAN S J Eld *MS* 15 Nov 1843

BOYNTON Jacob m STANLEY Mehitabel both of Brownfield ME on 8 Oct 1848 in Brownfield ME, HART E H Eld *MS* 15 Nov 1848

BOYNTON John m KNOWLES Maurice D of Thornton in Thornton *MS* 14 Mar 1838

BOYNTON John m SMITH Almira of Lowell MA on 8 Mar, WOODMAN J Eld *MS* 23 Aug 1843

BOYNTON Sylvester of Cornishville ME m NEVENS Sarah Jane of Sweden on 15 Dec, PIKE John Eld *MS* 22 Jan 1851

BOYNTON Waterman M m CHANDLER Rebecca both of Mercer ME on 30 ult, FULLER Rev *MS* 26 Nov 1834

BRACE Asahel of Winfield m YOUNG Eusebia N of Columbia on 16 Jan *MS* 24 May 1843

BRACE Lucius F of Winfield m YOUNG Margaret J of Columbia on 18 June at Poland Herkimer Co NY, McKOON D W Eld *MS* 2 Jul 1845

BRACKETT Amos m TEBBETTS Hannah B on 4th inst at Biddeford ME, BLAKE H M Rev *MFWBR* 11 May 1850

BRACKETT Benjamin m TUFTS Susan of New Gloucester ME on 1st inst at New Gloucester, TOBIE Ezra Esq *MFWBR* 4 Aug 1849

BRACKETT Daniel G m TUTTLE Roxanna of Lowell on Apr 1, THURSTON Nathaniel Eld *MS* 10 Apr 1839

BRACKETT Daniel of Limerick ME m LIBBY Mary of Limerick ME in Houlton ME *MS* 11 June 1828

BRACKETT David m FRANCIS Elizabeth of Durham on 8th Nov at New Market, FROST D S Eld *MS* 18 Nov 1846

BRACKETT Isaac m WEEKS Almira W of Parsonsfield ME on 17 May at Parsonsfield ME, MANSON B S Eld *MS* 7 Feb 1844

BRACKETT Jacob of Acton m SWASEY Abby P of Milton NH on 8 Oct

34

BRACKETT (Continued)

at Sanford ME, STEVENS T Eld *MS* 23 Oct 1844

BRACKETT John m GOURD Hannah M both of Colebrook NH on 17 Jan 1849, BEAN Benaiah Eld *MS* 7 Feb 1849

BRACKETT John of Milton m PITMAN Mary A of Great Falls NH on 22 Oct *MS* 4 Nov 1835

BRACKETT John of New Market NH m HARMON Martha E of Buxton ME on 1 Sept at Buxton ME, LIBBY C O Eld *MS* 16 Oct 1844

BRACKETT Joshua m GOODWIN Sarah A on 1 Apr at Kennebunkport ME, WITHAM L H Eld *MS* 23 Apr 1845

BRACKETT Lorenzo m STEVENS Elcy J of South Berwick ME on 17th inst at FWB meeting house at South Berwick ME, TRUE Ezekiel Eld *MS* 27 Jan 1847

BRACKETT Moses R of Cornish ME m WEEKS Mercy Ann of Parsonsfield ME on Jan 19, BUZZELL Alvah Eld *MS* 19 Feb 1840

BRACKETT Nathaniel m FOSS Pamelia on Jul 24, MANSON B S Eld *MS* 15 Jan 1840

BRACKETT Reuben G m LEIGHTON Orrilla on 24 Mar at Westbrook ME, HERSEY L Eld *MS* 1 June 1842

BRACKETT Rufus W Capt m HUSSEY Meriam L both of Acton ME on 28 Dec in Acton, STEVENS Enoch Eld *MS* 10 Jan 1838

BRACKETT Seth H of Portland ME m LIBBY Elizabeth A L on 7th inst, MOULTON A K Eld *MS* 20 Dec 1843

BRACKETT Timothy m DAVIS Sally W both of Limington ME on 20 Nov, MANSON B S Eld *MS* 15 Jan 1840

BRACKETT William H m CORSON Frances D at Bangor ME, CAVERNO A Eld *MS* 13 Sept 1843

BRADBURY Ammi R of Auburn ME m JOHNSON Caroline L on 20 Feb 1844 at Farmington, JOHNSON Timothy Eld *MS* 13 Mar 1844

BRADBURY Darius of Wentworth m HOBBS Emily on 1 Feb, MESSER Asa Eld *MS* 21 Feb 1844

BRADBURY Ebenezer H C of Biddeford m WAKEFIELD Mary J of Lyman on 9 Jan 1848 in Biddeford, WITHAM L H Eld *MS* 8 Mar 1848

BRADBURY Sam W Dr of Limington ME m BRACKETT Elizabeth of Parsonsfield ME on Christmas eve at Limington ME, TRIPP L S Rev *MFWBR* 15 Jan 1848

BRADEEN John P m PUGSLY Mary A both of Cornish on 8 Dec 1850 in Cornish ME, RAND J Eld *MS* 26 Feb 1851

BRADEEN Oliver of Waterborough ME m BOOTHBY Susanna of Limerick on 14 Sept 1848 in Limerick ME, RAND James Eld *MS* 29 Nov 1848

BRADEEN Samuel m STROUT Mary Mrs both of Standish ME on 430 Dec 1847, BAILEY J M Eld *MS* 12 Jan 1848

BRADFORD Charles G m PRENTISS Mary V both of St Albans on 15 Oct 1850 in St Albans ME, PERRY S Eld *MS* 22 Jan 1851

BRADLEY Alpheus m LONGFELLOW Mary Jane of Lowell, THUR-
STON N Eld *MS* 15 May 1839

BRADLEY Isaac of Haverhill MA m COURIER Caroline on Thanksgiving Eve in Danville, FULLONTON J Eld *MS* 12 Dec 1838

BRADLEY Nathaniel m VARNEY Achsah Mrs both of Alton NH on 16
Nov 1848, BROOKS N Eld *MS* 29 Nov 1848

BRADLEY William of Bedford MA m MORSE Sarah Ann of Sandwich
NH on 15 Apr 1849 in Sandwich, TASKER L B Eld *MS* 2 May
1849

BRAGDEN Edwin m FRENCH Susan P both of Corinth ME on 31
Aug 1848 in Corinth ME, HARDING E Eld *MS* 21 Feb 1849

BRAGDON Charles m ADAMS Rosamond P on 17th inst at Rochester, HUTCHINSON S Eld *MS* 30 Dec 1846

BRAGDON Eben W Capt m FRISBEE Betsey D in Gouldsborough
ME, HERVEY Hiram Esq *MS* 5 Feb 1840

BRAGDON Enoch m HUFF Hannah E of Kennebunk ME on 15 Jul
at Kennebunk, CRESSEY Rev *MFWBR* 28 Jul 1849

BRAGDON Gardner m BRAGDON Dorothy Ann at Bangor ME,
CAVERNO A Eld *MS* 13 Sept 1843

BRAGDON Issachar m BLACK Louisa, MANSON B S Eld *MS* 7 Feb
1844

BRAGDON Owen m SMITH Lydia both of Kennebunk ME on 21 Nov
in Kennebunk ME, BELKNAP P W Eld *MS* 29 Dec 1847

BRAGDON Samuel of Milton m CLEMENTS Lydia of Somersworth
NH *MS* 19 Dec 1833

BRAGDON Samuel of Windham m LATHAM Harriet of Gray ME on
16 Oct, WHITNEY G W Eld *MS* 10 May 1843

BRAGDON Seth P m WHITNEY Celinda both of Augusta in Augusta
ME, CURTIS Silas Eld *MS* 14 Mar 1838

BRAGDON Silas of Wells ME m HATCH Lucinda H of North Berwick
ME on 22 Jan, LORD D H Eld *MS* 3 May 1843 & *MS* 15 Feb 1843

BRAGDON Simon m WIMAN Rachel both of Freeport on 19 May in
Freeport ME, PURINTON A W Eld *MS* 13 Nov 1850

BRAGDON William of Kennebunk ME m WINN Emily of Wells ME on
28th ult at Charlestown, WETHERBEE I J Eld *MS* 9 Dec 1846

BRAGG Miles of Danby VT m ROW Mary of Woodstock VT on 2 Oct
in Danby VT, GREEN Orange *MS* 7 Nov 1838

BRAGG Milton B m MESSINGER Vesta A G at Bangor ME on 27th
ult *MFWBR* 9 Mar 1850

BRAGG Trustrum m TAYLOR Emily F both of Manchester on 5 Feb
1849 in Manchester, CILLEY D P Eld *MS* 14 Feb 1849

BRAIN Geo M m BICKFORD Malissa A both of Waterbury VT on 6
Dec in Waterbury VT, GRAY I Eld *MS* 23 Jan 1850

BRAINARD David W m CROOKS Hester Ann both of Barnston LC on
27 Nov 1836 *MS* 11 Jan 1837

BRAINARD John C of Bath ME m WEBBER Sarah Elizabeth of

BRAINARD (Continued)
Salem at Salem *MFWBR* 12 Oct 1850

BRAN Charles m DUNTON Phebe Ann both of Jefferson in Jefferson ME, STINSON R Eld *MS* 27 Apr 1842

BRAND Levi T m WAKEFIELD Martha Ann of Gardiner on 22nd ult, PERKINS Seth W Eld *MS* 16 Oct 1839

BRANSCOMB Charles Jr Capt m NORTON Elizabeth G both of Mt Desert on 14 Oct in Mt Desert, BROWN John Eld *MS* 2 Jan 1850

BREARD Nicholas of Sturbridge m 25 May EVANS Clarissa C of Barrington NH in Boston MA, BEECHER Edward Rev *MS* 17 June 1846

BREED Roger J of Woburn m SIMMONS Matilda J of Wilmington MA on 14th inst, DURGIN J M Eld *MS* 24 Jul 1844

BREWER Emery m MORSE Sarah C both of Freeport ME on 28 Dec 1847 in Brunswick ME, PAGE E G Eld *MS* 9 Feb 1848

BREWER Nathaniel m BABB Sarah Jane on 16th Mar at Strafford, PLACE E Eld *MS* 16 Apr 1845

BREWSTER Charles W H m CHAMBERLAIN Lydia A both of Portsmouth on 17 Jan 1850, BROOKS N Eld *MS* 30 Jan 1850

BRIAR Robert of Dutton m PENDEXTER Olive of Cornish on 2d inst, WEEKS James W *MS* 10 Feb 1832

BRIDGE Samuel H m SANBORN Julia A on 12 Dec in Litchfield ME, QUINNAM C Eld *MS* 8 Jan 1845

BRIDGES Robert J of Topsham m SNOW Priscilla Miss of Brunswick ME on 30th ult, BRIDGES A Eld *MS* 13 June 1833

BRIDGHAM Luther of Lowell MA m HADLEY Oliva L of Bethlehem on 12 Nov, BEAN Beniah Eld *MS* 4 Feb 1846

BRIER John m WORMWOOD Abigail at Cornish, HULL Alfred Esq *MS* 20 June 1833

BRIER Moses W Capt m TASKER Ann Eliza both of Monroe on 22 Feb 1848, ALLEN Ebenezer Eld *MS* 15 Mar 1848

BRIERLY Rev Mr of Dover NH m HARVELL Mary J of Amherst on 4th ult, CARPENTER Rev of Milford *MS* 9 Mar 1836

BRIGG William m WESTCOT Lucinda of Gorham ME on 5 June at Gorham ME, LIBBY C O Eld *MS* 17 Sept 1845

BRIGGS Ezra m FULLER Orpha of Brookfield on 18 April at West Brookfield, CLAFLIN Jehiel Eld *MS* 15 May 1839

BRIGGS George U of Windsor m McKINNEY Emeline of Wiscasset ME on 29 ult in Woolwich ME, PERKINS Seth W Eld *MS* 20 June 1838

BRIGGS Hiram D of Kittery ME m CANNEY Jane B of Farmington NH on 21 Dec at Rochester NH, MEADER Jesse Eld *MS* 30 Dec 1846

BRIGGS Phillip A of Auburn m HERRICK Hannah of Lewiston Falls ME on 28 Oct 1847 in Lewiston Falls ME, BEAN G W Eld *MS* 3 Nov 1847

BRIGGS Sumner m HADLEY Sophia both of Lowell MA on 1 June 1848 in Lowell MA, CURTIS S Eld *MS* 28 June 1848

BRIGGS William C m ANDREWS Lucinda of Corinna ME on 14 Apr 1839, COPP J B Eld *MS* 29 May 1839

BRIGHAM Albert m HARADON Harriet M on 19 Jul at Manchester, CILLEY D P Eld *MS* 23 Jul 1845

BRIMEJOHN Job m GROVER Margaret both of Richmond, SWETT Jesse Eld *MS* 27 Jan 1836

BRIRY James G m PARKS Margaret F of Richmond ME on 8 June at Richmond ME, QUINNAM C Eld *MS* 9 Jul 1845

BRITTON Mowry L m HALL Sarah D both of No Providence RI on 21st ult in RI, HUTCHINS Elias Eld *MS* 15 Jul 1835

BROADWAY Christopher m McGILL Susan both of Stephentown NY on 12 Nov in Stephentown, COLEMAN J B Eld *MS* 24 Apr 1844

BROCK James M m ROBERTS Elizabeth L of Acton ME at Dover NH *MS* 17 Apr 1839

BROCK James of Lowell MA m LEAVITT Elizabeth Jane of Gilford on 5 Feb in Alton, PINKHAM J Eld *MS* 8 Apr 1846

BROCKWAY John S m LANPHIER Rachel C of Stephenton NY on 11st ult at Stephenton NY, COLEMAN I B Eld *MS* 10 Aug 1842

BROOKINGS Samuel m McMURPHY Catharine on 31 Jul at Woolwich ME, FAIRFIELD S Eld *MS* 24 Aug 1842

BROOKS Archibald m COONS Rhoda on 8 Feb in York Union Co Ohio, HEATH J D Eld *MS* 22 May 1844

BROOKS Edward of Freedom m PATCH Sabrina D of Eaton on 28th ult at Eaton NH, ATKINSON King Eld *MFWBR* 16 Mar 1850

BROOKS Horatio G of Dunkirk NH m HAGGET Julia A of Edgecomb ME on 6 Mar in Edgecomb ME, PAGE E G Eld *MS* 2 Apr 1851

BROOKS James W of Boston m SWAIN Olive N of Chichester on 15 Nov in Chichester NH, SWAIN Wm Eld *MS* 5 Dec 1849

BROOKS John Eld of Wakefield NH m HARPER Sarah A on 24 Nov 1841 at Limerick ME, CHASE William P Eld *MS* 1 Dec 1841

BROOKS Joshua m SMITH Mary D on 9 Dec at Wakefield, BROOKS John Eld *MS* 24 Dec 1845

BROOKS Lebbeus m FREEMAN Olive Ann both of Great Falls NH on 28 Jul at Great Falls Freewill Bapt Meeting House, BROOKS N Eld *MS* 7 Aug 1850

BROOKS N Eld of Meredith Bridge m HARMON Rebecca L of Eaton, PINKHAM J Eld in Gilford *MS* 26 Sept 1838

BROOKS Nahum of Concord m WALTSON Emelin M of Great Falls NH at Great Falls *MS* 17 Feb 1836

BROOKS Robert G m REA Frances both of Perry Township Ohio on 2 Sept 1847 in Perry Township Logan Co Ohio, HEATH J D Eld *MS* 9 Feb 1848

BROOKS William E Jr m WALKER Emeline on 9 Jul at Naples, HUNTRESS D Eld *MS* 19 Jul 1843

BROOKS William W of Elliot ME m ALLARD Abigail F of Portsmouth NH on 31 Dec at Portsmouth NH, DAVIS Isaac G Eld *MS* 10 Jan 1844

BROWN Albert W of Newport m FELCH Hannah D of Newbury on 23 Sept in Newbury, EMERY A Eld *MS* 6 Oct 1847

BROWN Alfred B m YOUNG Sarah S of Deerfield on 16th ult, FERNALD S P Eld *MS* 3 Jul 1839

BROWN Ambrose m BURLEY Grace F on 23 Aug at Dover, PERKINS J Rev *MS* 2 Sept 1835

BROWN Amos Eld m COLLINS Lovell of Newbury NH at Wendell, DODGE William Eld *MS* 17 Feb 1847

BROWN Andrew J Exeter m DUDLEY Mary S of Brentwood on 26 Oct in Amesbury MA *MS* 13 Nov 1850

BROWN Arthur m at Foxcroft PACKARD Hannah *MS* 5 Dec 1833

BROWN Asa of Strafford VT m FLANDERS Lydia, PETTENGELL John Eld *MS* 1 Feb 1843

BROWN Asa of Sharon VT m WIGGIN Harriet W on 22 Feb at Moultonborough NH, BROOKS N Eld *MS* 12 Mar 1845

BROWN Benjamin D of N Hartford m WHITTAKER Eliza of Marcellus on 18 Feb at Whitestown Seminary, JORDAN Z Eld *MS* 12 Mar 1845

BROWN Benjamin F m STEVENS Martha on 6 Dec at Monhegan PLT ME, STARLING Joseph Esq *MS* 30 Dec 1846

BROWN Benjamin m NORTON Mary in Mt Desert ME, NORTON Lemuel Eld *MS* 9 Dec 1831

BROWN Benjamin of Tuftonborough m DOW Nancy A of Wolfborough on 2 inst in Dover, HUTCHINS E Eld *MS* 8 Apr 1846

BROWN Benjamin m ELLSWORTH Lydia S on 2 Mar 1847 at Wentworth NH, MEASER Asa Eld *MS* 14 Apr 1847

BROWN Bradbury D m BOWMAN Marilla D of Lowell MA on 20 Dec of Lowell MA, CURTIS S Eld *MS* 6 Jan 1847

BROWN Bradbury T m PHILBROOK Harriet R on 10 Feb at Sanbornton NH, MASON L Eld *MS* 11 Mar 1846

BROWN Caleb m TIBBETS Eliza Jane of Dover NH on 13 Nov at Dover NH, BROCK H H Eld *MS* 12 Nov 1845

BROWN Carlton m NUTTING Aura of Canton NY on 3d May at Canton NY, WHITFIELD W Eld *MS* 26 May 1847

BROWN Daniel B of Steubenville Ohio m PERKINS Catherine of Great Falls NH, CAVERNO A Eld *MS* 6 May 1835

BROWN Daniel m HANCOCK Juritia both of Freedom NY on 20 Feb 1848 in Freedom NY, FLYNN W H Eld *MS* 10 May 1848

BROWN Daniel m DUNNING Alice J C both of Roxbury MA in Roxbury MA, DAVIS J B Eld *MS* 13 May 1846

BROWN David Jr of No Hampton m LEAVITT Frances M of Hampton on 19 ult in Hampton, CILLEY D P Eld *MS* 3 Jan 1838

BROWN E K m DORE Sarah Jane both of Ossipee NH on 3 Jul at

BROWN (Continued)

Great Falls, BROOKS N Eld *MS* 11 Jul 1849

BROWN Eben H of North Kingston m SMART Clarissa A of Providence on 26 Apr in Providence RI, SCOTT E Eld *MS* 5 May 1846

BROWN Edward m PERKINS Mehitabel B of Hebron on 27 Nov at Holderness, SMITH Horace H Esq *MS* 13 Dec 1843

BROWN Elisha of Cornish ME m IRISH Mary S of Cornish ME on 15 May, HACKETT John O Eld *MS* 8 June 1842

BROWN Ezra m DODGE Nancy of Edgecomb ME on 10 Nov, PAGE E G Eld *MS* 7 Dec 1842

BROWN Franklin G m DIMOND Julia Ann both of Hopkinton on 19 May *MS* 22 June 1836

BROWN Gardner H of Lowell MA m TILTON Betsey T of New Hampton on 30 Oct, FISK E Eld *MS* 31 Jan 1844

BROWN George W m RANDALL Lucretia H both of Dover on 22 Jul in Farmington, PLACE E Eld *MS* 8 Aug 1849

BROWN Horace T of Parsonsfield ME m BABB Margaret A of Saccarrappa *MFWBR* 18 Jan 1851

BROWN Hartshorn R m BRADBURY Meroe [*sic*] A of Chesterville on 28 Jul 1844 at Chesterville, WHEELER Samuel Eld *MS* 14 Aug 1844

BROWN Henry of Boston m WIGGIN Martha of Portsmouth NY *MS* 7 Sept 1836

BROWN Henry of Moultonborough NH m MORRILL Patience of Gilford NH on 3 June 1849, FROST D S Eld in Gilford NH *MS* 9 Jan 1850

BROWN Herbert H m ROWE Tacy S [*sic*] both of South Adams MA on 9 Sept 1848 in Nassau, COLEMAN I B Eld *MS* 11 Oct 1848

BROWN Ira Jr m GARLAND Hannah both of Rye on 27th ult at Lamprey River, CILLEY D P Eld *MS* 5 Nov 1834

BROWN Isaac B m DAME Sophronia of Durham at New Market NH, HUTCHINS E Eld *MS* 8 June 1842

BROWN Isaac m WILLIAMS Sarah Ann both of Atkinson on 10th inst, HATHAWAY L Eld *MS* 18 May 1832

BROWN Isaac of Poplin m BEAN Mary Mrs of Danville on 28 Sept at Danville, GARLAND G D Eld *MS* 1 Nov 1843

BROWN Isreal G of Henniker m HUNKINS Lucy M of Groton NH on 14th inst, CILLEY James C Esq *MS* 28 Aug 1844

BROWN Ivory of Parsonsfield ME m HART Jane of Eaton NH on 6 Feb, KNOWLES Samuel Eld *MS* 11 May 1842

BROWN Jacob of Clinton m BROOKS Elizabeth on 24th ult in Thorndike, WARREN Charles Eld *MS* 12 June 1829

BROWN Jacob m JORDAN Sophronia on 17 Apr 1842 at Camden, ROBINSON N J Eld *MS* 15 June 1842

BROWN James H of Bristol NH m MUDGETT Mary M S of Bristol NH, BROWN A Eld *MS* 21 & 28 Feb 1844

BROWN Jefferson of Litchfield m ROBINSON Mary of Richmond at
Richmond ME *MS* 25 May 1836

BROWN Jeremiah of Hampton NH m LANE Martha Ann on 25 Feb,
BURBANK P S Eld *MS* 5 Feb 1845

BROWN John C m QUIMBY Philinda at Strafford VT, SWETT David
Eld *MS* 27 Feb 1839

BROWN John E m BOND Henrietta E both of Haverhill MA on 14
Nov 1847 in Haverhill MA, MERRIL Wm P Eld *MS* 8 Dec 1847

BROWN John H of Manchester m MAXFIELD Orissa of Goshen on 5
Feb in Manchester, CILLEY D P Eld *MS* 20 Feb 1850

BROWN John Jr of Cornish ME m BROWN Hannah C of Parsonsfield
ME on 26 Aug, HACKETT J O Eld *MS* 31 Mar 1847

BROWN John m SHIPP S Mrs both of Fowler NY on 18 Mar 1849,
JENKINS C Eld *MS* 4 Apr 1849

BROWN John of Clayton NY m GIDDINGS Rhoda of Weare on Sept
17, MOODY David Eld *MS* 12 Feb 1840

BROWN John of Loudon m NUTTER Sarah O of Farmington at
Rochester, MEADER Jesse Eld *MS* 24 Mar 1847

BROWN John of Westbrook ME m LIBBY Mary F of Gorham ME on
20 Nov 1848 in Gorham ME, HARRIMAN D P Eld *MS* 6 Dec 1848

BROWN Jonathan O m WALKER Susannah both of Tuftonborough
NH in Ossipee NH, WALKER John Eld *MS* 5 Apr 1837

BROWN Jonathan of Raymond m LADD Martha Mrs at Deerfield *MS*
30 June 1847

BROWN Joseph F m GOLDSMITH Melissa J on 1 Jan 1843 at
Ossipee NH, WALKER John Eld *MS* 31 May 1843

BROWN Joseph m EDWARDS Juliette both of West Poland in West
Poland ME, LIBBY James Eld *MS* 3 June 1846

BROWN Joseph of Sanbornton m McINTIRE Eliza Jane of Tuftonborough NH on 14 Feb 1849 in Tuftonborogh NH, BEAN Silas F
MS 9 May 1849

BROWN Joseph P m TAYLOR Rebecca C both of Deerfield on 24 Oct,
BURBANK P S Eld *MS* 14 Nov 1849

BROWN Josiah m GORDON Hannah of Candia at Deerfield, KIM-
BALL Eld *MS* 10 Sept 1834

BROWN Josiah m MUDGET Susan C on 14 Nov at Bristol, FISK E
Eld *MS* 31 Jan 1844

BROWN Levi Capt at Raymond m CRAM Abigail *MS* 28 Sept 1842

BROWN Lewis m ROLLINS Ann both of Concord on 29 Dec 1849 in
Concord NH, SMITH A D Eld *MS* 9 Jan 1850

BROWN Lorenzo m ROBINSON Sarah Abby of Portsmouth NH on
28th ult at Charlestown, WETHERBEE I J Eld *MS* 9 Dec 1846

BROWN Mark m NASH Elizabeth M on 12 Feb at Raymond ME,
KEENE J Eld *MS* 26 Mar 1845

BROWN Moody m RANKINS Lucy of Cornish ME on 10 Jul, HACK-
ETT John O Eld *MS* 9 Aug 1843

BROWN Moses F at Lowell m WHEELER Sophia, CURTIS S Eld *MS* 10 Sept 1845

BROWN Nathan m STEVENS Comfort both of Great Falls village NH on 12 inst *MS* 18 Mar 1835

BROWN Nathan m WEBSTER Elvira both of Albany on 18 Mar 1850 in Tamworth, NICKERSON Jona. Esq *MS* 3 Apr 1850

BROWN Nathaniel of Candia m PIPER Mary Ann of Manchester on 9 Dec 1848 in Manchester, CILLEY D P Eld *MS* 27 Dec 1848

BROWN Noah B of Sanbornton m SANBORN Jane of New Hampton on 7 June 1849, FISK E Eld *MS* 4 Jul 1849

BROWN Noah W of Sanbornton m ROBINSON Angeline of Meredith on 12 Aug in Meredith, MASON Lemuel Eld *MS* 30 Sept 1846

BROWN O S Eld m MARSH Julia on 11 Oct at Unadilla Forks NY, SPAULDING Joel Eld at Plainfield *MS* 8 Jan 1845

BROWN Obed of Porter divorced BROWN Abigail W *MS* 24 Feb 1832

BROWN Oliver Jr m TEBBETS Octavia both of Topsham on 7 Sept in Topsham ME, MERRILL Octavius A Esq *MS* 18 Sept 1850

BROWN Orren m PERKINS Mary Jane both of Manchester on 12 instin Manchester, CILLEY D P Eld *MS* 29 Apr 1846

BROWN Philo m COURTENAY Artemisea M at Milan Iowa, HA-THORN S Eld *MS* 5 June 1844

BROWN Reuben Jr m PHILBRICK Catharine both of Freedom on 10 Sept, ANDRUS Amos C Eld *MS* 26 Nov 1838

BROWN Robert in North Berwick m WEYMOUTH Mary Jane both of North Berwick on Jan 2nd 1842, LORD D H *MS* 19 Jan 1842

BROWN Robert m NISBET Ann on 5 Jan at Boston, GARLAND G D Eld *MS* 19 Mar 1845

BROWN S Daniel S m BEAN Mary H in Lowell, THURSTON N Eld *MS* 16 May 1838

BROWN Samuel m LINSCOTT Sarah in Limington ME, AYER Aaron Eld *MS* 20 June 1838

BROWN Samuel of Compton m PUTNEY Hannah of Hatley LC on 28 Aug, MOULTON Abial Eld *MS* 20 Sept 1837

BROWN Samuel of Goffstown m BUTTERS Elizabeth H on 24 Sept at Hooksett, CILLEY D P Eld *MS* 10 Oct 1844

BROWN Simeon m LINCOLN Susan both of Stanstead LC on 29 Oct last, MOULTON Abiel Eld *MS* 17 Feb 1836

BROWN Stephen MD m COLLINS Miriam F on 1 Feb at Deerfield, HIDDEN Rev *MS* 6 Sept 1843

BROWN Thomas W of Brownfield m LOUGEE Clara S of Parsons-field, BUZZELL John Rev *MFWBR* 5 Apr 1851

BROWN True W m PHILBRICK Lucinda H on 1st inst at Lowell MA, THURSTON N Eld *MS* 12 Nov 1835

BROWN W Joseph m, AYER Sarah both of Newbury on 14 Sept in Newbury, EMERY A Eld *MS* 6 Oct 1847

BROWN William J m HURD Mary Ann on 22 inst in Providence RI,

BROWN (Continued)

LEWIS J W Eld *MS* 5 Jul 1837

BROWN William of Starksboro' VT m JONES Lydia of Huntington VT on 1 June at Huntington VT, DIKE Orange Eld *MS* 19 Jul 1843

BROWN William P/T m GILMAN Hannah J both of Great Falls in Great Falls, CURTIS S Eld *MS* 4 Mar 1840

BROWN Zacheus of Hampton m NOYES Sarah L Mrs of Newburyport MA on 8th inst, BURBANK P S Eld *MS* 28 Dec 1842

BROWNELL Corland m SPENCER Harriet of Adams Jefferson Co NY on 18 Feb at Clayton, GRIFFETH Ansel Eld *MS* 10 Mar 1847

BROWNELL William A of Scituate m WILBUR Eliza of Smithfield on 4 ult at Smithfield RI, BURLINGAME M W Eld *MS* 30 Dec 1835

BROWNELL William B m JACKSON Eliza Jane both of Dover on 23 inst in Dover, HUTCHINS E Eld *MS* 3 May 1848

BRUELL James of Biddeford ME m GOLDTHWAITE Harriet A of Saco ME on 12th inst at Saco ME, DWIGHT Rev *MFWBR* 25 Sept 1847

BRYANT Henry C of Manchester NH m KENISTON Martha of Lowell on 30 ult in Lowell, THURSTON N Eld *MS* 14 Nov 1838

BRYANT James of Portsmouth NH m TAYLOR Betsey of Sanford on 6 inst in Sanford ME, LORD D H Eld *MS* 30 Aug 1837

BRYANT John S m HART Julia Ann both of Eaton NH, ATKINSON King Eld *MFWBR* 2 Feb 1850

BRYANT Joseph m HARRIMAN Sarah of Effingham NH on 26 Nov 1844, BUTLER O Eld *MS* 19 Feb 1845

BRYANT Samuel J m SOMER Nancy H both of Manchester on 4 Jul in Manchester, CILLEY D P Eld *MS* 11 Jul 1849

BRYANT Samuel L m ALLEN Hannah of Limerick ME *MS* 27 Sept 1827

BRYANT Samuel of Effingham m DURGIN Rhoda Ann of Eaton on 9 June in Effingham, FOSS N Eld *MS* 19 June 1850

BUBIER Benjamin of Lewiston ME m SMITH Lorenda of Hallowell ME on 28 Aug 1843, REDLON A Eld *MS* 27 Sept 1843

BUCK Gilman m COMSTOCK Eliza E on 18 Feb at Manchester, CILLEY D P Eld *MS* 24 Feb 1847

BUCKMAN Charles W of Lyndon VT m PHILBRICK Thankful T of Bath on 22 May, MOULTON F Eld *MS* 21 June 1843

BUCKMINISTER James m GEORGE Hannah L of Manchester NH on 6 Jan at Manchester NH, CILLEY D P Eld *MS* 20 Jan 1847

BUCKNAM J M m JOHNSON Louisa T on 19th inst at Falmouth ME *MFWBR* 28 Dec 1850

BUFFINGTON Chars A m BEAN Mary J both of Colebrook NH on 28 Nov in Colebrook, DEAN B Eld *MS* 11 Dec 1850

BUFFINTON Jeremiah of New Albion m SMITH Phena of Mansfield NY in Mansfield NY, TAYNTOR O Eld *MS* 14 Nov 1838

BUGBEE Horace m SAWYER Miriam Mrs on 3 Nov at Gilford, PERKINS Seth W Eld *MS* 16 Dec 1846

BUKER Daniel of Richmond m CORNISH Harriet M *MS* 22 May 1844

BUKER Jotham m LEIGHTON Abigail B both of Harmony on 26 Augin Harmony, STAFFORD Johnson L *MS* 11 Sept 1850

BUKER Valentine m WILLIAMS Susan P on 31 June at Bowdoin ME, RAYMOND J Eld *MS* 16 June 1847

BULINGAME Arnold H of Gloucester m BOSS Anny of Scituate on 15 ult in Scituate, ALLEN R Eld *MS* 18 Apr 1838

BULLARD Wm A of Northumberland Saratoga Co NY m CANEDY Hannah of Duxbury VT on 16 Oct Duxbury VT, GRAY I Eld in *MS* 23 Jan 1850

BULLIS Seymour L formerly of Ellenburg m GILLETT Eunice M on 22 Dec at Pamelia, PADDEN S B Eld *MS* 1 Feb 1843

BULLOCK D Gilbert D m FULLER Caroline E both of Rehoboth on 28 Nov 1850 in Rehoboth MA, CLARK G Eld *MS* 22 Jan 1851

BULLOCK Lowell m DAVIS Almira of Walworth on 20 June 1847 at Jericho VT, ALWOOD Mark Eld *MS* 21 Jul 1847

BULLOCK Warren m MARCH Sarah A of Bridgton ME on 9 Mar at Bridgton ME, JORDAN L Eld *MS* 23 Aug 1843

BUMP Everit of Mount Pleasant Wis m DOW Mary of Yorkshire NY on 25 Sept 1848 in Arcade NY, JACKSON N A Eld *MS* 1 Nov 1848

BUNDY Lewis of Mooers NY m EATON Maria, BUNDY Benjamin Eld *MS* 6 Apr 1847

BUNKER Enos A of Barnstead m MOULTON Martha of Sandwich, BROOKS N Eld *MS* 10 Oct 1844

BUNKER Ephraim Jr m BERRY Olive of Strafford, PLACE E Eld in Strafford *MS* 15 Nov 1837

BUNKER James M m CLARK Betsey J both of Manchester in Manchester, CILLEY D P Eld *MS* 19 Jan 1848

BUNKER John D m HARRIDEN Alice S T on 31 Jul at Woolwich ME, PAGE E G Eld *MS* 24 Sept 1845

BUNKER John m ABRAHAM Marion T on 13 Apr at Atkinson ME, HATHAWAY Leonard Eld *MS* 17 May 1843

BUNKER Joseph M m WENTWORTH Betsey at Strafford, PLACE Enoch Eld *MS* 24 Apr 1834

BUNKER Joseph m SMART Hannah both of Durham on 19 inst in Dover, HUTCHINS E Eld *MS* 22 Nov 1848

BUNKER Levi m STEVENS Elizabeth of Alton NH on 22d at Alton, PINKHAM J Eld *MS* 12 Feb 1845

BUNKER Nathaniel W m KENISTONE Emeline B of Gilmanton on 20 Nov at Pittsfield, CILLEY D P Eld *MS* 7 Dec 1842

BUNKER Obadiah Capt of Sutton VT m DROWN Jane of Barnston CE on 17 ult, HILL M Eld *MS* 13 Oct 1847

BUNKER Valentine of Durham NH m FREEMAN Lavina of Dover NH on 17 inst in Dover NH, CAVERNO A Eld *MS* 23 Jan 1850

BUNKER William m STILSON Hannah on 11 June at Lowell MA, SINCLAIR J L Eld *MS* 16 Aug 1843

BUNTON Levi m SARGENT Mehitabel Mrs both of Epsom NH on 16
Dec 1849 in Epsom NH, RAMSEY G P Eld *MS* 16 Jan 1850

BURBANK Abner m HARMON Eliza A both of Limerick ME, BUR-
BANK Samuel Eld *MS* 5 Apr 1837

BURBANK Adino J of Gilead m MURRAY Clara A of Lewiston Falls
on 30th ult at Auburn ME, ELLIOT Rev *MFWBR* 8 Sept 1849

BURBANK Alexander Dr of Shelburne NH m LOWELL Vesta of Lewiston ME on 7th inst at Lewiston ME *MFWBR* 24 Apr 1847

BURBANK Amos m MOOR Nancy on 14th inst at Newfield, BUR-
BANK Eld *MS* 22 Oct 1828

BURBANK Ezra m BOWLES Phebe both of Lisbon ME in Lisbon ME,
PETTENGILL John Eld *MS* 29 Dec 1847

BURBANK Luther m BUTLER Elenor both of Barnston on 9 Oct
1843 *MS* 1 May 1844

BURBANK Oscar F m CAWLEY Charlotte both of Manchester on 14
Nov in Manchester, CILLEY D P Eld *MS* 5 Dec 1849

BURBANK Porter S of Newfield ME m BURBANK Miriam B of Parsonsfield in Parsonsfield, BUZZELL John Eld *MS* 2 Aug 1837

BURBANK Thomas W m THOMAS Eliza Jane at Lowell MA *MS* 3 May
1843

BURBUNK James M m HILL Phebe both of Great Falls NH on 1 inst
at Waterboro ME, BURBANK Samuel Eld *MS* 18 Nov 1835

BURDICK Caleb L m PALMER Mary A both of Brookfield on 8 Apr in
Poolville NY, GARDNER S D Eld *MS* 1 May 1850

BURGESS Charles m GAGE Deborah both of Waterville ME on 9 Dec
1847 in Waterville ME, BURGESS J S Eld *MS* 19 Jan 1848

BURGESS J S Eld of Lewiston m GAGE Laura A of Waterville ME on
17 inst in Waterville ME, BEAN G W Eld *MS* 1 Nov 1848

BURGESS Thomas F m WING Sarah at Lowell MA, CURTIS Silas Eld
MS 9 Jul 1845

BURGESS Weeks m SMILEY Rebecca of Waterville ME, LEWIS
Daniel B Eld *MS* 15 Jan 1840

BURGESS William at Bangor ME m BICKFORD Belinda, CAVERNO
A Eld *MS* 13 Sept 1843

BURHAM Joseph m STACKPOLE Elizabeth both of Lowell in Lowell,
THURSTON N Eld *MS* 8 Jan 1840

BURKE James m FERREN Melissa of Eaton, GASKILL S Eld *MS* 21
Jan 1846

BURKS Charles H of Wolfborough NH m WENTWORTH Lucy B of
Lebanon ME on 29 Aug 1847, COWELL D B Eld *MS* 1 Dec 1847

BURLEIGH Benjamin m BEAN Huldah on 2 Dec 1843 at Sandwich,
McMURPHY B H Eld *MS* 5 June 1844

BURLEIGH John A Esq of Great Falls NH m COLCORD Emily A at
South Berwick ME *MFWBR* 13 Apr 1850

BURLESON Allen of Mich m NEWBARGE Mary L of Greenfield Ohio
on 30 Dec 1849, ROOT E Eld *MS* 20 Feb 1850

BURLEY Charles E m BEAN Mary both of Dover on 29 Feb at Dover
NH, PERKINS Rev *MS* 16 Mar 1836
BURLEY Cyrus of Bethlehem VT m QUIMBY Mehitabel of Lisbon on
5 Oct 1847 in Franconia, BLAKE C E Eld *MS* 10 Nov 1847
BURLEY Hiram m WHITEHOUSE Susan at Dover *MS* 13 Jul 1836
BURLINGAME Henry Otis of Gloucester MA m OLNEY Ratio of
Scituate on 12th inst, ALLEN R Eld *MS* 21 Sept 1842
BURLINGAME Thomas m COLLINS Mary Eliza both of No Scituate
RI on 4 Feb, NOYES E Eld *MS* 20 Feb 1850
BURNAB Gideon of Providence RI m DAHEG Patience E of Smithfield
on 12 Apr in Providence RI, SCOTT E Eld *MS* 21 June 1848
BURNE Edmond A m PORTER Sarah on 24th Mar at Charlestown
MA, WETHERBEE I J Eld *MS* 4 Aug 1847
BURNETT James F m WATSON Jane M on 20 Aug at Charlestown,
WETHERBEE I J Eld *MS* 9 Dec 1846
BURNHAM Alexander m STAPLES Susan A both of Biddeford on 19
Sept in Biddeford ME, WITHAM L H Eld *MS* 27 Oct 1847
BURNHAM Andrew W of Essex m BARNARD Mary Ann of Lowell in
Lowell, THURSTON N Eld *MS* 2 Jan 1839
BURNHAM Asa A m DAVIS Sabria G both of Reading VT on Feb 11
1840, WARNER William Eld *MS* 4 Mar 1840
BURNHAM Charles m WELCH Betsey on 17 Sept at Manchester,
CILLEY D P Eld *MS* 27 Sept 1843
BURNHAM Ingols m BROCK Martha both of Dover on 28 May,
BURBUNK P S Eld *MS* 20 June 1849
BURNHAM John m WALKER Susan both of Harrison ME on 9 Nov,
ROLLINS Eld *MS* 6 Jan 1836
BURNHAM John of Parsonsfield ME m ADAMS Sally *MFWBR* 20 Mar
1847
BURNHAM Joseph m STACKPOLE Elizabeth of Lowell, THURSTON N
Eld *MS* 8 Jan 1840
BURNHAM Mark m LORD Susan at Limerick, ROBERTS Eld *MS* 24
Oct 1833
BURNHAM Mark m PARKER Mary Ann both of Garland ME on 4
Aprin Garland ME, AMES M Eld *MS* 3 Jul 1850
BURNHAM Newton J of Meredith m BUZZELL Catharine L of Gilford,
WATSON Elijah Eld *MS* 2 Aug 1848
BURNHAM Simeon of Littleton m PHILLIPS Martha Mrs of Bethle-
hem in Franconia, BLAKE C E Eld *MS* 24 Jan 1849
BURNHAM William D of Biddeford m RICHARDS Roxanna of Saco on
5 Aug in Biddeford ME, WITHAM L H Eld *MS* 21 Nov 1849
BURPEE Cyrus B m GOODWIN Mary A both of Manchester on 9
June in Manchester, CILLEY D P Eld *MS* 24 June 1846
BURR Pyum of Hingham MA m HERSEY Anna C on 1st inst at
Hingham MA, RUSSELL Rev *MS* 7 June 1843
BURR William m McDONALD Frances S on Thurs morning last in

BURR (Continued)
Limerick ME *MS* 18 June 1828

BURR William T m NEAL Ann of Gardiner ME, GOODRICH Barnard Eld *MS* 4 Sept 1839

BURRIDGE Andrew B of Boston MA m BAKER Priscilla at Bowdoinham ME, QUINNAM C Eld *MS* 16 Oct 1839

BURROWS Benjamin m GILMAN Betsey both of Effingham NH, DAVIS Joseph Eld *MS* 1 Apr 1835

BURROWS Jabez m DIXON Fanny both of Dover, DOW Rev *MS* 16 Jul 1834

BURROWS Jiles W m VARNEY Susan E both of Milton on 12 Nov 1848 in Wakefield, SPINNEY Joseph Eld *MS* 3 Jan 1849

BURROWS Joseph Dea m BLAISDELL Lovey both of Lebanon on 1 Jul in Lebanon, BLAISDELL Edward Eld *MS* 5 Sept 1838

BUSSIEL Joseph C of Meredith NH m MARSTON Lucy Jane of Meredith NH, PITMAN Stephen J Eld *MS* 8 Dec 1841

BUSWELL Edmand D of Paris m HOLSTED Betsey B of Wheatland Wis on 29 Sept Wheatland Wis, COOMBS A Eld in *MS* 13 Nov 1850

BUSWELL Geo m WALKER Sarah Ann both of Paris on 24 Mar in Paris Wis, TANNER G W W Eld *MS* 22 May 1850

BUSWELL Samuel S m CHASE Lucinda both of Hopkinton on 18 Apr *MS* 8 May 1844

BUSWELL Smith D m MASON Rhoda on 27th at Manchester, BROOKS John Eld *MS* 24 Dec 1845

BUTLER Cornelius B m COBB Catharine F both of Portland ME on 1 inst in Portland ME, LIBBY Isaac Eld *MS* 9 Feb 1848

BUTLER John E of Dover NH m FARNHAM Lucinda J Eld on Aug 8th, DUNN Ransom Eld *MS* 14 Aug 1844

BUTLER John J teacher of the Biblical School at Whitestown m EVERETT Elizabeth former teacher in Clinton Seminary on 14 Nov at Steuben Oneida Co NY, EVERETT R Rev *MS* 27 Nov 1844

BUTLER Levi m VILES Susan at Norridgewock ME *MFWBR* 13 Oct 1849

BUTLER Nathan of Berwick m PAUL Sally W of Great Falls on 25 Feb at Great Falls, WOODMAN Jonathan Eld *MS* 4 Apr 1838

BUTLER Otis B m RIDGEWAY Ursula both of Farmington in Farmington ME, CHANEY John Eld *MS* 13 Dec 1837

BUTLER Simon m HEPPHERD Hannah on 23 Feb at Matildaville, WHITFIELD William Eld *MS* 3 May 1843

BUTMAN John T m POOL Sarah A formerly of Brunswick ME at Newburyport MA *MFWBR* 24 Mar 1849

BUTTERFIELD Albion KP of Danville m WYMAN Lucy S of Auburn ME on 17 inst in Lewiston Falls ME, BEAN G W Eld *MS* 26 Apr 1848

BUTTERFIELD Isaac m SEAVY Ruth T both of Lowell MA *MS* 11 Mar

BUTTERFIELD (Continued)
1835
BUTTERFIELD Jonas of Chesterville ME m ROBINSON Christiana J of Sidney ME at Sidney ME, LEWIS Daniel B Eld *MS* 25 Nov 1846
BUTTERS Ruel m BUTTERS Mary of Wilmington MA on 2 June, DURGIN J M Eld *MS* 26 June 1844
BUTTON Lyman m BROWN Polly both of Freedom NY on 29 June *MS* 31 Aug 1836
BUXTON David 2d m EASTMAN Miriam B both of So Weare 5 Jan 1848 in So Weare *MS* 8 Mar 1848
BUXTON David m EASTMAN Eliza B both of Weare on 26 ult in Weare, MOODY David Eld *MS* 24 Jan 1838
BUXTON Samuel m BUFFUM Ruth Ann both of Smithfield, BURLINGAME W W Eld *MS* 28 Feb 1838
BUZZELL Edmond m BACHELDOR Zeriah of New Chester *RI* Jan 1820 p 15
BUZZELL Eliphord of Dover m CAISBUING Lydia of Tamworth NH on 2 inst at Dover NH, SANBORN Abram Eld *MS* 12 Nov 1845
BUZZELL Gilman of Northwood m WATSON Eliza of Pittsfield on 29 Dec, CILLEY D P Eld *MS* 1 Feb 1843
BUZZELL Henry H m FRANCIS Mary Ann of Manchester on 14th inst at Durham, HUTCHINS E Eld *MS* 20 Nov 1844
BUZZELL Hezekiah D Eld m TIBBETTS Charlotte Mrs on 9 Jan 1849in Tuftonborough NH, COFFIN Stephen Eld *MS* 31 Jan 1849
BUZZELL Jacob Jr of Acton ME m ROGERS Catharine of Wakefield on 28 Dec in Wakefield, SPRING Joseph Eld *MS* 28 Feb 1838
BUZZELL John C m MURPHY Ann Eliza at Biddeford on 7th inst *MFWBR* 12 Jan 1850
BUZZELL John H Capt m FOSS Elizabeth on 28 May at Strafford, CAVERLY J Eld *MS* 14 June 1843
BUZZELL John R of Tamworth NH m CLARK Mary K of Holderness NH on 6 Dec, MERRRILL William S Eld *MS* 30 Dec 1846
BUZZELL Miles m ARLIN Elmira/Almira both of Dover on 27 Apr in Dover NH, SMITH A D Eld *MS* 9 May 1849 & *MFWBR* 12 May 1849
BUZZELL Miles of Strafford m HALL Deborah of Barnstead on 15th ult, CAVERLY John Eld *MS* 12 Jul 1843
BUZZELL Smith F m JENKINS Mary E of Lee NH on 24 Nov at Barrington, SHERBURNE S Eld *MS* 21 Jan 1846
BUZZELL True m THAYER Abby S of Roxbury MA at Gray ME, DURGIN J M Eld *MS* 16 Oct 1839
BUZZELL William (s/o Eld John Buzzell) of Parsonsfield ME m KIMBALL Harriet on 10 Nov at Dracut MA, CAVERLY Robert B Esq *MS* 26 Nov 1845
BUZZELL William Eld of Middleton m PINKHAM Jamson, BUZZELL H D Eld *MS* 18 Dec 1839

CABOT Dean m WARD Mary both of Windsor on 29 ult in Windsor VT, ADAMS Abel Eld *MS* 6 June 1838

CAGWIN Samuel G of Freedom m ALEXANDER Martha of Farmersville on 30 Oct *MS* 11 Dec 1850

CAHOON Albert B of Coventry m TAYLOR Sarah of Scituate on 9 Sept in Scituate RI, ALLEN R Eld *MS* 30 Oct 1850

CAIN David of Clinton ME m NOBLE Sarah of Salartacook on 9 Aug, BUKER Alvah J Eld *MS* 2 Dec 1846

CALDER Samuel of Vassalborough ME m STARRETT Mary Ann of China ME on 11 Jul in China ME, FOGG E T Eld *MS* 29 Sept 1847

CALEF Asa F of Lowell MA m NICHOLS Sarah on 6 Dec, CURTIS S Eld *MS* 6 Jan 1847

CALEF John L m DAVIS Laura Ann of Wilmington on 15th inst at Wilmington, DURGIN J M Eld *MS* 25 Oct 1843

CALEF Moses m THOMPSON Judith both of Salisbury on 8 inst in Andover, WATSON Elijah Eld *MS* 21 Nov 1838

CALL Henry S of Newton Lower Falls MA m WILLIAMS Harriet N in Kittery ME, PERKINS Seth W Eld *MS* 26 Mar 1851

CALL Warren of Bradford ME m POTTLE Martha Ann of Richmond ME on 10 Sept 1848 in Richmond ME, PURINGTON Collamore Eld *MS* 11 Oct 1848

CALLEY David of Plymouth NH m SMITH Mary Mooney on 23 Mar 1848 in Holderness, PERKINS Thomas Eld of New Hampton NH *MS* 12 Apr 1848

CALLEY Jeremiah M m SHEPHERD Mary P of Holderness on 4 Jan, PETTENGILL John Eld *MS* 26 June 1839

CALVIN Allen of Coventry m POTTER Eliza A of Scituate on 9 Nov 1848, CALVIN R Eld *MS* 17 Jan 1849

CAME Mark R of Old Town ME m HOBSON Sarah M of Standish ME on 4 Apr, HOBSON P M Eld *MS* 17 Apr 1844

CAMPBELL A S of Ellsworth m TRUE Anna M of Bangor on 30th ult, at Bangor ME *MFWBR* 9 Nov 1850

CAMPBELL Cyrus m LENFEST Adaline of Washington ME on 8 Dec at Bowdoin ME, PURINGTON Elisha Eld *MS* 13 Jan 1847

CAMPBELL Henry F of Strong ME m HILTON Sarah M of Anson ME, HARDING E Eld *MS* 18 Dec 1844

CAMPBELL James m BOWKER Letis both of Bowdoin ME, SWETT Jesse Eld *MS* 18 Mar 1835

CAMPBELL Joseph m EMMONS Hannah D both of Hill on 16 May in Hill, BROWN A Eld *MS* 19 June 1850

CAMPBELL Page m BUTTERFIELD Marilla both of Bedford on 12 Apr 1848 in Manchester, CILLEY D P Eld *MS* 26 Apr 1848

CAMPBELL Robert m ROGERS Catherine M both of Georgetown on March 30 in Georgetown ME, PERKINS Seth W Eld *MS* 27 Apr 1842

CAMPBELL Robert m NILES Sarah Jane both of Bowdoin on 25 Apr in Bowdoin ME, QUINNAM C Eld *MS* 1 May 1850

CANEY James M of Ossipee m HAM Lydia A of Great Falls on 24 Oct in Great Falls, BROOKS N Eld *MS* 31 Oct 1849

CANNEY James of Nottingham m SHERBURNE Lydia O of Barrington on 17 inst in Barrington, SHERBURNE S Eld *MS* 27 Sept 1848

CANOVAN Martin H of Boston MA m WALDRON Clarissa of Dover on 6 Nov in Dover, SMITH A D Eld *MS* 12 Dec 1838

CAPBELL Levi B m DEMORING June C both of Charleston ME on 5 Jan 1848 in Garland ME, AMES M Eld *MS* 2 Feb 1848

CAPRON Harford A of Pawtucket RI m THRASHER Rhoda P of Rehoboth MA on 21 Mar in Attleborough, CLARK G Eld *MS* 1 May 1850

CARD Albert m BRADBURY Sarah E both of Dover on 6 inst in Dover, HUTCHINS E Eld *MS* 10 Jan 1849

CARD Joel Jr m HALL Rebecca A in Litchfield, QUINNAM C Eld *MS* 8 Sept 1847

CAREY Calvin I m FOBES Ursula *MS* 19 May 1830

CAREY Thomas of Oxford m WATERHOUSE Julia A of Gray ME on 2d inst in Blakesburgh, DURGIN J M Eld *MS* 10 Jul 1839

CARGILL Charles of New Castle m KELLEY Catherine of Boothbay on 21 Sept at Boothbay ME, PAGE E G Eld *MS* 23 Nov 1842

CARIL Nathaniel m SMITH Clarissa both of Waterboro ME on 4th inst, HAMILTON Benjamin R Esq *MS* 14 Jan 1835

CARL Francis m WORCESTER Mary A on 6th inst at Dracut MA, CURTIS S Eld *MS* 24 Feb 1847

CARLISE Charles m LEWIS Eliza A on 4th Feb at Boothbay ME, MORRILL S P Eld *MS* 3 Mar 1847

CARLL James m SMALL Sarah at Lowell MA *MS* 5 Oct 1836

CARLTON Ephraim m HEDGE Lydia of Woolwich on 7 Nov at Woolwich ME, PAGE E G Eld *MS* 27 Dec 1843

CARLTON Sumner m FLANDERS Hannah of Warner on 7 ult of Hopkinton, SINCLAIR J Eld in Hopkinton *MS* 4 Apr 1838

CARMAN Enos of Wheatland Racine Co Wis m CARPENTER Mary on 15 Apr 1847, COCHRAN Warren Rev *MS* 12 May 1847

CARMAN John m CAMBURN Electa A both of Walworth NY on 8 Augin Walworth NY, HOLMES D G Eld *MS* 16 Oct 1850

CARMAN Wm H m MARTIN Adelia both of Sand Lake NY on 22 ult in Sand Lake NY, COLEMAN I B Eld *MS* 4 Sept 1850

CARPENTER Calvin of Seekonk m BENSLEY Ellen of Pawtucket in N Scituate, NOYES E Eld *MS* 1 May 1850

CARPENTER Dan Esq m MOSHIER Frances G at Saccarappa ME, CHAPMAN C Rev *MFWBR* 26 June 1847

CARPENTER Ebenezer G m JEWELL Renance of Lowell MA on 29 Jan 1843, WOODMAN J Eld *MS* 23 Aug 1843

CARPENTER Horace of Chichester m LAMPREY Sarah S of Deerfield on 3 inst, BURBANK P S Eld *MS* 17 Oct 1849

CARPENTER Olney C of Sutton MA m SMITH Louisa on 31 Jan 1843, FULLER W Eld *MS* 15 Feb 1843

CARR Chellis D Capt of Loudon m PRESCOTT Hannah B of Gilford on 25 Apr in Gilford, PINKHAM J Eld *MS* 22 May 1844

CARR Erastus W m DEAN Louisa A both of Stephentown NY on 9 Feb in Stephentown NY, COLEMAN I B Eld *MS* 13 Mar 1850

CARR Jeremiah at Manchester m NORTHEY Mary Ann of Manchester on 14 Oct, CILLEY D P Eld *MS* 25 Oct 1843

CARR John B m ARNOLD Betsey H both of Peru NY in Rockmanton NY, ELKINS David Eld *MS* 14 Feb 1838

CARR Levi m HASCAL Felitia of Campton on 15 Feb, MOULTON A Eld *MS* 13 Sept 1843

CARR Nelson m VENNA Eliza both of Edwards on 7 Sept in Fowler NY, JENKINS C Eld *MS* 21 Oct 1846

CARR Newell m DOWNER Mahala at Lowell, THURSTON N Eld *MS* 8 Jan 1840

CARSLEY Daniel of Sangerville m WESTON Emily of Foxcroft ME *MS* 5 Dec 1833

CARSLEY Freeman m PHINNEY Martha H on 31s ult, WHITE Joseph *MS* 17 Sept 1834

CARTER Abner of Dover m TEBBETS Caroline H of Dover on 30 June in Wolfborough, LUCAS W K Eld *MS* 24 Jul 1850

CARTER Alfred G of Woburn m SHELDON Caroline of Woburn at Wilmington MA, DURGIN J M Eld *MS* 22 Feb 1843

CARTER Benjamin F of Newtown m BAGLEY Sally of Candia *MS* 17 June 1835

CARTER Charles of Reading m FOSS Eliza Jane of Strafford on 9th inst at Strafford, PLACE E Eld *MS* 29 May 1844

CARTER Daniel P m TWOMBLY Mary E of Dover NH on 4th inst at Dover NH, PARKER S H Esq *MS* 13 Mar 1844

CARTER Ebenezer on 12 Nov 1848 EDGERLY Mary both of Great Falls, BROOKS N Eld in Great Falls *MS* 22 Nov 1848

CARTER Jesse of Randolph VT m SMITH Cornelia A of Tunbridge on 8 Feb 1849, SMITH C H Eld *MS* 28 Mar 1849

CARTER John M m WEBSTER Susan both of Sandwich on 25 Oct in Sandwich, BLAKE C E Eld *MS* 4 Nov 1846

CARTER Jonathan L m SWAIN Mary G on 30 Nov at Wilmington MA, DURGIN J M Eld *MS* 20 Dec 1843

CARTER Loudon of Virginia m PHILLIPS Nancy of Kittery ME on 10th inst, THURSTON Eld *MS* 27 Jan 1930

CARTER Samuel P of Newtown m FRENCH Judith of East Kingston on 15 inst Candia, MANSON B S Eld *MS* 1 Nov 1837

CARTER Sanborn of Sandford m FROST Maria A on 4 Aug 1839 at Springvale, LORD D H Eld *MS* 14 Aug 1839

CARVER Blany of Freeport ME m WOODMAN Eliza of Freeport ME on 20 Oct, PURINTON A W Eld *MS* 25 Nov 1846

CARVILLE Daniel W of Wales ME m DYER Drusilla of Lewiston ME on 4th instat Lewiston ME *MFWBR* 31 Aug 1850

CARVILLE Otis m DWELLEY H N on 13th inst at Lewiston ME, KNOX Rev *MFWBR* 24 Feb 1849

CARY Heman m DIMICK Susan on 25 Jan 1848 in Pierpont NY, WHITFIELD W Eld *MS* 15 Mar 1848

CARY Luther H MD m FERGUSON Arvil of Boston NY on 8 Oct at Boston Erie Co NY, LIGHTHALL William A Eld *MS* 25 Nov 1846

CARY Zenas m BAILEY Mary Ann of Maxfield on 23 June 1844 at Atkinson ME, HATHAWAY L Eld *MS* 21 Aug 1844

CASE Isaac m HALL Mary E on 15th inst at Belfast ME *MFWBR* 28 Jul 1849

CASH John m BUTLER Mary Ann both of Casco ME on 7 May in West Poland ME, LIBBY James Eld *MS* 3 June 1846

CASS David M m EATON Sarah B on 30 Nov at Manchester, CILLEY D P Eld *MS* 20 Dec 1843

CASS John F of Bridgewater m LOCK Jane of Bristol NH on 26 Dec 1843, BROWN Amos Eld *MS* 21 Feb 1844

CASS Levi m WIRE Sarah on 25 Feb 1844 *MS* 1 May 1844

CASS Lorenzo m BUTTERFIELD Abigail of Stanstead LC on 26 Aug 1841 of Stanstead LC, MOULTON A Eld *MS* 13 Apr 1842

CASS William E m STURDEY Sally W of Mendon on 27 Mar, BUR-LINGAME M W Eld *MS* 24 Apr 1839

CASWELL Minot of Auburn ME m BRIGGS Rhoda of Greene ME on 4 June 1843, EATON E G Eld *MS* 2 Aug 1843

CASWELL Richard W of Boston m WILLEY Martha T of Barnstead on 22 Mar Sabbath Eve in Barnstead, MORRELL James Eld *MS* 8 Apr 1846

CASWELL Thomas m TUFTS Ellen both of Dover on 17 inst in Dover, SMITH A D Eld *MS* 20 May 1846

CASWELL Willard W of Northwood m BASSETT Mary E both of Durham on 15 Jul, JOHNSON W D Eld *MS* 8 Aug 1849

CATE Alfred M m CHICK Mercy of Ossipee NH on 25 Dec, CHICK J Eld *MS* 14 Jan 1846

CATE David O m MARSHALL Susan E both of Somersworth on 17 Dec 1848 in Dover, SMITH A D Eld *MS* 3 Jan 1849

CATE Isaac m BURLEY Almira of Brookfield on 14 ult *MS* 1 Mar 1837

CATE William W of Payson m GREEN Sarah C on 26 Jul near Mt Sterling Brown Co IL, EGGLESTON A C Eld *MS* 25 Sept 1844

CATE Wm in Portsmouth m SHERBURNE Marena C *MS* 20 Mar 1834

CATER Richard B m HAYES Mahala W both of Somersworth last Sabbath morning in Dover, PINKHAM J Eld *MS* 13 Nov 1850

CATES Henry m STINSON Cordelia at Monroe ME, CILLEY Joseph L Eld *MS* 16 Aug 1843

CATES Levi m DUNHAM Harriet on 12 Sept 1847 in Dracut MA, CURTIS S Eld *MS* 22 Sept 1847

CATLIN S T Eld of Hopkinton NH m HURD Julia F of Concord NH on 9 Oct 1849 in Concord NH, CUMMINGS E E Rev *MS* 5 Dec 1849

CATLIN Samuel T Eld of Woolwich ME m MOORE Sarah Ann at Newfield, JORDAN Z Eld *MS* 20 May 1840

CATON Alphonso m DODSON Margaret at Middlebury NY, PLUMB H N Eld *MS* 27 Jan 1847

CAVERLY Abiel M of Loudon m AMES Caroline of Canterbury on 25 Mar at Canterbury, MOODY H Rev *MS* 9 Apr 1845

CAVERLY Asa of Strafford m YOUNG Abigail of Barrington *MS* 9 Sept 1835

CAVERLY Asa m PINKHAM Sally both of New Market NH on 1st inst at Lamprey River, CILLEY D P Eld *MS* 11 Mar 1835

CAVERLY Ephraim H m CRITCHET Mary Jane both of Barrington, PLACE E Eld *MS* 22 Apr 1840

CAVERLY Joel of Strafford m CAVERLY Mary S of Barrington on 30 ult *MS* 9 Nov 1836

CAVERLY John S m CAVERLY Nancy J of Barrington on 7 Apr 1747 [*sic*, 1847?], CLARK M Eld *MS* 12 May 1847

CAVERLY Thomas C m PLACE Susan Demeritt on 7th inst at Strafford, PLACE E Eld *MS* 24 May 1843

CHACE Charles of Wheelock m BRADLEY Mary Ann of Sheffield VT on 5 May 1842 at Sheffield VT, HARRIS H W Eld *MS* 12 Oct 1842

CHADBOURNE George of Gorham ME m BOYNTON Harriet at Cornish ME *MFWBR* 6 Mar 1847 & *MFWBR* 20 Feb 1847

CHADBOURNE Hiram H m BURROWS Elizabeth both of Great Falls on 4 Jul in Great Falls, BROOKS N Eld *MS* 10 Jul 1850

CHADBOURNE John Jr of Cornish ME m NORTON Adaline of Limington on 17 May at Fryeburg ME, PIKE J Eld *MS* 4 June 1845

CHADBOURNE William of Biddeford m WIGHT Sophronia L of Otisfield ME on 4 May in Otisfield ME, WIGHT J Eld *MS* 22 May 1850

CHADBOURNE Wm m SMITH Betsey both of Cornish on 23 Dec *MS* 17 Jan 1833

CHADDOCK Leverett m FREEMAN Maria on 24 Oct at Alexander, ROLLIN M L Eld *MS* 20 Nov 1844

CHADDOCK Seymour m LAMKIN Elizabeth on 17 Oct at Bethany NY, TAYLOR Eld *MS* 20 Nov 1844

CHADWICK Charles W of Gilford NH m BUCK Susan C at Augusta ME *MFWBR* 3 Nov 1849

CHADWICK John m CLARK Sarah on Wed last, ROOT Rev in Dover *MS* 8 Dec 1834

CHAFFEE Lyman m CLARK Clarissa both of Schroepple NY on 10th

CHAFFEE (Continued)
ult, GRIFFITH A Eld *MS* 6 Apr 1836

CHALLIES David of Newfield m SMITH Nancy of Newfield ME *MS* 19 Nov 1828

CHAMBERLAIN Albert B of Salem MA m HILL Sarah of Dover on 3 inst in Dover NH, HUTCHINS E Eld *MS* 5 May 1846

CHAMBERLAIN Alvah of Eaton NH m PROCTOR Louisa of Lowell MA on 23 Feb 1848 in Lowell MA, CURTIS S Eld *MS* 8 Mar 1848

CHAMBERLAIN Benjamin m BURNS Mary Jane of Lowell on 13th inst at Lowell, THURSTON N Eld *MS* 23 Oct 1839

CHAMBERLAIN C Mr of Madrid m BROOKS M Miss on 9 Dec at Pierpont, WHITFIELD Eld *MS* 6 Jan 1847

CHAMBERLAIN Chester of Foxcroft m WARREN Lucy Ann Y of Sangerville on Apr 7th at Sangerville ME, COMBS A Eld *MS* 29 May 1839

CHAMBERLAIN Edward B of Dover m COLCORD Abigail of Candia on 19th inst, FERNALD S P Eld *MS* 29 May 1839

CHAMBERLAIN Freeman m ADAMS Matilda S both of Dover on 3 Sept in Somersworth, PERKINS J Rev *MS* 13 Sept 1837

CHAMBERLAIN Moses m HAYES Ann of Roxbury MA on 7 Jan at Roxbury MA, DAVIS J B Eld *MS* 22 Jan 1845

CHAMBERLAIN Thomas of Lowell m FOLSOM Charlotte B of Gilmanton, LANCASTER Rev in Gilmanton *MS* 24 Jan 1838

CHAMBERLIN Abijah m JAQUITH Harriet on 20th at Manchester Iowa (Territory), HATHORN S Eld *MS* 27 Feb 1839

CHAMBERLIN Benjamin m MARDEN Hannah, THURSTON N Eld in Lowell MA *MS* 26 Aug 1835

CHAMBERLIN Eli R m BERRY Susan G at Somersworth NH *MFWBR* 9 Mar 1850

CHAMBERLIN Ellis E m FAIRBANKS Catherine on 10 Dec 1846 at Manchester Iowa, HATHORN Samuel Eld *MS* 27 Jan 1847

CHAMBERLIN Hammond of Brompton m AYERS Nancy of Hatley LC on 28 Feb, MOULTON A Eld *MS* 13 Sept 1843

CHAMBERLIN Robert S of Lowell m CHASE Maria J of Great Falls on 27 Nov 1843 at Great Falls, WEBBER Horace Eld *MS* 21 Feb 1844

CHAMBERLIN Samuel of Milton m FALL Mary E of Lebanon on 28th ult at Lebanon, *MFWBR* 14 Sept 1850

CHAMBERLIN Wm B m SANBORN Betsey C on 26 Dec at Brookfield, MEADER Eld *MS* 4 Jan 1837

CHAMBERS Wm H m DAVIS Lucy both of Chester ME, TURNER A Eld *MS* 8 Nov 1848

CHAMPION Cyrus K m GRANVILLE Sophronia A both of Effingham NH on 28 Nov, FOSS N Eld *MS* 12 Jan 1848

CHAMPION Lorenzo m MALOON Hannah both of Effingham on 13 Mar in Effingham, FOSS N Eld *MS* 26 Mar 1851

CHAMPION Moses J of Dover m TEBBETS Clara of Rochester on 27

CHAMPION (Continued)
ult in Dover, HUTCHINS E Eld *MS* 4 Dec 1850

CHAMPLIN Wm E of Watertown Jefferson Co NY m REED Charlotte of Three Mile Bay NY on 9 Nov 1847 in Three Mile Bay NY, PADDEN S B Eld *MS* 1 Dec 1847

CHAMPNEY Benjamin m ROLLINS Delila both of Belgrade ME on 4 Nov*MS* 10 Feb 1836

CHANDLER Benjamin Jr of Newbury NH m CROSS Aphia D in Springfield, CROSS Jesse Eld *MS* 26 Feb 1851

CHANDLER Calvin of Bangor m KNOWLES Elvina of Corinna ME on 1 Jan 1835, NASON S V Eld *MS* 11 Mar 1835

CHANDLER Christopher m SMITH Mary C of Portland ME on 12th inst at Portland ME, MOULTON A K Eld *MS* 19 June 1844

CHANDLER Ebenezer Jr of Temple m HARDY Lucinda of Wilton ME on 22d inst at Wilton, FOSTER Eld *MS* 2 Oct 1829

CHANDLER Ephraim A m WILKINSON Mary P on 30 Nov 1848, NOYES E Eld *MS* 13 Dec 1848

CHANDLER George H of Boston NY m DENNIS Lydia A of China NY on 1 June 1848 in China NY, LIGHTHALL W A Eld *MS* 5 Jul 1848

CHANDLER George m DAVENPORT Fanny M both of Ellington NY on 11 Oct in Ellington NY, LIGHTHALL W A Eld *MS* 6 Nov 1850

CHANDLER Hubbard Eld of Wilton m ROBBINS Susan of Phillips ME on 2nd inst in Phillips, HUTCHINGS Samuel Eld *MS* 16 Jul 1828

CHANDLER John H m LEWIS Esther P of Boothbay ME on 9 Nov at Boothbay, ROBINSON N J Eld *MS* 29 Nov 1843

CHANDLER John R of Manchester NH m GODFREY Elizabeth M, CILLEY D P Eld *MS* 10 Sept 1845

CHANDLER Luther of Colebrook m WHITTEMORE Olive Mrs of Dixville on 1 Dec 1847 in Dixville, BEAN Benaiah Eld *MS* Dec 15 1847

CHANDLER Nathaniel Capt m FIFIELD Ruth on 20 Dec at New Hampton, THOMPSON Samuel Eld at Holderness *MS* 15 Mar 1843

CHANDLER Solomon m BOWLES Mary Mrs on 13th Jul at Portsmouth NH in East Parsonsfield ME, MERRILL William P Eld *MS* 7 Sept 1845

CHANDLER Thomas of Augusta m BRAGG Hannah D of Sidney ME *MS* 15 Mar 1837

CHANEY Benjamin m KNOX Hannah of Lowell MA on 22 Sept, WOODMAN J Eld *MS* 19 Oct 1842

CHANEY Joseph of Springvale m ALLEN Lydia L of Cornish ME on 7 Nov 1847, HACKETT J O Eld *MS* 22 Dec 1847

CHANEY S Freeman Eld of Buxton m JOHNSON Acay D\Abigail Daggett of Farmington ME, JOHNSON Timothy Eld *MS* 3 Aug 1842

CHANNEL Abraham F J m DANIELS Dorothy B both of Durham on 26 May, SWETT Simeon Eld *MS* 8 June 1836

CHAPEL Ebenezer D Capt of Waterford CT m LOOK Margaret C Miss of Georgetown ME, WATERMAN D Eld *MS* 13 Feb 1834

CHAPIN Elmer D of Greenfield MA m BETTON Clarissa of Dover on Sun evening 1 inst in Dover NH, SMITH Eleazer Rev *MS* 11 Oct 1837

CHAPLIN William B m ANNIS Julia A, NOYES E Eld *MS* 15 Dec 1847

CHAPMAN Charles S m COLLINS Miriam both of Manchester on 9 Apr in Weare, MOODY David Eld *MS* 24 June 1846

CHAPMAN Ebenezer m HANAFORD Mary A all of New Market on Apr 17 in New Market, HUTCHINS E Eld *MS* 27 Apr 1842

CHAPMAN Eben'r m GRAFFAM Maria G both of Baldwin ME on 20 Jan, HART E H Eld *MS* 24 Jul 1850

CHAPMAN Emerson m GULLIVER Harriet on 15th inst at Bangor ME, POND Rev *MFWBR* 3 Mar 1849

CHAPMAN Gilbert m GROVER Mary A both of Bethel WHITNEY G W Eld in Bethel ME *MS* 17 June 1846

CHAPMAN Horace m PRESCOTT Emeline on 1 Feb at Manchester NH, CILLEY D P Eld *MS* 19 Feb 1845

CHAPMAN John C m GOULD Angenette on 12 June at Dracut MA, CURTIS S Eld *MS* 7 Jul 1847

CHAPMAN John H m CHURCHILL Sarah both of New Market on 13 inst in Dover, HUTCHINS E Eld *MS* 16 May 1849

CHAPMAN John m FOSS Louisa both of New Market on 18 Oct 1848, BURBANK P S Eld in Strafford NH *MS* 8 Nov 1848

CHAPMAN Nathaniel of Bangor m FRENCH Martha of Corinth ME on 10 Apr in Corinth ME, HARDING E Eld *MS* 29 Aug 1849

CHAPMAN Smith m FURNAL Harriet both of Newmarket Lamprey River NH on 26 Feb, CILLEY D P Eld *MS* 14 Mar 1833

CHAPMAN Smith of New Market m MESERVE Deborah of Durham in Dover NH, WILLIAMS Gibbon Rev *MS* 20 Mar 1834

CHAPMAN Timothy m FOSS Esther W on 5 Apr in New Market, FROST D S Eld *MS* 22 Apr 1846

CHAPMAN Wm m FOGG Vienna of Northwood on 24 Sept in Northwood NH, JOHNSON W D Eld *MS* 17 Oct 1849

CHASE Albert H m SMITH Minerva A of Foster RI on 25 Aug at Thompson CT, LEONARD L G Eld *MS* 11 Sept 1844

CHASE Alfred G m WARD Mary L, NOYES E Eld *MS* 6 Dec 1848

CHASE Ambrose m 14 May GOULD Joanna L both of Hopkinton *MS* 22 June 1836

CHASE Andrew of North Berwick ME m KNIGHT Mary of Parsonsfield ME on 19 Dec 1844 at Parsonsfield ME, JORDAN Z Eld *MS* 12 Mar 1845

CHASE Archibald M m GREEN Angerona on 7 Sept of Stephentown NY, COLEMAN I B Eld *MS* 4 Dec 1844

CHASE Augustus A m BURDICT Lovisa on 17 Feb 1848 in Pierpont
NY, WHITFIELD W Eld *MS* 15 Mar 1848

CHASE Caleb ae 74y m POOR Dorothay Mrs ae 48y both of Chester
in Chester, CHASE Paul Esq *MS* 1 Apr 1840

CHASE Charles A m CHASE Betsey S M of G on 14 Oct at Groton
MA, PECK Benjamin D *MS* 18 Jan 1843

CHASE Charles G of Dover NH m COTTLE Rhua L of Tisbury MA on
4 Aug 1843 *MS* 30 Aug 1843

CHASE Daniel m WENTWORTH Lovina S both of Somersworth on 15
inst Dover, HUTCHINS E Eld *MS* 25 Sept 1850

CHASE Dudly m SYLVESTER Mary C both of Bridgton on 13 Dec
1837 in Bridgton ME, WHITNEY George Eld *MS* 17 Jan 1837

CHASE Ebenezer C m PIKE Rhoda of Jay ME on 6 Apr at Chesterville, WHEELER S Eld *MS* 6 Aug 1845

CHASE George E of Pembroke m HILLIARD Clarissa E of Chichester
on 15 inst in Pittsfield, TRUE E Eld *MS* 21 Nov 1849

CHASE George W of Dover NH m MATHES Ann Miss of Lee on 31st
ult at Lee, THURSTON N Eld *MS* 3 Sept 1834

CHASE George W m STEVENS Eleanor on 5 Oct at Manchester NH,
CILLEY D P Eld *MS* 15 Oct 1845

CHASE Geroge W m MORRELL Mary K, THURSTON N Eld at Lowell
MA *MS* 14 Oct 1835

CHASE Horatio C m BROWN Mary M of Grafton MA on 2 Feb at
Grafton MA, PECK B D Eld *MS* 15 Mar 1843

CHASE Hosea of Meredith m GLINES Lucina on 14 Jan, PITMAN S J
Eld *MS* 12 Feb 1851

CHASE Ira S m SIMANDS Cordelia P both of Alexandria on 22 Mar
1849 in Bristol, BROWN D A Eld *MS* 11 Apr 1849

CHASE John D of North Berwick m LANGLEY Eliza P of South
Berwick on 16 April, JOHNSON W D Eld *MS* 3 May 1843

CHASE John Jr m RUSSELL Mary Ann, PITMAN S J Eld at Meredith
NH *MS* 25 Dec 1844

CHASE Jonathan Esq m REED Phebe Mrs of Danville ME? on 9 Nov
at Danville ME, PERRY S Eld *MS* 3 Dec 1845

CHASE Joseph of Blackstone MA m HARVELL Rachel W of Manchester NH on 21 June, CILLEY D P Eld *MS* 28 Jul 1847

CHASE Joseph m BRIAUT Abigail F of Waterboro' ME on 11 Aug at
Hollis ME, SINCLAIR J L Eld *MS* 11 Sept 1844

CHASE Luther M of Meredith m GORDON Roxana of N Hampton on
7 inst at New Hampton, HILL Eld *MS* 24 Feb 1836

CHASE Nathan M m MASON Elizabeth D both of Haverhill on 26
Mar 1846, *MS* 8 Apr 1846

CHASE Nelson m HARRIS Alzado both of Pascoag RI on 28 Jan 1848
in Pascoag RI, LORD D H Eld *MS* 23 Feb 1848

CHASE Paul Eld m DRAKE Polly Mrs of Plymouth on 3 May at
Holderness, THOMPSON Samuel Eld *MS* 28 May 1845

CHASE Pike m LUFKIN Hannah on 5th inst, SARGENT Rev *MS* 28 Mar 1833

CHASE Robert of Georgetown at Bath ME m FOGG Louisa Ann of Bath, *MS* 22 Oct 1834

CHASE Samuel Jr of Saco ME m McQUESTION Mary J of Biddeford at Saco, BATHRICK S Rev *MFWBR* 11 Jan 1851

CHASE Samuel m CARTER Betsey on 21 Mar 1847 in Albany, FLETCHER J Eld *MS* 25 Aug 1847

CHASE Simpson E of Berkshire VT m MUDGETT Louise of Jackson on 29 Sept 1847 in Jackson NH, LONG L A Eld *MS* 10 Nov 1847

CHASE Stephen B m HAZEN Hannah B both of Weare on 21 Nov in Gilmanton, MOODY D Eld *MS* 11 Dec 1850

CHASE Sumner B of Scarborough m COBB Almira B of Limington on 3 Sept in Limington, STEVENS T Eld *MS* 21 Oct 1846

CHASE Thomas Jr of Alton m PEARY Mary, GLINES Eld *MS* 22 Feb 1843

CHASE Timothy of Campton m HUSE Sally Mrs of Meredith on 19 Mar 1848, PITMAN S J Eld *MS* 21 June 1848

CHASE William P Eld at Warrensburgh NY m MOREHOUSE Sally Ann Miss of Warrensburgh *MS* 5 Aug 1835

CHASE Zachariah T Capt of Georgetown ME m BURGESS Philenia T of Phipsburgh ME, QUINNAM Constant Eld *MS* 25 Feb 1835

CHATLIN Charles of Brighton Monroe Co NY m WRIGHT Mary Ann of Parma on 17 Oct, CRANE E F Eld *MS* 15 Nov 1843

CHATMAN Eliphalet m COOK Adaline both of Tamworth NH on 19 inst in Tamworth, EMERY James Eld *MS* 12 Apr 1837

CHATMAN Emerson m EDGCOMB Lydia Ann both of Corinna ME on 12 Apr 1838 in Corinna, COPP John B Eld *MS* 9 May 1838

CHEESMAN James m DYE Emily both of Freedom NY on 2 Oct in Freedom NY *MS* 11 Dec 1850

CHELLIES Sumner of Newfield on Thurs last m MURRAY Susan, BURBANK S Eld in Limerick ME *MS* 25 Jan 1827

CHELLIS Ira m CLARK Betsy at Great Falls NH *MFWBR* 16 Oct 1847

CHELLIS Joseph H m QUINBY Sarah H in Danville, FULLONTON J Eld *MS* 2 Feb 1842

CHELLIS Seth m WILLIAMS Susan D of Parsonsfield ME on 24 Sept at Parsonsfield ME *MS* 18 Oct 1843

CHENEY A H Dr of Gorham m DOW E E of Buxton on 31 Mar in Buxton ME, BAILEY J M Eld *MS* 24 Apr 1850 & Eliza E *MFWBR* 27 Apr 1850

CHENEY Edmund W m JOHNSON Sally of Bridgewater, FISK Ebenezer Eld *MS* 15 Dec 1841

CHENEY Edmund W of Bristol m JOHNSON Hannah of Bridgewater NH on 5 Mar 1850 in Bridgewater NH, BROWN A Eld *MS* 27 Mar 1850

CHENEY John of New Berlin, Wiskinsan [*sic*] m PARMATER Mary

CHENEY (Continued)

Ann at Attica, Wyoming Co, NY on 13 Jul, LIGHTHALL William A Eld *MS* 6 Sept 1843

CHENEY Moses Jr of Peterboro' m RUNDLETT Rebecca L of Stratham on 10 May, BURBANK P S Eld *MS* 17 May 1843

CHENEY Oren B of Peterboro' m RUNDLETT Caroline A at Stratham, MERRILL A Eld *MS* 4 Mar 1840

CHENEY William of Wilmot m WATSON Pamelia P on 29 Apr at Andover, FROST D S Eld *MS* 14 May 1845

CHESLEY George W m BERRY Samson? on 3 Jan at Sheffield VT *MS* 16 Mar 1836

CHESLEY James C m LORD Sarah A of Lowell on 3 Feb, THURSTON N Eld *MS* 13 Feb 1839

CHESLEY James C of Barrington ROBERTSON Maria L, SHERBURNE S Eld *MS* 25 June 1845

CHESLEY Jeremiah of Palmyra ME m WIGGIN Deborah of Durham, CILLEY Daniel P Eld *MS* 13 Feb 1834

CHESLEY John Jr of Epsom m TIBBETS Joanna of Madbury on Thur last at Barrington, SHERBUNE Samuel Eld *MS* 27 Aug 1834

CHESLEY John of Epsom HOITT/ KEITH Charlotte of Northwood on 28th ult, CILLEY D P Eld *MS* 12 Dec 1833 & "This marriage was inserted in our paper of 12th inst and Bride's name was printed KEITH, but it should have been HOITT" *MS* 26 Dec 1833

CHESLEY John T of Lynn m PARMER Mary E of Lowell on 4 inst in Lowell MA *MS* 14 Sept 1836

CHESLEY Joseph H m EASTMAN Emeline D both of Manchester on 13 Sept Manchester, CILLEY D P Eld *MS* 23 Sept 1846

CHESLEY Moses H of New Durham NH m BERRY Abigail Ann, BERRY Nathaniel Eld *MS* 6 Sept 1843

CHESLEY Samuel of Berrington m SCRUTON Maria of Strafford on 26th ult, SHERBURN Samuel Eld *MS* 2 Jan 1834

CHESWELL Samuel of Durham ult m BRACKETT Betsey Mrs of New Market on 28 Jan in New Market, CILLEY D P Eld *MS* 7 Feb 1838

CHICK Amasa m WENTWORTH Leonora on 1 June at Ossipee NH, CHICK J Eld *MS* 25 June 1845

CHICK Harrison m NUTTER Elizabeth both of Ossipee on 10 Dec 1848, CHICK J Eld in Ossipee *MS* 25 Apr 1849

CHICK Lyman m WIGGIN Naomi on 21 Nov of Ossipee NH, CHICK J Eld *MS* 10 Jan 1844

CHICK Nathan of Limerick ME m FLANDERS Elizabeth C of Buxton ME on 23d inst in Limerick, STEVENS Theodore Eld *MFWBR* 29 May 1847

CHICK Robert m WENTWORTH Lydia of Ossipee NH on 31 Oct at Ossipee NH, HOBBS A W Eld *MS* 6 Dec 1843

CHICK Simon F Capt of Lebanon ME in that place m PRAY Ann B of Shapleigh ME *MS* 5 Jul 1837

CHICK William m LIBBEY Eliza Thursday last in Limington ME, SEAVY John Rev *MS* 10 Aug 1826

CHICK Winthrop F m DRAKE Huldah Jane on 23 Mar at Effingham NH, FOSS N Eld *MS* 6 Apr 1847

CHITTENDEN William m DABOLL Diadama of Stephentown on 24 Dec at Stephentown, COLEMAN I B Eld *MS* 6 Jan 1847

CHOAT George W of Hallowell m DAY Susan on 21 May of Hallowell ME, GATCHELL M Eld *MS* 19 Jul 1843

CHOUNARD Paschal m CARR Sarah Abigail Perthena of Stephentown on 30 Nov at Berlin, COLEMAN I B Eld *MS* 6 Jan 1847

CHUBB Jabez m EDWARDS Phebe C of Lowell MA on 21 May, WOODMAN J Eld *MS* 23 Aug 1843

CHURCH Henry m STRICKLAND Lucena both of Walworth on 25 Dec 1850 in Walworth NY, HOLMES D G Eld *MS* 15 Jan 1851

CHURCHILL Asaph K m BOUTWILL Eliza A both of Lowell on 24 Nov 1847 in Dracut, CURTIS S Eld *MS* 15 Dec 1847

CHURCHILL Charles of New Market m PURINTON Hyrena of Poplin on 6 Jul in Poplin, CILLEY D P Eld *MS* 2 Aug 1837

CHURCHILL Daniel m LANGLEY Eleanor both of Lamprey River MA on 29th ult, CILLEY D P Eld *MS* 7 May 1834

CHURCHILL Ezra Jr m MITCHELL Kezia A both of Montville ME on 19 Nov 1848 in Montville ME, ALLEN Nelson Esq *MS* 17 Jan 1849

CHURCHILL Geo H of Durham (formerly of Brookfield) m DANIELS Mary E of Durham on 10 inst in Dover NH, HUTCHINS E Eld *MS* 30 May 1849

CHURCHILL George m CASTOR Cynthia on 8th inst at Wolcott NY, MASON John B Eld *MS* 1 June 1842

CHURCHILL Ichabod D m QUINT Clarissa B both of Eaton on 30 Dec 1847 in Eaton, MILLS James E Eld *MS* 19 Jan 1848

CHURCHILL Mary C m THOMAS Albert at Augusta on 6th inst *MFWBR* 23 June 1849

CHURCHILL Thomas m BANKS Mary BUZZELL John Eld in Parsonsfield *MS* 24 Mar 1830

CHURCHILL Thomas T m HOIT Eunice B both of Greenland on 30 Nov in Greenland, CILLEY D P *MS* 13 Dec 1837

CHUTE Calvin m ABBOTT Dorcas C of Gorham ME on 17 Feb at Portland ME, MOULTON A K Eld *MS* 9 Jul 1845

CILBRITH - See also COLBATH

CILBRITH Lemuel of Maine at West Plymouth NH m WHITCHER Lavina E at West Plymouth NH, CHASE Paul Eld *MS* 4 Aug 1847

CILLEY Andrew Jackson Capt m SEVERANCE Nancy J of Andover NH on 24 Mar 1842 at Andover NH, WATSON Elijah Eld *MS* 20 May 1842

CILLEY B D m DALTON Sarah A of Gilmanton NH at Gilmanton NH of Kingston *MFWBR* 6 Feb 1847

CILLEY Daniel P Rev of New Market m HAINES Adelaide of Canter-

CILLEY (Continued)

bury on 13th inst, Principal of Female Seminary at Parsonsfield at Canterbury, DYER S B of Loudon *MS* 27 Jan 1836

CILLEY Ebenezer C Capt m CILLEY Phebe Ann both of Andover on 4 June in Salisbury NH *MS* 23 Sept 1846

CILLEY Elbridge G m HUNT Ruth on 27 May at Strafford VT, SHEPARD Almon Eld *MS* 24 Jul 1844

CILLEY Henry D Capt m FULLER Susan F at Andover on 19 Apr, WATSON Elijah Eld *MS* 6 May 1840

CILLEY John F of Tunbridge m CHAMBERLIN Sarah A of Strafford VT on 27 Mar, SHEPARD A Eld *MS* 14 May 1845

CILLEY John O at Nottingham NH m BUTLER Henrietta *MS* 9 Nov 1832

CILLEY Joseph L Esq of Nottingham m KELLEY Lavinia/ Lavina B on 22 ult at Exeter, SMITH Rev Mr *MS* 13 Dec 1837 & *MS* 24 Jan 1838

CILLEY Joseph W m BARTLETT Lydia both of Weare on 4 Feb in Weare, MOODY David Eld *MS* 11 Mar 1840

CILLEY Justin m DOLTON Mary R both of Deerfield NH on 7 June, BURBUNK P S Eld *MS* 20 June 1849

CILLEY Sewel m CLOUGH Temperance Ann both of Barnstead on 9 Nov 1848 in Strafford, HOLMES J C Eld *MS* 17 Jan 1849

CILLEY William Plumer m WHITNEY Emeline both of Epsom on Tues eve 11 inst, CILLEY Daniel P Eld *MS* 13 Feb 1834

CISSEY Robert H of Nassau m PHILIPS Diana of East Nassau on 16 Feb at Sand Lake, COLEMAN I B Eld *MS* 13 Mar 1850

CLAFLIN Charles J m BROWN Taudasa R both of Smithfield on 25 May at Johnston RI, HUTCHINS E Eld *MS* 9 Jul 1834

CLAFLIN Ephraim F m KENDALL Elvira of Brookfield on 10th inst at West Brookfield, CLAFLIN Jabiel Eld *MS* 17 Apr 1839

CLAFLIN Jehiel of Brookfield m STEELE Emily E of Roxbury on 3 inst in Brookfield VT, WILD Daniel Rev *MS* 20 Sept 1837

CLAGGETH Frederick of Newport m RICHARDSON Miriam of Cornish on 4th inst, WILLIAMS Gibbon Rev *MS* 8 June 1831

CLANCY M A of Boston m WILLEY L A Miss formerly of Dover NH on 12 inst in Boston, STOW Baron Rev *MS* 18 Sept 1850

CLARK - See CLARKE

CLARK Abrah S m KIMBALL Sarah F on 19 Dec at Farmington, MEADER Jesse Eld *MS* 12 Feb 1845

CLARK Alfred m BAKER Triphosa of Newbury at Newbury, ROW J Eld *MS* 28 Jul 1847

CLARK Amos F of Norfolk m CARPENTER Clarissa of Lawrence NY on 1 Jan 1849, SQUIRE L Eld *MS* 14 Feb 1849

CLARK Andrew J m WALLACE Catharine H of Dover on 8 inst in Dover NH, SMITH A D Eld *MS* 28 June 1848

CLARK Anthony m PAULS Sarah of Meredith NH on 17 Feb, PITMAN

CLARK (Continued)
Stephen Eld *MS* 24 Mar 1847

CLARK Asa m BATES Mary Ann of Waterville at Waterville ME,
LEWIS Daniel B *MS* 26 June 1839

CLARK Asahel m FRINK Nancy Maria on 3 Sept at Dover Lenawee Co
Mich, DREW E Eld *MS* 29 Nov 1843

CLARK Augustus O m APPLETON Elizabeth F at Alfred, ORR Rev
MFWBR 26 Oct 1850

CLARK B F m LIBBY Betsey on 8th inst at Belfast, FLETCHER Rev
MFWBR 24 Mar 1849

CLARK Benjamin F of Cornish ME m MORRISON Martha A P of
Cornish ME on 5 June at Parsonsfield ME, HACKETT J O Eld *MS*
31 Mar 1847

CLARK Calvin T in Danville SEAVER Martha both of Kingston,
FULLONTON J Eld *MS* 4 May 1842

CLARK Charles C m MOONEY Mary D both of Holderness on 25
Julin Holderness, PERKINS Thomas Eld *MS* 9 Aug 1837

CLARK Charles m BROWN Sarah J both of New Castle on 18 Jul
1849 in Edgecomb ME, PAGE E G Eld *MS* 15 May 1850

CLARK D Mr m HACKET Martha Jane on 2d inst at Dover NH,
HUTCHINS E Eld *MS* 13 Jan 1847

CLARK Daniel D m NASON Hannah both of Dover on 18 inst in
Dover, HUTCHINS E Eld *MS* 21 Oct 1846

CLARK Daniel D m MESERVE Sarah J on 7th inst at Dover NH,
HUNTINS E Eld *MS* 10 Feb 1847

CLARK Dexter m CHASE Mary of Grafton MA on 22 Dec at Groton,
PECK Benjamin D Eld *MS* 18 Jan 1843

CLARK Edward of Cambridge MA m BRACKET Elizabeth Mrs of
Limington ME, STEVENS T Eld *MS* 14 Jul 1847

CLARK George S m MOULTON Martha A at Dover NH *MFWBR* 22
Feb 1851

CLARK Gershom m GRANT Nancy of Dixmont on 6th ult, WHIT-
COMB A Jr Esq *MS* 16 Jan 1839

CLARK Hiram m BELLOWS Harriet C on 11 Jan at Manchester NH,
CILLEY D P Eld *MS* 21 Jan 1846

CLARK Ira m HARMON Mary in Limerick ME, LIBBEY E Eld *MS* 19
Sept 1833

CLARK J Smith m WENTWORTH Adaline J at Dover *MFWBR* 22 Dec
1849

CLARK James L m GERRISH A D L Mrs on 13 Mar at Nottingham,
TUTTLE A Eld *MS* 30 Apr 1845

CLARK James V of Strafford m NUTE Elizabeth of Dover NH on 15th
inst, PERKINS J Rev *MS* 29 Apr 1835

CLARK John m CLARK Love of Barrington, PLACE E Eld *MS* 6 Mar
1839

CLARK John m LIBBY Rebecca both of Great Falls on Sabbath Morn

CLARK (Continued)

26th ult, CURTIS S Eld *MS* 5 Jan 1842

CLARK John C at Dover NH m GILMAN Lucy D on 13 Jan of Dover NH, PERKINS S W Eld *MS* 22 Jan 1845

CLARK John m ROBERTS Martha N A both of Meredith in Meredith, PITMAN S J Eld *MS* 29 Aug 1838

CLARK John of Dover m YOUNG Caroline J of Barnstead on Jul 16 in Barnstead, GEORGE Enos Rev *MS* 24 Jul 1839

CLARK John of Olean NY m WINSOR Betsey M on 3 June at Franklinville, WINSOR Barnet Eld *MS* 4 Sept 1844

CLARK John S of Berwick ME m LINSCOTT Hannah W of Brownfield ME on 3 Jul 1848 at Great Falls NH, BROOKS N Eld *MS* 12 Jul 1848

CLARK Jonathan Jr m OTIS Hannah H on 25th inst at Dover NH, PERKINS Seth W *MS* 1 Oct 1845

CLARK Jonathan P m MUNSEY Mary J both of Manchester on 1 Jan 1848 in Manchester, CILLEY D P Eld *MS* 19 Jan 1848

CLARK Joseph H m GILE Mahala D of Gilmanton on 2 Feb, MASON Lemuel Eld *MS* 22 Feb 1843

CLARK Levi D m RICKER Mary E both of Dover on 25 inst 1847 in Dover, HUTCHINS E Eld *MS* 1 Dec 1847

CLARK Mayhew Jr m AMES Comfort Mrs of Gilford on 22 Oct, CLARK Mayhew Eld *MS* 31 Oct 1838

CLARK Moses m VARNEY Olive of Somersworth at Dover NH, WILLIAMS Gibbon Rev *MS* 5 Dec 1833

CLARK Nelson of Cavendish m WELLS Lucretia B of Springfield on 4 Oct at Windsor, ADAMS Abel Eld *MS* 16 Nov 1842

CLARK Peter of Gilmanton m WEARE Abigail of Dorchester MA on 13 Jul 1848 in Concord NH, KIMBALL J Eld *MS* 26 Jul 1848

CLARK Ransalear E of Boston MA m LEAVITT Elizabeth L of Effingham in Effingham NH, BUTLER O Eld *MS* 29 Jul 1846

CLARK Reuben of Saranac m BRADFORD Pervis of Berkshire VT on 3d Jul at Peru Clinton Co NY, FIELD T Esq *MS* 23 Jul 1845

CLARK Reuben m TOWLE Harriet N of Canaan on 5 Sept at Groton NH, CILLEY J C Esq *MS* 2 Oct 1844

CLARK Rufus F m GEORGE Harriet A both of Dover on 24 ult in Dover, CLARK Mayhew Eld *MS* 10 Jan 1849

CLARK S T Mr at Clinton m NETTLETON Hannah, SPAULDING Joel Eld *MS* 8 Jan 1845

CLARK Samuel m FOSS Mercy of Strafford on 11 Dec at Strafford, STRACY R B Eld *MS* 27 Dec 1843

CLARK Samuel S m TIBBETS Irena on 29 ult at Dover NH, PERKINS J Rev *MS* 9 Nov 1836

CLARK Thaddeus F of Bradford VT m PAGE Amoret J of Newbury VT on 17 Oct 1843 at Chabot VT *MS* 15 Nov 1843

CLARK Thomas C m KENT Elizabeth of Durham on 1 Jan at Dover

CLARK (Continued)
NH, CLARK M Eld *MS* 15 Jan 1845

CLARK Warner Esq of Francestown m HAM Sarah Mrs of Strafford on 9 Nov in Strafford, PLACE E Eld *MS* 13 Dec 1848

CLARK William m CLARK Susan on 11 Dec 1851 in Wells ME, KEENE J Eld Jr *MS* 8 Jan 1851

CLARK William R of Cambridge m WOOD Miriam L of Wellington ME on 29 Jan 1850 in Wellington ME, PRATT C S Eld *MS* 20 Mar 1850

CLARKE Charles of So Berwick m PINKHAM Sarah G of Berwick on 1 inst 1849 in Berwick, LITTLEFIELD Witham H Eld *MS* 18 Apr 1849

CLARKE Isaac F m FOLLANSBEE Harriet of Manchester on 14 Jan at Manchester, CILLEY D P Eld *MS* 14 Feb 1844

CLARKE John m LOW Mary V both of Great Falls on 29 ult, CAVERNO A Eld *MS* 9 Dec 1835

CLAY John m ALLEN Phebe at Wilmot NH *RI* Apr 1820 p 63

CLAY Jonathan of Buxton m CRESSEY Harriet H of Standish on 2 June in Standish, MITCHELL John Eld *MS* 28 Aug 1850

CLEAVELAND Aaron m WEYMOUTH Mary F on 21 Jan at Tunbridge VT, CALLEY D Eld *MS* 24 Feb 1847

CLEAVELAND Jonthan m CROCKER Huldah of Freedom NY on 10 Jan at Freedom NY, JACKSON N A Eld *MS* 21 Feb 1844

CLEAVELAND Levi m BALDWIN Zilpha both of Barnston on Feb 25, MOULTON A W Eld *MS* 15 Apr 1840

CLEAVELAND Simeon m DAVERSON Arthusu [*sic*] T both of Ware on 23 Feb at Pelham MA, PIERCE L Eld *MS* 6 Apr 1836

CLEMENT Benjamin of Moultonboro' m WILLIAMS Mary G of New Market on 9 May, CILLEY D P Eld *MS* 15 May 1839

CLEMENT Charles C m LATHAM Sarah S both of Lowell on 8 June in Lowell, CURTIS S Eld *MS* 24 June 1846

CLEMENT Daniel L of Moultonboro m HILL Polly A of Gilford on 13 Sept in Sandwich, PINKHAM John Eld *MS* 27 Sept 1837

CLEMENT George m CLARK Matilda of Holderness on 21 March at Holderness, MERRILL W S Eld *MS* 21 Apr 1847

CLEMENT J H of Gorham ME m BAKER Sarah C Miss of Somersworth NH at Somersworth, (by) BAKER Moses *MS* 12 Apr 1827

CLEMENT John B m CLIFFORD Clarissa of Barnston on 27th Feb 1839 *MS* 17 Apr 1839

CLEMENT Morrill m WEEKS Mahala both of Hopkinton on 13 Aug in Hopkinton NH, CATLIN S T Eld *MS* 5 Dec 1849

CLEMENTS Daniel m DOW Mary H both of Strafford on 5 Apr in Strafford VT, PETTINGILL John Eld *MS* 29 Apr 1846

CLEMENTS Henry m CURTIS Mary of Monroe on 8 Dec at Monroe *MS* 25 Jan 1843

CLEMENTS Richard at Meredith NH m HALL Mary Jane *MS* 24 Aug

CLEMENTS (Continued)
   MS 24 Aug 1836
CLEMENTS William m YOUNG Betsy on 6 May at Great Falls,
   BROOKS N Eld *MS* 16 May 1849
CLEMMENT Elijah G m RIDLEY Mary C both of Corinth ME on 10
   Dec 1848 in Corinth ME, HARDING E Eld *MS* 21 Feb 1849
CLEMONS Bartlett of Freedom NH m PLUMMER Sally Mrs of Brown-
   field ME on 8 Oct 1848 in Brownsfield ME, HART E H Eld *MS* 15
   Nov 1848
CLEMONS Sudrick m RICHARDSON Lucy, BRACKET D Eld at
   Hiram *MS* 8 Aug 1833
CLENDMAN William m BUTTERFIELD Eliza S, NOYES E Eld *MS* 15
   Dec 1847
CLENSLEY William m DEERING Mary of Edgecomb on 8 Nov at
   Edgecomb ME, PAGE E G Eld *MS* 7 Dec 1842
CLIFFORD Daniel m NORRIS Sarah F on 25 Nov at Manchester NH,
   CILLEY D P Eld *MS* 9 Dec 1846
CLIFFORD George B m REMINGTON Sarah both of Starksborough
   on 16 Dec 1847 in Starksborough VT, DIKE O Eld *MS* 19 Jan
   1848
CLIFFORD George W m ATWOOD Sally E on 1 Mar at Alexander,
   BROWN Amos Eld *MS* 26 Mar 1845
CLIFFORD George W on 7 Apr 1842 at Gilford m GLIDDEN Sarah S
   of Gilford, COOLEY T L Eld *MS* 11 May 1842
CLIFFORD Hiram m IRISH Martha Jane of Gorham ME at Gorham
   ME on Sun 15th inst, BUZZELL J M Eld *MFWBR* 21 Aug 1847
CLIFFORD John H m DREW Eliza S on 26 Mar at Manchester,
   CILLEY D P Eld *MS* 10 Apr 1844
CLIFFORD Josiah m FITTS Susan both of Candia in Candia,
   MANSON B S Eld *MS* 14 June 1837
CLIFFORD Micajah m MARTIN Patta Eliza of Hatley LC on 7 Dec,
   MOULTON A Eld of Stanstead LC *MS* 13 Apr 1842
CLIFFORD Nathan Esq Att at Law m AYER Hannah Miss on Thurs
   last in Newfield, BURBANK Eld *MS*26 Mar 1828
CLIFFORD Stewart m HAWKINS Margaret Ann at Dover NH *MFWBR*
   13 Apr 1850
CLINE Leonard m WHITMAN Melvina on 22 Sept at Three Mile Bay
   NY, PADDEN S B Eld *MS* 7 Dec 1842
CLOCK Josiah m DEWEY Mary Ann on 6 Sept 1846 at Three Mile
   Bay, PADDEN S B Eld *MS* 13 Jan 1847
CLOSE Aaron M of Bangor ME m GORDON Rhoda P on 23 Apr,
   SMALL William Eld *MS* 30 June 1847
CLOUDMAN Richard H m DUNTLEY Rhoda both of Milton on 1 Apr,
   WEDGWOOD Dearborn Eld *MS* 9 May 1849
CLOUGH Alexander m PERKINS Emeline A, NOYES E Eld *MS* 6 Dec
   1848

CLOUGH Charles of Barnstead m PLACE Mary E on 22 Nov, PALMER Abbot Rev *MS* 6 Dec 1843

CLOUGH Charles m PLACE Mary E "we learn that notice of the marriage of (the above) published in our last, was a hoax. No such union has been formed. The notice was forwarded from Barnstead postage paid; but the name was not given..." *MS* 13 Dec 1843

CLOUGH Charles of Barnstead on 3 Mar at Madbury m SAUNDERS Juliann of Madbury, STACY R B Eld *MS* 24 Mar 1847

CLOUGH Daniel m CLOUGH Hannah D both of Delaware, Walworth Co Wis on 26 Aug in that town, COOMBS Abner Eld *MS* 17 Oct 1849

CLOUGH David E m CLARK Nancy B on 2 Feb at Alton NH, FERNALD S P Eld *MS* 26 Feb 1845

CLOUGH David F m HUFF Isabella on 11th Dec at Kennebunkport ME, WITHAM L H Eld *MS* 1 Mar 1843

CLOUGH Henry C of Readfield me m TUCKER Elizabeth B of Mt Vernon at Mt Vernon ME, FOGG Dudley *MS* 29 June 1836

CLOUGH James of Readfield m DUDLEY Sarah of Mt Vernon ME, FOGG Dudley Esq *MS* 25 Mar 1835

CLOUGH Jeremiah m DREW Betsey B both of Loudon in Canterbury*MS* 19 Jan 1848

CLOUGH John m WHITEHOUSE Mehitabel both of Wolfborough NH on 27th ult, HOLMES H Eld *MS* 21 May 1834

CLOUGH John P of Gilmanton m WINKLEY Tamson H of Alton NH on Feb in Gilmanton, FERNALD S P Eld *MS* 22 May 1850

CLOUGH Jonathan S m STEVENS Susan A both of Alton NH in Alton NH, PINKHAM John Eld *MS* 20 Dec 1848

CLOUGH Jones L m HAINES Lydia O both of Biddeford ME in Saco ME, HALL T M Eld *MS* 13 Feb 1850

CLOUGH Joseph A of Strafford NH m WELLS Hannah M of Epson NH on 27 May in Epson NH, FOSS T Eld *MS* 10 June 1846

CLOUGH Joseph M m BUCKLIN Ahiah both of Manchester on 9 Aug in Manchester, CILLEY D P Eld *MS* 12 Sept 1849

CLOUGH Melville of Kennebunkport ME m KIMBALL Elizabeth J of Kennebunk ME on 18th inst at Biddeford ME, BLAKE H M Rev *MFWBR* 1 Dec 1849

CLOUGH Nathaniel D m MOORE Eliza A of Loudon NH on 27 Nov at Canterbury, CLOUGH Jeremiah Eld *MS* 11 Feb 1846

CLOUGH Willard m DUSTIN Charlotte both of Hopkinton on 24 Jul *MS* 12 Oct 1836

CLOUTMAN Eliphalet Esq 80y m BERRY Sarah Miss ae 40y of Rochester NH at Dover NH, THURSTON Nathaniel Eld *MS* 25 Apr 1833

CLOUTMAN Mark W m BURNETT Susan both of Gorham ME on 30th Sept, WHITE J Eld *MS* 12 Nov 1835

CLOWD William W m BEEBE Abigail on 26 Dec at Manchester, AYER Aaron Eld *MS* 8 Jan 1845

CLUFF Irony m McKENNY Phebe J on 11 May 1843 at Kennebunkport ME, WITHAM L H Eld *MS* 24 May 1843

CLUFF Nahum m CLUFF Mary on 30 Oct at Kennebunkport ME, WITHAM L H Eld *MS* 20 Nov 1844

CLUFF Shadrach m EMMONS Ann on 14 Oct at Kennebunkport ME, WITHAM L H Eld *MS* 20 Nov 1844

CLUM Edward R m SMITH Mercy A both of Walworth NY on 8 Jan in Walworth NY, HOLMES D G Eld *MS* 5 Mar 1851

COATS Charles G m TURNER Roxa R C of Concord on 15 Nov in Manchester, CILLEY D P Eld *MS* 5 Dec 1849

COBB Andrew of Limington m COLE Caroline D of Limerick ME on 3 Sept in Limington, STEVENS T Eld *MS* 21 Oct 1846

COBB Cyrus of Hiram ME m BLACK Abigail of Limington ME, RAND James Eld *MS* 8 Mar 1843

COBB Geo W m CUTTER Mary E on 29th ult at Portland ME, CARRUTHERS Dr Rev *MFWBR* 11 May 1850

COBB Jon L H m MORRILL L P Miss on 10th inst at Biddeford ME, FARRINGTON Rev *MFWBR* 30 Dec 1848

COBB Merritt N m LEWIS Louisa L of Portland ME on 8th inst at Portland *MFWBR* 21 Dec 1850

COBB N Mr m HART Jane on 17 March at Harrisburg Lewis Co NY, ABBY M H Eld *MS* 21 Apr 1847

COBB Samuel S m HODGKINS Deborah on 30 Nov at Westbrook ME, PERKINS Seth W Eld *MS* 20 Dec 1843

COBB Stephen M m BRADBURY Mary G of Limerick ME at West meeting house in Limington ME, LIBBY C O Eld *MS* 17 Sept 1845

COBB Thomas m COBB Louisa on 21 May at Portland ME, MOULTON A K Eld of Portland ME *MS* 9 Jul 1845

COBB Uriah m GODDWIN Martha on 16 Jan at Berwick ME, CAVERNO A Eld *MS* 6 Feb 1834

COBB William H of New Gloucester ME m THURLOW Emily Jane at Raymond ME, SMALL C Eld *MS* 25 Jan 1843

COBLEIGH Amos S of Sutton VT m LEAVETT Hannah of Sheffield on 3 Nov, CROSS D Eld *MS* 27 Nov 1850

COBURN Edward of Parkman ME m HANSON Elizabeth of Monmouth ME, FIELD A Eld *MS* 7 Feb 1833

COBURN Edwin m COOLBROTH Elizabeth both of Gorham ME on 7th ult in Standish ME, WHITE Joseph Eld *MS* 21 Jan 1835

COBURN Hiram S DOBIE m Sarah Ann both of West Sumner ME on 25 Nov at West Sumner *MFWBR* 8 Dec 1849

COBURN Isaiah of Greene ME m CUTLER Sarah of Bangor ME on 10th ult at Bangor ME *MFWBR* 2 Feb 1850

COBURN J Milton Eld (pastor of the Baptist Church) m MORSE Almira of Effingham NH on 21st inst at Effingham NH, HAYDEN L

COBURN (Continued)
Eld of Dover NH *MS* 3 Aug 1842
COBURN James M FULLER m Mary F both of West Brookfield VT on Sept 5 1841, CLAFLIN Jehiel Eld *MS* 5 Jan 1842
COBURN John C of Pittston m STINSON Margaret E of Arrowsic ME at Georgetown ME *MFWBR* 7 Aug 1847
CODMAN William W m MELLEN Dorcas both of Deering on 21 May in Weare, MOODY David Eld *MS* 24 June 1846
COE James m BARNS Jane Ann both of Davenport on 15 Jan in Meredith NY, GREENE D Eld *MS* 19 Feb 1851
COFFIN Benjamin Jr m CLARK Lucy S both of Alton NH, BUZZELL H D Eld *MS* 18 Dec 1839
COFFIN Charles of Dixfield ME m BENSON Abigail G of Peru ME, ALLEN John "a traveling preacher of the Methodist Episcopal church" *MS* 14 Apr 1847
COFFIN Enoch S m JONES Martha of Thorndike on 8th ult at Thorndike *MS* 20 Apr 1832
COFFIN George W NUTE m Sarah M at Dover NH *MFWBR* 27 Apr 1850
COFFIN Isaac P of Alton m CLOUGH Phebe E of Gilmanton NH on 3rd ult at Barnstead, GARLAND D Eld *MS* 13 Mar 1839
COFFIN James M m PHILBRICK Elizabeth H on 11 Mar in Thorndike ME *MS* 8 May 1850
COFFIN John of Leeds ME m TOWNSEND Lois of Auburn ME, LIBBEY Isaac Eld *MS* 27 Nov 1844
COFFIN Lorenzo S of Wolfboro NH m CURTIS Cynthia T of Warsaw NY on 24 Aug 1848 in Oberlin Ohio, WHIPPLE H E Eld *MS* 27 Dec 1848
COFFIN Morrill M m PALMER Mary A of Hampton on 5 Jul at Hampton, BURBANK P S Eld *MS* 14 Jul 1847
COFFIN Samuel S Capt m EDGERLY Sarah Jane of Barnstead on 1 Oct at Alton, FERNALD S P Eld *MS* 25 Oct 1843
COFFIN Sargent of Thorndike m EMERY Mary of Thorndike on 9th ult *MS* 29 Jul 1831
COFFIN Simeon of Thorndike m BOOTHBY Jane A of Unity on 10 May in Unity ME, ROBINSON N J Eld *MS* 27 May 1846
COFFIN Stephen of Wolfboro' NH m FOSS Caroline of Poughkeepsie, Dutchess Co, NY on 3rd inst at Barrington NH *MS* 10 Apr 1839
COFFIN William P m HUNT Abigail A on 5th inst at Portland ME, MOULTON A K Eld *MS* 13 Mar 1844
COFFING Abiel of Saco m WARREN Mary of Limerick ME on Monday at Limerick, LIBBY Eld *MS* 27 Dec 1827
COFFMAN Nicholas m STEBBENS Lucinda on 28 Feb 1850 in Lockport Erie Co PA, PAGE J B Eld *MS* 10 Apr 1850
COGSWELL Jonathan of Dorchester m FIFIELD Louisa L of Manchester in Deerfield NH, BURBANK P S Eld *MS* 18 Dec 1850

COLBATH - See also CILBRITH

COLBATH Isaac of Gardiner ME m SMALL Ruth Mrs of Bowdoinham ME on 13 Nov, QUINNAM C Eld *MS* 17 Dec 1845

COLBATH John m DORE Keziah both of Alton on 19 inst at Dover NH, MACK Enoch Eld *MS* 27 Jan 1836

COLBATH Lyman of Farmington NH m WENTWORTH Paulina of Lebanon on 26 Nov at Lebanon ME, CHENEY O B Eld "Accompanying this marriage notice was a liberal slice of cake ... Long life and a happy one to our young friends." *MS* 2 Dec 1846

COLBETH Franklin m GARLAND Dorothy T both of Middleton on 19 Nov, SMALL C Eld *MS* 8 Jan 1851

COLBURN Thomas of Wilton ME m HATHAWAY Rebecca of Wilton on 4th ult, HATHAWAY Leonard Eld *MS* 19 Aug 1831

COLBY Andrew P (printer) of Dover m PHILBRICK Huldah of Freedom NH on 3 Jul at Freedom, COBURN Rev *MS* 10 Jul 1844

COLBY Benjamin merchant of Dover NH m DEARBORN Harriet of Deerfield NH on 12 inst, KIMBALL J Eld *MS* 23 Sept 1835

COLBY Cyrus of Bow m BROWN Mehitabel of Gilford on 16 Sept 1848 in Canterbury, HARRIMAN J Eld *MS* 13 Dec 1848

COLBY Daniel m WILLIAMS Mary Ellen of Moultonboro' NH on 3 Dec at Effingham NH, HART E H Eld *MS* 30 Dec 1846

COLBY Edward of Athens ME m FOGG Mary Jane of Limerick ME on 23d ult, BURBANK Eld *MS* 1 Oct 1828

COLBY Elias Esq of Richmond ME m CHASE Margaret of Topsham ME on 6 Mar in Topsham ME, PURINGTON C Eld *MS* 27 Mar 1850

COLBY J B m MERRILL Catharine both of Manchester on 27 Jan 1848 in Manchester, CILLEY Daniel P Eld *MS* 2 Feb 1848

COLBY John of Bow NH m BROWN Mary Ann on 20 June at Gilford, PINKHAM John Eld *MS* 12 Oct 1842

COLBY John P of Danville m SKANE Hannah of Nashua, WATSON Elijah Eld *MS* 6 May 1840

COLBY Lucius m DAY Ruth both of Lowell on 6 Apr 1848 in Dracut MA, CURTIS S Eld *MS* 26 Apr 1848

COLBY Nehemiah Jr m COLCORD Betsey both of Candia on 18 ult in Candia, MANSON B S Eld *MS* 2 Aug 1837

COLBY Oliver m COOKLIN Hepzibah, COWING David Eld at Landaff NH *MS* 16 Jul 1828

COLBY Timothy m ELLIS Caroline E both of Haverhill MA on 7 Nov 1847 in Haverhill MA, MERRIL Wm P Eld *MS* 8 Dec 1847

COLCORD Steven of Candia m SMITH Sarah Ann of Meredith NH on 8th inst, PITMAN S J Eld *MS* 31 Jan 1833

COLE - see COE

COLE Bradford W m DAY Sarah I both of Brownfield on 4 Jul, HART E H Eld *MS* 24 Jul 1850

COLE Clark C of Cornish m BRIGGS Mary E of Cornish *MS* 18 Oct

COLE (Continued)
    1827

COLE Ephraim Jr of Etan m ARCHIBALD Sarah of Plymouth on 9 Sept in Plymouth, WHITCOMB A Esq *MS* 24 Oct 1838

COLE Harrison L m COLE Elmira S both of Lewiston ME on 23 June in Lewiston, LIBBY Isaac Eld *MS* 17 Oct 1838

COLE Henry C m CHICK Emily Ann both of Cornish on 10th inst, STEVENS John Eld *MS* 19 Oct 1832

COLE Hiram H m SHEHAN Martha on 28 Nov 1841 at Saco ME, WITHAM L H Eld *MS* 29 Dec 1841

COLE Ivory 2d m WALKER Cyrenia both of Brownfield on 16 June, HART E H Eld *MS* 24 Jul 1850

COLE J H Mr m LOWELL Jane of Hatley LC, MOULTON A Eld *MS* 13 Sept 1843

COLE James L m RANKINS Sarah both of Wells *MS* 27 Mar 1834

COLE James R Dr of Saccarappa ME m HAMILTON Martha A of Waterboro ME on 7th inst at Waterboro ME, DREW Ira T Esq *MFWBR* 13 Apr 1850

COLE Jeremiah of Lewiston ME m BAILEY Anna of Auburn ME on 8th inst at Lewiston ME, BURGESS J S Eld *MFWBR* 16 June 1849

COLE Jeremiah B of Waterborough ME m BROWN Theodate of Effingham in Effingham NH, COBURNS J Milton Rev *MS* 15 Jan 1840

COLE John T m LINSCOTT Mary G both of Brownfield on 4 Jul, HART E H Eld *MS* 24 Jul 1850

COLE John W m WOODMAN Rachel A both of Dover on 29 ult in Dover, HUTCHINS E Eld *MS* 1 Aug 1849

COLE John W merchant m HENRY Sila on 11 inst in Providence, CAVERNO A Eld *MS* 19 Dec 1838

COLE Joseph of Pawtucket m SMITH Louisa of Cumberland RI on 21 Sept at East Killingly CT, WILLIAMS D Eld *MS* 10 Oct 1844

COLE Joseph W m BOODY Hannah at Saco ME *MFWBR* 12 June 1847

COLE Kimball of New Market m STOCKWELL Mary of Athol MA on 17th inst, MERRIAM Asaph Eld *MS* 30 Mar 1842

COLE Mooers Eld of Salem m STEARNS Elizabeth S Mrs of Lowell on 11 inst in Lowell MA, MOULTON A K Eld *MS* 19 Mar 1851

COLE Ossian Z m CHANDLER Almira H at South Paris ME on 6th inst *MFWBR* 21 Jul 1849

COLE Pearl K m WHIDDEN Mary Jane both of Dover NH on Thurs last, THURSTON N Eld *MS* 5 Dec 1833

COLE Phinehas m BOWLES Julia Ann of Lisbon on 14 Nov at Franconia NH, GEORGE N K Eld *MS* 11 Dec 1844

COLE Samuel Jr of Shapleigh m DAVIS Sally of Newfield on Thursday last, BURBANK Eld *MS* 19 Nov 1828

COLE Samuel of Saco m CILLEY Louisa of Limerick ME, FOSS Eld
MS 26 Aug 1831

COLE Samuel of Wells m GARDINER Lucy of Biddeford ME on 10
Nov 1847 in Biddeford ME, WITHAM L H Eld MS 1 Dec 1847

COLE Solomon Jr formerly of Whitefield m PEASLEE Caroline E of
Nashville NY on 5 Nov at Nashville, PIKE J Rev MS 18 Nov 1846

COLEMAN Elisha E m JOHNSON Elizabeth on 9th Feb at Portsmouth NH, MERRILL William P Eld MS 26 Feb 1845

COLEMAN James m HOLMES Eliza of Portsmouth NH on 14 Dec at
Portsmouth NH, DAVIS Isaac G Eld MS 10 Jan 1844

COLEMAN Joseph m WOOD Sally of Smithstown on 3 Feb at
Smyrna NY, CARD E Eld MS 9 June 1847

COLEMAN Joseph W m GOODWIN May F both of Dover on 13 inst
in Dover, HUTCHINS E Eld MS 21 Feb 1849

COLESWORTHY William W of Dover NH m DOLBEAR Elizabeth of
Charlestown MS 21 Nov 1833

COLLEY Chase of Effingham NH divorced COLLEY Salley MS 3 Sept
1828

COLLEY Hiram m PEASLEY Polly both of Weare on Nov 14, MOODY
David Eld 12 Feb 1840

COLLEY Nathaniel m DURGIN Sarah both of Lowell MA MS 10 Aug
1836

COLLIER True H m ROGERS Lovina both of Lowell MA, THURSTON
N Eld MS 14 Oct 1835

COLLINS Alva B of Danville m ALLEN Mary A of Epsom NH on 15
Nov 1849, RAMSEY G P Eld in Epsom NH MS 16 Jan 1850

COLLINS Benjamin H of New London m SEWALL Hannah of Wilmot
on 1 Jan, BARTLETT J O D Eld MS 28 Jan 1846

COLLINS Charles P m LIBBY Abigail both of Lowell MA MS 12 Nov
1835

COLLINS David O of Amesbury MA m MOORE Achasah Ann of
Salisbury MA on 29 Sept at Deerfield MS 18 Nov 1835

COLLINS Frederick of Goffstown m CROSS Statira of Northfield NH
on 30 Sept in Northfield NH, CLOUGH Jeremiah Eld MS 14 Oct
1846

COLLINS John H m COLLINS Amy of Danville on 21 Nov at Danville
NH?, MERRILL William P Eld MS 20 Jan 1847

COLLINS Moses of Wilmington MA m TOWLE Mary of Hampton on
18th inst at Hampton, BURBANK P S Eld MS 5 Oct 1842

COLLINS Robert of Kittery ME m BLAKE Martha J of Kittery ME,
WETHERBEE K J Eld MS 1 Jan 1845

COLLY William B m FULLONTON Cyntha Jane on 1st inst at New
Market, HUTCHINS E Eld MS 19 Jul 1843

COLMAN Thomas C m BERRY Louisa Ann both of Durham on 6 inst
in Dover, HUTCHINS E Eld MS 13 June 1849

COLOMY Moses at Great Falls NH m DURGIN Irene of New Market

COLOMY (Continued)
NH, CURTIS S Eld *MS* 15 Mar 1843

COLVIN Welcome m BENNETT Malita both of Coventry, NOYES E
Eld *MS* 13 Nov 1850

COLWELL John W m WING Hannah W both of No Providence on 17
inst, HUTCHINS E Eld *MS* 7 Oct 1835

COMFORTH Oliver m CORSON Hannah of Waterville ME, LEWIS D
B Eld *MS* 25 Dec 1844

COMFORTH Robert 2d of Unity ME m CROSBY Rosetta, LEWIS D B
Eld at Unity ME *MS* 25 Dec 1844

COMSTOCK Ebenezer of Williamstown MA m ALLEN Susan M of
Stephentown NY on 14 Mar in Stephenton NY, COLEMAN I B Eld
MS 8 Apr 1846

CONANT George H of Charlestown MA m MOSES Harriet of Allenstown NH on 26 June, SWETT D Eld *MS* 23 Oct 1844

CONANT Nathan D m SIMPSON Elizabeth C on 17 Oct 1849 in
Roxbury MA, CURTIS S Eld *MS* 13 Feb 1850

CONANT Winslow of Auburn ME m ROBINS Olevia C of Lewiston ME
on 22 Oct at Lewiston ME, BEAN G W Eld *MS* 9 Dec 1846

CONDORE Joseph B m PIERCE Rosina both of Brunswick ME on 27
Aug 1848 in Brunswick ME, LIBBY Almon Eld *MS* 20 Sept 1848

CONEY George of Abington m LONG Caroline of Benton PA on 4
Julin Abington PA, CARPENTER R Eld MA 17 Jul 1850

CONFORTH Robert at Fairfield ME m WETHERSPOON Elizabeth,
LEWIS D B Eld *MS* 17 Apr 1844

CONGER Potter m JEWELL Mary both of Dickinson NY on 5 Apr in
Dickinson NY, SQUIRES Eld *MS* 17 June 1846

CONKEY Fortus of Canton m SACKETT Cornelia of Pierpont, WHIT-
FIELD Eld *MS* 18 Oct 1843

CONKLIN William m FREDRICK Julia on 24 Feb at Farmington NY,
HOLMES D G Eld *MS* 12 May 1847

CONNELL Wm of Gorham ME m PLAISTED Ann Miss of Standish
ME, HODSDON Caleb Esq *MS* 23 Nov 1832

CONNER Benjamin m BENNET Mary on 1 Jan 1845 at Alton NH,
BUZZELL H D Eld *MS* 19 Feb 1845

CONNER William H m PHILBROOK Mary P of Sanbornton NH on 10
Dec at New Hampton at New Hampton, MANSON L Eld *MS* 29
Jan 1845

CONNEY Samuel m BODGE Hannah of Dover NH on 2 Dec at Dover
NH, BROCK H H Eld *MS* 11 Dec 1844

CONNOR Asa m SARGEANT Cybil R on 24 inst at New Chester *MS*
11 May 1836

COOK Amos m ARCHIBALD Sally at Acton ME, FULLONTON J Eld
MS 18 Oct 1843

COOK Benjamin m ESTES Mary Mrs both of Dover on 9 inst in
Dover, HUTCHINS E Eld *MS* 12 Aug 1846

COOK Ebenezer R m DOLLOFF Sarah Jane on 2 Nov at Charlestown MA, WETHERBEE I J Eld *MS* 3 Dec 1845

COOK Edward H m DAVIS Clara A on Christmas Eve at Charlestown MA, WETHERBEE I J Eld *MS* 17 Feb 1847

COOK Elisha of Westford m LINDSAY Emeline A of Jericho on 12 Julin Jericho VT, PARMERLY S Rev *MS* 8 Aug 1849

COOK Hiram H of Westford m DAVIS Emeline of Jericho on 1 Jan in Jericho VT, DIKE O Eld *MS* 29 Jan 1851

COOK Jacob m KESTER Miss on 29 April at Hamburgh NY, PLUMB H N Eld *MS* 19 May 1847

COOK James McNorton m PAGE Nancy C on 9 Dec 1848 in Wakefield, SPINNEY Joseph Eld *MS* 3 Jan 1849

COOK John D of Biddeford m PIKE Rachel on 5th inst at Waterboro, EMERY Nathaniel Esq *MFWBR* 11 May 1850

COOK John Eld on 8 Nov 1846 at Garland ME m ADAMS Mary J of Garland ME, AMES M Eld *MS* 20 Jan 1847

COOK John m KINESTON Sally R both of Exeter ME on 29th ult, NASON Samuel V Eld *MS* 23 Jan 1834

COOK Joseph S m DEARBORN Almira P both of Danville on 16 Sept in Danville NH, MERRILL Wm P Eld *MS* 23 Sept 1846

COOK Moses of Boston m VARNEY Sarah T of Dover NH on 31st ult *MS* 8 Aug 1833

COOK P M m GOLDSMITH Mary at Ossipee on 8 ult, CHICK John Eld *MS* 22 Apr 1840

COOK Robinson m MAXFIELD Eliza Ann H both of Raymond ME, ROLLINS A Eld *MS* 12 Nov 1834

COOK Solomon m HAYES Susan A on 25 inst 1847 in Dover, HUTCHINS E Eld *MS* 1 Dec 1847

COOK Stephen S m RUSSELL Rosamond at Dover NH, THURSTON Nathaniel Eld *MS* 25 Apr 1833

COOK Thomas m EMERY Sarah Ann both of Dover NH on 17 ult in Dover NH, SMITH A D Eld *MS* 6 Sept 1837

COOKSON Reuben of Unity ME at Thorndike ME m WOOD Jane, LEWIS D B Eld *MS* 25 Dec 1844

COOL William P of Hebron m NEWTON Lois Mrs of Bingham PA on 7 Nov 1847 at Bingham Potter Co PA, JEFFERS WM Rev *MS* 1 Dec 1847

COOL Zebulon of Tamworth m MARCH Abigail of Eaton, SANBORN Thomas Eld *MS* 17 Jul 1839

COOLEY John L m WHITEHOUSE Abra K of Alton on 24 Oct, BUZZELL H D Eld *MS* 14 Nov 1833

COOLEY Ruel m BALDWIN Harriet Dyantha of Ellington NY on 12 Oct 1847 at F W Baptist Meeting House in Ellington NY, M'KAY J A Eld *MS* 9 Feb 1848

COOLEY Ward C m PRIEST Sally W both of Lisbon NH on 23 Feb at Lisbon (Sugar Hill) *MS* 15 Mar 1837

COOLY Jervis m LEONARD Rachel of Three Mile Bay on 29th Sept.
    PADDEN S B Eld *MS* 13 Jan 1847
COOMBS Albion P of Rochester Wis m AUGIR Harriet W of East Troy
    Wis on 5 Oct 1848 in East Troy Wis, AUGIR F P *MS* 29 Nov 1848
COOMBS David H of Chichester m DOE Nancy of Parsonsfield ME
    on 21 inst *MS* 28 Sept 1836
COOMBS Isaac m MARSHALL Temperance at Isleboro ME on Jan 2,
    FLETCHER Jabez Eld *MS* 25 Mar 1840
COOMBS John m BORNEY Julia, LIBBY A Eld in Durham ME *MS*
    12 Mar 1851
COOMBS Robert of Bowdoin ME m GRANT Elizabeth R of Richmond
    ME on 25th ult at Richmond ME, GRANT James W Esq *MS* 16
    Oct 1844
COOMBS William G of Lewiston ME m KINSLEY Clarinda A of
    Auburn ME, LIBBEY Isaac Eld *MS* 27 Nov 1844
COOMBS/COOMS William m MARR Jerusha S on 17 Dec at Bath
    ME, HOBSON P M Eld *MS* 17 Jan 1844
COON Dewitt C of Bradford m STILLMAN Mary Ann of Newport on
    29th Jan *MS* 24 May 1843
COONS Marlow of Stephentown m WOODBECK Hannah Mrs of
    Nassau NY on 27 Jan 1849 in Nassau NY, COLEMAN I B Eld *MS*
    2 May 1849
COOPER Charles on 3 Jan 1848 m ENNIS Deborah both of Burrill-
    ville RI, LORD D H Eld in Pascoag RI *MS* 23 Feb 1848
COOPER John P of Newcastle m BOARDMAN Ann G of Portsmouth
    NH, CLARK Rev on 21st ult at Portsmouth NH *MFWBR* 4 Dec
    1847
COPP Albert m BEAN Mary Jane both of Dover on 14 Jul in Ports-
    mouth, CAVERNO A Eld *MS* 22 Jul 1846
COPP George of Lawrence MA m EMERY Mary E of North Berwick
    ME on 19th ult at North Berwick, HOBBS Thomas I Esq *MFWBR*
    12 May 1849
COPP Henry A of Moultonboro' NH m HUTCHINS Lovinia S,
    BROOKS N Eld *MS* 2 June 1847
COPP Jeremiah L of Detroit m PRINCE Hannah L on 5 Nov, COPP E
    Eld *MS* 27 Dec 1843
COPP John B m PARKMAN Nathan T on 28 Mar at Corinna ME,
    COPP John B Eld *MS* 1 May 1839
COPP John of Chandlerville m MILLS Syrena on 9th inst at Water-
    boro ME, LIBBY E Eld *MS* 20 June 1833
COPP Samuel of Chandlerville ME m MILLS Betsey of Corinna on 30
    Dec 1838 at Corinna, COPP J B Eld *MS* 24 Apr 1839
COPPS William m GREEN Delilah on 21 Aug *MS* 7 Nov 1849
CORBET John C of Stewartstown NH m ALLARD Samantha of Straf-
    ford VT on 15 Oct 1848 in Strafford VT, CLARK E Eld *MS* 6 June
    1849

COREY Ralph of Albany m BEAN Malinda of Wheelock on Jan 4 1842 *MS* 2 Feb 1842

CORLESS Reuben m MASTON Sally of Lowell MA *MS* 3 May 1843

CORLISS Aaron m HALE Nancy Jane on 2 Feb at Manchester NH, CILLEY D P Eld *MS* 19 Feb 1845

CORLISS David B of Alexandria m SMITH Eliza A of East Livermore ME on 23 Jan in Amesbury MA, MERRILL W P Eld *MS* 12 Feb 1851

CORLISS Gilman m GILMAN Miriam both of Sandwich on 16 Feb, KENISTON T Eld *MS* 26 Mar 1851

CORLISS Joseph of Bath SMALL Jane M of Bowdoinham ME on 26th inst, LIBBY Aaron *MS* 17 May 1843

CORNER Moses of Parsonsfield ME m DURGIN Roxanna of Limerick ME on 19 June, HACKETT John O Eld *MS* 28 June 1843

CORNING John S WALCOTT Sarah A both of Brasher NY on 11 Sept in Brasher NY, WHITEFIELD W Eld *MS* 2 Oct 1850

CORNING Nathan m ADAMS Jane on 2 Nov at Lawrence NY, SWEAT J Eld *MS* 23 Dec 1846

CORNISH Lincoln of Bowdoin ME m WOODARD Sarah W of Lisbon ME on 27 Oct 1850 in Lisbon ME, BARD N Eld *MS* 8 Jan 1851

CORSON Benjamin m NOYES Mary both of Rochester on 24 Oct 1847 in Rochester NH, MEADER Jesse Eld *MS* 17 Nov 1847

CORSON Loring m HUSSEY Sarah of Waterville, LEWIS Daniel B Eld *MS* 30 Nov 1842

CORSON Phineas m WALLINGFORD Louisana both of Lebanon ME in Lebanon ME, CROWELL D B Eld *MS* 22 May 1850

CORY Harvey of Danby m LAKE Betsey Ann of Tinmouth VT on 23 Dec 1847 in Tinmouth VT, PRATT C N Eld *MS* 12 Jan 1848

COTRAL David C m DINGMAN Lydia in Poestenkill NY, HOAG I J Eld *MS* 15 Jan 1851

COTTLE Albert of Waterville ME m ABBOTT Abigail of Sidney ME, LEWIS Daniel B Eld *MS* 25 Nov 1846

COTTLE William of Dover NH m RANLET Mary L of Waltham MA in Wolfborough, PARIS C Eld *MS* 18 Apr 1849

COTTON ARIAL C m STEVENS Matilda T both of Troy on 5 Dec in Jackson ME, RINES J N Eld *MS* 25 Dec 1850

COTTON Daniel of Wolfboro m LANG Eliza H of Brookfield on 1 inst in Brookfield, WALKER J Eld *MS* 15 Aug 1838

COTTON Foss H m FOSS Harriet of Strafford *MS* 23 Nov 1836

COTTON John F of Wolfboro' m 27th ult YOUNG Mercy Miss of Effingham NH, HOLMES H Eld *MS* 21 Mar 1833

COTTON Mark F m HERBERT Mary A on 13 Nov at Haverhill, MOULTON F Eld *MS* 22 Jan 1845

COTTON Nelson of Holderness NH m LEE Mary of Lowell MA, CURTIS Sarah *MS* 9 Jul 1845

COTTON Oliver m JOHNSON Margary of Brownfield on 13th inst at

COTTON (Continued)
Brownfield ME, PEAVY S Eld *MS* 6 Sept 1843

COTTON Samuel of Wolfboro m HOBBS Abigail of Effingham NH on 16 Mar, JACKSON D Eld *MS* 20 Apr 1831

COTTON William m SUNBOWER Phebe on 6 Mar at Tyrone Fayette Co PA, WHEELER S Eld *MS* 26 Mar 1845

COTTON Wm Jr m STURGIS Maria both of Gorham on 23d ult in Standish ME, WHITE J Eld *MS* 8 Apr 1835

COTTRELL John C of Sand Lake m CHITTENDEN Rhoda on 16 Mar, COLEMAN I B Eld *MS* 24 Apr 1844

COUCH Samuel 2d m MOODY Sally of Boscawen on 15 Jul in Nashua, STEARNS S Eld *MS* 29 Jul 1846 5 Aug 1846

COUILLARD Alfred R m HOWARD Lois J both of Bangor ME on 16 ult in Bangor ME, ROBINSON N J Eld *MS* 7 June 1848

COUILLARD David on 21 Dec 1834 m COUILLARD Susan J both of Corinna ME, NASON S V Eld *MS* 11 Mar 1835

COURSON Michael E of Rochester m BUTLER Mary of Berwick ME on 11 inst in Dover NH, SMITH E Rev *MS* 20 Sept 1837

COURSON Willard of Rochester m WINGATE Lydia of Somersworth in Dover NH, SMITH Eleazer Rev *MS* 7 Feb 1838

COUSENS John of Kennebunk ME m HALEY Sylva M of Hollis ME on 12 May, SINCLAIR J L Eld *MS* 26 June 1844

COUSINS Samuel m DAVIS Olive of Dover on 24 Oct at Dover NH, BROCK H H Eld *MS* 30 Oct 1844

COWDRY Elias N m JOHNSON Eliza at Lowell, THURSTON N Eld *MS* 15 May 1839

COWELL George C m PERRY Eliza A both of Great Falls NH on 8 Jan in Great Falls, BROOKS N Eld *MS* 16 Jan 1850

COX Alfred m STEARNS Susan C both of New Market on 11 Oct in Durham, FROST D S Eld *MS* 14 Oct 1846

COX Charles H m BEAN Sarah E of Lowell MA on 10th inst at Dracut MA, CURTIS S Eld *MS* 18 Mar 1846

COX Charles of Hatley m RANDALL Sarah of Bolton on 26 Mar 1839 *MS* 17 Apr 1839

COX Charles S of Haverhill m NORRIS Betsey of Benton on 31 Dec at Benton, MOULTON F Eld *MS* 17 Jan 1844

COX Erastus m MAGOON Rhoda of Stanstead LC on 5 Mar, MOULTON Abial Eld *MS* 20 Sept 1837

COX John m PHILLIPS Abigail D both of Lowell on 10th in Lowell, THURSTON N Eld *MS* 20 June 1838

COX Oren F m DOW Betsey of Sandbornton NH, MASON S Eld *MS* 17 Mar 1847

COXE Sewell of Bowdoin ME m JOHNSON Charlotte of Durham on 11 Oct at Durham ME, BARD Nathaniel Eld *MS* 25 Oct 1843

COXETOR James E m GAGE Mary B both of Lowell on 6 Nov 1847 in Dracut, CURTIS S Eld *MS* 17 Nov 1847

COZZENS William W of Bangor m TWITCHELL Mahala Mrs of Waterville ME on 28 May in Waterville ME, LEWIS D B Eld *MS* 13 June 1849

CRABTREE Ephraim of Hancock ME m BADGER Maria L of Lowell MA on 27 Oct, CURTIS S Eld *MS* 6 Jan 1847

CRAIG Joseph S of Farmington ME m WHEELER Dorcas D of Chesterville ME, CURTIS S Eld *MS* 20 Oct 1830

CRAIGG Charles S of Farmington m GOWER Hannah A of New Sharon ME at Farmington on 5th inst *MFWBR* 16 Nov 1850

CRAKE George W m TOWLE Abigail D on 9 inst, HUTCHINS E Eld *MS* 15 Apr 1840

CRAM Benjamin m STEVENS Betsey both of Raymond at Deerfield NH *MS* 31 Oct 1833

CRAM John m BACHELDER Louisa both of Sanbornton NH on 15 June in Sanbornton, by FERNALD S P *MS* 2 Aug 1837

CRAM John W m BENSON Sabrina D both of Parsonsfield ME on 30 Aug in Parsonsfield ME, SMITH Wm Eld *MS* 31 Oct 1849

CRAM Jonathan Jr m ROGERS Isabella Y of Raymond on 26 Aug in Raymond, CHASE Paul Rev *MS* 13 Sept 1837

CRAM Josiah Capt m PALMER Mary Ann at Raymond *MS* 8 Dec 1841

CRAM Merrill m THOMPSON Nancy of Ossipee NH on 4 Jan 1847 at Effingham NH, HART E H Eld *MS* 5 May 1847

CRAM Philbrook of Raymond m TASKER Eliza Miss in Northwood NH *MS* 31 Oct 1833

CRANDALL Clark N of Stephentown m SIMPKINS Amy E of Berlin on 7 Nov, COLEMAN I B Eld *MS* 18 Nov 1846

CRANKITE Henry J m CHAMPON Eliza A both of Starkville on 13 Sept in Starkville, SMITH M H Eld *MS* 16 Jan 1850

CRANSON Theodore B of Pennfield, Calhoun Co m BLAISDELL Betsey E on 11 Apr at Assyria Barry Co Michigan, BROWNSON Rev *MS* 29 May 1844

CRAWFORD John m CUNNINGHAM Elizabeth in North Belmont, by WARD Cotton Esq *MS* 13 June 1849

CRESSEY Thomas of Newbury m JAMES Nancy Mrs of Manchester on 9 ult in Manchester, CILLEY D P Eld *MS* 31 Jan 1849

CRESSY Charles A of Lowell MA m WHITE Lucinda C of Lowell MA, CURTIS S Eld *MS* 24 Feb 1847

CREW Alonzo E of Farmington m PLACE Mary E of Great Falls on 7 Dec, BROOKS N Eld at Great Falls Freewill Baptist Church *MS* 18 Dec 1850

CRINKLAW Andrew of Lawrence m SHAW Lucinda L of Dickinson NY on 24 Jan 1849, SQUIRE L Eld *MS* 14 Feb 1849

CRITCHERSON Wm H m BURNHAM Eliza, HUTCHINS E Eld *MS* 19 Jan 1842

CROCKER F W m DREW Diana both of Barford on 4 Mar, MOULTON

CROCKER (Continued)
A W Eld *MS* 15 Apr 1840

CROCKER Joel of Corinth m SMITH Rhoda of Atkinson on 14 Nov in Atkinson, HATHAWAY L Eld *MS* 27 Dec 1837

CROCKETT Charles W SWAIN Nancy of Meredith NH on 10 Oct PITMAN S J Eld *MS* 15 Nov 1843

CROCKETT James M m QUIMBY Harriet both of Dover on 25 inst-HUTCHINS E Eld in Dover *MS* 28 Mar 1849

CROCKETT James at Windham HALL Mary P of Windham on 25 AprREDLON A Eld *MS* 5 June 1844

CROCKETT Joseph NASON Emily L of West Buxton ME on 1st inst at West Buxton ME, SINCLAIR J L Eld *MS* 11 Sept 1844

CROCKETT William E CURTIS Harriet E on 6 Apr at FWB meeting house, CILLEY D P Eld *MS* 16 Apr 1845

CROCKETT William T LEAVITT Susan R on 14 Nov at Meredith NH, PITMAN S J Eld *MS* 25 Dec 1844

CROOCKER William F of Bath ME WRIGHT Mary I of Phipsburg, FULLER Eld J in Phipsburg ME *MS* 11 Apr 1849 (see CROOKER)

CROOK Ransom m BOSTON Catherine at South Berwick ME *MFWBR* 1 Dec 1849

CROOKER F W m DREW Diana both of Barford on March 4, MOULTON A W Eld *MS* 15 Apr 1840

CROOKER John of Danville ME m BACHELDER Amoril L of Lewiston ME, DREW Rev on 1st ult at Augusta ME *MFWBR* 2 Feb 1850

CROOKER Josiah B of Bufford m WHEELER Lydia of Barnston on 3 Jan *MS* 22 Mar 1837

CROOKER William F of Bath m WRIGHT Mary J FULLER Rev at Phipsbury *MFWBR* 10 Mar 1849 (see CROOCKER)

CROSBY Charles S Esq of Bangor ME m OWEN Everlina at Brunswick ME on 18th ult *MFWBR* 6 Jul 1850

CROSBY Jonathan m SMART Sarah both of Swanville ME on 17 Oct 1847 in Dixmont ME, ALLEN Ebenezer Eld *MS* 17 Nov 1847

CROSBY Lemuel of Phillips m PORTER Thirza C of Strong ME on 30 Mar at Jay ME, WATERMAN D Eld *MS* 19 Apr 1843

CROSBY Tho H m CLARK Mehitabel C both of Stanstead LC on Nov 25, MOULTON A W Eld *MS* 15 Apr 1840

CROSMAN Sulivan m DOLLEY Margaret on 24 Oct 1847 in Meredith, DAVIS K R Eld *MS* 23 Feb 1848

CROSS James M m SPILLER Joanna D both of Bridgewater on 11 Jan 1849 *MS* 31 Jan 1849

CROSS Josiah D of Springfield m BROWN Sarah J of Wentworth on 22 Sept, JESSAMINE George W Eld *MS* 10 Oct 1844

CROSS Nathaniel at South Berwick ME m BIBBER Frances A of South Berwick ME, TRUE Ezekiel Eld *MS* 24 Feb 1847

CROSS Sylvester m BEAN Clarissa of Bridgewater, BROWN A Eld *MS* 28 Feb 1844

CROSSMAN C H of Gardiner m WITHAM Mary T of Phillips ME on 9th inst *MFWBR* 23 June 1849

CROSSWELL John W m RICH Adelia of Portland ME, BROWN Eld on 22d ult at Portland *MFWBR* 4 Aug 1849

CROUCH Daniel of Littleton m BRIANT Julia A on 7 Apr last at Bethlehem NH, BEAN Beniah Eld *MS* 4 Jan 1843

CROWELL Ethelbert m ELLIOT Mary A both of Corinna on 20 June 1845 in Corinna, ELLIOT J Eld *MS* 20 May 1846

CROWLEY David m FERRY Elizabeth both of Roxbury MA on 8 Dec 1849 in Roxbury MA, CURTIS S Eld *MS* 13 Feb 1850

CROWLEY James of Saco ME m WIGGIN Nancy of Saco ME, JACKSON Daniel Eld *MS* 6 Apr 1847

CROWLY William m PRICE Elsa Mrs both of Yorkshire NY on 24 May in Yorkshire NY, JACKSON N A Eld *MS* 15 Aug 1849

CROWN George W on 3 Sept m AUSTIN Venorma both of Lowell in Lowell, THURSTON N Eld *MS* 12 Sept 1838

CRUMB William Jr m LANGWORTHY Phebe Ann both of Brookfield on 1 inst Brookfield NY, GARDNER S D Eld *MS* 12 Feb 1851

CRUMENT Stephen B m LORD Mehitable E in Exeter *MS* 24 Jan 1838

CRUMMETT James R of Sebec ME at Bangor ME m TURNER Betsey B of Foxcroft ME on 5 Dec 1844, TURNER A Eld *MS* 9 Apr 1845

CUDWORTH Henry A of Boston MA m NESBITT Sophronia M of Readfield ME on 30 Oct 1848 in Readfield ME, LEWIS D B Eld *MS* 15 Nov 1848

CUMMINGS Daniel m WILLOUGHBY Esther Ann of Newport on 22 Feb at Newport *MS* 24 May 1843

CUMMINGS Silas A of Portland m WHITNEY Phebe A of Bethel ME on 14 Apr in Bethel ME, WHITNEY G W Eld *MS* 17 June 1846

CUMMINGS Simon m KIMBALL Sophronia G P both of Haynesville PLT ME on 8 Oct 1848 in Haynesville PLT ME, GELLERSON G W Eld *MS* 6 Dec 1848

CUMMINGS Warren of Belgrade ME m BROWN Sarah of Pittsfield ME at Waterville ME on 27th ult *MFWBR* 13 Jul 1850

CUMMINS James m STARBIRD Eunice of Greene on 10 Jul at Greene ME, EATON Eld *MS* 20 June 1842

CUNNINGHAM Charles R 2d m CUNNINGHAM Elizabeth on 5 Nov at Edgecomb ME, ROBINSON N J Eld *MS* 29 Nov 1843

CUNNINGHAM Daniel Jr m RICHARDSON Emily A both of Bradford on 4 Aug in Bradford ME, STROUT J Eld *MS* 16 Oct 1850

CUNNINGHAM Erastus m TRUNDY Sarah E both of Wiscassett ME on 26 Sept in Edgecomb ME, PAGE E G Eld *MS* 27 Nov 1850

CUNNINGHAM Freeman m LINDSEY Christina both of Topsham on 12 Sept in Topsham ME, SARGENT L Eld *MS* 9 Oct 1850

CUNNINGHAM John B of Manchester m CURRIER Frances M of Canaan in Manchester, CILLEY D P Eld *MS* 27 Sept 1848

CUNNINGHAM John of Newcastle m HEAL Harriet of Georgetown on 29 Dec, FULLER J Eld *MS* 27 Jan 1847

CUNNINGHAM Nathan Y of Penobscot m McFARLAND Elizabeth of Ellsworth at Ellsworth, WISWELL A Esq *MFWBR* 28 Apr 1849

CURRIER Abraham m SARGENT Judith both of Hopkinton on 26 Dec in Weare NH, KIMBALL J Eld *MS* 2 Apr 1851

CURRIER Augustus P B m ADAMS Sarah G of Gilmanton NH at Charlestown MA, SWETT D Eld *MS* 25 Dec 1844

CURRIER David B m HUNKINS Julia A both of Danville (ME?) or (NH?) in Raymond, FULLONTON J Eld *MS* 22 May 1850

CURRIER David Jr of Amesbury MA m PAGE Sarah Jane of Dover NH on 1 May at Dover NH, DYER B Eld *MS* 7 May 1845

CURRIER Ezra of Poplin m SPOFFORD Mary at Danville, FULLONTON J Eld *MS* 21 Dec 1842

CURRIER John P COX Latatia both of Manchester on 17 May in Manchester, CILLEY D P Eld *MS* 27 May 1846

CURRIER Joseph M of Boston m LARKIN Leah B of Macedon NY on 2 Dec in Walworth NY, HOLMES D G Eld *MS* 15 Jan 1851

CURRIER Lorenzo of Enfield m SMITH Elsea R of Grafton on 18 Oct 1849 in Grafton NH, TYLER Joc C Eld *MS* 19 June 1850

CURRIER Nathan M m ADAMS Jane M on 11 June 1838, MOULTON A W Eld *MS* 17 Apr 1839

CURRIER William of Amesbury MA m WILLEY Lydia Jane on 17th inst at Dover NH, SMITH A D Eld *MS* 30 Dec 1846

CURRIER Richard B of Deerfield NH m BROWN Mary Ann on 18 Dec at Candia, DAVIS K R Eld *MS* 7 Jan 1846

CURRIER True W m WHITTIER Abigail S both of Deerfield NH on 4 Feb, BURBANK P S Eld *MS* 14 Feb 1849

CURTIS Almon of Holland m KNIGHT Philena of Freedom NY on 20 Jan, ANDRUS A C Eld *MS* 4 Mar 1835

CURTIS Alonzo in Peru Ohio m EATON Martha A, CURTIS E Eld *MS* 16 Feb 1842

CURTIS David Jr m CURTIS Welthy M both of Monroe on 9 Dec in Monroe, CILLEY Joseph L Eld *MS* 19 Dec 1849

CURTIS David P of Monroe m STEVENS Jemima of Dixmont ME on 28 Sept 1847 in Dixmont ME, ALLEN Ebenezer Eld *MS* 17 Nov 1847

CURTIS George Jr of Minot m LANE Mary of Greene in Greene *MS* 16 Dec 1831

CURTIS Gideon m TRASK Nancy at Kingfield on Jan 8 1840, ABBOT William Eld *MS* 5 Feb 1840

CURTIS John m RAY Abigail both of Minot in Minot, PURRINGTON J Dr *MS* 1 May 1834

CURTIS Moses of Portsmouth NH m PERKINS Phebe of Wells ME on 27 Dec 1846, DAVIS J B Eld "Both deaf mutes; Wrote the marriage ceremony and both signed it, as they are well educated, and

CURTIS (Continued)

are capable of getting a good living. He has a good trade and is a good workman." *MS* 20 Jan 1847

CURTIS Robert G m SMITH Lydia F of Lowell MA on 11 Dec, CURTIS S Eld *MS* 24 Dec 1845

CURTIS Rufus of Newport ME? m YOUNG Susan of Corinna ME on 14th ult at Corinna ME, NASON S B Eld *MS* 30 Mar 1836

CURTIS Silas Eld of Minot m GOULD Patience Miss of Wayne in Wayne, BRIDGES A Eld *MS* 16 Dec 1831

CURTIS Thomas M of Freeport ME m WOODSIDE Anstress M of Brunswick ME at Brunswick ME, PAGE E G Eld *MS* 13 Jan 1847

CUSHING A m MITCHELL Lucy at Freeport ME on 21st ult *MFWBR* 8 Dec 1849

CUSHING James m LEE Narcissa of Holderness NH on 25 Jan, TRUE Ezekiel Eld *MS* 19 Apr 1843

CUSHMAN Lewis m EMERY Adaline of Poland ME on 5 Jan, LIBBEY James Eld *MS* 9 Apr 1845

CUSHMAN Samuel Esq of New Gloucester m LOCKE Betsey wid/o Eld Ward LOCKE *MS* 17 Mar 1830

CUTLER Dexter of Otiscon Mich m SLAYTON C Emeline formerly of Victor NY on 4 June 1848 in Grattan Kent Co Mich, CILLEY E G Eld *MS* 12 Jul 1848

CUTLER Horace A of N Killingly CT m HARRIS Lorinda M of Pennfield NY on 25 Aug at Pascoag RI, HARRIMAN D P Eld *MS* 4 Sept 1850

CUTTER Abiel Abbott m HALE Louisa F on 5th inst at Saccarrapee, ME *MFWBR* 8 Sept 1849

CUTTING A C of Strafford VT m LEGG Eliza R of Dover NH on 4 inst in this town, SMITH Eleazer Rev *MS* 11 Oct 1837

CUTTING John m WOODBURY Eliza S on 31 Dec at Haverhill, MOULTON F Eld *MS* 22 Jan 1845

CUTTS John m PEASLEY Martha Mrs both of Wendell NH on 19 Oct 1848 in Wendell NH, BARTLETT J O D Eld *MS* 20 Dec 1848

DAILY Selah m MERRILL Ploma/Pluma both of Stanstead LC on Jan 27, MOULTON A W Eld *MS* 15 Apr 1840

DAKE Erastus m THOMPSON Mary C Mrs on 23 ult at Napoli, TANNER F B Eld *MS* 20 May 1835

DALTON Benjamin m LIBBEY Lucinda B both of Great Falls on 24 June at Great Falls, BROOKS N Eld *MS* 11 Jul 1849

DALTON Edwin W of Roxbury MA m BARKLEFF Antonett P of Bath on 10 Mar, DAVIS Isaac G Eld *MS* 5 Apr 1843

DAM Daniel of Newfield m SAYWOOD Lucinda of Waterboro ME, BURBANK Eld *MS* 3 Nov 1830

DAM Hercules m STRAW Ruth in Waterboro ME, BAGLEY Orlando Esq *MS* 28 May 1828

DAM Richard of Portsmouth NH m JONES Margaret R of Somersworth NH at Great Falls NH *MFWBR* 19 Oct 1850

DAME Greenleaf of Nottingham m CHESWELL Charlotte of Durham NH on 24 ult in Dover NH, HUTCHINS E Eld *MS* 4 Oct 1848

DAME Jabez m BICKFORD Eliza at Parsonsfield, BUZZELL John Eld *MS* 26 Apr 1827

DAME John Jr of Jackson (NH?) m TUCKER Lydia of Durham on 9th inst at New Market, HUTCHINS E Eld *MS* 26 Apr 1843

DAME John O of Dover m MADDOX Harriet of Waterboro ME on 30th ult at Newmarket, HUTCHINS E Eld *MS* 20 Dec 1843

DAME Jonathan Jr m TASKER Susan both of Strafford *MS* 27 Jan 1836

DAME Leonard m ROLLINS Mehitabel of Farmington on 24 Sept at Farmington, WALDRON W H Eld *MS* 15 Nov 1843

DAME William m CATER Nancy *MS* 24 Apr 1834

DAMMON Esrael m RICH Lydia both of Exeter on 7 June in Exeter, PRATT Cyprian S Eld *MS* 8 Aug 1838

DAMON Frederick m STEWART Hannah F both of Manchester on 30 Dec 1847 in Manchester, CILLEY D P Eld *MS* 19 Jan 1848

DAMREN Isaac m KILLEY Elizabeth both of Belgrade ME on 24 Dec last *MS* 10 Feb 1836

DANA William B of New Hampton m MORSE Climena B of Holderness on 2d inst, TRUE Ezekiel Eld *MS* 26 Oct 1842

DANFORD Eldridge G of Thornton m DUFIN Mary of Williamstown VT on 28 Aug in East Williamstown VT, TUCKER Joshua Eld *MS* 13 Sept 1837

DANFORD Hiram m GRAY Hannah both of Dover on 31st ult in Dover, THURSTON N Eld *MS* 3 Sept 1834

DANFORTH Albridge m MARR Lydia H on 7 Dec at Litchfield ME, FROST Isaac Eld *MS* 17 Jan 1844

DANFORTH Henry m HORNE Hannah J both of Dover on 6 Nov 1847 in Dover NH, SMITH A D Eld *MS* 1 Dec 1847

DANFORTH Nathaniel C m BROWN Sophia C both of Lowell on 28th ult at Dover NH, THURSTON N Eld *MS* 8 Aug 1833

DANFORTH Parker R m BARNES Diana E both of Pittsburg on 7 Jul in Pittsburg NH, BEAN Benaiah Eld *MS* 11 Sept 1850

DANFORTH Phinehas of Warner NH m COPP Clara of New Hampton on 13 Nov 1850, PITMAN S J Eld *MS* 27 Nov 1850

DANFORTH Samuel of Porter ME m BROOKS Mary Ann on 15 Sept, HART E H Eld *MS* 23 Oct 1844

DANFORTH William m BACON Mary both of Framingham MA in Upper Gilmanton, MOODY David Eld *MS* 19 June 1850

DANFORTH Wm of Gardiner m HARRINGTON Mary J of Topsham, BEAN C Eld in Brunswick ME *MS* 19 Jan 1848

DANIEL Ira m DILNO Sarah A on 18th ult in Barnston *MS* 18 May 1836

DANIELS Israel m GRAY Rebecca both of Dover NH, HALE John Esq
MS 2 Jan 1834

DANIELS Jacob B m PAIGE Betsey B both of Manchester on 14 Feb
1848 in Manchester, CILLEY D P Eld MS 22 Mar 1848

DANIELSON Charles m DURGIN Nancy on 11 Jul at Northwood,
JOHNSON W D Eld MS 25 Sept 1844

DANIOLS Joseph Jr m HILL Eliza C both of Strafford NH, PLACE E
Eld MS 17 June 1835

DARLING Joshua m CARR Sarah both of Mendon on 18 Jan,
BURLINGAME W W Eld MS 28 Feb 1838

DARLING Samuel m FLAGG Susan at Auburn MFWBR 29 Mar 1851

DASHWOOD Henry m YOUNG Lavona on 22 Nov at Free Baptist
Church in Boston, NOYES E Eld MS 16 Dec 1846

DATON Nahum W m PAGE Mary in Sandown NH, ROBIE T Eld MS
30 Dec 1831

DAUGHERTY William Dr of Sebec ME m MITCHELL Louiza of Dover
ME on 5th ult at Dover, BARTLETT Flavel Eld MS 17 Sept 1834

DAVIDSON Samuel m ELLIOTT Theodate both of Manchester on 2
Dec in Manchester, CILLEY D P Eld MS 26 Dec 1849

DAVIS Aaron H of Reading m MORTON Susan of West Windsor on 1
Apr 1849 in Winslow VT, ADAMS A Eld MS 18 Apr 1849

DAVIS Abraham B m CARVER Ann both of Brunswick ME on 28
Aug, ROLLINS A Eld MS 2 Jan 1839

DAVIS Adams m PLAISTED Mary Jane on 17 Jan, CURTIS S Eld MS
10 Feb 1847

DAVIS Albion K P m MOULTON Mary J both of Newfield ME on 22
Sept in Parsonsfield ME, SMITH W Eld MS 30 Oct 1850

DAVIS Alfred L m WENTWORTH Susanna of Lowell MA on 29 May at
Lowell MA, WOODMAN J Eld MS 19 Oct 1842

DAVIS Almon m STEARNS Grace of Reading on 29 June at Reading,
ADAMS A Eld MS 6 Aug 1845

DAVIS Alonzo m WILSON Marion at Great Falls NH MFWBR 16 Oct
1847

DAVIS Alvah M m SMART Sarah A on 24 Oct at Parsonsfield ME,
SMART Moses M Eld MS 30 Oct 1844

DAVIS Amaziah H m GRAY Abigail on 2 inst at Great Falls NH,
CAVERNO A Eld MS 6 Feb 1834

DAVIS Amaziah m EMMONS Harriet on 3d Nov at Biddeford ME,
RAND James Eld MS 13 Nov 1844

DAVIS Amos S of Center Harbor m ROBINSON Sophronia A of New
Market, HUTCHINS E Eld MS 8 June 1842

DAVIS Bailey S of Hartland VT m OSMORE Frances E of Windsor on
Jan 5th, ADAMS Abel Eld MS 19 Jan 1842

DAVIS Cyrus m PIERCE Mary E at Manchester on 11 Dec, CILLEY D
P Eld MS 20 Dec 1843

DAVIS Daniel m SOPER Martha Jane of Livermore ME at Turner ME

DAVIS (Continued)

MFWBR 21 Jan 1849

DAVIS Daniel A m JAY Sarah both of Waterville ME on 28 Oct 1847, BURGESS J S Eld in Waterville ME *MS* 19 Jan 1848

DAVIS Daniel of Centre Harbor m SMITH Lydia Mrs of New Hampton on 21 May 1848, PERKINS Thomas Eld *MS* 31 May 1848

DAVIS Daniel of Meredith NH m HUCKINS Mary F of Centre Harbor on 1 Nov, PERKINS Thomas Eld *MS* 11 Nov 1846

DAVIS Daniel of Providence m ALGER Mary R of Newport RI at Newport RI, LORD D H Eld *MS* 17 Sept 1845

DAVIS Daniel m NASON Priscilla both of Great Falls NH on 8th Dec, DUNN R Eld *MS* 24 Dec 1845

DAVIS Daniel S m HEARD Lucy both of Newfield, BURBANK S Eld *MS* 23 Dec 1831

DAVIS David E m YORK Mary of Lee on 25th ult at Lee, HUTCHINS E Eld *MS* 15 Dec 1841

DAVIS David of Nottingham NH m DEARBORN Olive of Jackson NH on 26 Feb 1846 at Jackson NH, MESERVE George P Eld *MS* 11 Mar 1846

DAVIS David W Dr of Greenwood ME m GILMAN Mary Jane of Eaton, GASKILL S Eld *MS* 21 Jan 1846 & *MS* 22 Oct 1845

DAVIS Eleazer of Jackson m HOUSE Jerusha of Dixmont ME on 17 Feb, FLETCHER Jabez Eld *MS* 6 Mar 1839

DAVIS Erasmus D m PAIGE Harriet L of Nashua on 17 March at Manchester, CILLEY D P *MS* 10 Apr 1844

DAVIS Franklin A of Sidney m LEWIS D B Eld on New Year's Eve in Waterville ME *MS* 21 Mar 1849

DAVIS Franklin L of Sidney m LOTHROP Roxana K on Nov 28 at Chesterville, FOSTER J Eld *MS* 15 Jan 1840

DAVIS George O m GERRISH Joanna both of Lamprey River NH *MS* 8 Jul 1835

DAVIS George of Limington m HAMMONS Nancy of Cornish at Limington, STEVENS Eld *MS* 22 June 1836

DAVIS George W m HESS Eliza Ann both of Constantine Mich on 20 June 1848 in Constantine Mich, KETCHAM S Eld *MS* 12 Jul 1848

DAVIS Henry E of West Brookfield m BLANCHARD Roany on 14th inst, CLAFLIN Jehiel Eld *MS* 24 Apr 1839

DAVIS Hiram A m WATSON Sarah on 24 Mar in Farmington, WALDRON W H Eld *MS* 24 Apr 1844

DAVIS Hiram m DOE Caroline both of Nottingham on 1 Apr in Nottingham, SHERBURNE S Eld *MS* 29 Apr 1846

DAVIS Ira m HORN Kaziah on 13 Apr at Alexandria, BROWN A Eld *MS* 28 Feb 1844

DAVIS Isaac G of Roxbury MA m BULLOCK Almira of Lowell on 8 Aug, WOODMAN J Eld *MS* 23 Aug 1843

DAVIS Isaac N of Lewiston ME m LOMBARD Elizabeth D of Wales

DAVIS (Continued)

ME on 2 June in Wales ME, FILES Allen Eld *MS* 3 Jul 1850

DAVIS J E Eld of Gardiner ME m JUDKINS Sophia S of Lawrence MA on 27 June in Kingston, SWETLAND Ira A Rev *MS* 4 Jul 1849

DAVIS James P of Union m WORTHLEY Lydia S of Edgecomb on 5 May 1849 in Edgecomb ME, PAGE E G Eld *MS* 15 May 1850

DAVIS Joel m TERELL Lydia of Haverhill on 19 Mar 1844 at Haverhill, MOULTON F Eld *MS* 3 Apr 1844

DAVIS John C m FROST Mary J of Poland on 17 Aug at Poland ME, PERRY S Eld *MS* 3 Dec 1845

DAVIS John L of Lisbon ME m JORDAN Abigail of Lewiston ME on 10 Mar at Lewiston ME, BEAN G H Eld *MS* 31 Mar 1847

DAVIS John L m BICKFORD Clarinda on 14th Nov at Effingham NH, HOBBS A W Eld *MS* 30 Apr 1845

DAVIS John m SANBORN Sally both of Waterboro' ME *MS* 28 Dec 1832

DAVIS John M m JONES Lucy J Mrs on 22 Jan at Portsmouth NH, DAVIS Issac G Eld *MS* 7 Feb 1844

DAVIS John m MAXFIELD Rhoda F on 5 Dec 1843 at Chichester, SWAIN William Eld *MS* 29 May 1844

DAVIS John W of Somersworth NH m CORSON Mary of Lebanon ME on 19 Mar 1848 in Lebanon ME, CHENEY O B Eld *MS* 29 Mar 1848

DAVIS Joseph C of New Durham m BERRY Elizabeth of Alton on 15 May 1848 in Gilmanton, FERNALD S P Eld *MS* 21 June 1848

DAVIS Joseph P m EATON Hope M both of Concord NH on 28 May 1848 in Pittsfield NH, TRUE E Eld *MS* 5 Jul 1848

DAVIS Kinsman R of Epsom NH m BROOKS Sarah A of North Berwick ME on 20 Sept, GARLAND D Eld *MS* 10 Oct 1844

DAVIS Levi m TUTTLE Henrietta both of Nottingham in Nottingham, TUTTLE Rev Mr *MS* 21 Aug 1850

DAVIS Moses Jr m LELAND Harriet both of Lowell on 1 Dec in Dracut, CURTIS S Eld *MS* 15 Dec 1847

DAVIS Moses m COLE Mary Ann both of Manchester on 24 ult in Manchester, CILLEY D P Eld *MS* 1 Apr 1846

DAVIS Orin on 3 inst at Dover NH m HANSCOM Ruth N, PERKINS Seth W Eld *MS* 12 Nov 1845

DAVIS Philander of Newark VT m KIBBY Zillah M of Westmore VT at the dwelling of N K George in Franconia on 24 Sept, GEORGE N K Eld *MS* 6 Nov 1844

DAVIS Reuben m ALLEN Anstress at Lyman *MFWBR* 3 Mar 1849

DAVIS Robert m CLOUGH Meriam B both of Garland ME on Jan 27, AMES M Eld *MS* 4 May 1842

DAVIS Samuel A m HUNT Sarah R both of Dover on 26 Aug in Durham, EASTMAN C Allen *MS* 25 Sept 1850

DAVIS Samuel Jr m TWOMBLY Mary both of Madbury on 1 Jan

DAVIS (Continued)
   MS 1 Feb 1837

DAVIS Samuel m KEECH Laura M both of Mendon MA on 4 ult *MS* 4
   May 1836

DAVIS Samuel S m BENSON Clarissa both of Manchester NH on 19
   Jan 1840, JORDAN Z Eld *MS* 26 Feb 1840

DAVIS Stephen C m WINSLOW Sally T both of Pittsfield on 9 inst,
   TRUE E Eld *MS* 15 Aug 1849

DAVIS Stephen H m YORK Clarissa G of New Market on 29 Dec,
   HUTCHINS E Eld *MS* 4 Jan 1843

DAVIS Stephen m FOSTER Elizabeth S both of Gilford on Mar 13,
   PINKHAM John Eld *MS* 4 May 1842

DAVIS Thomas 2d m DURGIN Mary, BURBANK S Eld *MS* 15 Feb
   1827

DAVIS Thomas B of Effingham m BUSWELL Betsey of Ossipee NH
   MS 21 Dec 1836

DAVIS Thomas C merchant of Dover m ROGERS Hannah H of Portland ME on Thurs evening last, COLE Rev *MS* 7 Jan 1835

DAVIS Thomas m WILLIAMS Eliza in Atkinson, HARVY Nathaniel
   Eld *MS* 7 Feb 1828

DAVIS Timothy G m BARTLETT Mary D both of New Market on 16
   Nov 1848 in New Market, ALLEN C Eld *MS* 29 Nov 1848

DAVIS True B m LUCY Hannah T of Pittsfield on 3d inst, KNOWLES
   J Eld *MS* 17 Apr 1839

DAVIS William B m HAYWARD Martha E of Underhill VT on 27 Aug,
   SANBORN J Eld *MS* 6 Nov 1839

DAVIS William G m NEAL Rhoda on 4th inst at Portland ME, PECK
   Rev *MFWBR* 17 Mar 1849

DAVIS William Jr of Newfield m KNOX Olive of Newfield, BURBANK S
   Eld *MS* 13 Apr 1832

DAVIS William of Harmony m BUTLER Huldah Ann on 30 Mar at
   Farmington, WHEELER S Eld *MS* 6 Aug 1845

DAVIS William Y m VARNEY Betsey L of Manchester on 11 Mar at
   Manchester, CILLEY D P Eld *MS* 26 May 1847

DAVIS William m SHUMAN Lovina A both of Waldoboro' on 16 inst
   in Waldoboro', WALKER O B Rev *MS* 26 Apr 1848

DAVIS William of Boxford MA m JOHNSON Abigail of Sutton on 7
   Sept 1837 in Sutton VT, FLAGG Joseph Eld *MS* 14 Feb 1838

DAVIS Wyman K m ROBY Lucy A both of Fitchburg, THURSTON N
   Eld *MS* 25 May 1842

DAWLEY Charles H m BERRY Lovey A both of Dover on 24 inst in
   Dover, HUTCHINS E Eld *MS* 30 Oct 1850

DAWLEY William m JENKINS Abby C on 19 May at Dracut MA,
   CURTIS S Eld *MS* 2 June 1847

DAWS Samuel H m ADAMS Lucy A both of Harrison on 19 Jan in
   Harrison ME, LIBBY D Eld *MS* 19 Feb 1851

DAY Arad of Damariscotta m SPINNEY Margaret J of Boothbay on 16 Feb in Boothbay ME, PAGE E G Eld *MS* 26 Mar 1851

DAY Charles Col of Kennebunk Port m TAYLOR Elizabeth R of Lyman on 11 Apr in Lyman ME, RIDEOUT Uriel Eld *MS* 24 Apr 1850

DAY Israel m WALKER Sophia on 10 June at Waterboro ME, EMERY R Eld *MS* 18 June 1845

DAY John C m FOYE Lucinda P both of Augusta in Augusta, CURTIS S Eld *MS* 24 Jan 1838

DAY Joseph of Glover m MAGOON Eliza R of Wheelock VT on 5 Feb 1850 in Wheelock VT, GEORGE N K Eld *MS* 6 Mar 1850

DAY Nehemiah W of Naples ME m BROWN Esther M of Parsonsfield ME, HACKET John O Eld in East Parsonsfield ME *MS* 8 Mar 1848

DAY Oliver of Cornish m WATSON Abigail Sunday last at Limerick ME, LIBBY E Eld *MS* 1 June 1831

DAY Stephen 3d of Cornish ME m BERRY Catharine of Cornish ME on 13 May 1846 at Parsonsfield ME, HACKETT J O Eld *MS* 31 Mar 1847

DAY Sylvanus m PARROT Rebecca J of Portland ME on 26 Jan at Cape Elizabeth ME, LIBBY Almon Eld *MS* 26 Feb 1845

DAY Thadeus H of Hallowell ME m BRALEY Frances W on 18 Jan 1846, WEAVER Philip Eld *MS* 11 Mar 1846

DAY Theodore m GUPTIL Mary of Waterboro ME *MS* 28 May 1828

DAY Thomas of Cornish m DURGIN Susan Thurs last, REMICK Eld *MS* 31 Dec 1828

DAY Thomas m ALLEN Roxanna of Portland ME on 26 May at Wilmington MA, DURGIN J M Eld *MS* 26 June 1844

DEALING William m HOLBROOK Mary both of Harpswell in Harpswell ME, HERSEY L Eld *MS* 14 Feb 1849

DEAN Watson m JONES Mary on 9 Sept at Manchester, CILLEY D P Eld *MS* 18 Sept 1844

DEAN William H of Port Jackson m HUNTLEY Eunice Ann of Phoenix NY on 4 Apr 1849 in Phoenix NY, SMITH O W Eld *MS* 2 May 1849

DEANE Abial of Temple m RIDLEY Abigail of Farmington on 21st ult at Farmington, FOSTER John Eld *MS* 13 Jul 1832

DEARBORN Benjamin of Candia m FOLSOM Hannah N of Raymond NH on 25 inst in Raymond, SHELDON Anson Rev *MS* 4 Oct 1837

DEARBORN Daniel m CHILDS Diantha both of Corinth on 30 Jan in Corinth, SMITH A D Eld *MS* 16 Mar 1842

DEARBORN Dudley H m TITUS Mercy R of Monmouth ME at Wales ME, FILES A Eld *MS* 28 Feb 1844

DEARBORN Edmund of Bridgton ME m COBB Emma on 14th inst at Limington ME, McKENNEY H Esq *MS* 3 Apr 1839

DEARBORN George P of Jackson m DAVIS Abigail I of Nottingham on 19 Feb, TUTTLE A Eld *MS* 4 Mar 1846

DEARBORN George W of New Market m GARLAND Martha R of Hampton on 19 Sept in Hampton, CILLEY Daniel P Eld *MS* 26 Sept 1838

DEARBORN John m MARSTON Deborah both of Hampton on 28 Sept in Hampton, BURBANK P S Eld *MS* 7 Oct 1846

DEARBORN John of Effingham NH m HALE Eliza Ann on 1st inst in Limerick, FREEMAN Charles Rev *MS* 8 Nov 1827

DEARBORN John of Pembroke m JACKSON Elizabeth A of Gilford on 27 Dec, BROOKS N Eld *MS* 8 Feb 1843

DEARBORN John m LADD Sarah both of Saco ME on 7 Feb, JACKSON Daniel Eld *MS* 6 Apr 1847

DEARBORN Jonathan L of Sandbornton NH m CLAY Martha S on 14 Oct, MASON Lemuel Eld *MS* 16 Dec 1846

DEARBORN Joseph P m PHILBROOK Mary Y of Sanbornton NH on 29 Mar 1842 at Sanbornton, MASON L Eld *MS* 11 May 1842

DEARBORN Josiah Esq of Effingham ae 40y m on 14th inst QUARLES Belinda Miss of Ossipee NH ae 15y *MS* 31 May 1827

DEARBORN Sewall m SMALL Jane M both of Corinna on 1 Jan in Corinna, COPP John B Eld *MS* 9 May 1838

DEARBORN Sylvanus of Foxcroft m LOCKE Caroline H on 13th inst at Limerick ME, TRIPP L S Rev *MFWBR* 16 June 1849

DEARBORN Sylvanus m MEADER Mary both of Limerick on 25th ult, FREEMAN Rev *MS* 2 Sept 1831

DEARBORN Thomas I of Boston m DAME Sarah A of Dover on 20 Sept, CLARK M Eld *MS* 1 Oct 1845

DEARBORN Thomas of Candia m FOLSOM Delia L of Raymond *MS* 12 Nov 1835

DEARING Alpheas m HUTCHINS Hannah B *MS* 26 May 1830 & m by THURSTON Eld in Kittery *MS* 5 May 1830

DeCOSTER Axel of Waltham MA on 11 June at Falmouth ME m WATTS Lucy Ann of Falmouth on 5th inst at Kittery ME, PERKINS Seth W *MS* 6 Sept 1843

DEERING Abial of Edgecomb ME m ADAMS Elizabeth M on 25 Dec, PAGE E G Eld *MS* 4 Jan 1843

DEERING Arther of Bushnell's Basin m DEXTER Louisa of Middleville in Oct in Middleville, STARR Lovel B Eld *MS* 15 Nov 1848

DEERING Charles H m FOSS Lucretia both of Saco ME on 28 June, JACKSON Daniel Eld *MS* 30 Sept 1846

DEERING Erastus W of Denmark ME m JEWETT Joann I on 23 Mar, PIKE John Eld *MS* 13 Sept 1843

DEERING Rufus m EASTMAN Deborah of Limerick ME on 18 May at Limerick, CHANEY S Freeman Eld *MS* 31 May 1843

DEIGHKEL Daniel m 1848 KNARR Mary both of Berlin on 25 Mar in Sand Lake NY, COLEMAN I B Eld *MS* 12 Apr 1848

DELAITTUE George W m CUTTER Emeline of Sebec ME on 13 Apr at Sebec ME, GALLISON William F Eld *MS* 7 May 1845

DELAND William of Wolfboro m DELAND Sarah of Dover on 27 inst,
PERKINS J Rev *MS* 8 Mar 1837

DEMERIT C M Capt of Farmington m LANG Mary A of Brookfield on
1st inst at Rochester, MASON E Eld *MS* 8 Nov 1843

DEMERITT Benjamin F m BICKFORD Sarah Ann in Lowell, THUR-
STON N Eld *MS* 7 June 1837

DEMERITT Benjamin F of Effingham NH m MILLS Eunice of Eaton
on 31 Mar at Eaton NH, BUTLER O Eld *MS* 20 Apr 1842

DEMERITT Daniel m LEAVITT Evaline both of Effingham NH on 31
Mar in Effingham NH, FOSS N Eld *MS* 19 June 1850

DEMERITT Daniel m BATCHELDER Lorinda P on 3 Jul at Nottingham, TUTTLE A Eld *MS* 20 June 1842

DEMERITT Isaac of Eaton m CUSHING Priscilla of Freedom on 4
Octin Freedom, RUNNELS J Eld *MS* 11 Nov 1846

DEMERITT James Young m ROWE Marilda of Madbury on 27 Aug at
Strafford, PLACE E Eld *MS* 13 Sept 1843

DEMERITT John F m MILES Sarah A both of New Market on 13 inst
Sabbath eve in New Market, ALLEN C Eld *MS* 23 May 1849

DEMMON Truman G m ALLEN Rhoda P both of Chesterfield on 28
Nov 1848 in Chesterfield MA, KING Warren Eld *MS* 7 Feb 1849

DeMOUILPIED Nicholas of Mt Pleasant m HOSMER Ann L of Pike
Wis on 18 May at Pike Racine Co Wis, BIXBY Newell W Eld *MS* 23
June 1847

DENICK Charles of Brideton m 1839 LAKIN Scruilia of Plymouth VT
on 6 Oct, WARNER William Eld *MS* 4 Mar 1840

DENISON Albert m HIBBARD Mary on 6 June 1847 at Brookfield
NY, GARDINER S D Eld *MS* 23 June 1847

DENNELLS Zacariah m CHELLIES Mary of Newfield on 7th inst at
Newfield ME, LINSCOTT Henry Rev *MFWBR* 18 Dec 1847

DENNET Samuel of Augusta ME m LIBBY Sarah at Litchfield ME
MFWBR 13 Oct 1849

DENNETT Jeremiah W m NELSON Sophia D both of Portsmouth on
17 May in Portsmouth, CAVERNO A Eld *MS* 27 May 1846

DENNETT Mark A m FOSS Hannah of Pittsfield on 31 Oct at Pittsfield, CILLEY D P Eld *MS* 16 Nov 1842

DENNETT Samuel of Augusta ME m LIBBY Sarah at Litchfield
MFWBR 13 Oct 1849

DENNETT Winborn R m DURGIN Martha J both of So Berwick ME
on 15 inst 1849 in Dover, DAVIS J B Eld *MS* 25 Apr 1849

DENNIS Abraham of China m FISK Lucy of Freedom on 8 Oct in
Freedom NY *MS* 11 Dec 1850

DENNIS Hiram of Moscow ME m COLBY Charlotte on 8th ult at
Moscow ME, TURNER Sidney Rev *MFWBR* 1 May 1847

DENNIS Hobert of Dixmont ME m BALLETT Lydia of Unity ME at
Unity ME, LEWIS D B Eld *MS* 25 Dec 1844

DENNIS James/ S James of Manchester m BANGS Abby S of Dover

DENNIS (Continued)

    NH on 14th inst at Dover, HUTCHINS E Eld *MFWBR* 25 Jan 1851 & *MS* 22 Jan 1851

DENNISON Chester of Holland m STOW Triphena of Yorkshire, NY? *MS* 4 Mar 1835

DENNISON David H of Brunswick m DENNISON Nancy J of Freeport ME at Topsham ME, JACKSON Daniel Eld *MS* 24 Jul 1839

DENNISON Elijah B m RANSDELL Lydia W of Washington VT on 2 Dec 1838, GEORGE Nathaniel K Eld *MS* 15 May 1839

DENNISON John 3d of Freeport ME m SYLVESTER Louisa of Freeport ME on 8 Nov, PURINTON A W Eld *MS* 25 Nov 1846

DENSMORE Ebenezer S m TAYLOR Susan C of Windsor VT on 8 Apr at Windsor VT, ADAMS A Eld *MS* 21 Apr 1847

DEQUIO Joseph m McALLISTER Sarah Jane on 7th inst at Portland ME, MOULTON A K Eld *MS* 21 Nov 1843

DERBY Elmore m CHAMBERLAIN Mary of Lowell MA on 26 June, WOODMAN J Eld *MS* 23 Aug 1843

DERBY John of Stewartstown m FLETCHER Nancy D of Loudon NH on 30 Jan, CLOUGH Jeremiah Eld *MS* 14 Feb 1844

DERRILL Samuel E m KIMBALL Mary O of Clinton ME on 31 Oct, BUKER Alvah J Eld *MS* 2 Dec 1846

DESHON Samuel m CHASE Amy on 5 Dec at Waterboro' ME, EMERY Richard Eld *MS* 18 Dec 1844

DEUANS David S Dr m HATCH Mahala on 27 June at Gilford Village, PERKINS S W Eld *MS* 14 Jul 1847

DEVORE Henry Jr m DEVORE Elizabeth both of Nottingham Township PA on 13 Feb last *MS* 25 Apr 1833

DEXTER Amos m WHITCOMB Eliza both of Dunn Wis on 24 Sept 1848 in Dunn Wis, KNAPP Davis Eld *MS* 20 Dec 1848

DEXTER Parker of Norwich m CARPENTER Joann of Williamstown VT on 10 Mar 1850 in Williamstown VT, HARTSHORN Nelson Eld *MS* 10 Apr 1850

DIBBLE Daniel m GREEN Mary both of Freedom on 7 Mar 1849, JACKSON N A Eld at his residence in China NY *MS* 9 May 1849

DIBBLE Mason m FISK Mary both of Freedom NY on 15 Feb in Freedom NY, JACKSON N A Eld *MS* 25 Mar 1846

DICK W M Eld of Bytown CW m BALDWIN Maria L of Naugatuck CT at Waterbury CT, ALLEN A Rev *MS* 28 May 1845

DICKERMAN Moses W of Loudon NH m TILTON Abigail E of Alexandria NH on 14 Sept 1841 at Alexander NH, BROWN A Eld *MS* 4 May 1842

DICKERSON Daniel m DICKERSON Mary Jane on 10 ult in Mercer ME, WASHBURN H Eld *MS* 18 Jul 1838

DICKEY Alexander m HAMBLEN Louiza R of Monroe ME on 23 Nov at Dixmont ME, ALLEN E Eld *MS* 17 Jan 1844

DICKEY Morril m TUTTLE Betsey both of Strafford NH on 31 ult in

DICKEY (Continued)
Dover NH, SMITH A D Eld *MS* 21 Feb 1838

DICKEY Morrill of Epsom NH m WELLS Rachel of Lowell at So Berwick ME, THURSTON N Eld *MS* 25 Nov 1835

DICKSON Wm D m DEARBORN Mary last week in Parsonsfield ME, BUZZEL John Eld *MS* 9 Dec 1831

DICY Hazen of Gilmanton m BEAN Anna of Gilford on 3 Sept 1837 in Gilford, KNOWLES John D Eld *MS* 7 Feb 1838

DIGSBY David of Stow m ROLLINS Sally of Huntington on 12 inst in Huntington, DIKE O Eld *MS* 5 Sept 1838

DIKE Alexander of Auburn Theological Seminary m GLEASON Frances A of Kirkland Oneida Co NY on 26 Sept, PRATT Rev *MS* 26 Feb 1845

DIKE Arba C of Providence RI m HETHERINGTON of Providence RI on Thur 19th ult at Pawtucket RI, BENEDICT Rev *MS* 3 May 1827

DIKE Samuel of Sebago m CLAY Harriet in Buxton ME on Jan 30, HAMBLEN J F Eld *MS* 30 Mar 1842

DILL John A m GRATHAM Sarah on 3 Jul at Lowell MA, THURSTON N Eld *MS* 2 Nov 1842

DILLINGHAM Aremas of Lowell MA m DURGIN Mary Jane of Newfield, BURBANK S Eld *MS* 24 Aug 1832

DILLINGHAM Latinus m ABBOTT Sarah Ann both of Biddeford ME on 30 May in Biddeford ME, EATON E G Eld *MS* 3 Jul 1850

DIMOND Isaac N m HODGDON Adeline both of Manchester on March 24 at Meredith Bridge, BROOKS N Eld *MS* 27 Apr 1842

DIMOND Isaac of Gilford m SHAW Mary of Gilmanton on 28 Sept in Gilmanton, MOODY D Eld *MS* 11 Dec 1850

DIMOND Isreal of Danville m GARLAND Hannah S of Barnstead, GARLAND D Eld *MS* 17 Dec 1845

DINGLEY Levi m SPEAR Mary E both of Gardiner in Bowdoinham ME, QUINNAM C Eld *MS* 22 May 1844

DINGLEY Samuel m SHERMAN Sarah on 26 Aug at Charlestown MA, SWETT D Eld *MS* 23 Oct 1844

DINGLEY William B m LIBBY Eunice at Richmond ME *MFWBR* 13 Oct 1849

DINSMOOR William A of Lowell MA m FOLSOM Mary A on 9 Oct 1839 at Hopkinton, SINCLAIR J L Eld *MS* 6 Nov 1839

DINSMORE Charles W m COTTON Sarah both of Sandown on 5 inst in Sandown, BLORE J Eld *MS* 11 Dec 1850

DIX George Capt m PUMROY Sally at Mt Desert ME *MS* 9 Dec 1831

DIXMOND Orin m BRADLEY Mehitabel F in Danville, FULLONTON J Eld *MS* 27 Dec 1837

DIXON Harmon m MAXWELL Mary of Wales ME on 27 Feb at Wales ME, FILES A Eld *MS* 21 Apr 1847

DIXON Joseph W of Utica m EDWARDS Ann of New Hartford NY on 10 Dec 1850 in Checkerville NY, MARINER J Eld *MS* 1 Jan 1851

DIXON John m PRAY Ann both of Jay on 25 Jan in Jay ME, LIBBY Eld *MS* 14 Feb 1838

DIXON Joseph L m FERNALD Mary E of Wolfboro' NH on 31 Jul at Wolfboro', HOLMES John C Eld *MS* 4 Sept 1844

DIXON Luther m KNOX Elizabeth both of Lebanon ME on 7 Jan 1848 in Lebanon ME, CHENEY O B Eld *MS* 24 Jan 1849

DIXON Nathaniel m HOBBS Nancy both of Berwick ME *MS* 25 Feb 1835

DIXON Nathaniel m MAXWELL Lucy Ann of Wales ME at Wales ME, FILES A Eld *MS* 28 Feb 1844

DIXON Stephen Jr m JONES Sarah J both of Lebanon ME on 3 Feb 1849 in Lebanon ME, CHENEY O B Eld *MS* 21 Feb 1849

DIXON Thomas S m VARNEY Mary E both of Lebanon ME on 15 inst in Lebanon ME, CHENEY O B Eld *MS* 28 Aug 1850

DIXSON Mazianson m TAYLOR Mary, FILES A Eld at Hallowell ME *MS* 7 Feb 1833

DOBSON William O m GILINES Zanetta P on 4 Jul at Owego NY, BIXBY N W Eld *MS* 14 Aug 1839

DOCKHAM James W m FLOYD Lovinah S both of Biddeford on 14 Jul in Biddeford ME, WITHAM L H Eld *MS* 21 Nov 1849

DOCKUM Charles H m VINCENT Eliza H on 16th inst in Durham, HUTCHINS E Eld *MS* 19 Jan 1842

DODD John J m TRIPP Louisa both of Scarborough on 4 Apr in Scarborough ME, LANCASTER D Eld *MS* 1 Aug 1849

DODGE Alvah m MOREHOUSE Lydia Maria of Warrensburgh NY at Limerick ME, CHASE William P Eld *MS* 6 Jul 1842

DODGE Benjamin Jr of Monroe m at Monroe STEVENS Amanda B of Bath *MS* 9 May 1833

DODGE Calvin Eld m ALLEN Charlotte A of Union NY on 18 Dec in the town of Union in Broome Co NY, DODGE Asa Eld *MS* 15 Jan 1845

DODGE Charles B of Edgecomb m STONE Mary Ann of Boothbay on 29 Sept in Boothbay ME, PAGE E G *MS* 27 Nov 1850

DODGE Charles m at Lowell MA SARGEANT Martha Ann *MS* 18 Jan 1837

DODGE John L s/o William DODGE m STORY Mary A both of Hopkinton on 28 Dec 1837 in Hopkinton, SINCLAIR J L Eld *MS* 10 Dec 1838

DODGE John M m GLIDDEN Martha both of New Durham NH in Alton NH, PINKHAM John Eld *MS* 1 Nov 1848

DODGE Lot m PAGE Jane C both of Edgecomb on 15 Sept, PAGE E G Eld in Edgecomb ME *MS* 27 Nov 1850

DODGE Simeon S m DUDLEY Betsey A on 21 Jan 1847 at Newbury NH, DODGE William Eld *MS* 24 Feb 1847

DODGE Simon m DODGE Olive both of Edgecomb on 31 Oct in Edgecomb ME, PAGE E G Eld *MS* 27 Nov 1850

DODGE Washington m HAGGAETT Ann both of Edgecomb on 22 Dec 1847 in Edgecomb, PARKER Lowell Eld *MS* 12 Jan 1848

DOE Altern C m PERKINS Sarah both of China ME on 1 Oct *MS* 14 Nov 1833

DOE Amasa m PEASE Mary Jane both of Parsonsfield on 1 Jan in Parsonsfield, JORDAN Z Eld *MS* 22 Jan 1840

DOE Anthony E m BRYANT Betsey B both of Dover on 9 June in Dover, SMITH A D Eld *MS* 15 Jul 1846

DOE David Jr of Augusta m TUCK Hannah of Fayette ME on 6 Jan CHANEY J Jr Eld *MS* 6 Apr 1836

DOE Elijah E m BRYANT Hannah on 25th Apr at Dover NH, SMITH A D Eld *MS* 5 May 1847

DOE John of New Market m KENT Mary of Durham at Dover *MFWBR* 24 Mar 1849

DOGE Elias S m BERRY Narcissa both of Westbrook ME on 7 June in Saccarappa ME, MANSON B S Eld *MS* 22 Jul 1846

DOLE Albert of Bangor m McDONALD Miriam on Thurs last week, FREEMAN Charles Eld *MS* 1 May 1834

DOLE Leonard m WATERMAN Martha both of Richmond ME *MS* 29 June 1836

DOLIVER Benjamin S m MOORE Lydia J both of Mt Desert, BROWN John Jr *MS* 19 Jan 1842

DOLIVER Thomas of Tuftonboro' m DOLLOFF Ellice of Tuftonboro' on 16 June, BEAN Silas F *MS* 31 Jul 1839

DOLL Ephraim of Gray ME m NOBLE Frances Emerline of Casco ME on 7th inst at Casco, WIGHT A F *MFWBR* 27 Jul 1850

DOLLOFF Jerome B m STILSON Mary J both of Lowell on 5 Apr 1848 in Lowell, CURTIS S Eld *MS* 26 Apr 1848

DOLLOFF Joseph P m BLAKE Almira of Lowell MA on 26 Sept at Lowell MA, THURSTON N Eld *MS* 2 Nov 1842

DOLLOFF Lorenzo D m SMITH Susan P both of Meredith on 16 Feb 1848, PITMAN S J Eld *MS* 1 Mar 1848

DOLLOFF Salome of Bridgewater m SIMONS Kanly of Bristol on 1 May in Bristol, BROWN A Eld *MS* 19 June 1850

DONALDSON John m COLEMAN Cynthia P on 11 Jan at Stephentown NY, COLEMAN I B Eld *MS* 19 Mar 1845

DONNELL Benjamin m LEIGHTON Octavia on 2 May at Falmouth ME, BEAN C Eld *MS* 2 June 1847

DONNELL Jesse D of Webster ME m THOMPSON Sarah Ann of Monmouth ME at Wales ME, FILES A Eld *MS* 28 Feb 1844

DONNOCKER George m WILLET Hannah H on 3 Apr at Boston NY, LIGHTHALL W A Eld *MS* 9 June 1847

DOOLITTLE Alonzo of Cowlesville m HAWLEY Mary C of Sheldon on 26 Feb 1846 in Varysburgh NY, DICK A Eld *MS* 5 May 1846

DOOR John 3d m HALL Lucy both of Dover NH on Sunday last, MACK Enoch Eld *MS* 20 Jan 1836

DORE Brackett of Lebanon m MILLS Lydia of Rochester NH, BLAIS-
DELL E Eld *MS* 27 Nov 1844

DORE Charles m NASON Sarah Ann both of Great Falls on 23 ult in
Great Falls, WOODMAN J Eld *MS* 2 Aug 1837

DORE Charles of Great Falls m CHASE Sarah of North Berwick ME,
CURTIS S Eld *MS* 13 Nov 1839

DORE Ezekiel m QUINBY Melinda at Great Falls, CURTIS S Eld *MS*
18 Mar 1840

DORE Ezekiel of Dover m LEATHERS Diana of Brooks ME on 13
inst, HUTCHINS E Eld in Dover *MS* 16 Feb 1848

DORE Isaac m on 6 Feb 1848 HOWE Abby both of Milton NH in
Newfield ME, STONE J Rev F

DORE Jacob C m FERNALD Mary both of Ossipee on 13 Aug in
Ossipee, CHICK J Eld *MS* 7 Nov 1849

DORE Nathan of Milton NH m BUTLER Dorcas at Lebanon ME,
STRONG J E Rev *MS* 27 Nov 1844

DORE Samuel H at Sandwich m WEDGWOOD Mary M, BROOKS N
Eld *MS* 31 Dec 1845

DORE Wentworth m MEADER Sarah at Dover NH, THURSTON
Nathaniel Eld *MS* 25 Apr 1833

DORMAN Jabez m HEATH Naomi both of Great Falls on 14th inst,
CAVERNO Eld *MS* 24 June 1835

DORMAN James B of Tamworth m ELWELL Harriet S of Eaton on 1
Jan in Eaton, ROBERTSON Samuel Esq *MS* 15 Jan 1851

DORMAN John of Newfield ME m STANTON Sarah A on 15 Oct at
Wakefield, COOLEY John L Eld *MS* 25 Nov 1846

DORR John B of Milton Mills NH m MOULTON Martha Ann of Sanford ME on 24 Jan at Springvale ME, PEACOCK Rev Mr *MS* 3 Mar
1847

DORR Samuel m THOMPSON Betsey of Great Falls NH on 1 Dec at
North Berwick ME, HOBBS A W Eld *MS* 20 Jan 1847

DOTON John of Camden m COBB Polly of Harrisburg NY on 22 Feb
at Harrisburg NY, ABBEY M H Eld *MS* 13 Mar 1844

DOUGHTY Isaac L of Topsham m SMALLEN Mehitabel H of Lisbon
ME on 29 Dec 1851 in Lisbon ME, BARD N Eld *MS* 5 Feb 1851

DOUGLASS Benjamin B m BATES Rachel Jane of Richmond ME on
12 May at Litchfield ME, QUINNAM C Eld *MS* 2 June 1847

DOUGLASS Elias m MESERVE Sally both of Limington in Apr in
Limington, McKENNY Humphrey Esq *MS* 30 May 1838

DOUGLASS Elisha m MORTON Soloma of Limerick ME, MANSON B
S Eld *MS* 7 Feb 1844

DOUGLASS George m COOK Rebecca Mrs both of Bowdoin in
Bowdoin, QUINNAM C Eld *MS* 18 Apr 1838

DOUGLASS John Jr of Sebago m NORTON Abigail of Limington in
Limington ME, AYER Aaron Eld *MS* 20 June 1838

DOUGLASS Orin m WALKER Lydia Ann at Limington on Nov 21,

DOUGLASS (Continued)

MANSON B S Eld *MS* 15 Jan 1840

DOW Abraham m COUSENS Sarah of Hollis ME, McKENNY P Eld *MS* 14 June 1843

DOW Abram of Meredith m MOOERS Mary J of Alexandria on 8 Jan 1849, PITMAN Stephen J Eld *MS* 18 Apr 1849

DOW George A of Weare m KENESTON Nancy W of Pittsfield, KNOWLES J Eld *MS* 16 Oct 1839

DOW George O of North Hampton m PHILBRICK Mary E of Hampton on 2d inst at Hampton, BURBANK P S Eld *MS* 26 May 1847

DOW Henry W of Edgecomb ME m STOVER Matilda on 19 Nov "The fee received (two dollars) is herewith sent to aid the Mission cause - Wouldn't this be a good practice? - Administrator. " *MS* 16 Dec 1846

DOW Hezekiah B of Biddeford ME m GOODRICH Eliza A on 8th inst at Saco ME, STRICKLAND G G Rev *MFWBR* 20 Apr 1850

DOW Isaac W m MALOON Climena on 3d Dec at Manchester, CILLEY D P Eld *MS* 20 Dec 1843

DOW J R of Waterville m THAYER Margarette A of Portland ME on 23d ult at Portland ME *MFWBR* 4 May 1850

DOW Jacob at Raymond m DEARBORN Sarah D, PAGE Rev *MS* 11 Jan 1843

DOW James C of Dover NH m BACON Hannah G of Wilton ME on 25 June 1843, SANDERSON Eld *MS* 19 Jul 1843

DOW John 3d m DOW Betsey both of Gilmanton on 4 inst in Gilmanton, FERNALD Samuel P *MS* 24 Jan 1838

DOW Jonathan S m FRENCH Henrietta S, THURSTON Eld at Lowell MA *MS* 13 Apr 1836

DOW Lafayette of Yorkshire m CALCINS Loisa of China NY on 25 Mar in China NY, JACKSON N A Eld *MS* 9 May 1849

DOW Lorenzo of Newburyport MA m WINSLOW Elizabeth Ann of Nottingham NH on 31 May 1848 in New Market NH, EASTMAN C Allen Eld *MS* 7 June 1848

DOW Orchard m CROCKER Jane PARK Eld in Prospect *MS* 27 Jan 1830

DOW Parker of St Albans m SANBORN Clarissa Miss of Wales, FILES A Eld *MS* 21 Mar 1833

DOW Zebulon of Gilmanton m GILFORD Almira, BROOKS N Eld *MS* 8 Feb 1843

DOWD James m HAYES Nancy on 22 Oct at Attica NY, PLUMB H N Eld *MS* 18 Mar 1846

DOWLING James H m SMITH Betsey both of Bradford NH on 19 Mar in Bradford NH, HOLMES H Eld *MS* 19 June 1850

DOWNE Emerson of Portland m SNOW Mary E of Brunswick ME in Brunswick ME, BEAN C Eld *MS* 2 Aug 1848

DOWNES Nathaniel m MOODY Lucinda on 4 May at Lowell,

DOWNES (Continued)
CURTIS S Eld *MS* 2 June 1847

DOWNES Newell P of Newport m NYE Ruth H of Clinton ME on 1 Jan in Clinton, BUKER A J Eld *MS* 8 Apr 1846

DOWNING Ebenezer m GRAY Dorothy both of Somersworth NH on Sabbath last in this village (Dover NH?) SMITH Eleazar Rev *MS* 1 Nov 1837

DOWNING John m DREW Miss both of Holderness in Holderness, PETTINGILL John Eld *MS* 24 Jan 1838

DOWNS Aaron m TUTTLE Maria both of Lebanon in Lebanon, STEVENS T Eld *MS* 10 Jan 1838

DOWNS Aaron P 7 Oct m OLIVER Sarah A both of Boston in Boston, DUNN R Eld *MS* 17 Oct 1849

DOWNS Adams B m TOWLE Melinda N of Boston on 29 Nov, NOYES E Eld *MS* 16 Dec 1846

DOWNS Albert M m ATKINSON Hannah both of Lowell on 16 Mar 1848 in Lowell, CURTIS S Eld *MS* 26 Apr 1848

DOWNS George W m RICKER Lydia H both of Great Falls NH on 16 Dec, BROOKS N Eld *MS* 25 Dec 1850

DOWNS James m DOCKUM Mary Jane of Dover on 19th inst at Dover NH, HUTCHINS E Eld *MS* 25 Feb 1846

DOWNS Jonathan G m ARCHIBALD Mercy on 1 Mar at Acton ME, FULLONTON J Eld *MS* 18 Mar 1846

DOWNS Nathan P of Croydon m CHAMBERLIN Rhoda E on 7 May at Enfield, SMITH C H Eld *MS* 9 Jul 1845

DOWST Henry of Allenstown m DAVIS Hannah of Epsom NH on 2 May at Epsom NH, FOSS T Eld *MS* 12 May 1847

DRAKE - see DAKE

DRAKE Bradley of Hampton m NUDD Emeline S on 2d inst, BURBANK P S Eld *MS* 12 Apr 1843

DRAKE Charles J m STONE Maria E of Blackstone MA on 19 Jan, BURLINGAME M W Eld *MS* 5 Feb 1845

DRAKE George W m TOWLE Abigail D in Hampton on 9 inst, HUTCHINS E Eld *MS* 15 Apr 1840

DRAKE Ira m ALLARD Caroline on 24th at Effingham NH, FOSS N Eld *MS* 6 Apr 1847

DRAKE Lucius m GILMAN Caroline C on 1 Oct at Great Falls NH, WEBBER H Eld *MS* 18 Dec 1844

DRAKE S P Holt m DRAKE Abigail of Pittsfield on 27 Mar at Pittsfield, CILLEY D P Eld *MS* 20 May 1842

DRAPER Charles R of Roxbury MA m BURKE Mary A at Eaton NH, GASKILL S Eld *MS* 21 Jan 1846

DREW Alvan m FRENCH Elizabeth of Liberty at Belmont ME, WARD Cotton Esq *MS* 6 Nov 1839

DREW Ayer B m AUSTIN Mary H both of Tunbridge VT on 7 June 1848 in Tunbridge VT, SMITH C H Eld *MS* 21 June 1848

DREW Benjamin T of Eaton m MILLS Mary on May 27, RUNNELS J
Eld *MS* 30 June 1847 & 9 Feb 1848

DREW Ebenezer m RUSSELL Betsey B both of Manchester on 26 ult
in Manchester, CILLEY D P Eld *MS* 1 Apr 1846

DREW Ezekiel B m FOLSOM Relief S both of Dover on 7 inst in
Dover NH, HUTCHINS E Eld *MS* 11 Dec 1850

DREW Ezra Jr m BOWEN Matilda both of Bafford CE on 26 Jan in
Barnston CE, SAWYER G Eld *MS* 19 Feb 1851

DREW George W F m HANSCOM Eliza J both of Somersworth NH on
14 Apr in Somersworth NH, WEBBER H Eld *MS* 8 May 1844

DREW Hezekiah m SHAW Jane Mrs both of Dover on 28 ult in
Dover, HUTCHINS E Eld *MS* 4 Dec 1850

DREW Hiram m ROBINSON Mary Ann both of Barrington on 7th
inst *MS* 13 Jul 1836

DREW Isaac of Barnston m FLETCHER Henrietta on 8 June,
MOULTON A Eld *MS* 13 Sept 1843

DREW Joseph H of Berwick ME m NOWELL Mary Ann of York at
Biddeford ME, LORD T N Rev *MFWBR* 2 Nov 1850

DREW Joseph of Newfield ME m McKUSICK Charlotte of Limerick
ME on Sunday last, BURBANK S Eld at Limerick *MS* 27 June
1833

DREW Meshech m WOODBURY Elizabeth of New Market NH on 21st
Apr at New Market NH, FROST D S Eld *MS* 28 Apr 1847

DREW Moses m WHITE Joanna Miss on 3th ult in New Limerick ME
MS 15 Mar 1827

DREW Orvel m CROOKER Abigail both of Bafford LC on 27 Feb
1844*MS* 1 May 1844

DREW Samuel W m KNOX Esther W both of Newfield ME on 14
Mayat Great Falls, DREW Samuel W *MS* 22 May 1850

DREW Sargent S m TOWN Sally both of Newfield ME, BURBANK
Samuel Eld *MS* 24 June 1835

DREW Silas m CAVERLY Jane both of Barrington *MS* 23 Nov 1836

DREW Swain m HALL Matilda at Barrington *MS* 26 Dec 1833

DREW Timothy of Strafford m CAVERLY Sophia on 4 Mar *MS* 13 Mar
1834

DROWN Charles m SAWYER Hannah A on 13 Oct at Lowell MA at
Lowell MA, THURSTON N Eld *MS* 2 Nov 1842

DROWN Eliphalet G m CORNER Caroline M on 22 May of Lowell,
WOODMAN J Eld *MS* 19 Oct 1842

DROWN John G m FOWLER Deborah M of Boston MA on 27 Dec at
Gray ME, LIBBY James Eld *MS* 10 Feb 1847

DROWN John N m LEIGHTON Lydia both of Dover in Dover,
HUTCHINS E Eld *MS* 1 Jul 1846

DUDLEY Benjamin of Lyman m LOCKE Miss at Biddeford ME *MS* 15
June 1832

DUDLEY Benjamin of Mt Vernon ME m TUCKER Sarah in Raymond

DUDLEY (Continued)
NH *MS* 20 Sept 1827

DUDLEY David m KING Thankful, NOYES E Eld *MS* 15 Dec 1847

DUDLEY George W m SMITH Augusta A both of Augusta ME on 5 Dec 1847 in Augusta ME, DUDLEY Thomas J Eld *MS* 24 May 1848

DUDLEY Joseph m RIDEOUT Rebecca both of Pittsfield in Pittsfield, WEYMOUTH Nathaniel Esq *MS* 3 Jul 1850

DUDLEY Nelson m ELLIOT Betsey of Douglass on 3 May, FULLER W Eld *MS* 7 June 1843

DUDLEY Oren of Springfield MA m WALDRON Elizabeth Ann of Dover NH *MS* 13 Jul 1836

DUDLEY Samuel of Bethlehem VT m TEMPLE Jerusha of Littleton in Littleton, BLAKE C E Eld *MS* 18 Apr 1849

DUDLEY Sargent P of Alton m HANSON Betsey Y on 13 Feb, FERNALD S P Eld *MS* 26 Feb 1845

DUDLEY William of Brooks m HOYT Susan E of Lowell, THURSTON N Eld *MS* 11 Sept 1839

DUHEN Dennis m WEEKS Julia A on 3d in Kittery ME, WETHER-BEE K J Eld *MS* 1 Jan 1845

DULIN James Dr of Newton Union Co Ohio m HARTSHORN Sarah A on 29 Nov, HEATH J D Eld *MS* 23 Dec 1846

DUNBAR Ira of Bangor ME m SOUINS Judith of Newbury in Newbury NH, ROWE J Eld *MS* 20 Dec 1848

DUNBAR Jonathan N m BRUCE Mary Jane in Contoocookville NH? *MS* 8 May 1844

DUNGIN Samuel m on 1 inst BARTLETT Elizabeth H GATES on 5 Mar in Nottingham Square, Charles H Rev *MS* 15 Jan 1851

DUNHAM Alfred m LEIGHTON Emily C both of Falmouth ME in Falmouth ME, CROCKETT J Eld *MS* 24 Jan 1849

DUNHAM Ammi of Litchfield m FALES Olive of Hallowell ME on Dec 29 1841, GATCHELL Mark Eld *MS* 9 Mar 1842

DUNHAM Cyrenius of Bradley m HASKELL Clarinda P of Bangor ME on 9 Sept 1847 in Bangor ME, WEAVER P Eld *MS* 17 Nov 1847

DUNHAM Daniel J of Brunswick ME m SNOW Emily on 31 Dec at Brunswick ME, PAGE E G Eld *MS* 13 Jan 1847

DUNHAM Elliot M of Brunswick m WARD Mary Jane of Freeport ME on 30 Jul, ROLLINS A Eld *MS* 16 Aug 1837

DUNHAM John m HUSTON Elizabeth S of Falmouth on 31st ult, BEAN Charles Eld *MS* 27 Feb 1839

DUNHAM Nelson B of Nassau m GRIFFIN Palmyra B of Stephentown on 29 ult *MS* 1 Feb 1837

DUNLAP D S of New Gloucester m LATHAM Sarah T of Raymond ME on 11th inst at Raymond, FORD James Esq of Gray ME *MFWBR* 21 Apr 1849

DUNMELL Benjamin 2d m SMITH Mary Ann of Buxton ME on 17

DUNMELL (Continued)

Nov at Buxton ME, CARIL George Esq *MS* 21 Dec 1842

DUNN Alanson m TOWNSEND Hannah A on 5 June in Buxton ME, BAILEY J M Eld *MS* 3 Jul 1850

DUNN Albert J m CLAY Caroline B both of Buxton in Buxton ME, CROCKET J Eld *MS* 15 Jan 1851

DUNN Elias G m CASWELL Charity of West Sumner ME on 8th ult, CHANDLER R Esq *MFWBR* 24 Feb 1849

DUNN Isaiah m HACKETT Abby C of Windham ME on 27 May at Windham ME, BAILEY J M Eld *MS* 7 Jul 1847

DUNN Ranson Eld m EMERY Cyrena on 1 Sept in Great Falls NH, BROOKS N Eld *MS* 5 Sept 1849

DUNN Richard of Belgrade ME m WAILEIGH Susan A on 22 Nov, SPAULDING Joel Eld *MS* 8 Jan 1845

DUNN Samuel m HARMON Mary A E on 16 June in Buxton ME, BAILEY J M Eld *MS* 17 Jul 1850

DUNNELS Joseph Jr of Newfield ME m LANGLEY Hannah of Acton ME, BURBANK Eld *MS* 14 Apr 1830

DUNNING Robert of Brunswick ME m CHAMBERLAIN Mary J of Auburn ME on 26 Oct at Auburn ME, BEAN G W Eld *MS* 9 Dec 1846

DUNNING Wm m TRIM Loiz both of Charleston on 22d ult, HATH-AWAY L Eld *MS* 12 Nov 1834

DUNTON Andrew m DUNTON Alvina both of Westport, PHINNEY C Eld *MS* 14 Feb 1833

DUNTON Henry m TARBOX Ellis Ann in Westport ME, TARBOX Jordan Esq *MS* 16 May 1838

DUNTON Joseph m TARBOX Sabrina both of Westport ME on 13th inst, FAIRFIELD S Eld *MS* 30 Mar 1836

DUNTON Samuel Jr m HODGDON Harriet W of Westport ME on New Year's evening, TARBOX Jordan Esq *MS* 23 Jan 1839

DUPEE Job of Medway MA m CROSSMAN Clarissa M of Smithfield RI on 17 inst, HUTCHINS Eld *MS* 27 Jan 1836

DURAN David of Casco m GERRY Adaline of West Poland ME on 12 Apr in West Poland ME, LIBBY James Eld *MS* 3 June 1846

DURANT E C Mr m ELLIOT Abigail F A of Haverhill NH on 25 Mar at Corinth VT, MOULTON F Eld *MS* 19 May 1847

DURFEE John m TOOTHAKER Elizabeth of Charleston ME on 11 May at Garland ME, AMES M Eld *MS* 9 June 1847

DURGIN Alexander m APPLEBEE Phebe A of Minton NH on 22 Feb at Acton ME, FULLONTON J Eld *MS* 28 Feb 1844

DURGIN Ananias A m AVERY Abigail on 29 Nov 1843 at Sandwich NH, McMURPHY B H Eld *MS* 5 June 1844

DURGIN Clark m BRYANT Drusilla B on 3 Aug at Andover, FROST D Sidney Eld *MS* 14 Sept 1842

DURGIN David C of Limerick m WARREN Sabrina A of Limerick ME

DURGIN (Continued)

on 5th inst at Limerick ME, BUZZELL James Eld *MFWBR* 14 Sept 1850

DURGIN David of Strafford m DEMERITT Catharine of Barrington on Dec 5, CAVERLY J 4th Eld *MS* 29 Jan 1840

DURGIN Ephraim m WELCH Martha A on 31st ult in Limerick, FREEMAN Charles Rev *MFWBR* 8 Jul 1848

DURGIN Erastus m PROUTY Ester Ann both of Lowell in Lowell, THURSTON N Eld *MS* 10 May 1837

DURGIN Gershan of Andover m ROWE Mary of Wilmott in Andover, WATSON Elijah Eld *MS* 21 Nov 1838

DURGIN J M Eld m THAYER Harriet R of Gray ME, LIBBY Isaac Eld *MS* 18 Dec 1839

DURGIN Jacob m FLOYD Lucinda of Biddeford ME on Sun last, BLAKE H M Rev *MFWBR* 8 Feb 1851

DURGIN James H of Parsonsfield ME m VARNEY Jane H on 27 Oct, McMURPHY B H Eld *MS* 18 Dec 1844

DURGIN John m BYRUM Diana both of Portland ME, ABBOTT H B Rev on 16th inst at Portland ME *MFWBR* 29 June 1850

DURGIN John C of Haverhill MA m TUCKER Mary on 26 Feb at Orange, TYLER Job C *MS* 19 Mar 1845

DURGIN John W m YORK Roxana B of Lee on 6th inst at New Market, HUTCHINS E Eld *MS* 12 Mar 1845

DURGIN Joshua m KENERSON Mary in Freedom, RUNNELS J Eld *MS* 9 Feb 1848

DURGIN Leonard m TEBBETS Susan A of Farmington on 19 Feb 1843, HART E H Eld *MS* 1 Mar 1843

DURGIN Miles Esq m MOORE Sarah of Northwood on 10 Dec at Manchester NH, CILLEY D P Eld *MS* 1 Jan 1845

DURGIN Nathan of New Market m WIGGIN Frances of Durham on 19th ult at Durham, CILLEY D P Eld *MS* 1 Apr 1835

DURGIN Nathaniel of Northwood m HANSON Susan Mrs of Barnstead on 29 Mar, JOHNSON W D Eld *MS* 6 Apr 1847

DURGIN Newell m ELLIOT Mary of Dover at Farmington on 30 Jul, WALDRON W H Eld *MS* 13 Sept 1843

DURGIN Silas of Hiram ME m LOVERING Hannah of Freedom, EATON E G Eld *MS* 4 June 1834

DURGIN Silas m ROGERS Martha R on 23 Nov 1842 at Wolfboro' NH, PRESCOTT E T Eld *MS* 24 May 1843

DURGIN Wm C m MUDGETT Sophronia both of Dixmont ME on 8 Jan 1850, FLETCHER J Eld *MS* 22 May 1850

DURGIN Woodbury M m JAMES Abagail E both of Northwood NH on 16 Dec 1847, JOHNSON W D Eld in Northwood NH *MS* 12 Jan 1848

DURHAM David m FAIRBANKS Almena both of Hermon on 6 Sept in Fowler NY, JENKINS C Eld *MS* 21 Oct 1846

DURLAND Wm H m THING Sarah J both of Lynn MA on 13 Jul in Great Falls, BROOKS N Eld *MS* 31 Jul 1850

DURRELL George W Rev Dr of Kennebunkport ME m KNOWLTON Jane B of Brunswick ME at Brunswick ME *MFWBR* 31 Aug 1850

DURRELL John N of Durham m JEWELL Clara M of New Market on 1 Sept in New Market, FROST D S Eld *MS* 30 Sept 1846

DURRELL Nathan G m GOODRICH Rhoda both of Biddeford ME on 5 Feb 1848 in Biddeford, WITHAM L H Eld *MS* 8 Mar 1848

DURRELL Nathan G m WARREN Susan J on 9 Nov at Waterborough ME, EMERY Richard Eld *MS* 18 Dec 1844

DUSTIN Russell H m COLBURN Elzina of Tunbridge VT on 25th at Tunbridge VT, COLLEY D Eld *MS* 14 Jan 1846

DUSTON Lindley M m RANDEL Sarah M both of Poestenkill NY in Poestenkill NY, HOAG I J Eld *MS* 15 Jan 1851

DUTTON Oliver W of Chelsea m MARTIN Lydia of Williamstown VT on 13 Feb 1850 in Williamstown VT, HARTSHORN Nelson Eld *MS* 10 Apr 1850

DUTTON Thomas m both of Gray McDONALD Sarah on 18th ult, PURKIS John Eld *MS* 2 Feb 1831

DWINAL Cyrus C m BUCK Ruth R, COOMBS A Eld at Foxcroft ME *MS* 5 Dec 1833

DYER Barlow Eld m PAGE Rosaline A of New Sharon ME on 5 Dec at New Sharon ME, SLEEPER Hiram S Eld *MS* 18 Dec 1844

DYER C W m SOULE Harriet on 27th ult at New Sharon ME *MFWBR* 17 Mar 1849

DYER Daniel m TOOTHAKER Amelia, HERSEY L Eld in Harpswell ME *MS* 8 May 1850

DYER G of Gorham m BAKER Rebecca of Portland ME on 10th inst, PRATT J Rev *MFWBR* 23 June 1849

DYER George Capt of West Prospect m HIGGINS Joan of Freedom at Thorndike on Dec 25, TRUE John Eld *MS* 15 Jan 1840

DYER Joseph C son of Eld S B DYER of Deerfield m HARRIMAN Lucia on 7 May in Weare NH, MOODY D Eld *MS* 17 June 1846

DYER Orin m BARTLETT Dintha of New Portland on 31 Oct in New Portland, LENNAN John Eld *MS* 18 Dec 1839

DYER Watson of Jackson Brook (ME) m DAKIN Rebecca of Weston (ME) on 15 May at Weston ME, HASKELL G W Eld *MS* 5 Jul 1843

EADES Charles of Conway NH m STORER Louisa of Brownfield ME 30 Apr 1848 in Brownfield ME, HART E H Eld *MS* 5 Jul 1848

EAMES Daniel m RICHARDSON Lydia F on 28 Dec at Wilmington MA, PERKINS S W Eld *MS* 17 Jan 1844

EAMES Nathan S of Albany VT m SHERBURN Roxylany of Wheelock VT *MS* 1 Feb 1843

EAMES Thomas P of Wilmington m ALLEN Elona M of Billerica MA on 21 Dec 1843 at Billerica MA, PERKINS S W Eld

EAMES (Continued)
MS 17 Jan 1844

EARL Edmund m DOICK Mary I both of So Berwick on 15 Oct in So Berwick ME, JOHNSON W D Eld *MS* 23 Oct 1850

EARL Josiah m HASTY Hannah on 14th inst at South Berwick ME, TRUE Ezekiel Eld *MS* 24 Feb 1847

EARL William m GILFORD Hannah both of Biddeford ME on 29 Oct, BAILEY J M Eld *MS* 15 Nov 1848

EASTBROOK Leonard m COLLINS Mary of Charlestown MA on 17 Feb, JACKSON Daniel Eld *MS* 24 May 1843

EASTMAN Alfred of Concord m BRADLEY Hannah R of Canterbury NH on 13 Dec, CLOUGH Jeremiah Eld *MS* 14 Feb 1844

EASTMAN Benjamin m PETRIE Almira on 13 Nov, TALLMAN E P Eld *MS* 25 Dec 1850

EASTMAN David of Limerick ME m TRUE Charlotte E of Loudon NH on 10th inst, JONES Rev *MFWBR* 21 Jan 1849

EASTMAN David m STREETER Emily of Lisbon on 17 May 1843 at Lisbon NH, WITHAM L H Eld *MS* 13 Mar 1844

EASTMAN Eben Col m MUZZY Catherine L both of Whitefield on 29 Nov in Whitefield NH, SHEPHERD Simon Eld *MS* 26 Dec 1849

EASTMAN Ezra m WEEKS Emeline R both of Gilford on 13 June 1849 in Gilford NH, FROST D S Eld *MS* 9 Jan 1850

EASTMAN Francis P m PALMER Elizabeth on 2 June in Hollis ME, BAILEY J M Eld *MS* 3 Jul 1850

EASTMAN Geo A m EASTES Joanna both of Great Falls NH in Great Falls, BROOKS N Eld *MS* 16 Jan 1850

EASTMAN James M m JOHNSON Mary Ann on 19th ult at Parsonsfield ME, MOULTON S Eld *MFWBR* 1 Jan 1848

EASTMAN John F m McOLLISTER Elvira on 8 inst in Dover, HUTCHINS E Eld *MS* 17 Oct 1849

EASTMAN Jonathan G m JACKMAN Charlotte both of Hopkinton NH on 8 May *MS* 22 June 1836

EASTMAN Joseph K of Parsonsfield m DURGIN Dorcas of Cornish ME on 29 Nov *MS* 17 Jan 1833

EASTMAN Samuel of Boscawen m CUSHING Sarah of Hopkinton on 18 in Hopkinton, SINCLAIR J Eld *MS* 4 Apr 1838

EASTMAN Silas of Lyndon m MATHEWSON Hannah of Lyndon, MOULTON T P Eld *MS* 5 Apr 1843

EASTMAN Solomon of Stow m SAWYER Betsey of Cornish ME at Stow ME, RAND James Eld *MS* 8 Mar 1843

EASTMAN Walla [sic] B of Holderness NH on 10 Aug m LOUD Sarah B of Boston MA at Lowell MA, THURSTON N Eld *MS* 2 Nov 1842

EASTON Edward m HOWARD Abby S of Newport RI on 11 Jan 1846 at Newport RI, LORD D H Eld *MS* 11 Mar 1846

EASTWOOD Nelson m COLLINS Harriet of Pitt on 27 ult in Pitt, Washtenaw Co Mich, LIMBOCKER H S Eld *MS* 24 Oct 1838

EASTWOOD Palmer R m PULLEN Caroline of West Waterville ME at Sidney ME, LEWIS D B Eld *MS* 20 Apr 1842

EATON Charles M m WADE Deborah C of Topsham, BEAN C Eld in Brunswick ME *MS* 19 Jan 1848 & BEAN Rev on 28th ult at Topsham ME *MFWBR* 11 Dec 1847

EATON Charles S of Limerick ME m at Dedham FINNEY Abigail *MS* 1 Aug 1833

EATON Charles W m SWAIN Abigail M on 5 Dec at Manchester NH, CILLEY D P Eld *MS* 1 Jan 1845

EATON George of Newbury m PAGE Mary Ann on 26 Jan at Manchester, Cilley D P Eld *MS* 5 Feb 1845

EATON Horace of Wells ME m MORRILL Hannah J at Wilmington MA, DURGIN J M Eld *MS* 8 Mar 1843

EATON John L of Salisbury NH m BICKFORD Lovey of Lowell in Lowell, THURSTON N Eld *MS* 5 Apr 1837

EATON Marsena of Rome m McENTRYE Anna of New Lyme on 5 Nov 1848, HYDE Nelson Esq *MS* 3 Jan 1849

EATON Moses m JOHNSON Ruth both of Weare on 12 Jul in Weare NH, MOODY D Eld *MS* 14 Oct 1846

EATON Rufus of Bristol m JEWELL Mary J of Alexandria on 19 Sept 1848, CILLEY D Eld in Bristol NH *MS* 4 Oct 1848

EATON Samuel m CHASE Julia Ann both of Pittsfield on 24 inst in Strafford, CARVERNO A Eld *MS* 3 May 1837

EATON Samuel N of Sutton VT m BECKWITH Ann of Sutton VT, MOULTON T P Eld *MS* 5 Apr 1843

EATON William of Meredith m GORDON Mary Ann at New Hampton on 4th ult, PETTENGILL J Eld *MS* 10 Apr 1839

EATON Wm L of Dexter ME m HARE Charlotte of Lowell on 7 Jan in Lowell MA, WALDRON W H Eld *MS* 22 Jan 1851

EDDY Ambrose S m MASON Mary both of No Providence on 26 ult, HUTCHINS E Eld *MS* 16 Dec 1835

EDDY Darius of No Providence m REMINGTON Susan B of Cranston on 14th inst at Johnston RI *MS* 24 June 1835

EDDY Harviain T of Sutton m TAYLOR Sally W of Grafton, PECK Benjamin D Eld *MS* 13 Sept 1843

EDDY William G of Foster m KENYAM Eliza A of Coventry, NOYES E Eld *MS* 13 Nov 1850

EDGECOMB Charles m MANSON Isabella of Limington ME on 26 Dec, MANSON B S Eld *MS* 7 Feb 1844

EDGECOMB Edward of Bath m TRACY Anna B of Lewiston Falls ME on 2 inst in Lewiston Falls ME, BEAN G W Eld *MS* 26 Apr 1848

EDGECOMB Elizha of Limington ME m BABB Harriet C F of Buxton, ME CLAY Jonathan Eld *MS* 20 Nov 1844

EDGECOMB Jeremiah m PERRY Anna on 23d inst at Parsonsfield ME, MOULTON Silas Eld *MFWBR* 29 May 1847

EDGECOMB John of Saco ME m SEAVEY Sally E of Cornish ME on

EDGECOMB (Continued)

22 Apr, HACKETT John O Eld *MS* 8 June 1842

EDGECOMB Joseph Eld of Vienna m FOSS Eliza Mrs of Limington ME on 4 Mar in Limington ME, MANSON B S Eld *MS* 20 Mar 1850

EDGECOMB William of Hollis m USHER Elizabeth R of Limerick ME on 9th inst at Limington ME, STEVENS Eld *MFWBR* 16 Sept 1848

EDGERLY George W m BOOTHBY Sarah E on 1 Mar at Buxton ME, LIBBY C O Eld *MS* 18 Mar 1846

EDGERLY Hiram W of New Durham m YEATON Harriet of Strafford on 24 Jul in Rochester, MEADER Jesse Eld *MS* 21 Aug 1850

EDGERLY Ira C m LORD Louise of Northfield on 15 Dec 1846 at Sandbornton NH, MASON S Eld *MS* 17 Mar 1847

EDGERLY Jabez F of Barnstead m EATON Mary H of Dover formerly of Landaff NH, HODGE Rev in Gilmanton NH *MS* 24 Oct 1838

EDGERLY John G m STONE Rhoda L both of Salem on 23 June in Salem, EATON Rev *MS* 3 Jul 1850

EDGERLY Rook T m GOVE Sarah S Mrs both of Limington ME on 13 Jan 1848 in Limington ME, STEVENS T Eld *MS* 16 Feb 1848

EDGERLY Samuel Deacon of Limington ME m HASTLY Eliza Mrs on 25 Feb at Limerick ME *MS* 11 Mar 1846

EDGERLY Samuel N m MOULTON Cynthia P on 20 Oct at Gilmanton NH, HAM Ezra Eld *MS* 28 May 1845

EDGERLY Samuel m PINKHAM Abigail on 14 Mar at New Market NH, FROST D S Eld *MS* 6 Apr 1847

EDMONDS Aaron of Northwood NH m GRIFFIN Mary L of Epsom NH on 29 Nov 1849 in Epsom NH, RAMSEY G P Eld *MS* 16 Jan 1850

EDMONDS Joseph m GOODWIN Sarah on 17 Oct 1844 at Roxbury MA, DAVIS J B Eld *MS* 6 Nov 1844

EDMUNDS Lot of Lynn MA m EDMUNDS Sarah A of Lynn on 7 Aug at Saugus MA, MERRILL William P *MS* 14 Aug 1844

EDMUNDS Rhodolphus m BUNNEL Emily of Stanstead LC on 14 Feb, MOULTON A Eld *MS* 13 Sept 1843

EDSON James A of Brookline NH m GOULD Emily E of Lowell on 9 Sept in Lowell, CURTIS S Eld *MS* 14 Oct 1846

EDSON Truman of Barnston LC m WYMAN Amanda on 13 Jan 1842, MOULTON A Eld of Stanstead LC *MS* 13 Apr 1842

EDWARDS Almeran of West Hampton m DOLE Caroline A of Ashfield MA on Oct 1848 in Ashfield MA, KING Warren Eld *MS* 7 Feb 1849

EDWARDS Thomas Capt m JOHNSON Caroline S on 30 Mar in No Providence RI, HUTCHINS E Eld *MS* 19 Apr 1837

EFFLESTON Amos J m FRAZIER Salome E on 18 Nov 1847 in Hudson Mich, DREW Enoch Eld *MS* 2 Feb 1848

EGELISTON Benjamin m WHEELER Hannah of Barnston at Clifton *MS* 18 May 1836

ELBERT Charles C m DABOIS Augusta both of Concord NH on 10 Dec 1847 in Concord NH, CATLIN S T Eld *MS* 17 Jan 1849

ELDER Richard J of Windham m WASHBURN Roxcillana of Portland ME, BEAN C Eld *MS* 18 Apr 1838

ELDRIDGE Joseph m RICHARDSON Lydia, BRACKET D Eld at Hiram *MS* 8 Aug 1833

ELIAKIM Howard m LUCAS Ann Maria both of Dover on 25 inst in Dover *MS* 1 Feb 1837

ELIOT Winthrop m BATCHELDER Mary Mrs of Haverhill MA on 29 Jan at Haverhill, MOULTON F Eld *MS* 14 Feb 1844

ELISON Andrew N m JAMES Julia E both of Starksborough VT on 6 Jan 1848 in Starksborough VT, ATWOOD Mark Eld *MS* 5 Apr 1848

ELKINS Eben A of Thornton m GLIDDEN Emily of Gilmanton NH on 30 Jan at Gilmanton, GARLAND D Eld *MS* 13 Mar 1839

ELKINS Jonathan Jr m LEAVITT Eliza Mrs both of Hampton NH on 10 Oct in Hampton, MERRILL Wm P Eld *MS* 17 Oct 1849

ELLIOT Eli H of Barnstead NH m HAM Mary A of Gilmanton on 27 March, HAM Ezra Eld *MS* 19 June 1844

ELLIOT Henry G of Hebron m PEASLEY Martha Ann of Alexandria on 28 Oct 1847, BROWN Amos Eld *MS* Dec 15 1847

ELLIOT Hiram m LANPREY Plumy at Gilmanton NH, TUTTLE J G Eld *MS* 6 May 1840

ELLIOT Jason m COLLEY Mary E both of Lowell MA on 24 Nov in Dracut MA, CURTIS S Eld *MS* 15 Dec 1847

ELLIOT John m KATHAN Caroline both of Compton LC on 17 Dec, MOULTON A Eld *MS* 17 Feb 1836

ELLIOT Nathaniel m WELLMAN Hannah C both of New Portland ME on Wed 22 Dec last in Embden ME, GOULD Benjamin Eld *MS* 16 Feb 1842

ELLIOT William H m BUNKER Rosena of Barnstead on 15 May at Gilmanton, HAM Ezra Eld *MS* 19 June 1844

ELLIOTT Joseph Jr of Pittsfield NH m HUNT Mary B of Gilford on 16 Nov 1848 in Lewiston ME, LIBBY David Eld *MS* 29 Nov 1848

ELLIS Alfred G of Sanford ME m JONES Mary A of Alton NH on 5 Mar 1848 in Alton, PINKHAM John Eld *MS* 29 Mar 1848

ELLIS Cyrus m NORTON Achsah on 18 Apr in Clayton NY, GRIF-FETH A Eld *MS* 31 Jul 1850

ELLIS E C m STEVENS Sarah both of Stanstead LC? on 25 Feb *MS* 1 May 1844

ELLIS Ebenezer m WATSON Mary E both of Alton NH on 28 Nov 1848 in Alton NH, PINKHAM John Eld *MS* 20 Dec 1848

ELLIS George W m CHAMPELEN Ruth A H of South Kingston on 30 Nov at Providence RI, SCOTT E Eld *MS* 10 Dec 1845

ELLIS Joseph of Plymouth m KELLEY Mary J of Pembrook on 21 Oct 1847 in Pembrook, CATLIN S T Eld *MS* 17 Jan 1849

ELLIS Joshua of Alton NH m FOSS Mariah J of Rochester on 2 Dec,
PINKHAM J Eld *MS* 18 Dec 1844

ELLIS Lucius A m CUSHMAN Caroline F at Portsmouth NH *MFWBR*
29 Mar 1851

ELLIS Thomas m THURSTON Eliza Ann on 19 Apr at Eaton, ATKIN-
SON King Eld *MFWBR* 28 Apr 1849

ELLIS William m MORSE Zepina on 18 Oct 1843 at Haynesville ME,
GELLERSON George Eld *MS* 20 Dec 1843

ELLIS Wm B m ROBINSON Mary Ann both of Sidney ME, LEWIS D
B Eld *MS* 3 Apr 1850

ELLISON Andrew N m JAMES Julia E both of Starksborough VT on
6 Jan 1848 in Starksborough VT, ATWOOD Mark Eld *MS* 29 Mar
1848

ELWELL Jonias m BUTLER Sally on 20 Sept at South Berwick ME,
JOHNSON W D Eld *MS* 11 Oct 1843

ELWELL Joseph G m WEYMOUTH Clarisea both of No Berwick ME,
BURBANK Samuel Eld *MS* 5 Apr 1837

ELY Robert D m GREENLEAF Harriet R on 3 Oct 1847 in Abbot ME,
GALLISON W F Eld *MS* 24 Nov 1847

EMERSON Benj F m SAVAGE Rachel A both of Lowell MA on 26 Nov
1848 in Lowell MA, CURTIS S Eld *MS* 3 Jan 1849

EMERSON Benjamin J m VINCEN Sally both of New Market NH on 8
ult Sabbath eve in New Market, CILLEY D P Eld *MS* 25 Apr 1838

EMERSON Charles S m DUTTON Sally B both of Candia on 11 ult,
ROBIE T Eld *MS* 30 Dec 1835

EMERSON Edward of Boothbay m JENNESS Sarah of Edgecomb
ME, FAIRFIELD Smith Eld *MS* 12 June 1839

EMERSON Frances m TILTON Elizabeth L both of Haverhill MA on 2
Apr in Haverhill MA *MS* 26 Apr 1848

EMERSON Gideon L of Erie Monroe Co Mich m SEXTON Emeline D
of Bethany NY on 12 Nov 1848 in Bethany Genesee Co NY,
BLACKMARR H Eld *MS* 10 Jan 1849

EMERSON Hollis D of Ossipee NH m ABBOTT Mercy of Ossipee NH,
CHICK J Eld *MS* 13 Sept 1843

EMERSON Ira m ANGEL Ann on 21st at Manchester, CILLEY D P
Eld *MS* 17 Feb 1847

EMERSON Jesse of Windham m ROW Lucy B of Lowell in Lowell MA,
THURSTON Nathaniel Eld *MS* 18 Oct 1837

EMERSON Jonathan of Lyme m DODGE Amy of Clayton on 14 Feb
1847 at Clayton NY, PADDEN S B Eld *MS* 10 Mar 1847

EMERSON Joseph M m LAW Sarah Jane both of Manchester on 4
Jul 1848 in Manchester, CILLEY D P Eld *MS* 19 Jul 1848

EMERSON Joseph M m ALLEN Alimora P of Billerica MA on 2 June
at Wilmington MA, DURGIN J M Eld *MS* 26 June 1844

EMERSON Joseph m DOW Abigail Mrs of Strafford NH on 30 Oct of
Epsom NH, PLACE E Eld *MS* 16 Nov 1842

EMERSON Luther m COOPER Fidelia on 26 Nov of Boothbay ME, ROBINSON N J Eld *MS* 17 Jan 1844

EMERSON Moses H m HARVEY Caroline M of Wilmot on 21 Mar in Wilmot, SMITH C H Eld *MS* 1 May 1844

EMERSON Moses S of Georgetown m CURRIER Harriet of Lowell, CURTIS S Eld *MS* 26 Nov 1845

EMERSON Reuben of Wheelock VT m FOSS Lydia R of Stanstead *MS* 17 Apr 1839

EMERSON Samuel H m KENISTON Olive W both of Barnstead on 15 inst, TRUE E Eld *MS* 30 May 1849

EMERSON Thomas m FOLENSBY Mary E both of Edgecomb on 25 Dec in Edgecomb ME, PAGE E G Eld *MS* 26 Mar 1851

EMERSON Walter G merchant m FLANDERS Betsey both of Alton NH *MS* 8 Mar 1837

EMERSON William H m ATKINS Elizabeth W of Lowell MA on 27 Apr at Lowell MA, WOODMAN J Eld *MS* 11 May 1842

EMERSON William L m LEAVITT Susan S both of Alton on April 1, PINKHAM John Eld *MS* 4 May 1842

EMERTON Hervey of Columbia NH m CLEMENT Susan Maria of Barnston, MOULTON A Eld of Stanstead LC *MS* 13 Apr 1842

EMERY Alpheus S m CORBON Calesta A both of Manchester on 14 Feb 1848 in Manchester, CILLEY D P Eld *MS* 23 Feb 1848

EMERY Alvin of Hampton m WELCH Susan E of Effingham NH on 2d Jan, HUTCHINS E Eld *MS* 30 Jan 1839

EMERY Benjamin N of Pembroke m HAYES Hannah T *MS* 30 Dec 1835

EMERY Daniel Col of Hamden ME m EMERSON Lydia wid/o Wm EMERSON on 2nd inst at Limerick ME, FREEMAN Charles Rev *MS* 6 May 1826

EMERY Daniel of Limington ME m THOMPSON Nancy of Limington ME on 26 Apr, MANSON B S Eld *MS* 7 Feb 1844

EMERY David m WEBSTER Mary both of Gilmanton NH, LANCASTER Daniel Rev *MS* 14 Jan 1835

EMERY Elijah P m BLODGETT Ruth M both of Newbury on 18 Dec 1849, EMERY A Eld *MS* 2 Jan 1850

EMERY Enoch H m BALL Lydia A C both of Manchester on 21 Sept in Manchester, CILLEY D P Eld *MS* 6 Oct 1847

EMERY Gilbert of Barlett m LITTLEFIELD Nancy of Eaton on 25 Nov, PARIS C Eld *MS* 4 Jan 1843

EMERY Gilmore m CHALLIES Elizabeth A at Newfield ME, CHAPMAN E C Rev *MFWBR* 20 Mar 1847

EMERY James F m PORTER Lucy Y both of Dixmont ME on 3 Oct 1847 in Dixmont ME, ALLEN Ebenezer Eld *MS* 17 Nov 1847

EMERY James L m FOSS Caroline both of Saco ME on 3 Feb 1850 in Buxton ME, BAILEY J M Eld *MS* 27 Feb 1850

EMERY John of Somersworth m HILL May Jane of Dover *MFWBR* 12

EMERY (Continued)
May 1849

EMERY Jonathan Jr m LEATHERS Mary of St Albans on 1 Jan 1843 at St Albans, COPP J B Eld *MS* 29 Mar 1843

EMERY Joshua T of Portland ME m MOORE Sarah of Standish on 16th inst at Standish *MFWBR* 25 Sept 1847

EMERY Lorenzo m COBB Emily of Hampden ME, FLETCHER Jabez Eld on 11th ult *MS* 29 May 1839

EMERY Mark F m SILVER Cyrena of Bow on 5 Sept at Pittsfield, KNOWLES J Eld *MS* 16 Oct 1839

EMERY Nahum of Monroe ME m DODGE Mariah L on 20 Mar 1844, ALLEN Ebenezer Jr Eld *MS* 5 June 1844

EMERY Nathaniel m CLAY Eliza on 5th inst at Buxton, GOWER H B Rev *MFWBR* 18 Aug 1849

EMERY Rufus of Buxton m FELCH Sophia of Limerick in Limerick ME *MS* 12 Jul 1827

EMERY Samuel m HAYES Ann Maria in Limerick ME, FREEMAN Charles Rev *MS* 22 Mar 1827

EMERY Samuel m HEARD Rosanna both of Tamworth NH on 16 ult in Tamworth, EMERY James Eld *MS* 3 May 1837

EMERY Samuel of Biddeford m Sunday last HARPER Hannah of Limerick in Limerick, LIBBY E Eld *MS* 3 Nov 1830

EMERY Simeon m STEARNS Permelia both of Hatley LC *MS* 22 Mar 1837

EMERY Stephen W of Kirkland m HOLT Celia P of Bradford on 22 Sept in Bradford ME, STROUT J Eld Jr *MS* 16 Oct 1850

EMERY William of Newfield m DREW Sabrina of Parsonsfield ME in Parsonsfield, BURBANK Eld *MS* 6 Dec 1827

EMERY William S m LOCKE/LOCK Ann Maria on 22 Apr at Great Falls NH, DUNN R Eld *MS* 28 Apr 1847 & *MS* 7 Jul 1847

EMMONS Henry m SIMMONS Sally Maria both of Nassau on 6 May, COLEMAN I B Eld *MS* 4 Oct 1843

EMMONS Horace m TIBBETS Harriet R both of Lyman ME on 19 Dec 1850, WITHAM L H Eld in Lyman ME *MS* 22 Jan 1851

EMMONS J M R of Bristol m CHASE Eliza S at Bristol, FISK E Eld *MS* 31 Jan 1844

EMORY Nathan m FISH Sally both of Hatley on 20 Nov 1837, MOULTON A Eld *MS* 10 Jan 1838

ENGLISH R G W MD of Springfield MA m WIGGIN Mary P W of Durham on 6 Nov at New Market, FROST D S Eld *MS* 19 Nov 1845

ENOCH Wm m SWAIN Eunice, THURSTON Nathaniel Eld in Lowell *MS* 15 Jul 1835

ESTEE Indson [sic] m HAMMON Dianna on 4 Apr at Hamburgh NY, PLUMB H N Eld *MS* 19 May 1847

ESTES George m SOMES Susan C both of Dover on 9 inst in Dover,

ESTES (Continued)
HUTCHINS E Eld *MS* 13 Nov 1850

ESTES Isaac of Lebanon ME m MILLS Hannah of Somerworth NH on 23d inst in Dover, HUTCHINS E Eld *MS* 29 Sept 1847

ESTES ISRAEL H of Lisbon m SMITH Lydia W of Topsham on 5 Sept 1850 in Topsham ME, BARD N Eld *MS* 8 Jan 1851

ESTES Levi m CLOUDMAN Hannah L both of Gorham ME on 25 Feb 1849 in Gorham ME, HARRIMAN D P Eld *MS* 14 Mar 1849

ESTHERS John of Wolfboro' NH m MARDIN Emily Jane on 4 May 1843, PRESCOTT E T Eld *MS* 24 May 1843

ESTIS Richard O of Three Mile Bay m COLE Julia C of Amsterdam NY on 23 Dec 1847 in Three Mile Bay NY, PADDEN S B Eld *MS* 12 Jan 1848

EUSTIS Moses of Jay ME m CHANDLER Mary of Farmington ME on 24th ult, CURTIS S Eld *MS* 30 Mar 1831

EVANS/EVENS/EVINS

EVANS Albert m SWAIN Elizabeth A both of Dover NH on Monday eve 9 inst in Barrington, SHERBURNE S Eld *MS* 16 Jan 1850

EVANS Aaron m WOOD Amanda both of Dover NH on 29 Mar in East Randolph VT, MOULTON F Eld *MS* 27 June 1849

EVANS Benjamin Jr of Smithfield m BAKER Maria of Uxbridge MA on 1 inst at Johnston RI *MS* 11 Jan 1837

EVANS Daniel J of Farmington m FOSS Lavina of Rochester on 15 Nov in Strafford, PLACE E Eld *MS* 26 Dec 1849

EVANS Daniel of Portland ME m FERGUSON Sarah E on 18th inst at S Berwick ME, ALLEN Rev *MFWBR* 28 Aug 1847

EVANS Edward m STEVENS Ruth S of Barnston on 23 May, MOULTON A Eld *MS* 13 Sept 1843

EVANS I Mr m CENTER I Miss on 8 Nov at Potsdam NY, WHITFIELD Eld *MS* 6 Jan 1847

EVANS Jacob W m PINKHAM Mary E of Somersworth NH on 18th at Dover NH, SMITH A D Eld *MS* 24 Mar 1847

EVANS John K m WALKER Mary both of this town on 25 ult *MS* 5 Oct 1836

EVANS John m BOWEN Chloe Ann on 3 Jul at Owen NY, PECK P B Eld *MS* 14 Aug 1839

EVANS Joseph of Lowell MA m PRIEST Jane of Lowell MA on 27 Aug 1843, WOODMAN Jonathan Eld *MS* 6 Sept 1843

EVANS Jotham F m BURBANK Susannah both of Shelburn on 8th inst, WHEELER A Eld *MS* 26 Nov 1834

EVANS Nicholas m GEE Mary G both of Garland ME on 25 Feb 1849 in Garland ME, AMES M Eld *MS* 28 Mar 1849

EVANS William T m CLOUGH Adeline F on 10 Nov in Manchester, CILLEY D P Eld *MS* 1 Dec 1847

EVANS Zelotus m SHATTUCK Ann Jan both of Fowler NY in Fowler NY, JENKINS C Eld *MS* 15 Dec 1847

FAIRBANKS Asa m SAWYER Martha of Boston MA at Charlestown MA, SWETT D Eld *MS* 25 Dec 1844

FAIRBANKS George W m CROSBY Priscilla M of Grafton MA on 15 Aug, PECK Benjamin Eld *MS* 13 Sept 1843

FAIRFIELD Edmund B m JENISON Lucia on 28 Aug at Oberlin Ohio, MAHAN Pres *MS* 10 Sept 1845

FAIRFIELD Seth m BENSON Lydia on 21st inst at Biddeford *MFWBR* 3 Feb 1849

FAIRSERVICE Francis of Alna m DICKINSON Hannah of Wiscasset ME on 24 Sept, PAGE E G Eld *MS* 13 Nov 1844

FALL Isaac H of Lebanon ME m SWASEY Mary E on 23 Apr 1848 in Milton, COPELAND Rev Mr *MS* 17 May 1848

FALL Ivory Jr m FERNALD Abby on 5 Oct at Lebanon ME, FULLON-TON J Eld *MS* 15 Oct 1845

FALL Noah L m JAMES Amanda both of Lebanon on 3 Oct in Lebanon, LITTLEFIELD Wm H Eld *MS* 27 Oct 1847

FALL Tristram of Berwick m LIBBEY Katharine of Somerworth *MS* 19 Dec 1833

FALL Wilson T of North Berwick ME m HALL Sarah Ann on 10 Dec, TRUE Ezekiel Eld *MS* 30 Dec 1846 & at S Berwick _____ 17 Feb 1847

FALLET Charles W m THOMAS Minerva both of Exeter NY on 1 Sept in Exeter NY, CHANEY J Eld *MS* 30 Sept 1846

FARLEY John of Goldsborough m ABBY Susan of Mt Desert, BROWN John Jr *MS* 19 Jan 1842

FARMER Alexander m JONES Emily E both of Fowler NY on 12 Mar 1849, JENKINS C Eld *MS* 4 Apr 1849

FARMER Lemuel m MITCHELL Martha both of Temple on 6 Nov in Chesterville ME, MORRILL S P Eld *MS* 16 Jan 1850

FARMER Samuel m THOMAS Mary Ann both of Charleston ME on 10 Oct in Garland ME, AMES M Eld *MS* 7 Nov 1849

FARNAM John C of Manchester NH m KELLY Ester of Lowell, THURSTON N Eld *MS* 28 Aug 1839

FARNHAM Daniel m WIGGIN Sally W of Wakefield NH on 9 Oct of Wakefield NH, SPINNEY J Eld *MS* 2 Dec 1846

FARNHAM Ebenezer H m CRAIG Esther G both of Augusta on Thanksgiving evening, CURTIS S Eld *MS* 16 Dec 1835

FARNHAM Edward of Woolwich m HARRIS Mary of Wiscasset on 21 Nov, FAIRFIELD Smith Eld *MS* 8 Dec 1841

FARNHAM Ephraim of Belfast m ELWELL Jane N of Northport ME on 24 ult, RINES John N Eld *MS* 18 Nov 1835

FARNHAM George of Cato Addison County NY m ANGELL Hannah P of No Providence on 5 Nov 1837, HUTCHIN Elias Eld in No Providence RI *MS* 17 Jan 1838

FARNHAM John G m WHITTEN Louisa of Dover NH on 5 in Dover NH, MOULTON A K Eld *MS* 15 June 1842

FARNHAM Samuel W of Lewiston m FARNHAM Love W of Skowhegan ME, LIBBEY Isaac Eld *MS* 27 Nov 1844

FARNHAM William m QUIMBY Mary, at Andover NH IN 14 Mar *RI* Apr 1822 p 63

FARNHAM William K m WHITE Sarah of South Berwick ME on 27th ult, HUTCHINS E Eld *MS* 3 Dec 1845

FARNUM Caleb Jr Principal of Fruit Hill Seminary m BROWN Caroline of Gloucester on 26 ult *MS* 11 Jan 1837

FARNUM David m CASWELL Mary E of Manchester NH on 22 June at Manchester NH, CILLEY D P Eld *MS* 28 Jul 1847

FARR Roswell Esq of Cabot m HARVEY Fanny M of Monroe VT on Jan 18th at Monroe VT, McKAY William Eld *MS* 25 May 1842

FARRAR Sewell of Corinth m BAGLEY Elethe of Charleston ME on 18 Jul 1848 in Charleston ME, HARDING E Eld *MS* 21 Feb 1849

FARRAR William of Gilmanton NH a graduate of Dartmouth College m HILL Cylindia of Gilford on 23 Aug 1844, KNOWLES E G Eld *MS* 1 Jan 1845

FARRER James M m OSTRUM Catharine of Hastings NY on 21 Sept at Hastings NY, PADDEN S B Eld *MS* 29 Oct 1845

FARRIN Willliam J m THURLOW Ann E on 9 Jul at Litchfield ME, FROST Isaac Eld *MFWBR* 26 Jul 1848

FARROW John m KELSEY Sarah on 29 Oct 1843 at Charlestown, AMES M Eld *MS* 28 Feb 1844

FAUCHER Jay of WT m JONES Louisa of Attica NY on 4th inst, PLUMB H N Eld *MS* 18 Mar 1846

FAUNCE Nathaniel M of Oxford ME m HERRICK Jennett of Poland ME, LIBBEY James Eld *MS* 9 Apr 1845

FAVOR Moses G m HADLEY Anna L of Weare NH on 6 Jan at Manchester NH, SINCLAIR J L Eld *MS* 6 Apr 1842

FAYBENS Joshua of Leeds m HAM Mary of Monmouth, FILES Allen Eld *MS* 23 Mar 1836

FELCH Alson m ANSMORE Aurilla on 7 Jul at Sardinia NY *MS* 31 Aug 1836

FELCH Gideon D m BEAN Melvina on 9 May at Sutton NH, FROST D S Eld *MS* 24 Jul 1844 (*sic*) should be *MS* 31 Jul 1844

FELKER Elias of Dover NH m BURROWS Rebecca O on 19 Feb *MS* 8 Mar 1843

FELKER Michael of Searsport ME m VEAZIE Jane H on 15 Oct at Islesboro' ME, CLARK John Eld *MS* 18 Nov 1846

FELKER Samuel m VARNEY Hannah H on 7 March at Barrington, PLACE E Eld *MS* 27 Mar 1844

FELLOWS David A m SWAIN Sarah M on 28 Aug at Manchester NH, CILLEY D P Eld *MS* 10 Sept 1845

FELLOWS David F m COPP Mary J both of New Hampton on 19 Oct 1849, PITMAN Stephen Eld *MS* 18 Apr 1849

FELLOWS Ezekiel W m GORDON Caroline R both of Hebron on 13

FELLOWS (Continued)
Jan 1848, CHASE Paul Eld in Hebron *MS* 26 Jan 1848

FELLOWS George Eld of Chautauqua Co NY m BEAN Drusilla at Clay Onondaga Co NY on 15th inst, GRIFFITH A Eld *MS* 24 Aug 1842

FELLOWS Isaac N Col m KELLEY Sophia at Great Falls *MFWBR* 30 Dec 1848

FELLOWS James B of Concord NH m WEBSTER Betsey of Chichester on 11 inst, TRUE Ezekiel Eld *MS* 25 Oct 1848

FELLOWS Samuel Capt of Franklin m BRACKETT Eliza W of Lowell MA on 26 Mar at Manchester NH, CILLEY D P Eld *MS* 16 Apr 1845

FELLOWS Willard E m PHILLIPS Eliza on 30 June at Freedom NY, WINSOR Barnet Eld *MS* 15 Mar 1843

FELTCH Harris m CHASE Betsey P both of Manchester on 10 Sept in Manchester, CILLEY D P Eld *MS* 23 Sept 1846

FENDERSON Edward A m BABB Martha on 12 inst, THURSTON Nathaniel Eld both of Dover NH *MS* 23 May 1833

FENNER Hezekiah of Hebron NH m DURGIN Abigail R of Lowell, THURSTON Nathaniel Eld *MS* 18 Mar 1840

FENNER Thomas M of Lowell m ROBBENSON Ann S of Sandown NH on 4 Jul, THURSTON N Eld *MS* 17 Jul 1839

FERGUSON Daniel of Shapleigh m SMITH Nancy of Waterboro on 13th inst, THURSTON Eld *MS* 21 Aug 1829

FERNALD Eli B Rev of Topsham ME m ELLIOT Louisa on 27 Sept in New York City, FARRENT J F Eld *MS* 24 Oct 1849

FERNALD Eli of Lowell m FELCH Eliza Ann of Tamworth NH on 11 Jul at the First Unitarian Church, MILES Rev *MS* 28 Jul 1847

FERNALD John D m LUDDEN Remember S Mrs of Peru ME on 1 Jan at Peru ME, KNAPP Joseph Eld *MS* 26 Feb 1845

FERNALD John of Loudon m MARSHALL Sarah R of Bradford on 8 inst in Bradford, HOLMES H Eld *MS* 23 May 1849

FERNALD John Y of Ossipee m TUCKEY Sally of Waterboro on 23 Dec, EMERY N *MS* 9 Feb 1831

FERNALD Mark m LEAVER Judith B Mrs at Saco, WILLIAMS N M *MFWBR* 13 Apr 1850

FERNALD Samuel of Barrington m HILL Betsey of Strafford on 16 Feb, PLACE E Eld *MS* 13 Mar 1834

FERNALD Samuel P of Ossipee m PALMER Hannah of Tuftonborough in Tuftonborough, BEAN Silas Eld *MS* 25 Apr 1838

FERREN George W m SNELL Nancy D in Freedom, RUNNELS J Eld *MS* 9 Feb 1848

FERREN Jonathan of Thornton m HALL Mary V on 12 May at Sandwich, McMURPHY B H Eld *MS* 5 June 1844

FERREN Shepherd m THAYER Sylvia A in Alton, BUZZELL H D Eld *MS* 20 Jan 1836

FERRIN Francis m BEAN Harriet A of Dover NH on 10 Sept at Dover NH, BROCK H H Eld *MS* 17 Sept 1845

FERRIS William of Portland ME m SNELL Almaria C of Dedham MA on 21 Jan, WETHERBEE I J Eld *MS* 17 Feb 1847

FESSENDEN Nelson a licentiate of Owego Q M m BREED Hannah of Vestal Broom Co NY on 18 inst, GARDNER L G Eld at his residence *MS* 23 Sept 1846

FEZZEN Moses 3d m NORTON Elizabeth of Eaton NH on 24 Mar at Eaton, KNOWLES Samuel Eld *MS* 11 May 1842

FIELD Charles of Augusta m FOLSOM Mary C of Starks ME on 29th Jan at Starks, OLIVER Thomas J Eld *MFWBR* 14 Oct 1848

FIELD Edwain of Durham m DAY Isabel B of Biddeford on 30th ult, BLAKE H M Rev *MFWBR* 11 Jan 1851

FIELD Georg m JACKMAN Sarah both of Garland ME on 30 Sept in Garland ME, AMES M Eld *MS* 7 Nov 1849

FIELD Hiram of Elliot ME m LANGLEY Sally of Great Falls *MS* 8 Mar 1837

FIELD Jonathan of Buxton ME m ROBERTS Nancy of Waterboro ME, GREY James Eld at Waterboro ME *MFWBR* 8 May 1847

FIELDING John Jr of Lowell m EASTMAN Mary F of Dover at Dover *MFWBR* 22 Feb 1851

FIELDS James m HOYT Emily A both of Lowell MA *MS* 24 Aug 1836

FIFE Peter of Stowe ME m GORDON Loisa of Chatham NH on 18 Dec 1849 in Chatham NH, GUPTILL R W Esq *MS* 20 Feb 1850

FIFE Reuben m CLOUTMAN Betsey both of Concord on 6 ult at Deerfield, KIMBALL John Eld *MS* 22 Jul 1835

FIFIELD B M of New Hampton NH m BELL Mary Jane on 12th Nov, BUDDINGTON William Rev *MS* 4 Dec 1844

FIFIELD George E m WICCON Eliza J M both of Weare on March 31, MOODY David Eld 12 Feb 1840

FIFIELD Henry L of Manchester m PARKER Sarah A of Greenfield on 2 Nov 1847 in Manchester, CILLEY D P Eld *MS* 10 Nov 1847

FIFIELD Moses of Salisbury m BACHELDER Sally of this town at Andover NH *RI* Jan 1820 p 15

FILES Francis of Gorham ME m WATTS Hannah of Buxton on 29 Oct at Buxton ME, CLAY Jonathan Eld *MS* 20 Nov 1844

FILES Stephen of Gorham m FREEMAN Eunice B of Gorham, BAKER Daniel Esq *MS* 1 Nov 1827

FILES William S m DREW Huldah J both of Berwick ME at Somersworth NH *MFWBR* 3 Nov 1849

FILES William m LIBBY Roxana Miss of Gorham *MS* 4 Oct 1827

FILFIELD Isaac G m McLAUGHLIN Mary on 5 Dec 1844, AMES Moses Eld *MS* 29 Jan 1845

FIRMAN John N m HAZZARD Clarissa on 13 Dec 1846 at Huntington VT, HURIBUT William Eld *MS* 10 Feb 1847

FISH Stephen m RUSSELL Betsey on 24 Dec 1837 in Dexter, COPP

FISH (Continued)
John B Eld *MS* 9 May 1838
FISHER Barnard of Warwick MA m HATHAWAY Melissa of West Potsdam NY on 21 Sept, WHITFIELD Eld *MS* 18 Oct 1843
FISHER John m GARNSEY Mary of Ascott on 2 Mar of Ascott, MOULTON A Eld of Stanstead LC *MS* 13 Apr 1842
FISHER Lordon H of Kennebunk ME m TOOTHAKER Rebecca of Charleston ME on 1 Jan 1849 in Charleston ME, HARDING E Eld *MS* 21 Feb 1849
FISHER Waterman A of Killingly CT m BROWN Livina at Pelham MA *MS* 13 Jul 1836
FISK Charles B of Braintree m FULLER Betsey L of Brookfield at West Brookfield VT on Apr 7, CLAFLIN Jehiel Eld *MS* 29 May 1844
FISK Chester m KENDAL Melissa D of Yorkshire on 8 Oct in Freedom *MS* 11 Dec 1850
FISK Daniel B m SALESBURY Marcilia B both of Scituate on 28 Dec 1848, CALVIN R Eld *MS* 17 Jan 1849
FISK Dudly m McALISTER Amada A both of Phoenix NY on 1 Dec in Phoenix, SMITH O W Eld *MS* 22 Dec 1847
FISK George of Boston MA m HILL Abigail of Waterborough ME on 22 June 1847, EMERY Richard Eld *MS* 22 Dec 1847
FISK James m STIMPSON Mary both of Freedom NY in Freedom NY, JACKSON N A Eld *MS* 2 Sept 1844
FISK John G of Randolph m LOUGEE Mary Ann on 4 Dec at Tunbridge VT, CALLEY D Eld *MS* 14 Jan 1846
FISK Roswell C m GROSS Caroline H both of Manchester on 7 Dec in Manchester, CILLEY D P Eld *MS* 26 Dec 1849
FISK Samuel A m HOLMES Hannah both of Freedom NY on 15 Apr in Freedom NY, JACKSON N A Eld *MS* 13 May 1846
FISK Thomas G W m THURSTON Mary on 9 Oct at Lowell MA, THURSTON N Eld at Lowell MA *MS* 2 Nov 1842
FISKE John S m ANGELL Maria D both of Scituate on 6 Sept in Scituate RI, CILLEY D P Eld *MS* 25 Sept 1850
FITZ Andrew H of Brunswick m SPRAGUE Eleanor L of Chelsea VT on 9 Feb in Chelsea VT, SANBORN G Eld *MS* 22 Apr 1846
FLANDERS Dyer m DUDLEY Serene G on 24 Sept at Alton NH, FERNALD S P Eld *MS* 25 Oct 1843
FLANDERS George W m CILLEY Mary D both of Tunbridge VT on 8 Mar in Tunbridge VT, HENDERSON M C Eld *MS* 2 May 1849
FLANDERS Job m CHAMPION Abby C both of Lowell on 7 June in Lowell, CURTIS S Eld *MS* 24 June 1846
FLANDERS John m SAWYER Hannah of Alton on 13 Feb, COOLEY John L Eld *MS* 20 Feb 1839
FLANDERS Laugdon S of Concord m STEVENS Mary W of Stratham on 21 Nov, MERRILL Asa Eld *MS* 8 Jan 1845

FLANDERS Luther G of New Hampton m SMITH Mary E of Meredith on 21 Nov 1848 in Meredith, BEEDE H Eld *MS* 9 May 1849

FLANDERS Moses m PRATT Caroline on 12 Nov 1843, CALLEY David Eld *MS* 17 Apr 1844

FLANDERS Parker m MORRIL Louiza both of Lowell on 7 inst in Lowell MA, THURSTON N Eld *MS* 21 Mar 1838

FLANDERS Stephen B m DICKY Lydia A on 13 June at Gilmanton NH, FERNALD S P Eld *MS* 28 Jul 1847

FLANDERS True m COUCH Hannah both of Warner on 20 Dec 1837 in Hopkinton, SINCLAIR J L Eld *MS* 10 Jan 1838

FLANEGIN Charles m GOODRICH Cyntha on 20 June at Hume NY *MS* 31 Aug 1836

FLANSBURGH Wm H of Day NY m JOHNSON Rozina C of Hadley NY on 28 Feb 1849, ABBOTT Rev Mr *MS* 28 Mar 1849

FLATTEL Albert m ROBINSON Catharine of Sidney, LEWIS Daniel B Eld *MS* 15 Jan 1840

FLETCHER Eri of Dexter m CLOUGH Mary J of Garland ME on 8 Mar 1849 in Garland ME, AMES M Eld *MS* 28 Mar 1849

FLETCHER Henry A of Mt Vernon m GORDON Julia A of Augusta ME on 29 Feb 1848 in Mt Vernon ME, EDGCOMB J Eld *MS* 15 Mar 1848

FLETCHER Jeremiah of Lawrence formerly of Wilton ME m LADD Sarah of Lowell on 1 Sept 1847 in Dracut MA, CURTIS S Eld *MS* 8 Sept 1847

FLETCHER Joseph of Compton m WADLEY Lydia of Hatley LC on 5 May 1837, MOULTON A Eld *MS* 10 Jan 1837

FLETCHER Lorenzo m PATCH Melessa D of Kittery ME on 18 Dec at Kittery ME, WETHERBY I J Eld *MS* 28 Dec 1842

FLETCHER Samuel m FRENCH Lucy Jane at Lowell MA *MS* 25 May 1836

FLING William of Londonderry m EVANS Ann C on 4 Nov at Canterbury *MS* 29 Jan 1845

FLINT Charles W of Sweden ME m STEARNS Sarah F of Lovell on 3 Feb 1848 in Sweden ME, GARLAND D Esq *MS* 9 Feb 1848

FLINT John m BENNETT Eliza Ann of Sweden at Sweden ME *MS* 28 Feb 1844

FLINT John m BENNETT Eliza Ann of Sweden on 3 Jan at Sweden ME, HART E H Eld *MS* 13 Mar 1844

FLINT Nathaniel C m SPEAR Olevia N of East Thomaston on 13th inst at East Thomaston *MFWBR* 25 May 1850

FLINT Nathaniel Jr m MORRISON Dorothy C both of Sweden in Bridgton, WHITNEY G Eld *MS* 9 Feb 1842

FLOOD Jackson S m PIXLEY Sarah J on 6th inst at Lowell MA, CURTIS S Eld *MS* 24 Feb 1847

FLOOD John m HANSON Abigail on 6th inst, GOODWIN H Eld all of Hollis ME? *MS* 14 Oct 1831

FOBES Richard m TURNER Brittania on 4 Nov in Buckfield ME,
   PHINNEY Clement Eld *MS* 28 Nov 1849
FOBESH Ebenezer F m FARRINGTON Elizabeth T both of Livermore
   ME at Farmington ME, CHANEY John Eld *MS* 13 Dec 1837
FOGG Alvin m GOTT Susan both of Sandwich NH on 6 inst in
   Ossipee NH, LEAVITT Thomas Esq *MS* 18 Oct 1848
FOGG Charles H of Appleton ME m COLLINS Margaret A of Liberty
   ME on 26 Dec in Belmont ME, SMALL W Eld *MS* 15 Jan 1851
FOGG David C of Pittsfield m PAGE Mary of Epsom NH on 29 Sept at
   Epsom, CILLEY D P Eld *MS* 16 Oct 1839
FOGG Ezekiel T of Montville m STEVENS Eunice B of Limington ME
   on 22 Dec, STEVENS T Eld *MS* 3 Jan 1844
FOGG George of Greene m COLE Huldah H of Lewiston ME on 10
   Jul at Greene ME, EATON Eld *MS* 20 June 1842
FOGG Hezekiah T of Sandwich m ALLARD Almira of Albany on 17
   Feb at Albany, FLETCHER Jonathan Eld *MS* 4 Mar 1846
FOGG Ira D m HOIT Loisa M on 4 Jul 1847 in Garland ME, DORE T
   W Eld *MS* 15 Sept 1847
FOGG Isaac of this town m EDWARDS Tabathy in Parsonsfield ME,
   BURBANK Eld *MS* 7 Mar 1828
FOGG James Dr of Chesterville ME m EASTMAN Harriet of Limerick
   ME, FREEMAN Rev *MS* 27 Oct 1830
FOGG Jeremiah of Deerfield m CURRIER Chastina W of Enfield on
   21 May in Enfield NH, TYLER Job C *MS* 19 June 1850
FOGG John m GOODRIDGE Nancy both of Industry on 1 Nov 1837
   in Industry, LENNAN J Eld *MS* 10 Jan 1838
FOGG John m CLOUGH Betsey on 3 May in Durham, CILLEY D P
   Eld *MS* 16 May 1838
FOGG John of Portsmouth m SANKEY Sarah R of Dover NH *MS* 21
   Nov 1833
FOGG Jonathan m RUNNELS Hannah of Scarboro' 20th inst at
   Portland ME, BROWN S E Eld *MFWBR* 30 Nov 1850
FOGG Joseph of Raymond at Candia, COLBY Joe *MS* 8 Dec 1841
FOGG Joseph S m LITCHFIELD Amanda on 9 May at Manchester,
   CILLEY D P Eld *MS* 26 May 1847
FOGG Josiah of Readfield m SHAW Hannah W of Winthrop ME *MS*
   10 Jul 1839
FOGG Moses of Limerick ME m STONE Sarah E of Cornish on 26th
   ult, JOY Rev *MFWBR* 22 Feb 1851
FOGG Reuben m WOOD Mary at Wales ME, FILES A Eld *MS* 4 Mar
   1846
FOGG Timothy E m PRESCOTT Frances both of Raymond *MS* 5 Aug
   1835
FOLEY Michael m YEATS Mary B on 23 Jan at Charleston MA,
   JACKSON Daniel Eld *MS* 24 May 1843
FOLLANSBEE Joseph m WOODMAN Mary Jane of South Hampton

FOLLANSBEE (Continued)

on 18 Jan at Hampton, BURBANK P S Eld *MS* 7 Feb 1844

FOLLET Richard of Durham m HOITT Martha of Barrington on 20 June, SHERBURNE S Eld in Barrington *MS* 10 Jul 1850

FOLSOM Albert G of Meredith m ROBINSON Olive B of Gilford on 5 Jan, BROOKS N Eld *MS* 8 Feb 1843

FOLSOM Dudley of Sanbornton m CRIMBELL Meriam of Stratham, MERRILL A Eld *MS* 28 Jan 1846

FOLSOM Erastus C m BOSWELL Patience both of Ossipee NH on 10 Sept 1837 in Ossipee, CHICK John Eld *MS* 24 Jan 1838

FOLSOM H Maj of Limerick ME m DURGIN Sally W at Parsonsfield ME on 24 ult, BUZZELL Alvah Eld *MS* 29 Jan 1840

FOLSOM Ira F of Gilford m BLACKEY Sarah of Meredith NH, BROOKS N Eld *MS* 13 Sept 1843

FOLSOM John m ELLINWOOD Sally at Frankfort ME on Feb 6, RINES J N Eld *MS* 26 Feb 1840

FOLSOM John of East Sangerville ME m BEAN Hannah of Candia NH on 11 Jan, DYER S B Eld *MS* 1 Feb 1843

FOLSOM John of Newport ME m HICKS Phebe Mrs of Boston MA on 6 Dec 1841 at Boston MA, READ R W Eld *MS* 22 Dec 1841

FOLSOM John S m SEAWARD Martha F both of New Market NH on 1 Mar in New Market, CILLEY D P Eld *MS* 7 Mar 1838

FOLSOM John T m SANBORN Hannah M at Gilmanton NH on Nov 27 1839, TUTTLE John G Eld *MS* 19 Feb 1840

FOLSOM Josiah of Exeter m JAMES Elizabeth of Hampton on 21 Oct in Hampton, MERRILL W P Eld *MS* 31 Oct 1849

FOLSOM Josiah m BACHELDER Eleanor on 17 Mar at Northwood, JOHNSON W D Eld *MS* 9 Apr 1845

FOLSOM Josiah m DOE Sarah J (widow) of Newmarket on 27 June, HUTCHINS E Eld *MS* 5 Jul 1843

FOLSOM Kerm m HAMILTON Lovina on 13th inst, BAGLEY Orland Esq all of Waterboro ME *MS* 18 Nov 1831

FOLSOM Levi G m OSGOOD Leah of Gilford on 3 Jul of Quincy MA *MS* 13 June 1842

FOLSOM Lucien M at Dracut MA of Lowell ME m ATHERTON Elizabeth M, CURTIS S Eld *MS* 4 June 1845

FOLSOM Noah D m ESTES Lydia J both of Manchester on 28 Dec 1848 in Manchester, CILLEY D P Eld *MS* 17 Jan 1849

FOLSOM Samuel M of Boston MA m BUNKER Sarah C of Epping NH in Epping, PRESCOTT Rev Mr *MS* 9 Mar 1842

FOLSOM William MD of New York m LAMPREY Irene on 11 inst in Kensington, CILLEY D P Eld *MS* 20 Dec 1837

FOLSOM William R C m GOVE Elizabeth of Boston MA on 28 Mar, DAVIS I G Eld *MS* 10 Apr 1844

FOOT Samuel E m SWAIN Abigail both of Warren on 16 Nov 1845 in Wentworth, MESSER Asa Eld *MS* 25 Mar 1846

FORD Caleb J of Sebec ME m SNOW Hellen P of Atkinson ME on 28 Jan at Atkinson ME, HATHAWAY L Eld *MS* 24 Mar 1847

FORD Dan Y m WODBURY Charlotte A on 17 Sept in Newbury VT, SHIPMAN O Eld *MS* 7 Nov 1838

FORD E B Esq of Pierpont m Mar 6 in Monroe BUSHNEL Cordelia A of Monroe *MS* 24 Apr 1850

FORD H G Dr m JOHNSON Elvira of Whiting VT in Dover, WILLIAMS Gibbon Rev *MS* 26 Nov 1834

FORD Jefferson m CHURCH Tamson P of Biddeford ME at Dover NH *MFWBR* 28 Jul 1849

FORD Joseph of Lowell MA m FOLSOM Sarah Ann on 9 Feb, WOODMAN J Eld *MS* 23 Aug 1843

FORD Robert m SNOW Mary at Landaff NH *MS* 16 Jul 1828

FORD Thomas B m GILES Mahala of Dover NH on 7 May at South MEBerwick, JOHNSON W D Eld *MS* 17 May 1843

FORREST John W m ALLEN Lycia A both of Dover on 10 Aug in Dover, PINKHAM J Eld *MS* 28 Aug 1850

FORSAITH William Capt of Deering m GEORGE Relephe of Weare on 12th inst, HARRIMAN D Eld *MS* 4 May 1842

FOSDICK Lucina m DEXTER Almira both of Dracut on 18 Mar 1848 in Dracut MA, CURTIS S Eld *MS* 26 Apr 1848

FOSS Allen W m FROST Harriet N of Limington ME, KIMBALL J Rev *MS* 15 May 1839

FOSS Alvah m MEADER Joan both of Tamworth NH on 14 Oct in Tamworth, EMERY James Eld *MS* 21 Nov 1838

FOSS Alvin W m SMITH Athalinda at Lowell MA, THURSTON N Eld *MS* 29 Apr 1835

FOSS Andrew T Eld of Dover ult MORRILL Mary of Parsonsfield ME on 28th in Parsonsfield, BUZZELL John Eld *MS* 6 Feb 1829

FOSS Benjamin H of Gilmanton NH m RING Betsey of Loudon on 15 inst in Pittsfield, TRUE E Eli *MS* 21 Nov 1849

FOSS Benjamin of Rochester m 22d ult OTIS Joanna of Strafford in Strafford, PLACE E Eld *MS* 19 Apr 1837

FOSS Blake m MORSE Sally both of Alton NH on 17 Jul *MS* 17 Aug 1836

FOSS Charles V m NALEN Margaret both of Rochester on 4 Aug, MEADER Jesse Eld *MS* 21 Aug 1850

FOSS Cyrus m KEAY Mary E, WILLIAMS N M at Biddeford ME *MFWBR* 14 Apr 1849

FOSS Dennis Jr m PEAVEY Hannah on 16 Dec, SHERBURNE S Eld *MS* 21 Jan 1846

FOSS Dennis m SCRUTON Patience both of Strafford in Strafford, PLACE Enoch Eld *MS* 10 Jan 1838

FOSS Dyer m HARDLEY Polly both of Candia on 19 Dec 1850 in Chester, REYNOLDS T F Eld *MS* 8 Jan 1851

FOSS Ebenezer m CURRIER Sally L both of Meredith, MANSON

FOSS (Continued)

Benjamin S Eld *MS* 27 Feb 1834

FOSS Erastus D m MERRILL Frances M on 11 Jul at Strafford, PLACE E Eld *MS* 11 Aug 1847

FOSS George L m FOSS Elizabeth B on Nov 21 at Strafford, CAVER-LY J 4th Eld *MS* 29 Jan 1840

FOSS George W m BOODY Emily S both of Dover on 29 Apr, SMITH A D Eld in Dover NH *MS* 9 May 1849 & *MFWBR* 12 May 1849

FOSS George W m FOSS Jane S of Pownal ME on 9 Dec at Rochester, MEADER J Eld *MS* 24 Dec 1845

FOSS Ichabod m PIERCE Louiza both of Limerick ME, ROBERTS Eld *MS* 6 Jul 1832

FOSS Jeremiah L of Limington ME m GRANVILLE Elizabeth of Parsonsfield ME, STEVENS T Eld *MS* 14 Jul 1847

FOSS Joel S m FOSS Jane W both of Dover on 4th ult at Barrington, SHERBURNE S Eld *MS* 18 Feb 1835

FOSS John m BANGS Clarissa A both of Monmouth ME, FILES A Eld *MS* 29 Dec 1847

FOSS John of Strafford m VARNEY Olive of Dover on 23d ult in Rochester, PLACE E Eld *MS* 19 Apr 1837

FOSS Joseph M of Lynn MA m NEWHALL Abigail B of Henniker NH *MS* 23 Sept 1835

FOSS Joseph R of Strafford m BABB Delilah of Barnstead on 26 May, HAM Ezra Eld *MS* 19 June 1844

FOSS Leonard of Chelsea MA m RANDALL Nancy of Limington ME on 6th, SINCLAIR J L Eld *MS* 23 Jul 1845

FOSS Levi at Leeds ME m LEADBETTER Emeline of Leeds ME, EATON E G Eld *MS* 27 June 1842

FOSS Loren m MASON Mary Ann both of Moultonboro NH on 21 Apr at Sandwich, PICKHAM John Eld *MS* 15 June 1836

FOSS Moses of Great Falls NH m ALLARD Mary B on 22 Dec, MOULTON A K Eld *MS* 8 Feb 1843

FOSS Nathan R of Garland ME m FOSS Lucinda A of Charlestown on ?? Aug 1843, AMES M Eld *MS* 28 Feb 1844

FOSS Oliver m PERKINS Betsey on 2 Feb at Strafford, CLARK Mayhew Eld *MS* 12 Feb 1845

FOSS Robert m BOODY Sarah on 7th inst at Dover NH, SMITH A D Eld *MS* 20 Jan 1847

FOSS Samben B m GLIDDEN Judeth of Alton NH on 6 Jan, COOLEY John L Eld *MS* 20 Feb 1839

FOSS Samuel B of Kingsbury ME m WILKINSON Asenath C on 12 June, FOSS Joseph Eld *MS* 24 Jul 1844 (*sic*) should be *MS* 31 Jul 1844

FOSS Samuel m DEARBORN Betsey Thurs last week at Parsonsfield ME, BUZZELL John Eld *MS*9 Dec 1831

FOSS Silvanus C of Strafford m FOSS Lydia D, PLACE E Eld *MS* 14

FOSS (Continued)
Aug 1839

FOSS Tobias m SLOPER Margaret both of Strafford on 13 inst in Strafford, PLACE E Eld *MS* 19 Apr 1848

FOSS Zachariah B of Manchester m VEASIE Naomi of Dorchester on 1 Oct at F W Baptist meeting house, CILLEY D P Eld *MS* 11 Oct 1843

FOSTER Abner of Canton ME m NORTON Harriet of Barnston LC on 25 Jul, MOULTON Abial Eld *MS* 1 Jan 1840

FOSTER Asa m REED Mary Ann both of Manchester on 9 Aug in Manchester, CILLEY D P Eld *MS* 26 Aug 1846

FOSTER Elias m LIBBY Clarissa Ann of Gray ME on 28 June at Gray ME, WHITNEY G W Eld *MS* 12 Jul 1843 & on 2 Jul 1843 at Gray ME *MS* 17 Jan 1844

FOSTER Ezra of Jay m BEAN Mary on 16th inst in Jay ME, FOSTER John Eld *MS* 26 Mar 1828

FOSTER G W Eld of Canterbury m DOLE Clarissa of Grafton on 19 June, CLOUGH Jeremiah Eld *MS* 20 June 1842

FOSTER Isaiah W of Hillsboro m HOYT Abby of B on 25 Apr *MS* 15 May 1844

FOSTER James G Capt m GREAR Lucy V on 18 Aug at Monroe ME, ROBINSON N J Eld *MS* 24 Dec 1845

FOSTER John Eld of Jay m WILLARD Rhoda of Chesterville ME on 15 inst in New Sharon ME, JOHNSON Timothy Eld *MS* 30 Aug 1837

FOSTER Joseph A merchant of Pittsfield m KENNY Mary Ann of Loudon on 28 Nov in Loudon, SARGENT W A Eld *MS* 2 Apr 1851

FOSTER Nelson T N m TOWNSEND Harriet L of Hancock Berkshire Co MA on 5th inst at Sand Lake NY, COLEMAN I B Eld *MS* 24 Jul 1844 (*sic*) should be *MS* 31 Jul 1844

FOSTER Nicholas L of New Gloucester ME m FOSTER Mary S of Gray at New Gloucester, FOSTER S B Esq of Gray ME *MFWBR* 17 Mar 1849

FOSTER Peletiah H of Topsham m BRIERY Elizabeth of Bowdoin ME on 24 Nov in Bowdoin ME, QUINNAM C Eld *MS* 8 Dec 1847

FOSTER Solomon S m PETTY Susan both of Alexandria on 9 Aug, BROWN A Eld *MS* 28 Feb 1844

FOSTER Timothy of Richmond m MALLET Susan J of Topsham ME on 31 Jan 1850 in Tospham ME, BEAN C Eld *MS* 13 Feb 1850

FOSTER Wilson of Alexandria m KELLY Harriet of Hill on 31 Oct 1849 in Bristol NH, BROWN Amos Eld *MS* 16 Jan 1850

FOWELL Rufus H m STORY Belinda both of Bolton on 7 Oct in Waterbury VT, GRAY I Eld *MS* 23 Jan 1850

FOWLER Ava Esq of Concord m KNOX Mary D C on 13 inst in Epsom NH, DYER S G Eld *MS* 26 Jul 1837

FOWLER Benjamin T m HOBBS Ann both of Ossipee NH on 29 May

FOWLER (Continued)
MS 20 Jul 1836

FOWLER Daniel W m PLUMER Sarah E of Dover on 25 May at Meredith NH, PLUMER Parker Esq *MS* 18 June 1845

FOWLER Horatio J m WORTHING Caroline A on 8 May, CURTIS S Eld *MS* 2 June 1847

FOWLER Jesse of Dorchester m EATON Ruth of Bethlehem NH in Lowell, THURSTON N Eld *MS* 12 Dec 1838

FOWLER Josiah Eld of No Shenango m FULLER Mary A Mrs of Canneaut PA on 4 Jul, RITTENHOUSE W Eld *MS* 29 Jul 1846

FOWLER Nahum A of Greenbush ME m MILL Roxanna of Burlington ME? on 31 Oct 1847 in Greenbush ME, TAYLOR A Eld *MS* 29 Dec 1847

FOWLER Reuben A m PALFORD Mary of Rochester WT on 18 Jan at Rochester WT, COOMBS A Eld *MS* 23 Apr 1845

FOX Andrew W of Acton m FOX Mary B of Great Falls NH, GREENE Rev *MS* 4 Jan 1843

FOX John H m HAMILTON Mary B both of Manchester on 4 Nov 1848 in Manchester, CILLEY D P Eld *MS* 15 Nov 1848

FOX John m FROST Deborah of Bangor ME on 18 Feb at Bangor ME, SMALL William Eld *MS* 24 Mar 1847

FOX Lewis M m BROWN Eunice of Saco ME on 1 Nov, RAND James *MS* 25 Nov 1846

FOX William of Stanstead, Canada m GOOWIN Melissa [*sic*] (perhaps GOODWIN?) on 23 Feb, MOULTON A Eld *MS* 13 Sept 1843

FOY William L of Rye NH m WILLIAMS Hannah of Kittery ME *MS* 2 Feb 1831

FRANKLIN John of Cranston m SMITH Martha of Smithfield on 28th inst at Johnston, HUTCHINS Eld *MS* 3 Sept 1834

FRANKLIN Russell M m STEVERSON Eliza Jane both of Paris on 27 Mar in Paris Wis, TANNER G W W Eld *MS* 22 May 1850

FREDERICK John W m OLIVER Emily on 1 Jan 1844 at Starks ME *MS* 16 Apr 1845

FREEMAN Aaron H m HUSSEY Nancy J both of Dover on 7 Jan in Dover, PINKHAM John Eld *MS* 15 Jan 1851

FREEMAN Adam M of Brandon VT m HODGES Sophia L of Shelburn on the 20th inst, PRINDLE Mr *MS* 3 Jul 1839

FREEMAN Alexander m WATERHOUSE Sarah on 13 Sep 1843 at Gorham ME, CATLIN S T Eld *MS* 27 Sept 1843

FREEMAN Azariah ae 84y in Mansfield CT m THOMPSON Elizabeth ae 74y *MS* 23 Nov 1826

FREEMAN Charles Rev of L m ABBOT Salva of Temple *MS* 31 May 1827

FREEMAN Daniel m GARRETSON Rachael on 27 Feb in Sperry Fayette Co Iowa, GIFFORD H Eld *MS* 24 Apr 1850

FREEMAN Dexter m FULLER Maria both of Grafton on 16 Apr,

FREEMAN (Continued)

PECK B D Eld *MS* 1 May 1844

FREEMAN John Jr of Durham ME m MOODY Rebecca B of Auburn ME on 14 Oct, PERRY S Eld *MS* 3 Dec 1845

FREEMAN Miles m WILLEY Lucinda on 11 May at Barrington, SHERBURNE S Eld *MS* 2 Jul 1845

FREEMAN Peter (a black man) m FREEMAN Prudence Mrs (his 3rd wife) on 11 Dec at Greene ME, FULLER Jairus Eld *MS* 12 Feb 1845

FREEMAN Wilson m SOAPER Louisa on 1 Jan at Pierpont NY, WHITFIELD W Eld *MS* 25 Feb 1846

FRENCH Aaron m BROWN Catharine of Ossipee NH on 19th inst in Porter, MOULTON John Esq *MS* 24 June 1831

FRENCH Alfred m SMITH Sarah S of Candia NH on 2 Oct, FERNALD S P Eld *MS* 6 Nov 1839

FRENCH Charles m BURLEY Sarah F of Pittsfield on 21 May, CILLEY D P Eld *MS* 5 June 1839

FRENCH Charles L of Turner m BEALS Eliza on 8 Feb at Woolwich ME, PAGE E G Eld *MS* 20 Mar 1844

FRENCH Charles W m WILLEY Mary on 29 Nov 1846 at Alton NH, BUZZELL H D Eld *MS* 3 Mar 1847

FRENCH Ebenezer D m PARKER Hannah both of Garland ME on 5 June in Garland ME, AMES M Eld *MS* 3 Jul 1850

FRENCH Edmund m MATTHEWS Abigail on 16th ult of Exeter NH, NASON Eld both *MS* 14 Nov 1833

FRENCH Edward m CURTIS Corriscinda of Bath on 24 Oct at Bath ME, PAGE E G Eld *MS* 7 Dec 1842

FRENCH Elijah B of Canterbury NH m MOORE Julia D of Loudon NH on 18 Aug at Manchester NH, CILLEY D P Eld *MS* 27 Aug 1845

FRENCH Enoch m TURNER Sarah Ann of St Albans ME on 21 Mar, COPP J B Eld *MS* 7 June 1843

FRENCH Franklin of New Boston m WITHAM Sophia B L on 3 Dec at Milton, SPINNEY J Eld *MS* 7 Jan 1846

FRENCH James of Manchester m ALLEN Hannah D on 26 Nov, CILLEY D P Eld *MS* 6 Dec 1843

FRENCH John W of Dover NH m HART Sarah L of Conway NH at Conway NH *MFWBR* 9 Jan 1847 & *MS* 30 Dec 1846

FRENCH John W of Sanbornton NH m FOGG Ann M of New Hampton on 28 May 1848 in New Hampton, DANA Simeon Eld *MS* 14 Feb 1849

FRENCH Jonathan m PINKHAM Elizabeth of Dover NH on 30 Apr at Dover NH, PERKINS S W Eld *MS* 7 May 1845

FRENCH Jonathan m GILMAN Mary Ann on 9th inst at New Market NH, HUTCHINSON E Eld *MS* 19 Feb 1845

FRENCH Josiah H m MAXFIELD Martha A on 4 Dec at Lowell MA,

FRENCH (Continued)

THURSTON N Eld *MS* 25 May 1842

FRENCH Samuel Jr of Durham m HAM Martha of New Market NH *MS* 6 Mar 1834

FRENCH Thomas J of Nottingham m BASSETT Susan C of Dover on 8 Nov in New Market, EASTMAN C Allen *MS* 14 Nov 1849

FREY Warren on 12th Nov at Lyme m ROWE Frances, GRIFFETH Ansel Eld *MS* 10 Mar 1847

FRIEND Nathaniel of Alfred m PEABODY Abigail Miss of Kennebeck, ME *MS* 8 June 1832

FRISBEE Darius Jr m PERKINS Jane, THURSTON N Eld in Kittery *MS* 12 Aug 1831

FRISBEE James Jr m BUNKER Hannah J of Kittery ME on 31st March at Kittery, WETHERBY I J Eld *MS* 13 Apr 1842

FRISBEE Joseph m PHILIPS Lydia, PERRY Luther Eld in Kittery ME *MS* 26 Nov 1834

FROHOCK Jacob of Gilford NH m DAVIS Polly Jane of Gilford, PERKINS Seth W Eld *MS* 14 Apr 1847

FROST Amaza of Wentworth m CLAY Clarissa P of Canaan on 4 Jan in Canaan, JONES N Eld *MS* 5 Feb 1851

FROST Charles C (Brother of Eld D S FROST) m DOW Nancy S both of Manchester NH on 24 Jan 1849, FROST D S Eld in Manchester NH *MS* 7 Mar 1849

FROST Charles H m JONES Mary Ann of Brooks ME on 26 Feb at Brooks, CILLEY Joseph L Eld *MS* 16 Apr 1845

FROST D S Eld of Hopkinton m WATSON Minerva D on 12 May at Andover, BROOKS Eld *MS* 1 June 1842

FROST Daniel S of Clinton MA m DOLLOFF Sarah T of Sutton VT on 14 Oct, CROSS D Eld *MS* 27 Nov 1850

FROST George K m RIDLEY Huldah G both of Springvale ME on 2 Jul 1848 in Springvale ME, BRADBURY A R Eld *MS* 16 Aug 1848

FROST Joseph m GILMAN Hannah both of Tamworth NH on 24 ult in Tamworth, BLAISDELL Henry Rev *MS* 9 Apr 1851

FROST Joseph m ROSES Florentine of Leeds ME on 26 May at Leeds ME, LAMB E S Eld *MS* 10 Jul 1844

FROST O P of Leeds ME m STEVENS Susan of Green ME on 24 Oct 1847 in Leeds ME, LAMB E S Eld *MS* 10 Nov 1847

FROST Wm m MURPHY Maria both of Parsonsfield ME, FOSS Eld *MS* 26 Aug 1831

FRYE James E m WORD Martha J on 3 Oct 1849 in Wellington ME, PRATT C S Eld *MS* 20 Mar 1850

FRYE Joseph m DOE Abagail both of Lowell MA on 15 inst *MS* 25 May 1836

FRYE Lindsey Deacon m LEIGHTON Jane on Thanksgiving eve at Falmouth, PERKINS S W Eld *MS* 24 Jan 1844

FRYE Orrin m MURRY Jane T both of Durham on 20 Feb in Dur-

FRYE (Continued)
ham, BARD Nathaniel Eld *MS* 20 Mar 1850

FULLER Alden of Minot ME m WALKER A H of Paris ME at Paris on 14th inst *MFWBR* 28 Jul 1849

FULLER Artemus m LATHAM Susan S both of Smithfield on 1 Mar in Smithfield, ALLEN R Eld *MS* 18 Apr 1838

FULLER Cyrus of Stow VT m HALE Clarissa, GRAY Ira Eld *MS* 30 Nov 1842

FULLER Edwin of Chelsea VT m GRANT Nancy S of Meredith on 19 Oct 1842, PITMAN Stephen J *MS* 25 Jan 1843

FULLER Ezra B of Stowe m CARLTON Mahala D on 22 Sept at Brookfield VT, GRAY Ira Eld *MS* 15 Jan 1845

FULLER Frederick A Esq m GODFREY Margaret C on Wed eve at Stillwater, SPRINGER Rev *MS* 15 May 1839

FULLER Freeman of Worcester m PRENTICE Mary T of Northbridge on 15 Feb, FULLER W Eld *MS* 17 Apr 1844

FULLER J m McKENZIE Nancy on 30th ult at Portland ME, PRATT James Rev *MFWBR* 12 Jan 1850

FULLER Jarius in Topsham ME m CARGILL Sophia both of Bowdoinham ME, ROLLINS A Eld *MS* 12 Jan 1842

FULLER Joseph Jr of Lynn MA on 8 May m BROWN Martha of Ipswich MA, MERRILL William P Eld *MS* 29 May 1844

FULLER Nathan F of Searsport ME m VEAZIE Clarinda C of Islesboro' ME, CLARK John Eld *MS* 18 Nov 1846

FULLER Zadock P m WELLS Betsey R both of Brookfield on Jan 20 1842, CLAFLIN Jehiel Eld *MS* 23 Mar 1842

FULLONTON Ezekiel m BUNKER Adaline on 3 Oct at Epping NH, TUTTLE J G Eld *MS* 23 Oct 1844

FULLONTON Jeremiah Jr m FOLSOM Hannah P at Raymond, KIMBALL J Eld *MS* 12 Nov 1835

FULLONTON Joseph m ROBINSON Abigail at North Hampton, FRENCH Rev *MS* 4 Mar 1835

FULTON Robert of Thetford m LITTLE Rosetta of Waterbury in Waterbury, GRAY I Eld *MS* 8 Apr 1846

FURBER George Y m THOMPSON Jane, MEADER Jesse Eld in Wolfborough *MS* 27 Dec 1837

FURBER James T of Great Falls NH m KNOX Jane R of So Berwick ME in Chelsea MA, LANGWORTH Rev Mr *MS* 12 Mar 1851

FURBER Mack L m RICKER Eliza, THURSTON Nathaniel Eld *MS* 25 Apr 1833

FURBUSH/FURBISH - See FOBESH

FURBISH Calvin C m WILLIAMS Joanna both of Kittery ME on 14 inst in Kittery ME, PERKINS Seth W Eld *MS* 31 Oct 1849

FURBUSH Charles H m WINN Olive G of Lebanon on 24 Oct at Lebanon ME, BLAISDELL E Eld *MS* 27 Nov 1844

FURBUSH Franklin E of Salem m KIMBALL Muranda of Wells ME on

FURBUSH (Continued)
5 Jan in Salem MA, COLE M Eld *MS* 5 Mar 1851

FURBUSH Jesse L m CHARRIS Caroline E of Sanford ME on 16 Jul at Sanford ME, LORD D H Eld *MS* 30 Aug 1843

FURBUSH William of Lebanon ME m FURBUSH Rebecca of Great Falls NH on 11 Oct, BROOKS N Eld *MS* 24 Oct 1849

FURLONG Harrison C of Cornishville m PERRY Sarah W of Limerick ME on Wed last, LIBBY E Eld *MS* 31 Oct 1833

FURNALD Thomas m COFERAN Eliza K in Nottingham, TUTTLE A Eld *MS* 29 Nov 1848

FURNESS James R of Dorchester MA m GRAY Orpha of Sheffield on 29 Sept in Sheffield VT, RICHARDSON R E Eld *MS* 9 Oct 1850

GADSBY William of Haverhill MA m STEVENS Clarissa on 16th inst at Stratham, MERRILL Asa Eld *MS* 10 May 1843

GAGE Asa M on 21 Dec 1844 at Hopkinton of Boscawen NH m CALDWELL Sophia W of Boscawen, FROST D S Eld *MS* 8 Jan 1845

GAGE Daniel at Great Falls NH m HERSOM Sarah, DUNN R Eld *MS* 7 Jul 1847

GAGE Gerry R on 12th inst at Dover NH m TUTTLE Abigail of Dover, BARROWS Homer Rev *MS* 22 Oct 1845

GAGE James m FRENCH Doliser of Dover NH at Great Falls Village NH, STEVENS T Eld *MS* 23 Jan 1839

GAGE Joshua at Waterville ME m RICKER Sarah J, KEENE J Eld Jr *MS* 29 Dec 1841

GAGE Richard m KIMBALL Eliza of Bridgton ME on 5 Apr 1842 at Bridgton ME, HUNTRESS D Eld *MS* 27 Apr 1842

GAGE William m CLARK Alzina both of Austinburg Ohio on 25 Oct 1848 in Austinburg, COPP John B Eld *MS* 10 Jan 1849

GAGE William of Augusta ME m YEATON Lydia of Belgrade ME on 22 Sept, SPAULDING Joel Eld *MS* 8 Jan 1845

GALE Altah of New Portland ME m GALE Caroline A of Augusta ME on 7th inst *MFWBR* 16 June 1849

GALE Andrew m RICHARDSON Sylvia B at Great Falls NH, CURTIS S Eld *MS* 4 Mar 1840

GALE Henry m POTTER Mary Ann on 2 May at Bangor ME, SMALL William Eld *MS* 30 June 1847

GALE Horace B of Littleton NH m NEWTON Evaline of Lisbon NH on 27 Sept at Lisbon, GEORGE N K Eld *MS* 28 Dec 1842

GALE Jonathan T of East Kingston m JENNESS Sarah E of Epping NH on 23 June at Epping NH, BURGESS J S Eld *MS* 14 Jul 1847

GALIMON Joseph m PARKER Zeruiah of Barnston on April 2, MOULTON Abial Eld *MS* 1 Jan 1840

GALLUP Benjamin m BRADFORD Isabella both of Bangor ME on 22 Oct 1846 in Bangor ME, SMALL Wm Eld *MS* 4 Nov 1846

GALUSHA Florilla m ROBINSON Amanda at Augusta ME *MFWBR* 17 Mar 1849

GALUSHA Solon L of Detroit ME m PRINCE Honor D E A A on 30 Mar, COPP R Eld *MS* 7 June 1843

GAMMON Abial O of Naples m STINSON Susan D at Arrowsic ME on 7th inst *MFWBR* 23 June 1849

GAMMON Elden of Saco m FOGG Miriam Miss of Gorham ME *MS* 15 June 1832

GAMMON John Jr of Casco ME m EDWARDS Joanna at Casco ME *MFWBR* 14 Sep 1850

GARDENER John of Elba m SMITH Marinda of Middlebury NY on 21 Jul, ROLLIN D M L Eld *MS* 10 Aug 1842

GARDNER Aaron of Newburyport MA m GARLAND Leonora on 24 Dec, CILLEY D P Eld *MS* 1 Jan 1845

GARDNER Augustus N m CURRIER Rachel M both of Stephentown NY on 20 Jan 1848 in West Stephentown NY, COLEMAN I B Eld *MS* 12 Apr 1848

GARDNER James A B of Whitestown Sem m PHILLIPS Elizabeth sister of Rev J Phillips on 20 Feb in Little Meadows PA?, GARDNER S D Eld *MS* 6 Mar 1850

GAREY Daniel m BROWN Melissa H both of Saco ME on 7 June, JACKSON Daniel Eld *MS* 30 Sept 1846

GAREY Sumner m SHAW Julia A of Sebago, TYLER Rev *MFWBR* 21 Jan 1849

GARLAND Alexis Esq of Bartlett NH m CUMMINGS Nancy of Boston MA on 5 Apr 1843, LORD Isaac Rev *MS* 19 Apr 1843

GARLAND Benjamin F m WHITTEN Mary H both of Wolfborough NH in Brookfield, MEADER Jess Eld *MS* 19 Apr 1837

GARLAND Daniel H on 7 Oct m TUFTS Eliza in New Market both recent members of Shakers, EASTMAN C Allen *MS* 14 Nov 1849

GARLAND Daniel m BURNHAM Mary Elizabeth both of Nottingham on 18 inst in Nottingham, CILLEY D P Eld *MS* 28 June 1837

GARLAND David m HALEY Olive S on 30 May at Boston, NOYES E Eld *MS* 7 Jul 1847

GARLAND Ephraim M of Moultonboro' m MUDGETT Sarah H of Sandwich, McMURPHY B H Eld *MS* 18 Dec 1844

GARLAND Franklin of Wakefield m GOODWIN Mary of Milton on 25th ult at Milton NH, SPINNEY Joseph Eld *MS* 8 Dec 1841

GARLAND George W of Barnstead m BICKFORD Mary Jane of Alton NH on 21 Apr 1849 in Barnstead, GARLAND David Eld *MS* 2 May 1849

GARLAND Gilman D Eld of Boston m FARRINGTON Mary S of Lowell MA on 11 May at Lowell MA in the FWB church, CURTIS Silas Eld *MS* 21 May 1845

GARLAND Isaac m LAMPER Eliza M W of Gilmanton NH on 13 Oct at Barnstead, GARLAND D Eld *MS* 6 Nov 1844

GARLAND Jacob J of Rochester m BREWSTER Sabrina of Barrington on 7th ult, PLACE E Eld *MS* 8 Dec 1834

GARLAND Jacob P m SOWERSBY Eliza F of Dover NH on 3 June, PERKINS Seth W Eld *MS* 11 June 1845

GARLAND Joseph Jr of Rye m GARLAND Elizabeth of Nottingham on 4 Sept at Durham *MS* 14 Sept 1836

GARLAND Sherebiah m HOPKINS Eliza J at Dover NH *MFWBR* 14 Apr 1849 & *MS* 4 Apr 1849

GARNHAM G W m PRESSEY Nancy J both of Waterville ME in Waterville, BEAN G W Eld *MS* 2 Jan 1850

GARY Ephraim M of Dover ME m TATE Mary A of Corinth ME, AMES M Eld *MS* 20 Jan 1847

GASS John Jr m BROOKS Mary L of Lewiston ME on 11 Jul at Lewiston ME, BEAN G W Eld *MS* 4 Aug 1847

GASS Joseph T m STEARNS Lydia of Hooksett on 22d Jul at Manchester NH, CILLEY D P Eld *MS* 23 Jul 1845

GATCHELL Abiezer m STEVENS Susan Mrs of Brunswick ME on 1 Sept, PURINGTON C Eld *MS* 11 Sept 1850

GATCHELL Richard B m FULLER Elizabeth E both of Gardiner ME on Feb 1 1842, GATCHELL Mark Eld *MS* 9 Mar 1842

GATES Hiram N of Matilda WC m CHANEY Mary of Plainfield NY on 15 Sept in Unadilla Forks, CHANEY J Eld *MS* 30 Sept 1846

GATES Lyman m QUACKENBUSH Maria of Oneonta, Otsego Co, NY on 20th ult, RUSSELL Bishop A Eld *MS* 27 Nov 1839

GAUBERT John H m SOUTHARD Emeline M of Richmond on 3 Oct at Bowdoinham ME, QUINNAM C Eld *MS* 19 Oct 1842

GAULT Thomas E of Rollinsford m BROCK Julia J of Somersworth on 5 inst in Dover, HUTCHINS E Eld *MS* 14 Nov 1849

GAVIT Ezekiel m MAXFIELD Betsey C both of Smithfield on 18 Oct Smithfield RI, PHELON Benjamin Eld in *MS* 7 Nov 1838

GEAR Reuben N of New Market m STOCKBRIDGE Hannah W of Stratham on last evening, SHERBURNE S Eld; "A liberal slice of cake accompanied this notice." *MS* 18 Dec 1839

GEE Solomon of Durham m ELLIOT Lucy of Kingrey LC on 16 Dec, BARTLETT W Eld *MS* 30 Jan 1839

GEE Solomon m TWOMBLY Susan of Garland ME on 25 Apr at Garland ME, AMES M Eld *MS* 9 June 1847

GELLERSON James K m ANDERSON Sarah A both of Bancroft PLT Aroostook Co ME on 25 June 1848 in Weston ME, TAYLOR A Eld *MS* 6 Dec 1848

GELLERSON Warren W m MORSE Martha A both of Leavitt PLT ME? on 15 Oct 1848 in Weston ME, TAYLOR A Eld *MS* 6 Dec 1848

GENRLEMAN William Jr of Ottowa IL m CILLEY Rachel of Topsham in Topsham VT, SHIPMAN O Eld *MS* 7 Nov 1838

GEORGE Francis R of Strafford VT m WILLIAMS Edney on Mar 1844, PETTENGILL J Eld *MS* 11 Dec 1844

127

GEORGE James P Lucy A both of Strafford on 4 Jul m PIXLEY in Thetford VT, CLARK Eli Eld *MS* 21 Nov 1849

GEORGE Lewis m MARTIN Lucina G both of Lowell in Lowell, THURSTON N Eld *MS* 29 Aug 1838

GEORGE Robert m BOSFORD Abigail of Patton on 21 Mar of Patton, MOULTON A Eld of Stanstead LC *MS* 13 Apr 1842

GEORGE Samuel B of Richmond ME m PURINGTON Harriet Ann of Embden ME on 31 Jan 1848 in Embden, GOULD Benjamin Eld *MS* 19 Apr 1848

GEORGE Samuel m WALKER Martha on 21 Jan at Haverhill, MOULTON F Eld *MS* 14 Feb 1844

GEORGE Thomas m JONES Waity A, FULLONTON J Eld in Danville *MS* 21 Feb 1838

GEORGE William F of Nashua m BACHELDER Permilia at Chichester on Feb 12, CILLEY D P Eld *MS* 11 Mar 1840

GERMAN Read m DAVIS Arabel A both of Manchester in Manchester, CILLEY D P Eld *MS* 1 Apr 1846

GERRISH Albert H of Durham ME m LUNT Lydia Ann of Brunswick ME on 22 Apr, CROWELL E Eld *MS* 24 May 1843

GERRISH Andrew on 20 Nov m LUCY Angelina D both of Nottingham NH in Nottingham, TUTTLE A Eld *MS* 13 Dec 1837

GERRISH Charles F of Nottingham m BRYANT Hannah of Effingham NH on 13 Feb 1849, FOSS Nahum Eld *MS* 7 Mar 1849

GERRISH Daniel of Lebanon m HODGDON Sally on 27 Oct 1842 at Lebanon ME, COWELL D B Eld *MS* 16 Nov 1842

GERRISH Noah of Acton ME m WILSON Mary C of Canada on 18th inst, MURDOCK Rev *MS* 8 June 1842

GERRISH Paul m WINSLOW Mary Jane both of New Market NH on 21st ult in New Market, HUTCHINS E Eld *MS* 8 May 1844

GERRY John W of Boston MA m TARBOX Nancy H on 16 Sept at Hollis, SINCLAIR J L Eld *MS* 1 Oct 1845

GERRY Orman m CHITMAN Mercy both of West Poland ME on 22 Mar in West Poland ME, LIBBY James Eld *MS* 3 June 1846

GERRY Samuel of Portsmouth NH m FOSS S Lucretia of Somerworth NH on 8th inst at Dover NH, PERKINS Mr Rev *MS* 19 Aug 1835

GERRY William at Poland ME m KEEN Julia A of Poland ME on 10 Oct, LIBBY James Eld *MS* 8 Nov 1843

GETCHEL Daniel m HANSON Hannah H of Sanford ME on 28 May 1843 at Wakefield NH, BROOKS John Eld *MS* 13 Sept 1843

GETCHEL George I m DUTCH Hannah both of Brownfield ME on 11 June 1848 in Brownfield ME, HART E H Eld *MS* 15 Nov 1848 & *MS* 5 Jul 1848

GETCHEL Silas m SHAW Caroline of Woolwich ME on 28 Nov at Woolwich ME, PAGE E G Eld *MS* 8 Jan 1845

GETCHELL Asa of Litchfield ME m FULLER Lucy Ann of St Albans ME on 5 Dec 1841, COPP John B Eld *MS* 27 Apr 1842

GETCHELL Christopher m MOORE Amy both of Lewiston ME on 26
Apr in Lewiston ME, BURGESS J S Eld *MS* 6 June 1849

GETCHELL Isaac of Sanford ME m MORRELL Mary E of No Berwick
on 10 Oct in No Berwick ME, CLAY Daniel Eld *MS* 20 Nov 1850

GETCHELL Samuel m DOLE Sarah at Richmond *MS* 29 June 1836

GIBBS George W of Porter ME m KEZER Sally of Parsonsfield ME *MS*
17 Jan 1833

GIBBS John T Esq editor of the *Dover Gazette* m MARCH Ann T Mrs
on Thursday in Dover NH, PARKMAN Rev *MS* 1 May 1844

GIBBS Wm of Framingham MA m LULL Nancy M of Weare on the
13th of Jan 1842, HARRIMAN D Eld *MS* 4 May 1842

GIBSON Stanford C MD m CHURCH Sally A at Columbus NY,
GARDINER S D Eld *MS* 23 June 1847

GIBSON William W of West Rumney m SMITH Harriet P of Meredith
Village on 3 Dec 1839 in Meredith Village, QUINBY H Eld *MS* 12
Feb 1840

GIBSON Zechariah Rev m HOWARD Susanna in BrownfieldME ,
BISON Timothy Esq *MS* 7 Mar 1828

GIFFOR David P m HALLET Joanna both of Sidney ME, LEWIS D B
Eld *MS* 3 Apr 1850

GIFFORD William Henry of LeRoy IL m TISDATE Eunice of Beloit on
16 Jan in Beloit Wis, AUGIR F P Eld *MS* 19 Feb 1851

GILBERT Nathaniel of Lydon VT m CURRIER Lucretia W of Lowell
MA, EMERY James Eld *MS* 29 May 1844

GILCHRIST George C m HERSEY Mary E both of New Market on 4
inst at Dover *MS* 12 Oct 1836

GILCHRIST James R of Malden MA m LANGMAID Maris T of Strafford on 9 inst in Strafford, PLACE E Eld *MS* 15 Jul 1846

GILE Amos W D m COX Elizabeth at Lowell, THURSTON Nathaniel
Eld *MS* 18 Mar 1840

GILE George W m BARRETT Maria both of Rutland on 24 Nov 1850
in Rutland Ohio, BRANCH S S Eld *MS* 19 Mar 1851

GILE Jeremiah m KIMBALL Abigail on 4th in Alfred, ORR John Rev
MFWBR 24 Mar 1849

GILE Joseph of Nottingham m McDANIEL Rebecca of Barrington on
24 Aug at Barrington, SHERBURNE S Eld *MS* 13 Sept 1843

GILE William of Andover MA m HOWARD Elenor C of Eaton NH at
Eaton NH, DAVIS I Eld *MS* 25 May 1842

GILES David m HOWE Matilda on 11 Mar 1847 at Enfield NH,
SMITH C H Eld *MS* 5 May 1847

GILES George J m SOULE Martha J both of Woolwich ME on 6 May
1849 in Woolwich ME, AYER A Eld *MS* 11 Jul 1849

GILES Miron S m BARRETT Sarepta P both of Rutland on 2 Oct
1850 in Chester Ohio, BRANCH S S Eld *MS* 19 Mar 1851

GILES Thomas of Eaton m MANSON Jane, EATON E G Eld *MS* 12
Dec 1833

GILFORD Aaron m HAINES Isabella S on 15 May at Manchester, CILLEY D P Eld *MS* 5 June 1844

GILFORD Everett W m GOSS Elizabeth A both of Meredith NH on 26 Jan in Upper Gilmanton NH, KNOWLES E G Eld *MS* 19 Feb 1851

GILKEY Joseph of Limington m JACKSON Louisa of Limington ME on 16th inst, LIBBY Eld *MS* 24 Dec 1828

GILKEY Reuben of Limington ME m EDGECOMB Sarah on Nov ??, MANSON B S Eld *MS* 7 Feb 1844

GILKEY Samuel H of Saco ME m STEARNS Mehitable K on 27 Dec, JACKSON Daniel Eld *MS* 6 Apr 1847

GILLET Elias D m HENDRICK Rachel both of New Lebanon NY on 19 Mar in Stephenton NY, COLEMAN I B Eld *MS* 8 Apr 1846

GILMAN A G of Saco ME m WHITNEY Martha J of Casco ME on 20th ult at Biddeford ME, LORD T N Rev *MFWBR* 5 Oct 1850

GILMAN Alvah A m PRAY Lucinda both of Great Falls NH at Acton ME *MFWBR* 8 Feb 1851 & RAMSEY G P Eld *MS* 22 Jan 1851

GILMAN Amasa m SANBORN Mary Ann both of Gilmanton NH on Sept 13 in Gilmanton, FERNALD S P Eld *MS* 5 Jan 1842

GILMAN Amasa K Capt /GILMANTON Amasa K Capt on 14 Oct at Gilmanton m HILL Mehitable F/L Mrs, FERNALD S P Eld *MS* 3 Mar 1847 (correction *MS* 14 Apr 1847)

GILMAN Bracket H m WALKER Martha I both of Dover on 2 Jan 1849 in Dover, SMITH A D Eld *MS* 10 Jan 1849

GILMAN David F of Bethlehem m JACKSON Hannah of Gilford in Meredith, PITMAN S J Eld *MS* 29 Aug 1838

GILMAN Ebenezer m WHITEHOUSE Caroline S both of Dover NH on 30th ult, PERKINS Rev Mr *MS* 5 Nov 1834

GILMAN Ebenezer of Compton m EATON Lydia of Derby VT on 18 Feb, MOULTON A W Eld *MS* 15 Apr 1840

GILMAN Ebenezer of Foxcroft ME m PALMER Roxanna of Sebec ME in Sebec, BURNHAM R Eld *MS* 5 Aug 1831

GILMAN Edwin A m REYNOLDS Lucy P both of Monroe on 2 Sept in Jackson ME, RINES J N Eld *MS* 13 Nov 1850

GILMAN Ezekiel of Meredith m YOUNG Adaline P of Gilmanton NH on 24 Oct in Gilmanton, MASON L Eld *MS*12 Dec 1849

GILMAN George C m WHEELER Sophia in Boston on the 13th inst at the chapel in Causeway St, HOLMAN J W Eld *MS* 30 Mar 1842

GILMAN George H m THING Diana L both of Gilford on 17 June in Gilford, PERKINS Seth W Eld *MS* 8 Jul 1846

GILMAN John S of Gilmanton m PAGE Betsey on 3 Nov, FERNALD S P Eld *MS* 30 Nov 1842

GILMAN Jonathan of Sangerville ME m DAMMON Zeruiah of Sebec ME on 17 Sept in Kilmarnock ME, COOMBS A Eld *MS* 11 Oct 1837

GILMAN Josiah P m HANNAFORD Betsey, LORD W Eld in Parsonsfield ME *MS* 2 Aug 1827

GILMAN John S m GOSS Sally S both of Gilford on Thanksgiving Day in Gilford, PERKINS Seth W Eld *MS* 23 Feb 1848

GILMAN Levi W of Somersworth m JAMES Martha of Lebanon ME on 24 Dec 1848 Sabbath evening at Great Falls NH in Freewill meeting house, BROOKS N Eld *MS* 3 Jan 1849

GILMAN Lewis m DAVIS Caroline at Alton NH on 14 Jan, BUZZELL H D Eld *MS* 3 Mar 1847

GILMAN Lyman W m MORRISON Dorothy E of Gilford at Meredith NH, BROOKS N Eld *MS* 6 Sept 1843

GILMAN Manoah of Alton m GRANT Mercy of Gilford on 27 Nov, COOLEY John D Eld *MS* 25 Jan 1843

GILMAN Micajah m LIBBY Lydia L of Dover on 26th ult at Dover NH, HUTCHINS E Eld *MS* 4 Aug 1847

GILMAN Moses Jr of Dexter ME m GOULD Dorcas D of Dexter ME at Sangerville ME on 21 Sept, BRIDGES O W Eld *MS* 7 Dec 1842

GILMAN Moses m YOUNG Sarah Mrs both of Gilmanton on 18 Mar 1848 in Barnstead, GARLAND David Eld *MS* 26 Apr 1848

GILMAN Samuel D of Gilmanton m BUNKER Christina of Barnstead NH on 28 May 1848 in Gilmanton, FERNALD S P Eld *MS* 21 June 1848

GILMORE Alfred Hon m GRANT Louisa L on 19th inst at Hallowell ME *MFWBR* 30 Nov 1850

GILMORE Gilbert H m CHASE Elizabeth Ann both of Manchester on 4 Mar 1849 Sabbath eve in Manchester, CILLEY D P Eld *MS* 14 Mar 1849

GILMORE Nathan P m PEASLEY Julia Ann both of Weare on 10 June 1847 in Goshen, EMERY A Eld *MS* 6 Oct 1847

GILMORE Tristram m POWERS Maria Jane on 24th ult at Springvale *MFWBR* 4 Aug 1849

GILPATRICK Ara m FOGG Mercy Ann, FREEMAN C Rev on 8th inst at Limerick ME *MFWBR* 19 Jan 1848

GILPATRICK Jacob m PIERCE Susan H both of Limerick ME on 4 Apr 1950 in Limerick ME, RAND J Eld *MS* 10 Apr 1850

GILPATRICK John m YOUNG Abigail of Dover NH on 9th Sept, CILLEY D P Eld *MS* 16 Sept 1835

GILPATRICK Thomas of Limerick ME m LATHAM Charlotte S of Gray ME on 2 Jul in Gray ME, NEWELL David Eld *MS* 21 Aug 1850

GILPATRICK William of Newfield m DINNELS Lovina of Newfield ME *MS* 19 Nov 1828

GILSOM Abijah m McDONOLD Angeline on 25 Feb, WOODMAN J Eld *MS* 23 Aug 1843

GILSON Calvin B m WOOD Lucinda of Portland ME on 15th ult, MOULTON A K Eld *MS* 29 Nov 1843

GILSON Freeman of Compton LC m ROBINSON Sarah of Manchester on 22 Mar 1848 in Manchester, CILLEY D P Eld *MS* 5 Apr 1848

GILSON John of Ludlow m GATES Mary of Woodstock on 13 ult in

GILSON (Continued)
Reading VT, ADAMS A Eld *MS* 16 May 1849

GILSON Peter of Portland ME m SEAWARD Olive Mrs of Kittery ME *MS* 14 Dec 1836

GILSON William R of Abington MA m BICKNELL Nancy B at Augusta ME on 26th inst *MFWBR* 7 Aug 1847

GLALDEN Benj M m SMITH Betsey Ann both of Gilford on 23 Dec 1847 in Gilford, PERKINS Seth W Eld *MS* 23 Feb 1848

GLAZIER James of Haverhill m ELLIOTT Almire of Benton on 6 June 1845 in Benton, MOULTON F Eld *MS* 8 Apr 1846

GLEASON Andrew J of Raymond m LADD Mary of Deerfield on 5 Dec 1849 in Raymond, FOSS T Eld *MS* 23 Jan 1850

GLEDDEN Samuel W m WHITE Nancy J both of Bangor ME on 1 May in Garland ME, AMES M Eld *MS* 3 Jul 1850

GLIDDEN Bethuel m FLANDERS Elenor P Mrs of Alton NH and Gilford on 29 Oct 1843 at Alton, GLINES J Eld *MS* 10 Jan 1844

GILDDEN Daniel m BENNETT Mary W on 30 Apr *MS* 22 May 1844

GLIDDEN Daniel F m DUDLEY Elizabeth A of Alton NH on 18 Feb 1847 at Gilmanton NH, FERNALD S P Eld *MS* 14 Apr 1847

GLIDDEN Hosea of Alton NH m PERKINS Susan of Meredith on 28 Apr in Alton, FERNALD S P Elder *MS* 22 May 1844

GLIDDEN Jacob K m HAYES Lydia of Alton NH on 3 Mar, FERNALD S P Eld *MS* 14 Apr 1847

GLIDDEN Jeremiah m HAYNES Susan of Meredith NH on 13 June, PITMAN S J Eld *MS* 30 Oct 1844

GLIDDEN John L m FRENCH Sarah D of Meredith NH on 24 Dec, PITMAN Stephen J *MS* 25 Jan 1843

GLIDDEN John m JACKSON Sarah Ann both of Great Falls NH on 31 Oct in Great Falls Village, STEVENS T Eld *MS* 25 Dec 1839

GLIDDEN John P m TRUE Annett W on 11 Sept at East Randolph VT, SMITH A D Eld *MS* 29 Oct 1845

GLIDDEN Levi of Greensboro' VT m STREETER Susan of Lisbon on 11 Sept at Lisbon NH, GEORGE N K Eld *MS* 6 Nov 1844

GLINES Eli Capt m FERRIN Sarah Jane of Eaton on 5 Mar in Eaton, GASKELL Silas Eld *MS* 12 Aug 1846

GLINES Eli Col ae 75y 3d m PERKINS Mary Miss ae 65y 1m 10d at Eaton NH, KNOWLES Samuel Eld *MS* 11 May 1842

GLINES James F of Northfield m CHAPMAN Abigail of Gilmanton on 30 Nov at Gilmanton, MASON L Eld *MS* 27 Dec 1843

GLINES Truman G m KENNISON Mary Ann at Eaton NH, ATKINSON K Eld *MFWBR* 14 Apr 1849

GLOVER George m CLAY Hannah of Barrington NH on Sunday, SHERBURNE S Eld *MS* 14 June 1843

GLOVER William of Woodstock m RUSSELL Betsey Jane on 17 Apr at Franconia, GEORGE N K Eld *MS* 14 May 1845

GODDARD John m JOHNSON Lydia on 9th inst, LORD W Eld all of

GODDARD (Continued)
Parsonsfield ME *MS* 25 Nov 1831

GODDARD Levi m JOHNSON Almine H both of Durham on 14 June in Durham ME, BARD Nathaniel Eld *MS* 8 Jul 1846

GODDARF Joseph m CRAIGH Lorinda both of Switzerland Co Iowa on 15 Sept, FERRIS F Eld *MS* 2 Oct 1850

GODFREY Alfred m CRANDE Fanny W on 11 inst in Hampton, BURBANK P S Eld *MS* 1 May 1844

GODFREY Charles m HILL Maria both of Great Falls NH, BROOKS N ELD *MS* 18 Sept 1850

GODFREY Jason m DUDLEY Hannah D both of Candia on 29 Nov, MANSON B S Eld *MS* 12 Dec 1838

GODFREY Jonathan m HORNE Susanna both of Manchester on 3 Jul in Manchester, CILLEY D P Eld *MS* 11 Jul 1849

GODFREY Sylvester of Vershire VT m BACHELDER Clarinda of Vershire VT on 15 Jul 1849 in Vershire VT, HARTSHORN Nelson Eld *MS* 16 Jan 1850

GODING Amos of Jay ME m PIKE Lucinda of Livermore ME on 12 Feb at Livermore, FOSTER John Eld *MS* 6 Jul 1832

GODLEY Alphonso S of Saco ME m SPAULDING Eliza T of Frankfort ME on 7 Jul at Saco ME, NICHOLS Rev *MFWBR* 13 Jul 1850

GOFF Henry m MORSE Elizabeth of Gray ME on 9 Jan 1843, WHITNEY G W Eld *MS* 10 May 1843

GOFFREY Joseph m DRINKWATER Susan A on 10th inst at Rockland *MFWBR* 30 Nov 1850

GOLDSMITH Charles m GEARS Jane on 2 Nov at Providence RI, SCOTT E Eld *MS* 10 Dec 1845

GOLDTHWAIT G H m HARMON Sarah C on 23d ult at Biddeford ME, LORD T N Rev *MFWBR* 10 Nov 1849

GOLDTHWAITE Timoth H of Somersworth NH m JONES Hannah M of Lebanon in Lebanon ME, CHENEY O B Eld *MS* 15 Aug 1849

GOODALE Amos m ESTY Julia C both of Lowell on 30 May in Dracut MA, CURTIS S Eld *MS* 10 June 1846

GOODELL Charles m WOOD Sarah Ann both of Ashippun Wis on 13 Oct in Ashippun Wis, TANNER G W W Eld *MS* 14 Nov 1849

GOODENOW Daniel Esq m HOLMES Sarah Ann in Alfred ME *MS* 18 June 1828

GOODHUE Joseph m WORTHEN Sarah on 12 Mar at Enfield, SMITH C H Eld *MS* 16 Apr 1845

GOODIN Nelson A of Stanstead LC m KENNESON Rhoda of Barnston on 5 Jan *MS* 22 Mar 1837

GOODING Charles H of Portland ME m HANSON Mary A of Westbrook ME on 11 Oct in Saccarappa ME, MANSON B S Eld *MS* 23 Oct 1850

GOODING William A m COBB Rachael M both of Bridgton ME on 19 Dec, PIKE John Eld *MS* 22 Jan 1851

GOODNO W S Eld of Yates Quarterly Meeting m COLBY Rachel of
Portageville NY on 20 Dec, CRANE E R Eld *MS* 18 Jan 1843
GOODRICH Andrew m DUFFY Ellen on 16th inst at Biddeford ME,
BLAKE H M Rev *MFWBR* 22 June 1850
GOODRICH John R m STACY Mary both of Berwick ME on 10 Oct
1847 in Berwick ME, CLAY D Eld *MS* 3 Nov 1847
GOODRIDGE Jeremiah W of Canaan m BOWMAN Caroline of Sidney
ME, LEWIS D B Eld *MS* 17 Apr 1844
GOODWIN Amos S of Lowell m WHITE Abigail of Bradford in Lowell,
THURSTON Nathaniel Eld *MS* 4 Oct 1837
GOODWIN Blaisdel J m WORSTER Julia Ann both of Lebanon ME in
Lebanon ME, CHENEY O B Eld *MS* 20 June 1849
GOODWIN Charles m ROSE Joanna both of Biddeford ME on 22
June 1847 in Biddeford, WITHAM S H Eld *MS* 25 Aug 1847
GOODWIN David m HOLMES Abigail both of Barnstead NH on 28th
ult, GARLAND D Eld *MS* 18 Feb 1835
GOODWIN G W Capt of Foxcroft ME m PENNELL Sarah J of Dover
ME at Foxcroft [N.B. Now Dover and Foxcroft are one town called
Dover-Foxcroft, ME.] *MFWBR* 3 Mar 1849
GOODWIN Geo W m GLIDDEN Melissa Jane both of Tamworth NH
on 5 Oct 1848 in Tamworth NH, MERRIL Wm S Eld *MS* 1 Nov
1848
GOODWIN James B m STEVENS Betsey H of Farmington NH on 26
June at Farmington NH, HART E H Eld *MS* 31 Aug 1842
GOODWIN James Jr of Berwick ME m HANSON Sophia S of Som-
mersworth on 20 inst *MS* 27 May 1835
GOODWIN James K m HAYWARD Melvina both of Tunbridge VT on
25 Nov 1847 Tunbridge VT, HENDERSON M C Eld in *MS* 22 Dec
1847
GOODWIN Joel of Lebanon m HANSCOM Elizabeth of Great Falls NH
in Lebanon, STEVENS T Eld *MS* 10 Jan 1838
GOODWIN John D m CHASE Susan B both of New Market on 21 ult
at Durham, CILLEY D P Eld *MS* 4 Jan 1837
GOODWIN John G m HURD Joanna on 5 May at Dracut MA,
WOODMAN J Eld *MS* 19 Oct 1842
GOODWIN John P of Lyman m MADDOX Sarah Jane of Corinth on
18 Oct at Waterboro' ME, EMERY Richard Eld *MS* 6 Jan 1847
GOODWIN Levi of Ogden NY m BARLOW Ann of Batavia NY? on 11
inst in Bayron NY? *MS* 1 Feb 1837
GOODWIN Lewis B of Biddeford m LANE Ann B, at Buxton ME on
15th inst *MFWBR* 2 Nov 1850
GOODWIN Lewis m DODGE Eliza of Monroe ME on 5 Apr at Monroe
ME, ALLEN Ebenezer Eld *MS* 19 Apr 1843
GOODWIN Nahum G m GLIDDEN Melissa both of Lebanon ME on
14 Oct 1848 in Lebanon, LITTLEFIELD Wm H Eld *MS* 1 Nov 1848
GOODWIN Nehemiah m SPRINGER Philena of Litchfield on 9 Jul,

GOODWIN (Continued)

GATCHELL M Eld *MS* 19 Jul 1843

GOODWIN Oliver of Acton ME m BURBANK Lorinda J at Wakefield NH, COTTON Eld *MS* 29 Apr 1840

GOODWIN Seth B of East Machias ME m PERKINS Eliza A of Limerick ME on Wednesday last at Limerick, BURBANK Eld *MS* 29 Oct 1828

GOODWIN Sewall of Lebanon ME m GOODALL Susan of Farmington ME on 4 Jul 1844 at Farmington NH, WALDRON W H Eld *MS* 7 Aug 1844

GOODWIN Thomas R m PLUMMER Louisa H on 8 Aug at Charlestown MA, WETHERBEE Louisa H *MS* 22 Oct 1845

GOODWIN Timothy m GILFORD Clarissa both of Dover NH on 6 inst in Dover NH, SMITH A D Eld *MS* 19 Dec 1838

GOODWIN Urban D of Lebanon m HODGDON Augusta I of So Berwick on 29 Sept in So Berwick ME, JOHNSON W D Eld *MS* 23 Oct 1850 & *MFWBR* 2 Nov 1850

GOODWIN William of Shapleigh ME m GOODWIN Hannah of Lowell on 19 ult in Lebanon, BLAISDEL David Eld *MS* 3 Oct 1838

GOOGINS Samuel m LURVEY Eliza both of Buxton ME on 9 Aug 1848 in Hollis ME, BAILEY J M Eld *MS* 4 Oct 1848

GORDON Alonzo of Alexander NH m CURRIER Abigail of Vershire VT on 20 June at Bristol NH, BROWN Amos Eld *MS* 20 June 1842

GORDON Daniel Dr m MOULTON Mary on 22nd inst at Saco ME, STRICKLAND G G Rev *MFWBR* 27 Jul 1850

GORDON George M m FLANDERS Hannah both of New Hampton NH on 7 Mar in New Hampton, BEEDE H Eld *MS* 5 June 1850

GORDON George m PAMOT Harriet of Portland ME on 12 Sept at Cape Elizabeth, LIBBY Almon Eld *MS* 16 Oct 1844

GORDON Joseph M of Franklin ME m FOSS Mariah C of Biddeford ME on 18 June 1848 in Biddeford ME, WITHAM L H Eld *MS* 26 Jul 1848

GORDON Miles m JUDKINS Betsey of Phillips ME on 30 Jan at Jay ME, WATERMAN D Eld *MS* 19 Apr 1843

GORDON Stephen L of New Hampton m EATON Mary of Manchester on 7 May, CILLEY D P Eld *MS* 17 May 1843

GORDON Thomas m COMERON Jane on 9 Sept in Rochester, WHITCHER Eld *MS* 26 Sept 1849

GORDON Timothy W of Farmington ME m HILL Susan Jane of Dover NH on 1 Jul 1849 in Chesterville ME, MORRILL S P Eld *MS* 16 Jan 1850

GORDON William m CORNOR Catharine both of New Hampton/ Hampton at Holderness NH, PETTIGILL John Eld *MS* 18 Mar 1840

GORDON William E m DOLLOFF Lorint P of New Hampton on 26 Nov 1848 in Meredith NH, WELLS L S Eld *MS* 5 Apr 1848

GORHAM William E m GRAY Caskalicean W both of Boston on 11 June 1848 in Boston *MS* 28 June 1848

GOSS Daniel T of Pittsfield NH m GEORGE Alba W of Haverhill MA on 4 Dec. CUSHING Rev *MS* 18 Dec 1839

GOSS Dyer E of Poland m CLIFFORD Christianna C at Lewiston ME on 19th inst *MFWBR* 30 Nov 1850

GOSS George R m THOMPSON Phebe both of Gilford on 22 ult in Gilford, PINKHAM John Eld *MS* 10 Oct 1838

GOSS Guy C m RIGGS Mary at Bath ME on 8th inst *MFWBR* 25 May 1850

GOSS Stephen of Natick MA m BURLEY Elizabeth S of Dover NH on 21st ult at Dover NH, HUTCHINS E Eld *MFWBR* 1 June 1850 & *MS* 29 May 1850

GOTHAM Samuel R m BUNKER Sarah Ann both of New Market NH on 3 May *MS* 16 May 1838

GOTT Charles of Leeds ME m WOOD Anne of Norridgwock ME on 10 Oct at Livermore ME, MORRILL F Eld *MS* 2 Nov 1842

GOUGH Moses M m CROOK Amanda L of Washington VT on 18th ult, GEORGE Nathaniel K Eld *MS* 15 May 1839

GOULD Amos A m RANNCY Fylinda M of Lowell MA on 5 Dec. CURTIS S Eld *MS* 18 Dec 1844

GOULD Ancel m KNOWLTON Chloe of Edwards Co IL, SHURTLEFF James M Eld *MS* 20 Mar 1839

GOULD Austin m GAHAN Mary A both of Woolwich on 7 Apr 1850 in Woolwich ME, AVER A Eld *MS* 5 Feb 1851

GOULD Carlos m FINEX Almira T both of Colebrook NH on 14 Mar 1849, BEAN Benaiah Eld *MS* 14 Mar 1849

GOULD Daniel Jr m STEVENS Angeline O at Portland ME on 30th ult *MFWBR* 8 June 1850

GOULD David m SHERMAN Latesia both of Yorkshire NY on 17 Sept in Yorkshire NY, JACKSON N A Eld *MS* 7 Oct 1846

GOULD Elias L m TUKEY Abigail of Lowell MA at Dracut MA, CURTIS S Eld *MS* 24 Feb 1847

GOULD Hamilton of Wilton m BERRY Sally J of Wayne ME in Wayne, CURTIS Silas Eld *MS* 27 Jan 1836

GOULD Ira L m EARL Abigail at Bangor ME, CAVERNO A Eld *MS* 13 Sept 1843

GOULD Jacob m HINKLEY Rebecca on 6 Sept at Lisbon ME, FROST G G *MS* 28 Dec 1836

GOULD John B m PHILLIPS Eliza A on 5 Aug at Bangor ME, SKILLIN H Eld *MS* 30 June 1847

GOULD John m BLAISDELL Nancy F both of Mercer ME on 21 Apr in Mercer, TURNER A Eld *MS* 8 Dec 1844

GOULD Levi A m REED Betsey E of Lowell MA on 17 Jan at Dracut MA, CURTIS S Eld *MS* 18 Feb 1846

GOULD Luther of Great Falls NH m SHACKLEY Eliza of Shapleigh

GOULD (Continued)

ME on 27 Oct, CURTIS S Eld *MS* 9 Nov 1842

GOULD Stephen m PRINCE Lydia J both of Lisbon ME, WOODARD Wm *MS* 23 Jan 1834

GOULD William m WINGATE Laura J at Great Falls NH *MFWBR* 28 Dec 1850

GOVE John C m HARPER Nancy B of New Hampton NH on 11 Feb, PITMAN Stephen J Eld *MS* 26 Apr 1843

GOVE Mark m SARGENT Sarah of Henniker NH on 24 Oct, SIN-CLAIR J L Eld *MS* 6 Nov 1839

GOVE R B m MORSE Rosanna B on 29th ult at Portland ME, CHICKERING J W Rev *MFWBR* 8 Dec 1849

GOVE Richard m SMITH Mary Ann P both of Gilford on 27 in Gilford, PINKHAM John Eld *MS* 12 Sept 1838

GOVE Richard, watchmaker and jeweller of Meredith Bridge on 27 inst in morning m SMITH Mary Ann P in Gilford NH, PINKHAM John Eld *MS* 5 Sept 1838

GOVE Sanford D m THAYER Eliza B both of Manchester on 28 Dec 1848 in Manchster, CILLEY D P Eld *MS* 17 Jan 1849

GOVES Rufus m STILKEY Dorcas M both of Brunswick ME, HERSEY L Eld in Brunswick ME *MS* 8 Mar 1848

GOWEN Emilius L at Rochester NH m BICKFORD Abby A, PARKER D T Esq of Farmington NH *MS* 16 Apr 1845

GOWEN John m PERKINS Ellen both of Dover on 23 inst in Dover, HUTCHINS E Eld *MS* 27 Oct 1847

GOWEN Oren B m MILLS Martha R on 11 Jan in Lowell, CURTIS S Eld *MS* 2 Feb 1848

GOWEN Otis F of Boston MA m MILLS Lucy G of Lowell MA on 11 Mar 1849 in Eaton NH, MILLS James E Eld *MS* 4 Apr 1849

GOWEN Samuel Jr m SMITH Sarah Ann on 27 Oct 1841 at Sanford ME, BUZZELL Alvah Eld *MS* 15 Dec 1841

GOWING James Jr m CASWELL Elizabeth Jane both of Manchester on 28 June in Manchester, CILLEY D P Eld *MS* 11 Jul 1849

GRACE Patrick of Upper Canada m NEWTON Patty of Hamburgh NY on 14th Mar at Hamburgh NY, PLUMB H N Eld *MS* 19 May 1847

GRACE William H m CALL Mary Ann both of Kittery ME on Sabbath eve 25 Nov in Kittery ME, PERKINS Seth W Eld *MS* 5 Dec 1849

GRAND Paul Capt m JEWETT Miriam M both of Gilford NH in Gilford NH, FROST D S Eld *MS* 23 May 1849

GRANT Albion K P m SMALL Isabella W of Westbrook ME on 30th ult at Portland ME, STREETER R Rev *MFWBR* 10 Nov 1849

GRANT Alpheus C of Medway MA m BLISS Sarah of Washington VT on 23d ult at Kennebunk ME *MFWBR* 8 Feb 1851

GRANT Andrew M m WIGGIN Sarah C on 28 Aug at Epsom NH, RAMSEY G P Eld *MS* 19 Oct 1842

GRANT Elisha W of Meredith NH m ELKINS Martha of Gilford NH,

GRANT (Continued)
BROOKS N Eld *MS* 16 Nov 1842

GRANT Franklin m EARLE Elizabeth both of South Berwick on 8 ultin So Berwick ME, TRUE Ezekiel Eld *MS* 15 Apr 1846

GRANT George of Berwick m PIERCE Lydia H of So Berwick on 4 Jul So Berwick ME, TRUE Ezekiel Eld in *MS* 22 Jul 1846

GRANT Gideon m WHITE Prudence of Hodgdon on 20 May at Hodgdon ME, HASKELL G W Eld *MS* 5 Jul 1843

GRANT Granville m WADLEIGH Ann of Berwick ME on 16th inst at Dover NH, HUTCHINS E Eld *MFWBR* 1 Sept 1849 & *MS* 22 Aug 1849

GRANT John of Brighton m JUNKINS Hadarsa of No Berwick ME on 8th inst, CAVERNO A Eld *MS* 21 Jan 1835

GRANT Joseph of Sidney ME m SPEARS Emily W of Waterville ME, LEWIS Daniel B Eld *MS* 30 Nov 1842

GRANT Joshua m STACY Susan at Berwick ME *MFWBR* 24 Feb 1849

GRANT Joshua m STACY Susan both of Berwick on 28 Jan 1849 in North Berwick ME, CLAY D Eld *MS* 7 Feb 1849

GRANT Melatiah B m JACKSON Lydia of Hastings at Hastings Oswego Co NY, PADDEN S B Eld *MS* 28 Jan 1846

GRANT Noah m BROWN Sophia Ann on 14 Nov at Manchester NH, CILLEY D P Eld *MS* 27 Nov 1844

GRANT Oscar m JONES Mary Jane both of So Berwick ME on 22 ult in Dover, HUTCHINS E Eld *MS* 29 Dec 1847

GRANT Paul Capt m JEWETT Miriam M Mrs both of Gilford NH on 22 Apr 1849 in Gilford NH, FROST D S Eld *MS* 9 Jan 1850

GRANT Samuel F m HUFF Mary P both of St Albans on 30 Oct in St Albans ME, PERRY S Eld *MS* 22 Jan 1851

GRANT Samuel m WALTER Mary both of Dover on 24 inst in Dover, SMITH A D Eld *MS* 3 Jan 1849

GRANT Thomas J m JOY Sarah A at Great Falls NH *MFWBR* 28 Jul 1849 & at Somersworth NH *MFWBR* 4 Aug 1849

GRAVES Charles of Dover m QUINBY Elizabeth C of Dover on 16 Nov, AYER A Eld *MS* 27 Nov 1839

GRAVES Daniel Jr of Topsham m SUTHERLAND Zilpha of Lisbon ME, FROST G G Esq *MS* 23 Mar 1836

GRAVES Martin L of Buffalo m JOHNSTON Jane E of Hamburgh NY on 7 ult in Hamburgh, PLUMB H N Eld *MS* 28 June 1837

GRAVES Sewall H m HUTCHINSON Serena of Wayne ME on 29 Oct at Wayne ME, LOMBARD B L Esq *MS* 21 Nov 1843

GRAVES Tyler m CLARK Emily both of Underhill VT on 23 Nov 1848 in Underhill VT, ALWOOD Mark Eld *MS* 14 Feb 1849

GRAVES William H m KIMBALL Adeline E both of Scituate RI on 4 inst in Scituate RI, ALLEN R Eld *MS* 17 May 1848

GRAVES William m CURRIER Nancy H both of Manchester on 13

GRAVES (Continued)
    inst in Manchester, CILLEY D P Eld *MS* 29 Apr 1846
GRAVES William of Topsham m MERRIMAN Sarah of Brunswick ME
    on 10 Oct 1848 in Topsham ME, BEAN C Eld *MS* 17 Jan 1849
GRAY Daniel m SMITH Betsy of Hiram at the parsonage in Porter
    ME, STONE J Rev *MFWBR* 4 Jan 1851
GRAY Galon O of Bowdoinham ME m ORBSTON Martha Jane of
    Bowdoinham ME, QUINNAM C Eld *MS* 6 Sept 1843
GRAY George of Wilmot NH m PHILPOT Deborah H of NY on 31 ult
    in New York City, GRAHAM D M Eld *MS* 20 Nov 1850
GRAY George W m CHAMBERLIN Mary E of Dover NH at Dover NH
    on Sunday last, STEVENS Jacob Eld *MS* 20 Nov 1844
GRAY James M of Barrington m PERKINS Cordelia M of Strafford on
    27 Oct in Rochester, MEADER J Eld *MS* 8 Jan 1851
GRAY John of Waterboro ME m McKUSICK Hannah of Limerick ME,
    LIBBEY Elias Eld *MS* 28 Sept 1832
GRAY Joseph of Barrington m BERRY Joan of Strafford, MEADER
    Jesse Eld *MS* 11 Dec 1839
GRAY Joshua of Sheffield m DEAN Lucy of Sutton VT on 22 Nov,
    HILL Mark Eld *MS* 11 Jan 1843
GRAY Morrill of Barnston m HILL Maria on 7 Oct, MOULTON A Eld
    of Stanstead LC *MS* 13 Apr 1842
GRAY Robert B m BABB Hannah Jane both of Boston on 13 inst *MS*
    19 Oct 1836
GRAY Solomon T of Dover m PERKINS Lavina at Jackson, PETTEN-
    GILL Dudley Eld *MS* 25 Jan 1843
GRAY Thomas of Barnstead m DAVIS Olive S at Dover NH *MS* 18
    July 1833
GRAY Wells of Antwerp, Van Buren Co m LORD Amy of Volinia, Cass
    Co, Mich, JULIAN Samuel Eld *MS* 8 May 1839
GRAY William of Monmouth m TOOTHAKER Margaret of Richmond
    ME on 8 Oct 1848 in Richmond ME, PURINGTON Collamore Eld
    MS 22 Nov 1848
GRAY William P m FOSS Margaret E both of Strafford on 19 Mar
    1850 in Pittsfield, TRUE E Eld *MS* 10 Apr 1850
GRAY William m THOMPSON Mary Miss both of Barrington NH, *MS*
    11 Jan 1837
GREELEY Dennis P of Dover IL m HILLS Sarah H of Epping NH on
    2d Jul, HANSCOM P Eld *MS* 14 Jul 1847
GREELOW William m LUCAS S E at Phipsburg ME *MFWBR* 16 June
    1849
GREELY William m WHITE Harriet in Belfast ME *MS* 8 Dec 1830
GREEN Alfred A m DRAKE Sarah P both of Pittsfield on 15 Dec 1850
    in Pittsfield, TRUE E Eld *MS* 1 Jan 1851
GREEN Alvah Russell m OSBORNE Eliza of Loudon NH on 29 Jan at
    Pittsfield, CILLEY D P Eld *MS* 8 Feb 1843

GREEN Benjamin W m FENNER Mary E both of Smithfield on 1 Jan 1849, CALVIN R Eld *MS* 17 Jan 1849

GREEN Daniel m GREEN Catharine both of Barrington on 21 Apr Sunday eve in Barrington, SHERBURNE S Eld *MS* 8 May 1850

GREEN David L of Loudon m TILTON Hannah E of Pittsfield on 23 Jan in Pittsfield, TRUE E Eld *MS* 10 Apr 1850

GREEN Edward of Portland ME m BOLTON Eleanor Miss of Gorham on 7th inst, WHITE Joseph *MS* 18 apr 1833

GREEN Frederick E C of Plymouth NH m PALMER Lucinda of Campton NH on 6 Dec 1848 in Ramney NH, CHASE Paul Eld *MS* 20 Dec 1848

GREEN Hezekiah S of Sangersfield m CLARKE Thede E m on 17 Oct 1848 in Brookfield NY, GARDNER S D Eld *MS* 1 Nov 1848

GREEN Hiram of Henniker m STILES Harriet C of Bradford on 9 Jan 1849 of Bradford, WENTWORTH J J Eld *MS* 11 Apr 1849

GREEN James H m ABBOTT Ebner of Lowell MA on 17 Nov, WHITNEY G W Eld *MS* 10 May 1843

GREEN Loammi m OSBORNE Hannach C both of Loudon NH on 5 Dec Thanksgiving Day in Loudon, CILLEY D P Eld *MS* 25 Dec 1839

GREEN N L of Chichester at Hopkinton m ROBY Sarah Jane of Hopkinton on 21 Aug, FROST D Sidney Eld *MS* 14 Sept 1842

GREEN Noah m ROWE Sarah Jane of Smithfield ME on 16 Oct at Hallowell ME, WEAVER Phillip Eld *MS* 7 Jan 1846

GREEN Peter A of Granby LC m GORSLINE Silvina of Scriba NY on 4 Oct, COPP J B Eld *MS* 18 Nov 1846

GREEN Samuel m BROWN Lydia on 16 ult at Pittsfield, BEAN Silas Eld *MS* 2 Nov 1836

GREEN William H m BANGS Harriet F both of Sweden ME on 17 Oct 1847, PIKE J Eld *MS* 24 Nov 1847

GREENE William of Deerfield m LAKE Rachel of Newport on 5 Feb at Newport *MS* 24 May 1843

GREENHALGH Moses B m BOSTON Luranah A both of Sanford ME on 1 Dec, MILL Charles Eld *MS* 11 Dec 1850

GREENLAW Nathaniel m PERKINS Ann Mrs both of Brownfield ME on 25 Jan in Brownfield ME *MS* 9 Feb 1848

GREENLEAF Ezra L m ELLIOTT Mary Ann B both of Pittsfield on 12 inst in Pittsfield NH, TRUE E Eld *MS* 20 Dec 1848

GREENLEAF Hiram m POOL Ann on 29 Dec at Holderness NH *MS* 8 Feb 1837

GREENLEAF M P of Williamsburgh m HASKELL Lydia of Danville ME, LIBBY I Eld *MS* 10 Jul 1839

GREENLEAF Nathan S of Skowhegan ME m WOOD Charlotte E of Haverhill MA on 26 Sept *MS* 6 Oct 1847

GREENLEAF Nathaniel m FULLER Mary F both of Boothbay ME on 11 Oct in Boothbay ME, PAGE E G *MS* 15 May 1850

GREENLEAF Reuben of Hallowell m LEMAN Rosina of Augusta ME in Augusta, CURTIS S Eld *MS* 10 May 1837

GREENLEAF Stephen Esq m TAYLOR Fanny Miss *MS* 24 May 1827

GREENWOOD Joseph R m WATSON Sarah on 12 Nov, WATERMAN D Eld *MS* 23 Dec 1846

GREER Daniel A m SHIRLEY Mary both of Belmont in No Belmont, WARD Cotton Esq *MS* 13 June 1849

GREGORY Samuel O of Lanesboro MA m COMESTOCK Harriet of Arcadia NY at Stephentown NY on 24 Aug 1842, COLEMAN I B Eld *MS* 22 Feb 1843

GRIFFETH Laton m LANE Clarisa E both of Augusta ME in Augusta, CURTIS S Eld *MS* 20 June 1838

GRIFFIN Abner C of Boston m FLAGG Harriet D of Dover on 7 inst in Dover, BARROWS Rev Mr *MS* 13 Oct 1847

GRIFFIN Daniel B of West Stephenton m LAWRENCE Priscilla of Nassau NY on 15 Mar 1850 in Nassau NY, COLEMAN I B Eld *MS* 10 Apr 1850

GRIFFIN Eliphalet m PIPER Edith A both of Dover on 25 ult in Dover NH, CAVERNO A Eld *MS* 6 Mar 1850 & *MFWBR* 16 Mar 1850

GRIFFIN Erastus m CARPENTER Orpha of Stanstead LC on 30 Aug 1838 *MS* 17 Apr 1839

GRIFFIN Henry D of Rollinsford NH m CARR Sabrina K, FREEMAN C Rev on 26th inst at Limerick ME *MFWBR* 31 Aug 1850

GRIFFIN Ira m RICHARDSON Mary of Northwood on 13 Jul, ATWOOD Mark Eld *MS* 17 Dec 1845

GRIFFIN John H m DAVIS Mahala both of Manchester on 31 May in Manchester, CILLEY D P Eld *MS* 17 June 1846

GRIFFIN John of Exeter m DOE Lydia S of New Market on 10 inst in New Market, CILLEY D P Eld *MS* 23 May 1838

GRIFFIN Sylvanus Dea of H m LIBBY Olive of B on 5 Dec *MS* 1 May 1844

GRIFFIN W E of Somersworth m OSGOOD Sarah R of Pittsfield on 29 Oct in Pittsfield, RICHARDSON Rev *MS* 8 Nov 1837

GRIFFTHS David of Durham m JOY Sarah E of Manchester NH on 1 Feb at Manchester NH, CILLEY D P Eld *MS* 25 Feb 1846

GRIGGS William H m SCRUTON Martha E of Dover NH on 31 Jan at Dover NH, SMITH A D Eld *MS* 17 Feb 1847

GROSS Gilbert m STEVENS Abigail O on the 27th at Hallowell ME, WEAVER Phillip Eld *MS* 7 Jan 1846

GROUT Robert C of Monroe ME m STOWERS Experience E of Dixmont ME on Jan 1 1840, ALLEN Ebenezer Jr Eld *MS* 12 Feb 1840

GROVE Solomon of Edgecomb m BICKFORD Nancy of Boothbay ME in Boothbay ME, PAGE E G Eld *MS* 23 Feb 1842

GROVER Benjamin of Hallowell m COLLINS Lucinda of Gardiner ME on 26 inst *MS* 15 Feb 1837

GROVER Isaac m LEWIS Electa on 5 Oct at Brookfield NY, GARD-
NER S D Eld *MS* 15 Oct 1845

GROWES Dennis H m CALVIN Lydia Marandor Olney both of Scituate RI on 9 ult in Scituate RI, ALLEN R Eld *MS* 17 May 1848

GUILFORD Joseph m GORDON Elizabeth of Hollis ME, McKENNY P
Eld *MS* 14 June 1843

GUNDY John Lt m SANBORN Mary Ann both of New Hampton NH
on 2 Jul in New Hampton, FREEMAN Joseph Rev *MS* 5 Aug 1846

GUPPY George F m YORK Abigail F of Dover NH, PERKINS Rev *MS*
16 Dec 1835

GUPPY James B m BROCK Sophia both of Dover, PERKINS Rev *MS*
20 Jan 1836

GUPTIL C H Dr of Dover NH m CLEMENTS Harriet L of North Berwick ME on 11 inst at Dover, HAYDEN Lucian Rev *MS* 24 Jul
1839

GUPTILL Charles of Berwick ME m STILLINGS Olive of North Berwick on 14 Aug, LORD D H Eld *MS* 7 Sept 1842

GUPTILL Frost of Cornish ME m COBB Harriet of Limington ME on
14 Dec in Limington, TRUE Ezekiel *MS* 24 Jan 1838

GUPTILL George of Berwick ME m RICKER Eliza of Lebanon ME on
17 Aug at Lebanon ME, MARSTON James H Eld *MS* 27 Aug 1845

GUPTILL Granville m RICKER Betsey both of Berwick ME on 22 Dec
in Berwick, CLAY D Eld *MS* 15 Jan 1850

GUPTILL Hiram of Cornish ME m WEEKS Olive on 2 Jul, HACKETT
John O Eld *MS* 9 Aug 1843

GUPTILL Oliver H m HYDE Sarah both of Ossipee NH on 13 June in
Ossipee NH, CHICK J Eld *MS* 5 Jul 1848

GUPTILL Stephen of Cornish ME m WATERHOUSE Phebe of Limington ME on 5 Nov 1843, RAND I Eld *MS* 29 May 1844

GURDY Joel of Bristol m SANBORN Mary B of Alexandria NH on 5
Nov 1848 in Alexandria NH, BROWN Amos Eld *MS* 15 Nov 1848

GUSTIN Abijah L m BRUCE Lucinda both of Newark VT on 19 Mar
1849, GEORGE N K Eld *MS* 9 May 1849

HACKET John m QUINBY Dolly on 18 Apr at Sandwich NH,
McMURPHY B H Eld *MS* 5 June 1844

HACKETT Albert F of Sandwich m SMITH Susan A of Sandwich NH,
BROOKS N Eld *MS* 23 Jul 1845

HACKETT Andrew m HARMON Meranda on 5 Jan at Dracut MA,
CURTIS S Eld *MS* 10 Feb 1847

HACKETT Charles A m CLIFFORD Sophronia J on 29 Mar at Gilmanton, MOODY David Eld *MS* 21 June 1843

HACKETT George m DAME Charlotte J both of Jackson NH on 13
Aug 1848 in East Parsonsfield ME, HACKETT John O Eld *MS* 30
Aug 1848

HACKETT Isaac m BLAKE Lovina of Stanstead LC on Oct 22,

HACKETT (Continued)

MOULTON Abial Eld *MS* 1 Jan 1840

HACKETT J Carlton of Boston m HACKETT Eliza Ann of Gilmanton NH on 20 ult in Gilmanton, CLARK Peter Eld *MS* 5 Jul 1837

HACKETT John C of Somersworth m DUDLEY Julia A of Gilford on 8 Dec at Gilford NH *MS* 14 Dec 1842

HACKETT Luther A Esq m PIERSON Jane Ann on 6th inst at Johnstown NY, MONTEITH W J Rev *MS* 21 Feb 1844

HACKNEY Thomas m SEXTON Mary A both of Rochester Wis on 13 Apr 1848 in Rochester Wis, AUGIR F P Eld *MS* 28 June 1848

HADLEY Enoch Dea m GOVE Mary Ann both of Deering on 23 June in Weare, WENTWORTH J J Eld *MS* 5 Aug 1846

HADLEY Gilbert M m ANDREW Catherine on 2 Jul at Orange NH, TYLER Job C Eld *MS* 26 Jul 1843

HADLEY Joseph of Sandwich m BROWN Juda Mrs on 23 May, BROOKS N Eld *MS* 2 June 1847

HADLEY Moses C of Meredith m HADLEY Jane of Gilmanton NH on 15 Nov, PITMAN Stephen J *MS* 25 Jan 1843

HADLEY Uriah m ROLLINS Susan of Gilmanton on Thanksgiving day, PINKHAM John Eld *MS* 13 Feb 1839

HAFFORD Samuel m BROWN Betsey W of PLT Number Eight at Sangerville ME on 22 Apr, COMBS A Eld *MS* 29 May 1839

HAGBARM John m KENDALL Sarah Ann both of Hermon NY on 12 Dec 1847, JENKINS C Eld *MS* 19 Apr 1848

HAGGETT Edward M of Hartford m HODGDON Francis D of Farmington NH on 8th ult at Hartford, HALL T M Eld *MFWBR* 10 Nov 1849

HAGGETT Willard m DODGE Mary on 7th Nov at Edgecomb ME in the FWB meeting house, PAGE E G Eld *MS* 1 Dec 1841

HAGGETT William Jr m HAGGETT Lydia of Edgecomb ME on 22 Dec 1842, PAGE E G Eld *MS* 4 Jan 1843

HAILEY Samuel ae 76y m DROWN Hannah Mrs of Portsmouth NH ae 66y on 20 ult on Isle of Shoals (Gosport NH) *MS* 12 Oct 1836

HAILEY Samuel R of Tuftonboro' m COTTON Nancy M of Moultonboro' on 25 Jul, BEAN S F Eld *MS* 11 Sept 1844

HAINES Albert G of New Loudon NH m SUMMER Jane of Ithaca NY on 24 Mar at Ithaca NY, HENRY Rev *MS* 14 Apr 1847

HAINES Charles A m WEYMOUTH Martha J on 4 Dec of Great Falls NH, WEBBER H Eld at Great Falls NH *MS* 18 Dec 1844

HAINES James M m MATHES Nancy on 29 ult in Dover NH, HUTCHINS E Eld *MS* 5 Dec 1849

HAINES James Madison m TUTTLE Lydia S both of Nottingham NH on 4th inst at Lamprey River NH, CILLEY D P Eld *MS* 17 Dec 1834

HAINES John C of Moultonborough m MOULTON Judith R of Sandwich on 2 Jan 1848 at Center Sandwich Free-will Meeting

HAINES (Continued)
house, BROOKS N Eld *MS* 26 Jan 1848

HAINES John on 7th inst at New Market m NEAL Mary, HUTCHINS
E Eld *MS* 17 Apr 1844

HAINES Joshua B m ROBERTS Martha Jane both of Dover on 1 inst
in Dover, HUTCHINS E Eld *MS* 10 May 1848

HAINES Matthias M of Wolfboro' m HAINES Hannah L of Dover NH
on 1st inst at Dover, HUTCHINS E Eld *MS* 9 June 1847

HAINES Samuel G m HAINES Judith J both of Deerfield on 21 Feb
in Northwood NH, BICKFORD James *MS* 29 Mar 1848

HAINES Samuel of Saco m McFANNEN Minerva L of Embden ME on
6th inst at Saco, NICHOLS J T G Rev *MFWBR* 13 Jan 1849

HAINES Washington m FOLSOM Abigail H both of New Market NH
on 8 ult, WHITNEY S Eld *MS* 8 Apr 1840

HAINES William m LIBBY Jane both of Buxton ME in Portland ME,
LIBBY Isaac Eld *MS* 24 May 1848

HALE Amos m WHITE Harriet F on 6 Sept 1847 in Corinna ME,
ROBINSON N J Eld *MS* 6 Oct 1847

HALE Benj L m FROST Olive T both of Parsonsfield on 1 Sept in So
Parsonsfield ME, SMITH W Eld *MS* 30 Oct 1850

HALE Daniel m PAGE Phebe W at New Sharon ME *MS* 27 Feb 1834

HALE Kershy W m WATTS Sabrina C of Stow on 22 Sept at Brookfield VT, GRAY Ira Eld *MS* 15 Jan 1845

HALE Nathaniel of Denmark ME? m WHITNEY Mary of Bridgton
ME? on 25 Mar in Bridgton, WILLEY Eben C Eld *MS* 8 Apr 1846

HALE Simeon of Parsonsfield ME m DAVIS Julia Ann of Somersworth NH on 3 Feb, STEVENS T Eld *MS* 20 Feb 1839

HALEY Abel Hon of Tuftonborough m PINKHAM Lucinda Mrs of
Dover on 27 Oct in Dover NH, EASTMAN C A Eld *MS* 6 Nov 1850

HALEY Alvin B of Topsham m BRIERY Minerva of Bowdoin ME on 25
Nov 1847 in Bowdoin ME, QUINNAM C Eld *MS* 8 Dec 1847

HALEY Jesse D of Bath ME m BRINY Octavia Ann of Bowdoin ME on
6 Oct at Bowdoinham ME, QUINNAM C Eld *MS* 8 Jan 1845

HALEY John of Hollis m STROUT Hannah E of Limington ME,
MANSON B S Eld *MS* 7 Feb 1844

HALEY Parker of Chelsea MA m BRADEEN Almira W on 4 June at
Cornish ME, RAND J Eld *MS* 14 June 1843

HALEY William m GETCHELL Olive E on 12th inst at Saco ME,
BLAKE H M *MFWBR* 21 Sep 1850

HALEY William m MANSON Sarah Mrs both of Kittery ME in Kittery
ME on 13 Dec, PERKINS Seth W Eld *MS* 9 Jan 1850

HALL A C m GOODSPEED Eunice of Bafford LC on 22 Dec 1843 of
Bafford *MS* 1 May 1844

HALL Arthur William m HAMILTON Marilla J both of Windsor on 13
Oct in Windsor ME, STEVENS J Eld *MS* 11 Dec 1850

HALL Asa m DAVIS Tryphena both of Northwood on 12th inst on the

HALL (Continued)

Sabbath eve, CILLEY D P ELD *MS* 23 Jan 1834

HALL Clement M m NEWTON Elizabeth both of Dover NH on 18 Aug at South Boston MA, LITTLEFIELD William H Eld *MS* 28 Aug 1844

HALL Cushman m THAYER Mary Susan on 26th ult at Gray ME, DURGIN John M Eld *MS* 24 Apr 1839

HALL Daniel of Candia NH m MARKS Margaret of Salem on 11 Aug in Salem MA, COLE M Eld *MS* 16 Oct 1850

HALL Francis of Sandwich NH m STAUNTON Rebecca of Meredith NH on 27th, PITMAN Stephen Eld *MS* 24 Mar 1847

HALL George W m ABBOTT Adah H on 18 Jan at North Berwick ME, CLAY D Eld at North Berwick ME *MS* 28 Jan 1846

HALL Isaac G m MOODY Mary F both of Dover on 13 April 1848 in Dover NH, SMITH A D Eld *MS* 19 Apr 1848

HALL James Harvy on 6 Aug m VARNEY Adaline both of Dover in Rochester, SMITH A D Eld *MS* 12 Aug 1846

HALL James m LAKEMAN Harriet on 24th ult, HIGGINS Eld all of Thorndike ME *MS* 12 June 1829

HALL James M m HALL Dorcas A both of Bowdoinham in Litchfield ME, QUINNAM C Eld *MS* 8 Sept 1847

HALL John S m BROCK Hannah N both of Exeter NH on 26 ult at Dover NH, PERKINS Rev *MS* 4 Nov 1835

HALL Joseph D m LIBBEY Nancy on 20 Apr at Dover NH, DYER B Eld *MS* 30 Apr 1845

HALL Joseph Dea m SCRUTON Charlotte both of Strafford on 27 Oct in Strafford NH, PLACE E Eld *MS* 6 Nov 1850

HALL Joseph of Compton LC m REYNOLDS Polly of Stanstead LC on 20 Dec *MS* 22 Mar 1837

HALL Levi of Gorham ME m WHITE Elizabeth Mrs of Limerick ME on 24 Aug at Limerick ME, EMERY R Eld *MS* 1 Oct 1845

HALL Mark m RICHARDS Eliza of Dover on 25 June at Dover NH, PERKINS S W Eld *MS* 2 Jul 1845

HALL Marvin of Norway m WAFUL Rebecca of Newport NY on 5 Sept in Newport NY, TALLMAN E PE Eld *MS* 30 Oct 1850

HALL Moses m HORN Henrietta at Dover NH, THURSTON Nathaniel Eld *MS* 25 Apr 1833

HALL Oram R m WHITEHOUSE Laura G both of Dover in Dover NH, HUTCHENS E Eld *MS* 9 Jan 1850

HALL Philander m CARPENTER Adelia on 4 inst in Ogden *MS* 1 Feb 1837

HALL Samuel G of Litchfield m STINSON Julia Ann of Litchfield on 22d, GATCHELL Mark Eld *MS* 20 Dec 1843

HALL Samuel of Dover m LANGMAID Hannah at Strafford NH, PLACE E Eld *MS* 20 June 1833

HALL William H m DAY Relief H on 21 of May, GATCHELL M Eld

HALL (Continued)
MS 19 Jul 1843

HALL Winslow of Dover formerly of Gorham ME m STEVENSON Sophia of Wolfborough on 19 inst in Wolfborough NH, COLBY J Rev *MS* 29 Jul 1846

HALLOWELL George of Boothbay ME m REED Calista of Boothbay ME, MORRILL S P Eld *MS* 23 Dec 1846

HALLY Lorenzo m NICHOLS Polly on 5 Feb 1843 at Huntington VT, DIKE Orange Eld *MS* 12 Apr 1843

HALTON Edwards S m MORRISON Abigail both of Dover NH on 11th inst, THURSTON N Eld *MS* 26 Sept 1833

HAM Clement m HAM Margaret of Barrington on 28 Dec 1843 at Barrington, PLACE E Eld *MS* 27 Mar 1844

HAM Clement m CROOK Roxana B both of Somersworth NH on 18 inst Sabbath morning at Great Falls, BROOKS N Eld *MS* 28 June 1848

HAM George W of Pembroke m TILTON Mary Ann of Meredith, PITMAN S J Eld *MS* 30 Jan 1850

HAM James m THOMPSON Catherine M on 12 Sept at Brunswick ME, LANCASTER D Eld *MS* 2 Oct 1844

HAM Jonathan m KEECH Esther M of Bafford LC on 19 Apr, MOULTON A Eld *MS* 13 Sept 1843

HAM Joseph m CILLEY Abagail both of Brooks MEon 30 Aug, CILLEY Joseph L Eld *MS* 12 Dec 1849

HAM Joseph of Barrington m WATERHOUSE Dorothy K on 13 Oct, BROCK H H Eld *MS* 12 Nov 1845

HAM Joseph P m WILSON Eunice both of New Market on 4 Oct in New Market, FROST D S Eld *MS* 14 Oct 1846

HAM Joshua m ORCOTT Docia A both of Great Falls NH on 3 Nov 1848, BROOKS N Eld *MS* 20 Dec 1848

HAM Nathaniel m FOSS Clarissa Ann on 8 May, WINKLEY Jr Eld *MS* 29 June 1842

HAM Oliver P of Durham m SMITH Mehitable of Durham at New Market NH on 16 Mar, CILLEY D P Eld *MS* 29 Mar 1843

HAM Rufas R m BROWN Betsey D both of Dover on 10 inst at Great Falls NH, BROOKS N Eld *MS* 21 Aug 1850 & *MFWBR* 24 Aug 1850

HAM Samuel 3d merchant m MORRILL Sarah at Dover NH, THURSTON Nathaniel Eld *MS* 25 Apr 1833

HAM Samuel of Barrington m TIBBETTS Sally of Dover in Dover, PERKINS Rev *MS* 30 Mar 1835

HAM Samuel of Berwick ME m RICHARDS Sarah J on 12 Sept at Lebanon ME, GARLAND D Eld *MS* 10 Oct 1844

HAM Thomas of Manchester m SMITH Mary E of Meredith Village on 4th inst at Meredith Bridge, STEWART I D Eld *MS* 21 Aug 1844

HAM William A of Dover NH m WITHAM Martha A of Dover NH,

HAM (Continued)
SMITH A D Eld *MS* 5 May 1847

HAMBLEM Joseph F of Pownal ME m HALL Lois Jane of Falmouth at Falmouth ME in Dec, HERSEY L Eld *MS* 8 Jan 1845

HAMBLEN Joseph F of Gorham m STURGIS Temperance of Danville on Tues Feb 1st in Danville ME, BEAN C Eld *MS* 16 Feb 1842

HAMBLETON Joseph R of Swanville ME m YOUNG Emeline C of Jackson ME on 2d Nov, SAWYER J C Eld *MS* 13 Dec 1843

HAMBLETON Samuel C m FURLONG Ruth A at Biddeford ME *MFWBR* 4 Aug 1849

HAMBLIN Jacob m BUSSEY Sarah A of Bangor ME on 6 June at Newburgh, SKILLIN H Eld *MS* 30 June 1847

HAMILTON Daniel H of Gardiner m SAWYER Josephine B of Greene ME on 13 Sept 1846, FULLER J Eld *MS* 27 Jan 1847

HAMILTON James Jr of Elmira NY m WRIGHT Sarah Jane of Lewiston ME on 12 Sept 1847 in Lewiston ME, BEAN G W Eld *MS* 27 Oct 1847

HAMILTON John Capt Jr of Wales ME m LOMBARD Octavo H of Wales, FILES A Eld *MS* 10 Jul 1839

HAMILTON Wendal m BATCHELDER Hannah S both of N Yarmouth ME on 5 Jan 1848, CROCKETT J Eld *MS* 8 Mar 1848

HAMMON Allen of Springfield m BOOBER Charlotte of Lee in Lee ME *MS* 19 Nov 1834

HAMMOND Andrew J m BURGLEY Mary H of Rochester NH on 20, DAVIS J B Eld *MS* 27 Nov 1844

HAMMOND Daniel B m BLAKE Eliza M both of Ossipee in Ossipee ME, WALKER John Eld *MS* 27 Dec 1837

HAMMOND Henry H m ROBINSON Cordelia M on 25 Nov 1847 in Rochester NY, WHITCHER H Eld *MS* 8 Mar 1848

HAMMOND Jairus K m HOOPER Eliza of Paris in Paris ME *MFWBR* 10 Mar 1849

HAMMOND John S of Boston m COX Sarah J of Brunswick on 1 Sept in Brunswick ME, PURINTON A W Eld *MS* 13 Nov 1850

HAMMOND Nathan m BURGIS Phebe both of Yorkshire on 10 Oct, ANDRUS Amos C Eld *MS* 26 Dec 1838

HAMMOND Thomas m BRACKETT Olive of North Berwick ME on 5 May at North Berwick, STEVENS T Eld *MS* 2 Jul 1845

HAMMONDS Hiram W m PLUMER Caroline A both of Natick MA on 2 Jul 1848 in Milton *MS* 16 Aug 1848

HANDY John of Kittery ME m SACKETT Jane of Boston on 11 ult in Boston MA, PHOLON B Eld *MS* 11 Apr 1838

HANFORD Levi O m BROWNELL Betsey Ann both of Kartright NY on 23 May in Kartright NY, GREENE D Eld *MS* 27 June 1849

HANNAH Edward m SHEPHARD Eliza A of Portland ME on 5th inst at Portland, FREEMAN A N Rev *MFWBR* 14 Dec 1850

HANSCOM Charles m PRINCE Betsey of Minot ME on 13 Jan at

HANSCOM (Continued)

Portland ME, MOULTON A K Eld *MS* 29 Jan 1845

HANSCOM James E m GRAY Sarah Ann on 21st ult at Dover NH, HUTCHINS E Eld *MS* 1 Oct 1845

HANSCOM John of Waterville ME m LIBBY Emily of Waterville ME at Sidney ME, LEWIS D B Eld *MS* 20 Apr 1842

HANSCOM Josiah W of Hartland ME m PAGE Abigail of Sidney at Sidney, LEWIS D B Eld *MS* 20 Apr 1842

HANSCOM Lemuel E m BABB Eliza on 14 Jul at Barnstead *MS* 17 Aug 1836

HANSCOM Samuel Jr of N Berwick ME m MARSHALL Margaret J of South Berwick at North Berwick *MFWBR* 24 Mar 1849

HANSCOMB Ezra D of Biddeford ME m GOULD Amanda P of Biddeford ME on 7th inst at Biddeford, GRAY James Eld *MFWBR* 13 Feb 1847

HANSCOMB Samuel Jr of No Berwick m MARSHALL Margaret J of So Berwick on 4 Mar 1849 in North Berwick ME, CLAY D Eld *MS* 14 Mar 1849

HANSCOMB Seward M m RANKINS Mary A at Buxton ME, CLAY Jonathan Eld *MS* 20 Nov 1844

HANSON Avery of Elliot m WEEKS Almira of Kittery on 10th Dec, WETHERBEE I J Eld *MS* 27 Dec 1843

HANSON Caleb of Strafford m BENNET Lavina of Northwood on 4th inst, CILLEY D P Eld *MS* 21 Jan 1835

HANSON Caleb of Strafford NH m EVANS Louisa H of New Market NH on 28 Feb at New Market NH, HUTCHINS E Eld *MS* 13 Apr 1842

HANSON Charles of Sandwich m FOWLER Sarah E of Meredith on 15 Sept in Meredith NH, BEEDE H Eld *MS* 12 Dec 1849

HANSON Cyrus m WALKER Elizabeth H of Ossipee NH on 10 Mar at Ossipee NH, WALKER John Eld *MS* 20 Mar 1844

HANSON Daniel 3d m OSGOOD Eliza H both of Ossipee NH on 29 ult in Ossipee, WALKER John Eld *MS* 12 Dec 1838

HANSON Francis J m HOIT Sarah D of Northwood on 3 Dec at Northwood, JOHNSON W D Eld *MS* 6 Jan 1847

HANSON Frederick m CLAY Abby W both of Buxton ME on 21 Nov in Buxton ME, CROCKETT J Eld *MS* 15 Jan 1851

HANSON George S m YOUNG Sophia A of Barrington NH at Great Falls NH *MFWBR* 28 Jul 1849 & *MFWBR* 4 Aug 1849

HANSON Ivory m GARMON Emily both of Bafford LC on 12 Dec 1837, MOULTON A Eld *MS* 10 Jan 1828

HANSON James H of Harrison m CHOATE Catherine W of Otisfield ME on 28 Sept at Otisfield ME, BARROWS Worthy C Esq *MS* 19 Nov 1845

HANSON John D m FOSS Esther of Strafford on 30 Nov at Strafford NH, PLACE E Eld *MS* 3 Jan 1844

HANSON John T m ROLLINS Hannah M of Dover NH on 26 ult at Dover NH, HUTCHINS E Eld *MS* 2 Dec 1846

HANSON Joseph B m HANSON Lydia R both of Waterborough ME on 25 ult Sabbath eve, CAVERNE A Eld in Dover NH *MS* 5 Dec 1849

HANSON Nicholas Jr m BERRY Sarah both of Scarborough ME on 20 Jan 1850 in Scarborough ME, HALL T M Eld *MS* 13 Feb 1850

HANSON Rufus Capt of Wakefield m COOK Mary of Brookfield on 18 inst in Wakefield, MEADER Jesse Eld *MS* 28 Feb 1838

HANSON Samuel R of Rochester m FURBER Elizabeth C of Farmington NH on 30 June in Farmington NH, HUTCHINSON S Eld *MS* 29 Jul 1846

HANSON Stephen m FRANK Hannah both of Windham ME on 23 Jul in Gray, PURKIS John Eld *MS* 16 Aug 1837

HANSON William H m GLIDDEN Adaline L on 11th inst at Dover NH, HUTCHINS E Eld *MS* 17 Sept 1845

HANSON William m COLOMY Sarah both of Dover on 13 Nov, PERKINS J Rev *MS* 19 Nov 1834

HARBEY Benjamin m THOMPSON Keziah H both of Manchester in Manchester, CILLEY D P Eld *MS* 23 Sept 1846

HARDING Isaac Jr Capt of Haverhill MA m LAMPREY Anna M of Amesbury MA formerly of Hampton on 25 Nov in Hampton, MERRILL Wm P Eld *MS* 5 Dec 1849

HARDING Thomas P of Dover NH m FRINK Alice of Gorham ME on 28 Aug at Standish ME *MS* 28 Sept 1836

HARDING William B m EDWARDS Mary Ann in Gorham ME *MS* 4 Jan 1827

HARDING William H of Brooks m HARMON Priscilla C on 3 Nov, CLAY Jonathan Eld *MS* 20 Nov 1844

HARDY Abram m BAILEY Nancy E both of Manchester on 15 Dec in Manchester, CILLEY D P Eld *MS* 26 Dec 1849

HARDY James E of Nicketown ME? m HATCH Floretta of Chester ME, TURNER A Eld *MS* 8 Nov 1848

HARDY Jeremiah K m LEESLEE Betsey both of Hopkinton on 20 Oct *MS* 16 Nov 1836

HARDY John S m ABBOTT Clarissa M both of Manchester on 16 Aug in Manchester, CILLEY D P Eld *MS* 26 Aug 1846

HARDY Sylvester m EDWARDS Catherine on 4 Nov 1841 at Lowell MA, THURSTON N Eld *MS* 25 May 1842

HARFORD Jackson m HARFORD Elizabeth on 17 Nov 1842 at Georgetown ME *MS* 18 Jan 1843

HARGER Leonidas m HARGER Sally Mrs both of Nassau on 7 inst, COLEMAN I B Eld *MS* 23 Jan 1850

HARKER John C of Dover NH m WATSON Harriet A of Dover on 23d ult, HUTCHINS E Eld *MS* 1 Oct 1845

HARLEY Caleb B m GREEN Rozilla Mrs of Knox Co IL on 26th ult at Walnut Grove Knox Co IL, SHAW Samuel Eld *MS* 23 June 1847

HARMON Aaron F m CRAWFORD Sarah on 17th inst at Portland
ME, EATON J S Rev *MFWBR* 28 Jul 1849

HARMON Benjamin F of Thorndike m PLUMMER Elizabeth of
Gorham, BUZZELL Eld and Editor on Sun last in Gorham
MFWBR 24 Aug 1850

HARMON Gideon m JACKSON Susan G both of Durham on 14 June
in Durham ME, BARD Nathaniel Eld *MS* 8 Jul 1846

HARMON Henry M of Roxbury m GOODWIN Ruth L of Lawrence on
20 Oct in Lawrence MA, WOODMAN J Eld *MS* 27 Nov 1850

HARMON Reuben of Standish ME m LIBBY Eunice on 9 Dec at
Buxton, SINCLAIR J L Eld *MS* 7 Jan 1846

HARMON Samuel m MESERVE Delia L of Freedom on 30 Jan of
Freedom, BUTLER O Eld *MS* 19 Feb 1845

HARMON William m ATKINSON Abigail of Eaton NH on 21st Aug,
SANBORN Thomas Eld; "The Dover Enquirer is requested to copy"
MS 11 Sept 1839

HARMON William m CRAWFORD Huldah of Portland ME on 8th
inst, MOULTON A K Eld *MS* 28 June 1843

HARMON William 2d of Freedom NH m KENISON Louisa Mrs of
Lowell MA on 1 Feb 1849 in Lowell MA, CURTIS S Eld *MS* 21 Feb
1849

HARMON William J m GILBERT Lydia J on 3 Dec at Brunswick ME,
FOLSOM P Eld *MS* 6 Jan 1847

HARMON William V m THOMPSON Asenath of Harrison on 6 Jul at
Harrison ME, HUTCHINSON S Eld *MS* 24 Sept 1845

HARMON William of Charlestown MA m HALL Martha C of Bowdoin
ME in Topsham ME, BEAN C Eld *MS* 2 Aug 1848

HARPE John m STRATTON Rebecca both of Gerry NY on 4 Oct 1849
in Gerry NY, STARR N Eld *MS* 19 June 1850

HARPER Hiram m AMES Elmira of New Hampton on 4 Mar at New
Hampton, THOMPSON Samuel Eld *MS* 17 Apr 1844

HARPER Joseph P m MURPHY Abby J formerly of Jefferson ME in
Boston, NOYES E Eld *MS* 2 Feb 1848

HARPER Samuel Jr m LANG Mary A both of Limerick ME on 6 Dec
in Limerick ME, STEVENS T Eld *MS* 18 Dec 1850

HARRIMAN Cyrus m HARMON Mary S both of Eaton on 30 Sept in
Freedom, RUNNELS J Eld *MS* 11 Nov 1846

HARRIMAN David P of Burrillville RI m HOBSON Susan A on 8 May
at Buxton ME, SINCLAIR J L Eld *MS* 28 May 1845

HARRIMAN Joel of Newbury MA m JACOBS Ann of Manchester NH
on 28 Mar, CILLEY D P Eld *MS* 5 Apr 1843

HARRIMAN Obed of Chatham MA m BEAN Eliza M of Bethlehem NH
on 19 Dec Bethlehem NH, BEAN Beniah Eld *MS* 4 Jan 1843

HARRIMAN Samuel M m LOCKE Elizabeth both of Raymond on 6
Mar in Candia, MANSON B S Eld *MS* 19 Apr 1837

HARRINGTON Edward V m HAWKINS Eliza A both of No Providence

HARRINGTON (Continued)
RI on 12th inst at Johnston RI, HUTCHINS E Elder *MS* 18 Feb
1835
HARRINGTON Gardner Eld of Stephentown m DOOD Sally of Hinsdale MA on 10 Aug in Hinsdale MA, MERRY A Rev *MS* 23 Oct
1850
HARRINGTON Hiram m COOK Fanny of Wilmington MA on 16 May
at Wilmington MA, DURGIN J M Eld *MS* 26 June 1844
HARRINGTON James J m EDGERLY Hannah S both of Manchester
in Manchester, CILLEY Daniel P Eld *MS* 2 Feb 1848
HARRINGTON Josiah B m ALDRICH Huldah M both of No Scituate
on 6 Dec in No Scituate RI, ALLEN Reuben Eld *MS* 2 Jan 1830
HARRINGTON Leonard B of St Johnsbury VT m EASTMAN Nancy H
of Bath NH on 4 Sept 1842 at Swift Water Village, GEORGE N K
Eld *MS* 28 Dec 1842
HARRINGTON Mason A m TOLMAN Laura A both of New Ipswich MA
in New Ipswich MA, GUERNESEY J W Rev *MS* 27 Oct 1847
HARRINGTON Moses B m CURRIER Rebecca both of Concord on 14
inst 1849 in Concord ME, CATLIN S T Eld *MS* 21 Mar 1849
HARRINGTON Moses B of Pittsfield m MOORE Betsey P at Deerfield
NH, KIMBALL John Eld *MS* 3 Oct 1833
HARRINGTON Seth m MITCHELL Mary Ann both of No Providence
on 16 Jan in No Providence, HUTCHINS E Eld *MS* 7 Feb 1838
HARRIS Bela m HASELTINE Betsey of Lowell, THURSTON Nathaniel
Eld *MS* 10 Apr 1839
HARRIS Clark m FOSTER Judith N of Wentworth on 15 Dec at
Wentworth, MESSER Asa Eld *MS* 26 Feb 1845
HARRIS Eseck of Burrillville m MOWREY Almira T of Smithfield on 8
Dec in No Scituate RI, ALLEN R Eld *MS* 1 Jan 1851
HARRIS John A m SWETT Mary Ann both of Canaan NH on 22 June
1848 in Canaan NH, JONES N Eld *MS* 12 Jul 1848
HARRIS John D m BERRY Hannah W on 7 Mar 1843 at Holderness,
THOMPSON Samuel Eld *MS* 15 Mar 1843
HARRIS Matthew of Roxbury MA m FALL Elizabeth M of Ossipee NH
on 16 Mar in Ossipee, CHICK J Eld *MS* 24 June 1846
HARRIS Paul m LINNEKIN Mary Adaline of Boothbay on 25 Dec of
Boothbay ME, MORRILL S P Eld *MS* 4 Feb 1846
HARRIS Ralph m WHITMAN Mary E both of Scituate RI on 23 Dec in
Scituate RI, ALLEN Eld *MS* 15 Jan 1851
HARRIS Roswell A M former preceptor of Hampton NH Acad m
LEAVITT Matilda *MS* 19 Sept 1833
HARRIS Stephen Deacon m WEED Delia of Danville VT on 19 Mar at
Bethlehem NH, GEORGE N K Eld *MS* 14 May 1845
HARRIS William H m FREEMAN Hannah D both of Boston on 26 Apr
in Boston, NOYES E Eld *MS* 5 Aug 1846
HARRISON James M m NICHOLS Sarah W both of Woonsocket on

HARRISON (Continued)
28 Nov 1850 in No Scituate RI, ALLEN R Eld *MS* 1 Jan 1851

HARRISON Salmon of Addison m HAIGHT Amy E of Laurens on 14 Apr in Otsego NY, CADY S S Eld *MS* 8 May 1850

HART Edward of Milton NH m FOX Sally at Acton ME, FULLONTON J Eld *MS* 4 Oct 1843

HART Simon of Somersworth NH m WENTWORTH Mary Ann of South Berwick ME on 9 March, JOHNSON W D Eld *MS* 15 Mar 1843

HART William S of Lebanon m GOWIN Mary Ann of Shapleigh ME, STEVENS T Eld *MS* 25 Oct 1843

HARTFORD Edmunds m DAY Catherine of Brownfield ME on 18 Aug at Hiram ME, HOLMES J C Eld *MS* 31 Aug 1842

HARTILL Charles A m MILLER Caroline S of Charlestown MA on 3 Jul at Charlestown MA, SWETT D Eld *MS* 23 Oct 1844

HARTON James M m CLARK Betsey T on 28 Dec, KNOWLES John Eld *MS* 19 Mar 1845

HARTSHORN Anson H m BROWN Esther M both of Manchester on 4 Sept in Manchester, CILLEY D P Eld *MS* 12 Sept 1849

HARTWELL Lysander W m ROLLINS Lucy Ann on 30 Jan at St Albans ME, COPP John B Eld *MS* 17 Sept 1845

HARVEY Alonzo m BALINGER Rachel on 7 Aug at Perry Township Ohio, HARVEY E Eld *MS* 30 Oct 1844

HARVEY David S m WHITTEMORE J Miss on 6th May at Lowell MA, CURTIS S Eld *MS* 2 June 1847

HARVEY Howard Capt m YOUNG Ann C of Durham on 24 Aug of South Berwick ME, HUTCHINS E Eld *MS* 30 Aug 1843

HARVEY Jacob C m GOODRICH Sabrina H of Nottingham on 19 Jan at New Market, FROST D S Eld *MS* 28 Jan 1846

HARVEY Jacob S m PUTNEY Almira M both of Sutton on Nov 9 1841, MOODY David Eld *MS* 12 Jan 1842

HARVEY Joseph Eld m TASKER Emeline M on 18 Dec at Pittsfield, KNOWLES John Eld *MS* 19 Mar 1845

HARVEY Marshal m HAZARD Thirzah on 15 Dec 1842 at Huntington VT, DIKE Orange Eld *MS* 12 Apr 1843

HARVEY William m DELLAWARE Amanda M of Lowell, THURSTON N Eld *MS* 7 Aug 1839

HARVEY William m REDWAY Arminda of Barnston in May, MOULTON Abial Eld *MS* 1 Jan 1840

HARVY John m WHEELER Sarah on 13 Apr in Ruch Township Logan Co Ohio, HEATH J D Eld *MS* 22 May 1844

HASELTON Gilson of Moretown on 17 March at Waterbury VT m SIMONS Emily of Waterbury VT, GRAY Ira Eld *MS* 16 Apr 1845

HASKEL Rufus Capt m BURGESS Rachel Mrs both of Poland ME on 17 Mar in Lewiston ME, BEAN G W Eld *MS* 1 Apr 1846

HASKELL Isaac P of Bangor ME m COUILLARD Adeline of Bangor

HASKELL (Continued)

ME on 3 Dec, ALLEN Ebenezer Eld *MS* 13 Jan 1847

HASKELL Jabez of N Gloucester ME m HARRIS Miriam at Cumberland ME on 20th ult *MFWBR* 21 Apr 1849

HASKELL Jona L of New Gloucester ME m HASKELL Lydia of Poland ME at New Gloucester ME, JOHNSON Thomas Esq *MFWBR* 10 Apr 1847

HASKELL William H m NUTE Louisa B of Dover NH on 23 March at Dover NH, SMITH A D Eld *MS* 31 Mar 1847

HASKELL William m EMERY Jane of Poland on 5 Dec at West Poland ME, LIBBEY James Eld *MS* 9 Apr 1845

HASKINS Asa L m WEBSTER Mary Ann on 31 Dec 1846 at Enfield NH, SMITH C H Eld *MS* 5 May 1847

HASSOM Lewis of Northfield VT m BUZZELL Elizabeth on 23 Mar at Strafford, SANBORN G Eld *MS* 6 Apr 1847

HASTINGS Jonas m BAILEY Betsey both of Lowell m THURSTON N Eld *MS* 1 Nov 1837

HASTINGS Jonas at Newbury MA? m HASTINGS Lydia A (widow) of Newbury in Lowell MA, EMERY Amos Eld *MS* 10 Apr 1844

HATCH Alexander C of Nottingham m EVANS Terrasa W of Barrington NH on 15 May at Barrington, CILLEY D P Eld *MS* 21 May 1845

HATCH Benjamin m HATCH Pendorah on 10 Dec at Wells ME, SMALL C Eld *MS* 20 Jan 1847

HATCH David P m SWAIN Adaline N both of Meredith NH on 7 Nov, PITMAN S J Eld *MS* 15 Nov 1843

HATCH Dimon m TAYLOR Mary on 5 Dec in Wells ME, KEENE J Eld *MS* 8 Jan 1851

HATCH Eliab G m LEAVITT Jane of Guilford NH on 14 Nov at Alton NH, PINKHAM J Eld *MS* 18 Dec 1844

HATCH Franklin m SPENCER Mary of Roxbury on 7th inst at West Brooksfield, CLAFLIN Jehiel Eld *MS* 15 May 1839

HATCH Harvey m TOOTHAKER Rosina of Charlestown on 11 Jul 1844 at Corinth ME, AMES M Eld *MS* 21 Aug 1844

HATCH Henry M m WOODES Mary both of Dover on 3 inst in Dover, HUTCHINS E Eld *MS* 7 Mar 1849

HATCH Joel m SHIPLEY Elizabeth of Lowell MA on 31 Jul at Lowell MA, WOODMAN J Eld *MS* 19 Oct 1842

HATCH John C of West Winchester m ADAMS Charlotte of No Providence on 4 inst *MS* 12 Oct 1836

HATCH Joseph m BLUNT Philienia both of Boston MA, THURSTON N Eld *MS* 22 Jul 1835

HATCH Samuel M m WALTON Harriet N both of Lowell in Dracut MA, CURTIS S Eld *MS* 17 Nov 1847

HATCH Seth at Great Falls NH m DURGIN Eliza Ann, DUNN R Eld *MS* 7 Jul 1847

HATCH Sylvanus of Great Falls NH m GERRISH Mary Jane of Lebanon NH, CURTIS S Eld *MS* 9 Nov 1842

HATCH Sylvastine L m MORRILL Sarah Ann of North Berwick ME on 19 Jan 1843, LORD D H Eld *MS* 15 Feb 1843

HATCH William C m BATCHELDER Frances E at Portland ME *MFWBR* 1 Dec 1849

HATCH William Jr m DYER Mary of Portland on 29th ult at Portland ME, MOULTON A K Eld *MS* 8 Nov 1843

HATHAWAY Franklin of Potsdam m CLEAVELAND Martha on 10 Mar at Colten NY, WHITEFIELD Eld *MS* 6 Apr 1847

HATHORN Alexander G of Milford m HOWARD Abby W of Bangor ME on 18 May at Bangor ME, WEAVER Philip Eld *MS* 26 May 1847

HATHORN David Capt m HEDGE Thankful Hallet of Woolwich ME on 14 Nov at Woolwich ME, PAGE E G Eld *MS* 27 Dec 1843

HATHORN Samuel Eld m NEWELL Betsey, CURTIS Silas both of Bowdoinham ME *MS* 12 Oct 1832

HATHORN William W m HIGGINS Susan O both of Bowdoinham ME on 20 Feb in Providence RI *MS* 19 Mar 1851

HAWES George W m FERNALD Jane W of Lowell MA on 13th Dec at Lowell MA, CURTIS S Eld *MS* 24 Dec 1845

HAWKINS Alpheus of Albany m HARRIMAN Betsey of Conway NH, MERRILL Thomas Esq *MS* 27 May 1835

HAWKINS Benjamin T m SINCLAIR Nancy both of Center Harbor in Meredith Village, STEVENS Hiram *MS* 28 Nov 1838

HAWKINS George W m FOGG Susan R both of Center Harbor on 9 Oct, PITMAN S J Eld *MS* 30 Oct 1850

HAWKINS John S m LANE Betsey both of Dover NH on 26 June 1839 in Meredith Village, QUINBY H Eld *MS* 12 Feb 1840

HAWKINS Orson m MARTIN Mary both of Yorkshire on 14 Sept 1848 in Arcade NY, JACKSON N A Eld *MS* 1 Nov 1848

HAWKINS William P m CASWELL Deborah Jane both of Strafford in Strafford, PLACE Enoch Eld *MS* 10 Jan 1838

HAYDEN William H m BOWLES Mary Jane both of New Market on 5 ult in Durham, CILLEY D P Eld *MS* 25 Apr 1838

HAYES Alonzo of Dover m WHITE Olive of Effingham NH, DAVIS I Eld *MS* 25 May 1842

HAYES Andrew of Lebanon ME m HAYES Elizabeth on 3 Sept, ROTT David Rev *MS* 12 Oct 1836

HAYES Charles m DANFORTH Clara A both of New Durham NH on 3 Feb 1850 in Farmington, BODGE J Eld *MS* 13 Feb 1850

HAYES Charles H of Strafford m FOSS Sarah J of Rochester on 9 Mar in Rochester NH, PLACE E Eld *MS* 29 Mar 1848

HAYES Charles T m FOSS Betsey C both of Strafford on 12 Apr in Strafford, PLACE E Eld *MS* 22 Apr 1846

HAYES Chester G of Auburn Ohio m JEWELL Susan H of Tamworth

HAYES (Continued)

NH on 2 Oct, NEWELL Rev *MS* 26 Nov 1834

HAYES Cyrus W m FURBUSH Lydia on 1 May at Lebanon, BLAIS-
DELL E Eld *MS* 28 May 1845

HAYES Daniel m HALEY Joanna H of Dover on Sunday, WILLIAMS
Gibbon Rev *MS* 12 Nov 1834

HAYES David Jr of Farmington m BODGE Louisa M at Rochester,
WALDRON W H Eld *MS* 7 June 1843

HAYES David m ROBERTS Mary on 6th ult at Strafford *MS* 21 Dec
1836

HAYES Edmund Jr of Limerick m SANDS Eliza of Lyman at Lyman
MS 28 Dec 1826

HAYES Ezekial of Strafford NH m FOSS Susan of Strafford NH on 3d
March, FROST D S Eld *MS* 10 Mar 1847 & *MS* 6 Apr 1847

HAYES Hubbard m TURNER Mary Jane both of Nassau on 29 Jan
1846 in Sand Lake NY, COLEMAN I B Eld *MS* 8 Apr 1846

HAYES John m CROSS Eliza Ann *MS* 1 June 1836

HAYES John m EATON Louiza of Limerick on Sunday last, McDON-
ALD John *MS* 5 Aug 1831

HAYES Joseph m HAMILTON Eliza on 24th ult, FREEMAN Rev *MS* 3
Feb 1830

HAYES Joshua B m WILLEY Susan E of Somersworth NH at Effingham NH *MFWBR* 9 Mar 1850 & m on 4 Jan 1850 by TAYLOR
Elijah Esq in Effingham *MS* 27 Feb 1850

HAYES Luther S of Cambridge MA m SWETT Emeline of Limerick
ME on 12th inst at Limerick ME, FREEMAN C Rev *MFWBR* 17
Apr 1847

HAYES Moses H m HOIT Sarah F both of Great Falls NH on 18 inst
at Great Falls, BROOKS N Eld *MS* 28 Aug 1850

HAYES Samuel of Wolfboro m WENTWORTH Abigail R of Alton NH
on 7 Jul 1847 in Alton, PINKHAM John Eld *MS* 1 Sept 1847

HAYES Silas B on 5 Aug 1848 m TURNER Olive both of Nassau in
Sand Lake NY, COLEMAN I Eld *MS* 11 Oct 1848

HAYES Stephen W of Alton m RISS Abigail H at Gilmanton NH on 15
Nov 1843, ARNOLD S H Esq *MS* 20 Dec 1843

HAYES Washington E of Dover NH m REED Abigail A of Roxbury MA
in Roxbury MA, DAVIS J B Eld *MS* 24 June 1846

HAYES Wentworth of Rochester m BRACKETT Sally of Great Falls
NH on Sunday morning last 11 inst *MS* 21 Oct 1835

HAYNES Abraham S of Epsom NH m HAYNES Elizabeth of Manchester on 6 May CILLEY D P Eld *MS* 26 May 1847

HAYNES J S m HALL Louisa M both of Dover NH on 15 Nov at F B
Church in Manchester, CILLEY D P Eld *MS* 5 Dec 1849

HAYNES James m CURTIS Julia Ann on 4 Nov, WHITE William Esq
MS 17 Dec 1845

HAYNES John Esq m HARVEY Mary B both of Pittsburg on 22 Aug

HAYNES (Continued)
1847 in Pittsburg, BEAN Benaiah Eld *MS* 17 Nov 1847

HAYNES John of Stanstead Canada m ROBINSON Margaret of Hatley LC on 21 Mar, MOULTON A Eld *MS* 13 Sept 1843

HAYS Charles C of Farrington NH m POLLARD Elizabeth W of Somersworth NH on 24th ult at Dover NH, HUTCHINS E Eld *MS* 2 Dec 1846

HAYWOOD Gorham m DURELL Harriet M on 9 May at Charleston MA, JACKSON Daniel Eld *MS* 24 May 1843

HAYWOOD John S m BROWN Caroline A both of Manchester on 24 May in Manchester, CILLEY D P Eld *MS* 17 June 1846

HAZELTINE Benjamin L m BABB Sarah A of Buxton ME at Saco ME, WILLIAMS N M *MFWBR* 22 Feb 1851

HAZELTON Chesley D m CHANNELL Lydia B on 20th inst at Durham, HUTCHINS E Eld *MS* 27 Dec 1843

HAZELTON J Cutter "on 15th inst ... a merchant of the firm Haselton and Palmer" m HANSON Mary Elizabeth, HAYDEN Lucian Rev *MS* 23 Oct 1839

HAZELTON Stephen B m HAMILTON Mary E both of Conway NH on 2/23 Sept in Conway, LONG Larkin A Eld *MS* 20 Feb 1850 & *MS* 28 Nov 1849

HAZEN Ichabod E m ROWELL Ann both of Sutton on Nov 11, MOODY David Eld *MS* 12 Jan 1842

HAZEN Robert S m MOWRY Mary P both of Newport RI in Newport RI, LORD D H Eld *MS* 8 Apr 1846

HEAD Sampson of Conway m GRAY Betsey of Dover on 15 Jan in Eaton, GASKELL Silas Eld *MS* 12 Aug 1846

HEAD William m DAY Mercy, BURBANK Eld *MS* 2 Jul 1828

HEALD David of Boston m WHITTIER Lucy Ann both of Manchester on 10 Apr 1849 in Manchester, CILLEY D P Eld *MS* 25 Apr 1849

HEALD Samuel m MITCHELL Sarah N on 30 Dec 1847 in Dracut MA, CURTIS S Eld *MS* 2 Feb 1848

HEALEY Moses m TOWLE Esther both of Raymond on 12 Nov 1849 in Raymond, FOSS T Eld *MS* 23 Jan 1850

HEAPS Henry m PUGH Maria on 17 Dec at Dover, CLARK M Eld *MS* 25 Dec 1844

HEARD Francis m HEARD Mary of North Berwick ME at North Berwick ME, STEVENS T Eld *MS* 29 Mar 1843

HEARD John Capt of Newfield m FRENCH Eliza of Wakefield NH *MS* 23 Jul 1828

HEARD Wilder late of Newport m ELLIS Abigail of Barnston on 23 Nov at Barnston LC, MOULTON A Eld *MS* 17 Feb 1836

HEARL/HEARD Benjamin m HEARL/HEARD Dorcas "erronously printed HEARD in our paper week before last", JOHNSON W D Eld at South Berwick *MS* 3/17 May 1843

HEATH Daniel m ROW Dorothy both of Haverhill MA on 22 Feb 1848

HEATH (Continued)

in Haverhill MA, MERRILL W P Eld *MS* 8 Mar 1848

HEATH George of Stanstead LC m CLEAVELAND Ellen of Compton on 12 June, MOULTON A Eld *MS* 13 Sept 1843

HEATH J D Eld m REA Shady on 28 Feb at Perry Township Logan Co Ohio, BIRD James Eld *MS* 31 Mar 1847

HEATH John m BEAN Marinda on 3 Apr *MS* 1 May 1844

HEATH Jonathan D m RANDALL Mary at Ohio, DUDLEY Eld *MS* 3 Jul 1844

HEATH Stephen m ROBBINS Mary E both of Raymond on 13 Dec in Raymond, ROSS T Eld *MS* 23 Jan 1850

HEATH William T of Salisbury m SARGEANT Sarah in Danville, FULLONTON J Eld *MS* 23 Feb 1842

HEDDING Harley m SMITH Alvira of Lawrence on 18 Oct at Lawrence NY, WHITFIELD Eld *MS* 6 Dec 1843

HEDGE Barnabas Eld m HILTON Catherine Mrs in Wiscasset ME *MS* 29 Mar 1827

HEFFRON Daniel S, principal of the Whitestown Seminary m CHAPMAN D Mandane on 31 Jul at Plainfield Otsego Co NY, CHANEY John Eld *MS* 24 Sept 1845

HEKOK Channey J m MILLER Harriet A on 28 Feb in Mecca Ohio, ALDRICH S Eld *MS* 24 Apr 1850

HELEY Joseph m GARLAND Mary of Alexandria NH on 19 Sept at Alexandria NH, BROWN A Eld *MS* 4 May 1842

HELEY William of Alexandria NH m HILL Betsey of Haverhill NH, BROWN A Eld *MS* 4 May 1842

HEMENWAY Benjamin m COLE Rachel J both of East Nassau on 18 Apr in Nassau NY, COLEMAN I B Eld *MS* 27 May 1846

HEMINGWAY William R of Milton m SAWYER Hannah of Saco ME on 16th inst at Biddeford ME, FARRINGTON Rev *MFWBR* 28 Apr 1849

HENDERSON Aaron of Eaton NH m HUTCHINS Rebecca of Waterborough ME on 15 Aug 1847, EMERY Richard Eld *MS* 22 Dec 1847

HENDERSON Daniel S m MELDRUM Nancy J of Great Falls NH on 19th at Great Falls NH, CURTIS S Eld *MS* 29 Mar 1843

HENDERSON Samuel H Capt m GUPPY Sarah Ann in Dover NH on 5 inst Thursday *MS* 18 Jul 1838

HENERSON Seth m MOULTON Sarah J of Lowell MA on 6 Dec at Deerfield, CILLEY D P Eld *MS* 22 Dec 1841

HERBERT Sanders of NH m FISK Polly G 4 Jul at New Hampton, FISK Ebenezer Eld *MS* 24 Jul 1839

HERRINGTON Philo B m BRAND Sarah both of Loydsville on 16 Sept, CHANEY J Eld in Loydsville NY *MS* 30 Sept 1846

HERSEY Levi Eld m HERSEY Mary J of Minot ME on 18th ult at Minot ME, LIBBY Almon Eld *MS* 17 Apr 1844

HERSHAM Benjamin m RICKER Sarah H both of Lebanon on 8 Dec in Lebanon NH, STEVEN T Eld *MS* 25 Dec 1839

HERSOM Ebenezer of Acton ME m WENTWORTH Mahala of Effingham on 30 Mar 1847, FOSS N Eld *MS* 12 Jan 1848

HEWEY Arthur E m JORDAN Joanna H both of Topsham ME on 3 Nov in Bowdoin ME, PURINTON A W Eld *MS* 25 Dec 1850

HEYDON Parker m GOULD Permelia A both of Phoenix NY on 5 Dec 1847 in Phoenix, SMITH O W Eld *MS* 22 Dec 1847

HIBARD Joseph of Randolph m PRATT Olive on 16th March at Plymouth VT, CALLEY David Eld *MS* 17 Apr 1844

HIBBARD Albert of IL m MOULTON Pantha L of Conneaut Ohio on 15 Apr at Conneaut Ashtabula Co Ohio, BAKER Eld *MS* 6 Jul 1842

HIBBARD Hezekiah at Brookfield NY m MAIRU Elizabeth, GARDINER S D Eld *MS* 23 June 1847

HIBBARD Tanny m SANDERS Olive of Gilford NH on 16 Nov at Gilford, PINKHAM John Eld *MS* 28 Dec 1842

HIBBARD William of Alexandria Jefferson Co m JEPSON Terresa of Hammond NY St Lawrence Co on 16 Oct 1849 in Hammond NY, PADDEN S B Eld *MS* 25 Apr 1849

HICKOES Obadiah m PUTNAM Polly Mrs on 2 Sept in Rochester, WHITCHER Eld *MS* 26 Sept 1849

HICKS Elbridge D m JOHNSON Mary both of N Yarmouth ME on 23 Feb 1848, CROCKETT J Eld *MS* 8 Mar 1848

HICKS George W of Rumney NH m BLODGET Mary Jane on 27 June at West Plymouth, CHASE Paul Eld *MS* 7 Jul 1847

HICKS James m WELLS Agness both of Compton LC on 1st inst, MOULTON Eld *MS* 18 May 1836

HICKS Levi of Strongsville Cuyahoga Co Ohio m GILLS Olive M of Harrisville Medina Co Ohio on 7 March, VAUGHN Hiram Eld *MS* 10 Apr 1844

HICKS Ora m HASKELL Mehitabel S both of Harrison ME on 3 May in Harrison ME, BARROWS W C Esq *MS* 3 June 1846

HICKS Philander W of New Lebanon m GREEN Caroline A of Stephentown NY in Stephentown NY, COLEMAN I B Eld *MS* 31 Oct 1849

HIDDEN David S of Tamworth NH m LIBBY Mary Jane Mrs on Sept at Sandwich, McMURPHY B H Eld *MS* 16 Oct 1844

HIGGENS Jeremiah Capt of Lisbon ME m WILSON Rechel of Topsham on 18 Aug at Topsham ME, WHITEMORE John Eld *MS* 31 Aug 1842

HIGGINS Amos D m WILBER Flora both of Charleston on 20 Aug 1848 in Charleston ME, HARDING E Eld *MS* 21 Feb 1849

HIGGINS Daniel H Esq of Lisbon m JONES Mahala A of Webster ME on 8 Feb 1848 in Lisbon ME, WHITTEMORE John *MS* 23 Feb 1848

HIGGINS John C of Farmington m OLIVER Cordelia on 23 Feb *MS* 16 Apr 1845

HIGGINS John Jr m WOTTON Elmira both of Belmont, WARD Cotton Esq *MS* 31 May 1848

HIGGINS John m RACKLEFF Louisa J on 28 May 1848 in Lincoln-ville ME, KEENE J Eld *MS* 21 June 1848

HIGGINS Joseph Jr m HIGGINS Lousa W both of Thorndike ME on 3 May in Thorndike ME, ROBINSON N J Eld *MS* 27 May 1846

HIGHT Bryce of Bloomfield ME m HILTON Martha of N Anson ME *MFWBR* 8 Apr 1848

HILDRETH Oliver m STREETER Catherine on 19 Feb at Lisbon, GEORGE N K Eld *MS* 14 May 1845

HILL Andrew Capt of Strafford m MUDGET Plooma D, by LANCAS-TER Rev Mr *MS* 16 Jan 1834

HILL Archeaus W m CURTIS Lucy of Stanstead LC on 25 Apr, MOULTON Abial Eld *MS* 1 Jan 1840

HILL Asa M m HANSON Abigail both of Starksborough VT on 18 Mar in Starksborough VT, BIXBY Newell W Eld *MS* 8 Apr 1846

HILL Azariah B m HALL Hannah of Strafford NH on 4th inst at Straf-ford, PLACE E Eld *MS* 10 Apr 1839

HILL Benjamin C m COLLIER Cynthia H both of Lowell MA on 7 Apr *MS* 27 Apr 1842 & at Lowell MA by WOODMAN J Eld *MS* 19 Oct 1842

HILL Benjamin D of Northwood m PRESCOTT Mary J of Deerfield on 24 Oct in Deerfield NH, BURBANK P S Eld *MS* 27 Nov 1850

HILL Benjamin F m LOCK Sarah O D both of Great Falls NH on 14 Apr in Great Falls, BROOKS N Eld *MS* 8 May 1850

HILL Clark of Barrington m ROBERTS Melinda of Pittsfield on 27 Feb in Pittsfield, RICHARDSON J Rev *MS* 14 Mar 1838

HILL Daniel T m PLUMMER Augusta L of Great Falls NH, on 19th ult *MFWBR* 25 Jan 1851 & m by BROOKS N Eld at Great Falls in the Free Will Baptist Church *MS* 22 Jul 1851

HILL Edmund D Capt m FLETCHER Lavina A on 5 Nov 1843 at Canterbury NH, CLOUGH Jeremiah Eld *MS* 14 Feb 1844

HILL Edward Jr of Bartlett NH m WILLEY Dolly Miss of Sheffield on 21st ult *MS* 15 Jul 1835

HILL Freeman m CHADBORN Deborah of Sanford ME on 22d? ult at Berwick ME, SHAPLEIGH R Esq *MS* 3 Apr 1839

HILL Horace P of Lyman m WILSON Lydia Ann of Biddeford ME on 4 Mar, JACKSON Daniel Eld *MS* 6 Apr 1847

HILL Ichabod of Saco m SMITH Mary Mrs of Kennebunkport on 10 May in Biddeford ME, LIBBY Josiah Eld *MS* 3 June 1846

HILL Ira m HUBBARD Sarah of Barnston on 8 Jul, MOULTON A Eld *MS* 13 Sept 1843

HILL Ivory at Waterboro' m KNIGHT Abiah, EMERY R Eld *MS* 18 June 1845

HILL Japhet of Kennebunk ME m EMMONS Lucinda on 15 June, LORD D H Eld *MS* 5 Jul 1843

HILL Jehial m MOULTON Rosetta of Barnston on 29 Jan, MOULTON A Eld of Stanstead LC *MS* 13 Apr 1842

HILL John 2d m MAXFIELD Olive L of Starksboro VT on 23 Jan at Starksboro VT, BIXBY N W Eld *MS* 7 Feb 1844

HILL John C m WINCHELL Sophronia Miss on 25th Sept at Dover NH *MS* 3 Oct 1833

HILL John C m BARTLETT Rebecca J on 25th ult at Northwood NH, CILLEY D P Eld *MS* 23 May 1833

HILL John S m CATE Sophia on 30 Oct at Gilmanton, MOODY David Eld *MS* 18 Jan 1843

HILL Jonathan of Gilmanton NH m CHESLEY Eliza of No Durham, BUZZELL H D Eld *MS* 17 June 1835

HILL Joseph m WENTWORTH Susan M at Manchester NH, CILLEY D P Eld *MS* 9 Dec 1846

HILL Joseph G of Boston MA m EMERSON Eliza J on 30 June at Manchester, CILLEY D P Eld *MS* 16 Jul 1845

HILL Joseph H m SMALL Lucy Ann of Lowell MA on 25 May at Northwood, CILLEY D P Eld *MS* 11 June 1845

HILL Joseph m McKUSICK Lucinda both of Limerick ME on Mon last, BURBANK Eld *MS* 26 June 1829

HILL Levi G Dr of Gilmanton m SHACKFORD Abigail B of Barrington on 30 Jul in Strafford, PLACE E Eld *MS* 16 Aug 1837

HILL Levi m MORRISON Plooma A both of London NH on 4 Jul in Canterbury, CLOUGH Jeremiah Eld *MS* 17 Jul 1850

HILL Lorenzo of Bethany, Genesee Co, NY m BROWN Anna of Freedom NY on 4 Jan 1842, WINSOR Barnet Eld *MS* 15 Mar 1843

HILL Lyman H m HANSCOM Lois of Strafford NH at Northwood, FERNALD S P Eld *MS* 27 Feb 1839

HILL Mark formerly of Maine m RUGGLES Arvilla of Lyndon VT on 11th inst *MS* 29 Nov 1827

HILL Nathaniel Jr of Brownfield m RAND Eliza of Parsonsfield ME on 2nd Jan in Limington ME, RAND James Eld *MS* 2 Mar 1842

HILL Oliver m ROBINSON Nancy both of Meredith, PITMAN Stephen J Eld *MS* 5 Dec 1838

HILL Orin T m MATHEWS Hannah H on 2 Jan 1848 in Lowell, CURTIS S Eld *MS* 2 Feb 1848

HILL Stephen of Brighton MA m STEPHENS Lydia P on 7th inst *MFWBR* 18 Dec 1847

HILL Stephen of Cornish m EATON Caroline E of Portland ME in Cornish ME, WEEKS James W *MS* 27 Apr 1832

HILL Stephen P m HOLMES Lucy B both of Strafford on 1 Jan 1849 in Strafford, HOLMES J C Eld *MS* 17 Jan 1849

HILL Sylvanus m HANSON Mary both of Starksboro' VT on 26 Jan 1848 in Starksboro' VT, TUCKER Joshua Eld *MS* 23 Feb 1848

HILL Sylvester of Lyman m RICHARDS Rosilla of Saco ME on 29 ult in Biddeford ME *MS* 30 Oct 1850

HILL Thomas of Center Harbor m PERKINS Mary Elizabeth on 25 Aug at New Hampton *MS* 8 Nov 1843

HILL Thomas of Saco ME m CURRIER Hannah of Kennebunkport ME on 31st ult, DWIGHT Rev *MFWBR* 11 Jan 1851

HILL Timothy of N Berwick m BLAISDELL Rosamond of Great Falls NH on 15th ult, GOODWIN Joshua Eld *MS* 9 Jan 1834

HILL William Jr m LOCKE Abigail of Great Falls, CURTIS S Eld *MS* 23 Oct 1839

HILL Winthrop Y m CLIFFORD Nancy M on 4 Jul at Loudon NH, CLOUGH Jeremiah Eld *MS* 20 June 1842

HILL William 2d m HILL Lucy both of Starksboro VT on 26 Sept in Huntington VT, DIKE O Eld *MS* 20 Nov 1850

HILL William A of Cumberland m PARISH Lucy of Smithfield on 7 Feb last, BURLINGAME M W *MS* 9 Mar 1836

HILL William H of Deerfield NH m DURGIN Elizabeth W of Exeter on 23 Sept *MS* 18 Nov 1835

HILLS Henry m HUTCHENSON Harriet L on 20th inst at Boston, HOLMAN J W Eld *MS* 30 Mar 1842

HILLS James W Eld of Virgil m QUIVEY Clarissa of Cincinnatus both of Cortland Co NY on 9 Dec in Cincinnatus Cortland Co NY, BYER Wm C Eld *MS* 12 Jan 1848

HILTON Andrew m PAUL Eliza Ann both of Acton ME, PERRY Luther Eld *MS* 24 Sept 1834

HILTON Richard Jr m WENTWORTH Eunice both of Ossipee NH on 23 Feb 1842 in Ossipee, WALKER John *MS* 16 Mar 1842

HINES Barnum J both of Hartford ME m BARTLETT Abigail in Boston on the 20th inst, HOLMAN J W Eld *MS* 30 Mar 1842

HISERODT Andrew M m BLYE Mary A of Sand Lake on 13 Mar at Sand Lake, COLEMAN E B Eld *MS* 7 May 1845

HITCHCOCK Lemuel m BEEBE Delia of Sand Lake on 16 Oct, COLEMAN I B Eld *MS* 22 Feb 1843

HIZER James of Newport NY m WAFUL Mary of Norway on 1 Jan, KOON D W Eld *MS* 24 May 1843

HOAG Charles N m WHITCHER Marcia B on 24 May at Lockport NY, WHITCHER H Eld *MS* 16 June 1847

HOAG Chase of Lincoln VT m WRIGHT Rosina on 23 Dec, TUCKER Joshua Eld *MS* 10 Feb 1847

HOAG Horace of Rose Lewis Co m SMITH Adelia M on 24 Sept at Norway Herkimer Co NY, SMITH O W Eld *MS* 29 Jan 1845

HOAG Isaac J of Chatham m TIFFT Martha Ann of Nassau on afternoon 6 ult in Nassau, COLEMAN J B Eld *MS* 17 Oct 1838

HOBBS Abial W (a licensed preacher) of Wolfboro NH m DORE Lucinda of Ossipee NH on 7 Sept, CHICK John Eld *MS* 5 Oct 1842

HOBBS Euran m BENSON Sarah of Biddeford at Waterboro, HOBBS Henry Eld *MS* 24 June 1835

HOBBS Henry H of Norway Oxford Co ME m MOULTON Sarah P of Ossipee Carroll Co NH on 14 Dec 1847 in Ossipee NH, HART E H Eld *MS* 19 Apr 1848

HOBBS James Jr of South Berwick ME m GOODWIN Mary A of North Berwick at North Berwick, COOK Rev *MFWBR* 24 Feb 1849

HOBBS Joseph Jr m PINDER Nancy both of Ossipee on 19 ult in Ossipee, WALKER John Eld *MS* 10 Oct 1838

HOBBS Lewis of Livermore ME m LEATHERS Margaret of Hallowell ME on 22 Oct in Hallowell, TOBIE E M Elder *MS* 13 Dec 1837

HOBBS Oliver of Ossipee m JENNESS Deborah of Wolfboro NH on 4 Dec *MS* 21 Dec 1836

HOBBS Samuel of Parsonsfield m MORRISON Sevina of Saco ME on 5th ult, FOSS Eld *MS* 4 Aug 1830

HOBBS Thomas m HOBBS Fanny Miss at North Hampton NH *MS* 20 Jul 1832

HOBBS Wentworth H m HALL Patience both of Ossipee NH on 17 Oct 1847 in Ossipee NH, HART E H Eld *MS* 19 Apr 1848

HOBERT Atkinson m HELSEY Mary both of Charlestown ME on Dec 8 1841, AMES M Eld *MS* 4 May 1842

HOBSON Amos of Hollis ME m GOWELL Mary of Great Falls NH on 11 Oct 1848 at Great Falls, BROOKS N Eld *MS* 18 Oct 1848

HOBSON James G of Hollis m SWETT Sophronia B of Casco ME on 28 Jul Sunday morning in Casco ME, COOK O G Esq *MS* 21 Aug 1850

HOBSON Joseph L m JOHNSON Frances A both of Hollis in Hollis ME, BAILEY J M Eld *MS* 22 Jan 1851

HOBSON William F m PHINNEY Aurelia F on 19 June at Gorham ME, SINCLAIR J L Eld *MS* 23 Jul 1845

HODGDON Alexander W m WALKER Jane both of Epping NH on 27 May in New Market, ALLEN C Eld *MS* 6 June 1849

HODGDON Andrew J m TEBBETS Hannah both of Dover on Sunday Morning last in Dover NH, CAVERNO A Eld *MS* 5 June 1850

HODGDON Daniel of Hollis m DESHON Eliza of Waterboro *MS* 3 Feb 1832

HODGDON Daniel m WALKER Lucy at Barrington on 10 Dec, SHERBURNE S Eld *MS* 21 Jan 1846

HODGDON Dearborn T m GILMAN Apphia E on 9 Mar in Gilmanton MH, FERNALD S P Eld *MS* 1 May 1844

HODGDON Ebenezer Jr of Ossipee NH m TUTTLE Catharine of Effingham NH on 16th inst, DAVIS J Eld *MS* 27 Mar 1834

HODGDON Elisha of Lebanon ME m HAYES Hannah of Strafford in Strafford, PLACE E Eld *MS* 19 Dec 1838

HODGDON Freeman Capt m NEWBEGIN Mary Elizabeth of Boothbay ME on 14 Dec, ROBINSON N J Eld *MS* 17 Jan 1844

HODGDON James C m GLIDDEN Sarah on 21 Dec 1842 at Roxbury MA, DAVIS Isaac G Eld *MS* 1 Feb 1843

HODGDON John A m CASH Priscilla both of Raymond ME on 16 Apr in Raymond ME, KEENE J Eld Jr *MS* 5 May 1846

HODGDON John Capt 2d m DODGE Julia Mrs of Boothbay ME, MORRILL S P Eld *MS* 23 Dec 1846

HODGDON John m LOMBARD Adaline on 2 June at Gorham ME, LIBBY C O Eld *MS* 24 Jul 1844

HODGDON Josiah S m STARBIRD Joan W of Peru at Peru ME, ANDREWS Otis Eld *MS* 12 May 1847

HODGDON Josiah S of L m MOORE Sally in Canterbury NH *MS* 28 June 1827

HODGDON Moses m ROWE Olive both of West Poland on 14 May in West Poland ME, LIBBY James Eld *MS* 3 June 1846

HODGDON William m GRAY Eliza T both of Barrington NH *MS* 11 Jan 1837

HODGE Benjamin B of Sandwich m SMITH Mary A of Sandwich on 26 Nov, BROOKS N Eld *MS* 9 Dec 1846

HODGE Samuel in Ossipee NH m CHICK Mary *MS* 27 Jan 1832

HODGES Charles m PINKHAM Zelinda W both of Hallowell ME in Hallowell, TOBIE E M Eld *MS* 18 Apr 1838

HODGES Levi M m AMEDON Sarah both of Buffalo NY on 18 Nov 1847 in Buffalo NY, PLUMB H N Eld *MS* 19 Apr 1848

HODGES Samuel M m GATES Eliza Ann of Brookfield on 7 Oct at Poolville NY, CARLNER S D Eld *MS* 11 Nov 1846

HODGSDON Hiram m GLIDDEN Abby both of Great Falls NH on 17 Jan 1849 in Great Falls, BROOKS N Eld *MS* 31 Jan 1849

HODSDON Caleb Esq m BOULTON Martha both of Gorham ME, ROLLINS A Eld *MS* 12 Nov 1834

HODSDON William m SPRINGFIELD Drusilla on Apr 14 at Rochester, WALDRON W H Eld *MS* 24 Apr 1844

HODSKIN Benjamin of Rockford MA m PARSONS Amanda M of Biddeford, at Biddeford ME on 5th inst *MFWBR* 21 Jul 1849

HOIT/HOITT

HOITT Amos m PRIEST Lucy both of Weare NH on 5 Dec 1839, MOODY David Eld *MS* 12 Feb 1840

HOITT Benjamin B of Sandwich m QUINBY Caroline E, BROOKS N Eld *MS* 18 June 1845

HOITT Charles W m GOODWIN Eliza A of Lowell on 12th inst at Lowell, CURTIS S Eld *MS* 18 Mar 1846

HOITT David m FOSS Mary D both of Northwood on 20 Nov Thurs at Northwood, CILLEY D P Eld *MS* 26 Nov 1834

HOITT Enoch P m WIGGINS Mary Ann both of New Market NH on 15 ult in Dover, HUTCHINS E Eld *MS* 22 Nov 1848

HOITT James W of Northwood m CLARK Ellen B of N Market on 22 Dec at N Market, HUTCHINS E Eld *MS* 28 Dec 1842

HOITT Jeremiah B of Manchester NH m MAGOON Angeline on 17 Dec at Durham, FROST D S Eld *MS* 24 Dec 1845

HOITT Joseph of Gilmanton on 5th inst m BROOKS Sophia G of Wakefield at Meredith Bridge, BROOKS N Eld *MS* 23 Feb 1842

HOITT Nathan B m BENNETT Emely Ann on 19 ult, CILLEY D P Eld *MS* 9 Dec 1835

HOITT Nathan m HOOK Sally at Danville, FULLENTON J Eld *MS* 25 Mar 1840

HOITT Silvester m HALE Susan C of Vienna on 20th at Vienna ME?, EDGCOMB J Eld *MS* 16 Apr 1845

HOITT W H A m SWAIN Sarah C of New Market on 30th ult at New Market, HUTCHINS E Eld *MS* 5 Apr 1843

HOLBROOK Abram m SMITH Sarah on 20th inst at Walworth NY, HOLMES D G Eld *MS* 21 Jul 1847

HOLCOMB Simeon L m KENNEDY Martha both of Albia Village on 18 ult in West Stephentown NY, COLEMAN I B Eld *MS* 4 Sept 1850

HOLLIS Stephen I of Nassau m COONS C Lavantia of Sand Lake NY on 26 Feb 1848 in Sand Lake NY, COLEMAN I B Eld *MS* 12 Apr 1848

HOLLISTER Michael of Leon Cattaraugus Co NY m STEELE Esther of Boston NY, LIGHTHALL W A Eld *MS* 24 Mar 1847

HOLMAN S C of Boston MA m EMERY Sarah E, JUDD Rev on 11th inst *MFWBR* 24 Mar 1849

HOLMES Charles m GAGE Lydia, LEWIS Daniel B Eld at Waterville ME *MS* 15 Mar 1837

HOLMES Daniel G correction m CURRIER Huldah B both of Lowell MA *MS* 8 June 1836

HOLMES Elias B m CONE/CANE Susan on 9 Mar 1843 at Thornton NH, McMURPHY B H Eld *MS* 26 Apr 1843

HOLMES Elias B at Thornton m CONE/CANE Susan "erroneously printed CANE in our paper of week before last", McMURPHY B H Eld *MS* 10 May 1843

HOLMES Frederick of Derby VT m LEE Sarah W of Stanstead LC on June 25, MOULTON Abial Eld *MS* 1 Jan 1840

HOLMES George W m SMALL Orrilla L both of Hopkinson NH? on 12 Mar *MS* 8 May 1844

HOLMES Hiram Eld of Epsom NH m BROWN Susanna of Weare NH on 19 Oct in Weare, MOODY D Eld *MS* 13 Dec 1837

HOLMES Isaac of Dedham m DANFORTH Hannah of Somerville at Charleston MA, JACKSON Daniel Eld *MS* 24 May 1843

HOLMES James R President of the Portland Washingtonian Society m MITCHELL Theodosia on 5th inst at Portland ME m MOULTON A K Eld *MS* 15 Feb 1843

HOLMES John of Cornish m KIMBALL Hannah of Cornish in Cornish, LIBY Elias Eld *MS* 14 Dec 1826

HOLT Amos m PRIEST Lucy D both of Weare on Dec 5, MOODY David Eld *MS* 12 Feb 1840

HOLT Asa m BUZWELL Ann Mrs on 12 Aug in Dover, CLARK M Eld *MS* 26 Aug 1846

HOLT Daniel 2d of Pembroke m LEAVITT Hannah of Candia on 16 Nov 1848 in Manchester, CILLEY D P Eld *MS* 6 Dec 1848

HOLT Daniel m RANDELL Sarah both of New Market Lamprey River NH on 19 inst *MS* 1 Feb 1837

HOLT Henry S of Saco ME m MERROW Hannah W of Saco ME on 6 Oct, TRUE E Eld *MS* 15 Oct 1845

HOLT Horace m MAXFIELD Nancy E on 19 Mar, CILLEY D P Eld *MS* 26 Mar 1845

HOLT Luther of Exeter ME m SKINNER Cordelia K on 18 Jan 1847 at Garland ME, AMES M Eld *MS* 14 Apr 1847

HOLT Samuel W of Portland ME m PROCTOR Frances E, BROWN S E Eld on 27th ult at Portland ME *MFWBR* 6 Jul 1850

HOLT Stephen at Epping NH m JENNESS Mary Ann, HANSCOM P Eld *MS* 8 Dec 1841

HOLT Timothy K of Tewksbury m KIDDER Mary Ann on 13 Oct at Wilmington MA, DURGIN J M Eld *MS* 22 Feb 1843

HOLYOKE Joseph of Brewer m SMITH Eunice W of Brownville ME in Brewer ME, DOLE Rev Mr *MS* 15 Apr 1846

HOMBLEY Charles of Tiverton RI m HEALEY Rachel on 23 Oct at Little Compton RI, WHITTAMORE Joseph *MS* 8 Nov 1843

HOMES John H m CROCKET Mary Ann both of Buxton ME on 17 Jan 1848 in West Buxton ME *MS* 15 Mar 1848

HONLETT John 2d m STILES Susan H on 6 Jan 1843 at Bradford, HOLMES H Eld *MS* 20 Sept 1843

HOOD Charles m BRADSHAW Sarah of Chelsea on 21 Mar at Chelsea VT, SANBORN G Eld *MS* 6 Apr 1847

HOOK Abraham of Chester NH m SMITH Susan B at Manchester NH on 2 Aug, CILLEY D P Eld *MS* 9 Aug 1843

HOOK James m SANBORN Lavina in Danville, FULLONTON J Eld *MS* 20 Sept 1837

HOOK James of Concord m HOWE Harriet N of Canterbury on 28th ult, PATRICK William Rev *MS* 11 Feb 1835

HOOPER James G of South Berwick ME m TATTERSON Hannah on 10 Feb, TRUE E Eld *MS* 25 Feb 1846

HOOPER John of Waterboro m DAVIS Emily of Standish ME on 12th inst at Standish, HARRIS A D Rev *MFWBR* 21 Apr 1849

HOOPER Lyman m STANLEY Julia of Shapleigh on 18 Jan, RAMSEY G P Eld *MS* 28 Jan 1846

HOOPER Peter m ROBBINS Maria H both of Great Falls NH on 1 Oct Great Falls, BROOKS N Eld at *MS* 18 Oct 1848

HOOPER Robinson of Shapleigh ME m STANLEY Lovia Jane on 28 Nov, LORD D H Eld *MS* 11 Dec 1839

HOPE George W m BLANCHARD Mary F in Manchester, CILEY D P
Eld *MS* 1 May 1844

HOPE Royal M m CURRIER Lois M on 28 Sept at Manchester,
CILLEY D P Eld *MS* 10 Oct 1844

HOPKINS C Capt m PROUTY Eliza of Stanstead LC on Feb 14?,
MOULTON A Eld *MS* 13 Sept 1843

HOPKINS Gamaliel C m GROVER Rhoda of Kilmarhock ME on 14
Dec *MS* 1 Feb 1837

HOPKINS Simeon m PEACOCK Mary Ann on 30 Oct at Litchfield
ME, FOSS Alvin W Eld *MS* 4 Jan 1843

HOR Joseph of Lovel m FLINT Dorothy C Mrs of Sweden on 3 Mar,
PIKE John Eld *MS* 3 Apr 1850

HOR Lewis F m OTIS Hannah L, MEADER Jesse Eld on 4th Jul at
Rochester *MS* 24 Jul 1839

HORN - see MERRILL

HORN Aldin of Fairfield ME m WITHAM Katharine of Dearborn ME
at Waterville ME *MS* 15 Mar 1837

HORN Amasa m QUINBY Lydia on 3 Mar at Sandwich, MERRILL
William S Eld *MS* 19 June 1844

HORN Andres J m HAMILTON Martha C on 2d inst both of Dover
NH, THURSTON Nathaniel Eld *MS* 20 June 1833

HORN Benjamin m CHATMAN Mary both of Alexandria NH on 14
Mar 1850 in Alexandria NH, BROWN A Eld *MS* 27 mar 1850

HORN David J Capt of Lebanon m ROBINSON Abba G of Limington
ME, STEVENS T Eld *MS* 14 Jul 1847

HORN Gershom m HORN Eleanor at Dover NH, THURSTON Nathaniel Eld *MS* 25 Apr 1833

HORN Ira m MASON Eliza D at Wolfboro NH, COLBY John T G Eld
MS 17 Feb 1836

HORN John of Fairfield ME m GAGE Athala of Smithfield ME at
Smithfield ME, LEWIS D B Eld *MS* 20 Apr 1842

HORN Noah of Wakefield NH m SWETT Mary of Great Falls NH on
17 Oct at Great Falls NH, CURTIS S Eld *MS* 9 Nov 1842

HORN Richard of Roxbury MA m MERRILL Cynthia of Parsonsfield
ME on 16th inst in Parsonsfield ME, BUSSELL John Eld *MS* 19
Jan 1842

HORN Thomas of Smithfield ME m HUSSEY Cordelia of Smithfield
ME, LEWIS D B Eld *MS* 20 Apr 1842

HORN Thomas m WATSON Lucy of Dover NH on 10th inst at Dover
NH, HUTCHINS E Eld *MS* 18 June 1845

HORNE Jeremiah at Tuftonboro' m CANNEY Anne *MS* 6 Mar 1834

HORNE John 2d m ROBERTS Eunice of Dover on 6th inst at Dover
NH *MS* 17 Aug 1842

HORNE Jonathan W of Farmington m BODDGE Martha S of Rochester, WALDRON W H Eld *MS* 13 Sept 1843

HORNE Samuel F m PEARL Nancy both of Farmington NH on 25

HORNE (Continued)

Nov 1847 in Alton NH, PINKHAM J Eld *MS* 2 Feb 1848

HORSON Joseph m GOODWIN Nancy on 3d ult at Lebanon, PREBLE Thomas M Eld *MS* 17 Apr 1839

HORTON Simon of Grafton on 14 Apr m PURMORT Polly M of Enfield in Enfield, SMITH C H Eld *MS* 1 May 1844

HOIT Nathan m HOOK Sally N in Danville, FULLONTON J Eld *MS* 25 Mar 1840

HOUGH James R m HUBBARD Celynda F in Dover NH, SMITH Eleazer Rev *MS* 6 Dec 1837

HOUGHTALING William of Davenport m WHITE Margaret of Meredith NY on 2 May 1850 in Meredith NY, GREEN D Eld *MS* 5 June 1850

HOULTON William of Boothbay m FOYE Aphia H of Wiscasset on 6 Dec 1849 in Edgecomb, PAGE E G Eld *MS* 15 May 1850

HOUSE James L of Biddeford m BRYANT Belinda of Saco on 12 Jul, JACKSON Daniel Eld *MS* 30 Sept 1846 & *MS* 6 Apr 1847

HOUSTON Henry C m PACKARD Sally on 14 Jul at Thornton MA, DURGIN George W Esq *MS* 4 Sept 1844

HOVEY Chaney of Holland VT? m BISHOP Persis D of Holland VT on 24 Mar *MS* 1 May 1844

HOVEY Lewis P m PREBLE Catharine both of Hallowell on 7 Sept in Hallowell, TOBIE E M Eld *MS* 4 Oct 1837

HOVEY Lewis P m PEARSONS Abba C of Hallowell ME on 26 June at Hallowell ME, WEAVER Phillip Eld *MS* 24 Jul 1844

HOVEY Thomas C m DAVIS Naomi on 9 inst in Dover, HUTCHINS E Eld *MS* 17 Jul 1850

HOW George m BICKFORD Mary both of Parsonsfield ME, FOSS Eld *MS* 10 Mar 1830

HOW Josiah S of Dracutt MA m LANGLEY Betsey H on 30 June at Lowell MA, THURSTON N Eld *MS* 2 Nov 1842

HOW Orrin m SMALL Nancy of Bath ME on 9 March 1843 at Bath ME, SMITH O W Eld *MS* 22 Mar 1843

HOW Otis of Unity m COFFIN Phebe of Thorndike on 26th Apr, HIGGINS J Eld *MS* 1 June 1831

HOWARD Andrew P printer m JONES Rebecca in Dover NH on Thurs eve last, MACK Enoch Eld *MS* 5 Feb 1840

HOWARD George W m OTIS Sarah Ann on 8 Apr at Strafford, PLACE E Eld *MS* 16 Apr 1845

HOWARD Henry W m HURD Sarah A both of Great Falls NH on 12 Jan, BROOKS N Eld *MS* 22 Jan 1851

HOWARD Joseph Esq of Limerick m DANA Maria A at Fryeburg, HURD Carlton Rev *MS* 28 Dec 1826

HOWARD Luke m THAYER Hannah on 1 Dec 1842 at Landaff (NH?), GASKILL Silas Eld *MS* 19 Apr 1843

HOWARD Luther L m HUSSEY Sarah P both of Manchester on 29

HOWARD (Continued)
Mar in Manchester, CILLEY D P Eld *MS* 15 Apr 1846

HOWARD Orrin of Pierpont NY m TUPPER Susan on 16 Feb, WHIT-FIELD William Eld *MS* 3 May 1843

HOWARD Paul m HOBBS Sarah on Thurs in Dover NH, WILLIAMS Gibbon Rev *MS* 22 Oct 1834

HOWARD Samuel m WILLIAMS Sophronia E both of Pittsford Mich on 3 June in Pittsford Hillsdale Co Mich, FRAZIER Samuel Eld *MS* 19 Sept 1849

HOWARD William Jr m HARWOOD Alice N on 16th at the 1st FWB church in Charlestown MA, WETHERBEE I J Eld *MS* 3 Dec 1845

HOWE Aaron M Dr m BEAN Eleanor L of Sandwich NH on 31st Jul, BROOKS N Eld *MS* 6 Aug 1845

HOWE Horace F of Dracutt MA m SMITH Caroline on 14 Jul of Lowell MA, WOODMAN J Eld *MS* 19 Oct 1842

HOWE Jonas L of Farmington m NUTTER Abigail of Milton on 29 Dec, AYER Aaron Eld *MS* 8 Jan 1845

HOWE Joseph S m AYER Nancy both of Lowell in Lowell MA, THURSTON Nathaniel Eld *MS* 18 Oct 1837

HOWE Lewis of Fryburg m WATERHOUSE Sarah C of Sweden ME on 31 Jan 1849 in Sweden ME, PIKE J Eld *MS* 25 Apr 1849

HOWE William m WENTWORTH Margaret on 24 March at Jackson, CROSS Eld *MS* 7 Jul 1847

HOWEL Uriah m SMITH Nancy both of Yorkshire on Feb 18 1848 in Yorkshire NY, FLYNN W H Eld *MS* 10 May 1848

HOWLAND Charles W m SMITH Mary C both of Manchester on 26 Apr in Manchester, CILLEY D P Eld *MS* 5 May 1846

HOWLAND Richardson m QUINBY Martha both of Lisbon ME on 10 June 1847 in Lisbon ME, PETTENGILL John Eld *MS* 29 Dec 1847

HOYLE Asa m ALDERMAN Clarinda on 3 Jul at Middlebury NY, ROLLIN D M L Eld *MS* 10 Aug 1842

HOYT Avery A of Spring Prairie m HOYT Caroline of Rochester on 2 June at Rochester WT, COOMBS A Eld *MS* 14 Jul 1847

HOYT Francis F of Concord m SWAIN Arvilla A of Meredith on 25 June, PITMAN Stephen J Eld *MS* 26 Sept 1849

HOYT George F m SEVERANCE Mary Ann *MS* 10 Aug 1836

HOYT Joseph of Lyndon m SARGENT Sarah Jane of Danville on 28 May, GEORGE N K Eld *MS* 24 Feb 1847

HOYT Luther m HILL Betsey of Sheffield on 26 Nov at North Danville VT, GEORGE N K Eld *MS* 21 Jan 1846

HOYT Simeon of Meredith village m KNIGHT Abigail of Franconia on Sept 10, WITHAM L H Eld *MS* 13 Mar 1844

HOYT T Oliver m FRISBEE Jane of Kittery on Christmas eve at Kittery ME, WETHERBY I J Eld *MS* 11 Jan 1843

HOYT William of Tuftonboro' m CORSON Margaret of New Durham NH on 15 Sept 1844, BUZZELL H D Eld *MS* 19 Feb 1845

HOYT James m SIBLEY Clerrinda J both of Hopkinton on 3d inst, MOODY David Eld *MS* 13 Apr 1836

HUBBARD Aaron of Acton ME m LINSEY Polly *MS* 8 May 1844

HUBBARD Boyd of Alna m BAILEY Sarah of Woolwich ME on 17th ult, PERKINS Seth Eld *MS* 13 Feb 1839

HUBBARD Charles P MD of Passadumkeag ME? m PAGE Dorothy C on 8 Oct at Burlington ME, MURCH Dr (the postage on this notice was not paid) *MS* 19 Nov 1845

HUBBARD George I m CROSBEE Cornelia B on 3 Oct at Grafton MA *MS* 18 Oct 1843

HUBBARD James of Acton ME m ADAMS Hannah of Dover NH (Dover) last week, THURSTON N Eld *MS* 11 June 1834

HUBBARD John m MORGAN Deborah both of Dover NH *MS* 2 Sept 1835

HUBBELL Bishop B m DOPKINS Serena on 4th in Virgil, GARDNER L G Eld *MS* 15 Jan 1845

HUCKINS Daniel C m BROWN Abigail C of Dracut MA on 11 Sept at Lowell MA, THURSTON N Eld *MS* 2 Nov 1842

HUCKINS Ferdinand A of Effingham m JEWELL Nancy S of Tamworth NH on 19 Feb, MERRILL W S Eld *MS* 15 Mar 1843

HUCKINS Jonathan B at Meredith NH m SMITH Dorcas *MS* 24 Aug 1836

HUCKINS Randall m MEADER Betsey at Lowell MA *MS* 3 May 1843

HUCKINS Warren m MOULTON Lucretia Ann of Holderness on 7 Sept of Center Harbor, TRUE E Eld *MS* 16 Oct 1844

HUFF Charles W of Edgecomb m LEWIS Emily J of Boothbay in Boothbay ME, PAGE E G Eld *MS* 27 Nov 1850

HUFF Eben A m YORK Sarah A of Kennebunk on 12 Oct at Kennebunk ME, PERKINS S W Eld *MS* 27 Nov 1844

HUFF Ebenezer S m EARL Almira of Buxton ME on 16 Apr 1848 in Buxton ME *MS* 3 May 1848

HUFF Joseph Jr m BAILEY Eliza W at Gardiner ME *MFWBR* 17 Mar 1849

HUFF Thomas of Saco ME m YOUNG Eunice of Hollis ME on 30th ult in Hollis, ROBERT Rev Mr *MS* 4 Oct 1827

HUGGINS Nathaniel N m GOSS Sarah S in Boston, NOYES E Eld *MS* 2 Feb 1848

HUGHES Daniel of Winterford VT m HOIT Julia A of Whitefield NH on 4 Oct at Bethlehem NH, BEAN Beniah Eld *MS* 4 Jan 1843

HULETT Arnold m BROWN Unity of Dresden NY in Dresden New York, CHASE William P Eld *MS* 14 Feb 1838

HULL William of Crawford Co PA m DODGE Samantha of New Lyme on 17 Nov 1847 in New Lyme, HYDE Nelson Esq *MS* 29 Dec 1847

HUMHREY Jonas m DOLLY Lydia Miss both of Gray ME on 18th ult, PURKIS J Eld *MS* 3 Jan 1833

HUMPHREY Charles m SHIPMAN Maria of Bangor ME on 20 Jan at

HUMPHREY (Continued)
Bangor ME, SKILLIN Hiram Eld *MS* 4 Mar 1846

HUMPHREY William m PENNER Delia Ann both of Whitestown NY on New Years Eve in Whitestown NY, TALLMAN E P Eld *MS* 1 May 1850

HUNKINS Moses L of Manchester NH m JAMES Almira on 5 Dec, CURTIS S Eld *MS* 18 Dec 1844

HUNNAWILL Godfrey of Danville ME m KILBY Harriet of Freeport ME on 9 Feb at Freeport ME, PURINTON A W Eld *MS* 25 Feb 1846

HUNNEWELL James m FISH Mary Jane on 25 Oct 1846 at Woolwich, JORDAN Z Eld *MS* 13 Jan 1847

HUNT Albert m RUSSELL Mary Ann of Woodstock on 11 Jan in Woodstock, RUSSELL G W Eld *MS* 29 Jan 1851

HUNT Elias of Lincoln m GOVE Selina B of Readfield ME on 21 March at Readfield ME, BEAN G H Eld *MS* 31 Mar 1847

HUNT Franklin m LIBBY Mary of Biddeford ME at Saco ME on 6th inst *MFWBR* 12 June 1847

HUNT Hiram of Gilford m MERRILL Cyrena of Gilford on 23 Nov, COOLEY John D Eld *MS* 25 Jan 1843

HUNT James M m WEBSTER Sarah A C of Gray ME on 2 Nov, PERKINS S W Eld *MS* 17 Jan 1844

HUNT James S m SKOFFIELD Hannah M both of Brunswick ME on 8 Nov in Brunswick ME, LIBBY A Eld *MS* 23 Jan 1850

HUNT Jason at Gilford m GREEN Susan, PINKHAM J Eld *MS* 13 Dec 1843

HUNT Jeremiah Jr m WOODSIDE Salome G on 6th Mar at Brunswick ME, CROWELL E Eld *MS* 26 Apr 1843

HUNT John of Unity ME m CHANDLER Amanda M, LEWIS Daniel B Eld *MS* 21 Jan 1846

HUNT Mr N K m LEAVITT Sarah C on 27 Nov at Wolfborough, COLBY Eld *MS* 24 Dec 1845

HUNT Randall m SKINNER Phebe on 28 Oct 1847 in Norwich NY, CRANDALL J M Eld *MS* 19 Jan 1848

HUNT Ripley m LESTER Hila both of Nassau NY on 10 June in Nassau NY, COLEMAN I B Eld *MS* 22 Jul 1846

HUNT Robert G m MELCHER Sarah both of Brunswick on 15 Dec 1837 in Brunswick ME, ROLLINS Andrew Eld *MS* 21 Feb 1838

HUNT Stephen m LANE Mahala M on 27 Oct at Gilmanton NH, KNOWLES E G Eld *MS* 1 Jan 1845

HUNT Virgil O of Hiram Ohio m NORTON Mary S of Huntington VT on 3 Oct in Huntington VT, DIKE Orange Eld *MS* 6 Nov 1850

HUNTER Benjamin m SAYWARD Jane on 21 Feb of Lowell MA, WOODMAN J Eld *MS* 23 Aug 1843

HUNTER Manly m DARLING Mary J on 10 Jan at Manchester Iowa (Territory), HATHORN S Eld *MS* 27 Feb 1839

HUNTING Josiah H m BUNKER Lydia D on 18th of Charleston ME,

HUNTING (Continued)

AMES Moses Eld *MS* 29 Jan 1845

HUNTINGTON George W of Atkinson ME m POTTER Almira J of Lowell in Lowell, CURTIS S Eld *MS* 6 Dec 1848

HUNTINGTON James m BURBANK Rachel C both of Limerick? on 2 inst in Dracut MA, CURTIS S Eld *MS* 13 May 1846

HUNTINGTON Uriah m LEAVITT Emeline C both of Richmond ME on 7 Dec 1837 in Richmond ME, SWETT J Eld *MS* 7 Mar 1838

HUNTLEY Alson m BLODGETT Theoda both of Mooers NY in Mooers NY, BUNDY Benja Eld *MS* 23 Jan 1850

HUNTOON Peter of Waterville ME m EMERSON Hannah C of Fairfield ME, BURGESS J S Eld *MS* 14 Jul 1847

HUNTOON Warner of Bridgewater VT m NEWTON Almedia E on 6 Oct at Franconia NH, GEORGE N K Eld *MS* 21 Jan 1846

HUNTRESS Hubbard H of New Market m BANKS Hannah B of Nottingham NH, SHERBURNE S Eld *MS* 25 May 1842

HUNTRESS James K m KNIGHT Eunice on 31 Aug at Waterboro' ME, EMERY R Eld *MS* 1 Oct 1845

HUNTRESS Joseph MD m SARGENT Orra Ann on 9 Oct at Sandwich NH, BROOKS N Eld *MS* 15 Oct 1845

HUNTRESS Willard L m REYNOLDS Mary Jane of Lowell, THURSTON Nathaniel Eld *MS* 22 May 1839

HUNTRESS William C of Centre Harbor NH m PRESCOTT Laura of Meredith NH on 18th inst at Lowell MA, THURSTON N Eld *MS* 29 May 1839

HURD Amos H of Lowell MA m EDGERLY Betsey B of Great Falls NH on 23 ult, SMITH E Rev *MS* 9 Nov 1836

HURD Benjamin C m WAYMOUTH Olive Ann of North Berwick ME on Thanksgiving day at Lebanon, LORD D H Eld *MS* 8 Dec 1841

HURD Henry L m TIBBETS Mary A both of Alton on 6 Oct in Barnstead, GARLAND David Eld *MS* 6 Nov 1850

HURD Hiram S m MERRILL Hannah at Acton ME, FULLONTON J Eld *MS* 3 Jul 1844

HURD Jeremiah E m STEVENS Abigail on 23d ult at Lowell, THURSTON Nathaniel Eld *MS* 6 Feb 1839

HURD Jesse of New Durham NH m CLARK Eleanor of Dover on 13 Jan, DOW J M H Rev *MS* 20 Jan 1847

HURD John of Berwick m GUPPY Sophia of Rochester on 29th ult at Great Falls, CAVERNO Eld *MS* 7 May 1834

HURD John of Newfield m TUCKER Caroline of Ossipee NH on 7 inst in Ossipee, WALKER John Eld *MS* 27 Dec 1837

HURD John of Wendell m ROWEL Aurilla A of Goshen on 7 Mar 1850, EMERY A Eld *MS* 27 Mar 1850

HURD John S Esq of Farmington m BREWSTER Joanna H of Wolfborough NH on 16 Nov 1848 in Alton NH, PINKHAM John Eld *MS* 20 Dec 1848

HURD John W m STAPLES Harriet N of N Berwick ME on 14 Jan 1848 in North Berwick ME, CLAY D Eld *MS* 7 Feb 1849

HURD Jonathan B m GOODWIN Harriet both of Lowell on 11 Nov in Lowell, CURTIS S Eld *MS* 15 Dec 1847

HURD Peter m STILLINGS Mary of New Berwick on 12 Apr at Berwick ME, HOBBS A W Eld *MS* 20 Jan 1847

HURD Robert of Newport LC m BUNKER Sarah of Corinna ME on 13th inst, NASON Eld *MS* 30 Mar 1836

HURD Stephen N m WEBSTER Sarah J at Lowell MA, CURTIS S Eld *MS* 12 Nov 1845

HUREN Harmon m CORLIS Hannah G both of So Weare on 18 Jul 1847 in So Weare, MOODY D Eld *MS* 15 Sept 1847

HURSOM Benjamin m WITHAM Lovina Miss both of Dearborn ME at Waterville ME, LEWIS Daniel B *MS* 24 FEb 1836

HUSE Ebenezer ae 70y m SPEARS Elizabeth of Weare NH on 18th inst, HARRIMAN David Eld *MS* 25 apr 1833

HUSE Jesse of Lowell MA m BLANCHARD Rhoda on 10th, CURTIS S Eld *MS* 24 Feb 1847

HUSSEY Albert m WHITEHOUSE Elizabeth A of Lowell MA at Dracut MA, CURTIS S Eld *MS* 26 Nov 1845

HUSSEY John of Exeter ME m LOCK Mary of Great Falls NH on Sunday last, THURSTON N Eld *MS* 27 Aug 1834

HUSSEY John of Rochester m HANSON Abby E of Farmington on 3 inst, PLACE E Eld in Strafford *MS* 20 Nov 1850

HUSSEY Samuel m GLEASON Ann of Waterville ME, LEWIS Daniel B Eld *MS* 23 Jan 1839

HUSSEY William M m GOLATHWRIT [sic] Mary E on 14 Aug 1843 at Biddeford ME, WITHAM L H Eld *MS* 23 Aug 1843 & m GOLATT-WRIGHT [sic] Mary E of Biddeford, by WITHAM L H Eld *MS* 13 Mar 1844

HUSTEN Elijah m BLAKE Jane S both of New Gloucester on 28 June in New Gloucester ME, MORRELL F Eld *MS* 2 Sept 1846

HUTCHES John m CLARK Martha on 29 Nov at Putney NY, ARNOLD S H Esq *MS* 20 Dec 1843

HUTCHINGS John of Whitefield m SHERMAN Elizabeth on 2 Feb 1843 at Boothbay, PAGE E G Eld *MS* 1 Mar 1843

HUTCHINS Eias Eld m MARKS Marilla on 24th inst at Dover NH, DUNN Ransom Eld *MS* 30 Dec 1846

HUTCHINS Elias Eld m AMBROSE Lucy, PINKHAM J Eld all of Sandwich NH *MS* 20 Apr 1832

HUTCHINS Jeremiah of Fryeburg on 27 Nov 1843, HUBBARD Sarah D, PIKE John Eld *MS* 31 Jan 1844

HUTCHINS John L m TEWKSBURY Mary, HATHAWAY L Eld both of Atkinson ME *MS* 13 Feb 1834

HUTCHINS Solomon m CUSHING Sally Ann both of Wakefield on 25 Oct in Wakefield, SPINNEY Joseph Eld *MS* 21 Nov 1838

HUTCHINS William m STEARNS Mary H of Lovell on 11th inst, GAMMON E H Rev *MFWBR* 27 Apr 1850

HUTCHINS William B of Stewartstown m WHEEDEN Rachel E of Whitefield NH on 29 Nov in Whitefield, SHEPHERD Almon Eld NH *MS* 26 Dec 1849

HUTCHINSON Almon of Milan NH m WITHAM Martha M of Saco on 4 Jul at Kennebunkport ME, WITHAM L H Eld *MS* 13 June 1842

HUTCHINSON Asa Dea of Fayette ME m TUXBURY Hannah B of Salisbury MA on 4th inst, SHAW Elijah Eld *MS* 17 Sept 1834

HUTCHINSON Asa F of Bridgton m FRANK Elenor of Poland ME on 15 Oct in Minot ME, WHEELER A Eld *MS* 23 Oct 1850

HUTCHINSON Daniel of Turner ME m LIBBY Mary B of Poland ME on 2 Jul at West Poland ME, LIBBY James Eld *MS* 10 Feb 1847

HUTCHINSON Ebenezer (a licensed preacher in Otisfield QM) m DYER Frances B of Cape Elizabeth ME on 30 June, HERSEY L Eld *MS* 20 June 1842

HUTCHINSON James H of Dixfield ME m DAVIS Martha of Fayette ME on 24th ult, CURTIS S Eld *MS* 30 Mar 1831

HUTCHINSON Joseph of Hebron m DAVIS Celia A of Peru ME on 21 Apr, WOODSUM William Eld *MS* 15 May 1839

HUTCHINSON Orin m PARKER Sarah Maria on 13 May at Dracut MA, CURTIS S Eld *MS* 2 June 1847

HYDE Daniel A m PIPER Livonia D of Alton NH on 11 Jan, BUZZELL H D Eld *MS* 3 Mar 1847

HYDE Daniel m MATHES Mary Mrs of Ossipee NH on 24 June at Ossipee NH, CHICK J Eld *MS* 13 Sept 1843

IDE Frederick of Newpond LC? m GLOVER Atlanta of Burford LC? on 23 Oct, MOULTON Abial Eld *MS* 1 Jan 1840

ILLSLEY George of Thetford VT m AKERS Sarah A of Errol NH on 7 Feb 1849 in Strafford VT, CLARK E Eld *MS* 6 June 1849

ILSLEY Isaac m ILSELY Clementina Miss in Limerick ME , KINSMAN E P Eld *MS* 12 Apr 1827

ILSLEY Jeremiah of Portland ME m McDONALD Sarah of Limerick ME, FREEMAN C Rev *MS* 9 Mar 1831

INGALLS George I m NEWELL Hannah E both of Attleborough MA on 14 May, CLARKE G Eld in Attleborough *MS* 1 May 1850

INGALLS John C of Rochester m COLBY Emily T of Danville NH on 16 ult, PERKINS J Rev *MS* 1 Mar 1837

INGALS Jonathan m STEARNS Hannah M both of Goshen on 28 Feb 1850, EMERY A Eld *MS* 27 Mar 1850

INGERSOL Byron m CHASE Anna on 11 Sept at Warsaw NY, ROLLIN M L Eld *MS* 20 Nov 1844

INGLASS Spafford of Bridgton m WITHAM Sophronia R of Harrison ME on 25 inst in Harrison ME, PEIRCE Geo Esq *MS* 5 Jul 1848

IRELAND Osbert A of Stetson ME? m ELLIOT Dolly of Corinna ME

IRELAND (Continued)
on 28 Feb 1839 at Corinna, COPP J B Eld *MS* 24 Apr 1839

IRISH Dean of Limerick ME m SMALL Mehitabel of Limerick ME, BURBANK S Eld *MS* 7 Dec 1826

IRISH Levi at Waldo PLT ME m CALDERWOOD Lydia of Waldo PLT ME, WARD Cotton Esq *MS* 15 Jan 1845

IVES G W M on 5 Aug m WEATHERVEE Caroline E in Rochester, WHITCHER Eld *MS* 26 Sept 1849

JACK Nathan m WITHAM Abigail Maria both of Thorndike ME on 2 Jul in Thorndike ME, ROBINSON N J Eld *MS* 12 Aug 1846

JACKMAN Frederick B m GORDON Julia Ann at Lowell MA *MS* 8 Feb 1837

JACKMAN Richard m GILMAN Lydia on 2 Feb 1843, GASKILL Silas Eld *MS* 19 Apr 1843

JACKSON Abel G m BRANNEN Julia A both of Lewiston ME on 26 Dec 1847 in Lewiston ME, WILLEY E C Eld *MS* 23 Feb 1848

JACKSON Daniel Eld of Ossipee NH m KENNISON Mary of Eaton NH *MS* 4 Oct 1827

JACKSON Ivory of Eaton m ALLARD Adaline of Eaton, GASKILL S Eld *MS* 21 Jan 1846

JACKSON Leonard Esq m ANNAN Mary H Mrs both of Manchester on 31 Oct 1847 in Manchester, CILLEY D P Eld *MS* 10 Nov 1847

JACKSON Richard of Harrison m BARKER Irene H of Naples at Naples ME, EATON E G Eld *MS* 27 June 1842

JACKSON Wm W m RANDALL Elizabeth both of New Market on 21 Nov at Lamprey River, CILLEY D P Eld *MS* 2 Dec 1835

JACOB Charles R m JACOBS Ann both of Bridgeton *MS* 21 Dec 1836

JACOBS Moses m DOCKHAM Mary Ann of Saco on 22 Dec at Saco ME, RAND J Eld *MS* 5 Feb 1845

JAMES Alonzo G of Deerfield m KNOWLTON Eliza A of Northwood on 16 Nov 1848, JOHNSON W D Eld *MS* 29 Nov 1848

JAMES Annis C of Gilford m WEEKS Betsey, PINKHAM J Eld *MS* 13 Dec 1843

JAMES Charles A m HOLMES Adaline B of Dover NH on 26 Nov (Thanksgiving day), CILLEY D P Eld at Manchester NH *MS* 9 Dec 1846

JAMES Edward m WOODSIDE Caroline in Durham, LIBBY A Eld ME *MS* 12 Mar 1851

JAMES Ira H of Gilford m FREESE Augusta A of Moultonborough NH, BROOKS N Eld *MS* 29 Jan 1845

JAMES Ira of Hampton m LEAVITT Dolly of No Hampton on 2 Apr 1848 in Hampton, BURBANK P S Eld *MS* 12 Apr 1848

JAMES Isaiah Dea of Dearborn ME m OTIS Abigail P of Fairfield ME, LEWIS Daniel B Eld *MS* 30 Nov 1842

JAMES Jonathan L of Danville m GEORGE Sarah on 30 Nov,
FULLONTON J Eld *MS* 15 Dec 1841

JAMES Mortimer of Stephentown m HAYES Helen of Nassau on 5
Aug 1848 in Sand Lake NY, COLEMAN I Eld *MS* 11 Oct 1848

JAMES Moses G Lt of Northwood m HILL Dorothy S of Deerfield at
Deerfield, STEARNS Samuel Eld *MS* 12 Mar 1845

JAMES Samuel Jr m LAMPREY Martha on 18th ult at Hampton,
BURBANK P S Eld *MS* 30 Nov 1842

JAMES Samuel of Lebanon ME m BLAISDELL Caroline G on 23
May, BLAISDEL E Eld *MS* 23 June 1847

JAMES Samuel S Capt m HILL Martha G on 9 Jan at Deerfield,
JOHNSON W D Eld *MS* 12 Mar 1845

JAMES William H of Gilford m MARSH Mary J of Gilmanton NH on 4
Aug in Gilford, PINKHAM John Eld *MS* 12 Sept 1838

JAMES William m MORRISON Martha J of Portland ME on 23d inst,
MOULTON A K Eld *MS* 8 Mar 1843

JAMESON J W Col m ALBY Julia Mrs of Windsor ME on 20 Feb,
STEVENS J Eld *MS* 9 Apr 1845

JAMESON Mark of Somersworth NH m PATERSON Dorcas of Saco
ME on 15th inst, NICHOLAS J T G Rev *MFWBR* 24 Feb 1849

JAQUISH Franklin of Freedom m ROWLY Phebe of Yorkshire on 10
Sept in China NY, JACKSON N A Eld *MS* 11 Dec 1850

JARLIN Alron K of Sumner m RECORD Angeline C of Buckfield on 4
Jul *MS* 18 Jul 1849

JARVIS Alvah of Painsville Geauga Co Ohio m SCOTT Hannah M of
New Lyme on 12 Dec 1847, HYDE Nelson Esq in New Lyme *MS* 29
Dec 1847

JASPER Edwin E of Minot m ESTER Olive S of Lewiston ME on 30
Jul 1847 in Lewiston ME, WILLEY E C Eld *MS* 23 Feb 1848

JAY Benson m DUSTAN Aurilla R both of Sutton on Thanksgiving
Day in Sutton VT, RICHARDSON R D Eld *MS* 12 Dec 1849

JEDKINS David B of Lexington m SWIFT Emeline of Fayette, STIL-
SON C Eld *MS* 12 Aug 1835

JEFFERS James of Haverhill m SNOW Anna Mrs of Benton on 26
Dec, MOULTON F Eld *MS* 22 Jan 1845

JEFFERS Sylvester m ELLIOTT Roxana of Haverhill on 7 Feb at
Haverhill NH, MOULTON F Eld *MS* 21 Feb 1844

JEFFERSON Nathaniel W m BARRETT Martha A on 8th ult at
Charlestown, WETHERBEE I J Eld *MS* 9 Dec 1846

JEFFS Algernon P m WALTON Sarah D both of Salem on 24 ult in
Salem MA, COLE M Eld *MS* 27 Nov 1850

JELLESON Abel H m ROBERTS Betsey H both of Saco ME on 25
Aug, JACKSON Daniel Eld *MS* 30 Sept 1846

JELLESON Samuel m HODSDON Nancy both of Waterboro on 1st
inst Tuesday, EMERY Nathaniel *MS* 10 Jan 1833

JENKINS Austin m STEVENS Elizabeth on 26 Nov at Manchester

JENKINS (Continued)
NH, CILLEY D P Eld *MS* 9 Dec 1846

JENKINS George m RUSSELL Lydia J both of Manchester in Manchester, CILLEY D P Eld *MS* 27 Sept 1848

JENKINS Joel m HUTCHINS Jerusha of Goffstown at Manchester NH, CILLEY D P Eld *MS* 9 Dec 1846

JENKINS Leonard m GRAVES Abby A on 9 May in Kittery ME, PERKINS Seth W Eld *MS* 12 June 1850

JENKINS Oliver m WATERHOUSE Elizabeth on Sun eve at Somersworth NH, WILLIAMS Gibbon Rev *MS* 21 Jan 1835

JENKINS Stephen m HILL Sarah Ann K of Madbury on 19th inst at Madbury, MOULTON A K Eld "Cake recieved" *MS* 26 Oct 1842

JENKS Wm B m CATES Elecia both of Oneonta on 5 Dec 1849 in Oneonta NY, CADY S S Eld *MS* 2 Jan 1849

JENNE Alonzo of Hartland VT m HATHAWAY B Roene of Adams MA on 7 Oct in Windsor VT, ADAMS A Eld *MS* 21 Oct 1846

JENNE Seth Allen m BOYER Emeline both of Chester Mich on 12 Dec at Roxand Mich, ALLEN E Eld *MS* 17 Jan 1844

JENNESS Amos m PINKHAM Mary E on Sabbath morning 7 inst in Dover NH, PINKHAM John Eld *MS* 17 Jul 1850

JENNESS Charles of Tamworth m JENNESS Betsey of Meredith in Tamworth NH, MERRIL Wm S Eld *MS* 1 Nov 1848

JENNESS Cyrus m McDUFFEE Mercy of Rochester on 27 June at Rochester, MEADER Jesse Eld *MS* 27 Dec 1843

JENNESS George m HURD Lois E both of Lowell in Lowell, THURSTON Nathaniel Eld *MS* 11 Jul 1838

JENNESS George m CORSON Mary A H both of New Market on 11th inst in Durham, CILLEY D P Eld *MS* 17 Dec 1834

JENNESS Gilman m PLUMER Sarah Jane both of Alton NH on Thanksgiving eve in Dover, PINKHAM John Eld *MS* 28 Nov 1849

JENNESS Hiram m CHESLEY Asenath both of Sheffield VT on 31 Jan Monday *MS* 16 Mar 1836

JENNESS Ira H of Tamworth QUINT Eliza Ann of New Market on 1 Sept in New Market, FROST D S Eld *MS* 30 Sept 1846

JENNESS Isaac Col of Rochester m SANBORN Judith of Brookfield on 9 Oct, PLACE Enoch Eld *MS* 14 Oct 1831

JENNESS John J of Rochester m BERRY Abigail of Strafford, PLACE E Eld *MS* 3 June 1835

JENNESS Jonathan of Meredith NH m SMITH Mary J of Great Falls NH on 4 Oct, DUNN R Eld *MS* 24 Dec 1845

JENNESS Joshua of New Market NH m JENNESS Diantha E on 18th, FROST D S Eld *MS* 28 Apr 1847

JENNESS Luther S of Somersworth m TWOMBLY Susan M on 10 Aug at Alton, PRESCOTT E T Eld *MS* 17 Jan 1844

JENNESS Nathaniel m VARNEY Lydia on 1st inst both of Dover NH, THURSTON N Eld *MS* 9 Jan 1834

JENNESS Robert H of Boston MA m MARDIN Catharine of Wolfboro' NH on 9 Feb 1843, PRESCOTT E T Eld *MS* 24 May 1843

JENNESS Seth m BROCK Esther both of Rochester at Strafford, PLACE Eld *MS* 27 Jan 1836

JENNINGS Isaac of Leeds ME m STEVENS Lucy of Green ME on 13th inst *MS* 30 June 1830

JEPSON Leonard m DAVIS Rosanna on 4th inst at Lewiston ME, WAKEFIELD A Esq *MFWBR* 24 Feb 1849

JEROME Marshall of Berlin NY m HELMNS Aurelia of Stephentown on 1 May in Berlin NY, COLMAN I B Eld *MS* 13 June 1849

JERRIES William H m SMITH Mary S of Portland ME on 9th inst at Portland ME, MOULTON A K Eld *MS* 22 Mar 1843

JESSAMAN Ira of Franconia m YOUNG Betsey of Landaff on 4 May 1848 in Franconia, BLAKE C E Eld *MS* 24 May 1848

JEWELL John m EASTMAN Sarah of Cornish ME on 16 inst at Cornish ME, BURBANK P S Eld *MS* 18 Mar 1846

JEWETT Charles of Denmark ME m SARGEANT Ann of Brownfield ME on 17 Jul, WILLEY Eben C Eld *MS* 25 Jan 1843

JEWETT Florence m DUNTON Sarah K both of Westport ME, QUINNAM C Eld *MS* 7 May 1834

JEWETT H W of Gardiner ME m ATKINS Harriet A. at Gardiner *MFWBR* 14 Sep 1850

JEWETT James merchant m HAYES Sophia P both of Alton NH *MS* 8 Mar 1837

JEWETT Luther Esq of this port m JONES Charlotte P at Ellsworth ME on 1st inst *MFWBR* 11 May 1850

JEWETT Samuel N of Gilford m CATE Mary Jane of Gilmanton on 5 June, MOODY D Eld *MS* 21 Aug 1850

JEWETT Samuel S m JEWETT Edith A both of Gilford on 2 Aug in Gilford, PERKINS Seth W Eld *MS* 2 Sept 1846

JOHNS Joel S of Montpelier m McALLASTER Saphronia E of Stowe VT on 15 Feb 1849 in Stowe VT, M'ALLASTER Harvey Esq *MS* 25 Apr 1849

JOHNS Noble L of Huntington m NICHOLS Mariah S at Huntington, DIKE Orange Eld *MS* 11 Sept 1839

JOHNSON Aaron m QUINT Zabra Ann on 31 Dec at Brownfield ME, HART E H Eld *MS* 12 Feb 1845

JOHNSON Cyrus m NORTON Martha both of Boston NY on 23 Oct 1845, BELKNAP P W Eld *MS* 20 May 1846

JOHNSON Daniel Z m MARR Nancy L both of Topsham ME in Topsham ME, BEAN C Eld *MS* 2 Aug 1848

JOHNSON Dennis m PUGSLEY Lucinda F both of Limington ME on 29 Mar, BURBANK P S Eld *MS* 8 Apr 1846

JOHNSON Ebenezer S m JENKINS Ruth Ann on 7th Jul at Fowler NY, CILLEY D P Eld *MS* 28 Jul 1847

JOHNSON Elijah of Dover m JOHNSON Martha of Great Falls NH on

JOHNSON (Continued)

8 Sept, BROOKS N Eld *MS* 25 Sept 1849

JOHNSON Francis m RANKER Phebe Jane on 30 Aug at Lowell MA, THURSTON N Eld *MS* 2 Nov 1842

JOHNSON George I of Saco m CLARK Isabella P of Portland ME on 13th inst at Portland ME, DWIGHT Rev Dr *MFWBR* 23 June 1849

JOHNSON George of Jackson m GANNETT Jane of Great Falls NH on 2 Jul in Tamworth, AMES Charles G *MS* 17 Jul 1850

JOHNSON George W of Epping m CHAPMAN Sarah E of New Market on 7th inst, HUTCHINS E Eld *MS* 15 Feb 1843

JOHNSON Gowen W m STACKPOLE Eliza Ann on 4th inst at Dover NH, HUTCHINS E Eld *MS* 15 Oct 1845

JOHNSON Isaac m BACHELER Mary both of Franklin MA on 30 Jan, WILLIS S B Rev of So Baptist Church in Providence RI *MS* 20 Feb 1850

JOHNSON James I of Lowell m MILLER E H of Burlington ME on 5 Dec in Burlington ME, TAYLOR A Eld *MS* 29 Dec 1847

JOHNSON James m PROPHET Mariah on 25 inst in Providence RI, LEWIS J W Eld *MS* 5 Jul 1837

JOHNSON Jesse B of Kilmarnock m RALPH Harriet F of La Grange ME on 12 inst in La Grange, COOMBS A Eld *MS* 5 Sept 1838

JOHNSON Jesse m FOLSOM Betsey both of Lowell MA at Lowell MA, THURSTON N Eld *MS* 7 Jan 1835 & *MS* 24 Dec 1834

JOHNSON John m CLARK Elmira on 30th ult at North Berwick ME, TOBIE R B Eld *MFWBR* 9 Oct 1847

JOHNSON John B Esq of Hill m OBER Sylvia H of Manchester on 9 Oct 1848 in Manchester, CILLEY D P Eld *MS* 8 Nov 1848

JOHNSON John P of Concord m CROCKETT Sarah of Meredith on 27 Dec, PITMAN Stephen J Eld *MS* 25 Jan 1843

JOHNSON Jonathan H E of Stowe ME m JOHNSON Sarah E on 14 Nov at Strafford, PLACE E Eld *MS* 27 Nov 1844

JOHNSON Joshua E of Biddeford m LOUGEE Sarah Ann of Parsonsfield on 1 Sept 1848, SMITH Wm Eld in S Parsonsfield ME *MS* 8 Nov 1848

JOHNSON Noah W m BARTLETT Mary J both of Garland ME on 25 Dec 1848, AMES M Eld *MS* 10 Jan 1849

JOHNSON Oloro on 27 Apr m CHOPPEL Lucinda both of Smithfield in Garland ME, BURLINGAME M W Eld *MS* 24 May 1837

JOHNSON Richard at Dover NH m HARRIS Mary both of Somersworth NH *MS* 21 Nov 1833

JOHNSON Samuel m MARSH Sarah on 9 May at Hallowell ME *MS* 5 June 1844

JOHNSON Simon m HUDSON Rachel of Roxbury on 19 Nov at Roxbury, DAVIS J B Eld *MS* 27 Dec 1843

JOHNSON Thomas C m FOSTER Ellen on 20 ult in Sand Lake NY, COLEMAN I B Eld *MS* 12 June 1850

JOHNSON William 3rd of Gorham ME m HOBSON Nancy T of
Buxton ME, CHANEY S Freeman Eld *MS* 5 Jul 1843

JOHNSON William D of Northwood m MASON Louisa Q on 1 Oct,
McMURPHY B H Eld *MS* 16 Oct 1844

JOHNSON Wm M m GAGE Abigail A on 8th inst at Lowell *MS* 28
Sept 1836

JONES Alonzo on 15 March at Mount Pleasant WT, SECOR Rebecca
m BIXBY N W Eld *MS* 14 Apr 1847

JONES Benjamin L of Milbury MA m EDWARD Mehitabel P of Portland ME at Otisfield, WIGHT Joseph Esq *MS* 21 Jan 1846

JONES C P, A B of Genesee & Wyoming Seminary Alexander on 22
ult m NORTON Etta Juliana, HILL H F Rev in Groveland NY *MS* 4
Sept 1850

JONES Charles m HARTFORD Mary both of Dover on 25 inst *MS* 4
Jan 1837

JONES Cyrus Esq m RANDALL Sarah A at Great Falls NH *MFWBR* 1
Sept 1849

JONES Cyrus m MURCH Eliza Ann of Unity on 29 May at Unity,
SKILLIN H Eld *MS* 30 June 1847

JONES Daniel m ESTRUS Huldah both of Milton on 22 Nov 1848 in
Wakefield, SPINNEY Joseph Eld *MS* 3 Jan 1849

JONES Daniel m HEBARD Clarissa of East Randolph VT on 29 Nov
at East Randolph VT, SANBORN G Eld *MS* 4 Jan 1843

JONES David m BRANSON Sarah both of Perry Township Ohio on 4
Jul 1847, HEATH J D Eld in Perry Township, Logan Co Ohio *MS*
9 Feb 1848

JONES Ebenezer m FERNALD Parmelia both of Lebanon on 22 Dec
1849 in Lebanon, LITTLEFIELD William H Eld *MS* 9 Jan 1850

JONES Ebenezer m FOSS Hannah H both of Strafford on 27 Apr *MS*
18 May 1836

JONES Elias O m BROCKWAY Polly on 13 March at Stephentown
NY, COLEMAN I B Eld *MS* 4 Oct 1843

JONES Elijah of Epping m ROBIE Nancy of Raymond in Raymond,
PAGE Rev Mr *MS* 9 Mar 1842

JONES George W of Niles Mich m SMITH Priscilla on 12 Oct,
FELLOWS G Eld *MS* 26 Nov 1845

JONES Gershom m RICKER Mary both of Lebanon ME on 5 Jul in
Lebanon ME, LITTLEFIELD Wm H Eld *MS* 23 Sept 1846

JONES J B of Lewiston Falls ME m NASH Joan M of Minot ME,
LIBBY I Eld *MS* 10 Jul 1839

JONES James D of Gilmanton m WEEKS Sarah A of Canterbury on
23 Apr 1848 in Pittsfield NH, TRUE E Eld *MS* 3 May 1848

JONES James L of Lynn m SCRIBNER Deborah T of Harrison on 9
Oct at Harrison ME, BARROWS Worthy C *MS* 19 Nov 1845

JONES James M of Loudon m LOCKE Huldah P of Chichester on 8
June in Manchester, CILLEY D P Eld *MS* 24 June 1846

JONES Jephthah m WOODRUFF Mehitabel of Billerica MA on 16 May at Wilmington MA, DURGIN J M Eld *MS* 26 June 1844

JONES John G of Boston MA m McCORRISON Olive C of West Buxton on 1st inst at West Buxton, SINCLAIR J L Eld *MS* 11 Sept 1844

JONES John m ROLLINS Mary both of Lee on 16 Dec in Barrington, SHERBURNE S Eld *MS* 15 Jan 1851

JONES John of Somersworth NH m MARSTON Sally recently of Parsonsfield ME on 23d ult, BURBANK S Eld *MS* 11 Jul 1833

JONES John of Somerworth m DREW Lydia M of Alton NH on 15 ult at Barnstead, GEORGE Enos Rev *MS* 2 Dec 1835

JONES Jonathan m PILLSBURY Sarah both of Pittsfield on 9 May in Pittsfield, BEAN S F Eld *MS* 13 June 1838

JONES Joseph B m HALL Ann M of Lowell MA, THURSTON Eld *MS* 25 Sept 1839

JONES Joseph B m BROWN Vilara A L on 5 Oct at Dracut MA, CURTIS S Eld *MS* 6 Jan 1847

JONES Josiah B of Loudon m LEAVITT Mary of Gilmanton on 20th ult, CARLTON Eld *MS* 13 Feb 1839

JONES Nathan Dea of Wilmot m GILLINGHAM Lydia C widow of Bradford on Dec 30, MOODY David Eld *MS* 12 Jan 1842

JONES Nicholas of Gilmanton m FOLSOM Abigail M at the Friends Meeting House at Epping *MS* 2 Jul 1834

JONES Samuel of Bradford VT m CHASE Amanda at Lisbon on 8 ult, GEORGE N K Eld *MS* 29 Apr 1840

JONES Sanders m BUEL Lucinda on 22 Mar 1848 in Middlefield NY, CRANDAL R C Eld *MS* 5 Apr 1848

JONES Sewaver m RICKER Urana both of Lebanon ME on 19 Oct 1848 in Lebanon ME, LITTLEFIELD Wm H Eld *MS* 1 Nov 1848

JONES Stephen S m HOLMES Harriet on 29 June at Strafford, PLACE E Eld *MS* 9 Jul 1845

JONES William m BLODGET Julia Ann both of Ascott on 8 May, MOULTON Abial Eld *MS* 20 Sept 1837

JOOE Horace of Cooksville m ASHTON Gracia of Wanconia Wis on 16 Mar, KNAPP Davis Eld *MS* 16 June 1847

JORDAN Abijah of Topsham ME m BROOMER Louisa Mrs of Lisbon ME on 2 Jul at Lisbon, LEWIS John Eld *MFWBR* 26 Jul 1848

JORDAN Almon Libby m WOODBURY Mary A all of Cape Elizabeth Sept 12 1841 in Cape Elizabeth, LIBBY Almon Eld *MS* 19 Jan 1842

JORDAN Andrew S of Boston MA m CHASE Mary Jane of Dover NH on 31 Dec 1848 in Manchester, CILLEY D P Eld *MS* 17 Jan 1849

JORDAN Benjamin R m GOODWIN Hannah both of Parsonsfield, FOSS A T Eld *MS* 19 Oct 1832

JORDAN David Jr m CLARK Thankful in Raymond, JORDAN Z Eld *MS* 3 Jan 1828

JORDAN Edmund of Farmington m EMERY Charlotte B of Dover NH on 19 Feb, SMITH A D Eld *MS* 6 Mar 1839

JORDAN Ebenezer of Webster ME m STROUT Mary J of Wales ME, FILES A Eld *MS* 29 Dec 1847

JORDAN George H m WARD Elizabeth both of Freeport on 21 Mar in Brunswick ME, PURINTON A W Eld *MS* 15 May 1850

JORDAN James m SYMOND Sally on 24th ult both of Raymond, JORDAN Z Eld *MS* 17 Oct 1833

JORDAN Levi Capt of Raymond ME m WESCOTT Esther of Gorham on 12 Dec 1849 in Gorham ME, PARKER L Eld *MS* 16 Jan 1850

JORDAN Nathaniel of Bridgetown PLT m WHITEHOUSE Susan of Newfield ME, DAM Joseph Esq *MS* 1 Mar 1827

JORDAN Richworth Jr Capt of Biddeford ME m PIKE Hannah E of Hollis ME on 17 Feb 1848 in Hollis, WITHAM L H Eld *MS* 8 Mar 1848

JORDAN Z Eld m PAGE Sabrina at Parsonsfield ME, BRADBURY A R Eld *MS* 20 May 1840

JOSE Martin m GOODWIN Selinda on 29 Nov of Lyman, EMERY Richard Eld *MS* 6 Jan 1847

JOSLEN Chauncey m STEWARD Rosetta of Elk Creek on 25 Apr at Elk Creek PA, WINTON David Eld *MS* 26 May 1847

JOSLIN Thomas m HARRINGTON Rebecca both of New Hartford on 17 Nov in Checkerville NY, MARINER J Eld *MS* 1 Jan 1851

JOSS Hosea of Scarboro' ME m BENFORD Rebecca on 25 Jul at Baldwin ME, HOLMES J C Eld *MS* 31 Aug 1842

JOSSELYN Isaac M m SEAVEY Nancy P of Manchester NH on 29th, CILLEY D P Eld *MS* 7 May 1845

JOY Frederick D m LOUGEE Mary Ann of Strafford on 1 Nov 1846 at Strafford, PLACE E Eld *MS* 20 Jan 1847

JOY John m FOSS Julia A both of Limington ME at Limerick ME, BEAN Charles Eld *MS* 12 Nov 1835

JOY John W m DEMERITT Ann of New Market NH on 23rd inst at Nottingham, TUTTLE A Eld *MS* 8 May 1839

JOY William m ROLLINS Dorcas at Bangor ME, CAVERNO A Eld *MS* 13 Sept 1843

JOY William H m BALLINTINE Mary E at Fairfield ME, LEWIS D B Eld *MS* 17 Apr 1844

JUDD Orange W of Washington VT m WOODBRIDGE Almira of Bow NH on 12 Mar in Chelsea VT, SANBORN G Eld *MS* 29 Apr 1846

JUDKINS Daniel of Belgrade ME m MITCHEL Sarah of Rome ME on 11 Aug, SPAULDING Joel Eld *MS* 8 Jan 1845

JUDKINS J Judson of Lowell m HAYNES Evelin on Thanksgiving Day in Townsend, STOWELL Rev Mr *MS* 19 Dec 1838

JUDKINS Moses m BAYLEY Lorana at Poland, LIBBY James Eld *MS* 30 Jan 1839

JUDKINS S N m RICHARDSON M Jane on 13 June at Dracut MA,

JUDKINS (Continued)
  CURTIS S Eld *MS* 7 Jul 1847
JUDKINS Stephen B of Fayette ME m LUMBARD Thankful of Sidney
  ME *MS* 10 Feb 1836
JULIAN Samuel L m HILL Nancy L on Wed last both of Limerick ME,
  BURBANK S Eld *MS* 4 Nov 1831
JUNKINS Joseph m SMITH Lydia M both of Hollis ME on 3d inst at
  Hollis, FAYBAN Samuel Esq *MFWBR* 19 Oct 1850

KACEY Gordon C m STARBORD M S Mrs on 9 Dec 1849, KACEY R
  H Eld *MS* 27 Feb 1850
KAIME John Dea m RAND Parmelia both of Barnstead on 12th inst,
  GARLAND D Eld *MS* 29 Jul 1835
KAIME William W of Roxbury m ROBEY Rebekah G of Chichester NH
  at Jamaica Plaine Roxbury MA, CILLEY D P Eld *MS* 16 Dec 1835
KALER J S m RAISOR Eliza Ann at Waldoboro *MFWBR* 3 Mar 1849
KATHERN Lorinus of Shefford m WOOD Clarissa of Stanstead LC on
  1 Aug, MOULTON Abial Eld *MS* 20 Sept 1837
KAUL Thomas F m BURDICK Susan in Newport RI, RUNNELS J Eld
  MS 4 Apr 1849
KEATON Hartwill of Biddeford ME m GOULD Fanny of Saco ME on
  17 Jan, JACKSON Daniel Eld *MS* 6 Apr 1847
KEAY Albra m ROSS Lydia D both of Lebanon ME in Lebanon ME,
  LITTLEFIELD W H Eld *MS* 3 May 1848
KEAY William G m EMERY Olive J on 14th inst, SALTER Rev of
  Episcopal church at Dover NH *MFWBR* 1 Sept 1849
KEAZER David m MEADER Mahaley F both of Haverhill on 4 Apr in
  Haverhill, MOULTON F Eld *MS* 1 May 1844
KEAZER Frederick F m HOOKS Mehitabel S both of Lowell MA,
  THURSTON N Eld *MS* 4 Feb 1835
KEEFER Dean m SKEELES Sarah on 11 Nov at Greenfield Ohio,
  PARKER Benjamin Eld *MS* 25 Feb 1846
KEELE James of Clifton Park m HANSON Nancy M of Starkville on 1
  Jan in Starkville, SMITH M H Eld *MS* 16 Jan 1850
KEEN Amaziah m HODGDON Elenor of Poland ME on 27 Sept at
  West Poland ME, LIBBY James Eld *MS* 10 Feb 1847
KEENE Josiah Jr Eld m SMITH Everline M of Sidney ME, LEWIS
  Daniel B Eld *MS* 30 Nov 1842
KEITH Asa m STOREY Laura E both of East Randolph on 20 ult, *MS*
  2 Nov 1836
KEITH Ralph S m SANDERSON Mary J on 2d inst at Dover NH,
  PERKINS Seth W Eld *MS* 13 Aug 1845
KEITH Samuel m BENSON Milicent on 17 June at Strafford VT,
  MOULTON F Eld *MS* 30 June 1847
KEITH Samuel S Jr of Brooks m SEEKENS Lucy M of Swanville ME
  on 22d inst at Brooks, HARRIMAN W P Esq *MFWBR* 3 Feb 1849

KELLER Joseph A m MONSEL Nancy on 28 Jan of Perry Township, HEALTH J D Eld *MS* 30 June 1847

KELLEY Alpha J m ADAMS Mary E both of Windsor VT on 5 June 1848 in Windsor VT, ADAMS Abel Eld *MS* 14 June 1848

KELLEY Charles R m DEARBORN Jane of Meredith Bridge on 31 Jul, BROOKS N Eld *MS* 4 Sept 1839

KELLEY Samuel B of Orono m McCLURE E P of Bangor on 14th at Bangor ME, PRENTISS H E Esq *MFWBR* 24 Feb 1849

KELLEY Stephen m LIDDLE Mary Ann both of Spring Prairie Wis on 5 Oct 1848 in East Troy Wis, AUGIR F P *MS* 29 Nov 1848

KELLEY William L C Dr of Northwood m BUTLER Isabella F of Nottingham NH *MS* 12 Jan 1831

KELLEY William A of Lynn MA m EMERY Sarah T of Waterboro ME at Great Falls, BROOKS N Eld *MS* 31 Jul 1850

KELLOGG Charles C of Boston MA m CARLL Sophia W on 10 Aug, EMERY R Eld *MS* 27 Aug 1845

KELLY Amos m MERRILL Lydia J on 3d inst at Gardiner, FINNEY Eld Rev *MFWBR* 21 Apr 1849

KELLY Francis B of Salem m VITTUM Mary A of Sandwich on 6 Nov at Sandwich, BLAKE C E Eld *MS* 17 Dec 1845

KELLY James m JEPSON Elizabeth at Dover NH, THURSTON Nathaniel Eld *MS* 25 Apr 1833

KELSEY Charles m LOVERING Fidelia both of Lowell MA, THURSTON N Eld *MS* 4 Feb 1835

KELSEY Daniel Esq m HARBEY Lavina M of Nottingham on Dec 10 at Nottingham, TUTTLE A Eld *MS* 20 Dec 1843

KELSO David m GORSLINE Margaret on Oct 4 at Scriba Oswego Co NY, COPP J B Eld *MS* 18 Nov 1846

KENDAL Charles of Yorkshire m DIBBLE Malinda of Freedom NY on 15 Feb 1848 in Freedom NY, FLYNN W H Eld *MS* 10 May 1848

KENDALL James M of Phipsburgh ME m WHITTIER Emily R at Fairfield ME on 26 Jan, NYE J Eld *MS* 22 Mar 1843

KENDALL Joseph A m COLE Mariana at Norway ME 9th inst *MFWBR* 22 Dec 1849

KENDALL K R m LINNEL Lucinda H of Orrington ME on 21st ult at Bangor ME, ATWELL Rev *MFWBR* 3 Mar 1849

KENDALL Nathan T of Landaff NH m BALL Lois W on 24 Sept at the home of N K GEORGE in Franconia, GEORGE N K Eld *MS* 6 Nov 1844

KENDALL Robert of Nashua m RUSSELL Mary of Manchester in Lisbon, BLAKE C E Eld *MS* 2 Jan 1850

KENDRICK William H m HAMILTON Laura Ann at Bangor ME, CAVERNO A Eld *MS* 13 Sept 1843

KENDRICK William B m BROWN Harriet both of Deerfield NH on 3 Jan 1850 in Epsom NH, RAMSEY G P Eld *MS* 16 Jan 1850

KENERSON Francis m HEAD Mary Ann both of Tamworth NH on 21

KENERSON (Continued)
Apr Sabbath in Tamworth NH, AMES C G Eld *MS* 1 May 1850

KENERSON Job m HEAD Rhoda T W of Tamworth NH on 30 Nov at Tamworth NH, BROOKS John Eld *MS* 24 Dec 1845

KENERSON Nathan on 3 Dec m HAM Lucinda of Durham, WEBBER Horace Eld *MS* 21 Feb 1844

KENISTON Benj of Cabot m MARBLE Lucinda of Sutton on 7 Sept in Lyndon VT, QUIMBY D Eld *MS* 15 Nov 1837

KENISTON Bradbury of Bafford m CLARK Mary A of Barnston LC, MOULTON A Eld of Stanstead LC *MS* 13 Apr 1842

KENISTON Edwin of South Berwick ME m STACY Sally on 5th inst, DAVIS K R Eld *MS* 29 May 1844

KENISTON Freeman of Clappville MA m DAVIS Melissa A of New Market on 8th inst, HUTCHINS Elias Eld *MS* 18 Jan 1843

KENISTON Hiram B m MEARDEN Lucinda both of Alton NH on 22 Oct 1848 in Gilmanton, GARLAND David Eld *MS* 15 Nov 1848

KENISTON Ivory P m THOMPSON Mary J both of Wolfborough NH on 12 May in Wolfborough, COFFIN S Eld *MS* 22 May 1850

KENISTON Mark m CASWELL Asenath S both of New Market on 31 May in New Market, FROST D S Eld *MS* 8 Jul 1846

KENISTON of Franconia NH m MOODY Abagail L of Lisbon NH on 18 Oct, GEORGE N K Eld *MS* 28 Dec 1842

KENNARD Diamond of Brownfield ME m GILLERSON Nancy of Brownfield on 31 Aug at Harrison ME, PHINNEY Joseph H *MS* 8 Oct 1834

KENNARD Noah m PENDEXTER Betsey both of Parsonsfield ME on Dec 29 1841 in Parsonsfield, HACKETT J O Eld *MS* 19 Jan 1842

KENNEDY John L m LEAVITT Caroline A both of Bedford on 18 ult in Piscataqoug Village, CILLEY D P Eld *MS* 8 Jul 1846

KENNEY Henry of Lebanon m NASON Sabra of Lyman on 18 Dec, McKENNEY O Eld *MS* 28 Dec 1842

KENNEY John of Lagrange ME m WILLEY Elizabeth of Dover NH on 7th inst, PERKINS J Rev *MS* 13 May 1835

KENNEY John of Sutton m SMITH Irene A on 13 Oct 1843, FULLER W Eld *MS* 17 Apr 1844

KENNISON Ivory m LEAVITT Lucy on 12 Dec at Eaton, RUNNELS J Eld *MS* 19 Mar 1845

KENNISTON Henry of Andover m SHAW Sarah of New Market on 12 Apr 1848 in New Market NH, FROST D S Eld *MS* 3 May 1848

KENNNEY Joshua m DAVIS Weltha P of Lowell MA, CURTIS S Eld *MS* 26 Feb 1845

KENT J of Boston MA m TOWNSON Eliza G at Limerick ME, FREEMAN Charles Rev *MFWBR* 30 Dec 1848

KENT Josiah of Grandy Lower Canada m LUCAS Betsey C of Wolfboro' NH on 12 Oct at Wolfboro' NH, BUTLER O Eld *MS* 11 Feb 1846

KENYON B Franklin m FOX Mary S both of Ilion on 6 Oct in Burlington Flats NY, CADY S S Eld *MS* 27 Nov 1850

KENYON Daniel H m WATSON Hannah at Lowell on 12 Feb 1840, THURSTON N Eld

KENYON John of Batavia NY m DOW Amelia of Middlebury NY on 10 Dec at Middlebury NY, ROLLIN D M L Eld *MS* 11 Feb 1846

KEY William H of Ossipee NH m STATON Hannah M of Ossipee NH on 23 Oct, CHICK Eld *MS* 7 Dec 1842

KEYS Jonas C m HOYT Betsey J both of Manchester on 3 inst in Manchester, CILLEY D P Eld *MS* 23 Feb 1848

KEYS Peter Jr of Wolfboro m BURROWS Lavinia of Dover NH on 8 inst, MACK Enoch Eld *MS* 15 Mar 1837

KEYS Peter m ABBOTT Sarah Mrs on 18 Feb, CHICK J Eld *MS* 14 May 1845

KIBBEY Danforth B m HAYWOOD Maria Mrs of Montpeller VT on 3 Jan 1847 at Danville VT, GEORGE N K Eld *MS* 24 Feb 1847

KIDDAH James Jr m BROWN Hannah L both of Boston MA on 18 June, CHICK J Eld *MS* 7 Nov 1849

KIDDER Franklin of Tewksbury MA m PURVES Mary S of Lowell MA on 8 June 1843, DURGIN J M Eld *MS* 6 Sept 1843

KIDDER Joseph W m HILL Mary A at Skowhegan ME on 25th ult *MFWBR* 12 Jan 1850

KIDDER Leonard m SUTHERLAND Maria both of Topsham ME on Mon Dec 27 in Topsham, ROLLINS A Eld *MS* 12 Jan 1842

KIDDER Tyler m MORROW Louisa A at Dixfield *MFWBR* 22 May 1847

KILBORN Willard m MARTIN Hannah of Bridgton ME on 25 Nov 1841 at Bridgton ME, HUNTRESS D Eld *MS* 27 Apr 1842

KILBOURNE Samuel m WHITE Lydia of Barnston on Jul 21, MOULTON Abial Eld *MS* 1 Jan 1840

KIMBALL Abel T of Danville m FULLONTON Caroline, FOSS T Eld *MS* 8 Nov 1848

KIMBALL Albert R m HUTCHINS Rosannah of Moultonboro' NH at Sandwick NH, WEBBER H Eld *MS* 1 June 1842

KIMBALL Baxter R m CURRIER Mary A on 7 Mar at Manchester NH, CILLEY D P Eld *MS* 14 Apr 1847

KIMBALL Charles F m WHITNEY Mercy both of Lisbon ME *MS* 29 Jan 1836

KIMBALL Charles H of Weare NH m HOLMES Martha of Contoocookville on 13 Apr, FROST D S Eld of Contoocookville NH *MS* 26 Apr 1843

KIMBALL Charles S m HAYES Mary A both of Lowell on 29 Oct 1848 in Dracut, CURTIS S Eld *MS* 8 Nov 1848

KIMBALL Christopher C m RAND Hannah L of Lowell, THURSTON Nathaniel Eld *MS* 30 Jan 1839

KIMBALL Daniel D m KNIGHT Mary Jane on 1 Aug at Portland ME,

KIMBALL (Continued)
MOULTON A K Eld *MS* 21 Aug 1844

KIMBALL Daniel of Newark VT m FOREST Lucy Ann of Sutton on 7 June, CROSS D Eld *MS* 27 Nov 1850

KIMBALL George F of Poplin m FULLONTON Mary D on 4th inst at Raymond, McMURPHY B H Eld *MS* 18 Nov 1846

KIMBALL George H m BEAN Adelaide Q both of Manchester on 4 Sept in Manchester, CILLEY D P Eld *MS* 23 Sept 1846

KIMBALL George L m FLOYD Harriet W on 17 Aug at Hopkinton, DYER B Eld *MS* 17 Sept 1845

KIMBALL Heber Jr m WATSON Susan P of Saco ME on 14 Sept at Harrison ME, HUTCHINSON S Eld *MS* 24 Sept 1845

KIMBALL James L of Parkman m ROUNDS Anny Miss of Danville ME at Danville, STURGIS N G *MS* 13 Feb 1839

KIMBALL John of Dover m PRIME Eliza of Sanford ME at Dover NH, WILLIAMS Gibbon Rev *MS* 17 Sept 1834

KIMBALL John of Haverhill MA m HUSE Nancy of Portsmouth NH on 22 Feb at Portsmouth NH, MERRILL William P *MS* 21 May 1845

KIMBALL Josiah L m KIMBALL Ann P both of Hooksett on 9 Dec 1847 in Manchester, CILLEY D P Eld *MS* 29 Dec 1847

KIMBALL Moses L of Dover NH m EASTMAN Hannah F on 2d inst, HUTCHINS E Eld *MS* 8 Oct 1845

KIMBALL Moses W m KIMBALL Judith of Gilmanton NH on 6 May 1849 in Gilmanton, FERNALD S P Eld *MS* 6 June 1849

KIMBALL Nath F m LIBBY Susan both of New Market on 7 inst at Strafford, CAVERLY J Eld *MS* 23 Dec 1835

KIMBALL Obadiah of New Hampton m FLINT Elizabeth of Allenstown on 15 Mar 1848, PITMAN S J Eld *MS* 21 June 1848

KIMBALL Robert H m BOOTHBY Nancy on 19 Nov of Limington ME, MANSON B S Eld *MS* 7 Feb 1844

KIMBALL Rufus of Hollis m BURHAM Mary of Hollis, HALEY N Esq *MS* 9 Nov 1826

KIMBALL Stephen S m DOLLOFF Terzah Ann both of Meredith on 24 Nov 1847, PITMAN S J Eld *MS* 22 Dec 1847

KIMBALL William H m ADAMS Mary A both of Gilmanton on 5 Apr in Gilmanton, FERNALD S P Eld *MS* 6 June 1849

KINCAID Peter of Brunswick ME m CURTIS Sophia of Bowdoinham ME *MS* 13 Oct 1830

KINDALL Miram Mr m HIGGINS Amanda both of Middlebury on 15 ult in Middlebury NY, PLUMB H N Eld *MS* 20 May 1846

KINDAR William m HARGRAVES Maria, NOYES E Eld *MS* 13 Nov 1850

KING Henry C m HOWARD Mahitabel both of Boston in Strafford, PLACE E Eld *MS* 1 Aug 1838

KING Jeremiah m BILLINGS Mary both of No Providence on 3d ult, HUTCHINS Eld *MS* 4 May 1836

KING Joseph of Barre, MA m BURROWS Irena of Dover on 16 inst this town, HUTCINS E Eld *MS* 25 Mar 1846

KING Lewis D m MACOMBER Welthy A both of Monmouth ME, FILES A Eld *MS* 22 Apr 1840

KING Nathaniel Jr m WHITNEY Rebecca F on 15 Nov 1847 Tunbridge VT, HENDERSON Moses C Eld *MS* 24 Nov 1847

KING Rufus G m ALLEN Susan V on 19 March at Newport RI, LORD D H Eld *MS* 9 Apr 1845

KING Sylvester of Compton m TURNER Mary Ann of Hatley LC on 25 Nov, MOULTON A Eld of Stanstead LC *MS* 13 Apr 1842

KING Thomas of Bowdoinham ME on 23 Nov at Bowdoin ME m KELLEY Mary Jane of Hallowell ME, RAYMOND J Eld *MS* 18 Dec 1844

KING Walter W of Newport NH on 12 May m KIBBEY Nancy M of Newark, GEORGE N K Eld in Newark VT *MS* 19 June 1850

KINGMAN Nathan Col of Orford m BARNARD Lucy W of Enfield NH on Feb 21, FROST D Sidney Eld *MS* 23 Mar 1842

KINGSLEY Robert on 29 Jul m GOLDTHWAITE Susan both of Somersworth, CHENEY O B Eld in Lebanon ME *MS* 15 Aug 1849

KINISON Elisha M of Holderness NH on 8 Mar m RILL Lydia of Lyndon VT, QUINBY Daniel Eld *MS* 18 Apr 1838

KINNEY N S Mr on 23d ult both of Dixfield m PETERSON Patience B, CURTIS S Eld *MS* 20 Apr 1831

KINSMAN Denison m MARTIN Mary on 24 Nov at East Williamstown VT, HOLLIS N A Eld *MS* 18 Dec 1839

KINYAN Silas R of Richmond on 8 inst at No Providence RI m WILLIAMS Hannah O of No Providence RI *MS* 21 Sept 1836

KIRK Samuel P m PATTEE Mary both of Alexandria in Bristol April 19, BROWN A Eld *MS* 4 May 1842

KITTEL John J of Stephentown at Nassau NY on 12 Mar m DUNHAM Margaret V of Nassau NY, COLEMAN E B Eld *MS* 7 May 1845

KITTEREDGE Lucius S of New Lebanon on 1 inst m SEXBY Phebe Ann of Sand Lake, COLEMAN I B Eld in West Stephentown NY *MS* 26 Dec 1849

KITTREDGE Aaron Dr of Limerick ME m GOODHUE Martha, WARD Jonathan Rev at Hebron NH *MS* 6 May 1826

KITTREDGE Edmund F on 8th inst at Wilmington m RICHARDSON Harriet, DURGIN J M Eld *MS* 25 Oct 1843

KITTREDGE George H m HELD Eliza E both of Lowell, THURSTON N Eld in Lowell *MS* 8 Jan 1840

KITTREDGE Thomas W Esq on at Dover NH m TREDICK Adeline *MS* 21 Nov 1833

KNAPP Bennager of Dover MI on 21 Mar m ROBINSON Lucy of Rome MI, DREW Enoch Eld *MS* 12 May 1847

KNAPP George of Nashua on 14 May 1848 m FARROW Mary Jane of Gilmanton, MASON Lemuel Eld in Gilmanton NH

KNAPP (Continued)
MS 24 May 1848

KNAPP Joseph on 21 Apr m WINSOR Sally at Franklinville NY, WINSOR Barnet Eld MS 15 Mar 1843

KNIGHT Abner on 19 Nov 1848 m LAMB Rebecca, QUINNAM C Eld in Bowdoinham ME MS 13 Dec 1848

KNIGHT Albert of New Market m EMERSON Abigail MS 19 May 1847

KNIGHT Aldis E on 2 Feb 1848 m HILL Elizabeth D both of Starksboro' VT, TUCKER Joshua Eld in Starksboro' VT MS 23 Feb 1848

KNIGHT Allen W of Scituate RI on 9th inst at Conklin Broome Co NY m KNIGHT Elizabeth B, LONGSTREET George G Rev MS 31 Aug 1842

KNIGHT Alvin at Great Falls NH m HAMILTON Nancy of Waterboro', CURTIS S Eld MS 29 June 1842

KNIGHT Daniel m GREEN Susan G on 5th inst at Portland ME, MOULTON A K Eld MS 28 Feb 1844

KNIGHT Edmund of Corinna ME m PAGE Mary Mrs of Belgrade ME on 5th inst MS 3 June 1835

KNIGHT George M m CAHOON Elizabeth both of Scituate on 31 ult, CALVIN R Eld MS 17 Jan 1849

KNIGHT George m KNIGHT Mary (Pratt) Mrs (widow of Solomon Knight, who was brother of Geo K) on 2 Aug 1843 (& killed her Oct 1856), LIBBY James Eld MS 8 Nov 1843 & see p 76 Poole's History of Poland ME 1890

KNIGHT Henry W m MORSE J S of Portland on 27th ult MFWBR 8 Sept 1849

KNIGHT Isaac Capt m PIKE Ann E W of Saco ME on 16th ult at New York MFWBR 1 Feb 1851

KNIGHT James preacher m BAKER Nancy in Bethlehem NH, QUINBY Joshua Eld MS 10 Jul 1829

KNIGHT Joshua m PENDLETON Hannah of Parsonsfield ME on 4 June, BUZZELL A Eld MS 18 Sep 1839

KNIGHT Moses m WOODBURY Sarah P on 31 Dec at Haverhill, MOULTON F Eld MS 22 Jan 1845

KNIGHT Oliver m KNIGHT Sabina both of So Berwick ME on 16 inst in Dover, HUTCHINS E Eld MS 22 Nov 1848

KNIGHT P Deacon of Berwick ME m AUSTIN Adah of Great Falls NH on 18th inst at South Berwick, GRAY John Esq MFWBR 7 Apr 1849

KNIGHT Peter Dea of Berwick m AUSTIN Adah of Great Falls NH at South Berwick ME MFWBR 14 Apr 1849

KNIGHT Simeon of Waterborough m ROBERTS Betsey of Lyman on 4 Dec at Lyman ME, McKENNEY O Eld MS 28 Dec 1842

KNIGHT William of Wayne ME m KNIGHT Asenath of Falmouth ME on 28th ult at Buxton, BEAN Nathaniel C MS 17 Nov 1830

KNIGHT Zebulon m FLUENT Hannah E both of Buxton ME on 7 Dec

KNIGHT (Continued)

1848, BAILEY J M Eld *MS* 24 Jan 1849

KNIGHTS Frank of Westbrook ME m LORD Mary, HERSEY L Eld *MS* 1 June 1842

KNIGHTS Henry m KIMBALL Abigail on 21st ult at Saco ME, WILLIAMS N M (Esq?) *MFWBR* 3 Nov 1849

KNIGHTS Leonard m MORSE Nancy B on 6 Aug at Dixfield, BADGER W Eld *MS* 20 Aug 1845

KNOTT Robert Jr of Boston MA m ATKINSON Caroline of Lynn MA on 22 Jan, NOYES E Eld *MS* 8 Feb 1843

KNOW Isaac of Clinton m OBERTON Elvira A B of Litchfield on 5 May in Litchfield *MS* 22 May 1844

KNOW James of Lebanon ME m STAPLES Betsey of North Berwick ME on 29 Jan, BLAISDELL Edward Eld *MS* 11 Feb 1846

KNOWLES Charles H m TORR Mehitabel on 9th ult at Newmarket, KELLY S Eld *MS* 27 Dec 1843

KNOWLES David M m GRIFFIN Hannah on 22 Sept at Epsom NH, RAMSEY G P Eld *MS* 19 Oct 1842

KNOWLES Ithiel of Augusta m JEWETT Sarah of Readfield *MS* 1 Feb 1837

KNOWLES Jefferson of Northwood m BATCHELDER Abigail of Strafford VT on Dec 11 at Northwood, FERNALD S P Eld *MS* 27 Feb 1839

KNOWLES John a licentiate preacher of New Durham Q M m SANBORN Abigail at Guilford NH *MS* 21 Dec 1832

KNOWLES John Eld of Pittsfield NH m COLBY Abigail Mrs of Newburyport on 20 Nov 1849 in Andover *MS* 16 Jan 1850

KNOWLES Jonathan A at Epsom m BICKFORD Susan G, RAMSEY G P Eld *MS* 27 Sept 1843

KNOWLES Stephen S of Augusta m SMILEY Mary Ann of Sidney at Sidney ME on 8th inst *MFWBR* 16 June 1849

KNOWLES William m TASKER Ann Jane both of Northwood on 9 Oct in Northwood, FERNALD S P Eld *MS* 7 Nov 1838

KNOWLES William of Gilford m GILMAN Nancy of Epsom nh, MANSON B S Eld *MS* 26 Aug 1835

KNOWLTON Alonzo F m HUNCKINS Hannah B both of Northwood NH on 4 Nov in Northwood NH, JOHNSON W D Eld *MS* 17 Nov 1847

KNOWLTON Charles D m BUCK Harriet of Manchester NH on 17 Dec at Manchester NH, CILLEY D P Eld *MS* 1 Jan 1845

KNOWLTON Chase of Danby m SHAW Eliza of Holderness, PETTENGILL John Eld *MS* 4 Dec 1839

KNOWLTON Ebenezer of Northwood m HAINES Lydia J of Nottingham on 2d inst, CILLEY D P Eld *MS* 9 July 1834

KNOWLTON George H m CILLEY Hannah of Northwood on 6 inst in Northwood NH, JOHNSON W D Eld *MS* 14 Feb 1849

KNOWLTON Jacob m LOW Abigail, ALLEN E Jr both of Dixmont *MS* 9 May 1833

KNOWLTON James m DURGIN Nancy on 3 Sept at Northwood, JOHNSON W D Eld *MS* 25 Sept 1844

KNOWLTON Jonathan of Northwood m WILLEY Mary of Dover on 14 inst in Dover, SMITH A D Eld *MS* 24 Jul 1839

KNOWLTON Mayhew P m FOSS Hannah J both of Northwood NH on 21 in Gilmanton, FERNALD S P Eld *MS* 21 June 1848

KNOX Edward Jr of Ossipee NH m MASON Abigail of Eaton on 3 Nov 1844, KNOWLES Samuel Eld *MS* 13 Nov 1844

KNOX Hiram m SMITH Lovantia both of Mercer Co IL on 4 Jul in Illinois City, BEARDSLEY Elisha Eld *MS* 11 Sept 1850

KNOX Samuel m MOULTON Mary Mrs both of Albany on 23 Jan in Albany, MILLS James E Eld *MS* 24 Apr 1850

KNOX Thom T m FARRIS Abigail G on 22d inst at Biddeford ME, STRICKLAND G G Rev *MFWBR* 3 Mar 1849

KORTON Isaac m HOWARD Terresa both of Oakfield Wis on 7 Mar 1849 in Oakfield Wis, WRIGHT E N Eld *MS* 25 Apr 1849

KWEATKUSKE J Mr (a Polander) m KNOWLES Lavina both of Lowell MA on 4 inst *MS* 14 Sept 1836

KYES Perley m WOODBURY Polly on 22 in Moretown, CHATTERTON B Eld *MS* 23 Sept 1846

LABREE James m WORTHING Hannah both of Corinna ME on 30th ult, NASON S U Eld *MS* 24 Apr 1834

LADD Chester of Strafford VT m BROWN Charlotte, PETTENGILL J Eld *MS* 11 Dec 1844

LADD James of Saco ME m ROWE Caroline of Biddeford ME on 7th inst at Saco ME, FERNALD J Eld *MFWBR* 24 June 1848

LADD John Jr m MARSTON Betsey L in Brentwood, FULLENTON J Eld *MS* 5 Jan 1842

LADD Jonathan m ADAMS Catharine T both of Manchester on 14 Oct in Manchester, CILLEY D P Eld *MS* 24 Oct 1849

LAINE Daniel F of Gilmanton (NH)? m WEBSTER Marilla B of Boscawen NH *MS* 13 June 1842

LAKE Harman m SUTLIFF Abagail M on 7 Mar in Mecca Ohio, ALDRICH S Eld *MS* 24 Apr 1850

LAKE Joshua F at Epping m JENNESS Abigail *MS* 14 Jan 1835

LAMB Amos of Madison m JINKS Cornelia of Hamilton NY on 2 inst in Hamilton NY, GARDNER S D Eld *MS* 29 Dec 1847

LAMB Merrick of Green m SOULE Sarah S of Freeport ME on 3 Sept 1848 in Freeport ME, PURINTON A W Eld *MS* 1 Nov 1848

LAMBARD Charles A of Augusta ME m JOHNSON Frances E at Belfast ME *MFWBR* 9 Nov 1850

LAMBERT Abel M m PERRY Ann H of Camden on 22d in Farmington, ROGERS I Rev *MFWBR* 10 Mar 1849

LAMPHERE William m FARNUM Hannah both of Warner on 5 May in Hopkinton, SINCLAIR S L Eld *MS* 30 May 1838

LAMPREY Uriah of Gilmanton ME m BATCHELDER Abigail B of Meredith on 13 Feb, BROOKS N Eld *MS* 13 Mar 1839

LAMSON Silas m BROWN Malinda C both of Atkinson ME on 25 May 1848 in Atkinson ME, HATHAWAY L Eld *MS* 28 June 1848

LANCESTER David Eld of Corinna ME m CROCKETT Frances C of Deer Isle on 31 Oct at Brunswick ME, FULLER J Eld *MS* 18 Mar 1846

LANCIL Charles V Capt of Bangor ME m HARTFORD Louise of Dover NH on 2 inst in Lowell, THURSTON N Eld *MS* 14 June 1837

LAND John Capt m PARSONS Rebecca Mrs both of Boston on 16 Dec 1847 in Edgecomb, PARKER Lowell Eld *MS* 12 Jan 1848

LANE Edmund J bookseller of Dover NH m BARKER Elizabeth of Stratham, CUMMINGS Rev *MS* 13 Feb 1834

LANE Edward F m GOVER Sarah A both formerly of Maine on 13 Oct in Fairfield ME, GRIFFIN J Eld *MS* 13 Nov 1850

LANE Henry D of Raymond m WIGGIN Olive C of Moultonboro' NH, BROOKS N Eld *MS* 11 Nov 1846

LANE John K of Gloucester MA m GRIFFIN Mary Jane of Dover on Wednesday morn last in Dover NH, CAVERNO A Eld *MS* 13 Feb 1850

LANE John of Lee m CHESLEY Sarah of Dover on 21st inst, MACK Eld *MS* 27 Jan 1836

LANE Joseph at Bangor ME m TIBBETTS Naomi D, CAVERNO A Eld *MS* 13 Sept 1843

LANE Nathaniel H Lt of Hollis m HASKEL Martha *MS* 30 Nov 1826

LANE Peter of Chester m SIMPSON Sarah of Nottingham on 20th ult in Nottingham, CILLEY D P Eld *MS* 5 Jul 1837

LANE Reuben C m GREEN? Jane B at Pittsfield Dec 8 1839, KNOWLES John Eld *MS* 6 May 1840

LANE Thomas R Capt m CURTIS Mary L on 21 Oct at Freeport ME, PURINTON A W Eld *MS* 17 Dec 1845

LANE True W of Starksboro VT m HILL Abigail, TUCKER Joshua Eld *MS* 10 Feb 1847

LANE William of Sherburne MA m FOSS Vienna of Meredith on 8 Sept, PITMAN S J Eld *MS* 30 Sept 1846

LANE Winthrop M of Sandwich m MORRISON Francis Ann of Wakefield on 15 Sept in Wakefield, SPINNEY Joseph Eld *MS* 21 Nov 1838

LANE William G m HEATH Marietta both of Lowell on 29 May in Dracut MA, CURTIS S Eld *MS* 10 June 1846

LANE William Jr of Centreville m BENTON Laura of Hume NY *MS* 4 Mar 1835

LANG Daniel W of Brookfield m GLIDDEN Mary F of Ossipee NH on 16 Jan in Jackson, PINKHAM G H Eld *MS* 5 Mar 1851

LANG Edward 2d of Exeter m ELLISON Mary Jane of Dover on 14th inst, THURSTON N *MS* 26 Dec 1833

LANG John of Conway m MORRISON Elmira of Eaton NH, SANBORN Thomas Eld *MS* 17 Jul 1839

LANG Thomas E m MOULTON Susan B both of Meredith on 15 Jul, PITMAN Stephen J Eld *MS* 26 Sept 1849

LANGDON John T m LIBBY Sarah P both of Wolfborough NH on 16 inst in Dover, HUTCHINS E Eld *MS* 22 Mar 1848

LANGINALD Josiah Prentice m PERKINS Sarah P of Chichester on 20 Apr in Chichester *MS* 29 Apr 1840

LANGLEY Andrew m DOW Nancy at Wilmot NH *RI* 4 Dec 1819

LANGLEY Ephraim m ROBERTS Sarah B on 2 inst both of Alton NH, BUZZELL H D Eld *MS* 30 Jan 1834

LANGLEY Jonathan of Lee m FAIRFIELD Hannah at New Market on 3 inst, HUTCHINS E Eld *MS* 13 May 1840

LANGLEY Josiah m SMALL Susan of Nottingham on 30 Nov at Nottingham, TUTTLE A Eld *MS* 20 Dec 1843

LANGLEY Moses m GEAR Sarah A both of Dover on Tuesday morning 16 in Barrington, SHERBURNE S Eld *MS* 26 Sept 1849

LANGLEY Samuel m CURRIER Dolly at Andover NH *RI* Jan 1821 p 15

LANGLEY Samuel N m HATCH Abigail F both of Barnstead on Apr 12 at Pittsfield, CILLEY D P Eld *MS* 22 Apr 1840

LANGLEY Thomas W m ALLARD Charity H both of Lamprey River *MS* 11 Feb 1835

LANGLEY Valentine Jr of Acton m HEARD Betsey of Newfield, BURBANK S Eld *MS* 13 Apr 1832

LANGLEY William of Newfield m DEARBORN Sarah in Wakefield *MS* 18 June 1828

LANGMAID E K of Loudon NH m ROBINSON H of Dedham MA on 6 Apr 1848 in Concord, CATLIN S T Eld *MS* 17 Jan 1849

LANGMAID Josiah Prentice m PERKINS Sarah P at Chichester on Apr 20 *MS* 29 Apr 1840

LANGWORTHY William m LATHAM Lydia both of Warrensburgh NY, CHASE William P Eld *MS* 21 Oct 1835

LANNING Stephen of Gorham Ontario Co m BAKER Jane of Mito on 30 Sept in Mito NY, CRANE E F Eld *MS* 28 Nov 1838

LARA Daniel m COPELAND Celia at Turner ME *MFWBR* 28 Jul 1849

LARABEE Joseph m MULLOY Mary Ann both of Limington ME on 20 Jul 1839, MANSON B S Eld *MS* 15 Jan 1840

LARABEE Samuel Capt m IRISH Ann on 21st ult at Limington ME, TRIPP L S Rev *MFWBR* 15 Jan 1848

LARKID Norman of Nassau m WILLIAMS Emily on 4 Nov, COLEMAN I B Eld *MS* 18 Nov 1846

LARRABEE Benjamin m TOWLE Mercy on 12th inst in Porter, SAWYER James *MS* 28 June 1827

LARRABEE James Jr m PIKE E S of Gorham ME on 21st ult at Portland ME, HUSSEY L Rev *MFWBR* 3 Mar 1849

LARRABEE John G of New Market on 18 Apr m DYER Olive L of Nottingham in Barrington, SHERBURNE S Eld *MS* 29 Apr 1846

LASKEY Jonathan of Milton NH m BUZZELL Maria L of New Market NH in New Market NH, FROST D S Eld *MS* 3 May 1848

LATHAM Cyrus Deacon of Lowell MA m JORDAN Eliza of Raymond ME on 11 Mar at Raymond ME, LIBBY James Eld *MS* 26 May 1847

LAUGER Sylvester G m BUXLEY Reuhamah on 31 Dec, DAVIS J B Eld *MS* 22 Jan 1845

LAUGHTON Charles H of Boston MA m RICH Pamelia G of Roxbury on 8 Aug, DAVIS J B Eld *MS* 28 Aug 1844

LAWRENCE David M m KIMBALL Elenor of Eaton NH on 6 June at Eaton, MERRILL William S *MS* 23 June 1847

LAWRENCE David m YOUNG Jane Augusta on 2d inst at Dover NH, HAYDEN Lucian Rev *MS* 8 Dec 1841

LAWRENCE Elias H of Gardiner m CURTIS Hannah L of Richmond on 16 Nov 1848 in Bowdoinham ME, HATHORN S Eld *MS* 27 Dec 1848

LAWRENCE Farnsworth at Bangor ME m LAWRENCE Malinda B, CAVERNO A Eld *MS* 13 Sept 1843

LAWRENCE Noah Capt m MARSTON Polly both of Meredith on 25 Nov 1847, PITMAN S J Eld *MS* 22 Dec 1847

LAWRENCE Philip m MERRILL Caroline M both of Walworth on 18 Sept in Walworth, MERRILL Joseph Eld *MS* 16 Oct 1850

LAWRENCE Samuel m JONES Dorothy Ann on 3 Jul at Lowell MA at Lowell MA, THURSTON N Eld *MS* 2 Nov 1842

LAWRENCE William 2d of Gardiner ME m FANNIN Sarah of Bath ME on 26 Feb in Richmond, SWETT J Eld *MS* 7 Mar 1838

LAWTON George N m THOMPSON Rosetta A of Newport RI on 25 Jan at Newport RI, LORD D H Eld *MS* 11 Mar 1846

LEACH Thomas E of Kittery ME m RICHARDSON Eliza J of New Market in New Market, ALLEN C Eld *MS* 24 Jan 1849

LEAKE Isaac E m STEVENS Diana both of Janesville Wis on 16 Oct in Harmony Wis, POPE James R Eld *MS* 11 Dec 1850

LEARNED Calvin m WOOD Lois both of Dixfield ME on 2 Nov 1847 in Dixfield ME, POLLINS James Eld *MS* 9 Feb 1848

LEATHERS - see SEATHERS

LEATHERS Hiram G m WILLLIAMS Anna both of Barrington on 22 ult *MS* 1 Feb 1837

LEATHERS Loring of St Albans ME m BATES Martilla L, COPP J B Eld *MS* 7 June 1843

LEATHERS Nathaniel m BERRY Susan both of Great Falls NH in Rochester, HANSON John Esq *MS* 27 Mar 1834

LEAVETT Benjamin of Effingham NH m COBB Hannah of Limington

LEAVETT (Continued)
ME on 10th Feb at Limington, McKENNEY H Esq *MS* 3 Apr 1839

LEAVITT Alfred J m NUDD Abby M both of Haverhill MA on 1 Jul 1848 in Hampton NH, MERRILL William P Eld *MS* 12 Jul 1848

LEAVITT David H m PICKERING Abigail J on 28 Sept at Manchester, CILLEY D P Eld *MS* 10 Oct 1844

LEAVITT Ebenezer Capt of Pittsfield m BATCHELDER Nancy Mrs of Chichester on 16 Nov at Pittsfield, CILLEY D P Eld *MS* 7 Dec 1842

LEAVITT Ebenezer K m SEVERANCE Arsulia A both of Meredith, PITMAN Stephen J Eld *MS* 2 Feb 1842

LEAVITT Gideon P m THOMAS Sarah B both of Newburgh ME on 12 Nov in East Dixmont ME, ALLEN E Eld *MS* 5 Mar 1851

LEAVITT Gilman m MUNSEY Wealthy C of Gilford NH on 7 June, PERKINS Seth W Eld *MS* 23 June 1847

LEAVITT Jacob of Gilford NH m CONNER Sarah A of Gilford NH on New Year's Day, PINKHAM J Eld *MS* 21 Jan 1846

LEAVITT John B m SEAMMAN Martha C *MS* 15 June 1832

LEAVITT John B of Gilford m SWAIN Hannah M of Meredith NH on 21 Mar *MS* 12 Apr 1843

LEAVITT John C m TUTTLE Abigail H of Effingham NH on 1 Feb 1849, FOSS Nahum Eld *MS* 7 Mar 1849

LEAVITT John H m CHACE Lydia Jane both of Pittsfield on 12 Apr Sabbath Morn in Pittsfield, CILLEY D P Eld *MS* 22 Apr 1840

LEAVITT John m DOW Clara J both of Gilmanton NH on 4 May 1848 in Upper Gilmanton NH, MASON Lemuel Eld *MS* 17 May 1848

LEAVITT John of Boston MA m GILE Mary C of Gilmanton NH on 2 Dec 1847 in Sanbornton NH, MASON L Eld *MS* 12 Jan 1848

LEAVITT Jonathan 2d of Windham ME m HODGDON Joann M on 4 Dec at Gorham ME, MANSON B S Eld *MS* 31 Dec 1845

LEAVITT Oliver m LAMPREY Clarisa both of Hampton on 15 inst in Hampton, CILLEY D P Eld *MS* 8 Nov 1837

LEAVITT Samuel m EDGERLY Betsey Mrs both of Meredith on 23 Oct, PITMAN S J Eld *MS* 27 Nov 1850

LEAVITT Samuel Q m MOORE Elizabeth L both of Effingham NH, COBURNS Milton J Rev *MS* 15 Jan 1840

LEAVITT Silas m WOOD Eliza Ann both of Augusta ME on 30 Apr 1848 in Augusta ME, DUDLEY Thomas J Eld *MS* 24 May 1848

LEAVITT Simon m DEMERIT Betsey A both of Dover on 12 Jan in Effingham NH, FOSS N Eld *MS* 20 Mar 1850

LEAVITT Thomas C m HOBBS Mary in No Hampton NH *MS* 5 Aug 1831

LEAVITT Thomas Deacon m CRIMBALL Mary of Stratham on 27th ult, MERRILL Asa Eld *MS* 5 June 1839

LEAVITT Thomas of Boston m TORRENS Rebecca of Lowell MA on 7 inst, THURSTON N Eld *MS* 17 Feb 1836

LEAVITT Thomas m BERRY Lydia of Tamworth NH on 13 Feb at

LEAVITT (Continued)

Ossipee NH, KNOWLES Samuel Eld *MS* 3 Mar 1847

LEAVITT Thomas Hale m LAMPREY Eliza both of Hampton on 24 Sept in Hampton, BURBANK P S Eld *MS* 30 Sept 1846

LEAVITT U M of Boston MA m TUTTLE Sarah J of Effingham on 17 ult in Effingham NH, FOSS N Eld *MS* 4 Dec 1850

LEAVITT William m BUTLER Olive J of Sebago ME, TYLER Rev *MFWBR* 21 Jan 1849

LeBARN Horace m KINISON Charlotte both of Hatley LC on 18 Dec 1837, MOULTON A Eld *MS* 10 Jan 1837

LEE Hiram m HOW Mary A both of Holderness on 7 Dec 1849 in Holderness, THOMPSON S Eld *MS* 16 Jan 1850

LEE John of Dedham MA m PIERCE Mary Jane on 12th inst at Limerick ME, FREEMAN C Rev *MFWBR* 21 Sept 1850

LEE Newel m OLNEY Naomi Ann both of No Providence on 27 Aug, HUTCHINS E Eld *MS* 3 Spet 1834

LEE Thomas m LYFORD Julia W on 23d Oct at Dracut, CURTIS S Eld *MS* 18 Dec 1844

LEES Samuel of West Boylston MA m CATE Mary Ann of Northfield NH on 2 Aug in Northfield NH, CLOUGH Jeremiah Eld *MS* 14 Oct 1846

LEGRO Benjamin m LORD Betsey at Lebanon ME, COWELL D B Eld *MS* 19 Mar 1845

LEGRO David on 17 Nov at Dover NH m DORE Eunice of Dover, SMITH A D Eld *MS* 9 Dec 1846

LEGRO Ira m RUNEY Ellen both of Lebanon ME on 23 inst in Lebanon ME, CHENEY O B Eld *MS* 1 Nov 1848

LEGRO John S m LEWIS Mary Jane at Great Falls NH, DUNN R Eld *MS* 7 Jul 1847

LEIGHTON Andrew D Capt of Strafford m HACKETT Mary Jane of Upper Gilmanton NH on 1 Sept, CLARK Peter Eld *MS* 1 Oct 1834

LEIGHTON Charles m WENTWORTH Sally of Wakefield on 14 ult in Ossipee, WALKER John Eld *MS* 24 Oct 1838

LEIGHTON James L m DELAND Amanda M of Dover NH on 5th inst, MACK Enoch *MS* 13 Mar 1839

LEIGHTON Jethro N m COTTON Betsey T both of Gilmanton NH on 14 May 1848 in Gilmanton, FERNALD S P Eld *MS* 21 June 1848

LEIGHTON John J m CLARK Mark E of Dover NH on 3 Feb at Dover NH, CLARK M Eld *MS* 24 Feb 1847

LEIGHTON Lewis L of Milton m JONES Lucinda Jane of Lebanon ME in Lebanon ME, CHENEY O B Eld *MS* 19 Jul 1848

LEIGHTON Lorenzo m NUTT Phebe Ann on 23rd June at Exeter ME, COOK J Eld *MS* 10 Jul 1839

LEIGHTON Nelson of Westbrook ME m FROST Mary E of Wolfboro NH on 2 inst in Dover, HUTCHINS E Eld *MS* 11 Jul 1849 & *MFWBR* 21 Jul 1849

LEIGHTON William A of Brighton MA m STANTON Elizabeth M of Strafford on 16 Aug 1848 in Dover, SMITH A D Eld *MS* 18 Oct 1848

LEMONT Samuel W at Litchfield ME m BRIDGE Eliza, QUINNAM C Eld *MS* 7 Aug 1844

LEMONT Silas merchant of Gardiner m TOOTHAKER Phebe A of Litchfield ME on 4 Apr at Litchfield ME, QUINNAM C Eld *MS* 28 Apr 1847

LENNAN Moses m CAMPBELL Jane M both of Georgetown on Mar 30 at Georgetown, PERKINS Seth W Eld *MS* 27 Apr 1842

LENORD William m AXTELL Mary from Canada on Nov 21 1841 in Pierpont NY, WHITFIELD W Eld *MS* 2 Feb 1842

LEONARD Dwight L m CHADWICK Harriet A of Sutton MA on 25 Oct at Sutton MA, PECK Benjamin D *MS* 15 Nov 1843

LEONARD William H m ATCHINSON Laura Ann on 10 Sept at Purma NY, CRANE E F Eld *MS* 18 Oct 1843

LESTER Hiram L m BATEMAN Elizabeth of Nassau, COLEMAN I B Eld *MS* 22 Feb 1843

LEW Osmon of Lowell MA m TYNG Pamelia, CURTIS S Eld *MS* 10 Sept 1845

LEWIS Allen Capt m HODGDON Emeline P both of Boothbay on 5 Jan 1842 in Boothbay ME, STEVENS J Eld *MS* 2 Mar 1842

LEWIS Alvan B of Waterville ME m PARKER Caroline W of Waterville ME on 20th ult, BURGESS J S Eld *MS* 14 Jul 1847

LEWIS Asa of Waterville ME m GAGE Deborah of Hartland ME, LEWIS D B Eld *MS* 25 Dec 1844

LEWIS C W m CASWELL Sarah on 18 Sept at Boothbay ME, MORRILL S P Eld *MS* 22 Jan 1845

LEWIS Henry of Fryburg m JOHNSON Perthena R on 3 Dec 1846 at Brownfield, PIKE J Eld *MS* 21 Apr 1847

LEWIS James S m RICKER Sarah J both of Dover on 15 inst in Dover, HUTCHINS E Eld *MS* 22 Jul 1846

LEWIS James W m MORSE Elizabeth Ann on 8 Nov in Newbury NH, HOLMES H Eld *MS* 19 Feb 1851

LEWIS Jefferson m PERKINS Jerusha of Conway NH on 26 Jan 1842 at Conway NH, HAMILTON James Eld *MS* 6 Apr 1842

LEWIS John B of Waterborough m QUINT Nancy I of Brownfield on 29 Sept 1848 in Brownfield ME, HART E H Eld *MS* 15 Nov 1848

LEWIS Joshua W m LOWRY Betsey P both of Kittery ME on 6 Dec in Kittery ME, PERKINS Seth W Eld *MS* 9 Jan 1850

LEWIS Lincoln Eld m CHESLEY Ruth P both of Barnstead on 3 inst, TRUE E Eld *MS* 11 Apr 1849

LEWIS Lincoln of Burnham ME m SANBORN Eleanor of Ellsworth NH in Ellsworth NH, BLAKE I Eld *MS* 7 Mar 1828

LEWIS Russel m HODGDON Mary E both of Boothbay on 13 Sept 1849 in Boothbay ME, PAGE E G Eld *MS* 15 May 1850

LEWIS Tristram S of Waterboro m BROWN Olive J of Buxton ME on 21 Feb, MACOMBER H N Rev *MFWBR* 10 Mar 1849

LEWIS William B of Kittery ME m JONES Paulina on 12 Apr at Lebanon ME, BLAISDELL E Eld *MS* 28 May 1845

LEWIS William H m EMERSON Jane at Dover *MFWBR* 3 Nov 1849

LEWIS William m PICKERING Hannah both of Meredith in Meredith, PITMAN S J Eld *MS* 29 Aug 1838

LEWIS William of Boothbay m HARRINGTON Maria of Edgecomb on 7 Jan at Edgecomb ME, PAGE E G Eld *MS* 14 Feb 1844

LIBBEY David m JONES Dolly J both of Manchester on 26 Jul in Manchester Sabbath Eve, DEXTER Henry M Rev *MS* 5 Aug 1846

LIBBEY Eliab L m HOPKINS Sarah E both of Biddeford on 7 Nov 1848 in Biddeford ME, WITHAM L H Eld *MS* 24 Jan 1849

LIBBEY Hammond Capt m FOGG Ann Maria in Eliot ME *MS* 18 Jul 1838

LIBBEY Hanson m SHERMAN Elizabeth A of Monson on 27 May at Monson ME, BROWN B B Esq *MS* 16 June 1847

LIBBEY Horace B m TOWNSEND Mary both of Scarboro in Scarboro ME, LIBBY C O Eld *MS* 3 Jul 1850

LIBBEY J T S, printer m WINGATE Abby on 4 inst in Dover, HUTCH-INS E Eld *MS* 10 Oct 1849

LIBBEY Joseph of Bedford m WHITNEY Mary of Billerica MA on 14 Dec, DAVIS J B Eld *MS* 27 Dec 1843

LIBBEY Joseph T m CHAMBERLIN Elizabeth G both of New Durham on 16 Dec, GATES J R Esq *MS* 26 Dec 1849

LIBBEY Mark of Berwick m CHADBOURNE Eliza Ann of No Berwick on 22 Feb in No Berwick, CLAY D Eld *MS* 25 Mar 1846

LIBBEY Oscar F m GILMAN Lucinda R both of Lowell MA on 20 Feb 1848 in Lowell MA, CURTIS S Eld *MS* 8 Mar 1848

LIBBEY Phineas Rev m NOYES Mary E of Windham ME at Windham ME, COPELAND David Rev *MFWBR* 26 June 1847

LIBBY Abner C of Limerick ME m FELT Lucy S of Greenwood ME on 28th ult at Buxton ME, BARTLETT Rev *MFWBR* 1 Dec 1849

LIBBY Abner of Limerick ME m ALLEN Almira of Portland at Portland ME, RAND S Eld *MS* 29 Oct 1828

LIBBY Almon Eld of Poland ME m HALL Hannah H of Gorham ME on 19 Jan, HERSEY L Eld *MS* 1 Feb 1843

LIBBY Amos m HAINES Betsey F on 16th inst at Saco ME, STRICK-LAND G G Rev *MFWBR* 21 Jan 1849

LIBBY Amos m BOLTER Elizabeth on 14 Aug in West Buxton ME, BAILEY J M Eld *MS* 28 Aug 1850

LIBBY Andrew of Broom m DAVIS Nancy of Stanstead LC on 21 Mar, MOULTON A Eld of Stanstead LC *MS* 13 Apr 1842

LIBBY Andrew of Windham ME m HARDING Martha A of Standish ME on 7 May *MFWBR* 1 June 1850

LIBBY Asa m LIBBY Martha of Windham ME on 18 Nov at Falmouth

LIBBY (Continued)
ME, PERKINS Seth W Eld *MS* 20 Dec 1843

LIBBY Benjamin C m MEEDE Irene of Limington ME on 23d inst, BULLOCK John Eld *MS* 31 May 1827

LIBBY C E Dr m PURKIS Eliza A of Gray ME on 18 May 1843 at West Poland ME, LIBBY James Eld *MS* 8 Nov 1843

LIBBY Charles E m FOSTER Martha A both of Gray on 12 Sept 1848 in Gray ME, LANCASTER D Eld *MS* 1 Aug 1849

LIBBY Charles of Barnston m DRESSER Relief on 15 Sept, MOULTON A Eld of Stanstead LC *MS* 13 Apr 1842

LIBBY Cyrus m DYER Frances E both of Portland on 20 inst in Portland ME, LIBBY Isaac Eld *MS* 3 May 1848

LIBBY David Eld of Lewiston ME m SMITH Mary C of Lisbon ME on 12 inst in Lisbon ME, LIBBY Almon Eld *MS* 3 May 1848

LIBBY David m MOULTON Sally both of Newfield on 1 Dec in Newfield, JORDAN Z Eld *MS* 26 Feb 1840

LIBBY Edward divorced 27 Oct 1830 LIBBY Betsey *MS* 27 Oct 1830

LIBBY Beniah of Scarboro' m LIBBY Keziah of Portland ME on 27 Mar at Cape Elizabeth ME, LIBBY A Eld *MS* 16 Apr 1845

LIBBY Elbridge of Scarboro' m JOHNSON Mary on 31 Jan at Westbrook ME, LIBBY Almon Eld *MS* 17 Apr 1844

LIBBY Frederick W m COLBY Adelaide on 26th ult at East Thomaston *MFWBR* 8 Sept 1849

LIBBY Furber m STAPLES Betsey both of Monmouth ME, FILES A Eld *MS* 29 Dec 1847

LIBBY George of Scarboro m LIBBY Elizabeth of Standish ME on 3 inst in Standish ME, LIBBY C O Eld *MS* 27 Mar 1850

LIBBY Harrison J of Limerick ME m LIBBY Margaret Miss of Scarboro on Tues last at S, LIBBY John Eld *MS* 20 Jul 1832

LIBBY Henry of Portsmouth NH m MILIKEN Jane U of Buxton ME at Saco ME on 13th inst *MFWBR* 24 Aug 1850

LIBBY Isaac Eld m ALLEN Hannah J Mrs on 4 Sept 1848 in Gorham ME, LIBBY C O Eld *MS* 13 Sept 1848

LIBBY Isaac m MORRIS Elizabeth Payson on 31 ult in North Scarboro' ME, MANSON B S Eld *MS* 1 Dec 1847

LIBBY Isaac m MERRETT Harriet S of Brunswick ME on 5 June at Brunswick ME, ROLLINS Andrew Eld *MS* 29 June 1842

LIBBY Jacob m BUNKER Rebecca K both of Dover on 23 inst 1849 in Dover, HUTCHINS E Eld *MS* 2 May 1849

LIBBY James C of Ossipee m BRIARD Susan of Tuftonborough NH on 29 Dec 1848 in Tuftonborogh NH, BEAN Silas F *MS* 9 May 1849

LIBBY James m IRISH Esther Miss, HODSDON Caleb Esq *MS* 23 Nov 1832

LIBBY James m THAYER Betsey of Gray ME on 6 Aug at Gray ME, DURGIN J M Eld *MS* 16 Aug 1843

LIBBY John of Sandford ME m LITTLEFIELD Olive on 2 June at Springvale ME, LORD D H Eld *MS* 19 June 1839

LIBBY John W of Richmond ME m DINGLEY Betsey B of Bowdoin ME, QUINNAM C Eld *MS* 7 Feb 1849

LIBBY Joseph Jr m LIBBY Helena Miss at Limerick ME, FREEMAN C Rev *MS* 30 Nov 1832

LIBBY Levi m LIBBY Sarah D on 3 Jul 1842 at Scarboro ME, SMALL William Eld *MS* 20 June 1842

LIBBY Micah of Litchfield m BROWN Jane of Bowdoin ME in Bowdoin ME, QUINNAN C Eld *MS* 25 Jul 1838

LIBBY Nathaniel Esq of Limerick ME m BERY Catharine of Scarboro *MS* Dec 28 1826

LIBBY Parson m CASS Sophia both of S on 11 Apr 1844 *MS* 1 May 1844

LIBBY Samuel S of Limerick ME m COLE Huldah H of Limerick ME on 29 Jan 1843, MANSON B S Eld *MS* 7 Feb 1844

LIBBY Silas J of Scarborough ME m HAINES Hannah of Saco on 1 Nov in Saco ME, LIBBY Peter Eld *MS* 21 Nov 1838

LIBBY Simeon m COLE Louisa on 16 June 1844 at West Poland ME, LIBBEY James Eld *MS* 9 Apr 1845

LIBBY Solomon m SKOFFIELD Lucy A both of Brunswick in Brunswick ME, LIBBY A Eld *MS* 23 Jan 1850

LIBBY Tappan m CUMMINGS Catharine S of Cape Elizabeth on 5 June at Cape Elizabeth, LIBBY Almon Eld *MS* 17 Jul 1844

LIBBY Wentworth m MOULTON Mary B both of Newfield ME on 18 June in Parsonsfield, SMITH W Eld *MS* 17 Jul 1850

LIBBY Wilder M m LIBBY Betsey C of Gorham ME, LOMBARD Solomon Esq *MFWBR* 13 Apr 1850

LIBBY William H m MANNING Hannah on both of Dover NH on 19 Jan 1850 in new Market, EASTMAN C Allen Eld *MS* 30 Jan 1850

LIBBY Zebulon T of Scarboro ME m MOODY Charlotte of Cape Elizabeth ME at Cape Elizabeth ME, LIBBY C O Eld *MFWBR* 11 May 1850

LILIKIN Leander m MOULTON Susan A in Freedom, RUNNELS J Eld *MS* 9 Feb 1848

LILLY Patrick m RIX Sophronia both of Stanstead LC on 9 ult *MS* 18 May 1836

LINCOLN H B Esq m WEDENBURY Ann of Augusta at Providence RI *MFWBR* 2 Nov 1850

LINCOLN Rufus of Lewiston ME m JORDAN Mary N of Lisbon ME in Lisbon ME, WOODWARD William Esq *MS* 6 Sept 1837

LITCHFIELD A B of Manchester m GRANT Lucy P of Lyme on 23 Oct in Lyme, TENNEY Erdes Rev *MS* 30 Oct 1850

LITCHFIELD Ames Eld of Lewiston ME m BEAN Susan H of Montville ME on 17 Dec last, KNOWLTON E Eld *MS* 10 Apr 1834

LITCHFIELD Samuel m STANFORD Mary both of Lewiston ME,

LITCHFIELD (Continued)
BRIDGES A Eld *MS* 26 Sept 1833
LITCHFIELD Winslow A m McLITCHFIELD Nancy both of Boston on
11 June 1848 in Boston *MS* 28 June 1848
LITTLE Joseph R of Palmer m BARRETT Olive R of Manchester on 19
Oct 1848 in Manchester, CILLEY D P Eld *MS* 8 Nov 1848
LITTLE Moses m KINNAN Catharine both of Elmira on 29 June in
Enfield NY, EVANS S R Eld *MS* 25 Sept 1850
LITTLEFIELD Andrew G m RICE Mary of Hallowell ME on 19th Jul
at Litchfield ME, FROST Isaac Eld *MS* 16 Aug 1843
LITTLEFIELD Asa H m WINGATE Mary on 11th at Dover NH,
MOULTON A K Eld *MS* 17 Aug 1842
LITTLEFIELD Daniel m CARR Mahala W both of Dover NH on
Sunday last in this town, SMITH A D Eld *MS* 29 Aug 1838
LITTLEFIELD Daniel m PLUMMER Harriet B of Dover on 25th ult,
HUTCHINS E Eld *MS* 1 Oct 1845
LITTLEFIELD David A m JONES Sarah E both of Dover on 22 inst
Sunday morning in Dover NH, CAVERNO A Eld *MS* 25 Sept 1850
LITTLEFIELD Edmund P of Chesterville m BLACKWELL Albritaia on
4 Jul 1846, WHEELER S Eld *MS* 21 Apr 1847
LITTLEFIELD Edwin m GOWEN Angeline on 15 Nov at Wells ME,
SMALL C Eld *MS* 20 Jan 1847
LITTLEFIELD Ezekiel m SMITH Lydia of Biddeford ME on 3 Apr at
Kennebunkport ME, WITHAM L H Eld *MS* 18 May 1842
LITTLEFIELD Henry Jr of Wells m NEAL Alta G of No Berwick ME on
18 June 1848 in No Berwick ME, CLAY D Eld *MS* 16 Aug 1848
LITTLEFIELD Joseph H m HUSSEY Jane on Wed evening last in
Dover NH, MUCK E Eld *MS* 29 Aug 1838
LITTLEFIELD Joshua m MILLER Jenette Q on 29 June at Dover,
HUTCHINS E Eld *MS* 9 Jul 1845
LITTLEFIELD Robert S m HALL Louisa on 25th inst at Dover NH,
PERKINS Seth Eld *MS* 31 Dec 1845
LITTLEFIELD Solomon m LITTLEFIELD Ruth of Sanford ME on 14
Feb at Sanford ME, RAMSEY G P Eld *MS* 3 Mar 1847
LITTLEFIELD William H Eld m STEVENS Mary of Kennebunk ME on
20 Mar at Kennebunk ME, GOODWIN Joseph Eld *MS* 26 Mar
1845
LIVINGSTON R C of Gardiner MEm POTTER Abigail of Clinton,
LEWIS Daniel B Eld *MS* 15 Jan 1840
LOBDELL Miles C m LITTLEFIELD Sarah on 3d April at Hamburgh
NY, PLUMB H N Eld *MS* 12 June 1844
LOCK David m PHILBRICK Nancy P of Hampton on 28 March at
Hampton, BURBANK P S Eld *MS* 21 Apr 1847
LOCK George of Alexandria m CHENEY Elizabeth of Bristol on 7th
March at Bristol NH, BROWN A Eld *MS* 27 Mar 1844
LOCK Hamilton m GUPTIL Dorcas both of Wolfborough NH on 13

LOCK (Continued)

Oct in Wolfborough, PARIS C Eld *MS* 16 Oct 1850

LOCK Horace of Boston MA m SHORT Sarah A of Lowell MA on 19 June, WOODMAN J Eld *MS* 23 Aug 1843

LOCK Jethro of Barnstead m HANSCOM Lydia at Strafford on Nov 14, CAVERLY J 4th Eld *MS* 29 Jan 1840

LOCK Samuel W m ELKINS Irene both of Lowell MA on 17 Sept 1848 in Gilford NH, FROST D S Eld *MS* 11 Oct 1848

LOCK Varney of Boston m HUNTRESS Betsey of Strafford in Strafford, PLACE E Eld *MS* 19 Dec 1838

LOCKE Arthur C m BICKFORD Salina O both of Epsom NH on 23 Sept in Epsom, FOSS T Eld *MS* 13 Oct 1847

LOCKE Ephraim Dea of Epsom m COLLINS Rhoda in Guilford on Feb 15, PINKHAM John Eld *MS* 4 May 1842

LOCKE Ephraim Jr of Epsom m DYER Sarah C Miss on 19th ult *MS* 18 Feb 1835

LOCKE Reuben of Northboro MA m MERRILL Annah L of Craftsbury VT in Hartford CT *MS* 28 Mar 1849

LOCKE Samuel A m SHERBURNE Sophronia A on 28 Apr in Barrington, SHERBURNE S Eld *MS* 8 May 1850

LOCKE Thomas E m CROSS Sophia S both of Great Falls on 19 June in Great Falls, BROOKS N Eld *MS* 10 Jul 1850

LOCKWOOD Benajah T m WALKER Rhoda J both of Smithfield on 25 Dec 1848, CALVIN R Eld *MS* 17 Jan 1849

LOGAN John W m SARGENT Margaret S both of Searsport ME on 6th inst at Belfast ME, BEAN F A Rev *MFWBR* 19 June 1847

LONG Larkin A (a licensed preacher in Sandwick QM) m LEAVITT Harriet of South Conway on 9 Oct at South Conway NH, BROOKS John Eld *MS* 15 Oct 1845

LONG Viberus m LUNT Betsey of Eaton NH on 7 Nov, WILLEY E C Eld *MS* 20 Nov 1839

LOOK John J m WENDALL S L at Farmington ME *MFWBR* 16 June 1849

LOOK John J m WENDELL Susan L on 29th ult at Farmington, MILLER C Rev *MFWBR* 12 May 1849 & WENDALL S L *MFWBR* 16 June 1849

LOOK Richard m FISHER Lydia both of Georgetown ME, QUINNAM Constant Eld *MS* 7 Jan 1835

LOOKER Henry E of Wilmot m Van VORST Sophia T of Russia NY on 1st Jan at Russia Herkimer Co NY, McKOON D W Eld *MS* 5 Feb 1845

LORD Almon of Ossipee NH m MOULTON Mary of Parsonsfield ME on 25th ult, BURBANK Eld *MS* 1 Ocy 1828

LORD Andrew m ROGERS Mary E of Somersworth NH on 3d inst at Dover NH, HUTCHINS E Eld *MS* 12 May 1847

LORD Daniel m LORD Julia Ann both of Parsonsfield ME at Cornish

LORD (Continued)
ME, BUZZELL A Eld *MS* 29 Apr 1840

LORD David H Eld of Pascoag RI m MORRILL Annette of Parsonsfield ME on 9 inst in Roxbury MA, MOULTON A K Eld *MS* 29 Nov 1848

LORD David H Eld of Sanford ME m CLARK Almira of Dover NH on 4 Jan/Dec in Lebanon, STEVENS Enoch Eld *MS* 10 Jan 1838

LORD Davis B of Berwick ME m HALL Mary of Great Falls NH, CURTIS Silas Eld *MS* 9 Oct 1839

LORD Ebenezer at Berwick ME m FULLER Margaret A K of Berwick ME, BLAISDELL David Eld *MS* 8 Dec 1841

LORD Eli B m WENTWORTH Betsey on 7th inst at Lebanon ME, CHENEY O B Eld *MS* 17 Feb 1847

LORD George m BRYANT Mary Jane of Great Falls NH at Great Falls NH, CURTIS S Eld *MS* 4 Dec 1839

LORD Isaac m REDMAN Hannah on Thurs last in Parsonsfield ME, BUZZELL John Eld *MS* 2 Nov 1826

LORD Isaac m LORD Susan Miss *MS* 24 Mar 1830

LORD James m RENNETT Lydia A of Eaton, GASKILL S Eld *MS* 21 Jan 1846

LORD James of Limerick ME m WEEKS Hannah R at Parsonsfield ME on Dec 31, BUZZELL Alvah Eld *MS* 29 Jan 1840

LORD John 3rd m WEEKS Catherine P at Parsonsfield ME, BUZZELL John Eld *MFWBR* 27 Feb 1847

LORD John C of Pueblo San Jose CA m YOUNG Olive E of No Berwick on 14 Jul in No Berwick ME, CLAY D Eld *MS* 24 Jul 1850 & *MFWBR* 27 Jul 1850

LORD John m GREGORY Susan of Corinth ME on 24 Nov 1842 at Corinth ME, AMES M Eld *MS* 28 Feb 1844

LORD John m HILTON Sarah F of Sanford on Dec 2d at Sanford ME, BUZZELL Alvah Eld *MS* 15 Dec 1841

LORD Moses C m CALEFF Eliza Ann on 16 Mar 1848 in Dover NH, SMITH A D Eld *MS* 19 Apr 1848

LORD Nelson Capt merchant of Freedom m HURD Huldah of Eaton on 29 Jan in Eaton, GASKELL Silas Eld *MS* 12 Aug 1846

LORD Noah m COWELL Marianne on 6 June at Lebanon ME, CHENEY O B Eld *MS* 23 June 1847

LORD Samuel m BOOTHBY Miriam both of Parsonsfield ME on 18th inst, LIBBY E Eld *MS* 30 Nov 1832

LORD Samuel of Eaton NH m DOWNS Lydia of Kennebunk ME on 4 Jan at Tamworth's FW Baptist meeting house, BROOKS J Eld *MS* 18 Feb 1846

LORD Stephen m LORD Eliza of Hatley on 20 Mar, MOULTON A Eld *MS* 13 Sept 1843

LORD Tobias of Limerick m FENDERSON Catharine at Parsonsfield, BUZZELL Alvah Eld *MS* 20 May 1840

LORD William K m GAREY Abigail H on 31 Oct at Sanford ME,

LORD (Continued)

THING Samuel S Esq *MFWBR* 13 Nov 1847

LORD William of Limerick ME m AVERY Harriet, KINSMAN Eld in Limerick *MS* 31 Jan 1828

LORETTE Anthony F of Portland ME m BERRY Sarah at Portland ME, BEECHER Rev *MFWBR* 22 Jul 1848

LORING John S m WING Joanna both of Leeds on 25 Nov in Leeds ME, CATLIN S T Eld *MS* 9 Feb 1842

LOTHROP John C m HANSON Lydia B both of Rochester on 13 Dec 1848 in Rochester, WHITNEY G W Eld *MS* 7 Feb 1849

LOTHROP Urbane Dr m ORDAWAY Elicta of Strafford on 11 Jan at Chelsea VT, SANBORN G Eld *MS* 6 Apr 1847

LOUD Horace of Corinth m BENNETT Susan of Bangor ME on 12 May at Corinth ME, AMES M Eld *MS* 31 Aug 1842

LOUGEE George G m LEAVITT Sarah A both of Exeter NH on 26 Jan in Amesbury MA, MERRILL W P Eld *MS* 12 Feb 1851

LOUGEE James m WORK Eliza on 20 Oct at Sangerville ME, GILMAN Moses Esq *MS* 27 Nov 1844

LOUGEE John Jr of Parsonsfield m LIBBY Sally of Newfield *MS* 10 Mar 1820

LOUGEE Joseph B m EVANS Lucretia both of Strafford on 19 Apr 1849 in Strafford, GARLAND David Eld *MS* 2 May 1849

LOUGEE Lyman of Dover m DURGIN Nancy of Lee on 3d inst at Newmarket, HUTCHINS E Eld *MS* 13 Mar 1844

LOUGEE Samuel Jr m CLARK Mary Susan on 19th inst in Parsonsfield, McARTHUR J *MS* 27 Jan 1832

LOUGEE Taylor of Parsonsfield m HAYES Sabina on Sunday last in Limerick, FREEMAN Rev *MS* 12 Jul 1827

LOUGER Frederick C m HALL Mary A both of Manchester on 18 Aug in Manchester, CILLEY D P Eld *MS* 1 Sept 1847

LOVEJOY Azael m WOODWORTH Zintha Stutson of Brookline on 2 Nov at Boston MA, NOYES E Eld *MS* 21 Jan 1846

LOVEJOY Cyrus H of Landaff NH m GORDON Susan of Topsham on 17 ult in Topsham VT, SHIPMAN O Eld *MS* 7 Nov 1838

LOVEJOY Jonathan of Littleton NH m BLOSS Caroline of Sutton VT on 17 Jul, CROSS D Eld *MS* 27 Nov 1850

LOVEJOY Wesley m CRITCHET Arvilla at Candia, KIMBALL Eld *MS* 10 Sept 1834

LOVEJOY William m HAMILTON Lydia on 14 Nov at Great Falls NH, WEBBER H Eld *MS* 18 Dec 1844

LOVEJOY William O of Lawrence MA m BURKE Ellen of Dover in Dover NH, EASTMAN C A Eld *MS* 6 Nov 1850

LOVELESS Charles W m GRAHAM Lepheau both of Hadley LC on 23 Feb 1850 in Hadley, LOVELESS J H Eld *MS* 1 May 1850

LOVELESS Thomas S m JAMES Maanda (*sic* - Amanda?) on 22 Feb 1849 in Perry Township Logan Co Ohio, HEATH J D Eld

LOVELESS (Continued)
MS 28 Mar 1849

LOVELL Henry R of Boston m PATTEN Mehitabel of Candia on 15 Nov 1849 in Candia, ATWOOD M Eld *MS* 2 Jan 1850

LOVELL John L m HOWARD Mary Ann both of Westbrook ME on 26 Mar in Westbrook, NEVINS William Eld *MS* 8 May 1844

LOVEREIN Luke W m KIMBALL Clarissa S both of Lowell MA, THURSTON N Eld *MS* 16 Sept 1835

LOVERING John S m BEAN Ann both of Loudon NH on 27 Jan 1848 in Canterbury, CLOUGH Jeremiah Eld *MS* 16 Feb 1848

LOVERING Orville m LIBBY Susan E both of Colebrook NH on 31 Oct in Colebrook, BEAN Benaiah Eld *MS* 17 Nov 1847

LOVETT Lorenzo W of Gilford m PAGE Abba Amanda of Meredith on 19 Oct, PITMAN S J Eld *MS* 27 Nov 1850

LOVING Daniel R of Medford MA m GODFREY Martha Ann of Pittsfield on 14 Nov, DAVIS J B Eld *MS* 27 Nov 1844

LOW Ivory C m PULLEN Sophronia both of Waterville in Waterville ME, LEWIS Daniel B Eld *MS* 15 Jan 1840

LOW James of Sacarappa m DAVIS Susan M of Limington ME on 10th inst at Sacarappa, MANSON B S Eld *MFWBR* 16 June 1849

LOW James of Westbrook m DAVIS Susan M of Limington on 10 May, MANSON B S Eld *MS* 30 May 1849

LOW John m HILTON Sarah F on 2 Dec 1841 at Sanford ME, BUZZELL Alvah Eld *MS* 29 Dec 1841

LOW Seth m EASTMAN Flora G both of Warner on 25 Jan at Warner *MS* 8 May 1844

LOWD David m HARVEY Merriam S on 8 Oct at Portsmouth NH, DAVIS Isaac G Eld *MS* 10 Jan 1844

LOWD Sylvester m HANSON Dorcas on 4th inst at Acton ME, BUZZELL A Eld *MS* 17 May 1843

LOWELL Ambrose m MAINES Mary J both of Lawrence in Lawrence MA, CURTIS Eld S *MS* 3 Jan 1849

LOWELL Enoch of Newfield ME m DAM Eliza W of Shapleigh ME, BURBANK S Eld *MS* 13 Apr 1832

LOWELL Erastus m BOOKER Sarah on 30 Oct at Litchfield ME, FOSS Alvin W Eld *MS* 4 Jan 1843

LOWELL Harrison Hon m COLE Eliza D of Biddeford on 27th ult at Biddeford, LORD T N Rev *MFWBR* 9 Dec 1848

LOWELL Henry R of Boston m PATTEN Mehitable J of Candia in Candia on Thanksgiving eve *MS* 5 Dec 1849

LOWELL John W of Phipsburgh m OLIVER Louisa of Georgetown, WHITTEN S F Eld *MS* 21 Mar 1833

LOWELL Josiah B at Bangor ME m BLAISDELL Sophronia, CAVERNO A Eld *MS* 13 Sept 1843

LUCAS Daniel of Wolfboro' m CHESLEY Sarah F of New Durham NH 19 Apr 1842, PRESCOTT E T Eld *MS* 24 May 1843

LUCAS Mark C m GLIDDEN Tabitha both of Dover on 17 Apr in Dover NH, SMITH A D Eld *MS* 9 May 1849

LUCE Nelson C of Industry ME m BRUCE Lucena of Newark VT on 12 Nov 1848, GEORGE N K Eld *MS* 9 May 1849 & *MS* 10 Jan 1849

LUCE Sirah A of Winfield m WALKER Malina A of New Hartford on 11 Nov in Checkerville NY, MARINER J Eld *MS* 1 Jan 1851

LUDWIG Ephraim of Liberty ME m PEASE Elizabeth both of Hope ME in Hope, RINES J N Eld *MS* 25 Dec 1839

LUFKIN Nehemiah of Chester m HILL Sally on 24 Nov 1844 at Strafford, PLACE E Eld *MS* 29 Jan 1845

LUNNEY Richard m FORD Olive G of Sanford ME on 1 Nov at Sanford ME, RAMSEY G P Eld *MS* 25 Nov 1846

LUNT Bray of Berwick ME m LIBBY Asenath of Limerick ME on 1st inst at Great Falls NH, CAVERNO A Eld *MS* 18 Mar 1835

LUNT Israel B m GRANT Nancy at Mt Desert *MS* 9 Dec 1831

LUNT James Capt of Freeport m MORSE Hester Ann of Brunswick in Brunswick ME, BEAN C Eld *MS* 19 Jan 1848

LUNT William J m PRIDE Cynthia B 15 June at Westbrook ME, BEAN C Eld *MS* 30 June 1847

LUTHER Thomas of Manchester m WHEELER Esther of Eaton LC on 10 Nov in Manchester, CILLEY D PE Eld *MS* 5 Dec 1849

LYFORD Augustus formerly of Canterbury NH m EMERSON Abby formerly of Newburyport MA on 19 Oct 1842 at French Grove, Bureau Co IL, JULIAN S L Eld *MS* 19 Jul 1843

LYMAN Charles m WHITE Alma both formerly of Trenton NY on 23 Sept in Eldorado Wis, KEAVILL E J Eld *MS* 27 Nov 1850

LYMAN Robert A m HANSCOM Sarah Ann at South Berwick ME *MFWBR* 21 Sept 1850

LYMAN William B Capt of Milton m JONES Lydia Miss of Dover on Sunday last, WILLIAMS Gibbon Rev *MS* 2 Jan 1834

LYON Jonathan m HENIGEN Margaret both of Hume on 19 Nov *MS* 23 Dec 1835

MACK John G of Deerfield m GILMAN Harriet Mrs of Gilmanton on 8 Jul in Barnstead, GARLAND David Eld *MS* 7 Aug 1850

MACK John W of Corinth VT m WATERMAN Caroline M of Fairley on 21 Nov, MOULTON F Eld *MS* 17 Feb 1847

MACK Norman B of New Haven m TAYLOR Caroline P of Nelson on Jan 5th at Nelson NY, GARDINER S D Eld *MS* 12 Feb 1845

MACK William of Addison NY m KIMBALL Eliza of Wear NH on 10 Nov 1837 in Underhill VT, FAY E Eld *MS* 4 Apr 1838

MACK William of Strafford VT m TUCKER Lucinda of Sharon on 5 Nov 1848 in Strafford VT, CLARK E Eld *MS* 6 June 1849

MACOMBER George B m BALL Isabel D of Westport MA on 15 Oct at Tiverton RI, WHITTAMORE Joseph *MS* 8 Nov 1843

MACOMBER/MACUMBER Leander M m HAMILTON Lucinda of
Webster ME on 1st inst at Wales ME, FILES Allen Eld *MFWBR* 20
Mar 1847 & *MS* 21 Apr 1847

MACUMBER Charles F m FALL Celistia P both of Phoenix NY on 16
Apr in Phoenix Oswego Co NY, SMITH O W Eld *MS* 21 June 1848

MADDEN L J Eld of Lansing Mich m PERRY Catharine J of Concord
on 12 Jul in Spring Arbor Mich, FAIRFIELD E B Eld *MS* 22 Aug
1849

MADDOCKS Oliver m JOHNSON Caroline in Limerick, LIBBY Eld *MS*
27 Sept 1827

MADDOX John W of Cornish ME m BENEN Susan Miss of Parsonsfield on 8th inst, FOSS A T Eld *MS* 16 Nov 1832

MADDOX Thomas F m GREENLEAF Caroline G of Saco ME at Saco
ME on 14th inst *MFWBR* 4 May 1850

MAGOON Gilford of Stanstead LC m COX Sophronia of Hatley LC on
2 Jan*MS* 22 Mar 1837

MAGOON Henry C of Lowell m CLEMENTS Mehitable E on 24 Sept,
THURSTON N Eld *MS* 20 Nov 1839

MAGOON Josiah M of Wheelock VT m JACKSON Ruth of Hatley LC
on 23 Oct 1837, MOULTON A Eld *MS* 10 Jan 1838

MAGOON Wilder m BLAKE Lectina both of Stanstead LC on 3d inst
at Barnston *MS* 18 May 1836

MAHEW Wm of Foxcroft m SNOW Christiana of Kilmarnock ME on
12 ult at Kilmarnock ME, HATHAWAY L Eld *MS* 12 Nov 1834

MAHONY James J m LOCKE Elizabeth at Bangor ME, CAVERNO A
Eld *MS* 13 Sept 1843

MAJOR Thomas m HAYES Rachel K on 24 Sept at Manchester NH,
CILLEY D P Eld *MS* 1 Oct 1845

MAKEPEACE T L m THURBEE Mehitabel both of Newton MA on 31
Oct 1847 in Attleborough MA, CLARKE G Eld *MS* 8 Dec 1847

MALING Nathaniel G m BLAISDELL Eliza on 7 Jul at Charlestown
MA, WETHERBEE I J Eld *MS* 9 Dec 1846

MALLARD Asa of Meredith NH m CROCKETT Mary Ann of Meredith
NH, PITMAN Stephen J Eld *MS* 8 Dec 1841

MALLARY Jonathan of Center Harbor m BROCK Mahaly of Alexandria on 15 Aug in Alexandria, BROWN Amos Eld *MS* 12 Dec 1838

MALLETY Elisha P m SAWYER Elizabeth F both of Topsham ME on
23 May in Topsham ME, BEAN C Eld *MS* 15 Jan 1851

MALLET Isaac E of Topsham m BAKER Frances A of Litchfield ME
on 31 Dec in Bowdoinham ME, BEAN C Eld *MS* 15 Jan 1851

MALOY Dennis m YOUNG Ellen J of Great Falls NH on 27 Nov of
Great Falls NH, DUNN R Eld *MS* 24 Dec 1845

MANAHAN Harvey m MILLEN Rebecca G of Lowell MA on 6 Sept at
Lowell MA at Lowell MA, THURSTON N Eld *MS* 2 Nov 1842

MANCHESTER Niles of Smithfield m GORTON Sarah A of No Providence RI on 29th ult, HUTCHINS E Eld *MS* 18 Feb 1835

MANLEY Daniel W m RANDALL Mary L both of Charlestown MA on 7 inst in So Boston MA, TUTTLE E Eld *MS* 26 Mar 1851

MANN George W m WHITCHER Susan M of Benton MOULTON F Eld *MS* 21 June 1843 & *MS* 24 May 1843

MANNING Ezra C of Reading MA m KENDALL Frances R of Wilmington on 13 Apr 1843 at Benton, DURGIN J M Eld *MS* 23 Oct 1844

MANNING Jacob m THAYER Mehitabel A on 24 Jul at Wilmington MA, DURGIN J M Eld *MS* 13 Aug 1845

MANNING Jesse m MORGAN Elanor Mrs in Lowell, THURSTON N Eld *MS* 20 June 1838

MANNING John S of Big Bend Iowa m HAMMOND Maryett of Canal on 23 May, RITTENHOUSE W Eld *MS* 17 Jul 1844

MANSEIGH Lewis m ATKINSON Mary Ann both of Stanstead LC on 1 Jan *MS* 17 Feb 1836

MANSEIL Ira m BAKER Dorinda on 4 Apr 1847 in Garland ME, DORE T W Eld *MS* 15 Sept 1847

MANSER Darius m SANBORN Catharine both of Prospect *MS* 6 Apr 1831

MANSFIELD Jesse of Salisbury NH m LUFKIN Hannah of Dover on 3 Jul *MS* 13 Jul 1836

MANSFIELD John of Brownfield ME m McLELLAN Martha at Newfield ME, LIBBY Eld *MS* 14 Mar 1828

MANSON Benjamin Eld of Conway m BURNHAM Eliza Miss *MS* 27 Sept 1827

MANSON Charles H of Wilton m PETTEGROW Lucinda of Clinton of Conway NH, LEWIS Daniel B Eld *MS* 23 Jan 1839

MANSON George m BLAKE Sarah both of Kittery on 19 inst in Kittery, MILTON Nathan H Eld *MS* 22 Nov 1837

MANSON James m SHERBURNE Zerriah on Sun at Barrington, SHERBURNE S Eld *MS* 14 June 1843

MANSON Richard E m PETTIGREW Eliza A both of Clinton on 10 Nov, BUKER A J Eld *MS* 25 Dec 1850

MANSUR Horace m LEIGHTON Abigail T of Dover NH on 30 Oct at Dover NH, PERKINS Seth W Eld *MS* 5 Nov 1845

MANSUR James m BATCHELDER Adeline both of Newburyport MA on 7 May in Hampton NH, MERRILL W P Eld *MS* 15 May 1850

MANSUR William m HICKOFT Jerusha J of Methden on 30 Dec at Dracut MA, CURTIS Silas Eld *MS* 7 Jan 1846

MANTER Daniel E of Pittsfield m BAILY Sophronia F of Canaan on 25 Nov 1849 in Canaan, BUKER Alvah J Eld *MS* 16 Jan 1850

MANWELL Jacob H of East Livermore ME m EATON Harriet R of Chesterville ME on 7 Nov 1844, WHEELER S Eld *MS* 26 Mar 1845

MARBLE John Jr of Sutton m CROSBY Sabrey on 23 Aug, PECK Benjamin D *MS* 13 Sept 1843

MARCH Horace m EATON Elmira both of Plymouth VT on Jan 23 1840, WARNER William Eld *MS* 4 Mar 1840

MARCH William of Windham m RICHARDS Ellen M on 14 Sept at Falmouth ME, PERKINS Seth W Eld *MS* 20 Dec 1843

MARDEN Ebenezer Knowlton m HOYT Margaret W of Manchester NH on 11 Dec at Manchester NH, BROOKS John Eld *MS* 24 Dec 1845

MARDEN George of Chester m SANBORN Roxana of Danville, CLEMENT Jona Rev *MS* 6 Mar 1844

MARDEN Henry A of Epsom m LAKE Adaline C of Chichester on 1 inst in Pittsfield NH, TRUE E Eld *MS* 8 May 1850

MARDEN Israel m WALKER Hannah J B both of Portsmouth on 14 May in Portsmouth, CAVERNO A Eld *MS* 27 May 1846

MARDEN J Langdon of Rye NH m SEAWARD Sarah of Kittery ME on 1 Oct at Kittery ME, WETHERBY I J Eld *MS* 12 Oct 1842

MARDEN Jonathan m EATON Lavina on 26th ult, FOSTER John Eld *MS* 30 Jul 1828

MARDEN Samuel B of Wentworth m YOUNG Eleanor S of Epsom NH on 12 Sept at Epsom, RAMSEY G P Eld *MS* 11 Oct 1843

MARDIN Nathan m BURNHAM Mary M both of Epsom NH on 4 Apr 1849, RAMSEY G P Eld *MS* 18 Apr 1849

MARDIN True R m ROBERTS Marcialine R B both of Sharon VT on 1 Nov 1847 in Sharon VT, HOLT F Esq *MS* 15 Mar 1848

MARINOR William m CORLIS Relief on 21 Sept at Brunswick ME, PAGE E G Eld *MS* 13 Jan 1847

MARK James M C m FADDEN Catharine of Lowell, THURSTON N Eld *MS* 22 Jan 1840

MARR Henry Col of Wales ME m MARR Catharine of Webster ME, FILES A Eld *MS* 29 Dec 1847

MARR Horatio P m BLACKSTONE Eliza A at Dracut MA, CURTIS S Eld *MS* 12 Nov 1845

MARR Isaac of Limington ME m MORTON Eliza of Gorham ME, CLEMENT Daniel B *MFWBR* 27 Apr 1850

MARR Josiah F of Georgetown ME m WRIGHT Happy T of Lewiston ME, LIBBY I Eld *MS* 13 Nov 1839

MARR Thomas Esq of Georgetown ME m TAYLOR Nancy of Waterville ME on 14 Sept, WEBBER David Eld *MS* 24 Sept 1845

MARRINER John m CUNNINGHAM Abigail M both of Gardiner ME on 26 Dec 1847 in Pittston ME, QUINNAM C Eld *MS* 2 Feb 1848

MARRISON Dependence m HALL Sarah J both of Dover on 11 inst in Dover, HUTCHINS E Eld *MS* 22 Dec 1847

MARRYMAN Waitstell m PARKER Catharine M both of Brunswick ME on 28 Oct, ROLLINS A Eld *MS* 2 Jan 1839

MARSEY Timothy m COPP Eliza J both of Barrston on 14 Nov,MOULTON A W Eld *MS* 15 Apr 1840

MARSH Charles E Capt m CLOUGH Henrietta M on 27 June at Buffalo NY *MS* 7 Sept 1836

MARSH Leonard Eld of New Brunswick m HANDS Rebecca Ann of

MARSH (Continued)

Dixmont ME on 19 Feb, FLETCHER Jabez Eld *MS* 6 Mar 1839

MARSH Rolan of Yorkshire m OAKES Mary Ann of China on 9 Jul in China NY, JACKSON N A Eld *MS* 2 Sept 1846

MARSHALL Alfred of Portland ME m HASKELL Jane of Saco ME at Saco ME, DWIGHT Rev *MFWBR* 10 Apr 1847

MARSHALL George W m MUNFORD Rhoda Ann both of Macedon NY on 24 Oct in Macedon NY, HOLMES D G Eld *MS* 17 Nov 1847

MARSHALL Joel m BOODY Harriet of Lowell at Dracut, CURTIS S Eld *MS* 29 Jan 1845

MARSHALL Joel Capt of Buxton ME ult m MOULTON Mary Mrs of Freedom on Monday 20th at Freedom *MS* 8 Aug 1833

MARSHALL John B m WALTON Hannah D of Lowell MA on 30 Jul at Lowell MA, WOODMAN J Eld *MS* 19 Oct 1842

MARSHALL Reuben S m THOMPSON Lucy J of South Parsonsfield ME on 6 June 1847 at South Parsonsfield ME, WOODMAN J M Eld *MS* 21 Jul 1847

MARSTIN James of Lunenburg VT m DEARBON Lushia of Peeling on 29 ult in Peeling, RUSSELL George W Eld *MS* 10 May 1837

MARSTON Abram F of Effingham m PIPER Catharine R of Parsonsfield ME on 3 Oct in Parsonsfield ME, JORDAN Z Eld *MS* 3 Nov 1847

MARSTON David Col m DEARBORN Josephine A B on 8 June at Hampton, JOHNSON W D Eld *MS* 16 Jul 1845

MARSTON Edwin A m BATCHELDER Hannah H of North Hampton on 9th inst at New Market, HUTCHINS E Eld *MS* 19 Jul 1843

MARSTON Isaac of Nottingham m McDANIEL Asenath of Barrington in Barrington on Tues 15th, SHERBURNE S Eld *MS* 23 Feb 1842

MARSTON Jeremiah m DRAKE Elizabeth A both of Effingham NH on 18 Nov 1847, FOSS N Eld *MS* 12 Jan 1848

MARSTON Jeremiah of Ossipee NH m SHACKFORD Hannah of Tamworth NH on 27 Oct at Tamworth NH, HART E H Eld *MS* 30 Dec 1846

MARSTON John Jr m WORTHLEY Lydia both of N Yarmouth ME on 29 Dec 1847, CROCKETT J Eld *MS* 8 Mar 1848

MARSTON Jonathan C m DUSTIN Susan E at Manchester NH on 8 Apr, CILLEY D P Eld *MS* 3 May 1843

MARSTON Nathaniel B m BROWN Sarah A both of No Hampton on 9 Sept in Hampton, MERRILL Wm P Eld *MS* 19 Sept 1849

MARSTON Oren m EMERY Harriet J of Limerick ME *MFWBR* 18 Jan 1851

MARSTON Samuel m GREEN Lucenith P of Pittsfield on 27 Aug at Pittsfield, KNOWLES J Eld *MS* 10 Feb 1847

MARSTON Winthrop A Esq of Great Falls NH m WALDRON Mary Elizabeth Miss, LOTHROP Rev *MS* 13 Feb 1834

MARTIN Bartlett T m PRAY Eunice R at Roxbury MA, DAVIS J B Eld

MARTIN (Continued)
MS 7 Sept 1845

MARTIN Benjamin m BLOOD Miss both of Washington on 1 Sept 1847 in So Weare, MOODY D Eld *MS* 15 Sept 1847

MARTIN Benjamin P of Weare m PATTEN Abigail of Deering on 15 Oct 1839, MOODY David Eld *MS* 12 Feb 1840

MARTIN Caleb K m EMERSON Clarissa M both of Weare on Mar 31 [possibly 1839?], MOODY David Eld *MS* 12 Feb 1840

MARTIN Daniel m FRENCH Sarah of Hatley LCon 5 Feb 1839 *MS* 17 Apr 1839

MARTIN Edson of Williamstown m WILLEY Phivinna of Washington VT on 2d inst, GEORGE Nathaniel K Eld *MS* 15 May 1839

MARTIN Edward of New Castle m BERRY Sally of Dover at Strafford, PLACE E Eld *MS* 8 Dec 1841

MARTIN Edward m RANDALL Sarah Jane of Portsmouth on 14 Sept 1843 at Portsmouth NH, DAVIS Isaac Eld *MS* 10 Jan 1844

MARTIN Henry m NOURSE Roxalany on 31 Dec at Yorkshire NY, JACKSON N A Eld *MS* 27 Jan 1847

MARTIN Jacob m GORDON Charlotte of St Albans ME on 22 Mar of St Albans ME, COPP J B Eld *MS* 7 June 1843

MARTIN Jeremiah m CROSS Marietta Mrs both of Belmont, WARD Cotton Esq *MS* 31 May 1848

MARTIN Jeremiah of Portland ME m JAMESON Julia Octava of Westbrook ME on 16 Nov 1848 in Westbrook ME, CROCKETT J Eld *MS* 24 Jan 1849

MARTIN Jesse m SWAN Rhoda of Nashua on 19 Feb at Nashua, STEARNS S Eld *MS* 4 Mar 1846

MARTIN John G m MEAD Mary J on 4 Aug at Roxbury MA, DAVIS J B Eld *MS* 20 Aug 1845

MARTIN John L m JOHNSON Lydia M on Aug 1 1841, BROWN John Jr *MS* 19 Jan 1842

MARTIN Jonathan m MERRILL Roxanna both of Hopkinton on 27th ult, MOODY David Eld *MS* 13 Apr 1836

MARTIN Kimball m WILEY Delana both of Williamstown VT on 17 Mar 1850 in Williamstown VT, HARTSHORN Nelson Eld *MS* 10 Apr 1850

MARTIN Nathaniel H m EMERSON Frances J both of Bedford in Bedford, CILLEY D DP Eld *MS* 22 May 1844

MARTIN Robert A of Manchester m BARNEY Armintha of Grafton, CILLEY D P Eld *MS* 17 Jul 1844

MARTIN Samuel H m COOLEDGE Julia A both of Hillsboro on 19 June *MS* 12 Oct 1836

MARTIN Samuel m MURPHY Lucinda E on 1 June at Bridgeton Centre ME, NEVENS William P Eld *MS* 28 June 1843

MARVEL Joy of Norway m CHASE Mary Elizabeth of Salisbury NY on 23 Apr at Salisbury NY, SMITH O W Eld *MS* 9 Jul 1845

MARVEL William m BURWELL Amy Mrs both of Russia NY on 17 Aug 1847 in Russia NY, SMART M M Eld *MS* 1 Dec 1847

MARVIN Nathaniel D m MARSTON Tamar L both of Sand Lake NY on 27 ult in Sand Lake NY, COLEMAN I B Eld *MS* 21 June 1848

MASON Amos W of Sandwich m MOULTON Euphama, BROOKS N Eld *MS* 31 Mar 1847

MASON Artimus of Mason m BRACKETT Sarah of Harrison on 12 May in Harrison ME, BARROWS W C Esq *MS* 3 June 1846

MASON Asa M m REED MAry T at North Yarmouth *MFWBR* 7 Apr 1849

MASON Benjamin K of Chichester m RUNNELS Julia A of Gilmanton NH on 22 Oct in Gilmanton, BROOKS N Eld *MS* 7 Nov 1838

MASON C B of Pottersville MA m BARTON Amanda of Providence, NOYES E Eld *MS* 13 Nov 1850

MASON David T m HATCH Rosanna of Sandwich on 13th Sept at Holderness, PETTENGILL John Eld *MS* 2 Oct 1839

MASON Garland of Raymond m SEAVY Maria on 4th ult in Chester NH, ROBIE Thomas Eld *MS* 28 Mar 1833

MASON Henry P m ANDERSON Mary J of Bath on 21 Jul, PURING-TON C Eld *MS* 11 Sept 1850

MASON James L m BASS Desire E both of Plainfield NY on 19 Dec 1845 in Plainfield NY, CHANEY J Eld *MS* 29 Apr 1846

MASON Jeremiah M of this town m WOODMAN Martha W of Buxton on 9th inst at Buxton, GOWER H B Rev *MFWBR* 18 Aug 1849

MASON Jesse M m LEWIS Mary J both of Barnstead on 29 Dec 1849 in Barnstead, LEWIS L Eld *MS* 9 Jan 1850

MASON John m REYNOLDS Avis both of Dover on 28 ult in Dover, HUTCHINS E Eld *MS* 4 Nov 1846

MASON John of Salsbury m JOHNSON Charlotte of Hopkinton on 2 Dec in Hopkinton, SINCLAIR J L Eld *MS* 19 Dec 1838

MASON Joseph of Sanbornton m EATON Susan T at Manchester on Dec 22, SINCLAIR J L Eld *MS* 5 Feb 1840

MASON Levi S of Pittsfield m PHILBRICK Ruth M of Epsom on 1st inst in Epsom, HOMES H Eld *MS* 28 June 1837

MASON Nicholas of Roxbury MA formerly of Portsmouth NH m RANSON Sarah D of Roxbury formerly of Brunswick ME on 19 Feb 1850 in Brunswick ME, LIBBY A Eld *MS* 7 Aug 1850

MASON Thomas C m BOYNTON Hannah H of Dracut on 20 Aug 1843 at Lowell MA, WOODMAN Jonathan Eld *MS* 6 Sept 1843

MASON William H of Augusta ME m FARNAM Sarah L of Sidney ME, LEWIS D B Eld *MS* 17 Apr 1844

MASTA Joseph A Dr m BAKER Lucinda of Hatley on 21 Oct 1838 *MS* 17 Apr 1839

MASTEN Jeremiah Capt of Bridgewater m DRAKE Lydia wid of New Hampton on 8 June 1848 in New Hampton, DANA Simeon Eld *MS* 14 Feb 1849

MASTON Oliver G m SHERBURN Junia L of Pittsfield on 8th Feb,
DAVIS J E Eld *MS* 18 Feb 1846

MATHES Abraham m PRIEST Dorothy both of Lowell MA on Thanksgiving Day at Nottingham, CILLEY D P Eld *MS* 16 Dec 1835

MATHES Horace W m BATCHELDER Parmelia on 16 Jul 1843 at
Canterbury, CHASE William P Eld *MS* 31 Jan 1844

MATHES Reuben of Lee m BARTLETT Sally T of Nottingham on 29
May in New Market, EASTMAN C Allen Eld *MS* 5 June 1850

MATHES Timothy H m KNIGHT Julia F of New Market on 9th inst at
New Market *MS* 19 May 1847

MATHEWS Alfred m WENTWORTH Martha Mrs both of Boothbay on
28 Apr 1849 in Boothbay ME, PAGE E G Eld *MS* 15 May 1850

MATHEWS Joseph m FREEMAN Isabella both of Green ME on 18
Nov 1847 in Green ME, WILLEY E C Eld *MS* 23 Feb 1848

MATHEWS Joseph P m ALDRICH Nancy B of Manchester NH on 11
Jul at Manchester NH, CILLEY D P Eld *MS* 28 Jul 1847

MATISON Robert R of Stonington CT m BAKER Urania of Burrillville
RI on 22 Jan 1849 in Pascoag RI, DAVISON M N Eld *MS* 21 Mar
1849

MATTENLY John m NELSON Hannah both of Sutton on 12 Nov
1837 in Sutton VT, FLAGG Joseph Eld *MS* 14 Feb 1838

MATTENLY John Jr m SPAULDING Sarah both of Sutton VT on 28
Dec 1837 in Sutton VT, FLAGG Joseph Eld *MS* 14 Feb 1838

MATTESON James m WEAVER Persis both of Arkwright NY on 9
May in Arkwright NY, STARR N Eld *MS* 19 June 1850

MATTHEWS A m McCOBB Arinda on 10 Nov at Boothbay ME,
MORRILL S P Eld *MS* 22 Jan 1845

MATTHEWS John M m WILSON Frances E on 30 Oct at Nashua,
STEARNS S Eld *MS* 24 Dec 1845

MATTHEWSON William of Johnston m HAWKS Maria of No Providence on 6 inst at Johnston RI, SWEET Eld *MS* 16 Dec 1835

MAURN Gill of Melbourn LC m LEAVITT Mary on 20 Nov, BARTLETT
W Eld *MS* 30 Jan 1839

MAXFIELD Oliver of Gilmanton m TOWLE Sabrina at Manchester
MFWBR 2 Feb 1850

MAXFIELD Robert C of Cumberland m PAINE Harriet W of Pownal
ME on 28th ult at North Yarmouth ME, COBB A H Rev *MFWBR*
14 Dec 1850

MAXIM Jesse of Pleasant Ridge ME m BICKFORD Cyrena of Starks
ME on 19 June *MS* 2 Sept 1831

MAXWELL Charles Dea m CROSS Tammy both of Danville on 3d ult,
TRACY J Eld *MS* 4 May 1836

MAXWELL Daniel W of Windham m MOORE Abigail of Lewiston ME
on 25 Apr in Lewiston ME, BURGESS J S Eld *MS* 6 June 1849

MAXWELL James of Danville ME m McKENNEY Sarah D of Danville
ME, LIBBY Isaac Eld *MS* 14 Feb 1844

MAY Henry m WILDER Harriet of Sutton MA on 16th inst at Grafton
MA, PECK B D Eld *MS* 15 Mar 1843

MAY Silas m GOODWIN H C, NOYES E Eld *MS* 15 Dec 1847

MAY Sylvester m BEAN Eunice of Barnston LC on 6 Jul, MOULTON
A Eld *MS* 13 Sept 1843

MAYALL Joseph m STANLEY Eliza R both of Roxbury MA, CURTIS S
Eld in Roxbury MA *MS* 3 Apr 1850

MAYBERRY Merritt of Standish ME m MAYBERRY Margaret T of
Windham ME on 20 Apr at Windham ME, CLAY Daniel Eld *MS* 14
May 1845

MAYHEW John of Great Falls NH m CHAPMAN Sarah M in Limerick
ME on 18th inst, by BRADBURY A R *MS* 29 Jan 1840

MAYHUE William H of Stanford Dutchess Co NY m GERMOND Jane
of Farmington on 18 Apr at Farmington, HOLMES D G Eld *MS* 12
May 1847

MAYNARD John G of Lowell m ELLIOT Rebecca, THURSTON N Eld
MS 7 Aug 1839

MAYO Alphonso A m GRANT Emma H of Portland ME on 1st inst at
Portland ME, BROWN S E Eld *MFWBR* 9 Nov 1850

McALISTER Levi m SHAW Mary Mrs both of Harrison on 21 Jan in
Harrison ME, LIBBY D Eld *MS* 19 Feb 1851

McALLISTER Daniel m DWINELL Cynthia on 25 Dec at Stowe,
BIXBY L E Eld *MS* 21 Jan 1846

McALLISTER Robert m HATHORN Achsah both of Amoskeag NH on
28 Aug 1848 in Manchester, CILLEY D P Eld *MS* 6 Sept 1848

McALPINE George W m JOHNSON Maria C of Contoocookville NH on
16 Nov, FROST D Sidney Eld *MS* 30 Nov 1842

McCASLAND Cyrus m HERALD Lucene both of Palmyra on 7 inst,
COPP John Eld *MS* 20 Dec 1837

McCAUSLAND W B of Gardiner ME m FRENCH Melissa D of New
London NH on 22 inst in Sanbornton, CURTIS C Rev *MS* 31 May
1848

McCLERY David of Strong m COBBETT Mary of Farmington ME on
27 Jan 1848 in Farmington ME, MORRILL S P Eld *MS* 23 Feb
1848

McCLURE Andrew at Bangor ME m PUSHAW Lucy, CAVERNO A Eld
MS 13 Sept 1843

McCLURG Samuel Jr of Trenton NJ m FOSS Susan H of Rochester
on 14th Sept at Rochester, MEADER J Eld *MS* 15 Oct 1845

McCORRISON James F of Bath m WHITE Mary A of Litchfield in
Litchfield, QUINNAM C Eld *MS* 18 Jul 1849

McCOY Israel of Manchester NH m GRANT Elizabeth of Dover NH on
28 Nov, SMITH A D Eld *MS* 9 Dec 1846

McCRILLIS Calvin of Lowell MA m GOODWIN Fanny of Somersworth
NH in Great Falls, DUNN R Eld *MS* 1 Dec 1847

McCRILLIS Daniel m PETERS Mary on Sunday last at Dover NH,

McCRILLIS (Continued)

THURSTON N Eld *MS* 28 Nov 1833

McCRILLIS John H m BABB Maria both of Strafford on 24 Dec 1848in Strafford, HOLMES J C Eld *MS* 17 Jan 1849

McCRILLIS Philip m REYNOLDS Lydia at Dover NH, THURSTON Nathaniel Eld *MS* 25 Apr 1833

McCRILLIS Thomas m McCARTER Sophia both of Dover on 6 Aug in Dover, SMITH A D Eld *MS* 12 Aug 1846

McCRILLIS Thomas m WALDRON Elizabeth H of Dover NH on 20 Apr at Dover NH, DYER B Eld *MS* 30 Apr 1845

MCCULLOCK William Ensign m Mary Ann both of Grinville NY? on Jan 4 1840, PLUMB H N Eld *MS* 20 May 1840

McCULLY John of Wilton ME m THOMAS Diantha J of Wilton at Farmington ME on 3rd inst, DORR R H Rev *MFWBR* 15 May 1847 & 22 May 1847

McCUTCHEON James Eld of Pembroke m MORRILL Nancy Mrs on 22 Jan, SWAIN William Eld *MS* 29 May 1844

McDANIEL Noah m SHAW Mary B of Dover at So Berwick ME, TRICKEY Nathaniel H Eld *MS* 13 May 1835

McDONALD Andrew m KEEN Roann of Oxford ME on 30 Nov at West Poland ME, LIBBY James Eld *MS* 10 Feb 1847

McDONALD David m DUNNING Sarah Ann on 30 Nov at Roxbury, DAVIS J B Eld *MS* 27 Dec 1843

McDONALD John Maj of L m JEFFERDS Olive of Kennebunkport ME on Tuesday last *MS* 5 Jul 1827

McDONALD Joseph of Gray m McINTIRE Clara of Gloucester on 20 Dec 1847 in Gray ME, LANCASTER David Eld *MS* 26 Jan 1848

McDONGLE Charles m SHEARMAN Mary on 29 Dec, ROBINSON N J Eld *MS* 1 Feb 1843

McDUFFEE Maiquis of Great Falls m WIGGINS Dorothy E of New Market on 7 June in New Market, FROST D S Eld *MS* 8 Jul 1846

McDUFFIE Charles D of Rochester NH m DURGIN Laura B at Lowell *MFWBR* 11 Jan 1851

McDUFFIE Daniel m YORK Lydia C on 30 Oct at Rochester, HOLMES John C Eld *MS* 18 Dec 1844

McDUFFIE John H m HAM Julia both of Rochester NH on 28 Jan 1849 in Rochester NH, WHITNEY G W Eld *MS* 25 Apr 1849

McFADDEN David of Gardiner m POTTER Arabine of Litchfield on 27 Jan in Litchfield ME, QUINNAM C Eld *MS* 20 Feb 1850

McGILL Hugh m NEWTON Eunice Ann both of Stephentown NY on 26 Feb in Stephentown NY, COLEMAN I B Eld *MS* 13 Mar 1850

McGILL John m CAR Henrietta on 12 Nov at Stephentown NY, COLEMAN I B Eld *MS* 24 Apr 1844

McINTIRE John O m WILLEY Eliza J of Lowell on 28 Feb at Lowell, CURTIS S Eld *MS* 11 Mar 1846

McINTIRE Ralph M of Bath m BLITHEN Mercy D of Durham on 4

McINTIRE (Continued)

Dec 1850 in Durham ME, BARD N Eld *MS* 8 Jan 1851

McINTIRE Samuel m MATHEWS Lydia in Brunswick ME, LIBBY A Eld *MS* 12 Mar 1851

McINTIRE Warren m HARTFORD Sarah all of Manchester on 27 Septin Manchester, CILLEY D P Eld *MS* 7 Oct 1846

McKENNEY Charles m WOOD Olive of Danville ME, LIBBY Isaac Eld *MS* 14 Feb 1844

McKENNEY Cyrus B m LOWELL Elizabeth H on 3 June at Springfield ME, SCRIBNER Miles S Eld *MS* 24 Jul 1844

MCKENNEY D m BERRY Susan T of Saco on 11th inst at Saco ME, FERNALD J Eld *MFWBR* 24 June 1848

MCKENNEY Freeman m CHANEY Abigail Ann both of Limington ME on May 3, MANSON BS Eld m 13 May 1840

McKENNEY Joshua of Limington ME m BRADEEN Ann M of Cornish ME on 18 Feb at Cornish, RAND I Eld *MS* 29 May 1844

McKENNEY Sewell of Limington ME m MESERVE Eliza D of Limington ME, STEVENS T Eld *MS* 14 Jul 1847

McKENNEY Solomon m LITTLEFIELD Phebe at Great Falls NH *MFWBR* 24 Mar 1849

McKENNEY Wm m MURRAY Morgianna both of Danville on 17 Mar, LIBBY Isaac Eld *MS* 1 May 1844

McKENNY Henry H of Saco ME m EMERY Olive on 17th inst, EMERY Richard Eld *MS* 22 May 1829

McKOON Wm M of Schroepple m KENDALL Sarepta of Volney NY on 5 Oct 1848 in Volney NY, GRIFFETH A Eld *MS* 1 Nov 1848

McKUESICK Nahum of Limerick m GORDON Sally of Limerick ME on Sunday evening last, BURBANK Samuel Eld *MS* 24 May 1827

McKUSICK Nahum 2d of Limerick ME m BRACKETT Sarah C of Limerick ME, MANSON B S Eld *MS* 7 Feb 1844

McKUSICK Nahum, TARBOX Mary Jane of Limerick ME on 16 June 1842 at Limerick ME, CHASE William P Eld *MS* 6 Jul 1842

McLANE Charles of New Vineyard m SOPER Abigail M of New Sharon ME on 17 June at New Sharon ME, EDGECOMB Joseph Eld *MS* 9 Jul 1845

McLAUGHLIN Robert Jr Town clerk of Scarboro' ME m PARKER Harriet *MFWBR* 4 Jan 1851

McMASTER Samuel m POOR Mary A both of Strafford VT on 23 Nov 1848 in Strafford VT, CLARK E Eld *MS* 6 June 1849

McNEAL Jonathan m GARLAND Sarah J on 22 Sept at Barnstead, GARLAND D Eld *MS* 10 Oct 1844

McPHETERS Sanford J m GILMAN Sarah of Sangerville ME of Hermon on 1 May 1848 in Sangerville ME, GILMAN M Esq *MS* 5 Jul 1848

MEAD Franklin of Clarendon Mich m COOK Catherine of Eckford Mich on 26 Nov 1848 in Eckford Mich, WELLINGTON H Eld

MEAD (Continued)
   MS 27 Dec 1848
MEAD James H m MERRILL Abigail L both of Meredith *MS* 15 June
   1836
MEAD Potter m RAY Mary Ann, HARVEY Erastus Eld *MS* 3 Jul 1844
MEAD William m JEWETT Hannah of Gilford at Gilford NH, STRONG
   J E Rev *MS* 23 Jul 1845
MEADER Ephraim K of Dover m OTIS Lavina on 22 Jul in Strafford,
   PLACE E Eld *MS* 1 Aug 1838
MEADER George B m CROSS Martha M at Lowell MA *MS* 27 Apr
   1836
MEADER Gideon of Wales m DALE Clarissa of Richmond on 11 Dec,
   SWETT J Eld *MS* 28 Dec 1836
MEADER Jesse Eld, an itinerant preacher of New Durham Q M m
   YORK Hannah D Miss at Rochester NY *MS* 30 Nov 1832
MEADER John K m BASSETT Lucy D both of New Market on 17
   June Sabbath Eve in Newmarket, EASTMAN C Allen Eld *MS* 27
   June 1849
MEADER John of Gardiner m CHICK Joan E of Monmouth ME on
   2d ult in Monmouth, PERKINS Seth W Eld *MS* 19 Apr 1837
MEADER Levi m EASTMAN Armanda both of No Providence on 24
   Dec 1837 in No Providence RI, HUTCHINS Elias Eld *MS* 17 Jan
   1838
MEADER Otis C of Conway NH m WORMWOOD Ann M of Brownfield
   ME on 14 Nov, LONG L A Eld *MS* 27 Nov 1850
MEADER Stephen m KNIGHT Sarah both of So Berwick ME on 2 Jul
   1848 in No Berwick ME, CLAY D Eld *MS* 16 Aug 1848
MEADER Stephen m PINKHAM Mary Jane of New Market on 24 Aug
   at New Market, HUTCHINS E Eld *MS* 30 Aug 1843
MEADER Tobias merchant of Dover NH m MEADER Phebe H of No
   Berwick on 3d inst in Friend's Meeting House at No Berwick *MS* 9
   Dec 1835
MEANS Luther m NELSON Adaline both of Clinton on 23 Aug in
   Clinton ME, BUKER A J Eld *MS* 2 Oct 1850
MEARS Elijah of Chesterville m CARR Lovina P of Chesterville on 25
   Oct 1846, WHEELER S Eld *MS* 21 Apr 1847
MELALIN Asa of Charleston m BROWN Mercy of Dover on 6 inst,
   HATHAWAY Leonard Eld *MS* 8 May 1844
MELCHER Abner Jr Capt m ROSS Hannah M both of Brunswick ME
   on 23 Jul in Brunswick ME, ROLLINS A Eld *MS* 16 Aug 1837
MELCHER Jeremiah m MORSE Maria both of Brunswick on 18 Apr
   in Brunswick ME, LIBBY A Eld *MS* 22 Aug 1849
MELCHER Joseph Capt m STANWOOD Agness R both of Brunswick
   ME on 15 inst in Brunswick ME, ROLLINS Andrew Eld *MS* 30
   Aug 1837
MELCHER Osborn A of Brunswick ME m LORING Margaret Y on

MELCHER (Continued)

22d ult at Portland ME, PRATT J Rev *MFWBR* 2 Feb 1850

MELCHER William H M of Brunswick m ALEXANDER Sarah J M of Richmond on 14 June in Richmond ME, QUINNAM C Eld *MS* 22 Jul 1846

MELCHER William m BROWN Susan both of Dover on 14th inst at Dover, PERKINS J Rev *MS* 24 June 1835

MELLOON Joseph m CONNER Nancy of Dover on 20th inst at Dover NH, PERKINS S W Eld *MS* 26 Feb 1845

MELLOWS Aaron m ADAMS Lucretia at Alton NH on 3d Jan, BUZZELL H D Eld *MS* 3 Mar 1847

MELON Isaiah of Effingham NH m KENNET Eliza, HOBBS A W Eld *MS* 30 Apr 1845

MELOON Joseph P of Effingham NH m BUSWELL Sarah of Ossipee NH at Ossipee NH, CHICK John Eld *MS* 7 Aug 1839

MELVIN Abraham of Weare m COLBY Belinda of Lancaster on 4 June in Weare, KIMBALL J Eld *MS* 27 Nov 1850

MENNET David m MANCHESTER Freelove of Tiverton RI *MS* 4 May 1836

MERIAM Jesse W of No Providence m MINSOR Elizabeth M of Johnston on 18th ult, HUTCHINS E Eld *MS* 9 Jul 1834

MERRELL Seth m GRANT Betsey in Shapleigh, MARSH C Rev *MS* 23 Nov 1826

MERRIAM Zimri m LOVELAND Clarissa on 28 Dec 1848 in Clayton NY, GRIFFETH A Eld *MS* 24 Jan 1849

MERRICK Otis S m CHASE Lucy S on 23 Mar at Pittsfield, TURNER A Eld *MS* 9 Apr 1845

MERRIFIELD Stephen m DURGIN Dorothy on 18th inst, COLCORD David Esq all of Porter *MS* 13 Apr 1832

MERRIL Elihu C m BATCHELDER Harriet N both of Manchester on 1 Nov in Manchester, CILLEY D P Eld *MS* 14 Nov 1849

MERRIL John J s/o John MERRILL of Parsonsfield ME m BROWN H Josephine on 18 inst in even at residence of Mrs R HORN, CURTIS S Eld in Roxbury *MS* 1 May 1850

MERRIL Joseph W m McQUESTON Helen O both of Manchester on 9 Apr in Manchester, CILLEY D P Eld *MS* 26 Apr 1848

MERRILL Albert Capt of Conway NH m EASTMAN Emily of Limerick on 14th inst Wed, McDONALD J Esq *MS* 23 Sept 1831

MERRILL Albert Capt of Conway m OSGOOD Mary K of Northfield at Meredith Bridge, Brooks N Eld *MS* 27 Apr 1842

MERRILL Asa m PAGE Rachel F in Raymond NH *MS* 18 Nov 1831

MERRILL Benjamin m HOLT Abigail of Lowell MA on 22 Mar at Lowell MA, THURSTON N Eld *MS* 25 May 1842

MERRILL Brackett m HAYES Mary D on 5th ult *MS* 15 Feb 1843

MERRILL Calvin H of Roxbury m WILEY Abigail of Williamstown VT on 4 Jul 1848 in Williamstown VT, HARTSHORN Nelson Eld

MERRILL (Continued)
  MS 19 Jul 1848
MERRILL Charles of New Gloucester m BUCK Sarah S of Norway ME
  on 20th ult at Gray ME, HUMPHREY Meshach Esq *MFWBR* 3 Mar
  1849
MERRILL Charles W of Bowdoinham ME m HALL Priscilla of Bow-
  doin ME in Topsham ME, BEAN C Eld *MS* 2 Aug 1848
MERRILL David W of New Gloucester ME m SOULE Pamelia of
  Lewiston ME, LIBBEY Isaac Eld *MS* 27 Nov 1844
MERRILL Edward D of Saco ME m CHASE Sarah A of Scarboro' ME
  on 7 Dec 1847, CHASE S G Esq *MS* 29 Dec 1847
MERRILL Enoch of Andover m PLUMMER Susan at Danville,
  FULLONTON J Eld *MS* 18 Dec 1839
MERRILL Ezekiel E m SAWYER Hannah B both of So Hampton in So
  Hampton *MS* 23 May 1838
MERRILL Henry 3rd m WEEKS Mary J of Parsonsfield at East
  Parsonsfield ME, HACKETT J O Eld *MS* 18 Feb 1846
MERRILL Isaac m DOW Clarissa both of Hopkinton on 28 Dec at
  Concord, FROST D Sidney *MS* 8 May 1844
MERRILL Isaac m SHEPARD Esther of Holderness NH on 14 June
  1842 at Holderness NH, THOMPSON Samuel Eld *MS* 6 Jul 1842
MERRILL J M m YOUNG S Miss both of Stanstead LC on 26 Apr *MS*
  18 May 1836
MERRILL John A of Manchester NH m FARRINGTON Mary on 24
  Apr, THURSTON N Eld *MS* 25 May 1842
MERRILL John H Rev of Sedgwick ME RICHARDSON m Phebe P of
  Baldwin ME on 21st inst at Portland ME, CARRUTHERS Rev Dr
  MFWBR 30 Oct 1847
MERRILL John of Parsonsfield ME m TUFTS Olive H Mrs of Medford
  MA on 7 Sept 1848 in Parsonsfield ME, LORD D H Eld *MS* 27
  Sept 1848
MERRILL John T of New Gloucester ME m COLLIS Sybil of Bruns-
  wick ME, ROLLINS A Eld *MS* 2 Jan 1839
MERRILL Joseph T of Monmouth ME m BROWN Dorcas B of Free-
  port ME on 8 Nov, PURINTON A W Eld *MS* 19 Dec 1849
MERRILL Lorenzo m FISK Mary Ann of Contoocookville NH on 2 Nov,
  FROST D Sidney Eld *MS* 30 Nov 1842
MERRILL Nelson m WHITNEY Betsey both of Westbrook ME on 20
  Sept, WHITE J Eld *MS* 12 NOv 1835
MERRILL Phineas of Lawrence MA m CAVERLY Almira H of Dover
  NH *MFWBR* 4 Aug 1849
MERRILL Russell of Warren m BEAN Darrilla of Wilmot on 3 June in
  Wilmot, BARTLETT J O D Eld *MS* 24 June 1846
MERRILL Samuel D m MARSTON Jane P on 21 March at Holderness
  NH, MERRILL W S Eld *MS* 21 Apr 1847
MERRILL Samuel Esq of Buxton ME m THOMAS Catherine on 22d

MERRILL (Continued)
ult at Standish ME, GERRY E J Rev *MFWBR* 15 May 1847

MERRILL Samuel F m VESEY Mary J both of Deerfield NH on 1 Nov 1849 in Epsom NH, RAMSEY G P Eld *MS* 16 Jan 1850

MERRILL Samuel of Hudson NH m HOVEY Betsey C on 30 Dec at Lowell, CURTIS Silas Eld *MS* 7 Jan 1846

MERRILL Sumner B m RICKER Olive M at Manchester NH, CILLEY D P Eld *MS* 15 Oct 1845

MERRILL Timothy m CLARK Minerva M of Manchester at Manchester NH, CILLEY D P Eld *MS* 1 Oct 1845

MERRILL William of Dover m KENNEY Mary of Charlestown on 5 Nov 1843, AMES M Eld *MS* 28 Feb 1844

MERRILL William W of Meredith m MERRILL Sally M of Holderness. PITMAN Stephen J Eld *MS* 2 Feb 1842

MERRITT Henry S m LIBBY Sarah both of Pownal ME on 10 Jan 1850 in Durham ME, NEWELL David Eld *MS* 6 Mar 1850

MERRITT John S m TOOTHAKER Joan on 23 Sept at Brunswick ME, PAGE E G Eld *MS* 13 Jan 1847

MERROW Daniel G m MOODY Sarah both of Ossipee NH on 5 Oct 1848 in Ossipee, CHICK J Eld *MS* 15 Nov 1848

MERROW Elisha of Milton m MERROW Maria of Great Falls NH in Dover NH *MS* 27 June 1838

MERROW Harford of Dearborn ME m HUSSEY Lydia of Waterville, LEWIS Daniel B Eld *MS* 30 Nov 1842

MERROW Orrin m KENNEY Dorcas of Berwick ME, BLAISDELL Edward Eld *MS* 11 Feb 1846

MERROW Samuel D of Auburn ME m LORD Elcy of Norway ME on 30 June at Poland ME, PERRY S Eld *MS* 20 Aug 1845

MERROW William of Newfield ME m HODSDON Eliza A of Great Falls NH at Newfield on 26th ult *MFWBR* 16 Mar 1850

MERSERVE Daniel m HANSON Marsha all of Dover NH on Thurs eve last, THURSTON N Eld *MS* 4 June 1834

MERSERVE Henry m TUTTLE Elizabeth of Dover on 3d inst at Dover NH "Cake received" MOULTON A K Eld *MS* 12 Oct 1842

MESERVE Elijah B m WHITTEN Sarah E on 18 May at Hollis ME, McKENNY P Eld *MS* 14 June 1843

MESERVE George W m STAPLES Elizabeth D of Limington ME on 5 Oct, MANSON B S Eld *MS* 7 Feb 1844

MESERVE Harris B m LEACH Mary Jane both of Portland ME in Portland ME, STEVENS J Eld *MS* 30 May 1838

MESERVE James L at Limerick ME m FITZGERALD Emily B of Limerick ME on 8 May, CHASE William P Eld *MS* 18 May 1842

MESERVE Joseph of Limington ME m FOSS Olive M of Freedom on 2 Jan 1845, BUTLER O Eld *MS* 19 Feb 1845

MESERVE Samuel m HANSON Mary A on 5th inst both of Rochester NH, THURSTON Eld *MS* 12 Dec 1833

MESERVEY John E m LOVE Rocksalany both of Wheelock on Dec 2nd 1841 *MS* 2 Feb 1842

MESSER Hollis W of Newbury NH m BLODGETT Olive C on 14 Jan, CROSS Jesse Eld *MS* 27 Jan 1847

MESSER John A m STACY Mary J on 8 Feb at Lowell MA, CURTIS S Eld *MS* 18 Feb 1846

MESSER John m THOMAS Maribah H both of Waterville ME on 29 Nov in Waterville, BEAN G W Eld *MS* 2 Jan 1850

METCALF Abijan of Freeport ME m METCALF Rebecca of Lisbon ME *MS* 23 Mar 1836

METCALF Mason Jr of Litchfield m WELCH Hannah of Monmouth in Monmouth ME, CURTIS S Eld *MS* 26 Nov 1834

M'GARAHAN Ms "a female husband - At Albany on Saturday night, a new case came before the court, ... a woman named M'Garahan, was charged with marrying another woman, and committing other enormities. The fact of the marriage was clearly proved and the female husband committed for examination. *MS* 30 Nov 1842

MIDDAUGH George W of Ithaca m PRESTON Lamira S of Caroline on 11 ult in Caroline NY, DODGE A Eld *MS* 2 Oct 1850

MIGHEL Moses of Eaton NH m COLE Sarah of Brownfield ME on 19 Feb, HART E H Eld *MS* 24 Jul 1850

MIGHELS Jesse S Dr of Minot m RUST Evelina A of Norway at Norway *MS* 25 Jan 1827

MIGHLS Joseph d on 24 Oct 1847 m GUPTILL R I both of Limerick, HACKETT J O Eld in East Parsonsfield ME *MS* 22 Dec 1847

MILIKEN - see MILLIKIN

MILIKEN/MILLKIN Joseph m TRACY Sarah F Mrs at Farmington ME on 29th Nov *MFWBR* 2 Feb 1850 & *MS* 29 Jan 1850

MILLER Elisha m STONE Disnthy both of Stanstead on 25 Nov 1843 *MS* 1 May 1844

MILLER George of New Berlin m BARTHOLOMEW Eveline of Oxford NY on 29 June 1848 in Oneonta NY, WING Amos Eld *MS* 26 Jul 1848

MILLER Mark m KNOX Dorothy of Somersworth NH at Great Falls, CURTIS S Eld *MS* 8 June 1842

MILLER Nelson of Smithfield RI m BUXTON Lydia of Uxbridge on 16 ult in Waterford, BURLINGAME M W Eld *MS* 5 Sept 1838

MILLER R of Howland m SIMONTON Ann Maria of Hollis at Hollis *MS* 4 Aug 1830

MILLET Cyrus m GREENLEAF Ellen B on 10th inst at Saco ME, STRICKLAND G G Rev *MFWBR* 22 Feb 1851

MILLET Henry m [JAQUES] Katharine Miss on 9 inst in No Providence, ROBBINS Samuel Eld *MS* 26 Jul 1837 [N.B. The paper reads "of Jaques" but we think it should be her surname.]

MILLIKEN David m JOHNSON Jane Philena of Saco on 4 Apr at Saco ME, REDLON A Eld *MS* 17 Apr 1844

MILLIKIN Robert of Freedom m BUZZELL Mary of Ossipee NH, HOBBS A W Eld *MS* 3O Apr 1845

MILLS Elihu m DAVIS Hannah B on 30 June at Great Falls NH, WEBBER H Eld *MS* 18 Dec 1844

MILLS James of Waterboro ME m WEBBER Dorcas at Waterboro ME on 12th inst, GRAY J Eld *MFWBR* 21 Sep 1850

MILLS Jeremiah m FOSS Sarah both of Strafford on 27 Nov *MS* 14 Dec 1836

MILLS John of Rochester m COWELL Sally W of Lebanon on 18 inst in Lebanon ME, CHENEY O B Eld *MS* 31 Oct 1849 & *MFWBR* 3 Nov 1849

MILLS Simon H m SHERMAN Catherine both of Dedham in Lowell, THURSTON N Eld *MS* 5 Apr 1837

MINARD Silas A of Littleton m ALDRICH Sophia Jane of Lisbon on 19 Apr 1843 at Lisbon NH, WITHAM L H Eld *MS* 13 Mar 1844

MINER Benjamin of Ohio City m MINER Hertensia Gunelda of Otsego IN on 29 Sept 1847, MINER J H Eld in Otsego IN *MS* 13 Dec 1848

MINER Julius of Ellicottville NY m TAYLOR Eliza Ann of Dayton NY *MS* 22 Mar 1837

MITCHEL George A of Turner ME m PENLEY Sarah L of Danville ME on 16 Nov at Lewiston Falls ME, BEAN G W Eld *MS* 9 Dec 1846

MITCHELL Alonzo of Dover m LIBBEY Lydia S of Rochester on 2 inst in Dover NH, HUTCHINS E Eld *MS* 18 Dec 1850

MITCHELL Benjamin F m BROWN Roxcena S on 16 June in Manchester, CILLEY D P Eld *MS* 26 June 1850

MITCHELL Benjamin K m BULLARD Cyntha M at Charlestown MA, SWETT D Eld *MS* 23 Oct 1844

MITCHELL Charles Capt of Newfield m WENTWORTH Ruth of Kennebunk ME *MS* 9 Mar 1832

MITCHELL David of North Yarmouth ME m WOODS Hannah R MOULTON A K Eld of Portland ME *MS* 9 Jul 1845

MITCHELL Elijah of Waterville m BLAISDELL Catharine T of Sidney ME, LEWIS Daniel B Eld *MS* 24 Feb 1836

MITCHELL Elijah S of Monroe m CILLEY Mary E of Jackson on 1 Oct, CILLEY Joseph 1 Eld *MS* 12 Dec 1849

MITCHELL Galen O of Westport m MEADER Mary D of Westport on 11 Jan, MORRILL S P Eld *MS* 4 Feb 1846

MITCHELL John of Casco m LEAVITT Mary Ann of Naples on 1 Oct at Naples ME, HUNTRESS D Eld *MS* 20 Dec 1843

MITCHELL John W of Lewiston ME m FROST Mary E of Litchfield on 19 Apr at Litchfield ME, FROST Isaac Eld *MFWBR* 26 Jul 1848

MITCHELL Jonathan J of Holderness m SMITH Laura Ann of New Hampton on 15 Dec, TRUE E Eld *MS* 11 Jan 1843

MITCHELL Joseph B of Boston MA m COTE Rebecca P of Allenston on 2 Oct at Manchester NH, CILLEY D P Eld *MS* 10 Oct 1844

MITCHELL Joseph H m BEAN Clara A on 28 ult in Dover, HUTCH-
INS E Eld *MS* 1 Apr 1846

MITCHELL Orrin D of East Killingly CT m HAMMOND Phebe of
Danielsonville on 12 May at Danielsonville Killingly CT, HOUS-
TON Rev *MS* 4 June 1845

MITCHELL Thomas of Newfield ME m DAVIS Sarah of New Durham
NH on 29 Oct, WALDRON W H Eld *MS* 15 Nov 1843

MITTS John D m LONG Laura E both of Conway on 6 Nov 1849 in
Conway, LONG Larkin A *MS* 20 Feb 1850

MONROE Levi G of East Liberty Logan Co Ohio m KIRK Mary on 25
Mar, HEALTH J D Eld *MS* 30 June 1847

MONTARE Joseph A m FLETCHER Sarah F of Bath on 5 May at
Bath ME, HATHORN S Eld *MS* 18 May 1842

MONTGOMERY Drury R of Duxbury m MAYNARD Nancy M of Stow
VT on Feb 27, GRAY Ira Eld *MS* 30 Mar 1842

MONTGOMERY Jonathan H m STILES Sarah E both of Strafford on
25 ult in Dover, HUTCHINS E Eld *MS* 27 Nov 1850

MOODY Ager m WELLS Caroline Mrs on 20 May at Stowe, BIXBY L
E Eld *MS* 14 Jul 1847

MOODY Amos W m COFFIN Nancy M of Newburyport MA on 7 Dec
at Alton NH, PINKHAM J Eld *MS* 10 Mar 1847

MOODY Benjaman m LIBBY Catharine both of Limington ME on 21
inst in Limington, TRUE Ezekiel *MS* 28 Mar 1838

MOODY Caleb of Standish ME m WHITNEY Eunice on 6th inst *MS*
24 Jan 1828

MOODY David of Frankfort m JENKINS Mariah of Monroe ME *MS* 9
May 1833

MOODY Elbridge G m LIBBY Catharine F both of Scarboro ME on 14
inst in Scarboro ME, LIBBY C O Eld *MS* 27 Mar 1850

MOODY Henry H of Roxbury MA m STETSON Sarah M of Dorchester
MA on 12th, DAVIS J B Eld *MS* 7 May 1845

MOODY James M of Limington ME m WETHERBEE Lydia L of Effingham on 15 Feb at Effingham NH, HANSON Moses Eld *MFWBR*
10 Mar 1849 & *MS* 28 Feb 1849

MOODY Leander m McKENNEY Sally F of Limington on 9 Apr, AYER
A Eld *MS* 24 Apr 1839

MOODY Simon Capt m HUBBARD Harriet W formerly of Lebanon
NH at Limington ME *MS* 27 June 1833

MOODY Washington m MOODY Elizabeth at Ossipee NH, FERNALD
S P Eld *MS* 20 Jul 1836

MOONEY Fernando S m OAKES Chastina both of Franconia in
Franconia, BLAKE C E Eld *MS* 24 Jan 1849

MOONEY Geo W of Meredith m DRAKE Lydia J of New Hampton on
22 Nov 1849, PITMAN S J Eld *MS* 30 Jan 1850

MOONEY Joseph of Sandwich m GLIDDEN Nancy of Gilford on 3
Oct, PINKHAM John Eld *MS* 16 Oct 1839

MOONEY Newbegin of Parsonsfield m MERRILL Mary on Thursday in Newfield, BUZZELL J Eld *MS* 13 Dec 1827

MOONEY Samuel of Boston MA m GILPATRICK Ann M of Saco ME on 3rd inst at Saco, STRICKLAND G G Rev *MFWBR* 12 May 1849

MOONY Thomas m NILES Rebeccah of Danville VT on 11 Mar 1846 at Danville VT, TRUE Ezekiel Eld *MS* 24 Feb 1847

MOOR Benjamin C of Corinna m HILL Naomi S of Exeter ME on 31 Dec 1834, NASON S V Eld *MS* 11 Mar 1835

MOOR Henry of St Albans m CLOUGH Sarah Ann of Garland ME on Feb 8 in Garland ME, AMES M Eld *MS* 4 May 1842

MOORE Alexander m MERRILL Ruth of Haverhill on 7 Feb 1844 at Haverhill NH, MOULTON F Eld *MS* 21 Feb 1844

MOORE Charles m ROLLINS Priscilla of Gardiner ME on 22d ult at Gardiner, SHAW E Rev *MFWBR* 17 Mar 1849

MOORE Charles H of Canterbury m SANBORN Nancy T at Hampton on 10 inst, HUTCHINS E Eld *MS* 26 Feb 1840

MOORE Christopher m BENNETT Zady Ann both of Hallowell ME on 9 Jul 1846 in Hallowell, WEAVER Philip Eld *MS* 12 Aug 1846

MOORE Elijah m MULLICAN Sarah A of Salem MA at Portsmouth NH *MFWBR* 3 Feb 1849

MOORE Isaac m UPTON Nancy on 21 Mar Charleston MA, JACK-SON Daniel Eld *MS* 24 May 1843

MOORE Joseph of Newfield ME m CHADBOURNE Martha Jane of Parsonsfield ME on 27th ult at Parsonsfield ME, SANBORN Luther Esq *MS* 17 Jan 1844

MOORE Robert Jr of China ME m PORTER Lorana of Dixmont ME, ALLEN E Eld *MS* 19 Mar 1845

MOORES Joseph of Wilton ME m MOSHER Sarah of Temple ME, SMITH Oliver H Eld *MS* 15 Jan 1840

MORE John of Newfield ME m WEDGEWOOD Hannah of Parsonsfield ME, BURBANK S Eld *MS* 17 Oct 1833

MOREY Peter m CASE Harriet P both of Green on 23 Feb, ALDRICH S Eld *MS* 26 Mar 1851

MOREY Reuben Jr of Strafford m BROWN Rosetta M of Tunbridge VT on 11 May 1848 in Tunbridge VT, SMITH E Rev *MS* 5 Jul 1848

MOREY William m WILLIAMS Elizabeth of Edgecomb ME on 13 Oct at Edgecomb ME, PAGE E G Eld *MS* 23 Nov 1842

MORGAN H U M m POPE R S both of Salem on 29 Jan in Salem, COLE M Eld *MS* 5 Mar 1851

MORGAN Josiah S m DAVIS Harriet both of Sutton on 24 Nov 1847 in Newbury NH, NEWELL F P Eld *MS* 2 Feb 1848

MORGAN Levi of Dexter m POTTER Lucy of Corinna on 11 Dec 1838, COPP J B Eld *MS* 17 Apr 1839

MORGRIDGE Horatio N formerly of Corinth ME m RAWLAND Sarah A of Roxand Co Mich in Oneida Eaton Co Mich, CILLEY E G Eld *MS* 24 May 1848

MORRELL John A L of Cincinnati Ohio m GRIFFITH Lucille of New
York on 23d inst in the Presbyterian Church at Perth Amboy NJ,
CORY B Rev *MS* 4 Aug 1847

MORRELL Paul of Boston m VERRILL Tryphene P at Alexandria,
BROWN Amos Eld *MS* 3 Jul 1839

MORRELL Thomas m SHURTLIFF Belinda both of Raymond ME on
22 Mar in Raymond ME, KEENE J Eld *MS* 8 Apr 1846

MORRILL Alexander H m SEAVEY Eliza of Hallowell ME on 29 June
at Litchfield ME, QUINNAM C Eld *MS* 13 Aug 1845

MORRILL Benjamin m TALLANT Lucretia Mrs on 20 Apr of Canterbury NH, CATLIN S T Eld *MS* 5 May 1847

MORRILL Daniel J m STACKHOUS Susanna L at Philadelphia on
6th street of New York on 11th inst at Friends Meetinghouse,
QUAKER marriage? *MS* 19 Feb 1845

MORRILL David m MANNING Mary V of Manchester on 24 Dec,
CILLEY D P Eld *MS* 1 Jan 1845

MORRILL Elisha m ELDER Harriet N at Harpswell ME, CATLIN S T
Eld *MS* 25 Dec 1844

MORRILL Harrison m BROWN Maria on 27 Mar at Gilford NH,
PERKINS Seth W Eld *MS* 14 Apr 1847

MORRILL Isaac m EATON Ruhama C G on 29 May at Gilford NH,
PERKINS Seth W Eld *MS* 23 June 1847

MORRILL Jacob of Contoocookville m ABBOTT Sarah C on 30 Apr,
FROST D S Eld *MS* 14 May 1845

MORRILL John of Parsonsfield ME m MULLOY Mary of Limerick ME,
LIBBY Elias Eld *MS* 7 Dec 1826

MORRILL Joseph m COFFIN Betsey A of Canterbury on 25th ult,
PATRICK Wm Rev *MS* 11 Feb 1835

MORRILL Josiah R m WEEKS Flinda of Gilmanton NH on Jan 1844,
CHASE William P Eld *MS* 31 Jan 1844

MORRILL Nahum Esq of Lewiston ME m LITTLEFIELD Anna I at
Wells on 30th ult *MFWBR* 11 May 1850

MORRILL Nathaniel m GILE Eliza Miss of Hopkinton NH on Thanksgiving even, CAVERNO A Eld *MS* 24 Dec 1828

MORRILL Nathan m THOMAS Rachel P both of Waterville, CURTIS S
Eld *MS* 30 May 1833

MORRILL Reuben m McCOY Hannah both of Manchester NH on 25
June 1848 in Manchester NH, CILLEY D P Eld *MS* 5 Jul 1848

MORRILL Thomas C m GUPTILL Susannah W of Limerick ME on 28
Apr 1842 at Limerick ME, CHASE William P Eld *MS* 18 May 1842

MORRIS Charles James m MERRILL Clara Augusta on Thanksgiving
eve in North Scarboro' ME, MANSON B S Eld *MS* 1 Dec 1847

MORRISON Benjamin m MARSH Olive on 1 Jan at Gilmanton NH
MS 11 Jan 1837

MORRISON Caleb m HORNER Abigail at Dracut MA, CURTIS S Eld
MS 12 Nov 1845

MORRISON David m BROWN Mary N both of Haverhill MA on 28 Nov in Haverhill MA, MERRIL Wm P Eld *MS* 8 Dec 1847

MORRISON James H of Boston MA m STILES Abigail B on 6 Mar at Strafford, PLACE E Elder *MS* 12 Mar 1845

MORRISON John m CONVERS Mary of Barnston on Aug 16, MOULTON Abial Eld *MS* 1 Jan 1840

MORRISON John C of Bethlehem m EDWARDS Mary P at Meredith Bridge on 14th ult, BROOKS N Eld *MS* 2 Mar 1842

MORRISON John Jr m MOULTON Lydia of Moultonboro NH on 15 Jul, BEAN S F Eld *MS* 4 Aug 1847

MORRISON Jonathan M m PIERCE Lucinda of Boston MA on 1 Sept, WEBBER Horace Eld *MS* 14 Sept 1842

MORRISON Jonathan m BOOTHBAY Jane on 25 Dec at Parsonsfield ME, JORDAN Z Eld *MS* 4 Feb 1846

MORRISON Jonathan m GOULD Mary on 30 June at Tuftonboro', BEAN S F Eld *MS* 4 Aug 1847

MORRISON Robert m MORRISON Joanna S both of Sweden ME on 19 Jul in Sweden ME, WILLEY Eben C *MS* 2 Sept 1846

MORRISON Samuel C m WENTWORTH Abby A both of Great Falls NH on 14 Oct in Great Falls, BROOKS N Eld *MS* 31 Oct 1849

MORRISON Uriah of Gilford m ODELL Sarah of Meredith NH on 15 March at Lake Village, FAIRFIELD Smith Eld *MS* 24 Mar 1847

MORSE Abner m DOW Abigail of Gilmanton on 26 Mar at Gilmanton, FERNALD S P Eld *MS* 30 Apr 1845

MORSE George B of North Yarmouth ME m SARGENT Eunice H 18th inst at Pownal ME, DRESSER R Esq *MFWBR* 31 Jul 1847

MORSE Henry m LAWTON Sarah both of Grafton MA on 31 Jan in Grafton, PECK B D Eld *MS* 1 May 1844

MORSE Marvil Jr m HARRIS Louisa L both of Pascoag RI on 23 Mayin Pascoag RI, HARRIMAN D P Eld *MS* 5 June 1850

MORSE Nathaniel m SEWALL Harriet M A both of Bath on 2 inst in Bath ME, SKILLEN H Eld *MS* 19 Feb 1851

MORSE Oscar F of Hebron m SANBORN Eliza J of Bristol in Bristol NH, CALLEY D Eld *MS* 4 Oct 1848

MORSE Richard of Chester m SANBORN Mary M of Gilford, KNOWLES E G Eld *MS* 1 Jan 1845

MORSE Rufus W m COX Lucinda P on 27 Aug 1849 in Holderness, THOMPSON S Eld *MS* 16 Jan 1850

MORSE S Ambrose of Holderness m PLASTED Adeline of Boston MA on 16 Dec 1849 in Holderness, THOMPSON S Eld *MS* 16 Jan 1850

MORSE Stephen of Canton NH m GORDON Mehitabel of Lowell MA at Lowell MA, EMERY James Eld *MS* 29 May 1844

MORSE Timon M of Manchester m BOYNTON Hannah A both of Charlestown MA in Manchester, CILLEY D P Eld *MS* 14 Feb 1849

MORSE William m FOSS Martha J both of Lowell on 5 Sept in

MORSE (Continued)
Dracut, CURTIS S Eld *MS* 14 Oct 1846

MORSE Winslow of Bath ME m NASH Sarah A at Minot ME, LIBBY Isaac Eld *MS* 6 May 1840

MORTON Solomon m MURCH Mary both of Westbrook ME on Nov 25, LIBBY Almon Eld *MS* 19 Jan 1842

MORTON Stephen Jr m LANE Lydia both of New Portland ME, STILSON Cyrus Eld *MS* 31 Oct 1833

MORTON Thomas of Boston MA m GRAY Lydia H of Bowdoinham ME on 15 May at Bowdoinham ME, QUINNAM C Eld *MS* 1 June 1842

MOSES Abraham of Biddeford ME m FOSS Mary Ann on 22 Dec 1842 at Saco ME, BEAN C Eld *MS* 1 Feb 1843

MOSES Horace of Eaton m YOUNG Paulina *MS* 12 Dec 1833

MOSES Mark S m DOLBEER Eliza L M both of Epsom NH, MANSON B S Eld *MS* 17 June 1835

MOSES William 2nd m BREWSTER Eliza of Portsmouth NH on 20th ult, TRUE E Eld *MS* 8 May 1839

MOSES William Capt m BERRY Ann of Scarboro' on 31 Jan at Scarboro' ME, SMITH William Eld *MS* 22 Feb 1843

MOSHER Amos P m WEDGEWOOD Sylvia I at Belgrade ME *MFWBR* 24 Aug 1850

MOSHER Mark of Gorham SMITH Lydia on 11th inst at Biddeford ME, LORD T N Rev *MFWBR* 21 Jan 1849

MOSHIER Rufus m RICHARDSON Dolly F on 25 Dec at Gorham, WITHAM L H Eld *MS* 5 Feb 1845

MOSSMAN Albion K m HARRINGTON Harriet both of Thomaston in Camden ME on 6 Aug 1848, SMALL Wm Eld *MS* 30 Aug 1848 & *MS* 16 May 1849

MOTLEY George of Lowell MA m STOVER Harriet at Gorham ME *MFWBR* 28 Dec 1850

MOTT Miner of Lebanon CT m SIBLEY Polly of Uxbridge MA on 28 Feb, PECK B D Eld *MS* 15 Mar 1843

MOULTON Charles m KNOWLES Betsey both of Cornish on 13 Dec *MS* 17 Jan 1833

MOULTON Cyrus F of Boston MA m FOSS Olive M of Boston MA in Boston MA, YOUNG Rev Dr *MFWBR* 14 Sep 1850

MOULTON David W of Manchester NH m WALLACE Lama Ann, CILLEY D P Eld *MS* 17 Feb 1847

MOULTON George of Bath m DAY Jane on Thurs last, LIBBY E Eld *MS* 24 Nov 1830

MOULTON Gilman m QUIMBY Abby T both of Sandwich on 4 Jul in Sandwich, TASKER L B Eld *MS* 18 Jul 1849

MOULTON Grange T m PULISIFER Julia A at Union Broome Co NY, DODGE Asa Eld *MS* 15 Jan 1845

MOULTON Ira of Scarboro m BERRY Lydia H of Saco, STRICKLAND

MOULTON (Continued)
G G Rev *MFWBR* 4 Jan 1851

MOULTON James Jr of Freedom m LAMPER Sally of Effingham,
DAVIS Joseph Eld *MS* 1 Apr 1835

MOULTON Jeremiah of York ME m STACKPOLE Abigail of Dover NH,
PERKINS J Rev *MS* 29 Apr 1835

MOULTON Josiah of Meredith m MAXFIELD Lydia of Sandwich on
20 Mar in Sandwich, BLAKE C E Eld *MS* 15 Apr 1846

MOULTON Josiah m HILLIARD Elizabeth A both of Meredith on 22
Dec 1850, PITMAN S J Eld *MS* 12 Feb 1851

MOULTON Oliver m McKUSICK Susan on Sunday last, LIBBY Eld in
Limerick ME *MS* 18 Oct 1827

MOULTON Samuel 3d m KNOWLES Cyrene on Sunday at Parsonsfield ME, BUZZELL John Eld *MS* 19 Oct 1826

MOULTON Samuel Dea at age 76y m BICKFORD Sally age 76y on
14th ult in Parsonsfield ME, BUZZELL John *MS* 1 May 1829

MOULTON Thomas P Eld of Walden VT m MOORE Louisa of Hatley
LC on Jan 17, MOULTON A W Eld *MS* 15 Apr 1840

MOULTON Wentworth L m BENSON Sarah Ann of Parsonsfield on 8
Sept, BUZZEL A Eld *MS* 18 Sep 1839

MOUSEY Timothy m COPP Eliza J both of Barnston on Nov 14 1839,
MOULTON A W Eld *MS* 15 Apr 1840

MOWRY Lyman of Smithfield m WHITING Mary Ann of Mendon,
BURLINGAME M W Eld *MS* 11 Dec 1839

MOWRY Wm Jr m ALDRICH Patience both of Smithfield on 29 ult in
Smithfield, ALLEN R Eld *MS* 18 Apr 1838

MUDGET John W of Gilmanton NH m GILMAN Saphronia D of
Loudon NH, DYER S B *MS* 19 Dec 1933

MUDGET Levi of New Hampton m COX Eliza Ann of Holderness on
20 Dec, TRUE E Eld *MS* 11 Jan 1843

MUDGET Luther m PIERCE Margaret S both of Prospect, STOWE J
P Eld *MS* 19 Jan 1842

MUDGET Robert m EMERY Urana both of Newbury on 16 Apr 1848
in Newbury, EMERY A Eld *MS* 2 Aug 1848

MUDGET William D m CHENEY Mary both of Bristol on 20 Mar in
Bristol, BROWN A Eld *MS* 2 Apr 1851

MUDGETT Jesse m BURNHAM Jane on 4 Dec at Sandwich *MS* 4 Jan
1837

MUDGETT Joseph E m PICKERING Olive Jane on 23 Nov 1843,
PITMAN Stephen J Eld *MS* 14 Feb 1844

MUGFORD George m McCOLISTER Catharine on 30 May 1848 in
Dracut, BLAISDELL Henry Rev *MS* 7 June 1848

MUGIN Russell m MURRAY Elizabeth Ann both of Stockbridge MA
on 13 Sept 1835 *MS* 4 May 1836

MULLIKEN John F of Haverhill m PENNIMAN Charlotte of West
Plymouth on 20 May at West Plymouth NH, CHASE Paul Eld

MULLIKEN (Continued)
MS 16 June 1847

MUNN Seth m PERRY Eliza of Boston MA on 12th inst at the FWB church in Charlestown MA, WETHERBEE Louisa H *MS* 22 Oct 1845

MUNROE Henry G m CILLEY Ann T both of Dover NH on 2 inst in Dover NH, SMITH A D Eld *MS* 12 Jul 1848

MUNSELL Daniel m SKIDMORE Hope both of Perry Township Ohio on 28 Oct 1847 in Perry Township, Logan Co Ohio, HEATH J D Eld *MS* 9 Feb 1848

MUNSEY Andrew C of Lincoln m HOPKINS Mary Jane on of Litchfield ME on 7 Nov 1847 in Litchfield ME, QUINNAM C Eld *MS* 8 Dec 1847

MUNSEY David H m ROBERTS Betsey H on 28 Feb 1843 at Gilford, PINKHAM J Eld *MS* 12 Apr 1843

MURCH Benjamin m FAUNEE Mary B both of Foxcroft at Guilford ME *MS* 19 Nov 1834

MURCH George W m BURNHAM Julia N A W on 13th inst at Portland ME, STREETER Rev *MFWBR* 24 Feb 1849

MURPHEY John m BENNETT Jane Mrs both of Enfield on 23 May in Enfield NY, EVANS S R Eld *MS* 25 Sept 1850

MURPHY George F of Denmark m MARCH Lucinda E of Bridgeton on 14 Oct in Bridgeton ME, PHINNEY J H Eld *MS* 21 Nov 1838

MURPHY Jesse K of Denmark ME m BICKFORD Anna E of Biddeford ME at Biddeford ME 26th ult *MFWBR* 12 Oct 1850

MURPHY Thomas of Dorchester m MERRILL Lydia Jane of Rochester on 3 Nov, DAVIS J B Eld *MS* 27 Nov 1844

MURRAY Daniel m DORE Margaret on 8 inst Sunday in Dover, SMITH Eleazer Rev *MS* 25 Oct 1837

MURRAY William of Knox m McLAUGHLIN Sarah J of Freedom on Thanksgiving Day in So Montville ME, KNOWLTON E Eld *MS* 22 Jan 1851

MURRY James Capt Jr m HODGDON Frances, MORRILL S P Eld *MS* 23 Dec 1846

MUZZEY Asa A m CILLEY Abigail C of Lowell *MS* 8 Feb 1837

MUZZEY Eden m WAKEFIELD Sarah A both of Gardiner on 16 Dec Gardiner ME, LANCASTER D Eld *MS* 24 Apr 1950

MYERS Henry J m ROLFE Marianna of Bethany NY on 13 Feb 1848in Bethany NY, BLACKMARR H Eld *MS* 19 Jul 1848

MYERS Jacob of Goshen m WELLMAN Sarah Jane of Yankeytown Ohio on 30 Dec 1841, DUDLEY Moses Eld *MS* 2 Mar 1842

MYERS Sumner m CARNEY Abagail Mrs at Dresden *MFWBR* 13 Oct 1849

NASH Charles C of Sidney ME m TAYLOR Julia A of Waterville ME at Winslow ME, LEWIS Daniel B Eld *MS* 25 Nov 1846

NASH Charles W of Dover m TYLER Amaretta Miss of Portsmouth, DEMING Rev *MS* 19 Dec 1833

NASON Aaron of Wakefield m BEAN Mary S on 3 Nov 1844, BROOKS John Eld *MS* 1 Jan 1845

NASON Abraham m CLARKE Lydia both of Dixmont on 17 inst in Dixmont ME, WHITCOMB A Esq *MS* 31 Jan 1838

NASON Daniel L m SMITH Sabrina H of Lowell MA on 11 Sept at Lowell MA, WOODMAN J Eld *MS* 19 Oct 1842

NASON Elisha m JENNESS Julia Ann of Dover NH on 12 inst at Dover NH, HUTCHINS E Eld *MS* 22 Oct 1845

NASON Freeman m WHITTEN Eliza at Waterboro ME, DREW Ira T Esq *MFWBR* 23 Oct 1847

NASON Mark F m NUTE Marietta both of Dover on 26 Apr in Durham, TOBEY Alvan Rev *MS* 1 May 1850

NASON Nathan m WENTWORTH Mary in Limington ME, MITCHELL Isaac Esq *MS* 10 Aug 1826

NASON Rufus m STILSON Nancy at Waterville ME *MFWBR* 13 Oct 1849

NASON Seth C m WITHAM Olive of Danville ME on 24 Sept, LIBBY James Eld *MS* 8 Nov 1843

NASON Storer m DEARBORN Sarah both of Lowell in Lowell, THURSTON N Eld *MS* 21 Nov 1838

NASON William m DURGIN Mary A of Great Falls NH on 10 Jan at Great Falls, WEBBER Horace Eld *MS* 21 Feb 1844

NASON Zebulon of Milton NH m TIBBETTS Mary S of Acton ME on 13 Oct, STEVENS T Eld *MS* 23 Oct 1839

NEAL Hiram m CHADBOURN Clarissa Ann both of No Berwick on 31 Dec in North Berwick ME, CLAY D Eld *MS* 7 Feb 1849

NEAL James A of Dover m TAYLOR Sarah Jane of Effingham NH on 26 ult in Effingham, WATSON Elijah Eld *MS* 26 Jan 1848

NEAL John at Manchester m BODWELL Hannah, CILLEY D P Eld *MS* 20 Dec 1843

NEAL Julius m SEAVEY Sarah both of Hallowell ME *MS* 1 Feb 1837

NEAL Moses C m TILTON Sarah C both of Loudon on 5 Dec, CORSER Enoch Rev *MS* 19 Dec 1838

NEAL Oliver m SMITH Mel R at Great Falls *MFWBR* 24 Feb 1849

NEALLEY Joseph T of Monroe m COULLARD Lucy on 28 Nov, ALLEN E Eld *MS* 18 Dec 1844

NEFF Judson m FOWLER Celinda both of Rochester on 26 Aug in Rochester Racine Co Wis *MS* 17 Oct 1849

NELSON Henry D m MERRILL Elizabeth G on 4th Jul at Manchester NH, CILLEY D P Eld *MS* 28 Jul 1847

NELSON Hiram of Bristol m RANDALL Sarah M of Centre Harbor on 15 Oct, TRUE E Eld *MS* 21 Nov 1843

NELSON John of Portland ME m MERRILL Martha of Portland on 31st ult, MOULTON A K Eld *MS* 8 Feb 1843

NELSON John P of Deerfield m BROWN Sarah C of Candia NH on 15 ult in Candia NH, ATWOOD Mark Eld *MS* 6 June 1849

NELSON John S m TILTON Belinda of Bristol on 23 Nov at New Hampton, FISK E Eld *MS* 31 Jan 1844

NELSON Levi Jr m BATCHELDER Lucinda both of Bristol on 21 Apr in Bristol, BROWN A Eld *MS* 5 May 1846

NELSON Otis C m WHITNEY Martha W both of New Gloucester ME on 10 Feb 1848 in New Gloucester ME *MS* 23 Feb 1848

NEVENS Davis Jr m NASON Eliza of Lewiston ME on 7th inst at Danville, LIBBY Isaac Eld *MS* 27 Mar 1839

NEVENS William P m EASTMAN Phebe E of Limerick ME on 6 May at Limerick ME, LORD D H Eld *MS* 9 June 1847

NEWBEGIN Harvy of Newfield ME m LIBBY Hannah on Sunday last, BURBANK Eld *MS* 14 Mar 1828

NEWBEGIN John of Shapleigh ME m MURRAY Ann of Limerick ME on 6th inst, BURBANK S Eld *MS* 21 Dec 1832

NEWBEGIN Luke L of Newfield ME m LIBBEY Eliza A of Somersworth NH at Rochester NH *MFWBR* 27 Jul 1850

NEWCOMB Bangs D m BILLINGS Elizabeth H on 29 Oct at Newburgh ME, ALLEN E Eld *MS* 17 Jan 1844

NEWCOMB Otis m SMITH Margaret of Braintree MA on 3 Nov 1842 at Otisfield ME, HUNTRESS D Eld *MS* 16 Nov 1842

NEWELL David m BRACKETT Jane in Gorham, HODSDON Caleb Esq *MS* 7 Sept 1826

NEWELL Francis P of Sutton m RAMSEY Hannah B of New Hampton on 20 May 1847, FISK Ebenezer Eld *MS* 22 Sept 1847

NEWELL George W of Lawrence MA m GOODWIN Margaret L of Lebanon ME on 14 May 1848 at Freewill Baptist meeting house in Great Falls NH, BROOKS N Eld *MS* 24 May 1848

NEWELL Henry C m SPEAR Margaret both of Bowdoinham ME on 21 Dec 1847 in Bowdoinham ME, HATHORN S Eld *MS* 29 Dec 1847

NEWELL Lucius m CONVERS Perlina of Matildaville on 4 May at Matildaville NY, WHITFIELD Eld *MS* 12 Jul 1843

NEWELL William B m WEEKS Susannah K both of Durham on 16 June in Durham, NEWELL David Eld *MS* 10 Jul 1850

NEWHALL Albert of Lynn MA m KEAG Hannah S of Wolfboro NH on 3d ult, HOLMES Hiram Eld *MS* 7 Feb 1833

NEWHALL Frances of Lyme MA m FROST Sarah of Bridgton on 2 Oct 1842, WHITNEY G W Eld *MS* 10 May 1843

NEWHOLD Joshua m DAVIS Rebeccah on 27 May both of Washington township Fayette Co PA, WILLIAMS Samuel Eld *MS* 3 Aug 1832

NEWMAN Benjamin m CARTER Elizabeth B both of Sanford on 30 Dec 1841 in Sanford ME, BUZZELL Alvah Eld *MS* 16 Feb 1842

NEWTON Silas Jr m DALRYMPLE Seviah F both of Roscoe Winneba-

NEWTON (Continued)
go Co IL at Roscoe, GRIFFIN Jacob Eld *MS* 18 Oct 1848

NEWTON Wm C of Bolney NY m TURNER Emma of Schroeppel NY on 16 Sept 1847 in Schroeppel Oswego Co NY, KFAIN [KRAIN/KRUM?] S Eld *MS* 17 Nov 1847

NICHOLS Alfred of Reading MA m POTTER Hannah B of Gilford on 1 Jan in Gilford, FROST D S Eld *MS* 12 Feb 1851

NICHOLS Benjamin m NICHOLS Elanor both of Ossipee NH on 5 Dec in Ossipee, CHICK John Eld *MS* 15 Jan 1840

NICHOLS Daniel P of Bowdoin m HODGKINS Ruth of Lewiston ME on 17 Oct 1848 in Lewiston ME, LIBBY David Eld *MS* 29 Nov 1848

NICHOLS Dolphas m DIMICK Delight on 23 Jan 1848 in Pierpont NY, WHITFIELD W Eld *MS* 15 Mar 1848

NICHOLS H L Dr m EVANS Sarah on 7th inst at Augusta ME, JUDD Rev *MFWBR* 18 Sept 1847

NICHOLS J T G Rev of Saco ME m TUCKER Caroline M at Boston MA, YOUNG Rev Dr *MFWBR* 12 Oct 1850

NICHOLS Jacob W m KING Nancy on 19 Jul in Ossipee, PERKINS Levi Esq *MS* 12 Aug 1846

NICHOLS James B Capt of Searsport ME m RICH Esther G on 14 Dec, ROBINSON N J Eld *MS* 24 Dec 1845

NICHOLS Josiah of Lowell m MUIR Caroline of Portsmouth NH in Lowell MA, THURSTON Nathaniel *MS* 18 Oct 1837

NICHOLS Nathaniel of Vinalhaven m PENDLETON Cordelia of Islesboro ME, PAYNE J Dr *MS* 18 Nov 1835

NICHOLS Solomon M m GIFFORD Mary E on 16 Dec in Boardman Clayton Co Iowa, BIXBY N W Eld *MS* 16 Jan 1850

NICHOLS Thomas B m BICKFORD Climena both of Meredith on 18 Dec 1849, PITMAN S J Eld *MS* 30 Jan 1850

NICHOLS Timothy of Windsor VT m HUTCHINSON Catherine of Windsor, ADAMS Abel Eld *MS* 22 Mar 1843

NICHOLS William m LEAR Betsey both of Effingham NH on 16 Jan 1849 in Effingham NH, FOSS N Eld *MS* 7 Feb 1849

NICHOLS William S m ALEXANDER Margaret of Brunswick at Brunswick ME, CROWELL E Eld *MS* 26 Apr 1843

NICHOLS William of Meredith m ELLSWORTH Sarah of Sandbornton NH on 27 June in Sandbornton, BROOKS N Eld *MS* 11 Jul 1838

NICKERSON John E m SMITH Naamah on 1 May at Barrington, Shelburne Co, Nova Scotia, Canada, HENDERSON M C Eld *MS* 9 Jul 1845

NICKERSON Jonathan Jr of Albany m ALLARD Mary M of Eaton on 31st Oct, KNOWLES S Eld *MS* 27 Nov 1839

NICKERSON Luke of Eaton m TUTTLE Lydia A of Effingham NH on 9 Jan in Effingham, FOSS N Eld *MS* 26 Mar 1851

NICKERSON Robert m GLIDDEN Susan of Albany on 3 Mar at Eaton

NICKERSON (Continued)
  NH, KNOWLES Samuel Eld *MS* 11 May 1842
NICKERSON Watson m SEARS Lovina on 17 Apr at Barrington,
  Shelburne Co, Nova Scotia, Canada, HENDERSON M C Eld *MS* 9
  Jul 1845
NIXON James m SOANS Polly of Tecumseh, Lenawee Co, Michigan
  on 2 June, EASTWOOD Eld *MS* 18 Sep 1839
NOALLY John 2nd m DURGIN Mary A S both of Northwood on 20
  Nov, CILLEY D P Eld *MS* 26 Nov 1834
NOBLE Albert H of St Albans ME m QUIMBY Sophia M of Meredith
  Bridge NH on 8 Jan, GASKILL Silas Eld *MS* 17 Jan 1844
NOBLE Frederick A m SMITH Lydia Ann of Sandbornton on 24th at
  Bradford NH, HOLMES H Eld "N.B. The Christian Reflector will
  please copy this." *MS* 17 Mar 1847
NORRIS Arthur F L Esq of Pittsfield m WALLACE Olive W of Dover
  on 25 Jul in Chichester, SWAIN Wm Eld *MS* 21 Oct 1846
NORRIS Eliphalet of Newport VT m KILBOURN Lucy of Thetford VT
  on 3 Jul in Thetford, CLARK Eli Eld *MS* 21 Nov 1849
NORRIS George W of Moriah NY m HOUSE Harriet F of Nashua,
  STEARNS S Eld *MS* 4 Mar 1846
NORRIS Hiram of Epping m HARVEY Sally of Nottingham at Deer-
  field, HANSCOM P Eld *MS* 8 Dec 1841
NORRIS John A of Corinth m WALKER Susannah of Williamstown
  on 7 Nov 1849 in Williamstown, HARTSHORN Nelson Eld *MS* 16
  Jan 1850
NORRIS Joseph m PLUMER Nancy at Gilmanton Jan 20 1840,
  TUTTLE John G Eld *MS* 19 Feb 1840
NORRIS Samuel m ABBOT Esther of Ossipee NH on 2d ult at Ossi-
  pee NH, CHICK John Eld *MS* 21 Aug 1844
NORRIS Theophilus m FOLSOM Abigail at Epping *MS* 2 Jul 1834
NORRIS Trueworthy m BROWN Mary Jane at Pittsfield on Feb 11,
  CILLEY D P Eld *MS* 19 Feb 1840
NORRIS Wm B of Nashville m BLOOD Lucinda M of Newbury NH on
  3 Aug 1847 in Newbury NH, NEWELL F P Eld *MS* 2 Feb 1848
NORTHRUP Bushrod m DARLING Sarah on 1 June at Pierpont,
  WHITFIELD Eld *MS* 12 Jul 1843
NORTON B Mr m STEELE Eliza on 4 March at Boston Erie Co NY,
  LIGHTHALL W A Eld *MS* 24 Mar 1847
NORTON Ebenezer of Porter m SARGEANT Martha of Brownfield ME
  on 9 May at Limington ME, RAND I Eld *MS* 29 May 1844
NORTON George W m THOMPSON Elizabeth on 5 June in Alexan-
  dria NY, GRIFFETH A Eld *MS* 31 Jul 1850
NORTON Ivory m SAWYER Jane B both of Limington on Jan 20,
  RAND James Eld *MS* 2 Mar 1842
NORTON Martin m REYNOLDS Eliza Jane both of Oakfield on 16
  Feb 1848 in Fon du Lac Co Wis, WRIGHT E N Eld

NORTON (Continued)
    MS 26 Apr 1848
NORTON Reuben of West Enosburgh m DUNTON Caroline C of
    Swanton in Swanton VT, COFFRIN Joshua Eld *MS* 5 Feb 1851
NORTON William of New Market m JENKS Caroline of Madbury on
    21 Apr, CILLEY D P Eld *MS* 1 May 1839
NOTEWARE John Jr of Warsing Ulster Co NY m MAYHEW Phebe of
    Owego on 22 Jan 1849, GARDNER L G Eld *MS* 28 Mar 1849
NOURSE Phineas A of Lowell MA m EATON Elizabeth B of Hopkin-
    ton on 28 Apr in Hopkinton *MS* 8 May 1844
NOWELL Daniel m STEVENS Abigail both of Somersworth on 26th
    at Great Falls, THURSTON N Eld *MS* 5 Dec 1833
NOWELL John of Vassalborough m WILSON Mary J of Topsham in
    Topsham ME, FOLSOM P Eld *MS* 2 Sept 1846
NOYCES William M m SHIELDS Mary H on 29th ult at Portland ME,
    CARRUTHERS Rev Dr *MFWBR* 16 Nov 1850
NOYES Amos L m PEASLEY Hannah both of Manchester on 26 Jul
    in Manchester, CILLEY D P Eld *MS* 1 Aug 1849
NOYES Charles of Boscawen m ROBERTS Sarah of Andover on 19
    Jul at Andover, WATSON E Eld *MS* 3 Aug 1842
NOYES Eli Brother of Jefferson ME m PIERCE Clementina Sister of
    Portsmouth NH on 3 inst, CRAWFORD Mr Esq *MS* 17 June 1835
NOYES Harvey m ADAMS Caroline E both of Tunbridge VT 1 June
    1848 in Tunbridge VT, SMITH C H Eld *MS* 21 June 1848
NOYES John S m SMITH Louisa B both of Deerfield NH on Christ-
    mas Eve, BURBANK P S Eld *MS* 24 Jan 1849
NOYES Lyman m COOK Maria of Wheatland Mich on 27th Oct,
    WILCOX S H Eld *MS* 4 Dec 1839
NOYES Moses of Landaff m ROYCE Lydia of Benton on 23 Apr 1845
    in Benton, MOULTON F Eld *MS* 8 Apr 1846
NOYES William H of Gloucester MA m PARSLEY Sarah M of Straf-
    ford in Strafford on 14 May 1848, PLACE E Eld *MS* 24 May 1848
NOYS Horatio L m ANNIS Sarah B on 10 Jan at Great Falls NH,
    DUNN R Eld *MS* 20 Jan 1847
NUDD Benjamin B Capt m PERKINS Rebecca C of Loudon on 14 Nov
    at Canterbury NH, CLOUGH Jeremiah Eld *MS* 14 Feb 1844
NUDD Stephen W m PERKINS Caroline both of Roxbury on 25 ult,
    CURTIS S Eld in Roxbury MA *MS* 15 May 1850
NUTE Abraham m KING Almira of Ossipee NH on 22 Dec at Ossipee
    NH, HOLMES J C Eld *MS* 4 Jan 1843
NUTE Alfred m BEAN Judith at Candia *MS* 22 June 1836
NUTE David C m BROWNELL Lydia A on 24 Dec at Dover NH,
    BROCK H H Eld *MS* 8 Jan 1845
NUTE Hopley Y m PINDAR Lydia C on 7th inst at Dover NH, PER-
    KINS S W Eld *MS* 15 Oct 1845
NUTE Rufus M m BURROWS Abigail both of Middleton on 17 May

NUTE (Continued)
1849 in Farmington, BODGE J Eld *MS* 13 Feb 1850

NUTE Thomas J m BULLOCK Lavina on 14 Nov at Lowell MA, THURSTON N Eld *MS* 25 May 1842

NUTE Zenas H of Tuftonborough m STILLING Sarah Ann of Ossipee NH on 1 Dec in Ossipee, CHICK J Eld *MS* 15 Jan 1851

NUTT Samuel of Troy ME m CHURCH Sally of New Market on 27 Dec, HUTCHINS E Eld *MS* 4 Jan 1843

NUTTER Abner J at Dover NH m PITMAN Angeline of Dover, DYER B Eld *MS* 7 May 1845

NUTTER Abner J m ROBERTS Hannah both of Dover on 12 inst in Dover NH, HUTCHINS E Eld *MS* 19 Dec 1849

NUTTER Alphonso J m TAYLOR Betsey T on 27th ult at Dover NH, HUTCHINS E Eld *MS* 6 Aug 1845

NUTTER Asa N m NUTTER Mary A both of Alton NH on 20 Aug 1848 in Gilmanton NH, FERNALD S P Eld *MS* 6 Sept 1848

NUTTER Enos George m SMITH Betsey R of Pittsfield on 31 Oct at Pittsfield, CILLEY D P Eld *MS* 16 Nov 1842

NUTTER Ezra S m YOUNG Jane S on 24th inst in Gilmanton NH, GARLAND David Eld *MS* 21 Jan 1835

NUTTER George F of Palermo m HATHORN Mary T on 7 Nov at Bowdoinham ME, HATHORN S Eld *MS* 17 Dec 1845

NUTTER George m TWOMBLY Abigail at Tuftonboro' *MS* 6 Mar 1834

NUTTER Joseph P of Manchester m FOLSOM Betsey A of Gilford, BROOKS N Eld *MS* 26 Apr 1843

NUTTER Lewis m GRACE Betsy of Dover NH on 15 Nov at Dover NH, LEWIS L Eld *MS* 25 Nov 1846

NUTTER Oliver of Wakefield m WENTWORTH Roxannah C of Jackson NH on 27 June in Conway NH, CHASE J T Hon *MS* 11 Jul 1849 & *MFWBR* 21 Jul 1849

NUTTER Valentine of Ossipee m PRAY Sophia of Dover on 2 inst in Dover NH, CLARK Mayhew Eld *MS* 12 Apr 1837

NUTTER William Jr m GOTHAM Ann J W at Portsmouth NH *MFWBR* 18 Aug 1849

NUTTER William of Portsmouth NH m TODD Catherine of Kittery ME, WETHERBEE K J Eld *MS* 1 Jan 1845

NUTTING Edward D m GODING Esther S on 12th inst at Gardiner, SHAW Rev *MFWBR* 28 Apr 1849

NUTTING Harvey S of Wardsboro VT m BOLLES Emeline B of Bethlehem NH on 3 Oct in Bethlehem NH, BLAKE C E Eld *MS* 24 Oct 1849

OAKES David of Lisbon m MORRISON Lydia Ann of Bethlehem in Franconia, BLAKE C E Eld *MS* 24 Jan 1849

OAKES John m RICH Nancy J at Bangor ME, CAVERNO A Eld *MS* 13 Sept 1843

OAKS Oscar m BRUCE Louisa on 10 Aug at Nashua, STEARNS S Eld *MS* 22 Oct 1845

ODELL Ebenezer F of Sandbornton NH m BATCHELDER Louisa of Sandbornton, BROOKS N Eld *MS* 15 Nov 1843

ODIORNE Charles W m SPERLIN Esther at Dover NH, HUTCHINS E Eld *MS* 15 Oct 1845

ODLIME John W of Boston MA m JONES Nancy M of Portsmouth NH on 8 Jan 1847, DAVIS J B Eld *MS* 20 Jan 1847

ODWAY Walter of Belmont m WYMAN Saphrinia of Searsmont ME on 22 Mar 1849 in Searsmont ME, LAMB Henry A *MS* 18 Apr 1849

OLIVER Edward B of Hatley m FOSS Mary D of Stanstead LC *MS* 17 Apr 1839

OLIVER Gilbert of Industry m HUNNEWELL Sarah of Wiscasset ME on 13th inst at Westport, FAIRFIELD Eld *MS* 30 Mar 1836

OLIVER James D m OLIVER Nancy M of Georgetown ME on 3 Dec, ROBINSON N J Eld *MS* 17 Jan 1844

OLIVER James E m FREDRICK Rhoda both of Starks on Dec 7 1843 in Starks, Oliver John Esq *MS* 8 May 1844

OLIVER Jeremiah m HINKLEY Eliza at Georgetown ME, HINKLEY John Esq *MS* 5 June 1839

OLIVER John Jr m MANN Elcy on 23d inst at Phipsburgh ME, SMITH O W Eld *MS* 2 Aug 1843

OLIVER Mathew of Georgetown ME m OLIVER Salome of Phipsburgh on 13 Oct in Georgetown ME, WEBBER David Eld *MS* 30 Oct 1850

OLIVER Moses O m TRAFTON Emeline G both of Georgetown ME on 14 Feb 1850, PENDEXTER S Eld *MS* 27 Feb 1850

OLIVER Thomas Y of Starks m HERSOM Mary of Fairfield ME *MS* 15 Mar 1837

OLIVER Washington Capt m WINKLEY Mary Jane on 24 Nov 1842 at Georgetown ME, KEENE Josiah Jr Eld *MS* 8 Mar 1843

OLIVER Washington of Georgetown m OLIVER Mary Jane on 17 Nov, SPINNEY Zina W/H Esq *MS* 11 Dec 1839

OLIVER William 2d m OLIVER Mehitabel of Georgetown ME, QUINNAM Constant Eld *MS* 6 Feb 1834

OLIVER Zina H of Hallowell m LOWELL Prudence of Phipsburgh on 20 ult in Phipsburgh, LOWELL Tallman Esq *MS* 3 Oct 1838

OLMSTED Orrin O m WELLS Phebe on 17 Dec 1834, ANDRUS A D Eld *MS* 7 Jan 1835

OLNEY Edwin B of Gloucester m ALLEN Alnetriphanthem of No Providence RI on 21st ult, HUTCHINS E Eld *MS* 7 May 1834

ORDWAY Benjamin m AYERS Sarah A Mrs both of Kittery ME on 22 Dec 1849 in Kittery ME, PERKINS Seth W Eld *MS* 9 Jan 1850

ORDWAY Edson of Strafford m JOHNSON Lydia of Tunbridge in Tunbridge VT, SWETT David Eld *MS* 18 Apr 1838

ORDWAY Harry of Strafford m AVERY Sarah Ann C of Sharon in
Tunbridge, SWETT David Eld *MS* 18 Apr 1838

ORDWAY Joshua of Hopkinton m RION Martha Ann of Northfield on
23 Jan at Canterbury, CHASE William P Eld *MS* 31 Mar 1847

ORNE Joseph M of New Boston m BARTLETT Climena P of Deering
on 7 Mar in Manchester, CILLEY D P Eld *MS* 22 Mar 1848

ORR Hermon C m SAWYER Arabine T of Harpswell in Freeport ME,
HERSEY L Eld *MS* 24 Oct 1849

ORR Richard R m BLAKE Didama L both of Manchester on 24 Oct
1847 in Manchester, CILLEY D P Eld *MS* 10 Nov 1847

ORRELL Samuel R m CURREY Adeline both of Dover on Mon last,
THURSTON N Eld *MS* 3 Sept 1834

OSBORNE/OSBORN

OSBORNE Daniel m OSBORN Mercy P both of Dover on 29 ult in
Dover, HUTCHINS E Eld *MS* 5 June 1850 & *MFWBR* 8 June 1850

OSBORNE David C of Russel Ohio m ROBERTS Mary L on 14 May at
Munson Ohio, DUNN R Eld *MS* 11 June 1845

OSBORNE James L m WALLRON Lydia A on 2 Oct in Rochester,
WHITNEY G W Eld *MS* 1 Jan 1851

OSBORNE John S m BROWN Jane S R on 18 Sept at Loudon NH,
CILLEY D P Eld *MS* 12 Oct 1842

OSGOOD Aaron of Durham ME m NEVENS Eunice S of Lewiston ME
on 13 Jan 1848 in Lewiston ME, BEAN G W Eld *MS* 16 Feb 1848

OSGOOD B F m GOODWIN Sarah A both of Manchester on 7 Apr
1849 in Manchester, CILLEY D P Eld *MS* 25 Apr 1849

OSGOOD Calvin (printer) m CALEF Dorothy of Lowell on 25th,
THURSTON N Eld *MS* 28 Aug 1839

OSGOOD Charles H m HILL Matilda M both of Northwood on 25 Aug
in Northwood NH, MOULTON F Eld *MS* 6 Nov 1850

OSGOOD D L Marquis of Exeter ME m RAMSDEL Elizabeth B of
Garland on 1 Mar in Garland ME, DORE T W Eld *MS* 15 Sept
1847

OSGOOD Ebenezer of Raymond m FOX Abagail *MS* 19 Apr 1837

OSGOOD Ebenezer P of Concord m RANDALL Ann of Centre Harbor
on 25 Nov 1849, PITMAN S J Eld *MS* 30 Jan 1850

OSGOOD Edward of Canterbury NH m HODGDON Charlotte of
Northfield NH on 17 Sept in Canterbury, CLOUGH Jeremiah Eld
NH *MS* 14 Oct 1846

OSGOOD Enoch F Jr m BLAKE Mary at Raymond NH *MS* 9 Nov
1832

OSGOOD Enoch F of Gilford m WEBSTER Sally D of Gilford,
BROOKS N Eld *MS* 13 Sept 1843

OSGOOD George W m DIXON Maria on 15 Feb at Manchester NH,
SINCLAIR J L Eld *MS* 6 Apr 1842

OSGOOD James m GRANT Deborah A of Gilford NH at Meredith NH,
BROOKS N Eld *MS* 16 Nov 1842

OSGOOD John H of Gilmanton m DAVIS Martha B of Pittsfield NH on 22 Aug at Pittsfield NH, KNOWLES J Eld *MS* 30 Aug 1843

OSGOOD John P m COLBY Laura J on 4th inst at Dover NH, HUNTINS E Eld *MS* 10 Feb 1847

OSGOOD Reuben Capt of Salisbury m MOORE Abba (a widow) of Hampton on 28th ult, HUTCHING E Eld *MS* 13 Mar 1839

OSGOOD Samuel of Amesbury MA m BURRILL Elizabeth of Chester on 1 Jan 1844 at Manchester, CILLEY D P Eld *MS* 17 Jan 1844

OSGOOD Timothy m DOE Nancy B of Raymond NH on 1 Dec *MS* 14 Dec 1836

OSTRANDER Henry Jr m HIGHNS [*sic*] Sophia on 7 June 1835 *MS* 4 May 1836

OTIS Daniel m BANNISTER Kilany of Pierpont on 5 Nov 1842, WHITFIELD W Eld *MS* 1 Feb 1843

OTIS George K m ROLLINS Mary J of Berwick on 3 Jul, JOHNSON W D Eld *MS* 10 Jul 1850

OTIS Joseph G m BAKER Sarah E of Lowell MA on 21 Aug at Lowell MA, THURSTON N Eld *MS* 2 Nov 1842

OTIS Joshua Esq of Strafford m RICKER Rebecca F of Farmington on 11 May 1848 in Farmington, PLACE E Eld *MS* 24 May 1848

OTIS Paul m DROWN Polly widow both of Sheffield VT on 11 Oct in Sheffield VT, CROSS David Eld *MS* 24 Jan 1838

OTIS William M Capt m MELCHER Harriet M of Brunswick ME on 3 Sept, ROLLINS Andrew Eld *MS* 18 Sep 1839

OTIS William P m JOHNSON Elizabeth B of Somersworth at Rochester, MEADER Jesse Eld *MS* 24 Jul 1839

OTIS William P of Dover m WENTWORTH Mary on 7 ult in Dover, SMITH A D Eld *MS* 24 Jul 1839

OTIS William S of Somersworth NH m BERRY Betsey of Somersworth NH on 22 Oct, MEADER Jesse Eld *MS* 27 Dec 1843

OWEN Charles of Leeds m ADAMS Martha A of Litchfield in Litchfield ME, QUINNAM C Eld *MS* 18 Sept 1850

OWEN Levi m BARNES Elizabeth on 17 Mar in Laroy, Dodge Co., Wis, WRIGHT E N Eld *MS* 23 May 1849

OWEN Mark L H m HARMON Matilda both of Buxton ME on May 19 in Buxton ME, CROCKETT J Eld *MS* 28 Aug 1850

OWEN Robert M m STONE Cordelia L on 14th inst at Brunswick, BROOKS Rev *MFWBR* 21 Jan 1849

OWEN William m EMERY Roxanna at Buxton ME, CLAY Jonathan Eld *MS* 20 Nov 1844

PACKARD E "Heman" m REED J Willey both of Lowell MA on 20 Aug in Topsham VT, DICKEY H F Eld *MS* 11 Sept 1850

PACKARD Job C B Esq of Blanchard m BUCK Rosina of Buckfield on 28th ult at Hebron *MFWBR* 17 Mar 1849

PACKARD John A Jr m JACKSON Mary E of Lowell on 18th inst,

PACKARD (Continued)
THURSTON N Eld *MS* 27 Feb 1839

PAGE - see PAIGE

PAGE Abby m FLANDERS Nancy both of Weare on 2 Oct 1336 (*sic* - 1836) at Weare *MS* 16 Nov 1836

PAGE Benjamin G of Hallowell ME m DUNTON Julia A on 17 Nov at Westport ME, PAGE Benjamin G Esq *MS* 27 Dec 1843

PAGE Christopher m ATKINSON Sarah both of Stanstead LC on 5 Oct 1837, MOULTON A Eld *MS* 10 Jan 1837

PAGE Daniel M m PIKE Eliza both of Great Falls on 20 ult in Dover NH, SMITH A D Eld *MS* 6 Sept 1837

PAGE David S of Lowell m BUZWELL Elizabeth of Bradford on 29 Nov in Methuen, THURSTON N Eld *MS* 12 Dec 1838

PAGE Ezekiel G m BURLEY Mary G both of Farmington ME on 30 Mar in Farmington ME, CHANEY John Eld *MS* 17 May 1837

PAGE Ezekiel H s/o PAGE John Eld m BARTLETT Sarah at Garland ME, NASON Samuel V Eld *MS* 23 Jan 1834

PAGE Harrison m HUNT Emeline of Lowell *MS* 30 Jan 1839

PAGE Harvey m MASON Sarah M on 25 Dec at Bethel ME, DONHAM Rev *MS* 4 Feb 1846

PAGE Ira E m COTTON Nancy both of Gilmanton on 30 Mar in Gilmanton, FERNALD S P Eld *MS* 1 May 1844

PAGE Jacob m THOMPSON Esther on 28 Jan at Newfield, JORDAN Z Eld *MS* 4 Feb 1846

PAGE James m INGERSON Lucy M both of Farmington NH? *MS* 9 Sept 1835

PAGE John m LANE Mahala B of Pittsfield on 28 Aug, CILLEY D P Eld *MS* 11 Sept 1839

PAGE John A m DEARBORN Martha A both of Manchester on 1 Jan in Manchester, DAVIS J B Eld *MS* 26 Mar 1851

PAGE John B m DUDLEY Mary A both of Northwood on 5 Jan in Northwood NH, MOULTON F Eld *MS* 22 Jan 1851

PAGE John B of Boston MA m LOMBARD Ruth R of Boston, HOLMAN J W Eld *MS* 25 Jan 1843

PAGE John E of Gilmanton m FOSTER Eliza W of Gilmanton NH on 1 Feb, MASON Lemuel Eld *MS* 22 Feb 1843

PAGE John of Kensington m STILSON Susan C of Durham on 18 May at Durham, FROST D S Eld *MS* 11 June 1845

PAGE M W m HARMON Mary C both of Windham ME on 1 May, MANSON B S Eld *MS* 29 May 1850

PAGE Moses of Whitefield m APPLELY Morgan Miss of Landaff, GASKILL Silas Eld *MS* 19 Apr 1843

PAGE Robert m BARRETT Almena of Manchester NH on 26 Mar, SINCLAIR J L Eld *MS* 6 Apr 1842

PAGE Samuel B of Weare m FELCH Lois N both of Newbury on Nov 18, MOODY David Eld *MS* 12 Jan 1842

PAGE William D C of Newburyport MA m CROMWELL Martha S of Dexter ME on 6th inst at Augusta ME, KALLOCH Rev *MFWBR* 21 Jan 1849

PAGE William H m LAMPER Drusilla H on 22 Dec at Gilmanton NH, FERNALD S P Eld *MS* 11 Jan 1843

PAGE William P of Sidney ME m ALLEN Huldah on 15th ult at Augusta ME *MFWBR* 3 Mar 1849

PAGE William R Jr m ANDREWS Aphia both of Corinna ME on 30 Aug 1849 in Corinna ME, ROBINSON N J Eld *MS* 20 Feb 1850

PAGET Joseph m WHITE Rebecca H of South Boston on Apr 4 at South Boston MA, DAVIS J B Eld *MS* 17 Apr 1844

PAIGE Daniel L m TOWLE Mahala D both of Gilmanton NH on 6 Dec 1849 in Gilmanton, MASON L Eld *MS* 2 Jan 1850

PAINE - see PAYNE

PAINE Charles of Meredith m BENNETT Deborah of Gilford on 14 Feb 1848 in Gilford, PERKINS Seth W Eld *MS* 23 Feb 1848

PAINE Francis E m BROWN Nancy at Grafton MA, PECK B D Eld *MS* 4 Oct 1843

PAINE Henry L m TOWLE Mehitabel of Buxton, WIELD C E Esq *MFWBR* 21 Jan 1849

PAINE Joseph of Vershire m FRENCH Sarah of Strafford on 10 Apr at Strafford VT, PETTENGILL J Eld *MS* 11 May 1842

PALFREY John L m CURRIER Charity A both of Hopkinton on 31 May *MS* 22 June 1836

PALL Moses of Day m HYDE Eliza of Corinth on 7 Apr in Corinth, LOVELESS J H Eld *MS* 1 May 1850

PALMER Andrus m GILES Mary B of Northwood on 29 Nov at Northwood, FERNALD S P Eld *MS* 27 Feb 1839

PALMER Beniah D m ELLIS Fanny B on 21 Nov at Lowell MA, THURSTON N Eld *MS* 25 May 1842

PALMER Calvin L of Stewartstown m MELOON Lovina R of Moulton-borough on 12 inst in Moultonborough, MASON Samuel Eld *MS* 26 Sept 1838

PALMER Christopher m JOHNSON Sarah W on 25th ult at Dover NH, MOULTON A K Eld *MS* 2 Nov 1842

PALMER Daniel E MD of Tuftonboro' m DURGIN Anna of Gilmanton NH on 14 Mar, FERNALD S P Eld *MS* 14 Apr 1847

PALMER Dennis m WEEKS Sarah C on 10th ult in Dover NH, THURSTON Nathaniel Eld *MS* 22 Jul 1831

PALMER Elihu H of Cambridge m DREW Nancy M in Dover NH, BUCKINGHAM Rev *MS* 27 June 1838

PALMER G W of Bridgewater m LOOMIS Belinda of Plainfield NY on 11 Jan 1849 in Plainfield NY, BELKNAP P W Eld *MS* 28 Mar 1849

PALMER George F m VARNEY Sarah J on 11 Jan at Rochester, AYER A Eld *MS* 21 Jan 1846

PALMER Hiram of New Haven m BROWN Maria of Starksboro' VT on

PALMER (Continued)

3 Apr, BIXBY N W Eld *MS* 23 Apr 1845

PALMER Jacob m STAFFORD Betsey both of Danby on 30 ult in Danby VT, GREEN Orange Eld *MS* 7 Nov 1838

PALMER Jesse m YORK Anna on 15 Nov 1849, PRATT C S Eld *MS* 20 Mar 1850

PALMER John G of Lee on 26 inst Fri afternoon m COTTON Margaret E of Lee formerly of Yarmouth ME in Brighton ME, CAVERNO A Eld in Dover NH *MS* 1 May 1850

PALMER John m WILBOUR Susannah of Little Compton RI on 19 Mar *MS* 4 May 1836

PALMER Jonathan m BATCHELDER Nancy Mrs both of Pittsfield NH on 25 June 1848 in Pittsfield NH, TRUE E Eld *MS* 12 Jul 1848

PALMER Paul of Stephentown m TIFFT Nancy M of Nassau on 29 Sept afternoon in Nassau, COLEMAN J B Eld *MS* 17 Oct 1838

PALMER Ransom of Richmond m STEVENS Caroline M of Danbury on 14 Nov in Bolton VT, DIKE O Eld *MS* 18 Dec 1850

PALSEY Arlon M of Roxbury MA m HIGGINS Adrianna L of Lisbon ME on 3 Jul in Lisbon ME, BARD N Eld *MS* 24 Jul 1850

PARHAM Jonathan S m ABBOTT Fanny of Brookfield on 21st inst at West Brookfield, CLAFLIN Jabiel Eld *MS* 17 Apr 1839

PARKER Aaron of Standish m BINFORD Hannah of Baldwin ME in Gorham ME, HODSDON Caleb Esq *MS* 27 Nov 1850

PARKER Abial of Charlestown m HODGDON Elizabeth of Lowell in Lowell, THURSTON N Eld *MS* 17 Oct 1838

PARKER Alfred D m PENREE Julia Ann of Stephentown on 6 Apr at Sand Lake, COLEMAN E B Eld *MS* 7 May 1845

PARKER Alfred of Sheldon m FORDE Lucena of Attica NY on 31 Dec, ROLLIN D M L Eld *MS* 11 Feb 1846

PARKER Amasa J m ADAMS Sally at Stephentown on 31 Oct, COLEMAN I B Eld *MS* 18 Nov 1846

PARKER Amos A m PRATT Cynthia of Cavendish VT on 4 inst in Cavendish VT, ADAMS Abel Eld of Windsor *MS* 21 June 1837

PARKER Asa 2d m TWOMBLY Margaret C on 2 Jul at Monroe, McKENNEY O Eld *MS* 24 Jul 1844

PARKER B F m WHITTEN Harriet B both of Wolfborough NH on 22 Jul in Wolfborough, PARIS C Eld *MS* 21 Aug 1850

PARKER Benjamin F of Dracut m KING Sally Ann of Gilford NH on 10 Dec 1848 in Gilford NH, FROST D S Eld *MS* 10 Jan 1849

PARKER Charles of Buxton ME m BERRY Helen A on 15th inst at Standish, MITCHELL Rev *MFWBR* 1 Dec 1849

PARKER Daniel G of Kittery ME m TUTTLE Mary J of Strafford on 23 Jan in Strafford, PLACE E Eld *MS* 5 Feb 1851

PARKER Elihu Jr m GUPTILL Livona H on 11 Apr at Cornish, RAND I Eld *MS* 29 May 1844

PARKER George W of Scarboro' m HARMON Sarah C of Portland ME

PARKER (Continued)

on Thanksgiving Eve at Scarboro', ATKINS Rev *MFWBR* 12 Jan 1850

PARKER H James m COLE Eveline of Peru Huron Co Ohio on 18 Nov 1846 at Mansfield Ohio, PARKER Benjamin Esq *MS* 20 Jan 1847

PARKER Harrison G m GODFREY Lusette E on 11 Feb 1847 at Sheldon NY, FLYNN William H *MS* 6 Apr 1847

PARKER James M m RIDLEY Anna P both of Brunswick ME in Harpswell ME, HERSEY L Eld *MS* 7 Oct 1846

PARKER Joseph m BARKER Harriet both of Canton ME on 13 Jan 1848 in Canton ME, ROLLINS James Eld *MS* 9 Feb 1848

PARKER Mr m ABBOT Alice at Berrien, Berrien Co MI *MS* 5 Apr 1837

PARKER Oliver m HURD Love of Porter on 27th ult at Parsonsfield ME, BUZZELL John Rev *MFWBR* 6 Jul 1850

PARKER Osgood of Boston MA m BECK Sarah A at Charlestown on 14 Jan, WETHERBEE I J Eld *MS* 11 Feb 1846

PARKER William of Cornish ME m WATSON Mary of Limerick ME on 26th ult, LIBBY Elias Eld *MS* 3 Feb 1832

PARKER Zara of Douglass m HUNT Martha on 23 Mar, FULLER W Eld *MS* 7 June 1843

PARKHURST Phineas of Sharon m PRESTON Chloe A on 21 Apr at Strafford VT, SHEPARD Almon Eld *MS* 24 Jul 1844

PARKS Augustus R m GILSON Harriet of Lynn on 24 Nov at Lynn, WALDRON W H Eld *MS* 9 Dec 1846

PARKS Eliphalet R m SAYWARD Lucy of Parsonsfield ME on 8 Jan, BUZZEL A Eld *MS* 18 Sep 1839

PARKS John L m JAMES Elizabeth S both of New Market on 14 Jan 1849 in New Market, ALLEN C Eld *MS* 24 Jan 1849

PARKS Stephen m BUTLER Caroline A both of Bradford on 8 Sept in Bradford ME, STROUT J Eld Jr *MS* 16 Oct 1850

PARLIN William J of Bradley ME m COLLINS Elmira of Eddington ME at Bangor ME on 9th inst *MFWBR* 22 June 1850

PARMENTER William N m ARM Sarah both of Oneida NY on 17 Dec 1848, CURRIER S A Eld *MS* 24 Jan 1849

PARMERTER Joel D of Gananougua Canada W m McDONALD Rebecca of 3 Mile Bay NY on 7 Oct 1847 in 3 Mile Bay NY, PADDEN S B Eld *MS* 1 Dec 1847

PARSHLEY Albert A m LANGLEY Harriet E both of Northwood on 13 Oct in Northwood NH, MOULTON F Eld *MS* 6 Nov 1850

PARSHLEY John m WAKS Ann both of Brunswick in Brunswick ME, LIBBY A Eld *MS* 23 Jan 1850

PARSHLEY John W m FOSS Mary A on 15 inst at Strafford, PLACE Eld *MS* 30 Mar 1836

PARSHLEY Stephen S of Meredith NH m FOGG Mary Jane of Gilford on 5 Nov, BROOKS N Eld *MS* 16 Nov 1842

PARSLEY Albert of Barnstead m KIMBALL Martha E R of Alton NH on 6 Apr at South Alton, GEORGE Enos Rev *MS* 25 June 1845

PARSLEY William of Meredith m FELLOWS Lois E of New Hampton on 21 Jan 1843, PITMAN Stephen J Eld *MS* 26 Apr 1843

PARSON Elisha m SMART Hannah both of Belfast on 19 Dec 1839, ALLEN Ebenezer Eld Jr *MS* 12 Feb 1840

PARSON Enock m MOODY Elizabeth Q on 22 Feb in Parsonsfield *MS* 9 Mar 1832

PARSON Josiah of Plymouth m NUTTER Nancy of Exeter on 14 Nov 1839, ALLEN Ebenezer Eld Jr *MS* 12 Feb 1840

PARSON Stephen S m TOWN Sarah A both of Lawrence on 7 Feb 1849 in Dracut *MS* 21 Feb 1849

PARSONS Charles G m BRADBURY Clarissa Ann on 6th inst at Parsonsfield ME *MS* 21 Dec 1832

PARSONS Elisha m SMART Hannah both of Belfast ME on Dec 19, ALLEN Ebenezer Jr Eld *MS* 12 Feb 1840

PARSONS Enoch m PAGE Louisa at Parsonsfield ME *MS* 13 Feb 1834

PARSONS Jeremiah Jr of Farmington ME m PIKE Naomi of Livermore ME in Livermore, CHANEY John Eld *MS* 13 Dec 1837

PARSONS John Jr of Shapleigh ME m ANNIS Emeline of Somersworth NH on 7 Dec at Great Falls NH, WEBBER H Eld *MS* 18 Dec 1844

PARSONS Josiah of Plymouth m NUTTER Nancy of Exeter on Nov 14 1839, ALLEN Ebenezer Jr Eld *MS* 12 Feb 1840

PARTRIDGE Amos of Prospect ME m RIDLEY Mary of Prospect ME *MS* 29 Nov 1827

PARTRIDGE Jotham m BENNETT Martha Ann on 18 Aug at Westbrook ME, NEVINS William P Eld *MS* 11 Sept 1844

PASKO Cyrus m DILTZ Marilla of Racine WT on 2 March at Mount Pleasant WT, BIXBY N W Eld *MS* 14 Apr 1847

PATCH Burnam m WHITTEMORE Susan H of Lowell on 9th inst at Saco, THURSTON N Eld *MS* 20 Nov 1839

PATRICK L B m LANE Eliza, STRICKLAND Rev *MFWBR* 21 Apr 1849

PATRIDGE Franklin Esq m FOSTER Susan of Saccarrappa at Saccarrappa ME, CHAPMAN C Rev *MFWBR* 26 June 1847

PATTEE David m PATTEE Lucy of Jackson on 30 May, ALLEN E Eld *MS* 18 Jul 1838

PATTEN David P of Kennebunkport ME m SMITH Sarah A at Kennebunkport on 28th ult *MFWBR* 9 Dec 1848

PATTEN Robert of Alexandria m BROWN Ann of Bristol on 3 Dec 1848 in Bristol, BROWN A Eld *MS* 11 Apr 1849

PATTERSON Alfred Eld of Sebec m GILMAN Mary P of Sebec ME, GILMAN Moses Esq *MS* 27 Nov 1844

PATTERSON Dan H of Henniker m MORSE Hannah Miss of Henniker on 13th ult at Fishersfield NH, DODGE Wm Eld

PATTERSON (Continued)
MS 4 Apr 1833

PATTERSON Isaac of Limerick ME m BARKER Mary of Cornish ME on 7th ult at Cornish, RAND James Eld *MFWBR* 13 Feb 1847 & *MS* 17 Feb 1847

PATTERSON James W m PEASE Elizabeth N both of Swansville ME on 23 Jul 1848 in Jackson ME, RINES J N Eld *MS* 30 Aug 1848

PATTERSON Joab Esq (Town Clerk) m HERBERT Susan C of Hopkinson on 24 Dec at Hopkinson, FROST D S Eld *MS* 8 Jan 1845

PATTERSON John Jr m COLE Urana T of Saco ME 12 inst at Saco ME, FERNALD James Eld *MFWBR* 15 June 1850

PATTERSON Lewis of Sebec ME m SEARS Mehitabel Mrs of Dover ME on 20 Apr, BRIDGES O W Eld *MS* 5 May 1847

PATTERSON Peter m SEATTLE Mary E, RUNNELS J Eld in Newport RI *MS* 4 Apr 1849

PATTERSON Stephen of Saco ME m PIERCE Fanny of South Berwick ME, RAND J Eld *MS* 5 Feb 1845

PAUL Hiram L m RIX Normanda of Barnston LC on 8 May 1838, MOULTON A W Eld *MS* 17 Apr 1839

PAUL John A m MUDGET Julia Ann both of Acton ME on 9 Apr in Acton ME, NEVENS W P Eld *MS* 17 May 1848

PAUL Sidney m CHESLEY Louisa Ann of Dover NH on Thurs last, THURSTON N Eld *MS* 5 Dec 1833

PAUL Sylvester of Westbrook ME m WARREN Esther P at Biddeford ME on 2d inst *MFWBR* 22 Jul 1848

PAYNE Joshua W m HART Maria on 3 Jan at Meredith, HILL J Eld *MS* 24 Feb 1836

PAYNE Samuel of Mukwonago m HOYT Priscilla of Rochester WT on 1 May, COOMBS A Eld *MS* 21 May 1845

PEABAD Washburn m TASKER Ann M both of Dixmont ME, FLETCHER J Eld *MS* 22 May 1850

PEABODY Ezekiel m COLBY Lydia S at Lynn MA, CURTIS S Eld *MS* 31 Jan 1844

PEACE Charles of Tamworth NH m BENSON Almira of Parsonsfield ME on 27 Dec, BUZZEL A Eld *MS* 18 Sep 1839

PEACH Jonathan J m RICHARDSON Phebe Q both of Chelmsford on 9 Apr 1848 in Dracut, CURTIS S Eld *MS* 26 Apr 1848

PEARL Abraham m HOWARD Mary both of Rochester in Rochester NH, MEADER Jesse Eld *MS* 8 Mar 1848

PEARL Ichabod m CHICK Philena of Great Falls NH at Great Falls NH, CURTIS S Eld *MS* 15 Mar 1843

PEARL Isaac of Porter ME m KENNARD Ann of Cornish ME on 21 Nov, HACKETT J O Eld *MS* 31 Mar 1847

PEARL Thomas Fits m WILLIAMS Deborah on 7 Aug, MOULTON A Eld *MS* 13 Sept 1843

PEARSON Eben B of Lawrence MA m TOWN Cyrena of Newfield on

PEARSON (Continued)

14 Mar in Newfield ME, SMITH W Eld *MS* 5 June 1850

PEARSON William S of Concord NH m PAGE Sarah B on 12 June in Manchester, DAVIS J B Eld *MS* 26 June 1850

PEASE Alfred of Oswego m GORSELINE Mary of Scriba on 29 Nov 1848 in Scriba NY, KRUM S Eld *MS* 17 Jan 1849

PEASE Charles W of N Berwick m STILKLEY Olive J, LORD D H Eld *MS* 28 Dec 1842

PEASE Clinton A m WILLIAMS Julina of Wheatland on 8th at Wheatland Hillsdale Co Mich, AMES A S Eld *MS* 29 Nov 1843

PEASE Edwin of Freedom NH m SMART Harriet A of Parsonsfield ME on 13 Sept 1847, SMART M M Eld in Whitestown NY *MS* 1 Dec 1847

PEASE John Capt of Parsonsfield ME m MASON Hannah of Newfield ME, AYER James Jr Esq *MS* 20 Sept 1827

PEASE Joseph W on Christmas m HOYT Mary W both of Lowell in Lowell, WALDRON W H Rev *MS* 1 Jan 1851

PEASE Leonard m FULLONTON Hannah on 22 Oct 1848 in Raymond, FULLONTON J Eld *MS* 8 Nov 1848

PEASE Nathaniel m BATCHELDER Sally at Freedom, DAVIS Rev *MS* 1 Apr 1835

PEASE Sheperd m DOW Eliza both of Meredith on 21 Mar 1848 in Meredith NH, WELLS L S Eld *MS* 5 Apr 1848

PEASE Simeon D m BACHELDER Betsey E on 9 Feb, PITMAN Stephen J Eld *MS* 26 Apr 1843

PEASE Usher P m WILLIAMS Juliette of Parsonsfield on 12 Jan 1845 at Parsonsfield ME, JORDAN Z Eld *MS* 12 Mar 1845

PEASLEY George W m PEASLEY Ruth 2d both of Weare on 26 Dec in Weare NH, KIMBALL J Eld *MS* 2 Apr 1851

PEAT Thomas m GOODSELL Amelia both of Mooers NY on 7 inst in Mooers NY, TOWN G W Eld *MS* 27 Mar 1850

PEAVEY George W of Lubec m HARMON Sarah G on 17th inst at Limerick, FREEMAN C Rev *MFWBR* 26 Oct 1850

PEAVEY Hezekiah W m MANN Sarah M on 17 May at Manchester, CILLEY D P Eld *MS* 5 June 1844

PEAVEY James of Sardinia m STEEL Sarah of Freedom NY on 26 Apr in Freedom NY, JACKSON N A Eld *MS* 13 May 1846

PECK Alfred m COLVIN Cordelia both of No Providence on 24 ult at Johnston RI *MS* 18 May 1836

PECK Daniel of Boston MA m MOORE Margaret A of Northwood NH on 25 Dec 1848, JOHNSON W D Eld *MS* 10 Jan 1849

PECKER David m PRESCOTT Mary at Raymond *MS* 5 Aug 1835

PEIRCE - see PIERCE, PEARCE

PEIRCE Alpheus m ELLIS Lois both of Dover in Dover NH, SMITH A D Eld *MS* 9 May 1849

PEIRCE Andrew 3d m DUNAWAY Rebecca W on 16th inst in Dover,

PEIRCE (Continued)
WILLIAMS Rev *MS* 24 Apr 1834

PEIRCE Daniel m SHOREY Caroline on 18th ult both of Monmouth ME, CURTIS S Eld *MS* 25 Apr 1833

PEIRCE Daniel m PEIRCE Alice A of Barrington on 24 Dec at Rochester NH, HUTCHINSON S Eld *MS* 13 Jan 1847

PENDER Alexander of Somersworth m RECORD Sally B of Parsonsfield on 28 May at Parsonsfield, QUINBY Hosea Eld *MS* 5 June 1839

PENDER Nathaniel F of Portsmouth NH m LERVEY Susannah H of Portsmouth, DAVIS Issac G Eld *MS* 7 Feb 1844

PENDERGAST Levi E m JENKINS Sarah J both of Lee NH on 20 June in Barrington, SHERBURNE S Eld *MS* 10 Jul 1850

PENDERGAST Solomon of Durham m MATHES Judith Matilda of Lee on 29 May in New Market, EASTMAN C Allen Eld *MS* 5 June 1850

PENDEXTER Daniel E of Bartlett NH m CUSHMAN Harriet O of New Gloucester ME on 29 Oct at New Gloucester ME, PERRY S Eld *MS* 25 Nov 1846

PENDEXTER Oliver of Cornish ME m JOHNSON Clarissa of Cornish ME on 17 Jan, HACKETT J O Eld *MS* 31 Mar 1847

PENDEXTER Oliver T m BICKFORD Hannah of Baldwin on 19 Sept in Cornish ME, PENDEXTER S Eld *MS* 27 Nov 1850

PENDEXTER Samuel Jr Eld/Rev of Georgetown m WADSWORTH Ruth of Hiram on 3 Dec in Hiram ME, STONE J Rev *MS* 12 Dec 1849 & *MFWBR* 22 Dec 1849

PENDLEGRASS Martin of Chautauqua NY m HOLMES Phebe of Hamburg in Hamburg NY, PLUMB Horatio N Eld *MS* 12 Jan 1842

PENLEY William of Danville ME m MELCHER Maria of Brunswick ME on 10 June at Falmouth ME, BEAN C Eld "*Liberty Standard* please copy" *MS* 30 June 1847

PENNELL Thomas m SINCLAIR Elizabeth, STREETER R Rev on 5th inst at Portland ME *MFWBR* 18 Aug 1849

PENNEY Arioch W m GOODWIN Mary J on 9 Sept in Wells ME, KEENE J Eld Jr *MS* 8 Jan 1851

PENNEY James m McFADDEN Elizabeth on 20 Aug at Charlestown, WETHERBEE I J Eld *MS* 9 Dec 1846

PENNEY Leonard m MARSH Rosanna on 5 Sept at Unadilla Forks NY, SPAULDING Joel Eld *MS* 8 Jan 1845

PENNINGTON Joseph m AYRES Amanda of Macon on 17 Nov 1842 at Macon Mich, WILCOX S H Eld *MS* 14 Dec 1842

PENNY Arba of Waterville ME m PAINE Eunice of Augusta ME, LEWIS Daniel B *MS* 21 Jan 1846

PENNY George m BLANCHARD Jane both of Belgrade ME in Augusta, CURTIS S Eld *MS* 20 June 1838

PENNY Hiram m CURTIS Rebecca both of Minot, TRACY J Eld

PENNY (Continued)
  MS 20 Apr 1831
PENNY Samuel S m STAPLES Nancy H both of Boston on 9 Oct in
  Boston, DUNN R Eld *MS* 17 Oct 1849
PERCIVAL John F of Boston MA m WEBSTER Martha E of Dover on
  1 Nov in New Durham, BUTLER O Eld *MS* 7 Nov 1849
PERCY W G of Phipsburg ME m WHITMORE Minerva H on 24th ult
  at Bowdoinham, CONE C C Rev *MFWBR* 18 Sept 1847
PERKINS Albert A at Wolfboro' NH m BEAN Abby C of Ossipee NH,
  DOLDT James Eld *MS* 22 Oct 1845
PERKINS Albion W m RAND Susan M both of Epsom on 16 Sept in
  Pittsfield *MS* 29 Sept 1847
PERKINS Andrew H of Boston MA m MATHES Susan of Somers-
  worth on 5 Apr 1849 *MS* 18 Apr 1849
PERKINS Arthur D of Conway m PEASE Martha of Ellsworth NH on
  10 Feb at Ellsworth NH, MOULTON Jonathan Esq *MS* 24 Feb
  1847
PERKINS Daniel m MAGRAW Sarah Ann of Fairfield, LEWIS Daniel
  B Eld *MS* 23 Jan 1839
PERKINS Daniel m PATCH Elmira B on 19 Nov at Great Falls ME,
  HILL John C *MS* 29 Nov 1843
PERKINS Darius m HAM Leonora F of Strafford NH, PLACE E Eld
  MS 6 Mar 1839
PERKINS Dudley G m KIMBALL Eliza both of Danville on 9 inst in
  Dover NH, BLORE J Eld *MS* 20 Mar 1850
PERKINS Ebenezer A of Boston MA m HILTON Mary Ann, PAGE E G
  Eld *MS* 24 Sept 1845
PERKINS Ebenezer m LOTHROP Abby both of Edgecomb on 14 Oct
  1849 in Edgecomb ME, PAGE E G Eld *MS* 15 May 1850
PERKINS George of Saco m CLARK Joanna of Sanford ME on 4 Dec
  1848 at Saco ME, STRICKLAND G G Rev *MFWBR* 13 Jan 1849
PERKINS Hiram m YOUNG Mary of Strafford on 7 Nov at Strafford
  NH, STACY R B Eld *MS* 4 Dec 1844
PERKINS Horatio M of Chelsea m HACKETT Mary A of Tunbridge on
  5 Dec in Tunbridge VT, HENDER M C Eld *MS* 2 Jan 1850
PERKINS James of Limerick ME m SMITH Sarah A of Newfield on
  30th ult at Newfield, FREEMAN Charles Rev *MFWBR* 18 Dec 1847
PERKINS James S of Somersworth NH m WENTWORTH Eliza W of
  Berwick ME on 16 Nov 1848 in Dover NH, SMITH A D Eld *MS* 22
  Nov 1848
PERKINS James W of Fairfield ME m ROWE Sarah H of Norridge-
  wock ME, LEWIS D B Eld *MS* 25 Dec 1844
PERKINS John m ROBERTS Harriet E both of Colesville NY, WIL-
  KINS N D Eld *MS* 22 Dec 1847
PERKINS Joseph m HAYNES Nancy both of Epsom in Epsom NH,
  RAMSEY G P Eld *MS* 16 Jan 1850

PERKINS Joseph of Jackson m HEATH Mary of Ossipee NH on 15th
inst at Ossipee NH, FURNALD S P Eld *MS* 29 Aug 1833

PERKINS Lemuel m ROGERS Mahala both of Dover on 22 ult in
Dover, HUTCHINS E Eld *MS* 1 Mar 1848

PERKINS Luke of Newport m MOORE Marcia at Waterville ME on
28th ult *MFWBR* 14 Dec 1850

PERKINS Moses of Sandown m BROWN Sarah at Poplin, FULLER-
TON J Eld *MS* 1 Mar 1843

PERKINS Moses P m NUTE Elizabeth A both of Dover on 31 Oct
1847 in Dover NH, SMITH A D Eld *MS* 1 Dec 1847

PERKINS Nathaniel m CUMMINGS Charlotte A on 12th inst at
Portsmouth NH, TRUE E Eld *MS* 22 May 1839

PERKINS Noah m TURNER Nancy Mrs at Portsmouth *MS* 26 Dec
1833

PERKINS Orley m STAMBRO Mary Ann at Concord NY *MS* 6 Sept
1836

PERKINS Samuel of Bath ME m COFFIN Sarah P of Topsham ME on
7th inst at Topsham *MFWBR* 22 Dec 1849

PERKINS Samuel of Lowell m WILLEY Hannah Mrs of Conway on 12
Dec 1849 in Conway NH, MILLS James E Eld *MS* 24 Apr 1850

PERKINS Seth W Eld of Gardiner m DAMMAN Clarinda C of Belgrade at Waterville, LEWIS Daniel B Esq *MS* 26 June 1839

PERKINS Thomas Eld of New Hampton m DRAKE Abigail J on 25
Nov, WEBBER H Eld *MS* 17 Dec 1845

PERKINS William D m STOKOLL Mary Ann at Portsmouth NH
MFWBR 20 Apr 1850

PERKINS William M of Oxford m JORDAN Ruth M of Portland at
Poland on Jan 1, LIBBY James Eld *MS* 30 Jan 1839

PERKINS William m MORSE Almira on 14 Mar, EMERY Amos Eld
MS 10 Apr 1844

PERKINS William of Somersworth NH m HODGDON Mary E of
Somersworth NH on 25th, MEADER J Eld *MS* 15 Oct 1845

PERNO Nicholas B of Concord m PICKERING Martha Ann of Manchester on 3d Jul at Manchester NH, CILLEY D P Eld *MS* 28 Jul
1847

PERRY Allen of Cabot VT m PHILPOT Almira O of Limerick ME on 19
Nov 1846 at Limerick ME, RAND James Eld *MS* 23 Dec 1846

PERRY Charles m McKENNEY Sarah E on 3rd inst at Portland ME,
EATON Rev *MFWBR* 16 Nov 1850

PERRY Charles m GARVIN Susan A both of Lowell on 25 May in
Dracut MA, CURTIS S Eld *MS* 10 June 1846

PERRY Charles of Matildaville m WEARE Mary Ann of Pierpont on
20 Oct, WHITFIELD W Eld *MS* 1 Feb 1843

PERRY Daniel m PATCH Elizabeth J both of Kittery ME on 13 Dec in
Kittery ME, PERKINS Seth W Eld *MS* 9 Jan 1850

PERRY John of Parsonsfield m TAYLOR Mary of Porter at Porter on

PERRY (Continued)
21st Nov *MFWBR* 4 Jan 1851

PERRY John W m ALLEN Emily both of Bangor ME on 13 Sept 1848 in Bangor ME, AMES M Eld *MS* 22 Nov 1848

PERRY Joseph m KNIGHT Mary Mrs both of Parsonsfield ME on 30 Dec *MS* 17 Jan 1833

PERRY Joseph of Concord Mich m TEETER Rachel of Lansing on 1 Jul in Lansing Mich, MADEN L J Eld *MS* 22 Aug 1849

PERRY Luther C Eld m PRAY Caroline of Kittery at Dover NH, THURSTON Nathaniel Eld *MS* 9 May 1833

PERRY Nathan m FIELD Rachael both of Waterville ME on 13 Feb 1849 in Waterville ME, LEWIS D B Eld *MS* 21 Mar 1849

PERRY Samuel m WELLS Bethiah Clarissa both of PLT No Two on 20 Oct 1839 in PLT No Two, ABBOT William Eld *MS* 5 Feb 1840

PERRY William H m STONE Miss of Biddeford ME on 15th inst at Biddeford, LORD Thomas N Rev *MFWBR* 28 Apr 1849

PERSON Gilbert m BARNEY Lucy both of Barnston LC on 20 Apr, MOULTON Abial Eld *MS* 20 Sept 1837

PERSON William of Woodhull m McPHERSONS Amy of Cameron on 3 June in Jasper NY, McKENNY J B Eld *MS* 21 Aug 1850

PETTENGILL Dudley Eld of Sandwich m BOYNTON Hannah of Thornton on 2 June, PETTINGILL John Eld *MS* 22 June 1836

PETTENGILL Leonard of Ossipee NH m BUZZELL Leonora of Effingham on 27th ult, HOLMES Hiram Eld *MS* 10 Dec 1834

PEVERLY Freeman m TRICKEY Mary Ann Mrs of Portsmouth NH on 14 Mar at Portsmouth NH, DAVIS I G Eld *MS* 10 Apr 1844

PHELON Benjamin Eld of Center Village No Providence m GREENE W of Warwick RI on Wed morn 11 June in Olneyville RI, CHENEY Martin Eld *MS* 18 Jul 1838

PHELPS Almond of Sutton m HURD Sarah of Weare in Weare, KIMBALL John Eld *MS* 2 May 1849

PHILBROOK John M of Ossipee NH m HASLETT Ann Mariah in Ossipee NH, JACKSON Daniel *MS* 2 Jul 1828

PHILBRICK Alvin B m COOPER Mary J on 24 Feb at Wakefield, BROOKS J Eld *MS* 4 Sept 1844

PHILBRICK Christopher m DEARBORN Ann of Lowell MA on 19 Oct, CURTIS S Eld *MS* 6 Jan 1847

PHILBRICK David M of Epsom m STEARNS Sarah A of Deerfield on 28 Nov in Deerfield NH, BURBANK P S Eld *MS* 18 Dec 1850

PHILBRICK Ebenezer M of New Market m MATTHEWS Elizabeth D on 21 May, HUTCHINS E Eld *MS* 7 June 1843

PHILBRICK Edwain T m HAINES Sarah K of Exeter on 17 Feb at Exeter, WESTON J B Eld *MS* 3 Mar 1847

PHILBRICK George W of Hampton m SHAW Mary on 22d ult, BURBANK P S Eld *MS* 11 Jan 1843

PHILBRICK J Harvey Maj of Deerfield m SEAVEY Clara B of Green-

PHILBRICK (Continued)
land on 24 Oct 1847 in Greenland, FURBER Rev Mr *MS* 3 Nov 1847

PHILBRICK John of Freedom m FERNALD Irene A of Eaton on 14 Nov at Eaton, RUNNALS Eld *MS* 8 Jan 1845

PHILBRICK Thomas J of Sanbornton NH m LAWRENCE Eliza Ann of Meredith in Meredith on 21 Jan, KNOWLES John D Esq *MS* 7 Feb 1838

PHILBRICK William m WILLIAMS Abigail both of New Market at Lee, SHERBURN S Eld *MS* 5 Oct 1836

PHILLIPS Alexander Capt m SMITH Susan both of Barrington NS on 28 Apr in Barrington Nova Scotia, HENDERSON Moses C Eld *MS* 10 June 1846

PHILLIPS Asa of Bethlehem NH m SWETT Maria of Bethlehem NH at Bethlehem NH, BEAN Beniah Eld *MS* 4 Jan 1843

PHILLIPS Ebenezer m FRAZIER Eliza both of Henniker on 17 Mar *MS* 8 May 1844

PHILLIPS Gorham COLLINS Elizabeth M on 22d ult at Portland ME, CHICKERING Rev *MFWBR* 2 Oct 1847

PHILLIPS Joseph m WOODMAN Joanna in Kittery ME, THURSTON N Eld *MS* 3 Feb 1832

PHILLIPS Metaphor C m DAVIS Sarah J both of Biddeford on 8 June in Biddeford ME, WITHAM L H Eld *MS* 26 Jul 1848

PHILLIPS Oliver m HUTCHINS Shuah D on 30 Dec 1847 in Charlestown, WETHERBEE I J Eld *MS* 19 Jan 1848

PHILLIPS Samuel B m CHASE Harriet both of Bethlehem on 20 Mar in Bethlehem, BLAKE C E Eld *MS* 10 Apr 1850

PHILMORE John P m HOXIE Betsey both of Stephentown on 13 Mar in Stephenton NY, COLEMAN I B Eld *MS* 8 Apr 1846

PHILPOT Ichabod of Somersworth m EMERSON Minerva J of Barnstead on 1 Nov 1848 in Gilmanton, GARLAND David Eld *MS* 15 Nov 1848

PHILPOT Moses m THURSTON Mercy B at Limerick ME on 19th inst *MFWBR* 25 Nov 1848

PHONIS Richard of Hollis m DUDLEY Mary C of Buxton ME, LIBBY Isaac Esq *MS* 7 Nov 1849

PICKERING Cyrus C m CHURCHILL Betsey T of New Market on 26 Oct 1843, HUTCHINS Eld E *MS* 1 Nov 1843

PICKERING Leonard of Ann Arbor Mich m SIMOND Marilla of Lowell on 14 Oct in Lowell, THURSTON N Eld *MS* 7 Nov 1838

PICKERING Nathaniel Esq m HOWARD Jane Mrs of Barnstead at Strafford, PLACE E Eld *MS* 13 Sept 1843

PICKET Joseph m FRANKLIN Samantha of Hammond on 15 Sept at Hammond St Lawrence Co NY, PADDEN S B Eld *MS* 18 Dec 1844

PIDGIN William merchant m HUNTRISS Lovey H in Dover, WILLIAMS Gibbon Rev *MS* 3 Sept 1834

PIERCE - see PEIRCE, PEARCE

PIERCE Alpheus m WHITE Deborah of Dover NH on 5 Mar at Dover NH, CLARK M Eld *MS* 17 Mar 1847

PIERCE Andrus F of Westport m McKENNEY Ruth Ann of Georgetown on 3 Nov, SPINNEY Zina W Esq *MS* 11 Dec 1839

PIERCE Charles K of Limerick ME m LORD Euditha A on 30th ult in Limerick, BURBANK Abner Esq *MFWBR* 6 May 1848

PIERCE Charles m HALLEY Maria Mrs of Huntington on 27th Sept at Underhill VT, DIKE Orange Eld *MS* 2 Dec 1846

PIERCE Hall of Barrington m HALL Sally of Strafford *MS* 18 Apr 1838

PIERCE James A m COLE Catharine on 27 Feb 1848 in Theresa NY, GRIFFETH A Eld *MS* 21 June 1848

PIERCE Leonidas of Brooklin NH m GOULD Susanna of Lowell MA on 11 Sept at Lowell MA, WOODMAN J Eld *MS* 27 Sept 1843

PIERCE Mark W m BURBANK Harriet D both of Manchester on 30 Jul 1848 in Manchester, CILLEY D P Eld *MS* 16 Aug 1848

PIERCE Marshal of Colden m POMROY Rachel of Hamburgh NY on Christmas Day, PLUMB H N Eld *MS* 19 Feb 1845

PIERCE Melzar of Plymouth MA m TEWINY Caroline T of Newport on 15 Feb, LORD D H Eld *MS* 11 Mar 1846

PIERCE Nathan of Warsaw NY m BELKNAP Olive on 22 Oct, ROLLIN M L Eld *MS* 20 Nov 1844

PIERCE Nathaniel of Bangor ME m YOUNG Mary H of Augusta ME at Augusta ME on 12th inst *MFWBR* 25 May 1850

PIERCE Nathaniel of Tewksbury m FRANCIS Martha of Lowell, THURSTON N Eld *MS* 7 Aug 1839

PIERCE Samuel of New Haven m WILDER Jane Z of Chataugary on 7 Mar 1848 in Malone NY, TOWN G W Eld *MS* 29 Mar 1848

PIERCE Stephen William m PECK Emily Maria both of Smithfield in Gloucester RI, ALLEN R Eld *MS* 19 Jul 1848

PIERCE Sylvester of Gloucester m HURD Esther of Lowell, THURSTON Eld *MS* 28 Aug 1839

PIERCE William A m RAND Joanna at Lewiston ME on 18th ult *MFWBR* 8 Dec 1849

PIKE Asa O m WARREN Harriet of Fryeburg ME on 26 Dec, PIKE John Eld *MS* 31 Jan 1844

PIKE George H of Roxbury MA m BAKER Mary of Shapleigh ME on 8 Oct 1848 in Springvale, BRADBURY A R Eld *MS* 14 Feb 1849

PIKE James Jr m POOL Betsey B of Chelmsford, THURSTON Nathaniel Eld *MS* 22 May 1839

PIKE James m WIGGIN Lucy Ann both of Meredith on 27 Oct, PITMAN S J Eld *MS* 27 Nov 1850

PIKE Robert W L of Farmington m COTTLE Maria H of Brookfield on 31 Jan 1849 in Wolfborough, PARIS C Eld *MS* 18 Apr 1849

PIKE Stephen Jr of Bradford m TAYLOR Harriet of Haverhill MA on

PIKE (Continued)

21 Nov 1847 in Haverhill MA, MERRIL William P Eld *MS* 8 Dec 1847

PIKE William F m EARL Emeline of Hollis, SAWYER J H Rev on 8th inst at Buxton ME *MFWBR* 16 Oct 1847

PIKE William M of Meredith m ROBY Susan E of New Hampton on 19 Dec 1849, PITMAN S J Eld *MS* 30 Jan 1850

PILLSBURY David K m HILL Sarah J both of Elsworth on 7 Oct in Elsworth, WETHERBEE Josiah Eld *MS* 24 Oct 1849

PILLSBURY John D of Bradford MA m JOHNSON Sarah C of Great Falls on 16 Apr at Great Falls ME, BROOKS N Eld *MS* 16 May 1849

PILLSBURY John D of Shapleigh ME m LINSCOTT Eliza A of So Berwick ME on 15 Jul in So Berwick ME, TRUE Ezekiel Eld *MS* 22 Jul 1846

PINE Nelson J of Huntington VT m DOUGLASS Louisa R of Richmond VT on 2 Apr, DIKE O Eld *MS* 26 Nov 1845

PINGREE Henry B of Dracutt m COLBY Lomira L of Lowell MA on 22 May, THURSTON N Eld *MS* 2 Nov 1842

PINKHAM Burleigh m GRAY Hannah Jane on 17th inst at Dover NH, SMITH A D Eld *MS* 24 Mar 1847

PINKHAM Cyrus F Esq m JOHNSON Catherine C on 13 Jul 1842 at Jackson, PETTENGILL Dudley Eld *MS* 25 Jan 1843

PINKHAM Ezra m RUST Caroline P both of Wolfboro NH on 7 Aug *MS* 17 Aug 1836

PINKHAM Geo W of West Cambridge MA m LITTLEFIELD Dorothy of Dover on 29 Jul in Dover NH, SMITH A D Eld *MS* 22 Aug 1838

PINKHAM George C m GRAY Betsey Y of New Durham on 9 Nov 1842 at Farmington, HART E H Eld *MS* 1 Mar 1843

PINKHAM George E of Farmington m EMERSON Mary E of Great Falls on 18 Jan 1849 in Great Falls NH, BROOKS N Eld *MS* 31 Jan 1849

PINKHAM H C m GOSS Olive R, NOYES E Eld *MS* 15 Dec 1847

PINKHAM Isaiah of Raymond m MURRAY Mary D of Limerick ME on Thurs last, BURBANK Eld *MS* 6 Dec 1827

PINKHAM James m ROBBINS Elmira on 25 June at Lowell MA, THURSTON N Eld *MS* 2 Nov 1842

PINKHAM Jason m TIBBETTS Abagail on 18 ult in Boothbay, FAIRFIELD S Eld *MS* 26 Jul 1837

PINKHAM John m HILL Betsey in Waterboro *MS* 18 Sept 1829

PINKHAM Joseph m HUSSEY Lydia J both of Dover on 2 inst in Dover, VAN DAME B Eld *MS* 26 Jul 1848

PINKHAM Nathan m WILLEY Dorantha on 6 Sept in Dracut, CURTIS S Eld *MS* 22 Sept 1847

PINKHAM Oshea of Exeter NH m SMITH Jane P at Biddeford ME *MS* 15 June 1832

PINNEO James R Eld m LINSLEY Melissa E both of Prattsbury NY on 21 Feb Thursday eve in Prattsbury Steuben Co NY, SMITH D C Rev *MS* 27 Mar 1850

PIPER Daniel m PARSONS Hannah F of Parsonsfield on 16 inst in Parsonsfield ME, BUZZELL John Eld *MS* 26 Jul 1837

PIPER George S m COOPER Sarah F both of Sanford, RAMSEY G P Eld *MS* 28 Jan 1846

PIPER George W m PICKERING Mary Jane both of Meredith on 27 Oct 1849, PITMAN S J Eld *MS* 30 Jan 1850

PIPER Isaac B m CARLTON Rhoda of Lowell MA on 25 June, WOODMAN J Eld *MS* 23 Aug 1843

PIPER James of Holderness m PLAISTED Charlotte on 21 ult in Centre Harbor, THOMPSON Samuel Eld *MS* 7 Feb 1838

PIPER John of Meredith m MOSES Sarah H of Sanbornton NH, PITMAN Stephen J Eld m 13 May 1840

PIPER Jonathan E m DOTY Mary J both of Saco ME on 14 Nov 1847 in Dracut, CURTIS S Eld *MS* 15 Dec 1847

PIPER Joseph m LEIGHTON Mary Ann both of Northwood on 22 Sept in Northwood NH, MOULTON F Eld *MS* 6 Nov 1850

PIPER Joshua N of Moultonborough m JUDKINS Ann Maria of Freedom on 25 Nov, BUTLER O Eld *MS* 22 Dec 1847

PIPER Robert R m PIPER Jane S both of Holderness in Holderness on Dec 23 1841, THOMPSON S Eld *MS* 19 Jan 1842

PIPER Thomas H m WYATT Cyntha B both of Northfield NH in Northfield NH, CLOUGH Jeremiah Eld *MS* 19 Jan 1848

PITMAN Ebenezer Jr m SWAIN Eliza Jane Mrs both of Meredith on 16 Oct, PITMAN S J Eld *MS* 27 Nov 1850

PITMAN Ebenezer of Boston MA m LEAVITT Laura Ann of Meredith on 15 Jan, PITMAN S J Eld *MS* 12 Feb 1851

PITSINGER Ephraim m JOSLIN Rebecca both of Chesterfield on 30 Nov 1848 in Chesterfield MA, KING Warren Eld *MS* 7 Feb 1849

PITTS Nathaniel of Waterboro' m CHASE Almira on 27 Dec, EMERY Richard Eld *MS* 6 Jan 1847

PITTS Orren m THOMAS Martha W at New Portland ME *MFWBR* 13 Oct 1849

PIXLEY Orren m MONWARREN Orrilla on 10 Apr at Farmersville NY, WINSOR Barnet Eld *MS* 15 Mar 1843

PIXLEY Oscar of Bethany NY m PIXLEY Rosetta of Freedom NY on 28 Feb at Freedom, WINSOR Barnet Eld *MS* 15 Mar 1843

PLACE Allen S m PAPE Annah E both of Gloucester on 21 Oct 1847 in Chepachet, BRADBURY A R Eld *MS* 1 Dec 1847

PLACE Benjamin F m DOWNING Susan E at Great Falls NH *MFWBR* 20 Apr 1850

PLACE Demerit m FOSS Mary Jane on 13 inst in Strafford *MS* 19 Jul 1837

PLACE Harrel F m BLAISDELL Eliza of Dover NH on 30 ult *MS* 9 Nov

PLACE (Continued)
1836

PLACE James H m CHESLEY Lydia on Sunday morning last both of Dover NH, CUSHMAN Rev *MS* 23 Jan 1834

PLACE Moses m NOYES Harriet N both of Great Falls NH on 5 Mar 1850, BROOKS N Eld *MS* 20 Mar 1850 & *MFWBR* 16 Mar 1850

PLACE Robert m GREEN Clarissa both of Lowell MA in Lowell MA, THURSTON Nathaniel Eld *MS* 4 Oct 1837

PLAISTEAD Major m LIBBY Mary of Gorham on 10th inst at North Gorham, DORR K H Rev *MFWBR* 23 June 1849

PLAISTED Oren of New Hampton m HUCKINS Judith P on 8 Oct, TRUE E Eld *MS* 16 Oct 1844

PLAISTED Samuel m MARTIN Eliza on 6 Aug 1837 in Bridgeton ME, WHITNEY George Eld *MS* 17 Jan 1838

PLUMER Allen of Dover m PENDERGAST Abby J of Lee on Sunday morning 23 inst in Barrington, SHERBURNE S Eld *MS* 2 Feb 1842

PLUMER Francis of Somersworth m OTIS Almira of Strafford in Strafford, PLACE Enoch Eld *MS* 10 Jan 1838

PLUMER Libby Esq m EWERS Clarinda of Richmond on 23 May at Richmond ME, QUINNAM C Eld *MS* 2 June 1847

PLUMER Otis m STINSON Abigail M on 3 Dec at Richmond, QUINNAM C Eld *MS* 17 Dec 1845

PLUMMER Charles M of Portland ME m RIDLON Miranda S of Saco on 18th June at Saco, WILLIAMS Rev *MFWBR* 8 Jul 1848

PLUMMER Daniel m CUMMINGS Mary H, BEECHER Rev *MFWBR* 30 Oct 1847

PLUMMER Edwin of Norway ME, printer of the *Norway Advertiser* m NORTON Mary E of Portland ME at Portland ME on 11th inst, PRATT Rev *MFWBR* 30 Jan 1847

PLUMMER George of Lisbon m COFFIN Almira Jane of Webster ME on 4 Apr in Webster, BARD Nathaniel Eld *MS* 1 May 1850

PLUMMER Henry H of So Berwick m HALE Martha of Bradford MA on 17 Oct at So Berwick *MS* 25 Nov 1835

PLUMMER Henry m FULLER Mary Jane both of Manchester on 11 Nov 1847 in Manchester, CILLEY D P Eld *MS* 1 Dec 1847

PLUMMER Henry of Thornton m GILMAN Mahala of Bristol NH on 22 May, CHASE Moses Eld *MS* 2 Aug 1843

PLUMMER Horace P of Sanford ME m HOBBS Harriet N of Great Falls NH at Great Falls NH *MFWBR* 7 Aug 1847

PLUMMER James H m ROWELL Abigail P at Gilford, PINKHAM John Eld *MS* 4 Oct 1843

PLUMMER Jesse of Meredith m GOSS Lydia of New Hampton *MS* 8 Feb 1837

PLUMMER Jesse of Meredith m SANBORN Phebe of Hampton in Dover NH, PETTINGILL John Eld *MS* 8 Nov 1837

PLUMMER Joseph M of Gorham ME m HARMON Mary F on 26 Sept,
MANSON B S Eld *MS* 7 Feb 1844

PLUMMER Libby m SWETT Mary both of Richmond ME on 21 Sept,
SWETT Jesse Eld *MS* 18 Nov 1835

PLUMMER Richard of Milton m WIGGIN Mary Jane of Farmington
NH on 9 Nov 1848 in Farmington NH, BODGE Jacob Eld *MS* 31
Jan 1849

PLUMMER Richard of Sandwich NH m HUTCHINS Phylura W of
Gray on 6th inst, PURKIS Eld *MS* 23 Mar 1831

PLUMMER Samuel m MARSTIN Elizabeth Ann on 3d at Epping NH,
PRESCOTT Samuel Rev *MS* 6 Apr 1842

PLUMMER Silas of Lisbon m EASTE Emily both of Durham ME on
23 June in Durham ME, BARD N Eld *MS* 24 Jul 1850

PLUMMER Soloman H m BAILEY Lucy H both of Freeport on 14 Nov
1847 in Freeport ME, PURINTON A W Eld *MS* 8 Dec 1847

PLUMMER William m MORRISON Olive both of Sanford on 11 Nov in
Sanford, LORD D H Eld *MS* 21 Nov 1838

PLUMMER William m SMITH Lucy E both of Groton on 23 Apr in
Groton, CHASE D P Eld *MS* 5 May 1846

PLUMMER William G m DENHAM Susan both of Bowdoin on 6 Feb
in Bowdoin ME, WHITTEMORE J Esq *MS* 19 Feb 1851

POLAND Benjamin Esq m SANBORN Lucy both of Standish,
TENNEY Rev Mr *MS* 19 May 1830

POLAND Eliot formerly of Bristol m CROCKER Dolly of Prospect,
PARK Thomas Eld *MS* 29 Nov 1827

POLLARD Isaac of Lewiston ME m MERRILL Sophronia of Pownal at
Pownal ME *MFWBR* 27 Mar 1847

POMEROY Ashley D of New Hampton m CHICKERING Eliza Jane of
Gilford on 11 Jan, GASKILL Silas Eld *MS* 17 Jan 1844

POMEROY Luther m TIFFT Rebecca on 30 Oct at Stephentown,
COLEMAN I B Eld *MS* 11 Dec 1844

POND J Mr m SWEETSIR Harriet on 3rd inst at Sacoboro [Scar-
boro'?] ME, TOBEY William Rev *MFWBR* 21 Apr 1849

POND Julius of Hudson m SCOTT Sarah of Chester Ohio on 25 Jan
in Chester, Geauga Co Ohio, BRANCH D Eld *MS* 16 Feb 1848

POOL Albert H m ABBOTT Lucy of Woolwich ME on 19 Sept, FAIR-
FIELD Smith Eld *MS* 8 Dec 1841

POOL John of Edgecomb m DUNTON Mary Mrs of Boothbay ME,
ROBINSON N J Eld *MS* 1 Feb 1843

POOL Joshua m DUNTON Mary J both of Boothbay on 2 Feb in
Edgecomb ME, PAGE E G Eld *MS* 26 Mar 1851

POOLE Henry O of Mt Vernon m CARR Lozana E on 18 Mar at
Vienna, EDGCOMB J Eld *MS* 16 Apr 1845

POOR W B m ROBINSON Charlotte on 23 June at Great Falls NH,
WEBBER H Eld *MS* 18 Dec 1844

PORTER Benjamin F m BUFFUM Eliza A on 5 Aug at Manchester

PORTER (Continued)

NH, CILLEY D P Eld *MS* 21 Aug 1844

PORTER David of Dixmont ME m STILES Phebe Ann of Jackson on 24 Nov, ALLEN E Eld *MS* 18 Dec 1844

PORTER George N m HOYT Frances T of Boston MA at Charlestown MA, SWETT D Eld *MS* 25 Dec 1844

POTTER Benjamin m THURLOW Maranda on 28 May 1843 at Litchfield ME, FROST Isaac Eld *MS* 16 Aug 1843

POTTER George W of Loudon m MORRILL Mary J, CILLEY Daniel P Eld *MS* 24 Apr 1834

POTTER Isaac J m WOODMAN Roxana U of Richmond on 15 Aug, PURINGTON C Eld *MS* 11 Sept 1850

POTTER James A m HOPKINS Mary F both of Pascoag RI on 24 May in Pascoag RI, DAVISON M N Eld *MS* 10 Oct 1849

POTTER John of Gilford m EDGERLY Hannah B of Meredith in Meredith, PETTINGILL John Eld *MS* 24 Jan 1838

POTTER John W of Providence RI m ESTHERS Mary of Boston MA on 29 May in Providence RI, WHITTEMORE D R Eld *MS* 12 June 1850

POTTER L B of Spring Arbor m DAVIS Susan E sister of Eld J B DAVIS of Providence RI on 11 inst at Leoni Mich, THOMPSON L J Eld *MS* 31 Oct 1849

POTTER Moses O m CARPENTER Harriet A both of Scituate RI on 2 Jan in Scituate RI, ALLEN Eld *MS* 15 Jan 1851

POTTER Warren m SAYLES Malina F both of Burrillville RI on 21 Feb 1849 in Pascoag RI, DAVISON M N Eld *MS* 21 Mar 1849

POTTLE Joseph H m McNEAL Maranea J both of North Hampton in New Market, HUTCHINS E Eld *MS* 19 Jan 1842

POTTLE Samuel at Portsmouth NH m FRENCH Julia of Portsmouth on 14 Apr, MERRILL William P Esq *MS* 21 May 1845

POTTLER Orington of Richmond m CALL Louisa of Perkins on 7 Sept 1848 in Richmond ME, PURINGTON Collamore Eld *MS* 11 Oct 1848

POWERS Abner B m MANARD Polly at Montpelier VT on 2 Aug, GRAY Ira Eld *MS* 2 Oct 1844

POWERS Charles on New Year's Eve at Charlestown MA m BAKER Hannah I, WETHERBEE I J Eld *MS* 17 Feb 1847

POWERS Daniel S m JORDON Sarah F both of Boston MA on 3d inst in Biddeford *MS* 17 Jan 1828

POWERS Ichabod m WHITNEY Almira N both of Biddeford on 4 Jul, JACKSON Daniel Eld *MS* 30 Sept 1846

POWERS Jonathan Master ae 13y on in Pepperel MA m REED Prescilla C ae 13y *MS* 23 Nov 1826

POWERS Simon of Compton m JAMES Betsey of Ascott on 16 Nov, MOULTON A Eld of Stanstead *LCMS* 13 Apr 1842

PRATT Alva S of Ontario m TWITCHELL Lianda A of Walworth on 13

PRATT (Continued)
Nov in Walworth NY, HOLMES D G Eld *MS* 15 Jan 1851
PRATT Jeremiah m YOUNG Mary of Barnstow at Stanstead LC *MS* 18 May 1836
PRATT Matthew m FORD Hannah both of Braintree on Dec 12, CLAFLIN Jehiel Eld *MS* 5 Jan 1842
PRATT Moses m JENNE A Maria both of Hartland on 17 Apr 1848 in Windsor VT, ADAMS Abel Eld *MS* 26 Apr 1848
PRATT Mr of Oregon m CUSHING Mrs of Rutland WI on New Year's Day, PAINE J Eld *MS* 31 Jan 1849
PRATT Noah of Skowhegan ME m EATON Lydia of St Albans ME on 16 Feb, COPP John B Eld *MS* 27 Apr 1842
PRATT Thomas L of Rushford m HERRICK Sarah of Candea on 11 Nov 1847 in Candea, GOODNA W A Eld *MS* 1 Dec 1847
PRAY David m APPLEBEE Almira at Great Falls NH, CURTIS S Eld *MS* 7 June 1843 & *MS* 19 Jul 1843
PRAY Ephraim Capt m ____ Rebecca P both of Mt Desert ME, NORTON L Eld *MS* 11 Mar 1835
PRAY Franklin m COLBATH Sarah both of Gardiner in Litchfield, QUINNAM C Eld *MS* 8 Mar 1848
PRAY Humphrey of Rolinsford NH m STACKPOLE Eunice at South Berwick on 14th inst *MFWBR* 28 Dec 1850
PRAY Miles O m DEXTER Lydia A both of No Scituate RI on 24th ult in Killingly CT, WILLIAMS Daniel Eld *MS* 2 Jan 1839
PRAY T J W MD m WHEELER Sarah E on 20 inst in Dover NH, BARROWS Rev Mr *MS* 27 Nov 1850 & *MFWBR* 30 Nov 1850
PREBLE Daniel m RAYMOND Almira in Bowdoinham ME, HATHORN Eld *MS* 31 Jan 1838
PREBLE Dexter m COLMAN Elvira in Bowdoinham ME, HATHORN Eld *MS* 31 Jan 1838
PREBLE Levi T Dea m BEAN Cynthia both of Chesterville ME on 1 Jan in Chesterville, FOSTER J Eld *MS* 15 Jan 1840
PREBLE Nehemiah of Farmington m BUTLER Caroline R of Farmington on 28 Mar 1847, WHEELER S Eld *MS* 21 Apr 1847
PREBLE Otis of Wales m MAXWELL Naomi I of Wales ME on 19 Nov, GATCHELL Mark Eld *MS* 20 Dec 1843
PREBLE Sewell in Bowdoinham ME m COLEMAN Elizabeth on Oct 24, QUINNAM C Eld *MS* 5 Jan 1842
PREBLE Stephen of Bowdoinham m POTTLE Elizabeth C of Richmond on 27 Dec 1837 in Richmond ME, SWETT J Eld *MS* 7 Mar 1838
PREBLE T M of Parsonsfield ME m EATON H M of Weare on 14 Nov in Weare, MOODY D Eld *MS* 13 Dec 1837
PRESCOT Mr m PERSONS Mary both of Lexington on Feb 17 at Lexington, LENNAN John Eld *MS* 15 Apr 1840
PRESCOTT Alva m DAVENPORT Sylvia L on 6th ult at Conewango

PRESCOTT (Continued)

NY, WHITCHER Hiram Eld *MS* 23 Nov 1832

PRESCOTT Asa of Sandwich NH m COLE Anstres of Lowell MA, EMERY James Eld *MS* 29 May 1844

PRESCOTT Cyrus m BEAN Hannah on 26 Dec at Candia, ATWOOD M Eld *MS* 8 Jan 1845

PRESCOTT Daniel K of New Hampton NH m CURTIS Mary M on 26 Nov at Thetford VT, MASON James Eld *MS* 10 Mar 1847 & *MS* 6 Jan 1847

PRESCOTT Ebenezer Jr in Raymond m FOGG Eleanor *MS* 14 Jan 1835

PRESCOTT Edward P m COLLINS Rebecah on 30th ult, KIMBALL John Eld *MS* 18 Nov 1835

PRESCOTT Enoch B of Gilford m THING Hannah G of Pittsfield on 4 Dec in Pittsfield, CILLEY D P Eld *MS* 25 Dec 1839

PRESCOTT George M m QUINBY Julia M both of Lyndon VT on 5 Mar, QUINBY M A Eld *MS* 2 Apr 1851

PRESCOTT George W m BRACKET Eliza G at Acton, FULLONTON J Eld *MS* 27 Sept 1843

PRESCOTT J C m MORSE Sarah of Portland ME on 25 Feb, MOULTON A K Eld *MS* 8 Mar 1843

PRESCOTT James L m TRIPP Harriet M both of Epsom on 23 Dec 1847 in Epsom NH, RAMSEY G P Eld *MS* 26 Jan 1848

PRESCOTT John M m WEBSTER Mary Ann of Sandwich on 24 Nov, McMURPHY B H Eld *MS* 18 Dec 1844

PRESCOTT John O of Meredith m RANDALL Lydia B of Centre Harbor on 28 Nov, PITMAN S J Eld *MS* 11 Dec 1850

PRESCOTT Joshua C m BEATY Emeline L both of Holderness on 27 Mar in Holderness, SANBORN G Eld *MS* 9 Apr 1851

PRESCOTT Samuel of Alton NH m PAGE Susan of Gilmanton on 16 Apr 1849 in Alton NH, PINKHAM J Eld *MS* 16 May 1849

PRESCOTT Sewell of Acton m HEARSON Marilla M in Lebanon on 15 Sept, LITTLEFIELD William H Eld *MS* 24 Oct 1849

PRESCOTT William m JENNESS Elizabeth both of Meredith on 23 May 1849, PITMAN Stephen J Eld *MS* 26 Sept 1849

PRESCOTT William Y m FULLER Elana of Lowell MA, CURTIS S Eld *MS* 17 Jul 1844

PRESSEY G W Jr m BLACKWELL Harriet both of Waterville ME in Waterville, BEAN G W Eld *MS* 2 Jan 1850

PRESSEY George W Jr at Fairfield ME m EMERSON Mary M, LEWIS D B Eld *MS* 17 Apr 1844

PRESSEY John m KIMBALL Mary of Sutton on 9 June at Bradford, HOLMES H Eld *MS* 28 Jul 1847

PRESTON Benjamin F of Dover m DREW Olive H of Newfield on 19 Dec at Newfield ME, HAM Dr Esq *MS* 27 Dec 1843

PRESTON David D Jr m BROWN Silas (*sic*) on May 1842 at Strafford

PRESTON (Continued)
VT, PETTENGILL J Eld *MS* 6 Jul 1842
PRICE James M m KEAY Sarah A of Biddeford ME on 14th inst at Biddeford ME, BAKE H Rev *MFWBR* 20 Apr 1850
PRIEST Daniel m SPOONER Anniss W on 22 Feb 1844 of Franconia, WITHAM L H Eld *MS* 13 Mar 1844
PRIEST David of Lisbon m CARLTON Widow of Franconia on 10 Nov in Lisbon ME, PETTENGILL John Eld *MS* 29 Dec 1847
PRINCE George W of Limington ME m DURGIN Assenath of Cornish ME on 13 Aug in East Parsonsfield ME, HACKETT J O Eld *MS* 22 Dec 1847
PRINCE John of Detroit ME m DREW Abigail of Pittsfield ME on 26 May 1844, COPP Roger Eld *MS* 24 Jul 1844 (*sic*) should be *MS* 31 Jul 1844
PRINCE Roderic m HICKS Lucy Ann on 29th ult at Cumberland ME *MFWBR* 21 Apr 1849
PRINCE Seward M of Danville ME m CHAMBERLAIN Adaline on 16th ult at Auburn ME, BURGESS J S Eld *MFWBR* 8 June 1850
PRIOR Joseph m WILSON Lydia A both of Great Falls NH on 5 Jan in Great Falls, BROOKS N Eld *MS* 22 Jan 1851
PROCTOR James H of Dover m BROWN Eliza of Franklin NH *MS* 20 June 1833
PUGSLEY Edmund of Biddeford ME m MARTIN Sarah E of Saco ME in Saco on Jan 1st 1842 in Falmouth ME, BEAN C Jr Eld *MS* 12 Jan 1842
PUGSLEY John of Cornish m NORTON Hannah of Limington ME, RAND James Eld *MS* 8 Mar 1843
PUGSLEY Moses m WELCH Mercy both of Springvale on 1 Oct 1848 in Springvale, BRADBURY A R Eld *MS* 14 Feb 1849
PULCIVER Henry at Dracut m HAYDEN Eliza D of Manchester, CURTIS S Eld *MS* 17 Jul 1844
PULLEN Franklin C m HUSSEY Drusilla at Waterville ME, LEWIS D B Eld *MS* 16 Oct 1839
PURINGTON Collamore of Embden ME m KINCADE Laura W of Lexington 30 Jan at Lexington ME, HAYDEN Wentworth Eld *MS* 5 June 1844
PURINGTON Joseph m DINGLEY Caroline both of Lewiston ME, BRIDGES A Eld *MS* 12 Sept 1833
PURINTON Gollamore Eld of Embden Somerset Co ME m RANDALL Margaret E of Bowdoinham Lincoln Co ME on 19 inst in Bowdoin ME, PURINTON Stephen Eld *MS* 8 Jul 1846
PURKIS John Eld of Gray m LIBBY Hannah of Gorham on 18th inst at Scarboro, WHITE Joseph Eld *MS* 3 Dec 1828
PURMORT Mark m PACKARD Martha H on 7 Apr, SMITH C H Eld *MS* 16 Apr 1845
PURRINGTON Oliver of Epping NH m NEALEY Emeline of Newfield

PURRINGTON (Continued)
ME on 20 Jan in Newfield ME, SMITH W Eld *MS* 13 Mar 1850
PURRINGTON Stephen of Bowdoin ME m GREEN Susan of Lisbon ME, BEAN Charles Eld *MS* 27 Jan 1836
PUSHOR Peter of Plymouth m MORSE Hannah of G in Chesterville, CHANEY John Eld [N.B. The paper states Hannah as being from "G" but as Rev Chaney served the Franklin Co area, more likely it was "C" for Chesterville, ME.] *MS* 13 Dec 1837
PUTNAM Elbridge m EDMUNDS Hannah both of Weare on 7 ult in Weare, MOODY David Eld *MS* 24 Jan 1838
PUTNAM Henry S of Salem MA m DOWNS Mahala M of Great Falls NH on 16 Nov 1847 in Great Falls, DUNN R Eld *MS* 1 Dec 1847
PUTNAM Rufus Jr of Hopkinton m CLARK Apphia of Warner on 21 ult *MS* 7 Dec 1836
PUTNEY Almon m ANDRES Mehitabel K on 4 Apr in Bradford, HOLMES H Eld *MS* 15 May 1844
PUTNEY Henry Esq of Dunbarton NH m ALEXANDER Abigail M of Tunbridge VT on 22d ult *MS* 15 May 1839
PUTNEY John B m BACHELDER Lucy Jane both of Lowell on 29 Nov in Lowell, THURSTON N Eld *MS* 12 Dec 1838
PUTNEY Joseph of Wales m AUSTIN Calista of Hamburgh NY on 23 Jan at Hamburgh NY, PLUMB H N Eld *MS* 20 Mar 1844

QUACKINBUSH Jacob m BERGIN Phebe both of Oneonta NY on 15 June 1848 in Oneonta NY, WING Amos Eld *MS* 26 Jul 1848
QUENN John m WILLIS Martha on 3 Jul in Dracut, CURTIS S Eld *MS* 8 Sept 1847
QUENNAM Constant of Wiscasset ME m SWETT Betsey P in White-field *MS* 24 June 1831
QUICK John m SMITH Pauline of Biddeford on 22 Jan 1843 at Biddeford, WITHAM L H Eld *MS* 1 Mar 1843
QUIMBY Alpheus of Lyndon VT m QUIMBY Sarah of Sandwich NH *MS* 26 Jul 1843
QUIMBY David of Lisbon (NH?) m WEBSTER Sarah of Landaff at Landaff on 23 June 1842, GASKILL Silas Eld *MS* 19 Apr 1843
QUIMBY George W of Sandwich m FULLERTON Mary E of New Market on 7th inst at New Market, MOWRY J M Rev *MS* 20 Mar 1839
QUIMBY Hiram G m SMITH Hannah M both of Garland on 5 Sept in Garland ME, DORE T W Eld *MS* 15 Sept 1847
QUIMBY J O of Biddeford ME m PENDEXTER Mary of Biddeford on 16th inst at Saccarappa, HOBART J Rev *MFWBR* 25 Nov 1848
QUIMBY James m RADDEN Emily both of Franconia in Franconia, BLAKE C E Eld *MS* 4 Apr 1849
QUIMBY Joseph L of No Sandwich m NEAL Comford M of Loudon NH on 12 Nov, SMITH J Rev *MS* 19 Dec 1838

QUINBY Daniel W, merchant of Somersworth NH m JONES Laura A W at Great Falls NH, MERRILL William P Eld *MS* 7 Sept 1845

QUINBY Hosea of Sandwick NH m BURLEY Dorothy of Sandwick NH *MS* 14 May 1828

QUINBY Isaac F m BROWN Catherine G on 19th inst at Saccarappa ME, MOULTON A K Eld *MS* 29 May 1844

QUINBY John M of Sandwich m HAINES Sarah S of Moultonboro' NH, BROOKS N Eld *MS* 18 June 1845

QUINBY Lewis m TAYLOR Mary Jane on 2 Aug at Sandwich NH, WEBBER Horace Eld *MS* 14 Sept 1842

QUINT Benjamin B m JOHNSON Lucy Ann of Whitefield NH on 14 Jul at Whitefield NH, GEORGE Nathaniel K Eld *MS* 27 June 1842

QUINT George of Dover m HALL Sarah W of Barnstead NH in Barnstead NH, BERRY N Eld *MS* 20 Dec 1827

QUINT George W m EVANS Susan D on 28 Dec at Sanford ME, RAMSEY G P Eld *MS* 28 Jan 1846

QUINT George W m AYER Olive J of Manchester on 29 Nov at FWB meeting house at Manchester NH, CILLEY D P Eld *MS* 9 Dec 1846

QUINT Nathaniel V of Topsham m GODDARD Louise C of Brunswick ME on 25 Dec 1848 in Topsham ME, BEAN C Eld *MS* 17 Jan 1849

RACKCLIFFE Ezekiel m OLIVER Clementine at Starks on 8 Sept 1844 *MS* 16 Apr 1845

RACKIFF John M m MILLS Lydia C of Corinna ME on 28 Feb at St Albans, COPP J B Eld *MS* 29 Mar 1843

RACKLIEFF Alexander m SHAW Eliza both of Woolwich ME on 19 ult in Woolwich ME, PERKINS Seth W Eld *MS* 3 Jan 1838

RAFTON Pollerick m YOUNG Jane of Stanstead LC on 21 Oct, MOULTON Abial Eld *MS* 1 Jan 1840

RAMONS Ludden m BABCOCK Sarah on 2 Apr at Hamburgh NY, PLUMB H N Eld *MS* 12 June 1844

RAMSDELL William A m BATES Eliza Ann both of Richmond on 5 Nov 1848 in Litchfield ME, QUINNAM C Eld *MS* 15 Nov 1848

RAMSEY B Mr m ROBERTS Hannah at Lebanon ME, FULLONTON J Eld *MS* 21 Nov 1843

RAMSY William P m MILLER Tamson on 1 inst at Somerworth NH, WOODMAN Jonathan Eld *MS* 18 Jan 1837

RAND Bickford of Rochester m BERRY Abigail of Strafford *MS* 18 Apr 1838

RAND Charles D of Hopkinton m ANNIS Harriet N Mrs of Warner on 10 Oct 1843 in Warner, SIDNEY D Eld *MS* 8 May 1844

RAND Charles D of Hopkinton m WATSON Emily of Warner on 29 Nov in Warner, SINCLAIR J L Eld *MS* 19 Dec 1838

RAND Jacob B of Fryeburg ME m COLBY Ann of Denmark ME at Denmark on 15th ult *MFWBR* 30 Jan 1847

RAND James m FERNALD Dorothy both of Parsonsfield ME on 26 Dec in Parsonsfield, BUZZELL John Eld *MS* 15 Jan 1840

RAND Leonard of Haverville MA m GOODWIN Sarah A of Dover NH on 6th inst at Dover NH, HUTCHINS E Eld *MS* 12 May 1847

RAND Matthew P m HOLMES Sally A both of Hopkinton on 26 Dec in Hopkinton, SINCLAIR J L Eld *MS* 5 Feb 1840

RANDAL Gordon of Garland m HEYDEN Relief Mrs of Corinna on 2 inst in Corinna ME, COPP John B *MS* 20 Dec 1837

RANDAL James of Limerick m DAY Rachel of Cornish, LIBBY Eld *MS* 26 Nov 1828

RANDALL Andrew W m RECORD Cordelia W both of Roxbury on 14 Apr, DAVIS J B Eld *MS* 24 Apr 1844

RANDALL Daniel L of Farmington m TUFTS Lucretia H, PLACE E Eld *MS* 27 Nov 1844

RANDALL Daniel m THOMSON Lucy Mrs both of Great Falls NH in Great Falls, BROOKS N Eld *MS* 30 Oct 1850

RANDALL Daniel m SYLVESTER Rebecca both of Freeport on 10 Oct 1847 in Bowdoin ME, PURINTON A W Eld *MS* 17 Nov 1847

RANDALL Gordon P of Northfield m DREW Louisa of Strafford in West Brookfield on 31 Dec 1841, CLAFLIN Jehiel Eld *MS* 23 Mar 1842

RANDALL Haven of New Hampton m SMITH Lydia at Holderness, PETTENGILL John Eld *MS* 4 Dec 1839

RANDALL Heatherly Col of Bowdoinham ME m PAINE Caroline E of Litchfield ME on 22 Oct, QUINNAM C Eld *MS* 8 Jan 1845

RANDALL Henry A m BAXTER Eliza Ann of Charlestown MA on 15 Sept at Charlestown MA, SWETT D Eld *MS* 23 Oct 1844

RANDALL James of So Boston m WOOD Ellen of Charlestown MA, THURSTON N Eld *MS* 4 Feb 1835

RANDALL Jesse m JAMESON Betsey both of Bangor ME on 18 June 1848 in Bangor ME, ROBINSON N J Eld *MS* 5 Jul 1848

RANDALL Samuel A m DRAKE Abby both of Holderness NH on 28 ult, TRUE Ezekiel Eld *MS* 4 Nov 1846

RANDALL Sewall of New Durham m THOMPSON Eliza A of Gilman-ton on 2 inst in Gilmanton, FERNALD S P Eld *MS* 22 Mar 1848

RANDALL Silas m WEED Laura Ann of Danville VT on 11 Jan of Danville VT, GEORGE N K Eld *MS* 21 Jan 1846

RANDALL William B of Boston m DRAKE Mary E of Holderness on 2 Apr 1850 in New Hampton NH, PERKINS Thomas Eld *MS* 10 Apr 1850

RANDALL William m HALL Susan on 25th ult both of New Market *MS* 31 Aug 1836

RANDEL John m HAWKINS Adaline on 25 Sept 1842 of Center Harbor, PITMAN Stephen Eld *MS* 26 Oct 1842

RANDLETT Daniel m WEEKS Betsey K of Meredith, PITMAN Stephen J Eld *MS* 14 Feb 1844

RANDLETT John 3d of Meredith m BENNETT Polly M of New Hampton NH on 6 Feb in New Hampton NH, DANA Simeon Eld *MS* 16 Feb 1848

RANDLETT Stephen H m MARSHALL Arvilla P both of Manchester on 10 Dec 1848 in Manchester, CILLEY D P Eld *MS* 27 Dec 1848

RANKIN Jonathan Jr m COWELL Maria A at Lebanon *MFWBR* 22 Dec 1849

RANKINS Jonathan Jr m COWELL Maria A both of Lebanon on 13 Dec in Lebanon ME, CHENEY O B Eld *MS* 2 Jan 1850

RANKINS Oliver of Monmouth ME m RICHARDSON Lydia of Monmouth, GATCHELL M Eld *MS* 19 Jul 1843

RANKINS William H m CARIL Mary E of Buxton ME on 16 June at Buxton ME, CLAY Jonathan Eld *MS* 28 Jul 1847

RANLET Noah m BURNHAM Deborah both of Littleton NH on 8 Dec 1847 in Littleton NH, BLAKE C E Eld *MS* 19 Jan 1848

RASMITSSON Augustus m MANLY Catherine F on 19 Sept at Charlestown MA, WETHERBEE Louisa H *MS* 22 Oct 1845

RAWLINS Francis S m WHITTIER Mary A both of Deerfield NH on 22 Nov, BURBANK P S Eld *MS* 12 Dec 1849

RAWSON E m McLOUTH Mrs of Bedford on 18 Jan in Erie PA, THOMAS J Eld *MS* 19 Mar 1851

RAWSON Jasper of Douglass m BARDON Nancy of Sutton on 16 Mar, FULLER W Eld *MS* 7 June 1843

RAYMENT Norman m EGELSTON Mary on 7 Feb at Varysburgh NY, FLYNN William H Esq *MS* 6 Apr 1847

RAYMOND Kendall m TUCKER Clarissa of Parma NY, CRANE E F Eld *MS* 18 Oct 1843

RAYMONDY Samuel D m DAVIS Martha Jane sister of Davis J B Eld of Jackson on 17 Oct in JACKSON Mich, FOSTER Rev Mr *MS* 6 Nov 1850

READ Thomas B Esq m JELLERSON Margaret G of Bowdoinham ME on 30 June at Bowdoinham ME, RAYMOND J Eld *MS* 18 Dec 1844

READ Thomas J m BURTON Sarah A both of Mendon on 23, BURLINGAME M W Eld *MS* 5 Sept 1838

RECKORD Manning of Sand Lake m SHEPHERD Julia Ann of Stephentown NY on 21 Dec 1845 in Stephentown NY, COLEMAN I B Eld *MS* 8 Apr 1846

RECORD Cyrus m STRAW Mary Ann both of Newfield, BURBANK S Eld *MS* 30 Nov 1832

RECORD Nahum m ROBERTSON Sarah B both of Great Falls NH in Great Falls, BROOKS N Eld *MS* 4 Oct 1848

REDDING Isaac H m SPRING Harriet W of Grafton on 23 Sept at Grafton MA *MS* 18 Oct 1843

REDLON Albion m BROWN Caroline L in Milan Iowa, HATHORN S Eld *MS* 1 May 1850

REDLON William at Buxton ME m CLAY Grace, CLAY Jonathan Eld *MS* 20 Nov 1844

REED Alton Esq m SACKETT Lucy Mrs of Pierpont NY on 26 Mar 1842 at Pierpont NY, WHITFIELD W Eld *MS* 18 May 1842

REED Bailey Capt m LEWIS Mary E on 19 Dec at Boothbay ME, MORRILL S P Eld *MS* 22 Jan 1845

REED Elijah m POWERS Jane both of Dresden ME on 11 inst *MS* 2 Nov 1836

REED Francis formerly of Biblical School Whitestown m GOODWIN Apphia of Lowell on 5 inst in Lowell, MOULTON A K Eld *MS* 18 Jul 1849

REED Franklin m HOWARD Harriet both of Manchester on 22 Jan in Manchester, CHILLEY D P Eld *MS* 30 Jan 1850

REED James A m SHERMAN Joanna on 14 Nov at Edgecomb ME, PAGE E G Eld *MS* 8 Jan 1845

REED James G of Newburyport MA m PARSHLEY Hannah E of Strafford NH on 20 Oct in Strafford NH, PLACE E Eld *MS* 6 Nov 1850

REED John of No Berwick m CHICK Sarah of Berwick, BROOKS N Eld *MS* 22 Jan 1851

REED Lewis D m RANDALL Annette W both of Dover NH on 10 Sept, PERKINS Seth W Eld *MS* 17 Sept 1845

REED Merril N m STEMPSON Amanda M both of Manchester on 4 June in Manchester, CILLEY D P Eld *MS* 19 June 1850

REED Robert M m STEWART Mary on 29 June in Barrington, PLACE E Eld *MS* 19 Jul 1837

REED Sewall m HANSON Sarah Jane on 8th inst at Pownal ME, PURINTON A W Eld *MS* 29 Oct 1845

REED Warren of Dresden m JACK Harriet M of Richmond ME in the Union meeting house at Richmond Corner ME, QUINNAM C Eld *MS* 7 Jan 1846

REED Webber Jr m FEE Sally of Durham LC on 15 May, BARTLETT W Eld *MS* 30 Jan 1839

REED William Jr m ATHERTON Catharine both of Mt Desert on 29 Nov 1849 in Mt Desert, BROWN John Eld *MS* 2 Jan 1850

REED William m POTTER Rhoda both of Scituate on 24 Oct in Scituate RI, ALLEN R Eld *MS* 30 Jul 1850

RELLINS Aaron B of Sandwich m WENTWORTH Elizabeth A of Dover on 27th ult, PLACE E Eld *MS* 8 Dec 1834

REMICK Ai m DREW Mary P of Dover on 30 Jan, LOTHROP Rev Mr *MS* 6 Feb 1834

REMICK David m JACOBS Susan C of Manchester NH on 4 Apr at Manchester, KIMBALL John Eld *MS* 28 Apr 1847

REMICK George W m STEVENS Rebecca A on 24 Dec of Great Falls NH, DUNN R Eld *MS* 6 Jan 1847

REMICK John m ELLIOT Jane both of Parsonsfield *MS* 25 Nov 1831

REMICK John of Tamworth m STEVENS Hannah J of Somersworth on 3 Aug at Great Falls, BUTLER O Eld *MS* 11 Sept 1850

REMINGTON DeWitt C of Burrillville m HARRIS Adah M of No Scituate on 18 Nov in No Scituate, CILLEY D P Eld *MS* 4 Dec 1850

REMINGTON Joel of Huntington VT m HALL Armina, DIKE Orange Eld *MS* 6 Dec 1843

REMINGTON William m KEACH Emily both of Mendon MA on 22 Feb in Mendon MA, BURLINGAME M W Eld *MS* 28 Mar 1838

RENNET Suel of Effingham m MOULTON Cynthia of Eaton, GASKILL S Eld *MS* 21 Jan 1846

RENNETT Alvah of Effingham m STILLINGS Mary of Conway, GASKILL S Eld *MS* 21 Jan 1846

REVER Joseph of Boston m REXFORD Lydia of Hatley LC on 16 Nov last, MOULTON Eld *MS* 17 Feb 1836

REXFORD Samuel of Hatley m TOPLIN Joanna of Stanstead LC *MS* 17 Feb 1836

REYNOLDS John m SERGEANT Dorothy both of Portsmouth on 29 ult in Portsmouth, TRUE E Eld *MS* 10 Oct 1838

REYNOLDS Oliver N of Lubec m HARMON Ann A on 25th ult in the Congregational church in Limerick ME, FREEMAN C Rev *MFWBR* 1 Jul 1848

REYNOLDS Samuel R of Candia m DEARBORN Sarah Ann on 7 Dec on 7 Dec at Raymond, DAVIS K R Eld *MS* 7 Jan 1846

REYNOLDS Tent J m SHONTS Miriam A on 7 Jul at Rock Creek Kane Co IL, STARR D S Eld *MS* 27 Nov 1844

RHODES Schuyler m SHERMAN Amanda of Scriba NY on 30 Nov at N Scriba NY, PADDEN S B Eld *MS* 24 Dec 1845

RICE Algernon S D G m DAVIS Eliza at Unity ME, LEWIS D B Eld *MS* 25 Dec 1844

RICE George m HUBBARD Mary of Waterville at Waterville ME, LEWIS Daniel B Eld *MS* 25 Nov 1846

RICE John A of Sutton VT m KENNESON Elizabeth G Mrs of Tamworth in Tamworth, AMES Charles G Eld *MS* 17 Jul 1850

RICE John P of Phoenix m GRIFFETH Marinda of Schroeppel NY on 1 Feb 1849 in Schroeppel NY, SMITH O W Eld *MS* 2 May 1849

RICE Lewis of Marlborough MA m ALDRICH Elizabeth of Smithfield on 28 inst in Smithfield, ALLEN R Eld *MS* 18 Apr 1838

RICH Albert m SEVERENS Jane of Pierpont on 12 Jan 1843, WHIT-FIELD W Eld *MS* 1 Feb 1843

RICH Albin of Moretown m WHITNEY Susanna of Brookfield VT in Brookfield VT, HARRIS L T Eld *MS* 4 Jul 1849

RICH James M m VARNEY Abby C both of Jackson on 27 ult in Unity, SKILLIN H Eld *MS* 24 Nov 1847

RICH Joseph m WALKER Lorinda both of Exeter ME on 14th ult *MS* 11 Mar 1835

RICH Lemuel Esq of Standish m BANGS Ester of Buxton on 1st inst,

RICH (Continued)

BEAN Nathaniel Esq *MS* 23 Dec 1831

RICH Moses Dea m SHAW Mary Ann both of Exeter ME, NASON S U
Eld *MS* 24 Apr 1834

RICH Proctor m BROWN Edna of Strafford VT at Strafford VT,
SWETT David Eld *MS* 27 Feb 1839

RICH Stephen m EASTMAN Sarah T on 7 Dec 1848 in Freewill
Meeting House in Harpswell ME, HERSEY L Eld *MS* 14 Feb 1849

RICHARDS David m BRAGDON Catharine on 4 Apr in Scarborough
ME, LANCASTER D Eld *MS* 1 Aug 1849

RICHARDS Jacob m SMITH Abigail of Hallowell ME on 21 Dec,
WEAVER Phillip Eld *MS* 7 Jan 1846

RICHARDS John K m WOODS Sarah F on 6th inst in Saco *MS* 17
Jan 1828

RICHARDS Leonard J m GORDON Lydia A both of Lancaster MA on
25 Nov 1847 in Dracut, CURTIS S Eld *MS* 15 Dec 1847

RICHARDS Luther m BEAN Maria J of Lowell MA, THURSTON N Eld
on 28 Aug *MS* 11 Sept 1839

RICHARDSON Abram C m SAWYER Viola F in New Portland ME,
DENNIS J M Esq *MS* 26 Sept 1838

RICHARDSON Asa W M m CLARY Caroline of Dracut MA on 3 Nov of
Lowell MA, CURTIS S Eld *MS* 6 Jan 1847

RICHARDSON Charles J m HUBBARD Louisa D of Westbrook ME on
14 Mar at Porter, PIKE J Eld *MS* 21 Apr 1847

RICHARDSON Charles m SLEEPER Dorothy both of So Reading on 3
June in Boston, NOYES E Eld *MS* 5 Aug 1846

RICHARDSON Edson m HALL Emeline at Strafford VT, PETTENGILL
J Eld *MS* 11 Dec 1844

RICHARDSON Edward E of Dracut MA m HAYES Phebe W of Limerick ME on 4th inst at Limerick ME, FREEMAN Charles Rev
MFWBR 13 Apr 1850

RICHARDSON Edward m HODGDON Eliza S both of Northwood on
12 Jul in Northwood NH, JOHNSON W D Eld *MS* 11 Nov 1846

RICHARDSON Elbridge m GAMAGE Sally both of Anson ME on 24
ult, STILSON C Eld *MS* 16 Sept 1835

RICHARDSON George W m MINOT Ann R of Dracut MA on 27 Apr at
Lowell MA, WOODMAN J Eld *MS* 19 Oct 1842

RICHARDSON Henry of Waterville ME m WEBBER Ruth F of Vienna
ME on 18 Jul 1843 at Readfield ME, LOMBARD B S Rev *MS* 6
Sept 1843 & *MS* 21 Nov 1843

RICHARDSON Isaac G of Tunbridge VT m PERKINS Elvira A of
Chester VT on 5 Dec 1849 in Tunbridge VT, HENDER M C Eld *MS*
2 Jan 1850

RICHARDSON James A m EIRL Eunice both of Great Falls NH on 16
June in Great Falls, BROOK N Eld *MS* 10 Jul 1850 [see RICH-
MOND]

RICHARDSON James A of Dover m EVANS Harriet B of Barrington on 26 Sept in Manchester, CILLEY D P Eld *MS* 3 Oct 1849

RICHARDSON John of Boston MA m GLIDDEN Mary Jane of Meredith on 5 Oct 1843, PITMAN S J Eld *MS* 15 Nov 1843

RICHARDSON Martin P m BUKER Ann H at Cambridge VT of Underhill, DAVIS Isaac G *MS* 8 June 1842

RICHARDSON Nathaniel A Esq of Woburn MA m HALL Hannah on 17 Apr, SHERBURNE S Eld *MS* 25 June 1845

RICHARDSON Philip of Eaton m WHITAKER Rebecca of Conway on 9 Apr in Conway, GASKELL Silas Eld *MS* 12 Aug 1846

RICHARDSON Rockwell m RICHARDSON Comfort C both of Sutton VT on 5 June in Sutton VT, FOLSOM Moses Eld *MS* 28 June 1848

RICHARDSON Samuel of Baldwin ME m TOWLE Hannah of Newfield ME, BURBANK S Eld *MS* 14 Feb 1833

RICHARDSON Sargent H m WOODWARD Maria E on 2d inst at Sutton NH, NEWELL F P Eld *MS* 23 June 1847

RICHARDSON Sullivan m BRIER Elvira at Manchester NH on 1 Sept, CILLEY D P Eld *MS* 11 Sept 1844

RICHER Wentworth R m DOWNS Maria B both of Dover on 2 inst in Dover NH, SMITH A D Eld *MS* 12 Jul 1848

RICHMOND James A m EIRL Eunice both of Great Falls NH at Great Falls NH *MFWBR* 29 June 1850 [see RICHARDSON]

RICKARE Abner m POOL Sarah of Stanstead on 2 Jan 1839 *MS* 17 Apr 1839

RICKER Abial D m CHICK Sarah of Berwick on 3 Mar at Berwick ME, DAVIS K R Eld *MS* 29 May 1844

RICKER Asa H m RICKER Esther J both of Lebanon ME on 19 Dec 1850 in Lebanon ME, LITTLEFIELD William H Eld *MS* 8 Jan 1851

RICKER Benjamin F m JONES Sarah J both of Great Falls NH on 26 June in Great Falls, BROOKS N Eld *MS* 10 Jul 1850 & *MFWBR* 13 Jul 1850

RICKER Bradford Esq m MARR Catherine on 23 Oct at Brownfield, WILLEY Eben C Eld *MS* 25 Jan 1843

RICKER Carr of Acton ME m GARVIN Eliza Ann of NH on 5 inst in Milton, REMICK John Esq *MS* 21 Mar 1838

RICKER Daniel of Acton m HOWE Sarah of Wakefield on 2d ult in Wakefield, PERRY Luther Eld *MS* 26 Jul 1837

RICKER David m GODFREY Mary L on 18th inst at Manchester, CILLEY D P Eld *MS* 28 Aug 1839

RICKER Dominicus Jr m THOMPSON Caroline both of Parsonsfield ME on 20 Aug 1848 in S Parsonsfield ME, SMITH William Eld *MS* 8 Nov 1848

RICKER Ezekiel m JONES Martha Ann of Farmington NH on 7 Jan at Effingham NH, HART E H Eld *MS* 5 May 1847

RICKER George H A B of Parsonsfield m CHASE Harriet N of New-

RICKER (Continued)
field on 2 Dec 1847 in Newfield ME, STEVENS T Eld *MS* 29 Dec 1847

RICKER George of Waterville ME m TRAFTON Paulina of Waterville ME, LEWIS D B Eld *MS* 17 Feb 1847

RICKER George W m KNIGHT Olive E on 3d Aug at Waterboro', EMERY R Eld *MS* 27 Aug 1845

RICKER George William m BLAISDELL Lucy Ann both of Lyman on Sunday 21 ult in Lyman ME, NASON James Esq *MS* 5 Jan 1842

RICKER Gershom m HARMAN Susan W of Acton on 29 Sept, STEVENS T Eld *MS* 23 Oct 1839

RICKER Isaac m MORSE Anna on 23 Nov at Alton NH, PINKHAM J Eld *MS* 10 Mar 1847

RICKER Ivory m TRAFTON Harriet F both of Waterville ME in Waterville ME, LEWIS D B Eld *MS* 31 May 1848

RICKER Jeremiah m HAM Nancy of Shapleigh ME in Shapleigh ME, HOOPER Rev *MFWBR* 14 Sep 1850

RICKER Joseph P m GOULD Mary E both of Westbrook ME on 25 Dec 1848 in Saccarappa ME, HARRIMAN D P Eld *MS* 3 Jan 1849

RICKER Lewis H of Dedham m KENNEY Hannah J O of Dover ME on 31 Dec 1846 at Dover ME, GALLISON W F Eld *MS* 21 Apr 1847

RICKER Obadiah m HARMON Deborah both of Somersworth on 24 Mar in Great Falls, DUNN R Eld *MS* 15 Apr 1846

RICKER Samuel of Monroe on 17 Dec at Dixmont ME m FROST Martha Elizabeth at Dixmont, ALLEN E Eld *MS* 11 Feb 1846

RICKER William m VARNEY Caroline G of Dover, CURTIS S Eld *MS* 13 Nov 1839

RICKER William 2nd on 12th inst in Dover NH m GOODWIN Harriet E of Lebanon ME, STEVENS Hiram Eld *MS* 8 Mar 1843

RICKER William of Saco ME m LORD Dorothy of Great Falls at Great Falls NH *MFWBR* 7 Aug 1847

RIDEOUT Benjamin A m PENLEY Eleanor M on 11 Feb at Danville, MORRELL F Eld *MFWBR* 3 Mar 1849

RIDEOUT Nathan C on 4 Jul m ROBERTS Jane both of Lee in Lee ME, GATCHELL H Eld *MS* 25 Jul 1849

RIDEOUT Willard on 18 Jan of Munroe m HASKELL Lydia of Callis, McKAY William Eld *MS* 25 May 1842

RIDER Rexford Rowland m HOXIE Henriette on 30 Mar at Sand Lake, COLEMAN E B Eld *MS* 7 May 1845

RIDLEY David m CROWELL Sarah W of Bangor ME on 26 Dec at Bangor ME, SMALL William Eld *MS* 20 Jan 1847

RIDLON Lewis m WEBSTER Susan both of Saco in Biddeford ME on 5 June 1848, WITHAM L H Eld *MS* 26 Jul 1848

RIDLON Thomas E of Sweden m RIDLON Philinda D of Hollis ME on 4 Apr 1848 in Hollis *MS* 3 May 1848

RIGGS John A m WHITE S A Maria at Georgetown on 3rd inst

RIGGS (Continued)
MFWBR 23 June 1849

RIKE Jonathan R of Collinsville CT m GORDON Sarah A K of New Hampton on 25 Aug, FISK Ebenezer Eld *MS* 22 Sept 1847

RILEY Thomas P m TOBEY Mary A both of Kittery ME on 13 June in Kittery ME, PERKINS Seth W Eld *MS* 3 Jul 1850

RILEY William m WILLIAMS Eliza Ann both of Kittery ME on 17 inst *MS* 26 Oct 1836

RILEY William m BAKER Eveline on 13 Mar 1843 at French Grove, Bureau Co, IL, JULIAN S L Eld *MS* 19 Jul 1843

RING A C m FROST Ann R on 11th ult at Orono, LEONARD Rev *MFWBR* 3 Mar 1849

RING Hiram of Richmond m PURINTON Eleanor of Bowdoin ME on 5 Mar 1850 in Bowdoin ME, PURINTON Elisha Eld *MS* 3 Apr 1850

RING Richard m FESSENDEN Vialetta on 11 Jan at Little Meadow PA "postage on this marriage was unpaid", FESSENDEN N Eld *MS* 10 Feb 1847

RINGROSE William m WARD Jane C both of Freeport ME in Bowdoin ME, PURINTON A W Eld *MS* 17 Nov 1847

RION Samuel of Northfield m BALLARD Avis M of West Hartford on 2 Feb, CHASE William P Eld *MS* 31 Mar 1847

RIPLEY Cushing m HILL Livonia both of Topsfield on 19 June in Topsfield ME, GATCHELL H Eld *MS* 25 Jul 1849

RIPLEY Thomas B Rev m MAYO Martha Miss in Portland ME, PAYSON Rev Dr *MS* 3 May 1827

RIPLEY William M of Coventry VT m FARRER Julia A of Corinth on 16 Oct 1848 in Corinth ME, HARDING E Eld *MS* 21 Feb 1849

RISE Eber E at Brownfield ME m STOVER Caroline L of Brownfield ME, BEAN C B *MS* 21 Nov 1843

RIX William P m FOX Almeda of Stanstead LC on 13 Oct 1838 *MS* 17 Apr 1839

ROAKS Isaac of Appleton ME m VEAZIE Rachel at Isleborough ME, RINES J N Eld *MS* 26 Feb 1840

ROBBINS Ira T of Sutton MA m MILLER Ellathyna P of Northbridge on 13 Mar, FULLER W Eld *MS* 7 June 1843

ROBBINS Lloyd O m MITCHELL Elmira E both of Chesterville on 1 Mar 1849 in Chesterville, WHEELER S Eld *MS* 28 Mar 1849

ROBBINS Samuel Eld formerly of ME m PHILBRICK Lucinda Josena of Andover NH *MS* 10 Jul 1829

ROBBINS Sylvester m MARCH Abigail T of Bridgeton ME on 12 Oct 1837 in Bridgeton, WHITNEY George *MS* 17 Jan 1838

ROBERTS Benjamin of Meredith NH m LEAVITT Polly of Sheffield VT on 23 Feb *MS* 16 Mar 1836

ROBERTS Charles m ROBERTS Huldah R on 2 Apr in Lafayette WT, COOMBS A Eld *MS* 20 May 1846

ROBERTS Charles m BICKFORD Ellen J both of Pittsfield on 2 May,

ROBERTS (Continued)

TRUE E Eld *MS* 16 May 1849

ROBERTS Charles W m VARNEY Almira both of Dover on 1 inst in Dover NH, HUTCHINS E Eld *MS* 18 Dec 1850

ROBERTS David S m LORD Sabrina in Great Falls NH, DUNN R Eld *MS* 8 Dec 1847

ROBERTS G W of Lebanon m RICKER Mehitabel F of Acton ME, FULLONTON J Eld *MS* 13 Jan 1847

ROBERTS Gardiner m WAIR Mary M of Gardiner at Gardiner ME, GOODRICH Barnard Eld *MS* 10 Apr 1839

ROBERTS George of Haverhill m MORRISON Elizabeth B on 19 ult at Sanbornton *MS* 8 Mar 1837

ROBERTS John C formerly of Farmington m CLARK Elizabeth of Gilmanton on 4 inst in Gilmanton NH, CLARK Rev Mr *MS* 12 Sept 1838

ROBERTS John H m SPRINGER Clarinda of Alexandria on 19 Sept at Alexandria, PADDEN S B Eld *MS* 18 Dec 1844

ROBERTS John of Danvers MA m NASON Matilda of North Berwick on 16 Jul at North Berwick ME, LORD D H Eld *MS* 30 Aug 1843

ROBERTS John of Kennebunk ME m WATERHOUSE ____ of Lyman ME at Lyman on 28th ult *MFWBR* 25 May 1850

ROBERTS John m COLE Persis S of Stark on 6 June at Stark, SPENCER S W Rev *MS* 7 Jul 1847

ROBERTS Jonathan of Lowell MA m BODGE Avis Jane of Dover on 8 inst in Madbury, HUTCHINS E Eld *MS* 15 May 1850

ROBERTS Joshua Jr of Parsonsfield ME m MEAL Lucy B in Portland ME *MS* 4 Oct 1827

ROBERTS Joshua m SCRUTON Sarah both of Strafford in Rochester *MS* 28 Dec 1836

ROBERTS Levi B m YOUNG Ann J of Haverhill MA on 7th, CURTIS S Eld *MS* 24 Feb 1847

ROBERTS Nathaniel m WEST Eliza both of Portland ME on 21 inst, LIBBY Isaac Eld in Portland *MS* 8 Mar 1848

ROBERTS Sanburn m CATE Mary both of Meredith, PITMAN Stephen J Eld *MS* 5 Dec 1838

ROBERTS Sewall F of Alton NH m HURD Eliza Ellen on 18 inst in Dover NH, CAVERNO A Eld *MS* 25 Dec 1850

ROBERTS Warren m DRAKE Abigail of Meredith NH at Meredith NH on 24 Apr 1842, PITMAN Stephen J Eld *MS* 8 June 1842

ROBERTS West m ROWELL Hannah on 9th Jul at Strafford VT, CLARK Eli Eld *MS* 13 Jan 1847

ROBERTS William B m LOUGEE Elizabeth J of Farmington NH on 4 Jul at Gilmanton, FERNALD S P Eld *MS* 28 Jul 1847

ROBERTS William H of Natick MA m LOWD Mary B on 3d inst at Acton ME, FULLONTON J Eld *MS* 11 Sept 1844

ROBERTS William H of Portland m BENSON Martha J on 22d Sept

ROBERTS (Continued)
at Gorham, HOBSON A Eld *MS* 23 Oct 1839

ROBERTS William of Solon ME m KINSMAN Lucy of Cornville at Athens ME on 10 June "They subscribed for the Morning Star, though neither of them are professors of religion", RUSSELL S Eld *MS* 7 Jul 1847

ROBERTS William H m HALL Clarissa both of Somersworth Great Falls NH *MS* 23 Sept 1831

ROBERTSON Alexander of Starksborough VT m STEVENS G Sally of Bradford NH on 8 Aug in Bradford, WENTWORTH J J Eld *MS* 4 Sept 1850

ROBERTSON Charles N m PATCH Huldab D on 14 Nov in Manchester, DAVIS J B Eld *MS* 26 Mar 1851

ROBERTSON Ebenezer S of Meredith NH m SANBORN Lucy J of Loudon NH on 25 Nov, BROOKS N Eld *MS* 8 Dec 1841

ROBERTSON Giles m BRUCE Almira both of Randolph VT on 31 May 1848 in East Randolph VT, MOULTON F Eld *MS* 14 Feb 1849

ROBERTSON Charles m STORY Mary E both of East Randolph VT on 31 May 1848 in East Randolph VT, MOULTON F Eld *MS* 14 Feb 1849

ROBERTSON Samuel N m PARSON Sarah E both of Monroe on 25 Nov 1850 in East Bixmont ME, ALLEN E Eld *MS* 5 Mar 1851

ROBEY William of city of Manchester m CROSS Betsey B of Northfield NH on 30 Sept in Northfield NH, CLOUGH Jeremiah Eld *MS* 14 Oct 1846

ROBIE Charles H m MARTIN Ann C both of Goffstown on 5 Apr in Manchester, CILLEY D P Eld *MS* 29 Apr 1846

ROBIE Ichabod Jr m ROBIE Jenette G of Corinth VT on 31 Mar 1842 at Corinth VT, SMITH A D Eld *MS* 13 Apr 1842

ROBIE Thomas Eld of Raymond m HOYT Polly Miss at Chester NH *MS* 20 Jul 1832

ROBINSON Ansel of Springfield m LANGLEY Lydia at Andover NH *RI* 4 Dec 1819

ROBINSON Benjamin D of Meredith NH m HALL Lois of Sandwich on 5 Jan, PITMAN Stephen Eld *MS* 24 Mar 1847

ROBINSON Benjamin of East Bridgewater ME m COX Harriet A of Brunswick in Brunswick ME, PURINTON A W Eld *MS* 3 Oct 1849

ROBINSON Benjamin W m DUDLEY Louisa J on 7 Feb at Manchester NH, CILLEY D P Eld *MS* 17 Feb 1847

ROBINSON Daniel J m TILTON Jane both of Gilmanton on 12 Nov in Gilmanton, FERNALD S P Eld *MS* 20 Dec 1837

ROBINSON Daniel m SANBORN Deborah both of Meredith, PITMAN Stephen J *MS* 5 Dec 1838

ROBINSON David m SANBORN Sarah A both of Wales on 21 inst in Wales, FILES Allen Eld *MS* 4 Oct 1837

ROBINSON David of Lowell MA m PHILBRICK Clarisa P of Tewksbury on 3 Jul at Lowell MA, THURSTON N Eld *MS* 2 Nov 1842

ROBINSON Edward M of Exeter m JACOBS Oliva of Dover in Dover
NH *MS* 13 June 1838

ROBINSON Elbridge m QUINBY Jane, SMITH Eleazer Rev *MS* 7 Feb
1838

ROBINSON Elijah of East Bridgewater MA m CASE Mary A of
Brunswick on 13 May 1850 in Brunswick ME, PURINTON A W
Eld *MS* 15 May 1850

ROBINSON George I m STACKPOLE Helen M of Thomaston ME at
Thomaston ME *MFWBR* 22 June 1850

ROBINSON John P of Holderness m KENNY Lovina of Meredith on
30 Nov, TRUE E Eld *MS* 27 Dec 1843

ROBINSON John W at Bangor ME m KENEDY Susan Jane, CAVER-
NO A Eld *MS* 13 Sept 1843

ROBINSON Joseph Jr m LINCOLN Anstress W both of Gardiner ME
on 14 June in Gardiner, PERKINS Seth W Eld *MS* 2 Aug 1837

ROBINSON Joseph m LINCOLN Anstress W on 14 ult in Gardiner,
PERKINS Seth W Eld *MS* 26 Jul 1837

ROBINSON Joseph of Litchfield on 28 ult m GETCHELL Eliza Ann of
Richmond, SWETT Jesse *MS* 7 Sept 1836

ROBINSON Joseph of Stratham NH m CROSBY Abigail S of Haverhill
MA on 5 June 1848 in Haverhill MA, MERRILL William P Eld *MS*
12 Jul 1848

ROBINSON Joseph on Aug 22 m TINKER Lydia, BROWN John Jr
Esq *MS* 19 Jan 1842

ROBINSON Joseph W on 1 Jan m LAWRENCE Nancy, PITMAN S J
Eld *MS* 18 June 1845

ROBINSON Mellin of Litchfield m LINCOLN Angeline of Litchfield,
QUINNAM C Eld *MS* 16 Oct 1839

ROBINSON Nathan J of Sebec ME on 8 Oct m MOORE Clarinda B of
Corinna in Corinna, HATHAWAY S Eld *MS* 13 Dec 1837

ROBINSON Noah of Waterboro m PARKER Olive of N Berwick ME,
EMERY R Eld *MS* 18 June 1845

ROBINSON Prescott of Andover MA m DANFORTH Eliza A of Lowell
MA on 12 Dec at Lowell MA, CURTIS S Eld *MS* 6 Jan 1847

ROBINSON Reuben of Newburgh ME m ABBOTT Nancy of Ossipee
NH at Ossipee NH, CHICK John Eld *MS* 7 Aug 1839

ROBINSON Thomas J Capt m GILLIDEN Eliza both of Meredith,
PITMAN Stephen Eld *MS* 5 Dec 1838

ROBINSON William C m DOUGLAS Mary on 6 Aug of Denmark ME,
PIKE J Eld *MS* 31 Dec 1845

ROCKWAY Daman m GRIFFETH Lydia both of Schroeppel NY on 23
Sept in Schroeppel Oswego Co NY, SMITH O W Eld *MS* 17 Nov
1847

ROCKWOOD David of Remsen Oneida Co NY m OSBORNE Caroline

ROCKWOOD (Continued)
P on 21 Jan 1847, GRIFFETH Ansel Eld *MS* 10 Mar 1847

ROGERS Alpheus of Effingham m HODGDON Nancy of Barrington *MS* 23 Nov 1836

ROGERS Asel W of Ossipee m CLIFFORD Selvina of Belgrade ME on 7 Sept 1848 in Ossipee, CHICK J Eld *MS* 15 Nov 1848

ROGERS Daniel B m MERRILL Sarah A of Holderness NH on 24 Sept 1848 *MS* 21 Mar 1849

ROGERS Francis of Lowell VT m GEORGE Esther Ann of Sandbornton NH on 24 Feb 1843 at New Hampton, FISK E Eld *MS* 31 Jan 1844

ROGERS George W at Bridgeton ME m BLAKE Emeline of Newfield ME on 13 Oct 1842, HUNTRESS D Eld *MS* 16 Nov 1842

ROGERS Increase J m EMERY Lucinda C both of Goshen on 20 Nov 1849, EMERY A Eld *MS* 2 Jan 1850

ROGERS James S m ROGERS Deborah of Somersworth NH on 10 Mar at Great Falls NH, HILL John C Esq *MS* 19 Mar 1845

ROGERS Jeremy of Pamelia m ESTES Jane Ann of 3 Mile Bay at 3 Mile Bay, PADDEN S B Eld *MS* 1 Feb 1843

ROGERS Jeremy of Permela NY m PECK Mary of Harrisburg NY, ABBEY M H Eld *MS* 7 Feb 1844

ROGERS John C m FRY Lydia C both of Sandwich NH on 9 May 1848 in Sandwich NH, BROOKS N Eld *MS* 24 May 1848

ROGERS John of Phipsbury m BOND Merinda H of Lewiston ME on 14th inst at Lewiston ME, GOLDER J Eld *MFWBR* 23 June 1849

ROGERS Miller J m BLACKSTONE Angeline at Lowell MA, CURTIS S Eld *MS* 26 Feb 1845

ROGERS Samuel of Parsonsfield divorced ROGERS Betsey on 7 Mar *MS* 14 Mar 1828

ROGERS William C m BROOKS Fidelia both of Norridgewock ME on 27 Aug 1848 in Norridgewock ME, BOWDEN Stephen Eld *MS* 29 Nov 1848

ROGERS William M D of Dover m EMERY Lucretia of Gorham ME on 8 ult in Dover NH, SMITH A D Eld *MS* 21 Feb 1838

ROLLINS Alba m PALMER Nancy Mrs of Dover NH on 1st inst at Dover NH, PERKINS S W Eld *MS* 8 Oct 1845

ROLLINS Andrew Minster of the Gospel m FREEMAN Huldah on 17th inst, WHITE Joseph Eld *MS* 22 May 1829

ROLLINS Benjamin m COLOMY Nancy on 17 May at N Market, HUTCHINS E Eld *MS* 7 June 1843

ROLLINS Daniel C m MARSTON Jemima A both of Manchester on 14 Mar in Manchester, CILLEY D P Eld *MS* 1 Apr 1846

ROLLINS David Jr of Newport VT m WHITCOMB Almira K of Strafford VT on 29 Oct 1848 in Strafford VT, CLARK E Eld *MS* 6 June 1849

ROLLINS Hiram m CONNER Mary Ann at Augusta ME on 8th inst

ROLLINS (Continued)
MFWBR 19 June 1847

ROLLINS Joseph C m HAYDEN Mary Ann both of No Bangor ME on 2 Apt 1849 in No Bangor ME, AMES Moses Eld *MS* 2 May 1849

ROLLINS Joseph F m INGALLS Amanda J both of Bristol on 29 Oct 1848 in Bristol, CALLEY D Eld *MS* 29 Nov 1848

ROLLINS Joseph P m WOODMAN Anna on 27 Dec, PINKHAM J Eld *MS* 10 Mar 1847

ROLLINS Joseph S m CHADBOURN Sylvina A both of Somersworth NH on 30 ult in Dover, HUTCHINS E Eld *MS* 10 May 1848

ROLLINS Levi D of Lee m ELLIS Grace at Epping, TUTTLE A Eld *MS* 12 May 1847

ROLLINS Nicholas Jr m ROLLINS Louiza both of Stratham on 3 Oct in Stratham, MERRILL A Eld *MS* 10 Oct 1838

ROLLINS Noah S of New Hampton m BICKFORD Elvira of Meredith, PITMAN S J Eld *MS* 21 June 1848

ROLLINS Otis m EMERY Abigail both of Somersworth on 14 inst in Dover, HUTCHINS E Eld *MS* 18 Oct 1848

ROLLINS Sherburne B m ODIORNE Sarah of Pittsfield on 15 Feb at Pittsfield NH, CILLEY D P Eld *MS* 24 Feb 1847

ROLLINS Silas B m MAXWELL Sarah both of Mt Vernon ME, LEWIS D B Eld *MS* 3 Apr 1850

ROOD Marshall m FOSS Mary of Portsmouth NH on 11 Dec at Strafford, PLACE E Eld *MS* 7 Jan 1846

ROODE Miles m BISHOP Mariet both of Perry on 4 June in Perry NY, WHITCHER H Eld *MS* 5 Jul 1837

ROOT Filer m HOWARD Clarissa on 16th inst at Sweden NY, CRANE E F Eld *MS* 20 Nov 1844

ROOT Marshal of Russia m SMITH Harriet of Norway on 21 ult in Norway NY, TALLMAN E P Eld *MS* 15 Jan 1851

ROSE Horace P of Pike NY m LILIBRIDGE Amy of Greece Monroe Co NY on 3 Mar 1842, ROLLINS D M Eld *MS* 25 May 1842

ROSS Asa Jr m WHIPPLE Florella P both of Burrillville RI on 2 inst in Burrillville RI, HARRIMAN D P Eld *MS* 12 Feb 1851

ROSS Edmund m LARKINS Zeruiah on 29 Apr at Barrington, Shelburne Co, Nova Scotia, Canada, HENDERSON M C Eld *MS* 9 Jul 1845

ROSS James M m GRAVES Cynthia on 24 ult, SMITH E Rev in Dover NH *MS* 18 Jul 1838

ROSS Peter m FARNHAM Lovey H both of Lebanon ME on 26 May in New Market, ALLEN C Eld *MS* 6 June 1849

ROSS Robert of Saco m BOOTHBY Sally of Limerick on 10 Sept 1846 in Limerick ME, LORD D H Eld *MS* 14 Oct 1846

ROSS Samuel m ROSS Mary C on 17 Nov at Brunswick ME, PAGE E G Eld *MS* 13 Jan 1847

ROSS Thomas J m JOHNSON Hannah E of Coventry RI on 5 Dec at

ROSS (Continued)

Scituate *MS* 14 Dec 1842

ROUGEN James m HARRIMAN Emily *MS* 7 Sept 1832

ROUND Peleg m OLNEY Lydia H both of Scituate RI on 4 Jul in Scituate, ALLEN R Eld *MS* 30 Oct 1850

ROUNDS Nathaniel of Danville ME m LIBBY Susan of Poland ME on 30th Dec at Poland, LIBBY James Eld *MS* 30 Jan 1839

ROUNDS Samuel m BISHOPS Nancy both of Gorham ME on 4th inst, WHITE Joseph Eld *MS* 2 Jul 1830

ROUNSEFELT James m CHASE Mary E both of Manchester on 14 May 1848 in Manchester NH, CILLEY D P Eld *MS* 24 May 1848

ROWE Benj m STEVENS Mary in Georgetown ME, WEBBER D Eld *MS* 2 Jan 1839

ROWE Chauncey A of Stephentown m BELKNAP Jane Etta of Nassau on 18 Oct at West Stephentown, COLEMAN I B Eld *MS* 18 Nov 1846

ROWE David B m McCRILLIS Mary C on 3d inst at Pittsfield, BELKNAP P W Eld *MS* 21 Apr 1847

ROWE David S m TAPPAN Susan both of Sandwich on 12 Nov in Tamworth, MERRILL William S Eld *MS* 5 June 1850

ROWE George W m BAGLEY Emeline at Danville ME, FULLONTON J Eld *MS* 18 Sep 1839

ROWE Gilman of Gilmanton m DOCKHAM Lucy *MS* 13 June 1842

ROWE Jonathan H m MARTIN Elizabeth Ann on 28 May 1844 at Atkinson ME, HATHAWAY L Eld *MS* 21 Aug 1844

ROWE Josiah of Gilford m LEAVITT Hannah of Gilmanton on 6 Apr 1843 at Upper Gilmanton NH, TUTTLE J G Eld *MS* 3 May 1843

ROWE Leonard m CLERY Emily of Brooks on 2 Sept 1848, HAMIL-TON J Rev *MFWBR* 13 Jan 1849

ROWE Samuel of St Albans ME m TUTTLE Rea Sylva A of Palmyra on 12 Feb in Palmyra ME, HANSON T Eld *MS* 26 Mar 1851

ROWE Sergeant m MARR Lydia in Georgetown ME, WEBBER D Eld *MS* 2 Jan 1839

ROWE Shepherd of Gilford m TAYLOR Susan of Sanbornton NH on 27 Dec 1849 in Gilford NH, FROST D S Eld *MS* 9 Jan 1850

ROWE William of New Gloucester m WRIGHT Catharine of Lewiston ME, LIBBY Isaac Eld *MS* 15 Apr 1840

ROWELL Benjamin m BEAN Sarah both of Montville ME on 9th ult at Montville, ROBINSON N J Eld *MS* 8 Apr 1840

ROWELL Benjamin m MASON Abigail A on 4 May at French Grove, Bureau Co, IL, JULIAN S L Eld *MS* 19 Jul 1843

ROWELL Charles S m TRIPE Lovey both of Lowell MA, THURSTON N Eld *MS* 23 Sept 1835

ROWELL Chase H of Tunbridge m HILL Sarah A of East Randolph VT on 16th inst at East Randolph VT *MS* 31 Mar 1847

ROWELL Darius T m ROBERTS Emelius of Sharon on 23 Nov at

ROWELL (Continued)
Sharon VT, CLARK Eli Eld *MS* 13 Jan 1847

ROWELL John m SMITH Lucy both of Barnston on 19 Oct *MS* 1 May 1844

ROWELL John of Vershire m BUCK Eliza of West Fairlee on 31 Dec in West Fairlee, LEAVITT Stephen *MS* 7 Feb 1838

ROWELL Reuben m HOUSE Emily of Dixmont ME on 15 Sept in Plymouth, WHITCOMB A Esq *MS* 24 Sept 1838

ROYAL William B m ALLEN Nancy W of Paris at Norway ME on 19th ult *MFWBR* 1 Feb 1851

RUGG Cyrus F of Potter m ESTEN Dianna of Gorham NY on 13 Dec 1848 in Gorham NY, ESTEN H Eld *MS* 27 Dec 1848

RUGG David on 21 Sept 1837 m WHITCOMB Minerva both of Compton, MOULTON A Eld *MS* 10 Jan 1837

RUGGLES Ephraim H of Lyndon m STODDARD Susan of Sutton VT, MOULTON T P Eld *MS* 5 Apr 1843

RUGGLES Gardiner Esq of Barre, MA m GILMAN Eliza of Dover NH, ROOT Rev *MS* 16 Jul 1834

RUGGLES Lorenzo D of Sutton VT m TUTTLE Elvira B of Sandwich on 1 inst in Moltonborough, MASON Lemuel Eld *MS* 24 Oct 1838

RULTON Matthew m McCONKEY Elizabeth of Upper Canada on 27 Jan at Three Mile Bay, PADDEN S B Eld *MS* 5 Feb 1845

RUMERY Suel C m MURRAY Frances M on 24 inst in New Market, EASTMAN C Allen Eld *MS* 30 Oct 1850

RUMERY Thomas on 3 Dec m SAWYER Mehitabel of Saco ME of Biddeford ME, JACKSON Daniel Eld *MS* 6 Apr 1847

RUMMERY Jacob m CANEY Martha both of Effingham *MS* 1 Apr 1835

RUMMERY Jerome B of Dover m DYER Abigail F on 29 ult in Loudon, DYER S B Eld *MS* 11 Apr 1838

RUNDET Thomas N m ANDREWS Abby S on 4 Feb of New Market NH, FROST D S Eld *MS* 6 Apr 1847

RUNDLET Nathaniel of Lee m SIMPSON Mary G *MS* 4 May 1836

RUNDLET Thomas N m ANDREWS Abby S on 4th Feb at New Market NH, FROST D S Eld *MS* 10 Mar 1847

RUNDLETT Newall m MORRILL Alvira of Gilmanton NH on 26 Oct at Meredith Bridge, BROOKS N Eld *MS* 9 Nov 1842

RUNNELS Israel m LOWE Sarah both of Acton in Newfield ME, RUNNELS J Eld *MS* 6 Nov 1850

RUNNELS John Eld m STAPLES Huldah on 15 Dec at North Berwick ME, LORD D H Eld *MS* 28 Dec 1842

RUSS Nathaniel M m JONES Orena of Northfield on 10 Feb 1845 at Randolph VT, SMITH A D Eld *MS* 19 Feb 1845

RUSSEL Joel m DROWN Abigail G of Eaton NH on 27 Dec 1848, BLAISDELL Henry Rev *MS* 10 Jan 1849 & *MFWBR* 13 Jan 1849

RUSSEL Nelson R m REDLEY Elizabeth H on Oct 25 of Lowell MA,

RUSSEL (Continued)
   CURTIS S Eld *MS* 6 Jan 1847
RUSSEL Wellington of Barnstead m CARR Sarah of Loudon NH on 21 inst, TRUE E Eld *MS* 31 May 1848
RUSSEL William of Salem m COLBY Eliza of Manchester NH on 20 Sept in Salem MA, COLE M Eld *MS* 16 Oct 1850
RUSSELL Arthur of Lawrence MA m SPOONER Lucy Jane of Manchester on 16 Jan 1848 in Manchester, CILLEY Daniel P Eld *MS* 2 Feb 1848
RUSSELL Charles M of Newfield m BICKFORD Susan H of So Parsonsfield on 27 Sept in So Parsonsfield ME, WOODMAN J M Eld *MS* 7 Oct 1846
RUSSELL Edward of Salem MA m ROACH Mary Jane of Bath on 30 Nov, LIBBY Almon Eld *MS* 1 Feb 1843
RUSSELL Isreal C m SMITH Martha of Biddeford ME on 4th inst at Lower Biddeford, DRAKE S S Rev *MFWBR* 14 Apr 1849
RUSSELL Samuel B of Canaan m BEAN Betsey Miss of Jay on 3d ult in Jay *MS* 6 Mar 1829
RUSSELL True of Roxbury MA m PRATT Susan on 23d inst at North Yarmouth, JACOBS Rev *MFWBR* 3 Feb 1849
RYDER Amaziah H m JEFFERSON Emeline A both of Pawtucket RI on 25 Nov 1849 in Providence RI, WILLIAMS A D Eld *MS* 20 Mar 1850
RYMES William Gen m KENNARD Susan E at Portsmouth NH *MFWBR* 4 Sept 1847
RYTHER Ja [James] of Lyndon VT m HALL Mary of Ascott LC on 11 Dec, MOULTON A Eld *MS* 15 Apr 1840

SADDLER Joseph m RANDALL Eunice Mrs both of Bangor ME on 18 June 1848 in Bangor ME, ROBINSON N J Eld *MS* 5 Jul 1848
SAFFORD Daniel of Fayette m MORSE Roxannah of Carthage on 23 Nov 1849 in Carthage, MORSE W Eld *MS* 16 Jan 1850
SALEY Orin m WHITE A J both of Sherburn NY in Sherburn, MOORE H A Eld *MS* 21 Nov 1849
SALSBURY Mr of Weathersfield Springs m BLACKMAN Chloe of Warsaw NY on 13 Apr in Warsaw NY, WHITCHER H Eld *MS* 5 Jul 1837
SAMBERGER Augustus of Charlotte m EDSON Arminta of Bethany NY on 1 Jan, ROLLIN D M L Eld *MS* 11 Feb 1846
SAMPSON George A of Newburyport MA m PARKS Martha M of Great Falls NH on 19 Nov, DUNN R Eld *MS* 16 Dec 1846
SAMPSON Ivory P at Alton NH m FRENCH Mary M of New Durham NH, BUZZELL H D Eld *MS* 3 Mar 1847
SANBORN Moses m LOURION Susan both of Lowell MA *MS* 29 Apr 1835
SANBORN Abrahm of Deerfield m BICKFORD Keziah D of Epsom in

SANBORN (Continued)

Epsom on 16 Nov 1848, RAMSEY G P Eld *MS* 13 Dec 1848

SANBORN Abram S m FLANDERS Irena I both of Manchester on 3 Jan 1850 in Manchester, CILLEY D P Eld *MS* 23 Jan 1850

SANBORN Alonzo F m QUINBY Elvira B both of Sandwich NH on 31 Aug 1848 in Sandwich NH, TASKER L B Eld *MS* 20 Sept 1848

SANBORN Alvin m GREAR Lucinda on 16 Mar at Manchester, CILLEY D P Eld *MS* 26 Mar 1845

SANBORN B L Mr of Meredith m DEARBORN Dorothy of Plymouth in Meredith Village, NEVENS William P Eld *MS* 23 Sept 1846

SANBORN B P Mr at Sanbornton m MASON Maria J on 23 Apr, MASON L Eld *MS* 29 May 1844

SANBORN Benjamin m SHAW Mary Ann on 12 Jan at Manchester, CILLEY D P Eld *MS* 12 Feb 1845

SANBORN Benjamin Esq m MARSTON Lucinda both of Gilford on 16 Jul in Gilford, PINKHAM John Eld *MS* 13 Sept 1837

SANBORN Benjamin J m TASKER Martha both of Manchester on 5 inst 1849 in Northwood, JOHNSON W D Eld *MS* 25 Apr 1849

SANBORN Enoch H m GILMAN Maria P both of Gilford in Gilford NH on Thanksgiving Day, PINKHAM J Eld *MS* 16 Feb 1842

SANBORN Gilman Eld m MERRILL Annah of Corinth VT on 6th inst at Corinth VT, BOWLES Nathaniel Esq *MS* 20 Mar 1839

SANBORN Gilman Eld m OSGOOD Clarissa of Randolph on 15 Nov 1844 at E Randolph VT, SMITH A D Eld *MS* 19 Feb 1845

SANBORN Henry Jr at Epping m STEVENS Nancy Miss *MS* 6 Feb 1834

SANBORN Ira of Parsonsfield m HODGDON Hannah of Ossipee NH, SMALL Carlton Eld *MS* 31 Jan 1833

SANBORN J Mr m SPENCER Charlotte C of Corinth VT, MOULTON F Eld *MS* 17 Feb 1847

SANBORN Jacob K m SANBORN Sarah Ann of Loudon NH on 28 Sept at Gilmanton, TUTTLE John G Eld *MS* 25 Oct 1843

SANBORN James Jr m YEATON Sarah E both of Epsom on 19 inst in Epsom, FOSS T Eld *MS* 29 Sept 1847

SANBORN James m EDGERLY Diedina both of Hampton in Dover NH, PETTINGILL John Eld *MS* 8 Nov 1837

SANBORN James of Monmouth ME m ANDREWS Lydia of Wales ME, FILES A Eld *MS* 10 Jul 1839

SANBORN Jeremiah m BEAN Abigail of Gilmanton on 13 Nov at Alton NH, FERNALD S P Eld *MS* 25 Feb 1846

SANBORN John W of Deerfield NH m HOGNE Lydia A of Manchester NH, DAVIS J B Eld *MS* 12 June 1850 & *MS* 3 Jul 1850

SANBORN Jonathan m RUNDLETT Mary in Epping *MS* 9 Mar 1842

SANBORN Joseph Jr of Gilford m FARRAR Eliza Ann of Gilmanton NH in Gilmanton, MASON L Eld *MS* 12 Dec 1849

SANBORN Joseph m GRAY Elizabeth in Waterboro' ME *MS* 15 Mar

SANBORN (Continued)
1827

SANBORN Joseph M of Colombia m TOWLE Judith M of Ellsworth on 18 Aug in Colebrook, BEAN Benaiah Eld *MS* 11 Sept 1850

SANBORN Joseph of Waterboro ME m SMITH Polly of Shapleigh ME *MS* 5 Jan 1831

SANBORN Joshua B m APPLEBEE Esther I both of Acton on 18 Feb 1849 in Acton, JORDAN Z Eld *MS* 7 Mar 1849

SANBORN Lewis F m CLARK Mary Ann on 11 Oct at Gilford, PER-KINS Seth W Eld *MS* 16 Dec 1846

SANBORN Lewis m QUINBY Louisa both of Sandwich on 7 Mar in Sandwich, BLAKE C E Eld *MS* 1 Apr 1846

SANBORN Lewis m ABBOTT Mary Ann both of Westbrook ME on Jul 1 1841 in Falmouth, BEAN C Jr Eld *MS* 12 Jan 1842

SANBORN Lowell of Gilmanton m BEAN Sarah A of Sandwich on 27 June in Sandwich, TASKER L B Eld *MS* 10 Jul 1950

SANBORN Luther of Parsonsfield m HAYES Sally of Limerick ME on Thurs last at Limerick ME, FREEMAN Charles Rev *MS* 7 Dec 1826

SANBORN Marshal m SANBORN Mary C, HARVEY Erastus Eld *MS* 3 Jul 1844

SANBORN Moses L of Grafton m BURBANK Eliza Ann of Grafton on 17 Apr, RICHARDSON C S Eld *MS* 14 May 1845

SANBORN Moses of Wales ME m WARREN Lydia of Monmouth ME *MS* 10 Jul 1839

SANBORN Nathan P of Malden MA m SANDERS Mary Ann of San-bornton NH on 20 Nov in Sanbornton NH, MASON L Eld *MS* 12 Jan 1848

SANBORN Ranson m KENISON Emily, THURSTON N Eld *MS* 14 Oct 1835

SANBORN Reuben m SMITH Mary E both of Biddeford ME on 1 Jul 1848 in Biddeford ME, WITHAM L H Eld *MS* 26 Jul 1848

SANBORN Samuel m BICKFORD Sylvania S on 5 Sept at Meredith NH, PITMAN S J Eld *MS* 30 Oct 1844

SANBORN Samuel P of Meredith NH m PRESCOTT Sally S at Hold-erness NH on 23 Jul, TRUE E Eld *MS* 6 Sept 1843

SANBORN Tristram m BURLEIGH Hannah M both of Sandwich on 18 Aug in Sandwich, TASKER L B Eld *MS* 11 Sept 1850

SANBORN William A of Boston MA m WATSON Maria S Mrs of South Berwick ME at FWB meeting house at South Berwick ME on 14th inst, TRUE Ezekiel Eld *MS* 24 Feb 1847

SANBORN William B m "erson" (*sic*) Jane Miss on 20 Dec at Lowell MA, THURSTON N Eld *MS* 25 May 1842

SANBORN William D m COX Sabrina S on 13 Jul 1847, CURTIS S Eld in Dracut *MS* 8 Sept 1847

SANBORN William H m DAME Sally of Gilford, COOLEY L Eld

SANBORN (Continued)
MS 15 May 1839

SANBORN William m MURRAY Esther both of Dover on 31 Dec 1848 in Dover, SMITH A D Eld MS 10 Jan 1849

SANBORN William P m BIXBY Olive W both of Wilmot on 27 Sept in Danbury NH, BARTLETT J O D Eld MS 4 Nov 1846

SANBORN Winborn Capt m HOLT Lovina both of Gilford NH, GORDAN J Esq MS 12 Nov 1835

SANBOTH Calvin D m FLINT Maria both of Alexandria on 15 Jul in Alexandria, BROWN Amos Eld MS 12 Dec 1838

SANDERS Abram B m NASON Susan Amanda at Dover NH MFWBR 9 Dec 1848

SANDERS Angel m VAUGHN Mary W both of Gloucester on 22 ult in Smithfield, ALLEN R Eld MS 18 Apr 1838

SANDERS Joel H of Ossipee NH m SCATES Adaline of Ossipee NH on 22 Mar, WALKER John Eld MS 31 May 1843

SANDERS John m GRAY Maria L at Strafford, PLACE E Eld MS 13 Feb 1834

SANDERS Levi m DREW Anna both of Strafford in Strafford, PLACE E Eld MS 27 June 1838

SANDERS S Warren m RANDLET Serene of Meredith NH on 3 Dec at Meredith, BROOKS N Eld MS 14 Dec 1842

SANDERS Truman P of Clarkville m CHAMPLIN Amy of Hamilton NY on 2 inst in Hamilton NY, GARDNER S D Eld MS 29 Dec 1847

SANDERS William of Strafford m SANDERS Abigail M, PLACE E Eld MS 14 Aug 1839

SANDERS William J of Dover m HUCKINS Harriet E of Madbury on 1 inst in Dover NH, HUTCHINS E Eld MS 9 Jan 1850

SANDERSON George on 6th inst m HAYES Olive V, PERKINS Seth W Eld MS 16 Apr 1845

SANDFORD James M of Bowdoinham ME m STINSON Mary Jane of Litchfield ME, QUINNAM C Eld MS 20 May 1840

SANDFORD James W Gen of Anson ME m BROWN Eleanor of Bowdoin, QUINNAM C Eld MS 25 Mar 1846

SANFORD Charles B m TAYLOR Frances of Bangor ME at Bangor ME on 20th inst MFWBR 6 Jul 1850

SANFORD Ephraim of Tiverton RI m LAKE Betsey on 15 Oct, WHITTAMORE Joseph Esq MS 8 Nov 1843

SARGEANT Charles S at Andover NH m SEVERANCE Judith T of Andover NH on 30 Dec 1841, WATSON Elijah Eld MS 20 May 1842

SARGEANT Hiram of Raymond m PORTER Elizabeth Miss in Canaan NH MS 7 Sept 1832

SARGENT Albert of Bradford m JONES Eunice of Warner at Warner, HOLMES H Eld MS 17 Dec 1845

SARGENT Benjamin m HAZEN Sarah on 31 Oct in Hopkinton,

SARGENT (Continued)

KIMBALL J Eld *MS* 2 Apr 1851 & *MS* 27 Nov 1850

SARGENT Calvin m GOULD Lovey E both of Amesbury MA on 31 Dec 1850 in Amesbury MA, MERRILL W P Eld *MS* 8 Jan 1851

SARGENT E B of Pittsfield m PHILBRICK Abigail of Epsom NH on 9 ult in Pittsfield, TRUE E Eld *MS* 21 Nov 1849

SARGENT Edward L m COLBY Mary C on 18 Apr of Canterbury NH, CATLIN S T Eld *MS* 5 May 1847

SARGENT Harrison m TUCKER Eliza T both of Concord NH in Canterbury *MS* 19 Jan 1848

SARGENT Jaman m DAVIS Harriet E both of Parsonsfield on 16 Nov 1848 in East Parsonsfield ME, RAND James Eld *MS* 29 Nov 1848

SARGENT John G m BELLAMY Martha at Dover NH *MS* 21 Nov 1833

SARGENT Josiah m LIBBY Electra both of Hopkinton on 25 Mar in Hopkinton, SINCLAIR S L Eld *MS* 30 May 1838

SARGENT Reuben of Northfield m BOWEN Sally M of Holderness NH on 18th inst, PETTENGILL John Eld *MS* 26 June 1839

SARGENT Samuel of Chester m CHAMBERLIN Emeline of Manchester on 31 Mar 1848 in Manchester, CILLEY D P Eld *MS* 26 Apr 1848

SARGENT Thomas W m GAGE Jane E both of Haverhill MA on 23 Nov 1847 in Haverhill MA, MERRIL William P Eld *MS* 8 Dec 1847

SARGENT Thomas W of Hanniker m WAY Martha L of Hopkinton 31 Oct in Hopkinton NH, CATLIN S T Eld *MS* 5 Dec 1849

SARGENT Zebulon of Hopkinton m WATSON Betsey of Warner on 11 Sept *MS* 12 Oct 1836

SARLES Almon of Stanstead LC m DANFORTH Roxanna on 8 Feb, MOULTON Abial Eld *MS* 20 Sept 1837

SARLES Harry m ALDRICH Dianthy on 25 Jan 1844 *MS* 1 May 1844

SATERLAY Joseph T m BARTLETT Mary J on 24 Nov at Manchester, CILLEY D P Eld *MS* 9 Dec 1846

SAUDERS Robert m SWEET Truelove of Gloucester on 1 Dec at Gloucester *MS* 14 Dec 1842

SAUNDERS George B of Boston MA m WALTON Clarissa H of Lowell MA on 30 June at Lowell MA, THURSTON N Eld *MS* 2 Nov 1842

SAUNDERS Samuel of New Sharon m BACHELDER/BATCHELDER Nancy of Waterville on 5 May, EDGCOMB J Eld &/or BURGESS J S Eld *MS* 7/14 Jul 1847

SAVAGAE Isaac A Rev m CLARK Mary Ann on 14 Dec at Chester, CILLEY D P Eld *MS* 17 Jan 1844

SAVAGE James of Woolwich ME m MITCHEL Emily J of Bath ME on 28 Feb, JORDAN Z Eld *MS* 10 Mar 1847

SAVAGE Samuel m MITCHELL Mary both of Manchester on 1 Mar 1848, CILLEY D P Eld in Manchester *MS* 22 Mar 1848

SAVAGE Seth W m FRYE Sarah of Charlestown MA on 26 Feb, JACKSON Daniel Eld *MS* 24 May 1843

SAWTELL Jotham A of Sidney ME m YOUNG Ruth A of Starks ME on 4 Jul 1847 in Starks, WHEELER S Eld *MS* 29 Sept 1847

SAWTELLE Hannibal M m PHILPOT Lucinda on 29th ult in Limerick ME, FREEMAN Charles Rev *MFWBR* 8 Jul 1848

SAWYER Almon of Exeter NH m LIBBY Charlotte of Limington MR at Limington, LIBBY Eld *MS* 29 Oct 1828

SAWYER Alvin of Gardiner m CURTIS Zelamy B of Richmond on 23 Sept 1848 in Richmond ME, PURINGTON Collamore Eld *MS* 22 Nov 1848

SAWYER Amos of Amesbury m HAM Sarah J of Salisbury on 12 Dec of Salisbury MA, MERRILL William P Esq *MS* 25 Dec 1850

SAWYER Cyrus of Buxton ME m MOULTON Elizabeth P of Scarboro ME on 8 Nov, JACKSON Daniel Eld *MS* 6 Apr 1847

SAWYER Elijah P m PARISH Julia A both of Great Falls NH on 28 Nov, BROOKS N Eld *MS* 4 Dec 1850

SAWYER Francis L m KENNEY Esther W both of Lowell in Lowell MS on Mar 27, WOODMAN J Eld *MS* 27 Apr 1842

SAWYER Horace of Saco m MOULTON Lydia J on 22d ult at Saco ME, STRICKLAND G G Rev *MFWBR* 4 Jan 1851

SAWYER James MD of Saco ME m FOSS Sophia d/o John Foss of Limington ME on 18th ult at Limington ME, FREEMAN C Rev *MFWBR* 5 June 1847

SAWYER John C m HARVEY Betsey T of Atkinson ME on 27 Jan 1839, HATHAWAY L Eld *MS* 24 Apr 1839

SAWYER Joseph H m TARBOX Mary E of Hollis on 19 Feb 1849, BAILEY J M Eld *MS* 28 Mar 1849

SAWYER Joseph M of Bangor ME m PATTERSON Martha A of Saco ME on 22d ult at Biddeford ME, FARRINGTON Rev *MFWBR* 4 Sept 1847

SAWYER Josiah of Gilford m ELKINS Sally of Gilford on 3 Nov 1842, COOLEY John D Eld *MS* 25 Jan 1843

SAWYER Josiah of Salisbury MA m PAGE Abigail of Gilmanton NH on Dec 5, FERNALD S P Eld *MS* 5 Jan 1842

SAWYER Moses m RUSSELL Susan both of Manchester on 23 May in Manchester, CILLEY D P Eld *MS* 1 Apr 1846

SAWYER Nathan F m BUCK Hannah S on 30 Jul at Fryeburgh ME, PIKE John Eld *MS* 20 Aug 1845

SAWYER Samuel B m STROUT Elizabeth B of Gray ME on 28th ult at Gray ME, DORR R H Rev *MFWBR* 8 Sept 1849

SAWYER Silas H m SCOTT Charity at Lowell MA *MS* 3 May 1843

SAWYER Thomas E Hon m MOODY Elizabeth on 15 Oct 1848 in Dover NH, SMITH C N Rev *MS* 25 Oct 1848

SAWYER William of Bradford m HAYES Savilla of Strafford NH, SWETT David Eld *MS* 13 Mar 1839

SCALES Joseph m SHAW Sarah N both of Canterbury on 14 Apr, HARPER J M Hon *MS* 29 Apr 1835

SCALES Rufus D Capt of Concord NH m FOWLER Susan of Epsom NH on 27 Nov 1842, RAMSEY G P Eld *MS* 8 Feb 1843

SCAMMAN Stephen of Stratham m GORDAN Maria in Epping, SPAULDING Eld *MS* 26 Nov 1834

SCAMMON James F m ABBOTT Laura J at Portland *MFWBR* 21 Jul 1849

SCAMMON John F of Biddeford ME m WEYMOUTH Sarah Ann on 3 Jan at North Berwick, CLAY Daniel Eld *MS* 14 Jan 1846

SCAMMON R S m COBB Caroline both of Portland ME on 5 Dec in Portland ME, LIBBY I Eld *MS* 12 Jan 1848

SCATES Norton m COOK Lyntha Langton both of Dover on 2 inst in Dover, SMITH A D Eld *MS* 12 Dec 1838

SCEGGEL Benjamin Jr m DORE Belinda both of Ossipee NH on 19 ult, CHICK John Eld *MS* 8 June 1836

SCEGGEL Zachariah of Ossipee m DRAKE Mary of Effingham NH on 3 Oct in Effingham, FOSS N Eld *MS* 4 Dec 1850

SCHILINGER Daniel of Poland m MORTON Sarah of Gorham ME *MS* 6 Feb 1834

SCRIBNER Daniel m WOODWARD Hannah, EMERY Nathaniel Esq all of Waterboro *MS* 16 Sept 1831

SCRIBNER Daniel of Raymond m LANGFORD Ann in Candia *MS* 19 Apr 1837

SCRIBNER Daniel m RUSSELL Martha on 18 Sept at Manchester NH, CILLEY D P Eld *MS* 1 Oct 1845

SCRIBNER John Esq m PAGE Betsey of Raymond on 17 Jul *MS* 14 Aug 1839

SCRIGGINS Bradbury of Charlestown MA m BACHELDER Mary M of Dover NH on 1 May 1849 in Dover NH, SMITH A D Eld *MS* 9 May 1849

SCRIPTURE Andrew J m WEST Sarah of Lowell, THURSTON N Eld *MS* 8 Jan 1840

SCRIVNER Harrison of Topsham m EASTMAN Amanda Mrs of Orange on 29 Nov 1849 in Orange VT, CUMMINGS S Eld *MS* 9 Jan 1850

SCRUTON Benjamin m SHELLERD Sally Mrs both of Sheffield VT on 7 Dec 1848 in Sheffield VT, HILL M Eld *MS* 24 Jan 1849

SCRUTON Ezra A m SCRUTON Patience of Farmington NH on 17 Jan at Rochester, MEADER Jesse Eld *MS* 27 Jan 1847

SCRUTON Hiram W m ROBERTS Rachael of Dover NH at Farmington NH, PLACE E Eld *MS* 6 Apr 1842

SCRUTON Michael m STEWART Susan both of Barrington *MS* 27 Jan 1836

SCUITON Thomas C m ELKINE Love T both of Farmington on 30 Dec in Rochester, MEADER J Eld *MS* 8 Jan 1851

SEARL Edwin of Lowell m LITTLEFIELD Mahala of Wilmington MA on 20 Sept, DURGIN J M Eld *MS* 22 Feb 1843

SEARL Franklin V m BURDEN Adeline both of Scituate in No Scituate RI, ALLEN R Eld *MS* 1 Jan 1851

SEARL John H at Dracut MA m HINKLEY Jane on 6 Dec, CURTIS S Eld *MS* 24 Dec 1845

SEARS Reuben m KELLEY Joanna on 9 Apr in Barrington Nova Scotia, HENDERSON Moses C Eld *MS* 5 May 1846

SEATHERS /LEATHERS Jonathan m SAWYER Hannah both of Lowell in Lowell, THURSTON N Eld *MS* 20 Dec 1837

SEAVER Isaac of East Cambridge MA m EATON Clarissa at Alfred, EATON E G Eld *MS* 27 June 1842

SEAVERNS George W m FARWELL Lydia J C of Norway ME *MFWBR* 5 Apr 1851

SEAVEY Calvin of Farmington m CLARK Hyrenia of Rochester in Strafford, PLACE Eld *MS* 18 Apr 1838

SEAVEY Ebenezer of Rochester m SEAVEY Dorothy of Farmington on 2 Aug in Farmington, PLACE E Eld *MS* 16 Aug 1837

SEAVEY Frederick m DUTTON Hannah both of Chester at Raymond, ROBIE Thomas Eld *MS* 1 May 1834

SEAVEY Jacob D m CLARK Olive C both of Rochester on 30 Nov in Rochester, WHITNEY G W Eld *MS* 1 Jan 1851

SEAVEY Nathaniel H m HAM Sarah J both of Barrington on 29 Apr in Strafford, PLACE E Eld *MS* 22 May 1850

SEAVEY Warren m STAPLES Olive Ann on 24th at Dover NH, HUTCHINS E Eld *MS* 27 Jan 1847

SEAVEY Zephaniah H m SEAVEY Hannah N of Cornish ME on 7 Dec 1839, BUZZEL A Eld *MS* 18 Sept 1839

SEAVY Joseph S of Pittsfield m TOWLE Philinda of Epsom NH on 8th ult, BEAN S F Eld *MS* 29 June 1836

SEAVY Peter C of Pittsfield m ALLEN Lydia Jane of Gilmanton NH on 30 June 1836 *MS* 13 Jul 1836

SEAWARD John m THOMPSON Mary J at Manchester NH on 14 Jan, CILLEY D P Eld *MS* 21 Jan 1846

SEAWARDS Joel D of Strafford ME m SEAWARDS Lydia of New Market NH, HUTCHINS E Eld *MS* 13 Apr 1842

SEBRA Robert m EMERSON Mary Mrs on 9 Nov at French Grove, Bureau Co, IL, JULIAN S L Eld *MS* 19 Jul 1843

SEDGELY John m SMITH Eliza A both of Saco ME on 31 Dec in Limerick ME, McMELLAN Rev *MFWBR* 30 Jan 1847

SEDGERLY Levi m JOHNSON Martha on Nov 14, MANSON B S Eld *MS* 15 Jan 1840

SEDGLEY Edward m MACE Lucinda of Greene ME on 16 Jul, EATON E G Eld *MS* 2 Aug 1843

SEELEY George W of Shelby m COLBY Zeruah H of Darien NY on 2 Sept, BLACKMARR Henry Eld *MS* 17 Sept 1845

SELINHAM B M B of Thornton m CARR Ruth T of Gilford on 1 June in Meredith Lake Village, FAIRFIELD S Eld *MS* 1 Jul 1846

SENTER Matthew m EVANS Lydia E on 17 Sept at Manchester NH,
CILLEY D P Eld *MS* 25 Sept 1844
SERGANT Thomas T m NEWHALL Sarah both of Stowe, BIXBY L E
Eld *MS* 21 Jan 1846
SERGEANT Samuel at Raymond m STEVENS Mary Jane *MS* 1 June
1842
SEVERANCE Asa m BEAN Sarah C of Charlestown MA on 2 Apr at
Charleston MA, JACKSON Daniel Eld *MS* 24 May 1843
SEVERANCE Asa m WEBSTER Hannah M both of Sandwich on 20
Nov in Sandwich, TASKER L B Eld *MS* 15 Jan 1851
SEVERANCE Enoch Q m CURRIER Mary on 25 June at Lowell MA,
SINCLAIR J L Eld *MS* 16 Aug 1843
SEVERANCE John W m KAME Hannah J of Chichester in Chiches-
ter, BEAN S F Eld *MS* 5 Jan 1842
SEVERANCE Jonathan of Washington ME m COPP Harriet of
Hopkinton on 27 Nov in Hopkinton NH, CATLIN S T Eld *MS* 5 Dec
1849
SEVERANCE Ora P m STICKNEY Ruth Ann both of Kingston on 9
inst in Danville, BLORE J Eld *MS* 20 Nov 1850
SEWALL Caleb M Eld m TURNER Catherine S on 11th ult at Adams
Co IL, TAYLOR Rev *MS* 17 Sept 1845
SEWALL Levi W of Epping NH m JONES Lydia A of New Market,
FROST D S Eld *MS* 6 Apr 1847
SEWARD Charles B m GORDON Lydia D on 17 May at Dracut MA,
CURTIS S Eld *MS* 2 June 1847
SEWARD George H m DIKE Lucretta at Lowell, THURSTON N Eld 12
Feb 1840
SEWARD Isaac m TOBEY Betsey both of Kittery ME *MS* 5 Jan 1831
SEXTON James of Rochester, Racine Co Wis m CRAGA Melissa E of
Spring Prairie Wis on 20 June 1848 in Spring Prairie WI, AUGIE F
P Eld *MS* 23 Aug 1848
SEYMMS William of Newfield m THOMPSON Mary of Newfield,
FREEMAN Rev *MS* 6 Dec 1827
SHACKFORD Joseph E m PALMER Eliza Jane both of Eaton NH on
8 Feb 1849 in Eaton NH, BLAISDELL Henry Rev *MS* 7 Mar 1849
SHACKFORD S B Maj of Conway m PENDEXTER Lydia of Bartlet NH
on 18 inst in New Gloucester ME, BUTLER Henry Rev *MS* 26 Jul
1848
SHACKFORD Samuel B m HALE Martha S both of Barrington on 5th
inst in Barrington, PLACE E Eld *MS* 19 Apr 1837
SHACKFORD Thomas m MARSTON Rachel of Eaton, ATKINSON
King Eld *MFWBR* 3 Feb 1849
SHACKLEY Augustus of Portsmouth NH m TRIPP Eliza Ann of
Kennebunk ME on 16 Jul 1848, SMALL C Eld *MS* 9 Aug 1848
SHACKLEY Isaiah m STANLEY Clarissa both of Shapleigh ME on 11
Jan in Shapleigh, LORD D H Eld *MS* 24 Jan 1838

SHACKLEY Moses of Alfred m MORRISON Sarah of Sanford ME on 15 Nov in Sanford, Springvale, LORD D H Eld *MS* 20 Dec 1837

SHACKLEY Richard m MORRISON Bridget both of Sanford on ME April 5 at Lexington, LENNAN John Eld *MS* 15 Apr 1840

SHALLIES Chauncy of Boston MA m VARNEY Mary E of Dover on 20 inst in Dover NH, HUTCHINS E Eld *MS* 26 Sept 1849

SHANNON Nathaniel MD of Sandwich NH m CUMMINGS Lucy M in Cape Elizabeth, LIBBY C O Eld *MS* 27 June 1849

SHAPLEIGH Edwin of Lebanon ME m CARPENTER Abby H of Great Falls NH, DUNN R Eld *MS* 24 Dec 1845

SHAPLEIGH Howard m HARTFORD Mary Mrs at Great Falls NH *MFWBR* 21 Apr 1849 & *MFWBR* 14 Apr 1849

SHAPLEIGH Moses W of Lebanon ME m PERKINS Emeline M in New Hampton, PERKINS Thos Eld *MS* 19 June 1850

SHARPSTEEN Alfred of Springport NY m GILLET Lucia A of Huntington on 26 Sept in Huntington VT, DIKE Orange Eld *MS* 17 Oct 1849

SHATTUCK Milo m ETRICH Ellen both of Hermon NY on 26 Feb 1848, JENKINS C Eld *MS* 19 Apr 1848

SHATTUCK William L of Landaff m WOODBURY Ann C of Bethlehem on 26 Sept in Bethlehem, BLAKE C E Eld *MS* 6 Nov 1850

SHAVELIER Christian m WOODEN Jane on 15 Dec at Virgil, GARDNER L G Eld *MS* 15 Jan 1845

SHAW Albert of Kennebunk ME m EMERY Caroline D of Andover NH on 21 Dec 1848 in Andover NH, KNOWLES E G Eld *MS* 7 Mar 1849

SHAW Benjamin m NUDD Sarah of Hampton on 3 Sept in Hampton, BURBANK P S Eld *MS* 9 Sept 1846

SHAW Curtis m CROCKETT Tryphena on 6th inst at Windham, TOBIE Levi Esq *MFWBR* 16 June 1849

SHAW E M 21 Sept 1847 m GRANT Abigail J both of Brewer ME, WEAVER P Eld in Bangor ME *MS* 17 Nov 1847

SHAW Francis on 4 Nov 1848 m LEAVITT Rachael Jane both of Lowell, WELLS L S Eld in Meredith NH *MS* 5 Apr 1848

SHAW Isaac M m CHAMBERLAIN Louise both of Exeter ME, NASON S U Eld *MS* 24 Apr 1834

SHAW John m BRAGDON Mary Ann at York ME *MS* 24 Apr 1834

SHAW John m DREW Nancy Mrs at Holderness NH, SMITH James Jr Esq *MS* 11 May 1842

SHAW John m SHAW Susan both of Holderness on Feb 16 at Alexandria, BROWN A Eld *MS* 4 Mar 1840

SHAW Moses of Boston m DOW Elmary of North Hampton on 26 Jan 1848 in North Hampton, BURBANK P S Eld *MS* 1 Mar 1848

SHAW Samuel of York ME m EMERY Sally of Somersworth NH on 3 Mar, WEBBER H Eld *MS* 10 Apr 1844

SHAW Sargent of Windham m HANSON Cynthia on 29 Sept,

SHAW (Continued)

HOBSON A Eld *MS* 23 Oct 1839

SHAW Seth Harding m BROCKINGS Arlette Hilton both of Woolwich ME on 31 Aug, PERKINS S W Eld *MS* 20 Sept 1937

SHAW Timothy Hon of Sanford ME m ALLEN Roena C Mrs of Great Falls NH, WEBBER Horace Eld *MS* 21 Feb 1844

SHEARMAN Henry m VALLET Mary on 11 Jan in No Providence, HUTCHINS E Eld *MS* 7 Feb 1838

SHEARMAN Preserved of No Providence m ARMINGTON Esther of Smithfield on 6 Apr in Smithfield, BURLINGAME M W Eld *MS* 24 May 1837

SHEDD Azetes of Bolton NY m DAVIS Sabrina of Hinesburgh VT on 12 Sept in Huntington VT, DIKE Orange Eld *MS* 6 Nov 1850

SHEDD Edward D m BARNES Mary A on 11 Oct at the Free Baptist church in Charlestown, WETHERBEE I J Eld *MS* 9 Dec 1846

SHELDON Edmunds T m FISK Lovina on 17 Sept at Waterbury VT, GRAY Ira Eld *MS* 2 Oct 1844

SHELDON Milton E m STEWART Nancy I on 7 Jan in Oxford, PAKER B E Eld *MS* 29 Jan 1851

SHEPARD Freeman m LEIGHTON Susan of Strafford on 30 Jan at Strafford, PLACE E Elder *MS* 12 Mar 1845

SHEPARD Joseph W m DANA Frances A of New Hampton on 30 Nov 1843 at New Hampton, DANA S Eld *MS* 26 June 1844

SHEPARD Morrill Esq m PHILLIPS Mary of Gilmanton NH on 5 Oct at Pittsfield, CILLEY D P Eld *MS* 12 Oct 1842

SHEPHARD Joel of Stephentown m RECORD Charlotte of Sand Lake on 17 Feb, COLEMAN I B Eld *MS* 19 Mar 1845

SHEPHARD John W of Dover m ROWELL Eliza Jane of So Berwick ME, TRICKEY N H Eld *MS* 10 Feb 1836

SHEPHERD Luke m GROVER Mahitabel Jordon both of Bowdoin ME on 1 Jan 1850 in Bowdoin ME, PURINTON Elisha Eld *MS* 3 Apr 1850

SHEPLEY Leonard m CHASE Frances on 2nd inst at Portland ME, CHICKERING Rev *MFWBR* 12 May 1849

SHERBURNE - see SHURBON

SHERBURNE George W m YOUNG Mary Jane both of Pittsfield Dec 28th, CILLEY D P Eld *MS* 5 Jan 1842

SHERBURNE James m WILLIAMS Zelinda both of Gardiner ME in Bowdoinham ME, QUINNAM C Eld *MS* 22 May 1844

SHERBURNE Jeremiah M m MORRISON Harriet H both of Barrington on 19 inst in Barrington, SHERBURNE S Eld *MS* 29 Apr 1846

SHERBURNE John S of Chichester m PAGE Mary K of Epsom on 4 Dec 1849, TRUE E Eld *MS* 9 Jan 1850

SHERBURNE Tobias of Rochester m AUSTIN Elisabeth Mrs of No Berwick ME, BURBANK S Eld *MS* 2 Dec 1835

SHERBURNE William B of Northwood m DAVIS Sarah Ann of Epping

SHERBURNE (Continued)
NH on Monday 14th ult at Effingham NH, DAVIS J Eld *MS* 1 Oct 1834

SHERBURNE Zelotts of Wellington m BROWN Mary R on 26 Apr 1848 in La Grange Ohio, WHIPPLE H E Eld *MS* 14 June 1848

SHERMAN Charles E of Edgecomb m GILES Mary Jane of Boothbay on 8 Sept in Boothbay ME, PAGE E G Eld *MS* 27 Nov 1850

SHERMAN Charles H of Dover m SLEEPER Marinda S of Poplin on 9th inst at Brentwood in Baptist meeting house, FULLONTON J Eld *MS* 19 Oct 1842

SHERMAN Charles m LANGWORTHY Aurelia both of Warrensburgh NY *MS* 5 Aug 1835

SHERMAN Cyrus m FOSTER Betsey of Eaton on 24 May, PARIS C Eld *MS* 21 June 1843

SHERMAN Eleazer m BARTER Susan of Boothbay ME on 5 May at Boothbay ME, ROBINSON N J Eld *MS* 15 June 1842

SHERMAN Elias A m MERRY Ann Maria both of Edgecomb ME on 10 Oct 1847 in Edgecomb, PARKER Lowell Eld *MS* 12 Jan 1848

SHERMAN P R m WALKER Susan on 20th ult, WHALIN James H Rev *MS* 14 May 1834

SHERMAN Samuel of Weathersfield m LUMBARD Zeviah of Windsor VT on 8 inst in Windsor VT, WARNER William Eld *MS* 18 Jul 1838

SHERMAN Washington m MANSFIELD Mananda of Lowell on 3 Jul at Lowell MA, THURSTON N Eld *MS* 2 Nov 1842

SHERMAN Zachariah T of Boothbay ME m WATERMAN Sophia of Litchfield ME on 2 May at Litchfield ME, WATERMAN D Eld *MS* 4 Sept 1839

SHERWOOD Thomas W of Franklinville m PERRIGRO Abigail of Sandinia on 20 Feb at Humphrey NY, WINSOR Barnet Eld *MS* 4 Sept 1844

SHERWOOD William C T of Rockdale m MITCHEL Eunice of Venango PA on Mar 21 in Venango PA, STICKNEY W Eld *MS* 1 May 1844

SHICER William m FLANSBUSGH Susan both of Day NY on 25 Feb 1849 in Day NY, LOVELESS J H Eld *MS* 28 Mar 1849

SHILLIN Moses D m SKILLIN Jane D of Gray ME on 14 Nov 1847 in Gray ME, LANCASTER David Eld *MS* 26 Jan 1848

SHIRLEY John m VARNEY Lydia M of Lowell MA on 26 Mar, THURSTON N Eld *MS* 25 May 1842

SHITE William P of Newburyport MA m SHUTE Nancy M on 17 Dec 1844 at Northwood, JOHNSON W D Eld *MS* 9 Apr 1845

SHOMVEY Isaiah m MOULTON Orinda of Somersworth NH on 21 Mar, WEBBER H Eld *MS* 10 Apr 1844

SHORES John S m BADGER Irene C of New Hampton on 4 Jul, FISK E Eld *MS* 31 Jan 1844

SHORES Thomas m ANDERSON Susan Mrs. see *Madison Banner* (Indiana)? *MFWBR* 22 Feb 1851

SHOREY Henry L m DECATER Margaret A at Great Falls *MFWBR* 24 Mar 1849

SHOREY Hollis m WHEELER Fanny on 18 Mar *MS* 1 May 1844

SHORT George W of Boston m GARLAND Abby on 27 Nov at Barnstead, GARLAND D Eld *MS* 17 Dec 1845

SHORT James m BICKFORD Catherine W of Durham on 17 Aug at Durham, HUTCHINS E Eld *MS* 30 Aug 1843

SHUFF Robinson of Newbury MA at Hampton m BLAKE Harriet, BURBANK P S Eld *MS* 3 Apr 1844

SHUKLING Henry R m HANSON Harriet both of Great Falls NH, CURTIS S Eld at Great Falls *MS* 1 Apr 1840

SHUMAN Aaron of Waldoboro m WILLIAMS Olive Ann of Parsonsfield, JORDAN Z Eld *MS* 4 Feb 1846

SHUMWAY James m PICKERING Charlotte both of Dover on 5 inst, PERKINS J Rev *MS* 15 Jul 1835

SHURBON Daniel m KNOWLES Sarah both of No Hampton in No Hampton, LEAVITT E Eld *MS* 21 Mar 1838

SHURLING Henry R m HANSON Harriet both of Great Falls at Great Falls NH, CURTIS S Eld *MS* 1 Apr 1840

SHURTLEFF Luther B m ROCKWELL Julia A on 1 Feb 1848 in Rochester NY, WHITCHER H Eld *MS* 8 Mar 1848

SHUTE George G m HALL Nancy P of Lee on 14 Nov at Lee, SHERBURNE S Eld *MS* 11 Dec 1844

SHUTE Jeremiah of Northwood m RING Mary Jane of Deerfield, CILLEY D P Eld *MS* 11 June 1845

SIAS John B m PINKHAM Mary E both of Rochester NH on 16 Apr, WEBBER H Eld *MS* 8 May 1844 & *MS* 18 Dec 1844

SIAS Samuel m PARSONS Caroline F both of Rochester on 27 Aug 1848 in Rochester, WHITNEY G W Eld *MS* 7 Feb 1849

SIAS William P m EVENS Belinda both of Salem MA on 5 Apr in Springvale, LORD D H Eld *MS* 16 May 1838

SIBLEY Joel m RUMERY Abigail M of Effingham on 9 May at Effingham NH *MS* 19 May 1847

SILLA William m HICKS Mary in Gorham *MS* 4 Oct 1827

SILLAWAY Abram W of Kingston m HOIT Ann Maria of Rochester in Danville, FULLONTON J Eld *MS* 12 Jan 1842

SILVA Francis J m WALGROVE Hester of New York on 11th inst at New York City, GONSALVES M J Eld *MS* 21 Sept 1842

SILVA John of Madeira m GRAY Sarah Jane on 13th inst at New York City, GONSALVES M J Eld *MS* 21 Sept 1842

SILVER Samuel m CARD Margery of Bowdoinham on 3 Nov of Dexter ME, QUINNAM C Eld *MS* 8 Jan 1845

SIMMONS Holsey m SMITH Celinda W both of East Killingly on 7 inst in East Killingly CT, WILLIAMS Daniel Eld *MS* 22 Jan 1840

SIMMONS Loring of Boston m BATCHELDER Dorothy of Lowell, THURSTON N Eld *MS* 24 Aug 1836

SIMONDS Gideon Jr m SIDERS Lucy J both of Bangor ME on 16 June, SMALL William Eld *MS* 30 June 1847

SIMONDS Samuel G m GORDON Melinda of Hatley LC on 24 Jan at Landaff NH, MOULTON A Eld of Stanstead LC *MS* 13 Apr 1842

SIMPSON Charles H B of Roxbury MA m CORSON Mary E of Dover on Wednesday last at Medbury, SHERBURNE S Eld *MS* 15 Nov 1843

SIMPSON Hezekiah of Sheffield VT m WILLEY Adaline of Sutton, HILL Mark Eld *MS* 16 Jul 1845

SIMPSON James Esq of Hampton m DOW Harriet of Salem MA on 17 inst in Sanbornton, BODWELL Abraham Rev *MS* 25 Oct 1837

SIMPSON John C of Boston m EDWARDS Esther E of Lowell on 1 Sept in Lowell, CURTIS S Eld *MS* 8 Sept 1847

SIMPSON Samuel A m SLEEPER Jane both of Lowell on 11 inst in Lowell, THURSTON N Eld *MS* 25 Jul 1838

SIMPSON Woodbury M m SUMMER Eliza H at Dover NH, THURSTON Nathaniel Eld *MS* 25 Apr 1833

SINCLAIR Alex C of Center Harbor m MERRILL Betsey of Holderness NH on 19 Feb at Tamworth NH, MERRILL W S Eld *MS* 21 Apr 1847

SINCLAIR David of Waterboro m HASTY Mary on 20th inst, CLARK Eld *MS* 26 Mar 1828

SINCLAIR John L Eld of Lynn MA m HAYNES Olive E of Deerfield, KIMBALL John Eld *MS* 30 Aug 1837

SINCLAIR John T m SAVERY Milnerva of Roxbury MA on 27 Dec at Roxbury MA, DAVIS J B Eld *MS* 10 Jan 1844

SINCLAIR Noah m COTTON Hannah both of Meredith on 7 inst in Meredith *MS* 17 May 1837

SINDER Almond m DOLLOFF Elizabeth both of Charlestown MA on 11 Apr in Charlestown MA, WETHERBEE I J Eld *MS* 24 June 1846

SIVER Adam of Milford m CLARK Elmira C of Laurens on 31 Dec 1848 in Laurens NY, CADY S S Eld *MS* 7 Feb 1849

SKILLIN Hiram Eld of the Summer St FWB Church of Bangor m SHEPHERD Henrietta D D on 2 Dec at Herman ME, SHEPHERD M Eld *MS* 7 Jan 1846

SKILLIN James T of Biddeford m MAYO Emily J of Bridgton ME on 3 Sept 1848 in Bridgton ME, PAGE Mr Rev *MS* 27 Sept 1848

SKILLIN Josiah G m LAWRENCE Cyrene E on 26th ult at Gray, ME ORNE W G Esq *MFWBR* 8 Sept 1849

SKILLINGER Leonard m HAMILTON Mary S both of Garland ME on 22 Oct 1848 in Bangor ME, AMES M Eld *MS* 22 Nov 1848

SKILLINGS Cold m IRISH Esther at Gorham ME, HODSDON Caleb *MS* 6 Feb 1834

SKIMER Glover of Lynn m WIGGINS Betsey E of Tamworth NH on 24 Jul in Tamworth NH, MERRIL William S Eld *MS* 1 Nov 1848

SKINNER Daniel M Capt at Sandwich m STRATTON Sarah P, BROOKS N Eld *MS* 1 Oct 1845

SKINNER Lewis m KINNEY Julia both of Royalton on 8 inst in Royalton, DRAKE C B *MS* 22 Nov 1837

SLACK Ransom m BAHONUIN Diantha both of Washington VT on 30 Dec 1847 in Washington VT, SANBORN G Eld *MS* 22 Mar 1848

SLATE Lyman J of Manchester m WORTHEN Abby B of Candia on 12 Nov in Candia, ATWOOD M Eld *MS* 25 Dec 1850

SLATER Benjamin G of Dresden m GATES Semantha of Bolton NY on 10 June, CHASE William Eld *MS* 13 Jul 1836

SLEEPER Charles of Rye m MARSTON Mary D on 5 June at Hampton, BURBANK P S Eld *MS* 12 June 1844

SLEEPER David T m SANBORN Mary Ann of Danville NH on 23 Sept at Danville NH, MERRILL William P Eld *MS* 20 Jan 1847

SLEEPER Geo of Alton m LOCK Mary A of Gilford on 8 Apr, PINKHAM J Eld *MS* 22 May 1844

SLEEPER George of Andover m WALLACE Nancy P on 9 May at Wilmot, WATSON E Eld *MS* 29 May 1844

SLEEPER Hiram m m FRENCH Cordelia in New Sharon ME *MS* 27 Jan 1836

SLEEPER Jonathan m HOWE Harriet, CILLEY D P Eld *MS* 17 Feb 1847

SLEEPER Levi F of Loudon m CLIFFORD Ann Maria of Gilmanton on 3d Aug at Canterbury, FAIRFIELD E B Eld *MS* 13 Aug 1845

SLEEPER Nathan S m HARDY Sarah Ann both of Lowell, THURSTON N Eld *MS* 27 Jan 1836

SLOAN Lewis of Westfield m RAMSDELL Emily of Lafayette, Medina Co, Ohio in Lafayette on Oct 7 1841, VAUGHN Hiram Eld *MS* 26 Jan 1842

SLOAN Peter P m RUDE Sarah A both of Westfield, VAUGHN Hiram Eld *MS* 26 Jan 1842

SLOCUM Seth m BIDSELL Roselinda on 1 Feb 1848 in Hainburgh NY, PLUMB H N Eld *MS* 19 Apr 1848

SLOOM Alexander m GOODWIN Lydia Ann at Lowell MA *MS* 3 May 1843

SLOWMAN John of Woolwich ME m PERKINS Harriet of New Castle on 27 Jul in Woolwich, PERKINS S W Eld *MS* 20 Sept 1837

SLOWMAN Josiah m DREW Lucitta both of Richmond, QUINNAM C Eld *MS* 20 May 1840

SLUSSER Alonzo m LATHROP Julia on 18 Dec at Pike NY, CRANE E R Eld *MS* 18 Jan 1843

SMALL Almer H m FRANK Julia A on 5th inst at Gray ME, LINCOLN Allen Rev *MFWBR* 28 Apr 1849

SMALL Amasa merchant formerly of Alton NH m DOLLOFF Lourenia

SMALL (Continued)

formerly of Sanbornton NH in Lowell, THURSTON N Eld *MS* 5 Apr 1837

SMALL Charles B m SMALL Almira both of Raymond ME on 24 inst in Raymond ME, KEENE J Eld *MS* 8 Apr 1846

SMALL Edward A of Auburn ME m LITTLEFIELD Lydia M of Windham ME at Windham on 16th inst *MFWBR* 27 Mar 1847

SMALL Ezra m LOWELL Hannah N on 9 April, MANSON B S Eld *MS* 7 Feb 1844

SMALL Francis m ADAMS Sally both of Kingsbury ME on 16 June, FOSS Joseph Eld *MS* 24 Jul 1844 (*sic*) should be *MS* 31 Jul 1844

SMALL Ivory of Limington m BEAN Sally at Limington, STEVENS John Eld *MS* 1 Mar 1827

SMALL Jeremiah m PERRY Susan of Biddeford ME on 6th inst *MFWBR* 21 Dec 1850 & m by SMALL Rufus *MS* 18 Dec 1850

SMALL John Jr of Catlin m WOODRUFF Margaret R of Enfield on 19 Aug in Enfield Centre NY, EVENS S R Eld *MS* 10 Oct 1849

SMALL John Jr m JORDAN Esther F on 26 Nov at Raymond ME, KEENE J Eld *MS* 31 Dec 1845

SMALL John m TENNEY Sally Mrs on 26 ult in Raymond, PARKER L Eld *MS* 10 Oct 1849

SMALL Judah m CAMPBELL Diana on 21 Jan at Bowdoin ME, PURINTON Elisha Eld *MS* 10 Mar 1847

SMALL Rufus of Limington ME m STAPLES Harriet of Biddeford ME on Jul 4, AYER Aaron Eld *MS* 10 Jul 1839

SMALL Samuel m LUNT Sarah of Westbrook ME on 19 Feb at Saccarappa ME, HARRIMAN D P Eld *MFWBR* 17 Mar 1849 & *MS* 14 Mar 1849

SMALL T F Capt of Lisbon ME m SMALL Jane E of Freeport ME at North Yarmouth ME on 30th ult *MFWBR* 24 Feb 1849

SMALL William B m RIGGS Rebecca of Portland ME on 5th inst at Portland ME, MOULTON A K Eld *MS* 26 Mar 1845

SMALL William of Wales m RANDALL Melinda of Lewiston ME on 27 Oct, LIBBY I Eld *MS* 13 Nov 1839

SMART Charles m STACKPOLE Sabra both of Parsonsfield ME on 12 May at Great Falls, BROOKS N Eld *MS* 23 May 1849

SMART Charles m BURLEIGH Mary of New Market on 10th inst, HUTCHINS E Eld *MS* 17 Apr 1844

SMART Henry B of Plymouth m CROSBY Miriam R of Swanville ME on 17 Oct 1847 in Dixmont ME, ALLEN Ebenezer Eld *MS* 17 Nov 1847

SMART John of Freedom m JACKSON Amanda at Freedom NH, DAVIS Joseph Eld *MS* 3 May 1843

SMART Moulton B m BURLEIGH Sarah A both of New Market on 13 inst in New Market, CILLEY D P Eld *MS* 26 Apr 1837

SMART Moulton B of New Market NH m McDUFFEE Louisa Ann

SMART (Continued)

Augusta of Alton NH, BUZZELL H D Eld *MS* 3 Mar 1847

SMILEY Oren C m EMERSON Eliza S of Waterville at Waterville ME, LEWIS D B Eld *MS* 17 Feb 1847

SMILEY Simeon m BROWN Rebecca both of Dover on 5 inst, HUTCHINS E Eld in Dover *MS* 8 Jul 1846

SMITH Aaron B MD of Tuftonboro m LEAVITT Harriet M of Dover on 4th inst in Dover NH, PERKINS J Rev *MS* 17 May 1837

SMITH Aaron m JOHNSON Abiah both of West Fairlee VT on 18 Oct 1837 in West Fairlee VT, LEAVITT Stephen Eld *MS* 7 Feb 1838

SMITH Abraham m PEASE Martha of Parsonsfield ME on 9th ult at Kempville NY *MS* 12 Oct 1832

SMITH Alpheus D Eld of Dover NH m TRUE Emily B of Corinth in Corinth VT *MS* 11 Jul 1838

SMITH Amasa of Howard Mich m SPRAGUE Anna formerly of Hartford VT on 22 ult in Hambugh NY, PLUMB H N Eld *MS* 28 June 1837

SMITH Andrew H m BATES Sarah J of St Albans ME on 14 Nov at St Albans, COPP J B Eld *MS* 27 Dec 1843

SMITH Anthony m CRABB Mary E of Portland ME on 3d inst at Portland, ABBOTT H B Rev *MFWBR* 14 Apr 1849

SMITH Artemas m BALDWIN Polly both of Freedom NY on 15 Oct in Freedom NY, PLUMB H N Eld *MS* 20 Dec 1837

SMITH Asa m BEAN Deborah of Waterborough ME on 12 Nov, EMERY Richard Eld *MS* 18 Dec 1844

SMITH Bartlett m GEORGE Rosannah both of Holderness on 2 Apr in Sandwich, TASKER L B Eld *MS* 10 Jul 1850

SMITH Benj M of Farmington ME m BRACKETT Abby of Epsom on 27 Feb 1850 in Epsom NH, RAMSEY G P Eld *MS* 10 Apr 1850

SMITH Benjamin W of Gilmanton m NUTTER Lydia M of Alton NH on 19 Apr, FERNALD S P Eld *MS* 3O Apr 1845

SMITH C A m REYNOLDS Polly both of Lesslie Mich on 22 Feb 1849 in Lesslie, Ingham Co, Mich, DAVIS S H Eld *MS* 4 Apr 1849

SMITH Charles F of Raymond m CRAM Judith H of Deerfield, DAVIS I G Eld *MS* 25 Sept 1844

SMITH Charles M of New Market m JONES Betsey of Durham *MS* 30 Dec 1835

SMITH Curtis of New Hampton m MUDGETT Orinda M of Bristol on 29 June 1848 in Bristol, BROWN Amos Eld *MS* 15 Nov 1848

SMITH Cyrus K m DENNETT Louisa on 25th ult at Hollis, HEALD A Esq *MFWBR* 3 Nov 1849

SMITH Daniel m WILLONGBY Mary Ann of Holderness NH on 31 Jan, TRUE Ezekiel Eld *MS* 19 Apr 1843

SMITH Daniel K of Sandbornton m BENNETT Martha C of Holderness in Holderness, THOMPSON Samuel Eld *MS* 24 Jan 1838

SMITH Daniel m DAVISON Evelina of Starksboro VT on 9 June at

SMITH (Continued)

Starksboro' VT, DIKE Orange Eld *MS* 21 Sept 1842

SMITH David m JELLESON Miriam on 1 Feb 1844 at Saco ME, WITHAM L H Eld *MS* 13 Mar 1844

SMITH David Y of Meredith m POTTER Mary G on 28th ult at Gilford, MANSON Benj S Eld *MS* 4 June 1834

SMITH Ebenezer H m CRAM Sarah both of Meredith on 20 Sept in Meredith, PITMAN S J Eld *MS* 17 Oct 1838

SMITH Ebenezer Jr of Strafford m SMITH Mary of Barrington, PLACE Enoch Eld *MS* 24 Apr 1834

SMITH Ebenezer U of Meredith m CRAM Sarah of Center Harbor, PITMAN Stephen J Eld *MS* 5 Dec 1838

SMITH Edmund m BALDWIN Philenia both of Freedom NY on 15 Oct in Freedom NY, PLUMB H N *MS* 20 Dec 1837

SMITH Edwin A m LEIGHTON Lucinda both of Dover on 2 inst in Dover, HUTCHEINS E Eld *MS* 13 Sept 1848

SMITH Eli m MEECH Minerva both of Yorkshire NY on 28 Feb 1848 in Yorkshire NY, FLYNN W H Eld *MS* 10 May 1848

SMITH Elijah m MOWRY Elizabeth of Smithfield on 23 Nov at Scituate *MS* 14 Dec 1842

SMITH Enoch m HILL Asenath of Danville on 28 Dec of Sutton, GEORGE N K Eld *MS* 24 Feb 1847

SMITH F m WHITE Marilla both of N B on 18 Mar in New Berlin, NY, BYER William C Eld *MS* 2 Apr 1851

SMITH George B m LITCHFIELD Lucinda both of Lewiston ME in Lewiston, CURTIS S Eld *MS* 26 Sept 1838

SMITH George F of N Hampton m LEAVITT Ruth S of Meredith Bridge on 5 Jan, BROOKS N Eld *MS* 8 Feb 1843

SMITH George m FROST Hannah M of Sandwich on 4 June in Sandwich, TASKER L B Eld *MS* 10 Jul 1850

SMITH George of Barnstead m GREEN Rachel H of Pittsfield NH on 27 Mar at Manchester NH, SINCLAIR J L Eld *MS* 6 Apr 1842

SMITH George at Franconia (NH?) m ALDRICH Ann of Lisbon (NH?) on 12 Jul 1842, GASKILL Silas Eld *MS* 19 Apr 1843

SMITH George W Esq Att at Law & editor of *Herkimer Journal* m HADLEY Sarah B on 10 Dec at Salisbury NY, GREEN Rev J *MFWBR* 9 Jan 1847

SMITH Gordon T Eld of Meredith NH m SHERBURN Eliza of Wheelock VT on 3d inst in Wheelock VT, WOODMAN J Eld *MS* 19 Sept 1838

SMITH Harris K of Terre Haute Ind m ORCUT Milison of East Randolph on 22 Aug in East Randolph VT, MOULTON F Eld *MS* 24 Oct 1849

SMITH Herman C m PENNINGTON Mary of Macon Mich on 12 Dec 1845 in Macon Mich, REYNOLDS Ira A Eld *MS* 8 Apr 1846

SMITH Hezekiah m WATERHOUSE Harriette E of Portland ME at

SMITH (Continued)

Portland ME on 30th ult, CHICKERING Rev Mr *MFWBR* 25 May 1850

SMITH Horace of Alfred ME m COOK Hannah Mrs of Rochester on 3d Oct, MEADER Jesse Eld *MS* 27 Dec 1843

SMITH Horatio G m PINGREY Emily B both of Auburn ME on 15 Nov 1849 in Auburn, ATWOOD M Eld *MS* 2 Jan 1850

SMITH Hugh m BUTTERFIELD Lucy Ann on 25th ult at Standish ME, BERRY Asa Esq *MFWBR* 11 Dec 1847

SMITH Ira H m BODGE Bridgett Y of Barrington NH on 27 Mar at Strafford, PLACE E Eld *MS* 12 Apr 1843

SMITH Ira of Standish ME m DECKER Eunice of Gorham ME on 1st ult, WHITE Joseph Eld *MS* 7 Jan 1829

SMITH Isaac of Westbrook m STOVER Lucinda H of Limington ME on 2 Jul, MANSON B S Eld *MS* 7 Feb 1844

SMITH Isaac P m CADY Salome of Oxford, Chenango NY on 20th ult, RUSSELL B A Eld *MS* 24 Apr 1839

SMITH Israel B m WELLS Lucy of Landaff (NH?) on 22 Dec, GASKILL Silas Eld *MS* 19 Apr 1843

SMITH Issachar W m FIFIELD Martha A both of Lamprey River New Market, on 2d inst, CILLEY Daniel P Eld at Strathan *MS* 10 Sept 1834

SMITH Jacob B of Bradford m PARSHLEY Mary Ann of Strafford on 3 May 1849 in Strafford, PLACE E Eld *MS* 23 May 1849

SMITH James F m GLIDDEN Jerusha of Farmington on 10 Dec at Alton NH, FERNALD S P Eld *MS* 3 Mar 1847

SMITH James of Otisfield m FOGG Caroline M of Harrison ME on 9 June in Harrison ME, WIGHT J Eld *MS* 2 Oct 1850

SMITH James m AYER Abigail on 3 Jul at Lowell MA, SINCLAIR J L Eld *MS* 16 Aug 1843

SMITH James W m McNEAL Sarah A both of New Market on 21 Mar in New Market, EASTMAN C Ellea Eld *MS* 24 Apr 1851

SMITH Jesse D of Hollis ME m SMITH Sarah I of Malden MA on 22 June in Biddeford ME, WITHAM L H Eld *MS* 18 Jul 1849

SMITH Jesse W of Dutton ME m SMITH Lydia M of New Market on 20 ult at Lamprey River, CILLEY D P Eld *MS* 30 Dec 1835

SMITH John B of Wendell m FELCH Almira of Bewbury on 16 Nov 1843, MOODY D Eld *MS* 24 Apr 1844

SMITH John E of Hiram ME m HOBBS Miriam of Tamworth NH on 3d Aug, BROOKS John Eld *MS* 20 Aug 1845

SMITH John F S of Monmouth ME m NICKERSON Jedidah of Mercer ME on 2 Feb, JONES A F Esq *MS* 19 Feb 1845

SMITH John Jr m ROGERS Sally G both of Holderness NH on 5 Apr 1848 in Holderness NH *MS* 21 Mar 1849

SMITH John m ELLIOT Naomi both of Brunswick ME on 5 Nov 1849 in Brunswick ME, LIBBY A Eld *MS* 23 Jan 1850

SMITH John in Raymond m OSGOOD Mehitabel *MS* 13 Sept 1837

SMITH John M m EDGERLY Fanny W both of Meredith on 9 May *MS* 15 June 1836

SMITH John of Dover m SEAVEY Ruth E of Alton NH on 3 inst in Dover, HUTCHINS E Eld *MS* 12 June 1850 & *MFWBR* 22 June 1850

SMITH John of New London m JENKINS Hannah U of Pittsfield on 26 ult in Sanbornton, CURTIS C Rev *MS* 31 May 1848

SMITH John P of Centre Harbor m SMITH Eliza of New Hampton at Holderness on 15th inst, TRUE E Eld *MS* 29 May 1844

SMITH Joseph (author of the *Book of Mormon*) m HALE Emma *MS* 30 Jul 1834

SMITH Joseph C of Candia ae 80y m KING Sarah Mrs ae 88y of Hooksett in Hooksett *MS* 8 Aug 1838

SMITH Joseph Harris of Boston MA m FOSS Olive Ann on 26 June in Strafford, PLACE E Eld *MS* 10 Jul 1850

SMITH Joseph m SHANNON Betsey of Hollis on 8 Dec in Buxton ME, WITHAM Lewis H Eld *MS* 15 Jan 1840

SMITH Joseph of Sandwich m WHITEHOUSE Jane A of Dover on 22 Dec *MS* 4 Jan 1837

SMITH Joshua of Biddeford m BEAN Emily J of Brownfield on 23d at Brownfield, TENNEY T J Rev *MFWBR* 3 Feb 1849

SMITH Jutus E m BALL Nancy on 10 Oct at Dryden, GARDNER L G Eld *MS* 15 Jan 1845

SMITH Lewis E m BEAL Emeline S on 15th inst at Great Falls NH, DUNN R Eld *MS* 28 Jul 1847

SMITH Libbey of Brunswick m WHEELER Mary H of Brunswick ME in Bowdoin ME, BEAN C Eld *MS* 2 Aug 1848

SMITH Luther M of Tamworth NH m DOLLOFF Melissa A of Meredith on 4 Mar, BROOKS N Eld *MS* 15 Mar 1843

SMITH Martin H Eld of Huntsburg Ohio m HOLMES Mary Ann of Woster Otsego Co NY on 28 Mar 1849 in Oneonta NY, WING Amos Eld *MS* 6 June 1849

SMITH Morrill B m GARLAND Sarah on 27 Jan at Hampton, BURBANK P S Eld *MS* 5 Feb 1845

SMITH Moses B of Meredith m HUNT Susan M of Gilford on Dec 5, PINKHAM John Eld *MS* 29 Jan 1840

SMITH Moses of Bradley m FENDERSON Lydia A of Jackson on 6 Dec in Jackson ME, RINES J N Eld *MS* 26 Dec 1849

SMITH Moses of Patton m MAGOON Betsey of Stanstead LC *MS* 18 May 1836

SMITH Nahum of Roxbury MA m HILL Joanna C at Waterboro on 25th ult *MFWBR* 18 Dec 1847

SMITH Nathaniel T m WHITE Catherine on 22 Apr at Hodgdon ME, HASKELL G W Eld *MS* 17 May 1843

SMITH Oliver W m BEAN Ann Octavia both of Dexter on 19 Dec

SMITH (Continued)

1837 in Dexter, COPP John B Eld *MS* 9 May 1838

SMITH Orland of Lewiston ME m PEABODY Caroline B of Gorham ME on 20th inst *MFWBR* 30 Nov 1850

SMITH Paul m GOODWIN Abigail both of Lebanon ME in Lebanon ME, LITTLEFIELD W H Eld *MS* 3 May 1848

SMITH Perkins of Kennebunkport ME m WORTH Lois of Biddeford ME on 14 Dec, WITHAM L H Eld *MS* 5 Feb 1845

SMITH R K of Gilbert's Mills m FRINK Louisa of Middleville on 24 Sept in Middleville NY, *MS* 30 Oct 1850

SMITH Robie m PILLSBURY Hannah of Candia on 26 Dec at Candia, ATWOOD M Eld *MS* 8 Jan 1845

SMITH Rufus of Moultonboro m LOVEJOY Nancy P of Meredith, PITMAN Stephen J Eld *MS* 23 Mar 1842

SMITH Samuel A of Gilmanton m NUTE Maria L of Alton NH on 3 Dec 1848 in Gilmanton, FERNALD S P Eld *MS* 27 Dec 1848

SMITH Samuel m BEAN Susan E on 5 Mar at Lowell MA, THURSTON N Eld *MS* 25 May 1842

SMITH Simon of Effingham NH m STAPLES Maria of Newfield, BURBANK S Eld *MS* 1 Oct 1834

SMITH Stephen m SMITH Patience both of Strafford on 2 Mar *MS* 13 Mar 1834

SMITH Stephen L m HACKETT Nancy on 14 Nov in Dracut, CURTIS S Eld *MS* 15 Dec 1847

SMITH T H of Buxton ME m VARNEY Abby L of Windham ME on 10 May 1848, HOBBS A W Eld *MS* 14 June 1848

SMITH Theodore C of Corinna ME m BATCHELDER Sarah E of Garland ME in Bangor ME, AMES M Eld *MS* 22 Nov 1848

SMITH Theodore C m LANCASTER Sarah C of Corinna ME on 10 Jul at St Albans ME, COPP John B Eld *MS* 17 Sept 1845

SMITH Thomas 4th of Litchfield ME m GODFREY Hannah Miss of Wales ME *MS* 21 Mar 1833

SMITH Thomas T at Great Falls NH m GREAT Mary H, DUNN R Eld *MS* 7 Jul 1847

SMITH Timothy H m HODSDON Martha B in Hollis, GOODWIN Timothy Eld *MS* 3 Jul 1829

SMITH Warner m JACKSON Mary A of Freedom on 1 Sept at Freedom NH, PARIS C Eld *MS* 28 Sept 1842

SMITH Warren of Durham m DREW Mary Jane of New Market on 20 Nov, HUTCHINS E Eld *MS* 30 Nov 1842

SMITH Watson of Munroe m PATTE Rosilla of Jackson on 17 inst in Jackson, ALLEN Ebenezer Eld *MS* 4 Oct 1837

SMITH William H m MARBLE Catherine on 28 Aug at Freedom NY, WINSOR Barnet Eld *MS* 15 Mar 1843

SMITH William M m HAWKES Sarah C of Windham ME both of Windham ME, REDLON A Eld *MS* 17 Jul 1844

SMITH William of Hollis m LIBBEY Mary Ann of Scarboro place at
Scarboro ME on 4 May, BEAN C Eld *MS* 8 June 1842

SMITH William of Moretown m HEDGES Jerusha of Northfield VT on
21 Nov 1843, HENDERSON Moses C Eld *MS* 17 Jan 1844

SMITH William P of Concord NH m JOHNSON Mary A on 18 Sept at
Wentworth, MESSER Asa Eld *MS* 25 Oct 1843

SMITH Wilson m WHEELER Betsey both of Ashtabula Co Ohio on 13
Dec 1848 in Trumbull Ohio, COPP John B Eld *MS* 10 Jan 1849

SMITH William C m HOLDEN Abigail M R on 5 May in Otisfield ME,
HUNTRESS D Eld *MS* 15 May 1844

SMITH William D of Manchester m MANUEL Zilpha of Boston MA on
24 Dec 1848 in Manchester, CILLEY D P Eld *MS* 17 Jan 1849

SMITH William HOLMAN m FULLONTON Mary A J Eld in Raymond
MS Dec 15 1847

SMITH William of Kennebunkport ME on 23 June 1847 m GOULD
Hannah J of Biddeford on 25 Nov 1847 in Biddeford, WHITHAM S
H Eld *MS* 25 Aug 1847

SMITH William R m BUTTLES Mary Ann on 20 Feb in Mecca Ohio,
ALDRICH S Eld *MS* 24 Apr 1850

SMITH William W of Lynn MA m SANBORN Lavina of Lamprey River
NH on 7th inst, CILLEY Daniel P Eld *MS* 21 Mar 1833

SMITH Woodbury of Haverhill MA m MELOON Mary E of Dover on
11 Feb 1850 in Effingham, FOSS N Eld *MS* 20 Mar 1850

SMYTH Arthur L of Holderness m DANA Mary J of New Hampton on
2 June, DANA S Eld *MS* 26 June 1844

SNELL Everett m SHEPHERD Sally both of Lowell MA *MS* 11 Mar
1835

SNELL Jerome m LORD Hannah of Eaton at Eaton on 3 Aug,
BROOKS John Eld *MS* 20 Aug 1845

SNELL N Charles m McCRILLIS Mary Jane both of Lowell, BLAIS-
DELL Henry Rev *MS* 26 Jan 1848

SNELL William Jr m CLARK Sally of Eaton NH on 1 Jan at Lowell,
BLAISDELL Henry Rev *MS* 14 Jan 1846

SNOW David S m PULLEN Chloe A B both of Lowell on 10 Sept in
Dracut, CURTIS S Eld *MS* 14 Oct 1846

SNOW Elisha H m DURGIN Irene of Lowell MA on 6 Aug, WOODMAN
J Eld *MS* 23 Aug 1843

SNOW Isaac of Windsor m GREENLEAF Mary wid of late Dea Asa of
Hallowell in Hallowell, CURTIS S Eld *MS* 20 June 1838

SNOW Joseph Capt m MORSE Sarah both of Brunswick ME on 24
Aug 1848 in Brunswick ME, LIBBY Almon Eld *MS* 20 Sept 1848

SNOW Joseph Jr m PATCH Wethy [*sic*] on 11th inst at Eaton,
ATKINSON K Eld *MFWBR* 17 Mar 1849

SNOW Joshua of New Gloucester ME m MORRILL Sarah of Raymond
ME on 25 June 1843, LIBBY James Eld *MS* 8 Nov 1843

SNOW Stephen of Brunswick m PURINTON Thankful S of Bowdoin

SNOW (Continued)
in Bowdoin, ROLLINS A Eld *MS* 12 Jan 1842
SNOW Thomas of Harpswell ME m GIVEN Louiza of Wales ME, FILES A Eld *MS* 21 Jan 1835
SNOWMAN John m CAMPBELL Susan both of Georgetown ME, QUINNAM Constant Eld *MS* 25 Feb 1835
SOPER Henry of Dunkirk m RANSON Lydia in Hainburgh NY, PLUMB H N Eld *MS* 19 Apr 1848
SOUL Eugene m HOYT Martha J on 9 Jan, BELKNAP P W Eld *MS* 26 Mar 1851
SOUL Robert T Capt of Bath ME m WADE Isabella J of Freeport ME, PURINTON A W Eld *MS* 18 June 1845
SOULE Benjamin P m BROWN Almira of Freeport ME on 24 Jan at Freeport ME, PURINTON A W Eld *MS* 14 Apr 1847
SOULE Horace H merchant of Boston MA m HOBBS Elizabeth C at South Berwick *MFWBR* 15 June 1850
SOUTHWICK Jonathan of Northbridge MA m CARPENTER Miranda E of Sutton on 28 Mar in Northbridge MA, PECK B D Eld *MS* 1 May 1844
SPALDING A O of Vestal NY m MOULTON Louisa of Warren on 28 ult in Warren PA, MOULTON O T Eld *MS* 27 Nov 1850
SPARKS Nicholas Capt m GIVEN Silence both of Bowdoinham ME on 28 Oct 1847 in Bowdoinham ME, HATHORN S Eld *MS* 29 Dec 1847
SPARKS William W m WILLIAMS Louisa S of Gardiner on 15 Sept at Gardiner ME, QUINNAM C Eld *MS* 19 Oct 1842
SPAULDING Charles m OSBORNE Ordelia on 29th inst at Murry Orleans Co, CRANE E F Eld *MS* 20 Nov 1844
SPAULDING Joel Jr m TRASK Mary Ann on 1 Jan of Belgrade ME, SPAULDING Joel Eld *MS* 9 Apr 1845
SPEAR David m MAXFIELD Sarah C at Cumberland on 19th ult *MFWBR* 21 Apr 1849
SPEAR James of Roxbury MA m HART Ann of Boston MA on 27th, DAVIS J B Eld *MS* 7 May 1845
SPEAR John P m BLACKWELL Sarah J of Madison on 12th inst, Weston J B Rev *MFWBR* 28 Apr 1849
SPEAR Moses of Vershire m CHEENY Margaret of Washington VT on 3 Feb in Washington VT, SANBORN G Eld *MS* 22 Mar 1848
SPEAR Nathan of Bershire m SANBORN Betsey C of Chelsea VT on 29 Feb in Chelsea VT, SANBORN G Eld *MS* 29 Apr 1846
SPEAR Thomas P of Lancaster m BROWN Caroline M of Newbury on 23 Sept in Newbury, EMERY A Eld *MS* 6 Oct 1847
SPEAR William m POPE Emily of Gardiner ME *MS* 14 Dec 1836
SPENCER Eleazar of Farmersville m VANDOSAN Fanny E of Freedom NY on 22 Feb 1848 in Freedom NY, FLYNN W H Eld *MS* 10 May 1848

SPENCER Hiram P of New Lebanon Colombia Co NY m FOSTER H Lavinia of Hancock MA at Alna on 30 Dec, COLEMAN L B Eld *MS* 2 Mar 1842

SPENCER S J of China m COOK C D Miss on 1st inst at China NY, ANDRUS A C Eld *MS* 23 Jan 1839

SPERRY Philesten of Claremont m ELLIOT Cassandria of Pittsfield on 30 Sept in Pittsfield, BEAN Silas Eld *MS* 7 Nov 1838

SPICER Charles A of Houndsfield m HALL Phedelia of Clayton on 15 Nov at Clayton, GRIFFETH Ansel Eld *MS* 10 Mar 1847

SPILLER Samuel of Liberty m BOYNTON Dorothy of Belmont in Belmont, MEARS Geo Z Eld *MS* 31 May 1848

SPILLER, Wheeler ae 15y m GROSS Sally ae 50y at N Hampton NH *MS* 6 May 1826

SPINNEY David Capt m CHAMBER Sally of Milton on 8 Dec at Wakefield, DUSTIN Caleb Rev "If Mr Dustin wants any more notices published, he must not TAX US with the postage." *MS* 28 Dec 1842

SPINNEY Oliver P m WHITEHOUSE Nancy Ann in Dover, SMITH Eleazar Rev *MS* 29 Nov 1837

SPOKESFIELD Daniel of Campton NH m YEATON Mary O of Gilford NH on 22 Jan 1849 in Gilford NH, FROST D S Eld *MS* 7 Mar 1849

SPOONER Joel m EASTMAN Laura on 3d Mar at Franconia NH, BLAKE C E Eld *MS* 28 Apr 1847

SPRAGUE David D of Huntington m SWEET Mary Ann of Starksboro on 2 Feb in Huntington VT, DIKE O Eld *MS* 26 Feb 1851

SPRAGUE William L m MORSE Lucretia of Phipsburg on 8th inst, LOWELL Tallman Esq *MS* 16 Oct 1839

SPRINGER Andrew m WATSON Caroline both of Richmond in Richmond ME, SWETT Jesse Eld *MS* 22 Aug 1838

SPRINGER David T m ALLEN Martha of Freeport ME on 11 Nov, LIBBY Isaac Eld *MS* 15 Dec 1841

SPRINGER Stephen m HATHORN Eliza F Mrs both of Richmond on 23 Oct in Richmond ME, PURINGTON Collamore Eld *MS* 22 Nov 1848

SPRINGER William m BLAKE Abigail P at Saco ME, WILLIAMS N M Esq *MFWBR* 14 Apr 1849

SPRINGER William m EATON Joanna on 13 March at Mooers, BUNDY Benjamin Eld *MS* 6 Apr 1847

SPRINGFIELD Isaac W m NUTTER Clarinda on 7 Jan at Rochester, PADMAN Eld *MS* 17 Jan 1844

SPURIN Thomas m BROWN Lucy A of Dover NH on 2 Jan at Dover NH, BROCK H H Eld *MS* 8 Jan 1845

ST CERE John C m BOWEN Lydia E in N Scituate, NOYES E Eld *MS* 1 May 1850

ST CLAIR James of Lewiston ME m MOORE Elizabeth R of Saco ME on 18th inst at Saco ME, STRICKLAND G G Rev

ST CLAIR (Continued)
MFWBR 29 June 1850

ST CLAIR Thomas m MOULTON Abigail both of Holderness on 8 Nov 1849 in Tamworth, MERRILL WM S Eld *MS* 5 June 1850

STACEY Elisha S m HUBBARD Anna Maria at Acton on Sunday last, HUBBARD Stephen Esq *MS* 7 June 1843

STACKPOLE Charles m COOK Mary H of Wolfboro' NH on 28 Dec at Wolfboro' NH, BUTLER O Eld *MS* 11 Feb 1846

STACKPOLE Edwin L of Rollinsford m WELCH Mary Jane of So Berwick on 14 Jul in So Berwick ME, JOHNSON W D Eld *MS* 31 Jul 1850

STACKPOLE Ichabod of Kennebunk ME m JENKS Maria A of So Berwick ME on 23 June, JOHNSON W D Eld *MS* 10 Jul 1850

STACKPOLE Isaac of Lebanon m MARSTON Cyrena of Parsonsfield ME on 25th inst at Parsonsfield, LIBBY E Eld *MS* 30 Sept 1831

STACKPOLE Joshua m ALLEN Roseman both of Wolfboro on 5 May *MS* 18 May 1836

STACKPOLE Theodore m PITTS Eliza Miss both of Waterboro ME on 18th ult, HOBBS Eld *MS* 5 May 1830

STACKPOLE Tobias m OSGOOD Eliza at Dover NH *MFWBR* 1 Sept 1849

STACY Andrew m FOSS Elizabeth both of Dover on 27 June 1848 at Strafford Centre, BURBANK P S Eld *MS* 13 Sept 1848

STACY Daniel L of Berwick ME m HOBBS Elizabeth Ann of North Berwick on Thanksgiving at North Berwick ME, LORD D H Eld *MS* 6 Jan 1847

STACY E P m EMERSON Laura A both of Waterville ME on 19 inst in Waterville ME, BEAN G W Eld *MS* 7 Mar 1849

STACY George Jr of Elliot m GUPTIL Mary Ann on 12th inst, DAVIS K R Eld *MS* 29 May 1844

STACY S F of Saco m HARMON Julia A of Standish ME, LIBBY Isaac Eld *MS* 14 Feb 1849

STACY Samuel H K m EASTMAN Mary Jane on 11 Apr at Eaton, RUNNELS J Eld *MS* 30 June 1847

STACY Samuel m HERSOM Nancy on 27th ult at Waterville ME, BURGESS J S Eld *MS* 14 Jul 1847

STACY William 2nd of Berwick m WEYMOUTH Love of No Berwick, BURBANK Samuel Eld *MS* 5 Apr 1837

STAFFORD Charles m EDGELSTON Caroline on 7 Feb 1850 both of Lockport in Lockport Erie Co PA, PAGE J B Eld *MS* 10 Apr 1850

STAFFORD Johnson L on 19 Aug in St Albans ME m BRAND Mary both of Harland *MS* 11 Sept 1850

STANCLIFT Horace B of Saco m HANSCOM Sarah E of New Gloucester on 14 Jan 1849 in Saco ME, WITHAM L H Eld *MS* 24 Jan 1849

STANLEY Benjamin P of So Berwick m SPERLIN Mary Jane of Dover

STANLEY (Continued)

on Sunday last in Dover NH, CAVERNO A Eld *MS* 11 Jul 1849

STANLEY Benjamin P of South Berwick m SPURLIN Mary J *MFWBR* 28 Jul 1849

STANLEY James C m MURCH Mary E both of Lowell on 13 Nov 1847 in Dracut, CURTIS S Eld *MS* 15 Dec 1847

STANLEY Moses C of NY m PEASE Sarah of Wilton ME on 24 June, PREBLE H Eld *MS* 18 Jul 1849

STANLEY Stephen of Tamworth NH m MERRILL Nancy of Parsonsfield on Dec 30, HACKETT J O Eld *MS* 19 Jan 1842

STANTON Benjamin A B of Lebanon ME m COFFIN Catharine P of Wolfborough on 27 Sept 1848 in Wolfborough, COFFIN Stephen Rev *MS* 18 Oct 1848

STANTON Dudley m PRAY Betsey on 22 Sept at Great Falls NH, WEBBER H Eld *MS* 18 Dec 1844

STANTON James B of Lebanon m WHITE Catharine of Saco ME *MFWBR* 5 Apr 1851

STANTON Samuel of Barnston m McCOLLISTER Jane of Barnston LC on 7 Sept in Stanstead LC, MOULTON A Eld *MS* 13 Apr 1842

STANTON Stephen D m HORNE Mary E both of Manchester on 21 Nov 1847 in Manchester, CILLEY D P Eld *MS* 8 Dec 1847

STANWOOD Charles H of Newburyport MA m LAMPREY Rebecca of Hampton NH on 14th inst at Biddeford ME, LORD Rev *MFWBR* 24 Feb 1849

STANWOOD Samuel m WITHAM Amenty on 1st May at Bath ME, HATHORN S Eld *MS* 18 May 1842

STANYAN Newell Jr of Wentworth m BOSWORTH Lucinda of Enfield on 30 Jan 1848 in Enfield, SMITH C H Eld *MS* 1 Mar 1848

STAPLE Nathaniel m BRACKETT Dorcas on Oct 22, MANSON B S Eld *MS* 15 Jan 1840

STAPLES Charles of Ossipee m ABBOTT Lydia M of Dover on 6 inst in Dover, HUTCHINS E Eld *MS* 12 Mar 1851

STAPLES David of Green Lake Wis m LORD Mary C of Brighton ME on 11 Feb 1850 in Brighton ME, PRATT C S Eld *MS* 20 Mar 1850

STAPLES George of Limerick m EMERY Sally of Limington on 16th inst, STEVENS Eld *MS* 26 May 1830

STAPLES Hiram Jr of Limington m WEEKS Nancy B at Parsonsfield, JORDAN Z Eld *MS* 20 May 1840

STAPLES Horton m SIMMONS Eunice of Scituate on 20 Nov at Scituate RI, ALLEN R Eld *MS* 14 Dec 1842

STAPLES Isaac m STAPLES Louisa on 14th inst at Biddeford ME, WITHAM L H Eld *MFWBR* 21 Jan 1849 & *MS* 24 Jan 1849

STAPLES J L K of Gardiner m TRUE Abba on 23 May in Montville ME, KNOWLTON Ebenezer Eld *MS* 20 June 1849

STAPLES John P of Lebanon m LIBBEY Harriet of North Berwick ME on 20 Aug, REDLON A Eld *MS* 27 Sept 1843

STAPLES Josiah M m BLAKE Rachel C on 5 Nov 1849 in Topsham ME, BEAN C Eld *MS* 13 Feb 1850

STAPLES Nathaniel F m CLAPP Margaret A on 25th inst at Portland ME, ALLEN C F Rev *MFWBR* 3 Feb 1849

STAR Damon m VARBERD Susan both of Burns, WEBB George Eld *MS* 20 Sept 1837

STARBIRD Russell m SEAL Margaret A of Westbrook ME on 13th ult at Westbrook, HUSSEY L Rev *MFWBR* 8 Feb 1851

STARK Caleb N m TURNER Theodore M both of Schroeppel NY on 11 Sept, STERRICKER W W Eld *MS* 4 Dec 1850

STARLING Josiah of Monhegan Plantation m STEVENS Julia Ann of Georgetown on 4 Nov in Georgetown ME, DOUGLASS G Eld *MS* 11 Dec 1850

STEARNS Benjamin C m BOODY Loana Mrs on 16 June at Dracut MA, CURTIS S Eld *MS* 7 Jul 1847

STEARNS Daniel m SPRAGUE Fanny both of Hamburgh NY, PLUMB H N Eld *MS* 30 Jul 1834

STEARNS Frank m COOMBS Eliza both of Bradford on 10 Sept in Bradford ME, STROUT J Eld Jr *MS* 16 Oct 1850

STEARNS Isaac N m HALL Julia A of No Providence on 12 inst at Johnston RI *MS* 21 Sept 1836

STEARNS Lorenzo m WARNER Loovsa both of Grafton VT on 26 Nov in Houghtonville VT, EASTMAN C Allen Eld *MS* 11 Dec 1850

STEARNS Moses J m McLELLAN Bertha D at Thomaston ME on 1st inst *MFWBR* 14 Sept 1850

STEARNS Samuel Eld m LATHAM Elizabeth S at Dracut MA on 20 June, CURTIS S Eld *MS* 7 Jul 1847

STEARNS Varus m BALLOU Fanny on 11 Apr at Lowell MA, THURSTON N Eld *MS* 25 May 1842

STEARNS Warren m COPP Susan G both of Manchester on 13 Sept 1848 in Manchester, CILLEY D P Eld *MS* 27 Sept 1848

STEAVEY Dustin Eld of Peterborough m FELCH Mary P of Newbury on 4 Mar, EMERY A Eld *MS* 19 Mar 1851

STEBBINS Edward m BIRD Arminda in Chesterfield MA on Jan 25, CLAP Bela B Esq *MS* 9 Mar 1842

STEEL James Hon of Brownfield m PIKE Dolly M on 25th ult, REMICK Timothy Rev *MS* 1 Dec 1830

STEEL John S of Township Letter B m CORNISH Lucinda of Lisbon on 6 Oct *MS* 28 Dec 1836

STEELE Horace of Roxbury m BATCHELDER Lydia C on 5 June at West Brookfield, CLAFLIN Jehiel Eld *MS* 13 June 1842

STEERE Anthony m ROOK Susannah A of Smithfield on 24 Nov at Smithfield RI, ALLEN R Eld *MS* 14 Dec 1842

STEERE Martin J Eld m RANDALL Abby W of No Scituate on 17 Apr in Mendon, BURLINGAME M W Eld *MS* 23 May 1838

STEERE Wanton m TOURTELLOTT Sarah W on 25 Dec at Glouces-

STEERE (Continued)
ter RI, BRADBURY A R Eld *MS* 18 Feb 1846

STEPHEN James S of Gilford m STEPHEN Matilda of Gilmanton, FERNALD S P Eld *MS* 1 May 1844

STEPHENS Henry of Hallowell ME m COPP Jane B at Augusta ME on 23d ult *MFWBR* 13 Oct 1849

STERLING Seth of Portland in Kittery m TREFERTHERN Mary S of Kittery *MS* 3 Feb 1832

STETSON Allen m HOYT Emily of Rochester on 9 Apr at Rochester WT, COOMBS A Eld *MS* 21 May 1845

STETSON George D of Dorchester MA m COLE Harriet N of Lewiston ME, LIBBY I Eld *MS* 9 Apr 1845

STETSON Josiah H of Dover NH m BROWN Jane of Biddeford ME *MFWBR* 27 Apr 1850

STETSON William P m GIVEN Thankful of Brunswick ME, BEAN C Eld in Brunswick ME *MS* 19 Jan 1848

STEVENS Abial C m FALL Angeline both of Lebanon on 29 Sept in Lebanon, LITTLEFIELD William H Eld *MS* 24 Oct 1849

STEVENS Augustus J m ELLIS Mercy both of Lowell MA *MS* 21 Dec 1836

STEVENS Augustus L of Portland m TYLER Jane S of Brownfield on 28th ult at Portland, CUTLER Rev *MFWBR* 10 Mar 1849

STEVENS Benjamin m HUNT Mary Jane on 27th Jul at Washington VT, GEORGE N K Eld *MS* 14 Aug 1839

STEVENS D L Marquis m WIGGIN Mary both of Dover on Sun last *MS* 19 Oct 1836

STEVENS Daniel C m SEVERENS Ruth both of Salsbury on 20 Apr in Salsbury, KNOWLES E G Eld *MS* 21 June 1848

STEVENS Daniel m DURGIN Susan both of Dixmont, ALLEN Ebenezer Eld *MS* 28 May 1834

STEVENS Daniel of Bangor m SEAVER Lucetta of Corinna ME on 15 Nov 1849 in Corinna ME, ROBINSON N J Eld *MS* 20 Feb 1850

STEVENS David M of Enfield m EASTMAN Rosanna on 12 Feb at Grantham, SMITH C H Eld *MS* 19 Mar 1845

STEVENS Elbridge G m DAY Eliza both of Lowell on 21 Oct in Lowell, WHITNEY Samuel Eld *MS* 7 Nov 1838

STEVENS George A at Gilford m MERRILL Ann M of Gilford, BROOKS N Eld *MS* 30 Aug 1843

STEVENS Henry S of Waterboro m HAYS Elizabeth R of Limerick ME on 16th inst at Limerick, FREEMAN C Rev *MFWBR* 25 Nov 1848

STEVENS Hiram E m REED Julia both of Colebrook on 4 Apr 1849 in No Bangor ME, AMES Moses Eld *MS* 2 May 1849

STEVENS James m GRAY Delia of Monmouth ME at Monmouth ME, FILES A Eld *MS* 28 Feb 1844

STEVENS James D m WHITEHOUSE Sophia of Middleton on 18th inst, SCATES Alvan Esq *MS* 26 Dec 1833

STEVENS James Madison m SADLER Mary Jane Miss, QUINNAM Constant Eld all of Georgetown *MS* 6 Feb 1834

STEVENS John M m SWIFT Elizabeth at Dixmont ME, ALLEN E Eld *MS* 17 Jan 1844

STEVENS John M of Grafton m BATCHELDER Lydia D of Dover on 26 Sept in Dover NH, CAVERNO A Eld *MS* 2 Oct 1850

STEVENS John m AMEE Agnes of Gardiner on 23 May at FWB meeting house in Gardiner village, STAPLES J S K Eld *MS* 2 June 1847

STEVENS Joseph H m JOY Martha of Waterville ME on 24 Mar at Waterville ME, BURGESS J S Eld *MS* 14 Jul 1847

STEVENS Joseph W of Fryeburg ME m GORDON Sarah C of Chatham NH on 31 Dec 1849 in Chatham NH, GUPTILL R W Esq *MS* 20 Feb 1850

STEVENS Lawrence m DAVIS Sally at Raymond *MS* 8 Dec 1841

STEVENS Levi B m LEIGHTON Harriet B in Lowell, THURSTON N Eld *MS* 14 Feb 1838

STEVENS Milton of Smithfield m MERROW Catherine of Waterville ME, LEWIS D B Eld *MS* 25 Dec 1844

STEVENS Moses of Gilmanton m GOWDY Mary Mrs of Ossipee NH on 4 Sept in Wakefield, WALKER John Eld *MS* 14 Sept 1836

STEVENS Nathaniel F Capt m CHOAT Huldah A both of Sandwich on 19 ult in Sandwich, PINKHAM John Eld *MS* 12 Jul 1837

STEVENS Nathaniel of Belfast m FREEMAN Jane of Westbrook on 23d ult at Saccarappa, NEVINS William P Eld *MFWBR* 9 Nov 1850

STEVENS Philip m HOLT Eliza both of Pembroke on 5 Jul in Manchester, CILLEY D P Eld *MS* 11 Jul 1849

STEVENS Richard m SADLER Caroline on 3 Dec in Georgetown, WEBBER D Eld *MS* 2 Jan 1839

STEVENS Theodore Eld m BRACKET Susan both of Acton ME, STEVENS J Eld *MS* 6 Apr 1836

STEVENS William C m ALLEN Drusilla A on 16 Oct at Dixmont ME, ALLEN E Eld *MS* 17 Jan 1844

STEVENS William P of Gorham m LIBBY Mary of Sweden on 28 Dec 1837 in Sweden, WHITNEY George Eld *MS* 17 Jan 1838

STEVENSON W S Mr m PHILBRICK Diantha on 6 June at Lowell MA, CURTIS S Eld *MS* 7 Jul 1847

STEWARD S T Rev, Presbyterian minister of Connersville Indiana m HUGGINS Sophia G of Delaware on 5 Nov, KELLEY Richard Eld *MS* 25 Dec 1844

STEWART Asa of Kittery ME m CHANEY Emily of South Berwick ME on 6 May at South Berwick ME, CHANEY John Eld *MS* 14 May 1845

STEWART Cyrus K m EVANS Susan, SMITH C H Eld at Warner on 20 Feb *MS* 19 Mar 1845

STEWART David W of Garland ME m PACKARD Rebecca of Exeter

STEWART (Continued)
ME, AMES M Eld *MS* 14 Apr 1847

STEWART Isaac D Eld of Meredith NH m RICE Elizabeth G of Henniker of Contoocookville on 8th Feb, FROST D S Eld *MS* 26 Apr 1843

STEWART James m NORTON Persis at Middlebury NY on 25 Dec, ROLLIN D M L Eld *MS* 11 Feb 1846

STEWART James W m HAMILTON Hannah F in Garland ME on April 17, AMES M Eld *MS* 4 May 1842

STEWART Joseph M of Glenburn ME m HAMILTON Catharine E of Garland on 24 Sept 1848 in Bangor ME, AMES M Eld *MS* 22 Nov 1848

STEWART Thomas H of Center Square m STONE Effy of Harmony ME on 11 Jul 1848 in Harmony ME, WALKER G S Eld *MS* 2 Aug 1848

STICKNEY W Eld an itinerant preacher m CUMMINGS Clarissa H of Venango on 28 Aug in Venango PA, FOWLER Josiah Eld *MS* 26 Sept 1838

STILES John m THOMPSON Esther D of Lowell, CURTIS S Eld *MS* 17 Jul 1844

STILES Joseph m FOSS Hannah W both of Strafford on 10 Jan 1849, BURBANK P S Eld *MS* 24 Jan 1849

STILES Joseph m GOVE Hannah both of Portsmouth NH on 22 ult at Strafford, PLACE E Eld *MS* 15 Apr 1835

STILES Lewis m SLOPER Hannah S on 29 Jan at Strafford, PLACE E Eld *MS* 12 Mar 1845

STILES William m GOODWIN Mary A of Portsmouth NH on 26 Sept at Portsmouth NH, MERRILL William P Esq *MS* 10 Oct 1844

STILHAM Nathaniel m HERSEY Catherine of Lineus ME on 24 Apr at Hodgdon ME, HASKELL G W Eld *MS* 17 May 1843

STILL Abiel of Hatley m HOWE Hannah of Stanstead LC on 17 Jan *MS* 17 Feb 1836

STILL Benjamin m LIBBY Clarinda of Lowell on 2 Mar, THURSTON Nathaniel Eld *MS* 10 Apr 1839

STILLINGS Benjamin of No Berwick m SHOREY Pheby of Limington ME *MS* 4 Apr 1833

STILLINGS Daniel m WEBSTER Cynthia at Dover NH, THURSTON Nathaniel *MS* 25 Apr 1833

STILLINGS Leander of Boston m TIBBETTS Abigail of Lowell on 2 Dec in Lowell, THURSTON N Eld *MS* 12 Dec 1838

STILSON James m WATSON Harriet of New Market on 2 Sept at New Market, CILLEY D P *MS* 11 Sept 1839

STILSON James m CHAPMAN Viana D of New Market on 1 June at New Market, FROST D S Eld *MS* 11 June 1845

STILSON John R of Durham NH m JOHNSON Mary A of Portland on 8 Oct 1848 in Saccarappa ME, HARRIMAN D P *MS* 18 Oct 1848

STIMPSON Nathaniel of Bath m HUNT Abby of Brunswick ME on 5 inst in Brunswick ME, LIBBY A Eld *MS* 22 Aug 1849

STIMSON John N m DREW Hannah on Thurs last in Newfield, FREEMAN Charles Rev *MS* 28 June 1827

STIMSON Thomas T m EATON Eliza both of Limerick ME *MS* 29 Sept 1830

STIMSON Thomas T of Limerick ME m GILPATRICK Eliza on 21st ult in Limerick ME, FREEMAN C Rev *MFWBR* 3 Jul 1847

STIMSON William of Limerick m LORD Mary of Parsonsfield ME on 16th ult, MOULTON S Eld *MFWBR* 1 Jan 1848

STINNEFORD Nicholas m PATTEN Caroline on 9 Nov of Saco ME, JACKSON Daniel Eld *MS* 6 Apr 1847

STINSON William C 2d of Pittsfield m JACK Mary Jane of Monmouth ME in Litchfield, QUINNAM C Eld *MS* 8 Mar 1848

STOCKMAN Edward A Rev of Limington ME m THOMAS Elizabeth A of Standish (Steep Falls) on 26th inst at Steep Falls ME, Hobson A Eld *MFWBR* 30 Oct 1847

STODDARD George m WOOSTER Elizabeth both of Middleville on 21 inst in Middleville NY, TALLMAN E P Eld *MS* 15 Jan 1851

STODDARD George R m BOYNTON Laura E both of Walworth on 25 Oct in Walworth NY, HOLMES D G Eld *MS* 15 Jan 1851

STODDARD Henry R m NUTE Sophia both of Wolfborough NH on 30 June in Wolfborough, LUCAS W K Eld *MS* 24 Jul 1850

STODDARD Nelson m NICKERSON Abigail on 2 Apr in Barrington Nova Scotia, HENDERSON Moses C Eld *MS* 5 May 1846

STOKES Daniel m MEADER Martha of Lowell MA on 25 Dec at Lowell MA, THURSTON N Eld *MS* 25 May 1842

STOKES Daniel H m PARKER Mary Lucinda on Fast day eve at Dover NH, PERKINS S W Eld *MS* 23 Apr 1845

STOKES Dudley L m MERRILL Eliza W in Lowell, THURSTON N Eld *MS* 23 May 1838

STOKES Ebenezer m JONES Jane both of Starksboro in Huntington VT on 21 Nov 1841, DIKE Orange Eld *MS* 19 Jan 1842

STOKES Joel L m DeMYER Nancy D on 9 Oct at Lowell MA at Lowell MA, THURSTON N Eld *MS* 2 Nov 1842

STOKES Jonathan m HAM Sarah Jane both of Dover on last Saturday eve in Dover NH, CAVERNO A Eld *MS* 12 Dec 1849 & *MFWBR* 22 Dec 1849

STOKES Moses F m BROWN Patience C on 24 Jan at Starksborough VT, BIXBY N W Eld *MS* 23 Apr 1845

STONE Ansel m ADAMS Martha Ann of Unity on 1 Apr in Unity ME, WATERMAN D Eld *MS* 8 May 1850

STONE Asa P formerly of Newfield ME m DAY Louiza on 27 ult in Ipswich, FITZ Rev *MS* 6 June 1838

STONE Benj Jr of Dorchester MA m CLAY Ursula of Hooksett NH, MANSON B S Eld *MS* 12 Dec 1838

STONE Elisha F m TOWNSON Miriam at Limerick ME, FREEMAN C Rev *MFWBR* 24 Feb 1849

STONE George m KENNISON Elizabeth both of Berwick ME at No Berwick ME *MS* 8 Jul 1835

STONE George S m WILSON Mary M on 25 Nov at Dracut MA, CURTIS S Eld *MS* 18 Dec 1844

STONE H P of Lowell m BOWERS Mary of Dracut in Lowell, THURSTON N Eld *MS* 9 Aug 1837

STONE John B of Foster RI m GRASON Susan of Killingly CT, WILLIAMS D Eld *MS* 10 Oct 1844

STONE Joseph m GOODWIN Miranda on 18 Oct of Lowell at Wilmington MA, DURGIN J M Eld *MS* 22 Feb 1843

STONE Levi m HAZELTINE Elizabeth J on Sunday last in Limerick ME, LIBBY Eld *MS* 22 Nov 1827

STONE Nathan m JOHNSON Elizabeth on 14 Aug in Austinburg Ohio, COPP I B Eld *MS* 10 Oct 1849

STONE Royal of Andover NH m CURRIER Ruth of Canterbury on Apr 7 in Loudon, CLOUGH Jeremiah Eld *MS* 15 Apr 1840

STONE Samuel M of Biddeford m WHITTEN Abigail T of Cornish on 26 Apr 1849, RAND James Eld *MS* 16 May 1849

STONE William F of Auburn ME m HARRIS Olive R of North Yarmouth, LIBBEY Isaac Eld *MS* 27 Nov 1844

STONE William 3d m COOMBS Abigail both of Augusta on 21 Oct 1847 in Augusta ME, WEAVER P Eld *MS* 17 Nov 1847

STONE William C m RICHARDSON Eunice L on 21 Oct in Manchester, CILLEY D P Eld *MS* 14 Nov 1849

STONKS Josiah H m CLARK Deborah S of Lowell MA on 20 May, WOODMAN J Eld *MS* 23 Aug 1843

STORER Horace P of Portland ME m BARKER Mary T on 14th ult at Limerick ME, FREEMAN C Rev *MFWBR* 8 May 1847

STORER William of Limington m LORD Elizabeth of Limerick ME at Limerick, BURBANK Abner Esq *MFWBR* 18 Jan 1851

STORY Isaac S m BEAN Caroline A both of Underhill VT on 15 Sept in Underhill VT, FAY Edward Eld *MS* 6 Nov 1850

STORY Job m STORY Lucy *RI* Apr 1822 p 63

STORY Martin m TUPPER Alma M both of Underhill on 7 Jul 1850 in Underhill VT, DIKE O Eld *MS* 14 Aug 1850

STOWELL Joseph H m BEAN Mary at Bangor ME, CAVERNO A Eld *MS* 13 Sept 1843

STOWELL Luther J of Gray ME m DAY Mary J of Cumberland ME on 2d inst at Cumberland, BLAKE Mr Rev *MFWBR* 12 May 1849

STOWERS Francis of Farmington m BUTLER Lovina on 3d June 1846, WHEELER S Eld *MS* 21 Apr 1847

STRAFFORD John B m CROUCH Harriet L of Smithfield on 2nd inst at Johnston RI, HUTCHINS E Eld *MS* 19 Nov 1834

STRAFFORD Warren C m MERRILL Lovina on 26 Mar at Bath,

STRAFFORD (Continued)
    MOULTON F Eld *MS* 23 Apr 1845
STRATTON Jonathan m TETHERLY Nancy B both of Dover on 19
    inst in Dover, HUTCHINS E Eld *MS* 22 Nov 1848
STRATTON William m BERRY Jemima both of Dover in Dover on 20
    Mar 1842, MOULTON A K Eld *MS* 23 Mar 1842
STRAW Andrew W m CROSS Maranda in Hustisford Dodge Co Wis,
    JONES Almon Eld *MS* 4 Apr 1849
STRAW David R Esq of Gilford m AYER Caroline Augusta Miss of
    Sangerville ME, WILLIAMS T Rev *MS* 21 Nov 1833
STRAW Ezra m GLIDDEN Mercy on 24 Apr 1845 at Gilmanton NH,
    HAM Ezra Eld *MS* 28 May 1845
STRAW Gideon Jr of Newfield m STAPLE Lucy of Waterborough on
    Thurs last, BURBANK Eld *MS* 17 Jan 1828
STRAW Josiah m WYMAN Joanna both of Manchester in West
    Plymouth, CHASE Paul Eld *MS* 4 Oct 1848
STREETER Joel P of Scriba m JOHNSON Adaline of New Haven on 1
    Dec in New Haven NY, STANLEY M C Eld *MS* 12 Dec 1849
STREETER Warren m HILDRETH Mary A both of Lowell in Lowell,
    THURSTON N Eld *MS* 8 Jan 1840
STRICKLAND Lucius L of Waterway m ABBOT Saphronia H of Straf-
    ford VT, SWETT David Eld *MS* 13 Mar 1839
STRONG Richard W m CROWELL Emma Ann on 3 Apr at Boston,
    GARLAND G D Eld *MS* 16 Apr 1845
STROUT Albert D m KIMBALL Hannah Jane on 16 Jan 1845 at
    Cornish ME, RAND J Eld *MS* 5 Feb 1845
STROUT Albert m BICKFORD Eliza both of Charleston ME on 9 Sept
    1847 in Garland ME, AMES M Eld *MS* 2 Feb 1848
STROUT James of Raymond ME m BARTON Merande, SMALL C Eld
    MS 29 Nov 1843
STROUT Sewall C Esq of Bridgton m SHAW Octavia JP of Portland
    ME *MFWBR* 1 Dec 1849
STROUT Solomon Jr of Portland ME at Gorham ME m FILES Eunice
    of Gorham ME, SINCLAIR J L Eld *MS* 11 Feb 1846
STUBBS John of Cumberland ME m SAWYER Julia Ann of Gray ME
    on 8 Oct in Gray ME, LANCASTER David Eld *MS* 26 Jan 1848
STUFF Benj m RICHARDS Jane both of Jenner, Somerset Co PA on
    25 Apr, SMUTZ S G Eld *MS* 15 May 1844
STURDY William m KEECH Mary Ann both of Mendon on 17 ult *MS*
    4 May 1836
STURER John m TAYLER Julia Ann both of this town (Dover NH) on
    23d ult at Effingham, DAVIS Joseph Eld *MS* 20 Mar 1834
STURGIS Benjamin K m ELDER Keziah both of Gorham on 1 Nov at
    Windham, ROLLINS A Eld *MS* 6 Jan 1836
STURGIS Nathaniel G of Danville in Standish ME m MOORE Betsey
    A *MS* 12 Jul 1837

SUITS John P of Mindon m SMITH Sarah of Otsego on 4 Jan 1849 in Otsego NY, CADY S S Eld *MS* 7 Feb 1849

SULLIVAN Charles of Tuftonborough NH m TATE Nancy of Kennebunk ME on 4 Jan 1849 in Tuftonborough NH, BEAN Silas F *MS* 9 May 1849

SULLIVAN Joseph A m CARD Lydia M both of Charlestown RI on 13 Apr in Carolina Mills RI, WILLIAMS A D Eld *MS* 22 May 1850

SUMMER Farmer m CASE Emily both of Chester Dodge Co WT on 16 Dec 1847, WRIGHT E N ELD *MS* 16 Feb 1848

SUMMERS C T M m HATCH Adaline L both of Manchester in Manchester, CILLEY D P Eld *MS* 11 Jul 1849

SUTHERLAND George W m HALL Mary E at Saco ME *MFWBR* 23 June 1849

SUTTON John Capt m AMES Lydia on 20 Mar at Parsonsfield ME, JORDAN Z Eld *MS* 16 Apr 1845

SWAIN Abraham D of Chichester m EATON Almira of Pittsfield *MS* 13 Jul 1836

SWAIN Alvah T m WEEKS Sarah F on 3 Dec, PITMAN Stephen J Eld *MS* 14 Feb 1844

SWAIN Bennet E m SWAIN Martha J on 7 Jan 1849 in Barrington, SHERBURNE S Eld *MS* 31 Jan 1849

SWAIN Calvin m EVANS Nancy J both of Dover on 27 ult in Dover, CLARK Mayhew Eld *MS* 10 Jan 1849

SWAIN Charles F m WEEKS Caroline E both of Gilford on 22 Oct 1848 in Alton NH, PINKHAM John Eld *MS* 1 Nov 1848

SWAIN Dudley T of Denmark ME m BEAN Comfort Ann of Meredith on 15 June, PITMAN J Stephen Eld *MS* 26 Sept 1849

SWAIN George W m PITMAN Elizabeth Ann both of Meredith, PITMAN Stephen J Eld *MS* 13 May 1840

SWAIN George W SANDERS Mary C both of Epsom on 6 Sept in Epsom NH, SWAIN William Eld *MS* 5 Dec 1849

SWAIN Harrison Jr at Meredith NH m FARRAR Lovina B of Meredith NH, PITMAN Stephen J Eld *MS* 5 May 1847

SWAIN Hezekiah M m PITMAN Hannah on 28 Oct in Meredith, PITMAN Stephen J Esq *MS* 17 Nov 1847

SWAIN Jesse m THAYER Rachel both of Lowell in Lowell, THURSTON N Eld *MS* 20 June 1838

SWAIN John D m ROLLINS Elizabeth E both of Dover on 31 inst in Dover, HUTCHINS E Eld *MS* 3 Jan 1849

SWAIN John L of Meredith NH m BATCHELDER Olive C, PITMAN Stephen J Eld *MS* 27 Nov 1839

SWAIN John M L m FOLSOM Hannah L both of Meredith, PITMAN S J Eld *MS* 11 Dec 1850

SWAIN John Quincy Adams m SWAIN Sarah Jane both of Barrington on 12 Mar in Barrington, SHERBURNE S Eld *MS* 2 Apr 1851

SWAIN Richard m CHESLEY Betsey both of Barrington on 25th ult,

SWAIN (Continued)
SHERBURNE Samuel Eld *MS* 9 Dec 1835

SWAIN Samuel m CHESLEY Susan M both of New Market Lamprey River NH on 24th *MS* 4 May 1836

SWAIN Warren P of New Market NH m STILSON Ednah A of Durham on 24 Jul, HUTCHINS E Eld *MS* 3 Aug 1842

SWAIN William of Meredith NH m FRENCH Lucinda at Meredith NH, PITMAN S J Eld *MS* 25 Dec 1844

SWAN Horace T of New Hampton m LANE Betsey C on 24 May, FISK E Eld *MS* 31 Jan 1844

SWAN Joel Esq m DANIELS Abigail both of Strafford on 2nd inst, WINKLEY John Eld *MS* 18 Mar 1840

SWASEY Henry S of Milton Mills m KIMBALL Mary R on 25 Nov 1847 (Thanksgiving Eve) in Wakefield, BARKER Nathaniel Esq *MS* 8 Dec 1847

SWASEY Henry W m BLAISDELL Mary C of Gilford on 8 Nov at Gilford, PERKINS Seth W Eld *MS* 16 Dec 1846

SWASEY Rufus L m PINKHAM Laurana W on 12 Sept at Lowell MA, WOODMAN J Eld *MS* 19 Oct 1842

SWASY Frederick T m HAYES Julia Ann in Berwick ME, FREEMAN Charles Rev *MS* 3 Feb 1832

SWEAT Artemas K m MORRISON Maria L of Canaan on 12 Jul of Bethlehem, BEAN Beniah Eld *MS* 4 Feb 1846

SWEET Henry m SPRAGUE Lovina both of Huntington on 20 Sept in Huntington VT, DIKE Orange Eld *MS* 6 Nov 1850

SWEET Lorain B of Smithfield m MANCHESTER Lucy M of Providence RI on 28 Dec 1847 in Smithfield RI, STETSON J A Eld *MS* 2 Feb 1848

SWEET Lorenzo of Boston MA m LOVE Kepsa of Yorkshire NY on 26 Jul 1843 JACKSON N A Eld *MS* 9 Aug 1843

SWEET Samuel W m PIERCE Julia A both of Huntington VT on 18 Feb 1848 in Huntington VT, DIKE Orange Eld *MS* 5 Apr 1848

SWEETLAND James H on 6th inst m BURLENGAME Emelin in Johnston, HUTCHINS E Eld *MS* 15 Apr 1835

SWETT Bernice of Standish m THORN Jane of Portland ME at Portland ME, SHAW S Eld *MFWBR* 27 Mar 1847

SWETT Charles m GIVEN Mary L both of Wales, FILES A Eld *MS* 29 Dec 1847

SWETT Charles m HIGGINS Submit Miss both of Wales, CURTIS S Eld *MS* 3 Mar 1830

SWETT Daniel of Waterboro m WAKEFIELD Sarah C of Hollis on 29th ult, HOBBS H Eld *MS* 20 Apr 1832

SWETT David P of Windham ME m STURGIS Louann of Gorham ME on 31 ult at Windham *MS* 20 Jan 1836

SWETT Jesse Eld of Richmond m SANFORD Bernice of Bowdoinham ME on 24th ult *MS* 16 Jan 1834

SWIFT Dean of Sidney m HANSON Catherine of Mt Vernon in Mt Vernon ME, CURTIS Silas Eld *MS* 29 Mar 1837

SWINERTONS Amos m HARRIMAN Betsey both of Somerworth on 11 inst in Dover NH, GREEN Silas Rev *MS* 21 Nov 1838

SWITZER Gilman m SIMPSON Clarissa of Sheffield VT on 1 Jan, HILL Mark Eld *MS* 16 Jul 1845

SYLVESTER Joseph m YOUNG Thankful of Freeport ME on 27 Apr at Bowdoin ME, PURINTON A W Eld *MS* 18 June 1845

SYLVESTER Merritt m BRACKETT Roxanna both of Brunswick ME on 29 Oct 1848 in Brunswick ME, LIBBY Almon Eld *MS* 15 Nov 1848

SYLVESTER Parker of Phippsburg ME m OLIVER Patience of Georgetown, TODD Nathaniel Esq *MS* 9 Feb 1831

SYLVESTER Ruggles m HOWARD Harriet Newell both of Leeds ME *MS* 22 Apr 1840

SYLVESTER Sewall m FOSTER Mary J on 15 June at Chesterville ME, WHEELER S Eld *MS* 6 Aug 1845

SYMMES Eben m BOOTHBY Martha A both of Newfield on 30 Sept in Parsonsfield ME, SMITH William Eld *MS* 31 Oct 1849

SYMONDS Henry A m WHITE Abby F on 4 Dec at New Gloucester ME, KEENE J Eld *MS* 31 Dec 1845

TABOR Ebenezer m GRAY Phebe P of Montpelier VT on 14 Jul at Montpelier VT, GRAY Ira Eld *MS* 2 Oct 1844

TABOR John Jr m THOMPSON Sarah both of Great Falls NH on 7 May at Great Falls, BROOKS N Eld *MS* 16 May 1849

TAGGARD Cyrus H m PHILLIPS Ann E both of Boston on 6 inst in Hampton, MERRILL William P Eld *MS* 19 Sept 1849

TALLANT David m MOOR Lucretia both of Canterbury on 25th ult at Canterbury, HARPER J M Hon *MS* 9 Sept 1835

TALLANT Masten M of Canterbury m LOCK Annah L of Allenstown on 30 Nov 1848 in Concord, CATLIN S T Eld *MS* 17 Jan 1849

TANK James of Boston m SANBORN Elmira of Gilford on 8 June in Gilford, PINKHAM John Eld *MS* 12 Jul 1837

TANNER Geo W W of Ellington m SMITH Philena of Sheridan in Sheridan NY, BROWN Eld of Forrisville *MS* 8 Aug 1838

TAPLEY William T of Dedham MA m HALE Martha A of Litchfield ME on 4 June 1848 in Litchfield ME, QUINNAM C Eld *MS* 14 June 1848

TAPLIN Caleb of Corinth VT m COLBY Harriet K Mrs on 28 Feb at Franconia, BLAKE C E Eld *MS* 28 Apr 1847

TAPPAN Daniel m WITTUM Naomi both of Sandwich on 17 ult in Sandwich, PINKHAM John Eld *MS* 27 Sept 1837

TAPPAN Daniel m HADLEY Rhoda both of Sandwich on 7 Nov, BROOKS N Eld *MS* 1 Dec 1847

TARBOX Daniel Jr of Phillips ME m TAYLOR Hannah P of Jay on 21

TARBOX (Continued)
   Mar at Jay ME, WATERMAN D Eld *MS* 19 Apr 1843
TARBOX Joseph G m PATRICK Hannah W at Buxton ME on 2 Feb at
   Buxton ME, SINCLAIR J L Eld *MS* 11 Feb 1846
TARBOX Joseph m SMITH Abigail L of Hollis on 4 Dec at Hollis ME,
   SINCLAIR J L Eld *MS* 7 Jan 1846
TARBOX Moses m STAPLES Miriam on 16 Oct 1842 at Biddeford,
   WITHAM L H Eld *MS* 1 Mar 1843
TARBOX Samuel Jr m HODGDON Olive P both of Westport on 26 ult
   MS 4 Jul 1838
TARBOX Thomas of Limerick ME m BEEDELL Hannah of Parsons-
   field ME on Sunday last, BUZZELL John Eld *MS* 29 June 1826
TARR Benjamin of Hallowell m CURTIS Catharine of Whitefield at
   Whitefield, QUINNAM C Eld *MS* 10 Oct 1833
TARR Daniel M of Webster m GROVER Hannah of Bowdoin ME on
   11 Jan 1849 in Freeport ME, PURINTON A W Eld *MS* 24 Jan
   1849
TARR Isaac m WOODWARD Nancy on 30 Mar at Lewiston ME,
   WOODWARD William Esq *MS* 1 May 1834
TASKER Alfred m HILL Mary M both of Strafford, PLACE E Eld *MS*
   22 Apr 1840
TASKER Charles C of Strafford m KNOWLES Hannah C of North-
   wood NH on 4 Dec 1847 in Northwood NH, JOHNSON W D Eld
   MS 12 Jan 1848
TASKER Eben of Ossipee NH m PHILBROOK Elizabeth M of Man-
   chester on 13 June at Manchester, TILLOTSON Rev *MFWBR* 17
   Jul 1847
TASKER Elisha m WALDRON Hannah B (widow of the late Simon
   BATCHELDER of Northwood) on 3 Feb at Northwood, COGSWELL
   E C Rev *MS* 17 Feb 1847
TASKER Ichabod of Strafford m MARTIN Huldah O of Williamstown
   VT on 7 Dec 1847 in Williamstown VT, SANBORN G Eld *MS* 12
   Jan 1848
TASKER Jonathan m MOODY Louis both of Somersworth on 9 ult in
   Great Falls, STEVENS Theodore Eld *MS* 10 Oct 1838
TASKER Levi B of Strafford m CASWELL Hannah P of Northwood on
   19 Aug in Northwood, FERNALD S P Eld *MS* 7 Nov 1838
TASKER Paul Jr m HANSCOM Ruth S both of Strafford on 16 Nov
   1847 in Northwood NH, JOHNSON W D Eld *MS* 12 Jan 1848
TASKER Paul m HILL Polly both of Strafford on 20th *MS* 30 Mar
   1836
TASKER Vincent P of Strafford m WALKER Hannah W of Strafford
   on 27 Sept, PLACE E Eld *MS* 16 Nov 1842
TATE John of Corinth ME m GERRY Silvinia of Dover ME on 24,
   AMES M Eld *MS* 14 Apr 1847
TATE Joshua R at Corinth ME m WHITEAR Amanda of Corinth,

TATE (Continued)

AMES M Eld *MS* 20 Jan 1847

TATE Josiah m HULL Annar both of Dover NH on 12 inst *MS* 18 Jan 1837

TATMAN Elias Jr m WINTER Elmira both of Phipsburgh ME *MS* 25 Mar 1835

TATMAN Elias m WINTER Elmira, BOYINGTON John Rev in Phipsburgh *MS* 8 Apr 1835

TAUNTON P Folsom of Taunton MA m EATON Emily on 13 inst in South Reading, ROBBINS Lemuel Eld *MS* 26 Sept 1838

TAYLER Andrew S of W Stephentown m HICKS Mary Jane of Nassua NY on 18 Apr 1848 in Brainerd's Bridge, COLEMAN I B Eld *MS* 7 June 1848

TAYLOR A Eld of Burlington ME m SPRILLER Abigail S of Passadumkeag ME on 2 Dec in Passadumkeag ME, MESSER A P Rev *MS* 29 Dec 1847

TAYLOR Alexander m GELLERSON Philena on 30 Jul at Weston ME, GELLERSON George W *MS* 23 Aug 1843

TAYLOR Alfred m CATE Sally S *MS* 23 Nov 1836

TAYLOR Asher m GAFFIELD Miranda on 30 Dec at Roxbury MA, DAVIS J B Eld *MS* 22 Jan 1845

TAYLOR Benjamin m WILLEY Charlotte Mrs both of Dover on 20 inst in Dover, HUTCHINS E Eld *MS* 27 Dec 1848

TAYLOR Daniel of Porter m TOWLE Mary Jane of Freedom on 29 Dec, BUTLER O Eld *MS* 19 Feb 1845

TAYLOR Ephraim m PACKARD Delia Mrs of Livermore ME on 7 Aug 1843 at Livermore ME, MOULTON F Eld *MS* 3 Apr 1844

TAYLOR George W m BIGELOW Elizabeth on 22 Apr at Norridgewock ME, BOWDEN Stephen Eld *MS* 14 May 1845

TAYLOR John M m CHASE Louisa E of Waltham MA on 30 Nov at Northwood, ATWOOD Mark Eld *MS* 17 Dec 1845

TAYLOR John of So Weymouth MA m LEIGHTON Betsey Ann of Waterborough ME, EMERY Richard Eld *MS* 22 Dec 1847

TAYLOR John W m HANSON Abigail at Lyman *MFWBR* 3 Mar 1849

TAYLOR Jonathan of Lisbon m EASTMAN Susan of Whitefield NH on 30 Aug in Whitefield NH, SHEPHERD Almon Eld *MS* 26 Dec 1849

TAYLOR Justin m KIES Nancy of Windsor VT, ADAMS Abel Eld *MS* 6 Feb 1839

TAYLOR Nathaniel H m FREESE Phebe Ann both of Sandwich NH on 9 Feb 1848 in Sandwich NH, WETHERBEE Josiah Eld *MS* 26 Apr 1848

TAYLOR Orrin m MAXIM Betsey B of Fairfield ME at Dover NH *MFWBR* 18 Aug 1849

TAYLOR Samuel of Natick MA m CUTTER Mary Rosaline of Livermore on 31 Oct 1847 in Livermore ME, BADGER William Eld *MS* 1 Dec 1847

TAYLOR Stephen C m MORRISON Abigail B of Manchester NH,
CILLEY D P Eld *MS* 18 Sept 1844

TAYLOR T H m YOUNG M Miss of Sanford ME on 12 Oct at Wells
ME, SMALL C Eld *MS* 20 Jan 1847

TAYLOR Theodore m TOWLE Mary on Sunday last, BURBANK S Eld
MS 30 Nov 1826

TAYLOR William m SANBORN Mary Ann of Sandwich on 21 May
1843 at Freedom, PARIS C Eld *MS* 21 June 1843

TAYLOR William M m HAWLAN Maria both of Lisbon NH in Franconia, GEORGE N K Eld *MS* 9 Oct 1850

TEBBETS Edmund B m WEEKS Louisa of Brooksfield on 21 Dec at
Wolfboro' NH, PRESCOTT E T Eld *MS* 17 Jan 1844

TEBBETS Jeremiah of Lawrence MA m GERRY Lucinda of Somersworth NH on 22 Nov in Lawrence, DAVIS J E Eld *MS* 5 Jan 1848

TEBBETS John m SMITH Susan both of Belgrade on 10 inst in
Belgrade ME, PERKENS Seth W Eld *MS* 23 Dec 1835

TEBBETS John m BICKFORD Martha both of Monmouth ME *MS* 20
Jan 1832

TEBBETS Noah Esq of Parsonsfield ME m WOODMAN Mary E in
Rochester, WILLEY Rev Mr *MS* 18 June 1828

TEBBETTS Charles G of Wolfboro NH m FURBUSH Jane E of Lebanon ME, BLAISDELL E Eld *MS* 29 June 1842

TEBBETTS David H m MERCHANT Roxana both of Belgrade ME on
21 inst, PERKINS Seth W *MS* 6 Apr 1836

TEBBETTS Edmond m BEAN Ann Mrs of Wolfborough NH on 17
June in Ossipee NH, CHICK J Eld *MS* 7 Nov 1849

TEBBETTS James M m BRACKETT Hannah at Berwick ME on 30th
ult *MFWBR* 9 Nov 1850

TEBBETTS James m LUCE Hannah R on 26 May 1844 at Alton,
BUZZELL H D Eld *MS* 19 Feb 1845

TEBBETTS Mark m RHODES Lydia Ann of Waterboro ME on 28th
ult at Waterboro, WEST John D Eld *MFWBR* 12 Oct 1850

TEBBETTS Orland of Lebanon ME m [CLARK] Lydia Ann of Rochester NH *MS* 25 Dec 1844 [surname did not appear in this news-
paper article but was found on p.197 of the *Genealogical and
Family History of the State of New Hampshire*, published in 1908.]

TEBBETTS William of Boothbay ME m HUFF Mary Ann of Boothbay
ME, ROBINSON N J Eld *MS* 29 Nov 1843

TEBETTS Samuel of Porter ME m LAMPEAR Mary Miss of Effingham
NH on Sun 9th inst, DAVIS J Eld *MS* 27 Mar 1834

TEMPLE John F m RANDALL Elizabeth on 28 Nov at Bowdoinham
ME, QUINNAM C Eld *MS* 8 Jan 1845

TENNE David of Chester Mich m HAVENS Sarah of Madison Mich
(both deaf-mutes) on 23 June 1842, THOMAS John Eld *MS* 27
June 1842

TENNEY Henry Jr m SYMONDS Maria D at Raymond on 14 Jul at

TENNEY (Continued)

Raymond ME, SMALL Carlton Eld *MS* 7 Aug 1844

TERPNING John m YANORSDALL Mary M of Raisin at Dover Mich, WILLCOX S H Eld *MS* 5 Jul 1843

TERRIN James M of Hebron m FOSS Mary Frances of Alton on 2 Nov, FERNALD S P Eld *MS* 30 Nov 1842

TEWKSBURY Daniel of New Market m SHERBURNE Sarah Ann of Northwood NH on 2d inst, DEMERITT William Eld *MS* 30 May 1833

THATCHER Seth T m EMERSON Deborah Y on 22 Sept at Lowell MA, CURTIS S Eld *MS* 2 Oct 1844

THAYER Artemus Jr m THAYER Sylvia of Mendon on 18 Mar in Mendon, BURLINGAME W M Eld *MS* 18 Apr 1838

THAYER George W m GRANT Sarah Jane of Gray on 9 Oct at Gray ME, REDLON Amos Eld *MS* 26 Nov 1845

THAYER John of Sidney m SPINNEY Eveline M at Augusta, THOMP-SON Z Rev *MFWBR* 29 Mar 1851

THAYER Warren m GOFF Mary Ann of Gray (ME?) on 10 Nov, WHITNEY G W Eld *MS* 10 May 1843

THAYER Zeary m PARKER Mary both of Franconia on 29 Apr 1848 in Franconia, BLAKE C E Eld *MS* 24 May 1848

THING Charles m EMERY Catherine on 14 Dec at Waterboro ME, EMERY Nathaniel Esq *MFWBR* 30 Dec 1848

THING Eliezer of Waterboro m THING Hannah of Shapleigh ME on 5th inst, THURSTON N Eld *MS* 17 Apr 1829

THING George m BRIGGS Betsey Ann of Lowell on 26th ult, THUR-STON Nathaniel Eld *MS* 6 Mar 1839

THING Gilman of Waterboro m GOWEN Hannah on 13th inst in Waterboro, THURSTON N Eld *MS* 19 Nov 1828

THING Jeremiah B m DAVIS Hannah L of Gilmanton\Gilford on 30 Jan, PINKHAM John Eld *MS* 13\27 Feb 1839

THING Joseph of Woolwich m PLUMMER Martha of Richmond in Richmond ME, SWETT Jesse Eld *MS* 2 Aug 1837

THING Samuel S Esq m LORD Armine G at Springvale ME on 18th inst *MFWBR* 1 Dec 1849

THOITS Oren of Pownal m TRUE Jennett at Pownal ME on 25th ult *MFWBR* 8 May 1847

THOMAS Abel H m JACOBS Eliza A of Lowell MA on 4 Oct at Lowell MA, THURSTON N Eld at Lowell MA *MS* 2 Nov 1842

THOMAS Albert H m EMERY Lydia A on 26 Oct at Nashville, STEARNS S Eld *MS* 24 Dec 1845

THOMAS Allen of Nelson m SCHOBIE Susannah of Trenton NY on 18 Feb in Weare, MOODY David Eld *MS* 11 Mar 1840

THOMAS Amos of Compton m KENYEN Nancy of Hinesburgh VT on 16 Mar of Stanstead LC, MOULTON A Eld *MS* 13 Apr 1842

THOMAS Benjamin Jr m LEAVITT Sally L on 22d ult in Hingham MA

THOMAS (Continued)
MS 3 May 1827

THOMAS Charles H of Freeport ME m BURNHAM Octavia F of Pownal ME on 14 Sep at Pownal ME, PURINTON A W Eld *MS* 25 Nov 1846

THOMAS Daniel m WINTERS Melissa both of Clayton NY on 19 Sept in Clayton NY, GRIFFETH A Eld *MS* 9 Oct 1850

THOMAS Jedediah m BUTLER Clarissa M both of Gardiner on 8 Jan in Gardiner ME, LANCASTER D Eld *MS* 24 Apr 1850

THOMAS Jeffrey m SHEPHERD Susan U of Stephentown on 17 June at Nassau NY, COLEMAN I B Eld *MS* 10 Sept 1845

THOMAS John Eld of Dover Mich m TALLFORD Sarah E of Dover, WILLCOX S H Eld *MS* 5 Jul 1843

THOMAS John Jr m BENSON Mary E on 9th inst at Biddeford ME, MASSUERE F Rev *MFWBR* 22 Dec 1849

THOMAS John N m HAWKINS Elizabeth D on 14th at Providence RI, HENSHAW J P Rev *MFWBR* 24 Feb 1849

THOMAS John m YORK Charlotte both of Great Falls NH on 12 Nov, BROOKS N Eld *MS* 27 Nov 1850

THOMAS Josephus T of Montgomery VT m DYER Affy of Augusta ME on 20 ult in Woodstock VT, HAZEN Jasper Rev *MS* 7 Mar 1838

THOMAS Josiah L a printer m PARSONS Elizabeth on 29th ult at Portland ME, CARRUTHER Dr Rev *MFWBR* 8 Dec 1849

THOMAS Sandrus H m SNELL Julia D on 15 Jul at Roxbury MA, DAVIS J B Eld *MS* 28 Aug 1844

THOMAS Stephen of Waterville m BRAGG Eunice M of Sidney ME *MS* 15 Mar 1837

THOMAS William of Otsego NY m STRAIGHT Dillan of Oneonta NY in Oneonta NY, WING Amos Eld *MS* 6 June 1849

THOMAS William R merchant of Cincinnati Ohio m SMITH Mary E *MS* 19 Dec 1833

THOMES Amos m JOHNSON Eunice of Limington ME on 26 Nov, MANSON B S Eld *MS* 7 Feb 1844

THOMPSON A Whitney m STEVENS Frances E on 24th ult at Portland, STREETER R Rev *MFWBR* 4 Aug 1849

THOMPSON Aaron of Washington m SCRANTON Phebe of Goshen on 23 June 1848 *MS* 2 Aug 1848

THOMPSON Addison of Boston MA m GREENLAU Sarah of Brownfield on 19 Feb, HART E H Eld *MS* 13 Mar 1844

THOMPSON Alonzo m SAWYER Rebecca of Ossipee NH on 2 Jan, CHICK J Eld *MS* 5 Feb 1845

THOMPSON Alvin m REED Margaretta of Portland on 14th inst at Falmouth, DAM C Rev *MFWBR* 28 Apr 1849

THOMPSON Asa m THOMPSON Clarissa Mrs both of Bowdoinham on 26 Nov 1848 in Bowdoinham ME, QUINNAM C Eld *MS* 13 Dec 1848

THOMPSON Benjamin F m WIGGIN Hannah Mrs both of Wolfborough NH on 17 Sept 1848 in Alton NH, PINKHAM John Eld *MS* 1
Nov 1848

THOMPSON Calvin m DYER Martha both of Lowell MA on 15th inst
Sat, THURSTON N Eld *MS* 27 Aug 1834

THOMPSON Charles H m ROLFEE Sarah on 9 May at Wilmot,
SMITH C H Eld *MS* 29 May 1844

THOMPSON Daniel of Parsonsfield m DOE Betsy of Parsonsfield on
Thursday last in Parsonsfield, BUZZELL John Eld *MS* 9 Nov 1826

THOMPSON Enoch H at Gilford m PERKINS Mary Jane, PINKHAM
John Eld *MS* 4 Oct 1843

THOMPSON George m RICKER Nancy of Parsonsfield, TYLER S Rev
MS June 1831

THOMPSON Haron [sic] of Richmond m GOODWIN Elizabeth at
Gardiner ME, GOODRICH Barnard Eld *MS* 4 Sept 1839

THOMPSON Henry m AUSTIN Amanda on 22 Sept at Rushford NY,
ANDRUS A C Eld *MS* 24 Oct 1833

THOMPSON Hiram of Tuftonboro m BEACHAM Sabrina of Ossipee
on 3 Mar, WALKER John *MS* 16 Mar 1842

THOMPSON Hollis of Bristol m CASS Loventia J of Alexandria NH on
8 Aug 1847 in Alexandria NH, BROWN A Eld *MS* 3 Nov 1847

THOMPSON Horace m EVANS Mary Ann of Lynn MA on 29 Dec at
Lynn MA, WALDRON W H Eld *MS* 13 Jan 1847

THOMPSON Isaac of New Market m THOMPSON Abigail of Nottingham on 7 inst in Nottingham, CILLEY D P Eld *MS* 28 Mar 1838

THOMPSON J H m MANLEY Jane at Saco ME, WILLIAM N M (Eld?)
MFWBR 21 Apr 1849

THOMPSON James m PRIEST Susan A both of Nottingham on 12
May in New Market, FROST D S Eld *MS* 20 May 1846

THOMPSON Jonathan m DOE Mary Ann on 26 May at Manchester,
CILLEY D P Eld *MS* 5 June 1844

THOMPSON Joseph m HEARD Eleanor of Newfield on 15th ult at
Parsonsfield, FOSS Eld *MS* 12 Jan 1831

THOMPSON Josiah m WRIGHT Sophronia both of Nashua on 18
May 1848 in Manchester NH, CILLEY D P Eld *MS* 24 May 1848

THOMPSON Nathaniel S m COX Frances B both of Holderness NH
on 2 Jul 1848 in Holderness NH *MS* 21 Mar 1849

THOMPSON Oren m STOKES Polly of Starboro' VT on 2 Nov at
Huntington VT, DIKE Orange Eld *MS* 6 Dec 1843

THOMPSON Pelatiah of Searsmont ME m PRESCOTT Nancy of
Dixmont ME on 16 Jan at Dixmont ME, RINES J N Eld *MS* 20 Apr
1842

THOMPSON Person C of Holderness m WEBBER Lucy of Lisbon NH
on 28 Mar 1850 in Lisbon NH, WEBBER Horace Eld *MS* 10 Apr
1850

THOMPSON Prince of Strong m WILSON Harriet of New Gloucester

THOMPSON (Continued)
  on 22d ult at New Gloucester, HAWKS J Rev Jr *MFWBR* 3 Mar
    1849
THOMPSON Samuel m DAVIS Phebe C at Searsmont ME, INGRA-
  HAM John Esq *MS* 17 Mar 1847
THOMPSON Samuel P of Meredosia IL m BLAISDELL Ruhamah P of
  Holderness NH on 15 Sept at Holderness, PETTENGILL John Eld
  MS 2 Oct 1839
THOMPSON Stephen J Capt of Barnstead m FOSS Lucy Y in Dover
  NH on 17th inst, CURTIS Silas Eld *MS* 27 Apr 1842
THOMPSON Stephen of Copenhagen m NORTON Cyrene of Clayton
  NY on 6 Feb in Clayton NY, GRIFFITH A Eld *MS* 5 Mar 1851
THOMPSON Washington of Tuftonboro' NH m BEACHAM Joanna of
  Ossipee NH, WALKER John Eld *MS* 31 May 1843
THOMPSON William m FLANDERS Charity R on 20 Mar at Bow-
  doinham ME, QUINNAM C Eld *MS* 6 Apr 1847
THOMPSON William m MARRINER Elizabeth on 5 June at Bruns-
  wick ME, ROLLINS Andrew Eld *MS* 29 June 1842
THOMSON Charles m MELLEN Rachel on 5 Nov of Lowell MA,
  THURSTON N Eld *MS* 20 Nov 1839
THOMSON Prince of Strong m POTTER Saviah of Corinna ME on 7
  inst in Corinna ME, COPP John B Eld *MS* 29 Mar 1837
THORN William of Standish m DAVIS Desire of Buxton on 13th inst,
  BEAN N C Esq *MS* 26 Nov 1828
THORNTON Boyd m SCOTT Elizabeth J of Hale Ohio on 8th Sept of
  York Ohio, HEALTH J D Eld *MS* 25 Sept 1844
THORNTON Hiram of Rochester m REED Mary of Perinton NY on 13
  Mar, HOLMES D G Eld *MS* 12 May 1847
THRASHER George H of Rehoboth m FREEMAN Calista A of Attle-
  borough on 10 Apr in Attleborough MA, CLARK G Eld *MS* 1 May
  1850
THURBER John ae 63y of Tioga NY m LAYTON E H Wid ae 62y of
  Vesta on 13 inst 1849, GARDNER L G Eld *MS* 28 Mar 1849
THURBER William m HAYDEM Caroline S on 19 June at Lowell MA,
  THURSTON N Eld *MS* 2 Nov 1842
THURSTON Andrew m NAY Amelia S on 2 Jan 1848 in Charlestown,
  WETHERBEE I J Eld *MS* 19 Jan 1848
THURSTON Charles m LORD Priscilla W both of Corinth ME on 19
  Nov in Corinth ME, ROBINSON N J Eld *MS* 26 Dec 1838
THURSTON Elijah C m LUCY Lois M on 19 Feb in New Market,
  EASTMAN C A Eld *MS* 24 Apr 1950
THURSTON Henry C m WEDGEWOOD Drusilla both of Eaton,
  EATON E G Eld *MS* 4 June 1834
THURSTON James H m TOWLE Mary Jane both of Freedom on 8
  Apr 1849 in Eaton, BLAISDELL Henry Rev *MS* 2 May 1849
THURSTON Joseph H m SIMONDS Adaline both of Lowell in Lowell,

THURSTON (Continued)

THURSTON N Eld *MS* 29 Aug 1838

THURSTON Miles of Alton NH m RICKER Eliza on 13 Feb *MS* 12 Apr 1843

THURSTON Nathaniel C of Freedom m DURGIN Hannah of Eaton on 4 Feb 1849, BUTLER O Eld *MS* 28 Mar 1849

THURSTON Nathaniel Eld of Parsonsfield ME m SPAULDING Martha N Miss female preacher, WOODMAN J Eld *MS* 23 June 1830

THURSTON Stephen m WHITTEN Hannah both of Parsonsfield ME at Parsonsfield ME, BUZZELL John Eld *MFWBR* 27 Feb 1847

THURSTON Watson m SCOTT Harriet both of Lowell on 9 inst in Lowell, THURSTON N Eld *MS* 20 June 1838

TIBBETS Christopher C m THORN Caroline both of Somersworth NH on 27 May in So Berwick ME, TRUE Ezekiel Eld *MS* 22 Jul 1846

TIBBETS George F of Lawrence MA m PLACE Betsey of Somersworth NH in Great Falls, DUNN R Eld *MS* 1 Dec 1847

TIBBETS Jeremiah G of Rochester m DREW Mary of Dover on 3d inst, PERKINS S W Eld *MS* 10 Dec 1845

TIBBETS John F of Woolwich ME m McKENNEY Julia Ann of Wiscasset on 25 Jan 1848 in Wiscasset ME, PAGE E G Eld *MS* 9 Feb 1848

TIBBETS Samuel m PINDER Maria both of Ossipee NH on 17 Nov *MS* 21 Dec 1836

TIBBETTS Joseph H m CHESLEY Annette F both of New Market on 11 Feb in New Market, CILLEY D P Eld *MS* 21 Feb 1838

TIBBETTS Moses P m BUSWELL Clara A both of Ossipee NH on 3 May in Ossipee, CHICK J Eld *MS* 24 June 1846

TIBBETTS Richard m BRAY Priscilla both of Charlestown MA on 21 May in Charlestown MA, WETHERBEE I J Eld *MS* 24 June 1846

TIBBETTS William G m RIPLEY Loisa P both of Augusta in Augusta ME, CURTIS S Eld *MS* 24 Jan 1838

TIBBITS Edmund of Ossipee NH m BEAN Anna of Tuftonboro NH at Ossipee NH on 17th ult *MFWBR* 21 Jul 1849

TIFFANY Hiram m EVERETT Elizabeth J both of Walworth on 19 Sept in Walworth NY, HOLMES D G Eld *MS* 16 Oct 1850

TIFFANY Lewis of Naroge Shenango Co NY m MATHEWSON Miranda of Walworth NY in Walworth NY, HOLMES D G Eld *MS* 27 June 1849

TIFFT Spelman V m WHEELER Abigail on 29 Nov at Nassau NY, COLEMAN I B Eld *MS* 17 Dec 1845

TILDEN Friend m LEAVITT Abby P, NOYES E Eld *MS* 15 Dec 1847

TILDEN Timothy of Manchester NY m YERRINGTON Marcia of Norwich in Norwich, CLARK E Eld *MS* 6 June 1849

TILTON Charles F of Manchester m SWAIN Rachael E of Meredith on 6 Mar in Meredith, PITMAN Stephen J Eld *MS* 1 May 1850

TILTON Cornelius 3rd m HUSSEY Asenath C of Waterville ME at

TILTON (Continued)

Waterville ME, LEWIS D B Eld *MS* 12 May 1847

TILTON David m JONES Mary of East Kingston on 5 June at Epping, HANSCOM P Eld *MS* 19 June 1844

TILTON David P of Pittsfield m BUNKER Sarah R of Barnstead on 4 Sept at Pittsfield, WEBBER Horace Eld *MS* 14 Sept 1842

TILTON Elisha of Brentwood m FOSS Susan J of New Market on 4 ult at Northwood NH, CILLEY Daniel P Eld *MS* 18 Nov 1835

TILTON John W of Boscawen NH m SWETT Bernice S of Bowdoinham ME on 29 Oct at Bowdoinham ME, QUINNAM C Eld *MS* 16 Nov 1842

TILTON Luther of Newburyport MA m KIMBALL Martha of Loudon NH on 11 Oct at Canterbury, CLOUGH Jeremiah Eld *MS* 25 Nov 1846

TILTON Mark (formerly of Canada) m REYNOLDS Almira of Pierpont NY on 14 Feb 1842 at Pierpont NY, WHITFIELD W Eld *MS* 18 May 1842

TILTON Shurburn m FOSS Signorine M both of Charleston ME on 16 Apr in Garland ME, AMES M Eld *MS* 3 Jul 1850

TILTON Stephen S m SWAIN Mary P both of Manchester on 9 May in Manchester, CILLEY D P Eld *MS* 22 May 1844

TILTON Timothy F of Contoocookville m TEWKSBURY Eunice on 10 Jul, FROST D Sidney Eld *MS* 14 Sept 1842

TINCKOM Daniel m SALESBURY Eliza L on 30th ult at Scituate RI, ALLEN R Eld *MS* 21 Sept 1842

TINKHAM Harvy of Sherburne m PORTER Sarah of Hamilton on 14 Nov 1849 in Poolville NY, GARDNER S D Eld *MS* 28 Nov 1849

TISDALE Benjamin R m ALLEN Julia Ann both of No Providence RI on 25 ult at Johnston RI *MS* 11 Jan 1837

TITCOMB George of Portland ME m SAWYER Cordelia A of Saco on 26th ult at Saco ME, DWIGHT Rev *MFWBR* 13 Feb 1847

TITCOMB George W of Haverhill MA m THOMPSON Jane M at Dover NH *MFWBR* 4 May 1850

TITCOMB Hiram R of Great Falls m LESLIE Sarah C at Meredith NH *MFWBR* 21 Jul 1849

TITCOMB Joseph of Boston m TITCOMB Sally in Acton ME on 27 Jan, LITTLEFIELD William H Eld *MS* 27 Feb 1850 & *MFWBR* 9 Mar 1850

TITCOMB Joshua Jr of Effingham m FOGG Hannah R of Ossipee at Ossipee on 7 ult, CHICK J Eld *MS* 3 Aug 1836

TITCOMB Joshua of Effingham m COOPER Dorothy of Wakefield on 15 Mar 1849 in Wakefield, WALKER John Eld *MS* 4 Apr 1849

TITCOMB Nathan W at Effingham m FOGG L Miss *MS* 1 Apr 1835

TITCOMB Wingate m FOGG Lucady on 5 Mar at Parsonsfield ME, JACKSON Daniel Eld *MS* 1 Apr 1835

TITUS Horace m AVERY Enthemy both of Lowell MA *MS* 18 Jan

TITUS (Continued)
    1837
TOBEY George m WHIPPLE Ann Moriah both of No Providence on 30
    ult in No Providence, HUTCHINS E Eld *MS* 15 Apr 1835
TOBEY Hiram of Kittery m PHILLIPS Salome of Kittery *MS* 3 Feb
    1832
TOBEY James H of Coventry m POTTER Harriet R of No Providence
    RI on 15 inst in No Providence RI, HUTCHINS E Eld *MS* 28 Mar
    1838
TOBEY Nathaniel of Fairfield m BOWMAN Nancy Mrs of Sidney on
    30th inst, BURGESS J S Eld *MS* 14 Jul 1847
TOBEY William of Smithfield m ANGELL Sarah Ann of No Providence
    RI on 30 Mar, CHENEY M Eld *MS* 13 Apr 1836
TOBIE Edward P m HARMON Jane Elizabeth both of Lewiston ME
    on 9th inst, LIBBY Isaac Eld *MS* 11 Mar 1840
TODD John William at Bangor ME m CHASE Deborah, CAVERNO A
    Eld *MS* 13 Sept 1843
TODD Thomas Maj Proprietor of the *Eastern Argus* m GREENLEAF
    Susan Mrs in Portland *MS* 10 Aug 1826
TOLBUT Joshua m DAVIS Sarah both of Portsmouth on 10 ult in
    Portsmouth, TRUE E Eld *MS* 10 Oct 1838
TOOTHAKER Ebenezer of Litchfield ME at Bowdoinham ME m
    WILLIAMS Martha O, QUINNAM C Eld *MS* 7 Aug 1844
TOOTHAKER Horatio m WILSON Mary M of Harpswell ME on 9 May
    at Brunswick ME, PAGE E G Eld *MS* 26 May 1847
TOOTHAKER Jacob of Etna m RANDOLPH Caroline on 28 Dec,
    WHITCOMBS Esq *MS* 24 Jan 1838
TOOTHAKER John H m AUBENS Rebecca D of Brunswick ME at
    Brunswick ME, PAGE E G Eld *MS* 13 Jan 1847
TOOTHAKER John m TOTMAN Lucretia both of Richmond ME on 22
    Aug in Richmond ME, PURINGTON C Eld *MS* 8 Sept 1847
TOOTHAKER William H m DAWS Olive of Richmond ME on 10 May
    at Bowdoin ME, PURINTON A W Eld *MS* 16 June 1847
TOOTHHAKER Joel of Dexter ME m POTTER Nancy of Dexter on 28
    Sept at Corinna ME, COPP J B Eld *MS* 11 Dec 1839
TOTMAN David W m ADAMS Sophia L on 25 Sept at Cincinnatus
    NY, HILLS J W Eld *MS* 5 Nov 1845
TOTMAN Elias Jr m MEREEN Jane D Mrs on 8 Mar 1848 in Phips-
    burg ME *MS* 29 Mar 1848
TOWLE Amos Esq of Freedom Village m MARCH Sally of Eaton,
    GASKILL S Eld *MS* 21 Jan 1846
TOWLE David of Chichester m KEZER Nancy on 4 Jul in Canter-
    bury, CLOUGH Jeremiah Eld *MS* 15 Jul 1846
TOWLE Enoch W m PERKINS Susanna T Miss at Exeter NH *MS* 21
    Dec 1832
TOWLE Henry D m BROWN Cynthia F on 5 Oct at Nashua,

TOWLE (Continued)
STEARNS S Eld *MS* 22 Oct 1845

TOWLE Jabez Capt m WEDGEWOOD Susan on Thurs last at Parsonsfield ME, BUZZELL John Eld *MS* 19 Oct 1826

TOWLE Jesse S m LEAVITT Mary of Gilmanton on 13 Apr 1843 at Upper Gilmanton NH, TUTTLE J G Eld *MS* 3 May 1843

TOWLE John F Esq m DAVIS Abigail D of Lee on 3 Feb at Lee, TUTTLE A Eld *MS* 4 Mar 1846

TOWLE Levi of Epping m BARTLETT Caroline of New Market NH on 26 Nov at New Market, FROST D S Eld *MS* 9 Dec 1846

TOWLE Ransellaer of Freedom NH m GILMAN Caroline W of Effingham NH on 2 June, BUTLER O Eld *MS* 28 Aug 1844

TOWLE Samuel of Porter m RICH Abby of Monroe ME on 25 Aug in Monroe ME, RINES J N Eld *MS* 13 Nov 1850

TOWN Emory m HOLMES Emily of Stow on Dec 1843 at Waterbury VT, WHITBY George Rev *MS* 15 Jan 1845

TOWNS Francis W of Newfield ME m STAPLE Harriet N of Limington ME on Nov 21, MANSON B S Eld *MS* 15 Jan 1840

TOWNSEND Absolom A Esq of Shellsburg WT m WELLS Almira formerly of Lyman Jefferson Co NY on 31st Jul at Wards Precinct IL, NORTON Isaac Eld Jr *MS* 21 Aug 1844

TOWNSON Alba of Hollis m LANG Elizabeth of Limerick on 11th inst, LIBBY E Eld *MS* 17 Nov 1830

TOZIER Charles L m MANELL Rebecca G on 17 June in Waterville ME, BEAN G W Eld *MS* 29 Aug 1849

TOZIER Franklin of Waterville at Hallowell ME m NORCROSS Marion W, NOYES E Eld *MS* 27 Dec 1843

TRACY Ferdinand of Limerick ME m HOBBS Sylvia J of Waterboro ME on 19th inst, WEST John D Eld *MFWBR* 21 Dec 1850

TRACY G W m MORTON Ellen P both of Owego NY on 17 Apr 1849 in Owego NY, GARDNER L G Eld *MS* 2 May 1849

TRACY Harvey N m LINDSEY Mary on 19 Dec at Lowell MA, THURSTON N Eld *MS* 25 May 1842

TRACY Jonathan Eld m BRACKETT Mary of Auburn ME on 6 Dec, LIBBEY James Eld *MS* 9 Apr 1845

TRAFTON Isaac M m AYER Ann R on 19th ult at Newfield, CUMMINGS Rev *MFWBR* 15 June 1850

TREADWELL Thomas D of Cambridge MA m GOULD Elizabeth of Dover on 6th inst, WILLIAMS Gibbon Rev *MS* 12 Nov 1834

TRECETT Richard Mr m FRENCH Maria in Prospect ME, STOWE J P Eld *MS* 19 Jan 1842

TRECHER Robert of Richmond m GILPATRICK Sarah on 25th ult of Gardiner, PERKINS Seth Eld *MS* 13 Feb 1839

TREDICK Charles m GILES Hannah of Dover NH at Great Falls Village on 1 Jan, STEVENS T Eld *MS* 23 Jan 1839

TREDICK John m COPP Mary W on 23 inst Tuesday evening in

TREDICK (Continued)

Dover NH, BUCKINGHAM Rev Mr *MS* 7 Feb 1838

TRETREN John L m PENNIMAN Sarah both of Manchester on 7 June in Manchester, CILLEY D P Eld *MS* 24 June 1846

TRICKEY Nathan H Eld m MOODY Sarah on 19 ult at So Berwick ME, KELER Rev *MS* 10 Dec 1834

TRICKEY Shepard m COBB Persis of Poland ME on 5 Jan 1847, LIBBY James Eld *MS* 10 Feb 1847

TRICKEY William of Brookfield m NORRIS Martha of Dover on 13 inst at Dover, PERKINS Rev *MS* 20 Jan 1836

TRICKY Joseph S m RUSSELL Mary J both of Manchester NH on 7 Sept 1848 in Woodstock NH, RUSSELL G W Eld *MS* 8 Nov 1848

TRIPP George of Parsonsfield m STERLING Sarah of Ossipee on 9 Jul in Ossipee, WALKER John Eld *MS* 19 Jul 1837

TRIPP Lewis m SANBORN Caroline A on 2 June at St Albans ME, COPP John B Eld *MS* 17 Sept 1845

TRIPP Nathaniel M m GOODWIN Elizabeth on 3 Nov 1850 in Wells ME, KEENE J Eld Jr *MS* 8 Jan 1851

TROW Francis S m DAVIS Pamelia ME both of Sunipee NH on 27 Feb in Sunipee, DODGE William Eld *MS* 12 Mar 1851

TRUE Cyrus D of Pittsfield m GREEN Julia Ann of Loudon NH on 29 Apr, TRUE E Eld *MS* 16 May 1849

TRUE Elbridge A m WATSON Abigail of Pittsfield on 15 Sept at Pittsfield, CILLEY D P Eld *MS* 12 Oct 1842

TRUE Ezekiel Eld of Portsmouth NH m HOBBS Sylvia M of Wells ME at Great Falls NH, CURTIS S Eld *MS* 4 Dec 1839

TRUE Jacob of Guilford m BUCK Elmira of Foxcorft ME on 11 Nov in Foxcroft ME, GALLISON W F Eld *MS* 28 Nov 1849

TRUE Jacob of St Louis Mo m POWERS Abigail P on 10 Aug 1842 at Corinth VT, MARTIN Rev *MS* 31 Aug 1842

TRUE John Eld of Montville m TAYLOR Fanny on 8th ult, BRAY S Rev *MS* 20 Feb 1829

TRUE John of Holderness m TRUE Lucy S of Center Harbor on 4 Aug in Center Harbor, TASKER L B Eld *MS* 11 Sept 1850

TRUE Porter C m ADAMS Ursula both of Pittsfield on 11 inst in Pittsfield F B Church, TRUE E Eld *MS* 21 Nov 1849

TRUFANT John of Lisbon ME m SPARKS Alice of Bowdoinham ME on 30 March at Bowdoinham ME, QUINNAM C Eld *MS* 19 Apr 1843

TRULL Wyman m WHITCOMB Nancy both of Sweden on 24 Dec in Sweden, WHITNEY George Eld *MS* 17 Jan 1838

TRUMBALL William P m STEVENS Emeline C of Bridgton ME on 10 Feb, WILLEY Eben C Eld *MS* 7 May 1845

TRUMBULL Abial m JACKMAN Susan W both of Boscowen NH on 24 Dec in Hopkinton, SINCLAIR J L Eld *MS* 5 Feb 1840

TRY John Capt m DECKER Ann on 3d inst at Portland ME,

TRY (Continued)
MOULTON A K Eld *MS* 20 Dec 1843
TUBBS Charles of Phoenix m KELLER Elizabeth of Schroeppel on 29 Nov 1847 in Schroeppel, SMITH O W Eld *MS* 22 Dec 1847
TUCK George W m RILEY Helen both of Lowell MA on 25 Jan 1848 in Manchester, CILLEY Daniel P Eld *MS* 2 Feb 1848
TUCK John Jr m WIGGIN Harriet at Parsonsfield ME, TUCK Jonathan Esq *MS* 16 Apr 1845
TUCK Jonathan of Parsonsfield m PHILBRICK Mary Ann of Ossippe NH in Ossippe, JACKSON Daniel Eld *MS* 6 Dec 1827
TUCKER Andrew J m SEVERNS Harriet N both of Andover on 18 ult in Andover, SINCLAIR J L Eld *MS* 3 Oct 1838
TUCKER Andrew J of Alexandria m CHASE Hannah of Meredith on 1 Apr 1848, PITMAN S J Eld *MS* 21 June 1848
TUCKER Daniel B of Thornton m ELLIOT Elizabeth of Canaan on 11 ult in Canaan NH, RICHARDSON Caleb H Eld *MS* 1 May 1850
TUCKER David 2d of Henniker m STRAW Elizabeth on 7 Mar of Contoocookville, FROST D S Eld *MS* 26 Apr 1843
TUCKER Eber H m VALENTINE Mary Ann of Sand Lake NY on 5th Oct, COLEMAN I B Eld *MS* 11 Dec 1844
TUCKER George m SMITH Elizabeth on 2 inst in De Pauville NY, GRIFFITH A Eld *MS* 23 Feb 1848
TUCKER James of Boston MA m SAVAGE Mary E of Durham NH on 23 Dec 1847 in Durham NH, FROST D S Eld *MS* 3 May 1848
TUCKER James of New Chester NH m BAILEY Nancy in Enfield NH, CHASE Ebenezer Eld *RI* 20 Jul 1819
TUCKER Joel of Goffstown m GREEN Catherine Mrs of Manchester NH on 28 Apr at Manchester NH, CILLEY D P Eld *MS* 7 May 1845
TUCKER John A m HOWE Lucy W of Manchester NH on 7 Jul of Manchester, CILLEY D P Eld *MS* 17 Jul 1844
TUCKER John m JACK Rhoda Jane both of Litchfield ME, QUINNAM C Eld *MS* 20 May 1840
TUCKER Moses D of Roxbury MA m PRESCOTT Martha A of Candia on Thanksgiving Evening in Candia, CAVERNO A Eld *MS* 29 Nov 1848
TUCKER William m BOOTHBY Mary of Buxton on 8 Feb at Buxton ME, SINCLAIR J L Eld *MS* 25 Feb 1846
TUFTS Amos m GRAY Sarah A of Rochester NH on 21st ult at Dover NH, HUTCHINS E Eld *MS* 1 Oct 1845
TUKEY Charles m JENKINS Cordelia of Lowell on 9 Apr, WOODMAN J Eld *MS* 23 Aug 1843
TUKEY Nathaniel F m HOLMES Susan S of Lowell MA on 31 Jan at Dracut MA, CURTIS S Eld *MS* 10 Feb 1847
TURNELL Joseph S of Candia NH m LOVEJOY Hepzibah M of Lowell in Lowell, THURSTON N Eld *MS* 22 Jan 1840
TURNER Abel Eld of Exeter ME m FITZGERALD Emily of Manchester

TURNER (Continued)

NH on 6 Oct 1847 in Manchester NH *MS* 27 Oct 1847

TURNER Abel Eld of Foxcroft ME m NICHALS Lydia Ann of Corinth ME on 29 Aug in Corinth ME, HATHAWAY Eld *MS* 11 Oct 1837

TURNER Daniel of Roxbury MA m DANIELS Abigail of Boston on 6 Apr at Roxbury, DAVIS J B Eld *MS* 7 May 1845

TURNER David Maj m YOUNG Mary L both of Royalton VT on 9 inst in Royalton VT, DRAKE Cyrus B Rev *MS* 17 Jan 1838

TURNER Ezekiel of Providence m RANDALL Mary W of Johnson, NOYES E Eld *MS* 13 Nov 1850

TURNER Henry B of Pawtucket m MATHEWSON Mary Jane of Providence on 5 Mar 1850 in Johnston RI, ALLEN Reuben Rev *MS* 3 Apr 1850

TURNER Joseph S of Candia NH m LOVEJOY Hepzibah M of Lowell, THURSTON N Eld *MS* 22 Jan 1840

TURNER Leroy of Wilett m WHITMARSH Zipporah of Smithville NY on 9 Jan 1849 in Smithville NY, HILLS J W Eld *MS* 31 Jan 1849

TURNER Moses m ROBINSON Hannah on 1 Sept 1844 at Alton NH, FERNALD S P Eld *MS* 26 Feb 1845

TURNER William H m SMITH Mary Ann of Lowell MA, THURSTON N Eld *MS* 19 June 1839

TUTTLE Andrew m DEMERITT Susan both of Dover on 20th inst *MS* 23 Mar 1836

TUTTLE Dan m EASTMAN Nancy of Bennington NY on 4 Feb at Bennington NY, FLYNN William H *MS* 6 Apr 1847

TUTTLE David L m WHITTEN Ruth E, WILLIAMS N M at Saco ME *MFWBR* 19 Oct 1850

TUTTLE Elijah of Barrington m HANSON Hannah of Strafford on 11 Aug 1842 at Strafford, PLACE E Eld *MS* 16 Nov 1842

TUTTLE Elon of Clinton m HUMPHREYVILLE Orissa of Norway on 9 Feb *MS* 24 May 1843

TUTTLE Franklin of Dover m HAYES Elizabeth Jane of Nottingham on 13 inst Wednesday eve in Dover NH, CAVERNOR A Eld *MS* 20 Feb 1850

TUTTLE George of Durham ME m LUNT Mary F of Brunswick ME on 10 Oct 1848 in Brunswick ME, PURINTON A W Eld *MS* 1 Nov 1848

TUTTLE Jesse of Boston m CHENY Alice on 9th inst at Haverhill MA *MS* 24 Dec 1834

TUTTLE John m HODGDON Harriet on 5th inst at Saco ME, STRICKLAND G G Rev *MFWBR* 18 Aug 1849

TUTTLE John of Somersworth m FOX Hannah I of Wolfboro *MS* 17 Feb 1836

TUTTLE Jonas B m McCRILLIS Caroline both of Center Harbor on 27 Jan, PITMAN S J Eld *MS* 12 Feb 1851

TUTTLE Jonathan m WATERHOUSE Sarah A of Barrington on 13

TUTTLE (Continued)

Mar at Strafford NH, PLACE E Eld *MS* 6 Apr 1842

TUTTLE Joseph m HOWARD Mahala of Wakefield NH on 13 Jul 1848 in Strafford NH, PLACE E Eld *MS* 9 Aug 1848

TUTTLE Merari m MOSES Florenda at Lowell MA, THURSTON N Eld *MS* 7 Oct 1835

TUTTLE Nathaniel m VARNEY Mary both of Dover "on last afternoon" [N.B. on 8 Apr 1851] in Dover Village, CAVERNO A Eld *MS* 9 Apr 1851

TUTTLE Silas Jr m HALL Elizabeth S both of Strafford on 7 Nov in Strafford, PLACE E Eld *MS* 1 Dec 1847

TUTTLE Stoten D m TAYLOR Elizabeth I both of Nottingham on 12 May in Nottingham, TUTTLE A Eld *MS* 24 June 1846

TUTTLE William m PENDERGAST Charlotte both of Durham on 27th ult, HUTCHINS E Eld *MS* 5 Jan 1842

TUTTLE William N m FROST Almira B in Eaton, RUNNELS J Eld *MS* 9 Feb 1848

TWICHELL Josiah Jr of Burnham m SIMONS Mahaley of Pittsfield ME at Pittsfield, LEWIS Daniel B Eld *MS* 24 Feb 1836

TWISS William N of Auburn m NELSON Mary of Groton on 26 Oct, PECK Benjamin D Esq *MS* 15 Nov 1843

TWITCHELL Isaac J m FLINT Catharine of Scarboro' ME at Cape Elizabeth ME, NASON Rev *MFWBR* 24 Aug 1850

TWITCHELL John of Plymouth m DRAKE Lydia of Albion on 10 Oct in East Dixmont ME, ALLEN E Eld *MS* 5 Mar 1851

TWOMBLEY Reuben m McLUCUS Mary G *MFWBR* 24 Mar 1849

TWOMBLY Benjamin of Billerica m AYER Mary J *MS* 8 Jan 1840

TWOMBLY George G m DAWLING Caroline both of Dover on 16 inst in Dover, HUTCHINS E Eld *MS* 22 May 1850

TWOMBLY Jonathan J D m LANGLEY Deborah F both of Lowell on 8 Nov 1848 in Dracut, CURTIS S Eld *MS* 5 Dec 1848

TWOMBLY Luther of Freedom m FLENEGIN Jane of Hume, ANDRUS Amos C Eld *MS* 26 Dec 1838

TWOMBLY Meshech m GOODWIN Abigail Mrs on 24 Nov at Lowell MA, CURTIS S Eld *MS* 18 Dec 1844

TWOMBLY Nathaniel 2d of Dover m EVANS Sarah W of Barrington NH, CILLEY D P Eld *MS* 21 May 1845

TWOMBLY Reuben Jr m TWOMBLY Mary Jane both of Dover on 25 ult in Dover, HUTCHINS E Eld *MS* 2 Sept 1846

TWOMBLY Thomas B Jr m WEYMOUTH Hope Jane both of Dover on 31 Oct in Dover, CLARK M Eld *MS* 11 Nov 1846

TWOMBLY William m PETTY Lucy both of No Yarmouth ME on 16th inst at No Yarmouth, WHITE Joseph Eld *MS* 25 Mar 1835

TWOMBY Charles H m HAYES Joanna W of Dover NH on 4th May at Dover NH, PERKINS S W Eld *MS* 14 May 1845

TYLER Abram m LOVERING Mary Ann on 23 Oct at Freedom NH,

TYLER (Continued)

BUTLER O Eld *MS* 23 Nov 1842

TYLER John m ARLIN Martha both of Barrington on 10 inst in Barrington, SHERBURNE S Eld *MS* 20 June 1849

TYLER Joseph of Woburn MA m DAVIS Emeline M of Woburn MA on 16 Mar at Wilmington MA, OURGIN J M Eld *MS* 6 Apr 1842

TYLER Shubel m YOUNG Laure both of Manchester in Manchester, CILLEY D P Eld *MS* 5 Dec 1849

TYREL Moses Dustin of Bridgewater m PEASLEE Mary Maria in Holderness NH, THOMPSON S Eld *MS* 16 Jan 1850

ULMER George m WINSLOW Sarah A both of Boston in Boston MA, NOYES E Eld *MS* 4 Apr 1849

UMSTED Elijah m MEECH __ary both of China NY on 25 Sept, ANDRUS A C Eld *MS* 23 Dec 1835

UNDERWOOD Alfred B of Green m ALLEN Sally Mrs of Wayne on 27 Apr at Wayne Ashtabula Co Ohio, CARTER S S Eld *MS* 26 May 1847

UNDERWOOD Hanson m FOLSOM Mary S at Friends Meeting House at Epping *MS* 2 Jul 1834

UNDERWOOD Sardies D of Lowell MA m RICHARDSON Emily J of Limington ME at Limington ME on 17th ult, WITHAM L H Eld *MFWBR* 5 Oct 1850 & *MS* 30 Oct 1850

UPHAM Clement m BERRY Almira H of Lowell MA on 5 May 1842 at Lowell MA, THURSTON N Eld *MS* 2 Nov 1842 & m BARRY Elmira, THURSTON N Eld *MS* 25 May 1842

UPHAM Robert L of Sand Lake m HUNTINGTON Sophia on 13 Oct, COLEMAN I B Eld *MS* 22 Feb 1843

UPTON Henry of Norway ME m BAKER Harriot of Waterford ME at Bridgton on 31st ult *MFWBR* 24 Apr 1847

UPTON Rufus P of Presque Isle PLT, Aroostook Co ME m BENSON Julia F of Greene ME on 10 Jul, FULLER J Eld *MS* 18 Mar 1846

UPTON Thomas of Reading m CARTER Jane of Wilmington MA at Wilmington MA, DURGIN J M Eld *MS* 22 Feb 1843

URAN John m CHAPMAN Loranda Miss at North Hampton NH *MS* 21 Dec 1832

USHER George m TARBOX Lucy on 3 Dec at Hollis ME, SMITH William Eld *MS* 30 Dec 1846

USHER Sidney m LORD Mary F at Limerick ME 10th inst, BUZZELL James Eld *MFWBR* 19 Oct 1850

VAN RENSSELAER Stevens Esq of Poland m PORTER Paulina T formerly of Medford MA on 29 May at Boston *MS* 29 June 1836

VAN-ORDER James m HENRY Louisa on 1 Oct at Purma NY, CRANE E F Eld *MS* 18 Oct 1843

VANCE Hiram m FISHER Mary of Ascott on 14 Sept 1838

VANCE (Continued)
MS 17 Apr 1839

VANDERBERG John S m SUTS Lucretia both of Plesses NY on 1 Jan 1849 in Plesses, PADDEN S B Eld *MS* 25 Apr 1849

VARNEY Alfred N m FOSS Almira both of Dover on 30 ult in Dover NH, HUTCHINS E Eld *MS* 2 Jan 1850

VARNEY Ebenezer m HORN Abigail of Dover on 3 June at Dover NH, SMITH A D Eld *MS* 9 June 1847

VARNEY George W of Rochester m HODGDON Mirriam/ Merriam of Barrington on 13 Apr, PLACE Eld *MS* 1 June 1836 & *MS* 18 May 1836

VARNEY Ira m TUTTLE Mary of Barnstead NH on 14 Aug 1842 at Alton, FERNALD S P Eld *MS* 30 Nov 1842

VARNEY J L of Ossipee NH m KIMBALL Sarah of Kennebunkport ME on 28d ult at Ossipee NH, HOBBS Isaac Esq *MFWBR* 10 Nov 1849

VARNEY James A of Brooks m RICH Hannah A of Jackson on 27 ult in Unity, SKILLIN H Eld *MS* 24 Nov 1847

VARNEY Joshua m WHITTEN Hannah both of Dover NH on 28 ult, ROOT Rev *MS* 1 Jul 1835

VARNEY Lewis D m GRAY Lydia on 14 Sept 1842 at Rochester, GOODWIN Lemuel Eld *MS* 21 Sept 1842

VARNEY Moses m TEBBETTS Lucinda of Rochester NH, AYER A Eld *MS* 21 Jan 1846

VARNEY Moses M R of Dover NH m CANNEY Livona of Farmington NH on 5 Oct at Farmington NH, PERKINS S W Eld *MS* 15 Oct 1845

VARNEY Rufus m FOSS Sally both of Barrington on 21st inst, SHERBURNE Samuel Eld *MS* 31 Dec 1834

VARNEY Samuel m MOODY Sophia both of Dover on 20 inst in Dover NH, HUTCHINS E Eld *MS* 27 Sept 1848

VARNEY Seth of Rochester NH m HOWARD Lucy on 18 Jul, PLACE E Eld *MS* 11 Aug 1847

VARNEY Solomon m FELKER Rachel both of Barrington *MS* 27 Jan 1836

VARNEY William of Windham ME m ELDEN Harriet Frances of Buxton ME on 19 Jan, SMITH William Eld *MS* 3 Mar 1847

VARNON Ralph m SMALL Naoma both of Bowdoinham ME in Richmond, STINSON Robert Eld *MS* 17 Oct 1838

VARRELL John P m PINKHAM Susan E on 26 ult in Dover NH, ROOT Rev *MS* 15 Aug 1838

VEAZIE James Jr m STINSON Jane K both of Eaton on 18 Oct in Eaton, RUNNELS J Eld *MS* 11 Nov 1846

VESEY Joseph H of Deerfield NH m LOCKE Sarah E of Epsom on 10 Oct in Epsom NH, RAMSEY G P Eld *MS* 24 Oct 1849

VICKERY Edward m TINT Ursula C both of Nassau on 9 Apr in Nassau NY, COLEMAN I B Eld *MS* 27 May 1846

VICKERY Joshua m GREEN Mary both of Rochester on 2 May in Rochester, MEADER Jesse Eld *MS* 22 May 1850

VICKERY Nelson of Unity m COMFORTH Isabella at Unity ME, LEWIS D B Eld *MS* 25 Dec 1844

VILES Albert of Chelmsford MA m VARNUM Hannah E of Dracut on 18 Feb at Dracut MA, CURTIS S Eld *MS* 24 Mar 1847

VINAL Ezekiel of Camden ME m PACKARD Abtezary of Thomaston ME on 22 Feb 1849, SMALL Wm Eld *MS* 16 May 1849

VINCENT Samuel m ALLEN Huldah of Norway on Jan 3 *MS* 24 May 1843

VINING David of Durham m SMITH Betsey of Lisbon, BRIDGES A Eld *MS* 12 Sept 1833

VITTUM George D merchant of Meredith m PERKENS Caroline C of New Hampton on 1 Dec *MS* 1 Feb 1837

VITTUM Lindley of Meredith NH m DERBY Caroline C of Huntington VT on 2 Oct at Underhill VT, DIKE O Eld *MS* 26 Nov 1845

VITTUM Mark J m MUDGETS Julia M on 14 Feb 1844 at Sandwich, McMURPHY B H Eld *MS* 5 June 1844

VITTUM Stephen of Sandwich m WATSON Mary, BROOKS N Eld *MS* 29 Jan 1845

VITTUM Stephen m TAPPAN Ruth A of Sandwich NH on 30 March, BROOKS N Eld *MS* 9 Apr 1845

WADE Arnold H m PHILLIPS Angeline both of Stephentown NY on 6 Aug in W Stephentown NY, COLMAN I B Eld *MS* 29 Aug 1849

WADE Stephen of Hatley m BUTTERFIELD Mary of Stanstead LC on 26 Aug of Stanstead LC, MOULTON A Eld *MS* 13 Apr 1842

WADLEIGH Charles J of Sanbornton m RAMSEY Jennet of New Hampton on 19 Oct 1847 in Newbury NH, NEWELL F P Eld *MS* 2 Feb 1848

WADLEIGH Daniel F of Kensington m LILEE Lucinda of Epsom NH on 16 Dec, RAMSEY G P Eld *MS* 8 Feb 1843

WADLEIGH Elijah m COPP Charlotte King Atkinson on 9 Tuesday evening in Dover NH, BUCKINGHAM Rev *MS* 17 Oct 1838

WADLEIGH Erastus m FLANDERS Mary W both of Sutton on 5 Jan 1848 in Newbury NH, NEWELL F P Eld *MS* 2 Feb 1848

WADLEIGH George W m EDGECOMB Abigail S of Portland ME on 26 Aug at Parsonsfield ME, MOULTON S Eld *MFWBR* 2 Oct 1847

WADLEIGH John C m NEALLEY Mary A both of Meredith on New Years Eve in Meredith NH, SINCLAIR J L Eld *MS* 10 Jan 1849

WADLEY Thomas Capt m ROBY Lovina both of Sutton on 14 Jan 1838 in Sutton VT, FLAGG Joseph Eld *MS* 14 Feb 1838

WAGNER Jacob m JACKSON Eunice T both of Belmont in Belmont, WARD Cotton Esq *MS* 2 Feb 1842

WAIT Holton m GOULD Sybil W of Anson on 22 Jan 1843, GOULD Benjamin Eld *MS* 19 Apr 1843

WAKEFIELD Abner C of Brownfield m JACKSON Julia R of Eaton on 19 Feb, GASKELL Silas Eld in Eaton *MS* 12 Aug 1846

WAKEFIELD Alfred m BRAN Olive on 7 inst in Gardiner ME, ALBEE H Eld *MS* 24 Apr 1844

WAKEFIELD Daniel of Biddeford m MILER Sarah of Brownfield on 3 Nov 1847 in Biddeford ME, LIBBY Josiah Eld *MS* 29 Dec 1847

WAKEFIELD Edward B m STAPLES Mary both of Biddeford ME on 24 Mar in Biddeford ME, LIBBY Josiah Eld *MS* 3 June 1846

WAKEFIELD Thomas D m WADE Lucy H both of Bath on 1 inst in Freeport ME *MS* 15 Jan 1851

WAKEFIELD Utiley Jr of Randolph NY m ARNOLD Jenette A of Randolph NY on 4 Feb, JONES L O Eld *MS* 13 Mar 1844

WALBRIDGE Philander Capt m JONES Lucina both of East Randolph VT in East Randolph VT, GOODALE Stephen Rev *MS* 22 Nov 1837

WALDO H H m DAVIS S A both of Edneston NY on 5 Mar in Edneston NY, CADY S S Eld *MS* 2 Apr 1851

WALDO L of Canisteo m SOUTHWORTH E M of Burlington on 5 Mar in Burlington NY, CADY S S Eld *MS* 2 Apr 1851

WALDRON Daniel B m PARSHLEY Druzilla W at Strafford, SMALL Carlton Eld *MS* 6 May 1835

WALDRON Francis A of Portland m FURBUSH Harriet of Brunswick on 12 inst in Brunswick ME, PAGE E G Eld *MS* 22 Jul 1846

WALDRON John B m EMERSON Clarinda both of Dover on 28 May in Dover, SMITH A D Eld *MS* 8 Aug 1849

WALDRON John C m LANG Hannah H both of Wakefield on 14 Jan 1849, BUTLER O Eld *MS* 28 Mar 1849

WALDRON John m PATCH Priscella at Kittery ME *MS* 14 Dec 1836

WALDRON Jonathan C m PARSHLEY Emeline S both of Strafford on 2 Apr in Strafford, PLACE E Eld *MS* 22 Apr 1846

WALDRON Oliver of Barnstead m CHESLEY Marcia O of Durham NH, at Dover NH *MFWBR* 1 Dec 1849

WALDRON William Eld of Lynn MA m GREEN Mary S of Epsom NH on 5 Nov at Epsom NH, COPP J B Eld *MS* 18 Nov 1846

WALDRON William W m PEAVEY Mary E both of Strafford NH on 27 ult in Strafford NH, BURBANK P S Eld *MS* 20 Sept 1848

WALDRON William m WEEKS Lorana B on 15th inst both of Kittery ME, PERRY Luther C Eld *MS* 19 Dec 1833

WALKER Abial m REED Eliza of Woolwich ME on 7 Nov at Woolwich ME, PAGE E G Eld *MS* 14 Jan 1846

WALKER Alexander m CALHOUN Louisa M at Portland ME, HUSSEY L Rev *MFWBR* 3 Feb 1849

WALKER Almore m SNOW Mary both of Lowell on 5 inst in Lowell, THURSTON N Eld *MS* 14 June 1837

WALKER Andrew J m BOYNTON Susan T of Lowell MA at Dracut MA, CURTIS S Eld *MS* 12 Nov 1845

WALKER Benjamin m FARROW Mary E both of Corinth ME on Feb 8, AMES M Eld *MS* 4 May 1842

WALKER Curtis m MEGQUIER Emeline both of West Poland on 13 May in West Poland ME, LIBBY James Eld *MS* 3 June 1846

WALKER Dexter M m ROBINSON Lucinda H both of Lowell on 31 ult in Lowell, THURSTON N Eld *MS* 14 Nov 1838

WALKER E S Mr of North Yarmouth ME m LEWIS M R (Miss)? of Portland on 2d inst at Portland ME, ABBOTT H Rev *MFWBR* 14 Apr 1849

WALKER Edwin F of Champlain NY m MIX Mary S of Huntington VT on 31 ult in Huntington VT, DIKE O Eld *MS* 10 Nov 1847

WALKER Ezekiel Jr of Woolwich ME m McKENNY Lydia of Wiscasset ME on 31st ult, PERKINS Seth Eld *MS* 13 Feb 1839

WALKER George of Sherbrook village m WOODMAN Mary M of Hatley LC *MS* 17 FEb 1836

WALKER Henry m DELANA Margaret both of Woolwich ME on 29 ult in Westport, TARBOX Samuel Esq *MS* 20 June 1838

WALKER Henry of Standish ME m DORSETT Eliza of Gorham ME at Standish ME *MFWBR* 4 May 1850

WALKER Hiram of Rochester m OSBORN Elizabeth Ann of Dover NH on 8 inst in Dover, HUTCHINS E Eld *MS* 15 May 1850

WALKER James D m EASTMAN Margaret on 4th inst at Charlestown ME, TURNER A Eld *MS* 16 Jul 1845

WALKER Jason H m MINER Betsey both of Great Falls NH on 27 Feb in Great Falls, BROOKS N Eld *MS* 6 Mar 1850 & *MFWBR* 9 Mar 1850

WALKER John of Brownfield m STORER Melissa of Porter on 1 May 1849, HART E H Eld *MS* 24 Jul 1850

WALKER Joseph m HILDRUP Elizabeth on 13th inst at Dover NH, PERKINS Rev *MS* 16 Dec 1835

WALKER Samuel A of Embden ME m ROCKLIFF Emeline of Industry ME on 30 Nov 1842, GOULD Benjamin Eld *MS* 19 Apr 1843

WALL George m ADAMS Mary P on 13 Feb at Falmouth ME, HERSEY L Eld *MS* 1 June 1842

WALLACE Abraham m LOVEJOY Laura of Candia on 26 Jan at Candia, ATWOOD Mark Eld *MS* 5 Feb 1845

WALLACE Daniel R m MARTIN Almira of Andover on 10 Feb 1849, DAVIS J E Eld *MS* 7 Mar 1849

WALLACE David m HADLEY Emily of Holderness on 20 Nov 1842, THOMPSON Samuel Eld *MS* 15 Mar 1843

WALLACE George B m WATSON Jane on 2 Nov at Dover NH, DUNN Ransom Eld *MS* 8 Nov 1843

WALLACE James F m WALLACE Abigail M at Sandwich, BROOKS N Eld *MS* 27 Mar 1844

WALLACE Reuben Jr m NEWCOMB Olive E of South Danville NY on 10 May at South Danville NY, COBB A Eld *MS* 17 Aug 1842

WALLEY James m MARTIN Ellen at Portsmouth NH *MFWBR* 18 Aug 1849

WALLIN Ezra m MORRILL Louisa of Oneonta NY on 4 Jul 1848 in Oneonta NY, WING Amos Eld *MS* 26 Jul 1848

WALLINGFOR G M of Stanstead m LEBARRON E A of Hatley LC on 2 Oct 1843 in Stanstead, MOULTON A Eld *MS* 1 May 1844

WALLIS Abraham C m LOVEJOY Sophronia D of Candia on 22d ult at FWB meeting house in Candia, FERNALD S P Eld *MS* 2 Oct 1839

WALRATH Nathaniel m WALRATH Elizabeth on 1 Mar 1848 in Clayton NY, GRIFFETH A Eld *MS* 21 June 1848

WALRATH Sylvester m SPERRY Grace on 30 Dec 1847 in Clayton NY, GRIFFITH A Eld *MS* 23 Feb 1848

WALTER Horace of Dover NH m BURNHAM Martha C of Newfield in Newfield, BURBANK Rev *MS* 13 Dec 1827

WALVERTON Amos of Conquest m GRANT Margaret on 2d ult at Butler Wayne Co NY, ALDRICH Eld *MS* 13 June 1833

WARD Benjamin m PEASE Sally both of Meredith on 30 Jan, MANSON Benjamin S Eld *MS* 27 Feb 1834

WARD Chase of Hardwick VT m HOLMES Abigail of Dalton NH on 29 Dec 1849 in Whitefield NH, SHEPHERD Almond Eld *MS* 27 Feb 1850

WARD Cotton "Post Master of North Belmont ME" m CATE Abby of Sanbornton NH *MS* 26 May 1847

WARD David m STEEL Lucretia on 10 May in Middlesex VT, CHATTERTON B Eld *MS* 23 Sept 1846

WARD David S m HOIT Adaline C both of Freeport ME on 7 Dec 1848 in Freeport ME, PURINTON A W Eld *MS* 24 Jan 1849

WARD Erastus m WATSON Emily of Freedom NH on 17 Mar at Effingham Falls NH, BUTLER O Eld *MS* 2 Apr 1845

WARD Horace J m BOWMAN Almira B both of Bradford on 21 Mar, WENTWORTH J J Eld *MS* 22 May 1850

WARD Isaac m GRANT Mary both of Freeport ME on 1 Dec in Freeport ME *MS* 25 Dec 1850

WARD John C Eld of Monroe ME m STANLEY Susan S of Conway NH on 19 Feb in Eaton, MILLS James E Eld *MS* 24 Apr 1850

WARD John C of Monroe m STANLEY Susan S of Conway NH at Eaton *MFWBR* 4 May 1850

WARD John m WARD Mary E both of Freeport ME on 12 Dec 1847 in Freeport ME, PURINTON A W Eld *MS* 9 Feb 1848

WARD John m WEEKS Laura on 4 Dec of Danville VT, GEORGE N K Eld *MS* 21 Jan 1846

WARD Josiah m SMYTH Amy of Brunswick ME, MARELEN J Alonzo Esq *MFWBR* 5 Apr 1851

WARD Josiah m SMITH Sarah T of New Hampton on 22 May 1842 at Meredith NH, PITMAN Stephen J *MS* 15 June 1842

WARD Samuel of New Hampton m PEASE Nancy of Meredith on 6 June, PITMAN S J Eld *MS* 30 Oct 1844

WARD Silas H m HARRIMAN Elsa Jane on 3 Mar at Eaton, RUNNELS J Eld *MS* 18 Mar 1846

WARD Thomas M m ALLEN Lorana in Durham ME, LIBBY A Eld *MS* 12 Mar 1851

WARDSWORTH Joseph of Livermore m EATON Nancy F of Chesterville at Farmington ME, CHANEY John Eld *MS* 12 June 1839

WARDWELL Charles P S of Lowell MA m COLE Martia B of Gilford NH on 24 June 1849 in Gilford NH, FROST D S Eld *MS* 9 Jan 1850

WARE Ezekiel of Gardiner ME m SMITH Jane both of Webster ME on 25 Aug 1847 in Bowdoin ME, PURINTON A W Eld *MS* 17 Nov 1847

WARNER Charles m BACON Eliza both of Mendon in Waterford, BULINGAME M W Eld *MS* 5 Sept 1838

WARNER David E m TAYLOR Ruth S of Mendon on 29th inst, BURLINGAME M W Eld *MS* 24 Apr 1839

WARNER John m CAMPBELL Lettis at Georgetown ME, BERRY A L Esq *MFWBR* 10 Mar 1849

WARNER Matthew m FLUNKER Sally both of Warsaw NY on Oct 31 1839, PLUMB H N Eld *MS* 20 May 1840

WARNER Myron of Wales NY m MORSE Sophia M of Lowell MA in Holderness, PETTINGILL John Eld *MS* 28 June 1837

WARNER Richard m SLY Philena of Hainburgh in Hainburgh NY, PLUMB H N Eld *MS* 19 Apr 1848

WARREN Ambrose m BOYINGTON Martha on 2nd inst, at Bangor ME *MFWBR* 12 Jan 1850

WARREN C F M of Berwick m PINDLEY Mary F of So Berwick on 15 Sept, BROOKS N Eld *MS* 26 Sept 1849

WARREN Charles m BRACKETT Betsey C of Waterville ME on 16 Dec 1847 in Waterville ME, BURGESS J S Eld *MS* 19 Jan 1848

WARREN Henry M m KNIGHT Mary J of Pownal ME on 29 Sept at Pownal ME, HAMBLEN J F Eld *MS* 8 Jan 1845

WARREN Joseph F of Newmarket m YOUNG Mary Ann of Somersworth on 20 Jan, STEVENS T Eld *MS* 20 Feb 1839

WARREN Noah m PALMER Maria J both of Milton on 1 Jan 1849 in Farmington NH, BODGE Jacob Eld *MS* 31 Jan 1849

WARREN Peter m SARGENT Ann K on 15 Sept at Mantua Ohio, MILLER D Eld *MS* 17 Dec 1845

WARREN Samuel m COOK Susan W both of Dover on 5 inst in Dover, HUTCHINS E Eld *MS* 13 June 1849

WARRINEF Israel C of Buffalo m AMCEDON Julia of Hamburgh NY, PLUMB Horatio N *MS* 25 Nov 1835

WARRINER Washington L m KINGSBURY Clarissa C both of Roxbury on Nov 23 in Brookfield, CLAFLIN Jehiel Eld *MS* 5 Jan 1842

WASAN Thomas of Exeter m NORRIS Mary in Raymond *MS* 30 Mar 1842

WASHBURN George of Peterboro NH m CHENEY Abby M of Holderness on 16 Sept 1847 in Holderness, WEBBER H Eld *MS* 6 Oct 1847

WASHBURN Thomas m ROGERS Ann, THURSTON N Eld *MS* 15 May 1839

WASON John O m SCRIBNER Joia C both of Candia on 15 Dec in Candia, MANSON B S Eld *MS* 19 Apr 1837

WATERHOUSE Charles F of Durham m WATERHOUSE Olive of Limington ME on 26 Feb, MANSON B S Eld *MS* 7 Feb 1844

WATERHOUSE Daniel m CORSON Delia Mrs both of Barrington on 6 Sept in Barrington, PLACE E Eld *MS* 18 Sept 1850

WATERHOUSE Thomas m ESTES Miriam in Standish, HODSDON Caleb Esq *MS* 5 Jul 1827

WATERHOUSE William m CLARK Isabella S at Hollis, McDANIEL J Rev *MFWBR* 21 Apr 1849

WATERMAN Charles m OWEN Abigail B of Buxton ME, LIBBY Isaac Eld *MS* 14 Feb 1849

WATERMAN Dexter Eld of Boothbay m WENTWORTH Mahala of Bristol on 2nd inst at Bristol ME, BRIDGES A Eld *MS* 2 Jul 1834

WATERMAN F W m HOLT P Mrs on 15 Jul in Sherburne NY, MOORE H A Eld *MS* 21 Nov 1849

WATERMAN Isaac of Troy m WHEELER Lucy E of Nassau on 19 Oct in Nassau, COLMAN I B Eld *MS* 3 Jan 1849

WATERMAN Oliver m BROWN Clarissa both of Litchfield ME on 23 Nov in Litchfield, QUINNAM C Eld *MS* 25 Dec 1839

WATERMAN Robert of Belfast m RICH Mary at Brooks ME *MFWBR* 22 May 1847

WATERS John T of Portland ME m MINOT Harriet P Mrs on 19th inst at Portland ME, BROWN S E Eld *MFWBR* 27 Apr 1850

WATSON B F of Concord m WHIPPLE Mary A of Hebron on 16 Nov 1848 in Hebron, CALLEY D Eld *MS* 29 Nov 1848

WATSON Benjamin S m BATES Alvira on 14 Nov at Groton, PECK Benjamin D Eld *MS* 18 Jan 1843

WATSON Charles A m GREENWOOD Mary E on 12 Nov at Weld ME, WATERMAN D Eld *MS* 23 Dec 1846

WATSON Daniel Jr m BLAKE Mehitabel W both of Pittsfield on 4 Oct in Northwood NH, JOHNSON W D Eld *MS* 11 Nov 1846

WATSON Daniel Jr m TILTON Margaret A both of Pittsfield on 6 May, TRUE E Eld *MS* 16 May 1849

WATSON David Jr of Limerick ME m DAY Sally of Cornish ME on 29th ult, BULLOCK Jeremiah Eld *MS* 10 May 1827

WATSON David of Ossipee NH m WITHERAL Hannah of Effingham NH on 10 Mar 1850 in Effingham, FOSS N Eld *MS* 20 Mar 1850

WATSON Freeman m PLAISTED Olive M of Lowell MA on 3rd inst at

WATSON (Continued)

Saccarappa ME, NEVENS William P Esq *MS* 4 Oct 1843

WATSON Jacob m WHITCHER Rachel of Meredith NH, PITMAN Stephen J Eld *MS* 30 Jan 1839

WATSON Jonathan of Limerick on Sunday m NORRIS Jane, LIBBY Eld *MS* 27 Aug 1828

WATSON Joseph Jr m PIPER Sarah Ann Mrs on 2 Oct at Gilmanton NH, HAM Ezra Eld *MS* 28 Jan 1846

WATSON Joseph m BUMFORD Lydia both of Barrington on 28 Mar, *MS* 27 Apr 1836

WATSON Josiah of New Market m CUTTS Maria S of South Berwick ME on 8th inst, JORDAN Zachariah Eld *MS* 14 Aug 1839

WATSON Lysander B of Brooklyn NY m LOCKE Melinda B of Dover on 26 ult in Dover, HUTCHINS E Eld *MS* 4 Dec 1850

WATSON Nathaniel of Scarboro ME m PURKIS Mary Ann of Gray ME on 15th, PURKIS John Eld *MS* 22 June 1836

WATSON Reuben B of Northwood NH m RICHARDS Huldah J of Hope ME, LAMB H A Esq *MS* 18 Oct 1848

WATSON Solomon m TILTON Betsey on 17 inst at Pittsfield *MS* 31 Aug 1836

WATSON Stephen B m STAR Sarah Mrs both of Richmond RI on 5 Mar 1850 in Carolina Mills RI, WILLIAMS A D Eld *MS* 20 Mar 1850

WATSON Thomas J m CHADBOURNE Lydia C both of Fryeburg ME on 22 Mar in Fryeburg, WILLEY Eben C Eld *MS* 8 Apr 1846

WATSON William m DAVIS Maria Jane both of Pittsfield on 23 Jul in Pittsfield, KNOWLES John Eld *MS* 6 Sept 1837

WATSON Winthrop m BEAN Sally L on 22 Dec 1844, PINKHAM J Eld *MS* 12 Feb 1845

WATTS Chamber m HALE Mary Angeline on 27 Sept at Stow VT, GRAY Ira Eld *MS* 30 Nov 1842

WAYMAN Hiram at Waterville m BERRY Hannah, LEWIS D B Eld *MS* 17 Apr 1844

WEARE Gardiner M of Candia NH m YOUNG Abigail B of Manchester NH on 6 Oct, FERNALD S P Eld *MS* 30 Nov 1842

WEATHERBEE Benjamin of Dedham m JOHNSON Elizabeth A of Deerfield on Thanksgiving Eve in Deerfield, GARLAND G D Eld *MS* 8 Dec 1847

WEATHERBY Ansel C m ROBBINS Caroline V both of Pittsfield MA on 17 Jan 1849 at Stephentown NY, COLEMAN I B Eld *MS* 2 May 1849

WEATHERBY Willard m DOTY Eliza of Nassau on 7 May, COLEMAN I B Eld *MS* 4 Oct 1843

WEAVER Isaiah G m COOK Sarah C both of Smithfield on 18 ult in Smithfield, ALLEN R Eld *MS* 18 Apr 1838

WEAVER John of Arkwright m SINCLAIR Martha of Gerry on 5 May

WEAVER (Continued)
in Gerry NY, STARR N Eld *MS* 19 June 1850

WEAVER Philip Eld m COOMBS Margaret H on 26 March at Augusta ME *MS* 24 Jul 1844

WEBB John of Waterville m RICKER Maria W, LEWIS D B Eld *MS* 16 Oct 1839

WEBBER Bradford of Monroe ME m WHITNEY Cynthia of Newburgh ME on 1 Nov, ALLEN Ebenezer Eld *MS* 13 Jan 1847

WEBBER Elias S m JEPSON Clarisa Ann of Lewiston ME at Lewiston ME on 7th ult *MFWBR* 2 Feb 1850

WEBBER Jeremiah S m TOWN Roxana D on 29 Dec of Boscawen NH, SINCLAIR J L Eld *MS* 16 Jan 1839

WEBBER Samuel m MILLS Henritta on 24th inst in Waterboro ME, CLARK Eld *MS* 30 Apr 1828

WEBBER Shapleigh m TAYLOR Phoebe on Mar 26th ult in Kennebunk ME, ROBERTS Eld *MS* 9 Nov 1826

WEBBER William m SMITH Mary both of Holderness in Holderness NH, PETTINGILL John Eld *MS* 28 June 1837

WEBBS Samuel Esq m HEMINGWAY Cynthia on 21st at Brunswick ME *MFWBR* 3 Feb 1849

WEBSTER Alfred m DARLING Cyntha both of Woodstock NH on 5 Oct 1848 in Woodstock NH, RUSSELL G W Eld *MS* 8 Nov 1848

WEBSTER Benjamin Jr m STANLEY Sarah A on 16 May 1844 at Haverhill NH, MOULTON F Eld *MS* 24 Jul 1844 (*sic*) should be *MS* 31 Jul 1844

WEBSTER Benjamin m PERRY Lynthia on Sunday last at Limerick ME, BURBANK S Eld *MS* 20 June 1833

WEBSTER Daniel C of Manchester NH m TRUE Sarah of Moultonboro' NH, BROOKS N Eld *MS* 10 Oct 1844

WEBSTER Davidson merchant of Dover m DEARBORN Julia Ann of Portsmouth in 1st Baptist Ch, HOWE Rev *MS* 7 Jan 1835

WEBSTER Elbridge of Meredith m ALDRICH Caroline of Gilford on 5 May in Gilford, SINCLAIR J L Eld *MS* 30 May 1849

WEBSTER Lyman W m SMITH Eliza Jane at Sandwich, BROOKS N Eld *MS* 27 Mar 1844

WEBSTER Nathaniel D at Kingston m DAVIS Julia A F on 25 Nov, FULLONTON J Eld *MS* 15 Dec 1841

WEBSTER Royal F of Gray ME m EMERY Olive of Limington ME on 7 Dec, MANSON B S Eld *MS* 7 Feb 1844

WEBSTER Samuel of Waterville ME m WOOD Louisa of Sidney ME, LEWIS Daniel B *MS* 21 Jan 1846

WEBSTER Samuel S m PITMAN Mary J on 21 Nov 1833 both of Meredith, MANSON Benjamin S Eld *MS* 27 Feb 1834

WEBSTER William B of Industry ME m PALMER Eliza Jane at New Sharon ME on 6th inst, ELA R Eld *MS* 23 Oct 1844

WEBSTER William m DOLLOFF Nancy both of Meredith NH in

WEBSTER (Continued)

Meredith NH, PITMAN S J Eld *MS* 10 Nov 1847

WEDGEWOOD John m HOYT Caroline M on 26 May at Dracut MA, CURTIS S Eld *MS* 7 Jul 1847

WEDGWOOD Thatcher of Parsonsfield ME m EATON Belinda of Limerick ME on 4th inst, FOSS Eld *MS* 10 Mar 1830

WEED Benjamin F of Lowell m FIELD Mary E of Portland on 7th inst at Portland ME, EATON J S Rev *MFWBR* 16 June 1849

WEEKS Charles m WYMAN Sophia, LEWIS D B Eld *MS* 25 Dec 1844

WEEKS Edmund P m PENDEXTER Harriet L on 6 Sept at Bridgeton ME, WILLEY C Eld *MS* 30 Dec 1846

WEEKS George W of Boston MA m ROBINSON Betsey of Meredith, PITMAN Stephen J Eld *MS* 8 Dec 1841

WEEKS John P of Danville VT m WARD Hannah of Danville, GEORGE N K Eld *MS* 24 Feb 1847

WEEKS Jonathan T m JAMES Zoa M both of Gilford on 26 ult in Gilford, PINKHAM John Eld *MS* 10 Oct 1838

WEEKS Joseph m PLAISTED Susan M at Newhampton *MS* 17 Aug 1836

WEEKS Joshua of Conway m FARNHAM Maria of Albany on 20 Dec 1846, FLETCHER J Eld *MS* 25 Aug 1847

WEEKS Levi m WEEKS Anna Mrs on 23d inst in Parsonsfield ME, BUZZELL John Eld *MS* 27 Sept 1827

WEEKS Lorenzo L of Ossipee NH m MURPHY Alice of Parsonsfield ME on 4 Oct, BUZZELL Alvah Eld *MS* 21 Jan 1846

WEEKS Lorrain Dr m CLIFFORD Hannah T on 9 June 1844 at Gilmanton NH, CHASE W P Eld *MS* 29 Jan 1845

WEEKS Noah Esq m COBB Betsey on 7 May at Cornish ME, HACKETT J O Eld *MS* 17 May 1843

WEEKS Noah m GARLAND Elizabeth in Parsonsfield ME *MS* 27 Feb 1829

WEEKS Phineas I of Wakefield m HAYES Mercy B of Effingham NH on 25 Apr in Effingham *MS* 23 May 1849

WEEKS Robert Jr m LOMBARD Harriet S of Gorham ME on 14 Jul, LIBBY C O Eld *MS* 16 Oct 1844

WEEKS Samuel D m WEDGEWOOD Olive both of Lowell on 28 inst in Lowell, THURSTON Nathaniel *MS* 12 Sept 1838

WEEKS Samuel of Gilmanton m FRENCH Abigail T of Loudon NH on 21 Nov, DYER Samuel Eld *MS* 19 Dec 1838

WEEKS Stephen Jr m STEVENS Mary Adeline on 16th ult, SMALL Carlton Eld at Gilmanton *MS* 16 Jan 1839

WEEKS Stephen Jr of Gilmanton m HAINES Elizabeth W of Canterbury on 22 May, HARPER J M Eld *MS* 19 June 1844

WEEKS William Capt m DAVIS Rhoda O on 21 Sept at Gilford, BROOKS N Eld *MS* 2 Nov 1842

WEEMAN Obediah of Standish ME m ALLEN Eliza of Biddeford ME

WEEMAN (Continued)
MFWBR 12 May 1849

WEGWOOD Samuel C of Effingham NH m DAVIS Mary Ann of Dover NH on 14th inst at Dover NH, PERKINS Seth W Eld *MS* 18 Feb 1846

WELCH Bray of Athens m ROWELL Emily of Cornville ME on 8 Jul 1847 in Cornville ME, RUSSELL S Eld *MS* 25 Aug 1847

WELCH Cyrus B of Parsonsfield m HILL Abigail of Brownfield ME on 17 Sept in Brownfield ME, HACKETT J O Eld *MS* 24 Oct 1838

WELCH Edward Jr m FELT Elbina L on 9 Nov at Hallowell ME, WEAVER Phillip Eld *MS* 7 Jan 1846

WELCH Isaiah of Sanford ME m STANLEY Sally M on Dec 25 at Shapleigh ME, LORD D H Eld *MS* 8 Jan 1840

WELCH Joseph m RIDER Judith Ann both of No Yarmouth ME on 3 Nov 1847 in No Yarmouth, CROCKETT J Eld *MS* 17 Nov 1847

WELCH Joseph of Wakefield NH m CLOUGH Sarah of Parsonsfield ME on 7th inst, CHAPMAN Andrew M C Esq *MS* 13 Feb 1829

WELCH Lawrence m MOORE Rachel on Oct 16, BROWN John Jr *MS* 19 Jan 1842

WELCH Samuel E m HUNTOON Betsey of Lowell MA on 4 March, WOODMAN J Eld *MS* 23 Aug 1843

WELCH Samuel m PRESCOTT Mary Jane both of Dixmont ME in Dixmont, RINES J N Eld *MS* 25 Dec 1839

WELCH Samuel M m GRAY Dorothy C at Dover NH *MFWBR* 20 Apr 1850 & WELCH Samuel W on 3 inst m GRAY Dorothy O both of Dover, HUTCHINS E Eld *MS* 10 Apr 1850

WELCH Sewall m LIBBEY Abagail of Raymond ME on 13th ult at Raymond ME, JORDAN Anson Esq of Casco *MFWBR* 8 June 1850

WELCHER Allen of Spencer m HOLCOMB Lucetta of La Grange on 30 Jul in Pittsfield Ohio, KNIGHT A Eld *MS* 4 Sept 1850

WELLER William m STOW Maria of Lawrence on 22 Oct at Lawrence NY, WHITFIELD Eld *MS* 6 Dec 1843

WELLINGTON Horace Prof of Languages in Mich Cen College m LOCKE Helen E of West Cambridge MA on 9 Aug 1847 in West Cambridge MA, FAIRFIELD E B Eld *MS* 22 Sept 1847

WELLMAN Eben B of Boston MA m WILLIAMS Martha Ann of Lowell MA on 7 Oct at Lowell MA, THURSTON N Eld *MS* 2 Nov 1842

WELLS James S m QUIMBY Sarah of Franconia on 15 Sept at Franconia NH, GEORGE N K Eld *MS* 28 Dec 1842

WELLS John of Ipswich MA m STILES Eleanor of Portsmouth NH on 16 Dec at Portsmouth NH *MS* 7 Jan 1846

WELLS John of Strafford VT m BURBANK Lovey, PETTENGELL John Eld *MS* 1 Feb 1843

WELLS Jonathan m KILLAM Phebe F of Hillsborough on 9 Mar, CILLEY D P Eld *MS* 19 Mar 1845

WELLS Rodney S m GLIFFORD Lydia L both of Manchester on 25

WELLS (Continued)
Nov 1847 in Manchester, CILLEY D P Eld *MS* 8 Dec 1847

WELLS Samuel Capt m LOCK Mary S both of Epsom on 1 Dec *MS* 11 Jan 1837

WELLS Squire m WAY Fidelia on 28 Jan at Pierpont NY, WHITFIELD W Eld *MS* 25 Feb 1846

WELLS Thomas of Sutton at Alexandria NH m GALE Deborah of Alexandria NH on 19 Apr 1842, BROWN A Eld *MS* 4 May 1842

WENDAL Daniel H on Sunday morning last m JENNESSE Huldah in Limerick ME, MACK Enoch Eld *MS* 20 Sept 1837

WENTWORTH Amos m LOCKE Eliza M on last Sunday in Dover NH, WILLIAM Gibbon Rev *MS* 1 Oct 1834

WENTWORTH Benjamin L of Great Falls NH m WENTWORTH Laura J of So Berwick ME on 21 Jan, BROOKS N Eld *MS* 30 Jan 1850

WENTWORTH Benjamin R of Somersworth m HANSON Deborah S R at Rochester, CURTIS S Eld *MS* 22 Apr 1840

WENTWORTH Bennin m MEDER Hannah both of Dover in Dover, SMITH A D Eld *MS* 29 Nov 1837

WENTWORTH David Dea m DAVIS Mary widow both of Dover on 7 Aug in Portsmouth NH, SMITH A D Eld *MS* 22 Aug 1838

WENTWORTH Eri of Milton m SHUTE Mary Jane of Effingham NH on 30 June, BUTLER O Eld *MS* 28 Aug 1844

WENTWORTH Ezra m EMERY Sabrina of Boston MA on 28th ult at Hampton, BURBANK P S Eld *MS* 11 Oct 1843

WENTWORTH George G m ELKINS Mary R of Dover in Lowell, THURSTON N Eld *MS* 26 Jul 1837

WENTWORTH George of Dover NH m WOODSUM Abby H at Saco ME, WILLIAMS N M Esq *MFWBR* 16 Mar 1850

WENTWORTH Henry R m LITTLEFIELD Eliza S of Dover NH at Dover NH on 1st inst, PERKINS Seth W *MS* 7 Jan 1846

WENTWORTH Hiram m DEMERITT Mercy of Effingham NH on 16 June at Effingham, BUTLER O Eld *MS* 28 Aug 1844

WENTWORTH Israel P of Barrington m CLARK Mary Ann of Dover on Sunday 14 inst at Strafford, SHURBURNE Eld *MS* 24 Feb 1836

WENTWORTH James W m DREW Margaret W on 26 Dec of Great Falls NH, DUNN R Eld *MS* 6 Jan 1847

WENTWORTH Job L m WEBB Sarah at Portsmouth NH *MFWBR* 27 Apr 1850

WENTWORTH John of Andover m LOVREIGH Eliza L of Lowell MA on 24 ult *MS* 3 June 1835

WENTWORTH John of Dover m TUXBURY Mary of Tamworth NH in Tamworth, EMERY James Eld *MS* 21 Nov 1838

WENTWORTH Jonathan Y m LORD Hannah W of Lebanon ME on 23 June at Lebanon ME, CORSON Charles Eld *MS* 17 Jul 1844

WENTWORTH Joseph of Waterboro' ME m BROWN Sally of Great Falls NH on 5 Dec, CAVERNO A Eld *MS* 10 Dec 1834

WENTWORTH Levi H of Lebanon ME m MOODY Lydia Ann of Gilmanton on 10 Mar 1850 in Gilmanton, MOODY D Eld *MS* 24 Apr 1850

WENTWORTH Lewis B of Somersworth m McINTIRE Mary E of Alton NH on 5 May in Alton NH, PINKHAM J Eld *MS* 16 May 1849

WENTWORTH Lewis E m HAM Sarah both of Dover on 11 inst in Dover, SMITH A D Eld *MS* 22 Nov 1848

WENTWORTH Oliver W of Dover m WENTWORTH Sarah N of Somersworth on 15 Oct in Dover NH, PINKHAM J Eld *MS* 13 Nov 1850

WENTWORTH Phineas of Barrington m JEWEL Mary of New Market on 1 Mar, SHERBURNE S Eld *MS* 25 June 1845

WENTWORTH Robert B, State Printer of Madison Wis m PIKE Lydia H on 9 inst in Fryeburg ME, PIKE J Eld *MS* 20 Nov 1850 & *MFWBR* 26 Oct 1850

WENTWORTH Samuel G m YOUNG Louisa D of Manchester NH at Manchester NH, CILLEY D P Eld *MS* 27 Nov 1844

WENTWORTH Samuel P m ABBOTT Susan at Dover NH on 1 June, PERKINS Seth W Eld *MS* 4 June 1845

WENTWORTH Stephen m GILMAN E P of Sangerville ME on 3 Apr at Sangerville, BRIDGES O W Eld *MS* 4 June 1845

WENTWORTH William F of Lebanon ME m HALL Armine W of Berwick ME in Lebanon ME, CHENEY O B Eld *MS* 19 Jul 1848

WENTWORTH William married m ALLEN Mary at Wakefield NH, CLARK Mayhew Eld *MS* 27 Jul 1826

WESCOTT Arthur m TANNER Betsy both of Providence on 29 Sept in No Scituate RI, CILLEY D P Eld *MS* 16 Oct 1850

WESCOTT Josiah S of Manchester NH m FAVOUR Mary Ann, CILLEY D P Eld *MS* 15 Oct 1845

WESCOTT William m EDER Maria S both of Windham ME on 9 Apr, MANSON B S Eld *MS* 29 May 1850

WESLEY Joseph of Tiverton m BURT Delia Miss of Providence RI on 26th ult, HUTCHINS Elias *MS* 2 Jan 1834

WEST Albert M m GOVE Elizabeth of Strafford VT on 14 Sept, PETTENGELL/PETTINGILL John Eld *MS* 1 Feb 1843 & *MS* 19 Oct 1842

WEST John D of Limerick ME m TRACY Sophia A at Auburn ME on 25th ult *MFWBR* 4 Dec 1847

WEST William A m NASON Maria on 31st ult at Sebago ME, TRACY J Eld *MFWBR* 21 Jan 1849

WESTCOTT Stephen m JORDAN Emeline C on 26th inst at Gorham ME, BUZZELL J M Eld *MFWBR* 30 Oct 1847

WESTGATE Elzi W of Cornish NH m PEASE Lydia of Ellsworth on 22 Nov in Ellsworth ME, BUZZELL David R Esq *MS* 28 Nov 1849

WESTLY Wamule m McCRILLIS Joanna both of Lebanon ME on 30 Aug 1847, COWELL D B Eld *MS* 1 Dec 1847

WESTON Caleb of Foxcroft ME m WOODARD Jane of Guilford

WESTON (Continued)
MS 1 Feb 1837

WESTON Moses of Foxcroft ME m SOALE Betsey of Guilford *MS* 1 Feb 1837

WESTON Peley m THAYER Christiana at Foxcroft ME, COOMBS Abner Eld *MS* 19 Nov 1834

WESTON Simeon of Mt Vernon m BLANCHARD Lavinia of Wilton ME on 21 Jan 1847, BAXTER John E Rev *MS* 14 Jul 1847

WETHERBEE Daniel J m GILMAN Sarah A both of Sandwich on 9 Aug in Sandwich, WETHERBEE Josiah Eld *MS* 24 Oct 1849

WETHEREN/WETHERN Amos F of New Portland ME m PULLEN Julia A of Kingfield ME on 30 Mar 1848 in Kingfield ME, LONG-LEY James P Eld *MS* 24 May 1848 & *MFWBR* 29 Apr 1848

WEYMOUTH Cyrus C of Freeman m LANDER Nancy M of Kingfield on 31 Oct in Kingfield, LENNAN John Eld *MS* 18 Dec 1839

WEYMOUTH George Esq m SWAN Charlotte of Tunbridge VT on 29 Oct at Tunbridge VT, CALLEY D Eld *MS* 2 Dec 1846

WEYMOUTH Henry Dr of Andover NH m YOUNG Louisa of Gilmanton NH on 1 Jan 1844, TUTTLE John G Eld *MS* 17 Jan 1844

WEYMOUTH J S m DEARBORN Sarah B on 5 Feb at Gilmanton, MOODY David Eld *MS* 21 June 1843

WEYMOUTH John C Capt m EVANS Martha A both of Gilmanton at Meredith Bridge Jan 4 1842, BROOKS N Eld *MS* 2 Feb 1842

WEYMOUTH John m JOHNSON Mary both of N Berwick in North Berwick on Apr 13, LORD D H Eld *MS* 27 Apr 1842

WEYMOUTH Levi E m JOHNSON Ann B on 19th inst at Portland ME, MOULTON A K Eld *MS* 28 Feb 1844

WEYMOUTH Luther of Saco m FOSS Lettice A of Hollis on 20th inst *MFWBR* 1 Feb 1851

WEYMOUTH Moses of No Berwick ME m DICKSON Ann of Sandford ME, BURBANK Samuel Eld *MS* 5 Apr 1837

WEYMOUTH Nathaniel F of Pittsfield m SIMONS Judith P of Clinton, LEWIS Daniel B Eld *MS* 21 Jan 1846

WEYMOUTH William m HUBBARD Mariah H on 26 Dec at Roxbury MA, DAVIS J B Eld *MS* 10 Jan 1844

WHALEY Simeon O m KELLEY Orpha L both of Middlebury on 8 ult in Middlebury NY, PLUMB H N Eld *MS* 20 May 1846

WHEEDEN Edward m TUTTLE Hannah Mrs of Great Falls NH at Great Falls NH *MFWBR* 4 May 1850

WHEELER Abel of Hatley LC m STILL Lucy, MOULTON A Eld *MS* 13 Sept 1843

WHEELER Andrew I of Lowell m HOPKINS Keziah of Wilmington on 5 Oct, DURGIN J M Eld *MS* 22 Feb 1843

WHEELER Ezekiel H m TOWNS Mehitabel both of Lisbon on 15 ult in Lisbon, WILLIS O F Eld *MS* 27 Sept 1837

WHEELER George D of Royalton m DREW Maria L of Tunbridge on

WHEELER (Continued)
18 Mar 1849, SMITH C H Eld *MS* 28 Mar 1849

WHEELER Henry at Manchester NH m CHILDS Elzina M, BROOKS
John Eld *MS* 24 Dec 1845

WHEELER Hiram m SPRAGUE Elvira both of Barnston on Dec 31,
MOULTON A W Eld *MS* 15 Apr 1840

WHEELER James F of Hancock MA m DABELL Sarah Ann of Stephentown NY on 15 Feb in West Stephentown NY, COLEMAN I B
Eld *MS* 13 Mar 1850

WHEELER Jeremiah m ANDERSON Mary on 19 Jan at Manchester
NH, CILLEY D P Eld *MS* 17 Feb 1847

WHEELER John Eld m GREGORY Huldah both of Greenfield in
Greenfield Huron Co Ohio, ROOT E Eld *MS* 2 Jan 1850

WHEELER John m PERKINS Florina S on 11 Apr 1844 in Loudon
NH, CLOUGH Jeremiah Eld *MS* 1 May 1844

WHEELER Orren T m BLANCHARD Ann E both of Manchester on 2
Apr in Manchester, CILLEY D P Eld *MS* 15 Apr 1846

WHEELER Zopher m TIFFT Orsena K on 12 Oct at Stephentown NY,
COLEMAN I B Eld *MS* 17 Dec 1845

WHEELOCK James M of Milford m FULLER Maria L on 1 Aug at
Sutton MA, FULLER Willard Eld *MS* 14 Aug 1844

WHELDEN Henry m JONES Susan F of Belfast, at Montville ME
MFWBR 17 Mar 1849

WHIDDEN Nathaniel B of Denmark ME m LOVICE Martha of Fryeburg on 23 Nov, PIKE J Eld *MS* 31 Dec 1845

WHIPPLE Benjamin m ALLEN Mary on 2d inst at No Providence RI,
HUTCHINS Elias Eld *MS* 24 Apr 1834

WHIPPLE Job P of Springfield m VAN VALKENBURGH Nancy of
Sand Lake on 8 inst in Sand Lake NY, COLEMAN I B Eld *MS* 22
Jan 1851

WHIPPLE Joseph m EATON Hannah J both of Manchester on 27 Dec
1848 in Manchster, CILLEY D P Eld *MS* 17 Jan 1849

WHITCHER Hiram Eld an itinerant preacher m GREEN Louiza B
Miss on 9th inst of Conewanga, Cataraugus Co NY, JENKINS
Herman Eld *MS* 31 Aug 1832

WHITCHER Ira m ROYCE Lucy on 26 Nov at Haverhill, MOULTON F
Eld *MS* 17 Jan 1844

WHITCHER Joseph C of Danville m FERRENTON Lucretia W of
Waldin on 23 Oct 1849 in Waldin VT, GEORGE N K Eld *MS* 2 Jan
1850

WHITCOMB Aseph m TWOMBLY Mary both of Littleton on 20 Jul
1834, COWIN David Eld *MS* 7 Jan 1835

WHITCOMB Ephraim O m RICHARDSON Eliza P both of Lowell MA,
THURSTON N Eld *MS* 2 Jul 1834

WHITCOMB Lindya m DEXTER Abigail Maria of Bethlehem NH on
11 Jan, BEAN Benaiah Eld *MS* 20 Jan 1847

WHITCOMB Oren m QUIMBY Naoma at Fairfield ME, LEWIS D B Eld
MS 20 Apr 1842
WHITCOMB Stillman m PARSONS Eliza of Thorndike, LEWIS Daniel
B Eld MS 21 Jan 1846
WHITCOMB Uzziel of Essex m SHELDON Marilla of Jericho in
Richmond VT on March 9, LOVELL Rev MS 30 Mar 1842
WHITE Allen m LOUGEE Elizabeth R of Effingham NH on 4 Feb
1847 of Ossipee NH, BUTLER O Eld MS 28 Apr 1847
WHITE Benjamin L of Greenfield NH m WILKERSON Lucy Ann of
Nashua NH on 7 Oct, WOODMAN J Eld MS 19 Oct 1842
WHITE Charles m ROGERS Susan on 3d inst at Dover NH, BRIERLY
Rev MS 13 Jul 1836
WHITE Edwin A m WIGGIN Mary Ann G both of Deerfield NH in
Epsom NH, RAMSEY G P Eld MS 16 Jan 1850
WHITE Enoch m SMITH Mary Ann both of Windham on 11th inst,
WHITE Joseph Eld MS 21 Jan 1835
WHITE George m SPRAGUE Mary Ann both of Scituate RI on 26 Aug
at Backstone MA, BURLINGAME M W Eld MS 9 Sept 1846
WHITE George m GALUSHA Betsey of Palmyra on 8 Oct 1843, COPP
E Eld MS 27 Dec 1843
WHITE George W m WINSOR Eunice L both of Johnston RI on 3
Sept 1848 in Johnston RI, ALLEN R Eld MS 11 Oct 1848
WHITE John B of Backstone MA m HARKNES Miranda of Smithfield
RI on 26 Aug at Free Baptist Ch in Backstone MA, PECK B E Eld
MS 9 Sept 1846
WHITE John C Brother of Roxbury MA m STANTON Lydia B Sister of
Lebanon on 15 Mar in Lebanon ME, WETHERBEE Josiah Eld MS
15 Apr 1846
WHITE John Capt of Bowdoinham ME m REED Rebecca Mrs of
Dresden ME in Dresden MS 22 May 1844
WHITE John S of Cambridge MA m BARNS Mary A of Roxbury MA
on 14 Aug, DAVIS J B Eld MS 28 Aug 1844
WHITE Levi of Malden MA m DEMERITT Sarah J of Nottingham on 4
Jul, TUTTLE A Eld MS 20 June 1842
WHITE Nathaniel of Ossipee NH m TASKER Clarinda of Ossipee NH
on 31 Aug 1842, CHICK John Eld MS 5 Oct 1842
WHITE P H Mr of Biddeford ME m JONES Eliza of Portsmouth NH
on 15th ult at Charlestown, WETHERBEE I J Eld MS 9 Dec 1846
WHITE Philip m LESTER Cynthia of Nassau NY on 11 June at
Nassau NY, COLEMAN I B Eld MS 10 Sept 1845
WHITE Samuel Jr m SARGENT Martha A both of Monroe ME on 25
Jan 1849, ALLEN Ebenezer Eld MS 14 Feb 1849 & MS 21 Mar
1849
WHITE Solon H m RANDALL Margaret of Bowdoinham ME on 8 Apr
at Bowdoinham ME, QUINNAM C Eld MS 19 Apr 1843
WHITE Thomas Deacon m CILLEY Susan of Hopkinson on 27 Dec,

WHITE (Continued)
SINCLAIR J L Eld *MS* 16 Jan 1839

WHITE William H of Stoughton MA m MITCHELL Eliza J of Chesterville ME on 22 June at Chesterville ME, WHEELER S Eld *MS* 6 Aug 1845

WHITE William m RACKLIFF Olive both of Portsmouth on 27 June in Hampton, MERRIL William P Eld *MS* 17 Jul 1850

WHITE William of Hallowell m GOODWIN Mary of Pittston ME on 13 inst *MS* 23 Nov 1836

WHITEHEAD Charles of Boston MA m BAILEY Mary of Andover NH on 13 Feb 1849 in Andover NH, KNOWLES E G Eld *MS* 7 Mar 1849

WHITEHOUSE Andrew J m SMITH Maria J both of Great Falls NH on 12 Nov 1848, BROOKS N Eld *MS* 29 Nov 1848

WHITEHOUSE Andrew S m ROSS Hester A both of Brunswick in Brunswick ME, LIBBY A Eld *MS* 23 Jan 1850

WHITEHOUSE Charles C m JONES Susanna A both of Farmington NH on 4 Feb 1849 in Alton NH, PINKHAM John Eld *MS* 28 Feb 1849

WHITEHOUSE Edmond H of Great Falls m BOYLE Caroline E of Bucksport ME, BROOKS N Eld *MS* 18 Sept 1850

WHITEHOUSE Henry of So Berwick ME m DREW Lydia of Strafford, *MS* 23 Nov 1836

WHITEHOUSE Joseph M m HARVEY Catharine at Dover NY *MS* 13 Jul 1836

WHITEHOUSE Robert M m GEREISH Elizabeth T of Dover NH on 4th inst at Dover NH, THOMPSON Rev Dr *MS* 18 Nov 1846

WHITEHOUSE Samuel m GOULD Louisa on 27 Jan at Berwick ME, HART E H Eld *MS* 31 Aug 1842

WHITEHOUSE Thomas L m LORD Abigail of Dover NH on 26 Nov at Dover NH, SMITH A D Eld *MS* 9 Dec 1846

WHITEN Nathan B m MOONEY Judith P on 19 Mar at Holderness, TRUE E Eld *MS* 24 Apr 1844

WHITHAM Henry of Danville m BROWN Eliza of Pownal on 14 May in Pownal ME, NEWELL David Eld *MS* 19 June 1850

WHITLOCK John C m KNOWLES Myrta M both of Meredith on 26 Dec 1850 in Meredith NY, GREENE D Eld *MS* 19 Feb 1851

WHITMAN Isaiah J m CONNER Mary Mrs both of Dover on New Year's Eve in Dover NH, CAVERNO A Eld *MS* 16 Jan 1850

WHITMAN Willard K m FIELD Amanda both of Rochester on 7 Sept in Rochester Racine Co Wis, COOMBS A Eld *MS* 3 Nov 1847

WHITMORE Dexter m MARRINER Lydia Jane of Bowdoinham ME on 11 Sept at Bowdoinham, QUINNAM C Eld *MS* 19 Oct 1842

WHITMORE Simon m WITHAM Sarah H both of Biddeford ME on 9 Dec 1848 in Biddeford ME, WITHAM L H Eld *MS* 24 Jan 1849

WHITNEY Asa P of Bridgton m KNEELAND Eunice of Harrison on 18

WHITNEY (Continued)
Oct, WHITNEY G W Eld *MS* 10 May 1843

WHITNEY Benjamin F of Bridgton ME m BENNETT Susan L of Freedom, BUTLER O Eld *MS* 7 Feb 1844

WHITNEY Charles E of Concord m NEWELL Lydia A of Epsom on 25 Nov 1847 in Epsom, FOSS T Eld *MS* Dec 15 1847

WHITNEY Daniel m JESSAMAN Alzina both of Franconia in Franconia, BLAKE C E Eld *MS* 24 Jan 1849

WHITNEY Ebenezer m SMALL Sarah in Bowdoinham, by WOODARD Wm *MS* 23 Jan 1834

WHITNEY George R of Meredith m WING Mary, WILKINS N D Eld *MS* 1 Dec 1847

WHITNEY Henry m MEARS Emily both of Belmont in Waldo ME, MEARS George Z Eld *MS* 13 June 1849

WHITNEY James G m CARSLEY Betsey H of Harrison ME on 3 Jan 1847, PIKE J Eld *MS* 21 Apr 1847

WHITNEY John m TURNER Almira both of Lisbon on 9 ult in Lisbon ME, PURINTON A W Eld *MS* 8 May 1844

WHITNEY Jonathan W m EMERSON Mehitabel on 30 Nov at Dracut MA, CURTIS S Eld *MS* 24 Dec 1845

WHITNEY Joseph of Sardina m WARNER Arabella of Ashford, TAYNTOR O Eld *MS* 14 Feb 1844

WHITNEY Leonard S m DOLLOFF Rolina on 14 inst in Dover NH, SMITH Eleazer Rev *MS* 24 Jan 1838 & *MS* 14 Feb 1838

WHITNEY Nathan of Westminster m TOLMAN Mary S of Ashburnham on 27 Nov in Fitchburg MA, SAVAGE E Rev *MS* 12 Mar 1851

WHITTEMORE Albert m BEAN Shuah S both of Colebrook NH on 1 Jan in Colebrook, BEAN Benaiah Eld *MS* 16 Jan 1850

WHITTEMORE Daniel W of Boston MA m LOVERING Elanor of Loudon NH on Jan 26 1840, CLOUGH Jeremiah Eld *MS* 15 Apr 1840

WHITTEMORE David R Eld of North Providence RI m GILBERT Eliza Jane of Francestown NH on 29 Nov *MS* 4 Jan 1843

WHITTEMORE Enoch of Lisbon ME m FROST Rebecca P of Brunswick ME on 20 May, PAGE E G Eld *MS* 26 May 1847

WHITTEN George m POLLEY Abigail at Topsham ME on 30 May at Topsham ME, FOLSOM P Eld *MS* 31 Aug 1842

WHITTEN Henry A m DREW Lydia H both of Wolfborough NH in Wolfborough, PARIS C Eld *MS* 29 Dec 1847

WHITTEN Joseph m TUTTLE Mehitabel of Saco ME on 17th ult, DWIGHT Rev *MFWBR* 1 Feb 1851

WHITTEN Nathaniel m RICHARDSON Betsey at Dover NH, THURSTON Nathaniel Eld *MS* 25 Apr 1833

WHITTEN Oran m EASTMAN Mary E both of Rochester on 14 Apr in Rochester, PLACE E Eld *MS* 8 May 1850

WHITTIER Nathaniel m STRAW Mahala both of Meredith, PITMAN

WHITTIER (Continued)
S J Eld *MS* 12 Feb 1851

WHITTIER Nathaniel of Orange m HASTING Sophia of Bristol on 26 Nov 1847, BROWN Amos Eld *MS* 15 Dec 1847

WHITTON Ebenezer m RICKER Mary Mrs on 8th inst at Waterboro Center, ROWDYN Esq *MFWBR* 1 Sept 1849

WIDER Julius of Turin m MORFORD Loisa on 29 Feb at West Munroe NY of West Munroe NY, MORFORD J B *MS* 10 Apr 1844

WIGGIN Daniel m HASTINGS Elizabeth Jane on 25 ult at Lamprey River NH, BLODGETT C Rev *MS* 8 Jul 1835

WIGGIN Henry m BERRY Sarah W at Lowell MA, THURSTON N Eld *MS* 7 Jan 1835

WIGGIN Isaac m ABBOTT Julia A on 23 Feb 1850 in Ossipee NH, DORE Ezekiel Esq *MS* 13 Mar 1850

WIGGIN Janverin F of Dover NH m SAYWOOD Hannah F of Waterboro, BURBANK S Eld *MS* 18 May 1832

WIGGIN John of Moultonboro' NH m MOULTON Sally Mrs of Sandwich, BROOKS N Eld *MS* 13 Jan 1847

WIGGIN John W m DOWNS Louisa in Great Falls NH, DUNN R Eld *MS* 8 Dec 1847

WIGGIN Joseph F m STEVENS Mary Ann both of Stratham on 13 ult in Stratham, MERRILL A Eld *MS* 10 Oct 1838

WIGGIN Mark T of Wolfboro m GRAVES Angelina P of Tuftonborough NH on 24 Apr 1849 in Tuftonborogh NH, BEAN Silas F *MS* 9 May 1849

WIGGIN Nathan in 80th yr of his age m MILES Elizabeth Mrs in 60th yr of her age both of Parsonsfield in Parsonsfield, JORDAN Z Eld *MS* 25 Mar 1840

WIGGIN Nathaniel of North Chelmsford m SANBORN Lydia S of Gilmanton on 29 March, WOODMAN J Eld *MS* 23 Aug 1843

WIGGIN Noah L m SARGENT Harriet M H both of Lowell on 17 Feb in Dracut, CURTIS S Eld *MS* 28 Feb 1849

WIGGIN Samuel D of Sandwich NH m PIERCE Mehitabel, WEBBER Horace Eld *MS* 14 Sept 1842

WIGGIN Stephen P of Sanbornton NH m ROBERTS Patience E of Plymouth NH on 26 Oct 1847 in Plymouth NH, EASTMAN B H Esq *MS* 24 Nov 1847

WIGGIN Theophilus of Lee m ROBIE Sarah of Raymond in Raymond, FOSS Tobias Eld *MS* 6 Mar 1850

WIGGIN Thomas H of Wellington m CAMPBELL Achsah R of Brighton ME on 23 May 1848 in Bowdoinham ME, RAYMOND I Eld *MS* 21 June 1848

WIGGIN Waingate m PRESSON Ann of New Market on 31st ult at New Market, HUTCHINS E Eld *MS* 10 Aug 1842

WIGGINS Daniel m TUCK Mary on 5 Dec 1844 at Parsonsfield ME, TUCK Jonathan Esq *MS* 16 Apr 1845

WIGGINS Henry m BERRY Sarah W at Lowell MA, THURSTON N Eld
MS 24 Dec 1834

WIGGINS Jacob B of Newmarket m SMART Caroline on 5th inst,
HUTCHINS Elias Eld MS 18 Jan 1843

WIGGLESWORTH Samuel m MOORE Polly T both of Deerfield NH on
21 Nov in Deerfield NH, BURBANK P S Eld MS 18 Dec 1850

WILBOUR William m JAMES Caroline both of Scituate on 26 Nov in
No Scituate RI, ALLEN R Eld MS 1 Jan 1851

WILBUR Ellison K m HAWKINS Sarah A of Gloucester RI on 27 Nov
at Gloucester RI MS 14 Dec 1842

WILCOX Henry m FULLER Sarah A both of Unadilla Forks NY on 16
May in Unadilla Forks, BELKNAP P W Eld MS 8 Aug 1849

WILD Elijah m CLARK Achsah L Miss at Troy NY MS 18 Apr 1833

WILDES Jacob of Kennebunk Port married m MADDOCKS Mary of
Limerick ME MS 27 Sept 1827

WILEY Wiliam A m ROBERTS Mercy Ann on 18 inst, SMITH Eleazer
Rev MS 4 Oct 1837

WILKINS Almon H of Auburn m CLAY Mary A of Buxton on 4 June
in Buxton ME, CROCKETT J Eld MS 28 Aug 1850

WILKINSON Charles G m LEIGHTON Lucy J on 22 Nov at Effingham
NH, HOBBS Abiel W Eld MS 1 Feb 1843

WILKINSON James m HAM Phebe Ann of South Berwick ME on last
Sat at Dover NH, DAVIS I G Eld MS 14 Jan 1846

WILKINSON L D Esq m ELDER Frances M on 27th ult at Saco ME,
NICHOLS J T G Rev MFWBR 7 Apr 1849

WILLAND Edward of Ossipee NH on 7 Nov 1841 m BROWN Betsey of
Wolfboro' NH, CHICK John Eld MS 5 Oct 1842

WILLARD George K on 9 Nov 1848 m ALLOWAY Ann E both of
Dover, BROOKS N Eld MS 20 Dec 1848

WILLARD John F of Ossipee m JENKINS Lydia E of Tuftonboro' on
16 Mar, WALKER John Eld MS 31 May 1843

WILLARD William Capt m MANRAR Sarah R of Cape Elizabeth ME,
LIBBY Almon Eld MS 11 Dec 1844

WILLEY Alfred S m CLARK Susan of Pittsfield on 21 Jul 1844 at
Barnstead, HAM Ezra Eld MS 28 May 1845

WILLEY Aziah m DEARBORN Martha both of Rollinsford on 23 Nov,
BROOKS N Eld MS 4 Dec 1850

WILLEY David of Sutton m EASTMAN Elizabeth of Lyndon, MOUL-
TON T P Eld MS 5 Apr 1843

WILLEY Enoch T m HODGDON Sarah at Dover NH MS 13 Jul 1836

WILLEY James N at Dracut m KNOX Eliza, CURTIS S Eld MS 26 Feb
1845

WILLEY Lemuel m GAGE Martha on Wed at Dover NH, WILLIAMS
Gibbon Rev MS 22 Oct 1834

WILLEY Nathaniel merchant of Wolfboro m ROBERTS Harriet of
Alton NH MS 8 Mar 1837

WILLEY Samuel B of Dover m OTIS Dorothy Ann of Rochester on 6 Nov 1844 at Dover NH, BROCK H H Eld *MS* 20 Nov 1844

WILLEY Samuel L m RANDALL Lydia H both of Great Falls, BROOKS N Eld *MS* 27 Nov 1850

WILLEY Samuel S m RICKER Mary Jane both of Dover NH on 25 ult Tuesday evening in this town, SMITH A D Eld *MS* 10 Jan 1838

WILLEY Sol Jr of Topsham m NORRIS Sally C of Corinth VT on 4 Feb, MOULTON F Eld *MS* 17 Feb 1847

WILLEY Stephen A m BENNETT Mary A both of New Market on 1 Oct in New Market, CILLEY D P Eld *MS* 18 Oct 1837

WILLEY Thomas J m PICKER Elizabeth of Dover NH on 14 inst *MS* 28 Sept 1836

WILLIAM Daniel m GILSON Lucy both of Kittery in Kittery ME, MILTON Nathan H Eld *MS* 22 Nov 1837

WILLIAM Rev Mr ae 70y m CANDLE Polly ae 14y in New York *MS* 27 Jul 1826

WILLIAM William m PAYNE Mary Ann both of Lowell MA *MS* 27 Apr 1842

WILLIAMS A D Eld of Hamilton College, Carolina Mills RI m at Unionville MDHORN/HARN Sarah of Unionville MD, teacher at Cedar Hill Ladies Sem, Lancaster Co PA, on 25 Apr, HURLEY J H Rev *MS* 22/29 May 1850 & *MFWBR* 1 June 1850

WILLIAMS Alaric m CHAMPLIN Lucretia C both of Brookfield Madison Co NY on 11 Oct 1848 in Unadila Forks Otsego Co NY, CHANEY John Eld *MS* 11 Apr 1849

WILLIAMS Benjamin m WEED Anna J both of Freedom in So Montville ME, KNOWLTON E Eld *MS* 22 Jan 1851

WILLIAMS Elihu m BALCH Marilda Mrs both of Haverhill MA on 28 Feb 1848 in Haverhill MA, MERRILL W P Eld *MS* 8 Mar 1848

WILLIAMS Elijah H of Portland ME m MORRISON Catherine, MOULTON A K Eld *MS* 29 Jan 1845

WILLIAMS Ezra F m EMMONS Margaret C both of Georgetown ME on 14 Feb 1850, PENDEXTER S Eld *MS* 27 Feb 1850

WILLIAMS James of Winthrop ME m TENNEY Eliza A of Raymond ME, SMALL C Eld *MS* 13 Mar 1844

WILLIAMS Jesse F of Manchester NH at Wilmot m PEASLY Mary of Manchester on 27 Nov, BARTLETT J I D Eld *MS* 17 Dec 1845

WILLIAMS John G m FABER Lydia both of Atkinson ME on 2d ult, HATHAWAY L Eld *MS* 27 Mar 1834

WILLIAMS John m WIGGINS Elizabeth both of Ossipee in Ossipee, WALKER John Eld *MS* 5 apr 1837

WILLIAMS John of Phipsburg m McKENNEY Sarah Jane at Phipsburg on 18th inst *MFWBR* 31 Aug 1850

WILLIAMS Johnson m WADE Elizabeth on 7 Dec at Woolwich ME *MS* 27 Dec 1843

WILLIAMS Josiah in Kittery ME m RILEY Emeline both of Kittery on

WILLIAMS (Continued)
Wed Eve 23 inst, WETHERBY I J Eld *MS* 9 Mar 1842

WILLIAMS Josiah W of Northfield m SMITH Delight of Northfield on 11 Apr 1843, CLAFFIN Jehiel Eld *MS* 14 June 1843

WILLIAMS Minot of Webster ME m POLLEY Hannah of Webster ME on 12th inst at Bowdoin ME, PURINGTON Amos Esq *MFWBR* 25 Nov 1848

WILLIAMS Nicholas S m SHERBURNE Eleanor both of Gardiner in Bowdoinham ME, QUINNAM C Eld *MS* 22 May 1844

WILLIAMS Robert m GIBBS Elizabeth at Lowell MA *MS* 29 Apr 1835

WILLIAMS Stephen m KELEE Elizabeth of Fallowsfield Township PA *MS* 15 Feb 1837

WILLIAMS Washington merchant of Dover NH m AYER Charlotte of Concord at Concord *MS* 6 Mar 1834

WILLIAMS William H m BABCOCK Olive Ann both of Nassau NY on 10 inst in Nassau NY, COLEMAN I B Rev *MS* 25 Dec 1850

WILLIAMS William m PAYNE Mary Ann both of Lowell, WOODMAN J Eld *MS* 27 Apr 1842

WILLIAMSON Henry A B formerly of Hamilton College m BOARD-MAN Temperance S of Mercer ME on 14 Nov 1849 in Rochester NY, WHITCHER H Eld *MS* 14 Mar 1849 & *MS* 8 Mar 1848

WILLIAMSON Isaac G of Wiscasset m CUNTON Susan A of Boothbay in Edgecomb ME, PAGE E G Eld *MS* 26 Mar 1851

WILLIARD Samuel m GREY Margaret both of Sheffield on 4 Feb *MS* 15 Jul 1835

WILLIS G H m HOLDRIDGE M A both of Plainfield NY on 15 Mar 1849 in Plainfield NY, BELKNAP P W Eld *MS* 28 Mar 1849

WILLIS Hiram Eld m TURNER Achsa both of Rome on 12 Sept in Belgrade, SPAULDING J Eld *MS* 5 Dec 1849

WILLIS Joseph m HOOK Lydia A S both of Exeter in Great Falls *MS* 1 Nov 1837

WILLMAITH John L of Stamford VT m BROWN Anna H of Fairfield NY on 27th Feb, GROSS Eld A *MS* 27 Mar 1839

WILLOUGHBY E K m RICHARDS Georgianna F on 29 Aug 1847 in Lowell, CURTIS S Eld *MS* 8 Sept 1847

WILLOUGHBY John m GOULD Mary on 12 at Holderness NH *MS* 8 Mar 1837

WILLSON David W of New Hampton m BAKER Mary Jane of Holderness NH on 18 Nov 1847 in Holderness NH, WEBBER Horace Eld *MS* 19 Jan 1848

WILLSON James m ALDRICH Olive of Barnston on 9 Oct, MOULTON A Eld *MS* 10 Jan 1838

WILMARTH Eben m FULLER Ann of Attleboro' on 2 Nov at Rehoboth, CLARK G Eld *MS* 16 Dec 1846

WILMARTH Elisha m BOSWORTH Angeline of Attleboro' MA on 15 Dec at Rehoboth, CLARK G Eld *MS* 20 Jan 1847

WILMORTH Albert T of Providence m EDWARDS Henrietta of No Providence at Johnston RI *MS* 2 Dec 1835

WILNOT William A of Fabius NY m BARDEN Catharine M of Three Mile Bay NY on 19 Dec 1847 in Three Mile Bay NY, PADDEN S B Eld *MS* 12 Jan 1848

WILSON Albion m DENNET Maria both of Kittery ME on 14 Apr in Kittery, WEATHERBEE I J Eld *MS* 8 May 1844

WILSON Allen of Orangeville m MARTIN Eliza of China on 27 May last at China NY, CHAFEE C Eld *MS* 15 JUly 1835

WILSON Andrew S m PAGE Lucy D at Acton *MFWBR* 24 Feb 1849

WILSON Benjamin of Harpswell m OWEN Drusilla of Lewiston ME on 30 Sept in Lewiston, LIBBY Isaac Eld *MS* 17 oct 1838

WILSON Cyrus of Palmyra ME m NICKERSON Abigail of Litchfield ME at Bowdoin ME, QUINNAM C Eld *MS* 21 Aug 1839

WILSON Foxwell C of Kittery m DREW Hannah of Newfield on 10 June, GILLPATRICK J Rev *MS* 25 Jul 1849

WILSON George m EATON Martha Jane on 16 Dec at Candia, DAVIS K R Eld *MS* 7 Jan 1846

WILSON Horace of Bath ME m SNOW Sarah of Brunswick ME, ROLLINS A Eld *MS* 2 Jan 1839

WILSON John L m TITUS Emeline both of W Fairlee on 26 Jan in W Fairlee VT, LEAVITT Stephen Eld *MS* 7 Feb 1838

WILSON John m KNIGHT Rebecca of Franconia on 12 June 1843 at Franconia, WITHAM L H Eld *MS* 13 Mar 1844

WILSON Lowell G m CARD Hannah A Mrs at Bath ME, FARRING-TON Rev *MFWBR* 9 Mar 1850

WILSON Moses Dr of Whitefield m BURNHAM Martha of Limerick ME on 1st inst at Limerick ME *MFWBR* 30 Jan 1847

WILSON Peter of Lowell MA m CLAIN Hannah E of Clinton ME on 3 Feb 1849 in Dracut, CURTIS S Eld *MS* 21 Feb 1849

WILSON Robert of Richmond m SPARKS Rachel W of Bowdoinham ME on 3 Jul at Bowdoinham ME, QUINNAM C Eld *MS* 20 June 1842

WILSON Roswell of Eden NY m TYLER Sarah on 19th ult at Hamburgh NY, PLUMB H N Eld *MS* 4 Aug 1847

WILSON Sanford m MITCHELL Hannah Mrs both of Richmond ME in Richmond, SWETT/SWEAT Jesse Eld *MS* 12 Apr 1837 & *MS* 3 May 1837

WILSON Thomas E of Kittery ME m REMICK Britaia A of Elliot ME on 26 Oct, WETHERBEE I J Eld *MS* 27 Dec 1843

WILSON William Jr m PALMER Emily P on 30 Nov in Weare NH, KIMBALL J Eld *MS* 2 Apr 1851

WILSON William L m SNOW Sarah R on 17th inst at Portland ME, MOULTON A K Eld *MS* 27 Nov 1844 & *MS* 29 Jan 1845

WILSON William m WOODARD Eliza both of H (Hatley LC?) on 29 Nov 1843, *MS* 1 May 1844

WINCAPAW Alexander of Friendship ME m ORNE Betsey K of Edge-comb on 23 Oct, PAGE E G Eld *MS* 23 Nov 1842

WINCH William m DALY Adeline in Bethlehem, WILLIS O F Eld *MS* 6 June 1838

WINCHESTER Horace H of Malborough VT m FELKER Mary Ann of Barrington on 24 June in Barrington VT, PLACE E Eld *MS* 4 Jul 1849

WING John H of Canaan m MORRISON Sobrina K of Clinton on 31 May in Clinton ME, BAKER A J Eld *MS* 8 Jul 1846

WINGATE Daniel Jr m WIGGIN Abigail J both of Somersworth NH on 17 inst in Dover, SMITH A D Eld *MS* 20 May 1846

WINGATE James formerly of Williston VT m PHILBRICK Polly of Effingham NH, BENNETT Joseph Esq *MS* 16 Jul 1828

WINKLEY Darius of Barrington m DANIELS Maria G of Dover on 20 Oct in Barnstead, CARLAND David Eld *MS* 11 Nov 1846

WINKLEY David B of Concord NH m WEEKS Mary S of Strafford on 23 Jan 1848 in Strafford, PLACE E Eld *MS* 29 Mar 1848

WINKLEY Ebenezer P m WHITCOMB Eliza W both of Lowell MA on 14 Sept *MS* 21 Sept 1836 & *MS* 28 Sept 1836

WINKLEY John H m LOUGEE Hannah N on 1 Sept at Manchester, CILLEY D P Eld *MS* 11 Sept 1844

WINKLEY Paul J m OTIS Abigail K at Strafford *MS* 18 May 1836

WINKLEY Samuel P Capt m OLIVER Sarah Jane on 15 Jan 1843 at Georgetown ME, SPINNEY Lina W Esq *MS* 8 Mar 1843

WINN Hiram of York m GETCHELL Lucy of Sanford in Sanford ME on 27 Feb 1842, BUZZELL Alvah Eld *MS* 16 Mar 1842

WINSHIP George D m BAILEY Abigail both of Biddeford ME on 14 June, JACKSON Daniel Eld *MS* 30 Sept 1846

WINSLOW Amasa m ALLEN Elizabeth both of Freeport ME on 2 Jan 1848 in Freeport ME, PURINTON A W Eld *MS* 9 Feb 1848

WINSLOW Appleton m ALLEN Miriam H both of Freeport on 29 Aug 1847 in Bowdoin ME, PURINTON A W Eld *MS* 17 Nov 1847

WINSLOW Charles E m WATSON Hannah B both of Northwood on 6 Mar 1849, JOHNSON W D Eld *MS* 11 Apr 1849

WINSLOW John of Lyme NH m CLARK Polly of Strafford VT on 28 Dec 1842, CLARK Eli Eld *MS* 25 Jan 1843

WINSLOW Joseph m CLOUGH Mary P of Portland ME on 4th inst at Portland ME, MOULTON A K Eld *MS* 25 June 1845

WINSLOW Matthew F m SMALL Deborah of Casco ME on 27 Dec at Casco ME, LIBBY James Eld *MS* 10 Feb 1847

WINSOR Albert W of Lyndon m MEIGS Sally C of Lyndon at Sutton VT, MOULTON T P Eld *MS* 5 Apr 1843 & *MS* 21 Dec 1842

WINTWORTH Eli formerly of Wakefield NH m HODGMAN Julia Ann of Lowell MA *MS* 22 Oct 1834

WISE Asel m POWERS Bainey on 6th ult at Galen NY, SHEPHERD H Eld *MS* 13 June 1833

WISEPH Joseph O m NICHOLS Susan both of Concord on 25 Jul in Loudon NH, NORRIS J Eld *MS* 1 Sept 1847

WITHAM Aaron m UPTON Sarah both of Biddeford ME on 12 ult at Saco ME, FERNALD James Eld *MS* 12 Aug 1835

WITHAM Asa m FOX Mary D both of Meredith on 5 Apr, SINCLAIR J L Eld *MS* 30 May 1849

WITHAM Daniel S m LANDER Cyntha both of Fairfield on 9 Dec 1849 in Smithfield ME, BOWDON Stephen Eld *MS* 23 Jan 1850

WITHAM Daniel S of Smithfield m HORN Catherine at Fairfield, LEWIS D B Eld *MS* 17 Apr 1844

WITHAM Ira L m WITHAM Climera P on 4 inst in Milton Mills, SPINNEY Joseph Eld *MS* 21 Nov 1838

WITHAM Joseph m TAYLOR Catherine of Dover NH at Great Falls NH, CURTIS S Eld *MS* 29 June 1842

WITHAM Levi m HALEY Sally of Lincoln, STINSON Robert Eld *MS* 23 Oct 1839

WITHAM Philip m FILES Harriet both of Thorndike on 25th inst, HIGGINS Joseph *MS* 19 May 1830

WITHAM William of Acton m MILLER Mary A of Rollinsford NH on 19 Dec in Acton ME, RUNNELS J Eld *MFWBR* 11 Jan 1851 & *MS* 1 Jan 1851

WITHAM William of Smithfield ME m STANLEY Alvira C, LEWIS D B Eld *MS* 25 Dec 1844

WITHAM William m JONES Ruth of Acton on 26 Oct 1848, JORDAN Z Eld *MS* 29 Nov 1848

WITT Arza Dr of Sutton VT m EATON Caroline H of Great Falls NH on 9 ult *MS* Mar 1837

WOLF George m PATTERSON Susannah both of Pikerun PA on 12 ult in Pikerun township PA, NEWBOLD J Eld *MS* 19 Apr 1837

WOLSEY Richard of Perinton m PARKER Julia A on 11 Sept in Walworth NY, HOLMES D G Eld *MS* 16 Oct 1850

WOOD George W m SOULE Emily both of Waterville ME, LEWIS Daniel B Eld *MS* 15 Jan 1840

WOOD Ira D m VERESS Elmira M of Sweden on 3 Jul at Sweden, HUNTRESS D Eld *MS* 19 Jul 1843

WOOD Israel of Hatley LC m MOULTON Lydia on 18 Oct in Stanstead CE, MOULTON A Eld *MS* 28 Nov 1849

WOOD James m GREENLEAF Anna of Starks ME at Starks ME *MS* 11 Oct 1843

WOOD John B Jr of Great Falls on Sabbath Evening m GERRISH Abby Jane in Dover, PARKMAN Rev Mr *MS* 26 Jul 1848

WOOD John M m WINSLOW Sarah G at Bath ME, FISKE John O Rev *MFWBR* 14 Aug 1847

WOOD John m GORDON Alma Jane on 23 Nov at St Albans, COPP J B Eld *MS* 27 Dec 1843

WOOD John P m PARKER Jennette of Portland ME on 10th inst at

WOOD (Continued)

Portland ME, ABBOTT H B Rev *MFWBR* 23 June 1849

WOOD Josiah Jr of Auburn m SOUTHWICK Mary J A of Chester on 17 Sept 1848 in Manchester, CILLEY D P Eld *MS* 27 Sept 1848

WOOD Oliver C of Townsend MA m TWINING Lucina B of Lowell on 12 Nov, CURTIS S Eld *MS* 6 Jan 1847

WOOD Silas of Hopkinton m SMITH Sarah of Lawrenceville on 29 Jul in Lawrenceville NY, LEWIS John W Eld *MS* 15 Aug 1849

WOODARD Abram of Bangor ME m FULLER Jane of Lewiston ME on 15 May, LIBBY Isaac Eld *MS* 3 Jul 1844

WOODARD Barnet m ORDWAY Maria A of Boston MA on 22d Apr at Warsaw NY, COOKLIN Rev *MS* 10 Sept 1845

WOODARD Joseph m COWEN Dolly Mrs of Lewiston ME on 18 Jan at Lewiston Falls ME, BEAN G W Eld *MS* 27 Jan 1847

WOODARD Joseph W of Lisbon m LUNT Apphia A of Brunswick on 25 Oct in Brunswick ME, BARD N Eld *MS* 8 Jan 1851

WOODARD Winchel of Lisbon m BARKER Ellen of Lewiston ME on 16 inst in Lewiston ME, BURGESS J S Eld *MS* 24 Jan 1849

WOODBECK Joel m LARKIN Hannah both of Stephentown on 5 inst in Stephentown, COLEMAN I B Eld *MS* 23 Jan 1850

WOODBRIDGE James A m ALBEE Frances L on 21 May at Hallowell ME *MS* 5 June 1844

WOODBURY William Esq m EMERSON Hannah both of Danville in Danville ME on Tues Feb 1, STURGIS N G Eld *MS* 16 Feb 1842

WOODCOCK Gideon m KELLEY Matilda J of Lowell MA on 30 Jan at Lowell MA, THURSTON N Eld *MS* 25 May 1842

WOODFORD William m STEVENS Nancy on Thurs last at Westbrook, RAND S Eld *MS* 3 May 1827

WOODMAN Andrew J of Saco m HALEY Abby A of Cornish on 2 Feb in Cornish ME, RAND J Eld *MS* 26 Feb 1851

WOODMAN David m SINNOTT Martha of Saco on 5th inst at Saco, Nichols J T G Rev *MFWBR* 17 Mar 1849

WOODMAN David B m PATTEN Jane of Alexandria on 21 Nov in Alexandria, BROWN Amos Eld *MS* 12 Dec 1838

WOODMAN J of Southampton m KIMBALL Ann W of Alton NH on 14 Nov at Gilmanton Iron Works, McMURPHY B H Eld *MS* 27 Nov 1850

WOODMAN Jeremiah of Alton NH m CLOUGH Mary P of Gilmanton NH, BUZZELL H D Eld *MS* 18 Dec 1839

WOODMAN John P m BURTON Lucretia M both of Manchester on 14 Dec 1848 in Manchester, CILLEY D P Eld *MS* 27 Dec 1848

WOODMAN Jonathan Eld of Sutton VT m EATON Mercy Mrs of Danville VT on 6 Aug at Danville VT *MS* 28 Sept 1832

WOODMAN Joseph m DEARING Mary on 6 inst at Kittery ME *MS* 14 Dec 1836

WOODMAN Joshua at Strafford m HUCHINS Martha Ann *MS* 13 Feb

WOODMAN (Continued)
1834

WOODMAN Joshua S Esq of Hatley CE m BECKNELL Arthusa of Wolcott VT on 4 Jan in Wolcott VT, FOLSOM M Eld *MS* 6 Mar 1850

WOODMAN Levi m NUTE Joanna C *MS* 19 Apr 1837

WOODMAN R M of Orono ME m MERRILL Susan C at Minot ME on Dec 12, LIBBY Isaac Eld *MS* 22 Jan 1840

WOODMAN Samuel Jr of Deerfield m GILE Sarah of Nottingham at Lee, CHESLEY Israel Eld *MS* 28 May 1834

WOODMAN Seth W m GEEAR Louisa M of Barrington on New Year's Eve at Barrington, SHERBURNE S Eld *MS* 18 Jan 1843

WOODRUFF Calvin of Ashford NY m VENESS Harriet of Sugar Grove PA, TAYNTOR O Eld *MS* 14 Feb 1844

WOODS Charles H of Southborough m POTTER Adah W of Lowell on 30 Apr in Lowell, WALDRON W H Eld *MS* 30 May 1849

WOODS George L m STILLINGS Amanda M both of Manchester on 30 May 1848 in Manchester, CILLEY D P Eld *MS* 14 June 1848

WOODS William H m WHITTIER Martha J on 8 ult in Brighton, PRATT Cyprian *MS* 4 Apr 1838

WOODSUM Thompson of Greenbush m WOODWARD Suphronia of Lisbon on 31 Oct *MS* 28 Dec 1836

WOODWARD Asa F of Lisbon m BERRY Ellen L in Bath ME, FISK Rev Mr *MS* 7 Mar 1849 & *MS* 12 Feb 1845

WOODWARD Horace N of Stockholm m FELLOWS Mary A formerly of Franklin NH on 26 Nov at Hopkinson, SWEAT J Eld *MS* 23 Dec 1846

WOODWARD Johnson of Hollis m EMERY Olive of Waterboro ME on 6th inst *MS* 28 Dec 1832

WOODWARD Joseph of Sidney ME m ROBINSON Roxana, LEWIS Daniel B Esq *MS* 21 Jan 1846

WOODWARD Squire m YOUNG Mary of Hatley LC on 20 June, MOULTON A Eld *MS* 13 Sept 1843

WOODWARD William Deacon m CLOUGH Betsey on 19 Oct at Lewiston ME, PURINTON N Eld *MS* 25 Feb 1846

WOODWORTH Edward m ARNOLD Charlotte both of Dixmont on 15 Dec, FLETCHER J Eld *MS* 24 Jan 1838

WOODWORTH Horace G m JURNEY Frances J both of Fayetteville on 17 Oct 1847 in Fayetteville Wis, WHITFORD I F Rev *MS* 22 Dec 1847

WOODWORTH John Jr m TUCK Nancy both of Fayette ME, CURTIS S Eld *MS* 28 Nov 1833

WOODWORTH Nathan of Mineral Point Wis m BIDWILL Jerusha of Brainbridge Ohio in Chester Geauga Co Ohio, BRANCH D Eld *MS* 3 Jan 1849

WOODWORTH Phillip m ALLEN Esther H both of Jay in Jay ME,

WOODWORTH (Continued)
LIBBY Eld *MS* 14 Feb 1838

WORDEN Orin D of Middlebury m HERRICK Melissa M of Alden on 29 Aug in Alden NY, BLACKMARR Henry Eld *MS* 3 Oct 1849

WORDEN Seilas of Stephentown NY m LEWIS Ursula of Nassau NY on 14 Apr 1849 in Nassau NY, COLEMAN I B Eld *MS* 2 May 1849

WORKS William m CURTIS Sarah P both of Brunswick in Brunswick ME, HERSEY L Eld *MS* 8 Mar 1848

WORMWOOD John B of Brownfield ME m MEADER Dorothy An of Conway NH on 3 ult in Conway NH, LONG L A Eld *MS* 10 Nov 1847

WORMUTH William J of Starkville m WORMUTH Margaret of Palatine on 10 Nov 1849 in Starkville, SMITH M H Eld *MS* 16 Jan 1850

WORSTER Ebenezer of Somersworth m KEYS Mary A of Berwick ME at Great Falls NH *MFWBR* 5 Oct 1850

WORTH Stephen of Biddeford ME m BRADBURY Harriet of Kennebunkport ME on 7 Feb, WITHAM L H Eld *MS* 24 Feb 1847

WORTH Thomas C of Biddeford ME m HATCH Olive L of Wells ME on 3 Dec 1843, WITHAM L H Eld *MS* 13 Mar 1844

WORTHEN Gilman C m FRENCH Lucy S both of Manchester in Manchester, CILLEY D P Eld *MS* 6 Dec 1848

WORTHEN Jonathan m FRENCH Hannah A on 15 Oct at Lowell MA at Lowell MA, THURSTON N Eld *MS* 2 Nov 1842

WORTHEN William m PARKER Eliza Ann both of Holderness NH, PETTENGILL John Eld *MS* 12 Feb 1840

WORTHING Charles J of Charlestown MA m CRAM Rosannah S of Meredith NH, PITMAN Stephen J Eld *MS* 11 Sept 1839

WRIGHT Isaac F m OLIVER Diantha Miss at Georgetown *MS* 6 Feb 1834

WRIGHT James J of Lowell MA m REYNOLDS Sarah Ann of Lowell MA, THURSTON N Eld *MS* 25 May 1842

WRIGHT John B m WRIGHT Agness of Woolwich ME on 9 Mar 1843, PERKINS Seth W Eld *MS* 19 Apr 1843

WRIGHT Leven m THORNTON Sarah on 31 Aug at Washington Township Union Co Ohio, HARVEY E Eld *MS* 30 Oct 1844

WRIGHT Nathaniel F m LINSCOTT Caroline M both of Saco in Newfield ME , RUNNELS J Eld *MS* 6 Nov 1850

WRIGHT Nathaniel E m SAVAGE Clarinda T both of Farmington on 5 Jul in Farmington ME, CHANEY J Eld *MS* 12 Sept 1838

WRIGHT Solomon of Harpersfield m BRANCH Hannah M Mrs of Trumbull Ohio on 2 May 1848 in Trumbull Ohio, COPP J B Eld *MS* 30 Aug 1848

WRIGHT William m KELLEY Nancy both of Charlestown on 16 Mar in Charlestown, WETHERBEE I J Eld *MS* 25 Mar 1846

WRISLEY C Sanford of Waterbury m CHATTERTON Clara of Middle-

WRISLEY (Continued)
sex VT on 29 Jan in Middlesex VT, CHATTERTON B Eld *MS* 27 Mar 1850

WYLIE Parker Capt m CLARK Elizabeth on 21 Nov at Boothbay ME, MORRILL S P Eld *MS* 22 Jan 1845

WYLIE Sewell Capt m MATHEWS Rebecca both of Boothbay on 10 Mar 1850 in Boothbay ME, PAGE E G Eld *MS* 15 May 1850

WYMAN Daniel Jr m WOODBURY Rebecca S both of Dover on 7 inst in Dover ME, HATHAWAY Leonard Eld *MS* 8 May 1844

WYMAN Howard B of Sidney m ATKINSON Maria B of Madison ME on 14 Nov 1848 in Madison ME, HATHAWAY G W Rev *MS* 29 Nov 1848

WYMAN James W of Chester m ADAMS Elizabeth of Unity on 11 Oct 1849 in Unity ME, WATERMAN D Eld *MS* 8 May 1850

WYMAN Seth m CHANDLER Susan both of Chatham NH on 29 Nov 1849 in Chatham NH, GUPTILL R W *MS* 20 Feb 1850

WYMAN William of Unity m YOUNG Catharine of Thorndike ME at Unity ME, LEWIS D B Eld *MS* 25 Dec 1844

YEARNSHAW John Eld of Cranston RI m COLLINS Esther B of Attleboro MA on 4th inst in Providence RI, TOBEY Z Eld *MS* 27 Oct 1830

YEATON Andrew m GODDRIDGE Eliza Jane both of Belgrade ME on 3 inst *MS* 10 Feb 1836

YEATON Paul Jr m GOODRIDGE Lydia Ann of Belgrade on 28 Jul, SPAULDING Joel Eld *MS* 8 Jan 1845

YEATON Philip 2d m SPAULDING Caroline A both of Belgrade on 1 Jan in Belgrade ME, SPAULDING J Eld *MS* 9 Jan 1850

YEATON William of Epsom m STEARNS Mary J of Deerfield NH on 19 Mar in Deerfield NH, DAVIS I G Eld *MS* 15 Apr 1846

YEOMANS Vinson of Orangeville NY m GATES Malissa, FLYNN William H *MS* 6 Apr 1847

YORK Horace B m CHASE Eliza, PETTINGILL John Eld in Holderness *MS* 24 Jan 1838

YORK Joseph G m JELLISON Abigail of Lowell MA on 8 May at Lowell MA, WOODMAN J Eld *MS* 19 Oct 1842

YORK Levi m FROST Lucy both of Lowell in Lowell, THURSTON Nathaniel Eld *MS* 28 Feb 1838

YORK Thomas of Lee m BARTLETT Harriet of Exeter at Lee, CHESLEY Israel Eld *MS* 28 May 1834

YORK William D of Brookfield NY m CRUMB Mary Ann on 28 Sept, GARDNER S D Eld *MS* 15 Oct 1845

YOUNG Andrew J of Gilmanton m BLAKE Dorothy of Pittsfield NH on 20 Apr 1848 in Pittsfield NH, TRUE E Eld *MS* 3 May 1848

YOUNG Artemas S of Lowell MA m HARMON Sarah S on 13 Mar 1850 in Eaton, BLAISDELL Henry Rev *MS* 27 Mar 1850

YOUNG Caleb of Jackson m CILLEY Hannah of Brooks ME on 2 Dec 1842 at Brooks ME, CILLEY Joseph L Eld *MS* 25 Jan 1843

YOUNG Charles master ae 18y m GARDNER Esther Maria ae 16y of Higham MA at New Haven *MFWBR* 28 Apr 1849

YOUNG Charles S of Shapleigh ME m DURGIN Betsey H of Newfield ME in S Parsonsfield ME, SMITH Wm Eld *MS* 8 Nov 1848

YOUNG Daniel Jr of Freedom m ALLARD Elenor Jane on 22 Mar 1849 in Eaton NH, BLAISDELL Henry Rev *MS* 4 Apr 1849

YOUNG Daniel of Kingston m PAGE Mary J at Danville, FULLONTON J Eld *MS* 9 Oct 1839

YOUNG David Jr m BROWN Angeline both of Deerfield NH on 3 Jan 1850 in Epsom NH, RAMSEY G P Eld *MS* 16 Jan 1850

YOUNG Elbridge G of West Newbury MA m ROWELL Betsey of Nottingham on 14 Nov at Deerfield, ATWOOD M Eld *MS* 8 Jan 1845

YOUNG Furber m GOODELL Rhoda E on 25 Sept, BLAISDELL Edward Eld *MS* 11 Feb 1846

YOUNG George A m GILMAN Pamelia C of Gilford on 28 Mar at Concord, KIMBALL J Eld *MS* 28 Apr 1847

YOUNG George m PARKER Martha A of Biddeford ME on 14 June in Kennebunkport ME, MARSTON J G Eld *MS* 10 Jul 1850

YOUNG Henry m MORRILL Louisa O on 24 inst in Strafford, CAVERNO A Eld *MS* 3 May 1837

YOUNG Isaac D of Gilmanton m DORR Martha A of Ossipee NH on 9 Jul in Ossipee, CHICK J Eld *MS* 4 Dec 1850

YOUNG Ivory H of Wolfborough m UNDERWOOD Fanny A of Saxonville MA on 29 Jan in Wolfborough NH, LUCAS Wm K Eld *MS* 23 May 1849

YOUNG James M m KENISTON Emeline both of Great Falls NH on 3 Sept in Great Falls, BROODS N Eld *MS* 12 Sept 1849

YOUNG James M Rev of Strafford m BETTON Eliza of Dover NH on Sunday even 10 inst in this town, SMITH Elezer Rev *MS* 20 June 1838

YOUNG Jason of Foster m BROWN Susan of No Providence on 30 May in No Providence RI, HUTCHINS E Eld *MS* 21 June 1837

YOUNG Jeremiah of Freedom m ALLEY Jane of Eaton NH on 26 Jan, BUTLER O Eld *MS* 8 Feb 1843

YOUNG John B of Dover NH m BUZZELL Mary Jane of Barrington, PARKMAN Rev *MS* 5 Feb 1845

YOUNG John of Burlington m WOODWARD Mary of Blackberry on 29 Aug, STARR D S Eld *MS* 27 Nov 1844

YOUNG Jonathan Esq of Barrington m GRAY Martha F of Dover on 18 inst in Dover, SMITH A D Eld *MS* 26 Jul 1848

YOUNG Jonathan Jr m SANDERS Sally both of Strafford on 18th inst, PLACE Enoch Eld *MS* 31 Dec 1834

YOUNG Jonathan m BUZZELL Sarah both of Effingham NH on 29th ult in Effingham, HOLMES H Eld *MS* 11 Feb 1835

YOUNG Joseph at Raymond m DEARBORN Elizabeth *MS* 8 Dec 1841

YOUNG Joseph of Ossipee m ALLEN Hannah of Effingham NH, COBURNS Milton J Rev *MS* 15 Jan 1840

YOUNG Joshua Rev of New North Church Boston m PLYMPTON Mary E at Cambridge MA on 14th ult *MFWBR* 3 Mar 1849

YOUNG Moses Colby (Sr) of Ossipee NH [s/o Rodolpha & Nancy/Anna (Tarr) YOUNG] m TIBBETTS Mary on 20 May, CHICK J Eld *MS* 25 June 1845

YOUNG Orland of Madbury m PEAVEY Keziah A of Dover on 11 instin Dover, HUTCHINS E Eld *MS* 14 Nov 1849

YOUNG Philo m ABBOT Mary A both of Hatley LC on 4 Feb *MS* 17 Feb 1836

YOUNG Priest m OAKS Lucretia of Franconia NH on 4 Jul at Lisbon, GEORGE Nathaniel K Eld *MS* 27 June 1842

YOUNG Richard m NEALY Betsey both of Great Falls on Fast Day Even in Great Falls, CURTIS S Eld *MS* 22 Apr 1840

YOUNG Samuel m STEVENS Martha A both of Middleton on 3 Nov 1850, SMALL C Eld *MS* 8 Jan 1851

YOUNG Seth P of Smithfield m MORSE Lydia E on 28th ult at Waterford, BURLINGAME M W Eld *MS* 11 Dec 1839

YOUNG Soloman Tarr/T of Ossipee NH [s/o Rodolpha & Nancy/Anna (Tarr) Young] m GOWEN Lydia A of Biddeford ME on 5 Sept in Biddeford ME, WITHAM L H Eld *MS* 27 Oct 1847

YOUNG Solomon of Canterbury NH m PEVERLY Hannah of Canterbury NH, CLOUGH Jeremiah Eld *MS* 14 Feb 1844

YOUNG Stephen Jr of Pittsfield m GODFREY Hannah of Manchester on 24 Nov 1847 in Manchester, CILLEY D P Eld *MS* 8 Dec 1847

YOUNG Stephen of Starks ME m NEAL Emily B of Skowhegan ME on 10 Dec 1848 in Starks ME, WILLIAMSON S Eld *MS* 3 Jan 1849

YOUNG Stephen of Canterbury NH m MINOR Sophia on 14 Mar 1847, CATLIN S T Eld *MS* 5 May 1847

YOUNG T S m BENJAMIN Caroline both of Pierpont NY on 22 Sept 1847 at the residence of Dea R BENJAMIN in Pierpont NY, CLARK R Eld *MS* 3 Nov 1847

YOUNG William B of Livermore m YOUNG Fairrozzeway Miss on 28th June, STILSON C Eld *MS* 12 Aug 1835

YOUNG Zebina Eld of Sheffield m MEIGS Sally of Lyndon VT on 14 Jul, QUINBY Daniel Eld *MS* 31 Aug 1836

ABBOTT Abigail of Sidney ME m COTTLE Albert of Waterville ME *MS* 25 Nov 1846

ABBOTT Adah H m HALL George W on 18 Jan at North Berwick ME *MS* 28 Jan 1846

ABBOTT Alice m PARKER Mr in Berrien Berrien Co Mich *MS* 5 Apr 1837

ABBOTT Clarissa M m HARDY John S both of Manchester 16 Aug *MS* 26 Aug 1846

ABBOTT Dorcas C of Gorham ME m CHUTE Calvin on 17 Feb at Portland ME *MS* 9 Jul 1845

ABBOTT Ebner of Lowell MA m GREEN James H on 17 Nov *MS* 10 May 1843

ABBOTT Esther of Ossipee NH m NORRIS Samuel on 2d ult at Ossipee NH *MS* 21 Aug 1844

ABBOTT Fanny of Brookfield VT on 21st inst m PARHAM Jonathan S *MS* 17 Apr 1839

ABBOTT Joanna m ALLEN Samuel Esq *MFWBR* 18 Aug 1849

ABBOTT Julia A m WIGGIN Isaac 23 Feb 1850 *MS* 13 Mar 1850

ABBOTT Laura J m SCAMMON James F *MFWBR* 21 Jul 1849

ABBOTT Lucy of Woolwich ME m POOL Albert H on 19 Sept *MS* 8 Dec 1841

ABBOTT Lydia M of Dover m STAPLES Charles of Ossipee NH on 6 inst *MS* 12 Mar 1851

ABBOTT Mary A m YOUNG Philo both of Hatley LC 4 Feb *MS* 17 Feb 1836

ABBOTT Mary Ann m SANBORN Lewis both of Westbrook ME on Jul 1 1841 *MS* 12 Jan 1842

ABBOTT Mary Ann of Ossipee m BEAN Silas F of Tuftonborough NH 15 Mar 1848 *MS* 29 Mar 1848

ABBOTT Mercy of Ossipee NH m EMERSON Hollis D of Ossipee NH *MS* 13 Sept 1843

ABBOTT Nancy of Ossipee NH m ROBINSON Reuben of Newburgh ME *MS* 7 Aug 1839

ABBOTT Salva of Temple ME m FREEMAN Charles Rev of Limerick ME *MS* 31 May 1827

ABBOTT Saphronia H of Strafford VT m STRICKLAND Lucius L of Waterway *MS* 13 Mar 1839

ABBOTT Sarah Ann m DILLINGHAM Latinus both of Biddeford ME on 30 May *MS* 3 Jul 1850

ABBOTT Sarah C m MORRILL Jacob of Contoocookville NH? on 30 Apr *MS* 14 May 1845

ABBOTT Sarah Mrs m KEYS Peter on 18 Feb *MS* 14 May 1845

ABBOTT Susan at Dover NH m WENTWORTH Samuel P on 1 June *MS* 4 June 1845

ABBY Susan of Mt Desert ME m FARLEY John of Gouldsborough ME *MS* 19 Jan 1842

ABRAHAM Marion T at Atkinson ME m BUNKER John on 13 Apr *MS* 17 May 1843

ADAMS Caroline E m NOYES Harvey 1 June 1848 *MS* 21 June 1848

ADAMS Catharine T m LADD Jonathan both of Manchester 14 Oct *MS* 24 Oct 1849

ADAMS Charlotte of No Providence RI m HATCH John C of West Winchester MA on 4 inst *MS* 12 Oct 1836

ADAMS Elizabeth M on 25 Dec m DEERING Abial of Edgecomb ME *MS* 4 Jan 1843

ADAMS Elizabeth of Unity m WYMAN James W of Chester 11 Oct 1849 *MS* 8 May 1850

ADAMS Hannah of this town (Dover NH) m HUBBARD James of Acton ME last week *MS* 11 June 1834

ADAMS Jane m CORNING Nathan on 2 Nov at Lawrence NY *MS* 23 Dec 1846

ADAMS Jane M on 11 June 1838 m CURRIER Nathan M *MS* 17 Apr 1839

ADAMS Lucretia at Alton NH m MELLOWS Aaron on 3d Jan *MS* 3 Mar 1847

ADAMS Lucy A m DAWS Samuel H both of Harrison ME on 19 Jan *MS* 19 Feb 1851

ADAMS Martha A of Litchfield ME m OWEN Charles of Leeds ME *MS* 18 Sept 1850

ADAMS Martha Ann of Unity ME m STONE Ansel on 1 Apr *MS* 8 May 1850

ADAMS Mary A m KIMBALL William H both of Gilmanton NH 5 Apr *MS* 6 June 1849

ADAMS Mary E m KELLEY Alpha J both of Windsor VT on 5 June 1848 *MS* 14 June 1848

ADAMS Mary J of Garland ME m COOK John Eld on 8 Nov 1846 at Garland ME *MS* 20 Jan 1847

ADAMS Mary P m WALL George on 13 Feb at Falmouth ME *MS* 1 June 1842

ADAMS Matilda S m CHAMBERLAIN Freeman both of Dover on 3 Sept *MS* 13 Sept 1837

ADAMS Rosamond P m BRAGDON Charles on 17th inst at Rochester *MS* 30 Dec 1846

ADAMS Sally m BURNHAM John of Parsonsfield ME *MFWBR* 20 Mar 1847

ADAMS Sally of Kingsbury ME m SMALL Francis on 16 June *MS* 24 Jul 1844 (*sic*) should be *MS* 31 Jul 1844

ADAMS Sally m PARKER Amasa J at Stephenstown NY *MS* 18 Nov 1846

ADAMS Sarah G of Gilmanton NH m CURRIER Augustus P B *MS* 25 Dec 1844

ADAMS Sarah S m BARTLETT John both of Garland ME on 8 Oct 1848 *MS* 22 Nov 1848

ADAMS Sophia L m TOTMAN David W on 25 Sept at Cincinnatus NY *MS* 5 Nov 1845

ADAMS Ursula m TRUE Porter C both of Pittsfield on 11 inst *MS* 21 Nov 1849

AKERS Sarah A of Errol NH m ILLSLEY George of Thetford VT on 7 Feb 1849 *MS* 6 June 1849

ALBEE Frances L m WOODBRIDGE James A on 21 May at Hallowell ME *MS* 5 June 1844

ALBY Julia Mrs of Windsor ME m JAMESON J W Col on 20 Feb *MS* 9 Apr 1845

ALDERMAN Clarinda m HOYLE Asa at Middlebury NY on 3 Jul *MS* 10 Aug 1842

ALDRICH Ann of Lisbon (NH?) m SMITH George on 12 Jul 1842 at Franconia (NH?) *MS* 19 Apr 1843

ALDRICH Caroline of Gilford NH? m WEBSTER Elbridge of Meredith NH? 5 May *MS* 30 May 1849

ALDRICH Dianthy m SARLES Harry on 25 Jan 1844 *MS* 1 May 1844

ALDRICH Elizabeth of Smithfield m RICE Lewis of Marlborough MA on 28 inst *MS* 18 Apr 1838 [*sic*] [editors think it should have read "28 ult".]

ALDRICH Huldah M m HARRINGTON Josiah B both of No Scituate RI on 6 Dec *MS* 2 Jan 1830

ALDRICH Nancy B of Manchester NH m MATHEWS Joseph P on 11 Jul at Manchester NH *MS* 28 Jul 1847

ALDRICH Olive of Barnston LC m WILLSON James 9 Oct *MS* 10 Jan 1838

ALDRICH Patience m MOWRY Wm Jr both of Smithfield 29 ult *MS* 18 Apr 1838

ALDRICH Sophia Jane of Lisbon m MINARD Silas A of Littleton NH on 19 Apr 1843 at Lisbon NH *MS* 13 Mar 1844

ALEXANDER Abigail M of Tunbridge VT on 22d ult m PUTNEY Henry Esq of Dunbarton NH *MS* 15 May 1839

ALEXANDER Margaret of Brunswick ME m NICHOLS William S *MS* 26 Apr 1843

ALEXANDER Martha of Farmersville NY m CAGWIN Samuel G of Freedom NY? 30 Oct *MS* 11 Dec 1850

ALEXANDER Sarah J M of Richmond ME m MELCHER William H M of Brunswick ME 14 June *MS* 22 Jul 1846

ALGER Mary R of Newport RI m DAVIS Daniel of Providence RI at Newport RI *MS* 17 Sept 1845

ALLARD Abigail F of Portsmouth NH m BROOKS William W of Elliot ME on 31 Dec at Portsmouth NH *MS* 10 Jan 1844

ALLARD Adaline of Eaton m JACKSON Ivory of Eaton NH *MS* 21 Jan 1846

ALLARD Almira of Albany NY? m FOGG Hezekiah T of Sandwich NH on 17 Feb at Albany *MS* 4 Mar 1846

ALLARD Caroline m DRAKE Ira on 24th at Effingham NH *MS* 6 Apr 1847

ALLARD Charity H m LANGLEY Thomas W both of Lamprey River NH *MS* on 11 Feb 1835

ALLARD Elenor Jane d/o ALLARD Jacob Esq of Eaton NH m YOUNG Daniel Jr of Freedom 22 Mar 1849 *MS* 4 Apr 1849

ALLARD Harriet B of Eaton m BICKFORD Paul P on 1 Feb at Eaton NH *MS* 11 Feb 1846

ALLARD Mary B m FOSS Moses of Great Falls NH on 22 Dec *MS* 8 Feb 1843

ALLARD Mary M of Eaton NH? on 31st Oct m NICKERSON Jonathan Jr of Albany *MS* 27 Nov 1839

ALLARD Samantha of Strafford VT m CORBET John C of Stewartstown NH 15 Oct 1848 *MS* 6 June 1849

ALLEN Alimora P of Billerica MA m EMERSON Joseph M on 2 June at Wilmington MA *MS* 26 June 1844

ALLEN Almira of Portland ME m LIBBY Abner of Limerick *MS* 29 Oct 1828

ALLEN Alnetriphanthem of No Providence RI m OLNEY Edwin B of Gloucester 21st ult *MS* 7 May 1834

ALLEN Anstress m DAVIS Reuben *MFWBR* 3 Mar 1849

ALLEN Charlotte A of Union NY m DODGE Calvin Eld on 18 Dec at Union Broome Co NY *MS* 15 Jan 1845

ALLEN Drusilla A m STEVENS William C on 16 Oct at Dixmont ME *MS* 17 Jan 1844

ALLEN Eliza of Biddeford ME m WEEMAN Obediah of Standish ME *MFWBR* 12 May 1849

ALLEN Elizabeth m WINSLOW Amasa both of Freeport ME 2 on Jan 1848 *MS* 9 Feb 1848

ALLEN Elona M of Billerica MA m EAMES Thomas P of Wilmington on 21 Dec 1843 at Billerica MA *MS* 17 Jan 1844

ALLEN Emily m PERRY John W both of Bangor ME 13 Sept 1848 *MS* 22 Nov 1848

ALLEN Esther H m WOODWORTH Phillip both of Jay ME *MS* 14 Feb

ALLEN (Continued)
1838

ALLEN Hannah D on 26 Nov m FRENCH James of Manchester *MS* 6 Dec 1843

ALLEN Hannah J Mrs m LIBBY Isaac Eld 4 Sept 1848 *MS* 13 Sept 1848

ALLEN Hannah of Effingham NH m YOUNG Joseph of Ossipee NH *MS* 15 Jan 1840

ALLEN Hannah of Limerick ME m BRYANT Samuel L *MS* 27 Sept 1827

ALLEN Huldah of Norway ME on Jan 3 m VINCENT Samuel *MS* 24 May 1843

ALLEN Huldah on 15th ult m PAGE William P of Sidney ME *MFWBR* 3 Mar 1849

ALLEN Julia Ann m TISDALE Benjamin R both of No Providence RI 25 ult at Johnston RI *MS* 11 Jan 1837

ALLEN Lorana m WARD Thomas M *MS* 12 Mar 1851

ALLEN Lycia A m FORREST John W both of Dover 10 Aug *MS* 28 on Aug 1850

ALLEN Lydia Jane of Gilmanton NH m SEAVY Peter C of Pittsfield 30 June 1836 *MS* 13 Jul 1836

ALLEN Lydia L of Cornish ME m CHANEY Joseph of Springvale ME on 7 Nov 1847 *MS* 22 Dec 1847

ALLEN Martha of Freeport ME m SPRINGER David T on 11 Nov *MS* 15 Dec 1841

ALLEN Mary A of Epsom NH m COLLINS Alva B of Danville 15 Nov 1849 *MS* 16 Jan 1850

ALLEN Mary Eliza m ALLEY Ira on 25 Apr at Cornish ME? *MS* 29 May 1844

ALLEN Mary m WENTWORTH William *MS* 27 Jul 1826

ALLEN Mary m WHIPPLE Benjamin 2d inst *MS* 24 Apr 1834

ALLEN Miriam H m WINSLOW Appleton both of Freeport ME on 29 Aug 1847 *MS* 17 Nov 1847

ALLEN Nancy W of Paris m ROYAL William B *MFWBR* 1 Feb 1851

ALLEN Percis m ALLEN Elial both of Winthrop ME 9 Nov at Fayette ME *MS* 10 Feb 1836

ALLEN Phebe m CLAY John *RI* Apr 1820 p 63

ALLEN Rhoda P m DEMMON Truman G both of Chesterfield MA 28 Nov 1848 *MS* 7 Feb 1849

ALLEN Roena C Mrs of Great Falls NH m SHAW Timothy Hon of Sanford ME *MS* 21 Feb 1844

ALLEN Rosannah m ALLEN John both of Brunswick ME *MS* 23 Jan 1850

ALLEN Roseman m STACKPOLE Joshua both of Wolfboro NH 5 May *MS* 18 May 1836

ALLEN Roxanna of Portland ME m DAY Thomas on 26 May at

ALLEN (Continued)
Wilmington MA *MS* 26 June 1844

ALLEN Sally Mrs of Wayne ME m UNDERWOOD Alfred B of Green
ME on 27 Apr at Wayne Ashtabula Co Ohio *MS* 26 May 1847

ALLEN Susan M of Stephentown NY m COMSTOCK Ebenezer of
Williamstown MA 14 Mar *MS* 8 Apr 1846

ALLEN Susan V m KING Rufus G on 19 March at Newport RI *MS* 9
Apr 1845

ALLEY Jane of Eaton NH on 26 Jan m YOUNG Jeremiah of Freedom
NH *MS* 8 Feb 1843

ALLOWAY Ann E m WILLARD George K both of Dover 9 Nov 1848
MS 20 Dec 1848

AMBROSE Lucy m HUTCHINS Elias Eld *MS* 20 Apr 1832

AMCEDON Julia of Hamburgh NY m WARRINEF Israel C of Buffalo
NY *MS* 25 Nov 1835

AMEDON Sarah m HODGES Levi M both of Buffalo NY 18 Nov 1847
MS 19 Apr 1848

AMEE Agnes of Gardiner ME m STEVENS John on 23 May at FWB
meeting house in Gardiner village *MS* 2 June 1847

AMES Caroline of Canterbury NH m CAVERLY Abiel M of Loudon NH
on 25 Mar at Canterbury *MS* 9 Apr 1845

AMES Comfort Mrs of Gilford m CLARK Mayhew Jr 22 Oct *MS* 31
Oct 1838

AMES Elmira of New Hampton NH m HARPER Hiram on 4 Mar at
New Hampton *MS* 17 Apr 1844

AMES Lydia m SUTTON John Capt on 20 Mar at Parsonsfield ME
MS 16 Apr 1845

AMES Lydia W of Corinth ME m BEAN Daniel of Exeter ME on 23
Sept 1847 *MS* 2 Feb 1848

AMES Maria D of Fowler NY m BELLINS Rufus of Clark Township
CW *MS* 15 Dec 1847

ANDERSON Mary J of Bath m MASON Henry P on 21 Jul *MS* 11
Sept 1850

ANDERSON Mary m WHEELER Jeremiah on 19 Jan at Manchester
NH *MS* 17 Feb 1847

ANDERSON Sarah A m GELLERSON James K both of Bancroft PLT
ME 25 June 1848 *MS* 6 Dec 1848

ANDERSON Susan Mrs "united ages number over 140 yrs or 70yrs
each" m SHORES Thomas *MFWBR* 22 Feb 1851

ANDRES Mehitabel K m PUTNEY Almon 4 Apr *MS* 15 May 1844

ANDREW Catherine on 2 Jul at Orange NH m HADLEY Gilbert M *MS*
26 Jul 1843

ANDREWS Abby S m RUNDET/RUNDLET Thomas N on 4 Feb of
New Market NH *MS* 6 Apr 1847 & *MS* 10 Mar 1847

ANDREWS Aphia m PAGE William R Jr both of Corinna ME 30 Aug
1849 *MS* 20 Feb 1850

ANDREWS Lucinda of Corinna ME 14 Apr 1839 m BRIGGS William C *MS* 29 May 1839

ANDREWS Lydia of Wales ME m SANBORN James of Monmouth ME *MS* 10 Jul 1839

ANGEL Ann m EMERSON Ira on 21st at Manchester *MS* 17 Feb 1847

ANGELL Hannah P of No Providence RI m FARNHAM George of Cato Addison County NY [*sic*] on 5 Nov 1837 [N.B. Addison Co. is in VT; however, we found no listing of a Cato in NY or VT.] *MS* 17 Jan 1838

ANGELL Maria D m FISKE John S both of Scituate RI on 6 Sept *MS* 25 Sept 1850

ANGELL Sarah ae 56y in Smithfield RI m ANGELL Israel Col ae 86y *MS* 18 May 1826

ANGELL Sarah Ann of No Providence RI m TOBEY William of Smithfield on 30 Mar *MS* 13 Apr 1836

ANNAN Mary H Mrs m JACKSON Leonard Esq both of Manchester on 31 Oct 1847 *MS* 10 Nov 1847

ANNIS Emeline of Somersworth NH m PARSONS John Jr of Shapleigh ME on 7 Dec *MS* 18 Dec 1844

ANNIS Harriet N Mrs of Warner NH? m RAND Charles D of Hopkinton NH on 10 Oct 1843 *MS* 8 May 1844

ANNIS Julia A m CHAPLIN William B *MS* 15 Dec 1847

ANNIS Sarah B m NOYS Horatio L on 10 Jan at Great Falls NH *MS* 20 Jan 1847

ANSMORE Aurilla m FELCH Alson 7 Jul at Sardinia NY *MS* 31 Aug 1836

APPLEBEE Almira m PRAY David at Great Falls NH *MS* 7 June 1843 & *MS* 19 Jul 1843

APPLEBEE Esther I m SANBORN Joshua B both of Acton ME? 18 Feb 1849 *MS* 7 Mar 1849

APPLEBEE Phebe A of Minton NH m DURGIN Alexander on 22 Feb at Acton ME *MS* 28 Feb 1844

APPLELY Morgan Miss of Landaff NH m PAGE Moses of Whitefield NH? *MS* 19 Apr 1843

APPLETON Elizabeth F d/o Hon N D APPLETON m CLARK Augustus O *MFWBR* 26 Oct 1850

ARCHIBALD Mercy m DOWNS Jonathan G at Acton ME on 1 Mar *MS* 18 Mar 1846

ARCHIBALD Sally at Acton ME m COOK Amos *MS* 18 Oct 1843

ARCHIBALD Sarah of Plymouth ME m COLE Ephraim Jr of Etna ME 9 Sept *MS* 24 Oct 1838

ARLIN Almira/Elmira of Dover NH m BUZZELL Miles *MFWBR* 12 May 1849 & on 27 Apr *MS* 9 May 1849

ARLIN Martha m TYLER John both of Barrington 10 inst *MS* 20 June 1849

ARM Sarah m PARMENTER William N both of Oneida NY 17 Dec 1848 *MS* 24 Jan 1849

ARMINGTON Esther of Smithfield RI m SHEARMAN Preserved of No Providence RI on 6 Apr *MS* 24 May 1837

ARNOLD Adah m BATTY Caleb O both of Scituate RI? on 8 Nov *MS* 1 Jan 1851

ARNOLD Betsey H m CARR John B both of Peru New York *MS* 14 Feb 1838

ARNOLD Charlotte m WOODWORTH Edward both of Dixmont ME on 15 Dec *MS* 24 Jan 1838

ARNOLD Jenette A of Randolph NY m WAKEFIELD Utiley Jr of Randolph NY on 4 Feb *MS* 13 Mar 1844

ASHTON Gracia of Wanconia Wis m JOOE Horace on 16 Mar of Cooksville *MS* 16 June 1847

ATCHINSON Laura Ann m LEONARD William H on 10 Sept at Parma NY *MS* 18 Oct 1843

ATHERTON Catharine m REED William Jr both of Mt Desert ME on 29 Nov 1849 *MS* 2 Jan 1850

ATHERTON Elizabeth M m FOLSOM Lucien M of Lowell ME at Dracut MA *MS* 4 June 1845

ATKINS Elizabeth W of Lowell MA m EMERSON William H on 27 Apr at Lowell MA *MS* 11 May 1842

ATKINS Harriet A m JEWETT H W of Gardiner ME *MFWBR* 14 Sept 1850

ATKINSON Abigail of Eaton NH on 21st Aug m HARMON William "The *Dover Enquirer* is requested to copy" *MS* 11 Sept 1839

ATKINSON Caroline of Lynn MA on 22 Jan m KNOTT Robert Jr of Boston MA *MS* 8 Feb 1843

ATKINSON Hannah m DOWNS Albert both of Lowell on 16 Mar 1848 *MS* 26 Apr 1848

ATKINSON Lucinda M m BANKS Esreff H both of Saco ME *MFWBR* 13 Nov 1847

ATKINSON Maria B of Madison ME m WYMAN Howard B of Sidney ME 14 Nov 1848 *MS* 29 Nov 1848

ATKINSON Mary Ann m MANSEIGH Lewis both of Stanstead LC on 1 Jan *MS* 17 Feb 1836

ATKINSON Sarah m PAGE Christopher both of Stanstead LC on 5 Oct 1836 *MS* 10 Jan 1837

ATWOOD Sally E m CLIFFORD George W on 1 Mar at Alexander *MS* 26 Mar 1845

AUBENS Rebecca D of Brunswick ME m TOOTHAKER John H *MS* 13 Jan 1847

AUGIR Harriet W of East Troy Wis m COOMBS Albion P of Rochester Wis on 5 Oct 1848 *MS* 29 Nov 1848

AUSTIN Adah of Great Falls NH on 18th inst m KNIGHT Peter Dea of Berwick ME *MFWBR* 7 & 14 Apr 1849

AUSTIN Amanda m THOMPSON Henry 22 Sept *MS* 24 Oct 1833

AUSTIN Calista of Hamburgh NY m PUTNEY Joseph of Wales NY? on 23 Jan at Hamburgh NY *MS* 20 Mar 1844

AUSTIN Elisabeth Mrs of No Berwick ME m SHERBURNE Tobias of Rochester *MS* 2 Dec 1835

AUSTIN Mary H m DREW Ayer B both of Tunbridge VT 7 June 1848 *MS* 21 June 1848

AUSTIN Venorma m CROWN George W both of Lowell on 3 Sept *MS* 12 Sept 1838

AVERY Abigail m DURGIN Ananias A on 29 Nov 1843 at Sandwich NH?/MA? *MS* 5 June 1844

AVERY Enthemy m TITUS Horace both of Lowell MA *MS* 18 Jan 1837

AVERY Harriet E of Corinth VT m ALLEN Ira B on 2 Nov at Corinth VT *MS* 17 Feb 1847

AVERY Harriet m LORD William of Limerick ME *MS* 31 Jan 1828

AVERY Sarah Ann C of Sharon m ORDWAY Harry of Strafford *MS* 18 Apr 1838

AXTELL Mary late from Canada m LENORD William in Pierpont NY on Nov 21 1841 *MS* 2 Feb 1842

AYER Abigail m SMITH James on 3 Jul at Lowell MA *MS* 16 Aug 1843

AYER Ann R m TRAFTON Isaac M "the printer's fee was gratefully received" *MFWBR* 15 June 1850

AYER Caroline Augusta Miss of Sangerville ME m STRAW David R Esq of Gilford *MS* 21 Oct 1833

AYER Charlotte of Concord m WILLIAMS Washington merchant of Dover NH at Concord *MS* 6 Mar 1834

AYER Hannah Miss d/o AYER James Esq m CLIFFORD Nathan Esq on Thurs last *MS* 26 Mar 1828

AYER Mary J of Lowell m TWOMBLY Benjamin of Billerica MA *MS* 8 Jan 1840

AYER Nancy m HOWE Joseph S both of Lowell *MS* 18 Oct 1837

AYER Olive J of Manchester NH m QUINT George W on 29 Nov at FWB meeting house *MS* 9 Dec 1846

AYER Sarah m BROWN W Joseph both of Newbury 14 Sept *MS* 6 Oct 1847

AYERS Betsey of Albany m ADERSON [ANDERSON?] Timothy on 7 June at Conway NH *MS* 23 June 1847

AYERS Nancy of Hatley LC m CHAMBERLIN Hammond on 28 Feb of Brompton *MS* 13 Sept 1843

AYERS Sarah A Mrs m ORDWAY Benjamin both of Kittery ME on 22 Dec 1849 *MS* 9 Jan 1850

AYRES Amanda of Macon m PENNINGTON Joseph on 17 Nov 1842 at Macon Mich *MS* 14 Dec 1842

BABB Almira m BABB Ezekiel H both of Strafford on 22 Oct 1848 *MS* 17 Jan 1849

BABB Delilah of Barnstead NH m FOSS Joseph R of Strafford on 26 May *MS* 19 June 1844

BABB Eliza m HANSCOM Lemuel E on 14 Jul at Barnstead NH *MS* 17 Aug 1836

BABB Hannah Jane m GRAY Robert B both of Boston on 13 inst *MS* 19 Oct 1836

BABB Harriet C F of Buxton ME m EDGCOMB Elizha of Limington ME *MS* 20 Nov 1844

BABB Margaret A of Saccarrappa ME m BROWN Harace T of Parsonsfield ME *MFWBR* 18 Jan 1851

BABB Maria m McCRILLIS John H both of Strafford NH on 24 Dec 1848 *MS* 17 Jan 1849

BABB Martha m FENDERSON Edward A on 12 inst *MS* 23 May 1833

BABB Sarah A of Buxton ME m HAZELTINE Benjamin L *MFWBR* 22 Feb 1851

BABB Sarah Jane m BREWER Nathaniel on 16th Mar at Strafford *MS* 16 Apr 1845

BABCOCK Olive Ann m WILLIAMS William H both of Nassau NY on 10 inst *MS* 25 Dec 1850

BABCOCK Sarah m RAMONS Ludden on 2 Apr at Hamburgh NY *MS* 12 June 1844

BACHELDER Amoril L of Lewiston ME m CROOKER John of Danville ME *MFWBR* 2 Feb 1850

BACHELDER Betsey E on 9 Feb m PEASE Simeon D on 9 Feb *MS* 26 Apr 1843

BACHELDER Clarinda of Vershire VT m GODFREY Sylvester of Vershire VT on 15 Jul 1849 *MS* 16 Jan 1850

BACHELDER Eleanor m FOLSOM Josiah on 17 Mar at Northwood NH *MS* 9 Apr 1845

BACHELDER Hannah D of Strafford NH? m BEAN James M of Newbury NH on 26 Aug *MS* 21 Nov 1849

BACHELDER Louisa m CRAM John both of Sanbornton NH on 15 June *MS* 2 Aug 1837

BACHELDER Lucy Jane m PUTNEY John B both of Lowell on 29 Nov *MS* 12 Dec 1838

BACHELDER Mary M of Dover NH m SCRIGGINS Bradbury of Charlestown MA on 1 May 1849 *MS* 9 May 1849

BACHELDER Nancy of Waterville ME m SAUNDERS Samuel of New Sharon ME *MS* 14 Jul 1847

BACHELDER Permelia of Chichester NH? m GEORGE Wm F of Nashua NH? on 12 Feb *MS* 11 Mar 1840

BACHELDER Sally of Enfield NH m FIFIELD Moses of Salisbury *RI* Jan 1820 p 15

BACHELDOR of Bridgewater m AMES James M on 17 Feb *MS* 26

BACHELDOR (Continued)
Mar 1845

BACHELDOR Zeriah of New Chester m BUZZELL Edmond *RI* Jan 1820 p 15

BACHELER Mary m JOHNSON Isaac both of Franklin MA on 30 Jan *MS* 20 Feb 1850

BACON Eliza A of Sutton m BAILEY Henry D on 26 Oct *MS* 18 Jan 1843

BACON Eliza m WARNER Charles both of Mendon MA *MS* 5 Sept 1838

BACON Hannah G of Wilton ME on 25 June 1843 m DOW James C of Dover NH *MS* 19 Jul 1843

BACON Mary m DANFORTH William both of Framingham MA *MS* 19 June 1850

BADGER Irene C of New Hampton m SHORES John S on 4 Jul *MS* 31 Jan 1844

BADGER Maria L of Lowell MA m CRABTREE Ephraim of Hancock ME on 27 Oct *MS* 6 Jan 1847

BAGLEY Elethe of Charleston ME m FARRAR Sewell of Corinth ME on 18 Jul 1848 *MS* 21 Feb 1849

BAGLEY Emeline at Danville m ROWE George W *MS* 18 Sept 1839

BAGLEY Sally of Candia NH m CARTER Benjamin F of Newtown *MS* 17 June 1835

BAHONUIN Diantha m SLACK Ransom both of Washington VT on 30 Dec 1847 *MS* 22 Mar 1848

BAILEY Abigail m WINSHIP George D both of Biddeford on 14 June *MS* 30 Sept 1846

BAILEY Anna of Auburn ME? m COLE Jeremiah of Lewiston ME on 8 May *MS* 6 June 1849 & *MFWBR* 16 June 1849

BAILEY Betsey m HASTINGS Jonas both of Lowell *MS* 1 Nov 1837

BAILEY Eliza W m HUFF Joseph Jr *MFWBR* 17 Mar 1849

BAILEY Lucy H m PLUMMER Soloman H both of Freeport ME on 14 Nov 1847 *MS* 8 Dec 1847

BAILEY Mary Ann of Maxfield m CARY Zenas on 23 June 1844 at Atkinson ME *MS* 21 Aug 1844

BAILEY Mary of Andover NH m WHITEHEAD Charles of Boston MA on 13 Feb 1849 *MS* 7 Mar 1849

BAILEY Nancy d/o BAILEY John Dea m TUCKER James of New Chester NH *RI* 20 Jul 1819

BAILEY Nancy m BAILEY Terry both of Woolwich ME on 10 Apr *MS* 20 June 1838

BAILEY Nancy E m HARDY Abram both of Manchester on 15 Dec *MS* 26 Dec 1849

BAILEY Rebecca G on 12th inst m BAILEY John B of Woolwich ME *MS* 29 June 1842

BAILEY Sarah of Woolwich ME on 17th ult m HUBBARD Boyd of

BAILEY (Continued)
Alna ME *MS* 13 Feb 1839
BAILY Sophronia F of Canaan m MANTER Daniel E of Pittsfield on
25 Nov 1849 *MS* 16 Jan 1850
BAKER Adaline m BATCHELDER Joshua C both of Shapleigh ME on
4 Jul 1847 *MS* 12 Jan 1848
BAKER Dorinda m MANSEIL Ira on 4 Apr 1847 *MS* 15 Sept 1847
BAKER Eveline m RILEY William on 13 Mar 1843 *MS* 19 Jul 1843
BAKER Frances A of Litchfield m MALLET Isaac E of Topsham ME
on 31 Dec *MS* 15 Jan 1851
BAKER Hannah I m POWERS Charles on New Year's eve at Charles-
town MA *MS* 17 Feb 1847
BAKER Harriot of Waterford ME m UPTON Henry of Norway ME
MFWBR 24 Apr 1847
BAKER Jane of Mito ME m LANNING Stephen of Gorham Ontario Co
NY on 30 Sept *MS* 28 Nov 1838
BAKER Lucinda of Hatley LC on 21 Oct 1838 m MASTA Joseph A Dr
MS 17 Apr 1839
BAKER Maria of Uxbridge MA m EVANS Benjamin Jr of Smithfield
on 1 inst at Johnston RI *MS* 11 Jan 1837
BAKER Mary E of Attleborough MA m BOUKER Simeon of Exeter ME
on 1 Sept 1848 *MS* 13 Sept 1848
BAKER Mary Jane of Holderness NH m WILLSON David W of New
Hampton NH on 18 Nov 1847 *MS* 19 Jan 1848
BAKER Mary of Shapleigh ME m PIKE George H of Roxbury MA on 8
Oct 1848 *MS* 14 Feb 1849
BAKER Nancy m KNIGHT James preacher *MS* 10 Jul 1829
BAKER Priscilla at Bowdoinham ME m BURRIDGE Andrew B of
Boston MA *MS* 16 Oct 1839
BAKER Rebecca of Portland ME m DYER G of Gorham ME *MFWBR*
23 June 1849
BAKER Sarah C Miss of Somersworth NH m CLEMENT J H of
Gorham ME *MS* 12 Apr 1827
BAKER Sarah E of Lowell MA m OTIS Joseph G on 21 Aug at Lowell
MA *MS* 2 Nov 1842
BAKER Triphosa of Newbury m CLARK Alfred at Newbury NH? *MS*
28 Jul 1847
BAKER Urania of Burrillville RI m MATISON Robert R of Stonnington
CT on 22 Jan 1849 *MS* 21 Mar 1849
BALCH Marilda Mrs m WILLIAMS Elihu both of Haverhill MA on 28
Feb 1848 *MS* 8 Mar 1848
BALDWIN Harriet Dyantha of Ellington NY m COOLEY Ruel on 12
Oct 1847 *MS* 9 Feb 1848
BALDWIN Maria m BARKER Francis on 10 Nov 1847 *MS* 8 Dec 1847
BALDWIN Maria L of Naugatuck CT m DICK W M Eld of Bytown CW
at Waterbury CT *MS* 28 May 1845

BALDWIN Philenia m SMITH EDMUND both of Freedom NY on 15 Oct *MS* 20 Dec 1837

BALDWIN Polly m SMITH Artemas both of Freedom NY on 15 Oct *MS* 20 Dec 1837

BALDWIN Zilpah on Feb 25 m CLEAVELAND Levi both of Barnston *MS* 15 Apr 1840

BALINGER Rachel m HARVEY Alonzo on 7 Aug at Perry Township OH *MS* 30 Oct 1844

BALL Isabel D of Westport MA m MACOMBER George B on 15 Oct at TIVERTON RI *MS* 8 Nov 1843

BALL Lois W m KENDALL Nathan T of Landaff NH at the home of N K GEORGE in Franconia NH on 24 Sept *MS* 6 Nov 1844

BALL Lydia A C m EMERY Enoch H both of Manchester on 21 Sept *MS* 6 Oct 1847

BALL Nancy m SMITH Jutus E on 10 Oct at Dryden *MS* 15 Jan 1845

BALLARD Avis M of West Hartford m RION Samuel on 2 Feb of Northfield *MS* 31 Mar 1847

BALLETT Lydia of Unity ME m DENNIS Hobert of Dixmont ME *MS* 25 Dec 1844

BALLINTINE Mary E m JOY William H at Fairfield ME *MS* 17 Apr 1844

BALLOU Fanny m STEARNS Varus on 11 Apr at Lowell MA *MS* 25 May 1842

BANGS Abby S of Dover m DENNIS S James of Manchester on 14 inst *MS* 22 Jan 1851 & *MFWBR* 25 Jan 1851

BANGS Clarissa A m FOSS John both of Monmouth ME *MS* 29 Dec 1847

BANGS Ester of Buxton ME m RICH Lemuel Esq of Standish ME on 1st inst *MS* 23 Dec 1831

BANGS Harriet F m GREEN William H both of Sweden ME on 17 Oct 1847 *MS* 24 Nov 1847

BANKS Hannah B of Nottingham NH m HUNTRESS Hubbard H of New Market *MS* 25 May 1842

BANKS Mary m CHURCHILL Thomas *MS* 24 Mar 1830

BANNISTER Kilany of Pierpont NY m OTIS Daniel on 5 Nov 1842 *MS* 1 Feb 1843

BARDEN Catharine M of Three Mile Bay NY m WILNOT Wm A of Fabius NY on 19 Dec 1847 *MS* 12 Jan 1848

BARDON Nancy of Sutton Caledonia Co VT on 16 Mar m RAWSON Jasper of Douglass Essex Co NY *MS* 7 June 1843

BARGIN Sally W of Parsonsfield m FOLSOM H Maj of Limerick ME on 24 ult *MS* 29 Jan 1840

BARKER Elizabeth of Stratham m LANE Edmund J bookseller of Dover NH *MS* 13 Feb 1834

BARKER Ellen of Lewiston ME m WOODARD Winchel of Lisbon ME on 16 inst *MS* 24 Jan 1849

BARKER Harriet m PARKER Joseph both of Canton ME 13 Jan 1848 *MS* 9 Feb 1848

BARKER Irene H of Naples m JACKSON Richard of Harrison ME at Naples ME *MS* 27 June 1842

BARKER Mar? T d/o BARKER Simeon Hon of Limerick ME m STORER Horace P of Portland ME *MFWBR* 8 May 1847

BARKER Mary of Cornish m PATTERSON Isaac of Limerick ME on 7 Jan 1847 *MS* 17 Feb 1847 & *MFWBR* 13 Feb 1847

BARLOW Ann of Batavia NY m GOODWIN Levi of Ogden on 11 inst in Bayron *MS* 1 Feb 1837

BARNARD Lucy W of Enfield NH on Feb 21 m KINGMAN Nathan Col of Orford *MS* 23 Mar 1842

BARNARD Mary Ann of Lowell MA m BURNHAM Andrew W of Essex *MS* 2 Jan 1839

BARNES Diana E m DANFORTH Parker R both of Pittsburg on 7 Jul *MS* 11 Sept 1850

BARNES Elizabeth m OWEN Levi on 17 Mar *MS* 23 May 1849

BARNES Mary A m SHEDD Edward D on 11 Oct at the Free Baptist church in Charlestown *MS* 9 Dec 1846

BARNEY Armintha of Grafton m MARTIN Robert A of Manchester *MS* 17 Jul 1844

BARNEY Lucy m PERSON Gilbert both of Barnston KC on 20 Apr *MS* 20 Sept 1837

BARNS Jane Ann m COE James both of Davenport NY? on 15 Jan *MS* 19 Feb 1851

BARNS Mary A of Roxbury MA m WHITE John S on 14 Aug of Cambridge MA *MS* 28 Aug 1844

BARRETT Almena of Manchester NH m PAGE Robert on 26 Mar *MS* 6 Apr 1842

BARRETT Maria m GILE George W both of Rutland on 24 Nov 1850 *MS* 19 Mar 1851

BARRETT Martha A m JEFFERSON Nathaniel W on 8th ult *MS* 9 Dec 1846

BARRETT Olive R of Manchester m LITTLE Joseph R of Palmer on 19 Oct 1848 *MS* 8 Nov 1848

BARRETT Sarepta P m GILES Miron S both of Rutland on 2 Oct 1850 *MS* 19 Mar 1851

BARRKLEFF Antonett P of Bath m DALTON Edwin W of Roxbury MA on 10 Mar *MS* 5 Apr 1843

BARRY Eleanor m BAKESKEY Theodore both of Lowell *MS* 12 Apr 1837

BARRY Elmira of Lowell MA m UPHAM Clement on 5 May at Lowell MA *MS* 25 May 1842

BARTER Susan of Boothbay ME m SHERMAN Eleazer on 5 May at Boothbay ME *MS* 15 June 1842

BARTHOLOMEW Eveline of Oxford NY m MILLER George of New

BARTHOLOMEW (Continued)

Berlin on 29 June 1848 *MS* 26 Jul 1848

BARTLETT Abigail in Boston on the 20th inst m HINES Barnum J both of Hartford ME *MS* 30 Mar 1842

BARTLETT Caroline of New Market NH m TOWLE Levi of Epping NH on 26 Nov at New Market *MS* 9 Dec 1846

BARTLETT Cintha on 31 Oct m DYER Orin of New Portland ME *MS* 18 Dec 1839

BARTLETT Climena P of Deering m ORNE Joseph M of New Boston on 7 Mar *MS* 22 Mar 1848

BARTLETT Dintha of New Portland ME m DYER Orin on 31 Oct *MS* 18 Dec 1839

BARTLETT Elizabeth H d/o BARTLETT Joseph Esq m DUNGIN Samuel both of Nottingham on 1 inst *MS* 15 Jan 1851

BARTLETT Harriet of Exeter m YORK Thomas of Lee *MS* 28 May 1834

BARTLETT Lydia at Weare on Feb 4 m CILLEY Joseph W *MS* 11 Mar 1840

BARTLETT Mary D m DAVIS Timothy G both of New Market on 16 Nov 1848 *MS* 29 Nov 1848

BARTLETT Mary J m SATERLAY Joseph T on 24 Nov at Manchester *MS* 9 Dec 1846

BARTLETT Mary J m JOHNSON Noah W both of Garland ME on 25 Dec 1848 *MS* 10 Jan 1849

BARTLETT Rebecca J d/o BARTLETT Philip Esq m HILL John C on 25th ult *MS* 23 May 1833

BARTLETT Sally T of Nottingham m MATHES Reuben of Lee on 29 May *MS* 5 June 1850

BARTLETT Sarah d/o BARTLETT Josiah m PAGE Ezekiel H s/o PAGE John Eld *MS* 23 Jan 1834

BARTLETTE Drusilla m BATCHELDER Samuel Eaton on 16 Nov at Phipsburg ME *MS* 1 Dec 1841

BARTON Amanda of Providence m MASON C B of Pottersville (Bristol Co MA?) *MS* 13 Nov 1850

BARTON Merande m STROUT James of Raymond ME *MS* 29 Nov 1843

BASS Desire E m MASON James L both of Plainfield NY on 19 Dec 1845 *MS* 29 Apr 1846

BASSART Amenda of Pierpont NY on 2 Mar m BOCHART William *MS* 3 May 1843

BASSETT Lucy D m MEADER John K both of New Market on 17 June Sabbath Eve *MS* 27 June 1849

BASSETT Mary E m CASWELL Willard W both of Durham of Northwood on 15 Jul *MS* 8 Aug 1849

BASSETT Mercy H of Dexter ME on 5th inst m BAILEY Giles Rev "pastor of Universalist Society" *MFWBR* 21 Dec 1850

BASSETT Susan C of Dover m FRENCH Thomas J of Nottingham NH on 8 Nov *MS* 14 Nov 1849

BATCHELDER Abigail of Strafford VT on Dec 11 m KNOWLES Jefferson of Northwood NH *MS* 27 Feb 1839

BATCHELDER Abigail B of Meredith on 13 Feb m LAMPREY Uriah of Gilmanton NH *MS* 13 Mar 1839

BATCHELDER Adeline m MANSUR James both of Newburyport MA on 7 May *MS* 15 May 1850

BATCHELDER Dorothy of Lowell m SIMMONS Loring of Boston *MS* 24 Aug 1836

BATCHELDER Eliza Ann m BARTLET Joseiah Jr both of Garland ME on 23 Nov *MS* 13 Dec 1837

BATCHELDER Frances E m HATCH William C *MFWBR* 1 Dec 1849

BATCHELDER Hannah B (widow of the late Simon BATCHELDER of Northwood) d/o WALDRON Isaac Col of Barrington m TASKER Elisha on 3 Feb at Northwood *MS* 17 Feb 1847

BATCHELDER Hannah H of North Hampton m MARSTON Edwin A on 9th inst at New Market *MS* 19 Jul 1843

BATCHELDER Hannah S m HAMILTON Wendal both of N Yarmouth on 5 Jan 1848 *MS* 8 Mar 1848

BATCHELDER Harriet N m MERRIL Elihu C both of Manchester on 1 Nov *MS* 14 Nov 1849

BATCHELDER Lorinda P m DEMERITT Daniel on 3 Jul at Nottingham NH *MS* 20 June 1842

BATCHELDER Louisa of Sandbornton NH m ODELL Ebenezer F of Sandbornton *MS* 15 Nov 1843

BATCHELDER Lucinda m NELSON Levi Jr both of Bristol on 21 Apr *MS* 5 May 1846

BATCHELDER Lydia C m STEELE Horace of Roxbury on 5 June at West Brookfield *MS* 13 June 1842

BATCHELDER Lydia D of Dover m STEVENS John M of Grafton on 26 Sept *MS* 2 Oct 1850

BATCHELDER Mary Mrs of Haverhill m ELIOT Winthrop on 29 Jan at Haverhill *MS* 14 Feb 1844

BATCHELDER Nancy Mrs m PALMER Jonathan both of Pittsfield NH on 25 June 1848 *MS* 12 Jul 1848

BATCHELDER Nancy of Chichester Mrs m LEAVITT Ebenezer Capt of Pittsfield on 16 Nov at Pittsfield *MS* 7 Dec 1842

BATCHELDER Nancy of Waterville ME m SAUNDERS Samuel on 5 May of New Sharon ME *MS* 7 Jul 1847

BATCHELDER Olive C m SWAIN John L of Meredith NH *MS* 27 Nov 1839

BATCHELDER Parmelia m MATHES Horace W on 16 Jul 1843 at Canterbury NH *MS* 31 Jan 1844

BATCHELDER Sally m PEASE Nathaniel *MS* 1 Apr 1835

BATCHELDER Sarah E of Garland ME m SMITH Theodore C of

BATCHELDER (Continued)

Corinna ME *MS* 22 Nov 1848

BATEMAN Elizabeth of Nassau m LESTER Hiram L *MS* 22 Feb 1843

BATES Alvira m WATSON Benjamin S on 14 Nov at Groton *MS* 18 Jan 1843

BATES Eliza Ann m RAMSDELL William A both of Richmond on 5 Nov 1848 *MS* 15 Nov 1848

BATES Martilla L m LEATHERS Loring of St Albans ME *MS* 7 June 1843

BATES Mary Ann of Waterville m CLARK Asa *MS* 26 June 1839

BATES Polly and BATES Alexander divorced 27 Jul 1832 *MS* 24 Aug 1832

BATES Rachel Jane of Richmond ME m DOUGLASS Benjamin B on 12 May at Litchfield ME *MS* 2 June 1847

BATES Sarah J of St Albans m SMITH Andrew H on 14 Nov at St Albans *MS* 27 Dec 1843

BAXTER Eliza Ann of Charlestown MA m RANDALL Henry A on 15 Sept at Charlestown MA *MS* 23 Oct 1844

BAYLEY Lorana m JUDKINS Moses *MS* 30 Jan 1839

BEACHAM Joanna of Ossipee NH m THOMPSON Washington of Tuftonboro' NH *MS* 31 May 1843

BEACHAM Sabrina of Ossipee NH m THOMPSON Hiram of Tuftonboro NH 3 Mar *MS* 16 Mar 1842

BEADLE Angeline m BARNES Matthews L on 11 Oct at Cooperstown NY *MS* 18 Dec 1844

BEAL Emeline S m SMITH Lewis E on 15th inst at Great Falls NH *MS* 28 Jul 1847

BEALS Eliza m FRENCH Charles L of Turner ME on 8 Feb at Woolwich ME *MS* 20 Mar 1844

BEAMAN Mary R m BIBBER Ezra of Portland ME *MFWBR* 14 Aug 1847

BEAN Abby C of Ossipee NH m PERKINS Albert A at Wolfboro' NH *MS* 22 Oct 1845

BEAN Abigail of Gilmanton m SANBORN Jeremiah on 13 Nov at Alton NH *MS* 25 Feb 1846

BEAN Adelaide Q m KIMBALL George H both of Manchester on 4 Sept *MS* 23 Sept 1846

BEAN Ann m LOVERING John S both of Loudon NH on 27 Jan 1848 *MS* 16 Feb 1848

BEAN Ann Mrs/ Anna of Wolfborough/ Tuftonboro' NH m TEBBETTS/ TIBBITS Edmond on 17 June *MS* 7 Nov 1849 & *MFWBR* 21 Jul 1849

BEAN Ann Octavia m SMITH Oliver W both of Dexter ME on 19 Dec 1837 *MS* 9 May 1838

BEAN Anna of Gilford m DICY Hazen of Gilmanton NH on 3 Sept 1837 *MS* 7 Feb 1838

BEAN Betsey Miss of Jay ME m RUSSELL Samuel B of Canaan MEon 3d ult in Jay *MS* 6 Mar 1829

BEAN Caroline A m STORY Isaac S both of Underhill VT on 15 Sept *MS* 6 Nov 1850

BEAN Clara A m MITCHELL Joseph H on 28 ult *MS* 1 Apr 1846

BEAN Clarissa of Bridgewater m CROSS Sylvester *MS* 28 Feb 1844

BEAN Comfort Ann of Meredith m SWAIN Dudley T of Denmark ME on 15 June *MS* 26 Sept 1849

BEAN Cynthia of Chesterville ME at Jay ME on Jan 1 m PREBLE Levi T *MS* 15 Jan 1840

BEAN Darrilla of Wilmot NH m MERRILL Russell of Warren on 3 June *MS* 24 June 1846

BEAN Deborah of Waterborough ME m SMITH Asa on 12 Nov *MS* 18 Dec 1844

BEAN Drusilla of NH m FELLOWS George Eld of Chautauqua Co NY at Clay Onondaga Co NY on 15th inst *MS* 24 Aug 1842

BEAN Eleanor L of Sandwich m HOWE Aaron M Dr on 31st Jul *MS* 6 Aug 1845

BEAN Eliza M of Bethlehem NH on 19 Dec m HARRIMAN Obed of Chatham MA *MS* 4 Jan 1843

BEAN Emily J of Brownfield ME on 23d m SMITH Joshua of Biddeford ME *MFWBR* 3 Feb 1849

BEAN Eunice of Barnston LC m May Sylvester on 6 Jul *MS* 13 Sept 1843

BEAN Hannah of Candia NH m FOLSOM John of East Sangerville ME on 11 Jan *MS* 1 Feb 1843

BEAN Hannah m PRESCOTT Cyrus on 26 Dec at Candia *MS* 8 Jan 1845

BEAN Harriet A of Dover NH m FERRIN Francis on 10 Sept at Dover NH *MS* 17 Sept 1845

BEAN Huldah m BURLEIGH Benjamin on 2 Dec 1843 at Sandwich NH *MS* 5 June 1844

BEAN Judith m NUTE Alfred m at Candia *MS* 22 June 1836

BEAN Malinda of Wheelock m COREY Ralph of Albany on Jan 4 1842 *MS* 2 Feb 1842

BEAN Maria J of Lowell MA on 28 Aug m RICHARDS Luther *MS* 11 Sept 1839

BEAN Marinda m HEATH John on 3 Apr *MS* 1 May 1844

BEAN Mary m STOWELL Joseph H at Bangor ME *MS* 13 Sept 1843

BEAN Mary BEAN d/o BEAN Jeremy Eld m FOSTER Ezra both of Jay ME on 16th inst *MS* 26 Mar 1828

BEAN Mary m BURLEY Charles E both of Dover on 29 Feb *MS* 16 Mar 1836

BEAN Mary H m BROWN S Daniel S *MS* 16 May 1838

BEAN Mary J m BUFFINGTON Chars A both of Colebrook NH on 28 Nov *MS* 11 Dec 1850

BEAN Mary Jane m COPP Albert both of Dover on 14 Jul *MS* 22 Jul 1846

BEAN Mary Mrs of Danville m BROWN Isaac of Poplin NH on 28 Sept at Danville *MS* 1 Nov 1843

BEAN Mary S m NASON Aaron on 3 Nov 1844 of Wakefield *MS* 1 Jan 1845

BEAN Melvina m FELCH Gideon D on 9 May at Sutton NH *MS* 24 Jul 1844 (sic) should be *MS* 31 Jul 1844

BEAN Sally m BACHELOR Joseph of Raymond *MS* 10 Sept 1834

BEAN Sally m SMALL Ivory of Limington ME *MS* 1 Mar 1827

BEAN Sally L m WATSON Winthrop on 22 Dec 1844 *MS* 12 Feb 1845

BEAN Sarah A of Sandwich m SANBORN Lowell of Gilmanton NH on 27 June *MS* 10 Jul 1850

BEAN Sarah on 9th ult m ROWELL Benjamin both of Montville ME *MS* 8 Apr 1840

BEAN Sarah C of Charlestown MA m SEVERANCE Asa on 2 Apr *MS* 24 May 1843

BEAN Sarah E of Lowell MA m COX Charles H on 10th inst at Dracut MA *MS* 18 Mar 1846

BEAN Shuah S m WHITTEMORE Albert both of Colebrook NH on 1 Jan *MS* 16 Jan 1850

BEAN Susan m BLAISDELL Ira *MFWBR* 16 Oct 1847

BEAN Susan E m SMITH Samuel on 5 Mar at Lowell MA *MS* 25 May 1842

BEAN Susan H of Montville ME m LITCHFIELD Ames Eld of Lewiston on 17 Dec last *MS* 10 Apr 1834

BEATY Emeline L m PRESCOTT Joshua C both of Holderness NH on 27 Mar *MS* 9 Apr 1851

BECK Sarah A at Charlestown m PARKER Osgood of Boston MA on 14 Jan *MS* 11 Feb 1846

BECKNELL Arthusa of Wolcott VT m WOODMAN Joshua S Esq of Hatley CE on 4 Jan *MS* 6 Mar 1850

BECKWITH Ann of Sutton VT m EATON Samuel N of Sutton VT *MS* 5 Apr 1843

BEEBE Abigail m CLOWD William W on 26 Dec at Manchester *MS* 8 Jan 1845

BEEBE Delia of Sand Lake m HITCHCOCK Lemuel on 16 Oct *MS* 22 Feb 1843

BEEDELL Hannah of Parsonsfield m TARBOX Thomas of Limerick ME on Sunday last *MS* 29 June 1826

BELKNAP Jane Etta of Nassau m ROWE Chauncey A of Stephentown on 18 Oct at West Stephentown NY *MS* 18 Nov 1846

BELKNAP Olive m PIERCE Nathan of Warsaw NY on 22 Oct *MS* 20 Nov 1844

BELL Mary Jane m BELL Benjamin Dr of Charlestown MA FIFIELD B M of New Hampton NH on 12th Nov *MS* 4 Dec 1844

BELLAMY Martha m SARGENT John G at Dover NH *MS* 21 Nov 1833

BELLOWS Harriot C m CLARK Hiram on 11 Jan at Manchester NH *MS* 21 Jan 1846

BELLOWS Nancy m BEAN Freeman on 20 Mar of Barnston LC *MS* 13 Apr 1842

BELLOWS Polly of Hartley LC on 14 Feb 1839 m BEAN Freeman *MS* 17 Apr 1839

BENEDICT Louisa A of Underhill VT m AMES Dexter N of Ferrisburg VT on 1 Jan 1849 *MS* 21 Mar 1849

BENEN Susan Miss of Parsonsfield m MADDOX John W of Cornish ME on 8th inst *MS* 16 Nov 1832

BENFORD Rebecca m JOSS Hosea of Scarboro' ME on 25 Jul at Baldwin ME *MS* 31 Aug 1842

BENJAMIN Caroline m YOUNG T S both of Pierpont NY on 22 Sept 1847 at the residence of Dea R BENJAMIN *MS* 3 Nov 1847

BENJAMIN Laura Ann Mrs m BENJAMIN Samuel S on 16 Nov at Norway Herkimer Co NY *MS* 10 Dec 1845

BENNET Betsey of Strafford m ALLEN Samuel of Enfield NH *MS* 1 Feb 1843

BENNET Lavina of Northwood m HANSON Caleb of Strafford on 4th inst *MS* 21 Jan 1835

BENNET Mary m CONNER Benjamin on 1 Jan 1845 at Alton NH *MS* 19 Feb 1845

BENNETT Deborah of Gilford m PAINE Charles of Meredith on 14 Feb 1848 *MS* 23 Feb 1848

BENNETT Eliza Ann of Sweden m FLINT John on 3 Jan at Sweden ME *MS* 28 Feb 1844 & *MS* 13 Mar 1844

BENNETT Emely Ann m HOIT Nathan B on 19 ult *MS* 9 Dec 1835

BENNETT Jane Mrs m MURPHEY John both of Enfield NH on 23 May *MS* 25 Sept 1850

BENNETT Malita m COLVIN Welcome both of Coventry RI *MS* 13 Nov 1850

BENNETT Martha Ann m PARTRIDGE Jotham on 18 Aug at Westbrook ME *MS* 11 Sept 1844

BENNETT Martha C d/o BENNETT Joseph of Holderness NH m SMITH Daniel K of Sandbornton NH on 20 *MS* 24 Jan 1838

BENNETT Mary A m WILLEY Stephen A both of New Market NH on 1 Oct *MS* 18 Oct 1837

BENNETT Mary W m GILDDEN Daniel on 30 Apr *MS* 22 May 1844

BENNETT Polly M of New Hampton NH m RANDLETT John 3d of Meredith NH on 6 Feb *MS* 16 Feb 1848

BENNETT Susan L m WHITNEY Benjamin F of Bridgton ME *MS* 7 Feb 1844

BENNETT Susan of Bangor ME m LOUD Horace of Corinth on 12 May at Corinth ME *MS* 31 Aug 1842

BENNETT Zady Ann m MOORE Christopher both of Hallowell ME on

BENNETT (Continued)

9 Jul 1846 *MS* 12 Aug 1846

BENSLEY Ellen of Pawtucket RI m CARPENTER Calvin of Seekonk
on *MS* 1 May 1850

BENSON Abigail G of Peru ME m COFFIN Charles of Dixfield ME *MS*
14 Apr 1847

BENSON Almira of Parsonsfield ME on 27 Dec m PEACE Charles of
Tamworth NH *MS* 18 Sept 1839

BENSON Clarissa m DAVIS Samuel S both of Manchester NH on 19
Jan *MS* 26 Feb 1840

BENSON Julia F of Greene ME on 10 Jul m UPTON Rufus P of
Presque Isle Plantation Aroostook Co ME *MS* 18 Mar 1846

BENSON Lydia on 21st inst m FAIRFIELD Seth *MFWBR* 3 Feb 1849

BENSON Martha J on 22d Sept at Gorham ME m ROBERTS William
H of Portland ME *MS* 23 Oct 1839

BENSON Mary E m THOMAS John Jr *MFWBR* 22 Dec 1849

BENSON Milicent m KEITH Samuel on 17 June at Strafford VT *MS*
30 June 1847

BENSON Sabrina D m CRAM John W both of Parsonsfield ME on 30
Aug *MS* 31 Oct 1849

BENSON Sarah Ann of Parsonsfield ME on 8 Sept m MOULTON
Wentworth L *MS* 18 Sept 1839

BENSON Sarah of Biddeford m HOBBS Euran *MS* 24 June 1835

BENTON Laura of Hume NY m LANE Wm Jr of Centreville *MS* 4 Mar
1835

BERGIN Phebe m QUACKINBUSH Jacob both of Oneonta NY on 15
June 1848 *MS* 26 Jul 1848

BERRY Abigail Ann m CHESLEY Moses H of New Durham NH *MS* 6
Sept 1843

BERRY Abigail of Strafford m JENNESS John J of Rochester *MS* 3
June 1835

BERRY Abigail of Strafford m RAND Bickford of Rochester *MS* 18 Apr
1838

BERRY Almira H of Lowell MA m UPHAM Clement on 5 May 1842 at
Lowell MA *MS* 2 Nov 1842

BERRY Ann of Scarboro' m MOSES William Capt on 31 Jan at
Scarboro' ME *MS* 22 Feb 1843

BERRY Betsey NH m OTIS William S on 22 Oct both of Somersworth
NH *MS* 27 Dec 1843

BERRY Catharine of Cornish ME m DAY Stephen 3d of Cornish ME
on 13 May 1846 at Parsonsfield ME *MS* 31 Mar 1847

BERRY Elizabeth of Alton NH m DAVIS Joseph C of New Durham NH
on 15 May 1848 *MS* 21 June 1848

BERRY Ellen L m WOODWARD Asa F of Lisbon ME *MS* 7 Mar 1849

BERRY Hannah m WAYMAN Hiram at Waterville ME *MS* 17 Apr
1844

BERRY Hannah W m HARRIS John D on 7 Mar 1843 *MS* 15 Mar 1843

BERRY Helen A d/o BERRY Asa of Standish ME m PARKER Charles of Buxton ME *MFWBR* 1 Dec 1849

BERRY Jemima m in Dover William both of Dover 20 Mar 1842 *MS* 23 Mar 1842

BERRY Joan of Strafford m GRAY Joseph of Barrington *MS* 11 Dec 1839

BERRY Judith m BERRY Daniel F *MS* 9 Sept 1835

BERRY Judith of Sheffield VT m BERRY Freeman of Barnstead on 1 Oct 1848 *MS* 15 Nov 1848

BERRY Louisa Ann m COLMAN Thomas C both of Durham on 6 inst *MS* 13 June 1849

BERRY Louisa of Chesterville ME m BLAISDELL Nehemiah of Jay ME on 13 May *MS* 13 Jul 1832

BERRY Lovey A m DAWLEY Charles H both of Dover on 24 inst *MS* 30 Oct 1850

BERRY Lydia m BABB Ashel both of Strafford on 29th ult *MS* 18 Feb 1835

BERRY Lydia H of Saco ME m MOULTON Ira of Scarboro ME *MFWBR* 4 Jan 1851

BERRY Lydia of Tamworth NH m LEAVITT Thomas on 13 Feb at Ossipee NH *MS* 3 Mar 1847

BERRY Marcissa m DOGE Elias S both of Westbrook ME on 7 June *MS* 22 Jul 1846

BERRY Olive of Strafford m BUNKER Ephraim Jr *MS* 15 Nov 1837

BERRY Sally J of Wayne ME m GOULD Hamilton of Wilton ME *MS* 27 Jan 1836

BERRY Sally of Dover m MARTIN Edward of New Castle *MS* 8 Dec 1841

BERRY Samson? m CHESLEY George W on 3 Jan at Sheffield VT *MS* 16 Mar 1836

BERRY Sarah d/o BERRY William B m LORETTE Anthony F of Portland ME *MFWBR* 22 Jul 1848

BERRY Sarah m HANSON Nicholas Jr both of Scarborough ME on 20 Jan 1850 *MS* 13 Feb 1850

BERRY Sarah Miss ae 40y of Rochester NH m CLOUTMAN Eliphalet Esq ae 80y *MS* 25 Apr 1833

BERRY Sarah W m WIGGIN Henry *MS* 7 Jan 1835 & m WIGGINS Henry *MS* 24 Dec 1834

BERRY Susan m LEATHERS Nathaniel both of Great Falls NH *MS* 27 Mar 1834

BERRY Susan G m CHAMBERLIN Eli R *MFWBR* 9 Mar 1850

BERRY Susan T of Saco m McKENNEY D *MFWBR* 24 June 1848

BERY Catharine of Scarboro m LIBBY Nathaniel Esq of Limerick ME *MS* Dec 28 1826

BETTON Clarissa of Dover m CHAPIN Elmer D of Greenfield MA on Sun evening 1 inst *MS* 11 Oct 1837

BETTON Eliza of Dover NH m YOUNG James M Rev of Strafford on Sun eve 10 inst *MS* 20 June 1838

BIBBER Frances A of South Berwick ME m CROSS Nathaniel at South Berwick ME *MS* 24 Feb 1847

BICKFORD Abby A m GOWEN Emilius L at Rochester NH *MS* 16 Apr 1845

BICKFORD Anna E of Biddeford ME m MURPHY Jesse K of Denmark ME *MFWBR* 12 Oct 1850

BICKFORD Belinda m BURGESS William at Bangor ME *MS* 13 Sept 1843

BICKFORD Catherine W of Durham m SHORT James on 17 Aug at Durham *MS* 30 Aug 1843

BICKFORD Clarinda m DAVIS John L on 14th Nov at Effingham NH *MS* 30 Apr 1845

BICKFORD Climena m NICHOLS Thomas B both of Meredith on 18 Dec 1849 *MS* 30 Jan 1850

BICKFORD Cyrena of Starks m MAXIM Jesse of Pleasant Ridge on 19 June *MS* 2 Sept 1831

BICKFORD Eliza d/o BICKFORD Stephen of Parsonsfield ME m DAME Jabez *MS* 26 Apr 1827

BICKFORD Eliza m STROUT Albert both of Charleston ME on 9 Sept 1847 *MS* 2 Feb 1848

BICKFORD Ellen J m ROBERTS Charles both of Pittsfield on 2 May *MS* 16 May 1849

BICKFORD Elvira of Meredith m ROLLINS Noah S of New Hampton *MS* 21 June 1848

BICKFORD Hannah of Baldwin m PENDEXTER Oliver T on 19 Sept *MS* 27 Nov 1850

BICKFORD Isabella m ADAMS William H on 15 Apr at New Market NH *MS* 28 Apr 1847

BICKFORD Keziah D of Epsom m SANBORN Abraham of Deerfield on 16 Nov 1848 *MS* 13 Dec 1848

BICKFORD Lovey of Lowell m EATON John L of Salisbury NH *MS* 5 Apr 1837

BICKFORD Malissa A m BRAIN Geo M both of Waterbury VT on 6 Dec *MS* 23 Jan 1850

BICKFORD Martha m TEBBETS John both of Monmouth ME *MS* 20 Jan 1832

BICKFORD Mary m HOW George both of Parsonsfield ME *MS* 10 Mar 1830

BICKFORD Mary Jane of Alton NH m GARLAND George W of Barnstead on 21 Apr 1849 *MS* 2 May 1849

BICKFORD Nancy of Boothbay m GROVE Solomon of Edgecomb ME in Boothbay ME *MS* 23 Feb 1842

BICKFORD Salina O m LOCKE Arthur C both of Epsom NH on 23 Sept *MS* 13 Oct 1847

BICKFORD Sally age 76y m MOULTON Samuel Dea age 76y on 14th ult *MS* 1 May 1829

BICKFORD Sarah Ann m DEMERITT Benjamin F *MS* 7 June 1837

BICKFORD Susan G m KNOWLES Jonathan A at Epsom NH *MS* 27 Sept 1843

BICKFORD Susan H of So Parsonsfield ME m RUSSELL Charles M of Newfield on 27 Sept *MS* 7 Oct 1846

BICKFORD Sylvania S m SANBORN Samuel on 5 Sept *MS* 30 Oct 1844

BICKINSEAL Miss of Sutton VT on 30 Oct m BERRY Jonathan of Sheffield *MS* 11 Jan 1843

BICKNELL Nancy B m GILSON William R of Abington MA *MFWBR* 7 Aug 1847

BIDLON Mary m BISHOP Naaman *MS* 12 Oct 1832

BIDSELL Roselinda m SLOCUM Seth on 1 Feb 1848 *MS* 19 Apr 1848

BIDWILL Jerusha of Brainbridge Ohio m WOODWORTH Nathan of Mineral Point Wis *MS* 3 Jan 1849

BIGELOW Elizabeth m TAYLOR George W on 22 Apr at Norridgewock ME *MS* 14 May 1845

BILLINGS Elizabeth H m NEWCOMB Bangs D on 29 Oct at Newburgh ME *MS* 17 Jan 1844

BILLINGS Mary both of m KING Jeremiah No Providence on 3d ult *MS* 4 May 1836

BINFORD Hannah of Baldwin m PARKER Aaron of Standish ME *MS* 27 Nov 1850

BIRD Arminda m STEBBINS Edward in Chesterfield MA on Jan 25 *MS* 9 Mar 1842

BISBEE Celia D of Woonsocket RI m BISHOP Cyrus of Nashua NH on 21 inst *MS* 4 Jul 1849

BISHOP Mariet m ROODE Miles both of Perry on 4 June *MS* 5 Jul 1837

BISHOP Persis D of Holland VT m HOVEY Chaney of Holland VT on 24 Mar *MS* 1 May 1844

BISHOPS Nancy m ROUNDS Samuel both of Gorham ME on 4th inst *MS* 2 Jul 1830

BIXBY Lavinea L of Williamstown VT m AUGIR Franklin P Eld of Rochester Wis on 19 Sept 1847 *MS* 13 Oct 1847

BIXBY Olive W m SANBORN William P both of Wilmot on 27 Sept *MS* 4 Nov 1846

BLACK Abigail of Limington ME m COBB Cyrus of Hiram ME *MS* 8 Mar 1843

BLACK Louisa m BRAGDON Issachar *MS* 7 Feb 1844

BLACKEY Sarah of Meredith NH m FOLSOM Ira F of Gilford *MS* 13 Sept 1843

BLACKMAN Chloe of Warsaw NY m SALSBURY Mr of Weathersfield Springs on 13 Apr *MS* 5 Jul 1837

BLACKSTONE Angeline m ROGERS Miller J at Lowell MA *MS* 26 Feb 1845

BLACKSTONE Eliza A m MARR Horatio P at Dracut MA *MS* 12 Nov 1845

BLACKWELL Albritaia m LITTLEFIELD Edmund P on 4 Jul 1846 of Chesterville *MS* 21 Apr 1847

BLACKWELL Harriet m PRESSEY G W Jr both of Waterville ME *MS* 2 Jan 1850

BLACKWELL Sarah J of Madison ME on 12th inst m SPEAR John P *MFWBR* 28 Apr 1849

BLAIR Malissa of Richmond m ALGER Alonzo W on 31 Dec 1846 at Richmond VT *MS* 10 Mar 1847

BLAISDELL Betsey E at Assyria Barry Co Michigan on 11 Apr m CRANSON Theodore B of Pennfield Calhoun Co *MS* 29 May 1844

BLAISDELL Caroline G m JAMES Samuel on 23 May of Lebanon ME *MS* 23 June 1847

BLAISDELL Catharine T of Sidney ME m MITCHELL Elijah of Waterville *MS* 24 Feb 1836

BLAISDELL Eliza m MALING Nathaniel G on 7 Jul at Charlestown MA *MS* 9 Dec 1846

BLAISDELL Eliza of Dover NH m PLACE Harrel F on 30 ult *MS* 9 Nov 1836

BLAISDELL Elizabeth A of Lebanon m ALLEN Amasa of Rochester on 23 Jan *MS* 5 Feb 1851

BLAISDELL Lovey m BURROWS Joseph Dea both of Lebanon on 1 Jul *MS* 5 Sept 1838

BLAISDELL Lucy Ann m RICKER George Wm both of Lyman on Sun 21 ult in Lyman ME *MS* 5 Jan 1842

BLAISDELL Mary C of Gilford m SWASEY Henry W on 8 Nov at Gilford *MS* 16 Dec 1846

BLAISDELL Nancy F m GOULD John both of Mercer ME on 21 Apr *MS* 8 Dec 1844

BLAISDELL Rosamond of Great Falls m HILL Timothy of N Berwick ME on 15th ult *MS* 9 Jan 1834

BLAISDELL Ruhamah P of Holderness NH on 15 Sept m THOMPSON Samuel P of Meredosia IL *MS* 2 Oct 1839

BLAISDELL Sophronia m LOWELL Josiah B at Bangor ME *MS* 13 Sept 1843

BLAKE Abigail P m SPRINGER William *MFWBR* 14 Apr 1849

BLAKE Almira of Lowell MA m DOLLOFF Joseph P on 26 Sept at Lowell MA *MS* 2 Nov 1842

BLAKE Didama L m ORR Richard R both of Manchester on 24 Oct 1847 *MS* 10 Nov 1847

BLAKE Dorothy of Pittsfield NH m YOUNG Andrew J of Gilmanton

BLAKE (Continued)
NH on 20 Apr 1848 *MS* 3 May 1848

BLAKE Eliza M m HAMMOND Daniel B both of Ossipee NH *MS* 27 Dec 1837

BLAKE Emeline of Newfield ME m ROGERS George W at Bridgeton ME on 13 Oct 1842 *MS* 16 Nov 1842

BLAKE Harriet m SHUFF Robinson of Newbury MA at Hampton *MS* 3 Apr 1844

BLAKE Jane S m HUSTEN Elijah both of New Gloucester ME on 28 June *MS* 2 Sept 1846

BLAKE Lectina m MAGOON Wilder both of Stanstead LC on 3d inst at Barnston LC *MS* 18 May 1836

BLAKE Lovina of Stanstead LC m HACKETT Isaac on 22 Oct *MS* 1 Jan 1840

BLAKE Martha J of Kittery ME m COLLINS Robert of Kittery ME *MS* 1 Jan 1845

BLAKE Mary m OSGOOD Enoch F Jr m at Raymond NH *MS* 9 Nov 1832

BLAKE Mehitabel W m WATSON Daniel Jr both of Pittsfield on 4 Oct *MS* 11 Nov 1846

BLAKE Rachel C m STAPLES Josiah M on 5 Nov 1849 *MS* 13 Feb 1850

BLAKE Sally of Lisbon ME m BAKER Horace *MS* 24 Sept 1834

BLAKE Sarah m MANSON George both of Kittery on 19 inst *MS* 22 Nov 1837

BLANCHARD Ann E m WHEELER Orren T both of Manchester on 2 Apr *MS* 15 Apr 1846

BLANCHARD Jane m PENNY George both of Belgrade ME *MS* 20 June 1838

BLANCHARD Lavinia of Wilton ME m WESTON Simeon on 21 Jan 1847 of Mt Vernon ME *MS* 14 Jul 1847

BLANCHARD Mary F m HOPE Geo W on 11 Mar *MS* 1 May 1844

BLANCHARD Rhoda m HUSE Jesse on 10th of Lowell MA *MS* 24 Feb 1847

BLANCHARD Roany on 14th inst m DAVIS Henry E of West Brookfield *MS* 24 Apr 1839

BLETHEN Octavia m BLETHEN David on 26th Jan of Durham (ME?) *MS* 12 Feb 1845

BLISS Sarah of Washington VT on 23d ult m GRANT Alpheus C of Medway MA *MFWBR* 8 Feb 1851

BLISS Orlinda A m BLISS Albert T both of Huston PA on 1 Sept *MS* 16 Oct 1850

BLITHEN Mercy D of Durham m McINTIRE Ralph M of Bath on 4 Dec 1850 *MS* 8 Jan 1851

BLODGET Julia Ann m JONES Wm both of Ascott on 8 May *MS* 20 Sept 1837

BLODGET Mary Jane m HICKS George W of Rumney NH on 27 June at West Plymouth *MS* 7 Jul 1847

BLODGETT Olive C m MESSER Hollis W on 14 Jan of Newbury NH *MS* 27 Jan 1847

BLODGETT Ruth M m EMERY Elijah P both of Newbury on 18 Dec 1849 *MS* 2 Jan 1850

BLODGETT Theoda m HUNTLEY Alson both of Mooers NY *MS* 23 Jan 1850

BLOOD Lucinda M of Newbury NH m NORRIS Wm B of Nashville TN on 3 Aug 1847 *MS* 2 Feb 1848

BLOOD Miss m MARTIN Benjamin both of Washington on 1 Sept 1847 *MS* 15 Sept 1847

BLOOD Sarah A of Newbury VT m ALEZANDER Willeby C on 13 Apr 1848 *MS* 26 Apr 1848

BLOSS Caroline of Sutton VT m LOVEJOY Jonathan of Littleton NH on 17 Jul *MS* 27 Nov 1850

BLUNT Philienia m HATCH Joseph both of Boston MA *MS* 22 Jul 1835

BLYE Mary A of Sand Lake m HISERODT Andrew M on 13 Mar at Sand Lake *MS* 7 May 1845

BOARDMAN Ann G of Portsmouth NH m COOPER John P of Newcastle *MFWBR* 4 Dec 1847

BOARDMAN Temperance S of Mercer ME m WILLIAMSON Henry AB late of Hamilton College on 14 Nov 1847 *MS* 8/14 Mar 1848

BODDGE Martha S of Rochester m HORNE Jonathan W of Farmington *MS* 13 Sept 1843

BODGE Avis Jane of Dover m ROBERTS Jonathan of Lowell MA on 8 inst *MS* 15 May 1850

BODGE Bridgett Y of Barrington NH m SMITH Ira H on 27 Mar at Strafford *MS* 12 Apr 1843

BODGE Hannah of Dover NH m CONNEY Samuel on 2 Dec at Dover NH *MS* 11 Dec 1844

BODGE Louisa M ay Rochester m HAYES David Jr of Farmington *MS* 7 June 1843

BODWELL Hannah m NEAL John at Manchester *MS* 20 Dec 1843

BOLLES Emeline B of Bethlehem NH m NUTTING Harvey S of Wardsboro VT on 3 Oct *MS* 24 Oct 1849

BOLTER Elizabeth m LIBBY Amos on 14 Aug *MS* 28 Aug 1850

BOLTON Eleanor Miss of Gorham m GREEN Edward of Portland on 7th inst *MS* 18 Apr 1833

BOND Hannah of Lisbon (ME?) m WOODWARD Asa F on 5 Jan *MS* 12 Feb 1845

BOND Henrietta E m BROWN John E both of Haverhill MA on 14 Nov 1847 *MS* 8 Dec 1847

BOND Lavina T m BADGER Wells M both of Manchester on 21 Oct 1848 *MS* 8 Nov 1848

BOND Merinda H of Lewiston ME m ROGERS John of Phipsbury ME *MFWBR* 23 June 1849

BOOBER Charlotte of Lee m HAMMON Allen of Springfield at Lee ME *MS* 19 Nov 1834

BOODY Emily m FOSS George W *MFWBR* 12 May 1849 & on 29 Apr *MS* 9 May 1849

BOODY Hannah m COLE Joseph W *MFWBR* 12 June 1847

BOODY Harriet of Lowell m MARSHALL Joel at Dracut MA *MS* 29 Jan 1845

BOODY Loana Mrs m STEARNS Benjamin C on 16 June at Dracut MA *MS* 7 Jul 1847

BOODY Sarah m FOSS Robert on 7th inst at Dover NH *MS* 20 Jan 1847

BOOKER Laura A of Lisbon Little River village ME m BERRY Edward Jr *MFWBR* 25 Jan 1851

BOOKER Sarah on 30 Oct m LOWELL Erastus at Litchfield ME *MS* 4 Jan 1843

BOOTHBAY Hannah of Parsonsfield ME m BABB Rufus on 6 Feb at Parsonsfield of Scarboro' ME *MS* 12 Mar 1845

BOOTHBAY Jane m MORRISON Jonathan on 25 Dec at Parsonsfield ME *MS* 4 Feb 1846

BOOTHBY Jane A of Unity m COFFIN Simeon of Thorndike ME on 10 May *MS* 27 May 1846

BOOTHBY Lydia W m BOLTER Amaziah H at Unity ME *MS* 25 Nov 1846

BOOTHBY Martha A m SYMMES Eben both of Newfield on 30 Sept *MS* 31 Oct 1849

BOOTHBY Mary of Buxton m TUCKER William on 8 Feb at Buxton ME *MS* 25 Feb 1846

BOOTHBY Miriam m LORD Samuel on 18th inst *MS* 30 Nov 1832

BOOTHBY Nancy m KIMBALL Robert H on 19 Nov of Limington ME *MS* 7 Feb 1844

BOOTHBY Sally of Limerick m ROSS Robert of Saco ME on 10 Sept 1846 *MS* 14 Oct 1846

BOOTHBY Sarah E m EDGERLY George W on 1 Mar at Buxton ME *MS* 18 Mar 1846

BOOTHBY Susanna of Limerick m BRADEEN Oliver of Waterborough on 14 Sept 1848 *MS* 29 Nov 1848

BORNEY Julia m COOMBS John *MS* 12 Mar 1851

BOSFORD Abigail of Patton m GEORGE Robert on 21 Mar of Patton *MS* 13 Apr 1842

BOSS Anny of Scituate m BULINGAME Arnold H of Gloucester on 15 ult *MS* 18 Apr 1838

BOSTON Catherine m CROOK Ransom *MFWBR* 1 Dec 1849

BOSTON Luranah A m GREENHALGH Moses B both of Sanford ME on 1 Dec *MS* 11 Dec 1850

BOSWELL Patience m FOLSOM Erastus C both of Ossipee NH on 10 Sept 1837 *MS* 24 Jan 1838

BOSWORTH Angeline of Attleboro' MA m WILMARTH Elisha on 15 Dec at Rehoboth *MS* 20 Jan 1847

BOSWORTH Lucinda of Enfield m STANYAN Newell Jr of Wentworth on 30 Jan 1848 *MS* 1 Mar 1848

BOULTON Martha m HODSDON Caleb Esq both of Gorham ME *MS* 12 Nov 1834

BOUTWILL Eliza A m CHURCHILL Asaph K both of Lowell on 24 Nov 1847 *MS* 15 Dec 1847

BOWEN Chloe Ann on 3 Jul at Owen NY m EVANS John *MS* 14 Aug 1839

BOWEN Elizabeth S m BOWEN Allen both of Rehoboth on 8 Nov 1847 *MS* 8 Dec 1847

BOWEN Lydia E m ST CERE John C *MS* 1 May 1850

BOWEN Matilda m DREW Ezra Jr both of Bafford CE on 26 Jan *MS* 19 Feb 1851

BOWEN Sally M of Holderness on 18th inst m SARGENT Reuben of Northfield *MS* 26 June 1839

BOWERS Mary of Dracut m STONE H P of Lowell *MS* 9 Aug 1837

BOWKER Letis m CAMPBELL James both of Bowdoin ME *MS* 18 Mar 1835

BOWLES Julia Ann of Lisbon m COLE Phinehas on 14 Nov at Franconia NH *MS* 11 Dec 1844

BOWLES Louisa of Bethlehem m BOWLES James of Dalton NH on 26 Dec 1849 *MS* 10 Apr 1850

BOWLES Mary Jane m HAYDEN William H both of New Market on 5 ult *MS* 25 Apr 1838

BOWLES Mary Mrs m CHANDLER Solomon on 13th Jul at Portsmouth NH *MS* 7 Sept 1845

BOWLES Phebe m BURBANK Ezra both of Lisbon ME *MS* 29 Dec 1847

BOWMAN Almira B m WARD Horace J both of Bradford on 21 Mar *MS* 22 May 1850

BOWMAN Caroline of Sidney ME m GOODRIDGE Jeremiah W of Canaan *MS* 17 Apr 1844

BOWMAN Marilla D of Lowell MA m BROWN Bradbury D on 20 Dec of Lowell MA *MS* 6 Jan 1847

BOWMAN Nancy Mrs of Sidney m TOBEY Nathaniel of Fairfield on 30th inst *MS* 14 Jul 1847

BOYD Elizabeth Jane of Boothbay m BENNET Benjamin on 3 Nov at Boothbay ME *MS* 29 Nov 1843

BOYER Emeline of Roxand Mich m JENNE Seth Allen of Chester on 12 Dec at Roxand Mich *MS* 17 Jan 1844

BOYINGTON Martha m WARREN Ambrose *MFWBR* 12 Jan 1850

BOYLE Caroline of Bucksport ME m WHITEHOUSE Edmond H of

BOYLE (Continued)
Great Falls *MS* 18 Sept 1850

BOYNTON Dorothy of Belmont ME m SPILLER Samuel of Liberty ME *MS* 31 May 1848

BOYNTON Hannah A m MORSE Timon M both of Charlestown MA of Manchester *MS* 14 Feb 1849

BOYNTON Hannah H of Dracut m MASON Thomas C on 20 Aug 1843 at Lowell MA *MS* 6 Sept 1843

BOYNTON Hannah of Thornton m PETTENGILL Dudley Eld of Sandwich on 2 June *MS* 22 June 1836

BOYNTON Harriet of Cornish ME m CHADBOURNE George of Gorham ME *MFWBR* 6 Mar 1847 & *MFWBR* 20 Feb 1847

BOYNTON Laura E m STODDARD George R both of Walworth on 25 Oct *MS* 15 Jan 1851

BOYNTON Susan T of Lowell MA m WALKER Andrew J at Dracut MA *MS* 12 Nov 1845

BRACKET Abigail m AMOS Martin both of Augusta ME on 2 Oct 1847 *MS* 24 May 1848

BRACKET Eliza G m PRESCOTT George W at Acton *MS* 27 Sept 1843

BRACKET Elizabeth Mrs of Limington ME m CLARK Edward of Cambridge MA *MS* 14 Jul 1847

BRACKET Lodema of Bristol both formerly of Geauga Sem Ohio m BATES Charles D of Mecca on 1 inst *MS* 23 Oct 1850

BRACKET ____ [Susan, see p.321 *Early Families of Limington ME* 1991 by R.L. Taylor.] m STEVENS Theodore Eld both of Acton ME *MS* 6 Apr 1836

BRACKETT Abby of Epsom m SMITH Benj M of Farmington ME on 27 Feb 1850 *MS* 10 Apr 1850

BRACKETT Betsey C of Waterville ME m WARREN Charles on 16 Dec 1847 *MS* 19 Jan 1848

BRACKETT Betsey Mrs of New Market m CHESWELL Samuel of Durham on 28 Jan ult *MS* 7 Feb 1838

BRACKETT Dorcas m STAPLE Nathaniel both of Limington ME on 22 Oct *MS* 15 Jan 1840

BRACKETT Eliza W of Lowell MA m FELLOWS Samuel Capt of Franklin on 26 Mar at Machester NH *MS* 16 Apr 1845

BRACKETT Elizabeth of Parsonsfield ME m BRADBURY Sam W Dr of Limington ME *MFWBR* 15 Jan 1848

BRACKETT Hannah m TEBBETTS James M *MFWBR* 9 Nov 1850

BRACKETT Jane m NEWELL David *MS* 7 Sept 1826

BRACKETT Mary of Auburn ME m TRACY Jonathan Eld on 6 Dec *MS* 9 Apr 1845

BRACKETT Olive of North Berwick ME m HAMMOND Thomas on 5 May at North Berwick *MS* 2 Jul 1845

BRACKETT Roxanna m SYLVESTER Merritt both of Brunswick ME

BRACKETT (Continued)
on 29 Oct 1848 *MS* 15 Nov 1848

BRACKETT Sally of Great Falls m HAYES Wentworth of Rochester on Sunday morning last 11 inst *MS* 21 Oct 1835

BRACKETT Sarah C of Limerick ME m McKUSICK Nahum 2d of Limerick ME *MS* 7 Feb 1844

BRACKETT Sarah of Harrison m MASON Artimus of Mason on 12 May *MS* 3 June 1846

BRADBURY Clarissa Ann m PARSONS Charles G on 6th inst at Parsonsfield *MS* 21 Dec 1832

BRADBURY Harriet of Kennebunkport ME m WORTH Stephen of Biddeford ME on 7 Feb *MS* 24 Feb 1847

BRADBURY Mary G of Limerick ME m COBB Stephen M at West meeting house in Limington ME *MS* 17 Sept 1845

BRADBURY Meroe A of Chesterville ME m BROWN Hartshorn R on 28 Jul 1844 at Chesterville *MS* 14 Aug 1844

BRADBURY Sarah E m CARD Albert both of Dover on 6 inst *MS* 10 Jan 1849

BRADEEN Almira W on 4 June at Cornish ME m HALEY Parker of Chelsea MA *MS* 14 June 1843

BRADEEN Ann M of Cornish m McKENNEY Joshua on 18 Feb at Cornish of Limington *MS* 29 May 1844

BRADFORD Isabella m GALLUP Benjamin both of Bangor ME on 22 Oct 1846 *MS* 4 Nov 1846

BRADFORD Pervis of Berkshire VT m CLARK Reuben of Saranac on 3d Jul at Peru Clinton Co NY *MS* 23 Jul 1845

BRADLEY Hannah R of Canterbury NH m EASTMAN Alfred of Concord on 13 Dec *MS* 14 Feb 1844

BRADLEY Mary Ann of Sheffield VT m CHACE Charles of Wheelock on 5 May 1842 at Sheffeld VT *MS* 12 Oct 1842

BRADLEY Mehitabel F m DIXMOND Orin *MS* 27 Dec 1837

BRADSHAW Sarah of Chelsea m HOOD Charles on 21 Mar at Chelsea VT *MS* 6 Apr 1847

BRAGDON Catharine m RICHARDS David on 4 Apr *MS* 1 Aug 1849

BRAGDON Dorothy Ann at Bangor ME m BRAGDON Gardner *MS* 13 Sept 1843

BRAGDON Mary Ann m SHAW John at York ME *MS* 24 Apr 1834

BRAGG Eunice M of Sidney ME m THOMAS Stephen of Waterville ME *MS* 15 Mar 1837

BRAGG Hannah D of Sidney ME m CHANDLER Thomas of Augusta *MS* 15 Mar 1837

BRALEY Frances W m DAY Thadeus H of Hallowell ME on 18 Jan 1846 *MS* 11 Mar 1846

BRAN Olive of Gardiner m WAKEFIELD Alfred on 7th inst at Gardiner ME *MS* 24 Apr 1844

BRANCH Hannah M Mrs of Trumbull OHIO m WRIGHT Solomon of

BRANCH (Continued)
Harpersfield on 2 May 1848 *MS* 30 Aug 1848

BRAND Mary m STAFFORD Johnson L both of Harland ME on 19 Aug in St Albans ME *MS* 11 Sept 1850

BRAND Sarah m HERRINGTON Philo B both of Loydsville on 16 Sept *MS* 30 Sept 1846

BRANNEN Julia A m JACKSON Abel G both of Lewiston ME on 26 Dec 1847 *MS* 23 Feb 1848

BRANSON Sarah m JONES Davidboth of Perry Township Ohio on 4 Jul 1847 *MS* 9 Feb 1848

BRAY Charlotte A of Warren VT on 9 Jul m BEAN Samuel C of Vergenes *MS* 2 Aug 1843

BRAY Priscilla m TIBBETTS Richard both of Charlestown MA on 21 May *MS* 24 June 1846

BREED Hannah of Vestal Broom Co NY m FESSENDEN Nelson a licentiate of Owego Q M on 18 inst *MS* 23 Sept 1846

BREWER Sarah of Purma NY m BIGNALL James Eld formerly of Yates Quartly meeting on 13 Sept at Purma NY *MS* 18 Oct 1843

BREWSTER Eliza of Portsmouth on 20th ult m MOSES William 2nd *MS* 8 May 1839

BREWSTER Joanna H of Wolfborough NH m HURD John S Esq of Farmington on 16 Nov 1848 *MS* 20 Dec 1848

BREWSTER Maris E of Brookfield m BLAKELY Silas S of Chelsea on 16 June *MS* 4 Jul 1849

BREWSTER Sabrina of Barrington m GARLAND Jacob J of Rochester on 7th ult *MS* 8 Dec 1834

BRIANT Julia A m CROUCH Daniel of Littleton *MS* 4 Jan 1843

BRIARD Susan of Tuftonborough NH m LIBBY James C of Ossipee NH on 29 Dec 1848 *MS* 9 May 1849

BRIAUT Abigail F of Waterboro' m CHASE Joseph on 11 Aug at Hollis ME *MS* 11 Sept 1844

BRIDGE Eliza m LEMONT Samuel W at Litchfield ME *MS* 7 Aug 1844

BRIDGES Eliza of Bridgeton m ADAMS Jacob of Wales ME on Thur last *MS* 9 Mar 1831

BRIER Elvira at Manchester NH m RICHARDSON Sullivan on 1 Sept *MS* 11 Sept 1844

BRIERY Elizabeth of Bowdoin ME m FOSTER Peletiah H of Topsham ME on 24 Nov *MS* 8 Dec 1847

BRIERY Minerva of Bowdoin m HALEY Alvin B of Topsham on 25 Nov 1847 *MS* 8 Dec 1847

BRIGGS Betsey Ann of Lowell on 26th ult m THING George *MS* 6 Mar 1839

BRIGGS Mary E of Cornish m COLE Clark C of Cornish *MS* 18 Oct 1827

BRIGGS Rhoda of Greene ME on 4 June 1843 m CASWELL Minot of

BRIGGS (Continued)
Auburn ME *MS* 2 Aug 1843

BRINY Octavia Ann of Bowdoin ME m HALEY Jesse D of Bath ME on 6 Oct at Bowdoinham ME *MS* 8 Jan 1845

BROCK Betsey m BERRY David *MS* 27 Jan 1836

BROCK Esther m JENNESS Seth both of Rochester *MS* 27 Jan 1836

BROCK Hannah N m HALL John S both of Exeter NH on 26 ult *MS* 4 Nov 1835

BROCK Julia J of Somersworth NH m GAULT Thomas E of Rollinsford NH on 5 inst *MS* 14 Nov 1849

BROCK Mahaly of Alexandria m MALLARY Jonathan of Center Harbor on 15 Aug *MS* 12 Dec 1838

BROCK Martha m BURNHAM Ingols both of Dover on 28 May *MS* 20 June 1849

BROCK Sophia m GUPPY James B both of Dover *MS* 20 Jan 1836

BROCKINGS Arlette Hilton m SHAW Seth Harding both of Woolwich on 31 Aug *MS* 20 Sept 1937

BROCKWAY Polly m JONES Elias O on 13 March at Stephentown NY *MS* 4 Oct 1843

BROCKWAY Sally Ann of Stephentown NY m ALLEN Daniel Jr on 12 March at Stephentown NY *MS* 4 Oct 1843

BROOKS Clarissa of East Randolph m ARNOLD Sprague at East Randolph VT *MS* 4 Jan 1843

BROOKS Elizabeth m BROWN Jacob of Clinton on 24th ult *MS* 12 June 1829

BROOKS Fidelia m ROGERS William C both of Norridgewock ME on 27 Aug 1848 *MS* 29 Nov 1848

BROOKS M Miss m CHAMBERLAIN C Mr of Madrid on 9 Dec at Pierpont *MS* 6 Jan 1847

BROOKS Mary Ann m DANFORTH Samuel on 15 Sept of Porter ME *MS* 23 Oct 1844

BROOKS Mary J of Limerick ME m BANGS E B Dr of Saco ME *MFWBR* 13 Mar 1847

BROOKS Mary L of Lewiston ME m GASS John Jr on 11 Jul at Lewiston ME *MS* 4 Aug 1847

BROOKS Sarah A of North Berwick ME m DAVIS Kinsman R on 20 Sept of Epsom NH *MS* 10 Oct 1844

BROOKS Sophia G of Wakefield m HOIT Joseph of Gilmanton at Meredith Bridge on 5th inst *MS* 23 Feb 1842

BROOMER Louisa Mrs of Lisbon ME m JORDAN Abijah of Topsham ME *MFWBR* 26 Jul 1848

BROWN Abigail C of Dracut MA m HUCKINS Daniel C on 11 Sept at Lowell MA *MS* 2 Nov 1842

BROWN Abigail W and BROWN Obed of Porter divorced *MS* 24 Feb 1832

BROWN Almira of Freeport ME m SOULE Benjamin P on 24 Jan at

BROWN (Continued)
Freeport ME *MS* 14 Apr 1847

BROWN Angeline m YOUNG David Jr both of Deerfield NH on 3 Jan 1850 *MS* 16 Jan 1850

BROWN Ann m ALLEN Theodore of Buxton on 19th inst *MS* 27 Mar 1829

BROWN Ann of Bristol m PATTEN Robert of Alexandria on 3 Dec 1848 *MS* 11 Apr 1849

BROWN Anna of Freedom NY on 4 Jan 1842 m HILL Lorenzo of Bethany Genesee Co NY *MS* 15 Mar 1843

BROWN Anna H of Fairfield NY on 27th Feb m WILLMAITH John L of Stamford VT *MS* 27 Mar 1839

BROWN Betsey D m HAM Rufas R both of Dover on 10 inst *MS* 21 Aug 1850 & *MFWBR* 24 Aug 1850

BROWN Betsey of Wolfboro' NH m WILLAND Edward of Ossipee NH on 7 Nov 1841 *MS* 5 Oct 1842

BROWN Betsey W of PLT Number Eight m HAFFORD Samuel *MS* 29 May 1839

BROWN Caroline A m HAYWOOD John S both of Manchester on 24 May *MS* 17 June 1846

BROWN Caroline L m REDLON Albion *MS* 1 May 1850

BROWN Caroline M of Newbury m SPEAR Thomas P of Lancaster on 23 Sept *MS* 6 Oct 1847

BROWN Caroline of Gloucester m FARNUM Caleb Jr Principal of Fruit Hill Seminary on 26 ult *MS* 11 Jan 1837

BROWN Catharine of Ossipee NH m FRENCH Aaron on 19th inst *MS* 24 June 1831

BROWN Catherine G m QUINBY Isaac F on 19th inst at Saccarappa ME *MS* 29 May 1844

BROWN Charlotte on LADD Chester of Strafford VT *MS* 11 Dec 1844

BROWN Clarissa m WATERMAN Oliver both of Litchfield ME 23 Nov *MS* 25 Dec 1839

BROWN Cynthia F m TOWLE Henry D on 5 Oct at Nashua *MS* 22 Oct 1845

BROWN Dorcas B of Freeport ME m MERRILL Joseph T of Monmouth ME on 8 Nov *MS* 19 Dec 1849

BROWN Edna of Strafford VT m RICH Proctor *MS* 27 Feb 1839

BROWN Eleanor of Bowdoin m SANDFORD James W Gen of Anson ME *MS* 25 Mar 1846

BROWN Eliza of Franklin NH m PROCTOR James H of Dover *MS* 20 June 1833

BROWN Eliza of Pownal ME m WHITHAM Henry of Danville ME on 14 May *MS* 19 June 1850

BROWN Elsoy m BOSTON John on 27 ult *MS* 10 Oct 1849

BROWN Esther M m HARTSHORN Anson H both of Manchester on 4 Sept *MS* 12 Sept 1849

BROWN Esther M of Parsonsfield ME m DAY Nehemiah W of Naples ME *MS* 8 Mar 1848

BROWN Eunice of Saco ME m FOX Lewis M on 1 Nov *MS* 25 Nov 1846

BROWN H Josephine d/o BROWN Josiah of Brentwood NH m MERRIL John J of Parsonsfield ME on 18 inst in evening *MS* 1 May 1850

BROWN Hannah C of Parsonsfield ME m BROWN John Jr of Cornish ME on 26 Aug *MS* 31 Mar 1847

BROWN Hannah L m KIDDAH James Jr both of Boston MA on 18 June *MS* 7 Nov 1849

BROWN Harriet m KENDRICK Wm B both of Deerfield NH on 3 Jan 1850 *MS* 16 Jan 1850

BROWN Jane of Biddeford ME m STETSON Josiah H of Dover NH *MFWBR* 27 Apr 1850

BROWN Jane of Bowdoin ME m LIBBY Micah of Litchfield ME *MS* 25 Jul 1838

BROWN Jane S R m OSBORNE John S on 18 Sept at Loudon NH *MS* 12 Oct 1842

BROWN Juda Mrs m HADLEY Joseph on 23 May of Sandwich *MS* 2 June 1847

BROWN Livina d/o BROWN E Esq m FISHER Waterman A of Killing-ly CT at Pelham *MS* 13 Jul 1836

BROWN Lourana m BALDWIN Josiah M both of Ashtabula Co on 9 Sept *MS* 10 Oct 1849

BROWN Lucy A of Dover NH m SPURIN Thomas on 2 Jan at Dover NH *MS* 8 Jan 1845

BROWN Lydia m GREEN Samuel on 16 ult *MS* 2 Nov 1836

BROWN Malinda C m LAMSON Silas both of Atkinson ME on 25 May 1848 *MS* 28 June 1848

BROWN Maria m MORRILL Harrison on 27 Mar at Gilford NH *MS* 14 Apr 1847

BROWN Maria of Starksboro' VT m PALMER Hiram of New Haven on 3 Apr *MS* 23 Apr 1845

BROWN Martha of Ipswich MA on May 8 m FULLER Joseph Jr of Lynn MA *MS* 29 May 1844

BROWN Mary Ann m COLBY John of Bow NH on 20 June at Gilford *MS* 12 Oct 1842

BROWN Mary Ann m CURRIER Richard B of Deerfield NH on 18 Dec at Candia *MS* 7 Jan 1846

BROWN Mary Jane at Pittsfield on Feb 11 m NORRIS Trueworthy *MS* 19 Feb 1840

BROWN Mary M of Grafton MA m CHASE Horatio C on 2 Feb at Grafton MA *MS* 15 Mar 1843

BROWN Mary N m MORRISON David both of Haverhill MA on 28 Nov *MS* 8 Dec 1847

BROWN Mary R d/o BROWN Jonathan Esq formerly of La Grange Ohio m SHERBURNE Zelotts of Wellington on 26 Apr 1848 *MS* 14 June 1848

BROWN Mehitabel of Gilford m COLBY Cyrus of Bow NH on 16 Sept 1848 *MS* 13 Dec 1848

BROWN Melissa H m GAREY Daniel both of Saco ME on 7 June *MS* 30 Sept 1846

BROWN Mercy of Dover m MELALIN Asa of Charleston on 6 inst *MS* 8 May 1844

BROWN Nancy m PAINE Francis E at Grafton MA *MS* 4 Oct 1843

BROWN Olive m BENNET Winthrop both of Dover on 29 ult *MS* 9 Oct 1850

BROWN Olive J of Buxton on 21 Feb m LEWIS Tristram S of Waterboro *MFWBR* 10 Mar 1849

BROWN Patience C m STOKES Moses F on 24 Jan at Starksborough VT *MS* 23 Apr 1845

BROWN Polly m BUTTON Lyman both of Freedom NY on 29 June *MS* 31 Aug 1836

BROWN Rebecca m SMILEY Simeon both of Dover on 5 inst *MS* 8 Jul 1846

BROWN Rosetta M of Tunbridge VT m MOREY Reuben Jr of Strafford on 11 May 1848 *MS* 5 Jul 1848

BROWN Roxcena S m MITCHELL Benjamin F on 16 June *MS* 26 June 1850

BROWN Ruth M of Warwick RI m ALLEN Reuben of Warwick RI on 27 June 1848 *MS* 19 Jul 1848

BROWN Sally m BLAISDEL Jacob of Strafford VT *MS* 1 Feb 1843

BROWN Sally of Great Falls m WENTWORTH Joseph of Waterboro' ME on 5 Dec *MS* 10 Dec 1834

BROWN Sarah A m MARSTON Nathaniel B both of No Hampton on 9 Sept *MS* 19 Sept 1849

BROWN Sarah at Poplin m PERKINS Moses of Sandown *MS* 1 Mar 1843

BROWN Sarah C of Candia NH m NELSON John P of Deerfield on 15 ult *MS* 6 June 1849

BROWN Sarah J m CLARK Charles both of New Castle on 18 Jul 1849 *MS* 15 May 1850

BROWN Sarah J of Wentworth m CROSS Josiah D of Springfield on 22 Sept *MS* 10 Oct 1844

BROWN Sarah of Pittsfield ME m CUMMINGS Warren of Belgrade ME *MFWBR* 13 Jul 1850

BROWN _____ d/o Silas (*sic*) m PRESTON David D Jr on May 1842 at Strafford VT *MS* 6 Jul 1842

BROWN Sophia Ann m GRANT Noah on 14 Nov at Manchester NH *MS* 27 Nov 1844

BROWN Sophia C m DANFORTH Nathaniel C both of Lowell on 28th

BROWN (Continued)
ult *MS* 8 Aug 1833

BROWN Susan m MELCHER Wm both of Dover on 14th inst *MS* 24 June 1835

BROWN Susan of No Providence m YOUNG Jason of Foster on 30 May *MS* 21 June 1837

BROWN Susanna of Weare m HOLMES Hiram Eld of Epsom on 19 Oct *MS* 13 Dec 1837

BROWN Taudasa R m CLAFLIN Charles J both of Smithfield on 25 May *MS* 9 Jul 1834

BROWN Theodate of Effingham NH m COLE Jeremiah B of Waterborough ME *MS* 15 Jan 1840

BROWN Unity of Dresden N Y m HULETT Arnold on *MS* 14 Feb 1838

BROWN Vilara A L m JONES Joseph B on 5 Oct at Dracut MA *MS* 6 Jan 1847

BROWNELL Ann M m ANDREWS Wm A *MS* 13 Nov 1850

BROWNELL Betsey Ann m HANFORD Levi O both of Kartright NY on 23 May *MS* 27 June 1849

BROWNELL Lydia A m NUTE David C on 24 Dec at Dover NH *MS* 8 Jan 1845

BRUCE Almira m ROBERTSON Giles both of Randolph VT on 31 May 1848 *MS* 14 Feb 1849

BRUCE Louisa m OAKS Oscar on 10 Aug at Nashua *MS* 22 Oct 1845

BRUCE Lucena of Newark VT m LUCE Nelson C of Industry ME *MS* 10 Jan 1849 & on 12 Nov 1848 *MS* 9 May 1849

BRUCE Lucin m GUSTIN Abijah L both of Newark VT on 19 Mar 1849 *MS* 9 May 1849

BRUCE Mary Jane m DUNBAR Jonathan N on 5 Mar in Contoocookville *MS* 8 May 1844

BRUNNING Hannah of Hatley m BEAN Joseph on 20 June *MS* 1 Jan 1840

BRYANT Belinda of Saco m HOUSE James L of Biddeford ME on 12 Jul *MS* 30 Sept 1846 & *MS* 6 Apr 1847

BRYANT Betsey B m DOE Anthony E both of Dover on 9 June *MS* 15 Jul 1846

BRYANT Drusilla B d/o BRYANT Jeremiah m DURGIN Clark on 3 Aug at Andover *MS* 14 Sept 1842

BRYANT Hannah m DOE Elijah E on 25th Apr at Dover NH *MS* 5 May 1847

BRYANT Hannah of Effingham NH m GERRISH Charles F of Nottingham on 13 Feb 1849 *MS* 7 Mar 1849

BRYANT Mary Jane of Great Falls NH m LORD George *MS* 4 Dec 1839

BUCK Eliza of West Fairlee m ROWELL John of Vershire on 31 Dec *MS* 7 Feb 1838

BUCK Elmira of Foxcorft ME m TRUE Jacob of Guilford on 11 Nov

BUCK (Continued)
MS 28 Nov 1849

BUCK Hannah S m SAWYER Nathan F on 30 Jul at Fryeburgh ME *MS* 20 Aug 1845

BUCK Harriet of Manchester NH m KNOWLTON Charles D on 17 Dec at Manchester NH *MS* 1 Jan 1845

BUCK Melissa of Paris ME m BERRY George on 28 Jul 1844 at Paris ME *MS* 25 Sept 1844

BUCK Rosina of Buckfield on 28th ult m PACKARD Job C B Esq of Blanchard *MFWBR* 17 Mar 1849

BUCK Ruth R m DWINAL Cyrus C *MS* 5 Dec 1833

BUCK Sarah S of Norway ME m MERRILL Charles of New Gloucester ME *MFWBR* 3 Mar 1849

BUCK Susan C m CHADWICK Charles W of Gilford NH *MFWBR* 3 Nov 1849

BUCKLIN Ahiah m CLOUGH Joseph M both of Manchester on 9 Aug *MS* 12 Sept 1849

BUEL Lucinda m JONES Sanders on 22 Mar 1848 *MS* 5 Apr 1848

BUFFINGTON Harriet m BABCOCK George both of New Albion NY on 10 inst *MS* 21 Dec 1836

BUFFUM Eliza A m PORTER Benjamin F on 5 Aug at Manchester NH *MS* 21 Aug 1844

BUFFUM Ruth Ann m BUXTON Samuel both of Smithfield *MS* 28 Feb 1838

BUKER Ann H m RICHARDSON Martin P at Cambridge VT *MS* 8 June 1842

BULLARD Cyntha M m MITCHELL Benjamin K at Charlestown MA *MS* 23 Oct 1844

BULLOCK Almira of Lowell on 8 Aug m DAVIS Isaac G of Roxbury MA *MS* 23 Aug 1843

BULLOCK Lavina m NUTE Thomas J on 14 Nov at Lowell MA *MS* 25 May 1842

BUMFORD Lydia m WATSON Joseph both of Barrington on 28 Mar *MS* 27 Apr 1836

BUNKER Adaline m FULLONTON Ezekiel on 3 Oct at Epping NH *MS* 23 Oct 1844

BUNKER Adelia of Epping m FULLONTON Ezekiel on 3 Oct at Epping NH of Boston MA *MS* 4 Dec 1844

BUNKER Christina of Barnstead NH m GILMAN Samuel D of Gilmanton NH on 28 May 1848 *MS* 21 June 1848

BUNKER Hannah J of Kittery ME m FRISBEE James Jr on 31st March at Kittery *MS* 13 Apr 1842

BUNKER Lydia D m HUNTING Josiah H on 18th of Charleston ME *MS* 29 Jan 1845

BUNKER Rebecca K m LIBBY Jacob both of Dover on 23 inst 1849 *MS* 2 May 1849

BUNKER Rosena of Barnstead NH m ELLIOT William H on 15 May at
Gilmanton NH *MS* 19 June 1844

BUNKER Sarah Ann m GOTHAM Samuel R both of New Market NH
on 3 May *MS* 16 May 1838

BUNKER Sarah C of Epping NH m FOLSOM Samuel M of Boston MA
in Epping *MS* 9 Mar 1842

BUNKER Sarah of Corinna ME m HURD Robert of Newport LC on
13th inst *MS* 30 Mar 1836

BUNKER Sarah R of Barnstead m TILTON David P of Pittsfield on 4
Sept at Pittsfield *MS* 14 Sept 1842

BUNNEL Emily of Stanstead EC m EDMUNDS Rhodolphus on 14
Feb *MS* 13 Sept 1843

BURBANK Eliza Ann of Grafton MA m SANBORN Moses L of Grafton
MA on 17 Apr *MS* 14 May 1845

BURBANK Elizabeth m ALLEN C G *MFWBR* 10 Nov 1849

BURBANK Harriet D m PIERCE Mark W both of Manchester on 30
Jul 1848 *MS* 16 Aug 1848

BURBANK Lorinda J at Wakefield NH m GOODWIN Oliver of Acton
ME *MS* 29 Apr 1840

BURBANK Lovey m WELLS John of Strafford VT *MS* 1 Feb 1843

BURBANK Mary Jane of Parsonsfield ME m BEEDLE Henry of
Somersworth NH on 25 Nov 1847 *MS* 12 Jan 1848

BURBANK Miriam B of Parsonsfield m BURBANK Porter S of Newfield ME *MS* 2 Aug 1837

BURBANK Rachel C m HUNTINGTON James both of L on 2 inst *MS*
13 May 1846

BURBANK Susannah m EVANS Jotham F both of Shelburn on 8th
inst *MS* 26 Nov 1834

BURDEN Adeline m SEARL Franklin V both of Scituate *MS* 1 Jan
1851

BURDICK Susan m KAUL Thomas F *MS* 4 Apr 1849

BURDICT Louisa m CHASE Augustus A on 17 Feb 1848 *MS* 15 Mar
1848

BURGESS Philenia T of Phipsburgh ME m CHASE Zachariah T Capt
of Georgetown ME *MS* 25 Feb 1835

BURGESS Rachel Mrs m HASKEL Rufus Capt both of Poland ME?
on 17 Mar *MS* 1 Apr 1846

BURGIS Phebe m HAMMOND Nathan both of Yorkshire on 10 Oct
MS 26 Dec 1838

BURGLEY Mary H of Rochester NH m HAMMOND Andrew J on 20
MS 27 Nov 1844

BURHAM Mary of Hollis m KIMBALL Rufus of Hollis *MS* 9 Nov 1826

BURKE Ellen of Dover m LOVEJOY Wm O of Lawrence MA *MS* 6 Nov
1850

BURKE Mary A at Eaton NH m DRAPER Charles R of Roxbury MA
MS 21 Jan 1846

BURLEIGH Hannah M m SANBORN Tristram both of Sandwich NH on 18 Aug *MS* 11 Sept 1850

BURLEIGH Mary of New Market NH m SMART Charles on 10th inst *MS* 17 Apr 1844

BURLEIGH Sarah A m SMART Moulton B both of New Market NH on 13 inst *MS* 26 Apr 1837

BURLEIGH Sarah J m BODGE Joseph of Portsmouth in New Market *MS* 27 Mar 1834

BURLENGAME Emelin m SWEETLAND James H on 6th inst *MS* 15 Apr 1835

BURLEY Almira of Brookfield m CATE Isaac on 14 ult *MS* 1 Mar 1837

BURLEY Dorothy of Sandwich NH m QUINBY Hosea of Sandwich NH *MS* 14 May 1828

BURLEY Elizabeth S of Dover m GOSS Stephen of Natick MA on 21 inst *MS* 29 May 1850 & *MFWBR* 1 June 1850

BURLEY Grace F m BROWN Ambrose on 23 Aug *MS* 2 Sept 1835

BURLEY Mary G m PAGE Ezekiel G both of Farmington ME on 30 Mar *MS* 17 May 1837

BURLEY Sarah F of Pittsfield on 21 May m FRENCH Charles *MS* 5 June 1839

BURNETT Susan m CLOUTMAN Mark W both of Gorham ME on 30th Sept *MS* 12 Nov 1835

BURNHAM Deborah m RANLET Noah both of Littleton NH on 8 Dec 1847 *MS* 19 Jan 1848

BURNHAM Eliza m CRITCHERSON Wm H *MS* 19 Jan 1842

BURNHAM Eliza Miss of Conway NH m MANSON Benjamin Eld of Conway *MS* 27 Sept 1827

BURNHAM Jane m MUDGETT Jesse m 4 Dec at Sandwich NH *MS* 4 Jan 1837

BURNHAM Julia N A W on 13th inst m MURCH George W *MFWBR* 24 Feb 1849

BURNHAM Martha Ann of So Parsonsfield ME m BICKFORD Ira H of Boston on 10 Sept *MS* 7 Oct 1846

BURNHAM Martha C of Newfield m WALTER Horace of Dover NH *MS* 13 Dec 1827

BURNHAM Martha d/o BURNHAM John Esq (late) of Limerick ME m WILSON Moses Dr of Whitefield *MFWBR* 30 Jan 1847

BURNHAM Mary Elizabeth m GARLAND Daniel both of Nottingham on 18 inst *MS* 28 June 1837

BURNHAM Mary M m MARDIN Nathan both of Epsom NH on 4 Apr 1849 *MS* 18 Apr 1849

BURNHAM Octavia F of Pownal ME m THOMAS Charles H of Freeport ME on 14 Sept at Pownal ME *MS* 25 Nov 1846

BURNS Mary Jane of Lowell on 13th inst at Lowell m CHAMBERLAIN Benjamin *MS* 23 Oct 1839

BURRILL Elizabeth of Chester m OSGOOD Samuel of Amesbury MA on 1 Jan 1844 at Manchester *MS* 17 Jan 1844

BURROWS Abigail m NUTE Rufus M both of Middleton on 17 May 1849 *MS* 13 Feb 1850

BURROWS Elizabeth m CHADBOURN Hiram H both of Great Falls on 4 Jul *MS* 10 Jul 1850

BURROWS Irena of Dover m KING Joseph of Barre MA on 16 inst *MS* 25 Mar 1846

BURROWS Lavinia of Dover NH m KEYS Peter Jr of Wolfboro NH on 8 inst *MS* 15 Mar 1837

BURROWS Rebecca O m FELKER Elias of Dover NH on 19 Feb *MS* 8 Mar 1843

BURT Delia Miss of Providence RI m WESLEY Joseph of Tiverton RI on 26th ult *MS* 2 Jan 1834

BURTON Lucretia M m WOODMAN John P both of Manchester on 14 Dec 1848 *MS* 27 Dec 1848

BURTON Sarah A m READ Thomas J both of Mendon MA on 23rd *MS* 5 Sept 1838

BURWELL Amy Mrs m MARVEL William both of Russia NY on 17 Aug 1847 *MS* 1 Dec 1847

BUSHNEL Cordelia A of Monroe m FORD E B Esq of Pierpont NY on Mar 6 in Monroe *MS* 24 Apr 1850

BUSSEY Lydia A m BICKFORD Horace P both of Newburgh ME on 18 Jan 1848 *MS* 15 Mar 1848

BUSSEY Sarah A of Bangor ME m HAMBLIN Jacob on 6 June at Newburgh *MS* 30 June 1847

BUSWELL Betsey of Ossipee m DAVIS Thomas B of Effingham NH *MS* 21 Dec 1836

BUSWELL Clara A m TIBBETTS Moses P both of Ossipee NH on 3 May *MS* 24 June 1846

BUSWELL Sarah of Ossipee NH m MELOON Joseph P of Effingham NH *MS* 7 Aug 1839

BUTCH Hannah m GETCHEL George J both of Brownfield ME on 11 June 1848 *MS* 5 Jul 1848

BUTLER Caroline A m PARKS Stephen both of Bradford on 8 Sept *MS* 16 Oct 1850

BUTLER Caroline R of Farmington m PREBLE Nehemiah on 28 Mar 1847 of Farmington *MS* 21 Apr 1847

BUTLER Clarissa M m THOMAS Jedediah both of Gardiner ME on 8 Jan *MS* 24 Apr 1850

BUTLER Dorcas at Lebanon ME m DORE Nathan of Milton NH *MS* 27 Nov 1844

BUTLER Elenor m BURBANK Luther both of Barnston on 9 Oct 1843 *MS* 1 May 1844

BUTLER Henrietta m CILLEY John O at Nottingham NH *MS* 9 Nov 1832

BUTLER Huldah Ann m DAVIS William of Harmony ME at Farmington ME on 30 Mar *MS* 6 Aug 1845

BUTLER Isabella F of Nottingham NH m KELLEY William L C Dr of Northwood *MS* 12 Jan 1831

BUTLER Lovina m STOWERS Francis on 3d June 1846 of Farmington *MS* 21 Apr 1847

BUTLER Mary Ann m CASH John both of Casco ME on 7 May *MS* 3 June 1846

BUTLER Mary of Berwick ME m COURSON Michael E of Rochester on 11 inst *MS* 20 Sept 1837

BUTLER Olive J of Sebago m LEAVITT William *MFWBR* 21 Jan 1849

BUTLER Sally m ELWELL Jonias on 20 Sept at South Berwick ME *MS* 11 Oct 1843

BUTTERFIELD Abigail of Stanstead LC m CASS Lorenzo on 26 Aug 1841 *MS* 13 Apr 1842

BUTTERFIELD Eliza S m CLENDMAN William *MS* 15 Dec 1847

BUTTERFIELD Lucy Ann m SMITH Hugh *MFWBR* 11 Dec 1847

BUTTERFIELD Marilla m CAMPBELL Page both of Bedford on 12 Apr 1848 *MS* 26 Apr 1848

BUTTERFIELD Mary of Stanstead LC m WADE Stephen of Hatley LC on 26 Aug *MS* 13 Apr 1842

BUTTERS Elizabeth H m BROWN Samuel of Goffstown NH on 24 Sept at Hooksett NH *MS* 10 Oct 1844

BUTTERS Mary of Wilmington MA m BUTTERS Ruel on 2 June *MS* 26 June 1844

BUTTLES Mary Ann m SMITH Wm R on 20 Feb *MS* 24 Apr 1850

BUXLEY Reuhamah m LAUGER Syvester G on 31 Dec *MS* 22 Jan 1845

BUXTON Lydia of Uxbridge m MILLER Nelson of Smithfield RI on 16 ult *MS* 5 Sept 1838

BUZWELL Ann Mrs m HOLT Asa on 12 Aug *MS* 26 Aug 1846

BUZWELL Elizabeth of Bradford m PAGE David S of Lowell on 29 Nov *MS* 12 Dec 1838

BUZZELL Catharine L of Gilford NH m BURNHAM Newton J of Meredith NH *MS* 2 Aug 1848

BUZZELL Elizabeth m HASSOM Lewis of Northfield VT on 23 Mar at Strafford *MS* 6 Apr 1847

BUZZELL Leonora of Effingham m PETTENGILL Leonard of Ossipee NH on 27th ult *MS* 10 Dec 1834

BUZZELL Maria L of New Market NH m LASKEY Jonathan of Milton NH *MS* 3 May 1848

BUZZELL Mary Jane Mrs of Guilford NH m BLAKE John of Barnstead NH *MS* 19 Feb 1845

BUZZELL Mary Jane of Barrington m YOUNG John B of Dover NH *MS* 5 Feb 1845

BUZZELL Mary of Ossipee NH m MILLIKIN Robert of Freedom NH

BUZZELL (Continued)
MS 30 Apr 1845

BUZZELL Sarah m YOUNG Jonathan both of Effingham NH on 29th ult MS 11 Feb 1835

BYRUM Diana m DURGIN John both of Portland ME MFWBR 29 June 1850

CADY Eliza m ADAMS James on 20 Feb MS 3 May 1843

CADY Salome of Oxford Chenango NY on 20th ult m SMITH Isaac P MS 24 Apr 1839

CAHOON Elizabeth m KNIGHT George M both of Scituate on 31 ult MS 17 Jan 1849

CAISBUING Lydia of Tamworth NH m BUZZELL Eliphord of Dover NH on 2 inst at Dover NH MS 12 Nov 1845

CALCINS Loisa of China NY m DOW Lafayette of Yorkshire on 25 Mar MS 9 May 1849

CALDERWOOD Lydia of Waldo PLT m IRISH Levi at Waldo PLT ME MS 15 Jan 1845

CALDWELL Sophia W of Boscawen m GAGE Asa M on 21 Dec 1844 at Hopkinton of Boscawen MS 8 Jan 1845

CALEF Dorothy of Lowell on 25th m OSGOOD Calvin (printer) MS 28 Aug 1839

CALEFF Eliza Ann m LORD Moses C on 16 Mar 1848 MS 19 Apr 1848

CALHOUN Louisa M m WALKER Alexander MFWBR 3 Feb 1849

CALL Louisa of Perkins m POTTLER Orington of Richmond on 7 Sept 1848 MS 11 Oct 1848

CALL Mary Ann m GRACE William H both of Kittery on Sabbath eve 25 Nov MS 5 Dec 1849

CALVIN Lydia Marandor Olney m GROWES Dennis H both of Scituate RI on 9 ult MS 17 May 1848

CAMBURN Caroline m BENCROFT Seneca C both of Walworth NY MS 16 Oct 1850

CAMBURN Electa A m CARMAN John both of Walworth NY on 8 Aug MS 16 Oct 1850

CAMMETT Sally of Waterboro NH m BEAN Jeremiah of Belmont NH on Sun evening last MS 4 Nov 1831

CAMPBELL Achsah R of Brighton ME m WIGGIN Thomas H of Wellington on 23 May 1848 MS 21 June 1848

CAMPBELL Diana m SMALL Judah on 21 Jan at Bowdoin ME MS 10 Mar 1847

CAMPBELL Jane M m LENNAN Moses both of Georgetown ME on Mar 30 at Georgetown MS 27 Apr 1842

CAMPBELL Lettis m WARNER John MFWBR 10 Mar 1849

CAMPBELL Susan m SNOWMAN John both of Georgetown ME MS 25 Feb 1835

CANDLE Polly ae 14y in New York m WILLIAM Rev Mr ae 70y *MS* 27 Jul 1826

CANEDY Hannah of Duxbury VT m BULLARD Wm A of Northumberland Saratoga Co NY on 16 Oct *MS* 23 Jan 1850

CANEY Martha m RUMMERY Jacob both of Effingham NH *MS* 1 Apr 1835

CANNEY Anne m HORNE Jeremiah at Tuftonboro' NH *MS* 6 Mar 1834

CANNEY Eliza Jane of Dover NH on 1 Nov m BASSETT Daniel Jr of Wolfboro' NH *MS* 9 Nov 1842

CANNEY Jane B of Farmington NH m BRIGGS Hiram D of Kittery ME on 21 Dec at Rochester NH *MS* 30 Dec 1846

CANNEY Livona of Farmington NH on 5 Oct m VARNEY Moses M R of Dover NH at Farmington NH *MS* 15 Oct 1845

CARD Abigail m BARRETT William both of Portsmouth on 11 May *MS* 27 May 1846

CARD Hannah A Mrs m WILSON Lowell G *MFWBR* 9 Mar 1850

CARD Lydia M m SULLIVAN Joseph A both of Charlestown RI on 13 Apr *MS* 22 May 1850

CARD Margery of Bowdoinham m SILVER Samuel on 3 Nov of Dexter ME *MS* 8 Jan 1845

CARGILL Sophia m FULLER Jarius both of Bowdoinham in Topsham *MS* 12 Jan 1842

CARIL Mary E of Buxton ME m RANKINS William H on 16 June at Buxton ME *MS* 28 Jul 1847

CARLL [sic] Sophia W m KELLOGG Charles C of Boston MA on 10 Aug *MS* 27 Aug 1845

CARLTON Mahala D m FULLER Ezra B of Stowe at Broodfield VT on 22 Sept *MS* 15 Jan 1845

CARLTON Rhoda of Lowell MA m PIPER Isaac B on 25 June *MS* 23 Aug 1843

CARLTON Widow of Franconia m PRIEST David of Lisbon on 10 Nov *MS* 29 Dec 1847

CARNEY Abagail Mrs m MYERS Sumner *MFWBR* 13 Oct 1849

CARPENTER Abby H of Great Falls NH m SHAPLEIGH Edwin of Lebanon ME *MS* 24 Dec 1845

CARPENTER Adelia m HALL Philander on 4 inst in Ogden *MS* 1 Feb 1837

CARPENTER Clarissa of Lawrence NY m CLARK Amos F of Norfolk on 1 Jan 1849 *MS* 14 Feb 1849

CARPENTER Eliza A of Sherburne m ALBRIGHT William H on 17 Apr *MS* 5 May 1846

CARPENTER Harriet A m POTTER Moses O both of Scituate RI on 2 Jan *MS* 15 Jan 1851

CARPENTER Joann of Williamstown VT m DEXTER Parker of Norwich on 10 Mar 1850 *MS* 10 Apr 1850

CARPENTER Mary m CARMAN Enos on 15 Apr 1847 of Wheatland Racine Co Wisconsin *MS* 12 May 1847

CARPENTER Miranda E of Sutton m SOUTHWICK Jonathan of Northbridge MA on 28 Mar *MS* 1 May 1844

CARPENTER Orpha of Stanstead on 30 Aug 1838 m GRIFFIN Frastus *MS* 17 Apr 1839

CARR Elizabeth d/o CARR John on 11th inst m BARTON Albion of Rollinsford NH *MFWBR* 16 Nov 1850

CARR Henrietta m McGILL John on 12 Nov at Stephentown NY *MS* 24 Apr 1844

CARR Jennett of Manchester m BENNETT Joshua of Peacham VT *MS* 26 Mar 1851

CARR Lovina P of Chesterville m MEARS Elijah on 25 Oct 1846 of Chesterville *MS* 21 Apr 1847

CARR Lozana E m POOLE Henry O of Mt Vernon on 18 Mar at Vienna *MS* 16 Apr 1845

CARR Mahala W m LITTLEFIELD Daniel both of Dover NH on Sunday last *MS* 29 Aug 1838

CARR Ruth T of Gilford m SELINHAM B M B of Thornton on 1 June *MS* 1 Jul 1846

CARR Sabrina K d/o CARR John of Limerick ME m GRIFFIN Henry D of Rollinsford NH *MFWBR* 31 Aug 1850

CARR Sarah Abigail Perthena of Stephentown m CHOUNARD Paschal on 30 Nov at Berlin *MS* 6 Jan 1847

CARR Sarah m DARLING Joshua both of Mendon on 18 Jan *MS* 28 Feb 1838

CARR Sarah of Loudon NH m RUSSEL Wellington of Barnstead NH on 21 inst *MS* 31 May 1848

CARSLEY Betsey H of Harrison ME m WHITNEY James G on 3 Jan 1847 *MS* 21 Apr 1847

CARTER Betsey m CHASE Samuel on 21 Mar 1847 *MS* 25 Aug 1847

CARTER Elizabeth B m NEWMAN Benjamin both of Sanford in Sanford ME 30 Dec 1841 *MS* 16 Feb 1842

CARTER Jane of Wilmington MA m UPTON Thomas of Reading MA *MS* 22 Feb 1843

CARVER Ann m DAVIS Abraham B both of Brunswick on 28 Aug *MS* 2 Jan 1839

CASE Emily m SUMMER Farmer both of Chester Dodge Co WT on 16 Dec 1847 *MS* 16 Feb 1848

CASE Harriet P m MOREY Peter both of Green on 23 Feb *MS* 26 Mar 1851

CASE Mary A of Brunswick m ROBINSON Elijah of East Bridgewater MA on 13 May 1850 *MS* 15 May 1850

CASH Priscilla m HODGDON John A both of Raymond ME on 16 Apr *MS* 5 May 1846

CASS Judith on Mar 16 m ALDRICH Lewis both of Stanstead LC

CASS (Continued)
MS 15 Apr 1840

CASS Loventia J of Alexandria NH m THOMPSON Hollis of Bristol on 8 Aug 1847 *MS* 3 Nov 1847

CASS Sophia m LIBBY Parson both of S on 11 Apr 1844 *MS* 1 May 1844

CASTOR Cynthia m CHURCHILL George on 8th inst at Wolcott NY *MS* 1 June 1842

CASWELL Asenath S m KENISTON Mark both of New Market NH on 31 May *MS* 8 Jul 1846

CASWELL Charity of West Sumner ME on 8th ult m DUNN Elias G *MFWBR* 24 Feb 1849

CASWELL Deborah Jane m HAWKINS William P both of Strafford *MS* 10 Jan 1838

CASWELL Elizabeth Jane m GOWING James Jr both of Manchester on 28 June *MS* 11 Jul 1849

CASWELL Hannah P of Northwood m TASKER Levi B of Strafford on 19 Aug *MS* 7 Nov 1838

CASWELL Mary E of Manchester NH m FARNUM David on 22 June at Manchester NH *MS* 28 Jul 1847

CASWELL Sarah m LEWIS C W on 18 Sept at Boothbay ME *MS* 22 Jan 1845

CATE Abby of Sanbornton NH m WARD Cotton "Post Master of North Belmont ME" *MS* 26 May 1847

CATE Mary Ann of Northfield NH m LEES Samuel of West Boylston MA on 2 Aug *MS* 14 Oct 1846

CATE Mary m ROBERTS Sanburn both of Meredith *MS* 5 Dec 1838

CATE Mary Jane of Gilmanton NH m JEWETT Samuel N of Gilford NH on 5 June *MS* 21 Aug 1850

CATE Rosilla of Meredith m ANNES Wm S of Pittsfield on 9 Feb *MS* 27 Feb 1834

CATE Sally S youngest d/o CATE John Capt of Barrington m TAYLOR Alfred *MS* 23 Nov 1836

CATE Sophia m HILL John S on 30 Oct at Gilmanton NH *MS* 18 Jan 1843

CATER Nancy m DAME William *MS* 24 Apr 1834

CATES Elecia m JENKS Wm B both of Oneonta on 5 Dec 1849 *MS* 2 Jan 1849

CAVERLY Almira H of Dover NH m MERRILL Phineas of Lawrence MA *MFWBR* 4 Aug 1849

CAVERLY Jane m DREW Silas both of Barrington *MS* 23 Nov 1836

CAVERLY Mary S of Barrington m CAVERLY Joel of Strafford on 30 ult *MS* 9 Nov 1836

CAVERLY Nancy J of Barrington m CAVERLY John S on 7 Apr 1747 (sic) 1847? *MS* 12 May 1847

CAVERLY Sophia d/o CAVERLY Nathaniel of Barrington m DREW

CAVERLY (Continued)

Timothy of Strafford on 4 Mar *MS* 13 Mar 1834

CAVERNO Elizabeth A formerly a teacher in Foxcroft Academy ME m on 29 Nov at Charlestown MA AVERILL John P principal of the Institution at Woodstock CT *MS* 10 Dec 1845

CAWLEY Charlotte m BURBANK Oscar F both of Manchester on 14 Nov *MS* 5 Dec 1849

CENTER I Miss m EVANS I Mr on 8 Nov at Potsdam NY *MS* 6 Jan 1847

CHACE Lydia Jane m LEAVITT John H both of Pittsfield on 12 Apr Sabbath Morn *MS* 22 Apr 1840

CHADBORN Deborah of Sanford ME on 22d? ult m HILL Freeman *MS* 3 Apr 1839

CHADBOURN Clarissa Ann m NEAL Hiram both of No Berwick ME on 31 Dec *MS* 7 Feb 1849

CHADBOURN Sylvina A m ROLLINS Joseph S both of Somersworth on 30 ult *MS* 10 May 1848

CHADBOURNE Eliza Ann of No Berwick m LIBBEY Mark of Berwick ME on 22 Feb *MS* 25 Mar 1846

CHADBOURNE Lydia C m WATSON Thomas J both of Fryeburg ME on 22 Mar *MS* 8 Apr 1846

CHADBOURNE Martha Jane of Parsonsfield ME m MOORE Joseph of Newfield ME on 27th ult at Parsonsfield ME *MS* 17 Jan 1844

CHADBOURNE Sarah B of Waterboro m ANDREWS John of Wales ME *MFWBR* 20 May 1848

CHADWICK Harriet A of Sutton MA m LEONARD Dwight L on 25 Oct at Sutton MA *MS* 15 Nov 1843

CHAFFEE Rhoda d/o CHAFFEE C Eld m BLANCHARD Levi 22 Mar *MS* 16 May 1838

CHALLIES Elizabeth A m EMERY Gilmore *MFWBR* 20 Mar 1847

CHAMBER Sally of Milton m SPINNEY David Capt on 8 Dec at Wakefield *MS* 28 Dec 1842

CHAMBERLAIN Adaline m PRINCE Seward M of Danville ME *MFWBR* 8 June 1850

CHAMBERLAIN Louise m SHAW Isaac both of Exeter ME *MS* 24 Apr 1834

CHAMBERLAIN Lydia A m BREWSTER Charles W H both of Portsmouth on 17 Jan 1850 *MS* 30 Jan 1850

CHAMBERLAIN Mary J of Auburn ME m DUNNING Robert of Brunswick ME on 26 Oct at Auburn ME *MS* 9 Dec 1846

CHAMBERLAIN Mary of Lowell MA m DERBY Elmore on 26 June *MS* 23 Aug 1843

CHAMBERLAIN Miss of Dover m BICKFORD Stephen H on 24 Oct at Rochester *MS* 25 Nov 1846

CHAMBERLIN Elizabeth G m LIBBEY Joseph T both of New Durham on 16 Dec *MS* 26 Dec 1849

CHAMBERLIN Emeline of Manchester m SARGENT Samuel of Chester on 31 Mar 1848 *MS* 26 Apr 1848

CHAMBERLIN Mary E of Dover NH m GRAY George W at Dover NH on Sunday last *MS* 20 Nov 1844

CHAMBERLIN Rhoda E m DOWNS Nathan P of Croydon on 7 May at Enfield *MS* 9 Jul 1845

CHAMBERLIN Sarah A of Strafford VT m CILLEY John F on 27 Mar of Tunbridge VT *MS* 14 May 1845

CHAMPELEN Ruth A H of South Kinsgton m ELLIS George W on 30 Nov at Providence RI *MS* 10 Dec 1845

CHAMPION Abby C m FLANDERS Job both of Lowell on 7 June *MS* 24 June 1846

CHAMPLIN Amy of Hamilton NY m SANDERS Truman P of Clarkville on 2 inst *MS* 29 Dec 1847

CHAMPLIN Lucretia C m WILLIAMS Alaric both of Brookfield Madison Co NY on 11 Oct 1848 *MS* 11 Apr 1849

CHAMPON Eliza A m CRANKITE Henry J both of Starkville on 13 Sept *MS* 16 Jan 1850

CHANDLER Almira H m COLE Ossian Z *MFWBR* 21 Jul 1849

CHANDLER Amanda M m HUNT John of Unity ME *MS* 21 Jan 1846

CHANDLER Mary of Farmington ME m EUSTIS Moses of Jay ME on 24th ult *MS* 30 Mar 1831

CHANDLER Rebecca m BOYNTON Waterman M both of Mercer ME on 30 ult *MS* 26 Nov 1834

CHANDLER Susan m WYMAN Seth both of Chatham NH on 29 Nov 1849 *MS* 20 Feb 1850

CHANEY Abigail Ann on May 3 m MCKENNEY Freeman both of Limington ME *MS* 13 May 1840

CHANEY Emily of South Berwick ME m STEWART Asa of Kittery ME on 6 May at South Berwick ME *MS* 14 May 1845

CHANEY Mary of Plainfield NY m GATES Hiram N of Matilda WC on 15 Sept *MS* 30 Sept 1846

CHANNELL Lydia B m HAZELTON Chesley D on 20th inst at Durham *MS* 27 Dec 1843

CHAPEL Emeline S of Colebrook Ohio m BECKWITH Christopher of New Lyme on 24 Feb *MS* 24 Apr 1850

CHAPMAN Abigail of Gilmanton m GLINES James F of Northfield on 30 Nov at Gilmanton *MS* 27 Dec 1843

CHAPMAN D Mandane only d/o CHAPMAN Stephen m on 31 Jul at Plainfield Otsego Co NY HEFFRON Daniel S principal of the Whitestown Seminary *MS* 24 Sept 1845

CHAPMAN Loranda Miss m URAN John m at North Hampton NH *MS* 21 Dec 1832

CHAPMAN Sarah E of New Market on 7th inst m JOHNSON George W of Epping *MS* 15 Feb 1843

CHAPMAN Sarah M in Limerick on 18th inst m MAYHEW John of

CHAPMAN (Continued)
Great Falls NH *MS* 29 Jan 1840

CHAPMAN Viana D of New Market m STILSON James on 1 June at New Market *MS* 11 June 1845

CHARRIS Caroline E of Sanford ME m FURBUSH Jesse L on 16 Jul at Sanford ME *MS* 30 Aug 1843

CHASE Almira on 27 Dec m PITTS Nathaniel of Waterboro' *MS* 6 Jan 1847

CHASE Amanda at Lisbon on 8 ult m JONES Samuel of Bradford VT *MS* 29 Apr 1840

CHASE Amy m DESHON Samuel on 5 Dec at Waterboro' ME *MS* 18 Dec 1844

CHASE Anna m INGERSOL Byron on 11 Sept at Warsaw NY *MS* 20 Nov 1844

CHASE Betsey P m FELTCH Harris both of Manchester m 10 Sept *MS* 23 Sept 1846

CHASE Betsey S M of G m CHASE Charles A on 14 Oct at Groton MA *MS* 18 Jan 1843

CHASE Deborah m TODD John William at Bangor ME *MS* 13 Sept 1843

CHASE Eliza m YORK Horace B *MS* 24 Jan 1838

CHASE Eliza S at Bristol m EMMONS J M R of Bristol *MS* 31 Jan 1844

CHASE Elizabeth Ann m GILMORE Gilbert H both of Manchester on 4 Mar 1849 Sab eve *MS* 14 Mar 1849

CHASE Frances m SHEPLEY Leonard *MFWBR* 12 May 1849

CHASE Hannah of Meredith m TUCKER Andrew J of Alexandria on 1 Apr 1848 *MS* 21 June 1848

CHASE Harriet m PHILLIPS Samuel B both of Bethlehem on 20 Mar *MS* 10 Apr 1850

CHASE Harriet N of Newfield m RICKER George H, A.B., of Parsonsfield on 2 Dec 1847 *MS* 29 Dec 1847

CHASE Julia Ann m EATON Samuel both of Pittsfield on 24 inst *MS* 3 May 1837

CHASE Laura A d/o CHASE J T Hon m ABBOTT Hiram C *MFWBR* 6 Feb 1847

CHASE Louisa E of Waltham MA m TAYLOR John M on 30 Nov at Northwood *MS* 17 Dec 1845

CHASE Lucinda m BUSWELL Samuel S both of Hopkinton on 18 Apr *MS* 8 May 1844

CHASE Lucy S m MERRICK Otis S on 23 Mar at Pittsfield *MS* 9 Apr 1845

CHASE Margaret of Topsham ME m COLBY Elias Esq of Richmond ME on 6 Mar *MS* 27 Mar 1850

CHASE Maria J of Great Falls NH m CHAMBERLIN Robert S of Lowell on 27 Nov 1843 at Great Falls *MS* 21 Feb 1844

CHASE Mary Ann at Bristol on Dec 14 m BEEDE Hanson of Franklin *MS* 29 Jan 1840

CHASE Mary E m ROUNSEFELT James both of Manchester on 14 May 1848 *MS* 24 May 1848

CHASE Mary Elizabeth of Salisbury NY m MARVEL Joy of Norway on 23 Apr at Salisbury NY *MS* 9 Jul 1845

CHASE Mary Jane of Dover NH m JORDAN Andrew S of Boston MA on 31 Dec 1848 *MS* 17 Jan 1849

CHASE Mary of Grafton MA m CLARK Dexter on 22 Dec at Groton *MS* 18 Jan 1843

CHASE Sarah A of Scarboro' ME m MERRILL Edward D of Saco ME on 7 Dec 1847 *MS* 29 Dec 1847

CHASE Sarah of North Berwick ME m DORE Charles of Great Falls NH *MS* 13 Nov 1839

CHASE Susan B m GOODWIN John D both of New Market on 21 ult *MS* 4 Jan 1837

CHATMAN Mary m HORN Benjamin both of Alexandria NH on 14 Mar 1850 *MS* 27 Mar 1850

CHATTERTON Clara of Middlesex VT m WRISLEY C Sanford of Waterbury on 29 Jan *MS* 27 Mar 1850

CHEENY Margaret of Washington VT m SPEAR Moses of Vershire on 3 Feb *MS* 22 Mar 1848

CHELDON Clarinda m BOWERS Frederick both of Hamburgh on 7 Oct *MS* 20 Dec 1837

CHELLIES Mary of Newfield m DENNELLS Zacariah *MFWBR* 18 Dec 1847

CHELLIS Hannah at Kingston m ANDERSON Moses on 1 Dec *MS* 15 Dec 1841

CHENEY Abby M of Holderness m WASHBURN George of Peterboro NH on 16 Sept 1847 *MS* 6 Oct 1847

CHENEY Elizabeth of Bristol m LOCK George of Alexandria on 7th March at Bristol NH *MS* 27 Mar 1844

CHENEY Harriet of Lawrence m BOODY John W on 4 Feb 1849 *MS* 7 Mar 1849

CHENEY Mary m MUDGET William D both of Bristol on 20 Mar *MS* 2 Apr 1851

CHENEY Sarah B of Holderness m ABBOTT Stephen G of Antrim on 16 Apr *MS* 13 May 1846

CHENY Alice m TUTTLE Jesse of Boston on 9th inst at Haverhill MA *MS* 24 Dec 1834

CHESLEY Annette F m TIBBETTS Joseph H both of New Market on 11 Feb *MS* 21 Feb 1838

CHESLEY Asenath m JENNESS Hiram both of Sheffield VT on 31 Jan Monday *MS* 16 Mar 1836

CHESLEY Betsey m SWAIN Richard both of Barrington on 25th ult *MS* 9 Dec 1835

CHESLEY Eliza of No Durham m HILL Jonathan of Gilmanton NH *MS* 17 June 1835

CHESLEY Louisa Ann of Dover NH m PAUL Sidney on Thurs last *MS* 5 Dec 1833

CHESLEY Lydia m PLACE James H on Sunday morning last *MS* 23 Jan 1834

CHESLEY Marcia O of Durham NH m WALDRON Oliver of Barnstead *MFWBR* 1 Dec 1849

CHESLEY Ruth P m LEWIS Lincoln Eld both of Barnstead on 3 inst *MS* 11 Apr 1849

CHESLEY Sarah F of New Durham NH 19 Apr 1842 on LUCAS Daniel of Wolfboro' *MS* 24 May 1843

CHESLEY Sarah of Dover m LANE John of Lee on 21st inst *MS* 27 Jan 1836

CHESLEY Susan M m SWAIN Samuel both of New Market Lamprey River on 24th *MS* 4 May 1836

CHESLEY Susan of Holderness m AMBROSE Samuel of Tamworth NH *MS* 3 June 1846

CHESWELL Charlotte of Durham NH m DAME Greenleaf of Nottingham on 24 ult *MS* 4 Oct 1848

CHICK Emily Ann m COLE Henry C both of Cornish *MS* 19 Oct 1832

CHICK Joan E of Monmouth m MEADER John of Gardiner ME on 2d ult *MS* 19 Apr 1837

CHICK Mary m HODGE Samuel in Ossipee NH *MS* 27 Jan 1832

CHICK Mercy of Ossipee NH m CATE Alfred M on 25 Dec *MS* 14 Jan 1846

CHICK Patience m ANDERSON James in Berwick *MS* 27 Jan 1832

CHICK Philena of Great Falls NH m PEARL Ichabod at Great Falls NH *MS* 15 Mar 1843

CHICK Sarah of Berwick m REED John of No Berwick *MS* 22 Jan 1851

CHICK Sarah of Berwick m RICKER Abial D on 3 Mar at Berwick ME *MS* 29 May 1844

CHICKERING Eliza Jane of Gilford m POMEROY Ashley D of New Hampton on 11 Jan *MS* 17 Jan 1844

CHILDS Diantha m DEARBORN Daniel both of Corinth 30 Jan in Corinth *MS* 16 Mar 1842

CHILDS Elzina M m WHEELER Henry at Manchester NH *MS* 24 Dec 1845

CHITMAN Mercy m GERRY Orman both of West Poland ME on 22 Mar *MS* 3 June 1846

CHITTENDEN Rhoda of Stephentown m COTTRELL John C of Sand Lake on 16 Mar in Stephentown *MS* 24 Apr 1844

CHOAT Huldah A m STEVENS Nathaniel F Capt both of Sandwich on 19 ult *MS* 12 Jul 1837

CHOATE Catherine W of Otisfield ME m HANSON James H of

CHOATE (Continued)
Harrison on 28 Sept at Otisfield ME *MS* 19 Nov 1845

CHOPPEL Lucinda m JOHNSON Oloro both of Smithfield on 27 Apr *MS* 24 May 1837

CHURCH Sally A at Columbus NY m GIBSON Stanford C MD *MS* 23 June 1847

CHURCH Sally of New Market on 27 Dec m NUTT Samuel of Troy ME *MS* 4 Jan 1843

CHURCH Tamson P m FORD Jefferson *MFWBR* 28 Jul 1849

CHURCHILL Betsey T of New Market m PICKERING Cyrus C on 26 Oct 1843 *MS* 1 Nov 1843

CHURCHILL Sarah m CHAPMAN John H both of New Market on 13 inst *MS* 16 May 1849

CILLEY Abagail m HAM Joseph both of Brooks on 30 Aug *MS* 12 Dec 1849

CILLEY Abigail C of Lowell m MUZZEY Asa A *MS* 8 Feb 1837

CILLEY Ann T m MUNROE Henry G both of Dover NH on 2 inst *MS* 12 Jul 1848

CILLEY Arvilla Ann m BERRY James Monroe on 23 June at Manchester *MS* 17 Jul 1844

CILLEY Hannah of Brooks ME m YOUNG Caleb of Jackson ME on 2 Dec 1842 at Brooks ME *MS* 25 Jan 1843

CILLEY Hannah of Northwood m KNOWLTON George H on 6 inst *MS* 14 Feb 1849

CILLEY Louisa of Limerick ME m COLE Samuel of Saco ME on *MS* 26 Aug 1831

CILLEY Mary D m FLANDERS George W both of Tunbridge VT on 8 Mar *MS* 2 May 1849

CILLEY Mary E of Jackson m MITCHELL Elijah S of Monroe ME on 1 Oct *MS* 12 Dec 1849

CILLEY Phebe Ann m CILLEY Ebenezer C Capt both of Andover on 4 June in Salibury NH *MS* 23 Sept 1846

CILLEY Rachel of Topsham m GENRLEMAN William Jr of Ottowa IL *MS* 7 Nov 1838

CILLEY Susan of Hopkinson m WHITE Thomas Deacon *MS* 16 Jan 1839

CLAGGETT Charlotte Ann of Russel Ohio m BANKS Lewis C of Oswego NY on 7 Apr *MS* 1 May 1850

CLAIN Hannah E of Clinton ME m WILSON Peter of Lowell MA on 3 Feb 1849 *MS* 21 Feb 1849

CLAPP Margaret A on 25th inst m STAPLES Nathaniel F *MFWBR* 3 Feb 1849

CLARK Abiah W of New Market NH m ABBOTT Orin on 4 Nov 1846 at New Market NH *MS* 20 Jan 1847

CLARK Achsah L Miss m WILD Elijah at Troy NY *MS* 18 Apr 1833

CLARK Almira of Dover NH m LORD David H Eld of Sanford ME

CLARK (Continued)

MS 10 Jan 1838

CLARK Alzina m GAGE William both of Austinburg Ohio on 25 Oct 1848 *MS* 10 Jan 1849

CLARK Apphia of Warner m PUTNAM Rufus Jr of Hopkinton on 21 ult *MS* 7 Dec 1836

CLARK Betsey J m BUNKER James M both of Manchester *MS* 19 Jan 1848

CLARK Betsey T m HARTON James M on 28 Dec *MS* 19 Mar 1845

CLARK Betsy m CHELLIS Ira *MFWBR* 16 Oct 1847

CLARK Clarissa m CHAFFEE Lyman both of Schroepple NY on 10th ult *MS* 6 Apr 1836

CLARK Deborah S of Lowell MA m STONKS Josiah H on 20 May *MS* 23 Aug 1843

CLARK Eleanor of Dover on 13 Jan m HURD Jesse of New Durham NH *MS* 20 Jan 1847

CLARK Elizabeth m WYLIE Parker Capt on 21 Nov at Boothbay ME *MS* 22 Jan 1845

CLARK Elizabeth of Epsom m ABBOTT Orson of Pembroke on 25 Apr *MS* 23 May 1838

CLARK Elizabeth of Gilmanton m ROBERTS John C formerly of Farmington on 4 inst *MS* 12 Sept 1838

CLARK Ellen B of N Market m HOITT James W on 22 Dec at N Market of Northwood *MS* 28 Dec 1842

CLARK Elmira C of Laurens m SIVER Adam of Milford on 31 Dec 1848 *MS* 7 Feb 1849

CLARK Elmira m JOHNSON John *MFWBR* 9 Oct 1847

CLARK Emily m GRAVES Tyler both of Underhill VT on 23 Nov 1848 *MS* 14 Feb 1849

CLARK Frances E m ARLING George G both of Rochester on 30 Nov *MS* 1 Jan 1851

CLARK Hyrenia of Rochester m SEAVEY Calvin of Farmington *MS* 18 Apr 1838

CLARK Isabella P of Portland ME m JOHNSON George I of Saco ME *MFWBR* 23 June 1849

CLARK Isabella S m WATERHOUSE William *MFWBR* 21 Apr 1849

CLARK Joanna of Sanford on 4 Dec 1848 m PERKINS George of Saco *MFWBR* 13 Jan 1849

CLARK Lydia Ann m TEBBETTS Orland of Lebanon ME *MS* 25 Dec 1844

CLARK Love of Barrington m CLARK John *MS* 6 Mar 1839

CLARK Lucy S m COFFIN Benjamin Jr both of Alton *MS* 18 Dec 1839

CLARK Mark E of Dover NH m LEIGHTON John J on 3 Feb at Dover NH *MS* 24 Feb 1847

CLARK Martha m HUTCHES John on 29 Nov at Putney NY *MS* 20

CLARK (Continued)
Dec 1843

CLARK Mary A of Barnston m KENISTON Bradbury of Bafford LC *MS* 13 Apr 1842

CLARK Mary Ann d/o CLARK John Esq of Chester m SAVAGE Isaac A Rev on 14 Dec at Chester *MS* 17 Jan 1844

CLARK Mary Ann m SANBORN Lewis F on 11 Oct at Gilford *MS* 16 Dec 1846

CLARK Mary Ann of Dover m WENTWORTH Israel P of Barrington on Sunday 14 inst *MS* 24 Feb 1836

CLARK Mary K of Holderness NH m BUZZELL John R of Tamworth NH on 6 Dec *MS* 30 Dec 1846

CLARK Mary Susan m LOUGEE Samuel Jr on 19th inst *MS* 27 Jan 1832

CLARK Matilda of Holderness m CLEMENT George on 21 March at Holderness *MS* 21 Apr 1847

CLARK Mehitabel C on Nov 25 m CROSBY Tho H both of Stanstead*MS* 15 Apr 1840

CLARK Minerva M of Manchester m MERRILL Timothy at Manchester NH *MS* 1 Oct 1845

CLARK Nancy B m CLOUGH David E on 2 Feb at Alton NH *MS* 26 Feb 1845

CLARK Olive C m SEAVEY Jacob D both of Rochester on 30 Nov *MS* 1 Jan 1851

CLARK Patience m ARMSTRONG Morey both of Plainfield NY on 5 Mar 1846 *MS* 29 Apr 1846

CLARK Polly of Strafford VT m WINSLOW John of Lyme NH on 28 Dec 1842 *MS* 25 Jan 1843

CLARK Ruth m BICKFORD Ebenezer at Meredith NH *MS* 24 Aug 1836

CLARK Sally of Eaton NH m SNELL William Jr on 1 Jan at Lowell *MS* 14 Jan 1846

CLARK Sarah m CHADWICK John on Wed last *MS* 8 Dec 1834

CLARK Susan m CLARK William on 11 Dec 1851 *MS* 8 Jan 1851

CLARK Susan of Pittsfield m WILLEY Alfred S on 21 Jul 1844 at Barnstead *MS* 28 May 1845

CLARK Thankful m JORDAN David Jr *MS* 3 Jan 1828

CLARKE Lydia m NASON Abraham both of Dixmont ME on 17 inst *MS* 31 Jan 1838

CLARKE Thede E m GREEN Hezekiah S of Sangersfield on 17 Oct 1848 *MS* 1 Nov 1848

CLARY Caroline of Dracut MA m RICHARDSON Asa W M on 3 Nov of Lowell MA *MS* 6 Jan 1847

CLAY Abby W m HANSON Frederick both of Buxton ME on 21 Nov *MS* 15 Jan 1851

CLAY Caroline B m DUNN Albert J both of Buxton ME *MS* 15 Jan

CLAY (Continued)
MS 15 Jan 1851

CLAY Clarissa P of Cannan m FROST Amaza of Wentworth on 4 Jan *MS* 5 Feb 1851

CLAY Eliza m EMERY Nathaniel *MFWBR* 18 Aug 1849

CLAY Grace m REDLON William at Buxton ME *MS* 20 Nov 1844

CLAY Hannah of Barrington NH on Sunday m GLOVER George *MS* 14 June 1843

CLAY Harriet in Buxton ME d/o CLAY Jonathan Eld of Buxton m DIKE Samuel of Sebago on Jan 30 *MS* 30 Mar 1842

CLAY Martha S m DEARBORN Jonathan L on 14 Oct of Sandbornton *MS* 16 Dec 1846

CLAY Mary A of Buxton m WILKINS Almon H of Auburn ME on 4 June *MS* 28 Aug 1850

CLAY Ursula of Hooksett NH m STONE Benj Jr of Dorchester MA *MS* 12 Dec 1838

CLEAVELAND Ellen of Campton m HEATH George of Stanstead LC on 12 June *MS* 13 Sept 1843

CLEAVELAND Martha m HATHAWAY Franklin of Potsdam on 10 Mar at Colten NY *MS* 6 Apr 1847

CLEAVES Rhoda m BACHELDER Thomas *MFWBR* 24 Mar 1849

CLEMENT Susan Maria of Barnston m EMERTON Hervey of Columbia NH *MS* 13 Apr 1842

CLEMENTS Harriet L of North Berwick ME m GUPTIL C H Dr of Dover NH *MS* 24 Jul 1839

CLEMENTS Lydia of Somersworth m BRAGDON Samuel of Milton on *MS* 19 Dec 1833

CLEMENTS Mehitabel E on 24 Sept m MAGOON Henry C of Lowell *MS* 20 Nov 1839

CLERY Emily of Brooks m ROWE Leonard *MFWBR* 13 Jan 1849

CLIFFORD Ann Maria of Gilmanton m SLEEPER Levi F of Loudon on 3d Aug at Canterbury *MS* 13 Aug 1845

CLIFFORD Christianna C m GOSS Dyer E of Poland *MFWBR* 30 Nov 1850

CLIFFORD Clarissa of Barnston on 27th Feb 1839 m CLEMENT John B *MS* 17 Apr 1839

CLIFFORD Hannah T m WEEKS Lorrain Dr on 9 June 1844 at Gilmanton *MS* 29 Jan 1845

CLIFFORD Nancy M m HILL Winthrop Y on 4 Jul at Loudon *MS* 20 June 1842

CLIFFORD Selvina of Belgrade ME m ROGERS Asel W of Ossipee NH on 7 Sept 1848 *MS* 15 Nov 1848

CLIFFORD Sophronia J m HACKETT Charles A on 29 Mar at Gilmanton *MS* 21 June 1843

CLIFFORD Susan P m AUSTIN Samuel P both of Manchester on 25 Sept *MS* 13 Oct 1847

CLOUDMAN Hannah L m ESTES Levi both of Gorham ME on 25 Feb 1849 *MS* 14 Mar 1849

CLOUGH Adeline F m EVANS William T on 10 Nov *MS* 1 Dec 1847

CLOUGH Apphia S m AVERY David on 5th inst *MS* 13 Feb 1834

CLOUGH Betsey m FOGG John on 3 May *MS* 16 May 1838

CLOUGH Betsey m WOODWARD William Deacon on 19 Oct at Lewiston ME *MS* 25 Feb 1846

CLOUGH Hannah D m CLOUGH Daniel both of Delaware on 26 Aug *MS* 17 Oct 1849

CLOUGH Henrietta M m MARSH Charles E Capt on 27 June at Buffalo NY *MS* 7 Sept 1836

CLOUGH Mary J of Garland ME m FLETCHER Eri of Dexter ME on 8 Mar 1849 *MS* 28 Mar 1849

CLOUGH Mary P of Gilmanton m WOODMAN Jeremiah of Alton *MS* 18 Dec 1839

CLOUGH Mary P of Portland ME m WINSLOW Joseph on 4th inst at Portland ME *MS* 25 June 1845

CLOUGH Meriam B on Jan 27 m DAVIS Robert both of Garland ME *MS* 4 May 1842

CLOUGH Sarah Ann of Garland ME m MOOR Henry W of St Albans ME *MS* 4 May 1842

CLOUGH Phebe E of Gilmanton on 3rd ult m COFFIN Isaac P of Alton *MS* 13 Mar 1839

CLOUGH Sarah of Parsonsfield m WELCH Joseph of Wakefield NH on 7th inst *MS* 13 Feb 1829

CLOUGH Temperance Ann m CILLEY Sewel both of Barnstead on 9 Nov 1848 *MS* 17 Jan 1849

CLOUTMAN Betsey m FIFE Reuben both of Concord on 6 ult *MS* 22 Jul 1835

CLUFF Mary m CLUFF Nahum on 30 Oct at Kennebunkport ME *MS* 20 Nov 1844

COBB Almira B of Limington ME m CHASE Sumner B of Scarborough ME on 3 Sept *MS* 21 Oct 1846

COBB Betsey m WEEKS Noah Esq on 7 May at Cornish ME *MS* 17 May 1843

COBB Caroline m SCAMMON R S both of Portland ME on 5 Dec *MS* 12 Jan 1848

COBB Catharine F m BUTLER Cornelius B both of Portland ME on 1 inst *MS* 9 Feb 1848

COBB Emily of Hampden ME m EMERY Lorenzo *MS* 29 May 1839

COBB Emma on 14th inst m DEARBORN Edmund of Bridgton *MS* 3 Apr 1839

COBB Hannah of Limington ME m LEAVETT Benjamin of Effingham NH *MS* 3 Apr 1839

COBB Harriet of Limington m GUPTILL Frost of Cornish on 14 Dec *MS* 24 Jan 1838

COBB Louisa m COBB Thomas on 21 May at Portland ME *MS* 9 Jul 1845

COBB Persis of Poland ME m TRICKEY Shepard on 5 Jan 1847 *MS* 10 Feb 1847

COBB Polly of Harrisburg NY m DOTON John of Camden on 22 Feb at Harrisburg NY *MS* 13 Mar 1844

COBB Rachael M m GOODING William A both of Bridgton ME on 19 Dec *MS* 22 Jan 1851

COBBETT Mary of Farmington ME m McCLERY David of Strong ME on 27 Jan 1848 *MS* 23 Feb 1848

COFERAN Eliza K m FURNALD Thomas *MS* 29 Nov 1848

COFFIN Albarous F m ANDERSON John on 25 Mar at Limerick ME of Limington ME *MS* 6 Apr 1847

COFFIN Almira Jane of Webster ME m PLUMMER George of Lisbon ME on 4 Apr *MS* 1 May 1850

COFFIN Betsey A m MORRILL Joseph both of Canterbury on 25th ult *MS* 11 Feb 1835

COFFIN Catharine P of Wolfborough NH m STANTON Benjamin A B of Lebanon ME on 27 Sept 1848 *MS* 18 Oct 1848

COFFIN Louisa Jane of Waterboro m BEAN Bradford of Waterboro ME *MFWBR* 6 Feb 1847

COFFIN Nancy M of Newburyport MA m MOODY Amos W on 7 Dec at Alton NH *MS* 10 Mar 1847

COFFIN Phebe of Thorndike ME m HOW Otis of Unity ME *MS* 1 June 1831

COFFIN Sarah P of Topsham ME on 7th inst m PERKINS Samuel of Bath ME *MFWBR* 22 Dec 1849

COFRIN Caroline of Springville NY m ALBRO Emery Deacon formerly of Warsaw NY on 14th Feb at the QM in Boston NY *MS* 31 Mar 1847

COGGSWELL Hannah S of Landaff NH m BOWLES Chandler of Lisbon on 19th ult *MS* 18 May 1832

COLBATH Sarah m PRAY Franklin both of Gardiner *MS* 8 Mar 1848

COLBURN Elzina of Tunbridge VT m DUSTIN Russell H on 25th at Tunbridge VT *MS* 14 Jan 1846

COLBY Abigail Mrs of Newburyport m KNOWLES John Eld of Pittsfield NH on 20 Nov 1849 in Andover *MS* 16 Jan 1850

COLBY Adelaide on 26th ult m LIBBY Frederick W *MFWBR* 8 Sept 1849

COLBY Ann of Denmark ME m RAND Jacob B of Fryeburg ME *MFWBR* 30 Jan 1847

COLBY Belinda of Lancaster m MELVIN Abraham of Weare on 4 June *MS* 27 Nov 1850

COLBY Charlotte m DENNIS Hiram of Moscow ME *MFWBR* 1 May 1847

COLBY Eliza of Manchester NH m RUSSEL Wm of Salem on 20 Sept

COLBY (Continued)
MS 16 Oct 1850

COLBY Emily T of Danville NH m INGALLS John C of Rochester on 16 ult *MS* 1 Mar 1837

COLBY Harriet K Mrs m TAPLIN Caleb of Corinth VT on 28 Feb at Franconia *MS* 28 Apr 1847

COLBY Joe m FOGG Joseph of Raymond at Candia *MS* 8 Dec 1841

COLBY Laura J m OSGOOD John P on 4th inst at Dover NH *MS* 10 Feb 1847

COLBY Lomira L of Lowell MA m PINGREE Henry B of Dracutt MA on 22 May *MS* 2 Nov 1842

COLBY Lydia S m PEABODY Ezekiel at Lynn MA *MS* 31 Jan 1844

COLBY Mary C m SARGENT Edward L on 18 Apr of Canterbury NH *MS* 5 May 1847

COLBY Rache of Portageville NY on 20 Dec m GOODNO W S Eld of Yates QM *MS* 18 Jan 1843

COLBY Zeruah H of Darien NY m SEELEY George W on 2 Sept of Shelby *MS* 17 Sept 1845

COLCORD Abigail of Candia on 19th inst m CHAMBERLAIN Edward B of Dover *MS* 29 May 1839

COLCORD Betsey m COLBY Nehemiah Jr both of Candia on 18 ult *MS* 2 Aug 1837

COLCORD Emily A m BURLEIGH John A Esq of Great Falls NH *MFWBR* 13 Apr 1850

COLE Amanda M m BENSON Cyrus Ervin of Parsonsfield ME on 29 Oct 1848 *MS* 8 Nov 1848

COLE Ansters of Lowell MA m PRESCOTT Asa of Sandwich NH *MS* 29 May 1844

COLE Calista M of Nassau m BABCOCK Varnum M Jr on 11th Sept at Stephenstown NY *MS* 22 Oct 1845

COLE Caroline D of Limerick ME m COBB Andrew of Limington ME on 3 Sept *MS* 21 Oct 1846

COLE Catharine m PIERCE James A on 27 Feb 1848 *MS* 21 June 1848

COLE Eliza D of Biddeford m LOWELL Harrison Hon *MFWBR* 9 Dec 1848

COLE Elmira S m COLE Harrison L both of Lewiston ME on 23 June *MS* 17 Oct 1838

COLE Eveline of Peru Huron Co Ohio m PARKER H James on 18 Nov 1846 at Mansfield Ohio *MS* 20 Jan 1847

COLE Harriet N m STETSON George D of Dorchester MA of Lewiston ME *MS* 9 Apr 1845

COLE Huldah H of Lewiston ME m FOGG George of Greene on 10 Jul at Greene ME *MS* 20 June 1842

COLE Huldah H of Limerick m LIBBY Samuel S on 29 Jan 1843 of Limerick ME *MS* 7 Feb 1844

COLE Julia C of Amsterdam NY m ESTIS Richard of Three Mile Bay on 23 Dec 1847 *MS* 12 Jan 1848

COLE Louisa m LIBBY Simeon on 16 June 1844 at West Poland ME *MS* 9 Apr 1845

COLE Mariana m KENDALL Joseph A *MFWBR* 22 Dec 1849

COLE Martia B of Gilford NH m WARDWELL Charles P S of Lowell MA on 24 June 1849 *MS* 9 Jan 1850

COLE Mary Ann m DAVIS Moses both of Manchester on 24 ult *MS* 1 Apr 1846

COLE Persis S of Stark m ROBERTS John on 6 June at Stark *MS* 7 Jul 1847

COLE Rachel J m HEMENWAY Benjamin both of East Nassau on 18 Apr *MS* 27 May 1846

COLE Sarah of Brownfield ME m MIGHEL Moses of Eaton NH on 19 Feb *MS* 24 Jul 1850

COLE Urana T of Saco ME m PATTERSON John Jr *MFWBR* 15 June 1850

COLEMAN Cynthia P m DONALDSON John on 11 Jan at Stephen-town NY *MS* 19 Mar 1845

COLEMAN Elizabeth m PREBLE Sewell in Bowdoinham ME on Oct 24 *MS* 5 Jan 1842

COLLEY Mary E m ELLIOT Jason both of Lowell on 24 Nov *MS* 15 Dec 1847

COLLEY Salley and COLLEY Chase of Effingham NH divorced *MS* 3 Sept 1828

COLLIER Cyntha H m HILL Benjamin C on 7 Apr at Lowell MA *MS* 27 Apr 1842 & *MS* 19 Oct 1842

COLLINS Amy of Danville m COLLINS John H on 21 Nov at Danville NH? *MS* 20 Jan 1847

COLLINS Elizabeth M m PHILLIPS Gorham *MFWBR* 2 Oct 1847

COLLINS Elmira of Eddington ME m PARLIN William J of Bradley ME *MFWBR* 22 June 1850

COLLINS Esther B of Attleboro MA m YEARNSHAW John Eld of Cranston RI on 4th inst *MS* 27 Oct 1830

COLLINS Harriet m EASTWOOD Nelson on 27 ult *MS* 24 Oct 1838

COLLINS Lovell of Newbury NH m BROWN Amos Eld at Wendell *MS* 17 Feb 1847

COLLINS Lucinda of Gardiner ME m GROVER Benjamin of Hallowell ME on 26 inst *MS* 15 Feb 1837

COLLINS Margaret A of Liberty m FOGG Charles H of Appleton ME on 26 Dec *MS* 15 Jan 1851

·COLLINS Mary Eliza m BURLINGAME Thomas both of No Scituate RI on 4 Feb *MS* 20 Feb 1850

COLLINS Mary of Charlestown MA m EASTBROOK Leonard on 17 Feb *MS* 24 May 1843

COLLINS Miriam m CHAPMAN Charles S both of Manchester on

COLLINS (Continued)

9 Apr *MS* 24 June 1846

COLLINS Miruam F d/o COLLINS Samuel Col m BROWN Stephen MD on 1 Feb at Deerfield *MS* 6 Sept 1843

COLLINS Phebe S m BAKER Asa both of Smithfield *MS* 8 June 1836

COLLINS Rebecah m PRESCOTT Edward P on 30th ult *MS* 18 Nov 1835

COLLINS Rhoda in Guilford m LOCKE Ephraim Dea of Epsom on Feb 15 *MS* 4 May 1842

COLLIS Sybil of Brunswick ME m MERRILL John T of New Gloucester ME *MS* 2 Jan 1839

COLMAN Elvira m PREBLE Dexter *MS* 31 Jan 1838

COLOMY Nancy m ROLLINS Benjamin on 17 May at N Market *MS* 7 June 1843

COLOMY Sarah m HANSON Wm both of Dover on 13 Nov *MS* 19 Nov 1834

COLVIN Cordelia m PECK Alfred both of No Providence on 24 ult at Johnston RI *MS* 18 May 1836

COMERON Jane m GORDON Thomas on 9 Sept *MS* 26 Sept 1849

COMESTOCK Harriet of Arcadia NY at Stephentown NY m GREGORY Samuel O of Lanesboro MA on 24 Aug 1842 *MS* 22 Feb 1843

COMFORTH Isabella m VICKERY Nelson of Unity *MS* 25 Dec 1844

COMSTOCK Eliza E m BUCK Gilman on 18 Feb at Manchester *MS* 24 Feb 1847

CONE/CANE Susan "erroneously printed CANE in our paper of week before last" m HOLMS Elias B at Thornton *MS* 10 May 1843

CONE/CANE Susan on 9 Mar 1843 m HOLMES Elias B *MS* 26 Apr 1843

CONNER Mary Ann m ROLLINS Hiram *MFWBR* 19 June 1847

CONNER Mary Mrs m WHITMAN Isaiah J both of Dover on New Year's eve *MS* 16 Jan 1850

CONNER Nancy of Dover m MELLOON Joseph on 20th inst at Dover NH *MS* 26 Feb 1845

CONNER Sarah A of Gilford NH m LEAVITT Jacob on New Year's day of Gilford NH *MS* 21 Jan 1846

CONVERS Lydia of Barnston on 1 Jan 1839 m BALDWIN Levi *MS* 17 Apr 1839

CONVERS Mary of Barnston m MORRISON John on 16 Aug *MS* 1 Jan 1840

CONVERS Perlina of Matildaville m NEWELL Lucius on 4 May at Matildaville NY *MS* 12 Jul 1843

COOK Adaline m CHATMAN Eliphalet both of Tamworth NH on 19 inst *MS* 12 Apr 1837

COOK C D Miss m SPENCER S J of China *MS* 23 Jan 1839

COOK Catherine of Eckford MI m MEAD Franklin of Clarendon MI on 26 Nov 1848 *MS* 27 Dec 1848

COOK Emeline of Manchester m BELL John of Beverly MA on 4 Mar 1850 *MS* 10 Apr 1850

COOK Fanny of Wilmington MA m HARRINGTON Hiram on 16 May at Wilmington MA *MS* 26 June 1844

COOK Hannah Mrs of Rochester m SMITH Horace of Alfred ME on 3d Oct *MS* 27 Dec 1843

COOK Laura A m BEAN Rufus L both of Rollinsford on 2 inst *MS* 5 Dec 1849

COOK Lyntha Langton m SCATES Norton both of Dover on 2 inst *MS* 12 Dec 1838

COOK Maria of Wheatland Michigan m NOYES Lyman *MS* 4 Dec 1839

COOK Mary H of Wolfboro' m STACKPOLE Charles on 28 Dec at Wolfboro' NH *MS* 11 Feb 1846

COOK Mary of Brookfield m HANSON Rufus Capt of Wakefield on 18 inst *MS* 28 Feb 1838

COOK Meriam of Somersworth m BEACH Augustus of Saco ME on 6 inst *MS* 28 Nov 1838

COOK Rebecca Mrs m DOUGLASS George both of Bowdoin ME *MS* 18 Apr 1838

COOK Sarah C m WEAVER Isaiah G both of Smithfield on 18 ult *MS* 18 Apr 1838

COOK Susan of Dover m BENNETT James M of Moultonboro on 11 Nov *MS* 15 Jan 1851

COOK Susan W m WARREN Samuel both of Dover on 5 inst *MS* 13 June 1849

COOKLIN Hepzibah m COLBY Oliver *MS* 16 Jul 1828

COOLBROTH Elizabeth m COBURN Edwin both of Gorham on 7th ult *MS* 21 Jan 1835

COOLEDGE Julia A m MARTIN Samuel H both of Hillsboro on 19 June *MS* 12 Oct 1836

COOMBS Abigail m STONE Wm 3d both of Augusta ME on 21 Oct 1847 *MS* 17 Nov 1847

COOMBS Eliza m STEARNS Frank both of Bradford on 10 Sept *MS* 16 Oct 1850

COOMBS Margaret H m WEAVER Philip Eld on 26 March at Augusta ME *MS* 24 Jul 1844

COONS C Lavantia of Sand Lake NY m HOLLIS Stephen I of Nassau on 26 Feb 1848 *MS* 12 Apr 1848

COONS Rhoda m BROOKS Archibald on 8 Feb *MS* 22 May 1844

COOPER Dorothy of Wakefield m TITCOMB Joshua of Effingham NH on 15 Mar 1849 *MS* 4 Apr 1849

COOPER Fidelia m EMERSON Luther on 26 Nov of Boothbay ME *MS* 17 Jan 1844

COOPER Mary J m PHILBRICK Alvin B on 24 Feb at Wakefield *MS* 4 Sept 1844

COOPER Mary Jane of Sanford ME m BACHELDOR Lyman P of Holderness NH *MS* 25 Oct 1843

COOPER Sarah F m PIPER George S both of Sanford ME *MS* 28 Jan 1846

COPELAND Celia m LARA Daniel *MFWBR* 28 Jul 1849

COPP Charlotte King Atkinson d/o COPP Amasa Esq of Wakefield m WADLEIGH Elijah on Tuesday evening 9 Oct *MS* 17 Oct 1838

COPP Clara of New Hampton m DANFORTH Phinehas of Warner NH on 13 Nov 1850 *MS* 27 Nov 1850

COPP Eliza J m MARSEY Timothy both of Barrston on 14 Nov *MS* 15 Apr 1840

COPP Eliza J on Nov 14 1839 m MOUSEY Timothy both of Barston*MS* 15 Apr 1840

COPP Harriet of Hopkinton m SEVERANCE Jonathan of Washington ME on 27 Nov *MS* 5 Dec 1849

COPP Jane B m STEPHENS Henry of Hallowell ME *MFWBR* 13 Oct 1849

COPP Mary C of Pittsfield m ALLEN Charles of Gilmanton NH on 13 Nov at Pittsfield *MS* 27 Nov 1844

COPP Mary J m FELLOWS David F both of New Hampton on 19 Oct 1849 *MS* 18 Apr 1849

COPP Mary S of Manchester m BEBEE Geo W of New York City on 19 May *MS* 30 May 1849

COPP Mary W d/o COPP Amasa Esq of Wakefield TREDICK John on 23 inst Tuesday evening *MS* 7 Feb 1838

COPP Susan G m STEARNS Warren both of Manchester on 13 Sept 1848 *MS* 27 Sept 1848

CORBON Calesta A m EMERY Alpheus S both of Manchester on 14 Feb 1848 *MS* 23 Feb 1848

CORLIS Hannah G m HUREN Harmon both of So Weare on 18 Jul 1847 *MS* 15 Sept 1847

CORLIS Relief m MARINOR William on 21 Sept at Brunswick ME *MS* 13 Jan 1847

CORNER Caroline M m DROWN Eliphalet G on 22 May of Lowell *MS* 19 Oct 1842

CORNFORTH Elvira M m BENSON Geo B both of Waterville ME on 14 Aug *MS* 29 Aug 1849

CORNISH Harriet M m BUKER Daniel of Richmond *MS* 22 May 1844

CORNISH Lucinda of Lisbon m STEEL John S of Township Letter B on 6 Oct *MS* 28 Dec 1836

CORNOR Catharine at Holderness m GORDON William both of New Hampton *MS* 18 Mar 1840

CORSON Delia Mrs m WATERHOUSE Daniel both of Barrington on 6 Sept *MS* 18 Sept 1850

CORSON Frances D at Bangor ME m BRACKETT William H *MS* 13 Sept 1843

CORSON Hannah of Waterville ME m COMFORTH Oliver *MS* 25 Dec 1844

CORSON Harriet C of Dover NH m ASPINWALL Ellis on 8th inst at Dover NH *MS* 11 Mar 1846

CORSON Margaret of New Durham NH m HOYT William on 15 Sept 1844 of Tuftonboro' *MS* 19 Feb 1845

CORSON Mary A H m JENNESS George both of New Market on 11th inst *MS* 17 Dec 1834

CORSON Mary E of Dover on Wednesday last at Medbury m SIMPSON Charles H B of Roxbury MA *MS* 15 Nov 1843

CORSON Mary of Lebanon ME m BLAISDELL Samuel of Gilford on 27 Sept *MS* 7 Oct 1846

CORSON Mary of Lebanon ME m DAVIS John W of Somersworth NH on 19 Mar 1848 *MS* 29 Mar 1848

COTE Rebecca P of Allenston m MITCHELL Joseph B on 2 Oct of Boston MA at Manchester NH *MS* 10 Oct 1844

COTTLE Maria H of Brookfield m PIKE Robert W L of Farmington NH 31 Jan 1849 *MS* 18 Apr 1849

COTTLE Rhoda of Waterville m BOWMAN David 3d of Sidney ME *MS* 30 Nov 1842

COTTLE Rhua L of Tisbury MA m CHASE Charles G of Dover NH on 4 Aug 1843 *MS* 30 Aug 1843

COTTON Betsey T m LEIGHTON Jethro N both of Gilmanton on 14 May 1848 *MS* 21 June 1848

COTTON Hannah m SINCLAIR Noah both of Meredith on 7 inst in Meredith *MS* 17 May 1837

COTTON Margaret E of Lee formerly of Yarmouth ME m PALMER John G of Lee on 26 inst Fri afternoon *MS* 1 May 1850

COTTON Mary Jane of Moultonborough m AMBROSE Oliver L of Sandwich on 25 Nov 1847 *MS* 1 Dec 1847

COTTON Nancy m PAGE Ira E both of Gilmanton on 30 Mar *MS* 1 May 1844

COTTON Nancy M of Moultonboro' m HAILEY Samuel R of Tuftonboro' NH *MS* 11 Sept 1844

COTTON Sarah m DINSMORE Charles W both of Sandown on 5 inst *MS* 11 Dec 1850

COUCH Hannah m FLANDERS True both of Warner on 20 Dec 1837 *MS* 10 Jan 1838

COUILLARD Adeline m HASKELL Isaac P on 3 Dec both of Bangor ME *MS* 13 Jan 1847

COUILLARD Susan J m COUILLARD David both of Corinna ME on 21 Dec 1834 *MS* 11 Mar 1835

COULLARD Lucy m NEALLEY Joseph T on 28 Nov of Monroe *MS* 18 Dec 1844

COURIER Caroline m BRADLEY Isaac of Haverhill MA on Thanksgiving Even *MS* 12 Dec 1838

COURTENAY Artemisea M m BROWN Philo at Milan IA *MS* 5 June 1844

COUSENS Sarah of Hollis ME m DOW Abraham *MS* 14 June 1843

COWELL Maria A m RANKIN Jonathan Jr *MFWBR* 22 Dec 1849

COWELL Maria A m RANKINS Jonathan Jr both of Lebanon on 13 Dec *MS* 2 Jan 1850

COWELL Marianne m LORD Noah on 6 June at Lebanon ME *MS* 23 June 1847

COWELL Sally W of Lebanon m MILLS John of Rochester on 18 inst *MS* 31 Oct 1849 & *MFWBR* 3 Nov 1849

COWEN Dolly Mrs of Lewiston ME m WOODARD Joseph on 18 Jan at Lewiston Falls ME *MS* 27 Jan 1847

COX Eliza Ann of Holderness on 20 Dec m MUDGET Levi of New Hampton *MS* 11 Jan 1843

COX Elizabeth at Lowell m GILE Amos W D *MS* 18 Mar 1840

COX Frances B m THOMPSON Nathaniel S both of Holderness NH on 2 Jul 1848 in Holderness NH *MS* 21 Mar 1849

COX Harriet A of Brunswick m ROBINSON Benjamin of East Bridgewater ME *MS* 3 Oct 1849

COX Latatia m CURRIER John P both of Manchester on 17 May *MS* 27 May 1846

COX Lucinda P m MORSE Rufus W on 27 Aug 1849 *MS* 16 Jan 1850

COX Sabrina S m SANBORN William D on 13 Jul 1847 *MS* 8 Sept 1847

COX Sarah J of Brunswick m HAMMOND John S of Boston on 1 Sept *MS* 13 Nov 1850

COX Sophronia of Hatley m MAGOON Gilford of Stanstead LC on 2 Jan *MS* 22 Mar 1837

CRABB Mary E of Portland m SMITH Anthony *MFWBR* 14 Apr 1849

CRAGA Melissa E of Spring Prairie Wis m SEXTON James of Rochester Racine Co Wis on 20 June 1848 *MS* 23 Aug 1848

CRAIG Esther G m FARNHAM Ebenezer H both of Augusta on Thanksgiving evening *MS* 16 Dec 1835

CRAIGH Lorinda m GODDARF Joseph both of Switzerland Co Iowa on 15 Sept *MS* 2 Oct 1850

CRAM Abigail m BROWN Levi Capt at Raymond *MS* 28 Sept 1842

CRAM Judith H of Deerfield m SMITH Charles F of Raymond *MS* 25 Sept 1844

CRAM Rosannah S of Meredith NH m WORTHING Charles J of Charlestown MA *MS* 11 Sept 1839

CRAM Sarah m SMITH Ebenezer H both of Meredith on 20 Sept *MS* 17 Oct 1838 & Sarah of Center Harbor m SMITH Ebenezer U of Meredith *MS* 5 Dec 1838

CRANDE Fanny W m GODFREY Alfred on 11 inst *MS* 1 May 1844

CRAWFORD Huldah of Portland ME on 8th inst m HARMON William

CRAWFORD (Continued)
MS 28 June 1843

CRAWFORD Sarah m HARMON Aaron F *MFWBR* 28 Jul 1849

CRESSEY Harriet H of Standish m CLAY Jonathan of Buxton on 2 June *MS* 28 Aug 1850

CRIMBALL Mary of Stratham on 27th ult m LEAVITT Thomas Deacon *MS* 5 June 1839

CRIMBELL Meriam of Stratham m FOLSOM Dudley of Sanbornton NH *MS* 28 Jan 1846

CRITCHET Arvilla m LOVEJOY Wesley *MS* 10 Sept 1834

CRITCHET Mary Jane m CAVERLY Ephraim H both of Barrington*MS* 22 Apr 1840

CROCKER Dolly of Prospect m POLAND ELIOT formerly of Bristol *MS* 29 Nov 1827

CROCKER Huldah of Freedom NY m CLEAVELAND Jonathan on 10 Jan at Freedom NY *MS* 21 Feb 1844

CROCKER Jane m DOW Orchard *MS* 27 Jan 1830

CROCKET Mary Ann m HOMES John H both of Buxton on 17 Jan 1848 in West Buxton ME *MS* 15 Mar 1848

CROCKETT Frances C of Deer Isle m LANCESTER David Eld of Corinna ME on 31 Oct at Brunswick ME *MS* 18 Mar 1846

CROCKETT Mary Ann of Meredith NH m MALLARD Asa of Meredith NH *MS* 8 Dec 1841

CROCKETT Sarah of Meredith m JOHNSON John P of Concord on 27 Dec *MS* 25 Jan 1843

CROCKETT Tryphena m SHAW Curtis *MFWBR* 16 June 1849

CROMWELL Hannah A m BATES Gilead both of Lowell on 2 Nov 1847 *MS* 17 Nov 1847

CROMWELL Martha S of Dexter ME m PAGE William D C of Newburyport MA *MFWBR* 21 Jan 1849

CROOK Amanda L of Washington VT on 18th ult m GOUGH Moses M *MS* 15 May 1839

CROOK Roxana B m HAM Clement both of Somersworth on 18 inst *MS* 28 June 1848

CROOK Susan m BENCH Frederick both of Great Falls on Thursday last *MS* 4 Oct 1837

CROOKER Abigail m DREW Orvel both of Bafford on 27 Feb 1844 *MS* 1 May 1844

CROOKS Hester Ann m BRAINARD David W both of Barnston LC on 27 Nov 1836 *MS* 11 Jan 1837

CROSBEE Cornelia B m HUBBARD George I on 3 Oct at Grafton MA *MS* 18 Oct 1843

CROSBY Abigail S of Haverhill MA m ROBINSON Joseph of Stratham NH on 5 June 1848 *MS* 12 Jul 1848

CROSBY Miriam R of Swanville ME m SMART Henry B of Plymouth on 17 Oct 1847 *MS* 17 Nov 1847

CROSBY Priscilla M of Grafton MA m FAIRBANKS George W on 15 Aug *MS* 13 Sept 1843

CROSBY Rosetta m COMFORTH Robert 2d of Unity ME *MS* 25 Dec 1844

CROSBY Sabrey m MARBLE John Jr on 23 Aug of Sutton *MS* 13 Sept 1843

CROSS Aphia D d/o CROSS J Eld m CHANDLE Benjamin Jr of Newbury NH *MS* 26 Feb 1851

CROSS Betsey B of Northfield NH m ROBEY William of Manchester on 30 Sept *MS* 14 Oct 1846

CROSS Eliza Ann d/o CROSS Joseph Esq m HAYES John *MS* 1 June 1836

CROSS Maranda m STRAW Andrew W *MS* 4 Apr 1849

CROSS Marietta Mrs m MARTIN Jeremiah both of Belmont *MS* 31 May 1848

CROSS Martha M m MEADER George B m at Lowell MA *MS* 27 Apr 1836

CROSS Sophia S m LOCKE Thomas E both of Great Falls NH on 19 June *MS* 10 Jul 1850

CROSS Statira of Northfield NH m COLLINS Frederick of Goffstown on 30 Sept *MS* 14 Oct 1846

CROSS Tammy m MAXWELL Charles Dea both of Danville on 3d ult . *MS* 4 May 1836

CROSSMAN Clarissa M of Smithfield RI m DUPEE Job of Medway MA on 17 inst *MS* 27 Jan 1836

CROUCH Harriet L of Smithfield m STRAFFORD John B on 2nd inst *MS* 19 Nov 1834

CROWELL Emma Ann m STRONG Richard W on 3 Apr at Boston *MS* 16 Apr 1845

CROWELL Sarah W of Bangor ME m RIDLEY David on 26 Dec at Bangor ME *MS* 20 Jan 1847

CRUMB Mary Ann m YORK William D of Brookfield NY on 28 Sept *MS* 15 Oct 1845

CRUMB Mary on 4 Nov m ADAMS Levi H on Plainfield NY *MS* 17 Feb 1847

CUMMINGS Catharine S of Cape Elizabeth m LIBBY TAPPAN on 5 June at Cape Elizabeth *MS* 17 Jul 1844

CUMMINGS Charlotte A m PERKINS Nathaniel *MS* 22 May 1839

CUMMINGS Clarissa H of Venango m STICKNEY W Eld *MS* 26 Sept 1838

CUMMINGS Cynthia m ALLEN Lemuel both of Augusta *MS* 24 Jan 1838

CUMMINGS Lucy M d/o CUMMINGS Wm Dea late of Cape Elizabeth m SHANNON Nathaniel MD of Sandwich NH *MS* 27 June 1849

CUMMINGS Mary H d/o CUMMINGS Daniel of Portland ME m PLUMMER Daniel *MFWBR* 30 Oct 1847

CUMMINGS Nancy of Boston MA on 5 Apr 1843 m GARLAND Alexis Esq of Bartlett NH *MS* 19 Apr 1843

CUMMINGS Susan J of Manchester NH on 3 Apr m BAKER Stephen C of Holderness NH *MS* 19 Apr 1843

CUNNINGHAM Abigail M m MARRINER John both of Gardiner ME on 26 Dec 1847 *MS* 2 Feb 1848

CUNNINGHAM Elizabeth m CRAWFORD John *MS* 13 June 1849

CUNNINGHAM Elizabeth m CUNNINGHAM Charles R 2d on 5 Nov at Edgecomb ME *MS* 29 Nov 1843

CUNTON Susan A of Boothbay m WILLIAMSON Isaac G of Wiscasset ME *MS* 26 Mar 1851

CURREY Adeline m ORRELL Samuel R both of Dover on Mon last *MS* 3 Sept 1834

CURRIER Abigail of Vershire VT m GORDON Alonzo of Alexander NH on 20 June at Bristol NH *MS* 20 June 1842

CURRIER Charity A m PALFREY John L both of Hopkinton on 31 May *MS* 22 June 1836

CURRIER Chastina W of Enfield m FOGG Jeremiah of Deerfield NH on 21 May *MS* 19 June 1850

CURRIER Dolly m LANGLEY Samuel *RI* Jan 1821 p 15

CURRIER Frances M of Canaan m CUNNINGHAM John B of Manchester *MS* 27 Sept 1848

CURRIER Hannah B m ALEXANDER Nehemiah C both of Farmington *MS* 13 Dec 1837

CURRIER Hannah of Kennebunkport ME on 31st ult m HILL Thomas of Saco ME *MFWBR* 11 Jan 1851

CURRIER Harriet of Lowell m EMERSON Moses S of Georgetown *MS* 26 Nov 1845

CURRIER Huldah B m HOLMES Daniel G both of Lowell MA correction *MS* 8 June 1836

CURRIER Lois M m HOPE Royal M on 28 Sept at Manchester *MS* 10 Oct 1844

CURRIER Lucretia W of Lowell MA m GILBERT Nathaniel of Lydon VT *MS* 29 May 1844

CURRIER Mary m SEVERANCE Enoch Q on 25 June at Lowell MA *MS* 16 Aug 1843

CURRIER Mary A m KIMBALL Baxter R on 7 March at Manchester NH *MS* 14 Apr 1847

CURRIER Nancy H m GRAVES William both of Manchester on 13 inst *MS* 29 Apr 1846

CURRIER Rachel M m GARDNER Augustus N both of Stephentown NY on 20 Jan 1848 *MS* 12 Apr 1848

CURRIER Rebecca m HARRINGTON Moses B both of Concord on 14 inst 1849 *MS* 21 Mar 1849

CURRIER Ruth of Canterbury m STONE Royal of Andover NH on 7 Apr *MS* 15 Apr 1840

CURRIER Sally L m FOSS Ebenezer both of Meredith *MS* 27 Feb 1834

CURTIS Catharine of Whitefield m TARR Benjamin of Hallowell *MS* 10 Oct 1833

CURTIS Corriscinda of Bath m FRENCH Edward on 24 Oct at Bath ME *MS* 7 Dec 1842

CURTIS Cynthia T of Warsaw NY m COFFIN Lorenzo S of Wolfboro NH on 24 Aug 1848 *MS* 27 Dec 1848

CURTIS Emeline E of Bath m ALBEE Wilmot of Alna *MFWBR* 8 Sept 1849

CURTIS Hannah L of Richmond ME m LAWRENCE Elias H of Gardiner ME on 16 Nov 1848 *MS* 27 Dec 1848

CURTIS Harriet E m CROCKETT William E on 6 Apr at FW Baptist meeting house *MS* 16 Apr 1845

CURTIS Julia Ann m HAYNES Jas on 4 Nov *MS* 17 Dec 1845

CURTIS Lucy of Stanstead m HILL Archeaus W on 25 Apr *MS* 1 Jan 1840

CURTIS Mary L m LANE Thomas R Capt on 21 Oct at Freeport ME *MS* 17 Dec 1845

CURTIS Mary M m PRESCOTT Daniel K of New Hampton NH on 26 Nov at Thetford VT *MS* 10 Mar 1847 & *MS* 6 Jan 1847

CURTIS Mary of Monroe m CLEMENTS Henry on 8 Dec at Monroe *MS* 25 Jan 1843

CURTIS Rebecca m PENNY Hiram both of Minot ME *MS* 20 Apr 1831

CURTIS Sarah P m WORKS William both of Brunswick ME *MS* 8 Mar 1848

CURTIS Sophia of Bowdoinham m KINCAID Peter of Brunswick ME *MS* 13 Oct 1830

CURTIS Welthy M m CURTIS David Jr both of Monroe ME on 9 Dec *MS* 19 Dec 1849

CURTIS Zelamy B of Richmond ME m SAWYER Alvin of Gardiner ME on 23 Sept 1848 *MS* 22 Nov 1848

CUSHING Mrs of Rutland Wis m PRATT Mr of Oregon on New Year's Day *MS* 31 Jan 1849

CUSHING Priscilla of Freedom m DEMERITT Isaac of Eaton on 4 Oct *MS* 11 Nov 1846

CUSHING Sally Ann m HUTCHINS Solomon both of Wakefield on 25 Oct *MS* 21 Nov 1838

CUSHING Sarah of Hopkinton m EASTMAN Samuel of Boscawen NH *MS* 4 Apr 1838

CUSHMAN Caroline F d/o CUSHMAN Samuel Hon m ELLIS Lucius A *MFWBR* 29 Mar 1851

CUSHMAN Harriet O of New Gloucester ME m PENDEXTER Daniel E on 29 Oct at New Gloucester ME of Bartlett NH *MS* 25 Nov 1846

CUTLER Sarah of Bangor ME m COBURN Isaiah of Greene ME *MFWBR* 2 Feb 1850

CUTTER Emeline of Sebec ME m DELAITTUE George W on 13 Apr at Sebec ME *MS* 7 May 1845

CUTTER Mary E m COBB Geo W *MFWBR* 11 May 1850

CUTTER Mary Rosaline of Livermore m TAYLOR Samuel of Natick MA on 31 Oct 1847 *MS* 1 Dec 1847

CUTTS Maria S of South Berwick on 8th inst m WATSON Josiah of New Market *MS* 14 Aug 1839

DABELL Sarah Ann of Stephentown NY m WHEELER James F of Hancock MA on 15 Feb *MS* 13 Mar 1850

DABOIS Augusta m ELBERT Charles C both of Concord NH on 10 Dec 1847 *MS* 17 Jan 1849

DABOLL Diadama of Stephentown m CHITTENDEN William on 24 Dec at Stephentown *MS* 6 Jan 1847

DAHEG Patience E of Smithfield m BURNAB Gideon of Providence RI on 12 Apr *MS* 21 June 1848

DAKIN Rebecca of Weston (ME) on 15 May m DYER Watson of Jackson Brook (ME) *MS* 5 Jul 1843

DALE Clarissa of Richmond ME m MEADER Gideon of Wales ME on 11 Dec *MS* 28 Dec 1836

DALRYMPLE Seviah F m NEWTON Silas Jr both of Roscoe Winnebago Co IL *MS* 18 Oct 1848

DALTON Sarah A of Gilmanton NH m CILLEY B D of Kingston NH *MFWBR* 6 Feb 1847

DALY Adeline m WINCH William *MS* 6 June 1838

DAM Eliza W of Shapleigh m LOWELL Enoch of Newfield *MS* 13 Apr 1832

DAME Charlotte J m HACKETT George both of Jackson NH on 13 Aug 1848 *MS* 30 Aug 1848

DAME Sally of Gilford m SANBORN William H *MS* 15 May 1839

DAME Sarah A of Dover m DEARBORN Thomas I on 20 Sept of Boston *MS* 1 Oct 1845

DAME Sophronia of Durham m BROWN Isaac B at New Market NH *MS* 8 June 1842

DAMMAN Clarinda C of Belgrade m PERKINS Seth W Eld of Gardiner *MS* 26 June 1839

DAMMON Zeruiah of Sebca m GILMAN Jonathan of Sangerville ME on 17 Sept *MS* 11 Oct 1837

DANA Frances A of New Hampton m SHEPARD Joseph W on 30 Nov 1843 at New Hampton *MS* 26 June 1844

DANA Maria A d/o DANA Hon Judge of Fryeburg m HOWARD Joseph Esq of Limerick ME *MS* 28 Dec 1826

DANA Mary J of New Hampton m SMYTH Arthur L on 2 June of Holderness *MS* 26 June 1844

DANFORTH Clara A m HAYES Charles both of New Durham NH on 3 Feb 1850 *MS* 13 Feb 1850

DANFORTH Eliza A of Lowell MA m ROBINSON Prescott of Andover MA on 12 Dec at Lowell MA *MS* 6 Jan 1847

DANFORTH Hannah of Somerville m HOLMES Isaac of Dedham *MS* 24 May 1843

DANFORTH Mary of Somersworth on 22 Dec m BERRY George Jr of Strafford *MS* 11 Jan 1843

DANFORTH Roxanna m SARLES Almon of Stanstead LC on 8 Feb *MS* 20 Sept 1837

DANIEL Caroline A of Waterbury m BARRETT Benjamin on 16 Sept at Waterbury VT *MS* 2 Oct 1844

DANIELS Abagail d/o DANIELS Joseph Esq of Strafford m SWAN Joel Esq on 2 inst *MS* 18 Mar 1840

DANIELS Abigail d/o DANIELS Joseph Esq m SWAN Joel Esq both of Strafford on 2nd inst *MS* 18 Mar 1840

DANIELS Abigail of Boston m TURNER Daniel of Roxbury MA on 6 Apr at Roxbury *MS* 7 May 1845

DANIELS Diadamy E M C of Underhill m AUSTIN Isaac N of Westford on 5 Feb *MS* 25 Mar 1846

DANIELS Dorothy B m CHANNEL Abraham F J both of Durham on 26 May *MS* 8 June 1836

DANIELS Margaret M of Canaan ME m BINGHAM John on 9 Aug at Canaan ME *MS* 22 Oct 1845

DANIELS Maria G of Dover m WINKLEY Darius of Barrington on 20 Oct *MS* 11 Nov 1846

DANIELS Mary E m CHURCHILL Geo H (formerly of Brookfield) both of Durham on 10 inst *MS* 30 May 1849

DANIELS Sarah Jane of Dover m AMES Charles formerly of Geauga Seminary Ohio on 28 ult *MS* 3 Apr 1850

DARLING Cyntha m WEBSTER Alfred both of Woodstock NH on 5 Oct 1848 *MS* 8 Nov 1848

DARLING Mary J on 10 Jan at Manchester Iowa Territory m HUNTER Manly *MS* 27 Feb 1839

DARLING Sarah m NORTHRUP Bushrod on 1 June at Pierpont NY *MS* 12 Jul 1843

DAVENPORT Fanny M m CHANDLER George both of Ellington NY on 11 Oct *MS* 6 Nov 1850

DAVENPORT Sylvia L m PRESCOTT Alva on 6th ult *MS* 23 Nov 1832

DAVERSON Arthusu T m CLEAVELAND Simeon both of Ware on 23 Feb *MS* 6 Apr 1836

DAVIS Abigail D of Lee m TOWLE John F Esq on 3 Feb at Lee *MS* 4 Mar 1846

DAVIS Abigail I of Nottingham m DEARBORN George P of Jackson on 19 Feb *MS* 4 Mar 1846

DAVIS Almira of Walworth m BULLOCK Lowell on 20 June 1847 at Jericho VT *MS* 21 Jul 1847

DAVIS Arabel A m GERMAN Read both of Manchester *MS* 1 Apr

DAVIS (Continued)
1846

DAVIS Augusta H m BEARDSLEY Smith H on 15 June at Nottingham *MS* 2 Jul 1845

DAVIS Betsey of Epsom NH m BAILEY Paul on 25 Nov at Epsom NH "his 3rd wife her 4th husband" *MS* 22 Dec 1841

DAVIS Caroline at Alton NH m GILMAN Lewis on 14 Jan *MS* 3 Mar 1847

DAVIS Celia A of Peru ME on 21 Apr m HUTCHINSON Joseph of Hebron *MS* 15 May 1839

DAVIS Clara A m COOK Edward H on Christmas eve at Charlestown MA *MS* 17 Feb 1847

DAVIS Desire of Buxton m THORN William of Standish on 13th inst *MS* 26 Nov 1828

DAVIS Eliza m RICE Algernon S D G *MS* 25 Dec 1844

DAVIS Elizabeth of Centre Harbor m BARTLETT James *MS* 5 June 1839

DAVIS Emeline M of Woburn MA d/o DAVIS Joseph Esq of Limington ME m TYLER Joseph of Woburn MA on 16 Mar at Wilmington MA *MS* 6 Apr 1842

DAVIS Emeline of Jericho m COOK Hiram H of Westford on 1 Jan *MS* 29 Jan 1851

DAVIS Emily of Standish ME m HOOPER John of Waterboro ME *MFWBR* 21 Apr 1849

DAVIS Hannah B m MILLS Elihu on 30 June *MS* 18 Dec 1844

DAVIS Hannah L of Gilford on 30 Jan m THING Jeremiah B *MS* 13/27 Feb 1839

DAVIS Hannah of Epsom NH m DOWST Henry of Allenstown on 2 May at Epsom NH *MS* 12 May 1847

DAVIS Harriet m MORGAN Josiah S both of Sutton on 24 Nov 1847 *MS* 2 Feb 1848

DAVIS Harriet E m SARGENT Jaman both of Parsonsfield ME on 16 Nov 1848 *MS* 29 Nov 1848

DAVIS Julia A F m WEBSTER Nathaniel D at Kingston NH on 25 Nov *MS* 15 Dec 1841

DAVIS Julia Ann of Somersworth NH m HALE Simeon of Parsonsfield *MS* 20 Feb 1839

DAVIS Laura Ann of Wilmington m CALEF John L on 15th inst at Wilmington *MS* 25 Oct 1843

DAVIS Lovina of Jericho VT m ATWOOD Mark Eld of Northwood NH on 19 Jan *MS* 28 Jan 1846

DAVIS Lucy m CHAMBERS Wm H both of Chester ME *MS* 8 Nov 1848

DAVIS Mahala m GRIFFIN John H both of Manchester on 31 May *MS* 17 June 1846

DAVIS Maria Jane m WATSON William both of Pittsfield on 23 Jul

DAVIS (Continued)

MS 6 Sept 1837

DAVIS Martha B of Pittsfield NH m OSGOOD John H of Gilmanton on 22 Aug at Pittsfield NH *MS* 30 Aug 1843

DAVIS Martha Jane sister of Davis J B Eld of Jackson m RAYMON-DY Samuel D on 17 Oct *MS* 6 Nov 1850

DAVIS Martha of Fayette m HUTCHINSON James H of Dixfield on 24th ult *MS* 30 Mar 1831

DAVIS Mary Ann of Dover NH m WEGWOOD Samuel C of Effingham NH on 14th inst at Dover NH *MS* 18 Feb 1846

DAVIS Mary widow m WENTWORTH David Dea both of Dover on 7 Aug *MS* 22 Aug 1838

DAVIS Melissa A of New Market NH? m KENISTON Freeman of Clappville MA on 8th inst *MS* 18 Jan 1843

DAVIS Naomi m HOVEY Thomas C on 9 inst *MS* 17 Jul 1850

DAVIS Nancy of Stanstead LC m LIBBY Andrew of Broom on 21 Mar *MS* 13 Apr 1842

DAVIS Olive of Dover m COUSINS Samuel on 24 Oct at Dover NH *MS* 30 Oct 1844

DAVIS Olive S m GRAY Thomas of Barnstead on at Dover NH *MS* 18 Jul 1833

DAVIS Pamelia m TROW Francis S both of Sunippe NH? on 27 Feb *MS* 12 Mar 1851

DAVIS Phebe C m THOMPSON Samuel at Searsmont ME *MS* 17 Mar 1847

DAVIS Polly Jane of Gilford m FROHOCK Jacob of Gilford NH *MS* 14 Apr 1847

DAVIS Rebeccah m NEWHOLD Joshua on 27 May *MS* 3 Aug 1832

DAVIS Rhoda O m WEEKS William Capt on 21 Sept at Gilford *MS* 2 Nov 1842

DAVIS Rosanna on 4th inst m JEPSON Leonard *MFWBR* 24 Feb 1849

DAVIS S A m WALDO H H both of Edneston NY on 5 Mar *MS* 2 Apr 1851

DAVIS Sabria G m BURNHAM Asa A both of Reading VT on 14 Feb *MS* 4 Mar 1840

DAVIS Sabrina of Hinesburgh VT m SHEDD Azetes of Bolton NY on 12 Sept *MS* 6 Nov 1850

DAVIS Sally m COLE Samuel Jr of Shapleigh ME *MS* 19 Nov 1828

DAVIS Sally m STEVENS Lawrence at Raymond *MS* 8 Dec 1841

DAVIS Sally W m BRACKETT Timothy both of Limington ME on 20 Nov *MS* 15 Jan 1840

DAVIS Sarah Ann of Epping NH m SHERBURN Wm B of Northwood on Monday 14th ult *MS* 1 Oct 1834

DAVIS Sarah m TOLBUT Joshua both of Portsmouth NH on 10 ult *MS* 10 Oct 1838

DAVIS Sarah J m PHILLIPS Metaphor C both of Biddeford ME on 8 June *MS* 26 Jul 1848

DAVIS Sarah L m BEAN Rufus B both of Effingham NH on 2 Apr *MS* 22 Apr 1846

DAVIS Sarah of New Durham NH m MITCHELL Thomas of Newfield ME *MS* 15 Nov 1843

DAVIS Sophronia of Buxton m BICKFORD James of Saco ME on 13 inst *MS* 29 Mar 1848

DAVIS Susan E sister of Eld J B DAVIS of Providence RI m POTTER L B of Spring Arbor Mich on 11 inst *MS* 31 Oct 1849

DAVIS Susan M of Limington m LOW James of Sacarappa/Westbrook on 10 May *MFWBR* 16 June 1849 & *MS* 30 May 1849

DAVIS Tryphena m HALL Asa on 12th inst on the Sabbath eve *MS* 23 Jan 1834

DAVIS Weltha P of Lowell MA m KENNNEY Joshua *MS* 26 Feb 1845

DAVISON Evelina of Starksboro VT m SMITH Daniel on 9 June at Starksboro' VT *MS* 21 Sept 1842

DAWLING Caroline m TWOMBLY George G both of Dover on 16 inst *MS* 22 May 1850

DAWS Olive of Richmond ME m TOOTHAKER William H on 10 May at Bowdoin ME *MS* 16 June 1847

DAY Catherine of Brownfield ME m HARTFORD Edmunds on 18 Aug at Hiram ME *MS* 31 Aug 1842

DAY Eliza m STEVENS Elbridge G both of Lowell on 21 Oct *MS* 7 Nov 1838

DAY Isabel B of Biddeford on 30th ult m FIELD Edwain of Durham *MFWBR* 11 Jan 1851

DAY Jane d/o DAY Ebenezer of Limerick ME m MOULTON George of Bath on Thurs last *MS* 24 Nov 1830

DAY Louiza d/o DAY Abner Deacon of Ipswich m STONE Asa P formerly of Newfield ME on 27 ult *MS* 6 June 1838

DAY Mary J of Cumberland m STOWELL Luther J of Gray ME *MFWBR* 12 May 1849

DAY Mercy d/o DAY Thomas of Newfield m HEAD William *MS* 2 Jul 1828

DAY Rachel of Cornish m RANDAL James of Limerick ME *MS* 26 Nov 1828

DAY Relief H on 21 May m HALL William H *MS* 19 Jul 1843

DAY Ruth m COLBY Lucius both of Lowell on 6 Apr 1848 *MS* 26 Apr 1848

DAY Sally of Cornish m WATSON David Jr of Limerick ME on 29th ult *MS* 10 May 1827

DAY Sarah I m COLE Bradford W both of Brownfield on 4 Jul *MS* 24 Jul 1850

DAY Susan on 21 May m CHOAT George W both of Hallowell *MS* 19 Jul 1843

DEAN Louisa A m CARR Erastus W both of Stephentown NY on 9 Feb *MS* 13 Mar 1850

DEAN Lucy of Sutton VT on 22 Nov m GRAY Joshua of Sheffield *MS* 11 Jan 1843

DEARBON Lushia of Peeling m MARSTIN James of Lunenburg VT on 29 ult *MS* 10 May 1837

DEARBORN Almira P m COOK Joseph S both of Danville on 16 Sept *MS* 23 Sept 1846

DEARBORN Ann of Lowell MA m PHILBRICK Christopher on 19 Oct *MS* 6 Jan 1847

DEARBORN Betsey m FOSS Samuel on Thurs last week *MS* 9 Dec 1831

DEARBORN Dorothy Ann of Hampton m BATCHELDER Emery Capt on 18 inst *MS* 26 Dec 1838

DEARBORN Dorothy of Plymouth m SANBORN B L Mr *MS* 23 Sept 1846

DEARBORN Elizabeth m YOUNG Joseph at Raymond *MS* 8 Dec 1841

DEARBORN Harriet of Deerfield NH m COLBY Benjamin merchant of Dover NH on 12 inst *MS* 23 Sept 1835

DEARBORN Jane of Meredith Bridge on 31 Jul m KELLEY Charles R *MS* 4 Sept 1839

DEARBORN Josephine A B m MARSTON David Col on 8 June at Hampton *MS* 16 Jul 1845

DEARBORN Julia Ann of Portsmouth m WEBSTER Davidson merchant of Dover *MS* 7 Jan 1835

DEARBORN Martha A m PAGE John A both of Manchester on 1 Jan *MS* 26 Mar 1851

DEARBORN Martha m WILLEY Aziah both of Rollinsford on 23 Nov *MS* 4 Dec 1850

DEARBORN Mary m DICKSON Wm D last week *MS* 9 Dec 1831

DEARBORN Olive of Jackson NH m DAVIS David of Nottingham NH on 26 Feb 1846 at Jackson NH *MS* 11 Mar 1846

DEARBORN Sarah m LANGLEY William of Newfield in Wakefield *MS* 18 June 1828

DEARBORN Sarah Ann on 7 Dec m REYNOLDS Samuel R of Candia on 7 Dec at Raymond *MS* 7 Jan 1846

DEARBORN Sarah B m WEYMOUTH J S on 5 Feb at Gilmanton *MS* 21 June 1843

DEARBORN Sarah m NASON Storer both of Lowell *MS* 21 Nov 1838

DEARBORN Sarah D m DOW Jacob at Raymond *MS* 11 Jan 1843

DEARING Mary m WOODMAN Joseph on 6 inst at Kittery ME *MS* 14 Dec 1836

DECATER Margaret A m SHOREY Henry L *MFWBR* 24 Mar 1849

DECKER Ann m TRY John Capt on 3d inst at Portland ME *MS* 20 Dec 1843

DECKER Eunice of Gorham m SMITH Ira of Standish ME on 1st ult *MS* 7 Jan 1829

DEERING Mary of Edgecomb m CLENSLEY William on 8 Nov at Edgecomb ME *MS* 7 Dec 1842

DELANA Margaret m WALKER Henry both of Woolwich ME on 29 ult *MS* 20 June 1838

DELAND Amanda M of Dover NH m LEIGHTON James L *MS* 13 Mar 1839

DELAND Mary Ann of Hallowell m ANTHONY George W at Hallowell ME *MS* 11 Mar 1846

DELAND Sarah of Dover m DELAND William of Wolfboro NH on 27 inst *MS* 8 Mar 1837

DELANO Sophronia of Sidney m BARTLETT Ambrose H Capt of Waterville on 15 inst at Augusta ME *MS* 28 Dec 1836

DELLAWARE Amanda M of Lowell m HARVEY William *MS* 7 Aug 1839

DEMERIFT Mary Jane of Durham m BERRY Ivory F on 7th inst at Newmarket *MS* 18 Jan 1843

DEMERIT Betsey A m LEAVITT Simon both of Dover on 12 Jan *MS* 20 Mar 1850

DEMERIT Mary Ann Miss m BABB Horatio on at Dover NH *MS* 21 Nov 1833

DEMERITT Ann of New Market NH on 23rd inst m JOY John W *MS* 8 May 1839

DEMERITT Catharine M of Barrington NH m DURGIN David of Strafford on 5 Dec *MS* 29 Jan 1840

DEMERITT Mercy of Effingham NH m WENTWORTH Hiram on 16 June at Effingham *MS* 28 Aug 1844

DEMERITT Sarah J of Nottingham m WHITE Levi of Malden MA on 4 Jul *MS* 20 June 1842

DEMERITT Susan m TUTTLE Andrew both of Dover on 20th inst *MS* 23 Mar 1836

DEMORING June C m CAMPBELL Levi B both of Charleston ME on 5 Jan 1848 *MS* 2 Feb 1848

DEMYER Nancy D m STOKES Joel L on 9 Oct at Lowell MA *MS* 2 Nov 1842

DENHAM Catharine of Bowdoin ME m BENSON George F of Bath ME on 20 June 1848 *MS* 12 Jul 1848

DENHAM Susan m PLUMMER Wm G both of Bowdoin ME on 6 Feb *MS* 19 Feb 1851

DENNET Maria m WILSON Albion both of Kittery ME on 14 Apr *MS* 8 May 1844

DENNETT Louisa m SMITH Cyrus K *MFWBR* 3 Nov 1849

DENNIS Lydia A of China NY m CHANDLER George H of Boston NY on 1 June 1848 *MS* 5 Jul 1848

DENNISON Nancy J of Freeport m DENNISON David H of Brunswick

433

DENNISON (Continued)
ME *MS* 24 Jul 1839

DERBY Caroline C of Huntington VT m VITTUM Lindley of Meredith NH on 2 Oct at Underhill VT *MS* 26 Nov 1845

DESHON Eliza of Waterboro m HODGDON Daniel of Hollis ME *MS* 3 Feb 1832

DEVOE Lucy L at Bertrand Mich m BARBER John A on 14 Sept 1848 at Bertrand *MS* 8 Nov 1843

DEVORE Elizabeth m DEVORE Henry Jr both of Nottingham Township PA on 13 Feb last *MS* 25 Apr 1833

DEWEY Mary Ann m CLOCK Josiah on 6 Sept 1846 at Three Mile Bay *MS* 13 Jan 1847

DEXTER Abigail Maria of Bethlehem NH m WHITCOMB Lindya on 11 Jan *MS* 20 Jan 1847

DEXTER Almira m FOSDICK Lucina both of Dracut on 18 Mar 1848 *MS* 26 Apr 1848

DEXTER Louisa of Middleville m DEERING Arther of Bushnell's Basin on Oct *MS* 15 Nov 1848

DEXTER Lydia A m PRAY Miles O both of No Scituate RI on 24th ult *MS* 2 Jan 1839

DEXTER Mary Jane m BOWLES David on 22 Dec *MS* 19 Apr 1843

DIBBLE Malinda of Freedom NY m KENDAL Charles of Yorkshire on 15 Feb 1848 *MS* 10 May 1848

DICKERSON Mary Jane m DICKERSON Daniel on 10 ult *MS* 18 Jul 1838

DICKINSON Hannah of Wiscasset ME m FAIRSERVICE Francis of Alna *MS* 13 Nov 1844

DICKSON Ann of Sandford m WEYMOUTH Moses of No Berwick *MS* 5 Apr 1837

DICKY Lydia A m FLANDERS Stephen B on 13 June at Gilmanton on 13 June *MS* 28 Jul 1847

DIKE Lucretta at Lowell m SEWARD George H *MS* 12 Feb 1840

DILNO Sarah A m DANIEL Ira on 18th ult in Barnston *MS* 18 May 1836

DILTZ Marilla of Racine WT m PASKO Cyrus on 2 March at Mt Pleasant WT *MS* 14 Apr 1847

DIMICK Delight m NICHOLS Dolphas on 23 Jan 1848 *MS* 15 Mar 1848

DIMICK Susan m CARY Heman on 25 Jan 1848 *MS* 15 Mar 1848

DIMOND Julia Ann m BROWN Franklin G both of Hopkinton on 19 May *MS* 22 June 1836

DINGLEY Betsey B of Bowdoin ME m LIBBY John W of Richmond ME *MS* 7 Feb 1849

DINGLEY Caroline m PURINGTON Joseph both of Lewiston ME *MS* 12 Sept 1833

DINGMAN Lydia m COTRAL David C *MS* 15 Jan 1851

DINNELS Lovina of Newfield m GILPATRICK William of Newfield MS 19 Nov 1828

DIXON Fanny m BURROWS Jabez both of Dover MS 16 Jul 1834

DIXON Lydia of Lebanon ME m BLAISDELL Thomas on 12 Sept at Lebanon ME MS 23 Oct 1844

DIXON Maria m OSGOOD George W on 15 Feb at Manchester NH MS 6 Apr 1842

DOBIE Sarah Ann m COBURN Hiram S both of West Sumner*MFWBR* 8 Dec 1849

DOCKHAM Lucy m ROWE Gilman of Gilmanton MS 13 June 1842

DOCKHAM Mary Ann of Saco m JACOBS Moses on 22 Dec at Saco ME MS 5 Feb 1845

DOCKHAM Sally m BEAN Loammi of Gilford MS 15 Nov 1843

DOCKUM Mary Jane of Dover m DOWNS James on 19th inst at Dover NH MS 25 Feb 1846

DODGE Amy of Clayton m EMERSON Jonathan of Lyme on 14 Feb 1847 at Clayton NY MS 10 Mar 1847

DODGE Eliza of Monroe ME m GOODWIN Lewis on 5 Apr at Monroe ME MS 19 Apr 1843

DODGE Julia Mrs m HODGDON John Capt 2d of Boothbay ME MS 23 Dec 1846

DODGE Mariah L m EMERY Nahum on 20 Mar 1844 of Monroe ME MS 5 June 1844

DODGE Mary m HAGGETT Willard on 7th Nov at Edgecomb ME in the FWB meeting house MS 1 Dec 1841

DODGE Nancy of Edgecomb ME m BROWN Ezra on 10 Nov MS 7 Dec 1842

DODGE Olive m DODGE Simon both of Edgecomb on 31 Oct MS 27 Nov 1850

DODGE Sarah L of Munroe m BAGLEY Sewell D of Dixmont ME on 26 ult MS 15 Nov 1837

DODGE Semantha of New Lyme m HULL Wm of Crawford Co PA on 17 Nov 1847 MS 29 Dec 1847

DODSON Margaret at Middlebury NY m CATON Alphonso MS 27 Jan 1847

DOE Abagail m FRYE Joseph both of Lowell MA on 15 inst MS 25 May 1836

DOE Betsy m THOMPSON Daniel both of Parsonsfield Thursday last MS 9 Nov 1826

DOE Caroline m DAVIS Hiram both of Nottingham on 1 Apr MS 29 Apr 1846

DOE Lydia S of New Market m GRIFFIN John of Exeter on 10 inst MS 23 May 1838

DOE Mary Ann m THOMPSON Jonathan on 26 May at Manchester MS 5 June 1844

DOE Nancy B of Raymond NH m OSGOOD Timothy on 1 Dec MS 14

DOE (Continued)
Dec 1836

DOE Nancy of Parsonsfield ME m COOMBS David H of Chichester on 21 inst *MS* 28 Sept 1836

DOE Sarah J (widow) of Newmarket m FOLSOM Josiah on 27 June *MS* 5 Jul 1843

DOICK Mary I m EARL Edmund both of So Berwick ME on 15 Oct *MS* 23 Oct 1850

DOLBEAR Elizabeth of Charlestown m COLESWORTHY William W of Dover NH *MS* 21 Nov 1833

DOLBEER Eliza L M m MOSES Mark S both of Epsom NH *MS* 17 June 1835

DOLE Caroline A of Ashfield MA m EDWARDS Almeran of West Hampton on 19 Oct 1848 *MS* 7 Feb 1849

DOLE Clarissa of Grafton m FOSTER G W Eld of Canterbury on 19 June *MS* 20 June 1842

DOLE Sarah m GETCHELL Samuel on at Richmond *MS* 29 June 1836

DOLLEY Margaret m CROSMAN Sulivan both of Meredith NH on 24 Oct 1847 *MS* 23 Feb 1848

DOLLOFF Elizabeth m SINDER Almond both of Charlestown MA on 11 Apr *MS* 24 June 1846

DOLLOFF Ellice of Tuftonboro' m DOLIVER Thomas of Tuftonboro' *MS* 31 Jul 1839

DOLLOFF Laurett Jane of Meredith m m BENNETT William L of Bristol on 11 Nov 1847 *MS* 22 Dec 1847

DOLLOFF Lorint P of New Hampton m GORDON William E on 26 Nov 1848 *MS* 5 Apr 1848

DOLLOFF Lourenia formerly of Sanbornton NH m SMALL Amasa formerly of Alton NH *MS* 5 Apr 1837

DOLLOFF Melissa A of Meredith m SMITH Luther M of Tamworth NH on 4 March *MS* 15 Mar 1843

DOLLOFF Nancy m WEBSTER William both of Meredith NH *MS* 10 Nov 1847

DOLLOFF Rolina m WHITNEY Leonard S on 14 inst *MS* 24 Jan 1838 & at Dover NH *MS* 14 Feb

DOLLOFF Sarah Jane m COOK Ebenezer R on 2 Nov at Charlestown MA *MS* 3 Dec 1845

DOLLOFF Sarah T of Sutton VT m FROST Daniel S of Clinton MA on 14 Oct *MS* 27 Nov 1850

DOLLOFF Terzah Ann m KIMBALL Stephen S both of Meredith on 24 Nov 1847 *MS* 22 Dec 1847

DOLLY Lydia Miss m HUMPHREY Jonas on 18th ult *MS* 3 Jan 1833

DOLTON Mary R m CILLEY Justin both of Deerfield NH on 7 June *MS* 20 June 1849

DOOD Sally of Hinsdale MA m HARRINGTON Gardner Eld of Ste-

DODD (Continued)

phentown on 10 Aug *MS* 23 Oct 1850

DOPKINS Serena m HUBBELL Bishop B on 4th in Virgil *MS* 15 Jan 1845

DORE Belinda m SCEGGEL Benjamin Jr both of Ossipee NH on 19 ult *MS* 8 June 1836

DORE Eunice of Dover m LEGRO David on 17 Nov at Dover NH *MS* 9 Dec 1846

DORE Keziah m COLBATH John both of Alton on 19 inst *MS* 27 Jan 1836

DORE Lucinda of Ossipee NH m HOBBS Abial W on 7 Sept (a licensed preacher) of Wolfboro NH *MS* 5 Oct 1842

DORE Margaret m MURRAY Daniel on 8 inst Sunday *MS* 25 Oct 1837

DORE Mary of Great Falls NH m BAGLEY John A at Great Falls NH *MS* 29 Mar 1843

DORE Sarah Jane m BROWN E K both of Ossipee NH on 3 Jul *MS* 11 Jul 1849

DORR Martha A of Ossipee NH m YOUNG Isaac D of Gilmanton NH on 9 Jul *MS* 4 Dec 1850

DORSETT Eliza of Gorham ME m WALKER Henry of Standish ME *MFWBR* 4 May 1850

DOTY Eliza of Nassau m WEATHERBY Willard on 7 May *MS* 4 Oct 1843

DOTY Mary J m PIPER Jonathan E both of Saco ME on 14 Nov 1847 *MS* 15 Dec 1847

DOUGLAS Mary m ROBINSON William C on 6 Aug of Denmark ME *MS* 31 Dec 1845

DOUGLASS Louisa R of Richmond VT m PINE Nelson J of Huntington VT on 2 Apr *MS* 26 Nov 1845

DOW Abigail Mrs of Strafford m EMERSON Joseph on 30 Oct of Epsom NH *MS* 16 Nov 1842

DOW Abigail of Gilmanton m MORSE Abner on 26 Mar at Gilmanton *MS* 30 Apr 1845

DOW Amelia of Middlebury NY m KENYON John of Batavia NY on 10 Dec at Middlebury NY *MS* 11 Feb 1846

DOW Betsey m DOW John 3d both of Gilmanton on 4 inst *MS* 24 Jan 1838

DOW Betsey of Sandbornton m COX Oren F *MS* 17 Mar 1847

DOW Clara J m LEAVITT John both of Gilmanton NH on 4 May 1848 *MS* 17 May 1848

DOW Clarissa m MERRILL Isaac both of Hopkinton on 28 Dec *MS* 8 May 1844

DOW E E of Buxton m CHENEY A H MD of Gorham on 31 Mar *MS* 24 Apr 1850

DOW Eliza m PEASE Sheperd both of Meredith on 21 Mar 1848 *MS*

DOW (Continued)
   5 Apr 1848
DOW Eliza E d/o DOW Oliver Esq m CHENEY A H Dr of Gorham ME
   MFWBR 27 Apr 1850
DOW Elmary of North Hampton m SHAW Moses of Boston on 26 Jan
   1848 *MS* 1 Mar 1848
DOW Harriet of Salem MA m SIMPSON James Esq of Hampton on
   17 inst *MS* 25 Oct 1837
DOW Mary H m CLEMENTS Daniel both of Strafford on 5 Apr *MS* 29
   Apr 1846
DOW Mary of Yorkshire NY m BUMP Everit of Mount Pleasant Wis
   on 25 Sept 1848 *MS* 1 Nov 1848
DOW Nancy m LANGLEY Andrew *RI* 4 Dec 1819
DOW Nancy A of Wolfborough NH m BROWN Benjamin of Tufton-
   borough NH on 2 inst *MS* 8 Apr 1846
DOW Nancy S m FROST Charles C (brother of Eld D S FROST) both
   of Manchester NH 24 Jan 1849 *MS* 7 Mar 1849
DOWNER Mahala m CARR Newell both of Lowell *MS* 8 Jan 1840
DOWNING Susan E m PLACE Benjamin F *MFWBR* 20 Apr 1850
DOWNS Louisa m WIGGIN John W *MS* 8 Dec 1847
DOWNS Lydia of Kennebunk ME m LORD Samuel of Eaton NH on 4
   Jan at Tamworth's FW Baptist meeting house *MS* 18 Feb 1846
DOWNS Mahala M of Great Falls m PUTNAM Henry S of Salem MA
   on 16 Nov 1847 *MS* 1 Dec 1847
DOWNS Maria B m RICHER Wentworth R both of Dover on 2 inst
   MS 12 Jul 1848
DRAKE Abby m RANDALL Samuel A both of Holderness NH on 28
   ult *MS* 4 Nov 1846
DRAKE Abigail J m PERKINS Thomas Eld of New Hampton on 25
   Nov *MS* 17 Dec 1845
DRAKE Abigail of Meredith NH m ROBERTS Warren at Meredith NH
   on 24 Apr 1842 *MS* 8 June 1842
DRAKE Abigail of Pittsfield m DRAKE S P Holt on 27 Mar at Pittsfield
   MS 20 May 1842
DRAKE Elizabeth A m MARSTON Jeremiah both of Effingham on 18
   Nov 1847 *MS* 12 Jan 1848
DRAKE Huldah Jane m CHICK Winthrop F on 23 Mar at Effingham
   NH *MS* 6 Apr 1847
DRAKE Lydia J of New Hampton m MOONEY Geo W of Meredith on
   22 Nov 1849 *MS* 30 Jan 1850
DRAKE Lydia of Albion m TWITCHELL John of Plymouth on 10 Oct
   MS 5 Mar 1851
DRAKE Lydia Wid of New Hampton m MASTEN Jeremiah Capt of
   Bridgewater on 8 June 1848 *MS* 14 Feb 1849
DRAKE Mary E of Holderness m RANDALL William B of Boston on 2
   Apr 1850 *MS* 10 Apr 1850

DRAKE Mary of Effingham NH m SCEGGEL Zachariah of Ossipee NH on 3 Oct *MS* 4 Dec 1850

DRAKE Polly Mrs of Plymouth m CHASE Paul Eld on 3 May at Holderness *MS* 28 May 1845

DRAKE Sarah P m GREEN Alfred A both of Pittsfield on 15 Dec 1850 *MS* 1 Jan 1851

DRESSER Adelaide P m BERWICK James A *MFWBR* 22 Feb 1851

DRESSER Relief m LIBBY Charles on 15 Sept of Barnston *MS* 13 Apr 1842

DREW Abigail of Pittsfield ME m PRINCE John of Detroit ME on 26 May 1844 *MS* 24 Jul 1844 (*sic*) should be *MS* 31 Jul 1844

DREW Anna m SANDERS Levi both of Strafford *MS* 27 June 1838

DREW Betsey B m CLOUGH Jeremiah both of Loudon in Canterbury *MS* 19 Jan 1848

DREW Diana m CROCKER F W both of Barford *MS* 15 Apr 1840

DREW Eliza S m CLIFFORD John H on 26 Mar at Manchester *MS* 10 Apr 1844

DREW Hannah d/o DREW Winborn A m STIMSON John N on Thurs last *MS* 28 June 1827

DREW Hannah of Newfield m WILSON Foxwell C of Kittery ME on 10 June *MS* 25 Jul 1849

DREW Huldah J m FILES William S *MFWBR* 3 Nov 1849

DREW Louisa of Strafford m RANDALL Gordon P of Northfield in West Brookfield 31 Dec 1841 *MS* 23 Mar 1842

DREW Lucitta m SLOWMAN Josiah both of Richmond *MS* 20 May 1840

DREW Lydia H m WHITTEN Henry A both of Wolfborough NH *MS* 29 Dec 1847

DREW Lydia M of Alton m JONES John of Somerworth NH on 15 ult *MS* 2 Dec 1835

DREW Lydia of Strafford m WHITEHOUSE Henry of So Berwick ME *MS* 23 Nov 1836

DREW Margaret W m WENTWORTH James W on 26 Dec of Great Falls NH *MS* 6 Jan 1847

DREW Maria L of Tunbridge m WHEELER George D of Royalton on 18 Mar 1849 *MS* 28 Mar 1849

DREW Mary Jane of New Market on 20 Nov m SMITH Warren of Durham *MS* 30 Nov 1842

DREW Mary of Dover m TIBBETS Jeremiah G of Rochester *MS* 10 Dec 1845

DREW Mary P of Dover m REMICK Ai on 30 Jan *MS* 6 Feb 1834

DREW Miss m DOWNING John both of Holderness *MS* 24 Jan 1838

DREW Nancy M m PALMER Elihu H of Cambridge *MS* 27 June 1838

DREW Nancy Mrs m SHAW John at Holderness NH *MS* 11 May 1842

DREW Olive H of Newfield m PRESTON Benjamin F of Dover on 19 Dec at Newfield ME *MS* 27 Dec 1843

DREW Sabrina of Parsonsfield m EMERY William of Newfield *MS* 6 Dec 1827

DREW Salome m BEAN Charles Eld on 4 inst *MS* 17 Oct 1838

DREW Sarah Ann of Barrington m AYER Joseph of Somersworth NH *MS* 24 Sept 1834

DRINKWATER Susan A on 10th inst m GOFFREY Joseph *MFWBR* 30 Nov 1850

DROWN Abigail G of Eaton NH m RUSSEL Joel on 27 Dec 1848 *MS* 10 Jan 1849 & of Freedom *MFWBR* 13 Jan 1849

DROWN Hannah Mrs of Portsmouth ae 66y m HAILEY Samuel ae 76y on 20 ult on Isle of Shoals (Gosport NH) *MS* 12 Oct 1836

DROWN Jane of Barnston Canadia East m BUNKER Obadiah Capt of Sutton VT on 17 ult *MS* 13 Oct 1847

DROWN Phebe A of Saco m ALMY Charles on 17 Mar at Saco ME *MS* 2 Apr 1845

DROWN Polly widow m OTIS Paul both of Sheffield VT on 11 Oct *MS* 24 Jan 1838

DUDLEY Betsey A m DODGE Simeon S on 21 Jan 1847 at Newbury NH *MS* 24 Feb 1847

DUDLEY Elizabeth A of Alton NH m GLIDDEN Daniel F on 18 Feb 1847 at Gilmanton NH *MS* 14 Apr 1847

DUDLEY Hannah D m GODFREY Jason both of Candia on 29 Nov *MS* 12 Dec 1838

DUDLEY Julia A of Gilford m HACKETT John C of Somersworth on 8 Dec at Gilford NH *MS* 14 Dec 1842

DUDLEY Louisa J m ROBINSON Benjamin W on 7 Feb at Manchester NH *MS* 17 Feb 1847

DUDLEY Mary A m PAGE John B both of Northwood on 5 Jan *MS* 22 Jan 1851

DUDLEY Mary C of Buxton ME m PHONIS Richard of Hollis ME *MS* 7 Nov 1849

DUDLEY Mary E of Augusta m ADLE Cornelius of Readfield ME on 28 Sept at Hallowell ME *MS* 7 Jan 1846

DUDLEY Mary S of Brentwood m BROWN Andrew J of Exeter on 26 Oct in Amesbury MA *MS* 13 Nov 1850

DUDLEY Sarah of Mt Vernon ME m CLOUGH James of Readfield ME *MS* 25 Mar 1835

DUDLEY Serene G m FLANDERS Dyer on 24 Sept at Alton NH *MS* 25 Oct 1843

DUFFY Ellen m GOODRICH Andrew *MFWBR* 22 June 1850

DUFIN Mary of Williamstown VT m DANFORD Eldridge G of Thornton on 28 Aug *MS* 13 Sept 1837

DUKE Sabrah J of Dayton m ALDRICH Samuel of Rochester on 26 Jan at Dayton Cattaraugus Co NY *MS* 22 Mar 1837

DUNAWAY Rebecca W m PEIRCE Andrew 3d on 16th inst *MS* 24 Apr 1834

DUNHAM Harriet m CATES Levi on 12 Sept 1847 *MS* 22 Sept 1847

DUNHAM Margaret V of Nassau NY m KITTEL John J of Stephen-town at Nassau NY on 12 Mar *MS* 7 May 1845

DUNNING Alice J C m BROWN Daniel both of Roxbury MA on *MS* 13 May 1846

DUNNING Sarah Ann m McDONALD David on 30 Nov at Roxbury *MS* 27 Dec 1843

DUNTLEY Rhoda m CLOUDMAN Richard H both of Milton on 1 Apr *MS* 9 May 1849

DUNTON Alvina m DUNTON Andrew *MS* 14 Feb 1833

DUNTON Caroline C of Swanton m NORTON Reuben of West Enos-burgh *MS* 5 Feb 1851

DUNTON Julia A on 17 Nov at Westport ME m PAGE Benjamin G of Hallowell ME *MS* 27 Dec 1843

DUNTON Mary J m POOL Joshua both of Boothbay on 2 Feb *MS* 26 Mar 1851

DUNTON Mary Mrs of Boothbay m POOL John of Edgecomb *MS* 1 Feb 1843

DUNTON Phebe Ann m BRAN Charles both of Jefferson in Jefferson ME *MS* 27 Apr 1842

DUNTON Sarah K m JEWETT Florence both of Westport ME *MS* 7 May 1834

DURELL Harriet M m HAYWOOD Gorham on 9 May *MS* 24 May 1843

DURGIN Abigail R of Lowell m FENNER Hezekiah of Hebron NH *MS* 18 Mar 1840

DURGIN Anna of Gilmanton NH m PALMER Daniel E MD on 14 Mar of Tuftonboro' *MS* 14 Apr 1847

DURGIN Asenath of Cornish m PRINCE George W of Limington ME on 13 Aug *MS* 22 Dec 1847

DURGIN Betsey H of Newfield m YOUNG Charles S of Shapleigh ME *MS* 8 Nov 1848

DURGIN Dorcas of Cornish ME m EASTMAN Joseph K of Parsons-field on 29 Nov *MS* 17 Jan 1833

DURGIN Dorothy m MERRIFIELD Stephen on 18th inst *MS* 13 Apr 1832

DURGIN Elizabeth W of Exeter m HILL Wm H of Deerfield NH on 23 Sept *MS* 18 Nov 1835

DURGIN Eliza Ann m HATCH Seth at Great Falls NH *MS* 7 Jul 1847

DURGIN Hannah of Eaton m THURSTON Nathaniel C of Freedom on 4 Feb 1849 *MS* 28 Mar 1849

DURGIN Irene of Lowell MA m SNOW Elisha H on 6 Aug *MS* 23 Aug 1843

DURGIN Irene of New Market NH m COLOMY Moses at Great Falls NH *MS* 15 Mar 1843

DURGIN Laura B m McDUFFIE Charles D of Rochester NH *MFWBR*

DURGIN (Continued)
11 Jan 1851

DURGIN Martha J m DENNETT Winborn R both of So Berwick ME on 15 inst 1849 *MS* 25 Apr 1849

DURGIN Mary d/o DURGIN Wm m DAVIS Thomas 2d all of Newfield *MS* 15 Feb 1827

DURGIN Mary A of Great Falls m NASON William on 10 Jan at Great Falls *MS* 21 Feb 1844

DURGIN Mary A S m NOALLY John 2nd both of Northwood on 20 Nov *MS* 26 Nov 1834

DURGIN Mary Jane of Newfield m DILLINGHAM Aremas of Lowell MA *MS* 24 Aug 1832

DURGIN Nancy m DANIELSON Charles on 11 Jul at Northwood *MS* 25 Sept 1844

DURGIN Nancy m KNOWLTON James on 3 Sept at Northwood *MS* 25 Sept 1844

DURGIN Nancy of Lee m LOUGEE Lyman of Dover on 3d inst at Newmarket *MS* 13 Mar 1844

DURGIN Rhoda Ann of Eaton m BRYANT Samuel of Effingham NH on 9 June *MS* 19 June 1850

DURGIN Roxanna of Limerick ME m CORNER Moses of Parsonsfield ME on 19 June *MS* 28 June 1843

DURGIN Sally W at Parsonsfield on 24 ult m FOLSOM H Maj of Limerick ME *MS* 29 Jan 1840

DURGIN Sarah m COLLEY Nathaniel both of Lowell MA *MS* 10 Aug 1836

DURGIN Susan m DAY Thomas of Cornish on Thurs last *MS* 31 Dec 1828

DURGIN Susan m STEVENS Daniel both of Dixmont ME *MS* 28 May 1834

DUSTAN Aurilla R m JAY Benson both of Sutton on Thanksgiving Day *MS* 12 Dec 1849

DUSTIN Charlotte m CLOUGH Willard both of Hopkinton on 24 Jul *MS* 12 Oct 1836

DUSTIN Susan E at Manchester NH m MARSTON Jonathan C on 8 Apr *MS* 3 May 1843

DUTCH Hannah m GETCHEL George I both of Brownfield Oxford Co ME *MS* 15 Nov 1848

DUTTON Hannah m SEAVEY Frederick both of Chester *MS* 1 May 1834

DUTTON Sally B m EMERSON Charles S both of Candia on 11 ult *MS* 30 Dec 1835

DWELLEY H N on 13th inst m CARVILLE Otis *MFWBR* 24 Feb 1849

DWINELL Cynthia m McALLISTER Daniel on 25 Dec at Stowe *MS* 21 Jan 1846

DWINELLS Nancy E of Canterbury m ABBOTT William of Loudon on

DWINELLS (Continued)
9 Mar *MS* 15 Apr 1840

DYE Emily m CHEESMAN James both of Freedom NY on 2 Oct in Freedom NY *MS* 11 Dec 1850

DYER Abigail F d/o DYER S B Eld of Loudon m RUMMERY Jerome B of Dover on 29 ult *MS* 11 Apr 1838

DYER Affy of Augusta ME m THOMAS Josephus T of Montgomery VT on 20 ult *MS* 7 Mar 1838

DYER Drusilla of Lewiston ME m CARVILLE Daniel W of Wales ME *MFWBR* 31 Aug 1850

DYER Frances B of Cape Elizabeth ME m HUTCHINSON Ebenezer (a licensed preacher in Otisfield QM) on 30 June *MS* 20 June 1842

DYER Frances E m LIBBY Cyrus both of Portland on 20 inst *MS* 3 May 1848

DYER Martha m THOMPSON Calvin both of Lowell MA on 15th inst Sat *MS* 27 Aug 1834

DYER Mary of Portland m HATCH William Jr on 29th ult at Portland ME *MS* 8 Nov 1843

DYER Olive L of Nottingham m LARRABEE John G of New Market on 18 Apr *MS* 29 Apr 1846

DYER Sarah C Miss d/o DYER S D Eld of Loudon m LOCKE Ephraim Jr of Epsom on 19th ult *MS* 18 Feb 1835

EARL Abigail m GOULD Ira L at Bangor ME *MS* 13 Sept 1843

EARL Almira of Buxton ME m HUFF Ebenezer S on 16 Apr 1848 in Buxton ME *MS* 3 May 1848

EARL Emeline of Hollis m PIKE William F *MFWBR* 16 Oct 1847

EARL Theodosia A m ALLEN Holman P both of Portland ME on 18 ult *MS* 8 May 1844

EARLE Elizabeth m GRANT Franklin both of South Berwick ME on 8 ult *MS* 15 Apr 1846

EASTE Emily m PLUMMER Silas both of Durham ME at Lisbon ME on 23 June *MS* 24 Jul 1850

EASTES Joanna m EASTMAN Geo A both of Great Falls *MS* 16 Jan 1850

EASTMAN Amanda Mrs of Orange m SCRIVNER Harrison of Topsham on 29 Nov 1849 *MS* 9 Jan 1850

EASTMAN Armanda m MEADER Levi both of No Providence on 24 Dec 1837 *MS* 17 Jan 1838

EASTMAN Deborah of Limerick ME m DEERING Rufus on 18 May at Limerick ME *MS* 31 May 1843

EASTMAN Eliza B m BUXTON David both of Weare on 26 ult *MS* 24 Jan 1838

EASTMAN Elizabeth of Lyndon m WILLEY David of Sutton *MS* 5 Apr 1843

EASTMAN Emeline D m CHESLEY Joseph H both of Manchester on

EASTMAN (Continued)
   13 Sept *MS* 23 Sept 1846
EASTMAN Emily of Limerick m MERRILL Albert Capt of Conway NH
   on 14th inst Wed *MS* 23 Sept 1831
EASTMAN Flora G m LOW Seth both of Warner on 25 Jan at Warner
   MS 8 May 1844
EASTMAN Hannah F m KIMBALL Moses L on 2d inst of Dover NH
   MS 8 Oct 1845
EASTMAN Harriet of Limerick m FOGG James Dr of Chesterville ME
   MS 27 Oct 1830
EASTMAN Laura m SPOONER Joel on 3d Mar at Franconia NH *MS*
   28 Apr 1847
EASTMAN Margaret m WALKER James D on 4th inst at Charlestown
   ME *MS* 16 Jul 1845
EASTMAN Mary E m WHITTEN Oran both of Rochester on 14 Apr
   MS 8 May 1850
EASTMAN Mary F of Dover m FIELDING John Jr of Lowell *MFWBR*
   22 Feb 1851
EASTMAN Mary Jane m STACY Samuel H K on 11 Apr at Eaton *MS*
   30 June 1847
EASTMAN Miriam B m BUXTON David 2d both of So Weare on 5 Jan
   1848 in So Weare *MS* 8 Mar 1848
EASTMAN Nancy H of Bath NH m HARRINGTON Leonard B of St
   Johnsbury VT on 4 Sept 1842 at Swift Water Village *MS* 28 Dec
   1842
EASTMAN Nancy of Bennington NY m TUTTLE Dan on 4 Feb at
   Bennington NY *MS* 6 Apr 1847
EASTMAN Phebe E of Limerick ME m NEVENS William P on 6 May
   at Limerick ME *MS* 9 June 1847
EASTMAN Rosanna m STEVENS David M of Enfield on 12 Feb at
   Grantham *MS* 19 Mar 1845
EASTMAN Sarah of Cornish ME m JEWELL John on 16 inst at
   Cornish ME *MS* 18 Mar 1846
EASTMAN Sarah T d/o EASTMAN James Dea m RICH Stephen all of
   Harpswell ME on 7 Dec 1848 *MS* 14 Feb 1849
EASTMAN Susan of Whitefield NH m TAYLOR Jonathan of Lisbon on
   30 Aug *MS* 26 Dec 1849
EATON Almira of Pittsfield m SWAIN Abraham D of Chichester *MS*
   13 Jul 1836
EATON Belinda of Limerick m WEDGWOOD Thatcher of Parsonsfield
   on 4th inst *MS* 10 Mar 1830
EATON Caroline E of Portland ME m HILL Stephen of Cornish ME
   MS 27 Apr 1832
EATON Caroline H of Great Falls m WITT Arza Dr of Sutton VT on 9
   ult *MS* Mar 1837
EATON Clarissa m SEAVER Isaac of East Cambridge MA at Alfred

EATON (Continued)
  MS 27 June 1842

EATON Eliza m STIMSON Thomas T both of Limerick ME *MS* 29 Sept 1830

EATON Elizabeth B of Hopkinton m NOURSE Phineas A of Lowell MA on 28 Apr in Hopkinton *MS* 8 May 1844

EATON Elmira m MARCH Horace both of Plymouth VT on 23 Jan 1840 *MS* 4 Mar 1840

EATON Elmira m MARCH Horace both of Plymouth VT on Jan 23 1840 *MS* 4 Mar 1840

EATON Emily d/o EATON L of So Reading m TAUNTON P Folsom of Taunton MA on 13 inst *MS* 26 Sept 1838

EATON H M of Weare m PREBLE T M of Parsonsfield on 14 Nov *MS* 13 Dec 1837

EATON Hannah J m WHIPPLE Joseph both of Manchester on 27 Dec 1848 *MS* 17 Jan 1849

EATON Harriet R of Chesterville ME m MANWELL Jacob H on 7 Nov 1844 of East Livermore ME *MS* 26 Mar 1845

EATON Hope M m DAVIS Joseph P both of Concord NH on 28 May 1848 *MS* 5 Jul 1848

EATON Joanna m SPRINGER William on 13 March at Mooers *MS* 6 Apr 1847

EATON Lavina d/o EATON Daniel Dea of Vienna ME? m MARDEN Jonathan on 26th ult *MS* 30 Jul 1828

EATON Louiza of Limerick ME m HAYES John on Sunday last *MS* 5 Aug 1831

EATON Lydia of Derby VT m GILMAN Ebenezer of Compton on 18 Feb *MS* 15 Apr 1840

EATON Lydia of St Albans ME m PRATT Noah of Skowhegan ME on 16 Feb *MS* 27 Apr 1842

EATON Maria m BUNDY Lewis of Mooers NY *MS* 6 Apr 1847

EATON Martha A m CURTIS Alonzo in Peru Ohio *MS* 16 Feb 1842

EATON Martha Jane m WILSON George on 16 Dec at Candia *MS* 7 Jan 1846

EATON Mary H of Dover formerly of Landaff NH m EDGERLY Jabez F of Barnstead *MS* 24 Oct 1838

EATON Mary of Manchester on 7 May m GORDON Stephen L of New Hampton *MS* 17 May 1843

EATON Mercy Mrs of Danville VT m WOODMAN Jonathan Eld of Sutton VT M 6 Aug at Danville VT *MS* 28 Sept 1832

EATON Nancy F of Chesterville m WARDSWORTH Joseph of Livermore ME *MS* 12 June 1839

EATON Ruhama C G m MORRILL Isaac on 29 May at Gilford NH *MS* 23 June 1847

EATON Ruth of Bethlehem NH m FOWLER Jesse of Dorchester *MS* 12 Dec 1838

EATON Sarah B m CASS David M on 30 Nov at Manchester *MS* 20 Dec 1843

EATON Susan T of Manchester m MASON Joseph of Sanbornton on 22 Dec *MS* 5 Feb 1840

EDER Maria S m WESCOTT William both of Windham ME on 9 Apr *MS* 29 May 1850

EDGCOMB Lydia Ann m CHATMAN Emerson both of Corinna ME on 12 Apr 1838 *MS* 9 May 1838

EDGECOMB Abigail S of Portland ME m WADLEIGH George W *MFWBR* 2 Oct 1847

EDGECOMB Sarah m GILKEY Reuben on Nov 19? of Limington ME *MS* 7 Feb 1844

EDGELSTON Caroline m STAFFORD Charles both of Lockport PA on 7 Feb 1850 *MS* 10 Apr 1850

EDGERLY Betsey B of Great Falls m HURD Amos H of Lowell MA on 23 ult *MS* 9 Nov 1836

EDGERLY Betsey Mrs m LEAVITT Samuel both of Meredith on 23 Oct *MS* 27 Nov 1850

EDGERLY Diedina m SANBORN James both of Hampton *MS* 8 Nov 1837

EDGERLY Fanny W m SMITH John M both of Meredith on 9 May *MS* 15 June 1836

EDGERLY Hannah B of Meredith m POTTER John of Gilford *MS* 24 Jan 1838

EDGERLY Hannah S m HARRINGTON James J both of Manchester*MS* 2 Feb 1848

EDGERLY Mary m CARTER Ebenezer both of Great Falls on 12 Nov 1848 *MS* 22 Nov 1848

EDGERLY Sarah Jane of Barnstead m COFFIN Samuel S Capt on 1 Oct at Alton *MS* 25 Oct 1843

EDMUNDS Hannah m PUTNAM Elbridge both of Weare on 7 ult *MS* 24 Jan 1838

EDMUNDS Sarah A of Lynn m EDMUNDS Lot of Lynn MA on 7 Aug at Saugus MA *MS* 14 Aug 1844

EDSON Arminta of Bethany NY on 1 Jan m SAMBERGER Augustus of Charlotte *MS* 11 Feb 1846

EDWARD Mehitabel P of Portland ME m JONES Benjamin L of Milbury MA at Otisfield *MS* 21 Jan 1846

EDWARDS Ann of New Hartford NY m DIXON Joesph W of Utica NY on 10 Dec 1850 *MS* 1 Jan 1851

EDWARDS Catherine m HARDY Sylvester on 4 Nov 1841 at Lowell MA *MS* 25 May 1842

EDWARDS Esther E of Lowell m SIMPSON John C of Boston on 1 Sept *MS* 8 Sept 1847

EDWARDS Henrietta of No Providence m WILMORTH Albert T of Providence at Johnston RI *MS* 2 Dec 1835

EDWARDS Joanna m GAMMON John Jr of Casco ME *MFWBR* 14 Sept 1850

EDWARDS Juliette m BROWN Joseph both of West Poland ME *MS* 3 June 1846

EDWARDS Mary Ann m HARDING Wm B in Gorham *MS* 4 Jan 1827

EDWARDS Mary P m MORRISON John C of Bethlehem at Meredith Bridge 14th ult *MS* 2 Mar 1842

EDWARDS Phebe C of Lowell MA m CHUBB Jabez on 21 May *MS* 23 Aug 1843

EDWARDS Susan m ANDERSON George of Limington ME in Gorham ME *MS* 27 Jan 1832

EDWARDS Tabathy m FOGG Isaac of Limerick ME *MS* 7 Mar 1828

EGELSTON Mary m RAYMENT Norman on 7 Feb at Varysburgh NY *MS* 6 Apr 1847

EIRL Eunice m RICHMOND James A both of Great Falls ME *MFWBR* 29 June 1850 & on 16 June *MS* 10 Jul 1850

ELDEN Harriet Frances of Buxton ME m VARNEY William of Windham ME on 19 Jan *MS* 3 Mar 1847

ELDER Frances M on 27th ult m WILKINSON L D Esq *MFWBR* 7 Apr 1849

ELDER Harriet N m MORRILL Elisha at Harpswell ME *MS* 25 Dec 1844

ELDER Keziah m STURGIS Benjamin K both of Gorham on 1 Nov *MS* 6 Jan 1836

ELKINE Love T m SCUITON Thomas C both of Farmington on 30 Dec *MS* 8 Jan 1851

ELKINS Irene m LOCK Samuel W both of Lowell MA on 17 Sept 1848 *MS* 11 Oct 1848

ELKINS Martha of Gilfrod NH m GRANT Elisha W of Meredith NH *MS* 16 Nov 1842

ELKINS Mary R of Dover m WENTWORTH George G *MS* 26 Jul 1837

ELKINS Sally of Gilford m SAWYER Josiah of Gilford on 3 Nov 1842 *MS* 25 Jan 1843

ELLINWOOD Sally m FOLSOM John M both of Frankfort ME on 6 Feb *MS* 26 Feb 1840

ELLIOT Abigail F A of Haverhill NH m DURANT E C Mr on 25 Mar at Corinth VT *MS* 19 May 1847

ELLIOT Betsey of Douglass m DUDLEY Nelson on 3 May *MS* 7 June 1843

ELLIOT Cassandria of Pittsfield m SPERRY Philesten of Claremont on 30 Sept *MS* 7 Nov 1838

ELLIOT Dolly of Corinna on 28 Feb 1839 m IRELAND Osbert A of Stelson *MS* 24 Apr 1839

ELLIOT Elizabeth of Canaan m TUCKER Daniel B of Thornton on 11 ult *MS* 1 May 1850

ELLIOT Jane m REMICK John both of Parsonsfield ME *MS* 25 Nov

ELLIOT (Continued)
1831
ELLIOT Judith of Dover m BENNETT David on 4th inst at Dover NH
MS 14 Sept 1842
ELLIOT Louisa d/o ELLIOT V of New York City m FERNALD Eli B
Rev of Topsham ME on 27 Sept MS 24 Oct 1849
ELLIOT Lucy of Kingrey LC on 16 Dec m GEE Solomon of Durham
MS 30 Jan 1839
ELLIOT Mary A m CROWELL Ethelbert both of Corinna on 20 June
1845 MS 20 May 1846
ELLIOT Mary of Dover at Farmington m DURGIN Newell on 30 Jul
MS 13 Sept 1843
ELLIOT Naomi m SMITH John both of Brunswick ME on 5 Nov 1849
MS 23 Jan 1850
ELLIOT Rebecca m MAYNARD John G of Lowell MS 7 Aug 1839
ELLIOTT Almire of Benton m GLAZIER James of Haverhill on 6 June
1845 MS 8 Apr 1846
ELLIOTT Mary Ann B m GREENLEAF Ezra L both of Pittsfield on 12
inst MS 20 Dec 1848
ELLIOTT Roxana of Haverhill m JEFFERS Sylvester on 7 Feb at
Haverhill NH MS 21 Feb 1844
ELLIOTT Theodate m DAVIDSON Samuel both of Manchester on 2
Dec MS 26 Dec 1849
ELLIS Abigail of Barnston m HEARD Wilder late of Newport on 23
Nov MS 17 Feb 1836
ELLIS Caroline E m COLBY Timothy both of Haverhill MA on 7 Nov
1847 MS 8 Dec 1847
ELLIS Fanny B m PALMER Beniah D on 21 Nov at Lowell MA MS 25
May 1842
ELLIS Grace m ROLLINS Levi D at Epping of Lee MS 12 May 1847
ELLIS Lois m PEIRCE Alpheus both of Dover MS 9 May 1849
ELLIS Mercy m STEVENS Augustus J both of Lowell MA MS 21 Dec
1836
ELLISON Mary Jan of Dover m LANG Edward 2d of Exeter on 14th
inst MS 26 Dec 1833
ELLISWORTH Sally S m BLOOD Stephen C on 2 Mar at Wentworth
MS 16 Apr 1845
ELLSWORTH Lydia S m BROWN Benjamin on 2 Mar 1847 at
Wentworth NH MS 14 Apr 1847
ELLSWORTH Sarah of Sandbornton m NICHOLS Wm of Meredith on
27 June MS 11 Jul 1838
ELWELL Harriet S of Eaton m DORMAN James B of Tamworth on 1
Jan MS 15 Jan 1851
ELWELL Jane N of Northport ME m FARNHAM Ephraim of Belfast
on 24 ult MS 18 Nov 1835
EMERSON Abby formerly of Newburyport MA m LYFORD Augustus

EMERSON (Continued)
formerly of Canterbury NH *MS* 19 Jul 1843

EMERSON Abigail m KNIGHT Albert of New Market *MS* 19 May 1847

EMERSON Clarinda m WALDRON John B both of Dover on 28 May *MS* 8 Aug 1849

EMERSON Clarissa M m MARTIN Caleb K both of Weare on 14 May 1839 *MS* 12 Feb 1840

EMERSON Deborah Y m THATCHER Seth T on 22 Sept at Lowell MA *MS* 2 Oct 1844

EMERSON Eliza J m HILL Joseph G of Boston MA on 30 June at Manchester *MS* 16 Jul 1845

EMERSON Eliza S of Waterville m SMILEY Oren C at Waterville ME *MS* 17 Feb 1847

EMERSON Frances J m MARTIN Nathaniel H both of Bedford *MS* 22 May 1844

EMERSON Hannah m WOODBURY William Esq both of Danville in Danville ME Tues Feb 1 *MS* 16 Feb 1842

EMERSON Hannah C of Fairfield ME m HUNTOON Peter of Waterville ME *MS* 14 Jul 1847

EMERSON Jane m LEWIS William H *MFWBR* 3 Nov 1849

EMERSON Laura A m STACY E P both of Waterville ME on 19 inst *MS* 7 Mar 1849

EMERSON Lucinda E of Ossipee NH m ABBOTT John F on 9 Jul at Ossipee NH *MS* 13 Sept 1843

EMERSON Lydia (McDonald) wid/o Wm EMERSON d/o McDONALD John Gen m EMERY Daniel Col of Hamden ME on 2nd inst *MS* 6 May 1826

EMERSON Mary E of Great Falls m PINKHAM George E of Farmington on 18 Jan 1849 *MS* 31 Jan 1849

EMERSON Mary M m PRESSEY George W Jr at Fairfield ME *MS* 17 Apr 1844

EMERSON Mary Mrs m SEBRA Robert on 9 Nov *MS* 19 Jul 1843

EMERSON Mehitabel m WHITNEY Jonathan W on 30 Nov at Dracut MA *MS* 24 Dec 1845

EMERSON Minerva J of Barnstead m PHILPOT Ichabod of Somersworth on 1 Nov 1848 *MS* 15 Nov 1848

EMERSON Sophrona of Candia m ATHERTON Joseph of Roxbury MA on 3 inst *MS* 30 Dec 1835

EMERY Abigail m ROLLINS Otis both of Somersworth on 14 inst *MS* 18 Oct 1848

EMERY Adaline of Poland ME m CUSHMAN Lewis on 5 Jan *MS* 9 Apr 1845

EMERY Caroline D of Andover NH m SHAW Albert of Kennebunk ME on 21 Dec 1848 *MS* 7 Mar 1849

EMERY Catherine m THING Charles *MFWBR* 30 Dec 1848

EMERY Charlotte B of Dover NH m JORDAN Edmund of Farmington

EMERY (Continued)
MS 6 Mar 1839

EMERY Cyrena m DUNN Ranson Eld on 1 Sept *MS* 5 Sept 1849

EMERY Elizabeth of Howland ME m BAILEY Abner S of Mansfield on 12 Jul *MS* 5 Aug 1846

EMERY Harriet J of Limerick ME m MARSTON Oren *MFWBR* 18 Jan 1851

EMERY Jane of Poland m HASKELL William on 5 Dec at West Poland ME *MS* 9 Apr 1845

EMERY Lucinda C m ROGERS Increase J both of Goshen on 20 Nov 1849 *MS* 2 Jan 1850

EMERY Lucretia of Gorham ME m ROGERS William M D of Dover on 8 ult *MS* 21 Feb 1838

EMERY Lydia A m THOMAS Albert H on 26 Oct at Nashville TN *MS* 24 Dec 1845

EMERY Mary E of North Berwick ME m COPP George of Lawrence MA *MFWBR* 12 May 1849

EMERY Mary of Thorndike m COFFIN Sargent of Thorndike ME on 9th ult *MS* 29 Jul 1831

EMERY Olive d/o EMERY Eld of Waterboro m McKENNY Henry H of Saco ME on 17th inst *MS* 22 May 1829

EMERY Olive J on 14th inst m KEAY William G *MFWBR* 1 Sept 1849

EMERY Olive of Limington ME m WEBSTER Royal F of Gray ME on 7 Dec *MS* 7 Feb 1844

EMERY Olive of Waterboro m WOODWARD Johnson of Hollis ME on 6th inst *MS* 28 Dec 1832

EMERY Rachel of Hatley on Jan 6 1840 m ARCHILIES Jr B of Patton *MS* 15 Apr 1840

EMERY Roxanna m OWEN William at Buxton ME *MS* 20 Nov 1844

EMERY Sabrina of Boston MA m WENTWORTH Ezra on 28th ult at Hampton *MS* 11 Oct 1843

EMERY Sally of Limington m STAPLES George of Limerick ME on 16th inst *MS* 26 May 1830

EMERY Sally of Somersworth NH m SHAW Samuel of York ME on 3 Mar *MS* 10 Apr 1844

EMERY Sarah Ann m COOK Thomas both of Dover NH on 17 ult *MS* 6 Sept 1837

EMERY Sarah E d/o EMERY J D Esq (late) of Augusta m HOLMAN S C of Boston MA *MFWBR* 24 Mar 1849

EMERY Sarah T of Waterboro ME m KELLEY Wm A of Lynn MA *MS* 31 Jul 1850

EMERY Urana m MUDGET Robert both of Newbury on 16 Apr 1848 *MS* 2 Aug 1848

EMMONS Ann m CLUFF Shadrach on 14 Oct at Kennebunkport ME *MS* 20 Nov 1844

EMMONS Hannah D m CAMPBELL Joseph both of Hill on 16 May

EMMONS (Continued)
MS 19 June 1850

EMMONS Harriet m DAVIS Amaziah on 3d Nov at Biddeford ME *MS*
13 Nov 1844

EMMONS Lucinda m HILL Japhet of Kennebunk ME on 15 June *MS*
5 Jul 1843

EMMONS Margaret C m WILLIAMS Ezra F both of Georgetown MEon
14 Feb 1850 *MS* 27 Feb 1850

ENNIS Deborah m COOPER Charles both of Burrillville RI on 3 Jan
1848 *MS* 23 Feb 1848

ENSIGN Mary Ann on Jan 4 1840 m MCCULLOCK Wm both of
Grinville *MS* 20 May 1840

ERSON (*sic*) Jane Miss m SANBORN William B on 20 Dec at Lowell
MA *MS* 25 May 1842

ESTEN Dianna of Gorham NY m RUGG Cyrus F of Potter on 13 Dec
1848 *MS* 27 Dec 1848

ESTER Olive S of Lewiston ME m JASPER Edwin E of Minot on 30
Jul 1847 *MS* 23 Feb 1848

ESTES Eunice m AYER Albion P both of Westbrook ME on 6 Feb
1848 *MS* 16 Feb 1848

ESTES Jane Ann of 3 Mile Bay m ROGERS Jeremy of Pamelia at 3
Mile Bay *MS* 1 Feb 1843

ESTES Lydia J m FOLSOM Noah both of Manchester on 28 Dec
1848 *MS* 17 Jan 1849

ESTES Mary Mrs m COOK Benjamin both of Dover on 9 inst *MS* 12
Aug 1846

ESTES Miriam m WATERHOUSE Thomas *MS* 5 Jul 1827

ESTHERS Mary of Boston MA m POTTER John W of Providence RI
on 29 May *MS* 12 June 1850

ESTRUS Huldah m JONES Daniel both of Milton on 22 Nov 1848 *MS*
3 Jan 1849

ESTY Julia C m GOODALE Amos both of Lowell on 30 May *MS* 10
June 1846

ETRICH Ellen m SHATTUCK Milo both of Hermon NY on 26 Feb
1848 *MS* 19 Apr 1848

EUER Augusta Ann m BEAN Alonzo E on 19 Dec *MS* 29 Jan 1851

EVANS Ann C m FLING William of Londonderry on 4 Nov at Canterbury *MS* 29 Jan 1845

EVANS Ann Jeannette of Lowell MA m BAXTER John on 16 Dec of
Lowell MA *MS* 1 Jan 1845

EVANS Clarissa C of Barrington NH m BREARD Nicholas of Sturbridge on 25 May *MS* 17 June 1846

EVANS Harriet B of Barrington m RICHARDSON James A of Dover
on 26 Sept *MS* 3 Oct 1849

EVANS Louisa H of New Market NH m HANSON Caleb of Strafford
NH on 28 Feb at New Market NH *MS* 13 Apr 1842

EVANS Lucretia m LOUGEE Joseph B both of Strafford on 19 Apr 1849 *MS* 2 May 1849

EVANS Lydia E m SENTER Matthew on 17 Sept at Manchester NH *MS* 25 Sept 1844

EVANS Martha A m WEYMOUTH John C Capt both of Gilmanton at Meredith Bridge Jan 4 1842 *MS* 2 Feb 1842

EVANS Mary Ann of Lynn MA m THOMPSON Horace on 29 Dec at Lynn MA *MS* 13 Jan 1847

EVANS Nancy J m SWAIN Calvin both of Dover on 27 ult *MS* 10 Jan 1849

EVANS Sarah d/o COLE Samuel Esq (eldest dau) m NICHOLS H L Dr *MFWBR* 18 Sept 1847

EVANS Sarah W of Barrington NH d/o EVANS Levi m TWOMBLY Nathaniel 2d of Dover *MS* 21 May 1845

EVANS Susan m STEWART Cyrus K at Warner on 20 Feb *MS* 19 Mar 1845

EVANS Susan D m QUINT George W on 28 Dec at Sanford ME *MS* 28 Jan 1846

EVANS Terrasa W of Barrington NH m HATCH Alexander C of Nottingham on 15 May at Barrington *MS* 21 May 1845

EVENS Belinda m SIAS Wm P both of Salem MA on 5 Apr *MS* 16 May 1838

EVERETT Elizabeth J m TIFFANY Hiram both of Walworth NY on 19 Sept *MS* 16 Oct 1850

EVERETT Elizabeth former teacher in Clinton Seminary m BUTLER John J on 14 Nov at Steuben Oneida Co NY teacher of the Biblical School at Whitestown *MS* 27 Nov 1844

EWERS Clarinda of Richmond m PLUMER Libby Esq on 23 May at Richmond ME *MS* 2 June 1847

FABER Lydia m WILLIAMS John G both of Atkinson ME on 2d ult *MS* 27 Mar 1834

FADDEN Catharine m MARK James M C both of Lowell *MS* 22 Jan 1840

FAIRBANKS Almena m DURHAM David both of Hermon on 6 Sept *MS* 21 Oct 1846

FAIRBANKS Catherine m CHAMBERLIN Ellis E on 10 Dec 1846 at Manchester Iowa *MS* 27 Jan 1847

FAIRFIELD Hannah at New Market on 3 inst m LANGLEY Jonathan of Lee 13 May 1840

FALES Olive of Hallowell m DUNHAM Ammi of Litchfield on Dec 29 1841 *MS* 9 Mar 1842

FALL Augeline m STEVENS Abial C both of Lebanon on 29 Sept *MS* 24 Oct 1849

FALL Celistia P m MACUMBER Charles F both of Phoenix NY on 16 Apr *MS* 21 June 1848

FALL Elizabeth M of Ossipee m HARRIS Matthew of Roxbury MA on 16 Mar *MS* 24 June 1846

FALL Mary E of Lebanon m CHAMBERLIN Samuel of Milton *MFWBR* 14 Sep 1850

FANNIN Sarah of Bath ME m LAWRENCE Wm 2d of Gardiner ME on 26 Feb *MS* 7 Mar 1838

FARNAM Sarah L of Sidney m MASON William H of Augusta *MS* 17 Apr 1844

FARNHAM Love W of Skowhegan ME m FARNHAM Samuel W of Lewiston *MS* 27 Nov 1844

FARNHAM Lovey H m ROSS Peter both of Lebanon ME on 26 May *MS* 6 June 1849

FARNHAM Lucinda J Eld on Aug 8th m BUTLER John E of Dover NH *MS* 14 Aug 1844

FARNHAM Maria of Albany m WEEKS Joshua of Conway on 20 Dec 1846 *MS* 25 Aug 1847

FARNUM Hannah m LAMPHERE William both of Warner on 5 May *MS* 30 May 1838

FARRAR Eliza Ann of Gilmanton m SANBORN Joseph Jr of Gilford *MS* 12 Dec 1849

FARRAR Lovina B of Meredith NH m SWAIN Harrison Jr at Meredith NH *MS* 5 May 1847

FARRER Julia A of Corinth m RIPLEY Wm M of Coventry VT on 16 Oct 1848 *MS* 21 Feb 1849

FARRINGTON Elizabeth T m FOBESH Ebenezer F both of Livermore ME *MS* 13 Dec 1837

FARRINGTON Mary m MERRILL John A of Manchester NH on 24 Apr *MS* 25 May 1842

FARRINGTON Mary S of Lowell MA m GARLAND Gilman D Eld of Boston on 11 May at Lowell MA in the FWB church *MS* 21 May 1845

FARRIS Abigail G m KNOX Thom T *MFWBR* 3 Mar 1849

FARROW Mary E on Feb 8 m WALKER Benjamin both of Corinth ME *MS* 4 May 1842 '

FARROW Mary Jane of Gilmanton m KNAPP George of Nashua on 14 May 1848 *MS* 24 May 1848

FARWELL Lydia J C of Norway ME m SEAVERNS George W *MFWBR* 5 Apr 1851

FAUNEE Mary B m MURCH Benjamin both of Foxcroft at Guilford ME *MS* 19 Nov 1834

FAVOUR Mary Ann m WESCOTT Josiah S of Manchester NH *MS* 15 Oct 1845

FEE Sally of Durham L C m REED Webber Jr *MS* 30 Jan 1839

FELCH Almira of Bewbury m SMITH John B of Wendell on 16 Nov 1843 *MS* 24 Apr 1844

FELCH Eliza Ann of Tamworth NH m FERNALD Eli of Lowell on 11

FELCH (Continued)
Jul at the First Unitarian Church *MS* 28 Jul 1847

FELCH Hannah D of Newbury m BROWN Albert W of Newport on 23 Sept *MS* 6 Oct 1847

FELCH Lois N m PAGE Samuel B both of Newbury at Weare on Nov 18 *MS* 12 Jan 1842

FELCH Lois N m AYER Moses C on Nov 18 both of Newbury *MS* 12 Jan 1842

FELCH Mary P of Newbury m STEAVEY Dustin Eld of Peterborough on 4 Mar *MS* 19 Mar 1851

FELCH Sophia of Limerick ME m EMERY Rufus of Buxton in Limerick *MS* 12 Jul 1827

FELKER Martha J of Barrington m BERRY Benjamin T of Strafford on 15 Oct 1848 *MS* 15 Nov 1848

FELKER Mary Ann of Barrington m WINCHESTER Horace H of Marlborough VT on 24 June *MS* 4 Jul 1849

FELKER Rachel m VARNEY Solomon both of Barrington *MS* 27 Jan 1836

FELLOWS Lois E of New Hampton on 21 Jan 1843 m PARSLEY William of Meredith *MS* 26 Apr 1843

FELLOWS Mary A formerly of Franklin NH m WOODWARD Horace N of Stockholm on 26 Nov at Hopkinton *MS* 23 Dec 1846

FELLOWS Sarah of Haverhill MA m BEARDSLEE John S on 14 Aug 1847 Haverhill MA *MS* 6 Oct 1847

FELT Elbina L m WELCH Edward Jr on 9 Nov at Hallowell ME *MS* 7 Jan 1846

FELT Lucy S of Greenwood m LIBBY Abner C of Limerick ME *MFWBR* 1 Dec 1849

FENDERSON Catharine at Parsonsfield ME m LORD Tobias of Limerick ME *MS* 20 May 1840

FENDERSON Lydia A of Jackson m SMITH Moses of Bradley on 6 Dec *MS* 26 Dec 1849

FENNER Mary E m GREEN Benj W both of Smithfield on 1 Jan 1849 *MS* 17 Jan 1849

FERGUSON Arvil of Boston NY m CARY Luther H MD on 8 Oct at Boston Erie Co NY *MS* 25 Nov 1846

FERGUSON Sarah E d/o FERGUSON T Esq (late) of South Berwick m EVANS Daniel of Portland ME *MFWBR* 28 Aug 1847

FERNALD Abby m FALL Ivory Jr at Lebanon ME on 5 Oct *MS* 15 Oct 1845

FERNALD Dorothy m RAND James both of Parsonsfield on 26 Dec *MS* 15 Jan 1840

FERNALD Irene A of Eaton m PHILBRICK John on 14 Nov at Eaton of Freedom *MS* 8 Jan 1845

FERNALD Jane W of Lowell MA m HAWES George W on 13th Dec at Lowell MA *MS* 24 Dec 1845

FERNALD Mary m DORE Jacob C both of Ossipee 13 Aug *MS* 7 Nov 1849

FERNALD Mary E of Wolfboro' m DIXON Joseph L on 31 Jul at Wolfboro' *MS* 4 Sept 1844

FERNALD Parmelia m JONES Ebenezer both of Lebanon on 22 Dec 1849 *MS* 9 Jan 1850

FERREN Melissa of Eaton m BURKE James *MS* 21 Jan 1846

FERRENTON Lucretia W of Waldin m WHITCHER Joseph C of Danville on 23 Oct 1849 *MS* 2 Jan 1850

FERRIN Sarah Jane of Eaton m GLINES Eli Capt on 5 Mar *MS* 12 Aug 1846

FERRY Elizabeth m CROWLEY David both of Roxbury MA on 8 Dec 1849 *MS* 13 Feb 1850

FESSENDEN Vialetta m RING Richard on 11 Jan at Little Meadow PA "postage on this marriage was unpaid" *MS* 10 Feb 1847

FIELD Amanda m WHITMAN Willard K both of Rochester WI on 7 Sept *MS* 3 Nov 1847

FIELD Isabella J m BLACKSTONE William on 2d inst *MS* 29 Nov 1843

FIELD Mary E of Portland m WEED Benjamin F of Lowell *MFWBR* 16 June 1849

FIELD Rachael m PERRY Nathan both of Waterville ME on 13 Feb 1849 *MS* 21 Mar 1849

FIFIELD Louisa L of Manchester m COGSWELL Jonathan of Dorchester *MS* 18 Dec 1850

FIFIELD Martha A m SMITH Issachar W both of Lamprey River New Market on 2d inst *MS* 10 Sept 1834

FIFIELD Ruth m CHANDLER Nathaniel Capt on 20 Dec at New Hampton *MS* 15 Mar 1843

FILES ESTER W m BLAKE Ithiel both of Gorham on 28 ult *MS* 2 Jan 1839

FILES Eunice of Gorham ME m STROUT Solomon Jr of Portland ME at Gorham ME *MS* 11 Feb 1846

FILES Harriet m WITHAM Philip both of Thorndike on 25th inst *MS* 19 May 1830

FINEX Almira T m GOULD Carlos both of Colebrook NH on 14 Mar 1849 *MS* 14 Mar 1849

FINNEY Abigail m EATON Charles S of Limerick ME at Dedham *MS* 1 Aug 1833

FISH Mary Jane m HUNNEWELL James on 25 Oct 1846 at Woolwich *MS* 13 Jan 1847

FISH Sally m EMORY Nathan both of Hatley LC on 20 Nov 1837 *MS* 10 Jan 1838

FISHER Lydia m LOOK Richard both of Georgetown ME *MS* 7 Jan 1835

FISHER Mary of Ascott on 14 Sept 1838 m VANCE Hiram *MS* 17 Apr

FISHER (Continued)
1839

FISK Lovina m SHELDON Edmunds T on 17 Sept at Waterbury VT
MS 2 Oct 1844

FISK Lucy of Freedom m DENNIS Abraham of China on 8 Oct Freedom NY MS 11 Dec 1850

FISK Mary Ann of Contoocookville NH on 2 Nov m MERRILL Lorenzo
MS 30 Nov 1842

FISK Mary m DIBBLE Mason both of Freedom NY on 15 Feb MS 25
Mar 1846

FISK Polly G m HERBERT Sanders of NH MS 24 Jul 1839

FITTS Susan m CLIFFORD Josiah both of Candia MS 14 June 1837

FITZGERALD Emily B of Limerick ME m MESERVE James L at
Limerick ME MS 18 May 1842

FITZGERALD Emily of Manchester NH m TURNER Abel Eld of Exeter
ME on 6 Oct 1847 in Manchester NH MS 27 Oct 1847

FLAGG Harriet D of Dover m GRIFFIN Abner C of Boston on 7 inst
MS 13 Oct 1847

FLAGG Susan m DARLING Samuel MFWBR 29 Mar 1851

FLANDERS Betsey m EMERSON Walter G G merchant both of Alton
NH MS 8 Mar 1837

FLANDERS Charity R m THOMPSON William on 20 Mar at Bowdoinham ME MS 6 Apr 1847

FLANDERS Elenor P Mrs of Alton and Gilford m GLIDDEN Bethuel
on 29 Oct 1843 at Alton MS 10 Jan 1844

FLANDERS Elizabeth C of Buxton m CHICK Nathan of Limerick ME
MFWBR 29 May 1847 & MS 14 Jul 1847

FLANDERS Hannah m GORDON George both of New Hampton on 7
Mar MS 5 June 1850

FLANDERS Hannah of Warner m CARLTON Sumner of Hopkinton 7
ult MS 4 Apr 1838

FLANDERS Irena I m SANBORN Abram S both of Manchester on 3
Jan 1850 MS 23 Jan 1850

FLANDERS Lydia m BROWN Asa of Strafford VT MS 1 Feb 1843

FLANDERS Mary W m WADLEIGH Ernstus both of Sutton on 5 Jan
1848 MS 2 Feb 1848

FLANDERS Nancy m PAGE Abby both of Weare on 2 Oct 1336 (sic)
1836 at Weare MS 16 Nov 1836

FLANSBUSGH Susan m SHICER Wm both of Day NY on 25 Feb
1849 MS 28 Mar 1849

FLENEGIN Jane of Hume m TWOMBLY Luther of Freedom MS 26
Dec 1838

FLETCHER Henrietta m DREW Isaac on 8 June of Barnston MS 13
Sept 1843

FLETCHER Lavina A m HILL Edmund D Capt on 5 Nov 1843 at
Canterbury NH MS 14 Feb 1844

FLETCHER Nancy D of Loudon NH m DERBY John on 30 Jan of
Stewartstown *MS* 14 Feb 1844

FLETCHER Sarah F of Bath m MONTARE Joseph A on 5 May at
Bath ME *MS* 18 May 1842

FLINT Catharine of Scarboro' ME m TWITCHELL Isaac J *MFWBR* 24
Aug 1850

FLINT Dorothy C Mrs of Sweden m HOR Joseph of Lovel on 3 Mar
MS 3 Apr 1850

FLINT Elizabeth of Allenstown m KIMBALL Obadiah of New Hampton
on 15 Mar 1848 *MS* 21 June 1848

FLINT Maria m SANBOTH Calvin D both of Alexandria on 15 Jul *MS*
12 Dec 1838

FLOYD Harriet W m KIMBALL George L on 17 Aug at Hopkinton *MS*
17 Sept 1845

FLOYD Lovinah S m BECKHAM/DOCKHAM James W *MFWBR* 28
Jul 1849 & both of Biddeford on 14 Jul *MS* 21 Nov 1849

FLOYD Lucinda of Biddeford ME on Sun last m DURGIN Jacob
MFWBR 8 Feb 1851

FLUENT Hannah E m KNIGHT Zebulon both of Buxton ME on 7 Dec
1848 *MS* 24 Jan 1849

FLUNKER Sally on Oct 31 1839 m WARNER Matthew both of
Warsaw NY *MS* 20 May 1840

FOBES Ursula d/o FOBES John Esq m CAREY Calvin I on 2d inst in
Blakesburgh *MS* 19 May 1830

FOGG Ann M of New Hampton m FRENCH John W of Sanbornton
NH on 28 May 1848 *MS* 14 Feb 1849

FOGG Ann Maria m LIBBEY Hammond Capt in Eliot ME *MS* 18 Jul
1838

FOGG Caroline M of Harrison ME m SMITH James of Otisfield ME
on 9 June *MS* 2 Oct 1850

FOGG Eleanor m PRESCOTT Ebenezer Jr in Raymond *MS* 14 Jan
1835

FOGG Hannah R of Ossipee m TITCOMB Joshua Jr of Effingham NH
on 7 ult *MS* 3 Aug 1836

FOGG L Miss d/o FOGG Seth m TITCOMB Nathan W on at Effingham *MS* 1 Apr 1835

FOGG Louisa Ann of Bath m CHASE Robert of Georgetown at Bath
ME *MS* 22 Oct 1834

FOGG Lucady m TITCOMB Wingate on 5 Mar *MS* 1 Apr 1835

FOGG Mary Jane of Gilford m PARSHLEY Stephen S of Meredith NH
MS 16 Nov 1842

FOGG Mary Jane of Limerick m COLBY Edward of Athens ME on
23d ult *MS* 1 Oct 1828

FOGG Mercy Ann m GILPATRICK Ara *MFWBR* 19 Jan 1848

FOGG Miriam Miss of Gorham ME m GAMMON Elden of Saco ME
MS 15 June 1832

FOGG Perrfenda R at Readfield ME m BEAN George W Eld of Farmington ME on 14 May *MS* 12 June 1844

FOGG Susan R m HAWKINS George W both of Center Harbor on 9
Oct *MS* 30 Oct 1850

FOGG Vienna of Northwood m CHAPMAN Wm on 24 Sept *MS* 17 Oct
1849

FOLENSBY Mary E m EMERSON Thomas both of Edgecomb on 25
Dec *MS* 26 Mar 1851

FOLLANSBEE Harriet of Manchester m CLARKE Isaac F on 14 Jan
at Manchester *MS* 14 Feb 1844

FOLSOM Abigail H m HAINES Washington both of New Market on 8
ult *MS* 8 Apr 1840

FOLSOM Abigail M m JONES Nicholas of Gilmanton NH at the
Friends Meeting House at Epping *MS* 2 Jul 1834

FOLSOM Abigail m NORRIS Theophilus on at Epping *MS* 2 Jul 1834

FOLSOM Betsey A of Gilford m NUTTER Joseph P of Manchester *MS*
26 Apr 1843

FOLSOM Betsey m JOHNSON JESSE M both of Lowell MA *MS* 7 Jan
1835

FOLSOM Charlotte B of Gilmanton m CHAMBERLAIN Thomas of
Lowell *MS* 24 Jan 1838

FOLSOM Clarissa P m BALL Alvinea both of Manchester on 12 Aug
1847 *MS* 25 Aug 1847

FOLSOM Delia L of Raymond d/o FOLSOM John Esq m DEARBORN
Thomas of Candia *MS* 12 Nov 1835

FOLSOM Hannah L m SWAIN John M L both of Meredith *MS* 11 Dec
1850

FOLSOM Hannah N of Raymond NH m DEARBORN Benjamin of
Candia on 25 inst *MS* 4 Oct 1837

FOLSOM Hannah P m FULLONTON Jeremiah Jr *MS* 12 Nov 1835

FOLSOM Love m BARTLETT Belknap on 1 Jan at Gilmanton NH *MS*
18 Jan 1843

FOLSOM Mary A on 9 Oct 1839 at Hopkinton m DINSMOOR William
A of Lowell MA *MS* 6 Nov 1839

FOLSOM Mary C of Starks ME m FIELD Charles of Augusta ME
MFWBR 14 Oct 1848

FOLSOM Mary S m UNDERWOOD Hanson at Friends Meeting
House at Epping *MS* 2 Jul 1834

FOLSOM Relief S m DREW Ezekiel B both of Dover on 7 inst *MS* 11
Dec 1850

FOLSOM Sarah Ann m FORD Joseph on 9 Feb of Lowell MA *MS* 23
Aug 1843

FOOT Mary m BLAISDELL Nicholas both of Phipsburgh ME *MS* 25
Mar 1835 & *MS* 8 Apr 1835

FORD Hannah on Dec 12 m PRATT Matthew both of Braintree *MS* 5
Jan 1842

FORD Olive G of Sanford ME m LUNNEY Richard on 1 Nov at Sanford ME *MS* 25 Nov 1846

FORDE Lucena of Attica NY m PARKER Alfred of Sheldon on 31 Dec *MS* 11 Feb 1846

FOREST Lucy Ann of Sutton m KIMBALL Daniel of Newark VT on 7 June *MS* 27 Nov 1850

FORSSKOL Elizabeth R of Saco ME m BABCOCK Edward A of Portland ME *MFWBR* 26 Oct 1850

FOSS Abby P of Strafford m BICKFORD Samuel of Rochester NH on 27 Nov at Strafford NH (In the distribution of the "Bridal loaf" the printers were not forgotten) *MS* 3 Dec 1845

FOSS Almira both of Dover m VARNEY Alfred N on 30 ult *MS* 2 Jan 1850

FOSS Betsey C m HAYES Charles T both of Strafford on 12 Apr *MS* 22 Apr 1846

FOSS Caroline m EMERY James L both of Saco ME on 3 Feb 1850 *MS* 27 Feb 1850

FOSS Caroline of Poughkeepsie Dutchess Co NY on 3rd inst m COFFIN Stephen of Wolfboro' NH *MS* 10 Apr 1839

FOSS Clarissa Ann m HAM Nathaniel on 8 May *MS* 29 June 1842

FOSS Dorothy of Strafford m BARRY Ezra T of Loudon *MS* 15 Nov 1837

FOSS Eleanor B m BATCHELDER Benjamin both of Raymond on 11 Jul *MS* 1 Aug 1838

FOSS Eliza Jane of Strafford m CARTER Charles of Reading on 9th inst at Strafford *MS* 29 May 1844

FOSS Eliza Mrs of Limington ME m EDGECOMB Joseph Eld of Vienna on 4 Mar *MS* 20 Mar 1850

FOSS Elizabeth m BUZZELL John H Capt on 28 May at Strafford *MS* 14 June 1843

FOSS Elizabeth B at Strafford on Nov 21 m FOSS George L *MS* 29 Jan 1840

FOSS Elizabeth m STACY Andrew both of Dover on 27 June 1848 *MS* 13 Sept 1848

FOSS Elizabeth m FOSS George L both of Strafford on 21 Nov *MS* 29 Jan 1840

FOSS Esther of Strafford m HANSON John D on 30 Nov at Strafford NH *MS* 3 Jan 1844

FOSS Esther W m CHAPMAN Timothy on 5 Apr *MS* 22 Apr 1846

FOSS Hannah H m JONES Ebenezer both of Strafford on 27 Apr *MS* 18 May 1836

FOSS Hannah J m KNOWLTON Mayhew P both of Northwood NH on 21 *MS* 21 June 1848

FOSS Hannah of Pittsfield m DENNETT Mark A on 31 Oct at Pittsfield *MS* 16 Nov 1842

FOSS Hannah W m STILES Joseph both of Strafford on 10 Jan 1849

FOSS (Continued)
MS 24 Jan 1849

FOSS Harriet of Strafford m COTTON Foss H *MS* 23 Nov 1836

FOSS Jane S of Pownal ME m FOSS George W on 9 Dec at Rochester *MS* 24 Dec 1845

FOSS Jane W m FOSS Joel S both of Dover on 4th ult *MS* 18 Feb 1835

FOSS Julia A m JOY John both of Limington ME *MS* 12 Nov 1835

FOSS Lavina of Rochester m EVINS Daniel J of Farmington on 15 Nov *MS* 26 Dec 1849

FOSS Lettice A of Hollis ME on 20th inst m WEYMOUTH Luther of Saco ME *MFWBR* 1 Feb 1851

FOSS Loisa m CHAPMAN John both of New Market on 18 Oct 1848 *MS* 8 Nov 1848

FOSS Lucinda A of Charlestown m FOSS Nathan R of Garland ME on ?? Aug 1843 *MS* 28 Feb 1844

FOSS Lucretia m DEERING Charles H both of Saco ME on 28 June *MS* 30 Sept 1846

FOSS Lucy Y m THOMPSON Stephen J Capt of Barnstead on 17 inst *MS* 27 Apr 1842

FOSS Lydia D m FOSS Silvanus C of Strafford *MS* 14 Aug 1839

FOSS Lydia R of Stanstead m EMERSON Reuben of Wheelock VT *MS* 17 Apr 1839

FOSS Margaret E m GRAY William P both of Strafford on 19 Mar 1850 *MS* 10 Apr 1850

FOSS Mariah C of Biddeford ME m GORDON Joseph M of Franklin ME on 18 June 1848 *MS* 26 Jul 1848

FOSS Mariah J of Rochester on 2 Dec m ELLIS Joshua of Alton NH *MS* 18 Dec 1844

FOSS Martha J m MORSE William both of Lowell on 5 Sept *MS* 14 Oct 1846

FOSS Mary A m PARSHLEY John W on 15 inst *MS* 30 Mar 1836

FOSS Mary Ann on 22 Dec 1842 at Saco ME m MOSES Abraham of Biddeford ME *MS* 1 Feb 1843

FOSS Mary D m HOITT David both of Northwood on 20 Nov Thurs *MS* 26 Nov 1834

FOSS Mary D of Stanstead m OLIVER Edward B of Hatley LC *MS* 17 Apr 1839

FOSS Mary Frances of Alton on 2 Nov m TERRIN James M of Hebron *MS* 30 Nov 1842

FOSS Mary Jane d/o FOSS Wm Esq m PLACE Demerit on 13 inst in Strafford *MS* 19 Jul 1837

FOSS Mary of Portsmouth NH m ROOD Marshall on 11 Dec at Strafford *MS* 7 Jan 1846

FOSS Mercy of Strafford m CLARK Samuel on 11 Dec at Strafford *MS* 27 Dec 1843

FOSS Olive Ann d/o FOSS Isaac of Strafford NH m SMITH Joseph Harris of Boston MA on 26 June *MS* 10 Jul 1850

FOSS Olive B of Hollis m BARNHAM George C of Portland ME *MFWBR* 19 Oct 1850

FOSS Olive M of Boston MA m MOULTON Cyrus F of Boston MA *MFWBR* 14 Sep 1850

FOSS Olive M of Freedom m MESERVE Joseph on 2 Jan 1845 of Limington ME *MS* 19 Feb 1845

FOSS Pamelia m BRACKETT Nathaniel both of Limington on 24 Jul *MS* 15 Jan 1840

FOSS S Lucretia of Somerworth m GERRY Samuel of Portsmouth NH on 8th inst *MS* 19 Aug 1835

FOSS Sally m VARNEY Rufus both of Barrington on 21st inst *MS* 31 Dec 1834

FOSS Sarah m MILLS Jeremiah both of Strafford on 27 Nov *MS* 14 Dec 1836

FOSS Sarah J of Rochester m HAYES Charles H of Strafford on 9 Mar *MS* 29 Mar 1848

FOSS Signorine M m TILTON Shurburn both of Charleston ME on 16 Apr *MS* 3 Jul 1850

FOSS Sophia d/o John Foss of Limington ME m SAWYER James MD of Saco ME *MFWBR* 5 June 1847

FOSS Susan H of Rochester m McCLURG Samuel Jr of Trenton NJ on 14th Sept at Rochester *MS* 15 Oct 1845

FOSS Susan J of New Market m TILTON Elisha of Brentwood on 4 ult *MS* 18 Nov 1835

FOSS Susan of Strafford NH m HAYES Ezekial of Strafford NH on 3d March *MS* 10 Mar 1847 & *MS* 6 Apr 1847

FOSS Vienna of Meredith m LANE William of Sherburne MA on 8 Sept *MS* 30 Sept 1846

FOSTER Betsey of Eaton m SHERMAN Cyrus on 24 May *MS* 21 June 1843

FOSTER Eliza W of Gilmanton m PAGE John E of Gilmanton on 1 Feb *MS* 22 Feb 1843

FOSTER Elizabeth S m DAVIS Stephen both of Gilford on Mar 13 *MS* 4 May 1842

FOSTER Ellen m JOHNSON Thomas C on 20 ult *MS* 12 June 1850

FOSTER H Lavinia of Hancock MA m SPENCER Hiram P of New Lebanon Columbia Co NY at Alna on 30 Dec last *MS* 2 Mar 1842

FOSTER Judith N of Wentworth m HARRIS Clark on 15 Dec at Wentworth *MS* 26 Feb 1845

FOSTER Martha A m LIBBY Charles E both of Gray on 12 Sept 1848 *MS* 1 Aug 1849

FOSTER Mary J m SYLVESTER Sewall on 15 June at Chesterville ME *MS* 6 Aug 1845

FOSTER Mary S of Gray m FOSTER Nicholas L of New Gloucester

FOSTER (Continued)
MFWBR 17 Mar 1849

FOSTER Susan of Saccarrappa m PATRIDGE Franklin Esq *MFWBR* 26 June 1847

FOSTER Zilphia of Gray ME m BENSON Jabez C on 14 Jan at Gray ME *MS* 25 Feb 1846

FOWLER Celinda m NEFF Judson both of Rochester on 26 Aug in Rochester Racine Co Wis *MS* 17 Oct 1849

FOWLER Deborah M of Boston MA m DROWN John G on 27 Dec at Gray ME *MS* 10 Feb 1847

FOWLER Roxanna m ANDREWS James L both of Freedom on 2 Dec *MS* 22 Dec 1847

FOWLER Sarah E of Meredith m HANSON Charles of Sandwich on 15 Sept *MS* 12 Dec 1849

FOWLER Susan of Epsom on 27 Nov 1842 m SCALES Rufus D Capt of Concord NH *MS* 8 Feb 1843

FOX Abagail m OSGOOD Ebenezer Ton in Raymond *MS* 19 Apr 1837

FOX Almeda of Stanstead LC on 13 Oct 1838 m RIX William P *MS* 17 Apr 1839

FOX Hannah I of Wolfboro m TUTTLE John of Somersworth *MS* 17 Feb 1836

FOX Lucy C of Raymond m BATCHELDER James *MFWBR* 24 Mar 1849

FOX Mary Ann of Three Mile Bay NY m BARBER Marcus on 28 Mar at the village of Three Mile Bay NY *MS* 26 May 1847

FOX Mary B of Great Falls NH m FOX Andrew W of Acton *MS* 4 Jan 1843

FOX Mary D m WITHAM Asa both of Meredith on 5 Apr *MS* 30 May 1849

FOX Mary S m KENYON B Franklin both of Ilion on 6 Oct at Burlington Flats NY *MS* 27 Nov 1850

FOX Sally m HART Edward of Milton NH at Acton ME *MS* 4 Oct 1843

FOYE Aphia H of Wiscasset m HOULTON William of Boothbay on 6 Dec 1849 *MS* 15 May 1850

FOYE Lucinda P m DAY John C both of Augusta *MS* 24 Jan 1838

FRANCIS Elizabeth of Durham m BRACKETT David on 8th Nov at New Market NH *MS* 18 Nov 1846

FRANCIS Martha of Lowell m PIERCE Nathaniel of Tewksbury *MS* 7 Aug 1839

FRANCIS Mary Ann of Manchester m BUZZELL Henry H on 14th inst at Durham *MS* 20 Nov 1844

FRANK Elenor of Poland ME m HUTCHINSON Asa F of Bridgton ME on 15 Oct *MS* 23 Oct 1850

FRANK Hannah m HANSON Stephen both of Windham ME on 23 Jul *MS* 16 Aug 1837

FRANK Julia A m SMALL Almer H *MFWBR* 28 Apr 1849

FRANKLIN Samantha of Hammond m PICKET Joseph on 15 Sept at Hammond St Lawrence Co NY *MS* 18 Dec 1844

FRASIER Mary A m ANDREWS Joseph of Goffstown on 14 May at Manchester *MS* 31 May 1843

FRAZIER Eliza m PHILLIPS Ebenezer both of Henniker on 17 Mar *MS* 8 May 1844

FRAZIER Salome E m EFFLESTON Amos J on 18 Nov 1847 *MS* 2 Feb 1848

FREDRICK Julia m CONKLIN William on 24 Feb at Farmington NY *MS* 12 May 1847

FREDRICK Rhoda m OLIVER James E both of Starks on Dec 7 1843 *MS* 8 May 1844

FREEMAN Calista A of Attleborough m THRASHER George H of Rehoboth on 10 Apr *MS* 1 May 1850

FREEMAN Eunice B of Gorham m FILES Stephen of Gorham *MS* 1 Nov 1827

FREEMAN Hannah D m HARRIS Wm H both of Boston on 26 Apr *MS* 5 Aug 1846

FREEMAN Huldah d/o FREEMAN Samuel m ROLLINS Andrew Minster of Gospel both of Gorham on 17th inst *MS* 22 May 1829

FREEMAN Isabella m MATHEWS Joseph both of Green ME (both were black) on 18 Nov 1847 *MS* 23 Feb 1848

FREEMAN Jane of Westbrook m STEVENS Nathaniel of Belfast *MFWBR* 9 Nov 1850 & on 23 Oct *MS* 6 Nov 1850

FREEMAN Lavina of Dover NH m BUNKER Valentine of Durham NH on 17 inst *MS* 23 Jan 1850

FREEMAN Maria m CHADDOCK Leverett on 24 Oct at Alexander *MS* 20 Nov 1844

FREEMAN Olive Ann m BROOKS Lebbeus both of Great Falls NH on 28 Jul *MS* 7 Aug 1850

FREEMAN Prudence Mrs m FREEMAN Peter (a blackman) on 11 Dec at Greene ME (his 3rd wife) *MS* 12 Feb 1845

FREESE Augusta A of Moultonborough m JAMES Ira H of Gilford *MS* 29 Jan 1845

FREESE Phebe Ann m TAYLOR Nathaniel H both of Sandwich NH on 9 Feb 1848 *MS* 26 Apr 1848

FRENCH Abigail T of Loudon m WEEKS Samuel of Gilmanton on 21 Nov *MS* 19 Dec 1838

FRENCH Cordelia m SLEEPER Hiram in New Sharon ME *MS* 27 Jan 1836

FRENCH Doliser of Dover NH m GAGE James *MS* 23 Jan 1839

FRENCH Eliza of Wakefield NH m HEARD John Capt of Newfield *MS* 23 Jul 1828

FRENCH Elizabeth of Liberty at Belmont ME m DREW Alvan *MS* 6 Nov 1839

FRENCH Hannah A m WORTHEN Jonathan on 15 Oct at Lowell MA

FRENCH (Continued)
MS 2 Nov 1842

FRENCH Henrietta S m DOW Jonathan S *MS* 13 Apr 1836

FRENCH Judith of East Kingson m CARTER Samuel P of Newtown on 15 inst *MS* 1 Nov 1837

FRENCH Julia of Portsmouth m POTTLE Samuel at Portsmouth NH on 14 Apr *MS* 21 May 1845

FRENCH Lucinda m SWAIN William of Meredith NH *MS* 25 Dec 1844

FRENCH Lucy Jane m FLETCHER Samuel at Lowell MA *MS* 25 May 1836

FRENCH Lucy S m WORTHEN Gilman C both of Manchester *MS* 6 Dec 1848

FRENCH Marin m TRECETT Richard Mr in Prospect ME *MS* 19 Jan 1842

FRENCH Martha of Corinth ME m CHAPMAN Nathaniel of Bangor ME on 10 Apr *MS* 29 Aug 1849

FRENCH Mary M of New Durham NH m SAMPSON Ivory P at Alton NH *MS* 3 Mar 1847

FRENCH Melissa D of New London NH m McCAUSLAND W B of Gardiner ME 22 inst *MS* 31 May 1848

FRENCH Sarah D of Meredith NH m GLIDDEN John L on 24 Dec *MS* 25 Jan 1843

FRENCH Sarah of Hatley on 5 Feb 1839 m MARTIN Daniel *MS* 17 Apr 1839

FRENCH Sarah of Strafford m PAINE Joseph of Vershire VT on 10 Apr at Strafford VT *MS* 11 May 1842

FRENCH Sarah of Unity NH m ADAMS Ira A of Winslow VT on 30 Oct 1849 *MS* 18 Apr 1849

FRENCH Susan m BENSON G D *MFWBR* 28 Jul 1849

FRENCH Susan P m BRAGDEN Edwin both of Corinth ME on 31 Aug 1848 *MS* 21 Feb 1849

FRINK Alice of Gorham ME m HARDING Thomas P of Dover NH on at Standish ME 28 Aug *MS* 28 Sept 1836

FRINK Louisa of Middleville m SMITH R K of Gilbert's Mills on 24 Sept in Middleville NY *MS* 30 Oct 1850

FRINK Nancy Maria at Dover Lenawee Co Michigan m CLARK Asahel on 3 Sept *MS* 29 Nov 1843

FRISBEE Betsey D in Gouldsborough ME m BRAGDON Eben W Capt *MS* 5 Feb 1840

FRISBEE Jane of Kittery m HOYT T Oliver on Christmas eve at Kittery ME *MS* 11 Jan 1843

FRIZZLE Nancy J m ALLS Jacob M both of Colebrook on 22 Dec *MS* 5 Jan 1848

FROST Almira B m TUTTLE William N *MS* 9 Feb 1848

FROST Ann R on 11th ult m RING A C *MFWBR* 3 Mar 1849

FROST Deborah of Bangor ME m FOX John on 18 Feb at Bangor ME

FROST (Continued)
MS 24 Mar 1847

FROST Hannah M of Sandwich m SMITH George on 4 June *MS* 10 Jul 1850

FROST Harriet N of Limington ME m FOSS Allen W *MS* 15 May 1839

FROST Lucy m YORK Levi both of Lowell *MS* 28 Feb 1838

FROST Maria A on 4 Aug 1839 at Springvale m CARTER Sanborn of Sanford *MS* 14 Aug 1839

FROST Martha Elizabeth at Dixmont m RICKER Samuel of Monroe on 17 Dec at Dixmont ME *MS* 11 Feb 1846

FROST Mary Ann of Industry ME m ALLEN Dennis F of Farmington on 30 Mar *MS* 10 May 1837

FROST Mary E of Litchfield m MITCHELL John W of Lewiston ME *MFWBR* 26 Jul 1848

FROST Mary E of Wolfboro' NH m LEIGHTON Nelson of Westbrook ME *MFWBR* 21 Jul 1849 & on 2 inst *MS* 11 Jul 1849

FROST Mary J of Poland m DAVIS John C on 17 Aug at Poland ME *MS* 3 Dec 1845

FROST Olive T m HALE Benj L both of Parsonsfield me on 1 Sept *MS* 30 Oct 1850

FROST Rebecca P of Brunswick m WHITTEMORE Enoch of Lisbon ME on 20 May *MS* 26 May 1847

FROST Sarah of Bridgton m NEWHALL Frances of Lyme MA on 2 Oct 1842 *MS* 10 May 1843

FRY Lydia C m ROGERS John C both of Sandwich NH on 9 May 1848 *MS* 24 May 1848

FRY Mary Miss of Limington m BOODY Israel of Limington ME on Thurs last *MS* 7 Dec 1826

FRYE Sarah of Charlestown MA m SAVAGE Seth W on 26 Feb *MS* 24 May 1843

FULLER Ann of Attleboro' m WILMARTH Eben on 2 Nov at Rehoboth *MS* 16 Dec 1846

FULLER Betsey L of Brookfield at West Brookfield VT m FISK Charles B of Braintree on Apr 7 *MS* 29 May 1844

FULLER Caroline E m BULLOCK D Gilbert D both of Rehoboth on 28 Nov 1850 *MS* 22 Jan 1851

FULLER Elana of Lowell MA m PRESCOTT William Y *MS* 17 Jul 1844

FULLER Elizabeth E m GATCHELL Richard B both of Gardiner ME on Feb 1 1842 *MS* 9 Mar 1842

FULLER Jane of Lewiston ME m WOODARD Abram on 15 May of Bangor ME *MS* 3 Jul 1844

FULLER Lucy Ann of St Albans m GETCHELL Asa of Litchfield ME on 5 Dec 1841 *MS* 27 Apr 1842

FULLER Margaret A K of Berwick ME m LORD Ebenezer at Berwick ME *MS* 8 Dec 1841

FULLER Maria m FREEMAN Dexter both of Grafton on 16 Apr

FULLER (Continued)
   MS 1 May 1844
FULLER Maria L d/o FULLER Simeon of Sutton m WHEELOCK
   James M of Milford on 1 Aug at Sutton MA MS 14 Aug 1844
FULLER Mary A Mrs of Canneaut PA m FOWLER Josiah Eld of No
   Shenango on 4 Jul MS 29 Jul 1846
FULLER Mary F m GREENLEAF Nathaniel both of Boothbay ME on
   11 Oct MS 15 May 1850
FULLER Mary F on Sept 5 1841 m COBURN James M both of West
   Brookfield VT MS 5 Jan 1842
FULLER Mary Jane m PLUMMER Henry both of Manchester on 11
   Nov 1847 MS 1 Dec 1847
FULLER Orpha of Brookfield m BRIGGS Ezra MS 15 May 1839
FULLER Sapreta of West Brookfield VT m BAILEY Seth of Braintree
   on 4 inst MS 14 Nov 1838
FULLER Sarah A m WILCOX Henry both of Unadilla Fords NY on 16
   May MS 8 Aug 1849
FULLER Susan F at Andover on 19 Apr m CILLEY Henry D Capt MS
   6 May 1840
FULLERTON Mary E of N Market m QUIMBY George W of Sandwich
   MS 20 Mar 1839
FULLONTON Caroline m KIMBALL Abel T of Danville MS 8 Nov 1848
FULLONTON Cyntha Jane m COLLY William B on 1st inst at New
   Market NH MS 19 Jul 1843
FULLONTON Hannah m PEASE Leonard on 22 Oct 1848 MS 8 Nov
   1848
FULLONTON Mary D m KIMBALL George F of Poplin on 4th inst at
   Raymond MS 18 Nov 1846
FURBER Betsey of Northwood NH m BEAN Samuel of Deerfield on
   20 ult MS 7 Oct 1835
FURBER Elizabeth Cushing of Farmington NH d/o FURBER John W
   Esq m HANSON Samuel R of Rochester on 30 June MS 22 Jul
   1846 & on 30 June MS 29 Jul 1846
FURBER Mary J of Dover NH m ADAMS James T of New Market NH
   Sabbath Morn last MS 8 Nov 1837
FURBUSH Harriet of Brunswick m WALDRON Francis A of Portland
   ME on 12 inst MS 22 Jul 1846
FURBUSH Jane E of Lebanon ME m TEBBETTS Charles G of Wolf-
   boro NH MS 29 June 1842
FURBUSH Lydia m HAYES Cyrus W on 1 May at Lebanon MS 28
   May 1845
FURBUSH Rebecca of Great Falls m FURBUSH William of Lebanon
   ME on 11 Oct MS 24 Oct 1849
FURLONG Ruth A m HAMBLETON Samuel C MFWBR 4 Aug 1849
FURNAL Harriet m CHAPMAN Smith on 26 Feb MS 14 Mar 1833

GAFFIELD [sic] Miranda m TAYLOR Asher on 30 Dec at Roxbury MA
    MS 22 Jan 1845
GAGE Abigail A m JOHNSON Wm M on 8th inst at Lowell MS 28
    Sept 1836
GAGE Athala of Smithfield ME m HORN John of Fairfield ME at
    Smithfield ME MS 20 Apr 1842
GAGE Deborah m BURGESS Charles both of Waterville ME on 9 Dec
    1847 MS 19 Jan 1848
GAGE Deborah of Hartland ME m LEWIS Asa of Waterville ME MS
    25 Dec 1844
GAGE Jane E m SARGENT Thomas W both of Haverhill MA on 23
    Nov 1847 MS 8 Dec 1847
GAGE Laura A of Waterville ME m BURGESS J S Eld of Lewiston ME
    on 17 inst MS 1 Nov 1848
GAGE Lydia m HOLMES Charles MS 15 Mar 1837
GAGE Martha m WILLEY Lemuel on Wed MS 22 Oct 1834
GAGE Mary B m COXETOR James E both of Lowell on 6 Nov 1847
    MS 17 Nov 1847
GAHAN Mary A m GOULD Austin both of Woolwich ME on 7 Apr
    1850 MS 5 Feb 1851
GALE Caroline A of Augusta m GALE Altah of New Portland ME
    MFWBR 16 June 1849
GALE Deborah of Alexandria NH m WELLS Thomas on 19 Apr 1842
    of Sutton at Alexandria NH MS 4 May 1842
GALUSHA Betsey m WHITE George on 8 Oct 1843 of Palmyra ME
    MS 27 Dec 1843
GAMAGE Sally m RICHARDSON Elbridge both of Anson ME on 24
    ult MS 16 Sept 1835
GANNETT Jane of Great Falls NH m JOHNSON George of Jackson
    on 2 Jul MS 17 Jul 1850
GARDINER Lucy of Biddeford ME m COLE Samuel of Wells on 10
    Nov 1847 MS 1 Dec 1847
GARDNER Esther Maria ae 16y of Higham MA m YOUNG Charles
    Master ae 18y "this was a runaway match" MFWBR 28 Apr 1849
GAREY Abigail H m LORD William K MFWBR 13 Nov 1847
GARLAND Abby m SHORT George W on 27 Nov at Barnstead of
    Boston MS 17 Dec 1845
GARLAND Dorothy T m COLBETH Franklin both of Middleton on 19
    Nov MS 8 Jan 1851
GARLAND Elizabeth m WEEKS Noah T in Parsonsfield ME MS 27
    Feb 1829
GARLAND Elizabeth of Nottingham m GARLAND Joseph Jr of Rye
    NH on 4 Sept at Durham MS 14 Sept 1836
GARLAND Hannah m BROWN Ira Jr both of Rye on 27th ult MS 5
    Nov 1834
GARLAND Hannah S of Barnstead m DIMOND Isreal of Danville

GARLAND (Continued)
  MS 17 Dec 1845
GARLAND Leonora m GARDNER Aaron on 24 Dec of Newburyport
  MA *MS* 1 Jan 1845
GARLAND Martha R of Hampton m DEARBORN George W of New
  Market NH on 19 Sept *MS* 26 Sept 1838
GARLAND Mary of Alexandria NH m HELEY Joseph on 19 Sept at
  Alexandria NH *MS* 4 May 1842
GARLAND Sarah m SMITH Morrill B on 27 Jan at Hampton *MS* 5
  Feb 1845
GARLAND Sarah J m McNEAL Jonathan on 22 Sept at Barnstead
  MS 10 Oct 1844
GARMON Emily m HANSON Ivory both of Bafford LC on 12 Dec
  1837 *MS* 10 Jan 1828
GARNSEY Mary of Ascott m FISHER John on 2 Mar of Ascott *MS* 13
  Apr 1842
GARRETSON Rachael m FREEMAN Daniel on 27 Feb *MS* 24 Apr
  1850
GARVIN Eliza Ann d/o GARVIN Wentworth Esq of NH m RICKER
  Carr of Acton ME on 5 inst *MS* 21 Mar 1838
GARVIN Susan A m PERRY Charles both of Lowell on 25 May *MS* 10
  June 1846
GATES Caroline m BICKNELL Thomas on 11 Jan 1848 *MS* 15 Mar
  1848
GATES Eliza Ann of Brookfield m HODGES Samuel M on 7 Oct at
  Poolville NY *MS* 11 Nov 1846
GATES Malissa m YEOMANS Vinson of Orangeville NY *MS* 6 Apr
  1847
GATES Mary of Woodstock VT m GILSON John of Ludlow VT on 13
  ult *MS* 16 May 1849
GATES Semantha of Bolton NY m SLATER Benjamin G of Dresden
  on 10 June *MS* 13 Jul 1836
GAUBERT Harriet of Richmond m BLANCHARD Ansel at Bowdoin-
  ham ME *MS* 6 Apr 1842
GAULT Sarah Ann at Boston MA m BARON John on 13th inst *MS* 19
  Jul 1843
GEAR Sarah A m LANGLEY Moses both of Dover on Tuesday morn-
  ing 16 *MS* 26 Sept 1849
GEARS Jane m GOLDSMITH Charles on 2 Nov at Providence RI *MS*
  10 Dec 1845
GEE Mary G m EVENS Nicholas both of Garland ME on 25 Feb 1849
  MS 28 Mar 1849
GEEAR Louisa M of Barrington m WOODMAN Seth W on New Year's
  Eve at Barrington *MS* 18 Jan 1843
GELLERSON Philena m TAYLOR Alexander on 30 Jul at Weston ME
  MS 23 Aug 1843

GEORGE Alba W of Haverhill MA on 4 Dec m GOSS Daniel T of Pittsfield NH *MS* 18 Dec 1839

GEORGE Elizabeth of Richmond ME m BATES William of Bowdoinham ME *MS* 21 Aug 1839

GEORGE Esther Ann of Sandbornton NH m ROGERS Francis of
Lowell VT on 24 Feb 1843 at New Hampton *MS* 31 Jan 1844

GEORGE Hannah L of Manchester NH m BUCKMINSTER James on
6 Jan at Manchester NH *MS* 20 Jan 1847

GEORGE Harriet A m CLARK Rufus F both of Dover on 24 ult *MS* 10
Jan 1849

GEORGE Relephe of Weare m FORSAITH Wm Capt of Deering on
12th inst *MS* 4 May 1842

GEORGE Rosannah m SMITH Bartlett both of Holderness NH on 2
Apr *MS* 10 Jul 1850

GEORGE Sarah m JAMES Jonathan L of Danville on 30 Nov *MS* 15
Dec 1841

GERMOND Jane of Farmington m MAYHUE William H of Stanford
Dutchess Co NY on 18 Apr at Farmington *MS* 12 May 1847

GERRISH A D L Mrs m CLARK James L on 13 Mar at Nottingham
NH *MS* 30 Apr 1845

GERRISH Abby Jane d/o GERRISH Wm of Dover m WOOD John B
Jr of Great Falls NH on Sabbath Evening *MS* 26 Jul 1848

GERRISH Elizabeth T of Dover NH m WHITEHOUSE Robert M on
4th inst at Dover NH *MS* 18 Nov 1846

GERRISH Joanna m DAVIS George O both of Lamprey River NH *MS*
8 Jul 1835

GERRISH Mary Jane of Lebanon NH m HATCH Sylvanus of Great
Falls NH *MS* 9 Nov 1842

GERRY Adaline of West Poland ME m DURAN David of Casco ME on
12 Apr *MS* 3 June 1846

GERRY Lucinda of Somersworth NH m TEBBETS Jeremiah of
Lawrence MA on 22 Nov *MS* 5 Jan 1848

GERRY Silvinia of Dover ME m TATE John on 24 Mar of Cornith ME
MS 14 Apr 1847

GETCHELL Eliza Ann of Richmond m ROBINSON Joseph of Litchfield on 28 ult *MS* 7 Sept 1836

GETCHELL Lucy of Sanford m WINN Hiram of York in Sanford ME
27 Feb 1842 *MS* 16 Mar 1842

GETCHELL Olive E m HALEY William *MFWBR* 21 Sep 1850

GIBBS Elizabeth m WILLIAMS Robert on at Lowell MA *MS* 29 Apr
1835

GIBBS Elizabeth, d/o GIBBS Ezra, m BLAZO Ebenezer Esq in Porter
MS 24 June 1831

GIDDINGS Rhoda of Weare m BROWN John of Clayton NY on 17
Sept 1839 *MS* 12 Feb 1840

GIDMAN Hannah J m BROWN William P both of G Falls NH

GIDMAN (Continued)
MS 4 Mar 1840

GIFFORD Mary E only d/o GIFFORD H Eld m NICHOLS Solomon M on 16 Dec *MS* 16 Jan 1850

GILBERT Eliza Jane of Francestown NH on 29 Nov m WHITTEMORE David R Eld of North Providence RI *MS* 4 Jan 1843

GILBERT Lydia J m HARMON William J on 3 Dec at Brunswick ME *MS* 6 Jan 1847

GILE Eliza Miss of Hopkinton NH m MORRILL Nathaniel on Thanksgiving even *MS* 24 Dec 1828

GILE Mahala D of Gilmanton m CLARK Joseph H on 2 Feb *MS* 22 Feb 1843

GILE Mary C of Gilmanton NH m LEAVITT John of Boston MA on 2 Dec 1847 *MS* 12 Jan 1848

GILE Sarah of Nottingham m WOODMAN Samuel Jr of Deerfield *MS* 28 May 1834

GILES Hannah of Dover NH m TREDICK Charles *MS* 23 Jan 1839

GILES Mahala of Dover NH m FORD Thomas B on 7 May *MS* 17 May 1843

GILES Mary B of Northwood on 29 Nov m PALMER Andrus *MS* 27 Feb 1839

GILES Mary Jane of Boothbay m SHERMAN Charles E of Edgecomb on 8 Sept *MS* 27 Nov 1850

GILFORD Almira m DOW Zebulon of Gilmanton *MS* 8 Feb 1843

GILFORD Clarissa m GOODWIN Timothy both of Dover NH on 6 inst *MS* 19 Dec 1838

GILFORD Hannah m EARL Wm both of Biddeford ME on 29 Oct *MS* 15 Nov 1848

GILINES Zanetta P on 4 Jul at Owego NY m DOBSON William O *MS* 14 Aug 1839

GILLERSON Nancy of Brownfield m KENNARD Diamond of Brownfield ME on 31 Aug *MS* 8 Oct 1834

GILLET Lucia A of Huntington m SHARPSTEEN Alfred of Springport NY on 26 Sept *MS* 17 Oct 1849

GILLETT Eunice M on 22 Dec at Pamelia m BULLIS Seymour L formerly of Ellenburg *MS* 1 Feb 1843

GILLIDEN Eliza m ROBINSON Thomas J Capt both of Meredith *MS* 5 Dec 1838

GILLINGHAM Lydia C widow of Bradford m JONES Nathan Dea of Wilmot on Dec 30 *MS* 12 Jan 1842

GILLS Olive M of Harrisville Medina Co Ohio m HICKS Levi of Strongsville Cuyahoga Co Ohio on 7 March *MS* 10 Apr 1844

GILMAN Apphia E m HODGDON Dearborn T on 9 Mar *MS* 1 May 1844

GILMAN Betsey m BURROWS Benjamin both of Effingham NH *MS* 1 Apr 1835

GILMAN Betsey m BEAN John on 6 Nov 1843 both of Gilmanton NH
MS 24 Apr 1844

GILMAN Caroline C m DRAKE Lucius on 1 Oct *MS* 18 Dec 1844

GILMAN Caroline W of Effingham on 2 June m TOWLE Ransellaer of
Freedom NH on 2 June *MS* 28 Aug 1844

GILMAN E P of Sangerville m WENTWORTH Stephen on 3 Apr at
Sangerville ME *MS* 4 June 1845

GILMAN Eliza of Dover NH m RUGGLES Gardiner Esq of Barre MA
MS 16 Jul 1834

GILMAN Hannah m FROST Joseph both of Tamworth NH on 24 ult
MS 9 Apr 1851

GILMAN Hannah J m BROWN William T both of Great Falls NH *MS* 4
Mar 1840

GILMAN Harriet Mrs of Gilmanton m MACK John G of Deerfield on 8
Jul *MS* 7 Aug 1850

GILMAN Lucinda R m LIBBEY Oscar F both of Lowell MA on 20 Feb
1848 *MS* 8 Mar 1848

GILMAN Lucy D of Dover NH m CLARK John C at Dover NH on 13
Jan *MS* 22 Jan 1845

GILMAN Lydia m JACKMAN Richard on 2 Feb 1843 *MS* 19 Apr 1843

GILMAN Mahala of Bristol NH m PLUMMER Henry of Thornton on
22 May *MS* 2 Aug 1843

GILMAN Maria P m SANBORN Enoch H both of Gilford in Gilford NH
Thanksgiving Day *MS* 16 Feb 1842

GILMAN Mary Ann m FRENCH Jonathan on 9th inst at New Market
MS 19 Feb 1845

GILMAN Mary Jane of Eaton m DAVIS David W Doctor of Greenwood
ME *MS* 21 Jan 1846 & *MS* 22 Oct 1845

GILMAN Mary P of Sebec m PATTERSON Alfred Eld of Sebec ME *MS*
27 Nov 1844

GILMAN Miriam m CORLISS Gilman both of Sandwich on 16 Feb *MS*
26 Mar 1851

GILMAN Nancy of Epsom m KNOWLES Wm of Gilford *MS* 26 Aug
1835

GILMAN Pamelia C of Gilford m YOUNG George A on 28 Mar at
Concord *MS* 28 Apr 1847

GILMAN Saphronia D of Loudon m MUDGET John W of Gilmanton
MS 19 Dec 1933

GILMAN Sarah A m WETHERBEE Daniel J both of Sandwich on 9
Aug *MS* 24 Oct 1849

GILMAN Sarah of Sangerville ME m McPHETERS Sanford J of
Hermon on 1 May 1848 *MS* 5 Jul 1848

GILPATRICK Ann M of Saco m MOONEY Samuel of Boston MA
MFWBR 12 May 1849

GILPATRICK Eliza m STIMSON Thomas T of Limerick ME *MFWBR* 3
Jul 1847

GILPATRICK Sarah on 25th ult of Gardiner m TRECHER Robert of Richmond *MS* 13 Feb 1839

GILSON Harriet of Lynn m PARKS Augustus R on 24 Nov at Lynn MA *MS* 9 Dec 1846

GILSON Lucy m WILLIAM Daniel both of Kittery MA *MS* 22 Nov 1837

GIVEN Louiza of Wales ME m SMOW Thomas of Harpswell ME *MS* 21 Jan 1835

GIVEN Mary L m SWETT Charles both of Wales *MS* 29 Dec 1847

GIVEN Silence m SPARKS Nicholas Capt both of Bowdoinham ME on 28 Oct 1847 *MS* 29 Dec 1847

GIVEN Thankful of Brunswick ME m STETSON Wm P *MS* 19 Jan 1848

GLEASON Ann of Waterville ME m HUSSEY Samuel *MS* 23 Jan 1839

GLEASON Frances A of Kirkland Oneida Co NY on 26 Sept m DIKE Alexander of Auburn Theological Seminary *MS* 26 Feb 1845

GLIDDEN Abby m HODGSDON Hiram both of Great Falls NH on 17 Jan 1849 *MS* 31 Jan 1849

GLIDDEN Adaline L m HANSON William H on 11th inst at Dover NH *MS* 17 Sept 1845

GLIDDEN Emily of Gilmanton m ELKINS Eben A of Thornton *MS* 13 Mar 1839

GLIDDEN Jerusha of Farmington m SMITH James F on 10 Dec at Alton NH *MS* 3 Mar 1847

GLIDDEN Judeth of Alton on 6 Jan m FOSS Samben B *MS* 20 Feb 1839

GLIDDEN Julia Ann m BERRY John N both of Boston on 11 inst *MS* 14 Oct 1846

GLIDDEN Martha m DODGE John M both of New Durham *MS* 1 Nov 1848

GLIDDEN Mary F of Ossipee m LANG Daniel W of Brookfield on 16 Jan *MS* 5 Mar 1851

GLIDDEN Mary Jane of Meredith m RICHARDSON John of Boston MA on 5 Oct 1843 *MS* 15 Nov 1843

GLIDDEN Melissa m GOODWIN Nahum G both of Lebanon ME on 14 Oct 1848 *MS* 1 Nov 1848

GLIDDEN Melissa Jane m GOODWIN Geo W both of Tamworth NH on 5 Oct 1848 *MS* 1 Nov 1848

GLIDDEN Mercy m STRAW Ezra on 24 Apr 1845 at Gilmanton NH *MS* 28 May 1845

GLIDDEN Nancy of Gilford on 3 Oct m MOONEY Joseph of Sandwich *MS* 16 Oct 1839

GLIDDEN Sarah on 21 Dec 1842 at Roxbury MA m HODGDON James C *MS* 1 Feb 1843

GLIDDEN Sarah S of Gilford m CLIFFORD George W on 7 Apr 1842 at Gilford *MS* 11 May 1842

GLIDDEN Susan of Albany m NICKERSON Robert on 3 Mar at Eaton

GLIDDEN (Continued)
   NH *MS* 11 May 1842
GLIDDEN Tabitha m LUCAS Mark C both of Dover on 17 Apr *MS* 9
   May 1849
GLIFFORD Lylda L m WELLS Rodney S both of Manchester on 25
   Nov 1847 *MS* 8 Dec 1847
GLINES Lucina m CHASE Hosea of Meredith on 14 Jan *MS* 12 Feb
   1851
GLOVER Atlanta of Burford Canada m IDE Frederick of Newpond on
   23 Oct *MS* 1 Jan 1840
GLOVER Lucretia of Bafford m BALDWIN Isaac on 17 Jan of Bafford
   MS 13 Apr 1842
GODDARD Louise C of Brunswick ME m QUINT Nathl V of Topsham
   on 25 Dec 1848 *MS* 17 Jan 1849
GODDARD Marian m BISHOP Nicholas both of New Lyme on 19 Nov
   1848 *MS* 3 Jan 1849
GODDRIDGE Eliza Jane m YEATON Andrew both of Belgrade ME on
   3 ist *MS* 10 Feb 1836
GODDWIN Martha m COBB Uriah on 16 Jan *MS* 6 Feb 1834
GODFREY Betsey S m BARKER Andrew H both of Manchester on 6
   Feb 1849 *MS* 14 Feb 1849
GODFREY Elizabeth M m CHANDLER John R of Manchester NH *MS*
   10 Sept 1845
GODFREY Hannah Miss of Wales ME m SMITH Thomas 4th of Litch-
   field *MS* 21 Mar 1833
GODFREY Hannah of Manchester m YOUNG Stephen Jr of Pittsfield
   on 24 Nov 1847 *MS* 8 Dec 1847
GODFREY Lusette E m PARKER Harrison G on 11 Feb 1847 at
   Sheldon NY *MS* 6 Apr 1847
GODFREY Margaret C d/o GODFREY A Esq m FULLER Frederick A
   Esq *MS* 15 May 1839
GODFREY Martha Ann of Pittsfield m LOVING Daniel R of Medford
   MA on 14 Nov *MS* 27 Nov 1844
GODFREY Mary L on 18th inst at Manchester m RICKER David *MS*
   28 Aug 1839
GODING Esther S m NUTTING Edward D *MFWBR* 28 Apr 1849
GOFF Mary Ann of Gray (ME?) m THAYER Warren on 10 Nov *MS* 10
   May 1843
GOLATHWRIGHT Mary E m HUSSEY William M on 14 Aug 1843 at
   Biddeford ME *MS* 23 Aug 1843 & *MS* 13 Mar 1844
GOLDSMITH Harriet C m ABBOTT Moses C both of Ossipee NH on
   19 Dec *MS* 15 Jan 1851
GOLDSMITH Mary at Ossipee 8 ult m COOK P M *MS* 22 Apr 1840
GOLDSMITH Melissa J m BROWN Joseph F on 1 Jan 1843 at
   Ossipee NH *MS* 31 May 1843
GOLDTHWAITE Harriot A of Saco ME m BRUELL James of Biddeford

GOLDTHWAITE (Continued)
ME *MFWBR* 25 Sept 1847

GOLDTHWAITE Susan m KINGSLEY Robert both of Somersworth on 29 Jul *MS* 15 Aug 1849

GOODALE Phebe I of Limington ME m ADAMS John F of Buxton ME *MS* 7 Feb 1844

GOODALL Susan of Farmington ME m GOODWIN Sewall of Lebanon ME on 4 Jul 1844 at Farmington NH *MS* 7 Aug 1844

GOODELL Rhoda E m YOUNG Furber on 25 Sept *MS* 11 Feb 1846

GOODHUE Martha d/o GOODHUE Stephen of Hebron NH m KITTREDGE Aaron Dr of Limerick ME *MS* 6 May 1826

GOODRICH Cyntha m FLANEGIN Charles on 20 June at Hume NY *MS* 31 Aug 1836

GOODRICH Eliza A m DOW Hezekiah B of Biddeford ME *MFWBR* 20 Apr 1850

GOODRICH Rhoda m DURRELL Nathan G both of Biddeford on 5 Feb 1848 *MS* 8 Mar 1848

GOODRICH Sabrina H of Nottingham m HARVEY Jacob C on 19 Jan at New Market *MS* 28 Jan 1846

GOODRIDGE Lydia Ann of Belgrade m YEATON Paul Jr on 28 Jul *MS* 8 Jan 1845

GOODRIDGE Nancy m FOGG John both of Industry on 1 Nov 1837 *MS* 10 Jan 1838

GOODSELL Amelia m PEAT Thomas both of Mooers NY on 7 inst *MS* 27 mar 1850

GOODSMITH Mary m COOK P M on 8 ult *MS* 22 Apr 1840

GOODSPEED Eunice of B m HALL A C of B on 22 Dec 1843 *MS* 1 May 1844

GOODWILL Olive E of Berwick ME m ANDREWS Nathaniel of Water-boro' ME on 25 Sept *MS* 15 Sept 1834

GOODWIN Abigail m SMITH Paul both of Lebanon ME *MS* 3 May 1848

GOODWIN Abigail Mrs m TWOMBLY Meshech on 24 Nov at Lowell MA *MS* 18 Dec 1844

GOODWIN Apphia of Lowell m REED Francis of Biblical School Whitestown on 5 inst *MS* 18 Jul 1849

GOODWIN Eliza A of Lowell m HOIT Charles W on 12th inst at Lowell *MS* 18 Mar 1846

GOODWIN Elizabeth m TRIPP Nathaniel M on 3 Nov 1850 *MS* 8 Jan 1851

GOODWIN Elizabeth at Gardiner ME m THOMPSON Haron of Richmond *MS* 4 Sept 1839

GOODWIN Fanny of Somersworth m McCRILLIS Calvin of Lowell MA *MS* 1 Dec 1847

GOODWIN H C m MAY Silas *MS* 15 Dec 1847

GOODWIN Hannah m JORDAN Benjamin R *MS* 19 Oct 1832

GOODWIN Hannah of Lowell m GOODWIN Wm of Shapleigh ME on 19 ult *MS* 3 Oct 1838

GOODWIN Hannah S m BESSE Alexander on 22 Aug at Great Falls NH *MS* 9 Nov 1842

GOODWIN Harriet m HURD Jonathan B both of Lowell on 11 Nov *MS* 15 Dec 1847

GOODWIN Harriet E of Lebanon ME m RICKER William 2nd on 12th inst in Dover NH *MS* 8 Mar 1843

GOODWIN Lydia Ann at Lowell MA m SLOOM Alexander *MS* 3 May 1843

GOODWIN Margaret L of Lebanon ME m NEWELL George W of Lawrence MA on 14 May 1848 *MS* 24 May 1848

GOODWIN Mary A m BURPEE Cyrus B both of Manchester on 9 June *MS* 24 June 1846

GOODWIN Mary A of North Berwick m HOBBS James Jr of South Berwick ME *MFWBR* 24 Feb 1849

GOODWIN Mary A of Portsmouth NH m STILES William on 26 Sept at Portsmouth NH *MS* 10 Oct 1844

GOODWIN Mary J m PENNEY Arioch W on 9 Sept *MS* 8 Jan 1851

GOODWIN Mary of Milton m GARLAND Franklin of Wakefield on 25th ult at Milton NH *MS* 8 Dec 1841

GOODWIN Mary of Pittston ME m WHITE Wm of Hallowell ME on 13 inst *MS* 23 Nov 1836

GOODWIN May F m COLEMAN Joseph W both of Dover on 13 inst *MS* 21 Feb 1849

GOODWIN Mercy A m BLAISDELL Ira *MS* 6 Dec 1848

GOODWIN Miranda m STONE Joseph on 18 Oct of Lowell *MS* 22 Feb 1843

GOODWIN Nancy on 3d ult m HORSON Joseph *MS* 17 Apr 1839

GOODWIN Ruth L of Lawrence m HARMON Henry M of Roxbury on 20 Oct *MS* 27 Nov 1850

GOODWIN Sarah m EDMONDS Joseph on 17 Oct 1844 at Roxbury MA *MS* 6 Nov 1844

GOODWIN Sarah A m BRACKETT Joshua on 1 Apr at Kennebunkport ME *MS* 23 Apr 1845

GOODWIN Sarah A m OSGOOD B F both of Manchester on 7 Apr 1849 *MS* 25 Apr 1849

GOODWIN Sarah A of Dover NH m RAND Leonard of Haverville MA on 6th inst at Dover NH *MS* 12 May 1847

GOODWIN Selinda m JOSE Martin on 29 Nov of Lyman *MS* 6 Jan 1847

GOOWIN Melissa (perhaps GOODWIN?) m FOX William on 23 Feb of Stanstead Canada *MS* 13 Sept 1843

GORDAN Maria m SCAMMAN Stephen of Stratham *MS* 26 Nov 1834

GORDON Alma Jane m WOOD John on 23 Nov at St Albans ME *MS* 27 Dec 1843

GORDON Caroline R m FELLOWS Ezekiel W both of Hebron on 13 Jan 1848 *MS* 26 Jan 1848

GORDON Charlotte of St Albans ME m MARTIN Jacob on 22 Mar of St Albans ME *MS* 7 June 1843

GORDON Elizabeth of Hollis ME m GUILFORD Joseph *MS* 14 June 1843

GORDON Hannah of Candia m BROWN Josiah *MS* 10 Sept 1834

GORDON Julia A of Augusta m FLETCHER Henry A of Mt Vernon ME on 29 Feb 1848 *MS* 15 Mar 1848

GORDON Julia Ann m JACKMAN Frederick B on at Lowell MA *MS* 8 Feb 1837

GORDON Loisa of Chatham NH m FIFE Peter of Stowe ME on 18 Dec 1849 *MS* 20 Feb 1850

GORDON Lucy of Candia on 25 Jan m ANDREWSON Joseph F of Raymond *MS* 1 Feb 1843

GORDON Lydia A m RICHARDS Leonard J both of Lancaster MA on 25 Nov 1847 *MS* 15 Dec 1847

GORDON Lydia D m SEWARD Charles B on 17 May at Dracut MA *MS* 2 June 1847

GORDON Mary Ann at New Hampton on 4th ult m EATON William of Meredith *MS* 10 Apr 1839

GORDON Mehitabel of Lowell MA m MORSE Stephen of Canton NH at Lowell MA *MS* 29 May 1844

GORDON Melinda of Hatley m SIMONDS Samuel G on 24 Jan at Landaff NH *MS* 13 Apr 1842

GORDON Rhoda P m CLOSE Aaron M on 23 Apr of Bangor ME *MS* 30 June 1847

GORDON Roxana of N Hampton m CHASE Luther M of Meredith on 7 inst *MS* 24 Feb 1836

GORDON Sarah A K of New Hampton m RIKE Jonathan R of Collinsville CT on 25 Aug *MS* 22 Sept 1847

GORDON Sarah C of Chatham NH m STEVENS Joseph W of Fryeburg ME on 31 Dec 1849 *MS* 20 Feb 1850

GORDON Sally of Limerick m McKUESICK Nahum of Limerick ME on Sunday evening last *MS* 24 May 1827

GORDON Susan of Topsham m LOVEJOY Cyrus H of Landaff NH on 17 ult *MS* 7 Nov 1838

GORSELINE Mary of Scriba m PEASE Alfred of Oswego on 29 Nov 1848 *MS* 17 Jan 1849

GORSLINE Margaret m KELSO David on Oct 4 at Scriba Oswego Co NY *MS* 18 Nov 1846

GORSLINE Silvina of Scriba NY m GREEN Peter A of Granby on 4 Oct *MS* 18 Nov 1846

GORTON Sarah A of No Providence RI m MANCHESTER Niles of Smithfield on 29th ult *MS* 18 Feb 1835

GOSS Elizabeth A m GILFORD Everett W both of Meredith on 26 Jan

GOSS (Continued)
MS 19 Feb 1851

GOSS Lydia of New Hampton m PLUMMER Jesse of Meredith *MS* 8 Feb 1837

GOSS Olive R m PINKHAM H C *MS* 15 Dec 1847

GOSS Sally S m GILMAN John S both of Gilford on Thanksgiving Day *MS* 23 Feb 1848

GOSS Sarah S m HUGGINS Nathaniel N *MS* 2 Feb 1848

GOTHAM Ann J W m NUTTER William Jr *MFWBR* 18 Aug 1849

GOTT Susan m FOGG Alvin both of Sandwich NH on 6 inst *MS* 18 Oct 1848

GOULD Amanda P of Biddeford ME m HANSCOMB Ezra D of Biddeford ME *MFWBR* 13 Feb 1847

GOULD Angenette m CHAPMAN John C on 12 June at Dracut MA *MS* 7 Jul 1847

GOULD Climena of Lowell MA m BEAU Daniel R of Raymond NH on 9 Dec 1848 *MS* 3 Jan 1849

GOULD Dorcas D of Dexter ME m GILMAN Moses Jr at Sangerville ME on 21 Sept at Dexter ME *MS* 7 Dec 1842

GOULD Elizabeth of Dover m TREADWELL Thos D of Cambridge MA on 6th inst *MS* 12 Nov 1834

GOULD Emily E of Lowell m EDSON James A of Brookline NH on 9 Sept *MS* 14 Oct 1846

GOULD Fanny of Saco ME on 17 Jan m KEATON Hartwill of Biddeford ME *MS* 6 Apr 1847

GOULD Hannah J of Biddeford m SMITH Wm of Kennebunkport ME on 23 June 1847 *MS* 25 Aug 1847

GOULD Joanna L m CHASE Ambrose both of Hopkinton on 14 May *MS* 22 June 1836

GOULD Louisa m WHITEHOUSE Samuel on 27 Jan at Berwick ME *MS* 31 Aug 1842

GOULD Louisa of Dexter ME m BAILEY Martin L of Cambridge (ME?) *MS* 17 May 1843

GOULD Lovey E m SARGENT Calvin both of Amesbury MA on 31 Dec 1850 *MS* 8 Jan 1851

GOULD Mary m MORRISON Jonathan on 30 June at Tuftonboro' NH *MS* 4 Aug 1847

GOULD Mary m WILLOUGHBY John on 12 at Holderness *MS* 8 Mar 1837

GOULD Mary E m RICKER Joseph P both of Westbrook ME on 25 Dec 1848 *MS* 3 Jan 1849

GOULD Patience Miss of Wayne ME m CURTIS Silas Eld of Minot ME *MS* 16 Dec 1831

GOULD Permelia A m HEYDON Parker both of Phoenix NY on 5 Dec 1847 *MS* 22 Dec 1847

GOULD Sarah P of Dexter ME on 30th Mar m BEAN Arlo C of Exeter

GOULD (Continued)
ME *MS* 17 May 1843

GOULD Susanna of Lowell MA m PIERCE Leonidas of Brooklin NH on 11 Sept at Lowell MA *MS* 27 Sept 1843

GOULD Sybil W of Anson ME on 22 Jan 1843 m WAIT Holton *MS* 19 Apr 1843

GOURD Hannah M m BRACKETT John both of Colebrook NH 17 Jan 1849 *MS* 7 Feb 1849

GOVE Elizabeth m WEST Albert M on 14 Sept at Strafford VT *MS* 19 Oct 1842

GOVE Elizabeth of Boston MA m FOLSOM William R C on 28 Mar *MS* 10 Apr 1844

GOVE Elizabeth of Strafford VT m WEST Albert M on 14 Sept *MS* 1 Feb 1843

GOVE Hannah m STILES Joseph both of Portsmouth on 22 ult *MS* 15 Apr 1835

GOVE Mary Ann m HADLEY Enoch Dea both of Deering on 23 June *MS* 5 Aug 1846

GOVE Sarah Miss [Goodwin- name found in records of Robert Taylor of Danville ME] of Limington ME m EDGERLY Rook T on Dec 6th 1843 *MS* 7 Feb 1844

GOVE Sarah S Mrs (d/o John & Rebecca [Small] GOVE) m EDGER-LY Rook T on 13 Jan 1848 at Limington ME *MS* 16 Feb 48

GOVE Selina B of Readfield ME m HUNT Elias of Lincoln on 21 March at Readfield ME *MS* 31 Mar 1847

GOVER Sarah A both formerly of Maine m LANE Edward F on 13 Oct *MS* 13 Nov 1850

GOWDY Mary Mrs of Ossipee NH m STEVENS Moses of Gilmanton on 4 Sept *MS* 14 Sept 1836

GOWELL Mary B of Bowdoin ME m BOWDMAN Abijah of Topsham ME *MS* 10 Feb 1847

GOWELL Mary of Great Falls m HOBSON Amos of Hollis ME on 11 Oct 1848 *MS* 18 Oct 1848

GOWEN Anceline m LITTLEFIELD Edwin on 15 Nov at Wells ME *MS* 20 Jan 1847

GOWEN Hannah m THING Gilman of Waterboro on 13th inst *MS* 19 Nov 1828

GOWEN Lydia A of Biddeford m YOUNG Soloman Tarr [s/o Rodolpha & Nancy (Tarr) YOUNG] of Ossipee NH on 5 Sept *MS* 27 Oct 1847

GOWEN Mary m BEAN Joseph both of Waterborough ME on 30 Sept *MS* 22 Dec 1847 & *MFWBR* 23 Oct 1847

GOWER Hannah A of New Sharon ME m CRAIGG Charles S of Farmington *MFWBR* 16 Nov 1850

GOWIN Mary Ann of Shapleigh ME m HART William S of Lebanon *MS* 25 Oct 1843

GRACE Betsy of Dover NH m NUTTER Lewis on 15 Nov at Dover NH

GRACE (Continued)
MS 25 Nov 1846

GRAFFAM Maria G m CHAPMAN Eben'r both of Baldwin ME on 20 Jan *MS* 24 Jul 1850

GRAHAM Lepheau m LOVELESS Charles W both of Hadley on 23 Feb 1850 *MS* 1 May 1850

GRAND Eliza D of Bridgton m BOOTHBY Alexander of Unity on 9 Apr 1849 *MS* 25 Apr 1849

GRANDY Amandy m ABLEMAN Joseph C both of Johnstown W T *MS* 8 Dec 1847

GRANDY Lavina m ABLEMAN G L both of Johnstown W T *MS* 8 Dec 1847

GRANT Abigail J m SHAW E M both of Brewer ME 21 Sept 1847 *MS* 17 Nov 1847

GRANT Betsey m MERRELL Seth *MS* 23 Nov 1826

GRANT Deborah A of Gilford NH m OSGOOD James at Meredith NH *MS* 16 Nov 1842

GRANT Elizabeth of Dover NH m McCOY Israel of Manchester NH on 28 Nov *MS* 9 Dec 1846

GRANT Elizabeth R of Richmond ME m COOMBS Robert of Bowdoin ME on 25th ult at Richmond ME *MS* 16 Oct 1844

GRANT Emma H of Portland ME m MAYO Alphonso A *MFWBR* 9 Nov 1850

GRANT Louisa L on 19th inst m GILMORE Alfred Hon *MFWBR* 30 Nov 1850

GRANT Lucy P of Lyme m LITCHFIELD A B of Manchester on 23 Oct *MS* 30 Oct 1850

GRANT Lydia of Dover m BABB Isaac on 29 Mar at Dover NH *MS* 28 Apr 1847

GRANT Margaret m WALVERTON Amos of Conquest on 2d ult *MS* 13 June 1833

GRANT Mary m WARD Isaac both of Freeport ME on 1 Dec in Freeport ME *MS* 25 Dec 1850

GRANT Mercy of Gilford m GILMAN Manoah of Alton NH on 27 Nov *MS* 25 Jan 1843

GRANT Nancy m LUNT Israel B on at Mt Desert ME *MS* 9 Dec 1831

GRANT Nancy of Dixmont m CLARK Gershom *MS* 16 Jan 1839

GRANT Nancy S of Meredith on 19 Oct 1842 m FULLER Edwin of Cheslsea VT *MS* 25 Jan 1843

GRANT Sarah Jane of Gray m THAYER George W on 9 Oct at Gray ME *MS* 26 Nov 1845

GRANVILLE Elizabeth of Parsonsfield ME m FOSS Jeremiah L of Limington ME *MS* 14 Jul 1847

GRANVILLE Sophronia A m CHAMPION Cyrus K both of Effingham on 28 Nov *MS* 12 Jan 1848

GRASON Susan of Killingly CT m STONE John B of Foster RI

GRASON (Continued)
MS 10 Oct 1844

GRATHAM Sarah m DILL John A on 3 Jul at Lowell *MS* 2 Nov 1842

GRAVES Abby A m JENKINS Leonard on 9 May *MS* 12 June 1850

GRAVES Angelina P of Tuftonborough NH m WIGGIN Mark T of Wolfboro NH on 24 Apr 1849 *MS* 9 May 1849

GRAVES Cynthia m ROSS James M on 24 ult *MS* 18 Jul 1838

GRAVES Mary O m BEARDSLEY Ezra W both of Rochester Wis on 5 Sept in Rochester Racine Co Wis *MS* 17 Oct 1849

GRAY Abigail m DAVIS Amaziah H on 2 inst *MS* 6 Feb 1834

GRAY Betsey Y of New Durham m PINKHAM George C on 9 Nov 1842 at Farmington *MS* 1 Mar 1843

GRAY Betsey of Dover m HEAD Sampson of Conway NH on 15 Jan *MS* 12 Aug 1846

GRAY Caskalicean W m GORHAM William E both of Boston on 11 June 1848 in Boston *MS* 28 June 1848

GRAY Delia of Monmouth ME m STEVENS James at Monmouth ME *MS* 28 Feb 1844

GRAY Dorothy m DOWNING Ebenezer both of Somersworth NH on Sabbath last *MS* 1 Nov 1837

GRAY Dorothy O m WELCH Samuel W both of Dover on 3 inst *MS* 10 Apr 1850 & *MFWBR* 20 Apr 1850

GRAY Eliza T m HODGDON Wm both of Barrington NH *MS* 11 Jan 1837

GRAY Elizabeth m SANBORN Joseph in Waterboro' *MS* 15 Mar 1827

GRAY Hannah m DANFORD Hiram both of Dover on 31st ult *MS* 3 Sept 1834

GRAY Hannah Jane m PINKHAM Burleigh on 17th inst at Dover NH *MS* 24 Mar 1847

GRAY Lydia m VARNEY Lewis D on 14 Sept 1842 at Rochester *MS* 21 Sept 1842

GRAY Lydia H of Bowdoinham ME m MORTON Thomas of Boston MA on 15 May at Bowdoinham ME *MS* 1 June 1842

GRAY Maria L d/o GRAY Barber SANDERS John *MS* 13 Feb 1834

GRAY Martha F of Dover m YOUNG Jonathan Esq of Barrington NH on 18 inst *MS* 26 Jul 1848

GRAY Orpha of Sheffield m FURNESS James R of Dorchester MA on 29 Sept *MS* 9 Oct 1850

GRAY Phebe P of Montpelier VT m TABOR Ebenezer on 14 Jul at Montpelier VT *MS* 2 Oct 1844

GRAY Rebecca m DANIELS Israel on Fri *MS* 2 Jan 1834

GRAY Sarah A of Rochester NH m TUFTS Amos on 21st ult at Dover NH *MS* 1 Oct 1845

GRAY Sarah Ann m HANSCOM James E on 21st ult at Dover NH *MS* 1 Oct 1845

GRAY Sarah Jane m SILVA John of Madeira on 13th inst at New

GRAY (Continued)
York City *MS* 21 Sept 1842

GREAR Lucinda m SANBORN Alvin on 16 Mar at Manchester *MS* 26 Mar 1845

GREAR Lucy V m FOSTER James G Capt on 18 Aug at Monroe ME *MS* 24 Dec 1845

GREAT Mary H m SMITH Thomas T at Great Falls NH *MS* 7 Jul 1847

GREEN Amanda m BILLINS Joseph both of Danby VT on 17 Oct *MS* 7 Nov 1838

GREEN Angerona m CHASE Archibald M on 7 Sept of Stephentown NY *MS* 4 Dec 1844

GREEN Caroline A of Stephentown NY m HICKS Philander W of New Lebanon *MS* 31 Oct 1849

GREEN Catharine m GREEN Daniel both of Barrington on 21 Apr Sunday eve *MS* 8 May 1850

GREEN Catherine Mrs of Manchester NH m TUCKER Joel of Goffstown on 28 Apr at Manchester NH *MS* 7 May 1845

GREEN Clarissa m PLACE Robert both of Lowell MA *MS* 4 Oct 1837

GREEN Delilah d/o GREEN David Eld m COPPS William both of Meredith on 21 Aug *MS* 7 Nov 1849

GREEN Julia Ann of Loudon m TRUE Cyrus D of Pittsfield on 29 Apr *MS* 16 May 1849

GREEN Louiza B Miss of Conewanga Catarangus Co NY m WHITCHER Hiram Eld an itinerant preacher on 9th inst *MS* 31 Aug 1832

GREEN Lucenith P of Pittsfield m MARSTON Samuel on 27 Aug at Pittsfield *MS* 10 Feb 1847

GREEN Mary m DIBBLE Daniel both of Freedom on 7 Mar 1849 *MS* 9 May 1849

GREEN Mary m VICKERY Joshua both of Rochester on 2 May *MS* 22 May 1850

GREEN Mary S of Epsom NH m WALDRON William Eld of Lynn MA on 5 Nov at Epsom NH *MS* 18 Nov 1846

GREEN Rachel H of Pittsfield NH m SMITH George of Barnstead on 27 Mar *MS* 6 Apr 1842

GREEN Rozilla Mrs of Knox Co IL m HARLEY Caleb B on 26th ult at Walnut Grove Knox Co IL *MS* 23 June 1847

GREEN Sarah C d/o GREEN John Deacon of Brown Co formerly of New England m CATE William W of Payson on 26 Jul near Mt Sterling Brown Co IL *MS* 25 Sept 1844

GREEN Susan m HUNT Jason at Gilford *MS* 13 Dec 1843

GREEN Susan G m KNIGHT Daniel on 5th inst at Portland ME *MS* 28 Feb 1844

GREEN Susan of Lisbon ME m PURRINGTON Stephen of Bowdoin ME *MS* 27 Jan 1836

GREEN? Jane B at Pittsfield Dec 8 1839 m LANE Reuben C *MS* 6

GREEN? (Continued)
May 1840

GREENE W of Warwick RI m PHELON Benjamin Eld of Central Village No Providence on Wed morn 11 June *MS* 18 Jul 1838

GREENLAU Sarah of Brownfield m THOMPSON Addison of Boston MA *MS* 13 Mar 1844

GREENLEAF Anna of Starks ME m WOOD James at Starks ME *MS* 11 Oct 1843

GREENLEAF Caroline G of Saco ME m MADDOX Thomas F *MFWBR* 4 May 1850

GREENLEAF Ellen B on 10th inst at Saco ME m MILLET Cyrus *MFWBR* 22 Feb 1851

GREENLEAF Harriet R m ELY Robert D on 3 Oct 1847 *MS* 24 Nov 1847

GREENLEAF Mary wid of late Dea Asa of Hallowell m SNOW Isaac of Windsor *MS* 20 June 1838

GREENLEAF Susan Mrs in Portland m TODD Thomas Maj proprietor of the *Eastern Argus* paper *MS* 10 Aug 1826

GREENWOOD Mary E m WATSON Charles A on 12 Nov at Weld ME *MS* 23 Dec 1846

GREGORY Huldah m WHEELER John Eld both of Greenfield *MS* 2 Jan 1850

GREGORY Susan of Corinth ME m LORD John on 24 Nov 1842 at Corinth ME *MS* 28 Feb 1844

GREY Margaret m WILLIARD Samuel both of Sheffield on 4 Feb *MS* 15 Jul 1835

GRIFFETH Lydia m ROCKWAY Daman both of Schroeppel NY on 23 Sept *MS* 17 Nov 1847

GRIFFETH Marinda of Schroeppel Ny m RICE John P of Phoenix on 1 Feb 1849 *MS* 2 May 1849

GRIFFIN Hannah m KNOWLES David M on 22 Sept at Epsom NH *MS* 19 Oct 1842

GRIFFIN Hannah B m ALLEN Joseph H at Danville *MS* 11 Jan 1843 & *MS* 1 Feb 1843

GRIFFIN Mary Jane of Dover m LANE John K of Gloucester MA on Wednesday morn last *MS* 13 Feb 1850

GRIFFIN Mary L of Epsom NH m EDMONDS Aaron of Northwood NH on 29 Nov 1849 *MS* 16 Jan 1850

GRIFFIN Palmyra B of Stephentown m DUNHAM Nelson B of Nassau 29 ult *MS* 1 Feb 1837

GRIFFITH Lucille of New York m MORRELL John A L of Cincinnati Oh on 23d inst in the Presbyterian Church at Perth Amboy NJ *MS* 4 Aug 1847

GROSS Caroline H m FISK Roswell C both of Manchester on 7 Dec *MS* 26 Dec 1849

GROSS Sally ae 50y at N Hampton NH m SPILLER Wheeler ae 15y

GROSS (Continued)
MS 6 May 1826

GROUT Sarah J of Columbia m BEAN John C of Colebrook on 25 Nov 1847 *MS* 15 Dec 1847

GROVER Hannah of Bowdoin ME m TARR Daniel M of Webster ME on 11 Jan 1849 *MS* 24 Jan 1849

GROVER Mahitabel Jordon m SHEPHERD Luke both of Bowdoin MEon 1 Jan 1850 *MS* 3 Apr 1850

GROVER Margaret m BRIMEJOHN Job both of Richmond ME *MS* 27 Jan 1836 [N.B. Job may be the s/o Thomas "BRIMIJOIN" who came from Philadelphia PA and settled in Bowdoin ME.]

GROVER Mary A m CHAPMAN Gilbert both of Bethel *MS* 17 June 1846

GROVER Rhoda of Kilmarhock ME m HOPKINS Gamaliel C on 14 Dec *MS* 1 Feb 1837

GULLIVER Harriet on 15th inst m CHAPMAN Emerson *MFWBR* 3 Mar 1849

GUPPY Sarah Ann m HENDERSON Samuel H Capt in Dover NH 5 inst Thursday *MS* 18 Jul 1838

GUPPY Sophia of Rochester m HURD John of Berwick ME on 29th ult *MS* 7 May 1834

GUPTIL Dorcas m LOCK Hamilton both of Wolfborough NH on 13 Oct *MS* 16 Oct 1850

GUPTIL Mary Ann m STACY George Jr of Elliot ME on 12th inst *MS* 29 May 1844

GUPTIL Mary of Waterboro m DAY Theodore *MS* 28 May 1828

GUPTILL Livona H m PARKER Elihu Jr on 11 Apr at Cornish *MS* 29 May 1844

GUPTILL R I m MIGHLS [*sic*] Joseph D both of Limerick ME on 24 Oct 1847 *MS* 22 Dec 1847

GUPTILL Susannah W of Limerick ME m MORRILL Thomas C on 28 Apr 1842 at Limerick ME *MS* 18 May 1842

HACKET Martha Jane m CLARK D Mr on 2d inst at Dover NH *MS* 13 Jan 1847

HACKETT Abby C of Windham m DUNN Isaiah on 27 May at Windham ME *MS* 7 Jul 1847

HACKETT Eliza Ann of Gilmanton m HACKETT J Carlton of Boston on 20 ult *MS* 5 Jul 1837

HACKETT Mary A of Tunbridge m PERKINS Horatio M of Chelsea on 5 Dec *MS* 2 Jan 1850

HACKETT Mary Jane of Upper Gilmanton m LEIGHTON Andrew D Capt of Strafford on 1 Sept *MS* 1 Oct 1834

HACKETT Nancy m SMITH Stephen L on 14 Nov *MS* 15 Dec 1847

HADLEY Anna L of Weare NH m FAVOR Moses G on 6 Jan at Manchester NH *MS* 6 Apr 1842

HADLEY Emily m WALLACE David of Holderness on 20 Nov 1842 MS 15 Mar 1843

HADLEY Jane of Gilmanton m HADLEY Moses C of Meredith on 15 Nov MS 25 Jan 1843

HADLEY Oliva L of Bethlehem m BRIDGHAM Luther of Lowell MA on 12 Nov MS 4 Feb 1846

HADLEY Rhoda m TAPPAN Daniel both of Sandwich on 7 Nov MS 1 Dec 1847

HADLEY Sarah B d/o HALEY Dr Hiram & gd/o Eld H D BUZZELL of Alton NH m SMITH George W Esq Att at Law & editor of *Herkimer Journal* paper *MFWBR* 9 Jan 1847

HADLEY Sophia m BRIGGS Sumner both of Lowell MA on 1 June 1848 MS 28 June 1848

HAGGAETT Ann m DODGE Washington both of Edgecomb ME on 22 Dec 1847 MS 12 Jan 1848

HAGGET Julia A of Edgecomb ME m BROOKS Horatio G of Dunkirk NH on 6 Mar MS 2 Apr 1851

HAGGETT Lydia of Edgecomb ME on 22 Dec 1842 m HAGGETT William Jr MS 4 Jan 1843

HAIGHT Amy E of Laurens m HARRISON Salmon of Addison on 14 Apr MS 8 May 1850

HAINES Adelaide of Canterbury Principal of Female Seminary at Parsonsfield m CILLEY Daniel P Rev of New Market on 13th inst MS 27 Jan 1836

HAINES Betsey F m LIBBY Amos *MFWBR* 21 Jan 1849

HAINES Elizabeth W of Canterbury on 22 May m WEEKS Stephen Jr of Gilmanton MS 19 June 1844

HAINES Hannah L of Dover NH m HAINES Matthias M of Wolfboro' at Dover on 1st inst MS 9 June 1847

HAINES Hannah of Saco m LIBBY Silas J of Scarborough ME on 1 Nov MS 21 Nov 1838

HAINES Isabella S m GILFORD Aaron on 15 May at Manchester MS 5 June 1844

HAINES Judith J m HAINES Samuel G both of Deerfield on 21 Feb MS 29 Mar 1848

HAINES Lydia J of Nottingham m KNOWLTON Ebenezer MS 9 July 1834

HAINES Lydia O m CLOUGH Jones L both of Biddeford ME MS 13 Feb 1850

HAINES Sarah K of Exeter m PHILBRICK Edwain T on 17 Feb at Exeter MS 3 Mar 1847

HAINES Sarah S of Moultonboro' m QUINBY John M of Sandwich MS 18 June 1845

HALE Clarissa m FULLER Cyrus of Stow VT MS 30 Nov 1842

HALE Eliza Ann m DEARBORN John of Effingham on 1st inst MS 8 Nov 1827

HALE Emma d/o HALE Isaac of Harmony (PA?) Co of Susquehannah m SMITH Joseph (author of the Book of Mormon) *MS* 30 Jul 1834

HALE Louisa F on 5th inst m CUTTER Abiel Abbott *MFWBR* 8 Sept 1849

HALE Martha of Bradford MA m PLUMMER Henry H of So Berwick ME on 17 Oct *MS* 25 Nov 1835

HALE Martha A of Litchfield ME m TAPLEY Wm T of Dedham MA on 4 June 1848 *MS* 14 June 1848

HALE Martha S m SHACKFORD Samuel B both of Barrington on 5th inst *MS* 19 Apr 1837

HALE Mary Angeline m WATTS Chamber on 27 Sept at Stow VT *MS* 30 Nov 1842

HALE Nancy Jane m CORLISS Aaron on 2 Feb at Manchester NH *MS* 19 Feb 1845

HALE Susan C of Vienna m HOIT Silvester on 20th at Vienna *MS* 16 Apr 1845

HALEY Abby A of Cornish m WOODMAN Andrew J of Saco ME on 2 Feb *MS* 26 Feb 1851

HALEY Joanna H of Dover m HAYES Daniel on Sunday *MS* 12 Nov 1834

HALEY Olive S m GARLAND David on 30 May at Boston *MS* 7 Jul 1847

HALEY Sally of Lincoln m WITHAM Levi *MS* 23 Oct 1839

HALEY Sylva M of Hollis on 12 May m COUSENS John of Kennebunk ME *MS* 26 June 1844

HALL Ann M of Lowell MA m JONES Joseph B *MS* 25 Sept 1839

HALL Armina m REMINGTON Joel of Huntington VT *MS* 6 Dec 1843

HALL Armine W of Berwick ME m WENTWORTH William F of Lebanon ME *MS* 19 Jul 1848

HALL Clarissa m ROBERTS Wm H both of Somersworth Great Falls NH *MS* 23 Sept 1831

HALL Deborah of Barnstead m BUZZELL Miles of Strafford on 15th ult *MS* 12 Jul 1843

HALL Dorcas A m HALL James M both of Bowdoinham *MS* 8 Sept 1847

HALL Elizabeth Mrs of Litchfield ME m BATES Alexander of Richmond ME on 17 Dec 1848 *MS* 3 Jan 1849

HALL Elizabeth S m TUTTLE Silas Jr both of Strafford on 7 Nov *MS* 1 Dec 1847

HALL Emeline m RICHARDSON Edson at Strafford VT *MS* 11 Dec 1844

HALL Hannah m RICHARDSON Nathaniel A Esq of Woburn MA on 17 Apr Esq *MS* 25 June 1845

HALL Hannah H of Gorham ME on 19 Jan m LIBBY Almon Eld of Poland ME *MS* 1 Feb 1843

HALL Hannah of Strafford NH on 4th inst m HILL Azariah B *MS* 10

HALL (Continued)
Apr 1839

HALL Julia A of No Providence m STEARNS Isaac N on 12 inst at Johnston RI *MS* 21 Sept 1836

HALL Julia at Alfred d/o HALL Abiel Dr m APPLETON Nathan D Esq *MS* 4 Jan 1827

HALL Lois Jane of Falmouth m HAMBLEM Joseph F of Pownal ME at Falmouth ME in Dec *MS* 8 Jan 1845

HALL Lois of Sandwich on 5 Jan m ROBINSON Benjamin D of Meredith NH *MS* 24 Mar 1847

HALL Louisa m LITTLEFIELD Robert S on 25th inst at Dover NH *MS* 31 Dec 1845

HALL Louisa M m HAYNES J S both of Dover NH on 15 Nov at F B Church *MS* 5 Dec 1849

HALL Lucy m DOOR John 3d both of Dover NH on Sunday last *MS* 20 Jan 1836

HALL Martha C of Bowdoin ME m HARMON Wm of Charlestown MA *MS* 2 Aug 1848

HALL Mary A m LOUGER Frederick C both of Manchester on 18 Aug *MS* 1 Sept 1847

HALL Mary E m CASE Isaac *MFWBR* 28 Jul 1849

HALL Mary E m SUTHERLAND George W *MFWBR* 23 June 1849

HALL Mary Jane m CLEMENTS Richard on at Meredith NH *MS* 24 Aug 1836

HALL Mary of Ascott L C m RYTHER Ja of Lyndon VT on 11 Dec *MS* 15 Apr 1840

HALL Mary of Great Falls m LORD Davis B of Berwick ME *MS* 9 Oct 1839

HALL Mary P of Windham ME m CROCKETT James on 25 Apr at Windham *MS* 5 June 1844

HALL Mary V m FERREN Jonathan of Thornton on 12 May at Sandwich *MS* 5 June 1844

HALL Matilda m DREW Swain on at Barrington *MS* 26 Dec 1833

HALL Nancy P of Lee m SHUTE George G on 14 Nov at Lee *MS* 11 Dec 1844

HALL Patience m HOBBS Wentworth H both of Ossipee NH on 17 Oct 1847 *MS* 19 Apr 1848

HALL Phedelia of Clayton m SPICER Charles A on 15 Nov at Clayton of Houndsfield *MS* 10 Mar 1847

HALL Priscilla of Bowdoin m MERRILL Charles W of Bowdoinham *MS* 2 Aug 1848

HALL Rebecca A m CARD Joel Jr *MS* 8 Sept 1847

HALL Sally of Strafford m PIERCE Hall of Barrington *MS* 18 Apr 1838

HALL Sarah Ann m FALL Wilson T of North Berwick ME *MS* 17 Feb 1847 & on 10 Dec at South Berwick ME *MS* 30 Dec 1846

HALL Sarah D m BRITTON Mowry L both of No Providence RI on 21st ult *MS* 15 Jul 1835

HALL Sarah J m MORRISON Dependence both of Dover on 11 inst *MS* 22 Dec 1847

HALL Sarah W of Barnstead NH m QUINT George of Dover *MS* 20 Dec 1827

HALL Susan m RANDALL Wm both of New Market on 25th ult *MS* 31 Aug 1836

HALLET Joanna m GIFFORD David P both of Sidney ME *MS* 3 Apr 1850

HALLEY Maria Mrs of Huntington m PIERCE Charles on 27th Sept at Underhill VT *MS* 2 Dec 1846

HAM Jane m BEEDEL Joseph both of Dover on 19 Nov 1848 *MS* 7 Feb 1849

HAM Julia m McDUFFIE John H both of Rochester NH on 28 Jan 1849 *MS* 25 Apr 1849

HAM Leonora F of Strafford NH m PERKINS Darius *MS* 6 Mar 1839

HAM Lucinda of Durham m KENERSON Nathan on 3 Dec *MS* 21 Feb 1844

HAM Lydia A of Great Falls m CANEY James M of Ossipee on 24 Oct *MS* 31 Oct 1849

HAM Margaret of Barrington m HAM Clement on 28 Dec 1843 at Barrington *MS* 27 Mar 1844

HAM Martha of New Market m FRENCH Samuel Jr of Durham *MS* 6 Mar 1834

HAM Mary A of Gilmanton m ELLIOT Eli H of Barnstead on 27 Mar *MS* 19 June 1844

HAM Mary of Monmouth ME m FAYBENS Joshua of Leeds *MS* 23 Mar 1836

HAM Nancy of Shapleigh ME m RICKER Jeremiah *MFWBR* 14 Sep 1850

HAM Phebe Ann of South Berwick ME m WILKINSON James on last Sat at Dover NH *MS* 14 Jan 1846

HAM Sarah J m SEAVEY Nathaniel H both of Barrington on 29 Apr *MS* 22 May 1850

HAM Sarah J of Salisbury m SAWYER Amos of Amesbury on 12 Dec *MS* 25 Dec 1850

HAM Sarah Jane m STOKES Jonathan both of Dover on last Saturday eve *MS* 12 Dec 1849 & *MFWBR* 22 Dec 1849

HAM Sarah Mrs of Strafford m CLARK Warner Esq of Francestown on 9 Nov *MS* 13 Dec 1848

HAM Sarah m WENTWORTH Lewis E both of Dover on 11 inst *MS* 22 Nov 1848

HAMBLEN Louiza R of Monroe ME m DICKEY Alexander on 23 Nov at Dixmont ME *MS* 17 Jan 1844

HAMILTON Catharine E of Garland m STEWART Joseph M of

HAMILTON (Continued)
  Glenburn ME on 24 Sept 1848 *MS* 22 Nov 1848
HAMILTON Eliza m HAYES Joseph on 24th ult *MS* 3 Feb 1830
HAMILTON Hannah F in Garland ME Apr 17 m STEWART James W
  MS 4 May 1842
HAMILTON Laura Ann m KENDRICK William H at Bangor ME *MS* 13
  Sept 1843
HAMILTON Lovina m FOLSOM Kerm on 13th inst *MS* 18 Nov 1831
HAMILTON Lucinda of Webster ME m MACOMBER Leander M
  MFWBR 20 Mar 1847 & MACUMBER Leander M on 28 Feb of
  Montville ME *MS* 21 Apr 1847
HAMILTON Marilla J m HALL Arthur Wm both of Windsor on 13 Oct
  MS 11 Dec 1850
HAMILTON Martha A of Waterboro ME m COLE James R Dr of
  Saccarrappa ME *MFWBR* 13 Apr 1850
HAMILTON Martha C m HORN Andres J on 2d inst *MS* 20 June
  1833
HAMILTON Mary B m FOX John H both of Manchester on 4 Nov
  1848 *MS* 15 Nov 1848
HAMILTON Mary E m HAZELTON Stephen B both of Conway on 2
  Sept *MS* 20 Feb 1850
HAMILTON Mary S m SKILLINGER Leonard both of Garland on 22
  Oct 1848 *MS* 22 Nov 1848
HAMILTON Nancy of Waterboro' m KNIGHT Alvin at Great Falls NH
  MS 29 June 1842
HAMMON Dianna m ESTEE Indson [sic] on 4 Apr at Hamburgh NY
  MS 19 May 1847
HAMMOND Maryett of Canal m MANNING John S on 23 May of Big
  Bend Iowa *MS* 17 Jul 1844
HAMMOND Phebe of Danielsonville CT m MITCHELL Orrin D on 12
  May at Danielsonville, Killingly, CT of East Killingly CT [sic] *MS* 4
  June 1845
HAMMONS Nancy of Cornish m DAVIS George of Limington *MS* 22
  June 1836
HANAFORD Mary A m CHAPMAN Ebenezer both of New Market in
  New Market on Apr 17 *MS* 27 Apr 1842
HANCOCK Juritia m BROWN Daniel both of Freedom NY on 20 Feb
  1848 *MS* 10 May 1848
HANDS Rebecca Ann of Dixmont ME on 19 Feb m MARSH Leonard
  Eld of New Brunswick *MS* 6 Mar 1839
HANNAFORD Betsey m GILMAN Josiah P *MS* 2 Aug 1827
HANNAFORD Mary of Cape Elizabeth ME m BAKER James P Esq of
  Strong ME on 2 Jul Thursday eve *MS* 15 Jul 1846
HANSCOM Eliza J m DREW George W F both of Somersworth NH on
  14 Apr *MS* 8 May 1844
HANSCOM Elizabeth of Great Falls m GOODWIN Joel of Lebanon

HANSCOM (Continued)
MS 10 Jan 1838

HANSCOM Lois of Strafford NH m HILL Lyman H *MS* 27 Feb 1839

HANSCOM Lydia at Strafford on Nov 14 m LOCK Jethro of Barnstead *MS* 29 Jan 1840

HANSCOM Nancy on 25 May of Somersworth NH m BERRY Benjamin Jr of Strafford *MS* 7 June 1843

HANSCOM Ruth N m DAVIS Orin on 3 inst at Dover NH *MS* 12 Nov 1845

HANSCOM Ruth S m TASKER Paul Jr both of Strafford on 16 Nov 1847 *MS* 12 Jan 1848

HANSCOM Sarah Ann m LYMAN Robert A *MFWBR* 21 Sep 1850

HANSCOM Sarah E of New Gloucester ME m STANCLIFT Horace B of Saco ME on 14 Jan 1849 *MS* 24 Jan 1849

HANSON Abby E of Farmington m HUSSEY John of Rochester on 3 inst *MS* 20 Nov 1850

HANSON Abigail m FLOOD John on 6th inst *MS* 14 Oct 1831

HANSON Abigail m TAYLOR John W *MFWBR* 3 Mar 1849

HANSON Abigail m HILL Asa M both of Starksborough VT on 18 Mar *MS* 8 Apr 1846

HANSON Betsey Y on 13 Feb m DUDLEY Sargent P of Alton NH *MS* 26 Feb 1845

HANSON Catherine of Mt Vernon ME m SWIFT Dean of Sidney ME *MS* 29 Mar 1837

HANSON Charlotte A of Atkinson on Nov 4 m BALL William Jr of Sebec ME *MS* 8 Jan 1840

HANSON Cynthia on 29 Sept m SHAW Sargent of Windham *MS* 23 Oct 1839

HANSON Deborah S R at Rochester m WENTWORTH Benjamin R of Somersworth NH *MS* 22 Apr 1840

HANSON Dorcas on 4th inst at Acton ME m LOWD Sylvester *MS* 17 May 1843

HANSON Elizabeth of Monmouth ME m COBURN Edward of Parkman *MS* 7 Feb 1833

HANSON Hannah H of Sanford ME m GETCHEL Daniel on 28 May 1843 at Wakefield NH *MS* 13 Sept 1843

HANSON Hannah J m BLAISDELL C S on 29 June at Great Falls NH *MS* 18 Dec 1844

HANSON Hannah of Strafford m TUTTLE Elijah of Barrington on 11 Aug 1842 at Strafford *MS* 16 Nov 1842

HANSON Harriet m SHUKLING Henry R both of Great Falls *MS* 1 Apr 1840

HANSON Lucy C of Sanford m BENNET Rufus on 22 Dec at North Berwick ME of Alfred ME *MS* 8 Jan 1845

HANSON Lydia B m LOTHROP John C both of Rochester on 13 Dec 1848 *MS* 7 Feb 1849

HANSON Lydia R m HANSON Joseph B both of Waterborough ME on 25 ult Sabbath eve *MS* 5 Dec 1849

HANSON Marsha m MERSERVE Daniel both of Dover NH on Thurs eve last *MS* 4 June 1834

HANSON Mary A m MESERVE Samuel on 5th inst *MS* 12 Dec 1833

HANSON Mary A of Westbrook m GOODING Charles H of Portland on 11 Oct *MS* 23 Oct 1850

HANSON Mary m HILL Sylvanus both of Starksboro' on 26 Jan 1848 *MS* 23 Feb 1848

HANSON Mary Elizabeth d/o HANSON Joseph m HAZELTON J Cutter "on 15th inst...a merchant of the firm Haselton and Palmer *MS* 23 Oct 1839

HANSON Nancy M of Starkville m KEELE James of Clifton Park on 1 Jan *MS* 16 Jan 1850

HANSON Sarah Jane m REED Sewall on 8th inst at Pownal ME *MS* 29 Oct 1845

HANSON Sophia S of Sommersworth m GOODWIN James Jr of Berwick on 20 inst *MS* 27 May 1835

HANSON Susan Mrs of Barnstead m DURGIN Nathaniel on 29 Mar of Northwood *MS* 6 Apr 1847

HARADON Harriet M m BRIGHAM Albert on 19 Jul at Manchester *MS* 23 Jul 1845

HARBEY Lavina M of Nottingham m KELSEY Daniel Esq on Dec 10 at Nottingham *MS* 20 Dec 1843

HARDING Martha A of Standish ME m LIBBY Andrew of Windham ME on 7 May *MS* 29 May 1850 & *MFWBR* 1 June 1850

HARDLEY Polly m FOSS Dyer both of Candia on 19 Dec 1850 *MS* 8 Jan 1851

HARDY Charlotte S of Pierpont m ALDRICH Scuyler Eld of Mecca Ohio on 5 Mar in Pierpont *MS* 24 Apr 1850

HARDY Lucinda of Wilton m CHANDLER Ebenezer Jr of Temple on 22d inst *MS* 2 Oct 1829

HARDY Sarah Ann m SLEEPER Nathan S both of Lowell *MS* 27 Jan 1836

HARE Charlotte of Lowell m EATON Wm L of Dexter ME on 7 Jan *MS* 22 Jan 1851

HARFORD Elizabeth m HARFORD Jackson on 17 Nov 1842 at Georgetown ME *MS* 18 Jan 1843

HARGER Sally Mrs m HARGER Leonidas both of Nassau on 7 inst *MS* 23 Jan 1850

HARGRAVES Maria m KINDAR Wm *MS* 13 Nov 1850

HARKNES Miranda of Smithfield RI m WHITE John B of Blackstone MA on 26 Aug *MS* 9 Sept 1846

HARMAN Susan W of Acton on 29 Sept m RICKER Gershom *MS* 23 Oct 1839

HARMON Ann A d/o HARMON Daniel of Limerick ME m REYNOLDS

HARMON (Continued)

Oliver N of Lubec *MFWBR* 1 Jul 1848

HARMON Deborah m RICKER Obadiah both of Somersworth on 24 Mar *MS* 15 Apr 1846

HARMON Eliza A m BURBANK Abner both of Limerick ME *MS* 5 Apr 1837

HARMON Jane Elizabeth m TOBIE Edward P both of Lewiston ME on 9 inst *MS* 11 Mar 1840

HARMON Julia A of Standish ME m STACY S F of Saco ME *MS* 14 Feb 1849

HARMON Martha E of Buxton ME m BRACKETT John on 1 Sept at Buxton ME of New Market NH *MS* 16 Oct 1844

HARMON Mary m CLARK Ira *MS* 19 Sept 1833

HARMON Mary A E m DUNN Samuel on 16 June *MS* 17 Jul 1850

HARMON Mary C m PAGE M W both of Windham ME on 1 May *MS* 29 May 1850

HARMON Mary F m PLUMMER Joseph M of Gorham ME on 26 Sept *MS* 7 Feb 1844

HARMON Mary S m HARRIMAN Cyrus both of Eaton on 30 Sept *MS* 11 Nov 1846

HARMON Matilda m OWEN Mark L H both of Buxton ME on May 19 *MS* 28 Aug 1850

HARMON Mehitabel C m BLAKE Jesse both of Roxbury on 9 ult *MS* 5 June 1850

HARMON Meranda m HACKETT Andrew on 5 Jan at Dracut MA *MS* 10 Feb 1847

HARMON Priscilla C m HARDING William H on 3 Nov of Brooks *MS* 20 Nov 1844

HARMON Rebecca L of Eaton m BROOKS N Eld of Meredith Bridge *MS* 26 Sept 1838

HARMON Sarah C m GOLDTHWAIT G H *MFWBR* 10 Nov 1849

HARMON Sarah C of Portland m PARKER George W of Scarboro' *MFWBR* 12 Jan 1850

HARMON Sarah G d/o HARMON Daniel of Limerick ME m PEAVEY George W of Lubec *MFWBR* 26 Oct 1850

HARMON Sarah S m YOUNG Artemas S of Lowell MA on 13 Mar 1850 *MS* 27 Mar 1850

HARN Sarah of Unionville MD m WILLIAMS A D Eld of Carolina Mills RI *MFWBR* 1 June 1850

HARPER Hannah of Limerick m EMERY Samuel of Biddeford on Sunday last *MS* 3 Nov 1830

HARPER Nancy B of New Hampton on 11 Feb m GOVE John C *MS* 26 Apr 1843

HARPER Sarah A m BROOKS John Eld of Wakefield NH on 24 Nov 1841 at Limerick ME *MS* 1 Dec 1841

HARRIDEN Alice S T m BUNKER John D on 31 Jul at Woolwich ME

HARRIDEN (Continued)
  MS 24 Sept 1845
HARRIMAN Augusta Ann of Groton on 6 Apr at Holderness m ANNIS George W of Methuen MA *MS* 26 June 1839
HARRIMAN Azula m ADAMS Thomas J both of Bradford on 7 Nov 1848 *MS* 11 Apr 1849
HARRIMAN Betsey m SWINERTONS Amos both of Somerworth on 11 inst *MS* 21 Nov 1838
HARRIMAN Betsey of Conway m HAWKINS Alpheus of Albany *MS* 27 May 1835
HARRIMAN Elsa Jane m WARD Silas H on 3 Mar at Eaton *MS* 18 Mar 1846
HARRIMAN Emily m ROUGEN James *MS* 7 Sept 1832
HARRIMAN Lucia d/o HARRIMAN D Eld late of Weare m DYER Joseph C son of Eld SB DYER of Deerfield on 7 May *MS* 17 June 1846
HARRIMAN Sarah m BRYANT Joseph on 26 Nov 1844 of Effingham NH *MS* 19 Feb 1845
HARRINGTON Harriet m MOSSMAN Albion K both of Thomaston on 6 Aug 1848 *MS* 30 Aug 1848 & *MS* 16 May 1849
HARRINGTON Maria of Edgecomb m LEWIS William of Boothbay ME on 7 Jan at Edgecomb ME *MS* 14 Feb 1844
HARRINGTON Mary J of Topsham m DANFORTH Wm of Gardiner *MS* 19 Jan 1848
HARRINGTON Rebecca m JOSLIN Thomas both of New Hartford on 17 Nov *MS* 1 Jan 1851
HARRIS Adah M of No Scituate m REMINGTON DeWitt C of Burrillville 18 Nov *MS* 4 Dec 1850
HARRIS Alzado m CHASE Nelson both of Pascoag RI on 28 Jan 1848 *MS* 23 Feb 1848
HARRIS Frances Mary d/o HARRIS William C m BARTLETT James P *MFWBR* 29 June 1850
HARRIS Laure m ALDRICH Horatio both of Uxbridge on 1 Feb *MS* 28 Feb 1838
HARRIS Lorinda M of Pennfield NY m CUTLER Horace A of N Killingly CT on 25 Aug *MS* 4 Sept 1850
HARRIS Louisa L m MORSE Marvil Jr both of Pascoag RI on 23 May *MS* 5 June 1850
HARRIS Mary m JOHNSON Richard both of Somersworth NH on at Dover NH *MS* 21 Nov 1833
HARRIS Mary of Wiscasset m FARNHAM Edward of Woolwich ME on 21 Nov *MS* 8 Dec 1841
HARRIS Miriam m HASKELL Jabez of N Gloucester ME *MFWBR* 21 Apr 1849
HARRIS Olive R of North Yarmouth m STONE William F of Auburn ME *MS* 27 Nov 1844

HART Ann of Boston MA m SPEAR James on 27th of Roxbury MA *MS* 7 May 1845

HART Jane d/o HART S Eld COBB N Mr on 17 Mar at Harrisburg Lewis Co NY *MS* 21 Apr 1847

HART Jane of Eaton NH m BROWN Ivory on 6 Feb of Parsonsfield ME *MS* 11 May 1842

HART Julia Ann m BRYANT John S both of Eaton NH *MFWBR* 2 Feb 1850

HART Maria m PAYNE Joshua W on 3 Jan *MS* 24 Feb 1836

HART Sarah L of Conway NH m FRENCH John W of Dover NH *MFWBR* 9 Jan 1847 & on 22 Nov at Conway NH *MS* 30 Dec 1846

HARTFORD Louise of Dover NH m LANCIL Charles V Capt of Bangor on 2 inst *MS* 14 June 1837

HARTFORD Mary m JONES Charles both of Dover on 25 inst *MS* 4 Jan 1837

HARTFORD Mary Mrs m SHAPLEIGH Howard *MFWBR* 14/21 Apr 1849

HARTFORD Sarah m McINTIRE Warren both of Manchester on 27 Sept *MS* 7 Oct 1846

HARTSHORN Sarah A m DULIN James Doct on 29 Nov of Newton Union Co Ohio *MS* 23 Dec 1846

HARVELL Mary J of Amherst m BRIERLY Rev Mr of Dover NH on 4th ult *MS* 9 Mar 1836

HARVELL Rachel W of Manchester NH m CHASE Joseph of Blackstone MA on 21 June *MS* 28 Jul 1847

HARVEY Betsey T of Atkinson ME on 27 Jan 1839 m SAWYER John C *MS* 24 Apr 1839

HARVEY Caroline M of Wilmot m EMERSON Moses H on 21 Mar *MS* 1 May 1844

HARVEY Catharine m WHITEHOUSE Joseph M at Dover NY *MS* 13 Jul 1836

HARVEY Fanny M of Monroe VT m FARR Roswell Esq of Cabot at Monroe VT on Jan 18th *MS* 25 May 1842

HARVEY Mary B m HAYNES John Esq both of Pittsburg on 22 Aug 1847 *MS* 17 Nov 1847

HARVEY Merriam S m LOWD David on 8 Oct at Portsmouth NH *MS* 10 Jan 1844

HARVEY Sally of Nottingham m NORRIS Hiram of Epping at Deerfield *MS* 8 Dec 1841

HARWOOD Alice N d/o HARWARD James of Wilton ME m HOWARD William Jr on 16th at the First FWB Church in Charlestown MA *MS* 3 Dec 1845

HASCAL Felitia of Campton m CARR Levi on 15 Feb *MS* 13 Sept 1843

HASELTINE Betsey of Lowell m HARRIS Bela *MS* 10 Apr 1839

HASKEL Martha d/o HASKELL Beriah Capt of Limington ME m

HASKEL (Continued)

LANE Nathaniel H Lt of Hollis ME *MS* 30 Nov 1826

HASKELL Caroline H m ALLARD Daniel Jr both of Dover on 3 inst *MS* 7 Aug 1850

HASKELL Clarinda P of Bangor m DUNHAM Cyrenius of Bradley ME on 9 Sept 1847 *MS* 17 Nov 1847

HASKELL Jane of Saco ME m MARSHALL Alfred of Portland ME *MFWBR* 10 Apr 1847

HASKELL Lydia Callis VT m RIDEOUT Willard on 18 Jan of Munroe VT *MS* 25 May 1842

HASKELL Lydia of Danville ME m GREENLEAF M P of Williamsburgh ME *MS* 10 Jul 1839

HASKELL Lydia of Poland ME m HASKELL Jona L of New Gloucester ME *MFWBR* 10 Apr 1847

HASKELL Mehitabel S m HICKS Ora both of Harrison ME on 3 May *MS* 3 June 1846

HASKELL Rebecca m ABBOTT Albert P both of Stow ME *MS* 20 Feb 1850

HASLETT Ann Mariah m PHILBOORK John M of Ossipee NH *MS* 2 Jul 1828

HASTING Sophia of Bristol m WHITTIER Nathaniel of Orange on 26 Nov 1847 *MS* 15 Dec 1847

HASTINGS Elizabeth Jane m WIGGIN Daniel on 25 ult *MS* 8 Jul 1835

HASTINGS Lydia A (widow) of Newbury m HASTINGS Jonas at Newbury *MS* 10 Apr 1844

HASTLY Eliza Mrs m EDGERLY Samuel Deacon of Limington ME on 25 Feb at Limerick ME *MS* 11 Mar 1846

HASTY Hannah m EARL Josiah on 14th inst at South Berwick ME *MS* 24 Feb 1847

HASTY Mary m SINCLAIR David of Waterboro on 20th inst *MS* 26 Mar 1828

HASTY Susan of Limington m BOSWORTH Isaac of Dedham MA on 30 Sept *MS* 21 Oct 1846

HATCH Abigail m LANGLEY Samuel N both of Barnstead on 12 Apr *MS* 22 Apr 1840

HATCH Abigail F on Apr 12 m LANGLEY Samuel N both of Barnstead *MS* 22 Apr 1840

HATCH Adaline L m SUMMERS C T M both of Manchester *MS* 11 Jul 1849

HATCH Emma m AUSTIN David S both of No Berwick ME on 8 Mar 1848 *MS* 29 Mar 1848

HATCH Floretta of Chester ME m HARDY James E of Nicketown ME? on 27 Aug 1848 *MS* 8 Nov 1848

HATCH Lucinda H of New Berwick ME on 22 Jan m BRAGDON Silas of Wells ME *MS* 3 May 1843 & *MS* 15 Feb 1843

HATCH Mahala m DEUANS David S Dr on 27 June at Gilford Village *MS* 14 Jul 1847

HATCH Olive L of Wells ME m WORTH Thomas C of Biddeford ME on 3 Dec 1843 *MS* 13 Mar 1844

HATCH Pendorah m HATCH Benjamin on 10 Dec at Wells ME *MS* 20 Jan 1847

HATCH Rosanna of Sandwich on 13th Sept m MASON David T *MS* 2 Oct 1839

HATHAWAY B Roene of Adams MA m JENNE Alonzo of Hartland VT on 7 Oct *MS* 21 Oct 1846

HATHAWAY Melissa of West Potsdam NY on 21 Sept m FISHER Barnard of Warwick MA *MS* 18 Oct 1843

HATHAWAY Rebecca of Wilton m COLBURN Thomas of Wilton ME on 4th ult *MS* 19 Aug 1831

HATHORN Achsah m McALLISTER Robert both of Amoskeag NH on 28 Aug 1848 *MS* 6 Sept 1848

HATHORN Eliza F Mrs m SPRINGER Stephen both of Richmond on 23 Oct *MS* 22 Nov 1848

HATHORN Mary T m NUTTER George F of Palermo ME on 7 Nov at Bowdoinham ME *MS* 17 Dec 1845

HAVENS Sarah of Madison Michigan (both deaf & dumb) m TENNE David of Chester Michigan on 23 June 1842 *MS* 27 June 1842

HAWKES Sarah C of Windham ME m SMITH William M of Windham ME *MS* 17 Jul 1844

HAWKINS Adaline m RANDEL John on 25 Sept 1842 of Center Harbor *MS* 26 Oct 1842

HAWKINS Eliza A m HARRINGTON Edward V both of No Providence RI on 12th inst *MS* 18 Feb 1835

HAWKINS Elizabeth D on 14th d/o HAWKINS John (the temperance lecturer) m THOMAS John N *MFWBR* 24 Feb 1849

HAWKINS Margaret Ann m CLIFFORD Stewart *MFWBR* 13 Apr 1850

HAWKINS Sarah A of Gloucester RI m WILBUR Ellison K on 27 Nov at Gloucester RI *MS* 14 Dec 1842

HAWKS Maria of No Providence m MATTHEWSON Wm of Johnston on 6 inst *MS* 16 Dec 1835

HAWLAN Maria m TAYLOR Wm M both of Lisbon *MS* 9 Oct 1850

HAWLEY Mary C of Sheldon m DOOLITTLE Alonzo of Cowlesville on 26 Feb 1846 *MS* 5 May 1846

HAYDEM Caroline S m THURBER William on 19 June at Lowell MA *MS* 2 Nov 1842

HAYDEN Eliza D of Manchester m PULCIVER Henry at Dracut MA *MS* 17 Jul 1844

HAYDEN Mary Ann m ROLLINS Joseph C both of No Bangor ME on 2 Apt 1849 *MS* 2 May 1849

HAYES Ann Maria m EMERY Samuel *MS* 22 Mar 1827

HAYES Ann of Roxbury MA m CHAMBERLAIN Moses on 7 Jan at

HAYES (Continued)
Roxbury MA *MS* 22 Jan 1845

HAYES Elizabeth d/o HAYES John W Esq of Barrington m HAYES Andrew of Lebanon ME on 3 Sept *MS* 12 Oct 1836

HAYES Elizabeth Jane of Nottingham m TUTTLE Franklin of Dover on 13 inst Wednesday eve *MS* 20 Feb 1850

HAYES Hannah of Strafford m HODGDON Elisha of Lebanon ME *MS* 19 Dec 1838

HAYES Hannah T m EMERY Benjamin N of Pembroke *MS* 30 Dec 1835

HAYES Helen of Nassau m JAMES Mortimer of Stephentown on 5 Aug 1848 *MS* 11 Oct 1848

HAYES Joanna W of Dover NH m TWOMBY Charles H on 4th May at Dover NH *MS* 14 May 1845

HAYES Julia Ann m SWASY Frederick T *MS* 3 Feb 1832

HAYES Lovina C at Dover m BAKER Otis both of Dover *MS* 1 Apr 1840

HAYES Lydia of Alton m GLIDDEN Jacob K on 3 Mar *MS* 14 Apr 1847

HAYES Mahala W m CATER Richard B both of Somersworth NH on last Sabbath morning *MS* 13 Nov 1850

HAYES Mary A m KIMBALL Charles S both of Lowell on 29 Oct 1848 *MS* 8 Nov 1848

HAYES Mary D d/o HAYES Hanson Esq of Milton m MERRILL Brackett on 5th ult *MS* 15 Feb 1843

HAYES Mercy B of Effingham m WEEKS Phineas I of Wakefield on 25 Apr in Effingham *MS* 23 May 1849

HAYES Nancy m DOWD James on 22 Oct at Attica NY *MS* 18 Mar 1846

HAYES Olive V m SANDERSON George on 6th inst *MS* 16 Apr 1845

HAYES Phebe W of Limerick ME m RICHARDSON Edward E of Dracut MA *MFWBR* 13 Apr 1850

HAYES Rachel K m MAJOR Thomas on 24 Sept at Manchester NH *MS* 1 Oct 1845

HAYES Sabina d/o HAYES Edmund m LOUGEE Taylor of Parsonsfield on Sunday last *MS* 12 Jul 1827

HAYES Sally of Limerick ME m SANBORN Luther of Parsonsfield Tmar Thurs last *MS* 7 Dec 1826

HAYES Savilla of Strafford NH m SAWYER William of Bradford *MS* 13 Mar 1839

HAYES Sophia P m JEWETT James merchant both of Alton NH *MS* 8 Mar 1837

HAYES Susan A m COOK Solomon on 25 inst 1847 *MS* 1 Dec 1847

HAYNES Eleanor of Nottingham m BATCHELDER Joseph of Northwood *MS* 20 Mar 1839

HAYNES Elizabeth of Manchester m HAYNES Abraham S of Epsom

HAYNES (Continued)
NH on 6 May *MS* 26 May 1847

HAYNES Evelin d/o HAYNES Joseph of Townsend m JUDKINS J
Judson of Lowell on Thanksgiving Day *MS* 19 Dec 1838

HAYNES Louisa of Epsom NH on 23 Jan 1843 m ANDREWS Levi of
Exeter *MS* 8 Feb 1843

HAYNES Nancy m PERKINS Joseph both of Epsom *MS* 16 Jan 1850

HAYNES Olive E of Deerfield m SINCLAIR John L Eld of Lynn MA *MS*
30 Aug 1837

HAYNES Susan of Meredith NH m GLIDDEN Jeremiah on 13 June
MS 30 Oct 1844

HAYS Elizabeth R of Limerick ME m STEVENS Henry S of Waterboro
ME *MFWBR* 25 Nov 1848

HAYWARD Martha E of Underhill VT m DAVIS William B *MS* 6 Nov
1839

HAYWARD Melvina m GOODWIN James K both of Tunbridge VT on
25 Nov 1847 *MS* 22 Dec 1847

HAYWOOD Maria Mrs of Montpelier VT m KIBBEY Danforth B on 3
Jan 1847 at Danville VT *MS* 24 Feb 1847

HAZARD Thirzah m HARVEY Marshal on 15 Dec 1842 at Huntington
VT *MS* 12 Apr 1843

HAZELTINE Elizabeth J m STONE Levi on Sunday last *MS* 22 Nov
1827

HAZEN Hannah B m CHASE Stephen B both of Weare on 21 Nov *MS*
11 Dec 1850

HAZEN Sarah m SARGENT Benjamin on 31 Oct *MS* 27 Nov 1850 &
MS 2 Apr 1851

HAZZARD Clarissa m FIRMAN John N on 13 Dec 1846 at Huntington VT *MS* 10 Feb 1847

HAZZARD Irena of Huntington m BAKER Alnus on 3 Jul at Huntington VT of Starksboro' *MS* 21 Sept 1842

HEAD Mary Ann m KENERSON Francis both of Tamworth NH on 21
Apr Sabbath *MS* 1 May 1850

HEAD Rhoda T W of Tamworth NH m KENERSON Job on 30 Nov at
Tamworth NH *MS* 24 Dec 1845

HEAL Harriet of Georgetown m CUNNINGHAM John of Newcastle on
29 Dec *MS* 27 Jan 1847

HEALEY Rachel on 23 Oct m HOMBLEY Charles of Tiverton RI at
Little Compton RI *MS* 8 Nov 1843

HEARD Betsey of Newfield m LANGLEY Valentine Jr of Acton *MS* 13
APr 1832

HEARD Eleanor of Newfield m THOMPSON Joseph on 15th ult *MS*
12 Jan 1831

HEARD Lucy m DAVIS Daniel S both of Newfield *MS* 23 Dec 1831

HEARD Mary m BEDELL John H both of Sanford ME *MS* 25 Jul
1849

HEARD Mary of North Berwick ME m HEARD Francis at North Berwick ME *MS* 29 Mar 1843

HEARD Rosanna m EMERY Samuel both of Tamworth NH on 16 ult *MS* 3 May 1837

HEARL/HEARD Dorcas "erroneously printed Heard in our paper week before last" m HEARL/HEARD Benjamin *MS* 17 May 1843 & *MS* 3 May 1843

HEARSON Marilla M m PRESCOTT Sewell of Acton on 15 Sept *MS* 24 Oct 1849

HEATH Marietta m LANE Wm G both of Lowell on 29 May *MS* 10 June 1846

HEATH Mary of Ossipee NH m PERKINS Joseph of Jackson on 15th inst *MS* 29 Aug 1833

HEATH Naomi m DORMAN Jabez both of Great Falls on 14th inst *MS* 24 June 1835

HEATH Sally M m BICKFORD Orin both of Sheffield VT on 7 Sept 1848 *MS* 24 Jan 1849

HEBARD Clarissa of East Randolph VT m JONES Daniel on 29 Nov at East Randolph VT *MS* 4 Jan 1843

HEDGE Lydia of Woolwich m CARLTON Ephraim on 7 Nov at Woolwich ME *MS* 27 Dec 1843

HEDGE Thankful Hallet of Woolwich ME m HATHORN David Capt on 14 Nov at Woolwich ME *MS* 27 Dec 1843

HEDGES Jerusha of Northfield VT on 21 Nov 1843 m SMITH William of Moretown on 21 Nov 1843 *MS* 17 Jan 1844

HELD Eliza E m KITTREDGE George H both of Lowell *MS* 8 Jan 1840

HELMNS Aurelia of Stephentown m JEROME Marshall of Berlin NY on 1 May *MS* 13 June 1849

HELSEY Mary on Dec 8 1841 m HOBERT Atkinson both of Charlestown ME *MS* 4 May 1842

HEMINGWAY Cynthia on 21st m WEBBS Samuel Esq *MFWBR* 3 Feb 1849

HENDRICK Rachel m GILLET Elias D both of New Lebanon NY on 19 Mar *MS* 8 Apr 1846

HENIGEN Margaret m LYON Jonathan both of Hume on 19 Nov *MS* 23 Dec 1835

HENRY Louisa m VAN-ORDER James on 1 Oct at Purma NY *MS* 18 Oct 1843

HENRY Nancy m BLAKE Jesse at Roxbury MA *MS* 17 Jul 1844

HENRY Sila d/o HENRY Stephen Maj m COLE John W merchant both of Providence on 11 inst *MS* 19 Dec 1838

HEPPHERD Hannah m BUTLER Simon on 23 Feb at Matildaville NY *MS* 3 May 1843

HERALD Lucene m McCASLAND Cyrus both of Palmyra on 7 inst *MS* 20 Dec 1837

HERBERT Mary A m COTTON Mark F on 13 Nov at Haverhill *MS* 22 Jan 1845

HERBERT Susan C of Hopkinton m PATTERSON Joab Esq (Town Clerk) 24 Dec at Hopkinton *MS* 8 Jan 1845

HERRICK Hannah of Lewiston Falls ME m BRIGGS Phillip A of Auburn on 28 Oct 1847 *MS* 3 Nov 1847

HERRICK Jennett of Poland ME m FAUNCE Nathaniel M of Oxford ME *MS* 9 Apr 1845

HERRICK Mary C of Alfred ME m BARTON Isaac N of Boston MA *MFWBR* 25 Sept 1847

HERRICK Melissa M of Alden m WORDEN Orin D of Middlebury on 29 Aug *MS* 3 Oct 1849

HERRICK Sarah of Canadea m PRATT Thomas L of Rushford on 11 Nov 1847 *MS* 1 Dec 1847

HERSEY Anna C d/o HERSEY Seth Capt m BURR Pyum of Hingham MA on 1st inst *MS* 7 June 1843

HERSEY Catherine of Lineus ME m STILHAM Nathaniel on 24 Apr at Hodgdon ME *MS* 17 May 1843

HERSEY Mary E m GILCHRIST George C both of New Market on 4 inst at Dover *MS* 12 Oct 1836

HERSEY Mary J of Minot ME m HERSEY Levi Eld on 18th ult at Minot ME *MS* 17 Apr 1844

HERSOM Mary of Fairfield m OLIVER Thomas Y of Starks *MS* 15 Mar 1837

HERSOM Nancy m STACY Samuel on 27th ult at Waterville ME *MS* 14 Jul 1847

HERSOM Sarah m GAGE Daniel at Great Falls NH *MS* 7 Jul 1847

HESS Eliza Ann m DAVIS George W both of Constantine Mich on 20 June 1848 *MS* 12 Jul 1848

HETHERINGTON of Providence RI m DIKE Arba C of Providence RI on Thur 19th ult *MS* 3 May 1827

HEYDEN Relief Mrs of Corinna m RANDAL Gordon of Garland on 2 inst *MS* 20 Dec 1837

HIBBARD Mary m DENISON Albert on 6 June 1847 at Brookfield NY *MS* 23 June 1847

HICKOFT Jerusha J of Methden m MANSUR William at Dracut MA on 30 Dec *MS* 7 Jan 1846

HICKS Lucy Ann on 29th ult m PRINCE Roderic *MFWBR* 21 Apr 1849

HICKS Mary m SILLA William in Gorham *MS* 4 Oct 1827

HICKS Mary Jane of Nassua [*sic*] NY m TAYLER Andrew S of W Stephentown NY on 18 Apr 1848 *MS* 7 June 1848

HICKS Phebe Mrs of Boston MA m FOLSOM John of Newport ME on 6 Dec 1841 at Boston MA *MS* 22 Dec 1841

HIGGINS Adrianna L of Lisbon ME m PALSEY Arlon M of Roxbury MA on 3 Jul *MS* 24 Jul 1850

HIGGINS Amanda m KINDALL Miram Mr both of Middlebury on 15 ult *MS* 20 May 1846

HIGGINS Joan at Thorndike ME on Dec 25 m DYER George Capt of West Prospect *MS* 15 Jan 1840

HIGGINS Lousa W m HIGGINS Joseph Jr both of Thorndike ME on 3 May *MS* 27 May 1846

HIGGINS Submit Miss m SWETT Charles both of Wales ME *MS* 3 Mar 1830

HIGGINS Susan O m HATHORN William W both of Bowdoinham ME on 20 Feb in Providence RI *MS* 19 Mar 1851

HIGHNS [sic] Sophia m OSTRANDER Henry Jr on 7 June 1835 *MS* 4 May 1836

HILDRETH Mary A m STREETER Warren both of Lowell *MS* 8 Jan 1840

HILDRUP Elizabeth m WALKER Joseph on 13th inst *MS* 16 Dec 1835

HILL Abigail m LANE True W of Starksboro VT *MS* 10 Feb 1847

HILL Abigail of Brownfield ME m WELCH Cyrus B of Parsonsfield ME on 17 Sept *MS* 24 Oct 1838

HILL Abigail of Waterborough ME m FISK George of Boston MA on 22 June 1847 *MS* 22 Dec 1847

HILL Asenath of Danville m SMITH Enoch on 28 Dec of Sutton *MS* 24 Feb 1847

HILL Betsey m PINKHAM John in Waterboro ME *MS* 18 Sept 1829

HILL Betsey of Haverhill NH m HELEY William of Alexandria NH *MS* 4 May 1842

HILL Betsey of Sheffield m HOYT Luther on 26 Nov at North Danville VT *MS* 21 Jan 1846

HILL Betsey of Strafford m FERNALD Samuel of Barrington on 16 Feb *MS* 13 Mar 1834

HILL Cylindia of Gilford on 23 Aug 1844 m FARRAR William of Gilmanton NH a graduate of Dartmouth College *MS* 1 Jan 1845

HILL Dorothy S of Deerfield m JAMES Moses G Lt at Deerfield of Northwood *MS* 12 Mar 1845

HILL Eliza C m DANIELS Joseph Jr both of Strafford NH *MS* 17 June 1835

HILL Elizabeth D m KNIGHT Aldis E both of Starksboro' VT on 2 Feb 1848 *MS* 23 Feb 1848

HILL Joanna C d/o HILL John Capt of Waterboro m SMITH Nahum of Roxbury MA *MFWBR* 18 Dec 1847

HILL Livonia m RIPLEY Cushing both of Topsfield on 19 June *MS* 25 Jul 1849

HILL Lucy m HILL Wm 2d both of Starksboro on 26 Sept *MS* 20 Nov 1850

HILL Maria m GRAY Morrill on 7 Oct of Barnston *MS* 13 Apr 1842

HILL Maria m GODFREY Charles both of Great Falls *MS* 18 Sept

HILL (Continued)
1850

HILL Martha G m JAMES Samuel S Capt on 9 Jan at Deerfield *MS* 12 Mar 1845

HILL Mary A m KIDDER Joseph W *MFWBR* 12 Jan 1850

HILL Mary Jane of Dover m EMERY John of Somersworth *MFWBR* 12 May 1849

HILL Mary M m TASKER Alfred both of Strafford *MS* 22 Apr 1840

HILL Matilda M m OSGOOD Charles H both of Northwood on 25 Aug *MS* 6 Nov 1850

HILL Mehitabel F Mrs m GILMAN Amasa K Capt on 14 Oct at Gilmanton *MS* 3 Mar 1847 (correction *MS* 14 Apr 1847)

HILL Nancy L m JULIAN Samuel L on Wed last *MS* 4 Nov 1831

HILL Naomi S of Exeter ME m MOOR Benjamin C of Corinna on 31 Dec 1834 *MS* 11 Mar 1835

HILL Phebe m BURBUNK James M both of Great Falls NH on 1 inst *MS* 18 Nov 1835

HILL Polly A of Gilford m CLEMENT Daniel L of Moultonboro 13 Sept *MS* 27 Sept 1837

HILL Polly m TASKER Paul both of Strafford on 20th *MS* 30 Mar 1836

HILL Sally d/o HILL William Deacon m LUFKIN Nehemiah of Chester on 24 Nov 1844 at Strafford *MS* 29 Jan 1845

HILL Sarah A of East Randolph VT m ROWELL Chase H on 16th inst at East Randolph VT on 16th inst of Tunbridge *MS* 31 Mar 1847

HILL Sarah Ann K of Madbury "Cake recieved" m JENKINS Stephen on 19th inst at Madbury *MS* 26 Oct 1842

HILL Sarah J m PILLSBURY David K both of Elsworth on 7 Oct *MS* 24 Oct 1849

HILL Sarah of Dover m CHAMBERLAIN Albert B of Salem MA on 3 inst *MS* 5 May 1846

HILL Susan Jane of Dover NH m GORDON Timothy W of Farmington ME on 1 Jul 1849 *MS* 16 Jan 1850

HILLIARD Clarissa E of Chichester m CHASE George E of Pembroke on 15 inst *MS* 21 Nov 1849

HILLIARD Elizabeth A m MOULTON Josiah both of Meredith on 22 Dec 1850 *MS* 12 Feb 1851

HILLS Sarah H of Epping NH m GREELEY Dennis P on 2d Jul of Dover Illinois *MS* 14 Jul 1847

HILTON Catherine Mrs m HEDGE Barnabas Eld in Wiscasset *MS* 29 Mar 1827

HILTON Martha of N Anson ME m HIGHT Bryce of Bloomfield ME *MFWBR* 8 Apr 1848

HILTON Mary Ann m PERKINS Ebenezer A of Boston MA *MS* 24 Sept 1845

HILTON Sarah F of Sanford m LOW John on 2 Dec 1841 at Sanford

HILTON (Continued)
ME *MS* 29 Dec 1841 & Sarah F HILTON of Sanford m LORD John on Dec 2d at Sanford ME *MS* 15 Dec 1841

HILTON Sarah M of Anson ME m CAMPBELL Henry F of Strong ME *MS* 18 Dec 1844

HILTON Tempy m BODWELL Asa Esq in Acton *MS* 21 Apr 1830

HINKLEY Eliza m OLIVER Jeremiah *MS* 5 June 1839

HINKLEY Jane m SEARL John H on 6 Dec at Dracut MA *MS* 24 Dec 1845

HINKLEY Rebecca m GOULD Jacob on 6 Sept *MS* 28 Dec 1836

HOAGUE Lydia A of Manchester m SANBORN John W of Deerfield NH on 23 May *MS* 3 Jul 1850

HOBBS Abigail of Effingham m COTTON Samuel of Wolfboro NH on 16 Mar *MS* 20 Apr 1831

HOBBS Ann m FOWLER Benjamin T both of Ossipee NH on 29 May *MS* 20 Jul 1836

HOBBS Elizabeth Ann of North Berwick m STACY Daniel L of Berwick ME on Thanksgiving at North Berwick *MS* 6 Jan 1847

HOBBS Elizabeth C d/o HOBBS H H Esq m SOULE Horace H merchant of Boston MA *MFWBR* 15 June 1850

HOBBS Emily m BRADBURY Darius of Wentworth on 1 Feb *MS* 21 Feb 1844

HOBBS Fanny Miss m HOBBS Thomas at North Hampton NH *MS* 20 Jul 1832

HOBBS Harriet N of Great Falls NH m PLUMMER Horace P of Sanford ME *MFWBR* 7 Aug 1847

HOBBS Mary m LEAVITT Thomas C in No Hampton NH *MS* 5 Aug 1831

HOBBS Miriam of Tamworth NH on 3d Aug m SMITH John E of Hiram ME *MS* 20 Aug 1845

HOBBS Nancy m DIXON Nathaniel both of Berwick ME *MS* 25 Feb 1835

HOBBS Sarah m HOWARD Paul on Thurs *MS* 22 Oct 1834

HOBBS Sylvia J of Waterboro on 19th inst m TRACY Ferdinand of Limerick ME *MFWBR* 21 Dec 1850

HOBBS Sylvia M of Wells ME m TRUE Ezekiel Eld of Portsmouth NH *MS* 4 Dec 1839

HOBSON Ethelinda d/o HOBSON Joseph m BAILEY James R both of West Buxton ME on 14 inst *MS* 22 Sept 1847

HOBSON Lydia M of Buxton ME m ADAMS Ebenezer of Limerick ME on 11 Jan 1849 *MS* 24 Jan 1849

HOBSON Mary G m BANKS Samuel Jr both of Hollis ME on 29 Dec 1850 *MS* 22 Jan 1851

HOBSON Nancy T of Buxton ME m JOHNSON William 3rd of Gorham ME *MS* 5 Jul 1843

HOBSON Sarah M of Standish ME m CAME Mark R on 4 Apr of Old

HOBSON (Continued)

Town ME *MS* 17 Apr 1844

HOBSON Susan A m HARRIMAN David P of Burrillville RI on 8 May at Buxton ME *MS* 28 May 1845

HODFDON Sally m GERRISH Daniel of Lebanon on 27 Oct 1842 at Lebanon ME *MS* 16 Nov 1842

HODGDON Adeline m DIMOND Isaac N both of Manchester at Meredith Bridge on Mar 24 *MS* 27 Apr 1842

HODGDON Augusta I of So Berwick m GOODWIN Urban D of Lebanon on 29 Sept *MS* 23 Oct 1850 & *MFWBR* 2 Nov 1850

HODGDON Charlotte of Northfield NH m OSGOOD Edward of Canterbury NH on 17 Sept *MS* 14 Oct 1846

HODGDON Elenor of Poland ME m KEEN Amaziah on 27 Sept at West Poland ME *MS* 10 Feb 1847

HODGDON Eliza S m RICHARDSON Edward both of Northwood on 12 Jul *MS* 11 Nov 1846

HODGDON Elizabeth of Lowell m PARKER Abial of Charlestown *MS* 17 Oct 1838

HODGDON Emeline P m LEWIS Allen Capt both of Boothbay in Boothbay ME on 5 Jan 1842 *MS* 2 Mar 1842

HODGDON Frances m MURRY James Capt Jr *MS* 23 Dec 1846

HODGDON Francis D of Farmington NH m HAGGETT Edward M of Hartford *MFWBR* 10 Nov 1849

HODGDON Hannah of Ossipee NH m SANBORN Ira of Parsonsfield *MS* 31 Jan 1833

HODGDON Harriet m TUTTLE John *MFWBR* 18 Aug 1849

HODGDON Harriet W of Westport ME on New Year's evening m DUNTON Samuel Jr *MS* 23 Jan 1839

HODGDON Joann M m LEAVITT Jonathan 2d of Windham at Gorham ME on 4 Dec *MS* 31 Dec 1845

HODGDON Mary E m LEWIS Russel both of Boothbay on 13 Sept 1849 *MS* 15 May 1850

HODGDON Mary E of Somersworth NH m PERKINS William on 25th of Somersworth NH *MS* 15 Oct 1845

HODGDON Merriam/Mirriam of Barrington m VARNEY George W of Rochester on 13 Apr *MS* 18 May 1836 & *MS* 1 June 1836

HODGDON Nancy of Barrington m ROGERS Alpheus of Effingham *MS* 23 Nov 1836

HODGDON Olive P m TARBOX Samuel Jr both of Westport on 26 ult *MS* 4 Jul 1838

HODGDON Sarah m WILLEY Enoch T on at Dover NH *MS* 13 Jul 1836

HODGE Irena H m ABBOTT Solomon Jr at Ossipee NH *MS* 12 Apr 1843

HODGES Sophia L of Shelburn on the 20th inst m FREEMAN Adam M of Brandon VT *MS* 3 Jul 1839

HODGKINS Deborah m COBB Samuel S on 30 Nov at Westbrook ME MS 20 Dec 1843

HODGKINS Ruth of Lewiston ME m NICHOLS Daniel P of Bowdoin on 17 Oct 1848 MS 29 Nov 1848

HODGMAN Julia Ann of Lowell MA m WINTWORTH Eli formerly of Wakefield NH MS 22 Oct 1834

HODSDON Eliza A of Great Falls NH m MERROW William of Newfield ME MFWBR 16 Mar 1850

HODSDON Martha B d/o HODSDON Andrew m SMITH Timothy H MS 3 Jul 1829

HODSDON Nancy m JELLESON Samuel on 1st inst Tuesday MS 10 Jan 1833

HOGNE Lydia A of Manchester NH m SANBORN John W of Deerfield NH MS 12 June 1850

HOIT Adaline C m WARD David S both of Freeport ME on 7 Dec 1848 MS 24 Jan 1849

HOIT Ann Maria of Rochester m SILLAWAY Abram W of Kingston MS 12 Jan 1842

HOIT Eunice B m CHURCHILL Thomas T both of Greenland on 30 Nov MS 13 Dec 1837

HOIT Julia A of Whitefield NH m HUGHES Daniel of Winterford VT on 4 Oct MS 4 Jan 1843

HOIT Loisa M m FOGG Ira D on 4 Jul 1847 MS 15 Sept 1847

HOIT Mercy R of St Albans ME m BATES John on 2 Nov at St Albans ME MS 3 Dec 1845

HOIT Sarah D of Northwood m HANSON Francis J on 3 Dec at Northwood MS 6 Jan 1847

HOIT Sarah F m HAYES Moses H both of Great Falls NH on 18 inst MS 28 Aug 1850

HOITT Charlotte of Northwood m CHESLEY John of Epsom on 28th ult MS 26 Dec 1833

HOITT Martha of Barrington m FOLLET Richard of Durham on 20 June MS 10 Jul 1850

HOLBROKE Laura on 11 Nov 1841 at Farmerville m BANCROFT William MS 15 Mar 1843

HOLBROOK Mary m DEALING Wm both of Harpswell ME MS 14 Feb 1849

HOLCOMB Lucetta of Lagrange m WELCHER Allen of Spencer on 30 Jul MS 4 Sept 1850

HOLDEN Abigail M R m SMITH Wm C on 5 May MS 15 May 1844

HOLDRIDGE M A m WILLIS G H both of Plainfield NY on 15 Mar 1849 MS 28 Mar 1849

HOLLOWELL Rhoda m ADAMS James on 27 Dec at Boothbay ME MS 1 Feb 1843

HOLMAN Mary A m SMITH Wm on 25 Nov 1847 MS 15 Dec 1847

HOLMES Abigail m GOODWIN David both of Barnstead on 28th ult

HOLMES (Continued)
MS 18 Feb 1835

HOLMES Abigail of Dalton NH m WARD Chase of Hardwick VT on 29 Dec 1849 *MS* 27 Feb 1850

HOLMES Adaline B of Dover NH m JAMES Charles A on 26 Nov (Thanksgiving day) *MS* 9 Dec 1846

HOLMES Eliza of Portsmouth NH m COLEMAN James on 14 Dec at Portsmouth NH *MS* 10 Jan 1844

HOLMES Emily of Stow m TOWN Emory on Dec 1843 at Waterbury VT *MS* 15 Jan 1845

HOLMES Hannah m FISK Samuel A both of Freedom NY on 15 Apr *MS* 13 May 1846

HOLMES Harriet m JONES Stephen S on 29 June at Strafford *MS* 9 Jul 1845

HOLMES Lucy B m HILL Stephen P both of Strafford on 1 Jan 1849 *MS* 17 Jan 1849

HOLMES Mahala m BABB Ira on 13 Jul at Barnstead *MS* 17 Aug 1836

HOLMES Martha of Contoocookville on 13 Apr m KIMBALL Charles H of Weare NH *MS* 26 Apr 1843

HOLMES Mary Ann of Worcester Otsego Co NY m SMITH Martin H Eld of Huntsburg Ohio on 28 Mar 1849 *MS* 6 June 1849

HOLMES Phebe of Hamburg m PENDLEGRASS Martin of Chautauqua NY in Hamburg NY *MS* 12 Jan 1842

Holmes Sally A at Hopkinton on 26 m RAND Matthew P *MS* 5 Feb 1840

HOLMES Sarah Ann d/o HOLMES John Hon m GOODENOW Daniel Esq in Alfred *MS* 18 June 1828

HOLMES Susan S of Lowell MA m TUKEY Nathaniel F on 31 Jan at Dracut MA *MS* 10 Feb 1847

HOLSTED Betsey B of Wheatland Wis m BUSWELL Edmand D of Paris on 29 Sept *MS* 13 Nov 1850

HOLT Abigail of Lowell MA m MERRILL Benjamin on 22 Mar at Lowell MA *MS* 25 May 1842

HOLT Celia P of Bradford m EMERY Stephen W of Kirkland NY on 22 Sept *MS* 16 Oct 1850

HOLT Eliza m STEVENS Philip both of Pembroke on 5 Jul *MS* 11 Jul 1849

HOLT Lovina m SANBORN Winborn Capt both of Gilford NH *MS* 12 Nov 1835

HOLT P Mrs m WATERMAN F W on 15 Jul *MS* 21 Nov 1849

HOOK Lydia A S m WILLIS Joseph both of Exeter in Great Falls *MS* 1 Nov 1837

HOOK Sally at Danville m HOIT Nathan *MS* 25 Mar 1840

HOOKS Mehitabel S m KEAZER Frederick F both of Lowell MA *MS* 4 Feb 1835

HOOPER Eliza of Paris m HAMMOND Jairus K *MFWBR* 10 Mar 1849

HOPKINS Eliza J m GARLAND Sherebiah *MFWBR* 14 Apr 1849 & on 29 ult 1849 *MS* 4 Apr 1849

HOPKINS Keziah of Wilmington m WHEELER Andrew I on 5 Oct of Lowell *MS* 22 Feb 1843

HOPKINS Mary F m POTTER James A both of Pascoag RI on 24 May *MS* 10 Oct 1849

HOPKINS Mary Jane on of Litchfield ME m MUNSEY Andrew C of Lincoln on 7 Nov 1847 *MS* 8 Dec 1847

HOPKINS Sarah E m LIBBEY Eliab L both of Biddeford on 7 Nov 1848 *MS* 24 Jan 1849

HORN Abigail of Dover m VARNEY Ebenezer on 3 June at Dover NH *MS* 9 June 1847

HORN Abigail of Rochester m BLAISDELL David 2nd of Lebanon ME on 25th ult *MS* 4 Feb 1835

HORN Catherine at Fairfield m WITHAM Daniel S of Smithfield *MS* 17 Apr 1844

HORN Eleanor m HORN Gershom *MS* 25 Apr 1833

HORN Henrietta m HALL Moses *MS* 25 Apr 1833

HORN - see BROWN

HORN Kaziah m DAVIS Ira on 13 Apr at Alexandria *MS* 28 Feb 1844

HORN Sarah of Unionville MD m WILLIAMS A D Eld of Carolina Mills on 25 Apr *MS* 29 May 1850 & each at Cedar Hill Ladies Sem Lancaster Co PA m WILLIAMS A D of Carolina Mills RI 25 Apr grad of Hamilton College *MS* 22 May 1850

HORNE Hannah J m DANFORTH Henry both of Dover on 6 Nov 1847 *MS* 1 Dec 1847

HORNE Mary E m STANTON Stephen D both of Manchester on 21 Nov 1847 *MS* 8 Dec 1847

HORNE Susanna m GODFREY Jonathan both of Manchester on 3 Jul *MS* 11 Jul 1849

HORNER Abigail m MORRISON Caleb at Dracut MA *MS* 12 Nov 1845

HOSE Mary m BARTLET Lewis both of Weare on 14 Feb 1839 *MS* 12 Feb 1840

HOSMER Ann L of Pike Wis m DeMOUILPIED Nicholas at Pike Racine Co Wis on 18 May *MS* 23 June 1847

HOUSE Emily of Dixmont m ROWELL Reuben on 15 Sept *MS* 24 Sept 1838

HOUSE Harriet F of Nashua m NORRIS George W of Moriah NY *MS* 4 Mar 1846

HOUSE Jerusha of Dixmont ME on 17 Feb m DAVIS Eleazer of Jackson *MS* 6 Mar 1839

HOVEY Betsey C m MERRILL Samuel of Hudson NH on 30 Dec at Lowell *MS* 7 Jan 1846

HOVEY Mary Ann m BIXBY Urbane L both of Brookfield VT on 22 Apr *MS* 9 May 1849

HOW Mary A m LEE Hiram both of Holderness on 7 Dec 1849 *MS* 16 Jan 1850

HOWARD Abby S of Newport RI m EASTON Edward on 11 Jan 1846 at Newport RI *MS* 11 Mar 1846

HOWARD Abby W of Bangor ME m HATHORN Alexander G of Milford on 18 May at Bangor ME *MS* 26 May 1847

HOWARD Clarrisa m ROOT Filer on 16th inst at Sweden NY *MS* 20 Nov 1844

HOWARD Elenor C of Eaton NH m GILE William of Andover MA at Eaton NH *MS* 25 May 1842

HOWARD Harriet m REED Franklin both of Manchester on 22 Jan *MS* 30 Jan 1850

HOWARD Harriet Newell m SYLVESTER Ruggles [*sic*] both of Leeds in Leeds ME *MS* 22 Apr 1840

HOWARD Jane Mrs of Barnstead m PICKERING Nathaniel Esq at Strafford *MS* 13 Sept 1843

HOWARD Lois J m COUILLARD Alfred R both of Bangor on 16 ult *MS* 7 June 1848

HOWARD Lucy on 18 Jul m VARNEY Seth of Rochester NH *MS* 11 Aug 1847

HOWARD Mahala of Wakefield NH m TUTTLE Joseph on 13 Jul 1848 *MS* 9 Aug 1848

HOWARD Mahitabel m KING Henry C both of Boston *MS* 1 Aug 1838

HOWARD Mary Ann m LOVELL John L both of Westbrook on 26 Mar *MS* 8 May 1844

HOWARD Mary m PEARL Abraham both of Rochester *MS* 8 Mar 1848

HOWARD Susanna m GIBSON Zechariah Rev *MS* 7 Mar 1828

HOWARD Terresa m KORTON Isaac both of Oakfield Wis on 7 Mar 1849 *MS* 25 Apr 1849

HOWE Abby m DORE Isaac both of Milton NH on 6 Feb 1848 *MS* 16 Feb 1848

HOWE Hannah of Stanstead m STILL Abiel of Hatley on 17 Jan *MS* 17 Feb 1836

HOWE Harriet m SLEEPER Jonathan *MS* 17 Feb 1847

HOWE Harriet N of Canterbury m HOOK James of Concord on 28th ult *MS* 11 Feb 1835

HOWE Lucy W of Manchester NH m TUCKER John A on 7 Jul of Manchester *MS* 17 Jul 1844

HOWE Matilda m GILES David on 11 Mar 1847 at Enfield NH *MS* 5 May 1847

HOWE Sarah of Wakefield m RICKER Daniel of Acton on 2d ult *MS* 26 Jul 1837

HOWLAND Martha I of Franconia NH on Dec 8th m BAGLEY Jonathan R of Plymouth NH *MS* 28 Dec 1842

HOXIE Betsey m PHILMORE John P both of Stephentown on 13 Mar

HOXIE (Continued)
MS 8 Apr 1846
HOXIE Henriette m RIDER Rexford Rowland on 30 Mar at Sand Lake
MS 7 May 1845
HOYT Abby of B m FOSTER Isaiah W of Hillsboro on 25 Apr *MS* 15
May 1844
HOYT Anna m ADAMS Charles both of Readfield ME on 8 Oct last
MS 10 Feb 1836
HOYT Betsey J m KEYS Jonas C both of Manchester on 3 inst *MS* 23
Feb 1848
HOYT Caroline M on 26 May m WEDGEWOOD John on 26 May at
Dracut *MS* 7 Jul 1847
HOYT Caroline of Rochester m HOYT Avery A of Spring Prairie on 2
June at Rochester WT *MS* 14 Jul 1847
HOYT Emily A m FIELDS James both of Lowell MA *MS* 24 Aug 1836
HOYT Emily of Rochester m STETSON Allen on 9 Apr at Rochester
WT *MS* 21 May 1845
HOYT Frances T of Boston MA m PORTER George N *MS* 25 Dec 1844
HOYT Margaret W of Manchester NH m MARDEN Ebenezer of Knowl-
ton on 11 Dec at Manchester NH *MS* 24 Dec 1845
HOYT Martha J d/o HOYT T C Hon m SOUL Eugene both of Roches-
ter Wis on 9 Jan *MS* 26 Mar 1851
HOYT Mary W m PEASE Joseph W both of Lowell on Christmas *MS* 1
Jan 1851
HOYT Polly Miss at Chester NH m ROBIE Thomas Eld of Raymond
MS 20 Jul 1832
HOYT Priscilla of Rochester WT m PAYNE Samuel on 1 May of
Mukwonago *MS* 21 May 1845
HOYT Susan E of Lowell m DUDLEY William of Brooks *MS* 11 Sept
1839
HUBBARD Anna Maria m STACEY Elisha S at Acton ME on Sunday
last *MS* 7 June 1843
HUBBARD Celynda F m HOUGH James R *MS* 6 Dec 1837
HUBBARD Harriet W formerly of Lebanon NH m MOODY Simon
Capt at Limington ME *MS* 27 June 1833
HUBBARD Louisa D of Westbrook ME m RICHARDSON Charles J on
14 Mar at Porter *MS* 21 Apr 1847
HUBBARD Mariah H m WEYMOUTH William on 26 Dec at Roxbury
MA *MS* 10 Jan 1844
HUBBARD Mary of Waterville m RICE George at Waterville ME *MS*
25 Nov 1846
HUBBARD Sarah D m HUTCHINS Jeremiah on 27 Nov 1843 of
Fryeburg *MS* 31 Jan 1844
HUBBARD Sarah of Barnston m HILL Ira on 8 Jul *MS* 13 Sept 1843
HUBBARD Sarah of South Berwick ME m ATWOOD A P of Bangor
ME *MFWBR* 13 Jul 1850

HUCHINS Martha Ann m WOODMAN JOSHUA Ton at Strafford *MS* 13 Feb 1834

HUCKINS Harriet E of Madbury m SANDERS Wm J of Dover on 1 inst *MS* 9 Jan 1850

HUCKINS Judith P m PLAISTED Oren on 8 Oct of New Hampton *MS* 16 Oct 1844

HUCKINS Mary F of Centre Harbor on 1 Nov m DAVIS Daniel of Meredith NH *MS* 11 Nov 1846

HUDSON Rachel of Roxbury m JOHNSON Simon on 19 Nov at Roxbury *MS* 27 Dec 1843

HUFF Hannah E of Kennebunk m BRAGDON Enoch *MFWBR* 28 Jul 1849

HUFF Isabella m CLOUGH David F on 11th Dec at Kennebunkport ME *MS* 1 Mar 1843

HUFF Mary Ann of Boothbay ME m TEBBETTS William of Boothbay ME *MS* 29 Nov 1843

HUFF Mary P m GRANT Samuel F both of St Albans ME on 30 Oct *MS* 22 Jan 1851

HUGGINS Sophia G of Delaware on 5 Nov m STEWARD S T Rev Presbyterian minister of Connersville Indiana *MS* 25 Dec 1844

HULL Annar m TATE Josiah both of Dover NH on 12 inst *MS* 18 Jan 1837

HUMPHREYVILLE Orissa of Norway ME on 9 Feb m TUTTLE Elon of Clinton *MS* 24 May 1843

HUNCKINS Hannah B m KNOWLTON Alonzo F both of Northwood NH on 4 Nov *MS* 17 Nov 1847

HUNKINS Julia A m CURRIER David B both of Danville *MS* 22 May 1850

HUNKINS Lucy M of Groton NH on 14th inst m BROWN Isreal G of Henniker *MS* 28 Aug 1844

HUNNEWELL Sarah of Wiscasset ME m OLIVER Gilbert of Industry ME on 13th inst *MS* 30 Mar 1836

HUNT Abby of Brunswick ME m STIMPSON Nathaniel of Bath on 5 inst *MS* 22 Aug 1849

HUNT Abigail A m COFFIN William P on 5th inst at Portland ME *MS* 13 Mar 1844

HUNT Adelia M of Jackson ME m BARRETT Calvin of Springfield MA on 7 Aug *MS* 31 Aug 1842

HUNT Emeline of Lowell m PAGE Harrison *MS* 30 Jan 1839

HUNT Martha on 23 Mar m PARKER Zara of Douglass *MS* 7 June 1843

HUNT Mary B of Gilford m ELLIOTT Joseph Jr of Pittsfield NH on 16 Nov 1848 *MS* 29 Nov 1848

HUNT Mary Jane on 27th Jul at Washington VT m STEVENS Benjamin *MS* 14 Aug 1839

HUNT Ruth m CILLEY Elbridge G on 27 May at Strafford VT *MS* 24

509

HUNT (Continued)
Jul 1844

HUNT Sarah R m DAVIS Samuel A both of Dover on 26 Aug *MS* 25 Sept 1850

HUNT Sarepta E of Montpelier VT m BAKER Edward of Lawrence on 16 Nov 1847 *MS* 14 Feb 1849

HUNT Susan of Gilford m SMITH Moses B of Meredith on 5 Dec *MS* 29 Jan 1840

HUNTINGTON Sophia on 13 Oct m UPHAM Robert L of Sand Lake *MS* 22 Feb 1843

HUNTLEY Eunice Ann of Phoenix NY m DEAN William H of Port Jackson on 4 Apr 1849 *MS* 2 May 1849

HUNTOON Betsey of Lowell MA m WELCH Samuel E on 4 Mar *MS* 23 Aug 1843

HUNTRESS Betsey of Strafford m LOCK Varney of Boston *MS* 19 Dec 1838

HUNTRESS Lydia L m ABBOT Thomas H both of Effingham on 5 Dec *MS* 19 Dec 1849

HUNTRISS Lovey H m PIDGIN William merchant *MS* 3 Sept 1834

HURD Drusilla P m BERRY Nahum both of Sheffield on 25 Apr 1848 *MS* 28 June 1848 & *MS* 24 Jan 1849

HURD Eleanor of Somersworth NH m ALDEN Shadrack on 16th inst at Great Falls NH *MS* 29 Mar 1843

HURD Eliza Ellen m ROBERTS Sewall F of Alton on 18 inst *MS* 25 Dec 1850

HURD Esther of Lowell m PIERCE Sylvester of Gloucester *MS* 28 Aug 1839

HURD Huldah of Eaton m LORD Nelson Capt merchant of Freedom on 29 Jan *MS* 12 Aug 1846

HURD Joanna m GOODWIN John G on 5 May at Dracut MA *MS* 19 Oct 1842

HURD Julia F of Concord NH m CATLIN S T Eld of Hopkinton NH on 9 Oct 1849 *MS* 5 Dec 1849

HURD Lois E m JENNESS George both of Lowell *MS* 11 Jul 1838

HURD Love of Porter m PARKER Oliver *MFWBR* 6 Jul 1850

HURD Mary Ann m BROWN William J on 22 inst *MS* 5 Jul 1837

HURD Olive m ABBOTT Horace P at North Berwick ME *MS* 17 Feb 1847

HURD Sarah A m HOWARD Henry W both of Great Falls NH on 12 Jan *MS* 22 Jan 1851

HURD Sarah of Weare m PHELPS Almond of Sutton *MS* 2 May 1849

HUSE Mary on Feb 14 1839 m BARTLETT Lewis both of Weare NH *MS* 12 Feb 1840

HUSE Nancy of Portsmouth NH m KIMBALL John on 22 Feb at Portsmouth NH of Haverhill MA *MS* 21 May 1845

HUSE Sally Mrs of Meredith m CHASE Timothy of Campton on 19

HUSE (Continued)

Mar 1848 *MS* 21 June 1848

HUSSEY Asenath C of Waterville ME m TILTON Cornelius 3rd at Waterville ME *MS* 12 May 1847

HUSSEY Cordelia m HORN Thomas both of Smithfield ME *MS* 20 Apr 1842

HUSSEY Drusilla m PULLEN Franklin C *MS* 16 Oct 1839

HUSSEY Jane m LITTLEFIELD Joseph H on Wed evening last *MS* 29 Aug 1838

HUSSEY Lydia J m PINKHAM Joseph both of Dover on 2 inst *MS* 26 Jul 1848

HUSSEY Lydia of Waterville m MERROW Harford of Dearborn ME *MS* 30 Nov 1842

HUSSEY Meriam L m BRACKET Rufus W Capt both of Acton on 28 Dec *MS* 10 Jan 1838

HUSSEY Nancy J m FREEMAN Aaron H both of Dover on 7 Jan *MS* 15 Jan 1851

HUSSEY Sarah of Waterville m CORSON Loring *MS* 30 Nov 1842

HUSSEY Sarah P m HOWARD Luther L both of Manchester on 29 Mar *MS* 15 Apr 1846

HUSTON Elizabeth S of Falmouth m DUNHAM John *MS* 27 Feb 1839

HUTCHENSON Harriet L m HILLS Henry at Boston on 20th inst *MS* 30 Mar 1842

HUTCHINS Hannah B m DEARING Alpheas on 5th inst at Kittery ME *MS* 26 May 1830 & *MS* 5 May 1830

HUTCHINS Jerusha of Goffstown m JENKINS Joel *MS* 9 Dec 1846

HUTCHINS Lovinia S m COPP Henry A of Moultonboro' NH *MS* 2 June 1847

HUTCHINS Phylura W of Gray m PLUMMER Richard of Sandwich NH on 6th inst *MS* 23 Mar 1831

HUTCHINS Rebecca of Waterborough ME m HENDERSON Aaron of Eaton NH on 15 Aug 1847 *MS* 22 Dec 1847

HUTCHINS Rosannah of Moultonboro' NH m KIMBALL Albert R at Sandwick NH *MS* 1 June 1842

HUTCHINS Shuah D on 30 Dec 1847 m PHILLIPS Oliver on 30 Dec 1847 *MS* 19 Jan 1848

HUTCHINSON Catherine m NICHOLS Timothy both of Windsor VT *MS* 22 Mar 1843

HUTCHINSON Rosette m ASHTON Joshua of Pierpont NY *MS* 25 Feb 1846

HUTCHINSON Serena of Wayne ME m GRAVES Sewall H on 29 Oct at Wayne ME *MS* 21 Nov 1843

HYDE Eliza of Corinth m PALL Moses of Day on 7 Apr *MS* 1 May 1850

HYDE Sarah m GUPTILL Oliver H both of Ossipee NH on 13 June

HYDE (Continued)
MS 5 Jul 1848

ILSLEY Clementina Miss m ILSLEY Isaac *MS* 12 Apr 1827
INGALLS Amanda J m ROLLINS Joseph F both of Bristol on 29 Oct
1848 *MS* 29 Nov 1848
INGERSON Lucy M m PAGE James both of Farmington NH? *MS* 9
Sept 1835
INGRAM Kaltha of Putnam Livingston Co Mich on 4 Jul m BENNETT
Henry *MS* 18 Sep 1839
IRISH Ann m LARABEE Samuel Capt *MFWBR* 15 Jan 1848
IRISH Esther m SKILLINGS Cold *MS* 6 Feb 1834
IRISH Esther Miss m LIBBY James *MS* 23 Nov 1832
IRISH Martha Jane m CLIFFORD Hiram of Gorham ME *MFWBR* 21
Aug 1847
IRISH Mary S of Cornish ME m BROWN Elisha on 15 May of Cornish
ME *MS* 8 June 1842

JACK Harriet M of Richmond ME m REED Warren of Dresden *MS* 7
Jan 1846
JACK Mary Jane of Monmouth m STINSON William C 2d of Pittsfield
MS 8 Mar 1848
JACK Rhoda Jane m TUCKER John b/o Litchfield *MS* 20 May 1840
JACK Susan G of Litchfield ME m ALEXANDER Robert D on 21 Dec
MS 7 Jan 1846
JACKMAN Charlotte m EASTMAN Jonathan G both of Hopkinton on
8 May *MS* 22 June 1836
JACKMAN Sarah m FIELD George both of Garland ME on 30 Sept
MS 7 Nov 1849
JACKMAN Susan W m TRUMBULL Abial both of Boscowen on 24
Dec *MS* 5 Feb 1840
JACKSON Amanda m SMART John of Freedom *MS* 3 May 1843
JACKSON Eliza Jane m BROWNELL Wm B both of Dover on 23 inst
MS 3 May 1848
JACKSON Elizabeth A of Gilford on 27 Dec m DEARBORN John of
Pembroke *MS* 8 Feb 1843
JACKSON Elizabeth of Eaton m BANFILL Eli on 13 Jan 1842 at
Eaton *MS* 11 May 1842
JACKSON Eunice T m WAGNER Jacob both of Belmont in Belmont
MS 2 Feb 1842
JACKSON Hannah of Gilford m GILMAN David F of Bethleham *MS*
29 Aug 1838
JACKSON Julia R of Eaton m WAKEFIELD Abner C of Brownfield on
19 Feb *MS* 12 Aug 1846
JACKSON Louisa of Limington m GILKEY Joseph of Limington on
16th inst *MS* 24 Dec 1828

JACKSON Lucretia d/o JACKSON J Capt of China NY m BEEBE Hiram of Freedom Cattaraugus Co NY on 11 Dec 1834 *MS* 7 Jan 1835

JACKSON Lydia of Hastings m GRANT Melatiah B at Hastings Oswego Co NY *MS* 28 Jan 1846

JACKSON Mary A of Freedom m SMITH Warner on 1 Sept at Freedom NH *MS* 28 Sep 1842

JACKSON Mary E of Lowell m PACKARD John A Jr *MS* 27 Feb 1839

JACKSON Ruth of Hatley LC m MAGOON Josiah M of Wheelock VT on 23 Oct 1837 *MS* 10 Jan 1838

JACKSON Sarah Ann m GLIDDEN John both of Great Falls on 31 Oct *MS* 25 Dec 1839

JACKSON Susan G m HARMON Gideon both of Durham on 14 June *MS* 8 Jul 1846

JACOBS Ann m JACOB Charles R both of Bridgeton ME *MS* 21 Dec 1836

JACOBS Ann of Manchester NH m HARRIMAN Joel of Newbury MA on 28 Mar *MS* 5 Apr 1843

JACOBS Eliza A of Lowell MA m THOMAS Abel H on 4 Oct at Lowell MA *MS* 2 Nov 1842

JACOBS Hannah W of Manchester m BAILEY Alpha of Washington on 25 June *MS* 11 Jul 1849

JACOBS Oliva of Dover m ROBINSON Edward M of Exeter in Dover NH *MS* 13 June 1838

JACOBS Susan C of Manchester NH m REMICK David on 4 Apr at Manchester *MS* 28 Apr 1847

JACQUES - see JAQUES

JAMES Abagail E m DURGIN Woodbury M both of Northwood NH on 16 Dec 1847 *MS* 12 Jan 1848

JAMES Almira m HUNKINS Moses L of Manchester NH on 5 Dec *MS* 18 Dec 1844

JAMES Amanda m FALL Noah L both of Lebanon on 3 Oct *MS* 27 Oct 1847

JAMES Amanda m LOVELESS Thomas S on 22 Feb 1849 *MS* 28 Mar 1849

JAMES Betsey of Ascott m POWERS Simon on 16 Nov of Compton *MS* 13 Apr 1842

JAMES Caroline m WILBOUR William both of Scituate on 26 Nov *MS* 1 Jan 1851

JAMES Elizabeth of Hampton m FOLSOM Josiah of Exeter on 21 Oct *MS* 31 Oct 1849

JAMES Elizabeth S m PARKS John L both of New Market on 14 Jan 1849 *MS* 24 Jan 1849

JAMES Julia E m ELISON Andrew N both of Starksborough VT on 6 Jan 1848 *MS* 5 Apr 1848

JAMES Martha of Lebanon ME m GILMAN Levi W of Somersworth

JAMES (Continued)
NH on 24 Dec 1848 Sabbath evening *MS* 3 Jan 1849

JAMES Nancy Mrs of Manchester m CRESSEY Thomas of Newbury on 9 ult *MS* 31 Jan 1849

JAMES Zoa M m WEEKS Jonathan T both of Gilford on 26 ult *MS* 10 Oct 1838

JAMESON Betsey m RANDALL Jesse both of Bangor ME on 18 June 1848 *MS* 5 Jul 1848

JAMESON Julia Octava of Westbrook ME m MARTIN Jeremiah of Portland ME on 16 Nov 1848 *MS* 24 Jan 1849

JAQUES Katherine m MILLET Henry at North Providence RI *MS* 26 Jul 1837

JAQUITH Harriet on 20th at Manchester Iowa (Territory) m CHAMBERLIN Abijah *MS* 27 Feb 1839

JAY Sarah m DAVIS Daniel A both of Waterville ME on 28 Oct 1847 *MS* 19 Jan 1848

JEFFERDS Olive of Kennebunkport m McDONALD John Maj of Limerick ME on Tuesday last *MS* 5 Jul 1827

JEFFERSON Emeline A m RYDER Amaziah H both of Pawtucket RI on 25 Nov 1849 *MS* 20 Mar 1850

JELLERSON Margaret G of Bowdoinham ME m READ Thomas B Esq on 30 June at Bowdoinham ME *MS* 18 Dec 1844

JELLESON Miriam m SMITH David on 1 Feb 1844 at Saco ME *MS* 13 Mar 1844

JELLISON Abigail of Lowell MA m YORK Joseph G on 8 May at Lowell MA *MS* 19 Oct 1842

JENISON Lucia m FAIRFIELD Edmund B on 28 Aug at Oberlin Ohio *MS* 10 Sept 1845

JENKINS Abby C m DAWLEY William on 19 May at Dracut MA *MS* 2 June 1847

JENKINS Cordelia of Lowell m TUKEY Charles on 9 Apr *MS* 23 Aug 1843

JENKINS Hannah U of Pittsfield m SMITH John of New London on 26 ult *MS* 31 May 1848

JENKINS Lydia E of Tuftonboro' on 16 Mar m WILLARD John F of Ossipee *MS* 31 May 1843

JENKINS Mariah of Monroe ME m MOODY David of Frankfort ME *MS* 9 May 1833

JENKINS Mary E of Lee NH m BUZZELL Smith F on 24 Nov at Barrington *MS* 21 Jan 1846

JENKINS Ruth Ann m JOHNSON Ebenezer S on 7th Jul at Fowler NY *MS* 28 Jul 1847

JENKINS Sarah J m PENDERGAST Levi E both of Lee NH on 20 June *MS* 10 Jul 1850

JENKS Caroline of Madbury on 21 Apr m NORTON William of New Market *MS* 1 May 1839

JENKS Maria A of So Berwick ME m STACKPOLE Ichabod of Kennebunk ME on 23 June *MS* 10 Jul 1850

JENKS Sarah S of Middlebury NY m BAKER Johnson C of China *MS* 10 Aug 1842

JENNE A Maria m PRATT Moses both of Hartland on 17 Apr 1848 *MS* 26 Apr 1848

JENNESS Abigail m LAKE Joshua F at Epping *MS* 14 Jan 1835

JENNESS Belinda of Rochester m BERRY Alexander S of Strafford *MS* 3 June 1835

JENNESS Betsey of Meredith m JENNESS Charles of Tamworth NH *MS* 1 Nov 1848

JENNESS Deborah of Wolfboro NH m HOBBS Oliver of Ossipee NH on 4 Dec *MS* 21 Dec 1836

JENNESS Diantha E on 18th m JENNESS Joshua of New Market NH *MS* 28 Apr 1847

JENNESS Elizabeth m BICKFORD Robert both of Durham on 1 inst *MS* 14 Nov 1838

JENNESS Elizabeth m PRESCOTT William both of Meredith on 23 May 1849 *MS* 26 Sept 1849

JENNESS Julia Ann of Dover NH m NASON Elisha on 12 inst at Dover NH *MS* 22 Oct 1845

JENNESS Mary Ann m HOLT Stephen at Epping NH *MS* 8 Dec 1841

JENNESS Nancy m BICKFORD Thomas both of Meredith NH *MS* 9 Mar 1842

JENNESS of Edgecomb ME m EMERSON Edward of Boothbay ME *MS* 12 June 1839

JENNESS Sarah E of Epping NH m GALE Jonathan T of East Kingston at Epping NH on 23 June *MS* 14 Jul 1847

JENNESSE Huldah d/o JENNESS Solomon Dea m WENDAL Daniel H on Sunday morning last *MS* 20 Sept 1837

JEPSON Clarisa Ann of Lewiston ME m WEBBER Elias S *MFWBR* 2 Feb 1850

JEPSON Elizabeth m KELLY James *MS* 25 Apr 1833

JEPSON Terresa of Hammond NY St Lawrence Co m HIBBARD William of Alexandria Jefferson Co on 16 Oct 1849 *MS* 25 Apr 1849

JESSAMAN Alzina m WHITNEY Daniel both of Franconia NH *MS* 24 Jan 1849

JEWEL Mary of New Market m WENTWORTH Phineas of Barrington on 1 Mar *MS* 25 June 1845

JEWELL Clara M of New Market m DURRELL John N of Durham on 1 Sept *MS* 30 Sept 1846

JEWELL Mary m CONGER Potter both of Dickinson NY on 5 Apr *MS* 17 June 1846

JEWELL Mary J of Alexandria m EATON Rufus of Bristol on 19 Sept 1848 *MS* 4 Oct 1848

JEWELL Nancy S of Tamworth NH m HUCKINS Ferdinand A of

JEWELL (Continued)
Effingham on 19 Feb *MS* 15 Mar 1843
JEWELL Renance of Lowell MA m CARPENTER Ebenezer G on 29
Jan 1843 *MS* 23 Aug 1843
JEWELL Susan H of Tamworth m HAYES Chester G of Auburn Ohio
on 2 Oct *MS* 26 Nov 1834
JEWETT Edith A m JEWETT Samuel S both of Gilford NH on 2 Aug
MS 2 Sept 1846
JEWETT Hannah of Gilford m MEAD William at Gilford NH *MS* 23
Jul 1845
JEWETT Joann I m DEERING Erastus W on 23 Mar of Denmark ME
MS 13 Sept 1843
JEWETT Miriam M m GRAND/GRANT Paul Capt both of Gilford NH
MS 23 May 1849 & Mrs of Gilford NH m GRANT Paul Capt on 22
Apr 1849 *MS* 9 Jan 1850
JEWETT Sarah of Readfield ME m KNOWLES Ithiel of Augusta *MS* 1
Feb 1837
JINKS Cornelia of Hamilton NY m LAMB Amos of Madison on 2 inst
MS 29 Dec 1847
JOHNSON Abiah m SMITH Aaron both of West Fairlee VT on 18 Oct
1837 *MS* 7 Feb 1838
JOHNSON Abigail of Sutton m DAVIS Wm of Boxford MA on 7 Sept
1837 *MS* 14 Feb 1838
JOHNSON Acay D of Farmington ME m CHANEY S Freeman Eld of
Buxton *MS* 3 Aug 1842
JOHNSON Adaline of New Haven m STREETER Joel P of Scriba NY
on 1 Dec *MS* 12 Dec 1849
JOHNSON Almine H m GODDARD Levi both of Durham on 14 June
MS 8 Jul 1846
JOHNSON Ann B m WEYMOUTH Levi E on 19th inst at Portland ME
MS 28 Feb 1844
JOHNSON Caroline m MADDOCKS Oliver *MS* 27 Sept 1827
JOHNSON Caroline L m BRADBURY Ammi R of Auburn ME on 20
Feb 1844 at Farmington *MS* 13 Mar 1844
JOHNSON Caroline S m EDWARDS Thomas Capt on 30 Mar *MS* 19
Apr 1837
JOHNSON Catherine C m PINKHAM Cyrus F Esq on 13 Jul 1842 at
Jackson *MS* 25 Jan 1843
JOHNSON Charlotte of Durham m COXE Sewell of Bowdoin ME on
11 Oct *MS* 25 Oct 1843
JOHNSON Charlotte of Hopkinton m MASON John of Salsbury on 2
Dec *MS* 19 Dec 1838
JOHNSON Clarissa of Cornish ME m PENDEXTER Oliver of Cornish
ME on 17 Jan *MS* 31 Mar 1847
JOHNSON Eliza at Lowell m COWDRY Elias N *MS* 15 May 1839
JOHNSON Elizabeth m STONE Nathan on 14 Aug *MS* 10 Oct 1849

JOHNSON Elizabeth B of Somersworth NH m OTIS William P *MS* 24 Jul 1839

JOHNSON Elvira of Whiting VT m FORD H G Dr *MS* 26 Nov 1834

JOHNSON Eunice of Limington ME m THOMES Amos on 26 Nov *MS* 7 Feb 1844

JOHNSON Frances A m HOBSON Joseph L both of Hollis ME *MS* 22 Jan 1851

JOHNSON Frances E d/o JOHNSON Alfred Hon m LAMBARD Charles A of Augusta *MFWBR* 9 Nov 1850

JOHNSON Hannah E of Coventry m ROSS Thomas J on 5 Dec at Scituate *MS* 14 Dec 1842

JOHNSON Hannah of Bridgewater NH m CHENEY Edmund W of Bristol on 5 Mar 1850 *MS* 27 Mar 1850

JOHNSON Harriet of Gorham m BOOTHBY Enoch of Buxton *MS* 7 Feb 1828

JOHNSON Jane Philena of Saco m MILLIKEN David on 4 Apr at Saco ME *MS* 17 Apr 1844

JOHNSON Louisa T on 19th inst m BUCKNAM J M *MFWBR* 28 Dec 1850

JOHNSON Lucy Ann of Whitefield NH m QUINT Benjamin B on 14 Jul at Whitefield NH *MS* 27 June 1842

JOHNSON Lydia m GODDARD John on 9th inst *MS* 25 Nov 1831

JOHNSON Lydia M m MARTIN John L Aug 1 1841 *MS* 19 Jan 1842

JOHNSON Lydia of Tunbridge m ORDWAY Edson of Strafford *MS* 18 Apr 1838

JOHNSON Margaret A m BARTON George W on 25 Apr at Bath ME *MS* 29 May 1844

JOHNSON Margary of Brownfield m COTTON Oliver on 13th inst at Brownfield ME *MS* 6 Sept 1843

JOHNSON Maria C of Contoocookville NH m McALPINE George W on 16 Nov *MS* 30 Nov 1842

JOHNSON Martha m SEDGERLY Levi both of Limington ME on 14 Nov *MS* 15 Jan 1840

JOHNSON Martha of Great Falls m JOHNSON Elijah of Dover on 8 Sept *MS* 25 Sept 1849

JOHNSON Mary m LIBBY Elbridge of Scarboro' ME on 31 Jan at Westbrook ME *MS* 17 Apr 1844

JOHNSON Mary A m SMITH William P of Concord NH on 18 Sept at Wentworth *MS* 25 Oct 1843

JOHNSON Mary A of Portland m STILSON John R of Durham NH on 8 Oct 1848 *MS* 18 Oct 1848

JOHNSON Mary Ann m EASTMAN James M *MFWBR* 1 Jan 1848

JOHNSON Mary m WEYMOUTH John both of N Berwick ME in North Berwick Apr 13 *MS* 27 Apr 1842

JOHNSON Mary m HICKS Elbridge D both of N Yarmouth on 23 Feb 1848 *MS* 8 Mar 1848

JOHNSON Olive S of Conway NH m BAILEY Richard of Bartlett NH on 16 Mar at Brownfield ME *MS* 30 Apr 1845

JOHNSON Perthena R m LEWIS Henry of Fryburg on 3 Dec 1846 at Brownfield *MS* 21 Apr 1847

JOHNSON Rozina C of Hadley NY m FLANSBURGH Wm H of Day on 28 Feb 1849 *MS* 28 Mar 1849

JOHNSON Ruth m EATON Moses both of Weare on 12 Jul *MS* 14 Oct 1846

JOHNSON Sally of Bridgewater m CHENEY Edmund W *MS* 15 Dec 1841

JOHNSON Sarah C of Great Falls m PILLSBURY John D of Bradford MA on 16 Apr *MS* 16 May 1849

JOHNSON Sarah E m JOHNSON Jonathan H E of Stowe ME on 14 Nov at Strafford *MS* 27 Nov 1844

JOHNSON Sarah W m PALMER Christopher on 25th ult at Dover NH *MS* 2 Nov 1842

JOHNSTON Jane E of Hamburgh NY m GRAVES Martin L of Buffalo NY on 7 ult *MS* 28 June 1837

JONES Ann H m BARKER Andrew H both of Unity NH in Windsor VT Jan 1st 1842 *MS* 19 Jan 1842

JONES Betsey of Durham m SMITH Charles M of New Market *MS* 30 Dec 1835

JONES Charlotte P m JEWETT Luther Esq of this port *MFWBR* 11 May 1850

JONES Dolly J m LIBBEY David both of Manchester on 26 Jul *MS* 5 Aug 1846

JONES Dorcas of Lebanon m BEAN Jonathan H of Waterboro' ME at Lebanon *MS* 8 Dec 1841

JONES Dorothy Ann m LAWRENCE Samuel on 3 Jul at Lowell MA *MS* 2 Nov 1842

JONES Elanor m BLETHEN Joseph on 20 Apr at Lewiston ME *MS* 7 June 1843

JONES Eliza A S Mrs of Sweden ME m BOWERS James W of Whitestown on 24 Oct 1847 *MS* 1 Dec 1847

JONES Eliza of Portsmouth NH m WHITE P H Mr of Biddeford ME on 15th ult *MS* 9 Dec 1846

JONES Emily E m FARMER Alexander both of Fowler NY on 12 Mar 1849 *MS* 4 Apr 1849

JONES Eunice of Warner m SARGENT Albert of Bradford at Warner *MS* 17 Dec 1845`

JONES Hannah M of Lebanon m GOLDTHWAITE Timothy H of Somersworth NH *MS* 15 Aug 1849

JONES Jane m STOKES Ebenezer both of Starksboro in Huntington VT on 21 Nov 1841 *MS* 19 Jan 1842

JONES Laura A W d/o JONES Stephen Esq of Lebanon ME m QUINBY Daniel W merchant of Somersworth at Great Falls NH

JONES (Continued)
MS 7 Sept 1845

JONES Louisa of Attica NY m FAUCHER Jay on 4th inst of WT *MS* 18 Mar 1846

JONES Lucina m WALBRIDGE Philander Capt both of East Randolph VT *MS* 22 Nov 1837

JONES Lucinda Jane of Lebanon ME m LEIGHTON Lewis L of Milton *MS* 19 Jul 1848

JONES Lucy J Mrs m DAVIS John M on 22 Jan at Portsmouth NH *MS* 7 Feb 1844

JONES Lydia A of New Market m SEWALL Levi W of Epping NH *MS* 6 Apr 1847

JONES Lydia Miss of Dover m LYMAN Wm B Capt of Milton on Sudnay last *MS* 2 Jan 1834

JONES Lydia of Huntington VT on 1 June m BROWN William of Starksboro' VT *MS* 19 Jul 1843

JONES Mahala A of Webster ME m HIGGINS Daniel H Esq of Lisbon ME on 8 Feb 1848 *MS* 23 Feb 1848

JONES Margaret R of Somersworth NH m DAM Richard of Portsmouth NH *MFWBR* 19 Oct 1850

JONES Martha Ann of Farmington NH m RICKER Ezekiel on 7 Jan at Effingham NH *MS* 5 May 1847

JONES Martha of Thorndike m COFFIN Enoch S on 8th ult at Thorndike *MS* 20 Apr 1832

JONES Mary m DEAN Watson on 9 Sept at Manchester *MS* 18 Sept 1844

JONES Mary A of Alton NH m ELLIS Alfred G of Sanford ME on 5 Mar 1848 *MS* 29 Mar 1848

JONES Mary Ann of Brooks m FROST Charles H on 26 Feb at Brooks *MS* 16 Apr 1845

JONES Mary Jane m GRANT Oscar both of So Berwick ME on 22 ult *MS* 29 Dec 1847

JONES Mary of East Kingston m TILTON David on 5 June at Epping *MS* 19 June 1844

JONES Mercy R of Dracut MA m BEERS Franklin on 28 Dec *MS* 25 May 1842

JONES Nancy M of Belgrade ME m BLOOD Oliver of Augusta ME *MS* 10 May 1837

JONES Nancy M of Portsmouth NH m ODLIME John W of Boston MA on 8 Jan 1847 *MS* 20 Jan 1847

JONES Orena of Northfield m RUSS Nathaniel M on 10 Feb 1845 at Randolph VT *MS* 19 Feb 1845

JONES Paulina m LEWIS William B of Kittery ME on 12 Apr at Lebanon ME *MS* 28 May 1845

JONES Rebecca C m HOWARD Andrew P printer both of Dover on Thurs Even last *MS* 5 Feb 1840

JONES Ruth of Acton m WITHAM Wm on 26 Oct 1848 *MS* 29 Nov 1848

JONES Sarah E m LITTLEFIELD David A both of Dover on 22 inst Sunday morning *MS* 25 Sept 1850

JONES Sarah J m RICKER Benjamin F both of Great Falls NH on 26 June *MS* 10 Jul 1850 & *MFWBR* 13 Jul 1850

JONES Sarah J m DIXON Stephen Jr both of Lebanon ME on 3 Feb 1849 *MS* 21 Feb 1849

JONES Susan F of Belfast m WHELDEN Henry *MFWBR* 17 Mar 1849

JONES Susanna A m WHITEHOUSE Charles C both of Farmington NH on 4 Feb 1849 *MS* 28 Feb 1849

JONES Waity A m GEORGE Thomas *MS* 21 Feb 1838

JONSHSON Elizabeth A of Deerfield m WEATHERBEE Benjamin of Dedham on Thanksgiving Eve *MS* 8 Dec 1847

JONSON Elizabeth m COLEMAN Elisha E on 9th Feb at Portsmouth NH *MS* 26 Feb 1845

JORDAN Abigail of Lewiston ME m DAVIS John L of Lisbon ME on 10 Mar at Lewiston ME *MS* 31 Mar 1847

JORDAN Eliza C of Biddeford m ALLEN Charles *MFWBR* 28 Dec 1850

JORDAN Eliza of Raymond ME m LATHAM Cyrus Deacon of Lowell MA on 11 Mar at Raymond ME *MS* 26 May 1847

JORDAN Emeline C m WESTCOTT Stephen *MFWBR* 30 Oct 1847

JORDAN Esther F m SMALL John Jr on 26 Nov at Raymond ME *MS* 31 Dec 1845

JORDAN Joanna H m HEWEY Arthur E both of Topsham on 3 Nov *MS* 25 Dec 1850

JORDAN Lucy A of Saco ME m ADAMS Reuel B of Biddeford ME *MS* 5 Feb 1845

JORDAN Mary N of Lisbon ME m LINCOLN Rufus of Lewiston ME *MS* 6 Sept 1837

JORDAN Ruth M of Portland ME m PERKINS William M of Oxford ME *MS* 30 Jan 1839

JORDAN Sarah B of Gorham d/o JORDAN Charles Deacon m BABB Isaac W on 3 Aug at Gorham ME of Westbrook ME *MS* 17 Sept 1845

JORDAN Sarah F m POWERS Daniel S of Boston *MS* 17 Jan 1828

JORDAN Sophronia m BROWN Jacob on 17 Apr 1842 at Camden *MS* 15 June 1842

JOSE Martha of Biddeford ME m ALLEN Joseph G *MFWBR* 15 June 1850

JOSLIN Rebecca m PITSINGER Ephraim both of Chesterfield on 30 Nov 1848 *MS* 7 Feb 1849

JOY Martha of Waterville ME m STEVENS Joseph H on 24 Mar at Waterville ME *MS* 14 Jul 1847

JOY Sarah A m GRANT Thomas J *MFWBR* 28 Jul 1849

JOY Sarah E of Manchester NH m GRIFFTHS David of Durham on 1 Feb at Manchester NH *MS* 25 Feb 1846

JUDKINS Ann Maria of Freedom m PIPER Jsohua N of Moultonborough NH on 25 Nov *MS* 22 Dec 1847

JUDKINS Betsey of Phillips m GORDON Miles on 30 Jan *MS* 19 Apr 1843

JUDKINS Sophia S of Lawrence MA m DAVIS J E Eld of Gardiner ME on 27 June *MS* 4 Jul 1849

JUDSON Lovina E of Huntington m AUBERY Albert of Burlington VT on 26 Jan 1848 *MS* 5 Apr 1848

JUNKINS Hadarsa of No Berwick m GRANT John of Brighton on 8th inst *MS* 21 Jan 1835

JURNEY Frances J m WOODWORTH Horace G both of Fayetteville on 17 Oct 1847 *MS* 22 Dec 1847

KAME Hannah J of Chichester m SEVERANCE John W in Chichester *MS* 5 Jan 1842

KATHAN Caroline m ELLIOT John both of Compton on 17 Dec *MS* 17 Feb 1836

KEACH Emily m REMINGTON William both of Mendon MA on 22 Feb *MS* 28 Mar 1838

KEAG Hannah S of Wolfboro NH m NEWHALL Albert of Lynn MA on 3d ult *MS* 7 Feb 1833

KEAY Mary E m FOSS Cyrus *MFWBR* 14 Apr 1849

KEAY Sarah A of Biddeford ME m PRICE James *MFWBR* 20 Apr 1850

KEECH Esther M of Bafford m HAM Jonathan on 19 Apr *MS* 13 Sept 1843

KEECH Laura M m DAVIS Samuel both of Mendon MA on 4 ult *MS* 4 May 1836

KEECH Mary Ann m STURDY Wm both of Mendon on 17 ult *MS* 4 May 1836

KEEN Julia A of Poland ME m GERRY William at Poland ME on 10 Oct *MS* 8 Nov 1843

KEEN Roann of Oxford ME m McDONALD Andrew on 30 Nov at West Poland ME *MS* 10 Feb 1847

KEITH Charlotte of Northwood - see HOITT Charlotte for the correction *MS* 12 Dec 1833

KELEE Elizabeth of Fallowsfield Township PA m WILLIAMS Stephen *MS* 15 Feb 1837

KELLER Elizabeth of Schroeppel m TUBBS Charles of Phoenix NY on 29 Nov 1847 *MS* 22 Dec 1847

KELLEY Catherine of Boothbay ME m CARGILL Charles of New Castle on 21 Sept at Boothbay ME *MS* 23 Nov 1842

KELLEY Joanna m SEARS Reuben on 9 Apr *MS* 5 May 1846

KELLEY Lavina B d/o KELLEY John Esq of Exeter m CILLEY Joseph

KELLEY (Continued)
L Esq of Nottingham in Exeter NH *MS* 24 Jan 1838
KELLEY Mary J of Pembrook m ELLIS Joseph of Plymouth on 21 Oct
1847 *MS* 17 Jan 1849
KELLEY Mary Jane of Hallowell ME m KING Thomas of Bowdoinham
ME on 23 Nov at Bowdoin ME *MS* 18 Dec 1844
KELLEY Matilda J of Lowell MA m WOODCOCK Gideon on 30 Jan at
Lowell MA *MS* 25 May 1842
KELLEY Nancy m WRIGHT William both of Charlestown on 16 Mar
MS 25 Mar 1846
KELLEY Orpha L m WHALEY Simeon O both of Middlebury on 8 ult
MS 20 May 1846
KELLEY Sophia m FELLOWS Isaac N Col *MFWBR* 30 Dec 1848
KELLY Ester of Lowell m FARNAM John C of Manchester NH *MS* 28
Aug 1839
KELLY Harriet of Hill m FOSTER Wilson of Alexandria on 31 Oct
1849 *MS* 16 Jan 1850
KELLY Lavinia B d/o KILLY John Esq of Exeter m CILLEY Joseph L
Esq of Nottingham on 22 ult *MS* 13 Dec 1837
KELSEY Sarah m FARROW John on 29 Oct 1843 at Charlestown *MS*
28 Feb 1844
KENDAL Melissa D of Yorkshire m FISK Chester on 8 Oct in Free-
dom *MS* 11 Dec 1850
KENDALL Elvira of Brookfield on 10th inst m CLAFLIN Ephraim F
MS 17 Apr 1839
KENDALL Frances R of Wilmington m MANNING Ezra C of Reading
MA *MS* 23 Oct 1844
KENDALL Sarah Ann m HAGBARM John both of Hermon NY on 12
Dec 1847 *MS* 19 Apr 1848
KENDALL Sarepta of Volney NY m McKOON Wm M of Schroepple on
5 Oct 1848 *MS* 1 Nov 1848
KENEDY Susan Jane m ROBINSON John W at Bangor ME *MS* 13
Sept 1843
KENERSON Mary m DURGIN Joshua *MS* 9 Feb 1848
KENESTON Nancy W of Pittsfield m DOW George A of Weare *MS* 16
Oct 1839
KENISON Emily m SANBORN Ranson *MS* 14 Oct 1835
KENISTON Emeline m YOUNG James M both of Great Falls NH on 3
Sept *MS* 12 Sept 1849
KENISTON Martha of Lowell m BRYANT Henry C of Manchester NH
on 30 ult *MS* 14 Nov 1838
KENISTON Olive W m EMERSON Samuel H both of Barnstead on 15
inst *MS* 30 May 1849
KENISTONE Emeline B of Gilmanton m BUNKER Nathaniel W on 20
Nov at Pittsfield *MS* 7 Dec 1842
KENNARD Ann of Cornish ME m PEARL Isaac on 21 Nov of Porter

KENNARD (Continued)
ME *MS* 31 Mar 1847

KENNARD Susan E m RYMES William Gen *MFWBR* 4 Sept 1847

KENNEDY Martha m HOLCOMB Simeon L both of Albia Village on 18 ult *MS* 4 Sept 1850

KENNESON Elizabeth G Mrs of Tamworth m RICE John A of Sutton VT *MS* 17 Jul 1850

KENNESON Rhoda of Barnston m GOODIN Nelson A of Stanstead LC on 5 Jan *MS* 22 Mar 1837

KENNET Eliza m MELON Isaiah of Effingham NH *MS* 30 Apr 1845

KENNEY Dorcas of Berwick ME m MERROW Orrin *MS* 11 Feb 1846

KENNEY Esther W m SAWYER Francis L both of Lowell in Lowell *MS* Mar 27 *MS* 27 Apr 1842

KENNEY Hannah J O of Dover ME m RICKER Lewis H of Dedham on 31 Dec 1846 at Dover ME *MS* 21 Apr 1847

KENNEY Mary of Charlestown m MERRILL William of Dover on 5 Nov 1843 *MS* 28 Feb 1844

KENNISON Elizabeth m STONE George both of Berwick at No Berwick ME *MS* 8 Jul 1835

KENNISON Mary Ann m GLINES Truman G *MFWBR* 14 Apr 1849

KENNISON Mary of Eaton NH m JACKSON Daniel Eld of Ossipee NH *MS* 4 Oct 1827

KENNY Lovina of Meredith on 30 Nov m ROBINSON John P of Holderness *MS* 27 Dec 1843

KENNY Mary Ann of Loudon m FOSTER Joseph A merchant of Pittsfield on 28 Nov *MS* 2 Apr 1851

KENSION Louisa Mrs of Lowell MA m HARMON William 2d of Freedom NH on 1 Feb 1849 *MS* 21 Feb 1849

KENT Elizabeth of Durham m CLARK Thomas C on 1 Jan at Dover NH *MS* 15 Jan 1845

KENT Mary of Durham m DOE John of New Market *MFWBR* 24 Mar 1849

KENYAM Eliza A of Coventry m EDDY Wm G of Foster *MS* 13 Nov 1850

KENYEN Nancy of Hinesburgh VT m THOMAS Amos of Compton on 16 Mar *MS* 13 Apr 1842

KESTER Miss m COOK Jacob on 29 April at Hamburgh NY *MS* 19 May 1847

KEYS Mary A of Berwick ME m WORSTER Ebenezer of Somersworth *MFWBR* 5 Oct 1850

KEZER Nancy only d/o KEZER John Esq of Canterbury m TOWLE David of Chichester on 4 Jul *MS* 15 Jul 1846

KEZER Sally of Parsonsfield ME m GIBBS George W of Porter ME *MS* 17 Jan 1833

KIBBEY Nancy M of Newark m KING Walter W of Newport NH on 12 May *MS* 19 June 1850

KIBBY Zillah M of Westmore VT m DAVIS Philander of Newark VT at the dwelling of N K George in Franconia on 24 Sept *MS* 6 Nov 1844

KIDDER Mary Ann m HOLT Timothy K on 13 Oct of Tewksbury MA *MS* 22 Feb 1843

KIDDER Sarah of Newbury NH m ABBOT Stephen of Springfield on 24 Jan *MS* 10 Apr 1844

KIES Nancy of Windsor VT m TAYLOR Justin *MS* 6 Feb 1839

KILBOURN Lucy of Thetford VT m NORRIS Eliphalet of Newport VT on 3 Jul *MS* 21 Nov 1849

KILBY Harriet of Freeport ME m HUNNAWILL Godfrey of Danville ME on 9 Feb at Freeport ME *MS* 25 Feb 1846

KILLAM Phebe F of Hillsborough m WELLS Jonathan on 9 Mar *MS* 19 Mar 1845

KILLEY Elizabeth m DAMREN Isaac both of Belgrade ME on 24 Dec last *MS* 10 Feb 1836

KIMBALL Abigail m BABB Joseph T on 30 Jan at Strafford NH *MS* 27 Mar 1844

KIMBALL Abigail m GILE Jeremiah *MFWBR* 24 Mar 1849

KIMBALL Abigail m KNIGHTS Henry *MFWBR* 3 Nov 1849

KIMBALL Adeline E m GRAVES William H both of Scituate RI on 4 inst *MS* 17 May 1848

KIMBALL Ann P m KIMBALL Josiah L both of Hooksett on 9 Dec 1847 *MS* 29 Dec 1847

KIMBALL Ann W of Alton NH m WOODMAN J of Southampton on 14 Nov *MS* 27 Nov 1850

KIMBALL Clarissa S m LOVEREIN Luke W both of Lowell MA *MS* 16 Sept 1835

KIMBALL Elenor of Eaton NH m LAWRENCE David M on 6 June at Eaton *MS* 23 June 1847

KIMBALL Eliza m PERKINS Dudley G both of Danville on 9 inst *MS* 20 Mar 1850

KIMBALL Eliza of Bridgton ME m GAGE Richard on 5 Apr 1842 at Bridgton ME *MS* 27 Apr 1842

KIMBALL Eliza of Wear NH m MACK William of Addison NY on 10 Nov 1837 *MS* 4 Apr 1838

KIMBALL Elizabeth J of Kennebunk ME m CLOUGH Melville of Kennebunkport ME *MFWBR* 1 Dec 1849

KIMBALL Hannah Jane m STROUT Albert D on 16 Jan 1845 at Cornish ME *MS* 5 Feb 1845

KIMBALL Hannah of Cornish m HOLMES John of Cornish *MS* 14 Dec 1826

KIMBALL Harriet m BUZZELL William (s/o Eld John Buzzell) of Parsonsfield ME on 10 Nov at Dracut MA *MS* 26 Nov 1845

KIMBALL Judith of Gilmanton m KIMBALL Moses W on 6 May 1849 *MS* 6 June 1849

KIMBALL Martha E R of Alton NH m PARSLEY Albert on 6 Apr at South Alton NH of Barnstead *MS* 25 June 1845

KIMBALL Martha of Loudon NH m TILTON Luther on 11 Oct at Canterbury of Newburyport MA *MS* 25 Nov 1846

KIMBALL Mary O of Clinton ME m DERRILL Samuel E on 31 Oct *MS* 2 Dec 1846

KIMBALL Mary of Sutton m PRESSEY John on 9 June at Bradford *MS* 28 Jul 1847

KIMBALL Mary R d/o KIMBALL Noah of Wakefield m SWASEY Henry S of Milton Mills on 25 Nov 1847 (Thanksgiving Eve) *MS* 8 Dec 1847

KIMBALL Muranda of Wells ME m FURBUSH Franklin E of Salem on 5 Jan *MS* 5 Mar 1851

KIMBALL Sarah F m CLARK Abrah S on 19 Dec at Farmington *MS* 12 Feb 1845

KIMBALL Sarah of Kennebunkport ME m VARNEY J L of Ossipee NH *MFWBR* 10 Nov 1849

KIMBALL Sophronia G P m CUMMINGS Simon both of Haynesville PLT ME on 8 Oct 1848 *MS* 6 Dec 1848

KINCADE Laura W of Lexington m PURINGTON Collamore of Embden ME on 30 Jan at Lexington ME *MS* 5 June 1844

KINESTON Sally R m COOK John on 29th ult *MS* 23 Jan 1834

KING Almira of Ossipee NH m NUTE Abraham on 22 Dec at Ossipee NH *MS* 4 Jan 1843

KING Nancy m NICHOLS Jacob W on 19 Jul *MS* 12 Aug 1846

KING Sally Ann of Gilford NH m PARKER Benjamin F of Dracut MA on 10 Dec 1848 *MS* 10 Jan 1849

KING Sarah A m BAKER Peter H both of South Boston on 10 Sept 1848 *MS* 4 Oct 1848

KING Sarah Mrs ae 88y of Hooksett m SMITH Joseph C of Candia ae 80y in Hooksett *MS* 8 Aug 1838

KING Thankful m DUDLEY David *MS* 15 Dec 1847

KINGSBURY Clarissa C Nov 23 in Brookfield m WARRINER Washington L both of Roxbury *MS* 5 Jan 1842

KINISON Charlotte m LeBARN Horace both of Hatley LC on 18 Dec 1837 *MS* 10 Jan 1837

KINNAN Catharine m LITTLE Moses both of Elmira on 29 June *MS* 25 Sept 1850

KINNEY Julia m SKINNER Lewis both of Royalton on 8 inst *MS* 22 Nov 1837

KINSLEY Clarinda A of Auburn ME m COOMBS William G of Lewiston ME *MS* 27 Nov 1844

KINSMAN Lucy of Cornville m ROBERTS William of Solon ME at Athens ME on 10 June "They subscribed for the *Morning Star* though neither of them are professors of religion" *MS* 7 Jul 1847

KIRK Mary m MONROE Levi G 25 Mar of East Liberty Logan Co Ohio

KIRK (Continued)

MS 30 June 1847

KNAPP Martha K Miss of Newburyport m BARNES Benjamin of Dover NH *MS* 10 Apr 1834

KNAPP Ruth of Huntington m BIXBY Newell W Eld of Waterbury Center on 9 Nov at Starksboro' VT *MS* 23 Nov 1842

KNARR Mary m DEIGHKEL Daniel both of Berlin on 25 Mar 1848 *MS* 12 Apr 1848

KNEELAND Eunice of Harrison on 18 Oct m WHITNEY Asa P of Bridgton MA *MS* 10 May 1843

KNIGHT Abiah m HILL Ivory at Waterboro' *MS* 18 June 1845

KNIGHT Abigail of Franconia NH m HOYT Simeon of Meredith village NH on Sept 10 *MS* 13 Mar 1844

KNIGHT Asenath of Falmouth ME m KNIGHT William of Wayne ME on 28th ult *MS* 17 Nov 1830

KNIGHT Elizabeth B m KNIGHT Allen W of Scituate RI on 9th inst at Conklin Broome Co NY *MS* 31 Aug 1842

KNIGHT Emeline m BAILEY Wm both of Westbrook ME on 6 Feb 1850 *MS* 20 Mar 1850

KNIGHT Eunice m HUNTRESS James K on 31 Aug at Waterboro' ME *MS* 1 Oct 1845

KNIGHT Julia F of New Market m MATHES Timothy H on 9th inst at New Market *MS* 19 May 1847

KNIGHT Lurana S m BALLARD Josiah C of Westbrook ME on 20 Nov at Bridgton ME *MS* 14 Jan 1846

KNIGHT Mary (Pratt) Mrs (widow of Solomon KNIGHT who was brother of Geo K) m KNIGHT George on 2 Aug 1843 (& killed her in Oct 1856) *MS* 8 Nov 1843 & see p 76 Poole's History of Poland ME 1890

KNIGHT Mary J of Pownal ME m WARREN Henry M on 29 Sept at Pownal ME *MS* 8 Jan 1845

KNIGHT Mary Jane m KIMBALL Daniel D at Portland ME on 1 Aug *MS* 21 Aug 1844

KNIGHT Mary Mrs m PERRY Joseph both of Parsonsfield ME on 30 Dec *MS* 17 Jan 1833

KNIGHT Mary Mrs of Corinna m BAILEY Thomas of Dexter ME on 30 Jan 1842 at Corinna ME *MS* 6 Apr 1842

KNIGHT Mary of Parsonsfield ME m CHASE Andrew of North Berwick ME on 19 Dec 1844 at Parsonsfield ME *MS* 12 Mar 1845

KNIGHT Olive E m RICKER George W on 3d Aug at Waterboro' *MS* 27 Aug 1845

KNIGHT Philena of Freedom NY m CURTIS Almon of Holland NY? on 20 Jan *MS* 4 Mar 1835

KNIGHT Rebecca of Franconia NH m WILSON John on 12 June 1843 at Franconia *MS* 13 Mar 1844

KNIGHT Sabina m KNIGHT Oliver both of So Berwick ME on 16 inst

KNIGHT (Continued)
MS 22 Nov 1848

KNIGHT Sarah m MEADER Stephen both of So Berwick ME on 2 Jul 1848 *MS* 16 Aug 1848

KNOWLES Betsey m MOULTON Charles both of Cornish ME on 13 Dec *MS* 17 Jan 1833

KNOWLES Cyrene m MOULTON Samuel 3d on Sunday *MS* 19 Oct 1826

KNOWLES D Maurice D of Thornton m BOYNTON John in Thornton *MS* 14 Mar 1838

KNOWLES Elvina of Corinna m CHANDLER Calvin of Bangor ME on 1 Jan 1835 *MS* 11 Mar 1835

KNOWLES Hannah C of Northwood NH m TASKER Charles C of Strafford on 4 Dec 1847 *MS* 12 Jan 1848

KNOWLES Joan C at Thornton m BOYINGTON Royal *MS* 25 Mar 1840

KNOWLES Lavina m KWEATKUSKE J Mr (a Polander) both of Lowell MA on 4 inst *MS* 14 Sept 1836

KNOWLES Myrta M m WHITLOCK John C both of Meredith on 26 Dec 1850 *MS* 19 Feb 1851

KNOWLES Sarah m SHURBON Daniel both of No Hampton *MS* 21 Mar 1838

KNOWLTON Charlotte A of Portage Alleghany Co NY d/o KNOWLTON Benj Capt of Portage NY m BELKNAP Philander W of China ME a preacher on 1/9 Jan *MS* 29/22 Mar 1837

KNOWLTON Chloe of Edwards Co IL m GOULD Ancel *MS* 20 Mar 1839

KNOWLTON Eliza A of Northwood m JAMES Alonzo G of Deerfield on 16 Nov 1848 *MS* 29 Nov 1848

KNOWLTON Jane B of Brunswick ME m DURRELL George W Rev Dr of Kennebunkport *MFWBR* 31 Aug 1850

KNOWLTON Judith Ann m BERRY Joseph H both of Portsmouth on 22d ult *MS* 9 July 1834

KNOWLTON Lucy A m BLAKE Charles E on 22 May at New Market NH *MS* 8 June 1842

KNOX Dorothy of Somersworth NH m MILLER Mark at Great Falls NH *MS* 8 June 1842

KNOX Eliza m WILLEY James N at Dracut *MS* 26 Feb 1845

KNOX Elizabeth m DIXON Luther both of Lebanon ME on 7 Jan 1848 *MS* 24 Jan 1849

KNOX Esther W m DREW Samuel W both of Newfield ME on 14 May *MS* 22 May 1850

KNOX Hannah of Lowell MA m CHANEY Benjamin on 22 Sept *MS* 19 Oct 1842

KNOX Jane R of So Berwick ME m FURBER James T of Great Falls NH *MS* 12 Mar 1851

KNOX Julia Ann m BARKER Abijah on 23 Sept of Clinton *MS* 2 Dec
1846
KNOX Olive of Newfield m DAVIS William Jr of Newfield *MS* 13 Apr
1832
KNOX Patience of Gardiner m BLANCHARD Thomas of Pittston ME
MS 10 Apr 1839
KNOX Mary D C d/o KNOX Robert Esq of Epsom m FOWLER Ava
Esq of Concord on 13 inst *MS* 26 Jul 1837

LADD Martha Mrs m BROWN Jonathan of Raymond at Deerfield *MS*
30 June 1847
LADD Mary of Deerfield m GLEASON Andrew J of Raymond on 5 Dec
1849 *MS* 23 Jan 1850
LADD Sarah of Lowell m FLETCHER Jeremiah of Lawrence formerly
of Wilton ME on 1 Sept 1847 *MS* 8 Sept 1847
LADD Sarah of Saco ME m DEARBORN John on 7 Feb of Saco ME
MS 6 Apr 1847
LAKE Adaline C of Chichester m MARDEN Henry A of Epsom NH on
1 inst *MS* 8 May 1850
LAKE Betsey Ann of Tinmouth VT m CORY Harvey of Danby on 23
Dec 1847 *MS* 12 Jan 1848
LAKE Betsey on 15 Oct m SANFORD Ephraim of Tiverton RI *MS* 8
Nov 1843
LAKE Rachel of Newport m GREENE William of Deerfield on 5 Feb at
Newport *MS* 24 May 1843
LAKEMAN Harriet m HALL James on 24th ult *MS* 12 June 1829
LAKIN Scruilia of Plymouth VT on Oct 6 m DENICK/DEMEK Charles
of Brideton/Bridgewater *MS* 4 Mar 1840
LAMB Rebecca d/o LAMB John Eld m KNIGHT Abner both of Lin-
colnville ME on 19 Nov 1848 *MS* 13 Dec 1848
LAMKIN Elizabeth m CHADDOCK Seymour on 17 Oct at Bethany NY
MS 20 Nov 1844
LAMPEAR Mary Miss of Effingham m TEBETTS Samuel of Porter ME
on Sun 9th inst *MS* 27 Mar 1834
LAMPER Drusilla H m PAGE William H on 22 Dec at Gilmanton *MS*
11 Jan 1843
LAMPER Eliza M W of Gilmanton NH m GARLAND Isaac on 13 Oct
at Barnstead *MS* 6 Nov 1844
LAMPER Sally of Effingham m MOULTON James Jr of Freedom *MS* 1
Apr 1835
LAMPREY Anna M of Amesbury MA formerly of Hampton m HARD-
ING Isaac Jr Capt of Haverhill MA on 25 Nov *MS* 5 Dec 1849
LAMPREY Clarisa m LEAVITT Oliver both of Hampton on 15 inst *MS*
8 Nov 1837
LAMPREY Eliza m LEAVITT Thomas Hale both of Hampton on 24
Sept *MS* 30 Sept 1846

LAMPREY Irene d/o LAMPREY Smith Hon of Kensington m FOLSOM William MD of New York 11 inst *MS* 20 Dec 1837

LAMPREY Martha m JAMES Samuel Jr on 18th ult at Hampton *MS* 30 Nov 1842

LAMPREY Rebecca of Hampton NH m STANWOOD Charles H of Newburyport MA *MFWBR* 24 Feb 1849

LAMPREY Sarah S of Deerfield NH m CARPENTER Horace of Chichester on 3 inst *MS* 17 Oct 1849

LANCASTER Sarah C of Corinna ME m SMITH Theodore C on 10 Jul at St Albans ME *MS* 17 Sept 1845

LANDER Cyntha m WITHAM Daniel S both of Fairfield on 9 Dec 1849 *MS* 23 Jan 1850

LANDER Lucy A m BENSON Elias P on 8 June *MS* 29 Aug 1849

LANDER Nancy M of Kingfield ME m WEYMOUTH Cyrus C of Freeman ME on 31 Oct *MS* 18 Dec 1839

LANE Ann B d/o LANE Stephen L of Buxton ME m GOODWIN Lewis B of Biddeford ME *MFWBR* 2 Nov 1850

LANE Betsey m HAWKINS John S both of Dover NH on 26 June 1839 *MS* 12 Feb 1840

LANE Betsey C on 24 May m SWAN Horace T of New Hampton *MS* 31 Jan 1844

LANE Clarisa E m GRIFFETH Laton both of Augusta *MS* 20 June 1838

LANE Eliza m PATRICK L B *MFWBR* 21 Apr 1849

LANE Harriet F m BINGHAM Albert Esq in Belfast ME *MS* 8 Dec 1830

LANE Lydia m MORTON Stephen Jr *MS* 31 Oct 1833

LANE Lydia L m AUSTIN Wm B both of Manchester on 13 Aug *MS* 26 Aug 1846

LANE Mahala B of Pittsfield on 28 Aug m PAGE John *MS* 11 Sept 1839

LANE Mahala M m HUNT Stephen on 27 Oct at Gilmanton NH *MS* 1 Jan 1845

LANE Martha Ann m BROWN Jeremiah on 25 Feb of Hampton NH *MS* 5 Feb 1845

LANE Mary of Green ME m CURTIS George Jr of Minot ME in Greene *MS* 16 Dec 1831

LANG Eliza H of Brookfield m COTTON Daniel of Wolfboro NH on 1 inst *MS* 15 Aug 1838

LANG Elizabeth of Limerick ME m TOWNSON Alba of Hollis ME on 11th inst *MS* 17 Nov 1830

LANG Hannah H m WALDRON John C both of Wakefield on 14 Jan 1849 *MS* 28 Mar 1849

LANG Mary A m HARPER Samuel Jr both of Limerick ME on 6 Dec *MS* 18 Dec 1850

LANG Mary A of Brookfield on 1st inst at Rochester m DEMERIT C M

LANG (Continued)
Capt of Farmington *MS* 8 Nov 1843
LANG Olive of Freedom on 21 Dec m BENNET Sylvester of Freedom
NH *MS* 4 Jan 1843
LANGFORD Ann m SCRIBNER Daniel of Raymond in Candia *MS* 19
Apr 1837
LANGLEY Abiagil L of Alton NH m AKENS Jacob of Barnstead on 15
Sept *MS* 10 Oct 1844
LANGLEY Betsey H m HOW Josiah S on 30 June of Dracut MA *MS* 2
Nov 1842
LANGLEY Deborah F m TWOMBLY Jonathan J D both of Lowell on 8
Nov 1848 *MS* 5 Dec 1848
LANGLEY Eleanor m CHURCHILL Daniel both of Lamprey River NH
on 29th ult *MS* 7 May 1834
LANGLEY Eliza P of South Berwick on 16 April m CHASE John D of
North Berwick ME *MS* 3 May 1843
LANGLEY Hannah of Acton m DUNNELS Joseph Jr of Newfield *MS*
14 Apr 1830
LANGLEY Harriet E m PARSHLEY Albert A both of Northwood NH on
13 Oct *MS* 6 Nov 1850
LANGLEY Lydia m ROBINSON Ansel of Springfield *RI* 4 Dec 1819
LANGLEY Sally of Great Falls m FIELD Hiram of Elliot ME *MS* 8 Mar
1837
LANGMAID Hannah m HALL Samuel of Dover *MS* 20 June 1833
LANGMAID Maris T of Strafford m GLICHRIST James R of Malden
MA on 9 inst *MS* 15 Jul 1846
LANGMAID Sally of Yorkshire NY m BAILEY George on 17 June at
Yorkshire NY *MS* 4 Aug 1847
LANGWORTHY Aurelia m SHERMAN Charles both of Warrensburgh
NY *MS* 5 Aug 1835
LANGWORTHY Phebe Ann m CRUMB William Jr both of Brookfield
on 1 inst *MS* 12 Feb 1851
LANPHIER Rachel C of Stephenton NY m BROCKWAY John S on
11th ult at Stephenton NY *MS* 10 Aug 1842
LANPREY Plumy at Gilmanton m ELLIOT Hiram *MS* 6 May 1840
LARKIN Hannah m WOODBECK Joel both of Stephentown on 5 inst
MS 23 Jan 1850
LARKIN Leah B of Macedon NY m CURRIER Joseph M of Boston on
2 Dec *MS* 15 Jan 1851
LARKINS Zeruiah m ROSS Edmund on 29 Apr at Barrington Shel-
burne Co Nova Scotia Canada *MS* 9 Jul 1845
LATHAM Charlotte S of Gray m GILPATRICK Thomas of Limerick ME
on 2 Jul *MS* 21 Aug 1850
LATHAM Elizabeth S at Dracut MA m STEARNS Samuel Eld on 20
June *MS* 7 Jul 1847
LATHAM Harriet of Gray ME m BRAGDON Samuel of Windham ME

LATHAM (Continued)
on 16 Oct *MS* 10 May 1843

LATHAM Lydia m LANGWORTHY William both of Warrensburgh NY
MS 21 Oct 1835

LATHAM Sarah S m CLEMENT Charles C both of Lowell on 8 June
MS 24 June 1846

LATHAM Sarah T of Raymond m DUNLAP D S of New Gloucester ME
MFWBR 21 Apr 1849

LATHAM Susan S m FULLER Artemus both of Smithfield on 1 Mar
MS 18 Apr 1838

LATHROP Julia on 18 Dec m SLUSSER Alonzo on 18 Dec at Pike NY
MS 18 Jan 1843

LAW Sarah Jane m EMERSON Joseph M both of Manchester on 4
Jul 1848 *MS* 19 Jul 1848

LAWRENCE Cyrene E m SKILLIN Josiah G *MFWBR* 8 Sept 1849

LAWRENCE Eliza Ann of Meredith m PHILBRICK Thomas J of
Sanbornton NH on 21 Jan *MS* 7 Feb 1838

LAWRENCE Malinda B m LAWRENCE Farnsworth at Bangor ME *MS*
13 Sept 1843

LAWRENCE Nancy m ROBINSON Joseph W on 1 Jan *MS* 18 June
1845

LAWRENCE Priscilla of Nassau NY m GRIFFIN Daniel B of West
Stephenton on 15 Mar 1850 *MS* 10 Apr 1850

LAWRENCE Sarah of Meredith NH m BATCHELDER Alvin on 26
June at Meredith Bridge NH *MS* 13 June 1842

LAWTON Sarah m MORSE Henry both of Grafton MA 31 Jan *MS* 1
May 1844

LAYTON E H Wid of Vestal NY age 62yrs m THURBER John of Tioga
on 13 inst ae 63yr *MS* 28 Mar 1849

LEACH Mary Jane m MESERVE Harris B both of Portland ME *MS* 30
May 1838

LEADBETTER Emeline of Leeds ME m FOSS Levi at Leeds ME *MS* 27
June 1842

LEAR Betsey m NICHOLS William both of Effingham NH on 16 Jan
1849 *MS* 7 Feb 1849

LEATHERS Diana of Brooks ME m DORE Ezekiel of Dover on 13
inst *MS* 16 Feb 1848

LEATHERS Margaret of Hallowell ME m HOBBS Lewis of Livermore
ME on 22 Oct *MS* 13 Dec 1837

LEATHERS Mary of St Albans m EMERY Jonathan Jr on 1 Jan 1843
at St Albans *MS* 29 Mar 1843

LEAVER Judith B Mrs m FERNALD Mark *MFWBR* 13 Apr 1850

LEAVETT Hannah of Sheffield m COBLEIGH Amos S of Sutton VT on
3 Nov *MS* 27 Nov 1850

LEAVITT Abby P m TILDEN Friend *MS* 15 Dec 1847

LEAVITT Caroline A m KENNEDY John L both of Bedford on 18 ult

LEAVITT (Continued)
MS 8 Jul 1846

LEAVITT Dolly of No Hampton m JAMES Ira of Hampton on 2 Apr 1848 *MS* 12 Apr 1848

LEAVITT Dorcas of Scarboro' ME m ABBOTT George on 1 Dec 1844 at Saco ME *MS* 5 Feb 1845

LEAVITT Eliza Mrs m ELKINS Jonathan Jr both of Hampton on 10 Oct *MS* 17 Oct 1849

LEAVITT Elizabeth Jane of Gilford m BROCK James of Lowell MA on 5 Feb *MS* 8 Apr 1846

LEAVITT Elizabeth L of Effingham NH m CLARK RANSALEAR E of Boston MA *MS* 29 Jul 1846

LEAVITT Emeline C m HUNTINGTON Uriah both of Richmond ME on 7 Dec 1837 *MS* 7 Mar 1838

LEAVITT Evaline m DEMERITT Daniel both of Effingham NH on 31 Mar *MS* 19 June 1850

LEAVITT Frances M of Hampton m BROWN David Jr of No Hampton on 19 ult *MS* 3 Jan 1838

LEAVITT Hannah D of Gilford m ADAMS Benjamin of Campton [sic] on 22 Dec *MS* 29 Jan 1840

LEAVITT Hannah of Candia m HOLT Daniel 2d of Pembroke on 16 Nov 1848 *MS* 6 Dec 1848

LEAVITT Hannah of Gilmanton on 6 Apr 1843 m ROWE Josiah of Gilford *MS* 3 May 1843

LEAVITT Harriet M of Dover m SMITH Aaron B MD of Tuftonboro NH on 4th inst *MS* 17 May 1837

LEAVITT Harriet of South Conway m LONG Larkin A at South Conway NH on 9 Oct (a licensed preacher in Sandwick QM) *MS* 15 Oct 1845

LEAVITT Jane of Guilford NH m HATCH Eliab G on 14 Nov at Alton NH *MS* 18 Dec 1844

LEAVITT Laura Ann of Meredith m PITMAN Ebenezer of Boston MA on 15 Jan *MS* 12 Feb 1851

LEAVITT Lucy m KENNISON Ivory on 12 Dec at Eaton *MS* 19 Mar 1845

LEAVITT Lydia S of Guilford at Alton NH m BARBER William S on 12 Nov *MS* 18 Dec 1844

LEAVITT Mary Ann of Naples ME m MITCHELL John of Casco ME on 1 Oct at Naples ME *MS* 20 Dec 1843

LEAVITT Mary of Gilmanton NH on 13 Apr 1843 m TOWLE Jesse S *MS* 3 May 1843

LEAVITT Mary of Gilmanton on 20th ult m JONES Josiah B of Loudon *MS* 13 Feb 1839

LEAVITT Mary on 20 Nov m MAURN Gill of Melbourn LC *MS* 30 Jan 1839

LEAVITT Matilda m HARRIS Roswell AM former preceptor of Hamp-

LEAVITT (Continued)

ton NH Acad *MS* 19 Sept 1833

LEAVITT Polly of Sheffield VT m ROBERTS Benjamin of Meredith NH on 23 Feb *MS* 16 Mar 1836

LEAVITT Rachael Jane m SHAW Francis both of Lowell on 4 Nov 1848 *MS* 5 Apr 1848

LEAVITT Ruth S of Meredith Bridge on 5 Jan m SMITH George F of N Hampton *MS* 8 Feb 1843

LEAVITT Sally L m THOMAS Benjamin Jr on 22d ult in Hingham MA *MS* 3 May 1827

LEAVITT Sarah A m LOUGEE George G both of Exeter NH on 26 Jan *MS* 12 Feb 1851

LEAVITT Sarah C m HUNT Mr N K on 27 Nov at Wolfborough NH *MS* 24 Dec 1845

LEAVITT Susan R on 14 Nov m CROCKETT William T *MS* 25 Dec 1844

LEAVITT Susan S m EMERSON Wm L both of Alton NH on April 1 *MS* 4 May 1842

LEBARRON E A of Hatley m WALLINGFORD G M of Stanstead LC on 2 Oct 1843 *MS* 1 May 1844

LEE Mary of Lowell MA m COTTON Nelson of Holderness NH *MS* 9 Jul 1845

LEE Narcissa of Holderness NH on 25 Jan m CUSHING James *MS* 19 Apr 1843

LEE Sarah W of Stanstead m HOLMES Frederick of Derby VT on 25 June *MS* 1 Jan 1840

LEESLEE Betsey m HARDY Jeremiah K both of Hopkinton on 20 Oct *MS* 16 Nov 1836

LEGG Eliza R of Dover NH m CUTTING A C of Strafford VT on 4 inst *MS* 11 Oct 1837

LEIGHTON Abigail B m BUKER Jotham both of Harmony on 26 Aug *MS* 11 Sept 1850

LEIGHTON Abigail T of Dover NH m MANSUR Horace on 30 Oct at Dover NH *MS* 5 Nov 1845

LEIGHTON Betsey Ann of Waterborough ME m TAYLOR John of So Weymouth MA *MS* 22 Dec 1847

LEIGHTON Emily C m DUNHAM Alfred both of Falmouth ME *MS* 24 Jan 1849

LEIGHTON Harriet B m STEVENS Levi B *MS* 14 Feb 1838

LEIGHTON Jane m FRYE Lindsey Deacon on Thanksgiving eve at Falmouth *MS* 17 Jan 1844

LEIGHTON Lucinda m SMITH Edwin A both of Dover on 2 inst *MS* 13 Sept 1848

LEIGHTON Lucy J on 22 Nov at Effingham NH m WILKINSON Charles G *MS* 1 Feb 1843

LEIGHTON Lydia m DROWN John N both of Dover *MS* 1 Jul 1846

LEIGHTON Mary Ann m PIPER Joseph both of Northwood on 22 Sept *MS* 6 Nov 1850

LEIGHTON Octavia m DONNELL Benjamin on 2 May at Falmouth ME *MS* 2 June 1847

LEIGHTON Orrilla m BRACKET Reuben G on 24 Mar at Westbrook ME *MS* 1 June 1842

LEIGHTON Susan m AYERS Richard on Sunday last *MS* 6 Jan 1836

LEIGHTON Susan of Strafford m SHEPARD Freeman on 30 Jan at Strafford *MS* 12 Mar 1845

LELAND Harriet m DAVIS Moses Jr both of Lowell on 1 Dec *MS* 15 Dec 1847

LEMAN Rosina of Augusta m GREENLEAF Reuben of Hallowell *MS* 10 May 1837

LENFEST Adaline of Washington ME m CAMPBELL Cyrus on 8 Dec at Bowdoin ME *MS* 13 Jan 1847

LEONARD Rachel of Three Mile Bay m COOLY Jervis on 29th Sept *MS* 13 Jan 1847

LERVEY Susannah H of Portsmouth m PENDER Nathaniel F of Portsmouth NH *MS* 7 Feb 1844

LESLIE Sarah C m TITCOMB Hiram R of Great Falls NH *MFWBR* 21 Jul 1849

LESTER Cynthia of Nassau NY m WHITE Philip on 11 June at Nassau NY *MS* 10 Sept 1845

LESTER Hila m HUNT Ripley both of Nassau NY on 10 June *MS* 22 Jul 1846

LEWING Hannah of Lebanon NH m BLAISDELL Harvey of Strafford VT on 31 Oct 1843 *MS* 6 Mar 1844

LEWIS Betsy F of Pharsalia NY m BENTON Almon of Spencer NY on 20 ult *MS* 9 Feb 1848

LEWIS Electa m GROVER Isaac on 5 Oct at Brookfield NY *MS* 15 Oct 1845

LEWIS Eliza A m CARLISE Charles on 4th Feb at Boothbay ME *MS* 3 Mar 1847

LEWIS Emily J of Boothbay ME m HUFF Charles W of Edgecomb ME *MS* 27 Nov 1850

LEWIS Esther P of Boothbay ME m CHANDLER John H on 9 Nov at Boothbay *MS* 29 Nov 1843

LEWIS Louisa L of Portland m COBB Merritt N *MFWBR* 21 Dec 1850

LEWIS M R (Miss)? of Portland m WALKER E S Mr of North Yarmouth ME *MFWBR* 14 Apr 1849

LEWIS Mary E m REED Bailey Capt on 19 Dec at Boothbay ME *MS* 22 Jan 1845

LEWIS Mary J m MASON Jesse M both of Barnstead on 29 Dec 1849 *MS* 9 Jan 1850

LEWIS Mary Jane m LEGRO John S at Great Falls NH *MS* 7 Jul 1847

LEWIS Ursula of Nassau NY m WORDEN Silas of Stephentown NY on 14 Apr 1849 *MS* 2 May 1849

LIBBEY Abagail of Raymond m WELCH Sewall *MFWBR* 8 June 1850

LIBBEY Eliza m CHICK William on Thursday last *MS* 10 Aug 1826

LIBBEY Eliza A of Somersworth NH m NEWBEGIN Luke L of Newfield ME *MFWBR* 27 Jul 1850

LIBBEY Harriet of North Berwick ME m STAPLES John P of Lebanon on 20 Aug *MS* 27 Sept 1843

LIBBEY Katharine of Somersworth NH m FALL Tristram of Berwick ME *MS* 19 Dec 1833

LIBBEY Lucinda B m DALTON Benjamin both of Great Falls NH on 24 June *MS* 11 Jul 1849

LIBBEY Lydia S of Rochester m MITCHELL Alonzo of Dover on 2 inst *MS* 18 Dec 1850

LIBBEY Mary Ann m SMITH William of Hollis ME at Scarboro ME on 4 May *MS* 8 June 1842

LIBBEY Nancy m HALL Joseph D on 20 Apr at Dover NH *MS* 30 Apr 1845

LIBBY Abigail m COLLINS Charles P both of Lowell MA *MS* 12 Nov 1835

LIBBY Ann M m BENSON Benjamin both of Gray ME on 5 Sept 1847 *MS* 26 Jan 1848

LIBBY Asenath of Limerick m LUNT Bray of Berwick ME on 1st inst *MS* 18 Mar 1835

LIBBY Betsey and LIBBY Edward **divorced** 27 Oct 1830 *MS* 27 Oct 1830

LIBBY Betsey C of Gorham ME m LIBBY Wilder M *MFWBR* 13 Apr 1850

LIBBY Betsey on 8th inst m CLARK B F *MFWBR* 24 Mar 1849

LIBBY Catharine m MOODY Benjamin both of Limington on 21 inst *MS* 28 Mar 1838

LIBBY Catharine F m MOODY Elbridge G both of Scarboro ME on 14 inst *MS* 27 Mar 1850

LIBBY Catherine R m BEMIS Joseph K of Fryeburg ME on 29 Dec 1844 at Brownfield ME *MS* 12 Feb 1845

LIBBY Charlotte of Limington m SAWYER Almon of Exeter NH *MS* 29 Oct 1828

LIBBY Clarinda of Lowell on 2 Mar m STILL Benjamin *MS* 10 Apr 1839

LIBBY Clarissa Ann of G m FOSTER Elias S on 2 Jul at Gray ME *MS* 24 Jan 1844 & on 28 June at Gray ME *MS* 12 Jul 1843

LIBBY Electra m SARGENT Josiah both of Hopkinton on 25 Mar *MS* 30 May 1838

LIBBY Elizabeth A L on 7th inst m BRACKETT Seth H of Portland ME *MS* 20 Dec 1843

LIBBY Elizabeth of Standish ME m LIBBY George on of Scarboro on

LIBBY (Continued)
  3 inst *MS* 27 mar 1850
LIBBY Emily of Waterville ME m HANSCOM John of Waterville ME
  MS 20 Apr 1842
LIBBY Eunice m DINGLEY William B *MFWBR* 13 Oct 1849
LIBBY Eunice m HARMON Reuben of Standish ME on 9 Dec at
  Buxton *MS* 7 Jan 1846
LIBBY Hannah d/o LIBBY Azariah of Limerick ME m NEWBEGIN
  Harvy of Newfield on Sunday last *MS* 14 Mar 1828
LIBBY Hannah of Gorham ME m PURKIS John Eld of Gray ME on
  18th inst *MS* 3 Dec 1828
LIBBY Helena Miss m LIBBY Joseph Jr *MS* 30 Nov 1832
LIBBY Janes m HAINES William both of Buxton ME *MS* 24 May
  1848
LIBBY Keziah of Portland ME m LIBBY Beniah of Scarboro' ME on
  27 Mar at Cape Elizabeth ME *MS* 16 Apr 1845
LIBBY Lucinda T of Brownfield ME m AYER Francis C of Frankfort
  ME on 12 ult *MS* 27 Dec 1837
LIBBY Lydia L of Dover m GILMAN Micajah on 26th ult at Dover NH
  MS 4 Aug 1847
LIBBY Margaret Miss of Scarboro m LIBBY Harrison J of Limerick
  ME on Tues last *MS* 20 Jul 1832
LIBBY Martha of Windham ME m LIBBY Asa on 18 Nov at Falmouth
  ME *MS* 20 Dec 1843
LIBBY Mary B of Poland ME m HUTCHINSON Daniel of Turner ME
  on 2 Jul at West Poland ME *MS* 10 Feb 1847
LIBBY Mary F of Gorham ME m BROWN John of Westbrook ME on
  20 Nov 1848 *MS* 6 Dec 1848
LIBBY Mary Jane Mrs m HIDDEN David S of Tamworth NH on Sept
  at Sandwich *MS* 16 Oct 1844
LIBBY Mary of Biddeford ME m HUNT Franklin *MFWBR* 12 June
  1847
LIBBY Mary of Gorham m PLAISTEAD Major *MFWBR* 23 June 1849
LIBBY Mary of Limerick m BRACLET Daniel of Limerick ME in
  Houlton Aroostook Co ME *MS* 11 June 1828
LIBBY Mary of Sweden m STEVENS William P of Gorham on 28 Dec
  1837 *MS* 17 Jan 1838
LIBBY Olive of B m GRIFFIN Sylvanus Dea of H on 5 Dec *MS* 1 May
  1844
LIBBY Olive of Limerick m BOWDITCH G Mr of Portland ME *MFWBR*
  16 Sept 1848
LIBBY Rebecca m CLARK John both of Great Falls Sabbath Morn
  26th ult *MS* 5 Jan 1842
LIBBY Roxana Miss of Gorham m FILES Wm *MS* 4 Oct 1827
LIBBY Ruth Ann of Richmond ME m BEACKER Aaron of Bowdoin-
  ham ME *MS* 17 Oct 1838

LIBBY Sally of Newfield ME m LOUGEE John Jr of Parsonsfield ME
MS 10 Mar 1820

LIBBY Sarah m MERRITT Henry S both of Pownel [Pownal ME?] on
10 Jan 1850 *MS* 6 Mar 1850

LIBBY Sarah D m LIBBY Levi on 3 Jul 1842 at Scarboro ME *MS* 20
June 1842

LIBBY Sarah m DENNETT Samuel of Augusta ME *MFWBR* 13 Oct
1849

LIBBY Sarah of Windham ME m BLACK John at Falmouth ME *MS*
20 Dec 1843

LIBBY Sarah P m LANGDON John T both of Wolfborough on 16 inst
MS 22 Mar 1848

LIBBY Susan m KIMBALL Nath F both of New Market on 7 inst *MS*
23 Dec 1835

LIBBY Susan E m LOVERING Orville both of Colebrook NH on 31
Oct *MS* 17 Nov 1847

LIBBY Susan F of Scarboro' ME m BOOTHBY William M of Saco ME
MFWBR 22 Dec 1849

LIBBY Susan of Poland ME m ROUNDS Nathaniel of Danville ME *MS*
30 Jan 1839

LIDDLE Mary Ann m KELLEY Stephen both of Spring Prairie Wis on
5 Oct 1848 *MS* 29 Nov 1848

LILEE Lucinda of Epsom NH m WADLEIGH Daniel F of Kensington
on 16 Dec *MS* 8 Feb 1843

LILIBRIDGE Amy of Greece Monroe Co NY m ROSE Horace P of Pike
NY on 3 Mar 1842 *MS* 25 May 1842

LINCOLN Angeline of Litchfield m ROBINSON Mellin of Litchfield *MS*
16 Oct 1839

LINCOLN Anstress W m ROBINSON Joseph Jr on 14 ult *MS* 26 Jul
1837 & both of Gardiner ME on 14 June *MS* 2 Aug 1837

LINDSAY Emeline A of Jericho VT m COOK Elisha of Westford on 12
Jul *MS* 8 Aug 1849

LINDSEY Christina m CUNNINGHAM Freeman both of Topsham ME
on 12 Sept *MS* 9 Oct 1850

LINDSEY Mary m TRACY Harvey N on 19 Dec at Lowell MA *MS* 25
May 1842

LINNEKIN Mary Adaline of Boothbay ME m HARRIS Paul on 25 Dec
of Boothbay ME *MS* 4 Feb 1846

LINNEL Lucinda H of Orrington ME m KENDALL K R *MFWBR* 3 Mar
1849

LINOLN Susan m BROWN Simeon both of Stanstead LC on 29 Oct
last *MS* 17 Feb 1836

LINSCOTT Caroline M m WRIGHT Nathaniel F both of Saco *MS* 6
Nov 1850

LINSCOTT Eliza A of So Berwick ME m PILLSBURY John D of Shapleigh ME on 15 Jul *MS* 22 Jul 1846

LINSCOTT Hannah W of Brownfield ME m CLARK John S of Berwick ME on 3 Jul 1848 *MS* 12 Jul 1848

LINSCOTT Mary G m COLE John T both of Brownfield on 4 Jul *MS* 24 Jul 1850

LINSCOTT Sarah m BROWN Samuel *MS* 20 June 1838

LINSEY Polly m HUBBARD Aaron of Acton ME *MS* 8 May 1844

LINSLEY Melissa E m PINNEO James R Eld both of Prattsbury NY on 21 Feb Thursday eve *MS* 27 Mar 1850

LITCHFIELD Amanda m FOGG Joseph S on 9 May at Manchester *MS* 26 May 1847

LITCHFIELD Lucinda m SMITH George B both of Lewiston ME *MS* 26 Sept 1838

LITTLE Rosetta of Waterbury m FULTON Robert of Thetford *MS* 8 Apr 1846

LITTLEFIELD Amy m BENNETT Amos F at Dracut MA *MS* 10 Sept 1845

LITTLEFIELD Anna I m MORRILL Nahum Esq of Lewiston ME *MFWBR* 11 May 1850

LITTLEFIELD Dorothy of Dover m PINKHAM Geo W of West Cambridge MA on 29 Jul *MS* 22 Aug 1838

LITTLEFIELD Eliza S of Dover NH m WENTWORTH Henry R at Dover NH on 1st inst *MS* 7 Jan 1846

LITTLEFIELD Joanna W of Wilmington MA m BARNARD Cyrus G at Wilmington MA *MS* 18 May 1842

LITTLEFIELD Lydia M of Windham ME m SMALL Edward A of Auburn *MFWBR* 27 Mar 1847

LITTLEFIELD Mahala of Wilmington MA m SEARL Edwin of Lowell on 20 Sept *MS* 22 Feb 1843

LITTLEFIELD Nancy of Eaton on 25 Nov m EMERY Gilbert of Barlett *MS* 4 Jan 1843

LITTLEFIELD Olive on 2 June at Springvale ME m LIBBY John of Sanford ME *MS* 19 June 1839

LITTLEFIELD Phebe m McKENNEY Solomon *MFWBR* 24 Mar 1849

LITTLEFIELD Ruth of Sanford ME m LITTLEFIELD Solomon on 14 Feb at Sanford ME *MS* 3 Mar 1847

LITTLEFIELD Sarah m LOBDELL Miles C on 3d April at Hamburgh NY *MS* 12 June 1844

LOCK Ann Maria m EMERY William S at Great Falls NH *MS* 7 Jul 1847

LOCK Anna m BARTLETT John Col on 16th ult *MS* 25 Apr 1833

LOCK Annah L of Allenstown m TALLANT Masten M of Canterbury on 30 Nov 1848 *MS* 17 Jan 1849

LOCK Jane of Bristol m CASS John F of Bridgwater at Bristol NH *MS* 28 Feb 1844

LOCK Jane of Bristol NH m CASS John F of Bridgewater on 26 Dec 1843 *MS* 21 Feb 1844

LOCK Mary A of Gilford m SLEEPER Geo of Alton on 8 Apr *MS* 22 May 1844

LOCK Mary of Great Falls m HUSSEY John of Exeter ME on Sunday last *MS* 27 Aug 1834

LOCK Mary S m WELLS Samuel Capt both of Epsom on 1 Dec *MS* 11 Jan 1837

LOCK Sarah O D m HILL Benjamin F both of Great Falls NH on 14 Apr *MS* 8 May 1850

LOCKE Abigail M of Boston MA m BATCHELDER George E of Chichester on 7 Sept *MS* 24 Sept 1845

LOCKE Abigail of Great Falls m HILL William Jr *MS* 23 Oct 1839

LOCKE Adaline M of Sandwich m BEAN Horace F of Boston MA *MS* 29 Jan 1845

LOCKE Ann Maria m EMERY William S on 22 Apr at Great Falls NH *MS* 28 Apr 1847

LOCKE Betsey wid/o Eld Ward LOCKE m CUSHMAN Samuel Esq of New Gloucester ME *MS* 17 Mar 1830

LOCKE Caroline H d/o LOCK Jesse Esq m DEARBORN Sylvanus of Foxcroft ME *MFWBR* 16 June 1849

LOCKE Eliza M m WENTWORTH Amos on last Sunday *MS* 1 Oct 1834

LOCKE Elizabeth m MAHONY James J at Bangor ME *MS* 13 Sept 1843

LOCKE Elizabeth m HARRIMAN Samuel M both of Raymond on 6 Mar *MS* 19 Apr 1837

LOCKE Helen E of West Cambridge MA m WELLINGTON Horace Prof of Languages in Mich Cen College on 9 Aug 1847 *MS* 22 Sept 1847

LOCKE Huldah P of Chichester m JONES James M of Loudon on 8 June *MS* 24 June 1846

LOCKE Melinda B of Dover m WATSON Lysander B of Brooklyn NY on 26 ult *MS* 4 Dec 1850

LOCKE Miss d/o LOCKE Simon m DUDLEY Benjamin of Lyman at Biddeford ME *MS* 15 June 1832

LOCKE Sarah E of Epsom m VESEY Joseph H of Deerfield NH on 10 Oct *MS* 24 Oct 1849

LOMBARD Adaline m HODGDON John on 2 June at Gorham ME *MS* 24 Jul 1844

LOMBARD Elizabeth D of Wales ME m DAVIS Isaac N of Lewiston ME on 2 June *MS* 3 Jul 1850

LOMBARD Harriet S of Gorham ME m WEEKS Robert Jr on 14 Jul *MS* 16 Oct 1844

LOMBARD Octavo H of Wales m HAMILTON John Capt Jr of Wales ME *MS* 10 Jul 1839

LOMBARD Ruth R of Boston m PAGE John B of Boston MA *MS* 25 Jan 1843

LONG Caroline of Benton PA m CONEY George of Abington on 4 Jul *MS* 17 Jul 1850

LONG Laura E m MITTS John D both of Conway NH on 6 Nov 1849 *MS* 20 Feb 1850

LONGFELLOW Mary Jane of Lowell m BRADLEY Alpheus *MS* 15 May 1839

LOOK Margaret C Miss of Georgetown ME m CHAPEL Ebenezer D Capt of Waterford CT *MS* 13 Feb 1834

LOOMIS Belinda of Plainfield NY m PALMER G W of Bridgewater on 11 Jan 1849 *MS* 28 Mar 1849

LORD Abigail of Dover NH m WHITEHOUSE Thomas L on 26 Nov at Dover NH *MS* 9 Dec 1846

LORD Amy of Volinia Cass Co MI m GRAY Wells of Antwerp Van Buren Co Mich? *MS* 8 May 1839

LORD Armine G m THING Samuel S Esq *MFWBR* 1 Dec 1849

LORD Betsey m LEGRO Benjamin at Lebanon ME *MS* 19 Mar 1845

LORD Dorothy of Great Falls m RICKER William of Saco ME *MFWBR* 7 Aug 1847

LORD Elcy of Norway ME m MERROW Samuel D of Auburn ME on 30 June at Poland ME *MS* 20 Aug 1845

LORD Eliza of Hatley m LORD Stephen on 20 Mar *MS* 13 Sept 1843

LORD Elizabeth of Limerick ME m STORER William of Limington ME *MFWBR* 18 Jan 1851

LORD Euditha A m PIERCE Charles K of Limerick ME *MFWBR* 6 May 1848

LORD Hannah of Eaton m SNELL Jerome at Eaton on 3 Aug *MS* 20 Aug 1845

LORD Hannah W of Lebanon ME m WENTWORTH Jonathan Y on 23 June at Lebanon ME *MS* 17 Jul 1844

LORD Julia Ann m LORD Daniel both of Parsonsfield ME *MS* 29 Apr 1840

LORD Louise of Northfield m EDGERLY Ira C on 15 Dec 1846 at Sandbornton *MS* 17 Mar 1847

LORD Mary m KNIGHTS Frank of Westbrook ME *MS* 1 June 1842

LORD Mary A m BARTLETT Broughton both of Boston MA *MS* 4 Apr 1849

LORD Mary C of Brighton ME m STAPLES David of Green Lake Wis on 11 Feb 1850 *MS* 20 Mar 1850

LORD Mary F m USHER Sidney *MFWBR* 19 Oct 1850

LORD Mary of Parsonsfield ME m STIMSON William of Limerick ME *MFWBR* 1 Jan 1848

LORD Mehitabel E m CRUMENT Stephen B in Exeter *MS* 24 Jan 1838

LORD Priscilla W m THURSTON Charles both of Corinth ME on 19 Nov *MS* 26 Dec 1838

LORD Sabrina m ROBERTS David S *MS* 8 Dec 1847

LORD Sarah A of Lowell on 3 Feb m CHESLEY James C *MS* 13 Feb 1839

LORD Susan m BURNHAM Mark *MS* 24 Oct 1833

LORD Susan Miss m LORD Isaac *MS* 24 Mar 1830

LORING Margaret Y m MELCHER Osborn A of Brunswick ME *MFWBR* 2 Feb 1850

LOTHROP Abby m PERKINS Ebenezer both of Edgecomb ME on 14 Oct 1849 *MS* 15 May 1850

LOTHROP Roxana K at Chesterville ME on Nov 28 m DAVIS Franklin L of Sidney ME *MS* 15 Jan 1840

LOUD Sarah B of Boston MA m EASTMAN Walla B of Holderness NH on 10 Aug *MS* 2 Nov 1842

LOUGEE Clara S of Parsonsfield ME m BROWN Thomas W of Brownfield ME *MFWBR* 5 Apr 1851

LOUGEE Elizabeth J of Farmington NH m ROBERTS William B on 4 Jul at Gilmanton *MS* 28 Jul 1847

LOUGEE Elizabeth R of Effingham NH m WHITE Allen on 4 Feb 1847 of Ossipee NH *MS* 28 Apr 1847

LOUGEE Hannah N m WINKLEY John H on 1 Sept at Manchester *MS* 11 Sept 1844

LOUGEE Mary Ann m FISK John G of Randolph on 4 Dec at Tunbridge VT *MS* 14 Jan 1846

LOUGEE Mary Ann of Strafford m JOY Frederick D on 1 Nov 1846 at Strafford *MS* 20 Jan 1847

LOUGEE Sarah Ann of Parsonsfield m JOHNSON Joshua E of Biddeford on 1 Sept 1848 *MS* 8 Nov 1848

LOURION Susan m SANBORN Moses both of Lowell MA *MS* 29 Apr 1835

LOVE Kepsa of Yorkshire NY m SWEET Lorenzo of Boston MA on 26 Jul 1843 *MS* 9 Aug 1843

LOVE Rocksalany m MESERVEY John E both of Wheelock Dec 2nd 1841 *MS* 2 Feb 1842

LOVEJOY Hepzibah M of Lowell m TURNELL Joseph S of Candia NH *MS* 22 Jan 1840

LOVEJOY Laura of Candia m WALLACE Abraham on 26 Jan at Candia *MS* 5 Feb 1845

LOVEJOY Nancy P of Meredith m SMITH Rufus of Moultonboro NH *MS* 23 Mar 1842

LOVEJOY Sophronia D of Candia on 22d ult at FWB meeting house in Candia m WALLIS Abraham C *MS* 2 Oct 1839

LOVELAND Clarissa m MERRIAM Zimri on 28 Dec 1848 *MS* 24 Jan 1849

LOVERING Elanor of Loudon NH m WHITTEMORE Daniel W of Boston MA on 26 Jan *MS* 15 Apr 1840

LOVERING Fidelia m KELSEY Charles both of Lowell MA *MS* 4 Feb 1835

LOVERING Hannah of Freedom m DURGIN Silas of Hiram ME *MS* 4 June 1834

LOVERING Mary Ann m TYLER Abram on 23 Oct at Freedom NH *MS* 23 Nov 1842

LOVICE Martha of Fryeburg on 23 Nov m WHIDDEN Nathaniel B of Denmark ME *MS* 31 Dec 1845

LOVIT Margaret of Portland ME m AVERILL Gerry Cook on 8th inst at Portland ME *MS* 17 Apr 1844

LOVREIGH Eliza L of Lowell MA m WENTWORTH John of Andover on 24 ult *MS* 3 June 1835

LOW Abigail m KNOWLTON Jacob *MS* 9 May 1833

LOW Mary V m CLARKE John both of Great Falls on 29 ult *MS* 9 Dec 1835

LOWD Mary B m ROBERTS William H of Natick MA on 3d inst at Acton ME *MS* 11 Sept 1844

LOWE Sarah m RUNNELS Israel both of Acton *MS* 6 Nov 1850

LOWELL Elizabeth H m McKENNEY Cyrus B on 3 June at Springfield ME *MS* 24 Jul 1844

LOWELL Hannah N m SMALL Ezra on 9 April *MS* 7 Feb 1844

LOWELL Jane of Hatley m COLE J H Mr *MS* 13 Sept 1843

LOWELL Mary A of Gorham ME m ANDERSON Richard of Windham ME on 26 ult *MS* 27 Mar 1850

LOWELL Prudence of Phipsburgh m OLIVER Zina H of Hallowell on 20 ult *MS* 3 Oct 1838

LOWELL Vesta of Lewiston ME m BURBANK Aleander Dr of Shelburne NH *MFWBR* 24 Apr 1847

LOWRY Betsey P m LEWIS Joshua W both of Kittery ME on 6 Dec *MS* 9 Jan 1850

LOYON Sybil of Rutland VT m BIXBY Loren E Eld on 18 Jan at Pittsford VT *MS* 7 Feb 1844

LUCAS Ann Maria m ELIAKIM Howard both of Dover on 25 inst in Dover *MS* 1 Feb 1837

LUCAS Betsey C of Wolfboro' NH m KENT Josiah of Grandy Lower Canada on 12 Oct at Wolfboro' NH *MS* 11 Feb 1846

LUCAS S E m GREELOW William *MFWBR* 16 June 1849

LUCE Hannah R m TEBBETTS James on 26 May 1844 at Alton *MS* 19 Feb 1845

LUCY Angelina D m GERRISH Andrew both of Nottingham on 20 Nov *MS* 13 Dec 1837

LUCY Hannah T of Pittsfield on 3d inst m DAVIS True B *MS* 17 Apr 1839

LUCY Lois M m THURSTON Elijah C on 19 Feb *MS* 24 Apr 1950

LUDDEN Remember S Mrs of Peru ME m FERNALD John D on 1 Jan at Peru ME *MS* 26 Feb 1845

LUFKIN Hannah m CHASE Pike on 5th inst *MS* 28 Mar 1833

LUFKIN Hannah of Dover m MANSFIELD Jesse of Salisbury NH on

LUFKIN (Continued)
3 Jul MS 13 Jul 1836

LULL Malinda L m BENNETT Henry both of Manchester on 5 Dec MS 29 Dec 1847

LULL Nancy M of Weare m GIBBS Wm on the 13th of Jan 1842 of Framingham MA MS 4 May 1842

LULL Phebe A m BACHELDER Jonathan on 11 Aug at Manchester NH MS 20 Aug 1845

LUMBARD Thankful of Sidney ME m JUDKINS Stephen B of Fayette ME MS 10 Feb 1836

LUMBARD Zeviah of Windsor VT m SHERMAN Samuel of Weathersfield on 8 inst MS 18 Jul 1838

LUNT Apphia A of Brunswick ME m WOODARD Joseph W of Lisbon ME on 25 Oct MS 8 Jan 1851

LUNT Betsey of Eaton NH on 7 Nov m LONG Viberus MS 20 Nov 1839

LUNT Lydia Ann of Brunswick ME on 22 Apr m GERRISH Albert H of Durham ME MS 24 May 1843

LUNT Mary F of Brunswick ME m TUTTLE George of Durham ME on 10 Oct 1848 MS 1 Nov 1848

LUNT Sarah m SMALL Samuel both of Westbrook ME on 19 Feb 1849 MS 14 Mar 1849 & MFWBR 17 Mar 1849

LURVEY Eliza m GOOGINS Samuel both of Buxton ME on 9 Aug 1848 MS 4 Oct 1848

LYFORD Julia W m LEE Thomas on 23d Oct at Dracut MA MS 18 Dec 1844

MACE Lucinda of Greene ME m SEDGLEY Edward on 16 Jul MS 2 Aug 1843

MACOMBER Welthy A m KING Lewis D both of ME MS 22 Apr 1840

MADDOCKS Mary Limerick ME m WILDES Jacob of Kennebunk Port ME MS 27 Sept 1827

MADDOX Harriet of Waterboro ME m DAME John O of Dover on 30th ult at Newmarket MS 20 Dec 1843

MADDOX Sarah Jane of Corinth m GOODWIN John P of Lyman on 18 Oct at Waterboro' ME MS 6 Jan 1847

MAGOON Angeline m HOITT Jeremiah B of Manchester NH on 17 Dec at Durham MS 24 Dec 1845

MAGOON Betsey of Stanstead m SMITH Moses of Patton MS 18 May 1836

MAGOON Eliza R of Wheelock VT m DAY Joseph of Glover on 5 Feb 1850 MS 6 Mar 1850

MAGOON Rhoda of Stanstead LC m COX Erastus on 5 Mar MS 20 Sept 1837

MAGRAW Sarah Ann of Fairfield m PERKINS Daniel MS 23 Jan 1839

MAINES Mary J m LOWELL Ambrose both of Lawrence MS 3 Jan

MAINES (Continued)
1849

MAIRU Elizabeth m HIBBARD Hezekiah at Brookfield NY *MS* 23 June 1847

MALLET Susan J of Topsham ME m FOSTER Timothy of Richmond on 31 Jan 1850 *MS* 13 Feb 1850

MALOON Climena at Manchester m DOW Isaac W on 3d Dec *MS* 20 Dec 1843

MALOON Hannah m CHAMPION Lorenzo both of Effingham NH on 13 Mar *MS* 26 Mar 1851

MALOON Martha of Boston MA m BIXBY Levi R *MS* 19 Jul 1843

MANARD Polly at Mountpelier VT m POWERS Abner B on 2 Aug *MS* 2 Oct 1844

MANCHESTER Freelove of Tiverton RI m MENNET David *MS* 4 May 1836

MANCHESTER Lucy of Providence RI m SWEET Lorain B of Smithfield on 28 Dec 1847 *MS* 2 Feb 1848

MANCHESTER Rhoda m ABBEY Stephen July 19 *MS* 19 Jan 1842

MANELL Rebecca G m TOZIER Charles L on 17 June *MS* 29 Aug 1849

MANLEY Jane m THOMPSON J H *MFWBR* 21 Apr 1849

MANLY Catherine F m RASMITSSON Augustus on 19 Sept at Charlestown MA *MS* 22 Oct 1845

MANN Elcy m OLIVER John Jr on 23d inst at Phipsburgh ME *MS* 2 Aug 1843

MANN Louisa at Randolph VT on Mar 10 m AMIDON Wm H H of Marshfield *MS* 25 Mar 1840

MANN Sarah M m PEAVEY Hezekiah W on 17 May at Manchester *MS* 5 June 1844

MANNING Hannah m LIBBY Wm H both of Dover NH on 19 Jan 1850 *MS* 30 Jan 1850

MANNING Mary V of Manchester m MORRILL David on 24 Dec of Manchester *MS* 1 Jan 1845

MANRAR Sarah R of Cape Elizabeth ME m WILLARD William Capt *MS* 11 Dec 1844

MANSEY Ann S m BLAISDELL Jacob at Gilford *MS* 4 Oct 1843

MANSFIELD Mananda of Lowell m SHERMAN Washington on 3 Jul *MS* 2 Nov 1842

MANSON Isabella of Limington ME m EDGECOMB Charles on 26 Dec *MS* 7 Feb 1844

MANSON Jane d/o MANSON John Dea of Freedom NH m GILES Thomas of Eaton *MS* 12 Dec 1833

MANSON Sarah Mrs m HALEY Wm both of Kittery ME on 13 Dec *MS* 9 Jan 1850

MANUEL Zilpha of Boston MA m SMITH Wm D of Manchester on 24 Dec 1848 *MS* 17 Jan 1849

MANWARREN Palmyra m BENTLEY James both of Sand Lake Rensalear Co New York on morning of 6 ult *MS* 17 Oct 1838

MARBLE Catherine m SMITH William H on 28 Aug at Freedom NY *MS* 15 Mar 1843

MARBLE Lucinda of Sutton m KENISTON Benj of Cabot Washington Co UT on 7 Sept *MS* 15 Nov 1837

MARCH Abigail of Eaton m COOL Zebulon of Tamworth NH *MS* 17 Jul 1839

MARCH Abigail T of Bridgeton ME m ROBBINS Sylvester on 12 Oct 1837 *MS* 17 Jan 1838

MARCH Ann T Mrs m GIBBS John T Esq Ed of the *Dover Gazette* on Thursday *MS* 1 May 1844

MARCH Lucinda E of Bridgeton m MURPHY George F of Denmark on 14 Oct *MS* 21 Nov 1838

MARCH Sally of Eaton m TOWLE Amos Esq of Freedom Village *MS* 21 Jan 1846

MARCH Sarah A of Bridgton ME m BULLOCK Warren on 9 Mar at Bridgton ME *MS* 23 Aug 1843

MARDEN Hannah m CHAMBERLIN Benjamin *MS* 26 Aug 1835

MARDIN Catharine of Wolfboro' m JENNESS Robert H of Boston MA *MS* 24 May 1843

MARDIN Emily Jane on 4 May 1843 m ESTHERS John of Wolfboro' NH *MS* 24 May 1843

MARKS Margaret of Salem m HALL Daniel of Candia NH 11 Aug *MS* 16 Oct 1850

MARKS Marilla m HUTCHINS Eias Eld on 24th inst at Dover NH *MS* 30 Dec 1846

MARR Catharine of Webster ME m MARR Henry Col of Wales ME *MS* 29 Dec 1847

MARR Catherine m RICKER Bradford Esq on 23 Oct at Brownfield *MS* 25 Jan 1843

MARR Jerusha S m COOMBS/COOMS William on 17 Dec at Bath ME *MS* 17 Jan 1844

MARR Lydia m ROWE Sergeant *MS* 2 Jan 1839

MARR Lydia H m DANFORTH Albridge on 7 Dec at Litchfield ME *MS* 17 Jan 1844

MARR Nancy L m JOHNSON Daniel Z both of Topsham ME *MS* 2 Aug 1848

MARRINER Elizabeth m THOMPSON William on 5 June at Brunswick ME *MS* 29 June 1842

MARRINER Lydia Jane of Bowdoinham ME m WHITMORE Dexter on 11 Sept at Bowdoinham *MS* 19 Oct 1842

MARSH Julia m BROWN O S Eld on 11 Oct at Unadilla Forks N York *MS* 8 Jan 1845

MARSH Mary J of Gilmanton m JAMES William H of Gilford on 4 Aug *MS* 12 Sept 1838

MARSH Olive m MORRISON Benjamin on 1 Jan at Gilmanton *MS* 11 Jan 1837

MARSH Rosanna m PENNEY Leonard on 5 Sept at Unadilla Forks N York *MS* 8 Jan 1845

MARSH Sarah m JOHNSON Samuel on 9 May at Hallowell ME *MS* 5 June 1844

MARSHALL Arvilla P m RANDLETT Stephen H both of Manchester on 10 Dec 1848 *MS* 27 Dec 1848

MARSHALL Margaret J of So Berwick m HANSCOMB Samuel Jr of No Berwick on 4 Mar 1849 *MS* 14 Mar 1849 & *MFWBR* 24 Mar 1849

MARSHALL Sarah R of Bradford m FERNALD John of Loudon on 8 inst *MS* 23 May 1849

MARSHALL Susan E m CATE David O both of Somersworth on 17 Dec 1848 *MS* 3 Jan 1849

MARSHALL Temperance A m COOMBS Isaac both of Isleboro ME on 2 Jan *MS* 25 Mar 1840

MARSTIN Elizabeth Ann m PLUMMER Samuel 3d at Epping NH *MS* 6 Apr 1842

MARSTON Betsey L in Brentwood m LADD John Jr *MS* 5 Jan 1842

MARSTON Cyrena of Parsonsfield m STACKPOLE Isaac of Lebanon on 25th inst *MS* 30 Sept 1831

MARSTON Deborah m DEARBORN John both of Hampton on 28 Sept *MS* 7 Oct 1846

MARSTON Jane P m MERRILL Samuel D on 21 March at Holderness NH *MS* 21 Apr 1847

MARSTON Jemima A m ROLLINS Daniel C both of Manchester on 14 Mar *MS* 1 Apr 1846

MARSTON Lucinda m SANBORN Benjamin Esq both of Gilford on 16 Jul *MS* 13 Sept 1837

MARSTON Lucy Jane of Meredith NH m BUSSIEL Joseph C of Meredith NH *MS* 8 Dec 1841

MARSTON Mary D m SLEEPER Charles of Rye on 5 June at Hampton *MS* 12 June 1844

MARSTON Mary of Tamworth NH m BEAN Jacob of No Sandwich NH on 12 Nov *MS* 19 Dec 1838

MARSTON Polly m LAWRENCE Noah Capt both of Meredith on 25 Nov 1847 *MS* 22 Dec 1847

MARSTON Rachel of Eaton m SHACKFORD Thomas *MFWBR* 3 Feb 1849

MARSTON Sally recently of Parsonsfield ME m JONES John of Somersworth NH M 23d ult *MS* 11 Jul 1833

MARSTON Tamar L both of Sand Lake NY m MARVIN Nathaniel D on 27 ult *MS* 21 June 1848

MARTIN Adelia both of Sand Lake NY m CARMAN Wm H on 22 ult *MS* 4 Sept 1850

MARTIN Almira of Andover m WALLACE Daniel R on 10 Feb 1849 *MS* 7 Mar 1849

MARTIN Ann C both of Goffstown m ROBIE Charles H on 5 Apr *MS* 29 Apr 1846

MARTIN Eliza m PLAISTED Samuel on 6 Aug 1837 *MS* 17 Jan 1838

MARTIN Eliza of China m WILSON Allen of Orangeville on 27 May last *MS* 15 July 1835

MARTIN Elizabeth Ann m ROWE Jonathan H on 28 May 1844 at Atkinson ME *MS* 21 Aug 1844

MARTIN Ellen m WALLEY James *MFWBR* 18 Aug 1849

MARTIN Hannah of Bridgton ME m KILBORN Willard on 25 Nov 1841 at Bridgton ME *MS* 27 Apr 1842

MARTIN Huldah O of Williamstown VT m TASKER Ichabod of Strafford on 7 Dec 1847 *MS* 12 Jan 1848

MARTIN Jane of Stanstead LC m BAILEY Joseph of Compton on 15 May *MS* 20 Sept 1837

MARTIN Lucina G m GEORGE Lewis both of Lowell *MS* 29 Aug 1838 & on 21 *MS* 12 Sept 1838

MARTIN Lydia of Williamstown VT m DUTTON Oliver W of Chelsea on 13 Feb 1850 *MS* 10 Apr 1850

MARTIN Mary m HAWKINS Orson both of Yorkshire on 14 Sept 1848 *MS* 1 Nov 1848

MARTIN Mary on 24 Nov at East Williamstown VT m KINSMAN Denison *MS* 18 Dec 1839

MARTIN Patta Eliza of Hatley m CLIFFORD Micajah on 7 Dec *MS* 13 Apr 1842

MARTIN Sarah E of Saco ME m PUGSLEY Edmund of Biddeford ME in Saco on Jan 1st 1842 *MS* 12 Jan 1842

MARVIN Mariah m BERGIN Jasper both of Oneonta *MS* 1 Dec 1847

MASON Abigail A on 4 May m ROWELL Benjamin *MS* 19 Jul 1843

MASON Abigail of Eaton on 3 Nov 1844 m KNOX Edward Jr of Ossipee NH *MS* 13 Nov 1844

MASON Eliza D m HORN Ira *MS* 17 Feb 1836

MASON Elizabeth D m CHASE Nathan M both of Haverhill on 26 Mar 1846 *MS* 8 Apr 1846

MASON Hannah C m ABBOTT Solomon of Boston MA on 25 Oct at Wolfboro NH *MS* 2 Nov 1842

MASON Hannah of Newfield m PEASE John Capt of Parsonsfield ME *MS* 20 Sept 1827

MASON Louisa Q d/o MASON Nathan & Charlotte P of Sandwich m JOHNSON William D of Northwood on 1 Oct *MS* 16 Oct 1844

MASON Lydia of Hampton m BATCHELDER James L on 30 Dec at Hampton *MS* 6 Jan 1847

MASON Maria J m SANBORN B P Mr at Sanbornton on 23 Apr *MS* 29 May 1844

MASON Mary Ann m FOSS Loren both of Moultonboro NH on 21 Apr

MASON (Continued)
MS 15 June 1836

MASON Mary m EDDY Ambrose S both of No Providence on 26 ult *MS* 16 Dec 1835

MASON Rhoda m BUSWELL Smith D on 27th at Manchester *MS* 24 Dec 1845

MASON Sarah M m AVERY John C on 23 Nov of Sandwich *MS* 17 Dec 1845

MASON Sarah M m PAGE Harvey on 25 Dec at Bethel ME *MS* 4 Feb 1846

MASTON Sally of Lowell MA m CORLESS Reuben *MS* 3 May 1843

MATHES Ann Miss of Lee m CHASE George W of Dover NH on 31st ult *MS* 3 Sept 1834

MATHES Judith Matilda of Lee m PENDERGAST Solomon of Durham on 29 May *MS* 5 June 1850

MATHES Mary Mrs of Ossipee NH m HYDE Daniel on 24 June at Ossipee NH *MS* 13 Sept 1843

MATHES Nancy m HAINES James M on 29 ult *MS* 5 Dec 1849

MATHES Susan of Somersworth m PERKINS Andrew H of Boston MA on 5 Apr 1849 *MS* 18 Apr 1849

MATHEWS Hannah H m HILL Orin T on 2 Jan 1848 *MS* 2 Feb 1848

MATHEWS Lydia m McINTIRE Samuel *MS* 12 Mar 1851

MATHEWS Rebecca m WYLIE Sewell Capt both of Boothbay ME on 10 Mar 1850 *MS* 15 May 1850

MATHEWSON Hannah of Lyndon m EASTMAN Silas of Lyndon *MS* 5 Apr 1843

MATHEWSON Mary Jane of Providence m TURNER Henry B of Pawtucket on 5 Mar 1850 *MS* 3 Apr 1850

MATHEWSON Miranda of Walworth NY m TIFFANY Lewis of Naroge Shenango Co NY *MS* 27 June 1849

MATTHEWS Abigail m FRENCH Edmund on 16th ult *MS* 14 Nov 1833

MATTHEWS Elizabeth D on 21 May m PHILBRICK Ebenezer M of New Market *MS* 7 June 1843

MAXFIELD Betsey C m GAVIT Ezekiel both of Smithfield on 18 Oct *MS* 7 Nov 1838

MAXFIELD Eliza Ann H m COOK Robinson both of Raymond ME *MS* 12 Nov 1834

MAXFIELD Lydia of Sandwich m MOULTON Josiah of Meredith on 20 Mar *MS* 15 Apr 1846

MAXFIELD Martha A m FRENCH Josiah H on 4 Dec at Lowell MA *MS* 25 May 1842

MAXFIELD Nancy E m HOLT Horace on 19 Mar *MS* 26 Mar 1845

MAXFIELD Olive L of Starksboro VT on 23 Jan m HILL John 2d at Starksboro VT *MS* 7 Feb 1844

MAXFIELD Orissa of Goshen m BROWN John H of Manchester on

MAXFIELD (Continued)
5 Feb *MS* 20 Feb 1850

MAXFIELD Rhoda F m DAVIS John on 5 Dec 1843 at Chichester *MS* 29 May 1844

MAXFIELD Sarah C m SPEAR David *MFWBR* 21 Apr 1849

MAXIM Betsey B of Fairfield ME m TAYLOR Orrin *MFWBR* 18 Aug 1849

MAXWELL Lucy Ann of Wales ME m DIXON Nathaniel at Wales ME *MS* 28 Feb 1844

MAXWELL Mary of Wales ME m DIXON Harmon on 27 Feb at Wales ME *MS* 21 Apr 1847

MAXWELL Naomi I of Wales ME m PREBLE Otis on 19 Nov of Wales ME *MS* 20 Dec 1843

MAXWELL Sarah m ROLLINS Silas B both of Mt Vernon ME *MS* 3 Apr 1850

MAY Ruby of S m BALDWIN Oscar of Barnston on 7 Nov *MS* 1 May 1844

MAYBERRY Margaret T of Windham ME m MAYBERRY Merritt of Standish ME on 20 Apr at Windham *MS* 14 May 1845

MAYHEW Phebe of Owego m NOTEWARE John Jr of Warsing Ulster Co NY on 22 Jan 1849 *MS* 28 Mar 1849

MAYNARD Nancy M of Stow VT on Feb 27 m MONTGOMERY Drury R of Duxbury *MS* 30 Mar 1842

MAYO Emily J of Bridgton ME m SKILLIN James T of Biddeford ME on 3 Sept 1848 *MS* 27 Sept 1848

MAYO Martha Miss m RIPLEY Thomas B Rev *MS* 3 May 1827

McALISTER Amada A m FISK Dudly both of Phoenix NY on 1 Dec *MS* 22 Dec 1847

McALLASTER Saphronia E of Stowe VT m JOHNS Joel S of Montpelier on 15 Feb 1849 *MS* 25 Apr 1849

McALLISTER Elvira m EASTMAN John F on 8 inst *MS* 17 Oct 1849

McALLISTER Sarah Jane at Portland ME m DEQUIO Joseph on 7th inst at Portland ME *MS* 21 Nov 1843

McCALLAR Jane of Falmouth ME m ATKINS Nathaniel of Westbrook ME on 13 Dec *MS* 2 Jan 1839

McCARTER Sophia m McCRILLIS Thomas both of Dover on 6 Aug *MS* 12 Aug 1846

McCLURE E P of Bangor ME m KELLEY Samuel B of Orono ME *MFWBR* 24 Feb 1849

McCOBB Arinda m MATTHEWS A on 10 Nov at Boothbay ME *MS* 22 Jan 1845

McCOLISTER Catharine m MUGFORD George on 30 May 1848 *MS* 7 June 1848

McCOLLISTER Jane of Barnston m STANTON Samuel on 7 Sept of Barnston *MS* 13 Apr 1842

McCONKEY Elizabeth of Upper Canada m RULTON Matthew on

McCONKEY (Continued)
27 Jan at Three Mile Bay *MS* 5 Feb 1845

McCORRISON Olive C of West Buxton m JONES John G on 1st inst at West Buxton of Boston MA *MS* 11 Sept 1844

McCOY Hannah m MORRILL Reuben both of Manchester NH on 25 June 1848 *MS* 5 Jul 1848

McCRILLIS Caroline m TUTTLE Jonas B both of Center Harbor on 27 Jan *MS* 12 Feb 1851

McCRILLIS Joanna m WESTLY Wamule both of Lebanon ME on 30 Aug 1847 *MS* 1 Dec 1847

McCRILLIS Mary C m ROWE David B on 3d inst at Pittsfield *MS* 21 Apr 1847

McCRILLIS Mary Jane m SNELL N Charles both of Lowell *MS* 26 Jan 1848

MCDANIEL Asenath of Barrington m MARSTON ISAAC of Nottingham in Barrington on Tues 15th *MS* 23 Feb 1842

McDANIEL Rebecca of Barrington m GILE Joseph of Nottingham on 24 Aug at Barrington *MS* 13 Sept 1843

McDONALD Frances S m BURR William on Thurs morning last Limerick *MS* 18 June 1828

McDONALD Miriam d/o McDONALD John Gen late of Limerick ME m DOLE Albert of Bangor on Thurs last week *MS* 1 May 1834

McDONALD Rebecca of 3 Mile Bay NY m PARMERTER Joel D of Gananougua Canada West on 7 Oct 1847 *MS* 1 Dec 1847

McDONALD Sarah m DUTTON Thomas on 18th ult both of Gray *MS* 2 Feb 1831

McDONALD Sarah of Limerick m ILSLEY Jeremiah of Portland ME *MS* 9 Mar 1831

McDONALS Ruth of Lowell m ALLEN Otis on 20th inst *MS* 29 May 1839

McDONOLD Angeline m GILSOM Abijah on 25 Feb *MS* 23 Aug 1843

McDUFFEE Louisa Ann Augusta of Alton NH m SMART Moulton B of New Market NH *MS* 3 Mar 1847

McDUFFEE Mercy of Rochester m JENNESS Cyrus on 27 June at Rochester *MS* 27 Dec 1843

McENTRYE Anna of New Lyme m EATON Marsena of Rome on 5 Nov 1848 *MS* 3 Jan 1849

McFADDEN Elizabeth m PENNEY James on 20 Aug at Charlestown *MS* 9 Dec 1846

McFANNEN Minerva L of Embden ME on 6th inst m HAINES Samuel of Saco *MFWBR* 13 Jan 1849

McFARLAND Elizabeth of Ellsworth ME m CUNNINGHAM Nathan Y of Penobscot ME *MFWBR* 28 Apr 1849

McFARLAND Zetha m BLISS Orvis Z of Groton *MS* 18 Jan 1843

McGILL Susan m BROADWAY Christopher on 12 Nov 1843 at Stephentown NY *MS* 24 Apr 1844

McINTIRE Clara of Gloucester m McDONALD Joseph of Gray on 20 Dec 1847 *MS* 26 Jan 1848

McINTIRE Eliza Jane of Tuftonborough NH m BROWN Joseph of Sanbornton on 14 Feb 1849 *MS* 9 May 1849

McINTIRE Mary E of Alton NH m WENTWORTH Lewis B of Somersworth on 5 May *MS* 16 May 1849

McKENNEY Julia Ann of Wiscasset ME m TIBBETS John F of Woolwich ME on 25 Jan 1848 *MS* 9 Feb 1848

McKENNEY Ruth Ann of Georgetown on 3 Nov m PIERCE Andrus F of Westport *MS* 11 Dec 1839

McKENNEY Sally F of Limington on 9 Apr m MOODY Leander *MS* 24 Apr 1839

McKENNEY Sarah D m MAXWELL James of Danville ME *MS* 14 Feb 1844

McKENNEY Sarah E d/o McKENNEY Eleazer Esq m PERRY Charles *MFWBR* 16 Nov 1850

McKENNEY Sarah Jane m WILLIAMS John of Phipsburg ME *MFWBR* 31 Aug 1850

McKENNY Lydia of Wiscasset ME on 31st ult m WALKER Ezekiel Jr of Woolwich ME *MS* 13 Feb 1839

McKENNY Phebe J m CLUFF Irony on 11 May 1843 at Kennebunkport ME *MS* 24 May 1843

McKENZIE Nancy m FULLER J *MFWBR* 12 Jan 1850

McKINNEY Emeline of Wiscasset ME m BRIGGS George U of Windsor ME on 29 ult *MS* 20 June 1838

McKUSICK Charlotte of Limerick ME m DREW Joseph of Newfield ME on Sunday last *MS* 27 June 1833

McKUSICK Hannah of Limerick ME m GRAY John of Waterboro ME *MS* 28 Sept 1832

McKUSICK Lucinda m HILL Joseph both of Limerick ME on Mon last *MS* 26 June 1829

McKUSICK Susan m MOULTON Oliver Sunday last *MS* 18 Oct 1827

McLANGHLIN Sarah J of Freedom m MURRAY William of Knox on Thanksgiving Day *MS* 22 Jan 1851

McLAUGHLIN Mary m FILFIELD Isaac G on 5 Dec 1844 *MS* 29 Jan 1845

McLELLAN Bertha D m STEARNS Moses J *MFWBR* 14 Sep 1850

McLELLAN Martha m MANSFIELD John of Brownfield *MS* 14 Mar 1828

McLITCHFIELD Nancy m LITCHFIELD Winslow A both of Boston on 11 June 1848 in Boston *MS* 28 June 1848

McLOUTH Mrs of Bedford m RAWSON E on 18 Jan *MS* 19 Mar 1851

McLUCUS Mary G m TWOMBLEY Reuben *MFWBR* 24 Mar 1849

McMURPHY Catharine m BROOKINGS Samuel on 31 Jul at Woolwich ME *MS* 24 Aug 1842

McNEAL Maranea J m POTTLE Joseph H both of North Hampton in

McNEAL (Continued)

New Market *MS* 19 Jan 1842

McNEAL Sarah A m SMITH James W both of New Market on 21 Mar *MS* 24 Apr 1851

McPHERSONS Amy of Cameron m PERSON Wm of Woodhull on 3 June *MS* 21 Aug 1850

McQUESTION Mary J of Biddeford ME m CHASE Samuel Jr of Saco ME *MFWBR* 11 Jan 1851

McQUESTON Helen O m MERRIL Joseph W both of Manchester on 9 Apr *MS* 26 Apr 1848

MEAD Mary J m MARTIN John G on 4 Aug at Roxbury MA *MS* 20 Aug 1845

MEADER Betsey at Lowell MA m HUCKINS Randall *MS* 3 May 1843

MEADER Dorothy Ann of Conway NH m WORMWOOD John B of Brownfield ME on 3 ult *MS* 10 Nov 1847

MEADER Joan m FOSS Alvah both of Tamworth on 14 Oct *MS* 21 Nov 1838

MEADER Mahaley F m KEAZER David both of Haverhill on 4 Apr *MS* 1 May 1844

MEADER Martha of Lowell MA m STOKES Daniel on 25 Dec at Lowell MA *MS* 25 May 1842

MEADER Mary m DEARBORN Sylvanus of Limerick ME on 25th ult *MS* 2 Sept 1831

MEADER Mary D of Westport m MITCHELL Galen O on 11 Jan of Westport *MS* 4 Feb 1846

MEADER Phebe H of No Berwick m MEADER Tobias merchant of Dover NH on 3d int in Friend's Meeting House at No Berwick ME *MS* 9 Dec 1835

MEADER Sarah m DORE Wentworth *MS* 25 Apr 1833

MEADER Vienna of Rochester m BODGE James on 18th *MS* 15 Oct 1845

MEAL Lucy B m ROBERTS Joshua Jr of Parsonsfield ME in Portland ME *MS* 4 Oct 1827

MEARDEN Lucinda m KENISTON Hiram B both of Alton NH on 22 Oct 1848 *MS* 15 Nov 1848

MEARS Emily m WHITNEY Henry both of Belmont ME *MS* 13 June 1849

MEDCALF Eunice on 20 Feb m BARNES John Deacon in Freedom NY *MS* 15 Mar 1843

MEDER Hannah m WENTWORTH Bennin both of Dover *MS* 29 Nov 1837

MEECH Minerva m SMITH Eli both of Yorkshire NY on 28 Feb 1848 *MS* 10 May 1848

MEECH _ary m UMSTED Elijah both of China NY on 25 Sept *MS* 23 Dec 1835

MEEDE Irene of Limington ME m LIBBY Benjamin C on 23d inst

MEEDE (Continued)
MS 31 May 1827

MEGQUIER Emeline m WALKER Curtis both of West Poland ME on 13 May *MS* 3 June 1846

MEIGS Sally C of Lyndon m WINSOR Albert W on 7 Dec at Sutton VT *MS* 21 Dec 1842 & *MS* 5 Apr 1843

MEIGS Sally of Lyndon VT m YOUNG Zebina Eld of Sheffield on 14 Jul *MS* 31 Aug 1836

MELCHER Harriet M of Brunswick ME on 3 Sept m OTIS William M Capt *MS* 18 Sep 1839

MELCHER Maria of Brunswick ME m PENLEY William of Danville ME on 10 June at Falmouth ME *MS* 30 June 1847

MELCHER Sarah m HUNT Robert G both of Brunswick ME on 15 Dec 1837 *MS* 21 Feb 1838

MELDRUM Nancy J of Great Falls ME m HENDERSON Daniel S on 19th at Great Falls NH *MS* 29 Mar 1843

MELLEN Dorcas m CODMAN William W both of Deering on 21 May *MS* 24 June 1846

MELLEN Rachel on 5 Nov of Lowell MA m THOMSON Charles *MS* 20 Nov 1839

MELLOON Huldah m BECK George of Dover *MS* 12 Nov 1845

MELOON Lovina R of Moultonborough m PALMER Calvin L of Stewartstown on 12 inst *MS* 26 Sept 1838

MELOON Mary E of Dover m SMITH Woodbury of Haverhill MA on 11 Feb 1850 *MS* 20 Mar 1850

MERCHANT Roxana m TEBBETTS David H both of Belgrade ME on 21 inst *MS* 6 Apr 1836

MEREEN Jane D Mrs m TOTMAN Elias Jr on 8 Mar 1848 in Phipsburg ME *MS* 29 Mar 1848

MERRETT Harriet S of Brunswick ME m LIBBY Isaac on 5 June at Brunswick ME *MS* 29 June 1842

MERRIL Catharine m COLBY J B both of Manchester on 27 Jan 1848 *MS* 2 Feb 1848

MERRILL Abigail L m MEAD James H both of Meredith *MS* 15 June 1836

MERRILL Ann M of Gilford m STEVENS George A at Gilford "This notice was inavertently overlooked or it would have been published before" *MS* 30 Aug 1843

MERRILL Annah L of Craftsbury VT m LOCKE Reuben of Northboro MA in Hartford CT *MS* 28 Mar 1849

MERRILL Annah of Cornish on 6th inst m SANBORN Gilman Eld *MS* 20 Mar 1839

MERRILL Betsey of Holderness NH m SINCLAIR Alex C of Center Harbor on 19 Feb at Tamworth NH *MS* 21 Apr 1847

MERRILL Caroline M m LAWRENCE Philip both of Walworth on 18 Sept *MS* 16 Oct 1850

MERRILL Clara Augusta d/o MERRIL Seward of No Scarboro ME m
MORRIS Charles James on on Thanksgiving eve *MS* 1 Dec 1847
MERRILL Cynthia of Parsonsfield ME m HORN Richard of Roxbury
MA in Parsonsfield ME on 16th inst *MS* 19 Jan 1842
MERRILL Cyrena of Gilford m HUNT Hiram on 23 Nov of Gilford *MS*
25 Jan 1843
MERRILL Eliza W m STOKES Dudley L *MS* 23 May 1838
MERRILL Elizabeth G m NELSON Henry D on 4th Jul at Manchester
NH *MS* 28 Jul 1847
MERRILL Frances M m FOSS Erastus D on 11 Jul at Strafford NH
MS 11 Aug 1847
MERRILL Hannah m HURD Hiram S at Acton ME *MS* 3 Jul 1844
MERRILL Lovina m STRAFFORD Warren C on 26 Mar at Bath *MS* 23
Apr 1845
MERRILL Lydia J on 3d inst m KELLY Amos *MFWBR* 21 Apr 1849
MERRILL Lydia Jane of Rochester m MURPHY Thomas of Dorchester
on 3 Nov *MS* 27 Nov 1844
MERRILL Martha of Portland m NELSON John of Portland ME on
31st ult *MS* 8 Feb 1843
MERRILL Mary m MOONEY Newbegin of Parsonsfield ME on Thurs-
day *MS* 13 Dec 1827
MERRILL Nancy of Parsonsfield on Dec 30 m STANLEY Stephen of
Tamworth NH *MS* 19 Jan 1842
MERRILL Pluma m DAILY Selah both of Stanstead on 27 Jan *MS* 15
Apr 1840
MERRILL Roxanna m MARTIN Jonathan both of Hopkinton on 27th
ult *MS* 13 Apr 1836
MERRILL Ruth of Haverhill m MOORE Alexander on 7 Feb 1844 at
Haverhill NH *MS* 21 Feb 1844
MERRILL Sally M of Holderness m MERRILL William W of Meredith
MS 2 Feb 1842
MERRILL Sarah A of Holderness NH m ROGERS Daniel B on 24 Sept
1848 *MS* 21 Mar 1849
MERRILL Sophronia of Pownal ME m POLLARD Isaac of Lewiston
ME *MFWBR* 27 Mar 1847
MERRILL Susan C of Minot ME m WOODMAN R M of Orono ME on
12 Dec *MS* 22 Jan 1840
MERRIMAN Sarah of Brunswick ME m GRAVES Wm of Topsham ME
on 10 Oct 1848 *MS* 17 Jan 1849
MERROW Catherine of Waterville ME m STEVENS Milton of Smith-
field *MS* 25 Dec 1844
MERROW Hannah W of Saco ME m HOLT Henry S on 6 Oct of Saco
ME *MS* 15 Oct 1845
MERROW Maria of Great Falls NH m MERROW Elisha of Milton in
Dover NH *MS* 27 June 1838
MERROW Phebe A m BATCHELDER Isaac 2d at Eaton *MS* 30 June

MERROW (Continued)
1847

MERRY Ann Maria m SHERMAN Elias A both of Edgecomb on 10 Oct 1847 *MS* 12 Jan 1848

MESERVE Deborah of Durham m CHAPMAN Smith of New Market *MS* 20 Mar 1834

MESERVE Delia L of Freedom m HARMON Samuel on 30 Jan of Freedom *MS* 19 Feb 1845

MESERVE Eliza D of Limington ME m McKENNEY Sewell of Limington ME *MS* 14 Jul 1847

MESERVE Sally m DOUGLAS Elias both of Limington ME in Apr *MS* 30 May 1838

MESERVE Sarah J m CLARK Daniel D on 7th inst at Dover NH *MS* 10 Feb 1847

MESERVE Susan Mrs of Rochester NH m BICKFORD D Mr of Barrington at Rochester NH *MS* 13 Jan 1847

MESSER Betsey m BLAKE James H both of Landaff on 10 May *MS* 13 June 1838

MESSINGER Vesta A G m BRAGG Milton B *MFWBR* 9 Mar 1850

METCALF Rebecca of Lisbon ME m METCALF Abijan of Freeport ME *MS* 23 Mar 1836

MILER Sarah of Brownfield m WAKEFIELD Daniel of Biddeford ME on 3 Nov 1847 *MS* 29 Dec 1847

MILES Elizabeth (in 60th yr of age) at Parsonsfield ME m WIGGIN Nathan (in 80th yr of age) *MS* 25 Mar 1840

MILES Sarah A m DEMERITT John F both of New Market on 13 inst Sabbath eve *MS* 23 May 1849

MILIKEN Jane U of Buxton ME m LIBBY Henry of Portsmouth NH *MFWBR* 24 Aug 1850

MILL Roxanna of Burlington m FOWLER Nahum A of Greenbush ME on 31 Oct 1847 *MS* 29 Dec 1847

MILLEN Rebecca G of Lowell MA m MANAHAN Harvey on 6 Sept at Lowell MA *MS* 2 Nov 1842

MILLER Caroline S of Charlestown MA m HARTILL Charles A on 3 Jul at Charletown MA *MS* 23 Oct 1844

MILLER E H of Burlington ME m JOHNSON James I of Lowell on 5 Dec *MS* 29 Dec 1847

MILLER Ellathyna P of Northbridge m ROBBINS Ira T of Sutton MA on 13 Mar *MS* 7 June 1843

MILLER Frances of Shapleigh ME m ANDERSON John B of Portland ME *MFWBR* 13 Jul 1850

MILLER Harriet A m HEKOK Channey J on 28 Feb *MS* 24 Apr 1850

MILLER Jenette Q m LITTLEFIELD Joshua on 29 June at Dover *MS* 9 Jul 1845

MILLER Mary A of Rollinsford NH m WITHAM William of Acton *MFWBR* 11 Jan 1851 & on 19 Dec *MS* 1 Jan 1851

MILLER Tamson m RAMSY Wm P on 1 inst *MS* 18 Jan 1837

MILLS Betsey of Corinna ME on 30 Dec 1838 m COPP Samuel of Chandlersville ME *MS* 24 Apr 1839

MILLS Eliza of Lebanon m BLAISDELL Joseph of Rochester on 27 Mar at Lebanon ME *MS* 13 Apr 1842

MILLS Elizabeth m ALLEN Charles both of Sanford on 16 in Sanford *MS* 24 Jan 1838

MILLS Eunice of Eaton m DEMERITT Benjamin F of Effingham NH on 31 Mar at Eaton NH *MS* 20 Apr 1842

MILLS Hannah of Somerwroth NH m ESTES Isaac of Lebanon ME on 23d inst *MS* 29 Sept 1847

MILLS Henrietta m WEBBER Samuel on 24th inst *MS* 30 Apr 1828

MILLS Lucy G of Lowell MA m GOWEN Otis F of Boston MA on 11 Mar 1849 *MS* 4 Apr 1849

MILLS Lydia C of Corinna ME m RACKIFF John M on 28 Feb at St Albans *MS* 29 Mar 1843

MILLS Lydia of Rochester NH m DORE Brackett of Lebanon *MS* 27 Nov 1844

MILLS Martha R m GOWEN Oren B on 11 Jan *MS* 2 Feb 1848

MILLS Mary m DREW Benjamin T of Eaton *MS* 9 Feb 1848 & *MS* 30 June 1847

MILLS Syrena m COPP John of Chandlerville on 9th inst *MS* 20 June 1833

MILNER Frances Mrs of Shapleigh ME m ANDERSON John B of Portland ME *MFWBR* 6 Jul 1850

MINER Betsey m WALKER Jason H both of Great Falls on 27 Feb *MS* 6 Mar 1850 & *MFWBR* 9 Mar 1850

MINER Hertensia Gunelda of Otsego IND m MINER Benjamin *MS* 13 Dec 1848

MINOR Sophia m YOUNG Stephen on 14 Mar 1847 of Canterbury NH *MS* 5 May 1847

MINOT Ann R of Dracutt MA m RICHARDSON Geoorge W on 27 Apr at Lowell MA *MS* 11 May 1842 & *MS* 19 Oct 1842

MINOT Harriet P Mrs m WATERS John T of Portland ME *MFWBR* 27 Apr 1850

MINSOR Elizabeth M of Johnston m MERIAM Jesse W of No Providence on 18th ult *MS* 9 Jul 1834

MITCHEL Emily J of Bath ME m SAVAGE James of Woolwich ME on 28 Feb *MS* 10 Mar 1847

MITCHEL Eunice of Venango PA m SHERWOOD Wm C T of Rockdale on Mar 21 *MS* 1 May 1844

MITCHEL Sarah of Rome ME m JUDKINS Daniel of Belgrade ME *MS* 8 Jan 1845

MITCHELL Eliza J of Chesterville ME m WHITE William H of Stoughton MA on 22 June at Chesterville ME *MS* 6 Aug 1845

MITCHELL Elmira E m ROBBINS Lloyd O both of Chesterville ME on

MITCHELL (Continued)

1 Mar 1849 *MS* 28 Mar 1849

MITCHELL Hannah Mrs m WILSON Sanford both of Richmond on 14 Feb *MS* 3 May 1837 & *MS* 12 Apr 1837

MITCHELL Kezia A m CHURCHILL Ezra Jr both of Montville ME on 19 Nov 1848 *MS* 17 Jan 1849

MITCHELL Louiza of Dover ME m DAUGHERTY William Dr of Sebec ME on 5th ult *MS* 17 Sept 1834

MITCHELL Lucy m CUSHING A *MFWBR* 8 Dec 1849

MITCHELL Martha m FARMER Lemuel both of Temple on 6 Nov *MS* 16 Jan 1850

MITCHELL Mary Ann m HARRINGTON Seth both of No Providence on 16 Jan *MS* 7 Feb 1838

MITCHELL Mary m SAVAGE Samuel both of Manchester on 1 Mar 1848 *MS* 22 Mar 1848

MITCHELL Sarah C m BENSON Luther M both of Monroe ME on 14 Oct *MS* 27 Nov 1850

MITCHELL Sarah N m HEALD Samuel on 30 Dec 1847 *MS* 2 Feb 1848

MITCHELL Theodosia on 5th inst at Portland ME m HOLMES James R President of the Portland Washingtonian Society *MS* 15 Feb 1843

MIX Mary S of Huntington VT m WALKER Edwin F of Champlain NY on 31 ult *MS* 10 Nov 1847

MONSEL Nancy m KELLER Joseph A on 28 Jan of Perry Township *MS* 30 June 1847

MONTGOMERY Jane of Boothbay ME m BAKER Bradford Y on 25 Jan *MS* 4 Feb 1846

MONTGOMERY Nancy of Manchester NH m BALLOU George on 5 Oct at Bedford *MS* 15 Oct 1845

MONWARREN Orrilla m PIXLEY Orren on 10 Apr at Farmersville *MS* 15 Mar 1843

MOODY Abagail L of Lisbon NH m KENISTON of Franconia NH on 18 Oct *MS* 28 Dec 1842

MOODY Charlotte of Cape Elizabeth ME m LIBBY Zebulon T of Scarboro ME *MFWBR* 11 May 1850

MOODY Elizabeth m MOODY Washington *MS* 20 Jul 1836

MOODY Elizabeth m SAWYER Thomas E Hon on 15 Oct 1848 *MS* 25 Oct 1848

MOODY Elizabeth Q m PARSON Enock on 22 Feb in Parsonsfield ME *MS* 9 Mar 1832

MOODY Louis m TASKER Jonathan both of Somersworth on 9 ult *MS* 10 Oct 1838

MOODY Lucinda m DOWNES Nathaniel on 4 May at Lowell *MS* 2 June 1847

MOODY Lydia Ann of Gilmanton m WENTWORTH Levi H of Lebanon

MOODY (Continued)
ME on 10 Mar 1850 *MS* 24 Apr 1850

MOODY Mary F m HALL Isaac G both of Dover on 13 April 1848 *MS* 19 Apr 1848

MOODY Rebecca B of Auburn ME m FREEMAN John Jr of Durham ME on 14 Oct *MS* 3 Dec 1845

MOODY Sally of Boscawen m COUCH Samuel 2d on 15 Jul *MS* 29 Jul 1846 5 Aug 1846

MOODY Sarah m TRICKEY Nathan H Eld on 19 ult *MS* 10 Dec 1834

MOODY Sarah m MERROW Daniel G both of Ossipee NH on 5 Oct 1848 *MS* 15 Nov 1848

MOODY Sarah of Ossipee NH m ABBOTT Asa M on 21 May at Ossipee NH *MS* 13 Sept 1843

MOODY Sophia m VARNEY Samuel both of Dover on 20 inst *MS* 27 Sept 1848

MOOERS Mary J of Alexandria m DOW Abram of Meredith on 8 Jan 1849 *MS* 18 Apr 1849

MOONEY Judith P m WHITEN Nathan B on 19 Mar at Holderness *MS* 24 Apr 1844

MOONEY Mary D m CLARK Charles C both of Holderness on 25 Jul *MS* 9 Aug 1837

MOOR Joanna on 14 Nov m BLAISDELL John of Georgetown ME *MS* 11 Dec 1839

MOOR Locina of Waterville ME m BLAISDELL Joseph of Dexter ME *MS* 15 Mar 1837

MOOR Lucretia m TALLANT David both of Canterbury on 25th ult *MS* 9 Sept 1835

MOOR Nancy m BURBANK Amos on 14th inst *MS* 22 Oct 1828

MOORE Abba (a widow) of Hampton on 28th ult m OSGOOD Reuben Capt of Salisbury *MS* 13 Mar 1839

MOORE Abigail of Lewiston ME m MAXWELL Daniel W of Windham on 25 Apr *MS* 6 June 1849

MOORE Achasah Ann of Salsbury MA m COLLINS David O of Amesbury MA on 29 Sept at Deerfield *MS* 18 Nov 1835

MOORE Amy m GETCHELL Christopher S M both of Lewiston ME 26 Apr *MS* 6 June 1849

MOORE Ann of New Market m ABBOTT Benjamin F on 10 Apr at New Market NH *MS* 20 May 1842

MOORE Betsey A d/o MOORE Jonathan Esq of Standish ME m STURGIS Nathaniel G of Danville in Standish ME *MS* 12 Jul 1837

MOORE Betsey P d/o MOORE John of Deerfield NH m HARRINGTON Moses B of Pittsfield *MS* 3 Oct 1833

MOORE Caroline of Parsonsfield ME m AYER Amaza L of Limerick ME on 14 Sept *MS* 27 Sept 1848

MOORE Clarinda B of Corinna ME m ROBINSON Nathan J Eld of Sebec ME on 8 Oct *MS* 27 Dec 1837 & *MS* 13 Dec 1837

MOORE Eleanor of Georgetown ME m BLAISDELL Joseph of Phipsburgh ME on 5 Oct at Georgetown ME *MS* 2 Nov 1842

MOORE Eliza A of Loudon NH m CLOUGH Nathaniel D on 27 Nov at
Canterbury *MS* 11 Feb 1846

MOORE Elizabeth L m LEAVITT Samuel Q both of Effingham NH *MS*
15 on Jan 1840

MOORE Elizabeth R of Saco ME m ST CLAIR James of Lewiston ME
MFWBR 29 June 1850

MOORE Julia D of Loudon m FRENCH Elijah B of Canterbury on 18
Aug at Manchester NH *MS* 27 Aug 1845

MOORE Louisa m ATWOOD Norman both of Lincoln VT on 18 Sept
MS 16 Oct 1850

MOORE Louisa of Hatley m MOULTON Thomas P Eld of Walden VT
on 17 Jan *MS* 15 Apr 1840

MOORE Lydia J m DOLIVER Benjamin S both of Mt Desert ME *MS*
19 Jan 1842

MOORE Marcia m PERKINS Luke of Newport *MFWBR* 14 Dec 1850

MOORE Margaret A of Northwood NH m PECK Daniel of Boston MA
on 25 Dec 1848 *MS* 10 Jan 1849

MOORE Mary Jane of Parsonsfield ME m BERRY Erastus A of
Limington on 2 Dec 1847 *MS* 12 Jan 1848

MOORE Polly T m WIGGLESWORTH Samuel both of Deerfield NH on
21 Nov *MS* 18 Dec 1850

MOORE Rachel on Oct 16 m WELCH Lawrence *MS* 19 Jan 1842

MOORE Rebecca G of Concord m BLAISDELL Uriah Dea of Great
Falls NH *MS* 3 Oct 1849

MOORE Sally m HODGDON Josiah S of L in Canterbury NH *MS* 28
June 1827

MOORE Sarah Ann at Newfield m CATLIN Samuel T Eld of Woolwich
ME *MS* 20 May 1840

MOORE Sarah of Northwood m DURGIN Miles Esq on 10 Dec at
Manchester NH *MS* 1 Jan 1845

MOORE Sarah of Standish ME m EMERY Joshua T of Portland ME
MFWBR 25 Sept 1847

MOREHOUSE Lydia Maria of Warrensburgh NY m DODGE Alvah at
Limerick ME *MS* 6 Jul 1842

MOREHOUSE Sally Ann Miss of Warrensburgh m CHASE Wm P Eld
on at Warrensburgh NY *MS* 5 Aug 1835

MORFORD Loisa d/o MORFORD J B Eld m WIDER Julius of Turin
on 29 Feb at West Munroe NY *MS* 10 Apr 1844

MORGAN Deborah m HUBBARD John both of Dover NH *MS* 2 Sept
1835

MORGAN Delia m BEAN Hiram on 8 Dec 1843 at Sutton NH *MS* 10
Apr 1844

MORGAN Elanor Mrs m MANNING Jesse *MS* 20 June 1838

MORRELL Mary E of No Berwick ME m GETCHELL Isaac of Sanford

MORRELL (Continued)
ME on 10 Oct *MS* 20 Nov 1850

MORRELL Mary K m CHASE Geroge W *MS* 14 Oct 1835

MORRIL Louiza m FLANDERS Parker both of Lowell on 7 inst *MS* 21 Mar 1838

MORRILL Alvira of Gilmanton NH m RUNDLETT Newall on 26 Oct at Meredith Bridge *MS* 9 Nov 1842

MORRILL Annette of Parsonsfield ME m LORD David H Eld of Pascoag RI on 9 inst *MS* 29 Nov 1848

MORRILL Hannah J m EATON Horace of Wells ME at Wilmington MA *MS* 8 Mar 1843

MORRILL L P Miss m COBB Jon L H *MFWBR* 30 Dec 1848

MORRILL Louisa O m YOUNG Henry on 24 inst *MS* 3 May 1837

MORRILL Louisa of Oneonta NY m WALLIN Ezra on 4 Jul 1848 *MS* 26 Jul 1848

MORRILL Mary J d/o MORRILL S D of Northwood m POTTER George W of Loudon *MS* 24 Apr 1834

MORRILL Mary of Parsonsfield m FOSS Andrew T Eld of Dover on 28th ult *MS* 6 Feb 1829

MORRILL Nancy Mrs m McCUTCHEON James Eld on 22 Jan of Pembroke *MS* 29 May 1844

MORRILL Patience of Gilford NH m BROWN Henry of Moultonborough NH on 3 June 1849 *MS* 9 Jan 1850

MORRILL Rosanna m BICKET Barnard both of Candia on 4 ult *MS* 17 Oct 1838

MORRILL Sarah m HAM Samuel 3d merchant *MS* 25 Apr 1833

MORRILL Sarah Ann of New Berwick ME on 19 Jan m HATCH Salvastine L *MS* 3 May 1843 & *MS* 15 Feb 1843

MORRILL Sarah of Raymond ME on 25 June 1843 m SNOW Joshua of New Gloucester ME *MS* 8 Nov 1843

MORRIS Elizabeth Payson d/o MORRIS Charles Esq of No Scarboro' m LIBBY Isaac on 31 ult *MS* 1 Dec 1847

MORRISON Abigail m HALTON Edwards S on 11th inst *MS* 26 Sept 1833

MORRISON Abigail B of Manchester NH m TAYLOR Stephen C *MS* 18 Sept 1844

MORRISON Bridget on April 5 m SHACKLEY Richard both of Sanford *MS* 15 Apr 1840

MORRISON Catherine m WILLIAMS Elijah H of Portland ME *MS* 29 Jan 1845

MORRISON Dorothy C m FLINT Nathaniel Jr both of Sweden in Bridgton *MS* 9 Feb 1842

MORRISON Dorothy E of Gilford m GILMAN Lyman W at Meredith NH *MS* 6 Sept 1843

MORRISON Elizabeth B d/o MORRISON Jonathan m ROBERTS George of Haverhill on 19 ult at Sanbornton *MS* 8 Mar 1837

MORRISON Elmira of Eaton m LANG John of Conway *MS* 17 Jul 1839

MORRISON Francis Ann of Wakefield NH m LANE Winthrop M of Sandwich NH on 15 Sept *MS* 21 Nov 1838

MORRISON Harriet H m SHERBURNE Jeremiah M both of Barrington on 19 inst *MS* 29 Apr 1846

MORRISON Joanna S m MORRISON Robert both of Sweden ME on 19 Jul *MS* 2 Sept 1846

MORRISON Lydia Ann of Bethlehem NH m OAKES David of Lisbon NH *MS* 24 Jan 1849

MORRISON Maria L of Canaan m SWEAT Artemas K on 12 Jul of Bethlehem NH *MS* 4 Feb 1846

MORRISON Martha A P of Cornish ME m CLARK Benjamin F on 5 June of Cornish ME at Parsonsfield ME *MS* 31 Mar 1847

MORRISON Martha J of Portland ME m JAMES William on 23d inst *MS* 8 Mar 1843

MORRISON Mary m BODGE William on 9 Mar at Barrington *MS* 25 June 1845

MORRISON Olive m PLUMMER William both of Sanford ME on 11 Nov *MS* 21 Nov 1838

MORRISON Plooma A m HILL Levi both of London NH on 4 Jul *MS* 17 Jul 1850

MORRISON Sarah of Sanford m SHACKLEY Moses of Alfred ME on 15 Nov *MS* 20 Dec 1837

MORRISON Sevina of Saco m HOBBS Samuel of Parsonsfield ME on 5th ult *MS* 4 Aug 1830

MORRISON Sobrina K of Clinton ME m WING John H of Canaan on 31 May *MS* 8 Jul 1846

MORROW Louisa A m KIDDER Tyler *MFWBR* 22 May 1847

MORSE Almira of Effingham NH m COBURN J Milton Eld on 21st inst at Effingham NH (pastor of the Baptist church *MS* 3 Aug 1842

MORSE Almira m PERKINS William on 14 Mar *MS* 10 Apr 1844

MORSE Anna m RICKER Isaac on 23 Nov at Alton NH *MS* 10 Mar 1847

MORSE Climena B of Holderness m DANA William B on 2d inst of New Hampton *MS* 26 Oct 1842

MORSE Elizabeth Ann m LEWIS James W on 8 Nov *MS* 19 Feb 1851

MORSE Elizabeth of Gray ME m GOFF Henry on 9 Jan 1843 *MS* 10 May 1843

MORSE Elvira C m BENJAMIN Henry F both of Manchester on 7 June *MS* 24 June 1846

MORSE Hannah Miss of Henniker m PATTERSON Dan H of Henniker on 13th ult *MS* 4 Apr 1833

MORSE Hannah of G m PUSHOR Peter of Plymouth *MS* 13 Dec 1837

MORSE Hester Ann of Brunswick ME m LUNT James Capt of

MORSE (Continued)
Freeport ME *MS* 19 Jan 1848

MORSE J S of Portland on 27th ult m KNIGHT Henry W *MFWBR* 8 Sept 1849

MORSE Louiza of Rushford NY m BLACKMAR H Eld of Alabama NY on 13 June 1843 *MS* 3 Jan 1844

MORSE Lucretia of Phipsburg ME on 8th inst m SPRAGUE William L *MS* 16 Oct 1839

MORSE Lydia E on 28th ult at Waterford ME m YOUNG Seth P of Smithfield *MS* 11 Dec 1839

MORSE Maria m MELCHER Jeremiah both of Brunswick ME on 18 Apr *MS* 22 Aug 1849

MORSE Martha A m GELLERSON Warren W both of Leavitt PLT on 15 Oct 1848 *MS* 6 Dec 1848

MORSE Martha on 8 Feb 1843 at West Brookfield VT m BASS Eleazer *MS* 14 June 1843

MORSE Nancy B m KNIGHTS Leonard on 6 Aug at Dixfield *MS* 20 Aug 1845

MORSE Rosanna B m GOVE R B *MFWBR* 8 Dec 1849

MORSE Roxannah of Carthage ME m SAFFORD Daniel of Fayette ME on 23 Nov 1849 *MS* 16 Jan 1850

MORSE Sabrina of West Plymouth NH m BAGLEY David Dea of West Topsham VT on 24 Sept 1848 *MS* 4 Oct 1848

MORSE Sally m FOSS Blake both of Alton on 17 Jul *MS* 17 Aug 1836

MORSE Sarah Ann of Sandwich m BRADLEY William of Bedford MA on 15 Apr 1849 *MS* 2 May 1849

MORSE Sarah m SNOW Joseph Capt both of Brunswick ME on 24 Aug 1848 *MS* 20 Sept 1848

MORSE Sarah C m BREWER Emery both of Freeport ME on 28 Dec 1847 *MS* 9 Feb 1848

MORSE Sarah of Portland ME m PRESCOTT J C on 25 Feb *MS* 8 Mar 1843

MORSE Sophia M of Lowell MA m WARNER Myron of Wales NY *MS* 28 June 1837

MORSE Zepina m ELLIS William on 18 Oct 1843 at Haynesville ME *MS* 20 Dec 1843

MORSE Zeruiah S of Solon m BIGELOW Sila of Chester on 30 Aug *MS* 19 Sept 1849

MORTON Eliza of Gorham m MARR Isaac of Limington ME *MFWBR* 27 Apr 1850

MORTON Ellen P m TRACY G W both of Owego NY on 17 Apr 1849 *MS* 2 May 1849

MORTON Sarah of Gorham ME m SCHILINGER Daniel of Poland ME *MS* 6 Feb 1834

MORTON Soloma of Limerick ME m DOUGLASS Elisha *MS* 7 Feb

MORTON (Continued)
1844

MORTON Susan of West Windsor m DAVIS Aaron H of Reading on 1 Apr 1849 *MS* 18 Apr 1849

MOSES Elvira of Wellington ME m BISBY Rovert of Harmony on 28 Oct 1849 *MS* 20 Mar 1850

MOSES Florenda m TUTTLE Merari *MS* 7 Oct 1835

MOSES Harriet of Allenstown NH m CONANT George H of Charlestown MA on 26 June *MS* 23 Oct 1844 & *MS* 3 Jul 1844

MOSES Martha J oof Biddeford ME m BENSON James E of Parsonsfield ME at Saco ME *MS* 21 Dec 1842

MOSES Sarah H of Sanbornton m PIPER John of Meredith *MS* 13 May 1840

MOSHER Sarah of Temple m MOORES Joseph of Wilton ME *MS* 15 Jan 1840

MOSHIER Frances G m CARPENTER Dan Esq *MFWBR* 26 June 1847

MOSLEY Margaret M of Bowdoin m ALEXANDER Lewis P of Topsham on 13 Aug 1848 *MS* 17 Jan 1849

MOULTON Abigail m ST CLAIR Thomas both of Holderness on 8 Nov 1849 *MS* 5 June 1850

MOULTON Caroline M m BENNETT William I at Freedom *MS* 21 Jan 1846

MOULTON Cynthia of Eaton m RENNET Ruel of Effingham NH *MS* 21 Jan 1846

MOULTON Cynthia P m EDGERLY Samuel N on 20 Oct at Gilmanton *MS* 28 May 1845

MOULTON Elizabeth P of Scarboro ME m SAWYER Cyrus on 8 Nov of Buxton ME *MS* 6 Apr 1847

MOULTON Elvira of Sandwich m BANKS Israel of Parsonsfield ME on 24 June Sabbath eve *MS* 18 Jul 1849

MOULTON Euphama m MASON Amos W of Sandwich *MS* 31 Mar 1847

MOULTON Judith R of Sandwich m HAINES John C of Moultonborough on 2 Jan 1848 *MS* 26 Jan 1848

MOULTON Louisa of Warren m SPALDING A O of Vestal NY on 28 ult *MS* 27 Nov 1850

MOULTON Lucretia Ann of Holderness m HUCKINS Warren on 7 Sept of Center Harbor *MS* 16 Oct 1844

MOULTON Lucy of Tamworth NH m ALLARD Levi of Albany on 4 Apr *MS* 5 June 1850

MOULTON Lydia d/o MOULTON A Eld of Stanstead CE m WOOD Israel of Hatley on 18 Oct *MS* 28 Nov 1849

MOULTON Lydia J m SAWYER Horace of Saco *MFWBR* 4 Jan 1851

MOULTON Lydia of Moultonboro NH m MORRISON John Jr on 15 Jul *MS* 4 Aug 1847

MOULTON Martha A m CLARK George S *MFWBR* 22 Feb 1851

MOULTON Martha Ann of Sanford ME m DORR John B of Milton Mills NH on 24 Jan at Springvale ME *MS* 3 Mar 1847

MOULTON Martha of Sandwich m BUNKER Enos A of Barnstead *MS* 10 Oct 1844

MOULTON Mary m GORDON Daniel Dr *MFWBR* 27 Jul 1850

MOULTON Mary B m LIBBY Wentworth both of Newfield ME on 18 June *MS* 17 Jul 1850

MOULTON Mary J m DAVIS Albion K P both of Newfield ME on 22 Sept *MS* 30 Oct 1850

MOULTON Mary Mrs m KNOX Samuel both of Albany on 23 Jan *MS* 24 Apr 1850

MOULTON Mary Mrs of Freedom m MARSHALL Joel Capt of Buxton ME at Freedom Monday 20th ult *MS* 8 Aug 1833

MOULTON Mary of Parsonsfield m LORD Almon of Ossipee NH on 25th ult *MS* 1 Ocy 1828

MOULTON Miriam B m BEAN James M on 20 Sept at Manchester *MS* 1 Oct 1845

MOULTON Orinda of Somersworth NH m SHOMVEY Isaiah on 21 Mar *MS* 10 Apr 1844

MOULTON Pantha L of Conneaut Ohio m HIBBARD Albert of IL on 15 Apr at Conneaut Ashtabula Co Ohio *MS* 6 Jul 1842

MOULTON Rosetta of Barnston m HILL Jehial on 29 Jan *MS* 13 Apr 1842

MOULTON Sally at Newfield on Dec 1 m LIBBY David *MS* 26 Feb 1840

MOULTON Sally Mrs of Sandwich m WIGGIN John of Moultonboro' *MS* 13 Jan 1847

MOULTON Sarah J of Lowell MA m HENERSON Seth on 6 Dec at Deerfield *MS* 22 Dec 1841

MOULTON Sarah P of Ossipee Carroll Co NH m HOBBS Henry H of Norway Oxford Co ME on 14 Dec 1847 *MS* 19 Apr 1848

MOULTON Susan A m LILIKIN Leander *MS* 9 Feb 1848

MOULTON Susan B m LANG Thomas E both of Meredith on 15 Jul *MS* 26 Sept 1849

MOWREY Almira T of Smithfield m HARRIS Eseck of Burrillville on 8 Dec *MS* 1 Jan 1851

MOWRY Elizabeth of Smithfield m SMITH Elijah on 23 Nov at Scituate *MS* 14 Dec 1842

MOWRY Mary P m HAZEN Robert S both of Newport RI *MS* 8 Apr 1846

MUDGET Julia Ann m PAUL John both of Acton ME on 9 Apr *MS* 17 May 1848

MUDGET Mary M S m BROWN James H on 3 Nov at Bristol NH *MS* 21 Feb 1844

MUDGET Plooma D d/o MUDGET J Dea of Gilmanton m HILL

MUDGET (Continued)
Andrew Capt of Strafford *MS* 16 Jan 1834

MUDGET Susan C on 14 Nov at Bristol m BROWN Josiah on 14 Nov at Bristol *MS* 31 Jan 1844

MUDGETS Julia M m VITTUM Mark J on 14 Feb 1844 at Sandwich *MS* 5 June 1844

MUDGETT Clarissa A m AVERY Joshua E on 27 Feb at Sandwich *MS* 12 Mar 1845

MUDGETT Louise of Jackson m CHASE Simpson E of Bershire VT on 29 Sept 1847 *MS* 10 Nov 1847

MUDGETT Mary M S of Bristol NH m BROWN James H of Bristol NH *MS* 28 Feb 1844

MUDGETT Orinda M of Bristol m SMITH Curtis of New Hampton on 29 June 1848 *MS* 15 Nov 1848

MUDGETT Sarah H of Sandwich NH m GARLAND Ephraim M of Moultonboro' NH *MS* 18 Dec 1844

MUDGETT Sophronia m DURGIN Wm C both of Dixmont ME on 8 Jan 1850 *MS* 22 May 1850

MUIR Caroline of Portsmouth NH m NICHOLS Josiah of Lowell *MS* 18 Oct 1837

MULLICAN Sarah A of Salem MA m MOORE Elijah *MFWBR* 3 Feb 1849

MULLOY Hannah of Limerick ME m BANKS Jacob of Parsonsfield ME *MS* 27 May 1835

MULLOY Mary Ann m LARABEE Joseph both of Limington ME on 20 Jul 1839 *MS* 15 Jan 1840

MULLOY Mary of Limerick m MORRILL John of Parsonsfield ME *MS* 7 Dec 1826

MUNFORD Rhoda Ann m MARSHALL George W both of Macedon NY on 24 Oct *MS* 17 Nov 1847

MUNGER Lucy of Mukwanego m AUGIR Orlando of East Troy on 25 Dec 1850 *MS* 26 Mar 1851

MUNSEY Mary J m CLARK Jonathan P both of Manchester on 1 Jan 1848 *MS* 19 Jan 1848

MUNSEY Wealthy C of Gilford NH d/o MUNSEY G W Dr m LEAVITT Gilman on 7 June *MS* 23 June 1847

MURCH Eliza Ann of Unity m JONES Cyrus on 29 May at Unity *MS* 30 June 1847

MURCH Mary m MORTON Solomon both of Westbrook ME in Westbrook on Nov 25 *MS* 19 Jan 1842

MURCH Mary E m STANLEY James C both of Lowell on 13 Nov 1847 *MS* 15 Dec 1847

MURPHREY Catherine of Nassau m BEERS Philo on 14 Nov 1846 at Nassau *MS* 6 Jan 1847

MURPHY Abby J formerly of Jefferson ME m HARPER Joseph P *MS* 2 Feb 1848

MURPHY Alice of Parsonsfield ME m WEEKS Lorenzo L of Ossipee NH *MS* 21 Jan 1846

MURPHY Ann Eliza m BUZZELL John C *MFWBR* 12 Jan 1850

MURPHY Lucinda E m MARTIN Samuel on 1 June at Bridgeton Centre ME *MS* 28 June 1843

MURPHY Maria m FROST Wm both of Parsonsfield *MS* 26 Aug 1831

MURRAY Ann of Limerick m NEWBEGIN John of Shapleigh ME on 6th inst *MS* 21 Dec 1832

MURRAY Clara A of Lewiston Falls ME on 30th ult m BURBANK Adino J of Gilead *MFWBR* 8 Sept 1849

MURRAY Elizabeth Ann m MUGIN Russell both of Stockbridge MA on 13 Sept 1835 *MS* 4 May 1836

MURRAY Esther m SANBORN William both of Dover on 31 Dec 1848 *MS* 10 Jan 1849

MURRAY Frances M d/o MURRAY David Esq m RUMERY Ruel C both of New Market on 24 inst *MS* 30 Oct 1850

MURRAY Mary D of L m PINKHAM Isiah of Raymond on Thurs last *MS* 6 Dec 1827

MURRAY Morgianna m McKENNEY Wm both of Danville ME on 17 Mar *MS* 1 May 1844

MURRAY Susan m CHELLIES Sumner of Newfield on Thurs last *MS* 25 Jan 1827

MURRY Jane T m FRYE Orrin both of Durham on 20 Feb *MS* 20 Mar 1850

MUZZY Catherine L m EASTMAN Eben Col both of Whitefield on 29 Nov *MS* 26 Dec 1849

NALEN Margaret m FOSS Charles V both of Rochester on 4 Aug *MS* 21 Aug 1850

NASH Elizabeth M m BROWN Mark on 12 Feb at Raymond ME *MS* 26 Mar 1845

NASH Joan M of Minot m JONES J B of Lewiston Falls ME *MS* 10 Jul 1839

NASH Sarah A at Minot m MORSE Winslow of Bath *MS* 6 May 1840

NASON Eliza of Lewiston ME m NEVENS Davis Jr *MS* 27 Mar 1839

NASON Emily L of West Buxton ME m CROCKETT Joseph on 1st inst at West Buxton ME *MS* 11 Sept 1844

NASON Hannah m CLARK Daniel D both of Dover on 18 inst *MS* 21 Oct 1846

NASON Maria m WEST William A *MFWBR* 21 Jan 1849

NASON Matilda of North Berwick m ROBERTS John of Danvers MA on 16 Jul at North Berwick ME *MS* 30 Aug 1843

NASON Phebe on 10 Mar 1844 m BERRY Levi G at Biddeford ME *MS* 3 Apr 1844

NASON Priscilla of Great Falls NH m DAVIS Daniel on 8th Dec of Great Falls NH *MS* 24 Dec 1845

NASON Sabra of Lyman m KENNEY Henry of Lebanon on 18 Dec *MS* 28 Dec 1842

NASON Sarah Ann m DORE Charles both of Great Falls NH on 23 ult MS 2 Aug 1837

NASON Susan Amanda m SANDERS Abram B *MFWBR* 9 Dec 1848

NASON Ursula m BERRY James both of Dover on 8 Oct *MS* 18 Oct 1848

NAY Amelia S m THURSTON Andrew on 2 Jan 1848 *MS* 19 Jan 1848

NEAL Alta G of No Berwick ME m LITTLEFIELD Henry Jr of Wells on 18 June 1848 *MS* 16 Aug 1848

NEAL Ann of Gardiner ME m BURR William T *MS* 4 Sept 1839

NEAL Comford M of Loudon m QUIMBY Joseph L of No Sandwich on 12 Nov *MS* 19 Dec 1838

NEAL Emily B of Scowbegan m YOUNG Stephen of Starks ME on 10 Dec 1848 *MS* 3 Jan 1849

NEAL Mary m HAINES John on 7th inst at New Market *MS* 17 Apr 1844

NEAL Rhoda on 4th inst m DAVIS William G *MFWBR* 17 Mar 1849

NEALEY Emeline of Newfield ME m PURRINGTON Oliver of Epping NH on 20 Jan *MS* 13 Mar 1850

NEALLEY Mary A m WADLEIGH John C both of Meredith on New Years Eve *MS* 10 Jan 1849

NEALY Betsey m YOUNG Richard both of Great Falls NH on Fast Day Even *MS* 22 Apr 1840

NELSON Adaline m MEANS Luther both of Clinton on 23 Aug *MS* 2 Oct 1850

NELSON Hannah m MATTENLEY John both of Sutton on 12 Nov 1837 *MS* 14 Feb 1838

NELSON Mary of Groton on 26 Oct m TWISS William N of Auburn *MS* 15 Nov 1843

NELSON Sophia D m DENNETT Jeremiah W both of Portsmouth NH on 17 May *MS* 27 May 1846

NESBITT Sophronia M of Readfield ME m CUDWORTH Henry A of Boston MA on 30 Oct 1848 *MS* 15 Nov 1848

NETTLETON Hannah m CLARK S T Mr at Clinton *MS* 8 Jan 1845

NEVENS Eunice S of Lewiston ME m OSGOOD Aaron of Durham ME on 13 Jan 1848 *MS* 16 Feb 1848

NEVENS Sarah Jane of Sweden m BOYNTON Sylvester of Cornishville ME on 15 Dec *MS* 22 Jan 1851

NEWBARGE Mary L of Greenfield Ohio m BURLESON Allen of Mich on 30 Dec 1849 *MS* 20 Feb 1850

NEWBEGIN Mary Elizabeth of Boothbay ME m HODGDON Freeman Capt on 14 Dec *MS* 17 Jan 1844

NEWCOMB Olive E of South Danville NY m WALLACE Reuben Jr on 10 May at South Danville NY *MS* 17 Aug 1842

NEWELL Betsey m HATHORN Samuel Eld *MS* 12 Oct 1832

NEWELL Hannah E m INGALLS George I both of Attleborough on 14 May *MS* 1 May 1850

NEWELL Lucy A m BISHOP Joseph W *MS* Dec 15 1847

NEWELL Lydia A of Epsom m WHITNEY Charles E of Concord on 25 Nov 1847 *MS* 15 Dec 1847

NEWHALL Abigail B of Henniker NH m FOSS Joseph of Lynn MA *MS* 23 Sept 1835

NEWHALL Sarah of Stowe m SERGANT Thomas T of Stowe *MS* 21 Jan 1846

NEWTON Almedia E m HUNTOON Warner of Bridgewater VT on 6 Oct at Franconia NH *MS* 21 Jan 1846

NEWTON Elizabeth m HALL Clement M both of Dover NH on 18 Aug at South Boston MA *MS* 28 Aug 1844

NEWTON Eunice Ann m McGILL Hugh both of Stephentown NY on 26 Feb *MS* 13 Mar 1850

NEWTON Evaline of Lisbon NH m GALE Horace B of Littleton NH on 27 Sept at Lisbon *MS* 28 Dec 1842

NEWTON Lois Mrs of Bingham PA m COOL Wm P of Hebron on 7 Nov 1847 *MS* 1 Dec 1847

NEWTON Patty of Hamburgh NY m GRACE Patrick of Upper Canada on 14th Mar at Hamburgh NY *MS* 19 May 1847

NICHALS Lydia Ann of Corinth ME m TURNER Abel Eld of Foxcroft ME on 29 Aug *MS* 11 Oct 1837

NICHOLS Elanor m NICHOLS Benjamin both of Ossipee NH on 5 Dec *MS* 15 Jan 1840

NICHOLS Eleanor of Ossippee on Dec 5 m NICHOLS Benjamin *MS* 15 Jan 1840

NICHOLS Mariah S m JOHNS Noble L of Huntington *MS* 11 Sept 1839

NICHOLS Polly on 5 Feb 1843 m HALLY Lorenzo *MS* 12 Apr 1843

NICHOLS Sarah m CALEF Asa F on 6 Dec of Lowell MA *MS* 6 Jan 1847

NICHOLS Sarah W m HARRISON James M both of Woonsocket RI on 28 Nov 1850 *MS* 1 Jan 1851

NICHOLS Susan m WISEPH Joseph O both of Concord on 25 Jul *MS* 1 Sept 1847

NICKERSON Abigail m STODDARD Nelson on 2 Apr *MS* 5 May 1846

NICKERSON Abigail of Litchfield m WILSON Cyrus of Palmyra ME *MS* 21 Aug 1839

NICKERSON Jedidah of Mercer ME m SMITH John F S on 2 Feb of Monmouth ME *MS* 19 Feb 1845

NICOLS Lucy D of Lowell MA m ANDREWS Daniel H of Pelham *MS* 3 May 1843

NILES Harriet O m AYERS Albert G on 16 Feb 1848 *MS* 8 Mar 1848

NILES Rebeccah of Danville VT m MOONY Thomas on 11 Mar 1846 at Danville VT *MS* 24 Feb 1847

NILES Sarah Jane m CAMPBELL Robert both of Bowdoin ME on 25 Apr *MS* 1 May 1850

NISBET Ann m BROWN Robert on 5 Jan at Boston *MS* 19 Mar 1845

NOBLE Frances Emerline of Casco ME m DOLL Ephraim of Gray ME *MFWBR* 27 Jul 1850

NOBLE Rebecca M m BARNARD Barzell both of Perry NY on March 15 1840 *MS* 20 May 1840

NOBLE Sarah of Salartacook m CAIN David of Clinton ME on 9 Aug *MS* 2 Dec 1846

NORCROSS Marion W m TOZIER Franklin of Waterville at Hallowell ME *MS* 27 Dec 1843

NORRIS Betsey of Benton m COX Charles S of Haverhill at Benton on 31 Dec *MS* 17 Jan 1844

NORRIS Jane m WATSON Jonathan of Limerick ME on Sunday *MS* 27 Aug 1828

NORRIS Martha of Dover m TRICKEY Wm of Brookfield on 13 inst *MS* 20 Jan 1836

NORRIS Mary in Raymond m WASAN Thomas of Exeter *MS* 30 Mar 1842

NORRIS Sally C of Corinth VT m WILLEY Sol Jr of Topsham on 4 Feb *MS* 17 Feb 1847

NORRIS Sarah F m CLIFFORD Daniel on 25 Nov *MS* 9 Dec 1846

NORTHEY Mary Ann of Manchester m CARR Jeremiah on 14 Oct at Mancester *MS* 25 Oct 1843

NORTON Abigail of Limington ME m DOUGLASS John Jr of Sebago ME *MS* 20 June 1838

NORTON Achsah m ELLIS Cyrus on 18 Apr *MS* 31 Jul 1850

NORTON Adaline of Limington ME m CHADBOURN John Jr of Cornish ME on 17 May at Fryeburg ME *MS* 4 June 1845

NORTON Cyrene of Clayton NY m THOMPSON Stephen of Copenhagen on 6 Feb *MS* 5 Mar 1851

NORTON Elizabeth G m BRANSCOMB Charles Jr Capt both of Mt Desert ME on 14 Oct *MS* 2 Jan 1850

NORTON Elizabeth of Eaton NH m FEZZEN Moses 3d on 24 Mar at Eaton *MS* 11 May 1842

NORTON Etta Juliana d/o NORTON A Esq of Groveland m JONES C P, A.B. of Genesee & Wyoming Seminary Alexander on 22 ult *MS* 4 Sept 1850

NORTON Hannah of Limington ME m PUGSLEY John of Cornish ME *MS* 8 Mar 1843

NORTON Harriet of Barnston L C m FOSTER Abner of Canton ME on 25 Jul *MS* 1 Jan 1840

NORTON Martha m JOHNSON Cyrus both of Boston NY on 23 Oct 1845 *MS* 20 May 1846

NORTON Mary m BROWN Benjamin *MS* 9 Dec 1831

NORTON Mary E of Portland ME m PLUMMER Edwin of Norway ME

NORTON (Continued)
printer of the *Norway Advertiser* paper *MFWBR* 30 Jan 1847

NORTON Mary S of Huntington VT m HUNT Virgil O of Hiram Ohio on 3 Oct *MS* 6 Nov 1850

NORTON Persis at Middlebury NY m STEWART James on 25 Dec *MS* 11 Feb 1846

NOURSE Elizabeth B of Hopkinton m ADAMS Enoch C of Newbury NH on 26 Nov *MS* 23 Dec 1846

NOURSE Roxalany m MARTIN Henry on 31 Dec at Yorkshire NY *MS* 27 Jan 1847

NOWELL Mary Ann of York m DREW Joseph H of Berwick ME *MFWBR* 2 Nov 1850

NOYES Harriet N m PLACE Moses of Great Falls NH *MFWBR* 16 Mar 1850 & on 5 Mar 1850 *MS* 20 Mar 1850

NOYES Martha L m ANNIS Sheldon H both of Great Falls NH on 5 inst *MS* 22 Apr 1840

NOYES Mary m CORSON Benjamin both of Rochester on 24 Oct 1847 *MS* 17 Nov 1847

NOYES Mary E of Winham ME m LIBBEY Phineas Rev *MFWBR* 26 June 1847

NOYES Mary of Lisbon NH m ALDRICH Cyrus L of Franconia on 14 Nov at Lisbon NH *MS* 22 Dec 1841

NOYES Sarah L Mrs of Newburyport MA m BROWN Zacheus of Hampton on 8th inst *MS* 28 Dec 1842

NUDD Abby M m LEAVITT Alfred J both of Haverhill MA on 1 Jul 1848 *MS* 12 Jul 1848

NUDD Emeline S m DRAKE Bradley of Hampton *MS* 12 Apr 1843

NUDD Sarah of Hampton m SHAW Benjamin on 3 Sept *MS* 9 Sept 1846

NUTE Elizabeth A m PERKINS Moses P both of Dover on 31 Oct 1847 *MS* 1 Dec 1847

NUTE Elizabeth of Dover NH m CLARK James V of Strafford NH on 15th inst *MS* 29 Apr 1835

NUTE Joanna C m WOODMAN Levi *MS* 19 Apr 1837

NUTE Judith P Mrs m BATCHELDER Plummer P on Dec 1848 *MS* 10 Jan 1849

NUTE Louisa B of Dover NH m HASKELL William H on 23 March at Dover NH *MS* 31 Mar 1847

NUTE Maria L of Alton NH m SMITH Samuel A of Gilmanton on 3 Dec 1848 *MS* 27 Dec 1848

NUTE Marietta m NASON Mark F both of Dover on 26 Apr *MS* 1 May 1850

NUTE Sarah M m COFFIN George W *MFWBR* 27 Apr 1850

NUTE Sophia m STODDARD Henry R both of Wolfborough NH on 30 June *MS* 24 Jul 1850

NUTT Phebe Ann on 23rd June at Exeter ME m LEIGHTON Lorenzo

NUTT (Continued)
MS 10 Jul 1839

NUTTER Abigail of Milton m HOWE Jonas L on 29 Dec of Farmington MS 8 Jan 1845

NUTTER Clarinda m SPRINGFIELD Isaac W on 7 Jan at Rochester MS 17 Jan 1844

NUTTER Elizabeth m CHICK Harrison both of Ossipee NH on 10 Dec 1848 MS 25 Apr 1849

NUTTER Lydia M of Alton NH m SMITH Benjamin W of Gilmanton on 19 Apr MS 30 Apr 1845

NUTTER Mary A m NUTTER Asa N both of Alton on 20 Aug 1848 MS 6 Sept 1848

NUTTER Nancy of Exeter m PARSON Josiah of Plymouth on 14 Nov 1839 MS 12 Feb 1840

NUTTER Sarah O of Farmington at Rochester m BROWN John of Loudon MS 24 Mar 1847

NUTTING Aura of Canton NY m BROWN Carlton on 3d May at Canton NY MS 26 May 1847

NYE Ruth H of Clinton ME m DOWNES Newell P of Newport on 1 Jan MS 8 Apr 1846

OAKES Chastina m MOONEY Fernando S both of Franconia NH MS 24 Jan 1849

OAKES Mary Ann of China m MARSH Rolan of Yorkshire on 9 Jul MS 2 Sept 1846

OAKS Lucretia of Franconia NH m YOUNG Priest on 4 Jul at Lisbon MS 27 June 1842

OBER Sylvia H of Manchester m JOHNSON John B Esq of Hill on 9 Oct 1848 MS 8 Nov 1848

OBERTON Elvira A B of Litchfield m KNOW Isaac of Clinton on 5 May in Litchfield MS 22 May 1844

ODELL Sarah of Meredith NH m MORRISON Uriah on 15 March at Lake Village of Gilford MS 24 Mar 1847

ODIORNE Sarah of Pittsfield m ROLLINS Sherburne B on 15 Feb at Pittsfield NH MS 24 Feb 1847

OLIVER Clementine m RACKCLIFFE Ezekiel at Starks ME? on 8 Sept 1844 MS 16 Apr 1845

OLIVER Cordelia m HIGGINS John C of Farmington on 23 Feb MS 16 Apr 1845

OLIVER Diantha Miss m WRIGHT Isaac F on at Georgetown MS 6 Feb 1834

OLIVER Emily m FREDERICK John W on 1 Jan 1844 at Starks ME? MS 16 Apr 1845

OLIVER Louisa of Georgetown m LOWELL John W of Phipsburgh MS 21 Mar 1833

OLIVER Mary Jane on 17 Nov m OLIVER Washington of Georgetown

OLIVER (Continued)
MS 11 Dec 1839

OLIVER Mehitabel of Georgetown ME m OLIVER M on 2d *MS* 6 Feb 1834

OLIVER Nancy M of Georgetown ME m OLIVER James D on 3 Dec *MS* 17 Jan 1844

OLIVER Patience of Georgetown m SYLVESTER Parker of Phippsburg *MS* 9 Feb 1831

OLIVER Salome of Phipsburgh m OLIVER Mathew of Georgetown ME on 13 Oct *MS* 30 Oct 1850

OLIVER Sarah A m DOWNS Aaron P both of Boston on 7 Oct *MS* 17 Oct 1849

OLIVER Sarah Jane m WINKLEY Samuel P Capt on 15 Jan 1843 at Georgetown ME *MS* 8 Mar 1843

OLNEY Lydia H m ROUND Peleg both of Scituate RI on 4 Jul *MS* 30 Oct 1850

OLNEY Mary I of No Providence m BARTLETT Nehemiah of Garland ME on 25th ult at No Providence *MS* 9 Mar 1836

OLNEY Naomi Ann m LEE Newel both of No Providence on 27 Aug *MS* 3 Sept 1834

OLNEY Ratio of Scituate m BURLINGAME Henry Otis on 12th inst of Gloucester MA *MS* 21 Sept 1842

ORBSTON Martha Jane of Bowdoinham ME m GRAY Galon O of Bowdoinham ME *MS* 6 Sept 1843

ORCOTT Docia A m HAM Joshua both of Great Falls on 3 Nov 1848 *MS* 20 Dec 1848

ORCUT Milison of East Randolph m SMITH Harris K of Terre Haute Ind on 22 Aug *MS* 24 Oct 1849

ORDAWAY Elicta of Strafford m LOTHROP Urbane Dr on 11 Jan at Chelsea VT *MS* 6 Apr 1847

ORDWAY Maria A of Boston MA m WOODARD Barnet on 22d Apr at Warsaw NY *MS* 10 Sept 1845

ORNE Betsey K of Edgecomb m WINCAPAW Alexander on 23 Oct of Friendship ME *MS* 23 Nov 1842

OSBORN Elizabeth Ann of Dover NH m WALKER Hiram of Rochester on 8 inst *MS* 15 May 1850

OSBORN Mercey P Mrs m OSBORN Daniel of Dover *MFWBR* 8 June 1850 & on 29 ult *MS* 5 June 1850

OSBORNE Caroline P on 21 Jan 1847 m ROCKWOOD David of Remsen Oneida Co NY *MS* 10 Mar 1847

OSBORNE Eliza of Loudon m GREEN Alvah Russell on 29 Jan at Pittsfield *MS* 8 Feb 1843

OSBORNE Hannach C m GREEN Loammi both of Loudon on 5 Dec Thanksgiving Day *MS* 25 Dec 1839

OSGOOD Clarissa of Randolph m SANBORN Gilman Eld on 15 Nov 1844 at E Randolph VT *MS* 19 Feb 1845

OSGOOD Eliza m STACKPOLE Tobias *MFWBR* 1 Sept 1849

OSGOOD Eliza H m HANSON Daniel 3d both of Ossipee NH on 29 ult *MS* 12 Dec 1838

OSGOOD Leah of Gilford m FOLSOM Levi G on 3 Jul of Quincy MA *MS* 13 June 1842

OSGOOD Mary D m ANDREWS James on 24th ult of Charlestown *MS* 9 Dec 1846

OSGOOD Mary K of Northfield m MERRILL Albert Capt of Conway at Meredith Bridge *MS* 27 Apr 8142

OSGOOD Mehitabel m SMITH John in Raymond *MS* 13 Sept 1837

OSGOOD Sarah R of Pittsfield m GRIFFIN W E of Somersworth NH on 29 Oct *MS* 8 Nov 1837

OSBORNE Ordelia m SPAULDING Charles on 29th inst at Murry Orleans Co *MS* 20 Nov 1844

OSMORE Frances E of Windsor m DAVIS Bailey S of Hartland VT on Jan 5th *MS* 19 Jan 1842

OSTRUM Catharine of Hastings NY m FARRER James M on 21 Sept at Hastings NY *MS* 29 Oct 1845

OTIS Abigail K, d/o OTIS Job Hon youngest, m WINKLEY Paul J on at Strafford *MS* 18 May 1836

OTIS Abigail P of Fairfield ME m JAMES Isaiah Deacon of Dearborn ME *MS* 30 Nov 1842

OTIS Almira of Strafford m PLUMER Francis of Somersworth *MS* 10 Jan 1838

OTIS Dorothy Ann of Rochester m WILLEY Samuel B of Dover on 6 Nov 1844 at Dover NH *MS* 20 Nov 1844

OTIS Hannah H m CLARK Jonathan Jr at Dover NH on 25th inst *MS* 1 Oct 1845

OTIS Hannah L m HOR Lewis F *MS* 24 Jul 1839

OTIS Joanna of Strafford m FOSS Benjamin of Rochester on 22d ult *MS* 19 apr 1837

OTIS Lavina m MEADER Ephraim K of Dover on 22 Jul *MS* 1 Aug 1838

OTIS Sarah Ann, d/o OTIS Joshua Esq (his youngest dau), m HOWARD George W on 8 Apr at Strafford *MS* 16 Apr 1845

OWEN Abigail B of Buxton ME m WATERMAN Charles *MS* 14 Feb 1849

OWEN Drusilla of Lewiston ME m WILSON Benjamin of Harpswell ME on 30 Sept *MS* 17 oct 1838

OWEN Everlina m CROSBY Charles S Esq of Bangor ME *MFWBR* 6 Jul 1850

PACKARD Abtezary of Thomaston ME m VINAL Ezekiel of Camden ME on 22 Feb 1849 *MS* 16 May 1849

PACKARD Delia Mrs of Livermore ME m TAYLOR Ephraim on 7 Aug 1843 at Livermore ME *MS* 3 Apr 1844

PACKARD Hannah m BROWN Arthur at Foxcroft *MS* 5 Dec 1833

PACKARD Martha H m PURMORT Mark on 7 Apr *MS* 16 Apr 1845

PACKARD Rebecca of Exeter ME m STEWART David W of Garland ME *MS* 14 Apr 1847

PACKARD Sally m HOUSTON Henry C on 14 Jul at Thornton MA *MS* 4 Sept 1844

PAGE Abba Amanda of Meredith m LOVETT Lorenzo W of Gilford on 19 Oct *MS* 27 Nov 1850

PAGE Abigail of Gilmanton NH m SAWYER Josiah on Dec 5 of Salisbury MA *MS* 5 Jan 1842

PAGE Abigail of Sidney m HANSCOM Josiah W at Sidney of Hartland ME *MS* 20 Apr 1842

PAGE Amoret J of Newbury VT m CLARK Thaddeus F of Bradford VT on 17 Oct 1843 at Chabot VT *MS* 15 Nov 1843

PAGE Betsey m GILMAN John S of Gilmanton on 3 Nov *MS* 30 Nov 1842

PAGE Betsey of Raymond on 17 Jul m SCRIBNER John Esq *MS* 14 Aug 1839

PAGE Dorothy C youngest d/o PAGE Col m HUBBARD Charles P MD of Passadumkeag on 8 Oct at Burlington ME *MS* 19 Nov 1845

PAGE Huldah of Epsom NH m BACHELDER Smith of Northwood *MS* 31 Oct 1833

PAGE Jane C m DODGE Lot both of Edgecomb ME on 15 Sept *MS* 27 Nov 1850

PAGE Louisa m PARSONS Enoch on at Parsonsfield ME *MS* 13 Feb 1834

PAGE Lucy D m WILSON Andrew S *MFWBR* 24 Feb 1849

PAGE Mary m DATON Nahum W *MS* 30 Dec 1831

PAGE Mary Ann m EATON George of Newbury on 26 Jan at Manchester *MS* 5 Feb 1845

PAGE Mary J at Danville m YOUNG Daniel of Kingston *MS* 9 Oct 1839

PAGE Mary K of Epsom m SHERBURNE John S of Chichester on 4 Dec 1849 *MS* 9 Jan 1850

PAGE Mary Mrs of Belgrade m KNIGHT Edmund of Corinna ME on 5th inst *MS* 3 June 1835

PAGE Mary of Epsom NH on 29 Sept m FOGG David C of Pittsfield *MS* 16 Oct 1839

PAGE Nancy C d/o PAGE Daniel of Wakefield m COOK James McNorton on 9 Dec 1848 *MS* 3 Jan 1849

PAGE Phebe W m HALE Daniel on at New Sharon ME *MS* 27 Feb 1834

PAGE Rachel F m MERRILL Asa in Raymond NH *MS* 18 Nov 1831

PAGE Rosaline A of New Sharon ME m DYER Barlow Eld on 5 Dec at New Sharon ME *MS* 18 Dec 1844

PAGE Sabrina at Parsonsfield m JORDAN Z Eld *MS* 20 May 1840

PAGE Sarah B m PEARSON William S of Concord NH on 12 June *MS* 26 June 1850

PAGE Sarah Jane of Dover NH m CURRIER David Jr of Amesbury MA on 1 May at Dover NH *MS* 7 May 1845

PAGE Susan of Gilmanton m PRESCOTT Samuel of Alton on 16 Apr 1849 *MS* 16 May 1849

PAIGE Betsey B m DANIELS Jacob B both of Manchester on 14 Feb 1848 *MS* 22 Mar 1848

PAIGE Harriet L of Nashua m DAVIS Erasmus D on 17 March at Manchester *MS* 10 Apr 1844

PAINE Caroline E of Litchfield ME m RANDALL Heatherly Col on 22 Oct of Bowdoinham ME *MS* 8 Jan 1845

PAINE Eunice of Augusta m PENNY Arba of Waterville ME *MS* 21 Jan 1846

PAINE Harriet W of Pownal ME m MAXFIELD Robert C of Cumberland ME *MFWBR* 14 Dec 1850

PALFORD Mary of Rochester WT m FOWLER Reuben A on 18 Jan at Rochester WT *MS* 23 Apr 1845

PALMER Eliza Jane at New Sharon ME m WEBSTER William B of Industry ME on 6th inst *MS* 23 Oct 1844

PALMER Eliza Jane m SHACKFORD Joseph E both of Eaton NH on 8 Feb 1849 *MS* 7 Mar 1849 & *MFWBR* 24 Feb 1849

PALMER Elizabeth m EASTMAN Francis P on 2 June *MS* 3 Jul 1850

PALMER Emily P m WILSON William Jr on 30 Nov *MS* 2 Apr 1851

PALMER Exeaun m AVERY Oren both of Ellsworth NH on 23 Feb *MS* 26 Mar 1851

PALMER Hannah of Tuftonborough NH m FERNALD Samuel P of Ossipee NH *MS* 25 Apr 1838

PALMER Lucinda of Campton NH m GREEN Frederick E C of Plymouth NH on 6 Dec 1848 *MS* 20 Dec 1848

PALMER Maria J m WARREN Noah both of Milton on 1 Jan 1849 *MS* 31 Jan 1849

PALMER Martha H of South Berwick ME m ATKINSON Theodore Esq of Lawrence *MFWBR* 10 Nov 1849

PALMER Mary A m BURDICK Caleb L both of Brookfield on 8 Apr *MS* 1 May 1850

PALMER Mary A of Hampton m COFFIN Morrill M on 5 Jul at Hampton on 5 Jul *MS* 14 Jul 1847

PALMER Mary Ann m CRAM Josiah Capt at Raymond *MS* 8 Dec 1841

PALMER Nancy Mrs of Dover NH m ROLLINS Alba on 1st inst at Dover NH *MS* 8 Oct 1845

PALMER Roxanna of Sebec ME m GILMAN Ebenezer of Foxcroft ME *MS* 5 Aug 1831

PAMOT Harriet of Portland ME m GORDON George on 12 Sept at Cape Elizabeth *MS* 16 Oct 1844

PAPE Annah E m PLACE Allen S both of Gloucester on 21 Oct 1847 MS 1 Dec 1847

PARISH Julia A m SAWYER Elijah P both of Great Falls NH on 28 Nov MS 4 Dec 1850

PARISH Lucy of Smithfield m HILL Wm A of Cumberland on 7 Feb last MS 9 Mar 1836

PARISH Mary J of Lowell m BOSWELL William W of Newton NH on 27 Nov MS 15 Dec 1847

PARKER Caroline W of Waterville ME m LEWIS Alvan B on 20th ult of Waterville ME MS 14 Jul 1847

PARKER Catharine M m MARRYMAN Waitstell both of Brunswick ME on 28 Oct MS 2 Jan 1839

PARKER Eliza Ann m WORTHEN William both of Holderness NH MS 12 Feb 1840

PARKER Hannah m FRENCH Ebenezer D both of Garland ME on 5 June MS 3 Jul 1850

PARKER Harriet d/o PARKER John Esq of Saco ME on 17 Dec m McLAUGHLIN Robert Jr Town clerk of Scarboro' ME MFWBR 4 Jan 1851

PARKER Jennette of Portland ME m WOOD John P MFWBR 23 June 1849

PARKER Julia A d/o PARKER T Eld of Perinton m WOLSEY Richard of Perinton on 11 Sept MS 16 Oct 1850

PARKER Lucy M of Manchester m BAILEY Orlando H of Bedford on 30 Sept MS 13 Oct 1847

PARKER Martha A of Biddeford ME m YOUNG George G on 14 June MS 10 Jul 1850

PARKER Mary Ann m BURNHAM Mark both of Garland ME on 4 Apr MS 3 Jul 1850

PARKER Mary m THAYER Zeary both of Franconia NH on 29 Apr 1848 MS 24 May 1848

PARKER Mary Lucinda m STOKES Daniel H on Fast day eve at Dover NH MS 23 Apr 1845

PARKER Olive of N Berwick ME m ROBINSON Noah of Waterboro ME MS 18 June 1845

PARKER Sarah A of Greenfield m FIFIELD Henry L of Manchester on 2 Nov 1847 MS 10 Nov 1847

PARKER Sarah Maria m HUTCHINSON Orin on 13 May at Dracut MA MS 2 June 1847

PARKER Zeruiah of Barnston m GAHMON Joseph on 2 Apr MS 1 Jan 1840

PARKER Zeruiah of Barnston on April 2 m GALIMON Joseph MS 1 Jan 1840

PARKMAN Nathan T on 28 Mar at Corinna ME m COPP John B MS 1 May 1839

PARKMARD Mary A m ANDREWS Oliver E both of Great Falls on

PARKMARD (Continued)
    19 Sept *MS* 25 Sept 1850
PARKS Margaret F of Richmond ME m BRIRY [sic] James G on 8
    June at Richmond ME *MS* 9 Jul 1845
PARKS Martha M of Great Falls NH m SAMPSON George A on 19
    Nov of Newburyport MA *MS* 16 Dec 1846
PARMATER Mary Ann at Attica Wyoming Co NY m CHENEY John of
    New Berlin Wiskinsan (sic) on 13 Jul *MS* 6 Sept 1843
PARMER Mary E of Lowell m CHESLEY John T of Lynn in Lowell MA
    4 inst *MS* 14 Sept 1836
PARMERTER Mrs m BARKER William both of Oneida Eaton Co Mich
    on 10 Jan 1849 *MS* 11 Apr 1849
PARROT Rebecca J of Portland ME m DAY Sylvanus on 26 Jan at
    Cape Elizabeth ME *MS* 26 Feb 1845
PARSHLEY Druzilla W m WALDRON Daniel B *MS* 6 May 1835
PARSHLEY Emeline S m WALDRON Jonathan C both of Strafford on
    2 Apr *MS* 22 Apr 1846
PARSHLEY Hannah E of Strafford NH m REED James G of New-
    buryport MA on 20 Oct *MS* 6 Nov 1850
PARSHLEY Mary Ann of Strafford NH? m SMITH Jacob B of Bradford
    on 3 May 1849 *MS* 23 May 1849
PARSLEY Sarah M of Strafford m NOYES William H of Gloucester
    MA on 14 May 1848 *MS* 24 May 1848
PARSON Sarah m ROBERTSON Samuel N both of Monroe on 25 Nov
    1850 *MS* 5 Mar 1851
PARSONS Amanda M of Biddeford m HODSKIN Benjamin of Rock-
    ford MA *MFWBR* 21 Jul 1849
PARSONS Caroline F m SIAS Samuel both of Rochester on 27 Aug
    1848 *MS* 7 Feb 1849
PARSONS Eliza of Thorndike m WHITCOMB Stillman *MS* 21 Jan
    1846
PARSONS Elizabeth m THOMAS Josiah L a printer *MFWBR* 8 Dec
    1849
PARSONS Hannah F of Parsonsfield m PIPER Daniel on 16 inst *MS*
    26 Jul 1837
PARSONS Rebecca Mrs m LAND John Capt both of Boston on 16
    Dec 1847 *MS* 12 Jan 1848
PATCH Elizabeth J m PERRY Daniel both of Kittery ME on 13 Dec
    MS 9 Jan 1850
PATCH Elmira B m PERKINS Daniel on 19 Nov at Great Falls NH *MS*
    29 Nov 1843
PATCH Harriet m ALLARD David M both of Eaton 2 Jul *MS* 5 Aug
    1846
PATCH Huldab D m ROBERTSON Charles N on 14 Nov *MS* 26 Mar
    1851
PATCH Melessa D of Kittery ME m FLETCHER Lorenzo on 18 Dec at

PATCH (Continued)
Kittery ME *MS* 28 Dec 1842

PATCH Priscella m WALDRON John on at Kittery ME *MS* 14 Dec 1836

PATCH Sabrina D of Eaton m BROOKS Edward of Freedom *MFWBR* 16 Mar 1850

PATCH Wethy on 11th inst m SNOW Joseph Jr *MFWBR* 17 Mar 1849

PATCHEN Eliza m BABCOCK George on 4 Sept *MS* 9 Oct 1850

PATERSON Dorcas of Saco ME on 15th inst m JAMESON Mark of Somerswortth NH *MFWBR* 24 Feb 1849

PATRICK Hannah W at Buxton ME m TARBOX Joseph G on 2 Feb at Buxton ME *MS* 11 Feb 1846

PATTE Rosilla of Jackson ME m SMITH Watson of Munroe ME on 17 inst *MS* 4 Oct 1837

PATTEE Lucy of Jackson m PATTEE David on 30 May *MS* 18 Jul 1838

PATTEE Mary in Bristol both of Alexandria April 19 m KIRK Samuel P *MS* 4 May 1842

PATTEN Abigail of Deering m MARTIN Benjamin P of Weare on 15 Oct 1839 *MS* 12 Feb 1840

PATTEN Caroline m STINNEFORD Nicholas on 9 Nov of Saco ME *MS* 6 Apr 1847

PATTEN Jane of Alexandria m WOODMAN David B on 21 Nov *MS* 12 Dec 1838

PATTEN Mehitabel of Candia m LOVELL Herny R of Boston on 15 Nov 1849 *MS* 2 Jan 1850 & on Thanksgiving eve *MS* 5 Dec 1849

PATTERSON Martha A of Saco ME m SAWYER Joseph M of Bangor ME *MFWBR* 4 Sept 1847

PATTERSON S A m ABBOTT E W both of Hopkinton NH on 22 Dec 1847 *MS* 26 Jan 1848

PATTERSON Susannah m WOLF George both of Pikerun PA on 12 ult *MS* 19 Apr 1837

PAUL Eliza Ann m HILTON Andrew both of Acton ME *MS* 24 Sept 1834

PAUL Sally W of Great Falls NH m BUTLER Nathan of Berwick ME on 25 Feb *MS* 4 Apr 1838

PAULS Sarah of Meredith NH m CLARK Anthony on 17 Feb *MS* 24 Mar 1847

PAYNE Mary Ann m WILLIAMS Wm both of Lowell *MS* 27 Apr 1842

PEABODY Abigail Miss of Kennebuck ME m FRIEND Nathaniel of Alfred ME *MS* 8 June 1832

PEABODY Caroline B of Gorham ME on 20th inst m SMITH Orland of Lewiston ME *MFWBR* 30 Nov 1850

PEACOCK Mary Ann m HOPKINS Simeon on 30 Oct at Litchfield ME *MS* 4 Jan 1843

PEARL Hannah Liss [*sic*, Miss?] m BODGE Isaac both of Barrington on 12 ult *MS* 8 Apr 1835

PEARL Nancy m HORNE Samuel F both of Farmington NH on 25 Nov 1847 *MS* 2 Feb 1848

PEARSONS Abba C of Hallowell ME m HOVEY Lewis P on 26 June at Hallowell ME *MS* 24 Jul 1844

PEARY Mary d/o PEARY John Esq of New Durham on 29th ult m CHASE Thomas Jr of Alton *MS* 22 Feb 1843

PEASE Elizabeth m LUDWIG Ephraim both of Hope ME in Liberty ME *MS* 25 Dec 1839

PEASE Elizabeth N m PATTERSON James W both of Swansville ME on 23 Jul 1848 *MS* 30 Aug 1848

PEASE Lydia of Ellsworth m WESTGATE Elzi W of Cornish NH on 22 Nov *MS* 28 Nov 1849

PEASE Martha of Ellsworth NH m PERKINS Arthur D of Conway NH on 10 Feb at Ellsworth NH *MS* 24 Feb 1847

PEASE Martha of Parsonsfield m SMITH Abraham on 9th ult at Kempville NY *MS* 12 Oct 1832

PEASE Mary Jane at Parsonsfield ME on Jan 1 m DOE Amasa *MS* 22 Jan 1840

PEASE Nancy of Meredith m WARD Samuel of New Hampton on 6 June *MS* 30 Oct 1844

PEASE Sally m WARD Benjamin both of Meredith on 30 Jan *MS* 27 Feb 1834

PEASE Sarah of Wilton ME m STANLEY Moses C of NY on 24 June *MS* 18 Jul 1849

PEASE Sophia of Parsonsfield ME m ALLEN Amasa of Lee on 10 Nov at Parsonsfield ME *MS* 11 Dec 1844

PEASLEE Caroline E of Nashville m COLE Solomon Jr formerly of Whitefield on 5 Nov at Nashville *MS* 18 Nov 1846

PEASLEE Mary Maria m TYREL Moses Dustin of Bridgewater *MS* 16 Jan 1850

PEASLEY Hannah m BASSIT Samuel on at Epping NH *MS* 2 Jul 1834

PEASLEY Hannah m NOYES Amos L both of Manchester on 26 Jul *MS* 1 Aug 1849

PEASLEY Jerusha of Alexander m BABB Davis on 22 Dec at Alexander *MS* 18 Jan 1843

PEASLEY Julia Ann m GILMORE Nathan P both of Weare on 10 June 1847 *MS* 6 Oct 1847

PEASLEY Martha Ann of Alexandria m ELLIOT Henry G of Hebron on 28 Oct 1847 *MS* 15 Dec 1847

PEASLEY Martha Mrs m CUTTS John both of Wendell NH on 19 Oct 1848 *MS* 20 Dec 1848

PEASLEY Polly m COLLEY Hiram both of Weare on 14 Nov 1839 *MS* 12 Feb 1840

PEASLEY Ruth 2d m PEASLEY George W both of Weare NH on 26 Dec *MS* 2 Apr 1851

PEASLY Mary of Manchester m WILLIAMS Jesse F of Manchester NH at Wilmot on 27 Nov *MS* 17 Dec 1845

PEAVEY Hannah m FOSS Dennis Jr on 16 Dec *MS* 21 Jan 1846

PEAVEY Keziah A of Dover m YOUNG Orland of Madbury on 11 inst *MS* 14 Nov 1849

PEAVEY Mary E m WALDRON William W both of Strafford NH on 27 ult *MS* 20 Sept 1848

PEAVY Louisa of Barnston m BARNS D A on 30 Jan *MS* 15 Apr 1840

PEAVY Mary Jane (who was b 26 Feb 1798) d/o PEAVY Anthony Col m in 1816 BADGER Joseph Eld *RI* May 1820 p 77

PECK Emily Maria m PIERCE Stephen Wm both of Smithfield *MS* 19 Jul 1848

PECK Mary of Harrisburg NY m ROGERS Jeremy of Permela NY *MS* 7 Feb 1844

PEIRCE Alice A of Barrington m PEIRCE Daniel on 24 Dec at Rochester NH *MS* 13 Jan 1847

PELTON Harriet m BABCOCK William A both of Leonardsville NY on 9 Sept *MS* 30 Sept 1846

PENDERGAST Abby J of Lee m PLUMER Allen of Dover on Sunday morning 23 inst *MS* 2 Feb 1842

PENDERGAST Charlotte on 27th ult m TUTTLE William both of Durham *MS* 5 Jan 1842

PENDEXTER Betsey m KENNARD Noah both of Parsonsfield ME in Parsonsfield on Dec 29 1841 *MS* 19 Jan 1842

PENDEXTER Harriet L m WEEKS Edmund P on 6 Sept at Bridgeton ME *MS* 30 Dec 1846

PENDEXTER Lydia of Bartlet NH m SHACKFORD S B Maj of Conway NH on 18 inst *MS* 26 Jul 1848

PENDEXTER Mary Ann m BEAN Stephen D of Dover NH *MS* 7 June 1843

PENDEXTER Mary of Biddeford m QUIMBY J O of Biddeford ME *MFWBR* 25 Nov 1848

PENDEXTER Olive of Cornish m BRIAR Robert of Dutton on 2d inst *MS* 10 Feb 1832

PENDLETON Cordelia of Ilesboro ME m NICHOLS Nathaniel of Vinalhaven *MS* 18 Nov 1835

PENDLETON Hannah of Parsonsfield ME on 4 June m KNIGHT Joshua *MS* 18 Sep 1839

PENLEY Eleanor M on 11 Feb m RIDEOUT Benjamin A *MFWBR* 3 Mar 1849

PENLEY Sarah L of Danville ME m MITCHEL George A of Turner ME on 16 Nov at Lewiston Falls ME *MS* 9 Dec 1846

PENNELL Sarah J of Dover ME m GOODWIN G W Capt of Foxcroft ME *MFWBR* 3 Mar 1849

PENNER Delia Ann m HUMPHREY William both of Whitestown NY on New Years Eve *MS* 1 May 1850

PENNIMAN Charlotte of West Plymouth m MULLIKEN John F of Haverhill on 20 May at West Plymouth NH *MS* 16 June 1847

PENNIMAN Sarah m TRETREN John L both of Manchester on 7 June *MS* 24 June 1846

PENNINGTON Mary of Macon Mich m SMITH Herman C on 12 Dec 1845 *MS* 8 Apr 1846

PENREE Julia Ann of Stephentown m PARKER Alfred D on 6 Apr at Sand Lake *MS* 7 May 1845

PERKENS Caroline C of New Hampton m VITTUM George D merchant of Meredith on 1 Dec *MS* 1 Feb 1837

PERKINS Alice G of Strafford m BLAKE Josiah of Barnstead on 10 Sept 1848 *MS* 17 Jan 1849

PERKINS Ann Mrs m GREENLAW Nathaniel both of Brownfield ME on 25 Jan in Brownfield ME *MS* 9 Feb 1848

PERKINS Betsey m FOSS Oliver on 2 Feb at Strafford *MS* 12 Feb 1845

PERKINS Caroline m NUDD Stephen W both of Roxbury on 25 ult *MS* 15 May 1850

PERKINS Catherine of Great Falls m BROWN Daniel B of Steubenville Ohio *MS* 6 May 1835

PERKINS Cordelia M of Strafford m GRAY James M of Barrington on 27 Oct *MS* 8 Jan 1851

PERKINS Eliza A of Limerick ME m GOODWIN Seth B of East Machias ME on Wednesday last *MS* 29 Oct 1828

PERKINS Ellen m GOWEN John both of Dover on 23 inst *MS* 27 Oct 1847

PERKINS Elvira A of Chester VT m RICHARDSON Isaac G of Tunbridge VT on 5 Dec 1849 *MS* 2 Jan 1850

PERKINS Emeline A m CLOUGH Alexander *MS* 6 Dec 1848

PERKINS Emeline M d/o PERKINS T Eld m SHAPLEIGH Moses W of Lebanon ME *MS* 19 June 1850

PERKINS Florina S m WHEELER John on 11 Apr 1844 *MS* 1 May 1844

PERKINS Harriet of New Castle m SLOWMAN John of Woolwich ME on 27 Jul *MS* 20 Sept 1837

PERKINS Jane m FRISBEE Darius Jr *MS* 12 Aug 1831

PERKINS Jerusha of Conway NH m LEWIS Jefferson on 26 Jan 1842 at Conway NH *MS* 6 Apr 1842

PERKINS Lavina at Jackson m GRAY Solomon T of Dover *MS* 25 Jan 1843

PERKINS Mary D of Centre Harbor m BOYNTON Colburn B of New Hampton on 1 Nov 1843 *MS* 15 Nov 1843

PERKINS Mary Elizabeth d/o PERKINS Thomas Eld m HILL Thomas of Center Harbor on 25 Aug at New Hampton *MS* 8 Nov 1843

PERKINS Mary Jane m THOMPSON Enoch H at Gilford *MS* 4 Oct 1843

PERKINS Mary Jane m BROWN Orren both of Manchester on 12 inst *MS* 29 Apr 1846

PERKINS Mary Miss ae 65y 1 on 10d m GLINES Eli Col ae 75y 3d at Eaton NH *MS* 11 May 1842

PERKINS Mehitabel B of Hebron m BROWN Edward on 27 Nov at Holderness *MS* 13 Dec 1843

PERKINS Phebe of Wells ME m CURTIS Moses of Portsmouth NH on 27 Dec 1846 "Both deaf mutes Wrote the marriage ceremony and both signed it as they are well educated and are capable of getting a good living. He has a good trade and is a good workman." *MS* 20 Jan 1847

PERKINS Rebecca C of Loudon m NUDD Benjamin B Capt on 14 Nov at Canterbury NH *MS* 14 Feb 1844

PERKINS Sarah m DOE Altern C both of China ME on 1 Oct *MS* 14 Nov 1833

PERKINS Sarah P at Chichester on Apr 20 m LANGMAID Josiah Prentice *MS* 29 Apr 1840

PERKINS Susan of Meredith m GLIDDEN Hosea of Alton on 28 Apr *MS* 22 May 1844

PERKINS Susanna T Miss m TOWLE Enoch W on at Exeter NH *MS* 21 Dec 1832

PERRIGRO Abigail of Sandinia m SHERWOOD Thomas W of Franklinville on 20 Feb at Humphrey NY *MS* 4 Sept 1844

PERRY Ann H of Camden on 22d m LAMBERT Abel M *MFWBR* 10 Mar 1849

PERRY Anna m EDGCOMB Jeremiah *MFWBR* 29 May 1847

PERRY Catharine J of Concord m MADDEN L J Eld of Lansing Mich on 12 Jul *MS* 22 Aug 1849

PERRY Eliza A m COWELL George C both of Great Falls on 8 Jan *MS* 16 Jan 1850

PERRY Eliza of Boston MA m MUNN Seth on 12th inst at the FWB church in Charlestown MA *MS* 22 Oct 1845

PERRY Lynthia m WEBSTER Benjamin on Sunday last *MS* 20 June 1833

PERRY Sarah W of Limerick ME m FURLONG Harrison C of Cornishville ME on Wed last *MS* 31 Oct 1833

PERRY Susan m SMALL Jeremiah both of Biddeford ME on 6 Dec *MS* 18 Dec 1850

PERRY Susan of Biddeford ME on 6th inst m SMALL Jeremiah *MFWBR* 21 Dec 1850

PERSONS Mary m PRESCOT Mr both of Lexington ME on 17 Feb *MS* 15 Apr 1840

PETERS Mary m McCRILLIS Daniel on Sunday last *MS* 28 Nov 1833

PETERSON Patience B m KINNEY N S Mr on 23d ult both of Dixfield

PETERSON (Continued)
MS 20 Apr 1831

PETRIE Almira m EASTMAN Benjamin on 13 Nov *MS* 25 Dec 1850

PETTEGROW Lucinda of Clinton ME m MANSON Charles H of Wilton ME *MS* 23 Jan 1839

PETTIGREW Eliza A m MANSON Richard E both of Clinton on 10 Nov *MS* 25 Dec 1850

PETTY Lucy m TWOMBLY Wm both of No Yarmouth ME on 16th inst *MS* 25 Mar 1835

PETTY Susan m FOSTER Solomon S both of Alexandria on 9 Aug *MS* 28 Feb 1844

PEVERLY Hannah of Canterbury NH m YOUNG Solomon of Canterbury NH *MS* 14 Feb 1844

PHILBRICK Abigail of Epsom m SARGENT E B of Pittsfield on 9 ult *MS* 21 Nov 1849

PHILBRICK Catharine m BROWN Reuben Jr both of Freedom on 10 Sept *MS* 26 Nov 1838

PHILBRICK Clarisa P of Tewskbury m ROBINSON David of Lowell MA on 3 Jul *MS* 2 Nov 1842

PHILBRICK Diantha m STEVENSON W S Mr on 6 June at Lowell MA *MS* 7 Jul 1847

PHILBRICK Elizabeth H m COFFIN James M on 11 Mar in Thorndike ME *MS* 8 May 1850

PHILBRICK Huldah of Freedom NH m COLBY Andrew P (printer) of Dover on 3 Jul at Freedom *MS* 10 Jul 1844

PHILBRICK Lucinda H m BROWN True W on 1st inst *MS* 12 Nov 1835

PHILBRICK Lucinda Josena of Andover NH m ROBBINS Samuel Eld formerly of ME *MS* 10 Jul 1829

PHILBRICK Mary Ann of Ossippee NH m TUCK Jonathan of Parsonsfield ME *MS* 6 Dec 1827

PHILBRICK Mary E of Hampton m DOW George O on 2d inst at Hampton of North Hampton *MS* 26 May 1847

PHILBRICK Nancy P of Hampton m LOCK David on 28 March at Hampton *MS* 21 Apr 1847

PHILBRICK Polly of Effingham NH m WINGATE James formerly of Williston VT *MS* 16 Jul 1828

PHILBRICK Ruth M of Epsom m MASON Levi S of Pittsfield on 1st inst *MS* 28 June 1837

PHILBRICK Thankful T of Bath m BUCKMAN Charles W of Lyndon VT on 22 May *MS* 21 June 1843

PHILBROOK Elizabeth M of Manchester m TASKER Eben of Ossipee NH *MFWBR* 17 Jul 1847

PHILBROOK Harriet R on 10 Feb at Sanbornton ṁ BROWN Bradbury T *MS* 11 Mar 1846

PHILBROOK Mary P of Sanbornton m CONNER William H on 10 Dec

PHILBROOK (Continued)
at New Hampton *MS* 29 Jan 1845

PHILBROOK Mary Y of Sanbornton NH m DEARBORN Joseph P on 29 Mar 1842 at Sanbornton NH *MS* 11 May 1842

PHILLIPS Abigail D m COX John both of Lowell on 10th *MS* 20 June 1838

PHILLIPS Angeline m WADE Arnold H both of Stephentown NY on 6 Aug *MS* 29 Aug 1849

PHILLIPS Ann E m TAGGARD Cyrus H both of Boston on 6 inst *MS* 19 Sept 1849

PHILLIPS Diana of East Nassau m CISSEY Robert H of Nassau on 16 Feb *MS* 13 Mar 1850

PHILLIPS Eliza A m GOULD John B on 5 Aug at Bangor ME *MS* 30 June 1847

PHILLIPS Eliza m FELLOWS Willard E on 30 June at Freedom NY *MS* 15 Mar 1843

PHILLIPS Elizabeth sister of Rev J PHILLIPS m GARDNER James A.B. of Whitestown Sem on 20 Feb *MS* 6 Mar 1850

PHILLIPS Lydia m FRISBEE Joseph *MS* 26 Nov 1834

PHILLIPS Martha Mrs of Bethlehem m BURNHAM Simeon of Littleton *MS* 24 Jan 1849

PHILLIPS Mary of Gilmanton m SHEPARD Morrill Esq on 5 Oct at Pittsfield *MS* 12 Oct 1842

PHILLIPS Nancy of Kittery ME m CARTER Loudon of Virginia on 10th inst *MS* 27 Jan 1930

PHILLIPS Salome of Kittery m TOBEY Hiram of Kittery ME *MS* 3 feb 1832

PHILPOT Almira O of Limerick ME m PERRY Allen of Cabot VT on 19 Nov 1846 at Limerick ME *MS* 23 Dec 1846

PHILPOT Deborha H of NY m GRAY George of Wilmot NH on 31 ult *MS* 20 Nov 1850

PHILPOT Lucinda m SAWTELLE Hannibal M *MFWBR* 8 Jul 1848

PHINNEY Aurelia F m HOBSON William F on 19 June at Gorham ME *MS* 23 Jul 1845

PHINNEY Martha H d/o PHINNEY John all of Gorham ME m CARSLEY Freeman on 31s ult *MS* 17 Sept 1834

PICKER Elizabeth of Dover NH m WILLEY Thomas J on 14 inst *MS* 28 Sept 1836

PICKERING Abigail J m LEAVITT David H on 28 Sept at Manchester *MS* 10 Oct 1844

PICKERING Charlotte m SHUMWAY James both of Dover on 5 inst *MS* 15 Jul 1835

PICKERING Hannah m LEWIS William both of Meredith *MS* 29 Aug 1838

PICKERING Martha Ann of Manchester m PERNO Nicholas B of Concord on 3d Jul at Manchester NH *MS* 28 Jul 1847

PICKERING Mary Jane m PIPER George W both of Meredith on 27
Oct 1849 *MS* 30 Jan 1850

PICKERING Mary of Meredith NH m BEAN Laomi *MS* 11 Sept 1839

PICKERING Olive Jane m MUDGETT Joseph E on 23 Nov 1843 *MS*
14 Feb 1844

PIERCE Clementina Sister of Portsmouth m NOYES Eli Brother of
Jefferson ME on 3 inst *MS* 17 June 1835

PIERCE Fanny of South Berwick m PATTERSON Stephen of Saco
ME *MS* 5 Feb 1845

PIERCE Julia A m SWEET Samuel W both of Huntington VT on 18
Feb 1848 *MS* 5 Apr 1848

PIERCE Louiza m FOSS Ichabod *MS* 6 Jul 1832

PIERCE Lucinda of Boston MA m MORRISON Jonathan M on 1 Sept
MS 14 Sept 1842

PIERCE Lydia H of So Berwick m GRANT Geo of Berwick ME on 4
Jul *MS* 22 Jul 1846

PIERCE Margaret S m MUDGET Luther both of Prospect ME *MS* 19
Jan 1842

PIERCE Mary E at Manchester m DAVIS Cyrus on 11 Dec *MS* 20 Dec
1843

PIERCE Mary Jane d/o PIERCE Nicholas of Limerick ME m LEE
John of Dedham MA *MFWBR* 21 Sep 1850

PIERCE Mehitabel m WIGGIN Samuel D of Sandwich NH *MS* 14 Sept
1842

PIERCE Rosina m CONDORE Joseph B both of Brunswick ME on 27
Aug 1848 *MS* 20 Sept 1848

PIERCE Susan H m GILPATRICK Jacob both of Limerick ME on 4
Apr 1850 *MS* 10 Apr 1850

PIERSON Jane Ann d/o PIERSON James Esq of Johnstown NY m
HACKETT Luther A Esq on 6th inst at Johnstown NY *MS* 21 Feb
1844

PIKE Ann E W of Saco on 16th ult m KNIGHT Isaac Capt *MFWBR* 1
Feb 1851

PIKE Dolly M d/o PIKE Bennet Esq of Cornish ME m STEEL James
Hon of Brownfield on 25th ult *MS* 1 Dec 1830

PIKE E S of Gorham ME m LARRABEE James Jr *MFWBR* 3 Mar
1849

PIKE Eliza m PAGE Daniel M both of Great Falls NH on 20 ult *MS* 6
Sept 1837

PIKE Eliza G of Lowell MA m BEAN George of Deerfield *MS* 16 Sept
1835

PIKE Hannah E of Hollis m JORDAN Richworth Jr Capt of Biddeford
ME on 17 Feb 1848 *MS* 8 Mar 1848

PIKE Hannah of Wolfborough NH m BENNETT Albert of Alton NH on
29 Feb 1849 *MS* 18 Apr 1849

PIKE Lucinda of Livemore ME m GODING Amos of Jay ME on 12 Feb

PIKE (Continued)
MS 6 Jul 1832

PIKE Lydia H d/o PIKE J Eld m WENTWORTH Robert B State printer of Madison WI on 9 inst *MS* 20 Nov 1850 & *MFWBR* 26 Oct 1850

PIKE Naomi of Livermore ME m PARSONS Jeremiah Jr of Farmington ME *MS* 13 Dec 1837

PIKE Rachel m COOK John D of Biddeford ME *MFWBR* 11 May 1850

PIKE Rhoda of Jay ME m CHASE Ebenezer C on 6 Apr at Chesterville ME *MS* 6 Aug 1845

PILLSBURY Hannah of Candia m SMITH Robie on 26 Dec at Candia *MS* 8 Jan 1845

PILLSBURY Sarah m JONES Jonathan both of Pittsfield on 9 May *MS* 13 June 1838

PINDAR Lydia C m NUTE Hopley Y on 7th inst at Dover NH *MS* 15 Oct 1845

PINDER Maria m TIBBETS Samuel both of Ossipee NH on 17 Nov *MS* 21 Dec 1836

PINDER Nancy m HOBBS Joseph Jr both of Ossipee NH on 19 ult *MS* 10 Oct 1838

PINDLEY Mary F of So Berwick m WARREN C F M of Berwick ME on 15 Sept *MS* 26 Sept 1849

PINGREY Emily B m SMITH Horatio G both of Auburn on 15 Nov 1849 *MS* 2 Jan 1850

PINKHAM Abigail m EDGERLY Samuel on 14 Mar at New Market *MS* 6 Apr 1847

PINKHAM Elizabeth of Dover NH m FRENCH Jonathan on 30 Apr at Dover NH *MS* 7 May 1845

PINKHAM Jamson m BUZZELL William Eld of Middleton *MS* 18 Dec 1839

PINKHAM Laurana W m SWASEY Rufus L on 12 Sept at Lowell MA *MS* 19 Oct 1842

PINKHAM Lucinda Mrs of Dover m HALEY Abel Hon of Tuftonborough NH on 27 Oct *MS* 6 Nov 1850

PINKHAM Mary E d/o PINKHAM John Eld m JENNESS Amos on Sabbath morning 7 inst *MS* 17 Jul 1850

PINKHAM Mary E m SIAS John B both of Rochester NH on 16 Apr *MS* 8 May 1844 & at Somersworth Great Falls NH *MS* 18 Dec 1844

PINKHAM Mary E of Somersworth NH m EVANS Jacob W on 18th at Dover NH *MS* 24 Mar 1847

PINKHAM Mary Jane of New Market m MEADER Stephen on 24 Aug at New Market *MS* 30 Aug 1843

PINKHAM Sally m CAVERLY Asam both of New Market 1st inst *MS* 11 Mar 1835

PINKHAM Sarah G of Berwick m CLARKE Charles on of So Berwick on 1 inst 1849 *MS* 18 Apr 1849

586

PINKHAM Susan E m VARRELL John P on 26 ult *MS* 15 Aug 1838

PINKHAM Zelinda W m HODGES Charles both of Hallowell ME *MS* 18 Apr 1838

PIPER Catharine R of Parsonsfield ME m MARSTON Abram F of Effingham NH on 3 Oct *MS* 3 Nov 1847

PIPER Edith A m GRIFFIN Eliphalet *MFWBR* 16 Mar 1850 & both of Dover on 25 ult *MS* 6 Mar 1850

PIPER Elizabeth H of Great Falls NH m APPLEBY Joseph A of Brunswick ME *MFWBR* 25 Jan 1851

PIPER Jane S m PIPER Robert R both of Holderness in Holderness Dec 23 1841 *MS* 19 Jan 1842

PIPER Livonia D of Alton NH m HYDE Daniel A on 11 Jan *MS* 3 Mar 1847

PIPER Mary Ann of Manchester m BROWN Nathaniel of Candia on 9 Dec 1848 *MS* 27 Dec 1848

PIPER Sarah Ann Mrs m WATSON Joseph Jr on 2 Oct at Gilmanton NH *MS* 28 Jan 1846

PITMAN Angeline of Dover m NUTTER Abner J at Dover NH *MS* 7 May 1845

PITMAN Elizabeth Ann m SWAIN George W both of Meredith *MS* 13 May 1840

PITMAN Hannah m SWIAN Hezekiah M on 28 Oct *MS* 17 Nov 1847

PITMAN Mary A of Great Falls m BRACKETT John of Milton on 22 Oct *MS* 4 Nov 1835

PITMAN Mary J m WEBSTER Samuel S on 21 Nov 1833 both of Meredith *MS* 27 Feb 1834

PITTS Eliza Miss m STACKPOLE Theodore both of Waterboro ME on 18th ult *MS* 5 May 1830

PIXLEY Lucy A m GEORGE James P both of Strafford on 4 Jul *MS* 21 Nov 1849

PIXLEY Rosetta of Freedom NY m PIXLEY Oscar on 28 Feb of Bethany NY at Freedom *MS* 15 Mar 1843

PIXLEY Sarah J m FLOOD Jackson S on 6th inst at Lowell MA *MS* 24 Feb 1847

PLACE Betsey of Somersworth m TIBBETS George F of Lawrence MA *MS* 1 Dec 1847

PLACE Mary E m CLOUGH Charles *MS* 13 Dec 1843 [see Groom's Index, "Marriage was a hoax."]

PLACE Mary E d/o PLACE E Eld of Strafford m CLOUGH Charles of Barnstead on 22 Nov *MS* 6 Dec 1843

PLACE Mary E of Great Falls NH m CREW Alonzo E of Farmington on 7 Dec *MS* 18 Dec 1850

PLACE Susan Demeritt d/o PLACE E Eld m CAVERLY Thomas C on 7th inst at Strafford *MS* 24 May 1843

PLAISTED Ann Miss of Standish ME m CONNELL Wm of Gorham ME *MS* 23 Nov 1832

PLAISTED Charlotte d/o PLAISTED William of Centre Harbor m PIPER James of Holderness on 21 ult *MS* 7 Feb 1838

PLAISTED Mary Jane m DAVIS Adams on 17 Jan *MS* 10 Feb 1847

PLAISTED Olive M of Lowell MA m WATSON Freeman on 3rd inst at Saccarappa ME *MS* 4 Oct 1843

PLAISTED Susan M m WEEKS Joseph at Newhampton *MS* 17 Aug 1836

PLASTED Adeline of Boston MA m MORSE S Ambrose of Holderness on 16 Dec 1849 *MS* 16 Jan 1850

PLUMER Caroline A m HAMMONDS Hiram W both of Natick MA on 2 Jul 1848 in Milton *MS* 16 Aug 1848

PLUMER Nancy at Gilmanton Jan 20 1840 m NORRIS Joseph *MS* 19 Feb 1840

PLUMER Sarah E of Dover m FOWLER Daniel W on 25 May at Meredith NH *MS* 18 June 1845

PLUMER Sarah Jane m JENNESS Gilman both of Alton NH on Thanksgiving eve *MS* 28 Nov 1849

PLUMMER Abigail of Portland ME m BOOTHBY Arthur 2d of Limington ME on 11th inst at Portland ME *MS* 20 Mar 1844

PLUMMER Augusta L m HILL Daniel T both of Great Falls on Sabbath last *MS* 22 Jan 1851 & *MFWBR* 25 Jan 1851

PLUMMER Elizabeth of Gorham m HARMON Benjamin F of Thorndike *MFWBR* 24 Aug 1850

PLUMMER Harriet B of Dover m LITTLEFIELD Daniel on 25th ult *MS* 1 Oct 1845

PLUMMER Louisa H m GOODWIN Thomas R on 8 Aug at Charlestown MA *MS* 22 Oct 1845

PLUMMER Martha of Richmond m THING Joseph of Woolwich ME *MS* 2 Aug 1837

PLUMMER Mary Jane of Thornton m BATCHELDER Eder D of Bridgewater on 28 Jan *MS* 26 Mar 1851

PLUMMER Mehitabel of Wolfboro m BICKFORD Thomas C of Wolfboro NH *MS* 4 Sept 1844

PLUMMER Sally Mrs of Brownfield ME m CLEMONS Bartlett of Freedom NH on 8 Oct 1848 *MS* 15 Nov 1848

PLUMMER Susan m MERRILL Enoch of Andover *MS* 18 Dec 1839

PLUMMER Susan at Danville m MERRILL Enoch of Andover *MS* 18 Dec 1839

PLYMPTON Mary E eldest d/o PLYMPTON Sylvanus MD m YOUNG Joshua Rev of New North Church Boston *MFWBR* 3 Mar 1849

POLLARD Elizabeth W of Somersworth NH m HAYS Charles C of Farmington NH on 24th ult at Dover NH *MS* 2 Dec 1846

POLLEY Abigail at Topsham ME m WHITTEN George on 30 May at Topsham ME *MS* 31 Aug 1842

POLLEY Hannah of Webster ME m WILLIAMS Minot of Webster ME *MFWBR* 25 Nov 1848

POMROY Rachel of Hamburgh NY m PIERCE Marshal of Colden on Christmas day *MS* 19 Feb 1845

POOL Ann m GREENLEAF Hiram on 29 Dec at Holderness *MS* 8 Feb 1837

POOL Betsey B of Chelmsford m PIKE James Jr *MS* 22 May 1839

POOL Sarah A formerly of Brunswick m BUTMAN John T *MFWBR* 24 Mar 1849

POOL Sarah of Stanstead on 2 Jan 1839 m RICKARE Abner *MS* 17 Apr 1839

POOR Dorathy Mrs ae 48y m CHASE Caleb ae 74y both of Chester*MS* 1 Apr 1840

POOR Mary A m McMASTER Samuel both of Strafford VT on 23 Nov 1848 *MS* 6 June 1849

POPE Emily of Gardiner ME m SPEAR William *MS* 14 Dec 1836

POPE R S m MORGAN H U M both of Salem 29 Jan *MS* 5 Mar 1851

PORTER Elizabeth Miss in Canaan NH m SARGEANT Hiram of Raymond *MS* 7 Sept 1832

PORTER Lorana of Dixmont ME m MOORE Robert Jr of China ME *MS* 19 Mar 1845

PORTER Lucy Y m EMERY James F both of Dixmont ME on 3 Oct 1847 *MS* 17 Nov 1847

PORTER Mary m BARROWS Putnam *MFWBR* 29 June 1850

PORTER Paulina T formerly of Medford MA m VAN RENSSELAER Stevens Esq of Poland on 29 May at Boston *MS* 29 June 1836

PORTER Sarah m BURNE Edmond A on 24th Mar at Charlestown MA *MS* 4 Aug 1847

PORTER Sarah of Hamilton m TINKHAM Harvy of Sherburne on 14 Nov 1849 *MS* 28 Nov 1849

PORTER Thirza C of Strong ME on 30 Mar m CROSBY Lemuel of Phillips ME *MS* 19 Apr 1843

POST Emma A of LaGrange m ALDRICH O E Eld of Spencer on 28 Mar *MS* 24 Apr 1850

POTER Lydia of Thorndike m BACHELDER Daniel Jr *MFWBR* 13 Jan 1849

POTTER Abigail of Clinton m LIVINGSTON R C of Gardiner *MS* 15 Jan 1840

POTTER Adah W of Lowell m WOODS Charles H of Southborough on 30 Apr *MS* 30 May 1849

POTTER Almira J of Lowell m HUNTINGTON George W of Atkinson ME *MS* 6 Dec 1848

POTTER Arabine of Litchfield m McFADDEN David of Gardiner ME on 27 Jan *MS* 20 Feb 1850

POTTER Eliza A of Scituate m CALVIN Allen of Coventry RI on 9 Nov 1848 *MS* 17 Jan 1849

POTTER Hannah B of Gilford m NICHOLS Alfred of Reading MA on 1 Jan *MS* 12 Feb 1851

POTTER Harriet R of No Providence RI m TOBEY James H of Coventry on 15 inst *MS* 28 Mar 1838

POTTER Lucy of Corinna on 11 Dec 1838 m MORGAN Levi of Dexter *MS* 17 Apr 1839

POTTER Mary Ann m GALE Henry on 2 May at Bangor ME *MS* 30 June 1847

POTTER Mary G m SMITH David Y of Meredith on 28th ult *MS* 4 June 1834

POTTER Nancy of Dexter m TOOTHHAKER Joel of Dexter ME *MS* 11 Dec 1839

POTTER Rhoda m REED William both of Scituate on 24 Oct *MS* 30 Jul 1850

POTTER Rhoda M of Gilford m SMITH David Y of Meredith NH on 9 Nov at Gilford *MS* 28 Dec 1842

POTTER Saviah of Corinna ME m THOMSON Prince of Strong ME on 7 inst *MS* 29 Mar 1837

POTTLE Elizabeth C of Richmond m PREBLE Stephen of Bowdoinham ME on 27 Dec 1837 *MS* 7 Mar 1838

POTTLE Martha Ann of Richmond ME m CALL Warren of Bradford ME on 10 Sept 1848 *MS* 11 Oct 1848

POWELL Jane A m BAKER Oscar E Eld both of Marion on 13 Oct *MS* 27 Nov 1850

POWERS Abigail P d/o POWERS Peter Esq of Corinth VT m TRUE Jacob of St Louis MO on 10 Aug 1842 at Corinth VT *MS* 31 Aug 1842

POWERS Bainey m WISE Asel on 6th ult *MS* 13 June 1833

POWERS Jane m REED Elijah both of Dresden ME on 11 inst *MS* 2 Nov 1836

POWERS Livona G of New Durham m BARKER John W merchant of Alton NH *MS* 8 Mar 1837

POWERS Maria Jane d/o POWERS John Esq m GILMORE Tristram *MFWBR* 4 Aug 1849

POWERS Mary Jane of New Market m BATCHELDER Nathaniel Esq of No Hampton on 20 June *MS* 3 Jul 1850

PRATT Caroline m FLANDERS Moses on 12 Nov 1843 *MS* 17 Apr 1844

PRATT Cynthia of Cavendish VT m PARKER Amos A on 4 inst *MS* 21 June 1837

PRATT Olive on 16th March at Plymouth VT m HIBARD Joseph of Randolph *MS* 17 Apr 1844

PRATT Susan d/o PRATT Levi H m RUSSELL True of Roxbury MA *MFWBR* 3 Feb 1849

PRAY Ann B of Shapleigh m CHICK Simon F Capt of Lebanon ME in that place *MS* 5 Jul 1837

PRAY Ann m DIXON John both of Jay on 25 Jan *MS* 14 Feb 1838

PRAY Betsey m STANTON Dudley on 22 Sept *MS* 18 Dec 1844

PRAY Caroline m PERRY Luther C Eld of Kittery *MS* 9 May 1833

PRAY Eunice R m MARTIN Bartlett T at Roxbury MA *MS* 7 Sept 1845

PRAY Lucinda m GILMAN Alvah A both of Great Falls NH on 19 Dec 1850 *MS* 22 Jan 1851

PRAY Lucinda of Great Falls m GILMAN Alvah A *MFWBR* 8 Feb 1851

PRAY Mary F of Ossipee NH m BEAN Benjamin Jr of Tuftonboro on 15 Nov *MS* 21 Dec 1836

PRAY Sophia of Dover m NUTTER Valentine of Ossipee NH on 2 inst *MS* 12 Apr 1837

PREBBLE Elizabeth m ANDREWS Winthrop on 12 Nov at Boothbay ME *MS* 22 Jan 1845

PREBLE Catharine m HOVEY Lewis P both of Hallowell ME on 7 Sept *MS* 4 Oct 1837

PRENTICE Mary T of Northbridge m FULLER Freeman of Worcester on 15 Feb *MS* 17 Apr 1844

PRENTISS Mary V m BRADFORD Charles G both of St Albans ME on 15 Oct 1850 *MS* 22 Jan 1851

PRESCOTT Emeline m CHAPMAN Horace on 1 Feb at Manchester NH *MS* 19 Feb 1845

PRESCOTT Frances m FOGG Timothy E both of Raymond *MS* 5 Aug 1835

PRESCOTT Hannah B of Gilford m CARR Chellis D Capt of Loudon on 25 Apr *MS* 22 May 1844

PRESCOTT Laura of Meredith NH on 18th inst at Lowell MA m HUNTRESS William C of Centre Harbor NH *MS* 29 May 1839

PRESCOTT Martha A of Candia m TUCKER Moses D of Roxbury MA on Thanksgiving Evening *MS* 29 Nov 1848

PRESCOTT Martha S of Meredith m BATCHELDER N G of Manchester on 23 Jan *MS* 13 Feb 1850

PRESCOTT Mary m PECKER David on at Raymond *MS* 5 Aug 1835

PRESCOTT Mary J of Deerfield m HILL Benjamin D of Northwood on 24 Oct *MS* 27 Nov 1850

PRESCOTT Mary Jane m WELCH Samuel both of Dixmont ME *MS* 25 Dec 1839

PRESCOTT Nancy of Dixmont ME m THOMPSON Pelatiah of Searsmont ME on 16 Jan at Dixmont ME *MS* 20 Apr 1842

PRESCOTT Sally S on 23 Jul at Holderness NH m SANBORN Samuel of Meredith NH *MS* 6 Sept 1843

PRESSEY Nancy J m GARNHAM G W both of Waterville *MS* 2 Jan 1850

PRESSEY Sophronia E m BABB Moses M both of Manchester 3 Jan 1848 *MS* 19 Jan 1848

PRESSON Ann of New Market m WIGGIN Waingate on 31st ult at New Market *MS* 10 Aug 1842

PRESTON Chloe A m PARKHURST Phineas of Sharon on 21 Apr at Strafford VT *MS* 24 Jul 1844

PRESTON Lamira S of Caroline m MIDDAUGH George W of Ithaca NY on 11 ult *MS* 2 Oct 1850

PRICE Elsa Mrs m CROWLY Wm both of Yorkshire NY on 24 May *MS* 15 Aug 1849

PRIDE Cynthia B m LUNT William J on 15 June at Westbrook ME *MS* 30 June 1847

PRIEST Dorothy m MATHES Abraham both of Lowell MA on Thanksgiving Day *MS* 16 Dec 1835

PRIEST Hannah m ARCHY Moazing on 8th ult *MS* 6 June 1833

PRIEST Jane m EVANS Joseph on 27 Aug 1843 both of Lowell MA *MS* 6 Sept 1843

PRIEST Lucy D m HOIT Amos both of Weare on 5 Dec 1839 *MS* 12 Feb 1840

PRIEST Mary C of Nottingham m BARTLETT Joseph O D Eld of Wilmot on 10 Oct at Deerfield *MS* 17 Dec 1845

PRIEST Sally W m COOLEY Ward C both of Lisbon on 23 Feb at Lisbon (Sugar Hill) *MS* 15 Mar 1837

PRIEST Susan A m THOMPSON James both of Nottingham on 12 May *MS* 20 May 1846

PRIME Eliza of Sanford ME m KIMBALL John of Dover NH? *MS* 17 Sept 1834

PRINCE Betsey of Minot ME m HANSCOM Charles on 13 Jan at Portland ME *MS* 29 Jan 1845

PRINCE Hannah L m COPP Jeremiah L on 5 Nov of Detroit ME *MS* 27 Dec 1843

PRINCE Honor D E A A m GALUSHA Solon L of Detroit ME on 30 Mar *MS* 7 June 1843

PRINCE Lydia J m GOULD Stephen *MS* 23 Jan 1834

PROCTOR Frances E m HOLT Samuel W of Portland ME *MFWBR* 6 Jul 1850

PROCTOR Louisa of Lowell MA m CHAMBERLAIN Alvah of Eaton NH on 23 Feb 1848 *MS* 8 Mar 1848

PROPHET Mariah m JOHNSON James on 25 inst *MS* 5 Jul 1837

PROUTY Eliza of Stanstead EC m HOPKINS C Capt on Feb 14? *MS* 13 Sept 1843

PROUTY Ester Ann m DURGIN Erastus both of Lowell *MS* 10 May 1837

PROUTY Sophia m ARMSTRONG Sylvester on 6 Oct at Middlebury NY *MS* 30 Dec 1846 & *MS* 27 Jan 1847

PUGH Maria m HEAPS Henry on 17 Dec at Dover *MS* 25 Dec 1844

PUGSLEY Lucinda F m JOHNSON Dennis both of Limington ME on 29 Mar *MS* 8 Apr 1846

PUGSLY Mary A m BRADEEN John P both of Cornish ME on 8 Dec 1850 *MS* 26 Feb 1851

PULISIFER Julia A m MOULTON Grange T at town of Union in Broome County NY *MS* 15 Jan 1845

PULLEN Caroline of West Waterville ME m EASTWOOD Palmer R *MS* 20 Apr 1842

PULLEN Chloe A B m SNOW David S both of Lowell on 10 Sept *MS* 14 Oct 1846

PULLEN Julia A of Kingfield ME m WETHEREN Amos F of New Portland ME on 30 Mar 1848 *MS* 24 May 1848 & *MFWBR* 29 Apr 1848

PULLEN Sophronia m LOW Ivory C both of Waterville *MS* 15 Jan 1840

PUMROY Sally m DIX George Capt on at Mt Desert ME *MS* 9 Dec 1831

PURINGTON Harriet Ann of Embden m GEORGE Samuel B of Richmond ME on 31 Jan 1848 *MS* 19 Apr 1848

PURINTON Eleanor of Bowdoin ME m RING Hiram of Richmond on 5 Mar 1850 *MS* 3 Apr 1850

PURINTON Hyrena of Poplin m CHURCHILL Charles of New Market on 6 Jul *MS* 2 Aug 1837

PURINTON Thankful S of Bowdoin ME m SNOW Stephen of Brunswick ME *MS* 12 Jan 1842

PURKIS Eliza A of Gray ME m LIBBY C E Dr on 18 May 1843 at West Poland ME *MS* 8 Nov 1843

PURKIS Mary Ann of Gray m WATSON Nathaniel of Scarboro ME on 15th *MS* 22 June 1836

PURMORT Polly M of Enfield m HORTON Simon of Grafton on 14 Apr *MS* 1 May 1844

PURVES Mary S of Lowell MA m KIDDER Franklin of Tewksbury MA on 8 June 1843 *MS* 6 Sept 1843

PUSHAW Lucy m McCLURE Andrew at Bangor ME *MS* 13 Sept 1843

PUTNAM Mary Ann of Hallowell m BECK Joseph S Capt of Augusta on 12 Sept *MS* 4 Oct 1837

PUTNAM Polly Mrs m HICKOES Obadiah on 2 Sept *MS* 26 Sept 1849

PUTNEY Almira M m HARVEY Jacob S both of Sutton on Nov 9 1841 *MS* 12 Jan 1842

PUTNEY Hannah of Hatley m BROWN Samuel of Compton on 28 Aug *MS* 20 Sept 1837

QUACKENBUSH Maria of Oneonta Otsego Co NY on 20th ult m GATES Lyman *MS* 27 Nov 1839

QUARLES Abigail A m BEACHMAN Asa Esq on 23 Mar *MS* 14 May 1845

QUARLES Belinda Miss of Ossipee NH ae 15y m DEARBORN Josiah Esq of Effingham ae 40y on 14th inst *MS* 31 May 1827

QUIMBY Abby T m MOULTON Gilman both of Sandwich on 4 Jul *MS* 18 Jul 1849

QUIMBY Harriet m CROCKETT James M both of Dover on 25 inst *MS* 28 Mar 1849

QUIMBY Mary m FARNHAM William *RI* Apr 1822 p 63

QUIMBY Mehitabel of Lisbon m BURLEY Cyrus of Bethlehem VT on 5 Oct 1847 *MS* 10 Nov 1847

QUIMBY Naoma m WHITCOMB Oren at Fairfield ME *MS* 20 Apr 1842

QUIMBY Philinda m BROWN John C *MS* 27 Feb 1839

QUIMBY Sarah of Franconia m WELLS James S on 15 Sept at Franconia NH *MS* 28 Dec 1842

QUIMBY Sarah of Sandwich NH m QUIMBY Alpheus of Lyndon VT *MS* 26 Jul 1843

QUIMBY Sophia M of Meredith Bridge NH on 8 Jan m NOBLE Albert H of St Albans ME *MS* 17 Jan 1844

QUINBY Caroline E m HOIT Benjamin B of Sandwich NH *MS* 18 June 1845

QUINBY Dolly m HACKET John on 18 Apr at Sandwich NH *MS* 5 June 1844

QUINBY Elizabeth C of Dover on 16 Nov m GRAVES Charles of Dover *MS* 27 Nov 1839

QUINBY Elvira B m SANBORN Alonzo F both of Sandwich NH on 31 Aug 1848 *MS* 20 Sept 1848

QUINBY Jane m ROBINSON Elbridge *MS* 7 Feb 1838

QUINBY Julia M m PRESCOTT George M both of Lyndon VT on 5 Mar *MS* 2 Apr 1851

QUINBY Louisa m SANBORN Lewis both of Sandwich NH on 7 Mar *MS* 1 Apr 1846

QUINBY Lydia m HORN Amasa on 3 Mar at Sandwich NH *MS* 19 June 1844

QUINBY Martha m HOWLAND Richardson both of Lisbon ME on 10 June 1847 *MS* 29 Dec 1847

QUINBY Mary M Mrs of Dover m BACHELDER Nathaniel of Northampton on Tues last week *MS* 1 May 1834

QUINBY Melinda of Great Falls NH m DORE Ezekiel *MS* 18 Mar 1840

QUINBY Sarah H m CHELLIS Joseph H in Danville *MS* 2 Feb 1842

QUINT Clarissa B m CHURCHILL Ichabod D both of Eaton on 30 Dec 1847 *MS* 19 Jan 1848

QUINT Eliza Ann of New Market m JENNESS Ira H of Tamworth NH on 1 Sept *MS* 30 Sept 1846

QUINT Lydia m BICKFORD Dodavah on Sunday before last *MS* 30 Apr 1828

QUINT Nancy I of Brownfield m LEWIS John B of Waterborough ME on 29 Sept 1848 *MS* 15 Nov 1848

QUINT Zabra Ann m JOHNSON Aaron on 31 Dec at Brownfield ME *MS* 12 Feb 1845

QUIVEY Clarissa of Cincinnatus m HILLS James W Eld both of Cortland Co NY of Virgil on 9 Dec *MS* 12 Jan 1848

RACKLEFF Louisa J m HIGGINS John on 28 May 1848 *MS* 21 June 1848

RACKLIFF Olive m WHITE Wm both of Portsmouth NH on 27 June *MS* 17 Jul 1850

RADDEN Emily m QUIMBY James both of Franconia *MS* 4 Apr 1849

RAISOR Eliza Ann m KALER J S *MFWBR* 3 Mar 1849

RALPH Harriet F of La Grange m JOHNSON Jesse B of Kilmarnock on 12 inst *MS* 5 Sept 1838

RAMSDEL Elizabeth B of Garland m OSGOOD D L Marquia of Exeter on 1 Mar *MS* 15 Sept 1847

RAMSDELL Charlotte of Washington m BIGELOW Ashbill of Worcester on 16 Jul 1848 *MS* 25 Oct 1848

RAMSDELL Emily of Lafayette m SLOAN Lewis of Westfield in Lafayette Medina Co Ohio on Oct 7 1841, VAUGHN Hiram Eld *MS* 26 Jan 1842

RAMSEY Hannah B of New Hampton m NEWELL Francis P of Sutton on 20 May 1847 *MS* 22 Sept 1847

RAMSEY Jennet of New Hampton m WADLEIGH Charles J of Sanbornton NH on 19 Oct 1847 *MS* 2 Feb 1848

RAN Parmelia m KAIME John Dea both of Barnstead on 12th inst *MS* 29 Jul 1835

RAND Eliza of Parsonsfield m HILL Nathaniel Jr of Brownfield in Limington ME 2nd Jan *MS* 2 Mar 1842

RAND Hannah L of Lowell m KIMBALL Christopher C *MS* 30 Jan 1839

RAND Joanna m PIERCE William A *MFWBR* 8 Dec 1849

RAND Susan M m PERKINS Albion W both of Epsom on 16 Sept in Pittsfield *MS* 29 Sept 1847

RANDALL Abby W of No Scituate m STEERE Martin J Eld on 17 Apr *MS* 23 May 1838

RANDALL Ann of Centre Harbor m OSGOOD Ebenezer P of Concord on 25 Nov 1849 *MS* 30 Jan 1850

RANDALL Annette W of Dover NH m REED Lewis D of Dover NH on 10 Sept *MS* 17 Sept 1845

RANDALL Elizabeth m TEMPLE John F on 28 Nov at Bowdoinham ME *MS* 8 Jan 1845

RANDALL Elizabeth m JACKSON Wm W both of New Market on 21 Nov *MS* 2 Dec 1835

RANDALL Eunice Mrs m SADDLER Joseph both of Bangor ME on 18 June 1848 *MS* 5 Jul 1848

RANDALL Lucretia H m BROWN George W both of Dover on 22 Jul *MS* 8 Aug 1849

RANDALL Lydia B of Centre Harbor m PRESCOTT John O of Meredith on 28 Nov *MS* 11 Dec 1850

RANDALL Lydia H m WILLEY Samuel L both of Great Falls *MS* 27 Nov 1850

RANDALL Margaret E of Bowdoinham Lincoln CO ME m PURINTON Gollamore Eld of Embden Somerset Co ME on 19 inst *MS* 8 Jul 1846

RANDALL Margaret of Bowdoinham ME m WHITE Solon H on 8 Apr *MS* 19 Apr 1843

RANDALL Mary m HEATH Jonathan D at Ohio *MS* 3 Jul 1844

RANDALL Mary L m MANLEY Daniel W both of Charlestown MA on 7 inst *MS* 26 Mar 1851

RANDALL Mary W of Johnson m TURNER Ezekiel of Providence *MS* 13 Nov 1850

RANDALL Melinda of Lewiston ME on 27 Oct m SMALL William of Wales *MS* 13 Nov 1839

RANDALL Nancy of Limington ME m FOSS Leonard of Chelsea MA on 6th *MS* 23 Jul 1845

RANDALL Sarah A m JONES Cyrus Esq *MFWBR* 1 Sept 1849

RANDALL Sarah Jane of Portsmouth m MARTIN Edward on 14 Sept 1843 at Portsmouth NH *MS* 10 Jan 1844

RANDALL Sarah M of Centre Harbor m NELSON Hiram of Bristol on 15 Oct *MS* 21 Nov 1843

RANDALL Sarah of Bolton on 26 Mar 1839 m COX Charles of Hatley *MS* 17 Apr 1839

RANDEL Sarah M m DUSTON Lindley M both of Poestenkill NY*MS* 15 Jan 1851

RANDELL Sarah m HOLT Daniel both of New Market on 19 inst *MS* 1 Feb 1837

RANDLET Serene of Meredith NH m SANDERS S Warren on 3 Dec at Meredith *MS* 14 Dec 1842

RANDOLPH Caroline d/o RANDOLPH W Dea of Dixmont ME m TOOTHAKER Jacob of Etna ME on 28 Dec *MS* 24 Jan 1838

RANKER Phebe Jane m JOHNSON Francis on 30 Aug at Lowell MA *MS* 2 Nov 1842

RANKINS Lucy of Cornish ME m BROWN Moody on 10 Jul *MS* 9 Aug 1843

RANKINS Mary A m HANSCOMB Seward M at Buxton ME *MS* 20 Nov 1844

RANKINS Sarah m COLE James L both of Wells ME *MS* 27 Mar 1834

RANLET Mary L of Waltham MA m COTTLE William of Dover NH *MS* 18 Apr 1849

RANNCY Fylinda M of Lowell MA m GOULD Amos A on 5 Dec *MS* 18 Dec 1844

RANSDELL Lydia W of Washington VT on 2 Dec 1838 m DENNISON Elijah B *MS* 15 May 1839

RANSOM Sarah D of Roxbury formerly of Brunswick ME m MASON Nicholas of Roxbury MA formerly of Portsmouth NH on 19 Feb *MS* 7 Aug 1850

RANSON Lydia m SOPER Henry of Dunkirk *MS* 19 Apr 1848

RATHBON Eliza of Collins NY m BOSS Horace of Ashford on 16 Jan
    MS 14 Feb 1844

RAWLAND Sarah A of Roxand Co Mich m MORGRIDGE Horatio N
    formerly of Corinth ME *MS* 24 May 1848

RAY Abigail d/o RAY William both of Minot m CURTIS John *MS* 1
    May 1834

RAY Mary Ann m MEAD Potter *MS* 3 Jul 1844

RAYMOND Almira m PREBLE Daniel *MS* 31 Jan 1838

RAYNOLD Olive E m BARTLETT Benjamin F at Boston MA *MS* 19
    Jul 1843

REA Frances m BROOKS Robert G both of Perry Township Ohio on 2
    Sept 1847 *MS* 9 Feb 1848

REA Shady m HEATH J D Eld on 28 Feb at Perry Township Logan
    Co Ohio *MS* 31 Mar 1847

RECORD Angeline C of Buckfield ME m JARLIN Alron K of Sumner
    ME on 4 Jul in Buckfield *MS* 18 Jul 1849

RECORD Charlotte of Sand Lake m SHEPHARD Joel of Stephentown
    on 17 Feb *MS* 19 Mar 1845

RECORD Cordelia W m RANDALL Andrew W on 14 Apr *MS* 24 Apr
    1844

RECORD Sally B of Parsonsfield ME on 28 May m PENDER Alexan-
    der of Somersworth NH *MS* 5 June 1839

REDLEY Elizabeth H m RUSSELL Nelson R on Oct 25 of Lowell MA
    MS 6 Jan 1847

REDMAN Hannah m LORD Isaac on Thurs last *MS* 2 Nov 1826

REDWAY Arminda of Barnston m HARVEY William in May *MS* 1 Jan
    1840

REED Abigail A of Roxbury MA m HAYES Washington E of Dover NH
    MS 24 June 1846

REED Betsey E of Lowell MA m GOULD Levi A on 17 Jan at Dracut
    MA *MS* 18 Feb 1846

REED Calista of Boothbay ME m HALLOWELL George of Boothbay
    ME *MS* 23 Dec 1846

REED Charlotte H m BARWISE John of Garland ME *MFWBR* 13 Oct
    1849

REED Charlotte of 3 Mile Bay NY m CHAMPLIN Wm E of Watertown
    Jefferson Co NY on 9 Nov 1847 *MS* 1 Dec 1847

REED Eliza of Woolwich ME m WALKER Abial on 7 Nov at Woolwich
    ME *MS* 14 Jan 1846

REED Ester V of Lowell MA m BOWERS Darius Bowers of Dracutt
    MA on 20 Oct *MS* 2 Nov 1842

REED J Willey m PACKARD E Heman both of Lowell MA on 20 Aug
    MS 11 Sept 1850

REED Julia m STEVENS Hiram E both of Colebrook NH on 4 Apr
    1849 *MS* 2 May 1849

REED Margaretta of Portland m THOMPSON Alvin *MFWBR* 28 Apr

REED (Continued)
MFWBR 28 Apr 1849

REED Mary Ann m FOSTER Asa both of Manchester on 9 Aug *MS* 26 Aug 1846

REED Mary of Perinton m THORNTON Hiram on 13 Mar of Rochester *MS* 12 May 1847

REED Mary T m MASON Asa M *MFWBR* 7 Apr 1849

REED Phebe Mrs of Danville m CHASE Jonathan Esq on 9 Nov at Danville ME *MS* 3 Dec 1845

REED Prescilla C ae 13y m POWERS Jonathan Master ae 13y in Pepperel MA *MS* 23 Nov 1826

REED Rebecca Mrs of Dresden ME m WHITE John Capt of Bowdoinham ME in Dresden *MS* 22 May 1844

REMICK Britaia A of Elliot m WILSON Thomas E of Kittery ME on 26 Oct *MS* 27 Dec 1843

REMICK Sophia M m ABBOTT William H of North Berwick *MS* 17 Jan 1844

REMINGTON Sarah m CLIFFORD George B both of Starksborough on 16 Dec 1847 *MS* 19 Jan 1848

REMINGTON Susan B of Cranston m EDDY Darius of No Providence on 14th inst at Johnston RI *MS* 24 June 1835

RENNETT Lydia A of Eaton m LORD James *MS* 21 Jan 1846

REXFORD Lydia of Hatley LC m REVER Joseph of Boston on 16 Nov last *MS* 17 Feb 1836

REYNOLDS Almira of Pierpont NY m TILTON Mark (late of Canada) on 14 Feb 1842 at Pierpont NY *MS* 18 May 1842

REYNOLDS Avis m MASON John both of Dover on 28 ult *MS* 4 Nov 1846

REYNOLDS Eliza Jane m NORTON Martin both of Oakfield on 16 Feb 1848 *MS* 26 Apr 1848

REYNOLDS Lucy P m GILMAN Edwin A both of Monroe on 2 Sept *MS* 13 Nov 1850

REYNOLDS Lydia m McCRILLIS Philip *MS* 25 Apr 1833

REYNOLDS Mary Jane of Lowell m HUNTRESS Willard L *MS* 22 May 1839

REYNOLDS Polly m SMITH C A both of Lesslie Mich on 22 Feb 1849 *MS* 4 Apr 1849

REYNOLDS Polly of Stanstead m HALL Joseph of Compton LC on 20 Dec *MS* 22 Mar 1837

REYNOLDS Sarah Ann of Lowell MA m WRIGHT James J of Lowell MA *MS* 25 May 1842

RHODES Lydia Ann of Waterboro ME m TEBBETTS Mark *MFWBR* 12 Oct 1850

RICE Elizabeth G of Henniker m STEWART Isaac D Eld of Meredith NH *MS* 26 Apr 1843

RICE Mary at Hallowell ME m LITTLEFIELD Andrew G on 19th Jul

RICE (Continued)

at Litchfield ME *MS* 16 Aug 1843

RICH Abby of Monroe ME m TOWLE Samuel of Porter on 25 Aug *MS* 13 Nov 1850

RICH Adelia of Portland ME m CROSSWELL John W *MFWBR* 4 Aug 1849

RICH Esther G m NICHOLS James B Capt of Searsport ME on 14 Dec *MS* 24 Dec 1845

RICH Hannah A of Jackson ME m VARNEY James A of Brooks ME on 27 ult *MS* 24 Nov 1847

RICH Lydia m DAMMON Esrael both of Exeter on 7 June *MS* 8 Aug 1838

RICH Mary at Brooks ME m WATERMAN Robert of Belfast ME *MFWBR* 22 May 1847

RICH Nancy J m OAKES John at Bangor ME *MS* 13 Sept 1843

RICH Pamelia G of Roxbury on 8 Aug m LAUGHTON Charles H of Boston MA *MS* 28 Aug 1844

RICHARDS Eliza of Dover m HALL Mark on 25 June at Dover NH *MS* 2 Jul 1845

RICHARDS Ellen M m MARCH William of Windham ME on 14 Sept at Falmouth ME *MS* 20 Dec 1843

RICHARDS Georgianna F m WILLOUGHBY E K on 29 Aug 1847 *MS* 8 Sept 1847

RICHARDS Huldah J of Hope ME m WATSON Reuben B of Northwood NH *MS* 18 Oct 1848

RICHARDS Jane m STUFF Benj both of Jenner Somerset Co PA on 25 Apr *MS* 15 May 1844

RICHARDS Rosilla of Saco ME m HILL Sylvester of Lyman on 29 ult in Biddeford ME *MS* 30 Oct 1850

RICHARDS Roxanna of Saco m BURNHAM Wm D of Biddeford ME on 5 Aug *MS* 21 Nov 1849

RICHARDS Sarah J m HAM Samuel of Berwick ME on 12 Sept at Lebanon ME *MS* 10 Oct 1844

RICHARDSON Abigail m AVERY Daniel E both of Sandwich NH on 8 Dec *MS* 4 Jan 1837

RICHARDSON Betsey m WHITTEN Nathaniel *MS* 25 Apr 1833

RICHARDSON Comfort C m RICHARDSON Rockwell both of Sutton VT on 5 June *MS* 28 June 1848

RICHARDSON Dolly F m MOSHIER Rufus on 25 Dec at Gorham ME *MS* 5 Feb 1845

RICHARDSON Eliza J of New Market m LEACH Thomas E of Kittery ME *MS* 24 Jan 1849

RICHARDSON Eliza P m WHITCOMB Ephraim O both of Lowell MA *MS* 2 Jul 1834

RICHARDSON Emily A m CUNNINGHAM Daniel Jr both of Bradford on 4 Aug *MS* 16 Oct 1850

RICHARDSON Emily m BAKER Albion K P both of Litchfield ME *MS* 28 Mar 1849

RICHARDSON Emily J of Limington ME m UNDERWOOD Sardies D of Lowell MA *MFWBR* 5 Oct 1850 & on 17th ult *MS* 30 Oct 1850

RICHARDSON Eunice H m ABBOT William N in Mt Desert Jan 13 *MS* 19 Jan 1842

RICHARDSON Eunice L m STONE Wm C on 21 Oct *MS* 14 Nov 1849

RICHARDSON Harriet m KITTREDGE Edmund F on 8th inst at Wilmington *MS* 25 Oct 1843

RICHARDSON Lucy m CLEMONS Sudrick *MS* 8 Aug 1833

RICHARDSON Lydia m ELDRIDGE Joseph *MS* 8 Aug 1833

RICHARDSON Lydia F m EAMES Daniel on 28 Dec at Wilmington MA *MS* 17 Jan 1844

RICHARDSON Lydia of Monmouth m RANKINS Oliver of Monmouth ME *MS* 19 Jul 1843

RICHARDSON M Jane m JUDKINS S N on 13 June at Dracut MA *MS* 7 Jul 1847

RICHARDSON Mary of Northwood m GRIFFIN Ira on 13 Jul *MS* 17 Dec 1845

RICHARDSON Miriam of Cornish m CLAGGETH Frederick of Newport on 4th inst *MS* 8 June 1831

RICHARDSON Nancy of Westport m BEALS Levi of Georgetown ME on 16 Nov *MS* 4 Feb 1846

RICHARDSON Phebe P of Baldwin d/o RICHARDSON Joseph Deacon m MERRILL John H Rev of Sedgwick ME *MFWBR* 30 Oct 1847

RICHARDSON Phebe Q m PEACH Jonathan J both of Chelmsford MA on 9 Apr 1848 *MS* 26 Apr 1848

RICHARDSON Sylvia B at Great Falls NH m GALE Andrew *MS* 4 Mar 1840

RICKER Balancha B of Dover m BERRY Elvin of Strafford ME on last Thurs *MS* 18 June 1834

RICKER Betsey m GUPTILL Granville both of Berwick ME on 22 Dec *MS* 15 Jan 1850

RICKER Charlotte M of Turner ME on 4 Sept m BERRY Henry C of Hartford ME *MS* 7 Jan 1846

RICKER Eliza m FURBER Mack L *MS* 25 Apr 1833

RICKER Eliza of Lebanon ME m GUPTILL George of Berwick ME on 17 Aug at Lebabon ME *MS* 27 Aug 1845

RICKER Eliza on 13 Feb m THURSTON Miles of Alton NH *MS* 12 Apr 1843

RICKER Esther J m RICKER Asa H both of Lebannon ME on 19 Dec 1850 *MS* 8 Jan 1851

RICKER Harriet A of West Waterville ME m BATCHELDER Samuel S at Fairfield ME of West Waterville ME *MS* 20 Apr 1842

RICKER Lydia H m DOWNS George W both of Great Falls on 16 Dec

RICKER (Continued)
   MS 25 Dec 1850

RICKER Maria W m WEBB John of Waterville *MS* 16 Oct 1839

RICKER Mary m JONES Gershom both of Lebanon ME on 5 Jul *MS* 23 Sept 1846

RICKER Mary C m BABCOCK Samuel on Lowell MA *MS* 26 Oct 1836

RICKER Mary E m CLARK Levi D both of Dover on 25 inst 1847 *MS* 1 Dec 1847

RICKER Mary Jane m WILLEY Samuel S both of Dover NH on 25 ult Tuesday evening *MS* 10 Jan 1838

RICKER Mary Mrs m WHITTON Ebenezer *MFWBR* 1 Sept 1849

RICKER Mehitable F of Acton ME m ROBERTS G W of Lebanon *MS* 13 Jan 1847

RICKER Nancy of Parsonsfield m THOMPSON George *MS* June 1831

RICKER Olive M m MERRILL Sumner B at Manchester NH *MS* 15 Oct 1845

RICKER Rebecca F of Farmington m OTIS Joshua Esq of Strafford on 11 May 1848 *MS* 24 May 1848

RICKER Sarah Ann of Buckfield ME m BENSON James S on 7 Dec *MS* 7 Jan 1846

RICKER Sarah H m HERSHAM Benjamin both of Lebanon on 8 Dec *MS* 25 Dec 1839

RICKER Sarah J m GAGE Joshua at Waterville ME *MS* 29 Dec 1841

RICKER Sarah J m LEWIS James S both of Dover on 15 inst *MS* 22 Jul 1846

RICKER Urana m JONES Sewaver both of Lebanon ME on 19 Oct 1848 *MS* 1 Nov 1848

RIDEOUT Rebecca m DUDLEY Joseph both of Pittsfield *MS* 3 Jul 1850

RIDER Judith Ann m WELCH Joseph both of No Yarmouth ME on 3 Nov 1847 *MS* 17 Nov 1847

RIDGEWAY Ursula m BUTLER Otis B both of Farmington *MS* 13 Dec 1837

RIDLEY Abigail of Farmington ME m DEANE Abial of Temple ME on 21st ult *MS* 13 Jul 1832

RIDLEY Anna P m PARKER James M both of Brunswick ME *MS* 7 Oct 1846

RIDLEY Huldah G m FROST George K both of Springvale ME on 2 Jul 1848 *MS* 16 Aug 1848

RIDLEY Mary C m CLEMMENT Elijah G both of Corinth ME on 10 Dec 1848 *MS* 21 Feb 1849

RIDLEY Mary of Prospect ME m PARTRIDGE Amos of Prospect ME *MS* 29 Nov 1827

RIDLON Miranda S of Saco m PLUMMER Charles M of Portland ME *MFWBR* 8 Jul 1848

RIDLON Philinda D of Hollis ME m RIDLON Thomas E of Sweden ME

RIDLON (Continued)
on 4 Apr 1848 in Hollis *MS* 3 May 1848

RIGGS Mary m GOSS Guy C *MFWBR* 25 May 1850

RIGGS Rebecca of Portland ME m SMALL William B on 5th inst at Portland ME *MS* 26 Mar 1845

RILEY Emeline m WILLIAMS Josiah both of Kittery ME in Kittery ME on Wed Eve 23 inst *MS* 9 Mar 1842

RILEY Helen m TUCK George W both of Lowell MA on 25 Jan 1848 *MS* 2 Feb 1848

RILEY Martha J m BLAKE Mark both of Kittery on 14 Nov *MS* 5 Dec 1849

RILL Lydia of Lyndon VT m KINISON Elisha M of Holderness NH on 8 Mar *MS* 18 Apr 1838

RING Betsey of Loudon NH m FOSS Benjamin H of Gilmanton NH on 15 inst *MS* 21 Nov 1849

RING Mary Jane of Deerfield NH m SHUTE Jeremiah of Northwood NH *MS* 11 June 1845

RION Martha Ann of Northfield NH m ORDWAY Joshua on 23 Jan at Canterbury NH of Hopkinton *MS* 31 Mar 1847

RIPLEY Loisa P m TIBBETTS William G both of Augusta ME *MS* 24 Jan 1838

RISS Abigail H at Gilmanton NH m HAYES Stephen W of Alton NH on 15 Nov 1843 *MS* 20 Dec 1843

RIX Normanda of Barnston on 8 May 1838 m PAUL Hiram L *MS* 17 Apr 1839

RIX Sophronia m LILLY Patrick both of Stanstead LC on 9 ult *MS* 18 May 1836

ROACH Mary Jane of Bath m RUSSELL Edward of Salem MA on 30 Nov *MS* 1 Feb 1843

ROBBENSON Ann S of Sandown NH on 4 Jul m FENNER Thomas M of Lowell *MS* 17 Jul 1839

ROBBINS Betsey Mrs of Collins Eric Co m BOSS Charles Esq on 29 Oct 1843 of Ashford NY *MS* 14 Feb 1844

ROBBINS Caroline V m WEATHERBY Ansel C both of Pittsfield MA on 17 Jan 1849 *MS* 2 May 1849

ROBBINS Elmira m PINKHAM James on 25 June *MS* 2 Nov 1842

ROBBINS Maria H m HOOPER Peter both of Great Falls NH on 1 Oct *MS* 18 Oct 1848

ROBBINS Mary m BEALE Nathaniel both of Phillips ME on 8 Apr 1849 *MS* 18 Apr 1849

ROBBINS Mary E m HEATH Stephen both of Raymond on 13 Dec *MS* 23 Jan 1850

ROBBINS Susan of Phillips ME m CHANDLER Hubbard Eld of Wilton ME on 2nd inst *MS* 16 Jul 1828

ROBERTS Betsey H m MUNSEY David H *MS* 12 Apr 1843

ROBERTS Betsey H m JELLESON Abel H both of Saco on 25 Aug *MS*

ROBERTS (Continued)
30 Sept 1846 & *MS* 6 Apr 1847

ROBERTS Betsey of Lyman m KNIGHT Simeon of Waterborough ME on 4 Dec at Lyman ME *MS* 28 Dec 1842

ROBERTS Elizabeth L of Acton ME m BROCK James M *MS* 17 Apr 1839

ROBERTS Ellen E of Lyman m BEDELL Isaiah M of Sanford ME on 1 June *MS* 15 Jul 1846

ROBERTS Emelius of Sharon m ROWELL Darius T on 23 Nov at Sharon VT *MS* 13 Jan 1847

ROBERTS Eunice of Dover m HORNE John 2d on 6th inst at Dover NH *MS* 17 Aug 1842

ROBERTS Hannah at Lebanon ME m RAMSEY B Mr *MS* 21 Nov 1843

ROBERTS Hannah m NUTTER Abner J both of Dover on 12 inst *MS* 19 Dec 1849

ROBERTS Harriet E m PERKINS John both of Colesville NY *MS* 22 Dec 1847

ROBERTS Harriet of Alton NH m WILLEY Nathaniel merchant of Wolfboro NH *MS* 8 Mar 1837

ROBERTS Huldah R m ROBERTS Charles on 2 Apr *MS* 20 May 1846

ROBERTS Jane m RIDEOUT Nathan C both of Lee on 4 Jul *MS* 25 Jul 1849

ROBERTS Joan of Strafford NH m BLAKE Wm of Barrington NH *MS* 21 Dec 1836

ROBERTS Marcialine R B m MARDIN True R both of Sharon VT on 1 Nov 1847 *MS* 15 Mar 1848

ROBERTS Martha Jane m HAINES Joshua B both of Dover on 1 inst *MS* 10 May 1848

ROBERTS Martha N A m CLARK John both of Meredith NH *MS* 29 Aug 1838

ROBERTS Mary m HAYES David on 6th ult at Strafford NH *MS* 21 Dec 1836

ROBERTS Mary L m OSBORN David C of Russel Ohio on 14 May at Munson Ohio *MS* 11 June 1845

ROBERTS Melinda of Pittsfield m HILL Clark of Barrington (NH?) on 27 Feb *MS* 14 Mar 1838

ROBERTS Mercy Ann m WILEY William A on 18 inst *MS* 4 Oct 1837

ROBERTS Nancy of Waterboro ME m FIELD Jonathan of Buxton ME *MFWBR* 8 May 1847

ROBERTS Patience E of Plymouth NH m WIGGIN Stephen P of Sanbornton NH on 26 Oct 1847 *MS* 24 Nov 1847

ROBERTS Phebe T m BARKER Joseph on 2 Apr *MS* 20 May 1846

ROBERTS Rachael of Dover NH m SCRUTON Hiram W at Farmington NH *MS* 6 Apr 1842

ROBERTS Rebecca of Ossipee NH m BLAISDELL Martin of Tam-

ROBERTS (Continued)
worth NH *MS* 20 Apr 1831
ROBERTS Sarah B m LANGLEY Ephraim on 2 inst *MS* 30 Jan 1834
ROBERTS Sarah of Andover m NOYES Charles of Boscawen NH on 19 Jul at Andover *MS* 3 Aug 1842
ROBERTS Tamson of Ossipee NH m AYERS Stephen of Wolfborough NH on 11 inst *MS* 29 Sept 1847
ROBERTSON Maria L m CHESLEY James C of Barrington *MS* 25 June 1845
ROBERTSON Sarah B m RECORD Nahum both of Great Falls NH *MS* 4 Oct 1848
ROBEY Rebekah G of Chichester NH m KAIME Wm W of Roxbury MA *MS* 16 Dec 1835
ROBIE Jenette G of Corinth VT m ROBIE Ichabod Jr on 31 Mar 1842 at Corinth VT *MS* 13 Apr 1842
ROBIE Nancy of Raymond m JONES Elijah of Epping in Raymond *MS* 9 Mar 1842
ROBIE Sarah of Raymond m WIGGIN Theophilus of Lee *MS* 6 Mar 1850
ROBINS Olevia C of Lewiston ME m CONANT Winslow of Auburn ME on 22 Oct at Lewiston ME *MS* 9 Dec 1846
ROBINSON Abba G of Limington ME m HORN David J Capt of Lebanon *MS* 14 Jul 1847
ROBINSON Abigail m FULLONTON Joseph *MS* 4 Mar 1835
ROBINSON Amanda at Augusta ME m GALUSHA Florilla *MFWBR* 17 Mar 1849
ROBINSON Angeline of Meredith m BROWN Noah W of Sanbornton NH on 12 Aug *MS* 30 Sept 1846
ROBINSON Betsey of Meredith m WEEKS George W of Boston MA *MS* 8 Dec 1841
ROBINSON Catharine m FLATTEL Albert both of Sidney ME *MS* 15 Jan 1840
ROBINSON Charlotte m POOR W B on 23 June *MS* 18 Dec 1844
ROBINSON Christiana J of Sidney ME m BUTTERFIELD Jonas of Chesterville ME at Sidney ME *MS* 25 Nov 1846
ROBINSON Cordelia M m HAMMOND Henry H on 25 Nov 1847 *MS* 8 Mar 1848
ROBINSON Grace E of Sandwich m BODWELL Elisha A of Saco ME on 14 Nov *MS* 26 Dec 1849
ROBINSON H of Dedham MA m LANGMAID E K of Laudon on 6 Apr 1848 *MS* 17 Jan 1849
ROBINSON Hannah m TURNER Moses on 1 Sept 1844 at Alton *MS* 26 Feb 1845
ROBINSON Lucinda H m WALKER Dexter M both of Lowell on 31 ult *MS* 14 Nov 1838
ROBINSON Lucy of Rome Michigan m KNAPP Bennager of Dover

ROBINSON (Continued)

Michigan on 21 Mar *MS* 12 May 1847

ROBINSON Margaret of Hatley m HAYNES John of Stanstead LC on 21 Mar *MS* 13 Sept 1843

ROBINSON Mary Ann m DREW Hiram both of Barrington on 7th inst *MS* 13 Jul 1836

ROBINSON Mary Ann m ELLIS Wm B both of Sidney ME *MS* 3 Apr 1850

ROBINSON Mary of Richmond m BROWN Jefferson of Litchfield ME on at Richmond ME *MS* 25 May 1836

ROBINSON Nancy m HILL Oliver both of Meredith *MS* 5 Dec 1838

ROBINSON Olive B of Gilford m FOLSOM Albert G of Meredith on 5 Jan *MS* 8 Feb 1843

ROBINSON Roxana m WOODWARD Joseph of Sidney ME *MS* 21 Jan 1846

ROBINSON Sarah Abby m BROWN Lorenzo on 28th ult of Portsmouth NH *MS* 9 Dec 1846

ROBINSON Sarah C m BOYD William on 27 Nov at Manchester *MS* 24 Dec 1845

ROBINSON Sarah of Manchester m GILSON Freeman of Compton LC 22 Mar 1848 *MS* 5 Apr 1848

ROBINSON Sophronia A of New Market m DAVIS Amos S of Center Harbor *MS* 8 June 1842

ROBY Lovina m WADLEY Thomas Capt both of Sutton on 14 Jan 1838 *MS* 14 Feb 1838

ROBY Lucy A of Fitchburg m DAVIS Wyman K of Fitchburg *MS* 25 May 1842

ROBY Sarah Jane of Hopkinton m GREEN N L on 21 Aug of Chichester at Hopkinton *MS* 14 Sept 1842

ROBY Susan E of New Hampton m PIKE Wm M of Meredith on 19 Dec 1849 *MS* 30 Jan 1850

ROCKLIFF Emeline of Industry ME on 30 Nov 1842 m WALKER Samuel A of Embden ME *MS* 19 Apr 1843

ROCKWELL Julia A m SHURTLEFF Luther B on 1 Feb 1848 *MS* 8 Mar 1848

ROGERS Ann m WASHBURN Thomas *MS* 15 May 1839

ROGERS Betsey and ROGERS Samuel of Parsonsfield divorced 7 Mar *MS* 14 Mar 1828

ROGERS Catharine of Wakefield m BUZZELL Jacob Jr of Acton ME on 28 Dec *MS* 28 Feb 1838

ROGERS Catherine M m CAMPBELL Robert both of Georgetown in Georgetown ME on March 30 *MS* 27 Apr 1842

ROGERS Deborah of Somersworth NH m ROGERS James S on 10 March at Great Falls NH *MS* 19 Mar 1845

ROGERS Hannah H of Portland ME m DAVIS Thomas C merchant of Dover on Thurs even last *MS* 7 Jan 1835

ROGERS Hannah of Newfield m BLAKE Francis of Brownfield ME *MS* 6 Dec 1827

ROGERS Isabella Y of Raymond m CRAM Jonathan Jr on 26 Aug *MS* 13 Sept 1837

ROGERS Lovina m COLLIER True H both of Lowell MA *MS* 14 Oct 1835

ROGERS Lydia S m BATCHELDER Henry F both of Loudon merchant on 5 Dec *MS* 26 Dec 1849

ROGERS Mahala m PERKINS Lemuel both of Dover on 22 ult *MS* 1 Mar 1848

ROGERS Martha R m DURGIN Silas on 23 Nov 1842 at Wolfboro' NH *MS* 24 May 1843

ROGERS Mary E of Somersworth NH m LORD Andrew on 3d inst at Dover NH *MS* 12 May 1847

ROGERS Rhoda G of Wendell m BLODGETT Joshua B of Newbury *MFWBR* 24 Mar 1849

ROGERS Sally G m SMITH John Jr both of Holderness NH on 5 Apr 1848 in Holderness NH *MS* 21 Mar 1849

ROGERS Susan m WHITE Charles on 3d inst *MS* 13 Jul 1836

ROLFE Marianna of Bethany NY m MYERS Henry J on 13 Feb 1848 *MS* 19 Jul 1848

ROLFEE Sarah m THOMPSON Charles H on 9 May at Wilmot *MS* 29 May 1844

ROLLINS Ann m BROWN Lewis both of Concord on 29 Dec 1849 *MS* 9 Jan 1850

ROLLINS Delila m CHAMPNEY Benjamin both of Belgrade ME on 4 Nov *MS* 10 Feb 1836

ROLLINS Dorcas m JOY William at Bangor ME *MS* 13 Sept 1843

ROLLINS Elizabeth E m SWAIN John D both of Dover on 31 inst *MS* 3 Jan 1849

ROLLINS Hannah M of Dover NH m HANSON John T on 26 ult at Dover NH *MS* 2 Dec 1846

ROLLINS Louiza m ROLLINS Nicholas Jr both of Stratham on 3 Oct *MS* 10 Oct 1838

ROLLINS Lucy Ann m HARTWELL Lysander W on 30 Jan at St Albans *MS* 17 Sept 1845

ROLLINS Mary m JONES John both of Lee on 16 Dec *MS* 15 Jan 1851

ROLLINS Mary J of Berwick ME m OTIS George K on 3 Jul *MS* 10 Jul 1850

ROLLINS Mehitable of Farmington m DAME Leonard on 24 Sept at Farmington *MS* 15 Nov 1843

ROLLINS Priscilla of Gardiner ME m MOORE Charles *MFWBR* 17 Mar 1849

ROLLINS Sally of Huntington m DIGSBY David of Stow on 12 inst *MS* 5 Sept 1838

ROLLINS Susan of Gilmanton on Thanksgiving day m HADLEY Uriah *MS* 13 Feb 1839

ROOK Susannah A of Smithfield m STEERE Anthony on 24 Nov at Smithfield RI *MS* 14 Dec 1842

ROSE Joanna m GOODWIN Charles both of Biddeford on 22 June 1847 *MS* 25 Aug 1847

ROSES Florentine of Leeds ME m FROST Joseph on 26 May at Leeds ME *MS* 10 Jul 1844

ROSS Adelia M of Harrison ME m BAKER Thomas of Waterford ME on 4 Jan *MS* 19 Feb 1851

ROSS Hannah M m MELCHER Abner Jr Capt both of Brunswick ME on 23 Jul *MS* 16 Aug 1837

ROSS Hester A m WHITEHOUSE Andrew S both of Brunswick ME *MS* 23 Jan 1850

ROSS Lydia D m KEAY Albra both of Lebanon ME *MS* 3 May 1848

ROSS Mary C m ROSS Samuel on 17 Nov *MS* 13 Jan 1847

ROSS Rhoda W m BAKER Ahira Esq both of Shapleigh ME on 3 Sept 1848 *MS* 20 Sept 1848

ROUNDS Anny Miss of Danville ME m KIMBALL James L of Parkman ME *MS* 13 Feb 1839

ROW Dorothy m HEATH Daniel both of Haverhill MA on 22 Feb 1848 *MS* 8 Mar 1848

ROW Lucy B of Lowell m EMERSON Jesse of Windham ME *MS* 18 Oct 1837

ROW Mary of Woodstock VT m BRAGG Miles of Danby VT on 2 Oct *MS* 7 Nov 1838

ROWE Caroline of Biddeford ME m LADD James of Saco ME *MFWBR* 24 June 1848

ROWE Frances m FREY Warren on 12th Nov at Lyme *MS* 10 Mar 1847

ROWE Marilda of Madbury m DEMERITT James Young on 27 Aug at Straford *MS* 13 Sept 1843

ROWE Mary of Wilmott m DURGIN Gershan of Andover *MS* 21 Nov 1838

ROWE Olive m HODGDON Moses both of West Poland ME on 14 May *MS* 3 June 1846

ROWE Sarah H of Norridgewock ME m PERKINS James W of Fairfield ME *MS* 25 Dec 1844

ROWE Sarah Jane of Smithfield ME m GREEN Noah on 16 Oct at Hallowell ME *MS* 7 Jan 1846

ROWE Tacy S m BROWN Herbert H both of South Adams MA on 9 Sept 1848 *MS* 11 Oct 1848

ROWEL Aurilla A of Goshen m HURD John of Wendell on 7 Mar 1850 *MS* 27 Mar 1850

ROWELL Abigail P m PLUMMER James H at Gilford *MS* 4 Oct 1843

ROWELL Ann m HAZEN Ichabod E both of Sutton on Nov 11 *MS* 12

ROWELL (Continued)
Jan 1842

ROWELL Betsey of Nottingham m YOUNG Elbridge G of West Newbury MA on 14 Nov at Deerfield *MS* 8 Jan 1845

ROWELL Eliza Jane of So Berwick ME m SHEPHARD John W of Dover *MS* 10 Feb 1836

ROWELL Emily of Conrville ME m WELCH Bray of Athens on 8 Jul 1847 *MS* 25 Aug 1847

ROWELL Hannah m ROBERTS West on 9th Jul at Strafford VT *MS* 13 Jan 1847

ROWLEY Susan m BAILEY Mose both of Yorkshire NY on 13 inst *MS* 26 Sept 1849

ROWLY Phebe of Yorkshire m JAQUISH Franklin of Freedom on 10 Sept *MS* 11 Dec 1850

ROYCE Lucy m WHITCHER Ira on 26 Nov at Haverhill *MS* 17 Jan 1844

ROYCE Lydia of Benton m NOYES Moses of Landaff on 23 Apr 1845 *MS* 8 Apr 1846

RUDE Sarah A m SLOAN Peter P both of Westfield, VAUGHN Hiram Eld *MS* 26 Jan 1842

RUGGLES Arvilla of Lyndon VT m HILL Mark formerly of Maine on 11th int *MS* 29 Nov 1827

RUMERY Abigail M of Effingham m SIBLEY Joel on 9 May at Effingham NH *MS* 19 May 1847

RUNDLETT Caroline A at Stratham m CHENEY Oren B of Peterboro' *MS* 4 Mar 1840

RUNDLETT Dorothy P m BARCLAY Cyrus P on 17 Sept of Lowell MA *MS* 27 Sept 1843

RUNDLETT Lydia S m BARCLEY Cyrus P on 6 May at Dracut MA *MS* 2 June 1847

RUNDLETT Mary m SANBORN Jonathan in Epping *MS* 9 Mar 1842

RUNDLETT Rebecca L of Stratham on 10 May m CHENEY Moses Jr of Peterboro' *MS* 17 May 1843

RUNEY Ellen m LEGRO Ira both of Lebanon ME on 23 inst *MS* 1 Nov 1848

RUNNELS Hannah on 20th inst of Scarboro' m FOGG Jonathan *MFWBR* 30 Nov 1850

RUNNELS Julia A of Gilmanton m MASON Benjamin K of Chichester on 22 Oct *MS* 7 Nov 1838

RUSSELL Betsey m FISH Stephen on 24 Dec 1837 *MS* 9 May 1838

RUSSELL Betsey B m DREW Ebenezer both of Manchester on 26 ult *MS* 1 Apr 1846

RUSSELL Betsey Jane m GLOVER William of Woodstock on 17 Apr at Franconia *MS* 14 May 1845

RUSSELL Charlotte m BEAN Geo J both of Lowell on 25 Nov *MS* 15 Dec 1847

RUSSELL Deborah L Mrs of Madison ME m ADAMS Daniel of Nor-ridgewock ME *MFWBR* 8 Dec 1849

RUSSELL Lydia J m JENKINS George both of Manchester *MS* 27 Sept 1848

RUSSELL Martha m SCRIBNER Daniel on 18 Sept at Manchester NH *MS* 1 Oct 1845

RUSSELL Mary Ann m CHASE John Jr *MS* 25 Dec 1844

RUSSELL Mary Ann of Woodstock m HUNT Albert on 11 Jan *MS* 29 Jan 1851

RUSSELL Mary J m TRICKY Joseph S both of Manchester NH on 7 Sept 1848 *MS* 8 Nov 1848

RUSSELL Mary of Manchester m KENDALL Robert of Nashua *MS* 2 Jan 1850

RUSSELL Rosamond m COOK Stephen S *MS* 25 Apr 1833

RUSSELL Susan m SAWYER Moses both of Manchester on 23 May *MS* 1 Apr 1846

RUST Caroline P m PINKHAM Ezra both of Wolfboro on 7 Aug *MS* 17 Aug 1836

RUST Evelina A of Norway m MIGHELS Jesse S Dr of Minot ME on at Norway ME *MS* 25 Jan 1827

SACKETT Cornelia of Pierpont m CONKEY Fortus of Canton *MS* 18 Oct 1843

SACKETT Jane Boston m HANDY John of Kittery ME on 11 ult *MS* 11 Apr 1838

SACKETT Lucy Mrs of Pierpont NY m REED Alton Esq on 26 Mar 1842 at Pierpont NY *MS* 18 May 1842

SADLER Caroline m STEVENS Richard on 3 Dec *MS* 2 Jan 1839

SADLER Mary Jane Miss m STEVENS James Madison *MS* 6 Feb 1834

SALESBURY Eliza L m TINCKOM Daniel on 30th ult at Scituate RI *MS* 21 Sept 1842

SALESBURY Marcilia B m FISK Daniel B both of Scituate on 28 Dec 1848 *MS* 17 Jan 1849

SAMPSON Abigail Mrs at Strafford m BABB Thomas of New Durham *MS* 27 Nov 1844

SANBORN Abigail m KNOWLES John a licentiate preacher of New Durham Q M on at Guilford NH *MS* 21 Dec 1832

SANBORN Ann W of Meredith NH m BATCHELDER William W on 4 Oct *MS* 26 Oct 1842

SANBORN Arvilla W m BATCHELDER Benjamin on 28 Nov *MS* 25 Dec 1844

SANBORN Betsey C m CHAMBERLIN Wm B on 26 Dec *MS* 4 Jan 1837

SANBORN Betsey C of Chelsea VT m SPEAR Nathan of Bershire on 29 Feb *MS* 29 Apr 1846

SANBORN Caroline A m TRIPP Lewis on 2 June at St Albans ME *MS* 17 Sept 1845

SANBORN Catharine m MANSER Darius on both of Prospect *MS* 6 Apr 1831

SANBORN Clariss Miss of Wales m DOW Parker of St Albans *MS* 21 Mar 1833

SANBORN Deborah m ROBINSON Daniel both of Meredith *MS* 5 Dec 1838

SANBORN Eleanor of Ellsworth NH m LEWIS Lincoln of Burnham ME *MS* 7 Mar 1828

SANBORN Eliza J of Bristol m MORSE Oscar F of Hebron *MS* 4 Oct 1848

SANBORN Elmira of Gilford m TANK James of Boston on 8 June *MS* 12 Jul 1837

SANBORN Hannah M at Gilmanton NH on Nov 27 1839 m FOLSOM John T *MS* 19 Feb 1840

SANBORN Jane of New Hampton m BROWN Noah B of Sanbornton NH on 7 June 1849 *MS* 4 Jul 1849

SANBORN Judith of Brookfield m JENNESS Isaac Col of Rochester on 9 Oct *MS* 14 Oct 1831

SANBORN Julia A m BRIDGE Samuel H on 12 Dec in Litchfield ME *MS* 8 Jan 1845

SANBORN Lavina m HOOK James *MS* 20 Sept 1837

SANBORN Lavina of Lamprey River NH m SMITH Wm W of Lynn MA on 7th inst *MS* 21 Mar 1833

SANBORN Lucy m POLAND Benjamin Esq both of Standish ME *MS* 19 May 1830

SANBORN Lucy J of Loudon NH on 25 Nov m ROBERTSON Ebenezer S of Meredith NH *MS* 8 Dec 1841

SANBORN Lydia S of Gilmanton m WIGGIN Nathaniel of North Chelmsford MA on 29 March *MS* 23 Aug 1843

SANBORN Mary A of Lowell MA m ABBOTT William F of Belfast ME on 15 Jul at Knox ME *MS* 4 Aug 1847

SANBORN Mary Ann m GILMAN Amasa both of Gilmanton NH on Sept 13 in Gilmanton *MS* 5 Jan 1842

SANBORN Mary Ann m GUNDY John Lt both of New Hampton on 2 Jul *MS* 5 Aug 1846

SANBORN Mary Ann of Danville NH m SLEEPER David T on 23 Sept at Danville NH *MS* 20 Jan 1847

SANBORN Mary Ann of Sandwich m TAYLOR William on 21 May 1843 at Freedom *MS* 21 June 1843

SANBORN Mary B of Alexandria NH m GURDY Joel of Bristol on 5 Nov 1848 *MS* 15 Nov 1848

SANBORN Mary C m SANBORN Marshal *MS* 3 Jul 1844

SANBORN Mary M of Gilford m MORSE Richard of Chester *MS* 1 Jan 1845

SANBORN Nancy T at Hampton on 10 inst m MOORE Charles H of Canterbury *MS* 26 Feb 1840

SANBORN Phebe of Hampton m PLUMMER Jesse of Meredith *MS* 8 Nov 1837

SANBORN Roxana of Danville m MARDEN George of Chester *MS* 6 Mar 1844

SANBORN Sally m DAVIS John both of Waterboro ME *MS* 28 Dec 1832

SANBORN Sarah A m ROBINSON David both of Wales ME 21 inst *MS* 4 Oct 1837

SANBORN Sarah Ann of Loudon NH m SANBORN Jacob K on 28 Sept at Gilmanton *MS* 25 Oct 1843

SANDERS Abigail M m SANDERS William of Strafford NH *MS* 14 Aug 1839

SANDERS Mary Ann of Sanbornton NH m SANBORN Nathan P of Malden MA on 20 Nov *MS* 12 Jan 1848

SANDERS Mary C m SWAIN George W both of Epsom on 6 Sept *MS* 5 Dec 1849

SANDERS Olive of Gilford NH m HIBBARD Tanny on 16 Nov at Gilford *MS* 28 Dec 1842

SANDERS Sally m YOUNG Jonathan Jr both of Strafford NH on 18th inst *MS* 31 Dec 1834

SANDERSON Mary J m KEITH Ralph S on 2d inst at Dover NH *MS* 13 Aug 1845

SANDS Eliza of Lyman m HAYES Edmund Jr of Limerick ME on at Lyman *MS* 28 Dec 1826

SANFORD Bernice of Bowdoinham ME m SWETT Jesse Eld of Richmond on 24th ult *MS* 16 Jan 1834

SANKEY Sarah R of Dover NH m FOGG John of Portsmouth NH *MS* 21 Nov 1833

SARGEANT Ann of Brownfield ME m JEWETT Charles of Denmark ME on 17 Jul *MS* 25 Jan 1843

SARGEANT Cybil R m CONNOR Asa on 24 inst at New Chester *MS* 11 May 1836

SARGEANT Martha Ann m DODGE Charles at Lowell MA *MS* 18 Jan 1837

SARGEANT Martha of Brownfield ME m NORTON Ebenezer on 9 May at Limington ME of Porter ME *MS* 29 May 1844

SARGEANT Sarah m HEATH William T of Salisbury in Danville *MS* 23 Feb 1842

SARGENT Ann K m WARREN Peter on 15 Sept at Mantua Ohio *MS* 17 Dec 1845

SARGENT Eunice H m MORSE George B of North Yarmouth ME *MFWBR* 31 Jul 1847

SARGENT Harriet M H m WIGGIN Noah L both of Lowell on 17 Feb *MS* 28 Feb 1849

SARGENT Judith m CURRIER Abraham both of Hopkinton on 26 Dec *MS* 2 Apr 1851

SARGENT Margaret S m LOGAN John W *MFWBR* 19 June 1847

SARGENT Martha A m WHITE Samuel Jr both of Monroe ME on 25 Jan 1849 *MS* 14 Feb 1849

SARGENT Mehitable Mrs m BUNTON Levi both of Epsom NH on 16 Dec 1849 *MS* 16 Jan 1850

SARGENT Orra Ann m HUNTRESS Joseph MD on 9 Oct at Sandwich NH *MS* 15 Oct 1845

SARGENT Sarah Jane of Danville m HOYT Joseph on 28 May of Lyndon *MS* 24 Feb 1847

SARGENT Sarah of Henniker on 24 Oct m GOVE Mark *MS* 6 Nov 1839

SAUNDERS Jemima M of Dover ME m AMES Phinehas on 4 Jul at Dover ME *MS* 24 Jul 1844

SAUNDERS Juliann of Madbury m CLOUGH Charles of Bradstead on 3 Mar at Madbury *MS* 24 Mar 1847

SAVAGE Clarinda T m WRIGHT Nathaniel E both of Farmington on 5 Jul *MS* 12 Sept 1838

SAVAGE Mary E of Durham NH m TUCKER James of Boston MA on 23 Dec 1847 *MS* 3 May 1848

SAVAGE Rachel A m EMERSON Benj F both of Lowell MA on 26 Nov 1848 *MS* 3 Jan 1849

SAVERY Minerva of Roxbury MA m SINCLAIR John T on 27 Dec at Roxbury MA *MS* 10 Jan 1844

SAVERY Miranda m ADAMS JAmes P on 15 Mar 1844 at Stephentown NY *MS* 24 Apr 1844

SAWYER Arabine T of Harpswell m ORR Hermon C *MS* 24 Oct 1849

SAWYER Betsey of Cornish at Stow ME m EASTMAN Solomon of Stow *MS* 8 Mar 1843

SAWYER Cordelia A of Saco d/o SAWYER Mark m TITCOMB George of Portland ME *MFWBR* 13 Feb 1847

SAWYER Eliza A on 1st inst m BLANCHARD Abel *MFWBR* 17 Mar 1849

SAWYER Eliza B m ADAMS Benjamin Esq *MFWBR* 18 Aug 1849

SAWYER Elizabeth F m MALLET Elisha P both of Topsham ME on 23 May *MS* 15 Jan 1851

SAWYER H Susan only d/o SAWYER J of Deerfield NH m BEAN Francis G of Candia on 25 June *MS* 8 Jul 1846

SAWYER Hannah A m DROWN Charles on 13 Oct at Lowell MA *MS* 2 Nov 1842

SAWYER Hannah B m MERRILL Ezekiel E both of So Hampton in So Hampton *MS* 23 May 1838

SAWYER Hannah m SEATHERS/LEATHERS Jonathan both of Lowell *MS* 20 Dec 1837

SAWYER Hannah of Alton on 13 Feb m FLANDERS John *MS* 20 Feb

1839

SAWYER Hannah of Saco m HEMMINGWAY William R of Milton *MFWBR* 28 Apr 1849

SAWYER Jane B m NORTON Ivory both of Limington ME Jan 20 *MS* 2 Mar 1842

SAWYER Josephine B of Greene ME m HAMILTON Daniel H on 13 Sept 1846 of Gardiner *MS* 27 Jan 1847

SAWYER Julia Ann of Gray ME m STUBBS John of Cumberland ME on 8 Oct *MS* 26 Jan 1848

SAWYER Martha of Boston MA m FAIRBANKS Asa at Charlestown MA *MS* 25 Dec 1844

SAWYER Mehitabel of Saco ME m RUMERY Thomas on 3 Dec of Biddeford ME *MS* 6 Apr 1847

SAWYER Miriam Mrs m BUGBEE Horace on 3 Nov at Gilford *MS* 16 Dec 1846

SAWYER Rebecca of Ossipee NH m THOMPSON Alonzo on 2 Jan *MS* 5 Feb 1845

SAWYER Viola F m RICHARDSON Abram C *MS* 26 Sept 1838

SAYLES Malina F m POTTER Warren both of Burrillville RI on 21 Feb 1849 *MS* 21 Mar 1849

SAYWAD Sally m ABBOTT Nathan *MS* 21 Apr 1830

SAYWARD Jane m HUNTER Benjamin on 21 Feb of Lowell MA *MS* 23 Aug 1843

SAYWARD Lucy of Parsonsfield on 8 Jan m PARKS Eliphalet R *MS* 18 Sep 1839

SAYWOOD Hannah F of Waterboro m WIGGIN Janverin F of Dover NH *MS* 18 May 1832

SAYWOOD Lucinda of Waterboro m DAM Daniel of Newfield *MS* 3 Nov 1830

SCAMMON Rachel C m BOOTHBY Arthur *MFWBR* 24 Mar 1849

SCATES Adaline of Ossipee NH on 22 Mar m SANDERS Joel H of Ossipee NH *MS* 31 May 1843

SCHOBIE Susannah of Trenton NY [*sic*] m THOMAS Allen of Nelson on 18 Feb *MS* 11 Mar 1840

SCOTT Charity at Lowell MA m SAWYER Silas H *MS* 3 May 1843

SCOTT Elizabeth J of Hale Ohio m THORNTON Boyd on 8th Sept of York Ohio *MS* 25 Sept 1844

SCOTT Hannah M of New Lyme m JARVIS Alvah of Painesville Geauga Co Ohio on 12 Dec 1847 *MS* 29 Dec 1847

SCOTT Harriet m THURSTON Watson both of Lowell on 9 inst *MS* 20 June 1838

SCOTT Sarah of Chester Ohio m POND Julius of Hudson on 25 Jan *MS* 16 Feb 1848

SCOVELL Marietta of Poland NY on 4 Oct m ABBEY M H Eld of Harrisburgh *MS* 25 Oct 1843

SCRANTON Phebe of Goshen m THOMPSON Aaron of Washington on 23 June 1848 *MS* 2 Aug 1848

SCRIBNER Deborah T of Harrison m JONES James L of Lynn on 9 Oct at Harrison ME *MS* 19 Nov 1845

SCRIBNER Joia C m WASON John O both of Candia on 15 Dec *MS* 19 Apr 1837

SCRUTON Charlotte m HALL Joseph Dea both of Strafford on 27 Oct *MS* 6 Nov 1850

SCRUTON Maria of Strafford m CHESLEY Samuel of Berrington on 26th ult *MS* 2 Jan 1834

SCRUTON Martha E of Dover NH m GRIGGS William H on 31 Jan at Dover NH *MS* 17 Feb 1847

SCRUTON Patience m FOSS Dennis both of Strafford *MS* 10 Jan 1838

SCRUTON Patience of Farmington NH m SCRUTON Ezra A on 17 Jan at Rochester *MS* 27 Jan 1847

SCRUTON Sarah m ROBERTS Joshua both of Strafford in Rochester *MS* 28 Dec 1836

SEAL Margaret A of Westbrook ME on 13th ult m STARBIRD Russell *MFWBR* 8 Feb 1851

SEAMMAN Martha C m LEAVITT John B d in Saco ME *MS* 15 June 1832

SEARGANT Dorothy m REYNOLDS John both of Portsmouth on 29 ult *MS* 10 Oct 1838

SEARS Lovina m NICKERSON Watson on 17 Apr at Barrington Shelburne Co Nova Scotia Canada *MS* 9 Jul 1845

SEARS Mehitabel Mrs of Dover ME m PATTERSON Lewis of Sebec ME on 20 Apr *MS* 5 May 1847

SEATTLE Mary E m PATTERSON Peter at Newport RI, RUNNELS J Eld *MS* 4 Apr 1849

SEAVER Lucetta of Corinna ME m STEVENS Daniel of Bangor on 15 Nov 1849 *MS* 20 Feb 1850

SEAVER Martha m CLARK in Danville both of Kingston *MS* 4 May 1842

SEAVER Ruth E of Alton NH m SMITH John of Dover NH *MFWBR* 22 June 1850

SEAVEY Clara B of Greenland m PHILBRICK J Harvey Maj of Deerfield on 24 Oct 1847 *MS* 3 Nov 1847

SEAVEY Dorothy of Farmington m SEAVEY Ebenezer of Rochester on 2 Aug *MS* 16 Aug 1837

SEAVEY Eliza of Hallowell ME m MORRILL Alexander H on 29 June at Litchfield ME *MS* 13 Aug 1845

SEAVEY Eunice Miss of Milton formerly of Cornish m BAXTER Zimri on 27th ult *MS* 15 June 1832

SEAVEY Hannah N of Cornish ME on 7 Dec 1839 m SEAVEY Zephaniah H *MS* 18 Sep 1839

SEAVEY Nancy P of Manchester NH m JOSSELYN Isaac M on 29th
    MS 7 May 1845
SEAVEY Ruth E of Alton m SMITH John of Dover on 3 inst *MS* 12
    June 1850
SEAVEY Sally E of Cornish ME m EDGECOMB John on 22 Apr of
    Saco ME *MS* 8 June 1842
SEAVEY Sarah m NEAL Julius both of Hallowell *MS* 1 Feb 1837
SEAVEY Susan L of Manchester NH m BARTLETT Joseph M at
    Manchester NH *MS* 23 Jul 1845
SEAVEY Ursula A m BEAN Silas F both of Pittsfield NH *MS* 19 Oct
    1836
SEAVY Maria m MASON Garland of Raymond on 4th ult *MS* 28 Mar
    1833
SEAVY Ruth T m BUTTERFIELD Isaac both of Lowell MA *MS* 11 Mar
    1835
SEAWARD Martha F m FOLSOM John S both of New Market on 1
    Mar *MS* 7 Mar 1838
SEAWARD Olive Mrs of Kittery m GILSON Peter of Portland *MS* 14
    Dec 1836
SEAWARD Sarah of Kittery ME m MARDEN J Langdon of Rye NH on
    1 Oct at Kittery ME *MS* 12 Oct 1842
SEAWARDS Lydia of New Market NH m SEAWARDS Joel D of Straf-
    ford ME *MS* 13 Apr 1842
SECOR Rebecca m JONES Alonzo on 15 March at Mount Pleasant
    WT *MS* 14 Apr 1847
SEEKENS Lucy M of Swanville ME m KEITH Samuel S Jr of Brooks
    ME *MFWBR* 3 Feb 1849
SEHOBIE Susannah of Trenton NY on Feb 18 m THOMAS Allen of
    Nelson *MS* 11 Mar 1840
SEVERANCE Arsulia A m LEAVITT Ebenezer K both of Meredith *MS*
    2 Feb 1842
SEVERANCE Judith T of Andover NH d/o SEVERANCE James
    Deacon of Andover NH m SARGEANT Charles S on 30 Dec 1841
    at Andover NH *MS* 20 May 1842
SEVERANCE Mary Ann m HOYT George F *MS* 10 Aug 1836
SEVERANCE Nancy J of Andover NH d/o SEVERANCE James
    Deacon of Andover NH m CILLEY Andrew Jackson Capt on 24
    Mar 1842 at Andover NH *MS* 20 May 1842
SEVERENCE Dorothy of Lowell MA m ANDREWS Stephen on 30 Oct
    1842 at Lowell MA *MS* 28 Dec 1842
SEVERENS Jane of Pierpont m RICH Albert on 12 Jan 1843 *MS* 1
    Feb 1843
SEVERENS Ruth m STEVENS Daniel C both of Salsbury on 20 Apr
    MS 21 June 1848
SEVERNS Harriet N m TUCKER Andrew J both of Andover on 18 ult
    MS 3 Oct 1838

SEVERY Miranda m ADAMS James F both of Stephentown NY on 15 Mar *MS* 24 Apr 1844

SEWALL Hannah of Wilmot m COLLINS Benjamin H of New London on 1 Jan *MS* 28 Jan 1846

SEWALL Harriet M A m MORSE Nathaniel both of Bath on 2 inst *MS* 19 Feb 1851

SEXBY Phebe Ann of Sand Lake m KITTEREDGE Lucius S of New Lebanon on 1 inst *MS* 26 Dec 1849

SEXFON Emeline D of Bethany NY m EMERSON Gideon L of Erie Monroe Co MIC on 12 Nov 1848 *MS* 10 Jan 1849

SEXTON Mary A m HACKNEY Thomas both of Rochester Wis on 13 Apr 1848 *MS* 28 June 1848

SHACKFORD Abigail B of Barrington m HILL Levi G Dr of Gilmanton on 30 Jul *MS* 16 Aug 1837

SHACKFORD Hannah of Tamworth NH m MARSTON Jeremiah of Ossipee NH on 27 Oct at Tamworth NH *MS* 30 Dec 1846

SHACKLEY Eliza of Shapleigh m GOULD Luther of Great Falls NH on 27 Oct *MS* 9 Nov 1842

SHANNON Betsey of Hollis m SMITH Joseph on 8 Dec *MS* 15 Jan 1840

SHATTUCK Ann Jan m EVANS Zelotus both of Fowler NY *MS* 15 Dec 1847

SHATTUCK Martha A of Wiscasset m BAILEY Charles of Woolwich ME on 26 Dec 1850 *MS* 5 Feb 1851

SHAW Caroline of Woolwich ME m GETCHEL Silas on 28 Nov at Woolwich ME *MS* 8 Jan 1845

SHAW Cyntha m BENNETT Joseph *MS* 2 Jul 1834

SHAW Eliza m RACKLIEFF Alexander both of Woolwich ME on 19 ult *MS* 3 Jan 1838

SHAW Eliza of Holderness m KNOWLTON Chase of Danby *MS* 4 Dec 1839

SHAW Hannah W of Winthrop ME m FOGG Josiah of Readfield ME *MS* 10 Jul 1839

SHAW Jane Mrs m DREW Hezekiah both of Dover on 28 ult *MS* 4 Dec 1850

SHAW Julia A of Sebago m GAREY Sumner *MFWBR* 21 Jan 1849

SHAW Lovinia m BEAN Daniel *MS* 12 Apr 1843

SHAW Lucinda L of Dickinson NY m CRINKLAW Andrew of Lawrence on 24 Jan 1849 *MS* 14 Feb 1849

SHAW Mary m PHILBRICK George W of Hampton on 22d ult *MS* 11 Jan 1843

SHAW Mary A m BODGE Davis on 14 Nov of Pittston *MS* 8 Dec 1841

SHAW Mary Ann m SANBORN Benjamin on 12 Jan at Manchester *MS* 12 Feb 1845

SHAW Mary Ann m RICH Moses Dea both of Exeter ME *MS* 24 Apr 1834

SHAW Mary B of Dover m McDANIEL Noah *MS* 13 May 1835

SHAW Mary Mrs m McALISTER Levi both of Harrison on 21 Jan *MS* 19 Feb 1851

SHAW Mary of Gilmanton m DIMOND Isaac of Gilford on 28 Sept *MS* 11 Dec 1850

SHAW Octavia JP of Portland m STROUT Sewall C Esq of Bridgton *MFWBR* 1 Dec 1849

SHAW Ruth of Beckmantown Clinton Co NY m BOND Seth of Ellenburgh NY on 10 inst *MS* 27 Mar 1850

SHAW Sarah N m SCALES Joseph both of Canterbury on 14 Apr *MS* 29 Apr 1835

SHAW Sarah of New Market m KENNISTON Henry of Andover on 12 Apr 1848 *MS* 3 May 1848

SHAW Susan m SHAW John both of Holderness on 16 Feb *MS* 4 Mar 1840

SHEARMAN Mary m McDONGLE Charles on 29 Dec *MS* 1 Feb 1843

SHEHAN Martha m COLE Hiram H on 28 Nov 1841 at Saco ME *MS* 29 Dec 1841

SHELDON Caroline of Woburn m CARTER Alfred G of Woburn MA *MS* 22 Feb 1843

SHELDON Marilla of Jericho in Richmond VT on March 9 she was formerly of Calais VT m WHITCOMB Uzziel of Essex *MS* 30 Mar 1842

SHELLERD Sally Mrs m SCRUTON Benjamin both of Sheffield VT on 7 Dec 1848 *MS* 24 Jan 1849

SHEPARD Esther of Holderness NH m MERRILL Isaac on 14 June 1842 at Holderness NH *MS* 6 Jul 1842

SHEPHARD Eliza A of Portland m HANNAH Edward (*sic*) *MFWBR* 14 Dec 1850

SHEPHERD Henrietta D D m SKILLIN Hiram Eld of the Summer St FWB Church of Bangor ME on 2 Dec at Herman ME *MS* 7 Jan 1846

SHEPHERD Julia Ann of Stephentown NY m RECKORD Manning of Sand Lake on 21 Dec 1845 *MS* 8 Apr 1846

SHEPHERD Mary m BODLE William *MS* 18 Feb 1835

SHEPHERD Mary P of Holderness m CALLEY Jeremiah M on 4 Jan *MS* 26 June 1839

SHEPHERD Sally m SNELL Everett both of Lowell MA *MS* 11 Mar 1835

SHEPHERD Susan U of Stephentown m THOMAS Jeffrey on 17 June at Nassau NY *MS* 10 Sept 1845

SHERBURN Eliza of Wheelock VT m SMITH Gordon T Eld of Meredith NH 3d inst *MS* 19 Sept 1838

SHERBURN Junia L of Pittsfield m MASTON Oliver G on 8th Feb *MS* 18 Feb 1846

SHERBURN Roxylany of Wheelock VT m EAMES Nathan S of Albany

SHERBURN (Continued)
VT *MS* 1 Feb 1843

SHERBURNE Eleanor m WILLIAMS Nicholas S both of Gardiner *MS* 22 May 1844

SHERBURNE Lydia O of Barrington m CANNEY James of Nottingham on 17 inst *MS* 27 Sept 1848

SHERBURNE Marena C m CATE Wm in Portsmouth *MS* 20 Mar 1834

SHERBURNE Sarah Ann of Northwood NH m TEWKSBURY Daniel of New Market on 2d inst *MS* 30 May 1833

SHERBURNE Sophronia A d/o SHERBURNE S Eld m LOCKE Samuel A both of Barrington on 28 Apr *MS* 8 May 1850

SHERBURNE Zerriah m MANSON James at Barrington on Sun *MS* 14 June 1843

SHERMAN Amanda of Scriba NY m RHODES Schuyler on 30 Nov at N Scriba NY *MS* 24 Dec 1845

SHERMAN Catherine m MILLS Simon H both of Dedham *MS* 5 Apr 1837

SHERMAN Elizabeth A of Monson m LIBBEY Hanson on 27 May at Monson ME *MS* 16 June 1847

SHERMAN Elizabeth on 2 Feb 1843 at Boothbay m HUTCHINGS John of Whitefield *MS* 1 Mar 1843

SHERMAN Joanna m REED James A on 14 Nov at Edgecomb ME *MS* 8 Jan 1845

SHERMAN Latesia m GOULD David both of Yorkshire NY on 17 Sept *MS* 7 Oct 1846

SHERMAN Sarah m DINGLEY Samuel on 26 Aug at Charlestown MA *MS* 23 Oct 1844

SHIELDS Mary H on 29th ult at Portland m NOYCES William M *MFWBR* 16 Nov 1850

SHIPLEY Elizabeth of Lowell MA on 31 Jul m HATCH Joel on 31 Jul at Lowell MA *MS* 19 Oct 1842

SHIPMAN Maria of Bangor ME m HUMPHREY Charles on 20 Jan at Bangor ME *MS* 4 Mar 1846

SHIPP S Mrs m BROWN John both of Fowler NY on 18 Mar 1849 *MS* 4 Apr 1849

SHIRLEY Mary m GREER Daniel A both of Belmont ME *MS* 13 June 1849

SHONTS Miriam A m REYNOLDS Tent J on 7 Jul at Rock Creek Kane Co IL *MS* 27 Nov 1844

SHOREY Caroline m PEIRCE Daniel on 18th ult *MS* 25 Apr 1833

SHOREY Eliza T m APPLEBEE George both of Great Falls on 30th ult *MS* 6 Jan 1836

SHOREY Pheby of Limington ME m STILLINGS Benjamin of No Berwick ME *MS* 4 Apr 1833

SHORT Sarah A of Lowell MA on 19 June m LOCK Horace of Boston

SHORT (Continued)
   MA *MS* 23 Aug 1843

SHUMAN Lovina A m DAVIS Wm both of Waldoboro' ME on 16 inst
   MS 26 Apr 1848

SHURTLIFF Belinda m MORRELL Thomas both of Raymond ME on
   22 Mar *MS* 8 Apr 1846

SHUTE Mary Jane of Effingham NH m WENTWORTH Eri of Milton
   on 30 June *MS* 28 Aug 1844

SHUTE Nancy M m SHITE William P of Newburyport MA on 17 Dec
   1844 at Northwood *MS* 9 Apr 1845

SIBLEY Clerrinda J m HOYT James both of Hopkinton on 3d inst *MS*
   13 Apr 1836

SIBLEY Polly of Uxbridge MA m MOTT Miner of Lebanon CT on 28
   Feb *MS* 15 Mar 1843

SIDERS Lucy J of Bangor ME m SIMONDS Gideon Jr on 16 June of
   Bangor ME *MS* 30 June 1847

SILVER Cyrena of Bow NH on 5 Sept at Pittsfield m EMERY Mark F
   MS 16 Oct 1839

SIMANDS Cordelia P m CHASE Ira S both of Alexandria on 22 Mar
   1849 *MS* 11 Apr 1849

SIMMONS Eunice of Scituate m STAPLES Horton on 20 Nov at
   Scituate RI *MS* 14 Dec 1842

SIMMONS Matilda J of Wilmington MA m BREED Roger J of Woburn
   MA on 14th inst *MS* 24 Jul 1844

SIMMONS Sally Maria m EMMONS Henry both of Nassau on 6 May
   MS 4 Oct 1843

SIMOND Marilla of Lowell m PICKERING Leonard of Ann Arbor Mich
   on 14 Oct *MS* 7 Nov 1838

SIMONDS Adaline m THURSTON Joseph H both of Lowell *MS* 29
   Aug 1838

SIMONS Emily of Waterbury VT m HASELTON Gilson of Moretown
   on 17 March at Waterbury VT *MS* 16 Apr 1845

SIMONS Judith P of Clinton m WEYMOUTH Nathaniel F of Pittsfield
   MS 21 Jan 1846

SIMONS Kanly of Bristol m DOLLOFF Salome of Bridgewater on 1
   May *MS* 19 June 1850

SIMONS Mahaley of Pittsfield ME m TWICHELL Josiah Jr of Burnham *MS* 24 Feb 1836

SIMONS Nancy of Bristol m DOLLOFF Solom of Bridgewater on 1
   May *MS* 3 Jul 1850

SIMONTON Ann Maria of Hollis m MILLER R of Howland on at Hollis
   MS 4 Aug 1830

SIMPKINS Amy E of Berlin m CRANDALL Clark N on 7 Nov of Stephentown *MS* 18 Nov 1846

SIMPSON Clarissa of Sheffield VT m SWITZER Gilman on 1 Jan *MS*
   16 Jul 1845

SIMPSON Elizabeth C m CONANT Nathan D on 17 Oct 1849 *MS* 13 Feb 1850

SIMPSON Mary G m RUNDLET Nathaniel of Lee *MS* 4 May 1836

SIMPSON Sarah Nottingham m LANE Peter of Chester on 20th ult *MS* 5 Jul 1837 & on 20th in Nottingham *MS* 28 June 1837

SINCLAIR Elizabeth m PENNELL Thomas *MFWBR* 18 Aug 1849

SINCLAIR Martha of Gerry m WEAVER John of Arkwright NY on 5 May *MS* 19 June 1850

SINCLAIR Nancy m HAWKINS Benjamin T both of Center Harbor *MS* 28 Nov 1838

SINNOTT Martha of Saco m WOODMAN David *MFWBR* 17 Mar 1849

SKANE Hannah of Nashua m COLBY John P of Danville *MS* 6 May 1840

SKEELES Sarah m KEEFER Dean on 11 Nov at Greenfield Ohio *MS* 25 Feb 1846

SKIDMORE Hope m MUNSELL Daniel both of Perry Township Ohioon 28 Oct 1847 *MS* 9 Feb 1848

SKILLIN Jane D of Gray ME m SHILLIN Moses D on 14 Nov 1847 *MS* 26 Jan 1848

SKINNER Cordelia K m HOLT Luther of Exeter ME on 18 Jan 1847 at Garland ME *MS* 14 Apr 1847

SKINNER Phebe m HUNT Randall on 28 Oct 1847 *MS* 19 Jan 1848

SKOFFIELD Hannah M m HUNT James S both of Brunswick ME on 8 Nov *MS* 23 Jan 1850

SKOFFIELD Lucy A m LIBBY Solomon both of Brunswick *MS* 23 Jan 1850

SKOLFIELD Ruth m ALLEN Charles Capt both of Harpswell ME *MS* 7 Oct 1846

SLAYTON C Emeline formerly of Victor NY m CUTLER Dexter of Otiscon Mich on 4 June 1848 *MS* 12 Jul 1848

SLEEPER Cynthia P of Gilmanton m BEEDE William of Dalton NH on 21 Nov at Sanbornton *MS* 31 Dec 1845

SLEEPER Dorothy m RICHARDSON Charles both of So Reading on 3 June *MS* 5 Aug 1846

SLEEPER Jane m SIMPSON Samuel A both of Lowell on 11 inst *MS* 25 Jul 1838

SLEEPER Marinda S of Poplin m SHERMAN Charles H of Dover on 9th inst at Brentwood in Baptist meeting house *MS* 19 Oct 1842

SLOPER Hannah S m STILES Lewis on 29 Jan at Strafford NH *MS* 12 Mar 1845

SLOPER Margaret m FOSS Tobias both of Strafford NH on 13 inst *MS* 19 Apr 1848

SLY Philena of Hainburgh m WARNER Richard *MS* 19 Apr 1848

SMALL Almira m SMALL Charles B both of Raymond ME on 24 inst *MS* 8 Apr 1846

SMALL Deborah of Casco ME m WINSLOW Matthew F on 27 Dec at

SMALL (Continued)

Casco ME *MS* 10 Feb 1847

SMALL Isabella W of Westbrook ME m GRANT Albion K P *MFWBR* 10 Nov 1849

SMALL Jane E of Freeport ME m SMALL T F Capt of Lisbon ME *MFWBR* 24 Feb 1849

SMALL Jane M m DEARBORN Sewall both of Corinna on 1 Jan *MS* 9 May 1838

SMALL Jane M of Bowdoinham on 26th inst m CORLISS Joseph of Bath ME *MS* 17 May 1843

SMALL Lucy Ann of Lowell MA m HILL Joseph H on 25 May at Northwood *MS* 11 June 1845

SMALL Mary of Dover NH m BEAN Oran K of Danvers MA on 6 inst *MS* 14 June 1837

SMALL Mehitabel of Limerick m IRISH Dean of Limerick ME *MS* 7 Dec 1826

SMALL Nancy of Bath ME m HOW Orrin on 9 March 1843 at Bath ME *MS* 22 Mar 1843

SMALL Naoma m VARNON Ralph both of Bowdoinham ME *MS* 17 Oct 1838

SMALL Orrilla L m HOLMES George W both of Hopkinson? on 12 Mar *MS* 8 May 1844

SMALL Ruth Mrs of Bowdoinham ME m COLBATH Isaac on 13 Nov of Gardiner ME *MS* 17 Dec 1845

SMALL Sarah m CARLL James on at Lowell MA *MS* 5 Oct 1836

SMALL Sarah m WHITNEY Ebenezer *MS* 23 Jan 1834

SMALL Susan of Nottingham m LANGLEY Josiah on 30 Nov at Nottingham *MS* 20 Dec 1843

SMALLEN Mehitabel H of Lisbon ME m DOUGHTY Isaac L of Topsham ME on 29 Dec 1851 *MS* 5 Feb 1851

SMART Caroline on 5th inst m WIGGINS Jacob B of Newmarket *MS* 18 Jan 1843

SMART Clarissa A of Providence m BROWN Eben H of North Kingston on 26 Apr *MS* 5 May 1846

SMART Hannah m PARSON Elisha both of Belfast on 19 Dec 1839 *MS* 12 Feb 1840

SMART Hannah m BUNKER Joseph both of Durham on 19 inst *MS* 22 Nov 1848

SMART Harriet A of Parsonsfield ME m PEASE Edwin of Freedom NH on 13 Sept 1847 *MS* 1 Dec 1847

SMART Sarah A m DAVIS Alvah M on 24 Oct at Parsonsfield ME *MS* 30 Oct 1844

SMART Sarah m CROSBY Jonathan both of Swanville ME on 17 Oct 1847 *MS* 17 Nov 1847

SMART Seftonah of Freedom m ALLEY Leavitt of Eaton *MS* 3 May 1843

SMILEY Mary Ann of Sidney m KNOWLES Stephen S of Augusta
MFWBR 16 June 1849

SMILEY Rebecca of Waterville m BURGESS Weeks *MS* 15 Jan 1840

SMITH Abigail L of Hollis m TARBOX Joseph on 4 Dec at Hollis ME
MS 7 Jan 1846

SMITH Abigail of Hallowell ME m RICHARDS Jacob on 21 Dec *MS* 7
Jan 1846

SMITH Adaline of Salmon Falls m BENNET Levi W of Great Falls NH
on 21 Sept *MS* 25 Sept 1850

SMITH Adelia M m HOAG Horace of Rose Lewis Co on 24 Sept at
Norway Herkimer Co NY *MS* 29 Jan 1845

SMITH Almira of Lowell MA m BOYNTON John on 8 Mar *MS* 23 Aug
1843

SMITH Alvira of Lawrence m HEDDING Harley on 18 Oct at Lawrence NY *MS* 6 Dec 1843

SMITH Athalinda m FOSS Alvin W *MS* 29 Apr 1835

SMITH Augusta A m DUDLEY George W both of Augusta ME on 5
Dec 1847 *MS* 24 May 1848

SMITH Betsey m CHADBOURNE Wm both of Cornish on 23 Dec *MS*
17 Jan 1833

SMITH Betsey Ann m GLADEN Benj M both of Gilford 23 Dec 1847
MS 23 Feb 1848

SMITH Betsey m DOWLING James H both of Bradford NH on 19 Mar
MS 19 June 1850

SMITH Betsey of Lisbon ME? m VINING David of Durham ME? *MS*
12 Sept 1833

SMITH Betsey R of Pittsfield m NUTTER Enos George on 31 Oct at
Pittsfield *MS* 16 Nov 1842

SMITH Betsy of Hiram m GRAY Daniel *MFWBR* 4 Jan 1851

SMITH Caroline on 14 Jul of Lowell MA m HOWE Horace F of Dracutt MA *MS* 19 Oct 1842

SMITH Celinda at East Killingly on 7 inst m SIMMONS Holsey *MS* 22
Jan 1840

SMITH Clarisa Ann of Norway m AMES Edmund of Norway ME
MFWBR 13 Feb 1847

SMITH Clarissa m CARIL Nathaniel both of Waterboro ME on 4th
inst *MS* 14 Jan 1835

SMITH Cornelia A of Tunbridge m CARTER Jesse of Randolph VT on
8 Feb 1849 *MS* 28 Mar 1849

SMITH Delight of Northfield on 11 Apr 1843 m WILLIAMS Josiah W
of Northfield *MS* 14 June 1843

SMITH Dorcas m HUCKINS Jonathan B on at Meredith NH *MS* 24
Aug 1836

SMITH Eliza A of East Livermore ME m CORLISS David B of Alexandria on 23 Jan *MS* 12 Feb 1851

SMITH Eliza A of Saco m SEDGELY John of Saco ME *MFWBR* 30

SMITH (Continued)
Jan 1847

SMITH Eliza m BECK Thomas F both of Augusta *MS* 16 Nov 1836

SMITH Eliza Jane at Sandwich m WEBSTER Lyman W *MS* 27 Mar 1844

SMITH Eliza of New Hampton at Holderness m SMITH John P of Centre Harbor on 15th inst *MS* 29 May 1844

SMITH Elizabeth m TUCKER George on 2 inst *MS* 23 Feb 1848

SMITH Elsea R of Grafton m CURRIER Lorenzo of Enfield on 18 Oct 1849 *MS* 19 June 1850

SMITH Eunice W of Brownville m HOLYOKE Joseph of Brewer *MS* 15 Apr 1846

SMITH Everline M of Sidney ME m KEENE Josiah Jr Eld *MS* 30 Nov 1842

SMITH Hannah M m QIUMBY Hiram G both of Garland on 5 Sept *MS* 15 Sept 1847

SMITH Harriet of Charlestown MA m BLAISDELL Charles *MS* 24 May 1843

SMITH Harriet of Norway m ROOT Marshal of Russia on 21 ult *MS* 15 Jan 1851

SMITH Harriet P of Meredith Village m GIBSON Wm W of West Rumney on 3 Dec 1839 *MS* 12 Feb 1840

SMITH Irena of Raymond m BEDEE Taylor of Poplin *MS* 6 Feb 1839

SMITH Irene A m KENNEY John on 13 Oct 1843 of Sutton *MS* 17 Apr 1844

SMITH Jane of Webster m WARE Ezekiel of Gardiner on 25 Aug 1847 *MS* 17 Nov 1847 & *MS* 8 Sept 1847

SMITH Jane P m PINKHAM Oshea of Exeter NH on at Biddeford *MS* 15 June 1832

SMITH John of Gloucester m BOSS Henry D of Scituate *MS* 18 Dec 1844

SMITH Laura Ann of New Hampton m MITCHELL Jonathan J of Holderness on 15 Dec *MS* 11 Jan 1843

SMITH Lorenda of Hallowell ME m BUBIER Benjamin of Lewiston ME on 28 Aug 1843 *MS* 27 Sept 1843

SMITH Louisa m CARPENTER Olney C on 31 Jan 1843 of Sutton MA *MS* 15 Feb 1843

SMITH Louisa B m NOYES John S both of Deerfield NH on Christmas Eve *MS* 24 Jan 1849

SMITH Louisa of Cumberland RI m COLE Joseph of Pawtucket on 21 Sept at East Killingly CT *MS* 10 Oct 1844

SMITH Lovantia m KNOX Hiram both of Mercer Co IL on 4 Jul *MS* 11 Sept 1850

SMITH Lucy m ROWELL John both of Barnston on 19 Oct *MS* 1 May 1844

SMITH Lucy E m PLUMMER William both of Groton on 23 Apr

SMITH (Continued)
MS 5 May 1846

SMITH Lydia m MOSHER Mark of Gorham *MFWBR* 21 Jan 1849

SMITH Lydia Ann of Sandbornton m NOBLE Frederick A on 24th at Bradford NH "N.B. *The Christian Reflector* will please copy this." *MS* 17 Mar 1847

SMITH Lydia at Holderness m RANDALL Haven of New Hampton *MS* 4 Dec 1839

SMITH Lydia m BRAGDON Owen both of Kennebunk ME on 21 Nov *MS* 29 Dec 1847

SMITH Lydia F of Lowell MA m CURTIS Robert G on 11 Dec *MS* 24 Dec 1845

SMITH Lydia M m JUNKINS Joseph both of Hollis *MFWBR* 19 Oct 1850

SMITH Lydia M of New Market m SMITH Jesse W of Dutton ME on 20 ult *MS* 30 Dec 1835

SMITH Lydia Mrs of New Hampton m DAVIS Daniel of Centre Harbor on 21 May 1848 *MS* 31 May 1848

SMITH Lydia of Biddeford ME m LITTLEFIELD Ezekiel on 3 Apr at Kennebunkport ME *MS* 18 May 1842

SMITH Lydia W of Topsham m ESTES ISRAEL H of Lisbon ME on 5 Sept 1850 *MS* 8 Jan 1851

SMITH Margaret of Braintree MA m NEWCOMB Otis on 3 Nov 1842 at Otisfield ME *MS* 16 Nov 1842

SMITH Maria J m WHITEHOUSE Andrew J both of Great Falls NH on 12 Nov 1848 *MS* 29 Nov 1848

SMITH Marinda of Middlebury NY m GARDENER John on 21 Jul of Elba NY *MS* 10 Aug 1842

SMITH Martha of Biddeford ME m RUSSELL Isreal C *MFWBR* 14 Apr 1849

SMITH Martha of Smithfield RI m FRANKLIN John of Cranston RI on 28th inst *MS* 3 Sept 1834

SMITH Mary A of Sandwich NH m HODGE Benjamin B on 26 Nov of Sandwich *MS* 9 Dec 1846

SMITH Mary Ann m WHITE Enoch both of Windham ME on 11th inst *MS* 21 Jan 1835

SMITH Mary Ann of Buxton ME m DUNMELL Benjamin 2d on 17 Nov at Buxton ME *MS* 21 Dec 1842

SMITH Mary Ann of Lowell MA m TURNER William H *MS* 19 June 1839

SMITH Mary Ann P d/o SMITH John P Esq of Gilford/ granddau of Hon Daniel SMITH m GOVE Richard watchmaker and Jeweller of Meredith Bridge on 27 inst in morning *MS* 5 Sept 1838 & m GOVE Richard on 27 *MS* 12 Sept 1838

SMITH Mary m WEBBER William both of Holderness *MS* 28 June 1837

SMITH Mary C m HOWLAND Charles W both of Manchester on 26 Apr *MS* 5 May 1846

SMITH Mary C of Lisbon ME m LIBBY David Eld of Lewiston ME on 12 inst *MS* 3 May 1848

SMITH Mary C of Portland ME m CHANDLER Christopher on 12th inst at Portland ME *MS* 19 June 1844

SMITH Mary D m BROOKS Joshua on 9 Dec at Wakefield *MS* 24 Dec 1845

SMITH Mary E d/o SMITH Joseph Esq of Dover NH m THOMAS William R merchant of Cincinnati Ohio *MS* 19 Dec 1833

SMITH Mary E m SANBORN Reuben both of Biddeford ME on 1 Jul 1848 *MS* 26 Jul 1848

SMITH Mary E of Meredith m FLANDERS Luther G of New Hampton on 21 Nov 1848 *MS* 9 May 1849

SMITH Mary E of Meredith Village m HAM Thomas of Manchester on 4th inst at Meredith Bridge *MS* 21 Aug 1844

SMITH Mary G of Portland ME m BARNARD Edward S of Nantucket *MFWBR* 2 Oct 1847

SMITH Mary J of Great Falls NH m JENNESS Jonathan on 4 Oct of Meredith NH *MS* 24 Dec 1845

SMITH Mary Mooney d/o SMITH Obadiah Esq of Holderness NH m CALLEY David of Plymouth NH on 23 Mar 1848 *MS* 12 Apr 1848

SMITH Mary Mrs of Kennebunkport m HILL Ichabod of Saco ME on 10 May *MS* 3 June 1846

SMITH Mary of Barrington m SMITH Ebenezer Jr of Strafford NH *MS* 24 Apr 1834

SMITH Mary S of Portland ME m JERRIES William H on 9th inst at Portland ME *MS* 22 Mar 1843

SMITH Mehitable of Durham at New Market NH m HAM Oliver P of Durham on 16 Mar *MS* 29 Mar 1843

SMITH Mel R m NEAL Oliver *MFWBR* 24 Feb 1849

SMITH Mercy A m CLUM Edward R both of Walworth NY on 8 Jan *MS* 5 Mar 1851

SMITH Minerva A of Foster RI m CHASE Albert H on 25 Aug at Thompson CT *MS* 11 Sept 1844

SMITH Naamah m NICKERSON John E on 1 May at Barrington Shelburne Co Nova Scotia Canada *MS* 9 Jul 1845

SMITH Nancy m HOWEL Uriah both of Yorkshire on Feb 18 1848 *MS* 10 May 1848

SMITH Nancy of Newfield m CHALLIES David of Newfield *MS* 19 Nov 1828

SMITH Nancy of Waterboro m FERGUSON Daniel of Shapleigh ME on 13th inst *MS* 21 Aug 1829

SMITH Patience m SMITH Stephen both of Strafford'on 2 Mar *MS* 13 Mar 1834

SMITH Pauline of Biddeford ME m QUICK John on 22 Jan 1843 at

SMITH (Continued)
Biddeford *MS* 1 Mar 1843

SMITH Phena of Mansfield N Y m BUFFINTON Jeremiah of New Albion *MS* 14 Nov 1838

SMITH Philena of Sheridan m TANNER Geo W W of Ellington *MS* 8 Aug 1838

SMITH Polly of Shapleigh m SANBORN Joseph of Waterboro ME *MS* 5 Jan 1831

SMITH Priscilla m JONES George W on 12 Oct of Niles Mich *MS* 26 Nov 1845

SMITH Rhoda of Atkinson m CROCKER Joel of Corinth on 14 Nov *MS* 27 Dec 1837

SMITH Sabrina H of Lowell MA m NASON Daniel L on 11 Sept at Lowell MA *MS* 19 Oct 1842

SMITH Sarah m HOLBROOK Abram on 20th inst at Walworth NY *MS* 21 Jul 1847

SMITH Sarah A m PATTEN David P of Kennebunkport ME *MFWBR* 9 Dec 1848

SMITH Sarah A of Newfield m PERKINS James of Limerick ME *MFWBR* 18 Dec 1847

SMITH Sarah Ann m BORDMAN Joseph merchant at Exeter *MS* 26 Dec 1833

SMITH Sarah Ann m GOWEN Samuel Jr on 27 Oct 1841 at Sanford ME *MS* 15 Dec 1841

SMITH Sarah Ann of Meredith NH m COLCORD Steven of Candia on 8th inst *MS* 31 Jan 1833

SMITH Sarah I of Malden MA m SMITH Jesse D of Hollis ME on 22 June *MS* 18 Jul 1849

SMITH Sarah of Lawrenceville m WOOD Silas of Hopkinton on 29 Jul *MS* 15 Aug 1849

SMITH Sarah of Otsego (NY?) m SUITS John P of Mindon (NY?)on 4 Jan 1849 *MS* 7 Feb 1849

SMITH Sarah S of Candia on 2 Oct m FRENCH Alfred *MS* 6 Nov 1839

SMITH Sarah T of New Hampton m WARD Josiah on 22 May 1842 at Meredith NH *MS* 15 June 1842

SMITH Susan d/o SMITH John Esq m BLAISDELL Samuel S at Meredith NH *MS* 1 Feb 1843

SMITH Susan A of Sandwich m HACKETT Albert F of Sandwich NH *MS* 23 Jul 1845

SMITH Susan B at Mancester NH m HOOK Abraham of Chester NH on 2 Aug *MS* 9 Aug 1843

SMITH Susan B of Boston m BERRY William M on 27 Oct at Boston MA *MS* 20 Nov 1844

SMITH Susan m PHILLIPS Alexander Capt both of Barrington NS on 28 Apr *MS* 10 June 1846

SMITH Susan m TEBBETS John both of Belgrade ME on 10 inst *MS* 23 Dec 1835

SMITH Susan P m DOLLOFF Lorenzo D both of Meredith on 16 Feb 1848 *MS* 1 Mar 1848

SMITH Urana F m BERRY Morrill P both of Roxbury on 7 inst *MS* 27 Mar 1850

SMYTH Amy of Brunswick ME m WARD Josiah *MFWBR* 5 Apr 1851

SNELL Almaria C of Dedham MA m FERRIS William on 21 Jan of Portland ME *MS* 17 Feb 1847

SNELL Julia D m THOMAS Sandrus H on 15 Jul at Roxbury MA *MS* 28 Aug 1844

SNELL Nancy D m FERREN George W *MS* 9 Feb 1848

SNELL Sally B m BLAISDELL Nicholas C both of Eaton on 22 Sept at Dover NH *MS* 3 Oct 1833

SNOW Anna Mrs of Benton m JEFFERS James of Haverhill on 26 Dec *MS* 22 Jan 1845

SNOW Christiana of Kilmarnock ME m MAHEW Wm of Foxcroft ME on 12 ult *MS* 12 Nov 1834

SNOW Emily m DUNHAM Daniel J of Brunswick ME on 31 Dec *MS* 13 Jan 1847

SNOW Helen P of Atkinson ME m FORD Caleb J of Sebec ME on 28 Jan at Atkinson ME *MS* 24 Mar 1847

SNOW Mary m FORD Robert on at Landaff NH *MS* 16 Jul 1828

SNOW Mary m WALKER Almore both of Lowell on 5 inst *MS* 14 June 1837

SNOW Mary E of Brunswick ME m DOWNE Emerson of Portland ME *MS* 2 Aug 1848

SNOW Priscilla Miss of Brunswick m BRIDGES Robert J of Topsham on 30th ult *MS* 13 June 1833

SNOW Sarah of Brunswick m WILSON Horace of Bath *MS* 2 Jan 1839

SNOW Sarah R m WILSON William L on 17th inst at Portland ME *MS* 27 Nov 1844 & *MS* 29 Jan 1845

SOALE Betsey of Guilford m WESTON Moses of Foxcroft ME *MS* 1 Feb 1837

SOANS Polly of Tecumsch Lenawee Co Mich on 2 June m NIXON James *MS* 18 Sep 1839

SOAPER Louisa m FREEMAN Wilson on 1 Jan at Pierpont NY *MS* 25 Feb 1846

SOMER Nancy H m BRYANT Samuel J both of Manchester on 4 Jul *MS* 11 Jul 1849

SOMES Susan C m ESTES George both of Dover on 9 inst *MS* 13 Nov 1850

SOPER Abigail M of New Sharon m McLANE Charles on 17 June at New Sharon *MS* 9 Jul 1845

SOPER Martha Jane of Livermore ME m DAVIS Daniel *MFWBR* 21

SOPER (Continued)
MFWBR 21 Jan 1849

SOUINS Judith of Newbury m DUNBAR Ira of Bangor ME *MS* 20 Dec 1848

SOUL Wealthy of Waterville ME m AVERY Samuel at Waterville ME *MS* 25 Nov 1846

SOULE Emily m WOOD George W both of Waterville *MS* 15 Jan 1840

SOULE Harriet on 27th ult m DYER C W *MFWBR* 17 Mar 1849

SOULE Martha J m GILES George J both of Woolwich ME on 6 May 1849 *MS* 11 Jul 1849

SOULE Pamelia of Lewiston ME m MERRILL David W of New Gloucester ME *MS* 27 Nov 1844

SOULE Sarah S of Freeport ME m LAMB Merrick of Greene ME on 3 Sept 1848 *MS* 1 Nov 1848

SOUTHARD Emeline M of Richmond m GAUBERT John H on 3 Oct at Bowdoinham ME *MS* 19 Oct 1842

SOUTHARD Frances L of Richmond ME m ALEXANDER Isaac at Bowdoinham ME *MS* 6 Sept 1843

SOUTHWELL Mary A of Newburyport MA m ALLEN George E of Portland *MFWBR* 21 Dec 1850

SOUTHWICK Elizabeth W on 2d inst m ALDRICH Robert *MS* 16 Jan 1839

SOUTHWICK Mary J A of Chester m WOOD Josiah Jr of Auburn on 17 Sept 1848 *MS* 27 Sept 1848

SOUTHWORTH E M of Burlington NY m WALDO L of Canisteo NY on 5 Mar *MS* 2 Apr 1851

SOWERSBY Eliza F of Dover NH m GARLAND Jacob P on 3 June *MS* 11 June 1845

SPARKS Alice of Bowdoinham ME on 30 March m TRUFANT John of Lisbon (ME) *MS* 19 Apr 1843

SPARKS Rachel W of Bowdoinham ME m WILSON Robert of Richmond on 3 Jul at Bowdoinham ME *MS* 20 June 1842

SPAULDING Caroline A m YEATON Philip 2d both of Belgrade ME on 1 Jan *MS* 9 Jan 1850

SPAULDING Eliza T of Frankfort ME m GODLEY Alphonso S of Saco ME *MFWBR* 13 Jul 1850

SPAULDING Martha N Miss female preacher m THURSTON Nathaniel Eld of Parsonsfield *MS* 23 June 1830

SPAULDING Mary E m BEEDE Samuel *MS* 25 Apr 1833 & on 25th ult in Dover NH *MS* 8 June 1832

SPAULDING Sarah m MATTENLY John Jr both of Sutton VT on 28 Dec 1837 *MS* 14 Feb 1838

SPEAR Evalina m ADAMS Andrew both of Farmersville NY on 2 Sept *MS* 30 Sept 1846

SPEAR Margaret m NEWELL Henry C both of Bowdoinham ME on 21 Dec 1847 *MS* 29 Dec 1847

SPEAR Mary E m DINGLEY Levi both of Gardiner ME *MS* 22 May 1844

SPEAR Olevia N of East Thomaston m FLINT Nathaniel C *MFWBR* 25 May 1850

SPEARS Elizabeth of Weare NH m HUSE Ebenezer ae 70y on 18th inst *MS* 25 Apr 1833

SPEARS Emily W of Waterville m GRANT Joseph of Sindey ME *MS* 30 Nov 1842

SPEARS Sarah Mrs of Gardiner m AUSTIN Oliver O on 25 Dec 1842 at West Gardiner ME *MS* 18 Jan 1843

SPENCER Charlotte C of Corinth VT m SANBORN J Mr *MS* 17 Feb 1847

SPENCER Harriet of Adams Jefferson Co NY m BROWNELL Corland on 18 Feb at Clayton *MS* 10 Mar 1847

SPENCER Mary of Roxbury on 7th inst m HATCH Franklin *MS* 15 May 1839

SPERLIN Esther m ODIORNE Charles W at Dover NH *MS* 15 Oct 1845

SPERLIN Mary Jane of Dover m STANLEY Benjamin P of So Berwick ME on Sunday last *MS* 11 Jul 1849

SPERRY Grace m WALRATH Sylvester on 30 Dec 1847 *MS* 23 Feb 1848

SPILLER Joanna D m CROSS James M both of Bridgewater on 11 Jan 1849 *MS* 31 Jan 1849

SPINNEY Eveline M m THAYER John of Sidney *MFWBR* 29 Mar 1851

SPINNEY Margaret J of Boothbay m DAY Arad of Damariscotta ME on 16 Feb *MS* 26 Mar 1851

SPOFFORD Mary m CURRIER Ezra at Danville of Poplin *MS* 21 Dec 1842

SPOONER Anniss W m PRIEST Daniel on 22 Feb 1844 of Franconia NH *MS* 13 Mar 1844

SPOONER Lucy Jane of Manchester m RUSSELL Arthur of Lawrence MA on 16 Jan 1848 *MS* 2 Feb 1848

SPRAGUE Anna formerly of Hartford VT m SMITH Amasa of Howard Mich on 22 ult *MS* 28 June 1837

SPRAGUE Clarissa m ASH William B at Manchester on 22 Feb *MS* 4 Mar 1846

SPRAGUE Eleanor L of Chelsea VT m FITZ Andrew H of Brunswick on 9 Feb *MS* 22 Apr 1846

SPRAGUE Elvira m WHEELER Hiram both of Barnston on 31 Dec *MS* 15 Apr 1840

SPRAGUE Fanny m STEARNS Daniel both of Hamburgh NY *MS* 30 Jul 1834

SPRAGUE Lovina m SWEET Henry both of Huntington on 20 Sept *MS* 6 Nov 1850

SPRAGUE Mary Ann m WHITE George both of Scituate RI on 26 Aug

SPRAGUE (Continued)
MS 9 Sept 1846

SPRILLER Abigail S of Passadumkeag ME m TAYLOR A Eld of Burlington ME on 2 Dec *MS* 29 Dec 1847

SPRING Harriet W of Grafton m REDDING Isaac H on 23 Sept at Grafton MA *MS* 18 Oct 1843

SPRINGER Clarinda of Alexandria m ROBERTS John H on 19 Sept at Alexander *MS* 18 Dec 1844

SPRINGER Philena of Litchfield on 9 Jul m GOODWIN Nehemiah *MS* 19 Jul 1843

SPRINGFIELD Drusilla m HODSDON William on Apr 14 at Rochester *MS* 24 Apr 1844

SPURLIN Mary J m STANLEY Benjamin P of South Berwick ME *MFWBR* 28 Jul 1849

STACKHOUSE Susanna L at Philadelphia on 6th street d/o STACKHOUSE Powell m MORRILL Daniel J of New York on 11th inst at Friends Meeting house *MS* 19 Feb 1845

STACKPOLE Abigail of Dover NH m MOULTON Jeremiah of York ME *MS* 29 Apr 1835

STACKPOLE Eliza Ann m JOHNSON Gowen W on 4th inst at Dover NH *MS* 15 Oct 1845

STACKPOLE Elizabeth m BURHAM Joseph both of Lowell *MS* 8 Jan 1840

STACKPOLE Eunice m PRAY Humphrey of Rolinsford NH *MFWBR* 28 Dec 1850

STACKPOLE Helen M of Thomaston ME m ROBINSON George I *MFWBR* 22 June 1850

STACKPOLE Sabra m SMART Charles both of Parsonsfield ME on 12 May *MS* 23 May 1849

STACY Mary m GOODRICH John R both of Berwick ME on 10 Oct 1847 *MS* 3 Nov 1847

STACY Mary J m MESSER John A on 8 Feb at Lowell MA *MS* 18 Feb 1846

STACY Sally m KENISTON Edwin of South Berwick on 5th inst *MS* 29 May 1844

STACY Susan m GRANT Joshua *MFWBR* 24 Feb 1849 & both of Berwick ME on 28 Jan 1849 *MS* 7 Feb 1849

STAFFORD Betsey m PALMER Jacob both of Danby on 30 ult *MS* 7 Nov 1838

STAMBRO Mary Ann m PERKINS Orley on at Concord NY *MS* 6 Sept 1836

STANFORD Mary m LITCHFIELD Samuel both of Lewiston ME *MS* 26 Sept 1833

STANLEY Alvira C m WITHAM William of Smithfield ME *MS* 25 Dec 1844

STANLEY Clarissa m SHACKLEY Isaiah both of Shapleigh on 11 Jan

STANLEY (Continued)
MS 24 Jan 1838

STANLEY Eliza R m MAYALL Joseph both of Roxbury MA *MS* 3 Apr 1850

STANLEY Julia of Shapleigh m HOOPER Lyman on 18 Jan *MS* 28 Jan 1846

STANLEY Lovia Jane on 28 Nov m HOOPER Robinson of Shapleigh ME *MS* 11 Dec 1839

STANLEY Mehtiabel m BOYNTON Jacob both of Brownfield ME on 8 Oct 1848 *MS* 15 Nov 1848

STANLEY Sally M of Shapleigh m WELCH Isaiah of Sanford ME on 25 Dec *MS* 8 Jan 1840

STANLEY Sarah A m WEBSTER Benjamin Jr on 16 May 1844 at Haverhill NH *MS* 24 Jul 1844 (*sic*) should be *MS* 31 Jul 1844

STANLEY Susan S of Conway NH m WARD John C Eld of Monroe ME on 19 Feb *MS* 24 Apr 1850 & *MFWBR* 4 May 1850

STANTON Elizabeth M of Strafford m LEIGTHON Wm A of Brighton MA on 16 Aug 1848 *MS* 18 Oct 1848

STANTON Lydia B Sister of Lebanon m WHITE John C Brother of Roxbury MA on 15 Mar *MS* 15 Apr 1846

STANTON Sarah A m DORMAN John of Newfield ME on 15 Oct at Wakefield *MS* 25 Nov 1846

STANWOOD Agness R m MELCHER Joseph Capt both of Brunswick ME on 15 inst *MS* 30 Aug 1837

STAPLES Betsey m LIBBY Furber both of Monmouth ME *MS* 29 Dec 1847

STAPLES Betsey of North Berwick ME m KNOW James on 29 Jan of Lebanon ME *MS* 11 Feb 1846

STAPLES Elizabeth D of Limington ME m MESERVE George W on 5 Oct *MS* 7 Feb 1844

STAPLES Harriet N of Limington m TOWNS Francis W of Newfield on 21 Nov *MS* 15 Jan 1840

STAPLES Harriet N of N Berwick ME m HURD John W on 14 Jan 1848 *MS* 7 Feb 1849

STAPLES Harriet of Biddeford ME Jul 4 m SMALL Rufus of Limington ME *MS* 10 Jul 1839

STAPLES Huldah m RUNNELS John Eld on 15 Dec at North Berwick ME *MS* 28 Dec 1842

STAPLES Louisa m STAPLES Isaac both of Biddeford ME on 14 Jan 1849 *MS* 24 Jan 1849 & *MFWBR* 21 Jan 1849

STAPLES Lucy of Waterborough m STRAW Gideon Jr of Newfield ME on Thurs last *MS* 17 Jan 1828

STAPLES Maria of Newfield m SMITH SIMON of Effingham NH *MS* 1 Oct 1834

STAPLES Mary m WAKEFIELD Edward B both of Biddeford ME on 24 Mar *MS* 3 June 1846

STAPLES Miriam m TARBOX Moses on 16 Oct 1842 at Biddeford ME
MS 1 Mar 1843
STAPLES Nancy H m PENNY Samuel S both of Boston on 9 Oct MS
17 Oct 1849
STAPLES Olive Ann m SEAVEY Warren on 24th at Dover NH MS 27
Jan 1847
STAPLES Sarah S m BOON William on 22 Oct at the house of Col E
STAPLES in Poolville NY MS 11 Nov 1846
STAPLES Susan A m BURNHAM Alexander both of Biddeford on M
19 Sept MS 27 Oct 1847
STAR Sarah Mrs m WATSON Stephen B both of Richmond RI on 5
Mar 1850 MS 20 Mar 1850
STARBIRD Eunice of Greene m CUMMINS James on 10 Jul at
Greene ME MS 20 June 1842
STARBIRD Frances of Poland ME at Poland ME m AUSTIN Thomas
W of Danville ME on 12 Mar 1843 MS 5 Apr 1843
STARBIRD Joan W of Peru m HODGDON Josiah S at Peru ME MS
12 May 1847
STARBORD M S Mrs m KACEY Gordon C on 9 Dec 1849 MS 27 Feb
1850
STARRETT Mary Ann of China ME m CALDER Samuel of Vassalbor-
ough ME on 11 Jul MS 29 Sept 1847
STATON Hannah M of Ossipee NH m KEY William H on 23 Oct of
Ossipee NH MS 7 Dec 1842
STAUNTON Rebecca of Meredith NH m HALL Francis on 27th of
Sandwich NH MS 24 Mar 1847
STEARNS Elizabeth S Mrs of Lowell m COLE Mooers Eld of Salem on
11 inst MS 19 Mar 1851
STEARNS Grace of Reading m DAVIS Almon on 29 June at Reading
MS 6 Aug 1845
STEARNS Hannah M m INGALS Jonathan both of Goshen on 28 Feb
1850 MS 27 Mar 1850
STEARNS Lydia of Hooksett m GASS Joseph T on 22d Jul at Man-
chester NH MS 23 Jul 1845
STEARNS Mary H of Lovell m HUTCHINS William MFWBR 27 Apr
1850
STEARNS Mary J of Deerfield NH m YEATON William of Epsom on
19 Mar MS 15 Apr 1846
STEARNS Mehitable K m GILKEY Samuel H on 27 Dec of Saco ME
MS 6 Apr 1847
STEARNS Permelia m EMERY Simeon both of Hatley LC MS 22 Mar
1837
STEARNS Sarah A of Deerfield m PHILBRICK David M of Epsom NH
on 28 Nov MS 18 Dec 1850
STEARNS Sarah F of Lovell m FLINT Charles W of Sweden ME on 3
Feb 1848 MS 9 Feb 1848

STEARNS Susan C m COX Alfred both of New Market NH on 11 Oct *MS* 14 Oct 1846

STEBBENS Lucinda m COFFMAN Nicholas on 28 Feb 1850 *MS* 10 Apr 1850

STEEL Lucretia m WARD David on 10 May *MS* 23 Sept 1846

STEEL Sarah of Freedom NY m PEAVEY James of Sardinia NY on 26 Apr *MS* 13 May 1846

STEELE Eliza m NORTON B Mr on 4 March at Boston Erie Co NY *MS* 24 Mar 1847

STEELE Emily E of Roxbury m CLAFLIN Jehiel of Brookfield on 3 inst *MS* 20 Sept 1837

STEELE Esther of Boston NY m HOLLISTER Michael of Leon Cattaraugus Co NY *MS* 24 Mar 1847

STEMPSON Amanda M m REED Merril N both of Manchester on 4 June *MS* 19 June 1850

STEPHEN Abigail of Lynn MA m BARTON William on 30 Jul at Lynn MA *MS* 14 Aug 1844

STEPHEN Matilda of Gilmanton m STEPHEN James S of Gilford *MS* 1 May 1844

STEPHENS Hannah O of Lowell MA m BARTLETT Abijah on 17 Aug at Lowell MA *MS* 19 Oct 1842

STEPHENS Lydia P d/o STEPHENS James of Waterboro ME m HILL Stephen of Brighton MA *MFWBR* 18 Dec 1847

STERLING Sarah of Ossipee m TRIPP George of Parsonsfield on 9 Jul *MS* 19 Jul 1837

STETSON Sarah M of Dorchester MA m MOODY Henry H of Roxbury MA on 12th *MS* 7 May 1845

STEVENS Abigail m NOWELL Daniel D both of Somersworth on 26th *MS* 5 Dec 1833

STEVENS Abigail O on the 27th m GROSS Gilbert at Hallowell ME *MS* 7 Jan 1846

STEVENS Abigail on 23d ult at Lowell m HURD Jeremiah E *MS* 6 Feb 1839

STEVENS Amanda B of Bath m DODGE Benjamin Jr of Monroe on at Monroe *MS* 9 May 1833

STEVENS Angeline O m GOULD Daniel Jr *MFWBR* 8 June 1850

STEVENS Betsey m CRAM Benjamin both of Raymond on at Deerfield NH *MS* 31 Oct 1833

STEVENS Betsey H of Farmington NH m GOODWIN James B on 26 June at Farmington NH *MS* 31 Aug 1842

STEVENS Caroline M of Danbury m PALMER Ransom of Richmond on 14 Nov *MS* 18 Dec 1850

STEVENS Clarissa on 16th inst at Stratham m GADSBY William of Haverhill MA *MS* 10 May 1843

STEVENS Comfort m BROWN Nathan both of Great Falls village on 12 inst *MS* 18 Mar 1835

STEVENS Diana m LEAKE Isaac E both of Janesville Wis on 16 Oct *MS* 11 Dec 1850

STEVENS Elcy J of South Berwick ME m BRACKETT Lorenzo on 17th inst at FWB meeting house at South Berwick ME *MS* 27 Jan 1847

STEVENS Eleanor m CHASE George W on 5 Oct at Manchester NH *MS* 15 Oct 1845

STEVENS Elizabeth m BENNET Alden B on at Lowell MA *MS* 21 Dec 1836

STEVENS Elizabeth m JENKINS Austin on 26 Nov *MS* 9 Dec 1846

STEVENS Elizabeth of Alton m BUNKER Levi on 22d at Alton *MS* 12 Feb 1845

STEVENS Emeline C of Bridgton ME m TRUMBALL William P on 10 Feb *MS* 7 May 1845

STEVENS Eunice B of Limington ME m FOGG Ezekiel T of Montville ME on 22 Dec *MS* 3 Jan 1844

STEVENS Frances E m THOMPSON A Whitney *MFWBR* 4 Aug 1849

STEVENS G Sally of Bradford NH m ROBERTSON Alexander of Starksborough VT on 8 Aug *MS* 4 Sept 1850

STEVENS Hannah J of Somersworth m REMICK John of Tamworth NH on 3 Aug *MS* 11 Sept 1850

STEVENS Jemina of Dixmont ME m CURTIS David P of Monroe on 28 Sept 1847 *MS* 17 Nov 1847

STEVENS Julia Ann of Georgetown m STARLING Josiah of Monhegan PLT on 4 Nov *MS* 11 Dec 1850

STEVENS Lucy of Green ME m JENNINGS Isaac of Leeds ME on 13th inst *MS* 30 June 1830

STEVENS Martha m BROWN Benjamin F on 6 Dec at Monhegan PLT ME *MS* 30 Dec 1846

STEVENS Martha A m YOUNG Samuel both of Middleton on 3 Nov 1850 *MS* 8 Jan 1851

STEVENS Mary m ROWE Benj *MS* 2 Jan 1839

STEVENS Mary Adeline on 16th ult m WEEKS Stephen Jr *MS* 16 Jan 1839

STEVENS Mary Ann m WIGGIN Joseph F both of Stratham on 13 ult *MS* 10 Oct 1838

STEVENS Mary Jane m SERGEANT Samuel at Raymond *MS* 1 June 1842

STEVENS Mary of Kennebunk ME m LITTLEFIELD William H Eld on 20 Mar at Kennebunk ME *MS* 26 Mar 1845

STEVENS Mary W of Stratham m FLANDERS Laugdon S of Concord on 21 Nov *MS* 8 Jan 1845

STEVENS Matilda T m COTTON Arial C both of Troy on 5 Dec *MS* 25 Dec 1850

STEVENS Nancy m WOODFORD Wm on Thurs last *MS* 3 May 1827

STEVENS Nancy Miss m SANBORN Herny Jr on at Epping *MS* 6 Feb

STEVENS (Continued)
1834

STEVENS Rebecca A m REMICK George W on 24 Dec of Great Falls NH *MS* 6 Jan 1847

STEVENS Ruth S of Barnston m EVANS Edward on 23 May *MS* 13 Sept 1843

STEVENS Sarah m ELLIS E C both of S on 25 Feb *MS* 1 May 1844

STEVENS Susan A m CLOUGH Jonathan S both of Alton NH *MS* 20 Dec 1848

STEVENS Susan Mrs of Brunswick ME m GATCHELL Abiezer on 1 Sept *MS* 11 Sept 1850

STEVENS Susan of Green ME m FROST O P of Leeds ME on 24 Oct 1847 *MS* 10 Nov 1847

STEVENS Thankful H m BICKFORD Abner S *MFWBR* 9 Mar 1850

STEVENSON Sophia of Wolfborough m HALL Winslow of Dover formerly of Gorham ME on 19 inst *MS* 29 Jul 1846

STEVERSON Eliza Jane m FRANKLIN Russell M both of Paris on 27 Mar *MS* 22 May 1850

STEWARD Rosetta of Elk Creek m JOSLEN Chauncey on 25 Apr at Elk Creek PA *MS* 26 May 1847

STEWART Hannah F m DAMON Frederick both of Manchester on 30 Dec 1847 *MS* 19 Jan 1848

STEWART Mary m BICKFORD George W Capt *MS* 9 Feb 1848

STEWART Mary m REED Robert M on 29 June *MS* 19 Jul 1837

STEWART Nancy I m SHELDON Milton E on 7 Jan *MS* 29 Jan 1851

STEWART Susan m SCRUTON Michael both of Barrington *MS* 27 Jan 1836

STICKNEY Mary Jane of Chesterville ME m BAILEY Wm C of Farmington *MS* 27 Jul 1836

STICKNEY Ruth Ann m SEVERANCE Ora P both of Kinston on 9 inst *MS* 20 Nov 1850

STILES Abigail B m MORRISON James H of Boston MA on 6 Mar at Strafford *MS* 12 Mar 1845

STILES Eleanor of Portsmouth NH m WELLS John of Ipswich MA on 16 Dec at Portsmouth NH *MS* 7 Jan 1846

STILES Harriet C of Bradford m GREEN Hiram of Henniker on 9 Jan 1849 *MS* 11 Apr 1849

STILES Phebe Ann of Jackson m PORTER David of Dixmont ME on 24 Nov *MS* 18 Dec 1844

STILES Sarah E m MONTGOMERY Jonathan H both of Strafford on 25 ult *MS* 27 Nov 1850

STILES Susan H m HONLETT John 2d on 6 Jan 1843 at Bradford *MS* 20 Sept 1843

STILKEY Dorcas M m GOVES Rufus both of Brunswick ME *MS* 8 Mar 1848

STILKLEY Olive J m PEASE Charles W of N Berwick *MS* 28 Dec 1842

STILL Lucy m WHEELER Abel of Hatley *MS* 13 Sept 1843

STILLING Sarah Ann of Ossipee NH m NUTE Zenas H of Tuftonborough NH on 1 Dec *MS* 15 Jan 1851

STILLINGS Amanda M m WOODS George L both of Manchester on 30 May 1848 *MS* 14 June 1848

STILLINGS Mary of Conway m RENNETT Alvah of Effingham NH *MS* 21 Jan 1846

STILLINGS Mary of New Berwick ME m HURD Peter on 12 Apr at Berwick ME *MS* 20 Jan 1847

STILLINGS Olive of North Berwick on 14 Aug m GUPTILL Charles of Berwick ME *MS* 7 Sept 1842

STILLMAN Mary Ann of Newport on 29th Jan m COON Dewitt C of Bradford *MS* 24 May 1843

STILSON Ednah A of Durham m SWAIN Warren P of New Market NH on 24 Jul *MS* 3 Aug 1842

STILSON Hannah m BUNKER William on 11 June at Lowell MA *MS* 16 Aug 1843

STILSON Mary J m DOLLOFF Jerome B both of Lowell on 5 Apr 1848 *MS* 26 Apr 1848

STILSON Nancy m NASON Rufus *MFWBR* 13 Oct 1849

STILSON Susan C of Durham m PAGE John of Kensington on 18 May at Durham *MS* 11 June 1845

STIMPSON Mary m FISK James both of Freedom NY *MS* 2 Sept 1846

STINSON Abigail M m PLUMER Otis on 3 Dec at Richmond *MS* 17 Dec 1845

STINSON Asenath V m BADGER James W on 2 Sept *MS* 22 Sept 1847

STINSON Cordelia m CATES Henry at Monroe ME *MS* 16 Aug 1843

STINSON Jane K m VEAZIE James Jr both of Eaton on 18 Oct *MS* 11 Nov 1846

STINSON Julia Ann of Litchfield m HALL Samuel G on 22d of Litchfield *MS* 20 Dec 1843

STINSON Margaret E of Arrowsic ME m COBURN John C of Pittston ME *MFWBR* 7 Aug 1847

STINSON Mary Jane of Litchfield ME m SANDFORD James M of Bowdoinham ME *MS* 20 May 1840

STINSON Susan D m GAMMON Abial O of Naples *MFWBR* 23 June 1849

STOCKBRIDGE Hannah W of Stratham on last evening m GEAR Reuben N of New Market "A liberal slice of cake accompanied this notice." *MS* 18 Dec 1839

STOCKWELL Mary of Athol MA on 17th inst m COLE Kimball of New Market *MS* 30 Mar 1842

STODDARD A Miss m ALLEN Ephraim on 30 Oct 1843 at Harrisburg NY *MS* 7 Feb 1844

STODDARD Roxanna of Brookfield m ALLEN Amasa of Warren *MS*

STODDARD (Continued)
  18 Apr 1838
STODDARD Susan of Sutton VT m RUGGLES Ephraim H of Lyndon
  MS 5 Apr 1843
STOKES Dorothy m BARTLETT Michael on 19 Feb at Lowell MA MS
  25 May 1842
STOKES Polly of Starboro' VT m THOMPSON Oren on 2 Nov at
  Huntington VT MS 6 Dec 1843
STOKOLL Mary Ann m PERKINS William D MFWBR 20 Apr 1850
STONE Cordelia L m OWEN Robert M MFWBR 21 Jan 1849
STONE Disnthy m MILLER Elisha both of Stanstead on 25 Nov 1843
  MS 1 May 1844
STONE Effy of Harmony ME m STEWART Thomas H of Center
  Square on 11 Jul 1848 MS 2 Aug 1848
STONE Maria E of Blackstone MA m DRAKE Charles J on 19 Jan
  MS 5 Feb 1845
STONE Mary Ann of Boothbay ME m DODGE Charles B of Edge-
  comb ME on 29 Sept MS 27 Nov 1850
STONE Miss of Biddeford ME m PERRY William H MFWBR 28 Apr
  1849
STONE Rhoda L m EDGERLY John G both of Salem on 23 June MS
  3 Jul 1850
STONE Sarah E of Cornish on 26th ult m FOGG Moses of Limerick
  ME MFWBR 22 Feb 1851
STORER Louisa of Brownfield ME m EADES Charles of Conway NH
  on 30 Apr 1848 MS 5 Jul 1848
STORER Melissa of Porter m WALKER John of Brownfield on 1 May
  1849 MS 24 Jul 1850
STOREY Laura E m KEITH Asa both of East Randolph on 20 ult MS
  2 Nov 1836
STORY Belinda m FOWELL Rufus H both of Bolton on 7 Oct MS 23
  Jan 1850
STORY Lucy m STORY Job RI Apr 1822 p 63
STORY Lucy m BARNS D S both of Compton on 9 Nov at Stanstead
  LC MS 17 Feb 1836
STORY Mary A m DODGE John L both of Hopkinton s/o Wm
  DODGE on 28 Dec 1837 MS 10 Dec 1838
STORY Mary E m ROBERTSON Giles both of East Randolph VT on
  31 May 1848 MS 14 Feb 1849
STOVER Caroline L of Brownfield ME m RISE Eber E at Brownfield
  ME MS 21 Nov 1843
STOVER Harriet m MOTLEY George of Lowell MA MFWBR 28 Dec
  1850
STOVER Lucinda H of Limington ME m SMITH Isaac on 2 Jul of
  Westbrook MS 7 Feb 1844
STOVER Matilda m DOW Henry W on 19 Nov of Edgecomb ME "The

STOVER (Continued)
fee received (two dollars) is herewith sent to aid the Mission cause - Wouldn't this be a good practice? - Administrator." *MS* 16 Dec 1846

STOW Maria of Lawrence m WELLER William on 22 Oct at Lawrence NY *MS* 6 Dec 1843

STOW Triphena of Yorkshire NY? m DENNISON Chester of Holland *MS* 4 Mar 1835

STOWE Lydia of Morristown NY m BIXBY Luther on 1 Jan at Morristown NY *MS* 27 Mar 1844

STOWERS Experience E of Dixmont on Jan 1 1840 m GROUT Robert C of Monroe *MS* 12 Feb 1840

STRAIGHT Dillan of Oneonta NY m THOMAS William of Otsego NY *MS* 6 June 1849

STRAIT Martha m BEERS Elijah both of Stephentown NY on 19 Oct 1848 *MS* 3 Jan 1849

STRATTON Rebecca m HARPE [*sic*] John both of Gerry NY on 4 Oct 1849 *MS* 19 June 1850

STRATTON Sarah P m SKINNER Daniel M Capt at Sandwich *MS* 1 Oct 1845

STRAW Cyrene m AYER James 3d *MS* 26 Jul 1827

STRAW Elizabeth m TUCKER David 2d of Henniker on 7 Mar *MS* 26 Apr 1843

STRAW Mahala m WHITTIER Nathaniel both of Meredith *MS* 12 Feb 1851

STRAW Mary Ann m RECORD Cyrus *MS* 30 Nov 1832

STRAW Ruth m DAM Hercules *MS* 28 May 1828

STREETER Catherine m HILDRETH Oliver at Lisbon on 19 Feb *MS* 14 May 1845

STREETER Emily of Lisbon m EASTMAN David on 17 May 1843 at Lisbon NH *MS* 13 Mar 1844

STREETER Susan of Lisbon m GLIDDEN Levi of Greensboro' VT on 11 Sept at Lisbon NH *MS* 6 Nov 1844

STRICKLAND Lucena m CHURCH Henry both of Walworth on 25 Dec 1850 *MS* 15 Jan 1851

STROUT Elizabeth B of Gray ME m SAWYER Samuel B *MFWBR* 8 Sept 1849

STROUT Hannah E of Limington ME m HALEY John of Hollis *MS* 7 Feb 1844

STROUT Mary J of Wales ME m JORDAN Ebenezer of Webster ME *MS* 29 Dec 1847

STROUT Mary Mrs m BRADEEN Samuel both of Standish ME on 30 Dec 1847 *MS* 12 Jan 1848

STURDEY Sally W of Mendon on 27 Mar m CASS William E *MS* 24 Apr 1839

STURGIS Louann of Gorham m SWETT David P of Windham ME on

STURGIS (Continued)

31 ult at Windham *MS* 20 Jan 1836

STURGIS Maria m COTTON Wm Jr both of Gorham ME on 23d ult *MS* 8 Apr 1835

STURGIS Temperance of Danville m HAMBLEN Joseph F of Gorham in Danville ME on Tues Feb 1st *MS* 16 Feb 1842

SULLIVAN Louisa m BATCHELDER James S both of Manchester *MS* 15 Apr 1846

SUMMER Eliza H m SIMPSON Woodbury M *MS* 25 Apr 1833

SUMMER Jane of Ithaca m HAINES Albert G of New Loudon NH on 24 Mar at Ithaca NY *MS* 14 Apr 1847

SUNBOWER Phebe m COTTON William on 6 Mar at Tyrone Fayette Co PA *MS* 26 Mar 1845

SUTHERLAND Maria m KIDDER Leonard both of Topsham ME in Topsham on Mon Dec 27 *MS* 12 Jan 1842

SUTHERLAND Zilpha of Lisbon ME m GRAVES Daniel Jr of Topsham *MS* 23 Mar 1836

SUTLIFF Abigail M m LAKE Harman on 7 Mar *MS* 24 Apr 1850

SUTS Lucretia m VANDERBERG John S both of Plesse [Plessis/ Plesses] NY? on 1 Jan 1849 *MS* 25 Apr 1849

SWAIN Abigail m FOOT Samuel E both of Warren on 16 Nov 1845 *MS* 25 Mar 1846

SWAIN Abigail M m EATON Charles W on 5 Dec at Manchester NH *MS* 1 Jan 1845

SWAIN Adaline N m HATCH David P both of Meredith NH on 7 Nov *MS* 15 Nov 1843

SWAIN Arvilla A of Meredith m HOYT Francis F of Concord on 25 June *MS* 26 Sept 1849

SWAIN Eliza Jane Mrs m PITMAN Ebenezer Jr both of Meredith on 16 Oct *MS* 27 Nov 1850

SWAIN Elizabeth A m EVENS Albert both of Dover NH on Monday eve 9 inst *MS* 16 Jan 1850

SWAIN Eunice m ENOCH Wm *MS* 15 Jul 1835

SWAIN Hannah M of Meredith NH on 21 Mar m LEAVITT John B of Gilford *MS* 12 Apr 1843

SWAIN Martha J d/o SWAIN Mark Dea m SWAIN Bennet E both of Barrington on 7 Jan 1849 *MS* 31 Jan 1849

SWAIN Mary E of Meredith m BADGER Lewis D of Gilford on 23 Feb *MS* 1 May 1850

SWAIN Mary G m CARTER Jonathan L on 30 Nov at Wilmington MA *MS* 20 Dec 1843

SWAIN Mary P m TILTON Stephen S both of Manchester on 9 May *MS* 22 May 1844

SWAIN Nancy of Meredith NH m CROCKETT Charles W on 10 Oct *MS* 15 Nov 1843

SWAIN Olive N of Chichester m BROOKS James W of Boston on 15

SWAIN (Continued)
Nov *MS* 5 Dec 1849

SWAIN Rachael E of Meredith m TILTON Charles F of Manchester on 6 Mar *MS* 1 May 1850

SWAIN Sarah C of New Market m HOITT W H A on 30th ult at New Market *MS* 5 Apr 1843

SWAIN Sarah Jane m SWAIN John Quincy Adams both of Barrington on 12 Mar *MS* 2 Apr 1851

SWAIN Sarah M m FELLOWS David A on 28 Aug at Manchester NH *MS* 10 Sept 1845

SWAN Charlotte of Tunbridge VT m WEYMOUTH George Esq on 29 Oct at Tunbridge VT *MS* 2 Dec 1846

SWAN Rhoda of Nashua m MARTIN Jesse on 19 Feb at Nashua *MS* 4 Mar 1846

SWASEY Abby P of Milton NH m BRACKETT Jacob of Acton on 8 Oct at Sanford ME *MS* 23 Oct 1844

SWASEY Mary E d/o SWASEY Charles Dea of Milton m FALL Isaac H of Lebanon ME on 23 Apr 1848 *MS* 17 May 1848

SWEET Mary Ann of Starksboro m SPRAGUE David D of Huntington on 2 Feb *MS* 26 Feb 1851

SWEET Truelove of Gloucester m SAUDERS Robert on 1 Dec at Gloucester *MS* 14 Dec 1842

SWEETSIR Harriet m POND J Mr *MFWBR* 21 Apr 1849

SWETT Bernice S of Bowdoinham ME m TILTON John W of Boscawen NH on 29 Oct at Bowdoinham ME *MS* 16 Nov 1842

SWETT Betsey P m QUENNAM Constant of Wiscasset ME in Whitefield *MS* 24 June 1831

SWETT Emeline of Limerick ME m HAYES Luther S of Cambridge MA *MFWBR* 17 Apr 1847

SWETT Maria of Bethlehem NH m PHILLIPS Asa of Bethlehem NH *MS* 4 Jan 1843

SWETT Mary Ann m HARRIS John A both of Canaan NH on 22 June 1848 *MS* 12 Jul 1848

SWETT Mary m PLUMMER Libby both of Richmond ME on 21 Sept *MS* 18 Nov 1835

SWETT Mary of Great Falls NH m HORN Noah of Wakefield NH on 17 Oct at Great Falls NH *MS* 9 Nov 1842

SWETT Sophronia B of Casco ME m HOBSON James G of Hollis ME on 28 Jul Sunday morning *MS* 21 Aug 1850

SWIFT Elizabeth m STEVENS John M at Dixmont ME *MS* 17 Jan 1844

SWIFT Emeline of Fayette m JEDKINS David B of Lexington *MS* 12 Aug 1835

SWORD Betsey of Norway m ALCOTT Thomas J Col of York Mich on 29 Sept in Norway NY *MS* 30 Oct 1850

SYLVESTER Louisa of Freeport ME m DENNISON John 3d on 8 Nov

SYLVESTER (Continued)

of Freeport ME *MS* 25 Nov 1846

SYLVESTER Mary C m CHASE Dudly both of Bridgton on 13 Dec 1837 *MS* 17 Jan 1837

SYLVESTER Rebecca m RANDALL Daniel both of Freeport ME on 10 Oct 1847 *MS* 17 Nov 1847

SYMOND Sally m JORDAN James on 24th ult *MS* 17 Oct 1833

SYMONDS Maria D at Raymond m TENNEY Henry Jr on 14 Jul at Raymond ME *MS* 7 Aug 1844

TALBOT Harriet m ARRINGTON James W both of Smithfield on 27 ult *MS* 10 Feb 1836

TALLANT Lucretia Mrs m MORRILL Benjamin on 20 Apr of Canterbury NH *MS* 5 May 1847

TALLFORD Sarah E of Dover m THOMAS John Eld of Dover MICHIGAN *MS* 5 Jul 1843

TANNER Betsy m WESCOTT Arthur both of Providence on 29 Sept *MS* 16 Oct 1850

TAPPAN Ruth A of Sandwich NH m VITTUM Stephen on 30 March *MS* 9 Apr 1845

TAPPAN Susan m ROWE David S both of Sandwich NH on 12 Nov *MS* 5 June 1850

TARBOX Ellis Ann m DUNTON Henry *MS* 16 May 1838

TARBOX Lucy m USHER George on 3 Dec at Hollis ME *MS* 30 Dec 1846

TARBOX Mary E of Hollis m SAWYER Joseph H on 19 Feb 1849 *MS* 28 Mar 1849

TARBOX Mary Jane of Limerick ME m McKUSICK Nahum on 16 June 1842 at Limerick ME *MS* 6 Jul 1842

TARBOX Nancy H m GERRY John W of Boston MA on 16 Sept at Hollis *MS* 1 Oct 1845

TARBOX Sabrina m DUNTON Joseph both of Westport ME on 13th inst *MS* 30 Mar 1836

TARBOX Sirena m BLETHEN Elias I both of Hollis ME on 25 Nov 1847 *MS* 5 Jan 1848

TASKER Ann Eliza m BRIER Moses W Capt both of Monroe on 22 Feb 1848 *MS* 15 Mar 1848

TASKER Ann Jane m KNOWLES Wm both of Northwood on 9 Oct *MS* 7 Nov 1838

TASKER Ann M m PEABODY Washburn both of Dixmont ME *MS* 22 May 1850

TASKER Clarinda of Ossipee NH m WHITE Nathaniel on 31 Aug 1842 of Ossipee NH *MS* 5 Oct 1842

TASKER Eliza Miss m CRAM Philbrook of Raymond in Northwood NH *MS* 31 Oct 1833

TASKER Emeline M on 18 Dec at Pittsfield m HARVEY Joseph Eld

TASKER (Continued)
MS 19 Mar 1845

TASKER Martha M m SANBORN Benjamin J both of Manchester on 5 inst 1849 *MS* 25 Apr 1849

TASKER Susan m DAME Jonathan Jr both of Strafford NH *MS* 27 Jan 1836

TATE Mary A of Corinth ME m GARY Ephraim M of Dover ME *MS* 20 Jan 1847

TATE Nancy of Kennebunk ME m SULLIVAN Charles of Tuftonborough NH on 4 Jan 1849 *MS* 9 May 1849

TATTERSON Hannah m HOOPER James G on 10 Feb of South Berwick ME *MS* 25 Feb 1846

TAYLER Julia Ann m STURER John both of Dover NH on 23d ult *MS* 20 Mar 1834

TAYLOR Betsey of Sanford m BRYANT James of Portsmouth NH on 6 inst *MS* 30 Aug 1837

TAYLOR Betsey T m NUTTER Alphonso J on 27th ult at Dover NH *MS* 6 Aug 1845

TAYLOR Caroline P of Nelson m MACK Norman B of New Haven at Jan 5th at Nelson NY *MS* 12 Feb 1845

TAYLOR Catherine of Dover NH m WITHAM Joseph at Great Falls ME *MS* 29 June 1842

TAYLOR Eliza Ann of Dayton m MINER Julius of Ellicottsville Cattaraugus Co NY *MS* 22 Mar 1837

TAYLOR Elizabeth B at Portsmouth on 2nd inst m AYER John *MS* 19 Feb 1840

TAYLOR Elizabeth I m TUTTLE Stoten D both of Nottingham on 12 May *MS* 24 June 1846

TAYLOR Elizabeth R of Lyman m DAY Charles Col of Kennebunk Port ME on 11 Apr *MS* 24 Apr 1850

TAYLOR Emily F m BRAGG Trustrum both of Manchester on 5 Feb 1849 *MS* 14 Feb 1849

TAYLOR Fanny d/o TAYLOR Amos Capt of Vassalboro ME m TRUE John Eld of Montville ME on 8th ult *MS* 20 Feb 1829

TAYLOR Fanny Miss m GREENLEAF Stephen Esq *MS* 24 May 1827

TAYLOR Frances of Bangor ME m SANFORD Charles B *MFWBR* 6 Jul 1850

TAYLOR Hannah P of Jay on 21 Mar m TARBOX Daniel Jr of Phillips ME *MS* 19 Apr 1843

TAYLOR Harriet of Haverhill MA m PIKE Stephen Jr of Bradford on 21 Nov 1847 *MS* 8 Dec 1847

TAYLOR Julia A of Waterville ME m NASH Charles C of Sidney ME at Winslow ME *MS* 25 Nov 1846

TAYLOR Mary m DIXSON Mazianson *MS* 7 Feb 1833

TAYLOR Mary m HATCH Dimon on 5 Dec *MS* 8 Jan 1851

TAYLOR Mary Jane m QUINBY Lewis on 2 Aug at Sandwich NH *MS*

TAYLOR (Continued)
14 Sept 1842

TAYLOR Mary of Porter m PERRY John of Parsonsfield ME *MFWBR* 4 Jan 1851

TAYLOR Nancy of Waterville ME m MARR Thomas Esq of George-town ME on 14 Sept *MS* 24 Sept 1845

TAYLOR Phoebe m WEBBER Shapleigh on 26th ult *MS* 9 Nov 1826

TAYLOR Rebecca C m BROWN Joseph P both of Deerfield on 24 Oct *MS* 14 Nov 1849

TAYLOR Ruth S of Mendon on 29th inst m WARNER David E *MS* 24 Apr 1839

TAYLOR Sarah Jane of Effingham m NEAL James A of Dover on 26 ult *MS* 26 Jan 1848

TAYLOR Sarah of Scituate m CAHOON Albert B of Coventry RI on 9 Sept *MS* 30 Oct 1850

TAYLOR Sally W of Grafton m EDDY Harviain T of Sutton *MS* 13 Sept 1843

TAYLOR Susan C of Windsor VT m DENSMORE Ebenezer S on 8 Apr at Windsor VT *MS* 21 Apr 1847

TAYLOR Susan of Sanbornton NH m ROWE Shepherd of Gilford on 27 Dec 1849 *MS* 9 Jan 1850

TEBBETTS - see also TIBBETS, TIBBETTS

TEBBETS Caroline H of Dover m CARTER Abner of Dover on 30 June *MS* 24 Jul 1850

TEBBETS Clara of Rochester m CHAMPION Moses J of Dover on 27 ult *MS* 4 Dec 1850

TEBBETS Hannah m HODGDON Andrew J both of Dover on Sunday Morning last *MS* 5 June 1850

TEBBETS Octavia m BROWN Oliver Jr both of Topsham ME on 7 Sept *MS* 18 Sept 1850

TEBBETS Susan A of Farmington m DURGIN Leonard on 19 Feb 1843 *MS* 1 Mar 1843

TEBBETTS Eleanor M of Waterboro ME m BAGLEY George R *MFWBR* 18 Jan 1851

TEBBETTS Hannah B m BRACKETT Amos *MFWBR* 11 May 1850

TEBBETTS Lucinda of Rochester NH m VARNEY Moses *MS* 21 Jan 1846

TEETER Rachel of Lansing m PERRY Joseph of Concord Mich on 1 Jul *MS* 22 Aug 1849

TEMPLE Jerusha of Littleton m DUDLEY Samuel of Bethlehem VT *MS* 18 Apr 1849

TENNEY Eliza A of Raymond ME m WILLIAMS James of Winthrop ME *MS* 13 Mar 1844

TENNEY Hannah J of Raymond ME m ALLEN Joseph W at Raymond *MS* 8 June 1842

TENNEY Kesiah of Raymond ME m ARCHIBALD Nathaniel of Poland

TENNEY (Continued)
ME on 11 Dec *MS* 10 Feb 1847

TENNEY Sally Mrs m SMALL John on 26 ult *MS* 10 Oct 1849

TERELL Lydia of Haverhill m DAVIS Joel on 19 Mar 1844 at Haverhill *MS* 3 Apr 1844

TERRY Harriet of Newport NY m BOOTH Stephen D of Remson on Oct 28 *MS* 19 Jan 1842

TERRY Rebecca m BLAKE William both of Boston on 30 Jan *MS* 12 Feb 1851

TETHERLY Nancy B m STRATTON Jonathan both of Dover on 19 inst *MS* 22 Nov 1848

TEWINY Caroline T of Newport m PIERCE Melzar of Plymouth MA on 15 Feb *MS* 11 Mar 1846

TEWKSBURY Eunice m TILTON Timothy F of Contoocookville NH? 10 Jul *MS* 14 Sept 1842

TEWKSBURY Mary m HUTCHINS John L *MS* 13 Feb 1834

THAYER Abby S of Roxbury MA m BUZZELL True *MS* 16 Oct 1839

THAYER Abigail m ALEXANDER Dan both of Uxbridge on Thanksgiving Day *MS* 19 Dec 1838

THAYER Betsey of Gray ME m LIBBY James on 6 Aug at Gray ME *MS* 16 Aug 1843

THAYER Christiana m WESTON Peley *MS* 19 Nov 1834

THAYER Eliza B m GOVE Sanford D both of Manchester on 28 Dec 1848 *MS* 17 Jan 1849

THAYER Hannah on 1 Dec 1842 at Landaff (NH?) m HOWARD Luke *MS* 19 Apr 1843

THAYER Harriet R m DURGIN J M Eld both of Gray ME *MS* 18 Dec 1839

THAYER Margarette A of Portland ME m DOW J R of Waterville *MFWBR* 4 May 1850

THAYER Mary Susan on 26th ult at Gray ME m HALL Cushman *MS* 24 Apr 1839

THAYER Mehitabel A m MANNING Jacob on 24 Jul at Wilmington MA *MS* 13 Aug 1845

THAYER Rachel m SWAIN Jesse both of Lowell *MS* 20 June 1838

THAYER Sylvia A m FERREN Shepherd *MS* 20 Jan 1836

THAYER Sylvia of Mendon m THAYER Artemus Jr on 18 Mar *MS* 18 Apr 1838

THING Betsey d/o THING Deacon of Shapleigh ME m BEAN Israel of Waterboro on 24th ult *MS* 21 Aug 1829

THING Diana L m GILMAN Geo H both of Gilford on 17 June *MS* 8 Jul 1846

THING Hannah G of Pittsfield m PRESCOTT Enoch B of Gilford on 4 Dec *MS* 25 Dec 1839

THING Hannah of Shapleigh ME m THING Eliezer of Waterboro ME on 5th inst *MS* 17 Apr 1829

THING Sarah J m DURLAND Wm H both of Lynn MA on 13 Jul *MS* 31 Jul 1850

THOMAS Albert m CHURCHILL Mary C *MFWBR* 23 June 1849

THOMAS Catherine m MERRILL Samuel Esq of Buxton ME *MFWBR* 15 May 1847

THOMAS Diantha J m McCULLY John both of Wilton *MFWBR* 22 May 1847

THOMAS Eliza Jane at Lowell MA m BURBANK Thomas W *MS* 3 May 1843

THOMAS Elizabeth A of Standish (Steep Falls) ME m STOCKMAN Edward A Rev of Limington ME *MFWBR* 30 Oct 1847

THOMAS Maribah H m MESSER John both of Waterville on 29 Nov *MS* 2 Jan 1850

THOMAS Martha W m PITTS Orren *MFWBR* 13 Oct 1849

THOMAS Mary Ann m FARMER Samuel both of Charleston ME on 10 Oct *MS* 7 Nov 1849

THOMAS Minerva m FALLET Charles W both of Exeter NY on 1 Sept *MS* 30 Sept 1846

THOMAS Rachel P m MORRILL Nathan *MS* 30 May 1833

THOMAS Salata m ALDRICH Hiram both of Barnston CE on 8 Jan *MS* 19 Feb 1851

THOMAS Sarah B m LEAVITT Gideon P both of Newburgh ME on 12 Nov *MS* 5 Mar 1851

THOMPSON Abby F m ANGELL Eben Smith on 22 Sept at North Scituate RI *MS* 18 Dec 1844

THOMPSON Abigail of Nottingham m THOMPSON Isaac of New Market on 7 inst *MS* 28 Mar 1838

THOMPSON Arsina m BERMIS John both of Dracut on 9 inst in even *MS* 20 June 1838

THOMPSON Asenath of Harrison m HARMON William V on 6 Jul at Harrison ME *MS* 24 Sept 1845

THOMPSON Betsey of Great Falls NH m DORR Samuel on 1 Dec at North Berwick ME *MS* 20 Jan 1847

THOMPSON Caroline m RICKER Dominicus Jr both of Parsonsfield ME on 20 Aug 1848 *MS* 8 Nov 1848

THOMPSON Catherine M m HAM James on 12 Sept at Brunswick ME *MS* 2 Oct 1844

THOMPSON Clarissa Mrs m THOMPSON Asa both of Bowdoinham ME on 26 Nov 1848 *MS* 13 Dec 1848

THOMPSON Eliza A of Gilmanton NH m RANDALL Sewall of New Durham on 2 inst *MS* 22 Mar 1848

THOMPSON Elizabeth m NORTON George W on 5 June *MS* 31 Jul 1850

THOMPSON Elizabeth ae 74y m FREEMAN Azariah ae 84 Mar in Mansfield CT *MS* 23 Nov 1826

THOMPSON Esther m PAGE Jacob on 28 Jan at Newfield *MS* 4 Feb

THOMPSON (Continued)
1846
THOMPSON Esther D of Lowell m STILES John *MS* 17 Jul 1844
THOMPSON Jane m FURBER George Y *MS* 27 Dec 1837
THOMPSON Jane M m TITCOMB George W of Haverhill MA *MFWBR* 4 May 1850
THOMPSON Judith m CALEF Moses both of Salsbury on 8 inst *MS* 21 Nov 1838
THOMPSON Keziah H m HARBEY Benjamin both of Manchester *MS* 23 Sept 1846
THOMPSON Lucy H m BOYNTON Charles R both of Centre Harbor on 18 Dec 1849 *MS* 18 Apr 1849
THOMPSON Lucy J of South Parsonsfield m MARSHALL Reuben S on 6 June 1847 at South Parsonsfield ME *MS* 21 Jul 1847
THOMPSON Mary Miss m GRAY Wm both of Barrington NH *MS* 11 Jan 1837
THOMPSON Mary C Mrs m DAKE [sic] Erastus on 23 ult *MS* 20 May 1835
THOMPSON Mary J at Manchester NH m SEAWARD John on 14 Jan *MS* 21 Jan 1846
THOMPSON Mary J m KENISTON Ivory P both of Wolfborough NH on 12 May *MS* 22 May 1850
THOMPSON Mary of Newfield m SEYMMS William of Newfield ME *MS* 6 Dec 1827
THOMPSON Nancy m EMERY Daniel both of Limington ME on 26 Apr *MS* 7 Feb 1844
THOMPSON Nancy of Ossipee NH m CRAM Merrill on 4 Jan 1847 at Effingham NH *MS* 5 May 1847
THOMPSON Olive E m BEAN Francis E both of Dover on 10 inst *MS* 17 Oct 1849
THOMPSON Phebe m GOSS George R both of Gilford on 22 ult *MS* 10 Oct 1838
THOMPSON Rosetta A of Newport RI m LAWTON George N on 25 Jan at Newport RI *MS* 11 Mar 1846
THOMPSON Sarah Ann of Monmouth ME m DONNELL Jesse D of Webster ME at Wales ME *MS* 28 Feb 1844
THOMPSON Sarah m TABOR John Jr both of Great Falls on 7 May *MS* 16 May 1849
THOMSON Lucy Mrs m RANDALL Daniel both of Great Falls NH *MS* 30 Oct 1850
THORN Caroline m TIBBETS Christopher C both of Somersworth NH on 27 May *MS* 22 Jul 1846
THORN Hannah of Standish ME m BEAN Benjamin of Rollinsford NH on 19 inst *MS* 29 Aug 1849
THORN Jane of Portland ME m SWETT Bernice of Standish ME *MFWBR* 27 Mar 1847

THORNTON Sarah m WRIGHT Leven on 31 Aug at Washington Township Union Co Ohio *MS* 30 Oct 1844

THRASHER Rhoda P of Rehoboth MA m CAPRON Harford A of Pawtucket RI on 21 Mar *MS* 1 May 1850

THURBEE Mehitabel m MAKEPEACE T L both of Newton MA on 31 Oct 1847 *MS* 8 Dec 1847

THURLOW Ann E m FARRIN William J *MFWBR* 26 Jul 1848

THURLOW Emily Jane at Raymond ME m COBB William H of New Gloucester ME *MS* 25 Jan 1843

THURLOW Maranda m POTTER Benjamin on 28 May 1843 at Litchfield ME *MS* 16 Aug 1843

THURSTON Abigail m BLAISDELL Henry Rev both of Eaton NH on 22 Mar 1849 *MS* 4 Apr 1849

THURSTON Betsey of Pelham m BARNES Harmon of Greenwich on 24 Mar *MS* 6 Apr 1836

THURSTON Eliza Ann m ELLIS Thomas *MFWBR* 28 Apr 1849

THURSTON Hannah D of Parsonsfield m ALLEY Alonzo D of Eaton *MS* 11 Nov 1846

THURSTON Mary m FISK Thomas G W on 9 Oct at Lowell MA *MS* 2 Nov 1842

THURSTON Mary E of Meredith NH m ATWOOD Jeduthan *MS* 11 Sept 1839

THURSTON Mercy B m PHILPOT Moses *MFWBR* 25 Nov 1848

TIBBETS - see also TEBBETS, TEBBETTS

TIBBETS Eliza Jane of Dover NH m BROWN Caleb on 13 Nov at Dover NH *MS* 12 Nov 1845

TIBBETS Harriet R m EMMONS Horace both of Lyman ME on 19 Dec 1850 *MS* 22 Jan 1851

TIBBETS Irena m CLARK Samuel S on 29 ult *MS* 9 Nov 1836

TIBBETS Joanna of Madbury m CHESLEY John Jr of Epsom on Thur last *MS* 27 Aug 1834

TIBBETS Mary A m HURD Henry L both of Alton NH on 6 Oct *MS* 6 Nov 1850

TIBBETTS Abagail m PINKHAM Jason on 18 ult *MS* 26 Jul 1837

TIBBETTS Abigail of Lowell m STILLINGS Leander of Boston on 2 Dec *MS* 12 Dec 1838

TIBBETTS Charlotte Mrs m BUZZELL Hezekiah D Eld on 9 Jan 1849 *MS* 31 Jan 1849

TIBBETTS Mary d/o TIBBETTS Edmund of Farmington NH m YOUNG Moses Colby Sr on 20 May of Ossipee NH [s/o Rodolpha & Nancy/Anna (Tarr) YOUNG] *MS* 25 June 1845

TIBBETTS Mary S of Acton ME m NASON Zebulon of Milton NH on 13 Oct *MS* 23 Oct 1839

TIBBETTS Naomi D m LANE Joseph at Bangor ME *MS* 13 Sept 1843

TIBBETTS Sally of Dover m HAM Samuel of Barrington *MS* 30 Mar 1835

TIFFT Martha Ann of Nassau m HOAG Isaac J of Chatham on afternoon 6 ult *MS* 17 Oct 1838

TIFFT Nancy M of Nassau m PALMER Paul of Stephentown on 29
Sept afternoon *MS* 17 Oct 1838

TIFFT Orsena K m WHEELER Zopher on 12 Oct at Stephentown NY
MS 17 Dec 1845

TIFFT Rebecca m POMEROY Luther on 30 Oct at Stephentown *MS*
11 Dec 1844

TILLOTSON Nancy of Topsham m AVERY Philander of Corinth in
Topsham on 5 Dec 1841 *MS* 16 Mar 1842

TILTON Abigail E of Alexandria NH m DICKERMAN Moses W of
Loudon NH on 14 Sept 1841 at Alexander NH *MS* 4 May 1842

TILTON Belinda of Bristol m NELSON John S on 23 Nov at New
Hampton *MS* 31 Jan 1844

TILTON Betsey m WATSON Solomon on 17 inst at Pittsfield *MS* 31
Aug 1836

TILTON Betsey T of New Hampton m BROWN Gardner H of Lowell
MA *MS* 31 Jan 1844

TILTON Elizabeth L m EMERSON Frances both of Haverhill MA on 2
Apr in Haverhill MA *MS* 26 Apr 1848

TILTON Hannah E of Pittsfield m GREEN David L of Loudon on 23
Jan *MS* 10 Apr 1850

TILTON Jane m ROBINSON Daniel J both of Gilmanton on 12 Nov
MS 20 Dec 1837

TILTON Margaret A m WATSON Daniel Jr both of Pittsfield on 6 May
MS 16 May 1849

TILTON Mary Ann of Meredith m HAM George W of Pembroke *MS* 30
Jan 1850

TILTON Sarah C m NEAL Moses C both of Loudon on 5 Dec *MS* 19
Dec 1838

TINKER Lydia m ROBINSON Joseph on Aug 22 *MS* 19 Jan 1842

TINT Ursula C m VICKERY Edward both of Nassau on 9 Apr *MS* 27
May 1846

TISDALE Eunice of Beloit m GIFFORD Wm Henry of LeRoy IL on 16
Jan *MS* 19 Feb 1851

TITCOMB Sally m TITCOMB Joseph of Boston on 27 Jan *MS* 27 Feb
1850 & *MFWBR* 9 Mar 1850

TITUS Emeline m WILSON John L both of W Fairlee on 26 Jan *MS* 7
Feb 1838

TITUS Mercy R of Monmouth ME m DEARBORN Dudley H at Wales
ME *MS* 28 Feb 1844

TOBEY Betsey of Kittery m SEWARD Isaac of Kittery ME *MS* 5 Jan
1831

TOBEY Ellen Mrs of Pownal m ALLEN Isaac of Freeport on 7 Apr *MS*
15 May 1850

TOBEY Mary A m RILEY Thomas P both of Kittery ME on 13 June

TOBEY (Continued)
MS 3 Jul 1850

TODD Catherine of Kittery ME m NUTTER William of Portsmouth NH
MS 1 Jan 1845

TOLMAN Laura A m HARRINGTON Mason A both of New Ipswich
MA*MS* 27 Oct 1847/ *MS* 29 Mar 1848

TOLMAN Mary S of Ashburnham m WHITNEY Nathan of Westminster on 27 Nov *MS* 12 Mar 1851

TOMPKINS Adelia S of Hamilton m BASCOM Andrew P on 16 Sept at
Poolville NY *MS* 11 Nov 1846

TOMPKINS Margaret m BAKER Perry at Middleville *MS* 29 Jan 1845

TOOTHAKER Amelia d/o TOOTHAKER S Esq m DYER Daniel both of
Harpswell ME *MS* 8 May 1850

TOOTHAKER Elizabeth of Charleston ME m DURFEE John on 11
May at Garland ME *MS* 9 June 1847

TOOTHAKER Joan m MERRITT John S on 23 Sept *MS* 13 Jan 1847

TOOTHAKER Margaret of Richmond ME m GRAY William of
Monmouth ME on 8 Oct 1848 *MS* 22 Nov 1848

TOOTHAKER Phebe A of Litchfield ME m LEMONT Silas merchant of
Gardiner on 4 Apr at Litchfield ME *MS* 28 Apr 1847

TOOTHAKER Rebecca of Charleston ME m FISHER Lordon H of
Kennebunk on 1 Jan 1849 *MS* 21 Feb 1849

TOOTHAKER Rosina of Charlestown m HATCH Harvey on 11 Jul
1844 at Corinth ME *MS* 21 Aug 1844

TOPLIN Joanna of Stanstead m REXFORD Samuel of Hatley *MS* 17
Feb 1836

TORR Mehitabel m KNOWLES Charles H on 9th ult at Newmarket
MS 27 Dec 1843

TORRENS Rebecca of Lowell MA m LEAVITT Thomas of Boston on 7
inst *MS* 17 Feb 1836

TOTMAN Lucretia m TOOTHAKER John both of Richmond ME on 22
Aug *MS* 8 Sept 1847

TOURTELLOTT Sarah W m STEERE Wanton on 25 Dec at Gloucester RI *MS* 18 Feb 1846

TOWLE Abigail D m CRAKE/DRAKE George W on 9 inst *MS* 15 Apr
1840

TOWLE Esther m HEALEY Moses both of Raymond on 12 Nov 1849
MS 23 Jan 1850

TOWLE Hannah of Newfield m RICHARDSON Samuel of Baldwin *MS*
14 Feb 1833

TOWLE Harriet N of Canaan m CLARK Reuben on 5 Sept at Groton
NH *MS* 2 Oct 1844

TOWLE Judith M of Ellsworth m SANBORN Joseph M of Columbia
on 18 Aug *MS* 11 Sept 1850

TOWLE Mahala D m PAIGE Daniel L both of Gilmanton on 6 Dec
1849 *MS* 2 Jan 1850

TOWLE Mary d/o TOWLE Josiah Maj of Newfield m TAYLOR Theodore Sunday last *MS* 30 Nov 1826

TOWLE Mary Jane m THURSTON James H both of Freedom on 8 Apr 1849 *MS* 2 May 1849

TOWLE Mary Jane of Freedom m TAYLOR Daniel on 29 Dec of Porter *MS* 19 Feb 1845

TOWLE Mary of Hampton m COLLINS Moses of Wilmington MA on 18th inst at Hampton *MS* 5 Oct 1842

TOWLE Mehitable of Buxton m PAINE Henry L *MFWBR* 21 Jan 1849

TOWLE Melinda N of Boston m DOWNS Adams B on 29 Nov *MS* 16 Dec 1846

TOWLE Mercy d/o TOWLE William Esq m LARRABEE Benjamin on 12th inst *MS* 28 June 1827

TOWLE Philinda of Epsom m SEAVY Joseph S of Pittsfield on 8th ult *MS* 29 June 1836

TOWLE Sabrina m MAXFIELD Oliver of Gilmanton *MFWBR* 2 Feb 1850

TOWN Cyrena of Newfield m PEARSON Eben B of Lawrence MA on 14 Mar *MS* 5 June 1850

TOWN Mary m BAKER John Dr both of Weare NH on 1st ult *MS* 3 Oct 1833

TOWN Roxana D on 29 Dec of Boscawen m WEBBER Jeremiah S *MS* 16 Jan 1839

TOWN Sally m DREW Sargent S both of Newfield ME *MS* 24 June 1835

TOWN Sarah A m PARSON Stephen S both of Lawrence on 7 Feb 1849 in Dracut *MS* 21 Feb 1849

TOWNS Mehitabel m WHEELER Ezekiel H both of Lisbon on 15 ult *MS* 27 Sept 1837

TOWNSEND Hannah A m DUNN Alanson on 5 June *MS* 3 Jul 1850

TOWNSEND Harriet L of Hancock Bershire Co MA m FOSTER Nelson T N on 5th inst at Sand Lake NY *MS* 24 Jul 1844 (sic) should be *MS* 31 Jul 1844

TOWNSEND Lois of Auburn ME m COFFIN John of Leeds ME *MS* 27 Nov 1844

TOWNSEND Mary m LIBBEY Horace B both of Scarboro *MS* 3 Jul 1850

TOWNSEND Mary C m BACHELOR David S both of Franklin NH *MS* 21 June 1848

TOWNSON Eliza G d/o TOWNSON William T Capt of Limerick ME m KENT J of Boston MA *MFWBR* 30 Dec 1848

TOWNSON Miriam d/o TOWNSON William Capt of Limerick ME m STONE Elisha F *MFWBR* 24 Feb 1849

TRACY Anna B of Lewiston Falls ME m EDGECOMB Edward of Bath on 2 inst *MS* 26 Apr 1848

TRACY Sarah F Mrs m MILIKEN Joseph *MFWBR* 2 Feb 1850

TRACY Sophia A d/o TRACY Jonathan of Auburn m WEST John D of Limerick *MFWBR* 4 Dec 1847

TRAFTON Emeline G m OLIVER Moses O both of Georgetown ME on 14 Feb 1850 *MS* 27 Feb 1850

TRAFTON Hannah S m BEAN James Jr both of Alfred ME *MS* 19 Sept 1838

TRAFTON Harriet F m RICKER Ivory both of Waterville ME *MS* 31 May 1848

TRAFTON Mary Ann m BLAISDELL John 2d at Fairfield ME *MS* 17 Apr 1844

TRAFTON Paulina of Waterville ME m RICKER George of Waterville ME *MS* 17 Feb 1847

TRASK Mary Ann m SPAULDING Joel Jr on 1 Jan of Belgrade ME *MS* 9 Apr 1845

TRASK Nancy m CURTIS Gideon both of Kingfield on 8 Jan *MS* 5 Feb 1840

TREDICK Adeline m KITTREDGE Thomas W Esq on at Dover NH *MS* 21 Nov 1833

TREFERTHERN Mary S of Kittery m STERLING Seth of Portland in Kittery *MS* 3 Feb 1832

TRICKEY Adeline of Brookfield m ALLEN Charles of York ME *MS* 23 Jan 1834

TRICKEY Mary Ann Mrs of Portsmouth NH m PEVERLY Freeman on 14 Mar at Portsmouth NH *MS* 10 Apr 1844

TRIM Loiz m DUNNING Wm both of Charleston on 22d ult *MS* 12 Nov 1834

TRIPE Lovey m ROWELL Charles S both of Lowell MA *MS* 23 Sept 1835

TRIPP Eliza Ann of Kennebunk ME m SHACKLEY Augustus of Portsmouth NH on 16 Jul 1848 *MS* 9 Aug 1848

TRIPP Harriet M m PRESCOTT James L both of Epsom on 23 Dec 1847 *MS* 26 Jan 1848

TRIPP Louisa m DODD John J both of Scarborough on 4 Apr *MS* 1 Aug 1849

TRUE Abba d/o TRUE Paul Capt of Montville m STAPLES J L K of Gardiner on 23 May *MS* 20 June 1849

TRUE Anna M of Bangor m CAMPBELL A S of Ellsworth *MFWBR* 9 Nov 1850

TRUE Annett W m GLIDDEN John P at East Randolph VT on 11 Sept *MS* 29 Oct 1845

TRUE Charlotte E of Loudon m EASTMAN David of Limerick *MFWBR* 21 Jan 1849

TRUE Emily B of Corinth m SMITH Alpheus D Eld of Dover NH *MS* 11 Jul 1838

TRUE Jennett m THOITS Oren of Pownal ME *MFWBR* 8 May 1847

TRUE Lucy S of Center Harbor m TRUE John of Holderness on

TRUE (Continued)
   4 Aug *MS* 11 Sept 1850
TRUE Roxy Ann G on 26 Sept at Franklin m BAILEY Elbridge A of
   Weare NH "One of the guests was the great grandmother of the
   bride now in her 93rd year who came from another town to this
   festival. She has witnessed nine weddings and eight deaths in the
   same house; came to reside on the same spot more than 70 yrs
   being then a married woman." *MS* 30 Oct 1844
TRUE Sarah of Moultonboro' m WEBSTER Daniel C of Manchester
   NH *MS* 10 Oct 1844
TRUNDY Sarah E m CUNNINGHAM Erastus both of Wiscassett on
   26 Sept *MS* 27 Nov 1850
TUCK Hannah m DOE David Jr of Augusta ME on 6 Jan *MS* 6 Apr
   1836
TUCK Mary m WIGGINS Daniel on 5 Dec 1844 at Parsonsfield ME
   MS 16 Apr 1845
TUCK Nancy m WOODWORTH John Jr *MS* 28 Nov 1833
TUCKER Caroline M d/o TUCKER William Esq m NICHOLS J T G
   Rev of Saco ME *MFWBR* 12 Oct 1850
TUCKER Caroline of Ossipee m HURD John of Newfield on 7 inst *MS*
   27 Dec 1837
TUCKER Clarissa of Parma NY m RAYMOND Kendall *MS* 18 Oct
   1843
TUCKER Eliza T m SARGENT Harrison both of Concord NH in
   Canterbury *MS* 19 Jan 1848
TUCKER Elizabeth B of Mt Vernon ME m CLOUGH Henry C of
   Readfield ME *MS* 29 June 1836
TUCKER Lucinda of Sharon m MACK William of Strafford VT on 5
   Nov 1848 *MS* 6 June 1849
TUCKER Lucretia A of Buckfield ME m AMES Ira of Canton ME *MS*
   12 May 1847
TUCKER Lydia of Durnham on 9th inst at New Market m DAME
   John Jr of Jackson (NH?) *MS* 26 Apr 1843
TUCKER Mary m DURGIN John C of Haverhill MA on 26 Feb at
   Organge??? *MS* 19 Mar 1845
TUCKER Mary of Ossipee m AMES Marston of Parsonsfield on 14
   inst *MS* 24 May 1837
TUCKER Sarah m DUDLEY Benjamin of Mt Vernon ME in Raymond
   NH *MS* 20 Sept 1827
TUCKEY Sally of Waterboro m FERNALD John Y of Ossipee NH on
   23 Dec *MS* 9 Feb 1831
TUFTS Eliza both recent members of Shakers m GARLAND Daniel H
   on 7 Oct *MS* 14 Nov 1849
TUFTS Ellen m CASWELL Thomas both of Dover on 17 inst *MS* 20
   May 1846
TUFTS Lucretia H m RANDALL Daniel L of Farmington *MS* 27 Nov

TUFTS (Continued)
1844
TUFTS Olive H Mrs of Medford MA m MERRILL John of Parsonsfield
ME on 7 Sept 1848 *MS* 27 Sept 1848
TUFTS Susan of New Gloucester m BRACKETT Benjamin *MFWBR* 4
Aug 1849
TUKEY Abigail of Lowell MA m GOULD Elias L at Dracut MA *MS* 24
Feb 1847
TUPPER Alma M m STORY Martin both of Underhill on 7 Jul 1850
MS 14 Aug 1850
TUPPER Susan m HOWARD Orrin of Pierpont NY on 16 Feb *MS* 3
May 1843
TURNER Achsa m WILLIS Hiram Eld both of Rome on 12 Sept *MS* 5
Dec 1849
TURNER Almira m WHITNEY John both of Lisbon on 9 ult *MS* 8 May
1844
TURNER Betsey B of Foxcroft ME on 5 Dec 1844 m CRUMMETT
James R of Sebec ME at Bangor ME *MS* 9 Apr 1845
TURNER Brittania m FOBES Richard on 4 Nov *MS* 28 Nov 1849
TURNER Catherine S m SEWALL Caleb M Eld on 11th ult at Adams
Co IL *MS* 17 Sept 1845
TURNER Emma of Schroeppel NY m NEWTON Wm C of Bolney NY
on 16 Sept 1847 *MS* 17 Nov 1847
TURNER Mary Ann of Hatley m KING Sylvester of Compton LC on 25
Nov *MS* 13 Apr 1842
TURNER Mary Jane m HAYES Hubbard both of Nassau on 29 Jan
1846 *MS* 8 Apr 1846
TURNER Nancy Mrs m PERKINS Noah on at Portsmouth *MS* 26 Dec
1833
TURNER Olive m HAYES Silas B both of Nassau on 5 Aug 1848 *MS*
11 Oct 1848
TURNER Roxa R C of Concord m COATS Charles G on 15 Nov *MS* 5
Dec 1849
TURNER Sarah Ann of St Albans ME m FRENCH Enoch on 21 Mar
MS 7 June 1843
TURNER Theodorie M m STARK Caleb N both of Schroeppel NY on
11 Sept *MS* 4 Dec 1850
TUTTLE Abigail of Dover m GAGE Gerry R on 12th inst at Dover NH
MS 22 Oct 1845
TUTTLE Betsey m DICKEY Morril both of Strafford on 31 ult *MS* 21
Feb 1838
TUTTLE Catharine of Effingham m HODGDON Ebenezer Jr of Ossi-
pee NH on 16th inst *MS* 27 Mar 1834
TUTTLE Elizabeth of Dover "Cake received" m MERSERVE Henry on
3d inst at Dover NH *MS* 12 Oct 1842
TUTTLE Elvira B of Sandwich m RUGGLES Lorenzo D of Sutton VT

653

TUTTLE (Continued)
on 1 inst *MS* 24 Oct 1838

TUTTLE Hannah Mrs of Great Falls NH m WHEEDEN Edward *MFWBR* 4 May 1850

TUTTLE Lydia A of Effingham m NICKERSON Luke of Eaton on 9 Jan *MS* 26 Mar 1851

TUTTLE Lydia S m HAINES James Madison both of Nottingham on 4th inst *MS* 17 Dec 1834

TUTTLE Maria m DOWNS Aaron both of Lebanon *MS* 10 Jan 1838

TUTTLE Mary J of Strafford m PARKER Daniel G of Kittery ME on 23 Jan *MS* 5 Feb 1851

TUTTLE Mary of Barnstead NH m VARNEY Ira on 14 Aug 1842 at Alton *MS* 30 Nov 1842

TUTTLE Mehitabel of Saco on 17thth ult m WHITTEN Joseph *MFWBR* 1 Feb 1851

TUTTLE Nancy M of Boston MA on 31st ult m BOLTON Thomas of Portland ME *MFWBR* 13 Jan 1849

TUTTLE Rea Sylva A of Palmyra ME m ROWE Samuel of St Albans ME on 12 Feb *MS* 26 Mar 1851

TUTTLE Roxanna of Lowell on Apr 1 m BRACKETT Daniel G *MS* 10 Apr 1839

TUTTLE Sarah J of Effingham m LEAVITT U M of Boston MA on 17 ult *MS* 4 Dec 1850

TUTTTLE Abigail H of Effingham m LEAVITT John C on 1 Feb 1849 *MS* 7 Mar 1849

TUTTTLE Henrietta m DAVIS Levi both of Nottingham *MS* 21 Aug 1850

TUXBURY Hannah B of Salbury MA m HUTCHINSON Asa Dea of Fayette ME on 4th inst *MS* 17 Sept 1834

TUXBURY Mary of Tamworth m WENTWORTH John of Dover *MS* 21 Nov 1838

TWINING Lucina B of Lowell m WOOD Oliver C on 12 Nov of Townsend MA *MS* 6 Jan 1847

TWITCHELL Lianda A of Walworth m PRATT Alva S of Ontario on 13 Nov *MS* 15 Jan 1851

TWITCHELL Mahala Mrs of Waterville ME m COZZENS William W of Bangor on 28 May *MS* 13 June 1849

TWOMBLY Abigail m NUTTER George on at Tuftonboro' NH *MS* 6 Mar 1834

TWOMBLY Ann B m BARTLETT Enoch both of Monroe on 29 Nov *MS* 26 Dec 1849

TWOMBLY Margaret C m PARKER Asa 2d on 2 Jul at Monroe *MS* 24 Jul 1844

TWOMBLY Mary m WHITCOMB Aseph both of Littleton on 20 Jul 1834 *MS* 7 Jan 1835

TWOMBLY Mary m DAVIS Samuel Jr both of Madbury on 1 Jan

TWOMBLY (Continued)
    MS 1 Feb 1837
TWOMBLY Mary E of Dover NH m CARTER Daniel P on 4th inst at
    Dover NH *MS* 13 Mar 1844
TWOMBLY Mary Jane m TWOMBLY Reuben Jr both of Dover on 25
    ult *MS* 2 Sept 1846
TWOMBLY Susan M m JENNESS Luther S of Somersworth on 10
    Aug at Alton *MS* 17 Jan 1844
TWOMBLY Susan of Garland ME m GEE Solomon on 25 Apr at
    Garland ME *MS* 9 June 1847
TYLER Amaretta Miss of Portsmouth NH m NASH Charles W of
    Dover *MS* 19 Dec 1833
TYLER Jane S of Brownfield m STEVENS Augustus L of Portland
    MFWBR 10 Mar 1849
TYLER Sarah on 19th ult at Hamburgh NY m WILSON Roswell of
    Eden NY *MS* 4 Aug 1847
TYNG Pamelia m LEW Osmon of Lowell MA *MS* 10 Sept 1845

UNDERWOOD Fanny A of Saxonville MA m YOUNG Ivory H of
    Wolfborough NH on 29 Jan *MS* 23 May 1849
UNDERWOOD Laura m CHADDOCK Lewis on 19 Sept at Attica NY
    MS 20 Nov 1844
UPTON Nancy m MOORE Isaac on 21 Mar *MS* 24 May 1843
UPTON Sarah m WITHAM Aaron both of Biddeford on 12 ult *MS* 12
    Aug 1835
USHER Elizabeth R of Limerick ME m EDGECOMB William of Hollis
    ME *MFWBR* 16 Sept 1848

VALENTINE Mary Ann of Sand Lake NY m TUCKER Eber H on 5th
    Oct *MS* 11 Dec 1844
VALLET Mary m SHEARMAN Henry on 11 Jan *MS* 7 Feb 1838
VAN VALKENBURGH Nancy of Sand Lake m WHIPPLE Job P of
    Springfield on 8 inst *MS* 22 Jan 1851
VAN VORST Sophia T of Russia NY m LOOKER Henry E of Wilmot
    on 1st Jan at Russia Herkimer Co NY *MS* 5 Feb 1845
VANDOSAN Fanny E of Freedom NY m SPENCER Eleazar of Farm-
    ersville on 22 Feb 1848 *MS* 10 May 1848
VARBERD Susan m STAR Damon both of Burns (Steuben Co NY?)
    MS 20 Sept 1837
VARNEY Abby C m RICH James M both of Jackson on 27 ult *MS* 24
    Nov 1847
VARNEY Abby L of Windham m SMITH T H of Buxton ME on 10 May
    1848 *MS* 14 June 1848
VARNEY Achsah Mrs m BRADLEY Nathaniel both of Alton NH on 16
    Nov 1848 *MS* 29 Nov 1848
VARNEY Adaline m HALL James b/o Dover 6 Aug *MS* 12 Aug 1846

VARNEY Almira m ROBERTS Charles W both of Dover on 1 inst *MS* 18 Dec 1850

VARNEY Betsey L of Manchester NH m DAVIS William Y on 11 Mar at Manchester NH *MS* 14 Apr 1847 & *MS* 26 May 1847

VARNEY Caroline G of Dover m RICKER William *MS* 13 Nov 1839

VARNEY Elizabeth m BEEDE David both of Dover *MS* 30 Dec 1835

VARNEY Hannah H on 7 March m FELKER Samuel on 7 March at Barrington *MS* 27 Mar 1844

VARNEY Jane H m DURGIN James H of Parsonsfield ME on 27 Oct *MS* 18 Dec 1844

VARNEY Lydia m JENNESS Nathaniel on 1st inst *MS* 9 Jan 1834

VARNEY Lydia M of Lowell MA m SHIRLEY John on 26 Mar *MS* 25 May 1842

VARNEY Mary m TUTTLE Nathaniel both of Dover on last afternoon *MS* 9 Apr 1851

VARNEY Mary E m DIXON Thomas S both of Lebanon ME on 15 inst *MS* 28 Aug 1850

VARNEY Mary E of Dover m SHALLIES Chauncy of Boston MA on 20 inst *MS* 26 Sept 1849

VARNEY Mary J m ALLARD Henry *MS* 8 Dec 1847

VARNEY Olive of Dover m FOSS John of Strafford on 23d ult *MS* 19 Apr 1837

VARNEY Olive of Somersworth m CLARK Moses *MS* 5 Dec 1833

VARNEY Samson m BENNETT Luther on 22 Dec 1844 at Alton NH *MS* 12 Feb 1845

VARNEY Sarah m AUSTIN Stoten both of Dover NH *MS* 13 May 1835

VARNEY Sarah J m PALMER George F on 11 Jan at Rochester *MS* 21 Jan 1846

VARNEY Sarah T of Dover NH m COOK Moses of Boston on 31st ult *MS* 8 Aug 1833

VARNEY Susan E m BURROWS Jiles W both of Milton on 12 Nov 1848 *MS* 3 Jan 1849

VARNUM Hannah E of Dracut m VILES Albert of Chelmsford MA on 18 Feb at Dracut MA *MS* 24 Mar 1847

VAUGHN Mary W m SANDERS Angel both of Gloucester on 22 ult *MS* 18 Apr 1838

VEASIE Naomi of Dorchester m FOSS Zachariah B of Manchester on 1 Oct *MS* 11 Oct 1843

VEAZIE Clarinda C of Islesboro' m FULLER Nathan F of Searsport ME *MS* 18 Nov 1846

VEAZIE Jane H on 15 Oct at Islesboro' ME m FELKER Michael of Searsport ME *MS* 18 Nov 1846

VEAZIE Rachel at Isleborough ME m ROAKS Isaac of Appleton ME *MS* 26 Feb 1840

VENESS Harriet of Sugar Grove PA m WOODRUFF Calvin of Ashford NY *MS* 14 Feb 1844

VENNA Eliza m CARR Nelson both of Edwards on 7 Sept *MS* 21 Oct 1846

VERESS Elmira M of Sweden m WOOD Ira D on 3 Jul at Sweden *MS* 19 Jul 1843

VERRILL Tryphene P m MORRELL Paul of Boston *MS* 3 Jul 1839

VESEY Mary J m MERRILL Samuel F both of Deerfield NH on 1 Nov 1849 *MS* 16 Jan 1850

VILES Susan m BUTLER Levi *MFWBR* 13 Oct 1849

VINCEN Sally m EMERSON Benjamin J both of New Market on 8 ult Sabbath eve *MS* 25 Apr 1838

VINCENT Abby Ann on 20 Oct 1846 m BEEBE Sylvester on 20 Oct 1846 at Clayton NY *MS* 10 Mar 1847

VINCENT Eliza H m DOCKUM Charles H in Durham 16th inst *MS* 19 Jan 1842

VINCENT Laura Ann at Norway m BENJAMIN David on 3 Jan *MS* 24 May 1843

VINCENT Thankful H of Durham NH m BATCH Frederick B of Lancaster NH on 14 Mar 1848 *MS* 3 May 1848

VITTUM Mary A of Sandwich m KELLY Francis B of Salem on 6 Nov at Sandwich *MS* 17 Dec 1845

WADE Deborah C m EATON C M *MFWBR* 11 Dec 1847 & of Topsham m EATON Charles M *MS* 19 Jan 1848

WADE Elizabeth on 7 Dec m WILLIAMS Johnson on 7 Dec at Woolwich ME *MS* 27 Dec 1843

WADE Isabella J of Freeport ME m SOUL Robert T Capt of Bath ME *MS* 18 June 1845

WADE Lucy H m WAKEFIELD Thomas D both of Bath on 1 inst in Freeport ME *MS* 15 Jan 1851

WADLEIGH Ann m GRANT Granville both of So Berwick ME on 16 inst *MS* 22 Aug 1849 & of Berwick ME m GRANT Granville *MFWBR* 1 Sept 1849

WADLEIGH Mary R of Manchester NH m BARRETT William M *MS* 15 Nov 1843 .

WADLEY Lydia of Hatley m FLETCHER Joseph of Compton LC on 5 May 1837 *MS* 10 Jan 1837

WADSWORTH Ruth of Hiram m PENDEXTER Samuel Jr Eld of Georgetown on 3 Dec *MS* 12 Dec 1849 & *MFWBR* 22 Dec 1849

WADSWORTH Sarah S of Hiram m BENTON Albion P on 7 June *MS* 7 Feb 1844

WAFUL Mary of Norway m HIZER James of Newport NY 1 Jan *MS* 24 May 1843

WAFUL Rebecca of Newport NY m HALL Marvin of Norway on 5 Sept *MS* 30 Oct 1850

WAILEIGH Susan A m DUNN Richard on 22 Nov of Belgrade ME *MS* 8 Jan 1845

WAIR Mary M of Gardiner m ROBERTS Gardiner *MS* 10 Apr 1839

WAKEFIELD Martha Ann of Gardiner on 22nd ult m BRAND Levi T
MS 16 Oct 1839

WAKEFIELD Mary J of Lyman m BRADBURY Ebenezer H C of Biddeford on 9 Jan 1848 *MS* 8 Mar 1848

WAKEFIELD Sarah A m MUZZEY Eden both of Gardiner on 16 Dec
MS 24 Apr 1950

WAKEFIELD Sarah C of Hollis ME m SWETT Daniel of Waterboro
ME on 29th ult *MS* 20 Apr 1832

WAKS Ann m PARSHLEY John both of Brunswick *MS* 23 Jan 1850

WALCOTT Julia Ann of Bath m BARRON Richard B at Bath ME *MS*
19 Oct 1842

WALCOTT Sarah A m CORNING John S both of Brasher NY on 11
Sept *MS* 2 Oct 1850

WALDRON Clarissa of Dover m CANOVAN Martin H of Boston MA on
6 Nov *MS* 12 Dec 1838

WALDRON Elizabeth Ann of Dover NH m DUDLEY Oren of Springfield MA *MS* 13 Jul 1836

WALDRON Elizabeth H of Dover NH m McCRILLIS Thomas on 20
Apr at Dover NH *MS* 30 Apr 1845

WALDRON Hannah B (widow of the late Simon BATCHELDER of
Northwood) d/o WALDRON Isaac Col of Barrington m(2) TASKER
Elisha on 3 Feb at Northwood *MS* 17 Feb 1847

WALDRON Mary Elizabeth Miss d/o WALDRON Job C Col late of
Dover NH town m MARSTON Winthrop A Esq of Great Falls *MS*
13 Feb 1834

WALGROVE Hester of New York m SILVA Francis J on 11th inst at
New York City *MS* 21 Sept 1842

WALKER A H of Paris m FULLER Alden of Minot *MFWBR* 28 Jul
1849

WALKER Caroline E of Manchester m BECKER Martin F of
Surinam(e) South America on 28 Mar 1850 *MS* 10 Apr 1850

WALKER Cyrenia m COLE Ivory 2d both of Brownfield ME on 16
June *MS* 24 Jul 1850

WALKER Elizabeth H of Ossipee NH m HANSON Cyrus on 10 Mar at
Osseppee NH *MS* 20 Mar 1844

WALKER Emeline m BROOKS William E Jr on 9 Jul at Naples ME
MS 19 Jul 1843

WALKER Hannah J B m MARDEN Israel both of Portsmouth NH on
14 May *MS* 27 May 1846

WALKER Hannah W of Strafford m TASKER Vincent P on 27 Sept of
Strafford *MS* 16 Nov 1842

WALKER Jane m HODGDON Alexander W both of Epping NH on 27
May *MS* 6 June 1849

WALKER Lorinda m RICH Joseph both of Exeter ME on 14th ult *MS*
11 Mar 1835

WALKER Lucy at Barrington NH m HODGDON Daniel on 10 Dec *MS* 21 Jan 1846

WALKER Lydia Ann m DOUGLASS Orin both of Limington ME on 21 Nov *MS* 15 Jan 1840

WALKER Malina A of New Hartford m LUCE Sirah A of Winfield on 11 Nov *MS* 1 Jan 1851

WALKER Martha I m GILMAN Bracket H both of Dover on 2 Jan 1849 *MS* 10 Jan 1849

WALKER Martha m GEORGE Samuel on 21 Jan at Haverhill *MS* 14 Feb 1844

WALKER Mary Ann m BOOTHBY Leander both of Limington ME on 5 May 1850 *MS* 29 May 1850 & m BOOTHBY Leador *MFWBR* 1 June 1850

WALKER Mary m EVANS John K both of Dover NH on 25 ult *MS* 5 Oct 1836

WALKER Rhoda J m LOCKWOOD Benajah T both of Smithfield on 25 Dec 1848 *MS* 17 Jan 1849

WALKER Sarah Ann m BUSWELL Geo both of Paris on 24 Mar *MS* 22 May 1850

WALKER Sophia m DAY Israel on 10 June at Waterboro ME *MS* 18 June 1845

WALKER Susan d/o WALKER Elihu m SHERMAN P R both of Aurora Erie Co NY on 20th ult *MS* 14 May 1834

WALKER Susan m BURNHAM John both of Harrison ME on 9 Nov *MS* 6 Jan 1836

WALKER Susannah of Williamstown m NORRIS John A of Corinth on 7 Nov 1849 *MS* 16 Jan 1850

WALKLER Susannah m BROWN Jonathan O both of Tuftonborough NH *MS* 5 Apr 1837

WALLACE Abigail M m WALLACE James F at Sandwich *MS* 27 Mar 1844

WALLACE Catharine H of Dover m CLARK Andrew J on 8 inst *MS* 28 June 1848

WALLACE Lama Ann m MOULTON David W of Manchester NH *MS* 17 Feb 1847

WALLACE Nancy P m SLEEPER George of Andover on 9 May at Wilmot *MS* 29 May 1844

WALLACE Olive W of Dover m NORRIS Arthur F L Esq of Pittsfield on 25 Jul *MS* 21 Oct 1846

WALLACE Vienna m BOWLES Levi on 23 Mar at Franconia NH *MS* 28 Apr 1847

WALLINGFORD Judith of Lebanon ME m BERRY Jotham S on 17 Apr of Portsmouth NH *MS* 21 May 1845

WALLINGFORD Louisana m CORSON Phineas both of Lebanon ME *MS* 22 May 1850

WALLRON Lydia A m OSBORN James L on 2 Oct *MS* 1 Jan 1851

WALRATH Elizabeth m WALRATH Nathaniel on 1 Mar 1848 *MS* 21 June 1848

WALTER Mary m GRANT Samuel both of Dover on 24 inst *MS* 3 Jan 1849

WALTON Clarissa H of Lowell MA m SAUNDERS George B of Boston MA on 30 June *MS* 2 Nov 1842

WALTON Hannah D m MARSHALL John B both of Lowell on 30 Jul *MS* 19 Jul 1842

WALTON Harriet N m HATCH Samuel M both of Lowell *MS* 17 Nov 1847

WALTON Sarah D m JEFFS Algernon P both of Salem on 24 ult *MS* 27 Nov 1850

WALTSON Emelin M of Great Falls d/o WATSON Elijah Eld of Andover m BROOKS Nahum of Concord at Great Falls *MS* 17 Feb 1836

WARD Elizabeth A m BAILEY Chandler on 27 Nov at Nottingham *MS* 30 Dec 1846

WARD Elizabeth m JORDAN George H both of Freeport on 21 Mar *MS* 15 May 1850

WARD Hannah of Danville m WEEKS John P of Danville VT *MS* 24 Feb 1847

WARD Jane C m RINGROSE William both of Freeport ME *MS* 17 Nov 1847

WARD Mary m CABOT Dean both of Windsor on 29 ult *MS* 6 June 1838

WARD Mary E m WARD John both of Freeport ME on 12 Dec 1847 *MS* 9 Feb 1848

WARD Mary Jane of Freeport ME m DUNHAM Elliot M of Brunswick ME on 30 Jul *MS* 16 Aug 1837

WARD Mary L m CHASE Alfred G *MS* 6 Dec 1848

WARNER Arabella of Ashford m WHITNEY Joseph of Sardina *MS* 14 Feb 1844

WARNER Loovsa m STEARNS Lorenzo both of Grafton VT on 26 Nov *MS* 11 Dec 1850

WARREN Esther P m PAUL Sylvester of Westbrook ME *MFWBR* 22 Jul 1848

WARREN Harriet of Fryeburg m PIKE Asa O on 26 Dec *MS* 31 Jan 1844

WARREN Lucy Ann Y of Sangerville ME on Apr 7th m CHAMBER-LAIN Chester of Foxcroft ME *MS* 29 May 1839

WARREN Lydia of Monmouth ME m SANBORN Moses of Wales ME *MS* 10 Jul 1839

WARREN Mary of L m COFFING Abiel of Saco ME on Monday *MS* 27 Dec 1827

WARREN Sabrina A of Limerick ME m DURGIN David C of Limerick *MFWBR* 14 Sep 1850

WARREN Susan J m DURRELL Nathan G on 9 Nov at Waterborough ME *MS* 18 Dec 1844

WASHBURN Roxcillana of Portland ME m ELDER Richard J of Windham ME *MS* 18 Apr 1838

WATERHOUSE Dorothy K m HAM Joseph of Barrington on 13 Oct *MS* 12 Nov 1845

WATERHOUSE Elizabeth m JENKINS Oliver on Sun eve *MS* 21 Jan 1835

WATERHOUSE Harriette E of Portland ME m SMITH Hezekiah *MFWBR* 25 May 1850

WATERHOUSE Julia A of Gray ME m CAREY Thomas of Oxford ME *MS* 10 Jul 1839

WATERHOUSE of Lyman ME m ROBERTS John of Kennebunk ME *MFWBR* 25 May 1850

WATERHOUSE Olive of Limington ME m WATERHOUSE Charles F of Durham on 26 Feb *MS* 7 Feb 1844

WATERHOUSE Phebe of Limington ME m GUPTILL Stephen of Cornish ME on 5 Nov 1843 *MS* 29 May 1844

WATERHOUSE Sarah A of Barrington m TUTTLE Jonathan on 13 Mar at Strafford NH *MS* 6 Apr 1842

WATERHOUSE Sarah C of Sweden ME m HOWE Lewis of Fryburg ME on 31 Jan 1849 *MS* 25 Apr 1849

WATERHOUSE Sarah m FREEMAN Alexander on 13 Sep 1843 at Gorham ME *MS* 27 Sept 1843

WATERMAN Caroline M of Fairley m MACK John W on 21 Nov of Corinth VT *MS* 17 Feb 1847

WATERMAN Laura m ANGELL Nathaniel on 20th ult *MS* 24 Apr 1834

WATERMAN Martha m DOLE Leonard both of Richmond ME *MS* 29 June 1836

WATERMAN Sophia of Litchfield ME m SHERMAN Zachariah T of Boothbay ME *MS* 4 Sept 1839

WATSON Abigail m DAY Oliver of Cornish on Sunday last *MS* 1 June 1831

WATSON Abigail of Pittsfield m TRUE Elbridge A on 15 Sept at Pittsfield *MS* 12 Oct 1842

WATSON Betsey of Warner m SARGENT Zebulon of Hopkinton on 11 Sept *MS* 12 Oct 1836

WATSON Caroline m SPRINGER Andrew both of Richmond *MS* 22 Aug 1838

WATSON Charlotte of Manchester m BICKFORD Jerome of Concord on 22 Nov 1847 *MS* 8 Dec 1847

WATSON Eliza of Pittsfield on 29 Dec m BUZZELL Gilman of Northwood *MS* 1 Feb 1843

WATSON Emily of Freedom NH m WARD Erastus on 17 Mar at Effingham Falls NH *MS* 2 Apr 1845

WATSON Emily of Warner m RAND Charles D of Hopkinton NH on 29 Nov *MS* 19 Dec 1838

WATSON F Eld of Andover m FROST D S Eld on 12 May at Andover of Hopkinton *MS* 1 June 1842

WATSON Hannah B m WINSLOW Charles E both of Northwood on 6 Mar 1849 *MS* 11 Apr 1849

WATSON Hannah m KENYON Daniel H both of Lowell *MS* 12 Feb 1840

WATSON Harriet A of Dover m HARKER John C of Dover NH *MS* 1 Oct 1845

WATSON Harriet of New Market on 2 Sept m STILSON James *MS* 11 Sept 1839

WATSON Jane M on 20 Aug m BURNETT James F *MS* 9 Dec 1846

WATSON Jane m WALLACE George B on 2 Nov at Dover NH *MS* 8 Nov 1843

WATSON Lucy of Dover NH m HORN Thomas on 10th inst at Dover NH *MS* 18 June 1845

WATSON Maria S Mrs of South Berwick ME m SANBORN William A of Boston MA at FWB meeting house at South Berwick ME on 14th inst *MS* 24 Feb 1847

WATSON Mary Ann m AMES Lotan both of Lowell on 29 inst *MS* 16 May 1838

WATSON Mary E m ELLIS Ebenezer both of Alton NH on 28 Nov 1848 *MS* 20 Dec 1848

WATSON Mary m VITTUM Stephen of Sandwich *MS* 29 Jan 1845

WATSON Mary of Limerick m PARKER William of Cornish on 26th ult *MS* 3 Feb 1832

WATSON Minerva D d/o WATSON E Eld of Andover NH m FROST D S Eld *MS* 1 June 1842

WATSON Pamelia P m CHENEY William of Wilmot on 29 Apr at Andover *MS* 14 May 1845

WATSON Sarah m DAVIS Hiram A on 24 Mar *MS* 24 Apr 1844

WATSON Sarah m GREENWOOD Joseph R on 12 Nov *MS* 23 Dec 1846

WATSON Susan P of Saco ME m KIMBALL Heber Jr on 14 Sept at Harrison ME *MS* 24 Sept 1845

WATTS Hannah of Buxton m FILES Francis of Gorham ME on 29 Oct at Buxton ME *MS* 20 Nov 1844

WATTS Joanna of Hallowell ME m ADAMS Ivory of Wales ME *MS* 7 Feb 1833

WATTS Lucy Ann of Falmouth m DeCOSTER Axel of Waltham MA on 11 June at Falmouth ME *MS* 6 Sept 1843

WATTS Sabrina C of Stow m HALE Kershy W on 22 Sept at Brookfield VT *MS* 15 Jan 1845

WAUGHN Betsy of Brunswick O m ASHELY John of Greenfield on 22 Oct *MS* 15 Jan 1851

WAY Fidelia m WELLS Squire on 28 Jan *MS* 25 Feb 1846

WAY Martha L of Hopkinton m SARGENT Thomas W of Hanniker on 31 Oct *MS* 5 Dec 1849

WAYMOUTH Olive Ann of North Berwick ME m HURD Benjamin C on Thanksgiving day at Lebanon *MS* 8 Dec 1841

WEARE Abigail of Dorchester MA m CLARK Peter of Gilmanton on 13 Jul 1848 *MS* 26 Jul 1848

WEARE Mary Ann of Pierpont on 20 Oct m PERRY Charles of Matildaville *MS* 1 Feb 1843

WEATHERVEE Caroline E m IVES G W M 5 Aug *MS* 26 Sept 1849

WEAVER Persis m MATTESON James both of Arkwright NY on 9 May *MS* 19 June 1850

WEBB Sarah m WENTWORTH Job L *MFWBR* 27 Apr 1850

WEBBER Dorcas m MILLS James of Waterboro ME *MFWBR* 21 Sep 1850

WEBBER Lucy of Lisbon NH m THOMPSON Person C of Holderness on 28 Mar 1850 *MS* 10 Apr 1850

WEBBER Roxana of Holderness m BOWEN John on 30 Oct at Holderness *MS* 17 Dec 1845

WEBBER Ruth F of Chesterville at Readfield ME m RICHARDSON Henry of Waterville ME on 18 Jul *MS* 21 Nov 1843 & Ruth F of Vienna ME on 18 Jul 1843 m RICHARDSON Henry of Waterville ME *MS* 6 Sept 1843

WEBBER Sarah Elizabeth of Salem m BRAINARD John C of Bath ME *MFWBR* 12 Oct 1850

WEBSTER Betsey of Chichester m FELLOWS James B of Concord NH on 11 inst *MS* 25 Oct 1848

WEBSTER Cynthia m STILLINGS Daniel *MS* 25 Apr 1833

WEBSTER Elvira m BROWN Nathan both of Albany on 18 Mar 1850 *MS* 3 Apr 1850

WEBSTER Hannah M m SEVERANCE Asa both of Sandwich on 20 Nov *MS* 15 Jan 1851

WEBSTER Lucy of Newfield m ANDREW Abraham of Somersworth on 16th inst *MS* 26 Oct 1832

WEBSTER Marilla B of Boscawen m LAINE Daniel F of Gilmanton (NH)? *MS* 13 June 1842

WEBSTER Martha E of Dover m PERCIVAL John F of Boston MA on 1 Nov *MS* 7 Nov 1849

WEBSTER Mary Ann m HASKINS Asa L on 31 Dec 1846 at Enfield NH *MS* 5 May 1847

WEBSTER Mary Ann of Sandwich m PRESCOTT John M on 24 Nov *MS* 18 Dec 1844

WEBSTER Mary m EMERY David both of Gilmanton *MS* 14 Jan 1835

WEBSTER Sally D of Gilford m OSGOOD Enoch F of Gilford *MS* 13 Sept 1843

WEBSTER Sarah A C of Gray ME m HUNT James M on 2 Nov *MS* 17 Jan 1844

WEBSTER Sarah J m HURD Stephen N at Lowell MA *MS* 12 Nov 1845

WEBSTER Sarah of Landaff at Landaff NH m QUIMBY David of Lisbon (NH?) *MS* 19 Apr 1843

WEBSTER Sarah T m BARKER Wm H both of Newport RI on 8 Mar *MS* 8 Apr 1846

WEBSTER Susan m RIDLON Lewis both of Saco ME on 5 June 1848 *MS* 26 Jul 1848

WEBSTER Susan m CARTER John M both of Sandwich on 25 Oct *MS* 4 Nov 1846

WEDENBURY Ann of Augusta m LINCOLN H B Esq *MFWBR* 2 Nov 1850

WEDGE Syrena m BISHOP George W on 10 June 1841 at Freedom NY *MS* 15 Mar 1843

WEDGEWOOD Drusilla m THURSTON Henry C both of Eaton *MS* 4 June 1834

WEDGEWOOD Hannah of Parsonsfield m MORE John of Newfield *MS* 17 Oct 1833

WEDGEWOOD Olive m WEEKS Samuel D both of Lowell on 28 inst *MS* 12 Sept 1838

WEDGEWOOD Susan m TOWLE Jabez Capt on Thurs last *MS* 19 Oct 1826

WEDGEWOOD Sylvia I m MOSHER Amos P *MFWBR* 24 Aug 1850

WEDGWOOD Mary M m DORE Samuel H at Sandwich *MS* 31 Dec 1845

WEED Anna J m WILLIAMS Benjamin both of Freedom *MS* 22 Jan 1851

WEED Delia of Danville VT m HARRIS Stephen Deacon on 19 Mar at Bethlehem NH *MS* 14 May 1845

WEED Laura Ann of Danville VT m RANDALL Silas on 11 Jan of Danville VT *MS* 21 Jan 1846

WEEKS Almira of Kittery ME m HANSON Avery of Elliot ME on 10th Dec *MS* 27 Dec 1843

WEEKS Almira W of Parsonsfield ME m BRACKETT Isaac on 17 May at Parsonsfield ME *MS* 7 Feb 1844

WEEKS Anna Mrs m WEEKS Levi on 23d inst *MS* 27 Sept 1827

WEEKS Betsey m JAMES Annis C of Gilford *MS* 13 Dec 1843

WEEKS Betsey K of Meredith m RANDLETT Daniel *MS* 14 Feb 1844

WEEKS Caroline E m SWAIN Charles F both of Gilford on 22 Oct 1848 *MS* 1 Nov 1848

WEEKS Catherine P d/o WEEKS Levi Deacon m LORD John 3rd *MFWBR* 27 Feb 1847

WEEKS Emeline R m EASTMAN Ezra both of Gilford on 13 June 1849 *MS* 9 Jan 1850

WEEKS Flinda of Gilmanton NH m MORRILL Josiah R on Jan 1844 MS 31 Jan 1844

WEEKS Hannah R of Parsonsfield m LORD James of Limerick ME on 31 Dec MS 29 Jan 1840

WEEKS Julia A m DUHEN Dennis on 3d Kittery ME MS 1 Jan 1845

WEEKS Laura m WARD John on 4 Dec of Danville VT MS 21 Jan 1846

WEEKS Lorana B m WALDRON Wm on 15th inst MS 19 Dec 1833

WEEKS Louisa of Brooksfield m TEBBETS Edmund B on 21 Dec at Wolfboro' NH MS 17 Jan 1844

WEEKS Mahala m CLEMENT Morrill both of Hopkinton NH on 13 Aug MS 5 Dec 1849

WEEKS Mary J of Parsonsfield ME m MERRILL Henry 3rd at East Parsonsfield ME MS 18 Feb 1846

WEEKS Mary S of Strafford m WINKLEY David B of Concord NH on 23 Jan 1848 MS 29 Mar 1848

WEEKS Mercy Ann of Parsonsfield on Jan 19 m BRACKETT Moses R of Cornish MS 19 Feb 1840

WEEKS Nancy B at Parsonsfield m STAPLES Hiram Jr of Limington ME MS 20 May 1840

WEEKS Olive m GUPTILL Hiram of Cornish ME on 2 Jul MS 9 Aug 1843

WEEKS Sarah A of Canterbury m JONES James D of Gilmanton on 23 Apr 1848 MS 3 May 1848

WEEKS Sarah C m PALMER Dennis on 10th ult MS 22 Jul 1831

WEEKS Sarah F m SWAIN Alvah T on 3 Dec MS 14 Feb 1844

WEEKS Susannah K m NEWELL William B both of Durham on 16 June MS 10 Jul 1850

WEEKS Susannah of Parsonsfield m BARKER Nathaniel Jr of Cornish MS 15 Apr 1840

WELCH Betsey m BURNHAM Charles on 17 Sept at Manchester MS 27 Sept 1843

WELCH Hannah of Monmouth m METCALF Mason Jr of Litchfield MS 26 Nov 1834

WELCH Martha A m DURGIN Ephraim MFWBR 8 Jul 1848

WELCH Mary Jane of So Berwick m STACKPOLE Edwin L of Rollinsford on 14 Jul MS 31 Jul 1850

WELCH Mercy m PUGSLEY Moses both of Springvale on 1 Oct 1848 MS 14 Feb 1849

WELCH Sally m AYERS Levi both of Tuftonboro NH on 27 ult MS 23 Aug 1837

WELCH Susan E of Effingham on 2d Jan m EMERY Alvin of Hampton MS 30 Jan 1839

WELLMAN Hannah C m ELLIOT Nathaniel both of New Portland ME in Embden ME Wed 22 Dec last MS 16 Feb 1842

WELLMAN Sarah Jane of Yankeytown Ohio m MYERS Jacob of

WELLMAN (Continued)
Goshen on 30 Dec 1841 *MS* 2 Mar 1842

WELLS Abigail m BACHELDER George W on 11 inst *MS* 26 Apr 1837

WELLS Agness m HICKS James both of Compton on 1st inst *MS* 18 May 1836

WELLS Almira formerly of Lyman Jefferson Co NY m TOWNSEND Absolom A Esq of Shellsburg WT *MS* 21 Aug 1844

WELLS Bethiah Clarissa at PLT No Two on 20 Oct m PERRY Samuel *MS* 5 Feb 1840

WELLS Betsey R m FULLER Zadock P both of Brookfield on Jan 20 1842 *MS* 23 Mar 1842

WELLS Caroline Mrs m MOODY Ager on 20 May at Stowe *MS* 14 Jul 1847

WELLS Hannah M of Epson m CLOUGH Joseph A of Strafford on 27 May *MS* 10 June 1846

WELLS Lucretia B of Springfield m CLARK Nelson of Cavendish on 4 Oct at Windsor *MS* 16 Nov 1842

WELLS Lucy of Landaff (NH?) m SMITH Israel B on 22 Dec *MS* 19 Apr 1843

WELLS Phebe d/o WELLS Simon Capt of China Gen Co NY m OLMSTED Orrin O on 17 Dec 1834 *MS* 7 Jan 1835

WELLS Rachel of Lowell m DICKEY Morrill of Epsom NH *MS* 25 Nov 1835

WENDELL Susan L m LOOK John J *MFWBR* 12 May 1849 & *MFWBR* 16 June 1849

WENTWORTH Abby A m MORRISON Samuel C both of Great Falls on 14 Oct *MS* 31 Oct 1849

WENTWORTH Abigail R of Alton m HAYES Samuel of Wolfboro on 7 Jul 1847 *MS* 1 Sept 1847

WENTWORTH Adaline J m CLARK J Smith *MFWBR* 22 Dec 1849

WENTWORTH Angelesia C of Jackson NH m ADAMS Reuben L Esq Post Master of Lancaster on 20 inst *MS* 3 Nov 1847

WENTWORTH Betsey m BUNKER Joseph M *MS* 24 Apr 1834

WENTWORTH Betsey m LORD Eli B on 7th inst at Lebanon ME *MS* 17 Feb 1847

WENTWORTH Clara R m BICKFORD Newell J both of Great Falls NH on 26 Aug *MS* 5 Sept 1849

WENTWORTH Eliza W of Berwick ME m PERKINS James S of Somersworth NH on 16 Nov 1848 *MS* 22 Nov 1848

WENTWORTH Elizabeth A of Dover m RELLINS Aaron B of Sandwich NH on 27th ult *MS* 8 Dec 1834

WENTWORTH Eunice m HILTON Richard Jr both of Ossipee NH in Ossipee 23 Feb 1842 *MS* 16 Mar 1842

WENTWORTH Laura J of So Berwick m WENTWORTH Benjamin L of Great Falls on 21 Jan *MS* 30 Jan 1850

WENTWORTH Leonora m CHICK Amasa on 1 June at Ossipee NH

WENTWORTH (Continued)
MS 25 June 1845

WENTWORTH Lovina S m CHASE Daniel both of Somersworth on 15 inst MS 25 Sept 1850

WENTWORTH Lucy B of Lebanon ME m BURKS Charles H of Wolfborough NH on 29 Aug 1847 MS 1 Dec 1847

WENTWORTH Lydia of Ossipee NH m CHICK Robert on 31 Oct at Ossipee NH MS 6 Dec 1843

WENTWORTH Mahala of Bristol m WATERMAN Dexter Eld of Boothbay on 2nd inst MS 2 Jul 1834

WENTWORTH Mahala of Effingham m HERSOM Ebenezer of Acton ME on 30 Mar 1847 MS 12 Jan 1848

WENTWORTH Margaret m HOWE William on 24 March at Jackson MS 7 Jul 1847

WENTWORTH Martha Mrs m MATHEWS Alfred both of Boothbay on 28 Apr 1849 MS 15 May 1850

WENTWORTH Mary m NASON Nathan MS 10 Aug 1826

WENTWORTH Mary Ann of South Berwick ME m HART Simon of Somersworth NH on 9 March MS 15 Mar 1843

WENTWORTH Mary on 7 ult m OTIS William P of Dover MS 24 Jul 1839

WENTWORTH Paulina of Lebanon m COLBATH Lyman of Farmington NH on 26 Nov at Lebanon ME "Accompanying this marriage was a liberal slice of cake the name of the bridegroom as a scriber to the Star. Long life and a happy one to our young friends." MS 2 Dec 1846

WENTWORTH Roxannah C of Jackson NH m NUTTER Oliver of Wakefield on 27 June MS 11 Jul 1849 & MFWBR 21 Jul 1849

WENTWORTH Ruth of Kennebunk m MITCHELL Charles Capt of Newfield MS 9 Mar 1832

WENTWORTH Sally of Wakefield m LEIGHTON Charles on 14 ult MS 24 Oct 1838

WENTWORTH Sarah A of Boston m BARTLETT John A of Webster ME on 23 Jan MS 12 Feb 1851

WENTWORTH Sarah N of Somersworth m WENTWORTH Oliver W of Dover on 15 Oct MS 13 Nov 1850

WENTWORTH Susan M m HILL Joseph MS 9 Dec 1846

WENTWORTH Susanna of Lowell MA m DAVIS Alfred L on 29 May at Lowell MA MS 19 Oct 1842

WESCOTT Esther of Gorham ME m JORDAN Levi Capt of Raymond ME on 12 Dec 1849 MS 16 Jan 1850

WEST Eliza m ROBERTS Nathaniel both of Portland on 21 inst MS 8 Mar 1848

WEST Sarah m SCRIPTURE Andrew J both of Lowell MS 8 Jan 1840

WESTCOT Lucinda of Gorham ME m BRIGG William on 5 June at Gorham ME MS 17 Sept 1845

WESTON Emily of Foxcroft ME m CARSLEY Daniel of Sangerville *MS* 5 Dec 1833

WETHERBEE Lydia L of Effingham NH m MOODY James M of Limington ME on 15 Feb 1849 *MS* 28 Feb 1849 & *MFWBR* 10 Mar 1849

WETHERBY Elizabeth m BLOOD Jason G both of Haverhill in Haverhill Nov 27 *MS* 8 Apr 1846

WETHERSPOON Elizabeth m CONFORTH Robert at Fairfield ME *MS* 17 Apr 1844

WEYMOUTH Clarisea m ELWELL Joseph G both of No Berwick ME*MS* 5 Apr 1837

WEYMOUTH Hope Jane m TWOMBLY Thomas B Jr both of Dover on 31 Oct *MS* 11 Nov 1846

WEYMOUTH Love of No Berwick m STACY William 2nd of Berwick ME *MS* 5 Apr 1837

WEYMOUTH Martha J m HAINES Charles A on 4 Dec of Great Falls NH *MS* 18 Dec 1844

WEYMOUTH Mary m BARNES George W both of Lowell MA on 30 Nov 1848 *MS* 3 Jan 1849

WEYMOUTH Mary F m CLEAVELAND Aaron on 21 Jan at Tunbridge VT *MS* 24 Feb 1847

WEYMOUTH Mary Jane m BROWN Robert both of North Berwick ME in North Berwick Jan 2nd 1842 *MS* 19 Jan 1842

WEYMOUTH Sarah Ann m SCAMMON John F of Biddeford ME on 3 Jan at New Berwick *MS* 14 Jan 1846

WHEEDEN Rachel E of Whitefield NH m HUTCHINS Wm B of Stewartstown on 29 Nov *MS* 26 Dec 1849

WHEELER Abigail m TIFFT Spelman V on 29 Nov at Nassau *MS* 17 Dec 1845

WHEELER Betsey m SMITH Wilson both of Ashtabula Co Ohio on 13 Dec 1848 *MS* 10 Jan 1849

WHEELER Dorcas D of Chesterville m CRAIG Joseph S of Farmington *MS* 20 Oct 1830

WHEELER Esther of Eaton LC m LUTHER Thomas of Manchester on 10 Nov *MS* 5 Dec 1849

WHEELER Fanny m SHOREY Hollis on 18 Mar *MS* 1 May 1844

WHEELER Hannah of Barnston LC m EGELISTON Benjamin on at Clifton *MS* 18 May 1836

WHEELER Lucy E of Nassau m WATERMAN Isaac of Troy on 19 Oct *MS* 3 Jan 1849

WHEELER Lydia of Barnston m CROOKER Josiah B of Bufford on 3 Jan *MS* 22 Mar 1837

WHEELER Mary H of Brunswick ME m SMITH Libbey of Brunswick *MS* 2 Aug 1848

WHEELER Mereby of Ossipee m ANDREWS of Effingham in Ossipee NH Jan 30 *MS* 9 Mar 1842

WHEELER Sarah m HARVY John on 13 Apr *MS* 22 May 1844

WHEELER Sarah E d/o WHEELER John H Dr m PRAY T J W MD *MFWBR* 30 Nov 1850 & *MS* 27 Nov 1850

WHEELER Sophia m BROWN Moses F at Lowell *MS* 10 Sept 1845

WHEELER Sophia in Boston on the 13th inst at the chapel in Causeway St m GILMAN Geo C *MS* 30 Mar 1842

WHIDDEN Mary Jane m COLE Pearl K on Thurs last *MS* 5 Dec 1833

WHIPPLE Ann Moriah m TOBEY George both of No Providence on 30 ult *MS* 15 Apr 1835

WHIPPLE Florella P m ROSS Asa Jr both of Burrillville RI on 2 inst *MS* 12 Feb 1851

WHIPPLE Mary A of Hebron m WATSON B F of Concord on 16 Nov 1848 *MS* 29 Nov 1848

WHITAKER Rebecca of Conway NH m RICHARDSON Philip of Eaton NH on 9 Apr *MS* 12 Aug 1846

WHITAKER Susan M m MANN George W on 13 Apr 1843 at Benton VT *MS* 24 May 1843

WHITCHER Lavina E at West Plymouth NH m CILBRITH Lemuel of Maine at West Plymouth NH *MS* 4 Aug 1847

WHITCHER Marica B m HOAG Charles N on 24 May at Lockport NY *MS* 16 June 1847

WHITCHER Rachel of Meredith NH m WATSON Jacob *MS* 30 Jan 1839

WHITCHER Susan M of Benton m MANN George W on 13 Apr 1843 at Benton *MS* 21 June 1843

WHITCOMB Almira K of Strafford VT m ROLLINS David Jr of Newport VT on 29 Oct 1848 *MS* 6 June 1849

WHITCOMB Eliza m DEXTER Amos both of Dunn Wis on 24 Sept 1848 *MS* 20 Dec 1848

WHITCOMB Eliza W m WINKLEY Ebenezer P both of Lowell on 4th inst *MS* 28 Sept 1836 & m on 14 Sept *MS* 21 Sept 1836

WHITCOMB Minerva m RUGG David both of Compton on 21 Sept 1837 *MS* 10 Jan 1837

WHITCOMB Nancy m TRULL Wyman both of Sweden on 24 Dec *MS* 17 Jan 1838

WHITE A J m SALEY Orin both of Sherburn NY *MS* 21 Nov 1849

WHITE Abby F m SYMONDS Henry A on 4 Dec at New Gloucester ME *MS* 31 Dec 1845

WHITE Abigail of Bradford m GOODWIN Amos S of Lowell *MS* 4 Oct 1837

WHITE Alma both formerly of Trenton NY m LYMAN Charles on 23 Sept *MS* 27 Nov 1850

WHITE Catharine of Saco m STANTON James B of Lebanon *MFWBR* 5 Apr 1851

WHITE Catherine on 22 Apr at Hodgdon ME m SMITH Nathaniel T *MS* 17 May 1843

WHITE Deborah of Dover NH m PIERCE Alpheus on 5 Mar at Dover NH *MS* 17 Mar 1847

WHITE Elizabeth Mrs of Limerick ME wid/o WHITE Joseph Eld of Standish ME m HALL Levi of Gorham ME on 24 Aug at Limerick ME *MS* 1 Oct 1845

WHITE Harriet m GREELY William in Belfast ME *MS* 8 Dec 1830

WHITE Harriet F m HALE Amos on 6 Sept 1847 *MS* 6 Oct 1847

WHITE Harriet Y of Wiscasset ME m BAILEY Jotham C on 26 Sept 1848 *MS* 4 Oct 1848

WHITE Joanna Miss m DREW Moses on 3th ult in New Limerick *MS* 15 Mar 1827

WHITE Lucinda C of Lowell MA m CRESSY Charles A of Lowell MA *MS* 24 Feb 1847

WHITE Lydia of Barnston m KILBOURNE Samuel on 21 Jul *MS* 1 Jan 1840

WHITE Margaret of Meredith NY m HOUGHTALING Wm of Davenport on 2 May 1850 *MS* 5 June 1850

WHITE Marilla m SMITH F both of NB on 18 Mar *MS* 2 Apr 1851

WHITE Mary A of Litchfield m McCORRISON James F of Bath *MS* 18 Jul 1849

WHITE Nancy J m GLEDDEN Samuel W both of Bangor ME on 1 May *MS* 3 Jul 1850

WHITE Olive of Effingham NH m HAYES Alonozo of Dover *MS* 25 May 1842

WHITE Prudence of Hodgdon m GRANT Gideon on 20 May at Hodgdon ME *MS* 5 Jul 1843

WHITE Rebecca H of South Boston m PAGET Joseph on Apr 4 at South Boston MA *MS* 17 Apr 1844

WHITE S A Maria m RIGGS John A *MFWBR* 23 June 1849

WHITE Sarah of South Berwick ME m FARNHAM William K on 27th ult *MS* 3 Dec 1845

WHITEAR Amanda of Corinth m TATE Joshua R at Corinth ME *MS* 20 Jan 1847

WHITEHOUSE Abra K of Alton m COOLEY John L on 24 Oct *MS* 14 Nov 1833

WHITEHOUSE Caroline S m GILMAN Ebenezer both of Dover NH on 30th ult *MS* 5 Nov 1834

WHITEHOUSE Elizabeth A of Lowell MA m HUSSEY Albert at Dracut MA *MS* 26 Nov 1845

WHITEHOUSE Jane A of Dover m SMITH Joseph of Sandwich on 22 Dec *MS* 4 Jan 1837

WHITEHOUSE Laura G m HALL Oram R both of Dover *MS* 9 Jan 1850

WHITEHOUSE Mehitabel m CLOUGH John both of Wolfborough NH on 27th ult *MS* 21 May 1834

WHITEHOUSE Nancy Ann m SPINNEY Oliver P *MS* 29 Nov 1837

WHITEHOUSE Sophia of Middleton m STEVENS James D on 18th inst *MS* 26 Dec 1833

WHITEHOUSE Susan m BURLEY Hiram at Dover *MS* 13 Jul 1836

WHITEHOUSE Susan of Newfield ME m JORDAN Nathaniel of Bridgestown PLT *MS* 1 Mar 1827

WHITING Mary Ann of Mendon m MOWRY Lyman of Smithfield *MS* 11 Dec 1839

WHITMAN Mary E m RALPH Harris both of Scituate RI on 23 Dec *MS* 15 Jan 1851

WHITMAN Melvina m CLINE Leonard on 22 Sept at Three Mile Bay NY *MS* 7 Dec 1842

WHITMARSH Zipporah of Smithville NY m TURNER Leroy of Wilett on 9 Jan 1849 *MS* 31 Jan 1849

WHITMORE Betsey of Standish m ARNOLD Samuel of Shirby *MS* 21 Jan 1835

WHITMORE Minerva H d/o WHITMORE Benjamin of Bowdoinham ME m PERCY W G of Phipsburg ME *MFWBR* 18 Sept 1847

WHITNEY Almira N m POWERS Ichabod both of Biddeford ME on 4 Jul *MS* 30 Sept 1846

WHITNEY Betsey m MERRILL Nelson both of Westbrook ME on 20 Sept *MS* 12 NOv 1835

WHITNEY Celinda m BRAGDON Seth P both of Augusta *MS* 14 Mar 1838

WHITNEY Cynthia of Newburgh ME m WEBBER Bradford of Monroe ME on 1 Nov *MS* 13 Jan 1847

WHITNEY Emeline m CILLEY Wm Plumer on Tues eve 11 inst *MS* 13 Feb 1834

WHITNEY Eunice d/o WHITNEY Joseph of Standish ME m MOODY Caleb of Standish on 6th inst *MS* 24 Jan 1828

WHITNEY Isabel B m ARMSTRONG Charles on 6 Apr *MS* 9 Jul 1845

WHITNEY Martha J of Casco ME m GILMAN A G of Saco ME *MFWBR* 5 Oct 1850

WHITNEY Martha W m NELSON Otis C both of New Gloucester MEon 10 Feb 1848 in New Gloucester ME *MS* 23 Feb 1848

WHITNEY Mary of Billirica MA m LIBBEY Joseph of Bedford on 14 Dec *MS* 27 Dec 1843

WHITNEY Mary of Bridgton m HALE Nathaniel of Denmark on 25 Mar *MS* 8 Apr 1846

WHITNEY Mercy m KIMBALL Charles F both of Lisbon ME *MS* 29 Jan 1836

WHITNEY Phebe A of Bethel ME m CUMMINGS Silas A of Portland on 14 Apr *MS* 17 June 1846

WHITNEY Rebecca F m KING Nathaniel Jr on 15 Nov 1847 *MS* 24 Nov 1847

WHITNEY Susanna of Brookfield VT m RICH Albin of Moretown *MS* 4 Jul 1849

WHITON Susan A m BLOSSOM Thomas D editor of *Hingham Gazette* in Hingham *MS* 31 May 1837

WHITTAKER Eliza of Marcellus m BROWN Benjamin D on 18 Feb at Whitestown Seminary of N Hartford *MS* 12 Mar 1845

WHITTEMORE J Miss m HARVEY David S on 6th May at Lowell MA *MS* 2 June 1847

WHITTEMORE Mary Mrs m ANDREWS Simon *MFWBR* 16 Oct 1847

WHITTEMORE Olive Mrs of Dixville m CHANDLER Luther of Colebrook NH on 1 Dec 1847 *MS* Dec 15 1847

WHITTEMORE Susan H of Lowell m PATCH Burnam *MS* 20 Nov 1839

WHITTEN Abigail T of Cornish m STONE Samuel M of Biddeford ME on 26 Apr 1849 *MS* 16 May 1849

WHITTEN Eliza m NASON Freeman *MFWBR* 23 Oct 1847

WHITTEN Hannah m VARNEY Joshua both of Dover NH on 28 ult *MS* 1 Jul 1835

WHITTEN Hannah of Parsonsfield m THURSTON Stephen of Parsonsfield ME *MFWBR* 27 Feb 1847

WHITTEN Harriet B m PARKER B F both of Wolfborough on 22 Jul *MS* 21 Aug 1850

WHITTEN Louisa of Dover NH m FARNHAM John G on 5 Dover NH *MS* 15 June 1842

WHITTEN Mary H m GARLAND Benjamin F both of Wolfborough ME *MS* 19 Apr 1837

WHITTEN Ruth E m TUTTLE David L *MFWBR* 19 Oct 1850

WHITTEN Sarah E m MESERVE Elijah B on 18 May at Hollis ME *MS* 14 June 1843

WHITTIER Abigail S m CURRIER True W both of Deerfield NH on 4 Feb *MS* 14 Feb 1849

WHITTIER Emily R at Fairfield ME m KENDALL James M of Phipsburgh ME on 26 Jan *MS* 22 Mar 1843

WHITTIER Lucy Ann m HEALD David both of Manchester of Boston on 10 Apr 1849 *MS* 25 Apr 1849

WHITTIER Martha J m WOODS Wm H on 8 ult *MS* 4 Apr 1838

WHITTIER Mary A m RAWLINS Francis S both of Deerfield NH on 22 Nov *MS* 12 Dec 1849

WHITTIER R Brenda m ABBOTT William T *MFWBR* 8 Dec 1849

WICCON Eliza J M on March 31 m FIFIELD George E both of Weare *MS* 12 Feb 1840

WIGGIN Abigail J m WINGATE Daniel Jr both of Somersworth NH on 17 inst *MS* 20 May 1846

WIGGIN Deborah of Durham m CHESLEY Jeremiah of Palmyra ME *MS* 13 Feb 1834

WIGGIN Emily C of Sandwich m BEECH Israel B MD of Sharon Ohio *MS* 16 Oct 1844

WIGGIN Frances of Durham m DURGIN Nathan of New Market on

WIGGIN (Continued)

19th ult *MS* 1 apr 1835

WIGGIN Hannah Mrs m THOMPSON Benjamin F both of Wolfborough NH on 17 Sept 1848 *MS* 1 Nov 1848

WIGGIN Harriet m TUCK John Jr at Parsonsfield ME *MS* 16 Apr 1845

WIGGIN Harriet W m BROWN Asa on 22 Feb at Moultonborough NH of Sharon VT *MS* 12 Mar 1845

WIGGIN Lucy Ann m PIKE James both of Meredith NH? on 27 Oct *MS* 27 Nov 1850

WIGGIN Martha of Portsmouth NY m BROWN Henry of Boston *MS* 7 Sept 1836

WIGGIN Mary Ann G m WHITE Edwin A both of Deerfield NH *MS* 16 Jan 1850

WIGGIN Mary m STEVENS D L Marquis both of Dover on Sun last *MS* 19 Oct 1836

WIGGIN Mary D d/o WIGGIN David Esq of Durham m BEEDE Moses V of Lowell MA on evening 6 inst *MS* 14 Feb 1849

WIGGIN Mary Jane of Farmington NH m PLUMMER Richard of Milton on 9 Nov 1848 *MS* 31 Jan 1849

WIGGIN Mary P W of Durham on 6 Nov at New Market m ENGLISH R G W MD of Springfield MA *MS* 19 Nov 1845

WIGGIN Nancy of Saco ME m CROWLEY James of Saco ME *MS* 6 Apr 1847

WIGGIN Naomi m CHICK Lyman on 21 Nov of Ossipee NH *MS* 10 Jan 1844

WIGGIN Olive C of Moultonboro' m LANE Henry D of Raymond *MS* 11 Nov 1846

WIGGIN Sally W of Wakefield NH m FARNHAM Daniel on 9 Oct of Wakefield NH *MS* 2 Dec 1846

WIGGIN Sarah C m GRANT Andrew M on 28 Aug at Epsom NH *MS* 19 Oct 1842

WIGGIN Susan of Warner m AVERY Joshua of Manchester on 26 Jul 1848 *MS* 16 Aug 1848

WIGGINS Betsey E of Tamworth NH m SKIMER Glover of Lynn MA on 24 Jul *MS* 1 Nov 1848

WIGGINS Dorothy E of New Market m McDUFFEE Maiquis of Great Falls NH on 7 June *MS* 8 Jul 1846

WIGGINS Elizabeth m WILLIAMS John both of Ossipee NH *MS* 5 apr 1837

WIGGINS Mary Ann m HOITT Enoch P both of New Market on 15 ult *MS* 22 Nov 1848

WIGHT Sophronia L of Otisfield ME m CHADBOURN William of Biddeford ME on 4 May *MS* 22 May 1850

WILBER Flora m HIGGINS Amos D both of Charleston on 20 Aug 1848 *MS* 21 Feb 1849

WILBOUR Susannah of Little Compton RI m PALMER John on 19 Mar *MS* 4 May 1836

WILBUR Eliza of Smithfield m BROWNELL Wm A of Scituate on 4 ult *MS* 30 Dec 1835

WILDER Harriet A of Varysburgh NY m AINSWORTH Wyman H on 9 June 1842 at Varysburgh NY *MS* 29 June 1842

WILDER Harriet of Sutton MA m MAY Henry on 16th inst at Grafton MA *MS* 15 Mar 1843

WILDER Jane Z of Chataugary m PIERCE Samuel of New Haven 7 Mar 1848 *MS* 29 Mar 1848

WILDER Wealthy J m BIBBER Joel both of Portland ME *MS* 24 May 1848

WILEY Abgail of Williamstown VT m MERRILL Calvin H of Roxbury on 4 Jul 1848 *MS* 19 Jul 1848

WILEY Delana m MARTIN Kimball both of Williamstown VT on 17 Mar 1850 *MS* 10 Apr 1850

WILKERSON Lucy Ann of Nashua NH m WHITE Benjamin L of Greenfield NH on 7 Oct *MS* 19 Oct 1842

WILKIE Margaret m BALLENGER John on 2d Mar of East Liberty Logan Co Ohio *MS* 30 June 1847

WILKINSON Asenath C m FOSS Samuel B on 12 June of Kingsbury ME *MS* 24 Jul 1844 (*sic*) should be *MS* 31 Jul 1844

WILKINSON Mary P m CHANDLER Ephraim A on 30 Nov 1848 *MS* 13 Dec 1848

WILLARD Nancy A m ABBOTT Rufus L both of Candia on 28 Oct 1848 *MS* 8 Nov 1848

WILLARD Rhoda of Chesterville ME m FOSTER John Eld of Jay ME on 15 inst *MS* 30 Aug 1837

WILLET Hannah H m DONNOCKER George on 3 Apr at Boston NY *MS* 9 June 1847

WILLETS Ruth Jane of Rome Mich on 4 Jul m BACHELDOR James H of Ridgeway Orleans Co NY *MS* 24 Jul 1839

WILLEY Adaline of Sutton m SIMPSON Hezekiah of Sheffield VT *MS* 16 Jul 1845

WILLEY Betsey of New Durham NH m BARKER Dudley merchant of Alton NH *MS* 8 Mar 1837

WILLEY Charlotte Mrs m TAYLOR Benjamin both of Dover on 20 inst *MS* 27 Dec 1848

WILLEY Dolly Miss of Sheffield m HILL Edward Jr of Bartlett NH on 21st ult *MS* 15 Jul 1835

WILLEY Dorantha m PINKHAM Nathan on 6 Sept *MS* 22 Sept 1847

WILLEY Eliza J of Lowell m McINTIRE John O on 28 Feb at Lowell *MS* 11 Mar 1846

WILLEY Elizabeth of Dover NH m KENNEY John of Lagrange ME on 7th inst *MS* 13 May 1835

WILLEY Hannah Mrs of Conway m PERKINS Samuel of Lowell on

WILLEY (Continued)

12 Dec 1849 *MS* 24 Apr 1850

WILLEY L A Miss formerly of Dover NH m CLANCY M A of Boston on 12 inst *MS* 18 Sept 1850

WILLEY Lucinda m FREEMAN Miles on 11 May at Barrington *MS* 2 Jul 1845

WILLEY Lydia Jane on 17th inst at Dover NH m CURRIER William of Amesbury MA *MS* 30 Dec 1846

WILLEY Martha T of Barnstead m CASWELL Richard W of Boston on 22 Mar Sabbath Eve *MS* 8 Apr 1846

WILLEY Mary m FRENCH Charles W on 29 Nov 1846 at Alton NH *MS* 3 Mar 1847

WILLEY Mary of Dover on 14 inst m KNOWLTON Jonathan of Northwood *MS* 24 Jul 1839

WILLEY Phivinna of Washington VT m MARTIN Edson of Williamstown on 2d inst *MS* 15 May 1839

WILLEY Susan E m HAYES Joshua B both of Somersworth NH on 4 Jan 1850 *MS* 27 Feb 1850 & *MFWBR* 9 Mar 1850

WILLEY Wealthy L of Bremen ME m BLOSSOM Alden Doct of Boothbay ME on 23 Oct *MS* 27 Nov 1850

WILLIAMS Abigail m PHILBRICK William both of New Market *MS* 5 Oct 1836

WILLIAMS Anna m LEATHERS Hiram G both of Barrington on 22 ult *MS* 1 Feb 1837

WILLIAMS Deborah m PEARL Thomas Fits on 7 Aug *MS* 13 Sept 1843

WILLIAMS Edney m GEORGE Francis R on Mar 1844 of Strafford VT *MS* 11 Dec 1844

WILLIAMS Eliza Ann m RILEY William both of Kittery ME on 17 inst *MS* 26 Oct 1836

WILLIAMS Eliza m DAVIS Thomas *MS* 7 Feb 1828

WILLIAMS Elizabeth of Edgecomb ME m MOREY William on 13 Oct at Edgecomb ME *MS* 23 Nov 1842

WILLIAMS Emily m LARKID Norman on 4 Nov of Nassau *MS* 18 Nov 1846

WILLIAMS Hannah O of No Providence RI m KINYAN Silas R of Richmond on 8 inst at No Providence RI *MS* 21 Sept 1836

WILLIAMS Hannah of Kittery ME m FOY WM L of Rye NH *MS* 2 Feb 1831

WILLIAMS Harriet N d/o WILLIAMS John Capt of Kittery m CALL Henry S of Newton Lower Falls MA *MS* 26 Mar 1851

WILLIAMS Joanna m FURBISH Calvin C both of Kittery ME on 14 inst *MS* 31 Oct 1849

WILLIAMS Juliette of Parsonsfield m PEASE Usher P on 12 Jan 1845 at Parsonsfield ME *MS* 12 Mar 1845

WILLIAMS Julina of Wheatland m PEASE Clinton A on 8th at

WILLIAMS (Continued)
Wheatland Hillsdale Co Mich *MS* 29 Nov 1843

WILLIAMS Louisa S of Gardiner m SPARKS William W on 15 Sept at Gardiner ME *MS* 19 Oct 1842

WILLIAMS Martha Ann of Lowell MA on 7 Oct m WELLMAN Eben B of Boston MA *MS* 2 Nov 1842

WILLIAMS Martha O m TOOTHAKER Ebenezer of Litchfield ME at Bowdoinham ME *MS* 7 Aug 1844

WILLIAMS Mary Ellen of Moultonboro' NH m COLBY Daniel on 3 Dec at Effingham NH *MS* 30 Dec 1846

WILLIAMS Mary G of New Market on 9 May m CLEMENT Benjamin of Moultonboro' *MS* 15 May 1839

WILLIAMS Mary of Readfield ME m BOWMAN Oren of Sidney ME *MS* 21 Jan 1846

WILLIAMS Olive Ann of Parsonsfield m SHUMAN Aaron of Waldoboro ME *MS* 4 Feb 1846

WILLIAMS Sally of Moultonboro' NH m BLAKE Thomas I of Ossipee NH on 27 Nov 1847 *MS* 19 Apr 1848

WILLIAMS Sarah Ann m BROWN Isaac on 10th inst *MS* 18 May 1832

WILLIAMS Sophronia E m HOWARD Samuel both of Pittsford Mich on 3 June *MS* 19 Sept 1849

WILLIAMS Susan D of Parsonsfield ME m CHELLIS Seth on 24 Sept at Parsonsfield ME *MS* 18 Oct 1843

WILLIAMS Susan P m BUKER Valentine on 31 June at Bowdoin ME *MS* 16 June 1847

WILLIAMS Zelinda m SHERBURNE James both of Gardiner ME *MS* 22 May 1844

WILLIS Martha m QUENN John on 3 Jul *MS* 8 Sept 1847

WILLONGBY Mary Ann of Holderness NH m SMITH Daniel *MS* 19 Apr 1843

WILLOUGHBY Esther Ann of Newport m CUMMINGS Daniel on 22 Feb at Newport *MS* 24 May 1843

WILSON Betsey m ALLEN Henry of Cornish on 20th inst *MS* 26 Mar 1828

WILSON Eunice m HAM Joseph P both of New Market on 4 Oct *MS* 14 Oct 1846

WILSON Frances E m MATTHEWS John M on 30 Oct at Nashua *MS* 24 Dec 1845

WILSON Hannah P m ADAMS Israel G both of Bowdoin ME *MS* 28 Dec 1836

WILSON Harriet of New Gloucester ME m THOMPSON Prince of Strong ME *MFWBR* 3 Mar 1849

WILSON Lydia A m PRIOR Joseph both of Great Falls on 5 Jan *MS* 22 Jan 1851

WILSON Lydia Ann of Biddeford ME m HILL Horace P of Lyman on

WILSON (Continued)
4 Mar *MS* 6 Apr 1847

WILSON Marion m DAVIS Alonzo *MFWBR* 16 Oct 1847

WILSON Mary C of Canada m GERRISH Noah of Acton ME on 18th inst *MS* 8 June 1842

WILSON Mary J of Topsham ME m NOWELL John of Vassalborough ME *MS* 2 Sept 1846

WILSON Mary M m STONE George S on 25 Nov at Dracut MA *MS* 18 Dec 1844

WILSON Mary M of Harpswell ME m TOOTHAKER Horatio on 9 May at Brunswick ME *MS* 26 May 1847

WILSON Rechel of Topsham m HIGGENS Jeremiah Capt of Lisbon ME on 18 Aug at Topsham ME *MS* 31 Aug 1842

WILSON Sarah A of Kittery ME on 16 inst m AYER Thomas L of Boston MA *MS* 26 Apr 1843

WIMAN Rachel both Freeport m BRAGDON Simon on 19 May *MS* 13 Nov 1850

WINCHELL Sophronia Miss m HILL John C on 25th Sept at Dover NH *MS* 3 Oct 1833

WINDOVER Almira of Ohio m BLISS Clark on 23 Dec at Middleville of Norway NY *MS* 29 Jan 1845

WING Hannah W m COLWELL John W both of No Providence on 17 inst *MS* 7 Oct 1835

WING Joanna m LORING John S both of Leeds in Leeds ME 25 Nov *MS* 9 Feb 1842

WING Mary d/o WING A Eld of Oneonta m WHITNEY George R of Meredith *MS* 1 Dec 1847

WING Sarah m BURGES Thomas F at Lowell MA *MS* 9 Jul 1845

WINGATE Abby m LIBBEY J T S printer on 4 inst *MS* 10 oct 1849

WINGATE Laura J m GOULD William *MFWBR* 28 Dec 1850

WINGATE Lydia of Somersworth m COURSON Willard of Rochester *MS* 7 Feb 1838

WINGATE Mary m LITTLEFIELD Asa H on 11th at Dover NH *MS* 17 Aug 1842

WINKLEY Mary Jane m OLIVER Washington Capt on 24 Nov 1842 at Georgetown ME *MS* 8 Mar 1843

WINKLEY Tamson H of Alton m CLOUGH John P of Gilmanton on Feb *MS* 22 May 1850

WINN Emily of Wells ME m BRAGDON William on 28th ult of Kennebunk ME *MS* 9 Dec 1846

WINN Olive G of Lebanon m FURBUSH Charles H on 24 Oct at Lebanon ME *MS* 27 Nov 1844

WINSLOW Elizabeth Ann of Nottingham NH m DOW Lorenzo of Newburyport MA on 31 May 1848 *MS* 7 June 1848

WINSLOW Mary Jane m GERRISH Paul both of New Market on 21st ult *MS* 8 May 1844

WINSLOW Sally T m DAVIS Stephen C both of Pittsfield on 9 inst *MS* 15 Aug 1849

WINSLOW Sarah A m ULMER George both of Boston *MS* 4 Apr 1849

WINSLOW Sarah G m WOOD John M *MFWBR* 14 Aug 1847

WINSOR Betsey M m CLARK John of Olean NY on 3 June at Franklinville NY *MS* 4 Sept 1844

WINSOR Eunice L m WHITE George W both of Johnston RI on 3 Sept 1848 *MS* 11 Oct 1848

WINSOR Sally at Franklinville NY m KNAPP Joseph on 21 Apr *MS* 15 Mar 1843

WINSOR Tabitha B of Providence RI m ALDRICH John of Scituate *MS* 8 Jan 1851

WINTER Elmira m TATMAN Elias Jr *MS* 8 Apr 1835 & both of Phipsburgh ME *MS* 25 Mar 1835

WINTERS Melissa m THOMAS Daniel both of Clayton NY on 19 Sept *MS* 9 Oct 1850

WIRE Sarah m CASS Levi on 25 Feb 1844 *MS* 1 May 1844

WISNER Mary of Charlestown MA m BAILEY William N on 17th June *MS* 4 Aug 1847

WITCRAFT Elizabeth H m BOYD James W on 9 Feb 1850 *MS* 27 Mar 1850

WITHAM Abigail Maria m JACK Nathan both of Thorndike ME on 2 Jul *MS* 12 Aug 1846

WITHAM Amenty m STANWOOD Samuel on 1st May at Bath ME *MS* 18 May 1842

WITHAM Climera P m WITHAM Ira L on 4 inst *MS* 21 Nov 1838

WITHAM Katharine of Dearbon m HORN Aldin of Fairfield on at Waterville ME *MS* 15 Mar 1837

WITHAM Lovina Miss m HURSOM Benjamin both of Dearborn ME *MS* 24 Feb 1836

WITHAM Martha A of Dover NH m HAM William A of Dover NH *MS* 5 May 1847

WITHAM Martha M of Saco ME m HUTCHINSON Almon of Milan NH on 4 Jul at Kennebunkport ME *MS* 13 June 1842

WITHAM Mary T of Phillips ME m CROSSMAN C H of Gardiner ME *MFWBR* 23 June 1849

WITHAM Olive of Danville ME m NASON Seth C on 24 Sept *MS* 8 Nov 1843

WITHAM Sarah H m WHITMORE Simon both of Biddeford ME on 9 Dec 1848 *MS* 24 Jan 1849

WITHAM Sophia B L m FRENCH Franklin of New Boston on 3 Dec at Milton *MS* 7 Jan 1846

WITHAM Sophronis R of Harrison ME m INGLASS Spafford of Bridgton ME on 25 isnt *MS* 5 Jul 1848

WITHAM Tryphena m BAKER Isaac L both of Jackson ME on 11 Aug *MS* 13 Nov 1850

WITHERAL Hannah of Effingham NH m WATSON David of Ossipee NH on 10 Mar 1850 *MS* 20 Mar 1850

WITTUM Naomi m TAPPAN Daniel both of Sandwich NH 17 ult *MS* 27 Sept 1837

WOOD Amanda m EVANS Aaron both of Dover NH on 29 Mar *MS* 27 June 1849

WOOD Anne of Norridgwock ME m GOTT Charles of Leeds ME on 10 Oct at Livermore ME *MS* 2 Nov 1842

WOOD Charlotte E of Haverhill MA m GREENLEAF Nathan S of Skowhegan ME on 26 Sept *MS* 6 Oct 1847

WOOD Clarissa of Stanstead m KATHERN Lorinus of Shefford on 1 Aug *MS* 20 Sept 1837

WOOD Eliza Ann m LEAVITT Silas both of Augusta ME on 30 Apr 1848 *MS* 24 May 1848

WOOD Ellen of Charlestown MA m RANDALL James of So Boston *MS* 4 Feb 1835

WOOD Jane m COOKSON Reuben of Unity ME at Thorndike ME *MS* 25 Dec 1844

WOOD Lois m LEARNED Calvin both of Dixfield ME on 2 Nov 1847 *MS* 9 Feb 1848

WOOD Louisa of Sidney m WEBSTER Samuel of Waterville ME *MS* 21 Jan 1846

WOOD Lucinda of Portland ME m GILSON Calvin B on 15th ult *MS* 29 Nov 1843

WOOD Marcella of Warwick RI m BATLEY Josiah W of Cumberland *MS* 24 Apr 1839

WOOD Mary m FOGG Reuben at Wales ME *MS* 4 Mar 1846

WOOD Miriam L of Wellington ME m CLARK Wm R of Cambridge on 29 Jan 1850 *MS* 20 Mar 1850

WOOD Olive m McKENNEY Charles *MS* 14 Feb 1844

WOOD Sally of Smithstown m COLEMAN Joseph on 3 Feb at Smyrna NY *MS* 9 June 1847

WOOD Sarah Ann m GOODELL Charles both of Ashippun Wis on 13 Oct *MS* 14 Nov 1849

WOODARD Eliza m WILSON Wm both of H (Hatley?) on 29 Nov 1843 *MS* 1 May 1844

WOODARD Hannah on 13th inst at Lisbon ME m BARD Nathaniel *MS* 23 Oct 1839

WOODARD Jane of Guilford m WESTON Caleb of Foxcroft ME *MS* 1 Feb 1837

WOODARD Sarah W of Lisbon m CORNISH Lincoln of Bowdoin ME on 27 Oct 1850 *MS* 8 Jan 1851

WOODBECK Hannah Mrs of Nassau NY m COONS Marlow of Stephentown on 27 Jan 1849 *MS* 2 May 1849

WOODBRIDGE Almira of Bow NH m JUDD Orange W of Washington VT on 12 Mar *MS* 29 Apr 1846

WOODBURY Ann C of Bethlehem m SHATTUCK William L of Landaff on 26 Sept *MS* 6 Nov 1850

WOODBURY Charlotte A m FORD Dan Y on 17 Sept at Newbury VT *MS* 7 Nov 1838

WOODBURY Eliza S m CUTTING John on 31 Dec at Haverhill *MS* 22 Jan 1845

WOODBURY Elizabeth of New Market NH m DREW Meshech on 21st Apr at New Market NH *MS* 28 Apr 1847

WOODBURY Mary A m JORDAN Almon Libby both of Cape Elizabeth in Cape Elizabeth ME Sept 12 1841 *MS* 19 Jan 1842

WOODBURY Polly m KYES Perley on 22 *MS* 23 Sept 1846

WOODBURY Rebecca S m WYMAN Daniel Jr both of Dover on 7 inst *MS* 8 May 1844

WOODBURY Sarah P m KNIGHT Moses on 31 Dec at Haverhill *MS* 22 Jan 1845

WOODCOCK Elizabeth m BAKER Henry A both of Sidney ME on 8 inst *MS* 7 Mar 1849

WOODEN Jane m SHAVELIER Christian on 15 Dec at Virgil NY *MS* 15 Jan 1845

WOODES Mary m HATCH Henry M both of Dover on 3 inst *MS* 7 Mar 1849

WOODMAN Anna m ROLLINS Joseph P on 27 Dec *MS* 10 Mar 1847

WOODMAN Eliza of Freeport ME m CARVER Blany on 20 Oct of Freeport ME *MS* 25 Nov 1846

WOODMAN H N of Meredith m BATCHELDER J of Quinsey [Quincy? MA?] on 29 Nov *MS* 26 Dec 1838

WOODMAN Joanna m PHILLIPS Joseph *MS* 3 Feb 1832

WOODMAN Martha W of Buxton m MASON Jeremiah M of Limerick ME *MFWBR* 18 Aug 1849

WOODMAN Mary E d/o WOODMAN J E Esq of Rochester NH m TEBBETS Noah Esq of Parsonsfield ME *MS* 18 June 1828

WOODMAN Mary J on 20th inst at Saco m BERRY Ivory of Buxton *MFWBR* 29 Mar 1851

WOODMAN Mary Jane of South Hampton m FOLLANSBEE Joseph on 18 Jan at Hampton *MS* 7 Feb 1844

WOODMAN Mary M of Hatley LC m WALKER George of Sherbrook village *MS* 17 FEb 1836

WOODMAN Rachel A m COLE John W both of Dover on 29 ult *MS* 1 Aug 1849

WOODMAN Roxana U of Richmond m POTTER Isaac J on 15 Aug *MS* 11 Sept 1850

WOODRUFF Margaret R of Enfield m SMALL John Jr of Catlin on 19 Aug *MS* 10 Oct 1849

WOODRUFF Mehitabel of Billerica m JONES Jephthah on 16 May at Wilmington MA *MS* 26 June 1844

WOODS Hannah R m MITCHELL David of North Yarmouth ME *MS* 9

woods (Continued)
Jul 1845

WOODS Sarah F m RICHARDS John K on 6th inst in Saco ME *MS* 17 Jan 1828

WOODSIDE Austress M of Brunswick ME m CURTIS Thomas M of Freeport ME *MS* 13 Jan 1847

WOODSIDE Caroline m JAMES Edward *MS* 12 Mar 1851

WOODSIDE Salome G on 6th Mar m HUNT Jeremiah Jr *MS* 26 Apr 1843

WOODSUM Abby H m WENTWORTH George of Dover NH *MFWBR* 16 Mar 1850

WOODWARD Hannah m BEAN Richard 3d both of Waterboro ME *MS* 16 Sept 1831

WOODWARD Hannah m SCRIBNER Daniel *MS* 16 Sept 1831

WOODWARD Lucretia L d/o WOODWARD George of Lowell ALLEN Henry B of Chelsea VT on 21 ult *MS* 13 Jul 1836

WOODWARD Maria E m RICHARDSON Sargent H on 2d inst at Sutton NH *MS* 23 June 1847

WOODWARD Mary of Blockberry m YOUNG John of Burlington on 29 Aug *MS* 27 Nov 1844

WOODWARD Nancy m TARR Isaac on 30 Mar *MS* 1 May 1834

WOODWARD Suphronia of Lisbon ME m WOODSUM Thompson of Greenbush ME on 31 Oct *MS* 28 Dec 1836

WOODWORTH Zintha Stutson of Brookline m LOVEJOY Azael on 2 Nov at Boston MA *MS* 21 Jan 1846

WOOSTER Elizabeth m STODDARD George both of Middleville on 21 inst *MS* 15 Jan 1851

WORCESTER Mary A m CARL Francis on 6th inst at Dracut MA *MS* 24 Feb 1847

WORD Martha J m FRYE James E on 3 Oct 1849 *MS* 20 Mar 1850

WORK Eliza m LOUGEE James on 20 Oct at Sangerville ME *MS* 27 Nov 1844

WORMUTH Margaret of Palatine m WORMUTH William J of Starkville m 10 Nov 1849 *MS* 16 Jan 1850

WORMWOOD Abigail m BRIER John *MS* 20 June 1833

WORMWOOD Ann M of Brownfield ME m MEADER Otis C of Conway NH on 14 Nov *MS* 27 Nov 1850

WORSTER Julia Ann m GOODWIN Blaisdel J both of Lebanon ME *MS* 20 June 1849

WORTH Lois of Biddeford ME m SMITH Perkins of Kennebunkport ME on 14 Dec *MS* 5 Feb 1845

WORTHEN Abby B of Candia m SLATE Lyman J of Manchester on 12 Nov *MS* 25 Dec 1850

WORTHEN Sarah m GOODHUE Joseph on 12 Mar at Enfield *MS* 16 Apr 1845

WORTHING Caroline A m FOWLER Horatio J on 8 May *MS* 2 June

WORTHING (Continued)
1847

WORTHING Hannah m LABREE James both of Corinna ME on 30th ult *MS* 24 Apr 1834

WORTHLEY Lydia m MARSTON John Jr both of N Yarmouth on 29 Dec 1847 *MS* 8 Mar 1848

WORTHLEY Lydia S of Edgecomb m DAVIS James P of Union on 5 May 1849 *MS* 15 May 1850

WOTTON Elmira m HIGGINS John Jr both of Belmont *MS* 31 May 1848

WRIGHT Agness of Woolwich ME on 9 Mar 1843 m WRIGHT John B *MS* 19 Apr 1843

WRIGHT Catharine of Lewiston ME m ROWE William of New Gloucester ME *MS* 15 Apr 1840

WRIGHT Happy T of Lewiston ME m MARR Josiah F of Georgetown ME *MS* 13 Nov 1839

WRIGHT Mary Ann of Parma m CHATLIN Charles of Brighton Monroe Co NY on 17 Oct *MS* 15 Nov 1843

WRIGHT Mary I of Phipsburg m CROOCKER William F of Bath ME *MS* 11 Apr 1849

WRIGHT Mary J m CROOKER William F of Bath *MFWBR* 10 Mar 1849

WRIGHT Rosina m HOAG Chase of Lincoln VT on 23 Dec *MS* 10 Feb 1847

WRIGHT Sarah Jane of Lewiston ME m HAMILTON James Jr of Elmira NY on 12 Sept 1847 *MS* 27 Oct 1847

WRIGHT Sophronia m THOMPSON Josiah both of Nashua on 18 May 1848 *MS* 24 May 1848

WYATT Cyntha B m PIPER Thomas H both of Northfield NH *MS* 19 Jan 1848

WYMAN Amanda m EDSON Truman on 13 Jan 1842 of Barnston *MS* 13 Apr 1842

WYMAN Ester E m BAILEY Silas at Fairfield ME *MS* 17 Apr 1844

WYMAN Joanna m STRAW Josiah both of Manchester *MS* 4 Oct 1848

WYMAN Lucy S of Auburn ME m BUTTERFIELD Albion KP of Danville ME on 17 inst *MS* 26 Apr 1848

WYMAN Saphrinia of Searsmont ME m ODWAY Walter of Belmont ME on 22 Mar 1849 *MS* 18 Apr 1849

WYMAN Sophia m WEEKS Charles *MS* 25 Dec 1844

YANORSDALL Mary M of Raisin m TERPNING John at Dover Mich *MS* 5 Jul 1843

YEATON Harriet of Strafford m EDGERLY Hiram W of New Durham on 24 Jul *MS* 21 Aug 1850

YEATON Lydia of Belgrade ME m GAGE William of Augusta ME on

YEATON (Continued)
22 Sept *MS* 8 Jan 1845

YEATON Mary O of Gilford NH m SPOKESFIELD Daniel of Campton NH on 22 Jan 1849 *MS* 7 Mar 1849

YEATON Sarah E m SANBORN James Jr both of Epsom on 19 inst *MS* 29 Sept 1847

YEATON Susan of Chichester on Mar 5 m BECK Thomas of Loudon *MS* 15 Apr 1840

YEATS Mary B m FOLEY Michael on 23 Jan at Charleston MA *MS* 24 May 1843

YERRINGTON Marcia of Norwich m TILDEN Timothy of Manchester NY *MS* 6 June 1849

YORK Abigail F of Dover NH m GUPPY George F *MS* 16 Dec 1835

YORK Anna m PALMER Jesse on 15 Nov 1849 *MS* 20 Mar 1850

YORK Charlotte m THOMAS John both of Great Falls NH on 12 Nov *MS* 27 Nov 1850

YORK Clarissa G of New Market m DAVIS Stephen H on 29 Dec *MS* 4 Jan 1843

YORK Hannah D Miss m MEADER Jesse Eld Itinerant Preacher of New Durham Q M on at Rochester NY *MS* 30 Nov 1832

YORK Lydia C m McDUFFIE Daniel on 30 Oct at Rochester *MS* 18 Dec 1844

YORK Mary of Lee m DAVIS David E on 25th ult at Lee *MS* 15 Dec 1841

YORK Roxana B of Lee m DURGIN John W on 6th inst at New Market *MS* 12 Mar 1845

YORK Sarah A of Kennebunk m HUFF Eben A on 12 Oct at Kennebunk ME *MS* 27 Nov 1844

YOUNG Abigail B of Manchester NH m WEARE Gardiner M of Candia NH on 6 Oct *MS* 30 Nov 1842

YOUNG Abigail of Barrington m CAVERLY Asa of Strafford *MS* 9 Sept 1835

YOUNG Abigail of Dover NH m GILPATRICK John on 9th Sept *MS* 16 Sept 1835

YOUNG Adaline P of Gilmanton m GILMAN Ezekiel of Meredith on 24 Oct *MS* 12 Dec 1849

YOUNG Ann C of Durham m HARVEY Howard Capt on 24 Aug of South Berwick ME *MS* 30 Aug 1843

YOUNG Ann J of Haverhill MA m ROBERTS Levi B on 7th *MS* 24 Feb 1847

YOUNG Betsey of Landaff m JESSAMAN Ira of Franconia on 4 May 1848 *MS* 24 May 1848

YOUNG Betsy m CLEMENTS William on 6 May *MS* 16 May 1849

YOUNG Caroline J of Barnstead m CLARK John of Dover *MS* 24 Jul 1839

YOUNG Catharine of Thorndike ME m WYMAN William of Unity

YOUNG (Continued)
MS 25 Dec 1844

YOUNG Dorothy Y of Dover NH m ADAMS Joseph P of Springfield MA *MS* 27 Apr 1842

YOUNG Eleanor S of Epsom NH m MARDEN Samuel B of Wentworth on 12 Sept at Epsom *MS* 11 Oct 1843

YOUNG Ellen J of Great Falls NH m MALOY Dennis on 27 Nov of Great Falls NH *MS* 24 Dec 1845

YOUNG Emeline C of Jackson ME m HAMBLETON Joseph R on 2d Nov of Swanville *MS* 13 Dec 1843

YOUNG Eunice of Hollis m HUFF Thomas of Saco 30th ult *MS* 4 Oct 1827

YOUNG Eusebia N of Columbia on 16 Jan m BRACE Asahel of Winfield *MS* 24 May 1843

YOUNG Fairrozzeway Miss m YOUNG Wm B of Livermore ME on 28th June *MS* 12 Aug 1835

YOUNG Hannah H of Charleston ME on 17 Jul m BITTEN William D of Linneus Aroostook Co ME *MS* 25 Sept 1839

YOUNG Isabella of Somersworth NH m BEAN John Jr at Berwick ME *MS* 8 June 1842

YOUNG Jane Augusta m LAWRENCE David on 2d inst at Dover NH *MS* 8 Dec 1841

YOUNG Jane of Stanstead LC m RAFTON Pollerick on 21 Oct *MS* 1 Jan 1840

YOUNG Jane S m NUTTER Ezra S on 24th inst *MS* 21 JaN 1835

YOUNG Laure m TYLER Shubel both of Manchester *MS* 5 Dec 1849

YOUNG Lavinia H m ANDRUS Calvin N both of Chelsea VT on 31 Dec 1849 *MS* 10 Apr 1850

YOUNG Lavona m DASHWOOD Henry on 22 Nov at Free Baptist church Boston *MS* 16 Dec 1846

YOUNG Louisa D of Manchester NH m WENTWORTH Samuel G at Manchester NH *MS* 27 Nov 1844

YOUNG Mercy Miss of Effingham NH m COTTON John F of Wolfoboro' NH on 27th ult *MS* 21 Mar 1833

YOUNG Louisa of Gilmanton NH m WEYMOUTH Henry Dr on 1 Jan 1844 of Andover NH *MS* 17 Jan 1844

YOUNG Louisa W of Tuftonborough NH m BENCHAM Simon F of Ossipee NH on 19 ult *MS* 21 June 1837

YOUNG M Miss of Sanford ME m TAYLOR T H on 12 Oct at Wells ME *MS* 20 Jan 1847

YOUNG Margaret J of Columbia m BRACE Lucius F of Winfield on 18 June at Poland Herkimer Co NY *MS* 2 Jul 1845

YOUNG Mary Ann of Somersworth m WARREN Joseph F of Newmarket *MS* 20 Feb 1839

YOUNG Mary H of Augusta ME m PIERCE Nathaniel of Bangor ME *MFWBR* 25 May 1850

YOUNG Mary Jane Dec 28th m SHERBURNE George W both of Pittsfield *MS* 5 Jan 1842

YOUNG Mary L m TURNER David Maj both of Royalton VT on 9 inst
MS 17 Jan 1838

YOUNG Mary of Barnstow m PRATT Jeremiah at Stanstead LC *MS*
18 May 1836

YOUNG Mary of Hatley m WOODWARD Squire on 20 June *MS* 13
Sept 1843

YOUNG Mary of Strafford m PERKINS Hiram on 7 Nov at Strafford
NH *MS* 4 Dec 1844

YOUNG Mercy of Freedom m ALLEN Samuel of Parsonsfield ME on
28 Jan 1844 *MS* 7 Feb 1844

YOUNG Olive E m LORD John C of Pueblo San Jose California
MFWBR 27 Jul 1850 & on 14 Jul *MS* 24 Jul 1850

YOUNG P H Miss of Meredith NH m ATWELL C W of Portland ME
MFWBR 24 Aug 1850

YOUNG Paulina, d/o YOUNG Daniel of Freedom NH, m MOSES
Horace of Eaton *MS* 12 Dec 1833

YOUNG Ruth A of Starks m SAWTELL Jotham A of Sidney ME on 4
Jul 1847 *MS* 29 Sept 1847

YOUNG S Miss m MERRILL J M both of Stanstead LC 26 Apr *MS* 18
May 1836

YOUNG Sally of Wakefield NH on 26 Dec m BLAZO Ebenezer of
Bartlett *MFWBR* 13 Jan 1849

YOUNG Sarah A m BLAZO Albert M both of Middleton on 7 Jul *MS* 7
Aug 1850

YOUNG Sarah M at Lexington on Aug 4 1839 m ABBOT Benjamin F
of PLT No 2 *MS* 5 Feb 1840

YOUNG Sarah Mrs m GILMAN Moses both of Gilmanton on 18 Mar
1848 *MS* 26 Apr 1848

YOUNG Sarah S of Deerfield on 16th ult m BROWN Alfred B *MS* 3
Jul 1839

YOUNG Sophia A m HANSON George S *MFWBR* 28 Jul 1849 & of
Barrington m HANSON George S *MFWBR* 4 Aug 1849

YOUNG Susan m BOLO Rufus on at Milton *MS* 13 Feb 1834

YOUNG Susan of Corinna ME m CURTIS Rufus of Newport ME? on
14th ult *MS* 30 Mar 1836

YOUNG Thankful of Freeport ME m SYLVESTER Joseph on 27 Apr
at Bowdoin ME *MS* 18 June 1845

List of Ministers and Justices of the Peace

Below is a listing of the ministers and Justices of the Peace who are named in this publication. The number in parentheses ( ) stands for the approximate number of issues in which he was named. We also give the location of marriages & span of time the records were reported.

ABBEY Mason H Eld (4) New York State 1844-1847
ABBOTT William Eld (6) Somerset Co ME 1840
ABBOTT H B Rev (4) 1849-1850
ABBOTT Rev (1) 1849
ABBOTT Samuel Rev (1) 1846
ADAMS Abel Eld (15) 1837-1849
ALBEE H Eld (2) 1844
ALDRICH Schuyler Eld (8) Mecca, Henrietta, Pittsfield, and Macedonia Ohio & Buffalo, Bethany, Phoenix, Elmira, and Poland NY 1833-1850
ALLEN A Rev (1) 1845
ALLEN C Eld (6) in New Market 1848-1849
ALLEN C F Rev at Portland 1849
ALLEN Ebenezer Jr Eld (35) in Jackson & East Dixmont ME 1833-1851
ALLEN John (1) "a traveling preacher of the Methodist Episcopal church" 1847
ALLEN Nelson Esq (1) Montville ME 1849
ALLEN Reuben Eld (2) Gloucester RI 1848; (1) Johnston RI 1848; (5) Scituate RI 1838-1851; (11) No Scituate RI 1830-1851; (8) Scituate RI 1848-1850; (4) 1842; (5) Smithfield 1838; (1) Johnston RI 1850
ALLEN Rev (1) S Berwick ME 1847
ATWOOD Mark Eld (2) in Underhill VT 1847-1849
AMES A S Eld *MS* 29 Nov 1843
AMES Charles G Eld (5) Tamworth NH *MS* 1 May 1850
AMES Moses Eld (44) Bangor ME, Garland ME & No Bangor ME 1834-1849
ANDREWS Otis Eld (2) Bowdoin QM ME 1847
ANDRUS Amos Eld (8) Rushford & China NY 1833-1839
ARNOLD S H Esq (2) *MS* 20 Dec 1843
ATKINS Rev Scarboro' 1850
ATKINSON King Eld (6) Eaton NH 1849-1850

ATWELL Rev (1) Bangor ME 1849
ATWOOD Mark Eld (16) Auburn, Candia NH, Lincoln VT, Starksboro VT 1845-1850
AUGIR Franklin Page Eld (6) in Spring Prairie Wis, Beloit Wis, Rochester Wis, East Troy Wis 1848-1851
AYER A Eld (5) Woolwich ME 1849-1851; (4) 1839-1846
AYER Aaron Eld (6) in Limington & Brownfield 1837-1845
AYER James Jr Esq 1827
BADGER W Eld (2) Livermore ME 1845-1847
BAGLEY Orland Esq (2) Waterboro 1828-1831
BAILEY James M (20) West Buxton, Buxton & Hollis Cumberland Co QM 1847-1851
BAKE H Rev at Biddeford ME 1850
BAKER A J Eld in Clinton ME 1846
BAKER Ahira Esq in Shapleigh 1848
BAKER Daniel Esq 1827
BAKER Eld 1842
BAKER George W Eld (2) in Marion Ohio 1850
BARD Nathaniel Eld (14) Durham, Webster & Lisbon ME 1850-1851; (4) Brunswick & Topsham ME 1851
BARKER Nathaniel (1) Wakefield 1847
BARROWS Homer Rev (4) Dover NH 1845-1850
BARROWS Worthy C Esq (4) Harrison ME 1845-1846
BARTLETT Flavel Eld (1) Dover 1834
BARTLETT J O D Eld (5) Danbury NH, Wendell NH, Wilmot NH 1845-1848
BARTLETT Rev (4) Buxton ME 1839-1849
BATHRICK S Rev (1) Saco 1851
BAXTER John E Rev 1847
BURLINGAME M W Eld (1) Waterford 1838
BEAN Benaiah Eld (8) Colebrook NH 1847-1850; (1) Dixville 1847; (3) Pittsburg 1847-1850; (7) Bethlehem NH 1843-1847
BEAN C Eld (24) Bowdoinham, Bowdoin & Topsham ME 1842-1851; (5) Brunswick ME 1848; (3) Falmouth 1839-1842
BEAN Charles Eld (3) Limerick ME 1835-1839
BEAN F A Rev Belfast ME 1847
BEAN G H Eld (8) Lewiston Falls 1846-1848; (8) Waterville 1848-1850; (5) 1846-1847
BEAN Nathaniel C Esq (3) at Buxton 1828-1831
BEAN Silas F Eld (13) Pittsfield & Tuftonboro NH 1838-1849
BEARDSLEY Elisha Eld (2) IL City 1850
BEEBE W Eld (2) Brunswick Ohio 1851
BEECHER Edward Rev (1) Boston MA 1846
BEECHER Rev 1847
BEECHER Rev Portland ME 1848
BEEDE H Eld (2) Meredith 1849; (2) New Hampton 1850

BELKNAP P W Eld (5) Kennebunk ME & Painfield NY & Unadilla
   Forks 1844-1851
BENEDICT Rev at Pawtucket RI 1827
BENNETT Joseph Esq 1828
BERRY Asa L Esq (1) Georgetown ME 1849; (1) Standish 1847
BERRY N Eld (1) Barnstead NH 1827; BERRY Nathaniel Eld 1843
BICKFORD James (1) Northwood NH 1848
BIRD James Eld 1847
BISON Timothy Esq (1) Brownfield 1828
BIXBY L E Eld (5) Williamstown VT 1846-1847
BIXBY Newell Willard Eld (8) Boardman Clayton Co Iowa 1839-1850;
   (2) Starksborough VT 1846-1947
BLACKMARR H Eld (2) Bethany Genesee Co NY 1848-1849; (2)
   Alden NY 1845-1849
BLAISDEL David Eld (4) Lebanon 1838-1847
BLAISDELL E Eld (8) Lebanon 1838-1851
BLAISDELL Henry Rev (10) Eaton, Dracut & Tamworth 1846-1850
BLAISDELL William Eld 1842
BLAKE Charles E Eld (5) Bethlehem NH 1849-1850; (8) in Franconia
   NH 1847-1849; (1) in Lisbon ME 1850; (2) in Littleton NH 1848-
   1849; (3) Sandwich 1845-1847
BLAKE H M (6) Saco & Biddeford ME 1849-1851
BLAKE Israel Eld (1) in Ellsworth NH 1828
BLAKE Mr Rev (1) at Cumberland 1849
BLAISDELL Edward Eld (3) Lebanon 1846
BLODGETT C Rev (1) Lamprey River 1835
BLORE J Eld (2) Danville NH 1850; (1) Sandown 1850; (1) Farming-
   ton 1850
BODGE Jacob Eld (1) Farmington NH 1849
BODWELL Abraham Rev (1) Sanbornton 1837
BODWELL Elisha (1) Shapleigh 1830
BOWDEN Stephen Eld (3) Norridgewock & Smithfield ME 1845-1850
BOWLES Nathaniel (1) Corinth VT 1839
BOYINGTON John Rev (2) Phipsburgh 1835
BRACKET D Eld (2) Hiram 1833
BRADBURY A R (7) Chepacket, Limerick, Springvale ME 1840-1849
BRADBURY Abby F Eld (1) 1844
BRANCH Daniel Eld (3) in Chester Geauga Co Ohio, & Solon Ohio
   1848-1849
BRANCH S S Eld (2) Chester Ohio; (2) Rutland Ohio 1851
BRAY S Rev 1829
BRIDGES Abiezer Eld (6) Bristol & Wayne ME 1831-1834
BRIDGES Otis W Eld (3) Sangerville 1842-1847
BRIERLY Rev (1) Dover NH 1836
BROCK H H Eld (6) 1844-1845
BROOKS Nahum (7) Great Falls NH & Gilmanton NH 1838-1850

689

BROOKS John Eld (10) Acton ME & Ossipee NH 1843-1846

BROOKS Nahum (120) ME & NH 1841-1851; Center Sandwich 1848; Great Falls 1850; Meredith Bridge 1839; Meredith NH; Sanbornton 1838; Sandwich NH 1848-1850;

BROOKS Rev Brunswick 1849

BROWN Amos Eld (35) Alexandria, Bridgewater, Bristol, & Hill NH 1838-1850

BROWN B B Esq (1) 1847

BROWN Eld (1) Portland 1849

BROWN Eld (1) Forrisville in Sheridan NY 1838

BROWN John W Eld (1) Mt Desert 1850

BROWN John Jr (3) 1842

BROWN S E Eld (4) Portland 1850

BROWNSON Rev (1) 1844

BUCKINGHAM Rev (3) Dover NH 1838

BUDDINGTON William Rev (1) *MS* 4 Dec 1844

BUKER Alvah J Eld (8) Upper Kennebec Valley ME; Clinton & Canaan 1846-1850

BULLOCK Jeremiah Eld (1) York Co ME 1827

BULLOCK John Eld (1) 1827

BUNDY Benjamin Eld (3) Mooers NY 1847-1850

BUNKER Rev (1) Saco ME 1847

BURBANK Abner Esq (2) Limerick 1848-1851

BURBANK Samuel Eld (30) Newfield, Limerick, Parsonsfield 1827-1837

BURBANK Porter S Eld (30) Strafford Center, Deerfield NH, Hampton, North Hampton 1842-1850

BURGESS Joseph S Eld (4) Lewiston ME 1849; (10) Waterville ME 1847-1848; (1) Auburn ME 1850

BURLINGAME Maxcy W Eld (23) Backstone MA, Mendon MA, Smithfield RI, Waterford ME

BURNHAM Jesse Eld in Sebec 1831; moved to Wis in 1840

BUTLER Henry Rev in New Gloucester ME 1848

BUTLER Oliver Eld (24) Effingham NH, Freedom, Great Falls, Middleton, New Durham 1847-1850

BUTTS Orry Eld (1) 1839

BUZZELL A Eld (3) 1839; (3) Cornish 1840; (1) 1843

BUZZELL Alvah Eld (11) Parsonsfield 1840-1846

BUZZELL David R Esq Ellsworth ME 1849

BUZZELL Editor (1) Gorham 1850

BUZZELL Hezekiah D Eld (13) Alton NH 1833-1847

BUZZELL James Eld (3) Limerick ME 1850

BUZZELL John Eld (16) Parsonsfield 1826-1851

BUZZELL Silas Esq Hollis 1850

BYER Wm C Eld (2) Cincinnatus Cortland Co NY 1848, New Berlin NY 1851

CADY S S Eld (7) Burlington Flats NY, Edneston NY, Laurens NY, Oneonta NY, Otsego NY 1849-1851

CALLEY David Eld (2) Tunbridge VT 1846; (7) Bristol NH, Hebron 1844-1848

CALVIN R Eld (3) 1849

CARD E Eld (1) 1847

CARIL George Esq 1842

CARLAND David Eld (1) Barnstead 1846

CARLNER S D Eld (1) 1846

CARLTON Eld (1) 1839

CARPENTER R Eld (1) Abington PA 1850

CARPENTER Rev (1) Milford 1836

CARRUTHER Dr Rev (3) Portland ME 1847-1849

CARTER S S Eld *MS* (1) Wayne, Ashtabula Co OH 1847

CARVERNO A Eld (2) Strafford NH 1837-1845

COVERNO A Eld: *MS* 6 May 1835

CARY Richard M Eld (2) Turtle Prairie Walworth Co WT, Johnstown Rock Co WT 1847

CATLIN S T Eld (12) Concord, Hopkinton NH, Prembrook 1842-1849

CAVERLY John 4th Eld (8) Strafford 1835-1840

CAVERLY Robert B Esq 1845

CAVERNO Arthur Eld (50) Berwick ME, Candia, Dover NH, Great Falls, Portsmouth, Providence, Strafford 1834-1850

CHAFEE Chester Eld (1) China NY 1835

CHANDLER R Esq 1849

CHANEY John Eld (9) Chesterville, Exeter NY, Farmington ME, Leonardsville NY, Livermore, Lloydsville NY, Plainfield NY, Unadilla Forks Otsego Co NY 1838-1846

CHANEY S Freeman Eld (2) Buxton ME 1843

CHAPMAN Andrew M C Esq 1829

CHAPMAN C Rev (1) Sacarrappa ME 1847

CHAPMAN E C Rev at Newfield ME 1847

CHASE D P Eld in Groton 1846

CHASE Ebenezer Eld (1) Enfield NH 1819

CHASE J T Hon (2) Conway NH 1849

CHASE Moses Eld 1843

CHASE Paul Eld (9) Chester, Hebron, Ramney NH, Raymond, West Plymouth 1840-1848

CHASE S G Esq 1847

CHASE William P Eld (14) Limerick ME & NH & Dresden New York 1835-1847

CHATTERTON Benjamin Eld (2) Middlesex VT & Moretown 1846-1850

CHENEY Martin Eld Olneyville RI 1836-1838

CHENEY Oren B Eld (13) in Lebanon ME 1846-1850

CHESLEY Israel Eld (1) Lee 1834

CHICK John Eld (40) Ossipee NH 1836-1851
CHICKERING J W Rev (3) Portland 1849-1850
CILLEY Daniel Plumer Eld (1) Bedford '44; (1) Chichester '40; (6) Durham '35-38; (2) Epsom '34-39; (1) Greenland '37; (3) Hampton '37-38; (1) Jamaica Plaine Roxbury '35; (1) Kensington '37; (5) Lamprey River '34-35; (1) Loudon '39; (120) Manchester NH '33-47; (8) N Market 1839; (1) Lamprey River NH '33; (4) N Scituate RI '50; (4) Northwood NH '33-35; (4) Nottingham '35-CILLEY Daniel P 1838; (1) Piscataqoug Village 1846; (3) Pittsfield 1839-1840; (1) Poplin 1837(1) Scituate RI 1850; (1) Strathan 1834; (116) 1833-1847
CILLEY Elbridge Gerry Eld (1) Grattan Kent Co Mich; (1) Oneida Eaton Co Mich 1848
CILLEY James C Esq (2) 1844
CILLEY Joseph L Eld (4) Jackson, Monroe & Brooks 1843-1849
CLAFFIN Jehiel Eld (12) Randolph VT, West Brookfield 1839-1843
CLARK Atherton Eld 1831
CLARK Eli Eld (11) Strafford VT & Thetford, Norwich 1843-1849
CLARK Eld (2) Waterboro 1828
CLARK G Eld (2) Attleborough & Rehoboth MA 1850-51
CLARK G Eld 1846-1847
CLARK John Eld (1) (travelled Maine, 40,000 miles and married 60 couples) 1846
CLARK Mayhew Eld (12) Dover, Wakefield 1826-1846
CLARK Peter Eld (2) Gilmanton 1834-1838
CLARK Rev (1) Portsmouth NH 1847
CLARK Rufus Eld (1) Colebrook Ohio 1850; (1) Pierpont NY 1847
CLARKE Gardner Eld (3) Attleborough 1847-1850
CLAPP Bela B Esq 1842
CLAY Daniel Eld (12) North Berwick & Berwick ME 1845-1850
CLAY Jonathan Eld (3) Buxton ME 1844-1847
CLEMENT Daniel B 1850
CLEMENT Jona Rev 1844
CLIFFORD Aldin S Eld West Topsham VT 1848
CLOUGH Jeremiah Eld (14) Canterbury, Loudon, & Northfield NH 1840-1848
COBB A H Eld (2) North Yarmouth 1842-1850
COBURN Rev 1844
COBURN J Milton Rev (2) Effingham NH 1840
COCHRAN Warren Rev 1847
COE Rev 1835
COFFIN Stephen Eld ( ) Wolfborough 1850
COFFIN S Eld (3) Wolfborough & Tuftonboro' 1848-1850
COFFRIN Joshua Eld Swanton VT 1851
COGSWELL G W Esq 1832
COGSWELL E C Rev 1847

COLBY Eld 1845

COLBY John Rev (3) Wolfborough 1835-1846

COLE Mooers Eld (5) Salem 1850-1851

COLEMAN E B Eld (2) 1845

COLEMAN Isaiah Bangs Eld (60) Sand Lake NY; Stephentown NY; Brainerd's Bridge; Nassau NY; Sand Lake NY; West Stephentown NY; Berlin NY 1843-1850

COLEMAN J B Eld (6) Nassau, Stephentown NY 1838-1844

COLEORD David Esq Porter 1832

COMBS A Eld at Sangerville ME 1839

CONE C C Rev Bowdoinham *MFWBR* 18 Sept 1847 ?????

COOK J(ohn)? labor in ME? 1839

COOK O G Esq (1) Casco ME 1850

COOK Rev at North Berwick 1849

COOKLIN Rev 1845

COOLEY John Eld (4) 1839-1846

COOLEY L/T L Eld 1839-1842

COOMBS Abner Eld (10) Foxcroft ME, Delaware Walworth Co Wis, Kilmarnock, La Grange, Lafayette WT, Rochester Racine Co Wis, Wheatland Wis 1833-1850

COPELAND David Rev at Winham ME 1847

COPELAND Rev Milton 1848

COPP E Eld 1843

COPP John Blaisdell/I B Eld (23) Austinburg & Trumbull Ohio 1839-1849

COPP J B Eld (8) Corinna/Dexter 1837-1839

COPP Roger Eld (2) Detroit, Corinna ME 1843-1844

CORSER Enoch Rev (1): Loudon NH 1838

CORSON Charles Eld (1) Lebanon ME 1844

CORY B Rev 1847

COTTON Eld Wakefield NH 1840

COTTON Ward Esq 1848

COWELL D B Eld (4) NH & ME 1842-1847

COWING David Eld (2) Landaff NH 1828-1835

COX Eld Portland 1847

CRANDAL R C Eld Middlefield NY 1848

CRANDALL J M Eld (2) Norwich NY & Pharsalia Chenango Co NY 1848

CRANE E F Eld (4) Mito New York 1838-1843

CRANE E R Eld 1843

CRAWFORD (Oshea W)? Mr: 1835

CRESSEY Rev (1) Kennebunk 1849; (1) Conway NH 1847

CRESSEY E W Eld (1) Jackson NH 1847

CROCKETT James Eld (7) Buxton, Falmouth, & Westbrook ME 1847-1851

CROSS David Eld (1) Sutton VT 1850

CROSS David Eld (1) Sheffield VT 1838
CROSS Eld 1847
CROSS Jesse Esq (3) New London & Springfield 1849-1851
CROWELL D B Eld (1) Lebanon ME 1850
CROWELL E Eld (3) Brunswick ME 1843
CUMMINGS E E Rev Concord NH 1849
CUMMINGS Rev 1834
CUMMINGS Rev Newfield 1850
CUMMINGS S Eld in Orange VT 1850
CURRIER S A Eld New York State 1849
CURTIS C Rev in Sanbornton 1848
CURTIS E Eld: (1) Peru OH 1842
CURTIS Eld Rochester NH 1840
CURTIS Eld S (1) Lawrence MA 1849
CURTIS Silas Eld (50) 1835-1847; Fayette ME 1833; (10) Lowell
    1845-1849; (15) Dracut 1846-1849; (17) Augusta, Bowdoinham,
    Mt Vernon, Lewiston, Hallowell, Wayne 1832-1846; (1) Monmouth
    ME 1834; (2) Dover NH 1840-1842; (6) Great Falls 1839-1840; (6)
    Roxbury 1850; Waterville 1833
CUSHING Rev (2) Haverhill MA 1834-1839
CUSHMAN Rev Dover NH 1834
CUTLER Rev Portland 1849
DAM C Rev Falmouth 1849
DAM Joseph Esq 1827
DAMMON I Eld 1842
DANA S Eld 1844
DANA Simeon Eld (2) New Hampton 1849
DAVIS I G Eld (12) Deerfield NH & Underhill 1843-1846
DAVIS J B Eld (32) Roxbury, Dover & Manchester NH 1843-1850
DAVIS J E Eld (3) Lawrence 1846-1849
DAVIS Joseph Eld (4) Effingham/Freedom NH 1834-1843
DAVIS K R Eld (4) Meredith 1844-1848
DAVIS Rev (1) Freedom 1835
DAVIS S H Eld Lesslie Ingham Co Mich 1849
DAVISON M N Eld (2) Pascoag RI 1849
DEAN B Eld (1) Colebrook 1850
DEMERITT Wm Eld 1833
DEMING Rev 1833
DENNIS J M Esq (1) New Portland ME 1838
DEXTER Henry M Rev (1) Manchester 1846
DICK A Eld in Varysburgh NY: MS 5 May 1846
DICKEY H F Eld in Topsham VT 1850
DIKE Orange Eld (1) Bolton VT 1850; (17) Huntington VT 1838-
    1851; (1) Jericho VT 1851; (2) Starksborough VT 1848; (2)
    Underhill VT 1849-1850; (4) 1842-1847
DODGE Asa Eld (2) Caroline NY 1845-1850

DODGE William Eld (3) 1833-1851 Sunipee & Fishersfield NH
DOLDT James Eld 1845
DOLE Rev Mr Brewer ME 1846
DONHAM Rev 1846
DORE Ezekiel Esq in Ossipee NH 1850
DORE T W Eld Garland ME 1847; North Gorham 1849; Gray ME
    1849
DORR R H Rev Farmington ME 1847
DOUGLASS G Eld in Georgetown ME 1850
DOW J M H Rev 1847
DOW Rev 1834
DRAKE Cyrus B in Royalton VT 1837-1838
DRAKE S S Rev Lower Biddeford 1849
DRESSER R Esq Pownal 1847
DREW Enoch Eld (3) Hudson Mich 1843-1848
DREW Ira T Esq (2) Waterboro ME 1847-1850
DREW Rev Augusta ME 1850
DREW Samuel W Great Falls 1850
DUDLEY Moses Eld 1842-1844
DUDLEY Thomas J Eld Augusta ME 1848
DUNN Ranson Eld (25) Boston 1843-1849 Great Falls NH
DURGIN George W Esq 1844
DURGIN John M Eld (17) Gray, Gorham ME & Wilmington MA 1839-
    1844; Rev John Milton 1842 labored in ME, NH, and MA
DUSTIN Caleb Rev "If Mr Dustin wants any more notices published,
    he must not TAX US with the postage." *MS* 28 Dec 1842
DWIGHT Rev 1851; Saco ME 1847; Portland ME 1849
DYER B Eld Hopkinton NH 1845-1848
DYER Samuel B/G (6) Loudon/Canterbury & Epson 1833-1845
DYER S G Eld Epsom 1837
EASTMAN B H Esq Plymouth NH 1847
EASTMAN C Allen Eld in Dover NH 1850; New Market 1849; (5) New
    Market 1848-1850; (2) Durham 1849-1850; Houghtonville VT
    1850
EASTWOOD Eld 1839
EATON E G Eld (10) Biddeford 1833-1850
EATON J S Rev Portland 1849
EATON Rev Salem 1850
EDGECOMB Joseph (3) Eld Mt Vernon ME 1845-1848
EGGLESTON A C Eld 1844
ELA R Eld 1844
ELKINS David Eld (1) Rockmanton New York 1838
ELLIOT J Eld Corinna 1846
ELLIOT Rev Auburn ME 1849
ELLIOTT J E Rev 1851
EMERY Amos Eld (4) Goshen & Newbury 1844-1851

EMERY E Eld Waterboro 1847
EMERY James Eld (8) Tamworth 1838-1844
EMERY Nathaniel (4) Waterboro 1829-1850
EMERY Richard (18) 1844-1847
ESTEN H Eld Gorham NY 1848
EVANS S R Eld (3) Enfield NY 1849-1850
EVERETT R Rev 1844
FAIRFIELD E B Eld (4) Spring Arbor Mich 1847-1849, West Cambridge MA 1847,
FAIRFIELD Eld Westport 1836
FAIRFIELD Smith Eld Meredith Lake Village 1836-1846; Boothbay 1837
FARRENT J F Eld New York City 1849
FARRINGTON Rev Bath ME 1850; Biddeford 1847-1848
FAY Edward Eld (2) Underhill VT 1838-1850; Jericho VT 1846
FAYBAN John D Esq Scarboro' 1849
FAYBAN Samuel Hollis 1850
FELCH A Rev Limerick ME 1847
FELLOWS George Eld (2) 1843-1845
FERNALD James Eld (4) Saco ME 1835-1850
FERNALD Samuel P Eld (45) Gilmanton NH & Northwood & Ossipee NH & Alton NH & Sanbornton 1838-1850
FERRIS F Eld 1850
FESSENDEN N Eld 1847
FIELD T Esq 1845
FILES Allen Eld (20) Monmouth, Hallowell, Wales ME 1833-1850
FINNEY Eld Rev Gardiner 1849
FISK Ebenezer Eld (5) New Hampton 1839-1849
FISK Rev Bath ME 1849
FISKE John O Rev Bath ME 1847
FITZ Rev Ipswick 1838
FLAGG Joseph Eld Sutton VT 1838
FLANDERS A Eld 1829
FLETCHER Jabez Eld (7) Islesboro Belfast & Munroe ME 1837-1850
FLETCHER Jonathan Eld Sandwich QM NH 1846
FLETCHER J Eld (2) Albany 1847
FLYNN William H Eld (7) Freedom & Yorkshire NY 1847-1848
FOGG Dudley Esq (2) Mt Vernon 1835-1836
FOGG E T Eld China ME 1847
FOLSOM Moses Eld (2) Sutton & Wolcott VT 1848-1850
FOLSOM P Eld (4) Topsham ME 1842-1847
FORD James Esq Gray & Raymond 1849
FOSS A T Eld Parsonsfield 1832
FOSS Alvin W Eld 1843
FOSS Eld Parsonsfield 1830-1831
FOSS Joseph Eld 1844

FOSS Nahum Eld (16) Effingham NH 1847-1851

FOSS Tobias Eld (5) Epsom & Raymond 1846-1850

FOSTER Eld (1) Wilton 1829

FOSTER John Eld (6) Chesterville, Farmington, Jay & Livermore 1832-1840

FOSTER Rev (1) Jackson Mich 1850

FOSTER S B Esq Gray ME & New Gloucester 1849

FOWLER Josiah Eld Venango PA 1838

FRAZIER Samuel Eld Pittsford Hillsdale Co Mich 1849

FREEMAN A N Rev Portland 1850

FREEMAN Charles Rev (20) Limerick & Newfield ME 1827-1850

FREEMAN Joseph Rev New Hampton 1846

FRENCH Rev North Hampton 1835

FROST D Sidney Eld (40) Concord, Contoocookville, New Market, Gilford NH, Durham NH 1842-1850

FROST G G Esq Lisbon ME 1836

FROST Isaac Eld (4) Litchfield ME 1843-1848

FULLENTON J Eld 1840-1842

FULLER Eld James (4) Phipsburg ME 1834-1849

FULLER Jairus Eld 1845

FULLER W Eld (5) 1843-1844

FULLONTON J Eld (7) Danville 1837-1842; (4) Raymond 1847-1850; (20) 1839-1847

FURBER Rev Mr in Greenland 1847

GALLISON William F Eld (4) Abbot & Foxcroft ME 1847-1849

GAMMON E H Rev 1850

GARDINER S D Eld (3) 1845-1847

GARDNER L G Eld (5) Owego NY 1845-1849

GARDNER S D Eld (8) Brookfield NY Hamilton NY, Sherburne NY, Little Meadows & Poolville NY 1848-1851

GARLAND David Eld (19) Barnstead & Gilmanton & Strafford 1835-1849

GARLAND G D Eld (5) Deerfield 1843-1847

GARLNAD D Sweden ME 1848

GASKELL Silas Eld (8) Conway & Eaton 1841-1846

GATCHELL H Eld (2) Lee ME & Topsfield 1849

GATCHELL Mark Eld (5) 1842-1843

GATES Charles H Rev Nottingham Square 1851

GATES J R Esq 1849

GELLERSON G W Eld in Haynesville Plantation ME 1848

GELLERSON George Eld 1843

GEORGE Enos Rev (3) Barnstead 1835-1845

GEORGE Nathaniel K Eld (25) Wheelock VT, Franconia & Lisbon & Newark & Waldin VT 1839-1850

GERRY E J Rev on 22d ult at Standish ME: *MFWBR* 15 May 1847

GIFFORD H Eld in Sperry, Fayette Co. Iowa 1850

GILLPATRICK J Rev 1849
GILMAN Moses Esq (3) Sangerville ME 1844-1848
GLINES J Eld (2) 1843-1844
GOLDER J Eld (1) Lewiston ME 1849
GONSALVES M J Eld 1842
GOODALE S Eld (Rev Stephen H) (1) East Randolph VT 1837
GOODNA W A Eld (1) Candea MS 1 Dec 1847
GOODRICH Barnard Eld (2) Gardiner 1839
GOODWIN H Eld Hollis 1831
GOODWIN Joseph Eld 1845
GOODWIN Joshua Eld 1834
GOODWIN Lemuel Eld 1842
GOODWIN Timothy El Hollis 1829
GORDAN J Esq 1835
GOULD Benjamin Eld (3) Embden 1842-1848
GOWER H B Rev (2) Buxton 1849
GRAHAM D M Rev at Saco 1849-1850; New York City 1850
GRANT James W Esq 1844
GRAY Ira Eld (14) D) Duxbury VT, Waterbury 1842-1850
GRAY J Eld Waterboro ME 1850
GRAY James Eld Biddeford 1847
GRAY John Esq South Berwick 1849
GREEN D Eld Meredith NY 1850
GREEN Orange Eld Danby VT 1838
GREEN Rev J Salisbury NY 1847
GREEN Silas Rev 1838
GREENE D Eld Kartright NY & Meredith NY 1849-1851
GREENE Rev 1843
GREY James Eld (2) Waterboro ME 1847-1848
GRIFFETH Ansel Eld (15) Alexandria NY, De Pauville NY, Clayton
    NY, Theresa NY, Volney NY 1836-1850
GRIFFIN J Eld (1) Fairfield ME 1850
GRIFFIN Jacob Eld Roscoe Winnebago Co IL 1848
GROSS Eld A 1839
GUERNESEY J W Rev New Ipswich MA 1847; New Ipswich NH 1848
GUPTILL R W Esq (3) Chatham NH 1850
HACKETT John O Eld (13) East Parsonsfield ME 1842-1848; (1)
    Brownfield ME 1838
HAGGETT S M Eld (1) Monroe ME 1850
HALE John (1) Dover NH 1834
HALEY N Esq 1826
HALL T M Eld (3) Saco, Scarborough & Hartford ME 1849-1850
HAM Dr 1843
HAM Ezra Eld (4) Gilmanton NH 1844-1846
HAMBLEN J F Eld (2) 1842-1845
HAMILTON Benjamin R Esq 1835

HAMILTON James Rev (2) 1842-1849

HANSCOM P Eld (3) 1841-1847

HANSON Moses Eld (3) Effingham NH 1849

HANSON T Eld (2) Palmyra ME 1851

HANSON John Esq (1) Rochester 1834

HARDING E Eld (4) Charleston & Corinth ME 1849

HARDING E Eld 1844

HARPER Joseph M Eld (Dr M.D.) (3) Canterbury 1835-1844

HARRIMAN David P Eld (1) Burrillville RI 1851; (2) Gorham ME
   1848-1849; (3) Pascoag RI 1850; (3) Saccarappa ME 1848-1849

HARRIMAN David Eld (2) Deering NH 1833-1842

HARRIMAN J Eld Canterbury 1848

HARRIMAN W P Esq Brooks 1849

HARRIS A D Rev Standish 1849

HARRIS H W Eld 1842

HARRIS Lucius T Eld Brookfield VT 1849

HARRISMAN D P Eld in Saccarappa ME 1849

HART Ephraim H Eld (1) 1850; (8) 1843; (2) Brownfield ME 1848; (2)
   Ossipee NH 1848

HARTSHORN Nelson Eld (5) Washington VT & Williamstown 1848-
   1850

HARVEY Erastus Eld (2) 1844

HARVEY Hiram Esq Gouldsborough ME 1840

HARVY Nathaniel Eld (1) Atkinson 1828

HASKELL G W Eld (2) 1843

HATHAWAY G W Eld/Rev (1) Corinth ME 1837; (1) Madison ME
   1848

HATHAWAY Leonard Eld (16) Dover, Corinna, Atkinson, Kilmarnock
   ME 1831-1848

HATHORN Samuel Eld (10) Bowdoinham 1838-1847

HATHORN S Eld (1) Milan Iowa 1850

HAWKS J Rev Jr New Gloucester 1849

HAYDEN Lucian Eld (6) Dover NH 1839-1842

HAYDEN Wentworth Eld 1844

HAYES Robert Eld 1846

HAZEN Jasper Rev (1) Woodstock VT 1838

HEDGE Barnabas Eld (1) Wiscasset 1827

HEALD A (1) Hollis 1849

HEALTH J D Eld (10) Perry Township Logan Co Ohio, Peru Township
   Logan Co Ohio, Ruch Township Logan Co Ohio, York Union Co
   Ohio 1844-1850

HENDER Moses C Eld (9) Chelsea, Tunbridge VT, Barrington Nova
   Scotia Canada 1844-1850

HENRY Rev (1) 1847

HENSHAW J P Rev Providence RI 1849

HERSEY L Eld (9) Brunswick, Harpswell, & Freeport ME 1842-1850

HERVEY Hiram Esq 1840
HERVEY Russell Eld Rome Mich 1839
HIDDEN Rev 1843
HIGGINS Joseph Eld (4) Thorndike 1829-1847
HILL Eld (1) New Hampton 1836
HILL H F Rev (2) Groveland NY 1850
HILL John Eld (1) Meredith 1836
HILL John C Esq (2) 1843-1845
HILL Mark Eld (5) Sheffield VT 1845-1845
HILLS James Wightman Eld (2) Smithville NY 1845-1849
HINKLEY John Esq (2) Georgetown 1839-1842
HOAG I J Eld (2) Poestenkill NY 1851
HOBART J Rev (1) Saccarappa 1848
HOBBS Abiel W Eld (5) 1843-1847
HOBBS Eld (1) 1830
HOBBS Henry Eld (2) Waterboro ME 1832-1835
HOBBS Isaac Esq (1) Ossipee NH 1849
HOBBS Thomas I (1) North Berwick ME 1849
HOBSON Andrew Eld (2) Steep Falls 1839-1847
HOBSON Pelatiah M Eld (3) Steep Falls ME 1844
HODGE Rev (1) Gilmanton 1838
HODSDON Caleb Esq (4) Gorham ME 1827-1850
HOLLIS N A Eld(1) East Williamstown VT 1839
HOLMAN J W Eld (3) New England 1842-1843
HOLMES D G Eld (7) Macedon & Walworth NY 1847-1851
HOLMES Hiram Eld (14) Bradford, Newbury, Candia, Effingham,
    Raymond NH 1833-1851
HOLMES John C Eld (5) Strafford & Wakefield NH 1842-1849
HOLT F Esq (1) Sharon VT 1848
HOMES H Eld (1) Epsom 1837
HOOPER Rev (1) Shapleigh ME 1850
HOUSTON Rev (1) 1845
HOWE Rev (1) 1835
HUBBARD Stephen Esq 1843
HULL Alfred Esq (1) Cornish 1833
HUMPHREY Meshach Esq (1) Gray ME 1849
HUNTRESS D Eld (5) Otisfield ME 1842-1844
HURD Carlton Rev (1) Fryeburg 1826
HURIBUT William Eld (1) 1847
HURLEY J H Rev (3) Unionville MD 1850
HUSSEY L Rev (3) Portland & Westbrook ME 1849-1851
HUTCHENS/HUNTINS/HURCHINS Elias Eld (70) 1834-1850; (1)
    Hampton 1838; (5) Johnston RI 1834-1835; (2) Madbury 1850;
    (3) New Market 1842-1844; (12) No Providence RI 1834-1838; (99)
    Dover 1846-1851
HUTCHINGS Samuel Eld (1) Phillips ME 1828

HUTCHINSON S Eld (5) Farmington NH 1845-1847
HYDE Nelson Esq (3) New Lynn 1847-1849
INGRAHAM John Esq 1847
JACKSON D Eld (1) Charleston MA 1843; (1) Parsonsfield ME 1835;
    (1) Topsham ME 1839; (2) Ossipee NH 1827-1828; (4) 1831-1847
JACKSON Nelson A Eld (1) Arcade NY 1848; China NY 1846-1850;
    (1) Farmersville NY 1846; Freedom NY (3) 1846; (2) Yorkshire NY
    1846-1849; (4) 1843-1847
JACOBS Rev (1) North Yarmouth 1849
JEFFERS William Rev (1) Bingham Potter Co PA 1847
JENKINS C Eld (4) Fowler NY 1846-1849
JENKINS Herman Eld (1) 1832
JESSAMINE George W Eld 1844
JOHNSON Thomas Esq New Gloucester ME 1847
JOHNSON Timothy Eld (3) New Sharon ME 1837-1844
JOHNSON William D Eld (22) Northwood NH & South Berwick ME
    1843-1850
JONES A F Esq (1) 1845
JONES Almon Eld (1) Hustisford Dodge Co Wis 1849
JONES Joseph Esq (1) Farmington 1834
JONES L O Eld 1844
JONES N Eld (2) Canaan 1848-1851
JONES Rev (1) 1849
JORDAN Anson Esq (1) Casco/Raymond ME 1850
JORDAN L Eld (1) 1843
JORDAN Zachariah Eld (11) 1839-1848; (2) Raymond 1828-1833; (1)
    Acton 1849; (1) Newfield 1840; (5) Parsonsfield 1840-1847;
JOY Rev (1) 1851
JUDD Rev (2) Augusta 1847-1849
JULIAN Samuel L Eld (2) French Grove, Bureau Co IL 1843
KACEY R H Eld (1) 1850
KALLOCH Rev (1) Augusta ME (1) 1849
KEAVILL E J Eld (1) Eldorado Wis 1850
KEENE Josiah Jr Eld (5) 1841-1845; (1) Lincolnville ME 1848; (2)
    Raymond 1846; (1) Wells ME
KEEVILL E J Eld (1) Eldado Wis 1850
KELER Rev (1) So Berwick ME 1834
KELLEY Richard Eld (1) 1844
KELLY S Eld (1) 1843
KENISTON Thomas Eld (2) Hollis ME 1848-1851
KETCHAM S Eld (1) Constantine Mich 1848
KIMBALL John Eld (1) Candia 1834; (1) Concord NH 1848; (3) Deer-
    field NH 1833-1835; (2) Hopkinton 1850-1851; (1) Raymond
    1835; (3) Weare 1849-1851; (5) 1835-1847
KING Warren Eld (1) Ashfield MA 1849; (1) Chesterfield MA 1849
KINSMAN Ebenezer P Eld (3) Limerick & Newfield ME 1827-1828

KNAPP Davis Eld (2) Dunn Wis 1847-1848
KNAPP Joseph Eld (1) 1845
KNIGHT A Eld (1) Pittsfield Ohio 1850
KNOWLES Elbridge G Eld (5) Andover, Salsbury, Upper Gilmanton 1845-1851
KNOWLES John D Eld (9) Guilford, Pittsfield & Meredith NH 1834-1847
KNOWLES Samuel Eld (4) Ossipee NH 1839-1847
KNOWLTON Ebenezer Eld (3) So Montville ME 1834-1851
KNOX Rev (1) Lewiston ME 1849
KOON D W Eld (1) 1843
KRAIN S Eld (1) Schroeppel Oswego Co NY 1847
KRUM S Eld (1) Scriba NY 1849
LAMB E S Eld (2) Leeds ME 1844-1847
LAMB Henry A Esq (2) Searsmont ME 1848-1849
LANCASTER David Eld (5) Gardiner ME, Gray ME, Scarborough 1844-1850
LANCASTER Daniel Rev (1) 1835
LANCASTER Rev (2) Gilmanton 1834-1838
LANCY G Esq (1) Palmyra ME 1834
LANGWORTH Rev Mr (1) Chelsea MA 1851
LEAVITT E Eld (1) No Hampton 1838
LEAVITT Stephen Eld (1) W Fairlee VT 1838
LEAVITT Thomas Esq (1) Ossipee NH 1848
LENNAN John Eld (2) Industry ME 1837-1838; (1) Kingfield 1839; (1) Lexington 1840; (2) New Portland 1839
LEONARD L G Eld (1) 1844
LEONARD Rev (1) Orono 1849
LEWIS Daniel B Eld (16) 1839-1850; (1) Pittsfield 1836; (1) Readfield ME 1848; (1) Sidney ME 1842; (1) Unity ME 1844; (8) Waterville ME 1837-1849
LEWIS J W Eld (1) Providence RI 1837
LEWIS John Eld (1) Lisbon 1848
LEWIS John W Eld (1) Lawrenceville NY 1849
LEWIS L Eld (2) Barnstead 1846-1850
LIBBEY Elias Eld (2) Dover NH 1832-1833
LIBBEY Isaac Eld (1) 1844
LIBBEY James Eld (1) 1845
LIBBY Aaron (1) 1843
LIBBY Almon Eld (6) Brunswick ME 1848-1851; (1) Durham ME 1851; Lisbon ME 1848; (8) 1842-1845
LIBBY Charles O Eld (12) Cape Elizabeth, Gorham, Scarboro, & Standish ME 1844-1850
LIBBY David Eld (2) Lewiston & Harrison 1848-1851
LIBBY Elias (23) Jay, Limerick, Limington, Newfield, Parsonsfield, Waterboro 1827-1835

LIBBY Isaac Eld (1) Cornish 1826; (2) Danville ME 1839-1844; (1)
  Lewiston 1838; (1) Minot; (5) Portland ME 1848; (12) 1839-1849
LIBBY James Eld (8) West Poland ME 1839-1847
LIBBY John Eld (1) 1832
LIBBY Josiah Eld (2) Biddeford ME 1846-1847
LIBBY Peter Eld (1) Saco ME 1838
LIGHTHALL William A Eld (6) China NY & Ellington NY 1846-1850
LIMBOCKER H S Eld in Pitt, Washtenaw Co Mich 1838
LINCOLN Allen Rev (1) Gray ME 1849
LINSCOTT Henry Rev (1) Newfield ME 1847
LITTLEFIELD William H Eld (10) Acton, Lebanon ME & Shapleigh
  ME 1844-1850
LITTLEFIELD Witham H Eld (1) Berwick ME 1849
LOMBARD B L Esq (1) 1843
LOMBARD B S Rev (1) Readfield ME 1843
LOMBARD Solomon Esq (1) Gorham ME 1850
LONG Larkin A Eld (6) Conway NH & Jackson NH 1847-1850
LONGLEY James P Eld (1) Kingfield ME 1848
LONGSTREET George G Rev (1) 1842
LORD David H (1) Limerick ME 1846; (1) Newport RI 1846; (1)
  Parsonsfield ME 1848; (1) Pascoag RI 1848; (2) Sanford ME 1837-
  1840; (1) Shapleigh 1838; (2) Springvale 1838; (18) 1839-1847
LORD H Eld (1) Shapleigh ME 1840
LORD Isaac Rev (1) 1843
LORD Thomas N Rev (7) Biddeford ME 1848-1850
LORD W Eld (2) Parsonsfield ME 1827-1831
LORMAN John Eld (1) Lexington ME 1840
LOTHROP Rev (2) 1834
LOVELESS J H Eld (3) Corinth, Day NY, & Hadley 1849-1850
LOVELL Rev (1) 1842
LOWELL Tallman Esq (2) Phipsburgh 1838-1839
LUCAS William K Eld (2) Wolfborough 1849-1850
MACE Jeremiah Rev (1) 1843
MACK Enoch Eld (6) Dover NH 1836-1840
MACOMBER H N Rev (1) 1849
MADEN L J Eld (1) Lansing Mich 1849
MAHAN Pres (1) 1845
M'ALLASTER Harvey Esq (1) Stowe VT 1849
MANSON Benjamin S Eld (4) Candia 1837; (1) Gilford 1834; (1)
  Limington ME 1850; (1) North Scarboro' 1847; (3) Saccarappa ME
  1846-1850; (10) 1835-1850
MANSON L Eld (1) New Hampton 1845
MARELEN J Alonzo (1) 1851
MARINER J Eld (1) Checkerville NY 1851
MARK Enoch Eld (1) Dover 1836
MARKS David Eld (2) Milo NY 1833-1834

MARSH C Rev (1) Shapleigh 1826
MARSTON J G Eld (1) Kennebunkport ME 1850
MARSTON James H Eld (1) 1845
MARTIN Rev (1) 1842
MASON E Eld (1) 1843
MASON James Eld (2) 1847
MASON John B Eld (1) 1842
MASON Lemuel Eld (14) Gilmanton, Sanbornton NH, Upper Gilmanton NH, Meredith, Moultonborough 1838-1850
MASON S Eld (1) 1847
MASON Samuel Eld (1) Moultonborough 1838
MASSUERE F Rev (1) Biddeford ME 1849
McARTHUR J (1) Parsonsfield 1832
McDANIEL J Rev (1) Hollis 1849
McDONALD John Esq (2) Limerick ME 1831
McKAY William Eld (1) 1842
McKENNEY O Eld (2) 1842-1844
McKENNY Humphrey Esq (2) Limington 1838-1839
McKENNY J B Eld (1) Jasper NY 1850
McKENNY P Eld (1) 1843
MCKOON D W Eld (3) 1842-1845
McMELLAN Rev (1) Limerick ME 1847
McMURPHY B H Eld (7) Gilmanton Iron Works, Thornton 1843-1850
MEADER Eld (2) Brookfield 1837; (5) Rochester NH 1839-1851; (1) Wakefield 1838; (1) Wolfborough NH 1837; (8) 1839-1850
MEARS George Z Eld (2) Waldo ME, Belmont 1848-1849
MEASER Asa Eld (1) 1847
MERRIAM Asaph Eld (1) 1842
MERRILL Asa Eld (7) Stratham 1838-1846
MERRILL Joseph Eld (1) Walworth 1850
MERRILL Octavius A Esq (1) Topsham 1850
MERRILL Thomas Esq (1) 1835
MERRILL William P Eld (2) Amesbury MA 1851; (1) Danville NH 1846; (8) Hampton NH 1848-1850; (2) Haverhill MA 1848; (1) Salisbury MA 1850; (8) 1844-1847
MERRILL William S Eld (6) 1843-1847; (2) Tamworth NH 1848, 1850
MERRY A Rev in Hinsdale MA (1) 1850
MESERVE George P Elder (1) 1846
MESSER A P Rev in Passadumkeag ME 1847
MESSER Asa Eld (1) Wentworth 1846; (5) 1838-1845
MILES Rev (1) 1847
MILL Charles Eld (1) 1850
MILLER C Rev (1) Farmington 1849
MILLER D Eld (1) 1845
MILLS James E Eld (1) Albany 1850; (1) Conway NH 1850; (4) Eaton 1848-1850

MILTON Nathan H Eld (1) Kittery 1837
MINER J H Eld (1) Otsego Ind 1848
MITCHELL Isaac Esq (1) Limington 1826
MITCHELL John Eld (1) Standish 1850
MITCHELL Rev (1) Standish 1849
M'KAY J A Eld (1) Ellington NY 1848
MONTEITH W J Rev (1) 1844
MOODY David Eld (2) Gilmanton NH; (10) South Weare & Weare
    1840-1846; (10) 1836-1844; (1) Upper Gilmanton NH 1850
MOODY H Rev (1) 1845
MOORE H A Eld (1) Sherburn 1849
MORFORD J B (1) West Munroe NY 1844
MORGAN S Eld (1) Ellsworth NH 1851
MORRELL James Eld (1) Barnstead 1846
MORRILL Franklin Eld (1) Danville 1849; (1) New Gloucester 1846;
    (1) 1842
MORRILL Samuel P Eld (6) Chesterville & Farmington ME 1845-
    1850
MORSE W Eld (1) Carthage 1850
MOULTON Abial Eld (1) Barnston Lower Canada 1836; (6) Stanstead
    Lower Canada 1842; (9) 1828-1843; (1) Stanstead Canada East
    1849
MOULTON A K Eld (24) Lowell MA, Roxbury MA & Portland ME
    1842-1851
MOULTON Abial W Eld (5) Barford/Burford/Bufford?? 1840
MOULTON Frederick Eld (1) Benton 1846; (3) East Randolph VT
    1849; (2) Northwood NH 1850-1851; (11) 1843-1847; (1) Haverhill
    1844
MOULTON John Esq (1) Porter 1831
MOULTON Jonathan Esq (1) 1847
MOULTON O T Eld (1) 1850
MOULTON Silas Eld (4) Parsonsfield 1847-1848
MOULTON T P Eld (2) 1842-1843
MOWRY J M Rev (1) 1839
MUCK E Eld (1) 1838
MURCH Dr (1) 1845
MURDOCK Rev (1) 1842
NASON Eld (1) Exeter NH 1833
NASON Eld 1836
NASON James Esq 1842
NASON Rev (1) Cape Elizabeth ME 1850
NASON Samuel V Eld (4) Corinna, Exeter & Garland ME 1834-1836
NEVENS William P Eld (9) Acton ME, Meredith NH, Saccarappa &
    Westbrook 1843-1850
NEWBOLD J Eld in Pikerun township PA 1837
NEWELL David Eld (4) Durham, Gray & Pownal ME 1850

NEWELL F P Eld (2) Newbury NH 1848
NICHOLAS J T G Rev (5) Saco 1849-1850
NICKERSON Jona. Esq (1) Tamworth 1850
NORRIS J Eld (2) Gilmanton & Loudon 1847-1851
NORRIS Rev (1) 1846
NORTON Isaac Eld Jr (1) Wards Precinct IL 1844
NORTON Lemuel Eld (2) Mt Desert 1831-1835
NOYES Eli (13) Boston & North Scituate 1846-1851
NYE J Eld 1843
OLIVER John Esq (1) Starks 1844
OLIVER Thomas J Eld (1) Starks 1848
ORNE W G Esq (1) Gray 1849
ORR John Rev (2) Alfred 1849-1850
OURGIN???J M Eld 1842
PADDEN S B Eld (16) 3 Mile Bay NY, Plesses, & Hammond NY 1842-
    1848
PADMAN Eld 1844
PAGE Benjamin G 1843
PAGE E D Eld (25) Edgecomb, Boothbay, Brunswick, Wiscasset ME
    1841-1851
PAGE J B Eld (1) Lockport Erie Co PA 1850
PAGE Mr Rev (1) Bridgton ME 1848
PAINE J Eld 1849
PAKER B E Eld (1) Oxford 1851
PALMER Abbot Rev 1843
PARIS C Eld (8) Wolfborough 1843-1850
PARK Thomas Eld (2) Prospect 1827-1830
PARKER Benjamin E (2) 1846-1847
PARKER D T Esq (1) Farmington NH 1845
PARKER Lowell Eld (3) Gorham, Raymond, Edgecomb ME 1848-
    1850
PARKER S H Esq 1844
PARKMAN Rev (3) Dover 1844-1848
PARKS R Eld (1) Ellenbourgh NY 1850
PARMERLY S Rev (1) Jericho VT 1849
PATRICK Wm Rev 1835
PAYNE J Dr 1835
PAYSON Rev Dr (1) Portland ME 1827
PEACOCK Rev Mr 1847
PEASE A Eld (1) Phillips ME 1849
PEAVY S Eld (1) 1843
PECK Benjamin D Eld (7) Grafton, Backstone & Northbridge MA
    1843-1849
PECK P B Eld 1839
PECK Rev Portland ME 1849
PEIRCE Geo Esq (1) Harrison ME 1848

PENDEXTER S Eld (1) Cornish ME 1850

PERKINS J Rev (16) Dover & Somersworth NH 1835-1837

PERKINS Levi Esq (1) Ossipee NH 1846

PERKINS Seth W Eld (1) Belgrade ME 1835; (1) Monmouth 1837; (2) Gardiner 1837; (5) Kittery ME 1849-1851; (3) Woolwich ME 1837-1838; (3) Gilford 1846-1848; (30) 1837-1847

PERKINS Thomas Eld (5) New Hampton, Holderness 1837-1850

PERRY Luther C Eld (4) Kittery 1833-1837

PERRY S Eld (4) St Albans ME 1845-1851

PETTENGILL Dudley Eld (1) 1843

PETTENGILL John Eld (21) Lisbon ME & Meredith NH, Dover NH, Holderness NH & Strafford VT 1836-1847

PHELON Benjamin Eld (1) Boston MA & Smithfield RI 1838

PHINNEY Clement Eld (2) Westport & Buckfield ME 1833-1849

PHINNEY Joseph H Eld (2) Harrison, Bridgeton ME 1834-1838

PICKHAM John Eld 1836

PIERCE Eld 1836

PIERCE L Eld (1) Pelham MA 1836

PIERCE Luther Eld (1) Belchertown MA 1842

PIKE John Eld (12) Fryeburg ME, Sweden ME 1844-1850

PINKHAM G H Eld (1) Jackson 1851

PINKHAM John Eld (40) Alton, Dover, Gilford, Sandwich 1832-1850

PIPER Jonathan Esq 1828

PITMAN J Stephen Eld (43) Meredith NH 1841-1850

PLACE Enoch Eld (67) Strafford, Barrington, Farmington, Rochester 1834-1850

PLUMB Horatio N Eld (20) Warsaw, Buffalo NY, Hainburgh NY, Middlebury NY & Freedom NY 1834-1848

PLUMER Parker Esq 1845

POLLINS James Eld (1) Dixfield ME 1848

POND Rev (1) Bangor ME 1849

POPE James R Eld (1) Harmony Wis 1850

PRATT C N Eld (1) Tinmouth VT 1848

PRATT Cyprian S (3) Wellington ME & Exeter 1834-1850

PRATT James Rev (4) Portland ME 1845-1850

PREBLE H Eld 1849

PREBLE Thomas M Eld 1839

PRENTISS H E Esq Bangor ME 1849

PRESCOTT E T Eld (3) 1843-1844

PRESCOT Judith J (a female preacher) of Parsonsfield ME *Religious Informer* magazine Kennebunk ME Nov 1820 Vol 2 # 2

PRESCOTT Rev Mr - 1842

PRESCOTT Samuel Rev 1842

PRINDLE Mr 1839

PURINGTON Amos Esq - Bowdoin ME 1848

PURINGTON Collamore Eld (5) Richmond & Topsham ME 1847-1850

PURINGTON Elisha Eld (1) 1847
PURINTON A W Eld (27) Bowdoin, Brunswick, Freeport, Lisbon ME 1847-1850
PURINTON Elisha Eld (3) Bowdoin ME 1847-1850
PURINTON N Eld (1) 1846
PURINTON Stephen Eld (1) Bowdoin ME 1846
PURKIS John Eld (3) Gray 1831-1836
PURINTON A W Eld (1) 1845
PURRINGTON J Dr (1) Minot 1834
QUINBY Daniel Eld (3) Lyndon VT 1836-1838
QUINBY H Eld (1) Meredith Village 1840
QUINBY Hosea Eld (1) Parsonsfield 1839
QUINBY Joshua Eld (1) Bethlehem, NH 1829
QUINBY M A Eld (1) 1851
QUINNAM Constant Eld (23) 1834-1849; Bowdoin (4) 1838-1850; Bowdoinham (4) 1843-1848; Georgetown 1834; Litchfield (11) 1839-1850; Pittston 1848; Richmond (2) 1839-1846; Whitefield 1833
RAMSEY G P Eld (2) Acton 1851; (10) Epsom NH 1848-1850; (1) Sanford 1846; (13) 1841-1847
RAND I Eld (1) 1844
RAND James Eld (12) 1842-1851; (2) Limerick ME 1848-1850; (1) Cornish ME 1847; (1) East Parsonsfield ME 1848
RAND S Eld (2) Portland & Westbrook 1828
RAYMOND I Eld (1) Bowdoinham ME 1848
RAYMOND J Eld (3) 1844-1847
READ R W Eld (1) 1841
REDLON Amos Eld (6) 1843-1846
REMICK Eld (1) 1828
REMICK John Esq (1) Milton 1838
REMICK Timothy Rev (1) 1830
REYNOLLS Ira A Eld (1) Macon Mich 1846
REYNOLDS T F Eld (1) Chester 1851
RICHARDS A Rev (1) Lebanon ME 1846
RICHARDSON C S Eld 1845
RICHARDSON Caleb H (1) Canaan NH 1850
RICHARDSON J Rev (2) Pittsfield 1837-1838
RICHARDSON R D Eld (1) Sutton VT 1849
RICHARDSON R E Eld (1) Sheffield VT 1850
RIDEOUT Uriel Eld (1) Lyman ME 1850
RINES John N Eld (12) Dixmont, Frankfort, Islesboro, Jackson, Monroe 1839-1850
RITTENHOUSE W Eld (2) 1844-1846
ROBBINS Lemuel Eld (1) South Reading 1838
ROBBINS Samuel Eld (1) No Providence 1837
ROBERT Rev Mr (1) Hollis 1827

ROBERTS Eld (2) Limerick 1832-1833; (1) Kennebunk 1826
ROBERTSON Samuel Esq (1) Eaton 1851
ROBIE Thomas Eld (3) Sandown NH, Chester NH & Raymond 1831-1835
ROBINSON N J Eld (24) Bangor, Corinna, Garland, Montville, Thorndike, Unity 1838-1848
ROGERS I Rev at Farmington: *MFWBR* 10 Mar 1849
ROLLIN D M L Eld (2) 1842-1846
ROLLIN M L Eld (1) 1844
ROLLINS Andrew Eld (15) Bowdoin, Windham, Brunswick, 1834-1842
ROLLINS D M Eld (1) 1842
ROLLINS Eld (1) 1836
ROLLINS James Eld (1) Canton ME 1848
ROOT E Eld (1) 1850
ROOT E Eld (1) Greenfield Huron Co Ohio 1850
ROOT Rev (2) 1834-1835
ROOT Rev (1) Dover 1834-1838
ROSS T Eld (1) Raymond 1850
ROTT David Rev 1836
ROW J Eld 1847
ROWDYN Esq (1) Waterboro Center 1849
ROWE J Eld (1) Newbury NH 1848
RUNNELS J Eld (15) Acton, Eaton, Freedom, Newfield ME &, Newport RI 1846-1851
RUSSELL Bishop A Eld (1) 1839
RUSSELL G E Eld (1) Thornton 1840
RUSSELL George W Eld (4) Woodstock NH & Peeling (Ossipee) 1837-1848
RUSSELL M Rev (1) 1835
RUSSELL Rev (1) Hingham MA 1843
RUSSELL Stephen Eld (3) Cornville ME & Howland ME 1846-1847
SALTER Rev of Episcopal church (1) Dover NH 1849
SANBORN Abram Eld (1) 1845
SANBORN G Eld (5) Chelsea VT, Holderness VT, Washington VT, Williamstown VT 1843-1848
SANBORN J Eld (1) 1839
SANBORN Luther Esq (1) 1844
SANBORN Thomas Eld (2) 1839
SANDERSON Eld(1) 1843
SARGENT L Eld (1) Topsham ME 1850
SARGENT Rev 1833
SARGENT W A Eld (2) Loudon 1849-1851
SAVAGE E Rev (1) 1851
SAWYER G Eld (1) Barnston Canada East 1851
SAWYER J C Eld 1843

SAWYER J H Rev (1) Buxton ME 1847

SAWYER James (1) Porter 1827

SCATES Alvan Esq 1833

SCOTT E Eld (2) Providence RI 1845-1848

SCRIBNER Miles S Eld (1) 1844

SEAVY John Rev (1) Limington ME 1826

SHAPLEIGH R Esq (1) Berwick ME 1839

SHAW E Rev (2) Gardiner 1849

SHAW Elijah Eld (2) 1834-1844

SHAW Samuel Eld (2) Portland ME 1847

SHELDON Anson Rev (1) Raymond 1837

SHEPARD Almon Eld (4) Whitefield NH 1845-1850

SHEPHERD H Eld (1) Galen NY 1833

SHEPHERD M Eld (1) 1846

SHEPHERD Simon Eld (1) Whitefield NH 1849

SHERBURNE Samuel Eld (18) Barrington, Lee, Nottingham, Stratham 1834-1851

SHIPMAN O Eld (2) Topsham VT & Newbury VT 1838

SHURBURNE Eld (1) Strafford 1836

SHURTLEFF James M Eld (1) 1839

SIDNEY D Eld (1) Warner 1844

SINCLAIR J Eld (12) Hopkinton, Gilford, Manchester, Andover,
Warner Lake Village 1838-1850

SINCLAIR S L Eld (2) Hopkinton 1838

SKILLIN Hiram Eld (4) Bath ME & Unity 1844-1851

SLEEPER Hiram S Eld (1) 1844

SMALL Carlton Eld (10) Gilmanton & Strafford 1833-1851

SMALL Rufus (1) Biddeford ME 1850

SMALL William Eld (6) Bangor & Camden & Belmont ME 1842-1849

SMART Moses M Eld (2) Russia NY & Whitestown NY 1842-1847

SMITH A D Eld (40) Dover, Portsmouth, Rochester, Concord 1842-
1850

SMITH C H Eld (11) Enfield, Tunbridge VT, Enfield & Wilmot 1844-
1849

SMITH D C Rev (1) Prattsbury Steuben Co NY 1850

SMITH Eleazer Rev (13) Tunbridge VT & Dover NH 1836-1846

SMITH Horace H Esq 1843

SMITH J Rev (1) 1838

SMITH Jacob S (1) 1844

SMITH James Jr (1) 1842

SMITH M H Eld (1) Starkville 1850

SMITH O W Eld (10) Phoenix Oswego Co NY & Schroepel NY 1843-
1848

SMITH Oliver H Eld (1) 1840

SMITH Rev Mr (1) Exeter 1837

SMITH William Eld (2) Newfield ME 1850; (3) Parsonsfield 1849-1850; (3) South Parsonsfield 1848-1850

SMUTZ S G Eld 1844

SPAULDING Eld (1) Epping 1834

SPAULDING J Eld (2) Belgrade 1849-1850

SPAULDING Joel Eld (4) Plainfield 1836-1845

SPENCER S W Rev (1) 1847

SPINNEY J Eld (2) 1846

SPINNEY Joseph Eld (3) Milton Mills & Wakefield 1838-1849

SPINNEY Zina H/W Esq (2) Georgetown ME 1839, 1843

SPRING Joseph Eld (1) Wakefield 1838

SPRINGER Rev (1) Stillwater 1839

SQUIRE L Eld (1) 1849

SQUIRES Eld (1) Dickinson NY 1846

STACY R B Eld (2) 1847

STAFFORD Johnson L (1) Harmony 1850

STANLEY M C Eld (1) New Haven NY 1849

STAPLES J S K Eld (1) 1847

STARLING Joseph Esq (1) 1846

STARR D S Eld (1) 1844

STARR Lovel B Eld (1) Middleville 1848

STARR N Eld (2) Arkwright NY & Gerry NY 1850

STEARNS Samuel Eld (5) Nashua 1845-1846

STERRICKER W W Eld (1) 1850

STETSON J A Eld (1) Smithfield RI 1848

STEVEN T Eld (1) Lebanon 1839

STEVENS Enoch Eld (5) Acton, Lebanon, Limington ME 1830-1848

STEVENS Hiram Eld (2) Meredith Village 1838-1843

STEVENS J Eld (4) Windsor & Portland 1836-1850

STEVENS Jacob Eld (1) 1844

STEVENS John Eld (2) Limington & Cornish 1827-1832

STEVENS S Rev (1) China NY 1838

STEVENS Theodore Eld (17) Great Falls, Lebanon, Newfield, Limington, Limerick ME 1838-1850

STEWART I D Eld (1) 1844

STICKNEY W Eld (1) Venango PA 1844

STILES Dutton Eld (1) Huston PA 1850

STILSON Cyrus Eld (3) New Portland 1833-1835

STINSON Robert Eld (3) Richmond 1838-1842

STONE J Rev (3) Newfield, Hiram & Porter ME 1849-1851

STOW Baron Rev (1) Boston 1850

STOWE J P Eld (1) 1842

STOWELL Rev (1) Townsend 1838

STRACY R B Eld (1) 1843

STREETER R Rev (4) Portland 1847-1849

STRICKLAND G G Rev (10) Scarboro', Saco, Biddeford 1849-1851

STRONG J E Rev (2) 1844-1845

STROUT J Eld Jr (1) Bradford ME 1850

STROUT Simeon Esq (1) Limington 1826

STURGIS N G Esq\Eld (2) Danville ME [#43 v16 my name appeared at the altar of Hymen connected w/ title "Eld". Title is applied to Rev's and officers of the church, I have no connection w/ priesthood whatever, & didn't forward the notice for publication. Know not whether the mistake was from the pen or type." *MS* 20 Apr 1842] 1839-1842

SWAIN William Eld (4) Chichester & Epsom NH 1844-1849

SWEET Eld (1) Johnston RI 1835

SWETLAND Ira A Rev (1) Kingston 1849

SWETT David Eld (6) Charleston MA. Strafford & Tunbridge VT 1839-1844

SWETT Jesse Eld (10) Richmond ME 1835-1838

SWETT Simeon Eld (1) 1836

TALLMAN Ezra P Eld (5) Middleville NY, Norway NY, Newport NY 1850-1851

TANNER F B Eld (1) Napoli 1835

TANNER G W W Eld (3) Ashippun & Paris Wis 1849-1850

TARBOX Jordan Esq (2) Westport ME 1838-1839

TARBOX Samuel Esq (2) Westport 1838

TASKER L B Eld (8) Center Harbor & Sandwich 1848-1850

TAYLOR A Eld (3) Burlington ME, Greenbush ME, Weston ME 1847-1848

TAYLOR Eld (1) 1844

TAYLOR Elijah Esq (1) Effingham 1850

TAYLOR Rev 1845

TAYNTOR O Eld (2) Mansfield NY 1838-1844

TENNEY Erdes Rev (1) Lyme 1850

TENNEY Rev Mr (1) 1830

TENNEY T J Rev (1) Brownfield 1849

THING Samuel S Esq (1) Sanford ME 1847

THOMAS J Eld (1) Erie PA 1851

THOMAS John Eld (1) 1842

THOMPSON L J Eld (1) Leoni Mich 1849

THOMPSON Rev Dr (1) 1846

THOMPSON Samuel Eld (8) Holderness & Center Harbor 1838-1850

THOMPSON Z Rev (1) Augusta 1851

THURSTON Nathaniel Eld (210) So Berwick ME, Dover NH, Lee, Methuen, Waterboro, Rochester NH, Kittery ME, Great Falls, NH, & Lowell MA 1829-1842

TILLOTSON Rev (1) Manchester 1847

TITUS C H Rev (1) Woonsocket RI 1849

TOBEY Alvan Rev (1) Durham 1850

TOBEY William Rev (1) Sacoboro 1849

TOBEY Z Eld (1) Providence RI 1830

TOBIE E M Eld (3) Hallowell 1837-1838

TOBIE Ezra Esq (1) New Gloucester 1849

TOBIE Levi Esq (1) Windham 1849

TOBIE R B Eld (1) North Berwick 1847

TODD Nathaniel Esq (1) 1831

TOWN G W Eld (2) Malone NY & Mooers NY 1848-1850

TRACY J Eld (3) Sebago ME 1831-1849

TRICKEY Nathaniel H Eld (2) So Berwick ME 1835-1836

TRIPP L S Eld (4) Limerick & Limington 1848-1849

TRUE E Eld (24) Pittsfield, Portsmouth NH 1849-1851

TRUE E (1) Corinth VT 1838

TRUE Ezekiel Eld (12) Limington ME, So Berwick 1840-1847

TRUE John Eld (1) Freedom & Thorndike 1840

TUCK Jonathan Esq (1) 1845

TUCKER Joshua Eld (3) Starksboro' VT & East Williamstown VT
    1837-1848

TURNER A Eld (3) Mercer 1844-1848

TURNER N Esq (1) 1832

TURNER Sidney Rev (2) Concord ME & Moscow ME 1847-1849

TUTTLE Alexander Eld (8) Nottingham 1837-1848

TUTTLE Ezra Eld (3) Nottingham & So Boston 1848-1851

TUTTLE John G Eld (7) Upper Gilmanton 1840-1844

TYLER Job C (5) Enfield NH & Grafton NH 1843-1850

TYLER S Rev (1) 1831

VAN DAME B Eld (2) Dover & Epsom 1838-1848

VARNEY M Eld (1) Ossipee NH 1849

VAUGHN Hiram Eld (1) 1844

WAKEFIELD Archibald Esq (1) Lewiston ME 1849

WALDRON W H Eld (11) Lowell, Farmington, Rochester 1843-1849

WALKER G S Eld (1) Harmony ME 1848

WALKER John Eld (10) Brookfield, Ossipee, Wakefield 1838-1849

WALKER O B Rev (1) Waldoboro' 1848

WARD Cotton Esq (5) N Belmont 1845-1849

WARD Jonathan Rev (1) Hebron NH 1826

WARNER William Eld (3) Windsor VT 1838-1840

WARREN Charles Eld (1) Thorndike 1829

WASHBURN H Eld (1) Mercer 1838

WATERMAN D Eld (6) Jay, Litchfield, Unity 1843-1850

WATSON Elijah Eld (7) Andover & Effingham 1838-1848

WEATHERBEE I J Eld (1) Kittery 1844

WEAVER Philip Eld (6) Hallowell, Bangor, Augusta ME 1844-1847

WEBB George Eld (1) 1837

WEBBER David Eld (3) Georgetown ME 1839-1850

WEBBER Horace Eld (10) Great Falls, Holderness, Somersworth NH,
    Lisbon NH 1838-1847

WEDGWOOD Dearborn Eld (1) 1849
WEEKS James W (2) Cornish ME 1832
WELLINGTON H Eld (1) Eckford Mich 1848
WELLS L S Eld (1) Meredith NH 1848
WENTWORTH James J Eld (4) Bradford & Weare 1849-1850
WEST John D Eld (3) Waterboro' 1850-1851
WESTON J B Eld (2) 1847-1849
WETHERBEE I J Eld (8) Charlestown 1846-1848
WETHERBEE Josiah Eld (4) Elsworth, Lebanon ME, Sandwich
    1846-1849
WETHERBEE K J Eld (1) 1845
WETHERBY I J Eld (5) 1842-1843
WEYMOUTH Nathaniel Esq (1) Pittsfield 1850
WHALIN James H Rev (1) 1834
WHEELER Austin Eld (2) Minot ME 1834-1850
WHEELER Samuel Eld (6) Chesterville & Starks ME 1844-1849
WHIPPLE H E Eld (3) La Grange & Oberlin Ohio 1848-1850
WHITBY George Rev (1) 1845
WHITCHER Hiram Eld (10) Rochester, Ogden NY, Perry NY, Warsaw
    NY, Conewango NY 1832-1849
WHITCOMB A Esq (4) Dixmont ME & Plymouth ME 1838-1839
WHITE Joseph Eld (13) Standish, N Yarmouth, Scarboro, Standish,
    Gorham ME 1828-1835
WHITE William Esq (1) 1845
WHITEFIELD W Eld (3) Brasher NY 1847-1850
WHITEMORE John Eld (1) 1842
WHITFIELD William Eld (12) Pierpont NY 1843-1848
WHITFORD I F Rev (2) Fayetteville Wis 1847
WHITHAM S H Eld (1) Biddeford 1847
WHITNEY George W Eld (12) Bethel ME, Rochester NH, Bridgeton,
    Sweden 1842-1849
WHITNEY Samuel Eld (3) New Market & Lowell 1838-1840
WHITTAMORE Joseph (1) 1843
WHITTEMORE D R Eld (1) Providence RI (1) 1850
WHITTEMORE John Esq (3) Bowdoin & Lisbon ME 1848-1851
WHITTEN Samuel F Eld (2) 1833-1835
WIELD C E Esq (1) 1849
WIGHT A F (1) Casco 1850
WIGHT Joseph Eld (3) Harrison & Otisfield ME 1846-1850
WILCOX S H Eld (2) 1839-1842
WILD Daniel Rev (1) Brookfield VT 1837
WILKINS N D Eld (2) 1847
WILLIAMS Gibbon Rev (1) 1834
WILLCOX S H Eld (1) 1843
WILLEY C Eld (1) 1846

WILLEY Eben C Eld (9) Greene, Lewiston, Bridgton, Fryeburg, & Sweden ME 1839-1848

WILLEY Rev Mr (1) Rochester 1828

WILLIAM N M (Eld?) (1) Saco 1849

WILLIAMS A D Eld (2) Carolina Mills RI & Providence RI 1850

WILLIAMS Daniel (4) East Killingly CT 1839-1844

WILLIAMS Gibbon Rev (10) Dover NH & Somersworth NH 1831-1835

WILLIAMS N M (8) Saco & Biddeford 1849-1850

WILLIAMS Rev (1) Dover 1834

WILLIAMS Samuel Eld (1) Washington township Fayette Co PA 1832

WILLIAMS T Rev (1) 1833

WILLIAMSON S Eld (1) Starks ME 1849

WILLIS O F Eld (2) Lisbon & Bethlehem NH 1837-1838

WILLIS S B Rev (1) Providence RI 1850

WING A Eld (1) 1847

WING Amos Eld (1) Oneonta NY 1848

WINKLEY John Eld (3) Strafford 1840-1842

WINSOR Barnet Eld (2) 1843-1844

WINTON David Eld Wellsburg PA 1847

WISWELL A Esq (1) Ellsworth ME 1849

WITHAM John Eld (1) 1839

WITHAM Lewis H Eld Saco 1849; (1) Buxton 1840; (7) 1842-1847; (1) Hollis 1848; (3) Limington ME 1850; (1) Lyman 1851; (9) Biddeford 1847-1849;

WITHAM S H Eld (1) Biddeford 1847

WOODARD Wm (2) Lisbon ME & Bowdoinham 1834

WOODMAN Jonathan Eld (14) Lawrence, Great Falls, Wheelock VT, So Parsonsfield, Somersworth 1830-1842

WOODSUM William Eld (2) 1839

WOODWARD William Esq (2) Lewiston & Lisbon ME 1834-1837

WRIGHT E N Eld (4) Fon du Lac Co Wis, Oakfield Wis & Laroy Dodge Co Wis 1848-1849

YOUNG Rev Dr (2) Boston MA 1850

LOCATIONS

The following is a list of locations in this work. Many of the records referred only to the city or town and did not include where the town actually was. We have used old atlases and a few other resources to attempt to locate as many of these places as possible. The *Morning Star* was published in two different towns so any mention of "in this town" prior to 1 Nov 1833 refers to Limerick ME, and from Nov 1833 through 1851 it refers to Dover NH.

Abbott ME
Abington, Montgomery Co, PA
Abington, Plymouth Co, MA
Acton ME (3) 1849-1851
Adams, Jefferson Co, NY
Adams, MA
Addison, NY
Alabama NY
Albany
Alden NY
Allentown PA
Alexander, Washington Co?
  ME?
Alexandria NH
Alexandria NY
Alfred ME 1847
Alton NH
Amesbury MA
Amherst MA
Amoskeag, NH
Amsterdam NY
Andover NH (4) 1820
Anson ME
Antrim, Hillsborough Co, (NH?)
Antwerp, Van Buren Co (MI?)
Appleton ME
Arcadia NY
Arkwright NY
Arrowsic ME (1) 1849
Ascott

Ashfield MA
Ashford
Ashippun WI
Assyria, Barry Co, MI
Athens ME
Atkinson, ME
Attica NY
Attleborough MA
Auburn ME (2) 1847-1851
Augusta ME (6) 1847-1850
Austinburg OH
Bafford Lower Canada
Baldwin ME
Bancroft Plt ME
Bangor ME (3) 1850
Barnstead NH
Barnston Lower Canada
Barrington NH 1839
Barrington Nova Scotia Canada
Barrington VT
Bartlett NH
Batavia NY?
Bath ME (1) 1850
Bath NH
Bayron NY?
Bedford MA?
Belchertown MA
Belfast ME (1) 1850
Belgrade ME (2) 1849-1850
Belmont ME

Beloit WI
Benton VT
Berlin NY
Bershire VT
Bertrand MI
Berwick ME (2) 1849-1850
Bethany, Genesee Co NY
Bethel ME
Bethlehem NH
Biddeford ME (3) 1848-1869
Big Bend IA
Billerica MA
Bingham, Potter Co, PA
Blackstone MA
Blockberry
Boardman Clayton Co Iowa
Bolton VT
Boothbay ME
Boscawen NH
Boston MA
Boston NY
Bow NH
Bowdoin ME
Bowdoinham ME
Bradford, Merrimack Co, NH?
Bradford ME
Bradley, ME
Brainerd's Bridge NY?
Brasher NY
Bremen ME
Brewer ME
Bridgestown Plt
Bridgewater
Bridgton ME (2) 1847
Brighton, Monroe Co NY
Bristol ME
Brookfield VT
Brookline NH
Brooks ME 1848-1849
Brownfield ME
Brunswick ME 1849-1850
Brunswick OH (2)
Buckfield ME
Buffalo NY
Burford, Lower Canada?
Burlington Flatts NY

Burlington ME
Burlington NY
Burnham ME
Burns, Steuben Co NY
Burrillville RI
Bushnell's Basin (NY?)
Butler Wayne Co NY
Buxton ME 1850
Bytown, Canada West
Cabot, Washington Co VT
Callis/Calias VT
Cambridge MA 1849
Camden ME
Cameron WI?
Canaan NH
Candia NH
Canisteo NY
Canterbury NH
Canton ME
Cape Elizabeth ME
Carolina Mills RI
Caroline NY
Casco ME 1850
Cato Addison Co (VT?)
Cavendish VT
Chandlersville ME
Chataugary (Chateagay NY?)
Chatham NH
Checkerville NY
Chelmsford MA
Chelsea MA
Chelsea VT
Chepachet
Chester Geauga Co OH
Chesterfield MA
Chesterville ME
Chichester NH
China NY
Cincinnati OH
Cincinnatus, Cortland Co NY
Clappville NH?
Clark Township Canada West
Clayton NY
Clinton ME
Colden NY
Colebrook NH

718

Collins, Erie Co NY
Columbia & Winfield (in Ontario, Canada?)
Columbus NY
Compton Lower Canada
Concord ME
Concord NH
Conewango NY
Conquest
Constantine MI
Contoocookville NH?
Conway NH 1847
Cooksville WI?
Cooperstown NY?
Corinna ME
Corinth ME
Corinth VT
Cornish ME 1847
Cornishville ME
Cornville ME
Coventry RI
Cowlesville NY?
Craftsbury VT
Cranston RI
Crawford Co
Cumberland ME 1849
Dalton NH
Damariscotta ME
Danbury NH
Danby VT
Danielsonville, Killingly, CT
Danville ME
Danville NH
Danville VT
Davenport NY?
Day NY
Dayton Cattaraugus Co NY
De Pauville NY
Dearborn ME
Dedham MA
Deer Isle ME
Deerfield NH
Deering (ME?)
Delaware, Walworth Co WI
Denmark ME 1847
Dexter ME

Dickinson NY
Dixfield ME 1847
Dixmont ME 1850
Dixville NH?
Dorchester
Douglass Essex Co NY
Dover IL
Dover Lenawee Co. MI
Dover ME
Dover NH 1839-1849
Dracut MA
Dresden ME 1849
Dresden NY
Dryden
Dunkirk NH
Dunn WI
Durham ME
Dutton ME?
East Killingly CT
East Liberty Logan Co OH
East Livermore ME
East Machais ME
East Parsonsfield ME
East Randolph VT
East Thomaston ME 1849-1850
East Troy WI
Eaton NH 1850
Eckford MI
Edgecomb ME
Edneston NY
Edwards (NY?)
Effingham NH 1850
Elba NY?
Elderado WI
Elicottville Cattaraugus Co NY
Eliot ME
Elk Creek PA
Ellenbourgh NY
Ellington NY
Ellsworth ME
Elmira NY
Embden ME
Enfield Centre NY·
Enfield NH
Epping NH?

Epsom NH
Erie PA
Errol NH
Essex
Etna ME
Exeter NY
Fairfield ME
Fallowsfield Township PA
Falmouth ME 1850
Farmington ME 1849-1850
Farmington NH? 1847-1850
Farmsville NY
Fayette ME
Fayetteville WI
Ferrisbury VT
Fishersfield NH
Fitchburg MA
Fon du Lac Co WI
Forrisville in Sheridan NY
Fowler NY
Foxcroft ME 1849
Franconia NH
Frankfort ME
Frankinville NY
Franklin ME
Franklin NH
Freedom NH?
Freedom Cataraugus Co NY
Freeport ME (2) 1849
French Grove, Bureau Co ILL
Fruit Hill Seminary
Fryeburg ME
Galen NY
Gardiner ME (3) 1849-1850
Garland ME
Geauga Seminary OH
Georgetown ME 1839-1849
Gerry NY
Gilford NH
Gilmanston NH
Gilmanton Iron Works NH?
Gilmanton NH 1847
Gloucester RI
Goffstown NH
Gorham ME 1850
Gorham Ontario Co NY

Goshen (NH or NY?)
Gouldsboro' ME
Grafton MA
Granby Lower Canada
Grattan Kent Co Mich
Gray ME
Great Falls NH 1847-1850
Greenbush ME
Greene ME
Greenfield Huron Co OH
Greenland NH
Greenwich MA
Grinville
Groton NH?
Groveland NY
Hadley? NY? or Lower Canada?
Hainburgh NY
Hallowell ME 1849-1850
Hambugh NY
Hamden ME
Hamilton NY
Hammond NY
Hampton NH
Hancock Bershire Co Ma
Hancock ME
Harmony ME
Harmony WI
Harpswell ME
Harrison ME
Harrisville, Medinalo OH
Hartford CT
Hartland VT
Hastings NY
Hatley Lower Canada
Haverhill MA
Haynesville Plt ME
Hebron ME 1849
Henniker NH
Hermon NY?
Hinsdale MA
Hiram ME 1849
Hiram OH
Hodgdon ME
Holderness NH?
Holland VT
Hookset NH

Hope ME
Hopkinton NH
Houghtonville VT
Howland ME
Hudson MI
Hume NY(?)
Huntington VT
Hustisford Dodge Co WI
Huston PA
Industry ME
Ipswick MA
Isle of Shoals (Gosport NH)
Islesboro ME
Ithaca NY
Jackson Brook ME
Jackson ME
Jackson MI
Jackson NH
Jamaica Plaine NY
Janesville WI
Jasper NY
Jay ME
Jefferson ME
Jericho VT
Johnston RI
Johnstown Rock Co WT
Kartwright NY
Kennebunk ME 1851
Kennebunkport ME 1848
Kensington NH?
Killingly CT
Kilmarnock ME
Kingfield ME
Kingrey Lower Canada
Kingston NH
Kirkland, Penobscot Co (name
    changed to Hudson in 1855)
Kirkland Oneida Co NY
Kittery ME
Knox Co Ill
La Grange Ohio
Lafayette WT
Lamprey River NH
Landaff NH?
Lansing MI
Laroy Dodge Co WI

Laurens NY
Lawrence
Lawrenceville, NY
Leavitt Plt ME?
Lebanon ME
Lebanon NH? 1849-1850
Lee ME
Leeds ME
Leon Cattaraugus Co NY
Leonardsville NY
Leoni MI
LeRoy IL
Lesslie Ingham Co MI
Lewiston Falls ME
Lewiston ME 1847-1850
Lexington ME
Liberty ME
Limerick ME 1847-1848
Limington ME
Lincoln VT
Lincolnville ME
Linneus, Aroostook Co, ME
Lisbon ME
Litchfield ME 1849
Little Compton RI
Little Meadows PA
Littleton NH
Livermore ME
Lockport Erie Co PA
Lockport NY
Loudon NH
Lowell MA 1851
Lower Biddeford ME?
Loydsville NY
Ludlow VT
Lunenburg VT
Lyman, Jefferson Co NY
Lyman ME 1849
Lyme
Lyndon VT
Lynn MA
Macedon NY
Macon MI
Madbury
Madeira NY?
Madison ME 1849

Madison MI
Madrid (ME?)
Malden MA
Malone NY
Manchester IA
Manchester Iowa Territory
Manchester NH? 1850
Mansfield NY
Marcellus
Marion OH
Marshfield (MA?)
Matildda, Canada West
Mecca OH
Mendon MA
Mercer Co IL
Mercer ME
Meredith NH 1849
Meredith NY
Meredith Lake Village NH 1850
Methuen
Middlebury NY
Middlefield NY
Middlesex VT
Middleville NY
Milan IA
Milo NY
Milton Mills
Mineral Point WI
Minot ME
Minton NH
Mito NY
Mohegan Plt ME
Monmouth ME
Monroe ME
Monson ME
Montpelier VT
Montville ME 1849
Mooers NY
Moretown VT?
Morristown NY
Moscow ME
Mt Desert ME
Mt Pleasant WI
Mt Sterling Brown Co IL
Mt Vernon ME
Mukwanego WI?

Naples ME
Napoli (Naples, Italy)
Nashville NY
Nassau NY
Nelson NY
New Albion NY
New Berlin NY
New Boston
New Castle ME
New Chester
New Durham NH
New Gloucester ME
New Hampton NH
New Hampton NY
New Hartford NY
New Haven CT? 1849
New Haven NY
New Ipswich MA
New Limerick ME
New Lyme
New Market NH
New Portland ME 1849
New Sharon ME 1849
New Vineyard ME
New York NY 1851
Newark VT
Newburgh ME
Newbury NH
Newburyport MA 1849
Newfield ME? 1850
Newpond, Lower Canada?
Newport NY
Newport RI
Newton Lower Falls MA
Newton Union Co OH
Nicketow ME (other spellings:
    Nickatou, Nicatow, Niketow;
    former name of Medway,
    Penobscot Co, ME.)
Niles MI
No Bangor ME
No Scituate RI
Norfolk NY
Norridgewock ME 1849
North Berwick ME 1849
North Hampton NH

North Scarboro ME
North Shenago PA
North Yarmouth ME 1849
Northbridge MA
Northfield NH
Northumberland, Saratoga Co NY
Northwood NH
Norway ME 1847-1851
Norwich NY
Nottingham NH?
Nottingham Square NH?
No. Two ME
No. Eight ME (later called Willimantic, Piscataquis Co.)
Oakfield WI
Oberlin OH
Ogden NY
Oldtown ME
Olean NY
Olina NY
Olneyville RI
Oneida Eaton Co MI
Oneonta Eaton Co NY
Orange NH
Orange VT
Oregon (1849)
Orono ME
Orrington ME
Ossipee NH 1849
Otiscow MI
Otisfield ME
Otsego IND
Otsego NY
Ottowa IL
Owego NY
Oxford ME?
Oxford NY
Painfield NY
Palermo ME
Palmer
Palmyra ME
Paris ME 1849
Paris WI
Parma NY
Parsonsfield ME

Pascoag RI
Passadumkeag ME
Patton, Lower Canada?
Pawtocket RI
Peacham VT
Pelham MA
Pembroke NH?
Penobscot ME
Perinton NY?
Perry NY
Perry Township, Logan Co, OH
Perth Amoby NJ
Peru ME
Peru Township Logan Co OH
Peterboro
Pharsalia, Chenango Co NY
Philadelphia PA
Phillips ME
Phipsburg ME 1849-1850
Phoenix Oswego Co NY
Pierpont NY
Pikerun township PA
Piscataqoug Village NH?
Pitt Washtenaw Co MI
Pittsfield ME
Pittsfield NH
Pittsford, Hillsdale Co, MI
Plainfield NY
Pleasent Ridge Plt, Somerset Co ME
Plesses NY
Plymouth ME
Plymouth VT
Poestenkill NY
Poland, Herkiner Co, NY
Poland ME
Poolville NY
Poplin NH
Portage NY
Porter ME
Porter ME? 1851
Portland ME 1849-1851
Portsmouth NH 1847-1851
Pottersville, Bristol Co, MA
Pownal ME 1847
Prattsbury Steuben Co NY

Prembrook NH
Prospect ME
Providence RI 1850
Pueblo San Jose CA (1) 1850
Putney NY
Quinsey
Ramney NH
Randolph VT
Raymond ME
Raymond NH
Readfield ME
Reading VT
Rehoboth MA
Richmond ME 1849
Ridgeway Orleans Co NY
Rochester NH 1850
Rochester NY
Rochester Racine Co WI
Rockdale
Rockland ME 1850
Rockmanton NY
Rollinsford NH
Rome ME
Rome MI
Roscoe Winnebago Co IL
Roxbury MA
Royalton VT
Rozand Co MI
Ruch Township Logan Co OH
Rushford NY
Russel OH
Russia NY
Rutland OH
Saccarappa ME
Saco ME 1847-1850
Salartacook
Salem MA 1850
Salisbury MA
Salisbury NY
Sanbornton NH
Sand Lake NY
Sandwich MA?
Sandwich NH
Sanford ME
Sangersfield NY
Sangerville ME

Sardinia NY
Saugus MA
Scarboro' ME
Schroeppel Oswego Co NY
Scituate RI
Scriba NY
Searsmont ME
Sebago ME
Sebec ME
Sedgwick ME
Shapleigh ME 1849-1850
Sharon VT
Sheffield VT
Sheldon NY
Shellsburg WT
Sherburne NY
Sidney ME 1849
Skowhegan ME 1849-1850
Smithfield ME
Smithfield ME
Smithfield RI
Smithstown NY?
Smithville NY
Smyrna NY
So Berwick ME
So Montville ME
Solon OH
Somersworth NH 1849-1850
South Adams MA
South Berwick ME 1849-1850
South Paris ME 1849
South Reading MA
Sperry Fayette Co Iowa
Spring Arbor, Jackson Co, MI
Spring Arbor MI
Spring Prairie WI
Springfield ME
Springvale ME 1849
St Albans ME
St Johnsbury VT
Standish ME 1847-1850
Stanford Dutches Co NY
Stanstead Lower Canada
Starks ME
Starksboro VT
Starkville

Steep Falls ME
Stephenton NY
Stephentown NY
Stetson ME
Steubenville MA
Steubenville OH
Stewartstown NH?
Stockbridge MA
Stonnington CT
Stowe VT
Strafford Center NH
Strafford Organge Co VT
Strong ME
Strongsville, Cuyahoga Co OH
Sturbridge Ma
Sugar Hill (Lisbon NH)
Sumner ME
Sunipee NH?
Suriname, South America (1)
    1850
Sutton VT
Swanton VT
Swanville ME
Sweden
Swiftwater Village VT
Switzerland Co IA
Tamworth NH
Tecumseh Lenawee Co MI
Temple ME
Tewsbury MA
Theresa NY
Thetford
Thomaston ME 1850
Thompson CT
Thorndike ME
Three Mile Bay NY
Tinmouth VT
Tioga NY
Tiverton RI
Topsfield ME
Topsham ME 1849
Topsham VT
Trenton NJ
Trumbull OH
Tuftonborough NH
Tunbridge VT

Turner ME
Turner ME 1849
Turtle Prairie, Walworth Co WT
Tyrone Fayette Co PA
Unadila Forks Otsego Co NY
Underhill VT
Union Broome Co NY
Unionville MD
Unity ME
Upper Gilmanton NH
Utica NY
Uxbridge MA
Varysburgh NY
Venango PA
Vergenes VT?
Vershire VT
Vesta NY?
Vestal Broom Co NY
Victor NY
Vienna ME
Virgil NY
Virginia
Volinia Cass Cp MI
Volney NY
Wakefield NH
Waldin VT
Waldo ME
Waldoboro ME 1849
Wales ME
Wales NY
Walnut Grove Knox Co IL
Walworth NY
Wanconia WI
Wards Precinct IL
Warner NH?
Warren PA
Warrensburgh NY
Warsow NY
Washington ME
Washington township Fayette
    Co PA
Washington VT
Waterboro ME 1847
Waterford CT
Waterford ME
Watertown Jefferson Co NY

Waterville ME 1849-1850
Waterway
Wayne ME
Wayne OH
Weare NH
Webster ME
Wells ME 1850
West Boylston MA
West Brookfield
West Cambridge MA
West Fairlee VT
West Hartford
West Munroe NY
West Plymouth
West Poland ME
West Potsdam NY
West Prospect ME
West Stephentown NY
West Sumner ME
West Sumner ME 1849
West Waterville ME
West Winchester MA
Westbrook ME
Weston ME
Westport ME?
Wheatland WI
Wheelock VT
Whitefield ME?
Whitefield NH
Whitestown NY
Whiting VT
Wianconia WI
Willington MA
Williamsburgh ME
Williamstown VT
Wilmot NH 1819-1820
Wilton ME
Windham ME 1847
Windsor VT
Winslow VT
Winthrop ME
Wiscasset ME
Woburn MA
Wolcott VT
Wolfborough NH
Woodhull WI

Woodstock NH
Woodstock VT
Woolwich ME
Woonsocket RI
Worcester Otsego Co NY
Yankeytown OH
York ME
York MI
York Union Co OH
Yorkshire NY

Heritage Books by David C. Young and Elizabeth Keene Young:

Marriage and Divorce Records from Maine
Freewill Baptist Publications, 1819–1851

CD: *Marriage and Divorce Records from Maine*
Freewill Baptist Publications, 1819–1851

Stackpole's History of Winthrop, Maine
with Genealogical Notes

Vital Records from Maine Newspapers, 1785–1820

Heritage Books by David C. Young:

Abstracts of Death Notices (1833–1852) and
Miscellaneous News Items from the Maine Farmer *(1833–1924)*
David C. Young and Benjamin Lewis Keene

History of the Town of Leeds, Androscoggin County, Maine
from Its Settlement, June 10, 1780
J. C. Stinchfield, with New Material Added by David C. Young

Death Notices from
Freewill Baptist Publications, 1811–1851
David C. Young and Robert L. Taylor

CD: *Death Notices from*
Freewill Baptist Publications, 1811–1851

Heritage Books by Elizabeth Keene Young:

Marriage Notices from the Maine Farmer *1833*
Elizabeth Keene Young and Benjamin Lewis Keene

www.ingramcontent.com/pod-product-compliance
Lightning Source LLC
Chambersburg PA
CBHW072036020426
42334CB00017B/1293

* 9 780788 401367 *